Survey of Computer Information Systems

CIS105 for Glendale Community College

Author: David Beskeen, Carol M. Cram, Jennifer Duffy, Lisa Friedrichsen, Elizabeth Eisner Reding, Carol Cram, Lynn Wermers

CENGAGE
Learning·

Australia • Brazil • Japan • Korea • Mexico • Singapore • Spain • United Kingdom • United States

Survey of Computer Information Systems: CIS105 for Glendale Community College,

Illustrated Microsoft® Office 365 & Office 2016
David Beskeen, Carol M. Cram, Jennifer Duffy, Lisa Friedrichsen, Elizabeth Eisner Reding

©2017 Cengage Learning. All rights reserved.

Illustrated Microsoft® Office 365TM & Word 2016—Comprehensive
Jennifer Duffy, Carol Cram

©2017 Cengage Learning. All rights reserved.

Illustrated Microsoft® Office 365TM & Excel® 2016—Comprehensive
Elizabeth Eisner Reding, Lynn Wermers

©2017 Cengage Learning. All rights reserved.

Illustrated Microsoft® Office 365TM & Access® 2016—Comprehensive
Lisa Friedrichsen

©2017 Cengage Learning. All rights reserved.

For product information and technology assistance, contact us at
Cengage Learning Customer & Sales Support, 1-800-354-9706

For permission to use material from this text or product,
submit all requests online at **cengage.com/permissions**
Further permissions questions can be emailed to
permissionrequest@cengage.com

This book contains select works from existing Cengage Learning resources and was produced by Cengage Learning Custom Solutions for collegiate use. As such, those adopting and/or contributing to this work are responsible for editorial content accuracy, continuity and completeness.

Compilation © 2018 Cengage Learning

ISBN: 978-1-337-91006-4

Cengage Learning

Cengage Learning is a leading provider of customized learning solutions with office locations around the globe, including Singapore, the United Kingdom, Australia, Mexico, Brazil, and Japan. Locate your local office at:
www.international.cengage.com/region.

Cengage Learning products are represented in Canada by Nelson Education, Ltd.

For your lifelong learning solutions, visit **www.cengage.com/custom.**

Visit our corporate website at **www.cengage.com.**

Brief Contents

Productivity Apps for School and Work

Corinne Hoisington

Lochlan keeps track of his class notes, football plays, and internship meetings with OneNote.

Zoe is using the annotation features of Microsoft Edge to take and save web notes for her research paper.

Nori is creating a Sway site to highlight this year's activities for the Student Government Association.

Hunter is adding interactive videos and screen recordings to his PowerPoint resume.

© Rawpixel/Shutterstock.com

Being computer literate no longer means mastery of only Word, Excel, PowerPoint, Outlook, and Access. To become technology power users, Hunter, Nori, Zoe, and Lochlan are exploring Microsoft OneNote, Sway, Mix, and Edge in Office 2016 and Windows 10.

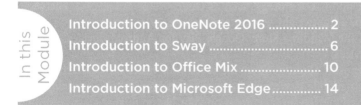

In this Module

Learn to use productivity apps!
Links to companion **Sways**, featuring **videos** with hands-on instructions, are located on www.cengagebrain.com.

Introduction to OneNote 2016

notebook | section tab | To Do tag | screen clipping | note | template | Microsoft OneNote Mobile app | sync | drawing canvas | inked handwriting | Ink to Text

As you glance around any classroom, you invariably see paper notebooks and notepads on each desk. Because deciphering and sharing handwritten notes can be a challenge, Microsoft OneNote 2016 replaces physical notebooks, binders, and paper notes with a searchable, digital notebook. OneNote captures your ideas and schoolwork on any device so you can stay organized, share notes, and work with others on projects. Whether you are a student taking class notes as shown in Figure 1 or an employee taking notes in company meetings, OneNote is the one place to keep notes for all of your projects.

Figure 1: OneNote 2016 notebook

Each **notebook** is divided into sections, also called **section tabs**, by subject or topic.

Use **To Do tags**, icons that help you keep track of your assignments and other tasks.

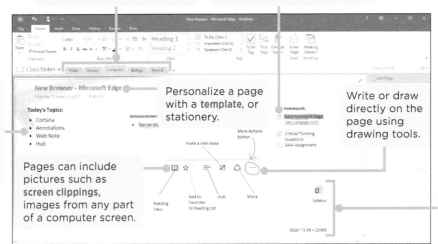

Type on a page to add a **note**, a small window that contains text or other types of information.

Personalize a page with a **template**, or stationery.

Write or draw directly on the page using drawing tools.

Pages can include pictures such as **screen clippings**, images from any part of a computer screen.

Attach files and enter equations so you have everything you need in one place.

Creating a OneNote Notebook

OneNote is divided into sections similar to those in a spiral-bound notebook. Each OneNote notebook contains sections, pages, and other notebooks. You can use OneNote for school, business, and personal projects. Store information for each type of project in different notebooks to keep your tasks separate, or use any other organization that suits you. OneNote is flexible enough to adapt to the way you want to work.

When you create a notebook, it contains a blank page with a plain white background by default, though you can use templates, or stationery, to apply designs in categories such as Academic, Business, Decorative, and Planners. Start typing or use the buttons on the Insert tab to insert notes, which are small resizable windows that can contain text, equations, tables, on-screen writing, images, audio and video recordings, to-do lists, file attachments, and file printouts. Add as many notes as you need to each page.

Syncing a Notebook to the Cloud

OneNote saves your notes every time you make a change in a notebook. To make sure you can access your notebooks with a laptop, tablet, or smartphone wherever you are, OneNote uses cloud-based storage, such as OneDrive or SharePoint. **Microsoft OneNote Mobile app**, a lightweight version of OneNote 2016 shown in Figure 2, is available for free in the Windows Store, Google Play for Android devices, and the AppStore for iOS devices.

If you have a Microsoft account, OneNote saves your notes on OneDrive automatically for all your mobile devices and computers, which is called **syncing**. For example, you can use OneNote to take notes on your laptop during class, and then open OneNote on your phone to study later. To use a notebook stored on your computer with your OneNote Mobile app, move the notebook to OneDrive. You can quickly share notebook content with other people using OneDrive.

Figure 2: Microsoft OneNote Mobile app

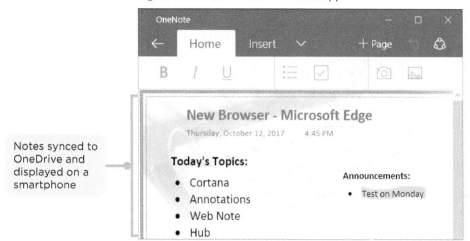

Notes synced to OneDrive and displayed on a smartphone

Taking Notes

Use OneNote pages to organize your notes by class and topic or lecture. Beyond simple typed notes, OneNote stores drawings, converts handwriting to searchable text and mathematical sketches to equations, and records audio and video.

OneNote includes drawing tools that let you sketch freehand drawings such as biological cell diagrams and financial supply-and-demand charts. As shown in **Figure 3**, the Draw tab on the ribbon provides these drawing tools along with shapes so you can insert diagrams and other illustrations to represent your ideas. When you draw on a page, OneNote creates a **drawing canvas**, which is a container for shapes and lines.

On the Job Now

OneNote is ideal for taking notes during meetings, whether you are recording minutes, documenting a discussion, sketching product diagrams, or listing follow-up items. Use a meeting template to add pages with content appropriate for meetings.

Figure 3: Tools on the Draw tab

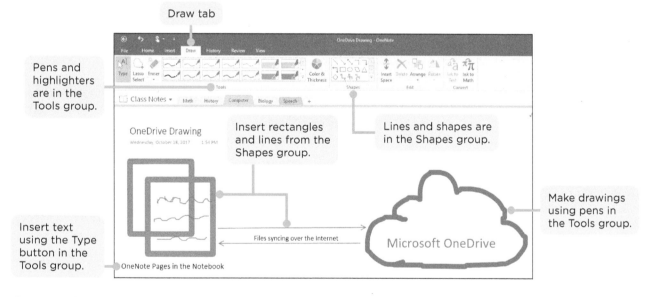

Draw tab

Pens and highlighters are in the Tools group.

Insert rectangles and lines from the Shapes group.

Lines and shapes are in the Shapes group.

Make drawings using pens in the Tools group.

Insert text using the Type button in the Tools group.

Converting Handwriting to Text

When you use a pen tool to write on a notebook page, the text you enter is called **inked handwriting**. OneNote can convert inked handwriting to typed text when you use the **Ink to Text** button in the Convert group on the Draw tab, as shown in **Figure 4**. After OneNote converts the handwriting to text, you can use the Search box to find terms in the converted text or any other note in your notebooks.

Figure 4: Converting handwriting to text

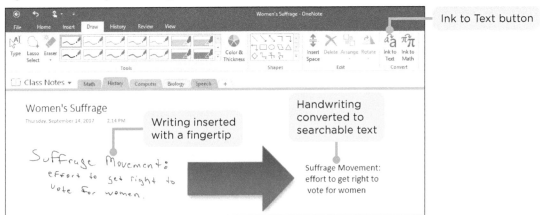

Ink to Text button

Women's Suffrage

Thursday, September 14, 2017   2:14 PM

Suffrage Movement: effort to get right to vote for women.

Writing inserted with a fingertip

Handwriting converted to searchable text

Suffrage Movement: effort to get right to vote for women

On the Job Now

Use OneNote as a place to brainstorm ongoing work projects. If a notebook contains sensitive material, you can password-protect some or all of the notebook so that only certain people can open it.

Recording a Lecture

If your computer or mobile device has a microphone or camera, OneNote can record the audio or video from a lecture or business meeting as shown in **Figure 5**. When you record a lecture (with your instructor's permission), you can follow along, take regular notes at your own pace, and review the video recording later. You can control the start, pause, and stop motions of the recording when you play back the recording of your notes.

Figure 5: Video inserted in a notebook

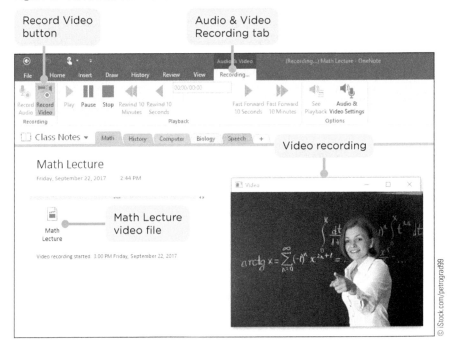

Record Video button

Audio & Video Recording tab

Video recording

Math Lecture

Friday, September 22, 2017   2:44 PM

Math Lecture video file

Math Lecture

Video recording started. 3:00 PM Friday, September 22, 2017

© iStock.com/petrograd99

Try This Now

Learn to use OneNote!
Links to companion **Sways**, featuring **videos** with hands-on instructions, are located on www.cengagebrain.com.

1: Taking Notes for a Week

As a student, you can get organized by using OneNote to take detailed notes in your classes. Perform the following tasks:

a. Create a new OneNote notebook on your Microsoft OneDrive account (the default location for new notebooks). Name the notebook with your first name followed by "Notes," as in **Caleb Notes**.
b. Create four section tabs, each with a different class name.
c. Take detailed notes in those classes for one week. Be sure to include notes, drawings, and other types of content.
d. Sync your notes with your OneDrive. Submit your assignment in the format specified by your instructor.

2: Using OneNote to Organize a Research Paper

You have a research paper due on the topic of three habits of successful students. Use OneNote to organize your research. Perform the following tasks:

a. Create a new OneNote notebook on your Microsoft OneDrive account. Name the notebook **Success Research**.
b. Create three section tabs with the following names:

   - **Take Detailed Notes**
   - **Be Respectful in Class**
   - **Come to Class Prepared**

c. On the web, research the topics and find three sources for each section. Copy a sentence from each source and paste the sentence into the appropriate section. When you paste the sentence, OneNote inserts it in a note with a link to the source.
d. Sync your notes with your OneDrive. Submit your assignment in the format specified by your instructor.

3: Planning Your Career

Note: This activity requires a webcam or built-in video camera on any type of device.

Consider an occupation that interests you. Using OneNote, examine the responsibilities, education requirements, potential salary, and employment outlook of a specific career. Perform the following tasks:

a. Create a new OneNote notebook on your Microsoft OneDrive account. Name the notebook with your first name followed by a career title, such as **Kara - App Developer**.
b. Create four section tabs with the names **Responsibilities, Education Requirements, Median Salary**, and **Employment Outlook**.
c. Research the responsibilities of your career path. Using OneNote, record a short video (approximately 30 seconds) of yourself explaining the responsibilities of your career path. Place the video in the Responsibilities section.
d. On the web, research the educational requirements for your career path and find two appropriate sources. Copy a paragraph from each source and paste them into the appropriate section. When you paste a paragraph, OneNote inserts it in a note with a link to the source.
e. Research the median salary for a single year for this career. Create a mathematical equation in the Median Salary section that multiplies the amount of the median salary times 20 years to calculate how much you will possibly earn.
f. For the Employment Outlook section, research the outlook for your career path. Take at least four notes about what you find when researching the topic.
g. Sync your notes with your OneDrive. Submit your assignment in the format specified by your instructor.

Introduction to Sway

Sway site | responsive design | Storyline | card | Creative Commons license | animation emphasis effects | Docs.com

Expressing your ideas in a presentation typically means creating PowerPoint slides or a Word document. Microsoft Sway gives you another way to engage an audience. Sway is a free Microsoft tool available at Sway.com or as an app in Office 365. Using Sway, you can combine text, images, videos, and social media in a website called a **Sway site** that you can share and display on any device. To get started, you create a digital story on a web-based canvas without borders, slides, cells, or page breaks. A Sway site organizes the text, images, and video into a **responsive design**, which means your content adapts perfectly to any screen size as shown in **Figure 6**. You store a Sway site in the cloud on OneDrive using a free Microsoft account.

Figure 6: Sway site with responsive design

You can display a Sway presentation in a web browser.

Sway uses responsive design to make sure pages fit perfectly on any device.

© iStock.com/marinello, © iStock.com/marekuliasz

Creating a Sway Presentation

You can use Sway to build a digital flyer, a club newsletter, a vacation blog, an informational site, a digital art portfolio, or a new product rollout. After you select your topic and sign into Sway with your Microsoft account, a **Storyline** opens, providing tools and a work area for composing your digital story. See **Figure 7**. Each story can include text, images, and videos. You create a Sway by adding text and media content into a Storyline section, or **card**. To add pictures, videos, or documents, select a card in the left pane and then select the Insert Content button. The first card in a Sway presentation contains a title and background image.

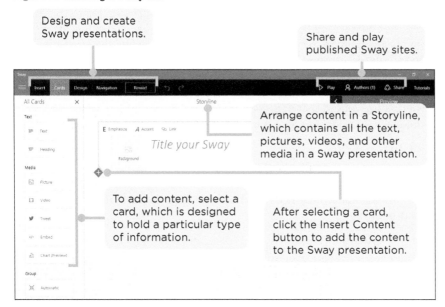

Design and create
Sway presentations.

Share and play
published Sway sites.

Arrange content in a Storyline,
which contains all the text,
pictures, videos, and other
media in a Sway presentation.

Title your Sway

To add content, select a
card, which is designed
to hold a particular type
of information.

After selecting a card,
click the Insert Content
button to add the content
to the Sway presentation.

Adding Content to Build a Story

As you work, Sway searches the Internet to help you find relevant images, videos, tweets, and other content from online sources such as Bing, YouTube, Twitter, and Facebook. You can drag content from the search results right into the Storyline. In addition, you can upload your own images and videos directly in the presentation. For example, if you are creating a Sway presentation about the market for commercial drones, Sway suggests content to incorporate into the presentation by displaying it in the left pane as search results. The search results include drone images tagged with a **Creative Commons license** at online sources as shown in **Figure 8**. A Creative Commons license is a public copyright license that allows the free distribution of an otherwise copyrighted work. In addition, you can specify the source of the media. For example, you can add your own Facebook or OneNote pictures and videos in Sway without leaving the app.

On the Job Now

If you have a Microsoft Word document containing an outline of your business content, drag the outline into Sway to create a card for each topic.

Figure 8: Images in Sway search results

Select the source
of media objects

Information about Creative
Commons licenses

Storyline title

The Market for
Commercial Drones

Drag an image to the
picture placeholder box

Suggested images in
the search results

Designing a Sway

Sway professionally designs your Storyline content by resizing background images and fonts to fit your display, and by floating text, animating media, embedding video, and removing images as a page scrolls out of view. Sway also evaluates the images in your Storyline and suggests a color palette based on colors that appear in your photos. Use the Design button to display tools including color palettes, font choices, **animation emphasis effects**, and style templates to provide a personality for a Sway presentation. Instead of creating your own design, you can click the Remix button, which randomly selects unique designs for your Sway site.

Publishing a Sway

Use the Play button to display your finished Sway presentation as a website. The Address bar includes a unique web address where others can view your Sway site. As the author, you can edit a published Sway site by clicking the Edit button (pencil icon) on the Sway toolbar.

Sharing a Sway

When you are ready to share your Sway website, you have several options as shown in Figure 9. Use the Share slider button to share the Sway site publically or keep it private. If you add the Sway site to the Microsoft **Docs.com** public gallery, anyone worldwide can use Bing, Google, or other search engines to find, view, and share your Sway site. You can also share your Sway site using Facebook, Twitter, Google+, Yammer, and other social media sites. Link your presentation to any webpage or email the link to your audience. Sway can also generate a code for embedding the link within another webpage.

Figure 9: Sharing a Sway site

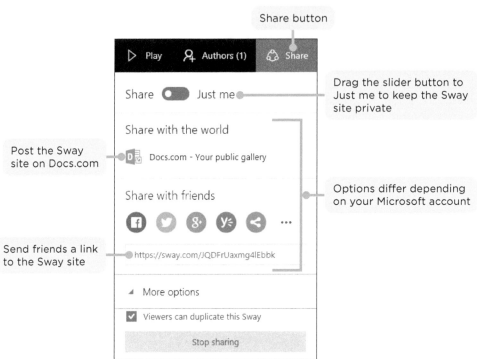

Try This Now

> **Learn to use Sway!**
> Links to companion **Sways**, featuring **videos** with hands-on instructions, are located on www.cengagebrain.com.

1: Creating a Sway Resume

Sway is a digital storytelling app. Create a Sway resume to share the skills, job experiences, and achievements you have that match the requirements of a future job interest. Perform the following tasks:

    a. Create a new presentation in Sway to use as a digital resume. Title the Sway Storyline with your full name and then select a background image.

    b. Create three separate sections titled **Academic Background, Work Experience**, and **Skills**, and insert text, a picture, and a paragraph or bulleted points in each section. Be sure to include your own picture.

    c. Add a fourth section that includes a video about your school that you find online.

    d. Customize the design of your presentation.

    e. Submit your assignment link in the format specified by your instructor.

2: Creating an Online Sway Newsletter

Newsletters are designed to capture the attention of their target audience. Using Sway, create a newsletter for a club, organization, or your favorite music group. Perform the following tasks:

    a. Create a new presentation in Sway to use as a digital newsletter for a club, organization, or your favorite music group. Provide a title for the Sway Storyline and select an appropriate background image.

    b. Select three separate sections with appropriate titles, such as Upcoming Events. In each section, insert text, a picture, and a paragraph or bulleted points.

    c. Add a fourth section that includes a video about your selected topic.

    d. Customize the design of your presentation.

    e. Submit your assignment link in the format specified by your instructor.

3: Creating and Sharing a Technology Presentation

To place a Sway presentation in the hands of your entire audience, you can share a link to the Sway presentation. Create a Sway presentation on a new technology and share it with your class. Perform the following tasks:

    a. Create a new presentation in Sway about a cutting-edge technology topic. Provide a title for the Sway Storyline and select a background image.

    b. Create four separate sections about your topic, and include text, a picture, and a paragraph in each section.

    c. Add a fifth section that includes a video about your topic.

    d. Customize the design of your presentation.

    e. Share the link to your Sway with your classmates and submit your assignment link in the format specified by your instructor.

Introduction to Office Mix

add-in | clip | slide recording | Slide Notes | screen recording | free-response quiz

To enliven business meetings and lectures, Microsoft adds a new dimension to presentations with a powerful toolset called Office Mix, a free add-in for PowerPoint. (An **add-in** is software that works with an installed app to extend its features.) Using Office Mix, you can record yourself on video, capture still and moving images on your desktop, and insert interactive elements such as quizzes and live webpages directly into PowerPoint slides. When you post the finished presentation to OneDrive, Office Mix provides a link you can share with friends and colleagues. Anyone with an Internet connection and a web browser can watch a published Office Mix presentation, such as the one in Figure 10, on a computer or mobile device.

Figure 10: Office Mix presentation

Adding Office Mix to PowerPoint

To get started, you create an Office Mix account at the website mix.office.com using an email address or a Facebook or Google account. Next, you download and install the Office Mix add-in (see Figure 11). Office Mix appears as a new tab named Mix on the PowerPoint ribbon in versions of Office 2013 and Office 2016 running on personal computers (PCs).

Figure 11: Getting started with Office Mix

Capturing Video Clips

A **clip** is a short segment of audio, such as music, or video. After finishing the content on a PowerPoint slide, you can use Office Mix to add a video clip to animate or illustrate the content. Office Mix creates video clips in two ways: by recording live action on a webcam and by capturing screen images and movements. If your computer has a webcam, you can record yourself and annotate the slide to create a **slide recording** as shown in Figure 12.

On the Job Now

Companies are using Office Mix to train employees about new products, to explain benefit packages to new workers, and to educate interns about office procedures.

Figure 12: Making a slide recording

Record your voice; also record video if your computer has a camera.

Use the Slide Notes button to display notes for your narration.

For best results, look directly at your webcam while recording video.

Choose a video and audio device to record images and sound.

Use inking tools to write and draw on the slide as you record.

When you are making a slide recording, you can record your spoken narration at the same time. The **Slide Notes** feature works like a teleprompter to help you focus on your presentation content instead of memorizing your narration. Use the Inking tools to make annotations or add highlighting using different pen types and colors. After finishing a recording, edit the video in PowerPoint to trim the length or set playback options.

The second way to create a video is to capture on-screen images and actions with or without a voiceover. This method is ideal if you want to show how to use your favorite website or demonstrate an app such as OneNote. To share your screen with an audience, select the part of the screen you want to show in the video. Office Mix captures everything that happens in that area to create a **screen recording**, as shown in Figure 13. Office Mix inserts the screen recording as a video in the slide.

On the Job Now

To make your video recordings accessible to people with hearing impairments, use the Office Mix closed-captioning tools. You can also use closed captions to supplement audio that is difficult to understand and to provide an aid for those learning to read.

Figure 13: Making a screen recording

Record the action on the screen within the red dashed outline.

Record audio while capturing your on-screen actions.

Select Area button

Inserting Quizzes, Live Webpages, and Apps

To enhance and assess audience understanding, make your slides interactive by adding quizzes, live webpages, and apps. Quizzes give immediate feedback to the user as shown in Figure 14. Office Mix supports several quiz formats, including a **free-response quiz** similar to a short answer quiz, and true/false, multiple-choice, and multiple-response formats.

Figure 14: Creating an interactive quiz

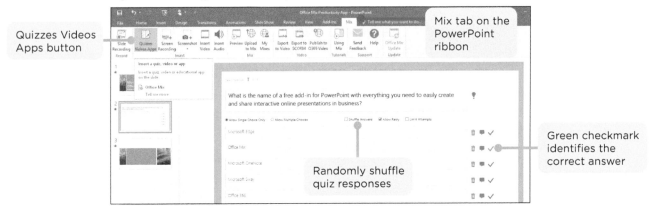

Quizzes Videos Apps button

Mix tab on the PowerPoint ribbon

Green checkmark identifies the correct answer

Randomly shuffle quiz responses

Sharing an Office Mix Presentation

When you complete your work with Office Mix, upload the presentation to your personal Office Mix dashboard as shown in Figure 15. Users of PCs, Macs, iOS devices, and Android devices can access and play Office Mix presentations. The Office Mix dashboard displays built-in analytics that include the quiz results and how much time viewers spent on each slide. You can play completed Office Mix presentations online or download them as movies.

Figure 15: Sharing an Office Mix presentation

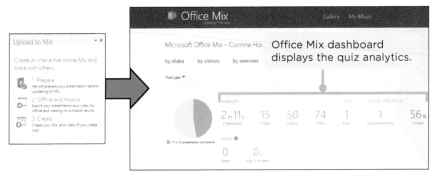

Office Mix dashboard displays the quiz analytics.

Try This Now

1: Creating an Office Mix Tutorial for OneNote

Note: This activity requires a microphone on your computer.

Office Mix makes it easy to record screens and their contents. Create PowerPoint slides with an Office Mix screen recording to show OneNote 2016 features. Perform the following tasks:

a. Create a PowerPoint presentation with the Ion Boardroom template. Create an opening slide with the title **My Favorite OneNote Features** and enter your name in the subtitle.
b. Create three additional slides, each titled with a new feature of OneNote. Open OneNote and use the Mix tab in PowerPoint to capture three separate screen recordings that teach your favorite features.
c. Add a fifth slide that quizzes the user with a multiple-choice question about OneNote and includes four responses. Be sure to insert a checkmark indicating the correct response.
d. Upload the completed presentation to your Office Mix dashboard and share the link with your instructor.
e. Submit your assignment link in the format specified by your instructor.

2: Teaching Augmented Reality with Office Mix

Note: This activity requires a webcam or built-in video camera on your computer.

A local elementary school has asked you to teach augmented reality to its students using Office Mix. Perform the following tasks:

a. Research augmented reality using your favorite online search tools.
b. Create a PowerPoint presentation with the Frame template. Create an opening slide with the title **Augmented Reality** and enter your name in the subtitle.
c. Create a slide with four bullets summarizing your research of augmented reality. Create a 20-second slide recording of yourself providing a quick overview of augmented reality.
d. Create another slide with a 30-second screen recording of a video about augmented reality from a site such as YouTube or another video-sharing site.
e. Add a final slide that quizzes the user with a true/false question about augmented reality. Be sure to insert a checkmark indicating the correct response.
f. Upload the completed presentation to your Office Mix dashboard and share the link with your instructor.
g. Submit your assignment link in the format specified by your instructor.

3: Marketing a Travel Destination with Office Mix

Note: This activity requires a webcam or built-in video camera on your computer.

To convince your audience to travel to a particular city, create a slide presentation marketing any city in the world using a slide recording, screen recording, and a quiz. Perform the following tasks:

a. Create a PowerPoint presentation with any template. Create an opening slide with the title of the city you are marketing as a travel destination and your name in the subtitle.
b. Create a slide with four bullets about the featured city. Create a 30-second slide recording of yourself explaining why this city is the perfect vacation destination.
c. Create another slide with a 20-second screen recording of a travel video about the city from a site such as YouTube or another video-sharing site.
d. Add a final slide that quizzes the user with a multiple-choice question about the featured city with five responses. Be sure to include a checkmark indicating the correct response.
e. Upload the completed presentation to your Office Mix dashboard and share your link with your instructor.
f. Submit your assignment link in the format specified by your instructor.

Introduction to Microsoft Edge

Reading view | Hub | Cortana | Web Note | Inking | sandbox

Bottom Line
- Microsoft Edge is the name of the new web browser built into Windows 10.
- Microsoft Edge allows you to search the web faster, take web notes, read webpages without distractions, and get instant assistance from Cortana.

Microsoft Edge is the default web browser developed for the Windows 10 operating system as a replacement for Internet Explorer. Unlike its predecessor, Edge lets you write on webpages, read webpages without advertisements and other distractions, and search for information using a virtual personal assistant. The Edge interface is clean and basic, as shown in Figure 16, meaning you can pay more attention to the webpage content.

Figure 16: Microsoft Edge tools

Forward button · New tab button · Web address in the Address bar · Add to favorites or reading list button · Back button · Reading view button · More button · Refresh (F5) button · Hub (Favorites, reading list, history, and downloads) button · Share Web Note button · Make a Web Note button

Learn to use Edge!
Links to companion **Sways**, featuring **videos** with hands-on instructions, are located on www.cengagebrain.com.

Browsing the Web with Microsoft Edge

One of the fastest browsers available, Edge allows you to type search text directly in the Address bar. As you view the resulting webpage, you can switch to **Reading view**, which is available for most news and research sites, to eliminate distracting advertisements. For example, if you are catching up on technology news online, the webpage might be difficult to read due to a busy layout cluttered with ads. Switch to Reading view to refresh the page and remove the original page formatting, ads, and menu sidebars to read the article distraction-free.

Consider the **Hub** in Microsoft Edge as providing one-stop access to all the things you collect on the web, such as your favorite websites, reading list, surfing history, and downloaded files.

Locating Information with Cortana

Cortana, the Windows 10 virtual assistant, plays an important role in Microsoft Edge. After you turn on Cortana, it appears as an animated circle in the Address bar when you might need assistance, as shown in the restaurant website in Figure 17. When you click the Cortana icon, a pane slides in from the right of the browser window to display detailed information about the restaurant, including maps and reviews. Cortana can also assist you in defining words, finding the weather, suggesting coupons for shopping, updating stock market information, and calculating math.

On the Job Now

Businesses started adopting Internet Explorer more than 20 years ago simply to view webpages. Today, Microsoft Edge has a different purpose: to promote interaction with the web and share its contents with colleagues.

Figure 17: Cortana providing restaurant information

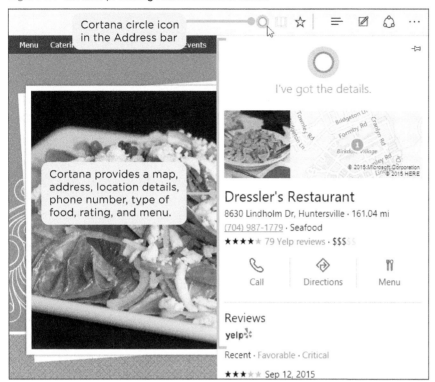

Cortana circle icon in the Address bar

Cortana provides a map, address, location details, phone number, type of food, rating, and menu.

I've got the details.

Dressler's Restaurant
8630 Lindholm Dr, Huntersville · 161.04 mi
(704) 987-1779 · Seafood
★★★★☆ 79 Yelp reviews · $$$$$

Call | Directions | Menu

Reviews
yelp⁑
Recent · Favorable · Critical
★★★☆☆ Sep 12, 2015

Annotating Webpages

One of the most impressive Microsoft Edge features are the **Web Note** tools, which you use to write on a webpage or to highlight text. When you click the Make a Web Note button, an **Inking** toolbar appears, as shown in **Figure 18**, that provides writing and drawing tools. These tools include an eraser, a pen, and a highlighter with different colors. You can also insert a typed note and copy a screen image (called a screen clipping). You can draw with a pointing device, fingertip, or stylus using different pen colors. Whether you add notes to a recipe, annotate sources for a research paper, or select a product while shopping online, the Web Note tools can enhance your productivity. After you complete your notes, click the Save button to save the annotations to OneNote, your Favorites list, or your Reading list. You can share the inked page with others using the Share Web Note button.

On the Job Now

To enhance security, Microsoft Edge runs in a partial sandbox, an arrangement that prevents attackers from gaining control of your computer. Browsing within the **sandbox** protects computer resources and information from hackers.

Figure 18: Web Note tools in Microsoft Edge

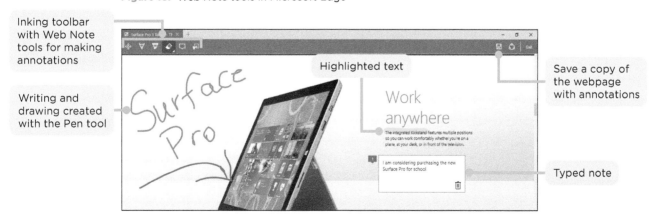

Inking toolbar with Web Note tools for making annotations

Writing and drawing created with the Pen tool

Highlighted text

Work anywhere

The integrated Kickstand features multiple positions so you can work comfortably whether you're on a plane, at your desk, or in front of the television.

I am considering purchasing the new Surface Pro for school

Save a copy of the webpage with annotations

Typed note

Try This Now

1: Using Cortana in Microsoft Edge

Note: This activity requires using Microsoft Edge on a Windows 10 computer.

Cortana can assist you in finding information on a webpage in Microsoft Edge. Perform the following tasks:

a. Create a Word document using the Word Screen Clipping tool to capture the following screenshots.

- Screenshot A—Using Microsoft Edge, open a webpage with a technology news article. Right-click a term in the article and ask Cortana to define it.
- Screenshot B—Using Microsoft Edge, open the website of a fancy restaurant in a city near you. Make sure the Cortana circle icon is displayed in the Address bar. (If it's not displayed, find a different restaurant website.) Click the Cortana circle icon to display a pane with information about the restaurant.
- Screenshot C—Using Microsoft Edge, type **10 USD to Euros** in the Address bar without pressing the Enter key. Cortana converts the U.S. dollars to Euros.
- Screenshot D—Using Microsoft Edge, type **Apple stock** in the Address bar without pressing the Enter key. Cortana displays the current stock quote.

b. Submit your assignment in the format specified by your instructor.

2: Viewing Online News with Reading View

Note: This activity requires using Microsoft Edge on a Windows 10 computer.

Reading view in Microsoft Edge can make a webpage less cluttered with ads and other distractions. Perform the following tasks:

a. Create a Word document using the Word Screen Clipping tool to capture the following screenshots.

- Screenshot A—Using Microsoft Edge, open the website **mashable.com**. Open a technology article. Click the Reading view button to display an ad-free page that uses only basic text formatting.
- Screenshot B—Using Microsoft Edge, open the website **bbc.com**. Open any news article. Click the Reading view button to display an ad-free page that uses only basic text formatting.
- Screenshot C—Make three types of annotations (Pen, Highlighter, and Add a typed note) on the BBC article page displayed in Reading view.

b. Submit your assignment in the format specified by your instructor.

3: Inking with Microsoft Edge

Note: This activity requires using Microsoft Edge on a Windows 10 computer.

Microsoft Edge provides many annotation options to record your ideas. Perform the following tasks:

a. Open the website **wolframalpha.com** in the Microsoft Edge browser. Wolfram Alpha is a well-respected academic search engine. Type **US$100 1965 dollars in 2015** in the Wolfram Alpha search text box and press the Enter key.
b. Click the Make a Web Note button to display the Web Note tools. Using the Pen tool, draw a circle around the result on the webpage. Save the page to OneNote.
c. In the Wolfram Alpha search text box, type the name of the city closest to where you live and press the Enter key. Using the Highlighter tool, highlight at least three interesting results. Add a note and then type a sentence about what you learned about this city. Save the page to OneNote. Share your OneNote notebook with your instructor.
d. Submit your assignment link in the format specified by your instructor.

Getting Started with Windows 10

CASE You are about to start a new job, and your employer has asked you to get familiar with Windows 10 to help boost your productivity. You'll need to start Windows 10 and Windows apps, work with on-screen windows and commands, get help, and exit Windows. *Note: With the release of Windows 10, Microsoft now provides ongoing updates to Windows instead of releasing new versions periodically. This means that Windows features might change over time, including how they look and how you interact with them. The information provided in this text was accurate at the time this book was published.*

Module Objectives

After completing this module, you will be able to:

- Start Windows 10
- Navigate the desktop and Start menu
- Point, click, and drag
- Start an app
- Work with a window
- Manage multiple windows
- Use buttons, menus, and dialog boxes
- Get help
- Exit Windows 10

Files You Will Need

No files needed.

Start Windows 10

Learning
Outcomes
• Power on a
  computer
• Log into
  Windows 10

Windows 10 is an **operating system**, a type of program that runs your computer and lets you interact with it. A **program** is a set of instructions written for a computer. If your computer did not have an operating system, you wouldn't see anything on the screen after you turned it on. Windows 10 reserves a special area called a **Microsoft account** where each user can keep his or her files. In addition, a Microsoft account lets you use various devices and services such as a Windows Phone or Outlook.com. You may have more than one Microsoft account. When the computer and Windows 10 start, you need to **sign in**, or select your Microsoft account name and enter a password, also called **logging in**. If your computer has only one Microsoft account, you won't need to select an account name. But all users need to enter a **password**, a special sequence of numbers and letters. Users cannot see each other's account areas or services without the other person's password, so passwords help keep your computer information secure. After you sign in, you see the Windows 10 desktop, which you learn about in the next lesson. **CASE** ➤ *You're about to start a new job, so you decide to learn more about Windows 10, the operating system used at your new company.*

STEPS

1. **Press your computer's** power button, **which might look like** 🔘 **or** 🔲, **then if the monitor is not turned on, press its** power button

   On a desktop computer, the power button is probably on the front panel. On a laptop computer it's likely at the top of the keys on your keyboard. After a few moments, a **lock screen**, showing the date, time, and an image, appears. See FIGURE 1-1. The lock screen appears when you first start your computer and also if you leave it unattended for a period of time.

2. **Press [Spacebar], or click once to display the sign-in screen**

   The **sign-in screen** shows your Windows account picture, name, and e-mail address, as well as a space to enter your Microsoft account password. The account may have your name assigned to it, or it might have a general name like "Student" or "Lab User."

3. **Type your** password, **as shown in** FIGURE 1-2, **using uppercase and lowercase letters as necessary**

   If necessary, ask your instructor or technical support person what password you should use. Passwords are **case sensitive**, which means that if you type any letter using capital letters when lowercase letters are needed, or vice versa, Windows will not let you use your account. For example, if your password is "booklet43+", typing "Booklet43+" or "BOOKLET43+" will not let you enter your account. For security, Windows substitutes bullets for the password characters you type.

4. **Click or tap the** Submit button →

   The Windows 10 desktop appears. See FIGURE 1-3.

Using a touch screen with Windows

Windows 10 was developed to work with touch-screen computers, including tablets and smartphones. See FIGURE 1-4. So if you have a touch-screen device, you'll find that you can accomplish many tasks with gestures instead of a mouse. A **gesture** is an action you take with your fingertip directly on the screen, such as tapping or swiping. For example, when you sign into Windows 10, you can tap the Submit button on the screen, instead of clicking it.

FIGURE 1-4: Touch-screen device

© vovan/Shutterstock.com

FIGURE 1-1: Lock screen with time and date

Your lock
screen contents
may differ

FIGURE 1-2: Typing your password

FIGURE 1-3: Windows 10 desktop

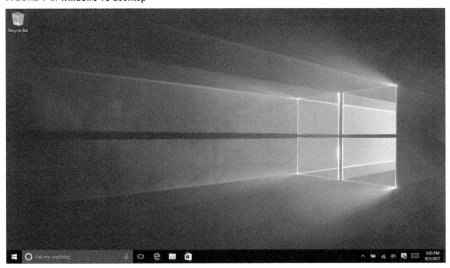

Navigate the Desktop and Start Menu

Every time you start your computer and sign in, the Windows 10 desktop appears. The **Windows 10 desktop** is an electronic work area that lets you organize and manage your information, much like your own physical desktop. The desktop contains controls that let you interact with the Windows 10 operating system. These controls are called its **user interface (UI)**. The Windows 10 user interface is called the **Windows 10 UI.** **CASE** *To become better acquainted with Windows 10, you decide to explore the desktop and Start menu.*

STEPS

1. **Examine the Windows 10 desktop**

   As shown in FIGURE 1-5, the desktop currently contains one item, an icon representing the **Recycle Bin**, an electronic wastepaper basket. You might see other icons, files, and folders placed there by previous users or by your school lab. The desktop lets you manage the files and folders on your computer. A **file** is a collection of stored information, such as a letter, video, or program. A **folder** is a container that helps you organize your files. A file, folder, or program opens in a window. You can open multiple windows on the desktop at once, and you can move them around so you can easily go back and forth between them. You work with windows later in this module. At the bottom of the screen is a bar called the **taskbar**, with buttons representing commonly used programs and tools. In a default Windows installation, the taskbar contains four buttons, described in TABLE 1-1. Also on the taskbar is the search box, which you can use to find an item on your computer or the Internet. On the right side of the status bar you see the **Notification area**, containing the time and date as well as icons that tell you the status of your computer. At the left side of the taskbar, you see the Start button. You click the **Start button** to display the **Start menu**, which lets you start the programs on your computer.

2. **Move the pointer to the left side of the taskbar, then click or tap the** Start button ⊞

   The Start menu appears, as shown in FIGURE 1-6. Your user account name and an optional picture appear at the top. The menu shows a list of often-used programs and other controls on the left, and variously-sized shaded rectangles called **tiles** on the right. Each tile represents an **app**, short for **application program**. Some tiles show updated content using a feature called **live tile**; for example, the Weather app can show the current weather for any city you choose. (Your screen color and tiles may differ from the figures shown here. Note that the screens in this book do not show live tiles.)

3. **Move the pointer near the bottom of the Start menu, then click or tap the** All apps button

   You see an alphabetical listing of all the apps on your computer. Only some of the apps are visible.

4. **Move the pointer into the list, until the gray scroll bar appears on the right side of the list, place the pointer over the** scroll box, **press and hold down the** mouse button, **then drag to display the remaining programs; on a touch screen, swipe the list to scroll**

5. **Click or tap the** Back button **at the bottom of the Start menu**

   The previous listing reappears.

6. **Move the pointer back up over the desktop, then click or tap once to close the Start menu**

FIGURE 1-5: Windows 10 desktop

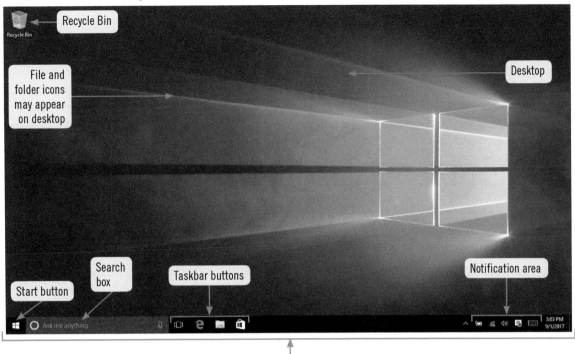

Recycle Bin

File and folder icons may appear on desktop

Desktop

Search box

Start button

Taskbar buttons

Notification area

Taskbar

FIGURE 1-6: Start menu

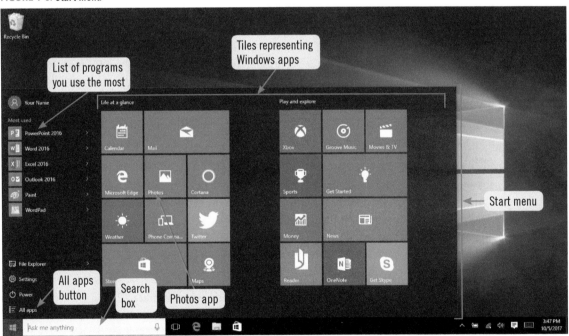

List of programs you use the most

Tiles representing Windows apps

Start menu

All apps button

Search box

Photos app

TABLE 1-1: Windows taskbar buttons

button	looks like	what it does
Task View		Shows miniatures of all open windows and lets you create multiple desktops, so you can switch from one to another
Microsoft Edge		Opens the Microsoft Edge web browser
File Explorer		Lets you explore the files in your storage locations
Store		Opens the Windows Store featuring downloadable apps, games, music, movies, and TV

Point, Click, and Drag

Learning Outcomes
- Point to, select, and deselect a desktop icon
- Move a desktop icon

You communicate with Windows 10 using a variety of pointing devices (or, with a touch-screen device, your finger). A **pointing device** controls the movement of the **pointer**, a small arrow or other symbol that moves on the screen. Your pointing device could be a mouse, trackball, graphics tablet, or touchpad. There are five basic **pointing device actions** you use to communicate with your computer; see TABLE 1-2. Touch-screen users can tap, press, and tap and hold. **CASE** *You practice the basic pointing device actions.*

STEPS

1. **Locate the pointer ⃕ on the desktop, then move your pointing device left, right, up, and down (or move your finger across a touch pad or screen)**
   The pointer shape ⃕ is the **Select pointer**. The pointer moves in the same direction as your device.

2. **Move your pointing device so the Select pointer is over the Recycle Bin (if you are using a touch screen, skip this step)**
   You are **pointing to** the Recycle Bin icon. The icon becomes **highlighted**, looking as though it is framed in a box with a lighter color background. (Note that touch-screen users cannot point to items.)

3. **While pointing to the Recycle Bin icon, press and quickly release the left mouse button once (or tap the icon once), then move the pointer away from the Recycle Bin icon**
   You click or tap a desktop icon once to **select** it, which signals that you intend to perform an action. When an icon is selected, its background changes color and maintains the new color even when you point away from it.

4. **With a pointing device, point to (don't click) the Microsoft Edge button 🅴 on the taskbar**
   The button becomes highlighted and an informational message called a **ScreenTip** identifies the program the button represents. ScreenTips are useful because they help you to learn about the tools available to you. **Microsoft Edge** is the new Microsoft web browser that lets you display and interact with webpages.

5. **If you are using a pointing device, move the pointer over the time and date in the notification area on the right side of the taskbar, read the ScreenTip, then click or tap once**
   A pop-up window appears, containing the current time and date and a calendar.

6. **Click or tap on the desktop, point to the Recycle Bin icon, then quickly click or tap twice**
   You **double-clicked** (or double-tapped) the icon. You need to double-click or double-tap quickly, without moving the pointer. A window opens, showing the contents of the Recycle Bin, as shown in FIGURE 1-7. The area at the top of the window is the title bar, which displays the name of the window. The area below the title bar is the **Ribbon**, which contains tabs, commands, and the Address bar. **Tabs** are groupings of **buttons** and other controls you use to interact with an object or a program.

7. **Click or tap the View tab**
   The buttons on that tab appear. Buttons act as **commands**, which instruct Windows to perform tasks. The **Address bar** shows the name and location of the item you have opened.

8. **Point to the Close button ✕ on the title bar, read the ScreenTip, then click or tap once**

9. **Point to the Recycle Bin icon, hold down the left mouse button, or press and hold the Recycle Bin image with your finger, move the mouse or drag so the object moves right as shown in FIGURE 1-8, release the mouse button or lift your finger, then drag the Recycle Bin back to its original location**

FIGURE 1-7: Recycle Bin window

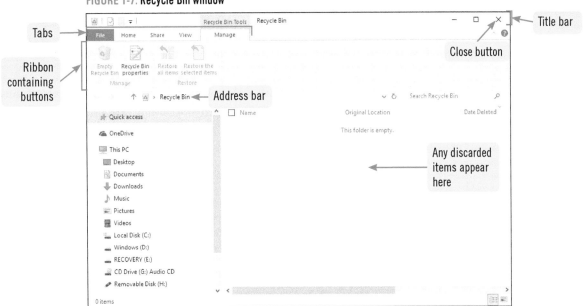

Tabs

Ribbon containing buttons

Address bar

Title bar

Close button

Any discarded items appear here

FIGURE 1-8: Dragging the Recycle Bin icon

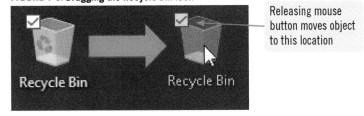

Releasing mouse button moves object to this location

TABLE 1-2: Basic pointing device actions

action	with a mouse	with a touch pad	use to
Point	Move mouse to position tip of pointer over an item	Move your finger over touch pad to position tip of pointer over an item	Highlight items or display small informational boxes called ScreenTips
Click	Press and release left mouse button once	Tap touch pad once	Select objects or commands, open menus or items on the taskbar
Double-click	Quickly press and release left mouse button twice	Tap touch pad twice in quick succession	Open programs, folders, or files represented by desktop icons
Drag	Point to an object, press and hold down left mouse button, move object to a new location, then release mouse button	Slide finger across touch pad to point to an object, press and hold left touch pad button, drag across touch pad to move object to new location, then release button	Move objects, such as icons, on the desktop
Right-click	Point to an object, then press and release right mouse button	Point to an object, then press and release right touchpad button	Display a shortcut menu containing options specific to the object

Selecting and moving items using touch-screen devices

If you use a touch-screen computer, a tablet, or a smartphone, you click desktop items by tapping them once on the screen. Tap an icon twice quickly to double-click and open its window. Press and hold an icon, then drag to move it. A touch-screen device does not let you point to an object without selecting it, however, as mice and touchpads do.

Start an App

Apps are programs that let you perform tasks. Windows 10 runs Windows apps and desktop apps. **Windows apps** are small programs that are available free or for purchase in the Windows Store, and can run on Windows desktops, laptops, tablets, and phones. Windows apps are also called **universal apps**. They are specially designed so they can stay open as you work without slowing down your computer, and often have a single purpose. Examples include the Photos app, which lets you view your photographs, and the OneDrive app, which lets you connect to files and programs you have stored on the Microsoft OneDrive website. **Desktop apps** are fully-featured programs; they may be available at an online store or on disk. For example, Microsoft Word allows you to create and edit letters, reports, and other text-based documents. Some smaller desktop apps called **Windows accessories**, such as Paint and Notepad, come already installed in Windows 10. **CASE** ▶ *To prepare for your new job, you start three apps.*

STEPS

1. **Click or tap the** Start button ⊞, **then click or tap the** Weather tile, **shown in** FIGURE 1-9
   The Weather app opens, letting you find the current weather in various locations.

2. **If you are asked to choose a location, begin typing your city or town, then click the full name if it appears in the drop-down list**
   The current weather for your selected city appears in Summary view. FIGURE 1-10 shows a forecast for Boston, MA.

3. **Click or tap the Weather app window's** Close button ✕

4. **Click or tap** ⊞, **then type** onenote
   Typing an app name is another way to locate an app. At the top of the Start menu, you see the OneNote Trusted Windows Store app listed, as shown in FIGURE 1-11. OneNote is a popular app that lets you create tabbed notebooks where you can store text, images, files, and media such as audio and video.

5. **Click or tap the** OneNote Trusted Windows Store app name
   The OneNote app opens, showing a blank notebook (or a notebook you have previously created).

6. **Click or tap the** Close button ✕ **in the upper right corner of the OneNote app window**
   You have opened two Windows apps, Weather and OneNote.

7. **Click or tap** ⊞, **then type** paint
   The top of the Start menu lists the Paint Desktop app, shown in FIGURE 1-12. Paint is a simple accessory that comes installed with Windows and lets you create simple illustrations.

8. **Click or tap the** Paint Desktop app name **at the top of the Start menu**
   Other accessories besides Paint and Notepad include the Snipping Tool, which lets you capture an image of any screen area, and Sticky Notes, that let you create short notes.

Using the Windows Store

The Windows Store is an app that lets you find all kinds of apps for use on Windows personal computers, tablets, and phones. You can open it by clicking or tapping its tile on the Start menu or by clicking or tapping the Store button on the taskbar. To use the Windows Store, you need to be signed in to your Microsoft account. You can browse lists of popular apps, games, music, movies, and TV including new releases; you can browse the top paid or free apps. Browse app categories to find a specific type of app, such as Business or Entertainment. To locate a specific app, type its name in the Search box. If an app is free, you can go to its page and click the Free button to install it on your computer. If it's a paid app, you can click or tap the Free trial button to try it out, or click or tap its price button to purchase it. Any apps you've added recently appear in the Recently added category of the Start menu.

FIGURE 1-9: Weather tile on the Start menu

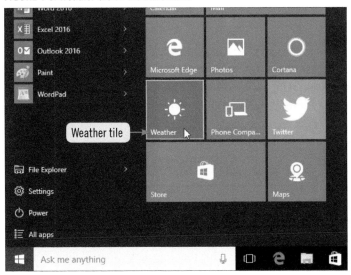

FIGURE 1-10: Weather app

FIGURE 1-11: OneNote Windows app name on Start menu

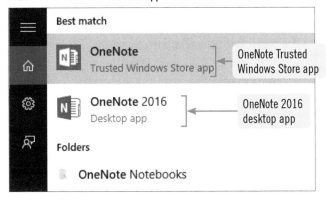

FIGURE 1-12: Paint Desktop app name on Start menu

Work with a Window

Learning
Outcomes
• Minimize, restore,
  and maximize a
  window
• Scroll a window
• Move a window

When you start an app, its **window**, a frame displaying the app's tools, opens. In many apps, a blank file also opens so you can start creating a new document. For example, in Paint, a blank document opens so you can start drawing right away. All windows in the Windows 10 operating system have similar window elements. Once you can use a window in one app, you will know how to work with windows in many other apps. **CASE** *To become more familiar with the Windows 10 user interface, you explore elements in the Paint window.*

DETAILS

Many windows have the following common elements. Refer to FIGURE 1-13:

- At the top of the window, you see a **title bar**, a strip that contains the name of the document and app. This document has not been saved, so it has the temporary name "Untitled" and the app name is "Paint."

- On the right side of the title bar, the **Window control buttons** let you control the app window. The **Minimize button** — temporarily hides the window, making it a button on the taskbar. The app is still running, but its window is temporarily hidden until you click its taskbar button or its miniature window in Task view to reopen it. The **Maximize button** ☐ enlarges the window to fill the entire screen. If a window is already maximized, the Maximize button changes to the **Restore Down button** ❐, which reduces it to the last non-maximized size. Clicking or tapping the **Close button** ☒ closes the app.

- Many windows have a **scroll bar** on the right side and/or the bottom of the window. You click (or press) and drag scroll bar elements to show additional parts of your document. See TABLE 1-3.

- Just below the title bar is the Ribbon, a bar containing tabs as well as a Help icon. The Paint window has three tabs: File, Home, and View. Tabs are divided into **groups** of buttons and tool palettes. The Home tab has five groups: Clipboard, Image, Tools, Shapes, and Colors. Many apps also include **menus** you click to show lists of commands, as well as **toolbars** containing buttons.

- The **Quick Access toolbar** lets you quickly perform common actions such as saving a file.

STEPS

1. **Click or tap the Paint window** Minimize button —
   The app is reduced to a taskbar button, as shown in FIGURE 1-14. The contrasting line indicates the app is still open.

2. **Click or tap the taskbar button representing the** Paint app 🎨 **to redisplay the app**

3. **Drag the gray** scroll box **down, notice the lower edge of the work area that appears, then click or tap the** Up scroll arrow 🔼 **until you see the top edge of the work area**

4. **Point to the** View tab, **then click or tap the** View tab **once**
   Clicking or tapping the View tab moved it in front of the Home tab. This tab has three groups containing buttons that let you change your view of the document window.

5. **Click the** Home tab, **then click or tap the Paint window** Maximize button ☐
   The window fills the screen, and the Maximize button becomes the Restore Down button ❐.

6. **Click the window's** Restore Down button ❐ **to return it to its previous size**

7. **Point to the** Paint window title bar **(if you are using a pointing device), then drag about an inch to the right to move it so it's centered on the screen**

FIGURE 1-13: **Typical app window elements**

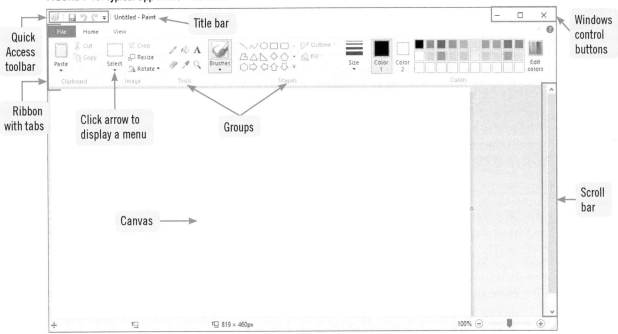

Quick Access toolbar

Title bar

Windows control buttons

Ribbon with tabs

Click arrow to display a menu

Groups

Scroll bar

Canvas

FIGURE 1-14: **Taskbar with minimized Paint program button**

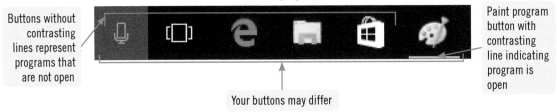

Buttons without contrasting lines represent programs that are not open

Paint program button with contrasting line indicating program is open

Your buttons may differ

TABLE 1-3: **Parts of a scroll bar**

name	looks like	to use
Scroll box	(Size may vary)	Drag to scroll quickly through a long document
Scroll arrows		Click or tap to scroll up, down, left, or right in small amounts
Shaded area	(Above, below, or to either side of scroll box)	Click or tap to move up or down by one screen

Using the Quick Access toolbar

On the left side of the title bar, the Quick Access toolbar lets you perform common tasks with just one click. The Save button saves the changes you have made to a document. The Undo button lets you reverse (undo) the last action you performed.

The Redo button reinstates the change you just undid. Use the Customize Quick Access Toolbar button to add other frequently used buttons to the toolbar, move the toolbar below the Ribbon, or minimize the Ribbon to show only tabs.

Manage Multiple Windows

Learning
Outcomes
• Open a second
  app
• Activate a window
• Resize, snap, and
  close a window

You can work with more than one app at a time by switching among open app windows. If you open two or more apps, a window opens for each one. You can work with app windows individually, going back and forth between them. The window in front is called the **active window**. Any open window behind the active window is called an **inactive window**. For ease in working with multiple windows, you can move, arrange, make them smaller or larger, minimize, or restore them so they're not in the way. To resize a window, drag a window's edge, called its **border**. You can use the taskbar to switch between windows. See TABLE 1-4 for a summary of taskbar actions. **CASE** ▷ *Keeping the Paint app open, you open the OneNote app and then work with both app windows.*

STEPS

1. **With Paint open, click or tap the Start button ▦, then the OneNote tile**

   The OneNote window appears as a second window on the desktop, as shown in FIGURE 1-15. The OneNote window is in front, indicating that it is the active window. The Paint window is the inactive window. On the taskbar, the contrasting line under the OneNote and Paint app buttons tell you both apps are open.

2. **Point to a blank part of the OneNote window title bar on either side of the app name (if you are using a pointing device), then drag the OneNote window down slightly so you can see more of the Paint window**

3. **Click or tap once on the Paint window's title bar**

   The Paint window is now the active window and appears in front of the OneNote window. You can make any window active by clicking or tapping it, or by clicking or tapping an app's icon in the taskbar.

4. **Point to the taskbar if you are using a pointing device, then click or tap the OneNote window button**

   The OneNote window becomes active. When you open multiple windows on the desktop, you may need to resize windows so they don't get in the way of other open windows.

TROUBLE
If you don't see the
lower-right corner of
the window, drag the
window up slightly
by its title bar.

5. **Point to the lower-right corner of the OneNote window until the pointer changes to ⬉, if you are using a pointing device, or tap and press the corner, then drag down and to the right about an inch to make the window larger**

   You can also point to any edge of a window until you see the ⟷ or ↕ pointer, or tap and press any edge, then drag to make it larger or smaller in one direction only.

QUICK TIP
To display Task view
using the keyboard,
press and hold ▦
and press [Tab]. You
can also move among
open windows by
pressing [Alt] + [Tab].

6. **Click or tap the Task View button ▣ on the taskbar, click or tap the Paint window, click or tap ▣ again, then click or tap the OneNote window**

   The **Task View button** is another convenient way to switch among open windows.

7. **Point to the OneNote window title bar if you are using a pointing device, drag the window to the left side of the screen until the pointer or your finger reaches the screen edge and you see a vertical line down the middle of the screen, then release the mouse button or lift your finger from the screen**

   The OneNote window instantly fills the left side of the screen, and any inactive windows appear on the right side of the screen. This is called the **Snap Assist** feature. You can also drag to any screen corner to snap open app windows to quarter-screen windows.

8. **Click or tap anywhere on the reduced-size version of the Paint window**

   The Paint window fills the right side of the screen. Snapping makes it easy to view the contents of two windows at the same time. See FIGURE 1-16.

9. **Click or tap the OneNote window Close button ✕, then click or tap the Maximize button ▢ in the Paint window's title bar**

   The OneNote app closes. The Paint app window remains open.

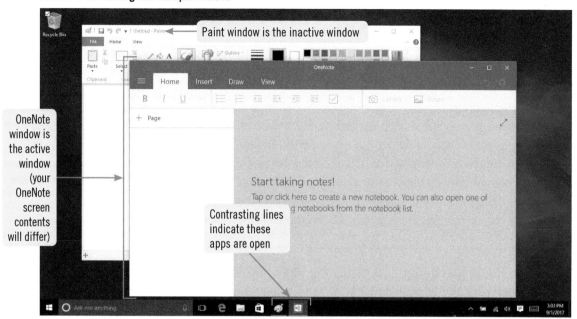

FIGURE 1-15: Working with multiple windows

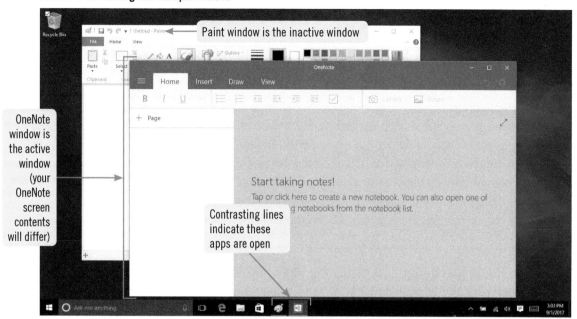

Paint window is the inactive window

OneNote
window is
the active
window
(your
OneNote
screen
contents
will differ)

Contrasting lines
indicate these
apps are open

FIGURE 1-16: OneNote and Paint windows snapped to each side of the screen

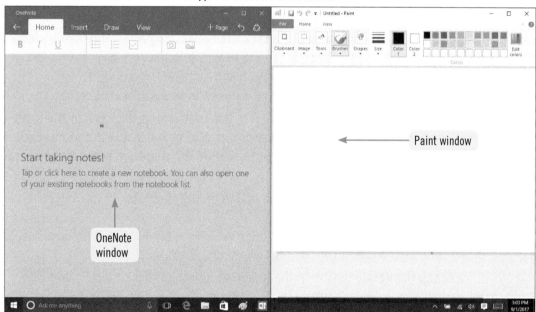

Paint window

OneNote
window

TABLE 1-4: Using the taskbar

to	do this
Add buttons to taskbar	Open an app, right-click or press its icon on the taskbar, then click or tap Pin this program to taskbar
Change order of taskbar buttons	Drag any icon to a new taskbar location
See a list of recent documents opened	Right-click or press taskbar app button
Close a document using the taskbar	Point to taskbar button, point to document image, then click its Close button
Minimize/Redisplay all open windows	Click or press Show desktop button (the thin bar) to the right of taskbar date and time
See preview of documents in taskbar	With a pointing device, point to taskbar button for open app
Bring a minimized window to the front	Click or press the Task View button, then click or tap the window or desktop you want in front
Rearrange windows on the desktop	Right-click taskbar, click Cascade Windows, Show windows stacked, or Show windows side by side

Learning Outcomes
- Use a button and a menu
- Work in a dialog box

Use Buttons, Menus, and Dialog Boxes

When you work in an app, you communicate with it using buttons, menus, and dialog boxes. **Buttons** let you issue instructions to modify app objects. Buttons are often organized on a Ribbon into tabs, and then into groups like those in the Paint window. Some buttons have text on them, and others show only an icon that represents what they do. Other buttons reveal **menus**, lists of commands you can choose. And some buttons open up a **dialog box**, a window with controls that lets you tell Windows what you want. TABLE 1-5 lists the common types of controls you find in dialog boxes. **CASE** *You practice using buttons, menus, and dialog boxes to create some simple graphics in the Paint app.*

STEPS

QUICK TIP
You might see a Shapes button instead of a gallery. If so, click the button, then click or tap △.

1. **In the Shapes group, click or tap the** More button ⏷ **just to the right of the shapes, then click the** Triangle button △

2. **Click or tap the** Turquoise button ▣ **in the Colors group, move the pointer or your finger over the white drawing area, then drag down and to the right, to draw a** triangle **similar to the one in** FIGURE 1-17

   The white drawing area is called the **canvas**.

QUICK TIP
If you need to move the selected object, use the keyboard arrow keys to move it left, right, up, or down while it is still selected.

3. **In the Shapes group, click or tap** ⏷**, click the** down scroll arrow **if necessary, click or tap the** Five-point star button, **click or tap the** Indigo color button ▣ **in the Colors group, then drag a star shape near the triangle, using** FIGURE 1-17 **as a guide**

   Don't be concerned if your object isn't exactly like the one in the figure, or in exactly the same place.

4. **Click or tap the** Fill with color button ⬥ **in the Tools group, click or tap the** Light turquoise color button ▢ **in the Colors group, click or tap inside the** triangle, **click or tap the** Purple color button ▣, **click or tap inside the** star, **then compare your drawing to** FIGURE 1-17

QUICK TIP
Windows apps generally do not have a menu bar; all the tools you need are included on the tabs.

5. **Click or tap the** Select list arrow **in the Image group, then click or tap** Select all, **as shown in** FIGURE 1-18

   The Select all command selects the entire drawing, as indicated by the dotted line surrounding the white drawing area. Other commands on this menu let you select individual elements or change your selection.

6. **Click or tap the** Rotate button **in the Image group, then click or tap** Rotate 180°

   You often need to use multiple commands to perform an action—in this case, you used one command to select the items you wanted to work with, and another command to rotate them.

7. **Click or tap the** File tab, **then click or tap** Print

   The Print dialog box opens, as shown in FIGURE 1-19. This dialog box lets you choose a printer, specify which part of your document or drawing you want to print, and choose how many copies you want to print. The **default**, or automatically selected, number of copies is 1, which is what you want.

8. **Click or tap** Print, **or if you prefer not to print, click or tap** Cancel

   The drawing prints on your printer. You decide to close the app without saving your drawing.

9. **Click or tap the** File tab, **click or tap** Exit, **then click or tap** Don't Save

   You closed the file without saving your changes, then exited the app. Most apps include a command for closing a document without exiting the program. However, Paint allows you to open only one document at a time, so it does not include a Close command.

FIGURE 1-17: **Triangle and star shapes filled with color**

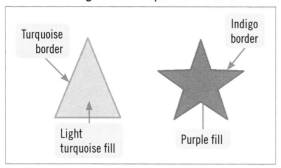

Turquoise border

Indigo border

Light turquoise fill

Purple fill

FIGURE 1-18: **Select menu options**

Select list arrow

Select menu

Select all command

FIGURE 1-19: **Print dialog box**

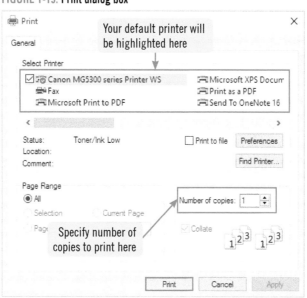

Your default printer will be highlighted here

Specify number of copies to print here

TABLE 1-5: **Common dialog box controls**

element	example	description
Text box	1 - 27	A box in which you type text or numbers
Spin box	1	A box with up and down arrows; you can click or tap arrows or type to increase or decrease value
Option button	⊙	A small circle you click or tap to select the option; only one in a set can be selected at once
Check box	☑	A small box that turns an option on when checked or off when unchecked; more than one in a set can be selected at once
List box		A box that lets you select from a list of options
Button	Save	A button you click or tap to issue a command

Get Help

As you use Windows 10, you might feel ready to learn more about it, or you might have a problem and need some advice. You can use the Windows 10 Getting Started app to learn more about help options. You can also search for help using Cortana, which you activate by using the search box on the taskbar. **CASE** *You explore Windows 10 help using the Get Started app and Cortana.*

STEPS

Note: Because Help in an online resource, topics and information are liable to change over time. If your screen choices do not match the steps below exactly, be flexible by exploring the options that are available to you and searching for the information you need.

1. Click or tap the Start button ⊞, then in the Explore Windows section click or tap the Get Started tile; if the Explore Windows section does not appear on your Start menu, begin typing Get Started, then click or tap Get Started Trusted Windows Store app in the list

   The Get Started app window opens. The window contains a menu expand button ≡ in the upper left and a bar containing buttons on the left side.

2. Click or tap the Menu Expand button ≡, move the pointer over the list of topics, then scroll down to see the remaining topics

3. Click or tap the Search and help topic, click the Search for anything, anywhere tile, then read the information, as shown in FIGURE 1-20, scrolling as necessary

4. Click or tap the Back button ← in the top-left corner of the window, click the Search for help tile, then read the Search for help topic and watch any available videos

5. Click or tap ≡, click or tap a topic that interests you, then read the information or click or tap one of the tiles representing a subtopic if one is available

6. After you have read the information, click or tap the Get started window's Close button ✕

   As the Help topic explained, you can also search the web for help with Windows using Cortana.

7. Click in the search box on the taskbar, then type windows help

   As you type, Cortana begins a search, and shows results on the Start menu. See FIGURE 1-21. Your results may also include topics from the Microsoft Store, the web, Store apps, and OneDrive, your online storage location.

8. Click any web option that interests you

9. When you are finished, click or tap the window's Close button ✕ to return to the desktop

FIGURE 1-20: Get Started Search and Help topic

Menu Expand button →

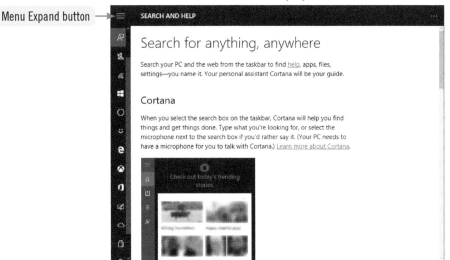

FIGURE 1-21: Search results information

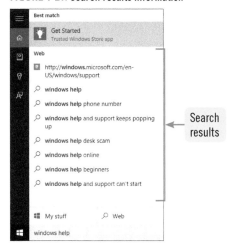

Search results →

Using Cortana

Cortana is the digital personal assistant that comes with Windows 10 and Windows phones. You can interact with Cortana typing or using your voice. Use Cortana to search the web, remind you of events or appointments, set alarms, change computer settings, get directions, get current news and weather, track airline flights, play, and even identify music. **FIGURE 1-22** shows Cortana's response to "What's the weather in New York?" which may also give a voice response. You call Cortana by saying, "Hey Cortana," or by clicking or tapping the microphone icon on the right side of the taskbar search box, and then asking a question or saying a command. Depending on your request, Cortana may reply out loud, display results in the Start menu, or display results in a Microsoft Edge web browser window. You may need to set up Cortana on your computer and answer security questions before you use it. The first time you use Cortana, you may be asked to answer questions to help the assistant recognize your voice or solve issues with your computer's microphone.

FIGURE 1-22: Using Cortana to check the weather

Symbol indicates Cortana is standing by

Cortana's response to a request for the weather

Information requested

Voice request appears in search box

Exit Windows 10

Learning
Outcomes
• Exit Windows and
 shut down

When you finish working on your computer, you should close any open files, exit any open apps, close any open windows, and exit (or **shut down**) Windows 10. TABLE 1-6 shows options for ending your Windows 10 sessions. Whichever option you choose, it's important to shut down your computer in an orderly way. If you turn off or unplug the computer while Windows 10 is running, you could lose data or damage Windows 10 and your computer. If you are working in a computer lab, follow your instructor's directions and your lab's policies for ending your Windows 10 session. **CASE** *You have examined the basic ways you can use Windows 10, so you are ready to end your Windows 10 session.*

STEPS

QUICK TIP

Instead of shutting down, you may be instructed to sign out, or log out, of your Microsoft account. Click or tap Start, click or tap your account name, then click or tap Sign out.

1. **Click or tap the** Start button ⊞**, then click or tap** Power

   The Power button menu lists shut down options, as shown in FIGURE 1-23.

2. **If you are working in a computer lab, follow the instructions provided by your instructor or technical support person for ending your Windows 10 session; if you are working on your own computer, click or tap** Shut down **or the option you prefer for ending your Windows 10 session**

QUICK TIP

If you are using a Windows 10 tablet, press the lock button on your tablet to bring up the lock screen, swipe the lock screen, then click or tap the Shut down button to power off your computer.

3. **After you shut down your computer, you may also need to turn off your monitor and other hardware devices, such as a printer, to conserve energy**

Getting Started with Windows 10

FIGURE 1-23: **Shutting down your computer**

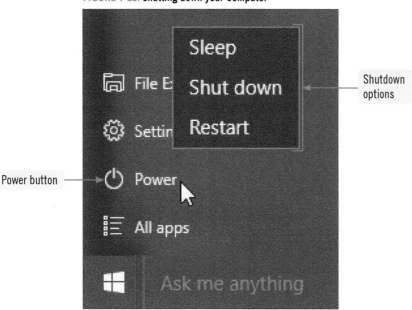

Power button →

Shutdown options

TABLE 1-6: **Power options**

option	description
Sleep	Puts computer in a low-power state while keeping any open apps open so you can return immediately to where you left off
Shut down	Closes any open apps and completely turns off the computer
Restart	Closes any open apps, shuts down the computer, then restarts it

Installing updates when you exit Windows

Sometimes, after you shut down your machine, you might find that your machine does not shut down immediately. Instead, Windows might install software updates. If you see an option on your Power menu that lets you update, you can click or tap it to update your software. If you see a window indicating that updates are being installed, do not unplug or press the power switch to turn off your machine. Let the updates install completely. After the updates are installed, your computer will shut down, as you originally requested.

Practice

Concepts Review

Label the elements of the Windows 10 window shown in FIGURE 1-24.

FIGURE 1-24

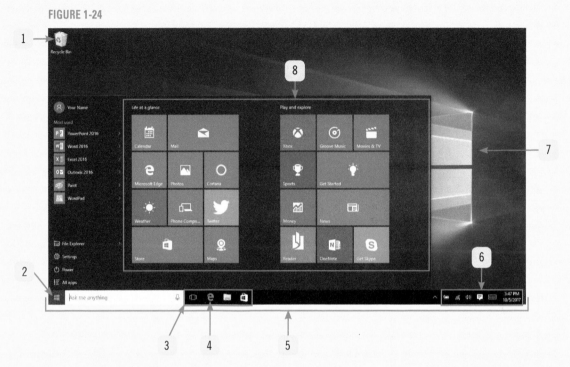

Match each term with the statement that best describes it.

9. Cortana
10. Snap Assist
11. Desktop app
12. Microsoft account
13. User interface
14. Operating system
15. Windows app

a. A special area of the operating system where your files and settings are stored
b. Controls that let you interact with an operating system
c. The personal digital assistant in Windows 10
d. Full-featured program that is installed on a personal computer
e. Feature that displays windows at full height next to each other on the screen
f. Available from the Windows store, it runs on Windows laptops, tablets, and phones
g. A program necessary to run your computer

Select the best answer from the list of choices.

16. The bar containing buttons and other elements at the bottom of the Windows 10 desktop is called the _____.
    a. title bar
    b. address bar
    c. scroll bar
    d. taskbar

17. Paint is an example of a(n) _____.
    a. group
    b. accessory
    c. active window
    d. operating system

18. **Which of the following is in the upper-left corner of a program window, and lets you perform common actions?**
   a. Application program
   b. Quick Access toolbar
   c. Operating system
   d. Accessory program

19. **The new Microsoft web browser is called Microsoft _____.**
   a. Paint
   b. WordPad
   c. Edge
   d. File Explorer

Skills Review

1. **Start Windows 10.**
   a. If your computer and monitor are not running, press your computer's and (if necessary) your monitor's power buttons.
   b. If necessary, select the user name that represents your user account.
   c. Enter your password, using correct uppercase and lowercase letters.

2. **Navigate the desktop and Start menu.**
   a. Examine the Windows 10 desktop.
   b. Open the Start menu.
   c. Display all the apps using a command on the Start menu, and scroll the list.
   d. Return to the Start menu.
   e. Close the Start menu.

3. **Point, click, and drag.**
   a. On the Windows 10 desktop, click or tap to select the Recycle Bin.
   b. Point to display the ScreenTip for Microsoft Edge in the taskbar, and then display the ScreenTip for each of the other icons on the taskbar.
   c. Double-click or double-tap to open the Recycle Bin window, then close it.
   d. Drag the Recycle Bin to a different corner of the screen, then drag it back to its original location.
   e. Click or tap the Date and Time area to display the calendar and clock, then click or tap it again to close it.

4. **Start an app.**
   a. Open the Start menu, then start the Maps app. (If asked to allow Windows to access your location, do so if you like.)
   b. Click or tap the icons on the left side of the Maps app window and observe the effect of each one.
   c. Close the Maps app.
   d. Reopen the Start menu, then type and click or tap to locate and open the Sticky Notes accessory.
   e. Click or tap the Sticky Notes Close button, clicking or tapping Yes to delete the note.
   f. Open the Weather Windows app.

5. **Work with a window.**
   a. Minimize the Weather window, then use its taskbar button to redisplay the window.
   b. Use the Weather app window's scroll bar or swiping to view the information in the lower part of the window, and then scroll or swipe up to display the top of it. (*Hint*: You need to move the pointer over the Weather app window, or swipe it, in order to display the scroll bar.)
   c. Click or tap the menu expand button, then click Historical Weather.
   d. Read the contents of the window, then click or tap two other menu buttons and read the contents.
   e. Maximize the Weather window, then restore it down.

6. **Manage multiple windows.**
   a. Leaving the Weather app open, go to the Start menu and type to locate the Paint app, open Paint, then restore down the Paint window if necessary.
   b. Click or tap to make the Weather app window the active window.
   c. Click or tap to make the Paint window the active window.
   d. Minimize the Paint window.

Skills Review (continued)

   e. Drag the Weather app window so it's in the middle of the screen.

   f. Redisplay the Paint window.

   g. Drag the Paint window so it automatically fills the right side of the screen.

FIGURE 1-25

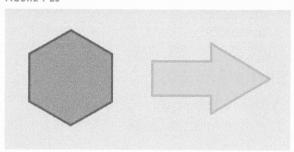

   h. Click or tap the Weather app window image so it snaps to the left side of the screen.

   i. Close the Weather app window, maximize the Paint window, then restore down the Paint window.

7. Use buttons, menus, and dialog boxes.

   a. In the Paint window, draw a Dark red Hexagon shape, similar to the one shown in FIGURE 1-25.

   b. Use the Fill with color button to fill the hexagon with a brown color.

   c. Draw an Orange right arrow to the right of the hexagon shape, using the figure as a guide.

   d. Use the Fill with color button to fill the orange arrow with a lime color.

   e. Fill the drawing background with Light turquoise color, as shown in the figure.

   f. Use the Select list arrow and menu to select the entire drawing, then use the Rotate command to rotate the drawing 180°.

   g. Open the Print dialog box, print a copy of the picture if you wish, then close the Paint app without saving the drawing.

8. Get help.

   a. Open the Get Started app, then use the menu expand button to display the available help topics.

   b. Use the Menu button to display help for Cortana.

   c. Click or tap a tile representing a Cortana help topic that interests you, read the help text, scrolling or swiping as necessary.

   d. Display the Search and Help topic, then close the Get Started window.

   e. In the search box on the taskbar, type Help Microsoft Account, then click the help Microsoft account result to search the web.

   f. In the Microsoft Edge browser window, select a help topic that interests you, read the information (ignore any commercial offers), then click or tap the Microsoft Edge window's Close button.

9. Exit Windows 10.

   a. Sign out of your account, or shut down your computer using the Shut down command in the Start menu's Power command or the preferred command for your work or school setting.

   b. Turn off your monitor if necessary.

Independent Challenge 1

You work for Chicago Instruments, a manufacturer of brass instruments. The company ships instruments and supplies to music stores and musicians in the United States and Canada. The owner, Emerson, wants to know an easy way for his employees to learn about the new features of Windows 10, and he has asked you to help.

   a. Start your computer if necessary, sign in to Windows 10, then use the search text box to search for **what's new in Windows 10**.

   b. Click or tap the Search the web link in the Best match section at the top of the Help menu, then in the Microsoft Edge browser window, click or tap a search result that interests you.

   c. Open the Getting Started app and review the new features listed there.

   d. Using pencil and paper, or the Notepad accessory if you wish, write a short memo to Emerson summarizing, in your own words, three important new features in Windows 10. If you use Notepad to write the memo, use the Print button to print the document, then use the Exit command on the File tab to close Notepad without saving your changes to the document.

Independent Challenge 1 (continued)

e. Close the browser window, then sign out of your account, or shut down your computer using the preferred command for your work or school setting. Turn off your monitor if necessary.

Independent Challenge 2

You are the new manager of Katharine Anne's Garden Supplies, a business that supplies garden tools to San Diego businesses. Some of their tools are from Europe and show metric sizes. For her American customers, Katharine Anne wants to do a simple calculation and then convert the result to inches.

a. Start your computer and log on to Windows 10 if necessary, then type to locate the Windows app called Calculator, and start it.

b. Click or tap to enter the number 96 on the Calculator.

c. Click or tap the division sign (÷) button.

d. Click or tap the number 4.

e. Click or tap the equals sign button (=), and write down the result shown in the Calculator window. (*Hint*: The result should be 24.)

f. Select the menu expand button in the Calculator window, then under CONVERTER, select Length.

g. Enter 24 centimeters, and observe the equivalent length in inches.

h. Start Notepad, write a short memo about how Calculator can help you convert metric measurements to inches and feet, print the document using the Print command on the File tab, then exit Notepad without saving.

i. Close the Calculator, then sign out of your account, or shut down your computer using the preferred command for your work or school setting. Turn off your monitor if necessary.

Independent Challenge 3

You are the office manager for Erica's Pet Shipping, a service business in Dallas, Texas, that specializes in air shipping of cats and dogs across the United States and Canada. It's important to know the temperature in the destination city, so the animals won't be in danger from extreme temperatures when they are unloaded from the aircraft. Erica has asked you to find a way to easily monitor temperatures in destination cities. You decide to use a Windows app so you can see current temperatures in Celsius on your desktop. (Note: To complete the steps below, your computer must be connected to the Internet.)

a. Start your computer and sign in to Windows 10 if necessary, then on the Start menu, click or tap the Weather tile.

b. Click or tap the Search icon in the location text box, then type **Toronto**.

c. Select Toronto, Ontario, Canada, in the drop-down list to view the weather for Toronto.

d. Search on and select another location that interests you.

e. Close the app.

f. Open Notepad, write Erica a memo outlining how you can use the Windows Weather app to help keep pets safe, print the memo if you wish, close Notepad, then sign out, or shut down your computer.

Independent Challenge 4: Explore

Cortana, the Windows 10 personal digital assistant, can help you with everyday tasks. In this Independent Challenge, you explore one of the ways you can use Cortana.

a. Click or tap the microphone icon, to the right of the search box in the Windows 10 taskbar, to activate Cortana and display its menu. (*Note*: If you have not used Cortana before, you will not see the microphone icon until you answer some preliminary questions and verify your user account; you may also need to first help Cortana to understand your speaking voice.) Cortana displays a pulsating circle, indicating that she is listening for speech, and then shows you a greeting and some general information.

Independent Challenge 4: Explore (continued)

FIGURE 1-26

b. In the list of icons on the left side of the menu, click the menu expand button to show the names of each one, as shown in FIGURE 1-26.

c. Click or tap the Reminders button, then click the plus sign at the bottom of the menu. Click or tap Remember to..., then enter information for a to-do item, such as "Walk the dog." Click or tap the time box and use the spin boxes to set the time for one or two minutes from now. Click or tap the check mark, then click Remind to set the reminder. Click or tap the Reminders icon again to see your reminder listed, then click the desktop. When the reminder appears, click Complete.

d. Click or tap the microphone icon again, and when you see the pulsating circle, speak into your computer microphone and tell Cortana to remind you to do something in one minute. Click or tap Remind, then close the Cortana window. When the reminder appears, click or tap Complete.

e. Click or tap the Close button on the Cortana menu, then sign out of your account, or shut down your computer.

Visual Workshop

Using the skills you've learned in this module, open and arrange elements on your screen so it looks similar to FIGURE 1-27. Note the position of the Recycle Bin, and the size and location of the Notepad and Weather app windows, as well as the city shown. In Notepad, write a paragraph summarizing how you used pointing, clicking (or tapping), and dragging to make your screen look like the figure. Print your work if you wish, close Notepad and the Weather app without saving changes, then sign out or shut down your computer.

FIGURE 1-27

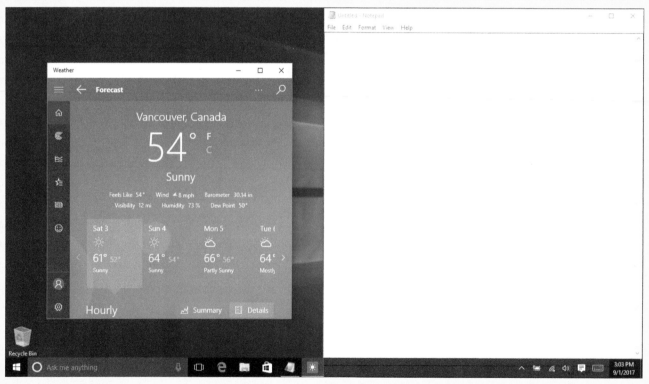

Understanding File Management

CASE ▶ Now that you are familiar with the Windows 10 operating system, your new employer has asked you to become familiar with **file management**, or how to create, save, locate and delete the files you create with Windows apps. You begin by reviewing how files are organized on your computer, and then begin working with files you create in the WordPad app. *Note: With the release of Windows 10, Microsoft now provides ongoing updates to Windows instead of releasing new versions periodically. This means that Windows features might change over time, including how they look and how you interact with them. The information provided in this text was accurate at the time this book was published.*

Module Objectives

After completing this module, you will be able to:

- Understand files and folders
- Create and save a file
- Explore the files and folders on your computer
- Change file and folder views

- Open, edit, and save files
- Copy files
- Move and rename files
- Search for files and folders
- Delete and restore files

Files You Will Need

No files needed.

Understand Files and Folders

Learning
Outcomes
• Analyze a file
  hierarchy
• Examine files and
  folders

As you work with apps, you create and save files, such as letters, drawings, or budgets. When you save files, you usually save them inside folders to help keep them organized. The files and folders on your computer are organized in a **file hierarchy**, a system that arranges files and folders in different levels, like the branches of a tree. FIGURE 2-1 shows a sample file hierarchy. **CASE** ▸ *You decide to use folders and files to organize the information on your computer.*

DETAILS

Use the following guidelines as you organize files using your computer's file hierarchy:

• **Use folders and subfolders to organize files**

  As you work with your computer, you can add folders to your hierarchy and name them to help you organize your work. As you've learned, folders are storage areas in which you can group related files. You should give folders unique names that help you easily identify them. You can also create **subfolders**, which are folders that are inside other folders. Windows 10 comes with several existing folders, such as Documents, Music, Pictures, and Videos, that you can use as a starting point.

QUICK TIP

When you open File Explorer, you see a list of recently opened files and frequently used folders in the Quick Access area that helps you go directly to files and locations.

• **View and manage files in File Explorer**

  You can view and manage your computer contents using a built-in program called **File Explorer**, shown in FIGURE 2-2. A File Explorer window is divided into **panes**, or sections. The **Navigation pane** on the left side of the window shows the folder structure on your computer. When you click a folder in the Navigation pane, you see its contents in the **File list** on the right side of the window. To open File Explorer from the desktop, click the File Explorer button ▣ on the taskbar. To open it from the Start menu, click the File Explorer shortcut.

QUICK TIP

The name "File Explorer" only appears in the title bar when you first open it. As you navigate, you'll see the current folder name instead.

• **Understand file addresses**

  A window also contains an **Address bar**, an area just below the Ribbon that shows the address, or location, of the files that appear in the File list. An **address** is a sequence of folder names, separated by the ▸ symbol, which describes a file's location in the file hierarchy. An address shows the folder with the highest hierarchy level on the left and steps through each hierarchy level toward the right; this is sometimes called a **path**. For example, the Documents folder might contain subfolders named Work and Personal. If you clicked the Personal folder in the File list, the Address bar would show Documents ▸ Personal. Each location between the ▸ symbols represents a level in the file hierarchy. If you see a file path written out, you'll most likely see it with backslashes. For example, in FIGURE 2-1, if you wanted to write the path to the Brochure file, you would write "Documents\Reason2Go\Marketing\Brochure.xlsx. File addresses might look complicated if they may have many levels, but they are helpful because they always describe the exact location of a file or folder in a file hierarchy.

QUICK TIP

Remember that in the Address bar and Navigation pane you single-click a folder or subfolder to show its contents, but in the File list you double-click it.

• **Navigate up and down using the Address bar and File list**

  You can use the Address bar and the File list to move up or down in the hierarchy one or more levels at a time. To **navigate up** in your computer's hierarchy, you can click a folder or subfolder name to the left of the current folder name in the Address bar. For example, in FIGURE 2-2, you can move up in the hierarchy three levels by clicking once on This PC in the Address bar. Then the File list would show the subfolders and files inside the This PC folder. To **navigate down** in the hierarchy, double-click a subfolder in the File list. The path in the Address bar then shows the path to that subfolder.

• **Navigate up and down using the Navigation pane**

  You can also use the Navigation pane to navigate among folders. Move the mouse pointer over the Navigation pane, then click the small arrows to the left of a folder name to show ▸ or hide ▾ the folder's contents under the folder name. Subfolders appear indented under the folders that contain them, showing that they are inside that folder.

FIGURE 2-1: **Sample folder and file hierarchy**

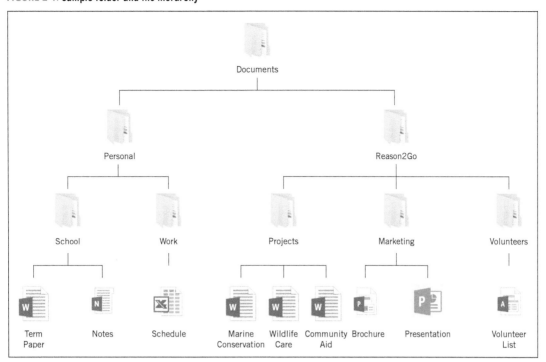

FIGURE 2-2: **File Explorer window**

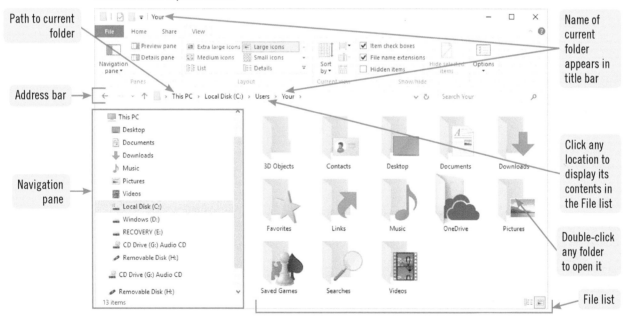

Path to current folder

Name of current folder appears in title bar

Address bar

Click any location to display its contents in the File list

Navigation pane

Double-click any folder to open it

File list

Plan your file organization

As you manage your files, you should plan how you want to organize them. First, identify the types of files you work with, such as images, music, and documents. Think about the content, such as personal, business, clients, or projects. Then think of a folder organization that will help you find them later. For example, you can use subfolders in the Pictures folder to separate family photos from business photos or to group them

by location or by month. In the Documents folder, you might group personal files in one subfolder and business files in another subfolder. Then create additional subfolders to further separate sets of files. You can always move files among folders and rename folders. You should periodically reevaluate your folder structure to make sure it continues to meet your needs.

Understanding File Management

Create and Save a File

Learning
Outcomes
• Start WordPad
• Create a file
• Save a file

After you start a program and create a new file, the file exists only in your computer's **random access memory (RAM)**, a temporary storage location. RAM contains information only when your computer is on. When you turn off your computer, it automatically clears the contents of RAM. So you need to save a new file onto a storage device that permanently stores the file so you can open, change, and use it later. One important storage device is your computer's hard drive built into your computer. You might want to store your files online in an online storage location like Microsoft OneDrive. Or you might use a **USB flash drive**, a small, portable storage device that you plug into a USB port on your computer. **CASE** *You create a document, then save it.*

STEPS

1. **Click or tap the Start button, then type** word
   Available apps with "word" in their names are listed. See FIGURE 2-3.

2. **Click the** WordPad Desktop app listing, **then maximize the WordPad window if necessary**
   Near the top of the WordPad window you see the Ribbon containing buttons, similar to those you used in Paint in Module 1. The Home tab appears in front. A new, blank document appears in the document window. The blinking insertion point shows you where the next character you type will appear.

3. **Type** Company Overview, **then press [Enter] twice, type** Conservation, **press [Enter], type** Community Work, **press [Enter], type** Research, **press [Enter] twice, then type your name**
   See FIGURE 2-4.

4. **Click the** File tab, **then click** Save
   The first time you save a file using the Save button, the Save As dialog box opens. You use this dialog box to name the file and choose a storage location for it. The Save As dialog box has many of the same elements as a File Explorer window, including an Address bar, a Navigation pane, and a File list. Below the Address bar, the **toolbar** contains buttons you can click to perform actions. In the Address bar, you can see the Documents folder, which is the **default**, or automatically selected, storage location. But you can easily change it.

QUICK TIP
On a laptop computer, the USB port is on the left or right side of your computer.

5. **If you are saving to a USB flash drive, plug the drive into a USB port on your computer, if necessary**

TROUBLE
If you don't have a USB flash drive, you can save the document in the Documents folder on OneDrive, or you can ask your instructor which storage location is best.

6. **In the Navigation pane scroll bar, click the** down scroll arrow ⌄ **as needed to see This PC and any storage devices listed under it**
   Under This PC, you see the storage locations available on your computer, such as Local Disk (C:) (your hard drive) and Removable Disk (H:) (your USB drive name and letter might differ). Above This PC, you might see your OneDrive listed. These storage locations are like folders in that you can open them and store files in them.

7. **Click the name of your USB flash drive, or the folder where you store your Data Files**
   The files and folders in the location you chose, if any, appear in the File list. The Address bar shows the location where the file will be saved, which is now Removable Disk (H:) or the name of the location you clicked. You need to give your document a meaningful name so you can find it later.

TROUBLE
If your Save As dialog box does not show the .rtf file extension, click Cancel, open File Explorer, click the View tab, then in the Show/hide group, click the File name extensions check box to select it.

8. **Click in the** File name text box to select the default name Document.rtf, **type** Company Overview, **compare your screen to** FIGURE 2-5, **then click** Save
   The document is saved as a file on your USB flash drive. The filename Company Overview.rtf appears in the title bar. The ".rtf" at the end of the filename is the file extension that Windows added automatically. A **file extension** is a three- or four-letter sequence, preceded by a period, which identifies a file to your computer, in this case **Rich Text Format**. The WordPad program creates files in RTF format.

9. **Click the** Close button ⊠ **on the WordPad window**
   The WordPad program closes. Your Company Overview document is now saved in the location you specified.

Understanding File Management

FIGURE 2-3: Results at top of Start menu

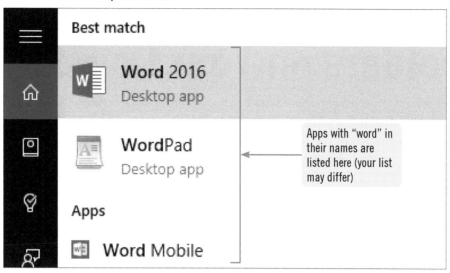

FIGURE 2-4: WordPad document

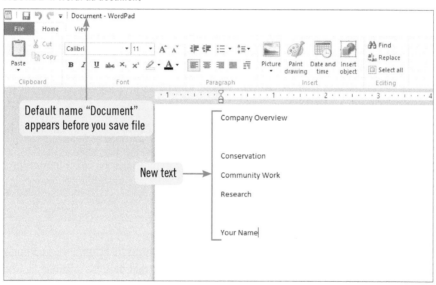

FIGURE 2-5: Save As dialog box

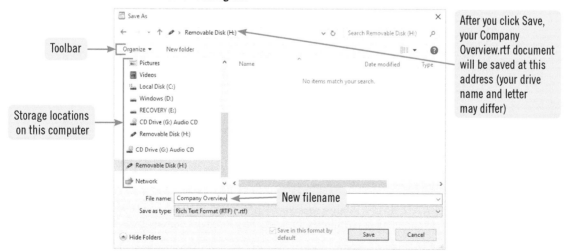

Understanding File Management

Explore the Files and Folders on Your Computer

In a File Explorer window, you can navigate through your computer contents using the File list, the Address bar, and the Navigation pane. Examining your computer and its existing folder and file structure helps you decide where to save files as you work with Windows 10 apps. **CASE** *In preparation for organizing documents at your new job, you look at the files and folders on your computer.*

STEPS

1. **At the Windows desktop, click the** File Explorer button 📁 **on the taskbar, then in the File Explorer Navigation pane, click** This PC

TROUBLE
If you don't see the colored bars, click the View tab, click Tiles in the Layout group.

2. **If you do not see a band of buttons near the top of the window, double-click the** View tab

The band containing buttons is called the **Ribbon**. Your computer's storage devices appear in a window, as shown in FIGURE 2-6. These include hard drives; devices with removable storage, such as CD and DVD drives or USB flash drives; portable devices such as smartphones or tablets; and any network storage locations. Colored bars shows you how much space has been taken up on your drives. You decide to move down a level in your computer's hierarchy and see what is on your USB flash drive.

3. **In the File list, double-click** Removable Disk (H:) **(or the drive name and letter for your USB flash drive)**

You see the contents of your USB flash drive, including the Company Overview.rtf file you saved in the last lesson. You decide to navigate one level up in the file hierarchy.

TROUBLE
If you do not have a USB flash drive, click the Documents folder instead.

4. **In the Address bar, click** This PC, **or if This PC does not appear, click the far-left** address bar arrow ▸ **in the Address bar, then click** This PC

You return to the This PC window showing your storage locations.

5. **In the File list, double-click** Local Disk (C:)

The contents of your hard drive appear in the File list.

6. **In the File list, double-click the** Users folder

The Users folder contains a subfolder for each user account on this computer. You might see a folder with your user account name on it. Each user's folder contains that person's documents. User folder names are the names that were used to log in when your computer was set up. When a user logs in, the computer allows that user access to the folder with the same user name. If you are using a computer with more than one user, you might not have permission to view other users' folders. There is also a Public folder that any user can open.

7. **Double-click the folder with your user name on it**

Depending on how your computer is set up, this folder might be labeled with your name; however, if you are using a computer in a lab or a public location, your folder might be called Student or Computer User or something similar. You see a list of folders, such as Documents, Music, and OneDrive. See FIGURE 2-7.

QUICK TIP
In the Address bar, you can click ▸ to the right of a folder name to see a list of its subfolders; if the folder is open, its name appears in bold in the list.

8. **Double-click** Documents **in the File list**

In the Address bar, the path to the Documents folder is This PC ▸ Local Disk (C:) ▸ Users ▸ *Your User Name* ▸ Documents.

9. **In the Navigation pane, click** This PC

You once again see your computer's storage locations. You can also move up one level at a time in your file hierarchy by clicking the Up arrow ⬆ on the toolbar, or by pressing [Backspace] on your keyboard. See TABLE 2-1 for a summary of techniques for navigating through your computer's file hierarchy.

Windows 10

FIGURE 2-6: **File Explorer window showing storage locations**

Click this arrow if necessary to navigate to a different location

Storage locations on this PC

Colored bars show how full drives are

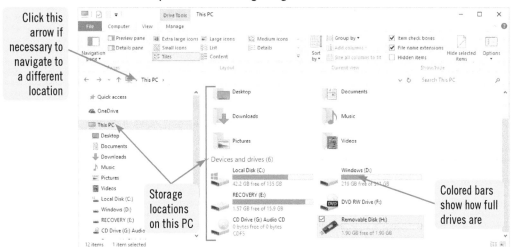

FIGURE 2-7: **Your user name folder**

Path to your user name folder contents

OneDrive

Your user name folder contents and view may differ

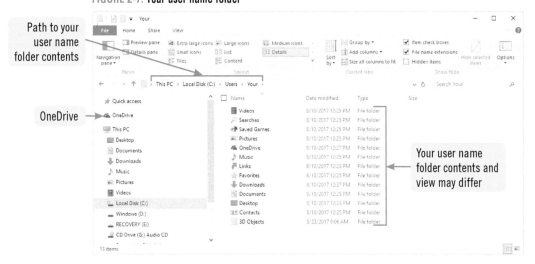

TABLE 2-1: **Navigating your computer's file hierarchy**

to do this	Navigation pane	Address bar	File list	keyboard
Move up in hierarchy	Click a drive or folder name	Click an item to the left of ▷ or Click the **Up to** button ↑		Press [**Backspace**]
Move down in hierarchy	Click a drive or folder name that is indented from the left	Click an item to the right of ▷	Double-click a folder	Press ↑ or ↓ to select a folder, then press [**Enter**] to open the selected folder
Return to previously viewed location		Click the **Back to** button ← or **Forward** button →		

Using and disabling Quick Access view

When you first open File Explorer, you see a list of frequently-used folders and recently used files, called Quick access view. Quick Access view can save you time by giving you one-click access to files and folders you use a lot. If you want File Explorer to open instead to This PC, you can disable Quick Access View. To do this, open a File Explorer window, click the View tab, click the Options button on the right side of the Ribbon, then click Change folder and search options. On the General tab of the Folder Options dialog box, click the Open File Explorer to list arrow, click This PC, then click OK.

Understanding File Management

Change File and Folder Views

As you view your folders and files, you can customize your **view**, which is a set of appearance choices for files and folders. Changing your view does not affect the content of your files or folders, only the way they appear. You can choose from eight different **layouts** to display your folders and files as different sized icons, or as a list. You can change the order in which the folders and files appear, and you can also show a preview of a file in the window. **CASE** ▷ *You experiment with different views of your folders and files.*

STEPS

1. **In the File Explorer window's Navigation pane, click** Local Disk (C:); **in the File list double-click** Users, **then double-click the** folder **with your user name**

   You opened your user name folder, which is inside the Users folder.

2. **Click the** View tab **on the Ribbon if necessary, then if you don't see eight icons in the Layout list, click the** More button ⤓ **in the Layout group**

   The list of available layouts appears, as shown in FIGURE 2-8.

3. **Click** Extra large icons **in the Layout list**

   In this view, the folder items appear as very large icons in the File list. This layout is especially helpful for image files, because you can see what the pictures are without opening each one.

4. **On the View tab, in the Layout list, point to the other layouts while watching the appearance of the File list, then click** Details

   In Details view, shown in FIGURE 2-9, you can see each item's name, the date it was modified, and its file type. It shows the size of any files in the current folder, but it does not show sizes for folders.

5. **Click the** Sort by button **in the Current view group**

   The Sort by menu lets you **sort**, or reorder, your files and folders according to several criteria.

6. **Click** Descending **if it is not already selected with a check mark**

   Now the folders are sorted in reverse alphabetical order.

7. **Click** Removable Disk (H:) **(or the location where you store your Data Files) in the Navigation pane, then click** Company Overview.rtf **in the File list**

8. **Click the** Preview pane button **in the Panes group on the View tab if necessary**

   A preview of the selected Company Overview.rtf file you created earlier appears in the Preview pane on the right side of the screen. The WordPad file is not open, but you can still see the file's contents. See FIGURE 2-10.

9. **Click the** Preview pane button **again to close the pane, then click the window's Close button** ✕

Using the Windows Action Center

The Windows Action Center lets you quickly view system notifications and selected computer settings. To open the Action Center, click the Notifications button on the right side of the taskbar. The Action Center pane opens on the right side of the screen. Any new notifications appear in the upper part of the pane, including messages about apps, Windows tips, and any reminders you may have set. In the lower part of the pane, you see Quick Action buttons, shown in FIGURE 2-11, for some commonly-used Windows settings. For example, click Note to open the OneNote app; click the Brightness button repeatedly to cycle though four brightness settings; click the Airplane mode button to place your computer in airplane mode,

which turns off your computer's wireless transmission; click Quiet hours to silence your computer's notification sounds. Clicking the All settings button opens the Settings windows, where you can access all Windows settings categories. Note that the buttons available will vary depending on your hardware and software configuration.

FIGURE 2-11: **Quick Action buttons**

FIGURE 2-8: Layout options for viewing folders and files

FIGURE 2-9: Your user name folder contents in Details view

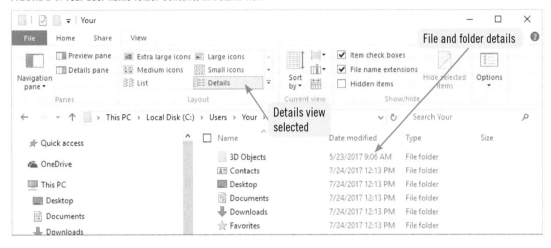

FIGURE 2-10: Preview of selected Company Overview.rtf file

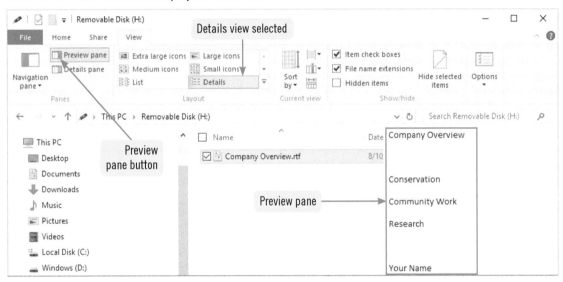

Customizing Details view

When you use File Explorer to view your computer contents in Details view, you see a list of the files and folders in that location. At the top of the list you see each item's Name, Size, Type, and Date Modified. If the list of file and folder details doesn't show what you need, you can customize it. To change a column's location, drag a column heading to move it quickly to a new position. To change the order of, or **sort**, your files and folders, click any column header to sort the list by that detail; click it a second time

to reverse the order. To show only a selected group of, or **filter**, files, click the ✔ icon to the right of the Name, Size, Type, or Date Modified, column headers, and select the check boxes for the type of items you want to include. To change the kind of details you see, right-click or tap-hold a column heading in Details view, then click or tap the detail you want to show or hide. To see more details or to change the list order, right-click or tap-hold a column title, then click or tap More.

Understanding File Management

Open, Edit, and Save Files

Learning Outcomes
• Open a file
• Edit a file
• Save a file

Once you have created a file and saved it with a name to a storage location, you can easily open it and **edit** (make changes to) it. For example, you might want to add or delete text or add a picture. Then you save the file again so the file contains your latest changes. Usually you save a file with the same filename and in the same location as the original, which replaces the existing file with the most up-to-date version. To save a file you have changed, you use the Save command. **CASE** > *You need to complete the company overview list, so you need to open the new Company Overview file you created earlier.*

STEPS

QUICK TIP
When you double-click a file in a File Explorer window, the program currently associated with that file type opens the file; to change the program, right-click a file, click Open with, click Choose another app, click the program name, select the Always use this app to open [file type] files check box, then click OK.

1. **Click the Start button, begin typing** wordpad, **then click the WordPad program if it is not selected or, if it is, simply press [Enter]**
   The WordPad program opens on the desktop.

2. **Click the File tab, then click Open**
   The Open dialog box opens. It contains a Navigation pane and a File list like the Save As dialog box and the File Explorer window.

3. **Scroll down in the Navigation pane if necessary until you see This PC and the list of computer locations, then click Removable Disk (H:) (or the location where you store your Data Files)**
   The contents of your USB flash drive (or the file storage location you chose) appear in the File list, as shown in FIGURE 2-12.

QUICK TIP
You can also double-click a file in the File list to open it.

4. **Click Company Overview.rtf in the File list, then click Open**
   The document you created earlier opens.

5. **Click to the right of the "h" in Research, press [Enter], then type Outreach**
   The edited document includes the text you just typed. See FIGURE 2-13.

QUICK TIP
To save changes to a file, you can also click the Save button 🖫 on the Quick Access toolbar (on the left side of the title bar).

6. **Click the File tab, then click Save, as shown in** FIGURE 2-14
   WordPad saves the document with your most recent changes, using the filename and location you specified when you previously saved it. When you save changes to an existing file, the Save As dialog box does not open.

7. **Click the File tab, then click Exit**
   The Company Overview document and the WordPad program close.

Comparing Save and Save As

Many apps, including Wordpad, include two save command options—Save and Save As. The first time you save a file, the Save As dialog box opens (whether you choose Save or Save As). Here you can select the drive and folder where you want to save the file and enter its filename. If you edit a previously saved file, you can save the file to the same location with the same file-name using the Save command. The Save command updates the stored file using the same location and filename without opening the Save As dialog box. In some situations, you might want to save a copy of the existing document using a different filename or in a different storage location. To do this, open the document, click the Save As command on the File tab, navigate to the location where you want to save the copy if necessary, and/or edit the name of the file.

FIGURE 2-12: **Navigating in the Open dialog box**

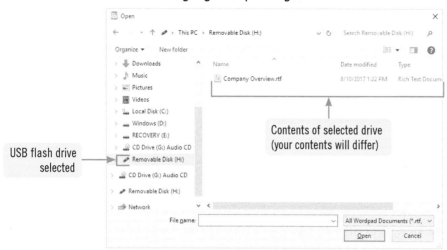

USB flash drive selected

Contents of selected drive (your contents will differ)

FIGURE 2-13: **Edited document**

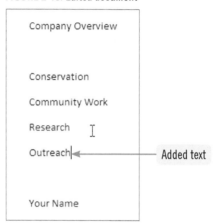

Company Overview

Conservation

Community Work

Research

Outreach

Added text

Your Name

FIGURE 2-14: **Saving the updated document**

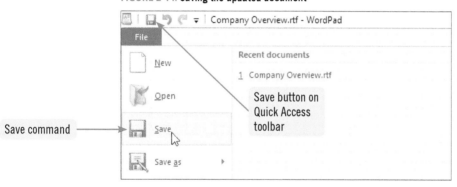

Save command

Save button on Quick Access toolbar

Using Microsoft OneDrive

Microsoft OneDrive is a location on the World Wide Web where you can store your files. Because OneDrive is an online location instead of a disk or USB device, it's often called a **cloud storage location**. When you store your files on OneDrive, you can access them from different devices, including laptops, tablets, and smartphones. Any changes you make to a file stored "in the cloud" are automatically made on OneDrive; this is known as **file syncing**. For example, if you make changes to a file from your laptop, and then open it on your tablet, you will see the changes. You can share OneDrive folders with others so they can view or edit files using a web browser such as Microsoft Edge or Internet Explorer. You can even have multiple users edit a document simultaneously. In Windows 10, OneDrive appears as a storage location in the navigation bar in File Explorer, and in the Open and Save As dialog boxes in Windows apps, so you can easily open, modify, and save files stored there. You can also download the free OneDrive Windows app from the Windows Store to help manage your OneDrive files from all your devices.

Copy Files

Learning Outcomes
- Create a new folder
- Copy and paste a file

Sometimes you need to make a copy of an existing file. For example, you might want to put a copy on a USB flash drive so you can open the file on another machine or share it with a friend or colleague. Or you might want to create a copy as a **backup**, or replacement, in case something happens to your original file. You can copy files and folders using the Copy command and then place the copy in another location using the Paste command. You cannot have two copies of a file with the same name in the same folder. If you try to do this, Windows asks you if you want to replace the first one, and then gives you a chance to give the second copy a different name. **CASE** *You want to create a backup copy of the Company Overview document that you can store in a folder for company publicity items. First you need to create the folder, then you can copy the file.*

STEPS

1. **On the desktop, click the** File Explorer button 🗔 **on the taskbar**

QUICK TIP
You can also create a new folder by clicking the New folder button on the Quick Access toolbar (on the left side of the title bar).

2. **In the Navigation pane, click** Removable Disk (H:) **(or the location where you store your Data Files)**

   First you create the new folder you plan to use for storing publicity-related files.

3. **In the New group on the Home tab, click the** New folder button

   A new folder appears in the File list, with its default name, New folder, selected.

4. **Type** Publicity Items, **then press** [Enter]

   Because the folder name was selected, the text you typed, Publicity Items, replaced it. Pressing [Enter] confirmed your entry, and the folder is now named Publicity Items.

QUICK TIP
You can also copy a file by right-clicking the file in the File list and then clicking Copy, or you can use the keyboard by pressing and holding [Ctrl], pressing [C], then releasing both keys.

5. **In the File list, click the** Company Overview.rtf **document you saved earlier, then click the** Copy button **in the Clipboard group, as shown in** FIGURE 2-15

   After you select the file, its check box becomes selected (the check box appears only if the Item check boxes option in the Show/Hide group on the View tab is selected). When you use the Copy command, Windows places a duplicate copy of the file in an area of your computer's random access memory called the **clipboard**, ready to paste, or place, in a new location. Copying and pasting a file leaves the file in its original location.

6. **In the File list, double-click the** Publicity Items folder

   The folder opens. Nothing appears in the File list because the folder currently is empty.

QUICK TIP
To paste using the keyboard, press and hold [Ctrl] and press [V], then release both keys.

7. **Click the** Paste button **in the Clipboard group**

   A copy of the Company Overview.rtf file is pasted into the Publicity Items folder. See FIGURE 2-16. You now have two copies of the Company Overview.rtf file: one on your USB flash drive in the main folder, and another in your new Publicity Items folder. The file remains on the clipboard until you end your Windows session or place another item on the clipboard.

Copying files using Send to

You can also copy and paste a file using the Send to command. In File Explorer, right-click the file you want to copy, point to Send to, then in the shortcut menu, click the name of the device you want to send a copy of the file to. This leaves the original file on your hard drive and creates a copy in that location. You can send a file to a compressed file, the desktop, your Documents folder, a mail recipient, or a drive on your computer. See TABLE 2-2.

FIGURE 2-15: Copying a file

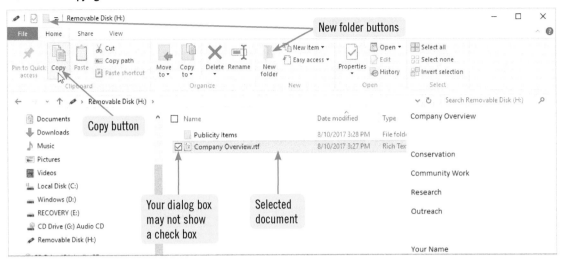

FIGURE 2-16: Duplicate file pasted into Publicity items folder

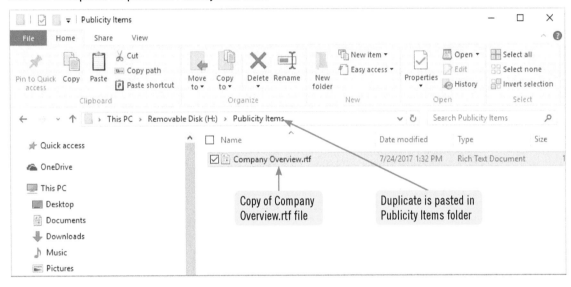

TABLE 2-2: Selected Send to menu commands

menu option	use to
Compressed (zipped) folder	Create a new, compressed (smaller) file with a .zip file extension
Desktop (create shortcut)	Create a shortcut (link) for the file on the desktop
Documents	Copy the file to the Documents library
Fax recipient	Send a file to a fax recipient
Mail recipient	Create an e-mail with the file attached to it (only if you have an e-mail program on your computer)
DVD RW Drive (D:)	Copy the file to your computer's DVD drive (your drive letter may differ)
CD Drive (G:) audio CD	Copy the file to your computer's CD drive (your drive letter may differ)
Removable Disk (H:)	Copy the file to a removable disk drive (your drive letter may differ)

Move and Rename Files

As you work with files, you might need to move files or folders to another location. You can move one or more files or folders at a time, and you can move them to a different folder on the same drive or to a different drive. When you **move** a file, the file is transferred to the new location, and unlike copying, it no longer exists in its original location. You can move a file using the Cut and Paste commands. Before or after you move a file, you might find that you want to change its name. You can easily rename it to make the name more descriptive or accurate. **CASE** ▶ *You decide to move your original Company Overview.rtf document to your Documents folder. After you move it, you edit the filename so it better describes the file contents.*

STEPS

1. **In the Address bar, click** Removable Disk (H:) **(or the name of the location where you store your Data Files) if necessary**

2. **Click the** Company Overview.rtf **document to select it**

3. **Click the** Cut button **in the Clipboard group on the Ribbon, as shown in** FIGURE 2-17

4. **In the Navigation Pane, under This PC, click** Documents
   You navigated to your Documents folder.

5. **Click the** Paste button **in the Clipboard group**
   The Company Overview.rtf document appears in your Documents folder and remains selected. See FIGURE 2-18. The filename could be clearer, to help you remember that it contains a list of company goals.

6. **With the Company Overview.rtf file selected, click the** Rename button **in the Organize group**
   The filename is highlighted. The file extension isn't highlighted because that part of the filename identifies the file to WordPad and should not be changed. If you deleted or changed the file extension, WordPad would be unable to open the file. You decide to change the word "Overview" to "Goals."

7. **Move the** I **pointer after the "w" in "Overview", click to place the insertion point, press [Backspace] eight times to delete** Overview, **type** Goals **as shown in** FIGURE 2-19, **then press [Enter]**
   You changed the name of the pasted file in the Documents folder. The filename now reads Company Goals.rtf.

8. **Close the File Explorer window**

Using Task View to create multiple desktops

As you have learned in Module 1, you can have multiple app windows open on your desktop, such as WordPad, Paint, and OneNote. But you might need to have a different set of apps available for a different project. Instead of closing all the apps and opening different ones, you can use Task View to work with multiple desktops, each containing its own set of apps. Then, when you need to work on another project, you can switch to another desktop to quickly access those apps. To open Task View, click the **Task View** button 🔲 on the taskbar. The current desktop becomes smaller and a New desktop button appears in the lower-right corner of the screen. Click the New desktop button. A new desktop appears in a bar at the bottom of the screen, which you can click to activate and work with its

apps. See FIGURE 2-20. To switch to another desktop, click the Task View button and click its icon.

FIGURE 2-20: **Working with multiple desktops in Task view**

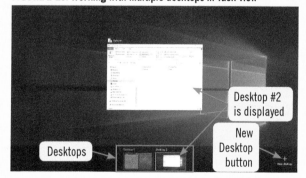

Desktops

Desktop #2 is displayed

New Desktop button

FIGURE 2-17: Cutting a file

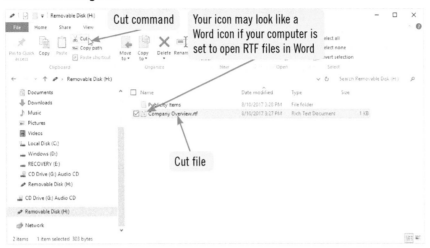

FIGURE 2-18: Pasted file in Documents folder

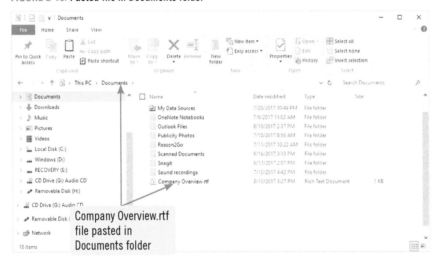

FIGURE 2-19: Renaming a file

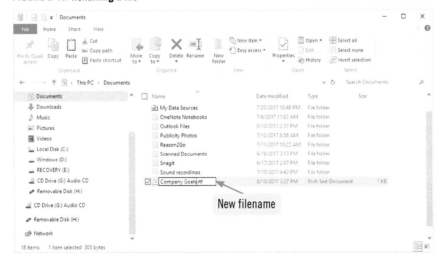

Search for Files and Folders

Windows Search helps you quickly find any app, folder, or file. You can search from the Search box on the taskbar to locate applications, settings, or files. To search a particular location on your computer, you can use the Search box in File Explorer. You enter search text by typing one or more letter sequences or words that help Windows identify the item you want. The search text you type is called your **search criteria**. Your search criteria can be a folder name, a filename, or part of a filename. **CASE** *You want to locate the Company Overview.rtf document so you can print it for a colleague.*

STEPS

1. **Click in the search box on the taskbar**
   The Cortana menu opens.

2. **Type company**
   The Search menu opens with a possible match for your search at the top, and some other possible matches below it. You may see results from The Windows Store, the Internet, or your computer settings.

3. **Click My stuff, near the bottom of the menu**
   This limits your search to the files and folders in your storage locations on this device. It includes documents with the text "company" in the title or in the document text.

4. **Scroll down if necessary to display search results under This Device, including the Company Goals.rtf file you stored in your Documents folder**
   See FIGURE 2-21. It does not find the Company Overview.rtf file stored on your Flash drive because it's searching only the items on this device. To open the found file, you could click its listing. You can also search using File Explorer.

5. **Click the File Explorer button ▨ on the taskbar, then click This PC in the Navigation pane**

6. **Click in the Search This PC box to the right of the Address bar, type company, then press [Enter]**
   Windows searches your computer for files that contain the word "company" in their title. A green bar in the Address bar indicates the progress of your search. After a few moments, the search results, shown in FIGURE 2-22, appear. Windows found the renamed file, Company Goals.rtf, in your Documents folder, and the original Company Overview.rtf document on your removable drive, in the Publicity Items folder. It may also locate shortcuts to the file in your Recent folder. It's good to verify the location of the found files, so you can select the right one.

7. **Click the View tab, click Details in the Layout group then look in the Folder column to view the path to each file, dragging the edge of the Folder column header with the ⟷ pointer to widen it if necessary**

8. **Double-click the Company Overview.rtf document in your file storage location**
   The file opens in WordPad or in another word-processing program on your computer that reads RTF files.

9. **Click the Close button ☒ on the WordPad (or other word-processor) window**

Using the Search Tools tab in File Explorer

The **Search Tools tab** appears in the Ribbon as soon as you click the Search text box, and it lets you narrow your search criteria. Use the commands in the Location group to specify a particular search location. The Refine group lets you limit the search to files modified after a certain date, or to files of a particular kind, size, type, or other property. The Options group lets you repeat previous searches, save searches, and open the folder containing a found file.

FIGURE 2-21: Found file

FIGURE 2-22: Apps screen and Search pane

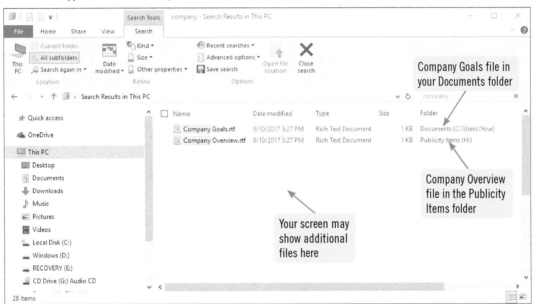

Using Microsoft Edge

When you search for files using the search box on the Windows taskbar and click Web, the new web browser called **Microsoft Edge** opens. You can also open Edge by clicking its icon 🅴 on the taskbar. Created to replace the older Internet Explorer browser, Edge is a Windows app that runs on personal computers, tablets, and smartphones. Edge features a reading mode that lets you read a webpage without ads. It also lets you annotate pages with markup tools such as a pen or highlighter, and add typed notes, as shown in FIGURE 2-23. You can also add pages to a Reading list or share them with OneNote or a social networking site.

FIGURE 2-23: Web page annotated in Microsoft Edge

Delete and Restore Files

Learning Outcomes
- Delete a file
- Restore a file
- Empty the Recycle Bin

If you no longer need a folder or file, you can delete (or remove) it from the storage device. By regularly deleting files and folders you no longer need and emptying the Recycle Bin, you free up valuable storage space on your computer. Windows places folders and files you delete from your hard drive in the Recycle Bin. If you delete a folder, Windows removes the folder as well as all files and subfolders stored in it. If you later discover that you need a deleted file or folder, you can restore it to its original location, as long as you have not yet emptied the Recycle Bin. Emptying the Recycle Bin permanently removes deleted folders and files from your computer. However, files and folders you delete from a removable drive, such as a USB flash drive, do not go to the Recycle Bin. They are immediately and permanently deleted and cannot be restored. **CASE** *You decide to delete the Company Goals document that you stored in your Documents folder.*

STEPS

1. **Click the** Documents folder **in the File Explorer Navigation pane**
   Your Documents folder opens.

2. **Click** Company Goals.rtf **to select it, click the** Home tab, **then click the** Delete list arrow ⊠ **in the Organize group; if the Show recycle confirmation command does not have a check mark next to it, click** Show recycle confirmation **(or if it does have a check mark, click** ⊠ **again to close the menu)**
   Selecting the Show recycle confirmation command tells Windows that whenever you click the Delete button, you want to see a confirmation dialog box before Windows deletes the file. That way you can change your mind if you want, before deleting the file.

3. **Click the** Delete button ⊠ **in the Organize group**
   The Delete File dialog box opens so you can confirm the deletion, as shown in FIGURE 2-24.

4. **Click** Yes
   You deleted the file. Because the file was stored on your computer and not on a removable drive, it was moved to the Recycle Bin.

5. **Click the** Minimize button — **on the window's title bar, examine the Recycle Bin icon, then double-click the** Recycle Bin icon **on the desktop**
   The Recycle Bin icon appears to contain crumpled paper, indicating that it contains deleted folders and/or files. The Recycle Bin window displays any previously deleted folders and files, including the Company Goals.rtf file.

6. **Click the** Company Goals.rtf **file to select it, then click the** Restore the selected items **button in the Restore group on the Recycle Bin Tools Manage tab, as shown in** FIGURE 2-25
   The file returns to its original location and no longer appears in the Recycle Bin window.

7. **In the Navigation pane, click the** Documents folder
   The Documents folder window contains the restored file. You decide to permanently delete this file after all.

8. **Click the file** Company Goals.rtf, **click** ⊠ **in the Organize group on the Home tab, click** Permanently delete, **then click** Yes **in the Delete File dialog box**

9. **Minimize the window, double-click the** Recycle Bin, **notice that the Company Goals.rtf file is no longer there, then close all open windows**

FIGURE 2-24: Delete File dialog box

FIGURE 2-25: Restoring a file from the Recycle Bin

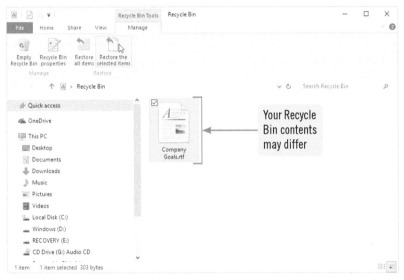

Your Recycle Bin contents may differ

More techniques for selecting and moving files

To select a group of items that are next to each other in a window, click the first item in the group, press and hold [Shift], then click the last item in the group. Both items you click and all the items between them become selected. To select files that are not next to each other, click the first file, press and hold [Ctrl], then click the other items you want to select as a group. Then you can copy, cut, or delete the group of files or folders you selected. **Drag and drop** is a technique in which you use your pointing device to drag a file or folder into a different folder and then drop it, or let go of the mouse button, to place it in that folder. Using drag and drop does not copy your file to the clipboard. If you drag and drop a file to a folder on a different drive, Windows *copies* the file. However, if you drag and drop a file to a folder on the same drive, Windows *moves* the file into that folder

instead. See FIGURE 2-26. If you want to move a file to another drive, hold down [Shift] while you drag and drop. If you want to copy a file to another folder on the same drive, hold down [Ctrl] while you drag and drop.

FIGURE 2-26: Moving a file using drag and drop

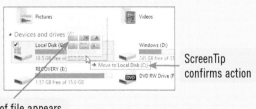

ScreenTip confirms action

Image of file appears as you drag

Practice

Concepts Review

Label the elements of the Windows 10 window shown in FIGURE 2-27.

FIGURE 2-27

Match each term with the statement that best describes it.

7. **View**

8. **File extension**

9. **Address bar**

10. **Path**

11. **Clipboard**

12. **Snap Assist**

a. A series of locations separated by small triangles or backslashes that describes a file's location in the file hierarchy

b. A feature that helps you arrange windows on the screen

c. An area above the Files list that contains a path

d. A three- or four-letter sequence, preceded by a period, that identifies the type of file

e. A set of appearance choices for files and folders

f. An area of a computer's RAM used for temporary storage

Select the best answer from the list of choices.

13. **Which part of a window lets you see a file's contents without opening the file?**
  a. File list
  b. Address bar
  c. Navigation pane
  d. Preview pane

14. **The new Microsoft web browser is called Microsoft _____.**
  a. View
  b. Task
  c. Edge
  d. Desktop

15. **The text you type in a Search text box is called:**
  a. Sorting.
  b. RAM.
  c. Search criteria.
  d. Clipboard.

16. **Which of the following is not a visible section in a File Explorer window?**
  a. Clipboard
  b. Navigation pane
  c. File list
  d. Address bar

Skills Review

1. Understand files and folders.

a. Create a file hierarchy for an ice cream manufacturing business, using a name that you create. The business has departments for Product Development, Manufacturing, and Personnel. Product development activities include research and testing; manufacturing has facilities for ice cream and frozen yogurt; and Personnel handles hiring and payroll. How would you organize your folders and files using a file hierarchy of three levels? How would you use folders and subfolders to keep the documents related to these activities distinct and easy to navigate? Draw a diagram and write a short paragraph explaining your answer.

b. Use tools in the File Explorer window to create the folder hierarchy in the Documents folder on your computer.

c. Open NotePad and write the path of the Hiring folder, using backslashes to indicate levels in the hierarchy. Do the same for the Testing folder.

2. Create and save a file.

a. Connect your USB flash drive to a USB port on your computer, then open WordPad from the Start menu.

b. Type **Advertising Campaign** as the title, then start a new line.

c. Type your name, press [Enter] twice, then create the following list:

Menu ads

Email customers

Web page specials

Local TV spots

d. Save the WordPad file with the filename **Advertising Campaign.rtf** in the location where you store your Data Files, view the filename in the WordPad title bar, then close WordPad.

3. Explore the files and folders on your computer.

a. Open a File Explorer window.

b. Use the Navigation pane to navigate to your USB flash drive or the location where you store your Data Files.

c. Use the Address bar to navigate to This PC.

d. Use the File list to navigate to your local hard drive (C:).

e. Use the File list to open the Users folder, and then open the folder that represents your user name.

f. Open the Documents folder. (*Hint*: The path is This PC\Local Disk (C:) \Users\Your User Name\Documents.)

g. Use the Navigation pane to navigate back to This PC.

4. Change file and folder views.

a. Navigate to your Documents folder or the location of your Data Files using the method of your choice.

b. Use the View tab to view its contents as large icons.

c. View the folder's contents in the seven other views.

d. Sort the items in this location by date modified in ascending order.

e. Open the Preview pane, view a selected item's preview, then close the Preview pane.

5. Open, edit, and save files.

a. Start WordPad, then use the Open dialog box to open the Advertising Campaign.rtf document you created.

b. After the text "Local TV spots," add a line with the text **Social media**.

c. Save the document and close WordPad.

6. Copy files.

a. In the File Explorer window, navigate to the location where you store your Data Files if necessary.

b. Copy the Advertising Campaign.rtf document.

c. Create a new folder named **Advertising** on your USB flash drive or the location where you store your Data Files (*Hint*: Use the Home tab), then open the folder.

d. Paste the document copy in the new folder.

7. Move and rename files.

a. Navigate to your USB flash drive or the location where you store your Data Files.

b. Select the Advertising Campaign.rtf document located there, then cut it.

Skills Review (continued)

c. Navigate to your Documents folder, then paste the file there.

d. Rename the file **Advertising Campaign - Backup.rtf**.

8. **Search for files and folders.**

a. Use the search box on the taskbar to search for a file using the search text **backup**. (*Hint*: Remember to select My stuff.)

b. If necessary, scroll to the found file, and notice its path.

c. Open the Advertising Campaign - Backup document from the search results, then close WordPad. (*Hint*: Closing the program automatically closes any open documents.)

d. Open a File Explorer window, click in the search box, search your USB flash drive using the search text **overview**.

e. Open the found document from the File list, then close WordPad.

9. **Delete and restore files.**

a. Navigate to your Documents folder.

b. Verify that your Delete preference is Show recycle confirmation, then delete the Advertising Campaign - Backup.rtf file.

c. Open the Recycle Bin, and restore the document to its original location.

d. Navigate to your Documents folder, then move the Advertising Campaign - Backup.rtf file to the Advertising folder on your USB flash drive (or the location where you store your Data Files).

Independent Challenge 1

To meet the needs of gardeners in your town, you have opened a vacation garden care business named GreenerInc. Customers hire you to care for their gardens when they go on vacation. To promote your new business, your website designer asks you to give her selling points to include in a web ad.

a. Connect your USB flash drive to your computer, if necessary.

b. Create a new folder named **GreenerInc** on your USB flash drive or the location where you store your Data Files.

c. In the GreenerInc folder, create two subfolders named **Handouts** and **Website**.

d. Use WordPad to create a short paragraph or list that describes three advantages of your business. Use **GreenerInc Selling Points** as the first line, followed by the paragraph or list. Include your name and email address after the text.

e. Save the WordPad document with the filename **Selling Points.rtf** in the Website folder, then close the document and exit WordPad.

f. Open a File Explorer window, then navigate to the Website folder.

g. View the contents in at least three different views, then choose the view option that you prefer.

h. Copy the Selling Points.rtf file, then paste a copy in the Documents folder.

i. Rename the copied file **Selling Points Backup.rtf**.

j. Cut the Selling Points Backup.rtf file from the Documents folder, and paste it in the GreenerInc\Website folder in the location where you store your Data Files, then close the File Explorer window.

Independent Challenge 2

As a freelance webpage designer for nonprofit businesses, you depend on your computer to meet critical deadlines. Whenever you encounter a computer problem, you contact a computer consultant who helps you resolve the problem. This consultant has asked you to document, or keep records of, your computer's available drives.

a. Connect your USB flash drive to your computer, if necessary.

b. Open File Explorer and go to This PC so you can view information on your drives and other installed hardware.

c. View the window contents using three different views, then choose the one you prefer.

d. Open WordPad and create a document with the text **My Drives** and your name on separate lines. Save the document as **My Drives.rtf**.

Independent Challenge 2 (continued)

e. Use Snap Assist to view the WordPad and File Explorer windows next to each other on the screen. (*Hint*: Drag the title bar of one of the windows to the left side of the screen.)

f. In WordPad, list the names of the hard drive (or drives), devices with removable storage, and any other hardware devices installed on the computer as shown in the Devices and Drives section of the window.

g. Switch to a view that displays the total size and amount of free space on your hard drive(s) and removable storage drive(s), and edit each WordPad list item to include the amount of free space for each one (for example, 22.1 GB free of 95.5 GB).

h. Save the WordPad document with the filename **My Drives** on your USB flash drive or the location where you store your Data Files.

i. Close WordPad, then maximize the File Explorer window. Navigate to your file storage location, then preview your document in the Preview pane, and close the window.

Independent Challenge 3

You are an attorney at Garcia and Chu, a large accounting firm. You participate in the company's community outreach program by speaking at career days in area schools. You teach students about career opportunities available in the field of accounting. You want to create a folder structure to store the files for each session.

a. Connect your USB flash drive to your computer (if necessary), then open the window for your USB flash drive or the location where you store your Data Files.

b. Create a folder named **Career Days**.

c. In the Career Days folder, create a subfolder named **Valley Intermediate**. Open this folder, then close it.

d. Use WordPad to create a document with the title **Accounting Jobs** at the top of the page and your name on separate lines, and the following list of items:
Current Opportunities:
Bookkeeper
Accounting Clerk
Accountant
Certified Public Accountant (CPA)

e. Save the WordPad document with the filename **Accounting Jobs.rtf** in the Valley Intermediate folder. (*Hint*: After you switch to your USB flash drive in the Save As dialog box, open the Career Days folder, then open the Valley Intermediate folder before saving the file.) Close WordPad.

f. Open WordPad and the Accounting Jobs document again, add **Senior Accountant** after Accountant, then save the file and close WordPad.

g. Store a copy of the file using the Save As command to your Documents folder, renaming it **Accounting Jobs - Copy.rtf**, then close WordPad.

h. In File Explorer, delete the document copy in your Documents folder so it is placed in the Recycle Bin, then restore it.

i. Open the Recycle Bin window, snap the File Explorer to the left side of the screen and the Recycle in to the right side, then verify that the file has been restored to the correct location.

j. Cut the file from the Documents folder and paste it in the Career Days\Valley Intermediate folder in your Data File storage location, then close all windows.

Independent Challenge 4: Explore

Think of a hobby or volunteer activity that you do now, or one that you would like to start. You will use your computer to help you manage your plans or ideas for this activity.

a. Using paper and pencil, sketch a folder structure with at least two subfolders to contain your documents for this activity.

b. Connect your USB flash drive to your computer, then open the window for your USB flash drive.

Independent Challenge 4: Explore (continued)

c. In File Explorer, create the folder structure for your activity, using your sketch as a reference.

d. Think of at least three tasks that you can do to further your work in your chosen activity.

e. Start a new WordPad document. Add the title **Next Steps** at the top of the page and your name on the next line.

f. Below your name, list the three tasks. Save the file in one of the folders created on your USB flash drive, with the title **To Do.rtf**.

g. Close WordPad, then open a File Explorer window and navigate to the folder where you stored the document.

h. Create a copy of the file, place the copied file in your Documents folder, then rename this file with a name you choose.

i. Delete the copied file from your Documents folder, restore it, then cut and paste the file into the folder that contains your To Do.rtf file, ensuring that the filename of the copy is different so it doesn't overwirte the To Do.rtf file.

j. Open Microsoft Edge using its button on the taskbar, click in the search text box, then search for information about others doing your desired hobby or volunteer activity.

k. Click the Make a Web Note button ✎ at the top of the window, click the Highlighter tool, then highlight an item that interests you.

l. Click the Share button ⌂, click Mail, choose your desired email account, then send the annotated page to yourself. You will receive an email with an attachment showing the annotated page.

m. Close Edge, your email program, and any open windows.

Visual Workshop

Create the folder structure shown in FIGURE 2-28 on your USB flash drive (or in the location where you store your Data Files). Create a WordPad document containing your name and today's date, type the path to the Midsize folder, and save it with the filename **Midsize.rtf** in a Midsize folder on your USB Flash drive or the location where you store your Data Files.

FIGURE 2-28

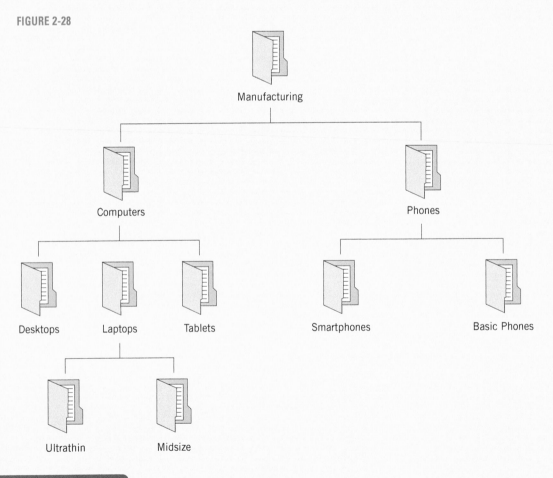

Understanding File Management

Getting Started with Microsoft Office 2016

CASE ▶ This module introduces you to the most frequently used programs in Office, as well as common features they all share.

Module Objectives

After completing this module, you will be able to:

- Understand the Office 2016 suite
- Start an Office app
- Identify Office 2016 screen elements
- Create and save a file

- Open a file and save it with a new name
- View and print your work
- Get Help, close a file, and exit an app

Files You Will Need

OF 1-1.xlsx

Understand the Office 2016 Suite

Learning
Outcomes
• Identify Office
  suite components
• Describe the
  features of each
  app

Microsoft Office 2016 is a group of programs—which are also called applications or apps—designed to help you create documents, collaborate with coworkers, and track and analyze information. You use different Office programs to accomplish specific tasks, such as writing a letter or producing a presentation, yet all the programs have a similar look and feel. Microsoft Office 2016 apps feature a common, context-sensitive user interface, so you can get up to speed faster and use advanced features with greater ease. The Office apps are bundled together in a group called a **suite**. The Office suite is available in several configurations, but all include Word, Excel, PowerPoint, and OneNote. Some configurations include Access, Outlook, Publisher, Skype, and OneDrive. **CASE** > *As part of your job, you need to understand how each Office app is best used to complete specific tasks.*

DETAILS

The Office apps covered in this book include:

QUICK TIP
In this book, the terms "program" and "app" are used interchangeably.

* **Microsoft Word 2016**

  When you need to create any kind of text-based document, such as a memo, newsletter, or multipage report, Word is the program to use. You can easily make your documents look great by using formatting tools and inserting eye-catching graphics. The Word document shown in FIGURE 1-1 contains a company logo and simple formatting.

* **Microsoft Excel 2016**

  Excel is the perfect solution when you need to work with numeric values and make calculations. It puts the power of formulas, functions, charts, and other analytical tools into the hands of every user, so you can analyze sales projections, calculate loan payments, and present your findings in a professional manner. The Excel worksheet shown in FIGURE 1-1 tracks checkbook transactions. Because Excel automatically recalculates results whenever a value changes, the information is always up to date. A chart illustrates how the monthly expenses are broken down.

* **Microsoft PowerPoint 2016**

  Using PowerPoint, it's easy to create powerful presentations complete with graphics, transitions, and even a soundtrack. Using professionally designed themes and clip art, you can quickly and easily create dynamic slide shows such as the one shown in FIGURE 1-1.

* **Microsoft Access 2016**

  Access is a relational database program that helps you keep track of large amounts of quantitative data, such as product inventories or employee records. The form shown in FIGURE 1-1 can be used to generate reports on customer invoices and tours.

Microsoft Office has benefits beyond the power of each program, including:

* **Note-taking made simple; available on all devices**

  Use OneNote to take notes (organized in tabbed pages) on information that can be accessed on your computer, tablet, or phone. Share the editable results with others. Contents can include text, web page clips (using OneNote Clipper), email contents (directly inserted into a default section), photos (using Office Lens), and web pages.

* **Common user interface: Improving business processes**

  Because the Office suite apps have a similar **interface**, your experience using one app's tools makes it easy to learn those in the other apps. Office documents are **compatible** with one another, so you can easily **integrate**, or combine, elements—for example, you can add an Excel chart to a PowerPoint slide, or an Access table to a Word document.

  Most Office programs include the capability to incorporate feedback—called **online collaboration**—across the Internet or a company network.

FIGURE 1-1: Microsoft Office 2016 documents

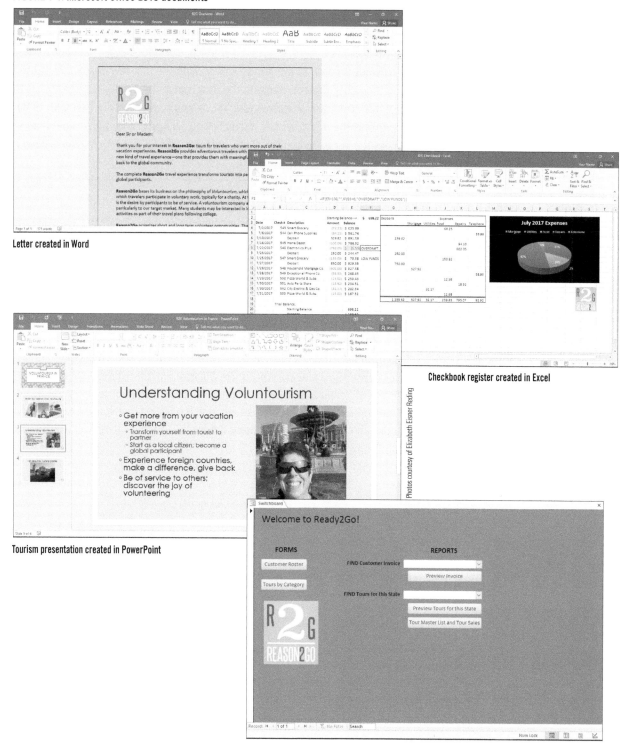

Letter created in Word

Checkbook register created in Excel

Tourism presentation created in PowerPoint

Form created in Access

What is Office 365?

Until recently, most consumers purchased Microsoft Office in a traditional way: by buying a retail package from a store or downloading it from Microsoft.com. You can still purchase Microsoft Office 2016 in this traditional way—but you can also now purchase it as a subscription service called Microsoft Office 365, which is available in a wide variety of configurations.

Depending on which configuration you purchase, you will always have access to the most up-to-date versions of the apps in your package and, in many cases, can install these apps on multiple computers, tablets, and phones. And if you change computers or devices, you can easily uninstall the apps from an old device and install them on a new one.

Office 2016

Start an Office App

Learning
Outcomes
• Start an Office app
• Explain the purpose
  of a template
• Start a new blank
  document

To get started using Microsoft Office, you need to start, or **launch**, the Office app you want to use. An easy way to start the app you want is to press the Windows key, type the first few characters of the app name you want to search for, then click the app name In the Best match list. You will discover that there are many ways to accomplish just about any Windows task; for example, you can also see a list of all the apps on your computer by pressing the Windows key, then clicking All Apps. When you see the app you want, click its name. **CASE** ➤ *You decide to familiarize yourself with Office by starting Microsoft Word.*

STEPS

QUICK TIP
You can also press
the Windows key on
your keyboard to
open the Start menu.

1. **Click the** Start button ⊞ **on the Windows taskbar**

   The Start menu opens, listing the most used apps on your computer. You can locate the app you want to open by clicking the app name if you see it, or you can type the app name to search for it.

2. **Type** word

   Your screen now displays "Word 2016" under "Best match", along with any other app that has "word" as part of its name (such as WordPad). See FIGURE 1-2.

QUICK TIP
In Word, Excel, and
PowerPoint, the
interface can be
modified to automat-
ically open a blank
document, work-
book, or presenta-
tion. To do this, click
the File tab, click
Options, in the Start
up options section
click Show the Start
screen when this
application starts
(to deselect it), then
click OK. The next
time the program
opens, it will open a
blank document.

3. **Click** Word 2016

   Word 2016 launches, and the Word **start screen** appears, as shown in FIGURE 1-3. The start screen is a landing page that appears when you first start an Office app. The left side of this screen displays recent files you have opened. (If you have never opened any files, then there will be no files listed under Recent.) The right side displays images depicting different templates you can use to create different types of documents. A **template** is a file containing professionally designed content and formatting that you can easily customize for your own needs. You can also start from scratch using the Blank Document template, which contains only minimal formatting settings.

Enabling touch mode

If you are using a touch screen with any of the Office 2016 apps, you can enable the touch mode to give the user interface a more spacious look, making it easier to navigate with your fingertips. Enable touch mode by clicking the Quick Access toolbar list arrow, then clicking Touch/Mouse Mode to select it. Then you'll see the Touch Mode button 👆 in the Quick Access toolbar. Click 👆, and you'll see the interface spread out.

Using shortcut keys to move between Office programs

You can switch between open apps using a keyboard shortcut. The [Alt][Tab] keyboard combination lets you either switch quickly to the next open program or file or choose one from a gallery. To switch immediately to the next open program or file, press [Alt][Tab]. To choose from all open programs and files, press and hold [Alt], then press and release [Tab] without releasing [Alt]. A gallery opens on screen, displaying the filename and a thumbnail image of each open program and file, as well as of the desktop. Each time you press [Tab] while holding [Alt], the selection cycles to the next open file or location. Release [Alt] when the program, file, or location you want to activate is selected.

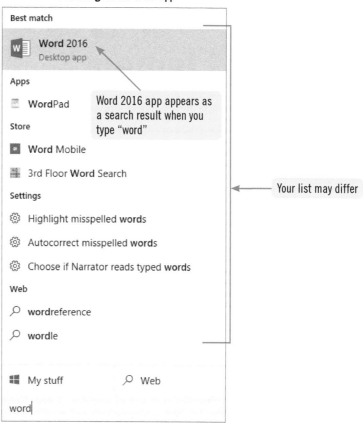

FIGURE 1-2: **Searching for the Word app**

Word 2016 app appears as a search result when you type "word"

Your list may differ

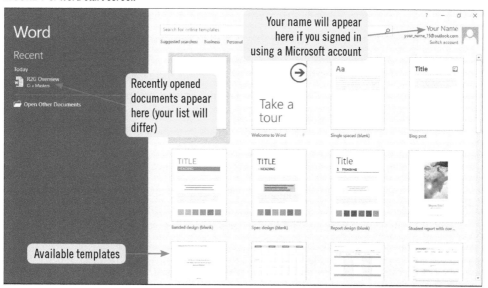

FIGURE 1-3: **Word start screen**

Your name will appear here if you signed in using a Microsoft account

Recently opened documents appear here (your list will differ)

Available templates

Using the Office Clipboard

You can use the Office Clipboard to cut and copy items from one Office program and paste them into others. The Office Clipboard can store a maximum of 24 items. To access it, open the Office Clipboard task pane by clicking the dialog box launcher in the Clipboard group on the Home tab. Each time you copy a selection, it is saved in the Office Clipboard. Each entry in the Office Clipboard includes an icon that tells you the program it was created in. To paste an entry, click in the document where you want it to appear, then click the item in the Office Clipboard. To delete an item from the Office Clipboard, right-click the item, then click Delete.

Identify Office 2016 Screen Elements

Learning Outcomes
• Identify basic components of the user interface
• Display and use Backstage view
• Adjust the zoom level

One of the benefits of using Office is that its apps have much in common, making them easy to learn and making it simple to move from one to another. All Office 2016 apps share a similar user interface, so you can use your knowledge of one to get up to speed in another. A **user interface** is a collective term for all the ways you interact with a software program. The user interface in Office 2016 provides intuitive ways to choose commands, work with files, and navigate in the program window. **CASE** *Familiarize yourself with some of the common interface elements in Office by examining the PowerPoint program window.*

STEPS

1. **Click the Start button ⊞ on the Windows taskbar, type** pow, **click** PowerPoint 2016, **then click** Blank Presentation

   PowerPoint starts and opens a new file, which contains a blank slide. Refer to FIGURE 1-4 to identify common elements of the Office user interface. The **document window** occupies most of the screen. At the top of every Office program window is a **title bar** that displays the document name and program name. Below the title bar is the **Ribbon**, which displays commands you're likely to need for the current task. Commands are organized onto **tabs**. The tab names appear at the top of the Ribbon, and the active tab appears in front. The **Share button** in the upper-right corner lets you invite other users to view your cloud-stored Word, Excel, or Powerpoint file.

2. **Click the** File tab

   The File tab opens, displaying **Backstage view**. It is called Backstage view because the commands available here are for working with the files "behind the scenes." The navigation bar on the left side of Backstage view contains commands to perform actions common to most Office programs.

3. **Click the** Back button ⊙ **to close Backstage view and return to the document window, then click the** Design tab **on the Ribbon**

   To display a different tab, click its name. Each tab contains related commands arranged into **groups** to make features easy to find. On the Design tab, the Themes group displays available design themes in a **gallery**, or visual collection of choices you can browse. Many groups contain a **launcher**, which you can click to open a dialog box or pane from which to choose related commands.

4. **Move the mouse pointer ⬚ over the** Ion Boardroom theme **in the Themes group as shown in** FIGURE 1-5, **but** *do not click* **the mouse button**

   The Ion Boardroom theme is temporarily applied to the slide in the document window. However, because you did not click the theme, you did not permanently change the slide. With the **Live Preview** feature, you can point to a choice, see the results, then decide if you want to make the change. Live Preview is available throughout Office.

5. **Move ⬚ away from the Ribbon and towards the slide**

   If you had clicked the Ion theme, it would be applied to this slide. Instead, the slide remains unchanged.

6. **Point to the** Zoom slider `— ———I——— + 100%` **on the status bar, then drag to the right until the Zoom level reads** 166%

   The slide display is enlarged. Zoom tools are located on the status bar. You can drag the slider or click the Zoom In or Zoom Out buttons to zoom in or out on an area of interest. **Zooming in** (a higher percentage), makes a document appear bigger on screen but less of it fits on the screen at once; **zooming out** (a lower percentage) lets you see more of the document at a reduced size.

7. **Click the** Zoom Out button `⊟` **on the status bar to the left of the Zoom slider until the Zoom level reads** 120%

FIGURE 1-4: PowerPoint program window

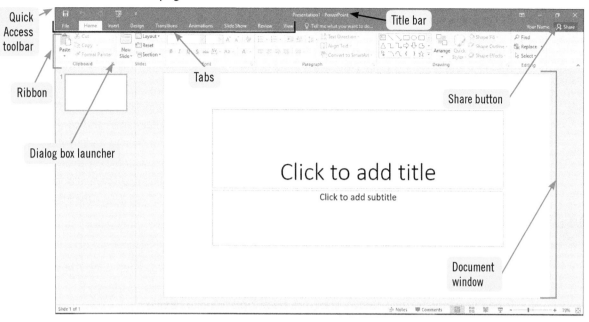

Quick Access toolbar

Title bar

Ribbon

Tabs

Share button

Dialog box launcher

Click to add title

Click to add subtitle

Document window

FIGURE 1-5: Viewing a theme with Live Preview

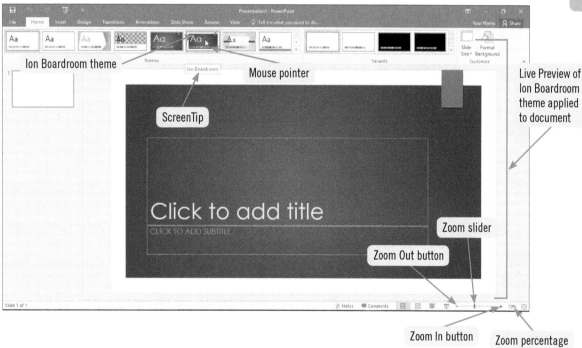

Ion Boardroom theme

Mouse pointer

Live Preview of Ion Boardroom theme applied to document

ScreenTip

Click to add title

CLICK TO ADD SUBTITLE

Zoom slider

Zoom Out button

Zoom In button

Zoom percentage

Using Backstage view

Backstage view in each Microsoft Office app offers "one stop shopping" for many commonly performed tasks, such as opening and saving a file, printing and previewing a document, defining document properties, sharing information, and exiting a program. Backstage view opens when you click the File tab in any Office app, and while features such as the Ribbon, Mini toolbar, and Live Preview all help you work *in* your documents, the File tab and Backstage view help you work *with* your documents. You can click commands in the navigation pane to open different places for working with your documents, such as the Open place, the Save place, and so on. You can return to your active document by clicking the Back button.

Create and Save a File

Learning
Outcomes
• Create a file
• Save a file
• Explain OneDrive

When working in an Office app, one of the first things you need to do is to create and save a file. A **file** is a stored collection of data. Saving a file enables you to work on a project now, then put it away and work on it again later. In some Office programs, including Word, Excel, and PowerPoint, you can open a new file when you start the app, then all you have to do is enter some data and save it. In Access, you must create a file before you enter any data. You should give your files meaningful names and save them in an appropriate location, such as a folder on your hard drive or OneDrive so they're easy to find. **OneDrive** is a Microsoft cloud storage system that lets you easily save, share, and access your files from anywhere you have Internet access. **CASE** *Use Word to familiarize yourself with creating and saving a document. First you'll type some notes about a possible location for a corporate meeting, then you'll save the information for later use.*

STEPS

1. **Click the** Word button 🔳 **on the taskbar, click** Blank document, **then click the** Zoom In button ➕ **until the level is** 120%, **if necessary**

2. **Type** Locations for Corporate Meeting, **then press [Enter] twice**
   The text appears in the document window, and the **insertion point** blinks on a new blank line. The insertion point indicates where the next typed text will appear.

3. **Type** Las Vegas, NV, **press** [Enter], **type** Chicago, IL, **press** [Enter], **type** Seattle, WA, **press** [Enter] **twice, then type your name**

4. **Click the** Save button 💾 **on the Quick Access toolbar**
   Because this is the first time you are saving this new file, the Save place in Backstage view opens, showing various options for saving the file. See FIGURE 1-6. Once you save a file for the first time, clicking 💾 saves any changes to the file *without* opening the Save As dialog box.

5. **Click** Browse
   The Save As dialog box opens, as shown in FIGURE 1-7, where you can browse to the location where you want to save the file. The Address bar in the Save As dialog box displays the default location for saving the file, but you can change it to any location. The File name field contains a suggested name for the document based on text in the file, but you can enter a different name.

6. **Type** OF 1-Possible Corporate Meeting Locations
   The text you type replaces the highlighted text. (The "OF 1-" in the filename indicates that the file is created in Office Module 1. You will see similar designations throughout this book when files are named.)

7. **In the Save As dialog box, use the Address bar or Navigation Pane to navigate to the location where you store your Data Files**
   You can store files on your computer, a network drive, your OneDrive, or any acceptable storage device.

8. **Click** Save
   The Save As dialog box closes, the new file is saved to the location you specified, and the name of the document appears in the title bar, as shown in FIGURE 1-8. (You may or may not see the file extension ".docx" after the filename.) See TABLE 1-1 for a description of the different types of files you create in Office, and the file extensions associated with each.

TABLE 1-1: Common filenames and default file extensions

file created in	is called a	and has the default extension
Word	document	.docx
Excel	workbook	.xlsx
PowerPoint	presentation	.pptx
Access	database	.accdb

FIGURE 1-6: **Save place in Backstage view**

Saves to your OneDrive account

Click to display a list of recently accessed locations on this PC

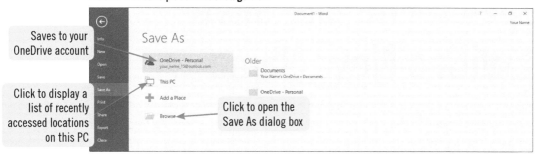

Click to open the Save As dialog box

FIGURE 1-7: **Save As dialog box**

Navigation pane; your links and folders may differ

File name field; your computer may not display file extensions

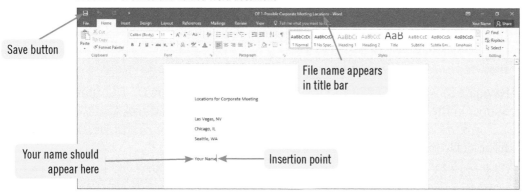

Address bar; your location may differ

Save as type list

FIGURE 1-8: **Saved and named Word document**

Save button

Your name should appear here

File name appears in title bar

Insertion point

Saving files to OneDrive

All Office programs include the capability to incorporate feedback—called **online collaboration**—across the Internet or a company network. Using **cloud computing** (work done in a virtual environment), you can store your work in the cloud. Using OneDrive, a file storage service from Microsoft, you and your colleagues can create and store documents in the cloud and make the documents available anywhere there is Internet access to whomever you choose. To use OneDrive, you need a Microsoft Account, which you obtain at onedrive.live.com. Pricing and storage plans vary based on the type of Microsoft account you have. When you are logged into your Microsoft account and you

save a file in any of the Office apps, the first option in the Save As screen is your OneDrive. Double-click your OneDrive option, and the Save As dialog box opens displaying a location in the address bar unique to your OneDrive account. Type a name in the File name text box, then click Save and your file is saved to your OneDrive. To sync your files with OneDrive, you'll need to download and install the OneDrive for Windows app. Then, when you open Explorer, you'll notice a new folder called OneDrive has been added to your folder. In this folder is a sub-folder called Documents. This means if your Internet connection fails, you can work on your files offline.

Office 2016

Office 2016
Module 1

Learning
Outcomes
• Open an existing file
• Save a file with a new name

Open a File and Save It with a New Name

In many cases as you work in Office, you need to use an existing file. It might be a file you or a coworker created earlier as a work in progress, or it could be a complete document that you want to use as the basis for another. For example, you might want to create a budget for this year using the budget you created last year; instead of typing in all the categories and information from scratch, you could open last year's budget, save it with a new name, and just make changes to update it for the current year. By opening the existing file and saving it with the Save As command, you create a duplicate that you can modify to suit your needs, while the original file remains intact. **CASE** *Use Excel to open an existing workbook file, and save it with a new name so the original remains unchanged.*

STEPS

1. **Click the** Start button ⊞ **on the Windows taskbar, type** exc, **click** Excel 2016, **click** Open Other Workbooks, This PC, **then click** Browse

   The Open dialog box opens, where you can navigate to any drive or folder accessible to your computer to locate a file.

2. **In the Open dialog box, navigate to the location where you store your Data Files**

   The files available in the current folder are listed, as shown in FIGURE 1-9. This folder displays one file.

3. **Click** OF 1-1.xlsx, **then click** Open

   The dialog box closes, and the file opens in Excel. An Excel file is an electronic spreadsheet, so the new file displays a grid of rows and columns you can use to enter and organize data.

4. **Click the** File tab, **click** Save As **on the navigation bar, then click** Browse

   The Save As dialog box opens, and the current filename is highlighted in the File name text box. Using the Save As command enables you to create a copy of the current, existing file with a new name. This action preserves the original file and creates a new file that you can modify.

5. **Navigate to where you store your Data Files if necessary, type** OF 1-Corporate Meeting Budget **in the File name text box, as shown in** FIGURE 1-10, **then click** Save

   A copy of the existing workbook is created with the new name. The original file, OF 1-1.xlsx, closes automatically.

6. **Click cell** A18, **type your name, then press** [Enter], **as shown in** FIGURE 1-11

   In Excel, you enter data in cells, which are formed by the intersection of a row and a column. Cell A18 is at the intersection of column A and row 18. When you press [Enter], the cell pointer moves to cell A19.

7. **Click the** Save button 🖫 **on the Quick Access toolbar**

   Your name appears in the workbook, and your changes to the file are saved.

Exploring File Open options

You might have noticed that the Open button in the Open dialog box includes a list arrow to the right of the button. In a dialog box, if a button includes a list arrow you can click the button to invoke the command, or you can click the list arrow to see a list of related commands that you can apply to the currently selected file. The Open list arrow includes several related commands, including Open Read-Only and Open as Copy.

Clicking Open Read-Only opens a file that you can only save with a new name; you cannot make changes to the original file. Clicking Open as Copy creates and opens a copy of the selected file and inserts the word "Copy" in the file's title. Like the Save As command, these commands provide additional ways to use copies of existing files while ensuring that original files do not get changed by mistake.

FIGURE 1-9: Open dialog box

FIGURE 1-10: Save As dialog box

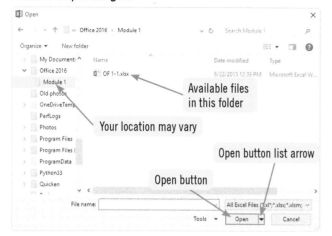

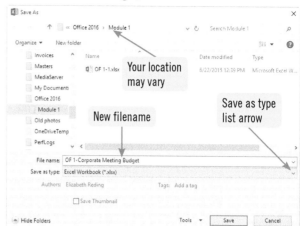

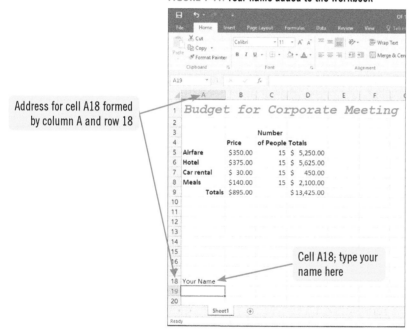

FIGURE 1-11: Your name added to the workbook

Working in Compatibility Mode

Not everyone upgrades to the newest version of Office. As a general rule, new software versions are **backward compatible**, meaning that documents saved by an older version can be read by newer software. To open documents created in older Office versions, Office 2016 includes a feature called Compatibility Mode. When you use Office 2016 to open a file created in an earlier version of Office, "Compatibility Mode" appears in the title bar, letting you know the file was created in an earlier but usable version of the program. If you are working with someone who may not be using the newest version of the software, you can avoid possible incompatibility problems by saving your file in another, earlier format. To do this in an Office program, click the File tab, click Save As on the navigation bar, then click Browse. In the Save As dialog box, click the Save as type list arrow in the Save As dialog box, then click an option in the list. For example, if you're working in Excel, click Excel 97-2003 Workbook format in the Save as type list to save an Excel file so it can be opened in Excel 97 or Excel 2003.

Office 2016

View and Print Your Work

Learning Outcomes
- Describe and change views in an app
- Print a document

Each Microsoft Office program lets you switch among various **views** of the document window to show more or fewer details or a different combination of elements that make it easier to complete certain tasks, such as formatting or reading text. Changing your view of a document does not affect the file in any way, it affects only the way it looks on screen. If your computer is connected to a printer or a print server, you can easily print any Office document using the Print button in the Print place in Backstage view. Printing can be as simple as **previewing** the document to see exactly what the printed version will look like and then clicking the Print button. Or, you can customize the print job by printing only selected pages. You can also use the Share place in Backstage view or the Share button on the Ribbon (if available) to share a document, export to a different format, or save it to the cloud. **CASE** *Experiment with changing your view of a Word document, and then preview and print your work.*

STEPS

1. **Click the** Word program button **on the taskbar**

   Word becomes active, and the program window fills the screen.

QUICK TIP
To minimize the display of the buttons and commands on tabs, click the Collapse the Ribbon button ⌃ on the lower-right end of the Ribbon.

2. **Click the** View tab **on the Ribbon**

   In most Office programs, the View tab on the Ribbon includes groups and commands for changing your view of the current document. You can also change views using the View buttons on the status bar.

3. **Click the** Read Mode button **in the Views group on the View tab**

   The view changes to Read Mode view, as shown in FIGURE 1-12. This view shows the document in an easy-to-read, distraction-free reading mode. Notice that the Ribbon is no longer visible on screen.

4. **Click the** Print Layout button **on the Status bar**

   You return to Print Layout view, the default view in Word.

QUICK TIP
Office 2016 apps default to print to OneDrive.

5. **Click the** File tab, **then click** Print **on the navigation bar**

   The Print place opens. The preview pane on the right displays a preview of how your document will look when printed. Compare your screen to FIGURE 1-13. Options in the Settings section enable you to change margins, orientation, and related options before printing. To change a setting, click it, and then click a new setting. For instance, to change from Letter paper size to Legal, click Letter in the Settings section, then click Legal on the menu that opens. The document preview updates as you change the settings. You also can use the Settings section to change which pages to print. If your computer is connected to multiple printers, you can click the current printer in the Printer section, then click the one you want to use. The Print section contains the Print button and also enables you to select the number of copies of the document to print.

QUICK TIP
You can add the Quick Print button to the Quick Access toolbar by clicking the Customize Quick Access Toolbar button, then clicking Quick Print. The Quick Print button prints one copy of your document using the default settings.

6. **If your school allows printing, click the** Print button **in the Print place (otherwise, click the** Back button ⊙**)**

   If you chose to print, a copy of the document prints, and Backstage view closes.

Customizing the Quick Access toolbar

You can customize the Quick Access toolbar to display your favorite commands. To do so, click the Customize Quick Access Toolbar button ▽ in the title bar, then click the command you want to add. If you don't see the command in the list, click More Commands to open the Quick Access Toolbar tab of the current program's Options dialog box. In the Options dialog box, use the Choose commands from list to choose a category, click the desired command in the list on the left, click Add to add it to the Quick Access toolbar, then click OK. To remove a button from the toolbar, click the name in the list on the right in the Options dialog box, then click Remove. To add a command to the Quick Access toolbar as you work, simply right-click the button on the Ribbon, then click Add to Quick Access Toolbar on the shortcut menu. To move the Quick Access toolbar below the Ribbon, click the Customize Quick Access Toolbar button, and then click Show Below the Ribbon.

FIGURE 1-12: Read Mode view

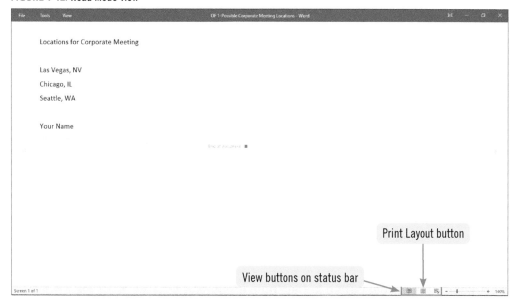

Print Layout button

View buttons on status bar

FIGURE 1-13: Print settings on the File tab

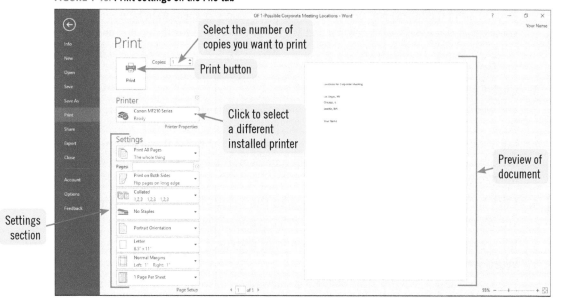

Select the number of copies you want to print

Print button

Click to select a different installed printer

Preview of document

Settings section

Creating a screen capture

A **screen capture** is a digital image of your screen, as if you took a picture of it with a camera. For instance, you might want to take a screen capture if an error message occurs and you want a Technical Support person to see exactly what's on the screen. You can create a screen capture using the Snipping Tool, an accessory designed to capture whole screens or portions of screens. To open the Snipping Tool, click the Start button on the Windows taskbar, type "sni", then click the Snipping Tool when it appears in the left panel. On the Snipping Tool toolbar, click New, then drag the pointer on the screen to select the area of the screen you want to capture. When you release the mouse button, the screen capture opens in the Snipping Tool window, and you can save, copy, or send it in an email. In Word, Excel, and PowerPoint 2016, you can capture screens or portions of screens and insert them in the current document using the Screenshot button in the Illustrations group on the Insert tab. Alternatively, you can create a screen capture by pressing [PrtScn]. (Keyboards differ, but you may find the [PrtScn] button in or near your keyboard's function keys.) Pressing this key places a digital image of your screen in the Windows temporary storage area known as the **Clipboard**. Open the document where you want the screen capture to appear, click the Home tab on the Ribbon (if necessary), then click the Paste button in the Clipboard group on the Home tab. The screen capture is pasted into the document.

Get Help, Close a File, and Exit an App

Learning
Outcomes
• Display a
  ScreenTip
• Use Help
• Close a file
• Exit an app

You can get comprehensive help at any time by pressing [F1] in an Office app or clicking the Help button on the title bar. You can also get help in the form of a ScreenTip by pointing to almost any icon in the program window. When you're finished working in an Office document, you have a few choices for ending your work session. You close a file by clicking the File tab, then clicking Close; you exit a program by clicking the Close button on the title bar. Closing a file leaves a program running, while exiting a program closes all the open files in that program as well as the program itself. In all cases, Office reminds you if you try to close a file or exit a program and your document contains unsaved changes. **CASE** ▸ *Explore the Help system in Microsoft Office, and then close your documents and exit any open programs.*

STEPS

1. **Point to the Zoom button in the Zoom group on the View tab of the Ribbon**

   A ScreenTip appears that describes how the Zoom button works and explains where to find other zoom controls.

   QUICK TIP
   You can also open Help (in any of the Office apps) by pressing [F1].

2. **Click the Tell me box above the Ribbon, then type Choose a template**

   As you type in the Tell me box, a Smart list anticipates what you might want help with. If you see the task you want to complete, you can click it and Word will take you to the dialog box or options you need to complete the task. If you don't see the answer to your query, you can use the bottom two options to search the database.

   QUICK TIP
   If you are not connected to the Internet, the Help window displays on the Help content available on your computer.

3. **Click Get Help on "choose a template"**

   The Word Help window opens, as shown in FIGURE 1-14, displaying help results for choosing a template in Word. Each entry is a hyperlink you can click to open a list of topics. The Help window also includes a toolbar of useful Help commands such as printing and increasing the font size for easier readability, and a Search field. Office.com supplements the help content available on your computer with a wide variety of up-to-date topics, templates, and training.

4. **Click the Where do I find templates link in the results list Word Help window**

   The Word Help window changes, and a more detailed explanation appears below the topic.

5. **If necessary, scroll down until the Download Microsoft Office templates topic fills the Word Help window**

   The topic is displayed in the Help window, as shown in FIGURE 1-15. The content in the window explains that you can create a wide variety of documents using a template (a pre-formatted document) and that you can get many templates free of charge.

   QUICK TIP
   You can print the entire current topic by clicking the Print button 🖶 on the Help toolbar, then clicking Print in the Print dialog box.

6. **Click the Keep Help on Top button ⊷ in the lower-right corner of the window**

   The Pin Help button rotates so the pin point is pointed towards the bottom of the screen: this allows you to read the Help window while you work on your document.

7. **Click the Word document window, notice the Help window remains visible**

8. **Click a blank area of the Help window, click 📌 to Unpin Help, click the Close button ☒ in the Help window, then click the Close button ☒ in the Word program window**

   Word closes, and the Excel program window is active.

9. **Click the Close button ☒ in the Excel program window, click the PowerPoint app button 📰 on the taskbar if necessary, then click the Close button ☒ to exit PowerPoint**

   Excel and PowerPoint both close.

FIGURE 1-14: **Word Help window**

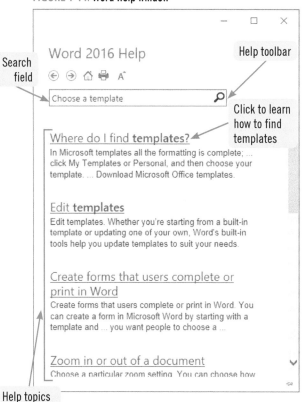

FIGURE 1-15: **Create a document Help topic**

Using sharing features and co-authoring capabilities

If you are using Word, Excel, or PowerPoint, you can take advantage of the Share feature, which makes it easy to share your files that have been saved to OneDrive. When you click the Share button, you will be asked to invite others to share the file. To do this, type in the name or email addresses in the Invite people text box. When you invite others, you have the opportunity to give them different levels of permission. You might want some people to have read-only privileges; you might want others to be able to make edits. Also available in Word, Excel, and PowerPoint is real-time co-authoring capabilities for files stored on OneDrive. Once a file on OneDrive is opened and all the users have been given editing privileges, all the users can make edits simultaneously. On first use, each user will be prompted to automatically share their changes.

Recovering a document

Each Office program has a built-in recovery feature that allows you to open and save files that were open at the time of an interruption such as a power failure. When you restart the program(s) after an interruption, the Document Recovery task pane opens on the left side of your screen displaying both original and recovered versions of the files that were open. If you're not sure which file to open (original or recovered), it's usually better to open the recovered file because it will contain the latest information. You can, however, open and review all versions of the file that were recovered and save the best one. Each file listed in the Document Recovery task pane displays a list arrow with options that allow you to open the file, save it as is, delete it, or show repairs made to it during recovery.

Practice

Concepts Review

Label the elements of the program window shown in FIGURE 1-16.

FIGURE 1-16

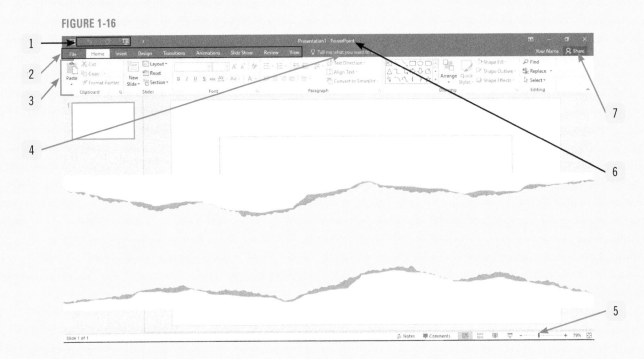

Match each project with the program for which it is best suited.

8. Microsoft PowerPoint   **a.** Corporate convention budget with expense projections

9. Microsoft Word   **b.** Presentation for city council meeting

10. Microsoft Excel   **c.** Business cover letter for a job application

11. Microsoft Access   **d.** Department store inventory

Independent Challenge 1

You just accepted an administrative position with a local independently owned insurance agent who has recently invested in computers and is now considering purchasing a subscription to Office 365. You have been asked to think of uses for the apps and you put your ideas in a Word document.

     a. Start Word, create a new Blank document, then save the document as **OF 1-Microsoft Office Apps Uses** in the location where you store your Data Files.

     b. Change the zoom factor to 120%, type **Microsoft Access**, press [Enter] twice, type **Microsoft Excel**, press [Enter] twice, type **Microsoft PowerPoint**, press [Enter] twice, type **Microsoft Word**, press [Enter] twice, then type your name.

     c. Click the line beneath each program name, type at least two tasks you can perform using that program (each separated by a comma), then press [Enter].

     d. Save the document, then submit your work to your instructor as directed.

     e. Exit Word.

Creating Documents with Word 2016

CASE You have been hired to work in the Marketing Department at Reason2Go (R2G), a company that provides adventurous travelers with meaningful project options for giving back to the global community. Shortly after reporting to your new office, Mary Watson, the vice president of sales and marketing, asks you to use Word to create a memo to the marketing staff and a letter to one of the project hosts.

Module Objectives

After completing this module, you will be able to:

- Understand word processing software
- Explore the Word window
- Start a document
- Save a document
- Select text
- Format text using the Mini toolbar and the Ribbon
- Use a document template
- Navigate a document

Files You Will Need

WD 1-1.docx

Learning
Outcomes
• Identify the
features of Word
• State the benefits
of using a word
processing
program

Understand Word Processing Software

A **word processing program** is a software program that includes tools for entering, editing, and formatting text and graphics. Microsoft Word is a powerful word processing program that allows you to create and enhance a wide range of documents quickly and easily. FIGURE 1-1 shows the first page of a report created using Word and illustrates some of the Word features you can use to enhance your documents. The electronic files you create using Word are called **documents**. One of the benefits of using Word is that document files can be stored on a hard disk, flash drive, or other physical storage device, or to OneDrive or another Cloud storage place, making them easy to transport, share, and revise. **CASE** *Before beginning your memo to the marketing staff, you explore the editing and formatting features available in Word.*

DETAILS

You can use Word to accomplish the following tasks:

• **Type and edit text**

The Word editing tools make it simple to insert and delete text in a document. You can add text to the middle of an existing paragraph, replace text with other text, undo an editing change, and correct typing, spelling, and grammatical errors with ease.

• **Copy and move text from one location to another**

Using the more advanced editing features of Word, you can copy or move text from one location and insert it in a different location in a document. You also can copy and move text between documents. This means you don't have to retype text that is already entered in a document.

• **Format text and paragraphs with fonts, colors, and other elements**

The sophisticated formatting tools in Word allow you to make the text in your documents come alive. You can change the size, style, and color of text, add lines and shading to paragraphs, and enhance lists with bullets and numbers. Creatively formatting text helps to highlight important ideas in your documents.

• **Format and design pages**

The page-formatting features in Word give you power to design attractive newsletters, create powerful résumés, and produce documents such as research papers, business cards, brochures, and reports. You can change paper size, organize text in columns, and control the layout of text and graphics on each page of a document. For quick results, Word includes preformatted cover pages, pull quotes, and headers and footers, as well as galleries of coordinated text, table, and graphic styles. If you are writing a research paper, Word makes it easy to manage reference sources and create footnotes, endnotes, and bibliographies.

• **Enhance documents with tables, charts, graphics, screenshots, and videos**

Using the powerful graphics tools in Word, you can spice up your documents with pictures, videos, photographs, screenshots, lines, preset quick shapes, and diagrams. You also can illustrate your documents with tables and charts to help convey your message in a visually interesting way.

• **Use Mail Merge to create form letters and mailing labels**

The Word Mail Merge feature allows you to send personalized form letters to many different people. You can also use Mail Merge to create mailing labels, directories, e-mail messages, and other types of documents.

• **Share documents securely**

The security features in Word make it quick and easy to remove comments, tracked changes, and unwanted personal information from your files before you share them with others. You can also add a password or a digital signature to a document and convert a file to a format suitable for publishing on the web.

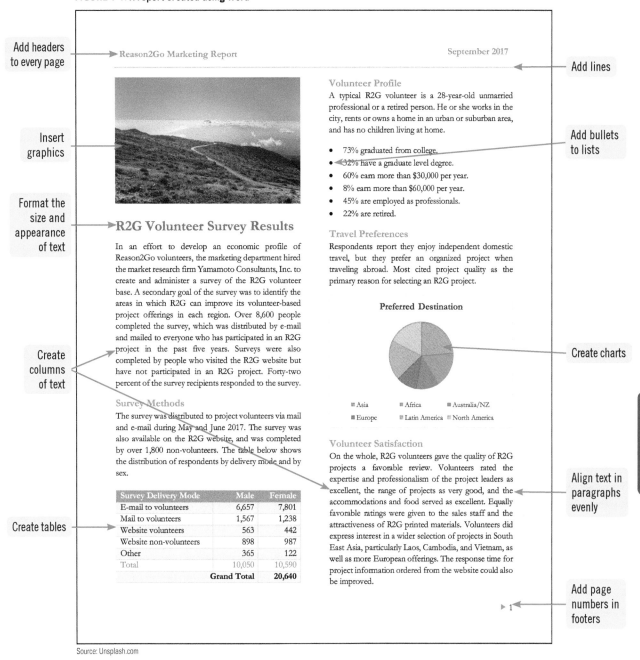

Source: Unsplash.com

The figure is labeled with the following callouts:

- Add headers to every page
- Insert graphics
- Format the size and appearance of text
- Create columns of text
- Create tables
- Add lines
- Add bullets to lists
- Create charts
- Align text in paragraphs evenly
- Add page numbers in footers

The report content shown:

Reason2Go Marketing Report — September 2017

Volunteer Profile

A typical R2G volunteer is a 28-year-old unmarried professional or a retired person. He or she works in the city, rents or owns a home in an urban or suburban area, and has no children living at home.

- 73% graduated from college.
- 32% have a graduate level degree.
- 60% earn more than $30,000 per year.
- 8% earn more than $60,000 per year.
- 45% are employed as professionals.
- 22% are retired.

Travel Preferences

Respondents report they enjoy independent domestic travel, but they prefer an organized project when traveling abroad. Most cited project quality as the primary reason for selecting an R2G project.

Preferred Destination

Asia — Africa — Australia/NZ
Europe — Latin America — North America

Volunteer Satisfaction

On the whole, R2G volunteers gave the quality of R2G projects a favorable review. Volunteers rated the expertise and professionalism of the project leaders as excellent, the range of projects as very good, and the accommodations and food served as excellent. Equally favorable ratings were given to the sales staff and the attractiveness of R2G printed materials. Volunteers did express interest in a wider selection of projects in South East Asia, particularly Laos, Cambodia, and Vietnam, as well as more European offerings. The response time for project information ordered from the website could also be improved.

R2G Volunteer Survey Results

In an effort to develop an economic profile of Reason2Go volunteers, the marketing department hired the market research firm Yamamoto Consultants, Inc. to create and administer a survey of the R2G volunteer base. A secondary goal of the survey was to identify the areas in which R2G can improve its volunteer-based project offerings in each region. Over 8,600 people completed the survey, which was distributed by e-mail and mailed to everyone who has participated in an R2G project in the past five years. Surveys were also completed by people who visited the R2G website but have not participated in an R2G project. Forty-two percent of the survey recipients responded to the survey.

Survey Methods

The survey was distributed to project volunteers via mail and e-mail during May and June 2017. The survey was also available on the R2G website, and was completed by over 1,800 non-volunteers. The table below shows the distribution of respondents by delivery mode and by sex.

Survey Delivery Mode	Male	Female
E-mail to volunteers	6,657	7,801
Mail to volunteers	1,567	1,238
Website volunteers	563	442
Website non-volunteers	898	987
Other	365	122
Total	10,050	10,590
Grand Total		20,640

1

Planning a document

Before you create a new document, it's a good idea to spend time planning it. Identify the message you want to convey, the audience for your document, and the elements, such as tables or charts, you want to include. You should also think about the tone and look of your document—are you writing a business letter, which should be written in a pleasant, but serious, tone and have a formal appearance, or are you creating a flyer that must be colorful, eye-catching, and fun to read? The purpose and audience for your document determine the appropriate design. Planning the layout and design of a document involves deciding how to organize the text, selecting the fonts to use, identifying the graphics to include, and selecting the formatting elements that will enhance the message and appeal of the document. For longer documents, such as newsletters, it can be useful to sketch the layout and design of each page before you begin.

Explore the Word Window

When you start Word, the Word start screen opens. It includes a list of recently opened documents and a gallery of templates for creating a new document. **CASE** ➤ *You open a blank document and examine the elements of the Word program window.*

STEPS

1. Start Word, **then click** Blank document

A blank document opens in the **Word program window**, as shown in FIGURE 1-2. The blinking vertical line in the document window is the **insertion point**. It indicates where text appears as you type.

2. Move the mouse pointer around the Word program window

The mouse pointer changes shape depending on where it is in the Word program window. You use pointers to move the insertion point or to select text to edit. TABLE 1-1 describes common pointers in Word.

3. Place the mouse pointer over a button on the Ribbon

When you place the mouse pointer over a button or some other elements of the Word program window, a ScreenTip appears. A **ScreenTip** is a label that identifies the name of the button or feature, briefly describes its function, conveys any keyboard shortcut for the command, and includes a link to associated help topics, if any.

DETAILS

Using FIGURE 1-2 **as a guide, find the elements described below in your program window:**

• The **title bar** displays the name of the document and the name of the program. Until you give a new document a different name, its temporary name is Document1. The left side of the title bar contains the **Quick Access toolbar**, which includes buttons for saving a document and for undoing, redoing, and repeating a change. The right side of the title bar contains the **Ribbon Display Options button**, which you use to hide or show the Ribbon and tabs, the resizing buttons, and the program Close button.

• The **File tab** provides access to **Backstage view** where you manage files and the information about them. Backstage view includes commands related to working with documents, such as opening, printing, and saving a document. The File tab also provides access to your account and to the Word Options dialog box, which is used to customize the way you use Word.

• The **Ribbon** contains the Word tabs. Each **tab** on the Ribbon includes buttons for commands related to editing and formatting documents. The commands are organized in **groups**. For example, the Home tab includes the Clipboard, Font, Paragraph, Styles, and Editing groups. The Ribbon also includes the **Tell Me box**, which you can use to find a command or access the Word Help system, and the **Share button**, which you can use to save a document to the Cloud.

• The **document window** displays the current document. You enter text and format your document in the document window.

• The rulers appear in the document window in Print Layout view. The **horizontal ruler** displays left and right document margins as well as the tab settings and paragraph indents, if any, for the paragraph in which the insertion point is located. The **vertical ruler** displays the top and bottom document margins.

• The **vertical** and **horizontal scroll bars** are used to display different parts of the document in the document window. The scroll bars include **scroll boxes** and **scroll arrows**, which you use to scroll.

• The **status bar** displays the page number of the current page, the total number of pages and words in the document, and the status of spelling and grammar checking. It also includes the view buttons, the Zoom slider, and the Zoom level button. You can customize the status bar to display other information.

• The **view buttons** on the status bar allow you to display the document in Read Mode, Print Layout, or Web Layout view. The **Zoom slider** and the **Zoom level button** provide quick ways to enlarge and decrease the size of the document in the document window, making it easy to zoom in on a detail of a document or to view the layout of the document as a whole.

FIGURE 1-2: Elements of the Word program window

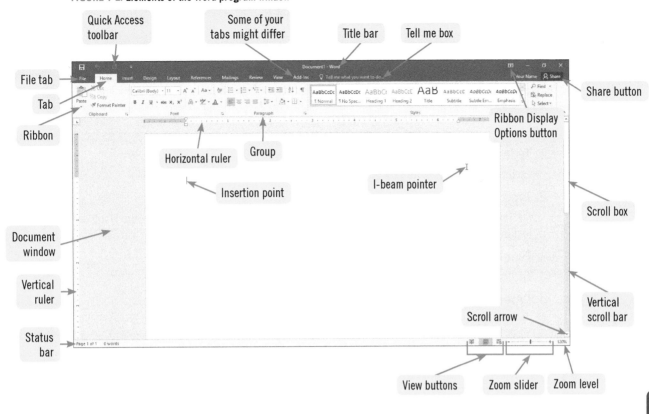

Quick Access toolbar

Some of your tabs might differ

Title bar

Tell me box

File tab

Tab

Ribbon

Share button

Horizontal ruler

Group

Ribbon Display Options button

Insertion point

I-beam pointer

Scroll box

Document window

Vertical ruler

Vertical scroll bar

Status bar

Scroll arrow

View buttons

Zoom slider

Zoom level

TABLE 1-1: Common mouse pointers in Word

name	pointer	use to
I-beam pointer	I	Move the insertion point in a document or to select text
Click and Type pointers, including left-align and center-align	I≡ I	Move the insertion point to a blank area of a document in Print Layout or Web Layout view; double-clicking with a Click and Type pointer automatically applies the paragraph formatting (alignment and indentation) required to position text or a graphic at that location in the document
Selection pointer	▷	Click a button or other element of the Word program window; appears when you point to elements of the Word program window
Right-pointing arrow pointer	⬁	Select a line or lines of text; appears when you point to the left edge of a line of text in the document window
Hand pointer	⬆	Open a hyperlink; appears when you point to a hyperlink in a task pane or when you press [Ctrl] and point to a hyperlink in a document
Hide white space pointer	⊣⊢	Hide the white space in the top and bottom margins of a document in Print Layout view
Show white space pointer	⊤⊥	Show the white space in the top and bottom margins of a document in Print Layout view

Creating Documents with Word 2016

Start a Document

You begin a new document by simply typing text in a blank document in the document window. Word uses **word wrap**, a feature that automatically moves the insertion point to the next line of the document as you type. You only press [Enter] when you want to start a new paragraph or insert a blank line. **CASE** *You type a quick memo to the marketing staff.*

STEPS

1. **Type Reason2Go, then press [Enter] twice**

   Each time you press [Enter] the insertion point moves to the start of the next line.

2. **Type TO:, then press [Tab] twice**

   Pressing [Tab] moves the insertion point several spaces to the right. You can use the [Tab] key to align the text in a memo header or to indent the first line of a paragraph.

3. **Type R2G Managers, then press [Enter]**

   The insertion point moves to the start of the next line.

4. **Type:** FROM: [Tab] [Tab] Mary Watson [Enter]

   DATE: [Tab] [Tab] March 13, 2017 [Enter]

   RE: [Tab] [Tab] Marketing Meeting [Enter] [Enter]

   Red or blue wavy lines may appear under the words you typed, indicating a possible spelling or grammar error. Spelling and grammar checking is one of the many automatic features you will encounter as you type. TABLE 1-2 describes several of these automatic features. You can correct any typing errors you make later.

5. **Type The next marketing staff meeting will be held on the 17th of March at 2 p.m. in the conference room on the ground floor., then press [Spacebar]**

   As you type, notice that the insertion point moves automatically to the next line of the document. You also might notice that Word automatically changed "17th" to "17th" in the memo. This feature is called **AutoCorrect**. AutoCorrect automatically makes typographical adjustments and detects and adjusts typing errors, certain misspelled words (such as "taht" for "that"), and incorrect capitalization as you type.

6. **Type Heading the agenda will be the launch of our new Sea Turtle Conservation Project, a rewarding opportunity to supervise hatcheries, count and release baby turtles, and patrol the nighttime shores of Costa Rica. The project is scheduled for September 2017.**

   When you type the first few characters of "September," the Word AutoComplete feature displays the complete word in a ScreenTip. **AutoComplete** suggests text to insert quickly into your documents. You can ignore AutoComplete for now. Your memo should resemble FIGURE 1-3.

7. **Press [Enter], then type Sam Roiphe is in Tamarindo hammering out the details. A preliminary draft of the project brochure is attached. Bring your creative ideas to the meeting.**

   When you press [Enter] and type the new paragraph, notice that Word adds more space between the paragraphs than it does between the lines in each paragraph. This is part of the default style for paragraphs in Word, called the **Normal style**.

8. **Position the I pointer after for (but before the space) in the last sentence of the first paragraph, then click to move the insertion point after "for"**

9. **Press [Backspace] three times, then type to begin in**

   Pressing [Backspace] removes the character before the insertion point.

10. **Move the insertion point before staff in the first sentence, then press [Delete] six times to remove the word "staff" and the space after it**

    Pressing [Delete] removes the character after the insertion point. FIGURE 1-4 shows the revised memo.

FIGURE 1-3: Memo text in the document window

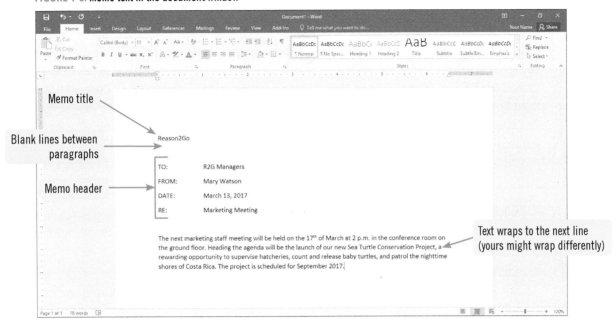

Memo title

Blank lines between paragraphs

Memo header

Text wraps to the next line (yours might wrap differently)

FIGURE 1-4: Edited memo text

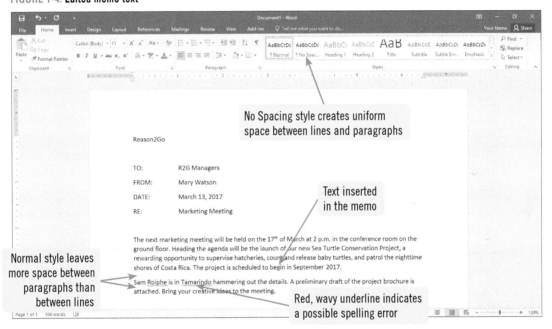

No Spacing style creates uniform space between lines and paragraphs

Text inserted in the memo

Normal style leaves more space between paragraphs than between lines

Red, wavy underline indicates a possible spelling error

TABLE 1-2: Automatic features that appear as you type in Word

feature	what appears	to use
AutoComplete	A ScreenTip suggesting text to insert appears as you type	Press [Enter] to insert the text suggested by the ScreenTip; continue typing to reject the suggestion
AutoCorrect	A small blue box appears when you place the pointer over text corrected by AutoCorrect; an AutoCorrect Options button appears when you point to the blue box	Word automatically corrects typos, minor spelling errors, and capitalization, and adds typographical symbols (such as © and ™) as you type; to reverse an AutoCorrect adjustment, click the AutoCorrect Options list arrow, then click the option that will undo the action
Spelling and Grammar	A red wavy line under a word indicates a possible misspelling or a repeated word; a blue wavy line under text indicates a possible grammar error	Right-click red- or blue-underlined text to display a shortcut menu of correction options; click a correction option to accept it and remove the wavy underline

Save a Document

Learning Outcomes
- Save a file using a descriptive filename
- Use the Save As dialog box

To store a document permanently so you can open it and edit it at another time, you must save it as a **file**. When you **save** a document you give it a name, called a **filename**, and indicate the location where you want to store the file. Files created in Word 2016 are automatically assigned the .docx file extension to distinguish them from files created in other software programs. You can save a document using the Save button on the Quick Access toolbar or the Save command on the File tab. Once you have saved a document for the first time, you should save it again every few minutes and always before printing so that the saved file is updated to reflect your latest changes. **CASE** ▶ *You save your memo using a descriptive filename and the default file extension.*

1. **Click the Save button 🖫 on the Quick Access toolbar**

   The first time you save a document, the Save As screen opens. The screen displays all the places you can save a file to, including OneDrive, your PC, or a different location.

2. **Click Browse in the Save As screen**

   The Save As dialog box opens, similar to FIGURE 1-5. The default filename, Reason2Go, appears in the File name text box. The default filename is based on the first few words of the document. The default file type, Word Document, appears in the Save as type list box. TABLE 1-3 describes the functions of some of the buttons in the Save As dialog box.

3. **Type WD 1-Sea Turtle Memo in the File name text box**

   The new filename replaces the default filename. Giving your documents brief descriptive filenames makes it easier to locate and organize them later. You do not need to type .docx when you type a new filename.

4. **Navigate to the location where you store your Data Files**

   You can navigate to a different drive or folder in several ways. For example, you can click a drive or folder in the Address bar or the navigation pane to go directly to that location. You can also double-click a drive or folder in the folder window to change the active location. When you are finished navigating to the drive or folder where you store your Data Files, that location appears in the Address bar. Your Save As dialog box should resemble FIGURE 1-6.

5. **Click Save**

   The document is saved to the drive and folder you specified in the Save As dialog box, and the title bar displays the new filename, WD 1-Sea Turtles Memo.docx.

6. **Place the insertion point before conference in the first sentence, type large, then press [Spacebar]**

   You can continue to work on a document after you have saved it with a new filename.

7. **Click 🖫**

   Your change to the memo is saved. After you save a document for the first time, you must continue to save the changes you make to the document. You also can press [Ctrl][S] to save a document.

FIGURE 1-5: **Save As dialog box**

Active folder or drive (yours might differ)

Folders and files in the active folder or drive (yours might differ)

Default filename and file extension are selected

Click to change the file type

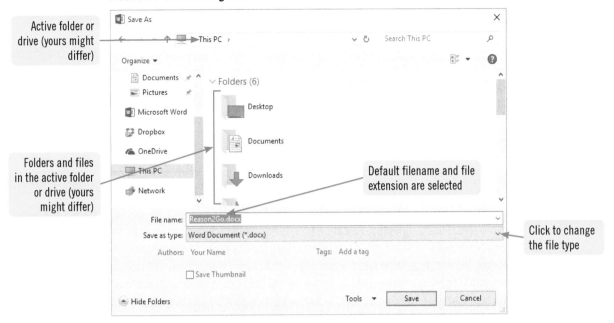

FIGURE 1-6: **File to be saved to the Mod 1 folder**

Click to create a new folder in the active folder or drive

Save location (yours might differ)

Your dialog box might list the files and folders in the active drive or folder here

New filename

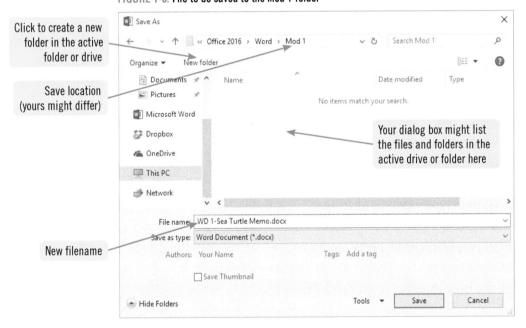

TABLE 1-3: **Save As dialog box buttons**

button	use to
Back	Navigate back to the last location shown in the Address bar
Forward	Navigate to the location that was previously shown in the Address bar
Up to	Navigate to the location above the current location in the folder hierarchy
Organize	Open a menu of commands related to organizing the selected file or folder, including Cut, Copy, Delete, Rename, and Properties
New folder	Create a new folder in the current folder or drive
Change your view	Change the way folder and file information is shown in the folder window in the Save As dialog box; click the Change your view button to toggle between views, or click the list arrow to open a menu of view options

Select Text

Before deleting, editing, or formatting text, you must **select** the text. Selecting text involves clicking and dragging the I-beam pointer across the text to highlight it. You also can click in the margin to the left of text with the ⚓ pointer to select whole lines or paragraphs. TABLE 1-4 describes the many ways to select text. **CASE** *You revise the memo by selecting text and replacing it with new text.*

STEPS

1. **Click the** Show/Hide ¶ **button** ¶ **in the Paragraph group**

   Formatting marks appear in the document window. **Formatting marks** are special characters that appear on your screen but do not print. Common formatting marks include the paragraph symbol (¶), which shows the end of a paragraph—wherever you press [Enter]; the dot symbol (·), which represents a space—wherever you press [Spacebar]; and the arrow symbol (▲), which shows the location of a tab stop—wherever you press [Tab]. Working with formatting marks turned on can help you to select, edit, and format text with precision.

2. **Click before** R2G Managers, **then drag the** I **pointer over the text to select it**

   The words are selected, as shown in FIGURE 1-7. For now, you can ignore the floating toolbar that appears over text when you first select it.

3. **Type** Marketing Staff

   The text you type replaces the selected text.

4. **Double-click** Mary, **type your first name, double-click** Watson, **then type your last name**

   Double-clicking a word selects the entire word.

5. **Place the pointer in the margin to the left of the RE: line so that the pointer changes to** ⚓, **click to select the line, then type** RE: [Tab] [Tab] Launch of new Sea Turtle Conservation Project

   Clicking to the left of a line of text with the ⚓ pointer selects the entire line.

6. **Select** supervise **in the third line of the first paragraph, type** build, **select** nighttime shores, **then type** moon-lit beaches

7. **Select the sentence** Sam Roiphe is in Tamarindo hammering out the details. **in the second paragraph, then press** [Delete]

   Selecting text and pressing [Delete] removes the text from the document.

8. **Click** ¶, **then click the** Save button 💾 **on the Quick Access toolbar**

   Formatting marks are turned off, and your changes to the memo are saved. The Show/Hide ¶ button is a **toggle button**, which means you can use it to turn formatting marks on and off. The edited memo is shown in FIGURE 1-8.

FIGURE 1-7: Text selected in the memo

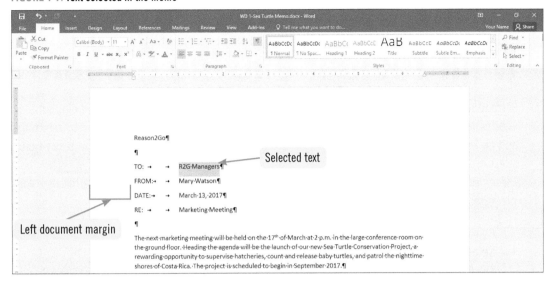

FIGURE 1-8: Edited memo with replacement text

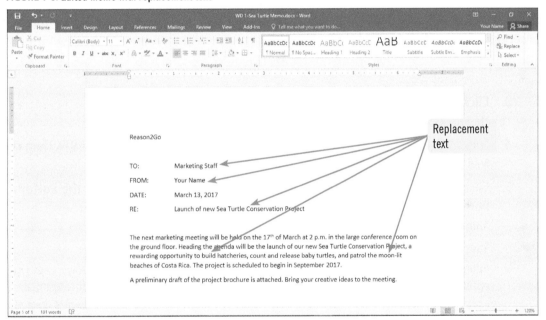

TABLE 1-4: Methods for selecting text

to select	use the pointer to
Any amount of text	Drag over the text
A word	Double-click the word
A line of text	Move the pointer to the left of the line, then click
A sentence	Press and hold [Ctrl], then click the sentence
A paragraph	Triple-click the paragraph or double-click with the pointer to the left of the paragraph
A large block of text	Click at the beginning of the selection, press and hold [Shift], then click at the end of the selection
Multiple nonconsecutive selections	Select the first selection, then press and hold [Ctrl] as you select each additional selection
An entire document	Triple-click with the pointer to the left of any text; press [Ctrl][A]; or click the Select button in the Editing group on the Home tab, and then click Select All

Format Text Using the Mini Toolbar and the Ribbon

Learning Outcomes
- Apply bold to text
- Increase the font size of text
- Print a document

Formatting text is a fast and fun way to spruce up the appearance of a document and highlight important information. You can easily change the font, color, size, style, and other attributes of text by selecting the text and clicking a command on the Home tab. The **Mini toolbar**, which appears above text when you first select it, also includes commonly used text and paragraph formatting commands. **CASE** *You enhance the appearance of the memo by formatting the text using the Mini toolbar. When you are finished, you preview the memo for errors and then print it.*

STEPS

1. **Select Reason2Go**

   The Mini toolbar appears over the selected text, as shown in FIGURE 1-9. You click a formatting option on the Mini toolbar to apply it to the selected text. TABLE 1-5 describes the function of the buttons on the Mini toolbar. The buttons on the Mini toolbar are also available on the Ribbon.

2. **Click the Increase Font Size button Å on the Mini toolbar six times, then click the Bold button B on the Mini toolbar**

   Each time you click the Increase Font Size button the selected text is enlarged. Applying bold to the text makes it thicker.

3. **Click the Center button in the Paragraph group on the Home tab**

   The selected text is centered between the left and right margins.

4. **Select TO:, click B, select FROM:, click B, select DATE:, click B, select RE:, then click B**

   Bold is applied to the memo header labels.

5. **Click the blank line between the RE: line and the body text, then click the Bottom Border button ⊞ in the Paragraph group**

   A single-line border is added between the heading and the body text in the memo.

6. **Save the document, click the File tab, then click Print**

   Information related to printing the document appears on the Print screen in Backstage view. Options for printing the document appear on the left side of the Print screen and a preview of the document as it will look when printed appears on the right side, as shown in FIGURE 1-10. Before you print a document, it's a good habit to examine it closely so you can identify and correct any problems.

7. **Click the Zoom In button + on the status bar five times, then proofread your document carefully for errors**

   The document is enlarged in print preview. If you notice errors in your document, you need to correct them before you print. To do this, press [Esc] or click the Back button in Backstage view, correct any mistakes, save your changes, click the File tab, and then click the Print command again to be ready to print the document.

8. **Click the Print button on the Print screen**

   A copy of the memo prints using the default print settings. To change the current printer, change the number of copies to print, select what pages of a document to print, or modify another print setting, you simply change the appropriate setting on the Print screen before clicking the Print button.

9. **Click the File tab, then click Close**

   The document closes, but the Word program window remains open.

FIGURE 1-9: **Mini toolbar**

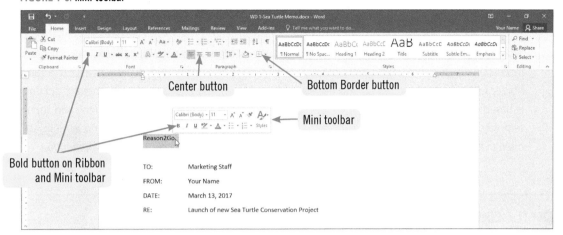

FIGURE 1-10: **Preview of the completed memo**

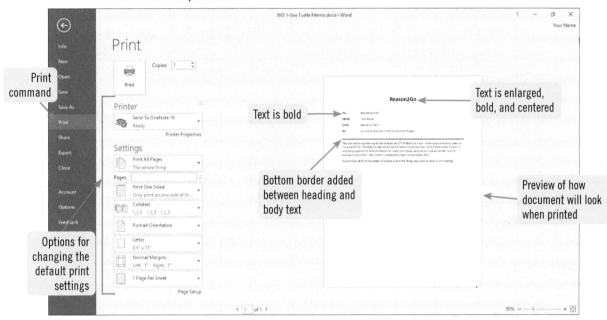

TABLE 1-5: **Buttons on the Mini toolbar**

button	use to	button	use to
Calibri (Body) ▾	Change the font of text	**B**	Apply bold to text
11 ▾	Change the font size of text	*I*	Apply italic to text
A^	Make text larger	U	Apply an underline to text
A˅	Make text smaller	aby ▾	Apply colored highlighting to text
✔	Copy the formats applied to selected text to other text	A ▾	Change the color of text
A Styles	Apply a style to text	⋮≡ ▾	Apply bullets to paragraphs
		≣ ▾	Apply numbering to paragraphs

Use a Document Template

Learning Outcomes
- Search for templates
- Customize a template
- Use content controls

Word includes many templates that you can use to create letters, reports, brochures, calendars, and other professionally designed documents quickly. A **template** is a formatted document that contains place-holder text and graphics, which you replace with your own text and graphics. To create a document that is based on a template, you use the New command on the File tab in Backstage view, and then select a template to use. You can then customize the document and save it with a new filename. **CASE** *You use a template to create a cover letter for a contract you will send to the Rainforest Hotel in Tamarindo.*

STEPS

> **QUICK TIP**
> You must have an active Internet connection to search for templates.

1. **Click the** File tab, **then click** New

   The New screen opens in Backstage view, as shown in FIGURE 1-11. You can select a template from the gallery shown in this window, or use the search box and links in the Suggested Searches section to find other templates.

> **TROUBLE**
> Templates change over time. If this template is not available, select another Cover Letter template or just read the steps to understand how to work with templates.

2. **Scroll down until you find the** Cover Letter (blue) **thumbnail on the New screen, click it, preview the template in the preview window that opens, then click** Create

   The Cover Letter (blue) template opens as a new document in the document window. It contains placeholder text, which you can replace with your own information. Your name might appear at the top of the document. Don't be concerned if it does not. When a document is created using this template, Word automatically enters the username from the Word Options dialog box at the top of the document and in the signature block.

3. **Click** [Date] **in the document**

   The placeholder text is selected and appears inside a content control. A **content control** is an interactive object that you use to customize a document with your own information. A content control might include placeholder text, a drop-down list of choices, or a calendar.

4. **Click the** [Date] **list arrow**

   A calendar opens below the content control. You use the calendar to select the date you want to appear on your document—simply click a date on the calendar to enter that date in the document.

5. **Click the** Today **button on the calendar**

   The current date replaces the placeholder text.

> **QUICK TIP**
> You can delete any content control by right-clicking it, and then clicking Remove Content Control on the menu that opens.

6. **Click** [Recipient Name], **type** Ms. Yana Roy, **press** [Enter], **type** Manager, **press** [Enter], **type** Rainforest Lodge, **press** [Enter], **type** P.O. Box 4397, **press** [Enter], **then type** Tamarindo 50309, COSTA RICA

   You do not need to drag to select the placeholder text in a content control, you can simply click it. The text you type replaces the placeholder text.

7. **Click** [Recipient], **then type** Ms. Roy

   The text you type replaces the placeholder text in the greeting line.

8. **Click the** File tab, **click** Save As, **then save the document as** WD 1-Rainforest Letter **to the location where you store your Data Files**

   The document is saved with the filename WD 1-Rainforest Letter, as shown in FIGURE 1-12.

FIGURE 1-11: **New screen in Backstage view**

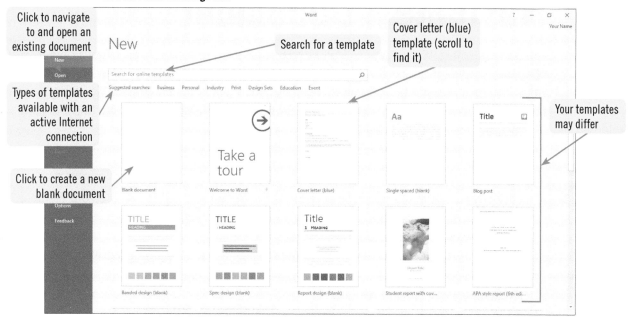

Click to navigate to and open an existing document

Types of templates available with an active Internet connection

Click to create a new blank document

Search for a template

Cover letter (blue) template (scroll to find it)

Your templates may differ

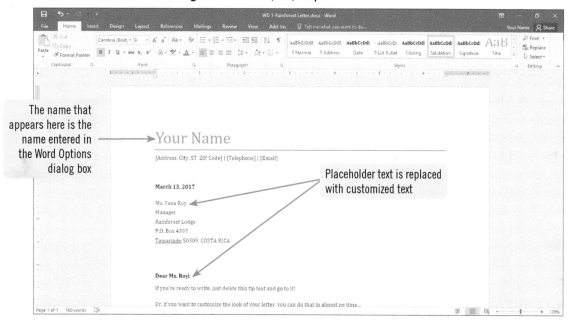

FIGURE 1-12: **Document created using the Cover Letter (blue) template**

The name that appears here is the name entered in the Word Options dialog box

Placeholder text is replaced with customized text

Word 2016

Using the Undo, Redo, and Repeat commands

Word remembers the editing and formatting changes you make so that you can easily reverse or repeat them. You can reverse the last action you took by clicking the Undo button 🔙 on the Quick Access toolbar, or you can undo a series of actions by clicking the Undo list arrow 🔙 ▾ and selecting the action you want to reverse. When you undo an action using the Undo list arrow, you also undo all the actions above it in the list—that is, all actions that were performed after the action you selected. Similarly, you can keep the change you just reversed by using the Redo button ↩

on the Quick Access toolbar. The Redo button appears only immediately after clicking the Undo button to undo a change.

If you want to repeat an action you just completed, you can use the Repeat button 🔄 on the Quick Access toolbar. For example, if you just typed "thank you," clicking 🔄 inserts "thank you" at the location of the insertion point. If you just applied bold, clicking 🔄 applies bold to the currently selected text. You also can repeat the last action you took by pressing [F4].

Navigate a Document

Learning Outcomes
- Remove a content control
- Zoom, scroll, and use Word views

The Zoom feature in Word lets you enlarge a document in the document window to get a close-up view of a detail or reduce the size of the document in the document window for an overview of the layout as a whole. You zoom in and out on a document using the tools in the Zoom group on the View tab or you can use the Zoom level buttons and Zoom slider on the status bar. **CASE** *You find it is helpful to zoom in and out on the document as you finalize the letter.*

STEPS

TROUBLE
If your name does not appear in the content control, replace the text that does.

1. **Click your name in the upper-left corner of the document, right-click the** Your Name **content control, click** Remove Content Control **on the menu that opens, select your name, then type** Reason2Go

   Removing the content control changes the text to static text that you can then replace with other text.

TROUBLE
If you do not see the vertical scroll box, move the pointer to the right side of the document window to display it.

2. **Drag the** vertical scroll box down **until the body of the letter and the signature block are visible in your document window**

   You **scroll** to display different parts of the document in the document window. You can also scroll by clicking the scroll arrows above and below the scroll bar, or by clicking the scroll bar.

3. **Select the** four paragraphs **of placeholder body text, type** Enclosed please find a copy of our contract for the Sea Turtle Conservation Project. We look forward to working with you.**, then, if the name in the signature block is not your name, select the text in the content control and type your name**

   The text you type replaces the placeholder text, as shown in FIGURE 1-13.

4. **Click the** View tab, **then click the** Page Width button **in the Zoom group**

   The document is enlarged to the width of the document window. When you enlarge a document, the area where the insertion point is located appears in the document window.

QUICK TIP
You can also click the Zoom button in the Zoom group on the View tab to open the Zoom dialog box.

5. **Click the** Zoom level button 154% **on the status bar**

   The Zoom dialog box opens. You use the Zoom dialog box to select a zoom level for displaying the document in the document window.

6. **Click the** Whole page option button, **then click** OK **to view the entire document**

QUICK TIP
You can also move the Zoom slider by clicking a point on the Zoom slide, or by clicking the Zoom Out and Zoom In buttons.

7. **Click** Reason2Go **to move the insertion point to the top of the page, then move the Zoom slider to the right until the Zoom percentage is approximately 230%**

   Dragging the Zoom slider to the right enlarges the document in the document window. Dragging the zoom slider to the left allows you to see more of the page at a reduced size.

8. **Click the** [Address...] content control, **type** Travel, **click** [Telephone], **type** Volunteer, **click** [Email], **type** www.r2g.com, **then press** [Tab]

   You can replace placeholder text with information that is different from what is suggested in the content control.

9. **Click the** Read Mode button 📖 **on the status bar**

   The document appears in the document window in Read Mode view. Read Mode view hides the tabs and ribbon to make it easier to read documents on screen. Read Mode view is useful for reading long documents.

QUICK TIP
You can also click View on the menu bar, then click Edit Document to return to Print Layout view.

10. **Click the** Print Layout view button 📄 **on the status bar, click the** Zoom Out button ➖ **on the status bar until the zoom level is 100%, then save the document**

    The completed cover letter is displayed at 100% zoom level in Print Layout view, as shown in FIGURE 1-14.

11. **Submit the document to your instructor, close the file, then exit Word**

FIGURE 1-13: Replacement text and Zoom slider

FIGURE 1-13: Replacement text and Zoom slider

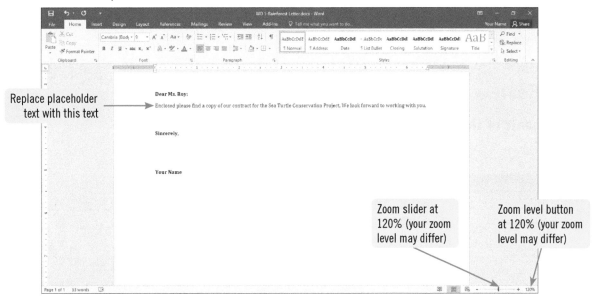

Replace placeholder text with this text

Zoom slider at 120% (your zoom level may differ)

Zoom level button at 120% (your zoom level may differ)

FIGURE 1-14: Completed letter

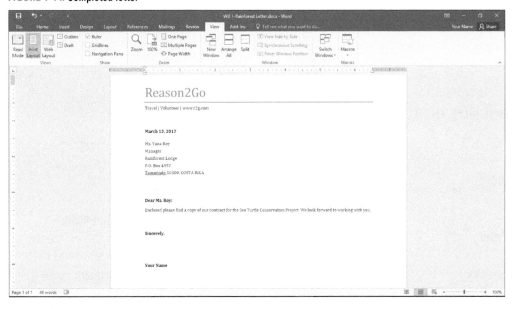

Using Word document views

Document **views** are different ways of displaying a document in the document window. Each Word view provides features that are useful for working on different types of documents. The default view, **Print Layout view**, displays a document as it will look on a printed page. Print Layout view is helpful for formatting text and pages, including adjusting document margins, creating columns of text, inserting graphics, and formatting headers and footers. Also useful is **Read Mode view**, which displays document text so that it is easy to read on screen. Other Word views are helpful for performing specialized tasks. **Web Layout view** allows you to format webpages or documents that will be viewed on a computer screen. In Web Layout view,

a document appears just as it will when viewed with a web browser. **Outline view** is useful for editing and formatting longer documents that include multiple headings. Outline view allows you to reorganize text by moving the headings. Finally, **Draft view**, shows a simplified layout of a document, without margins, headers and footers, or graphics. When you want to quickly type and edit text, it's often easiest to work in Draft View. You switch between views by clicking the view buttons on the status bar or by using the commands on the View tab. Changing views does not affect how the printed document will appear. It simply changes the way you view the document in the document window.

Word 2016

Practice

Concepts Review

Label the elements of the Word program window shown in FIGURE 1-15.

FIGURE 1-15

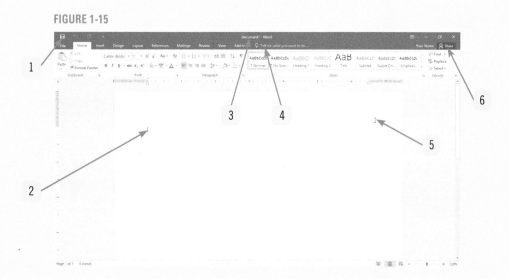

Match each term with the statement that best describes it.

7. **Ribbon**   **a.** A formatted document that contains placeholder text

8. **AutoCorrect**   **b.** Suggests text to insert into a document

9. **AutoComplete**   **c.** Fixes certain errors as you type

10. **Zoom slider**   **d.** Provides access to Word commands

11. **Status bar**   **e.** Special characters that appear on screen but do not print

12. **Horizontal ruler**   **f.** Displays tab settings and paragraph indents

13. **Template**   **g.** Enlarges and reduces the document in the document window

14. **Formatting marks**   **h.** Displays the number of pages in the current document

Select the best answer from the list of choices.

15. **Which of the following shows the number of words in the document?**
    - **a.** The title bar
    - **b.** The Ribbon
    - **c.** The status bar
    - **d.** The Mini toolbar

16. **Which tab includes buttons for formatting text?**
    - **a.** View
    - **b.** Page Layout
    - **c.** Insert
    - **d.** Home

17. **Which element of the Word window shows the top and bottom document margins settings?**
    - **a.** Status bar
    - **b.** View tab
    - **c.** Vertical ruler
    - **d.** Vertical scroll bar

18. **What is the default file extension for a document created in Word 2016?**
    - **a.** .doc
    - **b.** .dot
    - **c.** .dotx
    - **d.** .docx

19. Which of the following is not included in a ScreenTip for a command?

a. Link to a help topic on the command

c. Keyboard shortcut for the command

b. Alternative location of the command

d. Description of the function of the command

20. Which view is best for reading text onscreen?

a. Print Layout view

c. Read Mode view

b. Outline view

d. Draft view

Skills Review

1. Explore the Word program window.

a. Start Word and open a new, blank document.

b. Identify as many elements of the Word program window as you can without referring to the module material.

c. Click the File tab, then click the Info, New, Save, Open, Save As, Print, Share, and Export commands.

d. Click the Back button in Backstage view to return to the document window.

e. Click each tab on the Ribbon, review the groups and buttons on each tab, then return to the Home tab.

f. Point to each button on the Home tab and read its ScreenTip.

g. Click the view buttons to view the blank document in each view, then return to Print Layout view.

h. Use the Zoom slider to zoom all the way in and all the way out on the document, then return to 120%.

2. Start a document.

a. In a new blank document, type **Summer of Music Festivals** at the top of the page, then press [Enter] two times.

b. Type the following, pressing [Tab] as indicated and pressing [Enter] at the end of each line:

To: [Tab] [Tab] **Michael Mellon**

From: [Tab] [Tab] **Your Name**

Date: [Tab] [Tab] **Today's date**

Re: [Tab] [Tab] **Reservation confirmation**

Pages: [Tab] [Tab] **1**

Fax: [Tab] [Tab] **(603) 555-5478**

c. Press [Enter] again, then type **Thank you for your interest in our summer music festival weekend package, which includes accommodations for three nights, continental breakfast, and a festival pass. Rooms are still available during the following festivals: International Jazz Festival, Americana Festival, Classical Fringe Festival, and the Festival of Arts. Please see the attached schedule for festival dates and details.**

d. Press [Enter], then type **To make a reservation, please call me at (617) 555-7482 or visit our website. Payment must be received in full by the 3rd of June to hold a room. No one knows how to celebrate summer like music-lovers!**

e. Insert **Summer Strings Festival,** before International Jazz Festival.

f. Using the [Backspace] key, delete **1** in the Pages: line, then type **2**.

g. Using the [Delete] key, delete **festival** in the last sentence of the first paragraph.

3. Save a document.

a. Click the Save button on the Quick Access toolbar.

b. Save the document as **WD 1-Mellon Fax** with the default file extension to the location where you store your Data Files.

c. After your name, type a comma, press [Spacebar], then type **Reservations Manager**

d. Save the document.

4. Select text.

a. Turn on formatting marks.

b. Select the **Re:** line, then type **Re:** [Tab] [Tab] **Summer Music Festival Weekend Package**

Skills Review (continued)

    c. Select **three** in the first sentence, then type **two**.

    d. Select **3rd of June** in the second sentence of the last paragraph, type **15th of May**, select **room**, then type **reservation**.

    e. Delete the sentence **No one knows how to celebrate summer like music-lovers!**

    f. Turn off the display of formatting marks, then save the document.

5. Format text using the Mini toolbar.

    a. Select **Summer of Music Festivals**, click the Increase Font Size button on the Mini toolbar six times, then apply bold.

    b. Center **Summer of Music Festivals** on the page.

    c. Apply a bottom border under **Summer of Music Festivals**.

    d. Apply bold to the following words in the fax heading: **To:**, **From:**, **Date:**, **Re:**, **Pages:**, and **Fax:**.

    e. Read the document using the Read Mode view.

    f. Return to Print Layout view, zoom in on the document, then proofread the fax.

    g. Correct any typing errors in your document, then save the document. Compare your document to FIGURE 1-16.

    h. Submit the fax to your instructor, then close the document.

FIGURE 1-16

Summer of Music Festivals

To:	Michael Mellon
From:	Your Name, Reservations Manager
Date:	April 11, 2017
Re:	Summer Music Festival Weekend Package
Pages:	2
Fax:	(603) 555-5478

Thank you for your interest in our summer music festival weekend package, which includes accommodations for two nights, continental breakfast, and a festival pass. Rooms are still available during the following festivals: Summer Strings Festival, International Jazz Festival, Americana Festival, Classical Fringe Festival, and the Festival of Arts. Please see the attached schedule for dates and details.

To make a reservation, please call me at (617) 555-7482 or visit our website. Payment must be received in full by the 15th of May to hold a reservation.

6. Create a document using a template.

    a. Click the File tab, click New, then scroll the gallery of templates.

    b. Create a new document using the Fax cover sheet (Professional design) template.

    c. Click the "Company Name" placeholder text, type **Summer of Music Festivals**, delete the "Street Address" and "City..." content controls, click the "Phone number" placeholder text, type **Tel: 617-555-7482**, click the "Fax number" placeholder text, type **Fax: 617-555-1176**, click the website placeholder text, then type **www.summerofmusic.com**.

    d. Type **Jude Lennon** to replace the "To:" placeholder text; type **555-2119** to replace the "Fax:" placeholder text; click the "Phone:" placeholder text, then press [Delete]; then type **Summer of Music Festivals** to replace the "Re:" placeholder text.

    e. If your name is not on the From line, select the text in the From content control, then type your name.

    f. Insert today's date using the date content control.

    g. Delete the "Pages:" and "cc:" placeholder text.

    h. Save the document with the filename **WD 1-Lennon Fax** to the location where you store your Data Files, clicking OK if a warning box opens.

7. View and navigate a document.

    a. Scroll down until Comments is near the top of your document window.

    b. Replace the Comments placeholder text with the following text: **Packages for the following summer music festivals are sold out: Chamber Music Festival, Solstice Festival, and Dragonfly Festival. We had expected these packages to be less popular than those for the bigger festivals, but interest has been high. Next year, we will increase our bookings for these festivals by 30%.**

Skills Review (continued)

FIGURE 1-17

c. Use the Zoom dialog box to view the Whole Page.

d. Use the Zoom slider to set the Zoom percentage at approximately 100%.

e. Read the document using the Read Mode view.

f. Return to Print Layout view, zoom in on the document, then proofread the fax.

g. Preview the document, then correct any errors, saving changes if necessary. Compare your document to FIGURE 1-17. Submit the document to your instructor, close the file, then exit Word.

Independent Challenge 1

Yesterday you interviewed for a job as marketing director at Rose Design Services. You spoke with several people at the company, including Yuko Picard, chief executive officer, whose business card is shown in FIGURE 1-18. You need to write a follow-up letter to Ms. Picard, thanking her for the interview and expressing your interest in the company and the position. She also asked you to send her some samples of your marketing work, which you will enclose with the letter.

a. Start Word and save a new blank document as **WD 1-Picard Letter** to the location where you store your Data Files.

b. Begin the letter by clicking the No Spacing button in the Styles group. You use this button to apply the No Spacing style to the document so that your document does not include extra space between paragraphs.

c. Type a personal letterhead for the letter that includes your name, address, telephone number, and e-mail address. If Word formats your e-mail address as a hyperlink, right-click your e-mail address, then click Remove Hyperlink. (*Note: Format the letterhead after you finish typing the letter.*)

FIGURE 1-18

d. Three lines below the bottom of the letterhead, type today's date.

e. Four lines below the date, type the inside address, referring to FIGURE 1-18 for the information. Include the recipient's title, company name, and full mailing address.

f. Two lines below the inside address, type **Dear Ms. Picard:** for the salutation.

g. Two lines below the salutation, type the body of the letter according to the following guidelines:

- In the first paragraph, thank her for the interview. Then restate your interest in the position and express your desire to work for the company. Add any specific details you think will enhance the power of your letter.

- In the second paragraph, note that you are enclosing three samples of your work, and explain something about the samples you are enclosing.

- Type a short final paragraph.

h. Two lines below the last body paragraph, type a closing, then four lines below the closing, type the signature block. Be sure to include your name in the signature block.

i. Two lines below the signature block, type an enclosure notation. (*Hint*: An enclosure notation usually includes the word "Enclosures" or the abbreviation "Enc." followed by the number of enclosures in parentheses.)

j. Format the letterhead with bold, centering, and a bottom border.

k. Save your changes, preview the letter, submit it to your instructor, then close the document and exit Word.

Independent Challenge 2

Your company has recently installed Word 2016 on its company network. As the training manager, it's your responsibility to teach employees how to use the new software productively. Now that they have begun working with Word 2016, several employees have asked you about sharing documents with colleagues using OneDrive. In response, you wrote a memo to all employees explaining the Share feature. You now need to format the memo before distributing it.

a. Start Word, open the file **WD 1-1.docx** from the location where you store your Data Files, clicking the Enable Editing button if prompted to do so, then read the memo to get a feel for its contents. Switch to Print Layout view if the document is not already displayed in Print Layout view.

b. Save the file as **WD 1-Share Memo** to the location where you store your Data Files.

c. Replace the information in the memo header with the information shown in FIGURE 1-19. Make sure to include your name in the From line and the current date in the Date line.

d. Apply bold to **To:**, **From:**, **Date:**, and **Re:**.

e. Increase the size of **WORD TRAINING MEMORANDUM** to match FIGURE 1-19, center the text on the page, add a border below it, then save your changes.

f. Preview the memo, submit it to your instructor, then close the document and exit Word.

FIGURE 1-19

WORD TRAINING MEMORANDUM

To:	All employees
From:	Your Name, Training Manager
Date:	Today's date
Re:	Sharing documents

Independent Challenge 3

You are an expert on climate change. The president of the National Parks Association, Isabella Meerts, has asked you to be the keynote speaker at an upcoming conference on the impact of climate change on the national parks, to be held in Grand Teton National Park. You use one of the Word letter templates to write a letter to Ms. Meerts accepting the invitation and confirming the details. Your letter to Ms. Meerts should reference the following information:

- The conference will be held September 17–19, 2017, at the Jackson Lake Lodge in the park.
- You have been asked to speak for an hour on Saturday, September 18, followed by one-half hour for questions.
- Ms. Meerts suggested the lecture topic "Melting Glaciers, Changing Ecosystems."
- Your talk will include a 45-minute slide presentation.
- The National Parks Association will make your travel arrangements.
- Your preference is to arrive at Jackson Hole Airport on the morning of Friday, September 17, and to depart on Monday, September 20. You would like to rent a car at the airport for the drive to the Jackson Lake Lodge.
- You want to fly in and out of the airport closest to your home.

a. Start Word, click the File tab, click New, and then search for and select an appropriate letter template. Save the document as **WD 1-Meerts Letter** to the location where you store your Data Files.

b. Replace the placeholders in the letterhead with your personal information. Include your name, address, phone number, and e-mail address. Delete any placeholders that do not apply. (*Hints:* Depending on the template you choose, the letterhead might be located at the top or on the side of the document. You can press [Enter] when typing in a placeholder to add an additional line of text. You can also change the format of text typed in a placeholder. If your e-mail address appears as a hyperlink, right-click the e-mail address and click Remove Hyperlink.)

Independent Challenge 3 (continued)

c. Use the [Date] content control to select the current date.

d. Replace the placeholders in the inside address. Be sure to include Ms. Meerts title and the name of the organization. Make up a street address and zip code.

e. Type **Dear Ms. Meerts:** for the salutation.

f. Using the information listed previously, type the body of the letter:
   - In the first paragraph, accept the invitation to speak.
   - In the second paragraph, confirm the important conference details, confirm your lecture topic, and provide any relevant details.
   - In the third paragraph, state your travel preferences.
   - Type a short final paragraph.

g. Type **Sincerely,** for the closing, then include your name in the signature block.

h. Adjust the formatting of the letter as necessary. For example, remove bold formatting or change the font color of text to a more appropriate color.

i. Proofread your letter, make corrections as needed, then save your changes.

j. Submit the letter to your instructor, close the document, then exit Word.

Independent Challenge 4: Explore

Word includes a wide variety of templates that can help you create professional-looking documents quickly, including business letters, business cards, résumés, calendars, faxes, memos, labels, reports, blog posts, posters, invitations, certificates, newsletters, and holiday and party cards. In this independent challenge, you will explore the variety of Word templates available to you, and use a template to make a document that is helpful to you in your business or personal life. You might create business cards for yourself, a poster for an event, a letter for a job search, a new résumé, or an invitation to a party. Choose a template that allows you to personalize the text.

a. Start Word, click the File tab, click New, then click each link after Suggested searches: (Business, Personal, Industry, Print, Design Sets, Education, Event) to explore the templates available to you.

b. Preview all the templates for the type of document you want to create, and then select one to create a new document.

c. Save the document as **WD 1-Template Document** to the location where you store your Data Files.

d. Replace the placeholders in the document with your personal information. Delete any placeholders that do not apply. (*Hints:* You can press [Enter] when typing in a placeholder to add an additional line of text. If an e-mail or web address appears as a hyperlink in your document, right-click the e-mail or web address and then click Remove Hyperlink.)

e. Use the [Pick the date] content control to select a date if your document includes a date placeholder.

f. Experiment with changing the font of the text in your document by using the Font list arrow on the Mini toolbar or in the Font group on the Home tab. (*Note:* Remember to use the Undo button immediately after you make the change if you do not like the change and want to remove it.)

g. Experiment with changing the font size of the text in your document by using the Font Size list arrow on the Mini toolbar or in the Font group on the Home tab.

h. Experiment with changing the color of text in your document using the Font Color button on the Mini toolbar or in the Font group on the Home tab.

i. Make other adjustments to the document as necessary, using the Undo button to remove a change you decide you do not want to keep.

j. Save your changes to the document, preview it, submit it to your instructor, then close the document and exit Word.

Visual Workshop

Create the cover letter shown in FIGURE 1-20. Before beginning to type, click the No Spacing button in the Styles group on the Home tab. Add the bottom border to the letterhead after typing the letter. Save the document as **WD 1-Davidson Cover Letter** to the location where you store your Data Files, submit the letter to your instructor, then close the document and exit Word.

FIGURE 1-20

Your Name
82 Genesee Street, Madison, WI 53701
Tel: 608-555-7283; E-mail: yourname@gmail.com

November 8, 2017

Ms. Marta Davidson
Davidson Associates
812 Jefferson Street
Suite 300
Madison, WI 53704

Dear Ms. Davidson:

I read of the opening for a public information assistant in the November 4 edition of wisconsinjobs.com, and I would like to be considered for the position. I am a recent graduate of the University of Wisconsin-Madison (UW), and I am interested in pursuing a career in public relations.

My interest in a public relations career springs from my publicly acknowledged writing and journalism abilities. For example, at UW, I was a reporter for the student newspaper and frequently wrote press releases for campus and community events.

I have a wealth of experience using Microsoft Word in professional settings. Last summer, I worked as an office assistant for the architecture firm Mason & Greenbush, where I used Word to create newsletters, brochures, and financial reports. During the school year, I also worked part-time in the UW Office of Community Relations, where I used the Word mail merge feature to create form letters and mailing labels.

My enclosed resume details my skills and experience. I welcome the opportunity to discuss the position and my qualifications with you. I can be reached at 608-555-7283.

Sincerely,

Your Name

Enc.

Editing Documents

CASE ▶ You have been asked to edit and finalize a press release for an R2G promotional lecture series. The press release should provide information about the series so that newspapers, radio stations, and other media outlets can announce it to the public. R2G press releases are disseminated via the website and by e-mail. Before distributing the file electronically to your lists of press contacts and local R2G clients, you add several hyperlinks and then strip the file of private information.

Module Objectives

After completing this module, you will be able to:

- Cut and paste text
- Copy and paste text
- Use the Office Clipboard
- Find and replace text

- Check spelling and grammar
- Research information
- Add hyperlinks
- Work with document properties

Files You Will Need

WD 2-1.docx   WD 2-5.docx
WD 2-2.docx   WD 2-6.docx
WD 2-3.docx   WD 2-7.docx
WD 2-4.docx

Cut and Paste Text

Learning
Outcomes
- Open a document and save it with a new filename
- Edit text using formatting marks
- Cut and paste text

The editing features in Word allow you to move text from one location to another in a document. Moving text is often called **cut and paste**. When you **cut** text, it is removed from the document and placed on the **Clipboard**, a temporary storage area for text and graphics that you cut or copy from a document. You can then **paste**, or insert, text that is stored on the Clipboard in the document at the location of the insertion point. You cut and paste text using the Cut and Paste buttons in the Clipboard group on the Home tab. You also can move selected text by dragging it to a new location using the mouse. This operation is called **drag and drop**. **CASE** *You open the press release, save it with a new filename, and then reorganize the information in the press release using the cut-and-paste and drag-and-drop methods.*

STEPS

1. **Start** Word, **click** Blank document, **click the** File tab, **click** This PC on the Open screen, **click** Browse **to open the Open dialog box, navigate to the location where you store your Data Files, click** WD 2-1.docx, **then click** Open

   The document opens in Print Layout view. Once you have opened a file, you can edit it and use the Save or the Save As command to save your changes. You use the **Save** command when you want to save the changes you make to a file, overwriting the stored file. You use the **Save As** command when you want to leave the original file intact and create a duplicate file with a different filename, file extension, or location.

2. **Click the** File tab, **click** Save As, **click** Computer, **click** Browse **to open the Save As dialog box, type** WD 2-Lecture PR **in the File name text box, then click** Save

   You can now make changes to the press release file without affecting the original file.

3. **Replace** Mary Watson **with your name, scroll down until the headline "Pedro Soares to Speak..." is at the top of your document window, then click the** Show/Hide ¶ button ¶ **in the Paragraph group on the Home tab to display formatting marks**

4. **Select** Alaskan guide Michael Coonan, **(including the comma and the space after it) in the third body paragraph, then click the** Cut button **in the Clipboard group**

   The text is removed from the document and placed on the Clipboard. Word uses two different clipboards: the **system clipboard**, which holds just one item, and the **Office Clipboard** (the Clipboard), which holds up to 24 items. The last item you cut or copy is always added to both clipboards.

5. **Place the insertion point before** African **(but after the space) in the first line of the third paragraph, then click the** Paste button **in the Clipboard group**

   The text is pasted at the location of the insertion point, as shown in FIGURE 2-1. The Paste Options button appears below text when you first paste it in a document. For now you can ignore the Paste Options button.

6. **Press and hold** [Ctrl], **click the sentence** Ticket prices include lunch. **in the fourth paragraph, then release** [Ctrl]

   The entire sentence is selected. You will drag the selected text to a new location using the mouse.

7. **Press and hold the mouse button over the selected text, then drag the** pointer's vertical line **to the end of the fifth paragraph (between the period and the paragraph mark) as shown in** FIGURE 2-2

   You drag the insertion point to where you want the text to be inserted when you release the mouse button.

8. **Release the mouse button**

   The selected text is moved to the location of the insertion point. Text is not placed on the Clipboard when you drag and drop it.

9. **Deselect the text, then click the** Save button 🖫 **on the Quick Access toolbar**

FIGURE 2-1: Moved text with Paste Options button

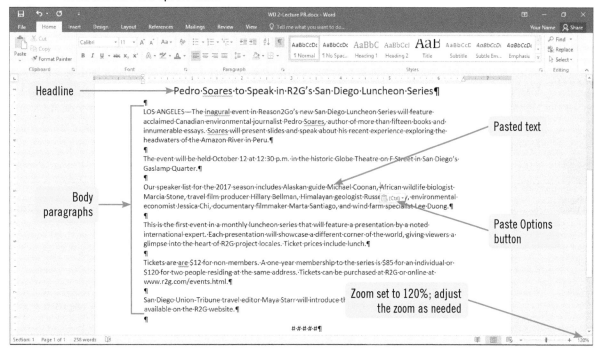

FIGURE 2-2: Dragging and dropping text in a new location

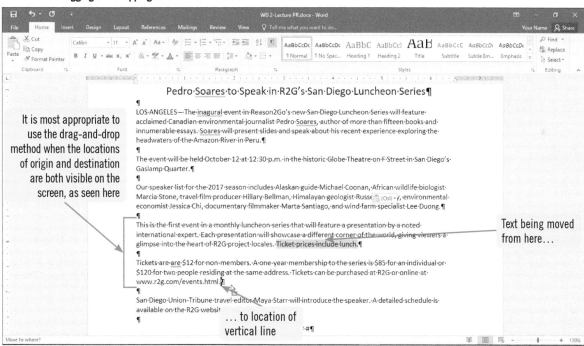

Using keyboard shortcuts

A **shortcut key** is a function key, such as [F1], or a combination of keys, such as [Ctrl][S], that you press to perform a command. For example, instead of using the Cut, Copy, and Paste commands on the Ribbon or the Mini toolbar, you can use the **keyboard shortcuts** [Ctrl][X] to cut text, [Ctrl][C] to copy text, and [Ctrl][V] to paste text. You can also press [Ctrl][S] to save changes to a document instead of clicking the Save button on the Quick Access toolbar or clicking Save on the File tab. Becoming skilled at using keyboard shortcuts can help you quickly accomplish many of the tasks you perform in Word. If a keyboard shortcut is available for a command, then it is listed in the ScreenTip for that command.

Copy and Paste Text

Copying and pasting text is similar to cutting and pasting text, except that the text you **copy** is not removed from the document. Rather, a copy of the text is placed on the Clipboard, leaving the original text in place. You can copy text to the Clipboard using the Copy button in the Clipboard group on the Home tab, or you can copy text by pressing [Ctrl] as you drag the selected text from one location to another. **CASE** *You continue to edit the press release by copying text from one location to another using the copy-and-paste and drag-and-drop methods.*

STEPS

1. **Select** San Diego Luncheon **in the headline, then click the** Copy button **in the Clipboard group on the Home tab**

   A copy of the selected text is placed on the Clipboard, leaving the original text you copied in place.

2. **Place the insertion point before** season **in the third paragraph, then click the** Paste button **in the Clipboard group**

   "San Diego Luncheon" is inserted before "season," as shown in FIGURE 2-3. Notice that the pasted text is formatted differently than the paragraph in which it was inserted.

3. **Click the** Paste Options button, **move the mouse over each button on the menu that opens to read its ScreenTip, then click the** Keep Text Only (T) button

   The formatting of "San Diego Luncheon" is changed to match the rest of the paragraph. The buttons on the Paste Options menu allow you to change the formatting of pasted text. You can choose to keep the original formatting (Keep Source Formatting), match the destination formatting (Merge Formatting), or paste as unformatted text (Keep Text Only).

4. **Select** www.r2g.com **in the fifth paragraph, press and hold [Ctrl], then drag the pointer's vertical line to the end of the last paragraph, placing it between** site **and the period**

   As you drag, the pointer changes to ⬚, indicating that the selected text is being copied and moved.

5. **Release the mouse button, then release [Ctrl]**

   The text is copied to the last paragraph. Since the formatting of the text you copied is the same as the formatting of the destination paragraph, you can ignore the Paste Options button. Text is not copied to the Clipboard when you copy it using the drag-and-drop method.

6. **Place the insertion point before** www.r2g.com **in the last paragraph, type** at **followed by a space, then save the document**

   Compare your document with FIGURE 2-4.

Splitting the document window to copy and move items in a long document

If you want to copy or move items between parts of a long document, it can be useful to split the document window into two panes. This allows you to display the item you want to copy or move in one pane and the destination for the item in the other pane. To split a window, click the Split button in the Window group on the View tab, and then drag the horizontal split bar that appears to the location you want to split the window. Once the document window is split into two panes, you can use the scroll bars in each pane to display different parts of the document. To copy or move an item from one pane to another, you can use the Cut, Copy, and Paste commands, or you can drag the item between the panes. When you are finished editing the document, double-click the split bar to restore the window to a single pane, or click the Remove Split button in the Window group on the View tab.

FIGURE 2-3: **Text pasted in document**

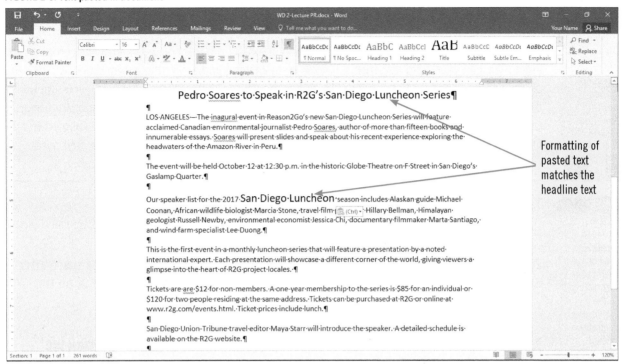

Formatting of pasted text matches the headline text

FIGURE 2-4: **Copied text in document**

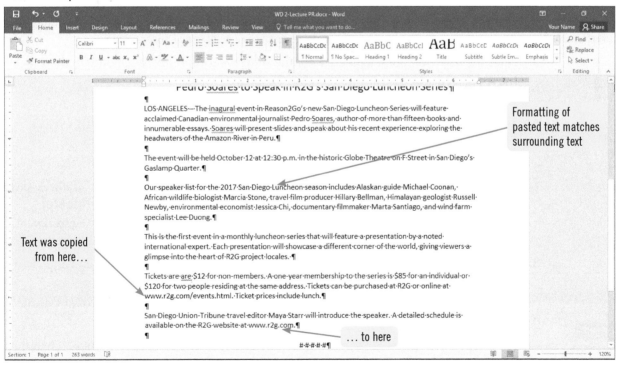

Formatting of pasted text matches surrounding text

Text was copied from here...

... to here

Use the Office Clipboard

Learning Outcomes
• Copy and cut items to the Clipboard
• Paste items from the Clipboard

The Office Clipboard allows you to collect text and graphics from files created in any Office program and insert them into your Word documents. It holds up to 24 items and, unlike the system clipboard, the items on the Office Clipboard can be viewed. To display the Office Clipboard (the Clipboard), you simply click the launcher in the Clipboard group on the Home tab. You add items to the Office Clipboard using the Cut and Copy commands. The last item you collect is always added to both the system clipboard and the Office Clipboard. **CASE** ▸ *You use the Office Clipboard to move several sentences in your press release.*

STEPS

QUICK TIP
You can set the Clipboard pane to open automatically when you cut or copy two items consecutively by clicking Options on the Clipboard pane, and then selecting Show Office Clipboard Automatically.

1. **Click the launcher ⬚ in the Clipboard group on the Home tab**
   The Office Clipboard opens in the Clipboard pane. It contains the San Diego Luncheon item you copied in the last lesson.

2. **Select the sentence San Diego Union-Tribune travel editor... (including the space after the period) in the last paragraph, right-click the selected text, then click Cut on the menu that opens**
   The sentence is cut to the Clipboard.

3. **Select the sentence A detailed schedule is... (including the ¶ mark), right-click the selected text, then click Cut**
   The Clipboard displays the items you cut or copied, as shown in FIGURE 2-5. The icon next to each item indicates the items are from a Word document. The last item collected is displayed at the top of the Clipboard pane. As new items are collected, the existing items move down the Clipboard.

QUICK TIP
If you add a 25th item to the Clipboard, the first item you collected is deleted.

4. **Place the insertion point at the end of the second paragraph (after "Quarter." but before the ¶ mark), then click the San Diego Union-Tribune... item on the Clipboard**
   Clicking an item on the Clipboard pastes the item in the document at the location of the insertion point. Items remain on the Clipboard until you delete them or close all open Office programs.

5. **Place the insertion point at the end of the third paragraph (after "Duong."), then click the A detailed schedule is... item on the Clipboard**
   The sentence is pasted into the document.

6. **Select the fourth paragraph, which begins with the sentence This is the first event... (including the ¶ mark), right-click the selected text, then click Cut**
   The paragraph is cut to the Clipboard.

7. **Place the insertion point at the beginning of the third paragraph (before "Our..."), click the Paste button in the Clipboard group on the Home tab, then press [Backspace]**
   The sentences from the "This is the first..." paragraph are pasted at the beginning of the "Our speaker list..." paragraph. You can paste the last item collected using either the Paste command or the Clipboard.

8. **Place the insertion point at the end of the third paragraph (after "www.r2g.com." and before the ¶ mark), then press [Delete] twice**
   Two ¶ symbols and the corresponding blank lines between the third and fourth paragraphs are deleted.

QUICK TIP
To delete an individual item from the Clipboard, click the list arrow next to the item, then click Delete.

9. **Click the Show/Hide ¶ button ¶ on in the Paragraph group**
   Compare your press release with FIGURE 2-6. Note that many Word users prefer to work with formatting marks on at all times. Experiment to see which method you prefer.

10. **Click the Clear All button on the Clipboard pane to remove the items from the Clipboard, click the Close button ✕ on the Clipboard pane, press [Ctrl][Home], then save the document**
    Pressing [Ctrl][Home] moves the insertion point to the top of the document.

FIGURE 2-5: **Office Clipboard in Clipboard pane**

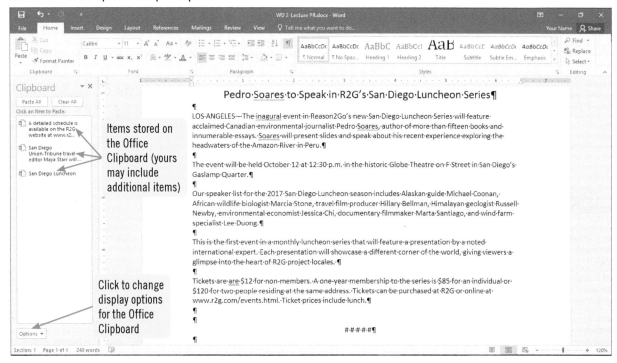

FIGURE 2-6: **Revised press release**

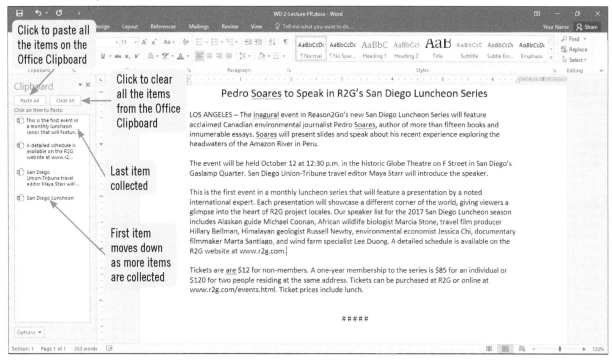

Copying and moving items between documents

You can also use the Clipboard to copy and move items between documents. To do this, open both documents and the Clipboard pane. With multiple documents open, copy or cut an item from one document and then switch to the other document and paste the item. To switch between open documents, point to the Word icon ⬜ on the taskbar, and then click the document you want to appear in the document window. You can also display more than one document at the same time by clicking the Arrange All button or the View Side by Side button in the Window group on the View tab.

Find and Replace Text

Learning Outcomes
• Replace text
• Find text with the Navigation pane
• Navigate a document

The Find and Replace feature in Word allows you to automatically search for and replace all instances of a word or phrase in a document. For example, you might need to substitute "tour" for "trip." To manually locate and replace each instance of "trip" in a long document would be very time-consuming. Using the Replace command, you can find and replace all occurrences of specific text at once, or you can choose to find and review each occurrence individually. Using the Find command, you can locate and highlight every occurrence of a specific word or phrase in a document. **CASE** *R2G management has decided to change the name of the lecture series from "Travel Luncheon Series" to "Travel Lecture Series." You use the Replace command to search the document for all instances of "Luncheon" and replace them with "Lecture."*

STEPS

TROUBLE
If any of the Search Options check boxes are selected in your Find and Replace dialog box, deselect them. If Format appears under the Find what or Replace with text box, click in the text box, then click the No Formatting button.

1. **Click the Replace button in the Editing group, then click More in the Find and Replace dialog box**

   The Find and Replace dialog box opens and expands, as shown in FIGURE 2-7.

2. **Type Luncheon in the Find what text box**

   "Luncheon" is the text that will be replaced.

3. **Press [Tab], then type Lecture in the Replace with text box**

   "Lecture" is the text that will replace "Luncheon."

4. **Click the Match case check box in the Search Options section to select it**

   Selecting the Match case check box tells Word to find only exact matches for the uppercase and lowercase characters you entered in the Find what text box. You want to replace all instances of "Luncheon" in the proper name "San Diego Luncheon Series." You do not want to replace "luncheon" when it refers to a lunchtime event.

QUICK TIP
To find, review, and replace each occurrence individually, click Find Next.

5. **Click Replace All**

   Clicking Replace All changes all occurrences of "Luncheon" to "Lecture" in the press release. A message box reports three replacements were made.

6. **Click OK to close the message box, then click the Close button in the Find and Replace dialog box**

   Word replaced "Luncheon" with "Lecture" in three locations, but did not replace "luncheon."

QUICK TIP
Alternately, you can also use the Find tab in the Find and Replace dialog box to find text in a document.

7. **Click the Find button in the Editing group**

   Clicking the Find button opens the Navigation pane, which is used to browse a longer document by headings, by pages, or by specific text. The Find command allows you to quickly locate all instances of text in a document. You use it to verify that Word did not replace "luncheon."

8. **Type luncheon in the search text box in the Navigation pane, then scroll up until the headline is at the top of the document window**

   The word "luncheon" is highlighted and selected in the document, as shown in FIGURE 2-8.

9. **Click the Close button in the Navigation pane**

   The highlighting is removed from the text when you close the Navigation pane.

10. **Press [Ctrl][Home], then save the document**

FIGURE 2-7: **Find and Replace dialog box**

Replace only exact matches of uppercase and lowercase characters

Find only complete words

Use wildcards (*) in a search string

Find words that sound like the Find what text

Find and replace all forms of a word

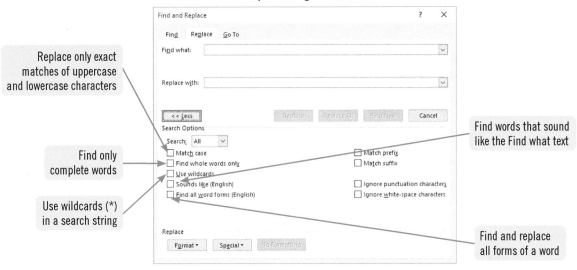

FIGURE 2-8: **Found text highlighted in document**

Navigation pane

Search text box

List shows each match and its surrounding text

Found text is highlighted and selected

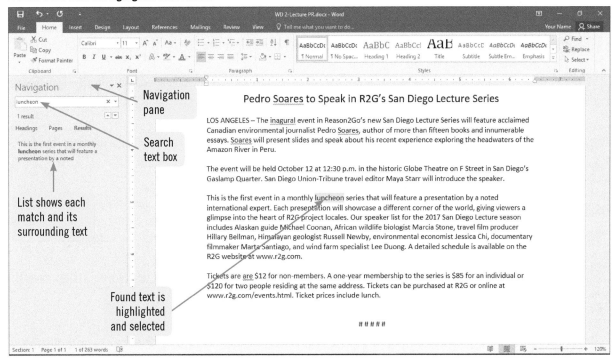

Navigating a document using the Navigation pane and the Go To command

Rather than scrolling to move to a different place in a longer document, you can use the Navigation pane to quickly move the insertion point to a specific page or a specific heading. One way to open the Navigation pane is by clicking the Page number button on the status bar, then clicking the link in the Navigation pane for the type of item you want to use to navigate the document.

To move to a specific page, section, line, table, graphic, or other item in a document, you use the Go To tab in the Find and Replace dialog box. On the Go To tab in the Find and Replace dialog box, select the type of item you want to find in the Go to what list box, enter the relevant information about that item, and then click Next to move the insertion point to the item.

Check Spelling and Grammar

Learning
Outcomes
•Ignore correctly
 spelled words
•Correct spelling
 errors
•Correct grammar
 errors

When you finish typing and revising a document, you can use the Spelling and Grammar command to search the document for misspelled words and grammar errors. The Spelling and Grammar checker flags possible mistakes, suggests correct spellings, and offers remedies for grammar errors such as subject–verb agreement, repeated words, and punctuation. **CASE** *You use the Spelling and Grammar checker to search your press release for errors. Before beginning the search, you set the Spelling and Grammar checker to ignore words, such as Soares, that you know are spelled correctly.*

STEPS

1. **Right-click** Soares **in the headline**

   A menu that includes suggestions for correcting the spelling of "Soares" opens. You can correct individual spelling and grammar errors by right-clicking text that is underlined with a red or blue wavy line and selecting a correction. Although "Soares" is not in the Word dictionary, it is spelled correctly in the document.

2. **Click** Ignore All

   Clicking Ignore All tells Word not to flag "Soares" as misspelled.

3. **Press** [Ctrl][Home]**, click the** Review tab**, then click the** Spelling & Grammar button **in the Proofing group**

   The Spelling pane opens, as shown in FIGURE 2-9. The pane identifies "inagural" as misspelled and suggests a possible correction for the error. The word selected in the suggestions box is the correct spelling.

4. **Click** Change

   Word replaces the misspelled word with the correctly spelled word. Next, the pane indicates that "are" is repeated in a sentence.

5. **Click** Delete

   Word deletes the second occurrence of the repeated word, and the Spelling pane closes. Keep in mind that the Spelling and Grammar checker identifies many common errors, but you cannot rely on it to find and correct all spelling and grammar errors in your documents, or to always suggest a valid correction. Always proofread your documents carefully.

6. **Click** OK **to complete the spelling and grammar check, press** [Ctrl][Home]**, then save the document**

Using Smart Lookup

The Smart Lookup feature gives you quick access to information about document text, including definitions, images, and other material from online sources. For example, you might use Smart Lookup to see the definition of a word used in a document or to hear the word pronounced. To use Smart Lookup, select the text you want to look up in your document, then click the Smart Lookup button in the Insights group on the Review tab. The Insights pane opens and includes the Explore and Define tabs. The Explore tab includes images and web links related to the selected text. The Define tab includes a dictionary definition of the selected text and a link you can click to hear the selected text pronounced.

FIGURE 2-9: **Spelling pane**

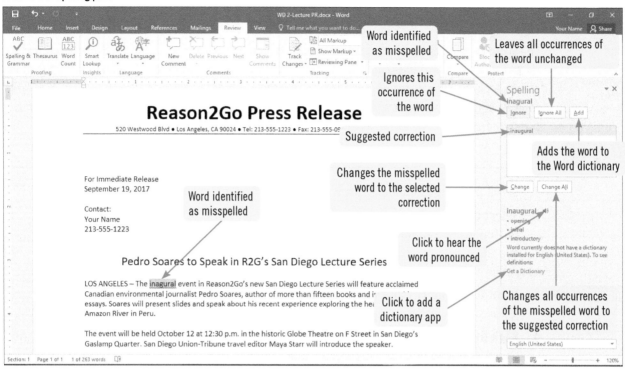

Inserting text with AutoCorrect

As you type, AutoCorrect automatically corrects many commonly misspelled words. By creating your own AutoCorrect entries, you can set Word to insert text that you type often, such as your name or contact information, or to correct words you misspell frequently. For example, you could create an AutoCorrect entry so that the name "Mary T. Watson" is automatically inserted whenever you type "mtw" followed by a space. You create AutoCorrect entries and customize other AutoCorrect and AutoFormat options using the AutoCorrect dialog box. To open the AutoCorrect dialog box, click the File tab, click Options, click Proofing in the Word Options dialog box that opens, and then click AutoCorrect Options. On the AutoCorrect tab in the AutoCorrect dialog box, type the text you want to be corrected automatically in the Replace text box (such as "mtw"), type the text you want to be inserted in its place automatically in the With text box (such as "Mary T. Watson"), and then click Add. The AutoCorrect entry is added to the list. Click OK to close the AutoCorrect dialog box, and then click OK to close the Word Options dialog box. Word inserts an AutoCorrect entry in a document when you press [Spacebar] or a punctuation mark after typing the text you want Word to correct. For example, Word inserts "Mary T. Watson" when you type "mtw" followed by a space. If you want to remove an AutoCorrect entry you created, simply open the AutoCorrect dialog box, select the AutoCorrect entry you want to remove in the list, click Delete, click OK, and then click OK to close the Word Options dialog box.

Research Information

Learning Outcomes
- Find synonyms using the Thesaurus
- Check word count

The Word research features allow you to quickly search reference sources and the web for information related to a word or phrase. Among the reference sources available are a Thesaurus, which you can use to look up synonyms for awkward or repetitive words, as well as dictionary and translation sources. **CASE** ▸ *After proofreading your document for errors, you decide the press release would read better if several adjectives were more descriptive. You use the Thesaurus to find synonyms.*

STEPS

1. **Scroll until the headline is displayed at the top of your screen**

2. **Select noted in the first sentence of the third paragraph, then click the Thesaurus button in the Proofing group on the Review tab**

   The Thesaurus pane opens, as shown in FIGURE 2-10. "Noted" appears in the search text box, and possible synonyms for "noted" are listed under the search text box.

QUICK TIP
To look up synonyms for a different word, type the word in the search text box, then click the search button.

3. **Point to prominent in the list of synonyms**

   A shaded box containing a list arrow appears around the word.

4. **Click the list arrow, click Insert on the menu that opens, then close the Thesaurus pane**

   "Prominent" replaces "noted" in the press release.

5. **Right-click innumerable in the first sentence of the first paragraph, point to Synonyms on the menu that opens, then click numerous**

   "Numerous" replaces "innumerable" in the press release.

6. **Select the four paragraphs of body text, then click the Word Count button in the Proofing group**

   The Word Count dialog box opens, as shown in FIGURE 2-11. The dialog box lists the number of pages, words, characters, paragraphs, and lines included in the selected text. Notice that the status bar also displays the number of words included in the selected text and the total number of words in the entire document. If you want to view the page, character, paragraph, and line count for the entire document, make sure nothing is selected in your document, and then click Word Count in the Proofing group.

7. **Click Close, press [Ctrl][Home], then save the document**

8. **Click the File tab, click Save As, navigate to the location where you store your files, type WD 2-Lecture PR Public in the File name text box, then click Save**

   The WD 2-Lecture PR file closes, and the WD 2-Lecture PR Public file is displayed in the document window. You will modify this file to prepare it for electronic release to the public.

Publishing a blog directly from Word

A **blog**, which is short for weblog, is an informal journal that is created by an individual or a group and available to the public on the Internet. A blog usually conveys the ideas, comments, and opinions of the blogger and is written using a strong personal voice. The person who creates and maintains a blog, the **blogger**, typically updates the blog regularly. If you have or want to start a blog, you can configure Word to link to your blog site so that you can write, format, and publish blog entries directly from Word.

To create a new blog post, click the File tab, click New, then double-click Blog post to open a predesigned blog post

document that you can customize with your own text, formatting, and images. You can also publish an existing document as a blog post by opening the document, clicking the File tab, clicking Share, and then clicking Post to Blog. In either case, Word prompts you to log onto your personal blog account. To blog directly from Word, you must first obtain a blog account with a blog service provider. Resources, such as the Word Help system and online forums, provide detailed information on obtaining and registering your personal blog account with Word.

FIGURE 2-10: **Thesaurus pane**

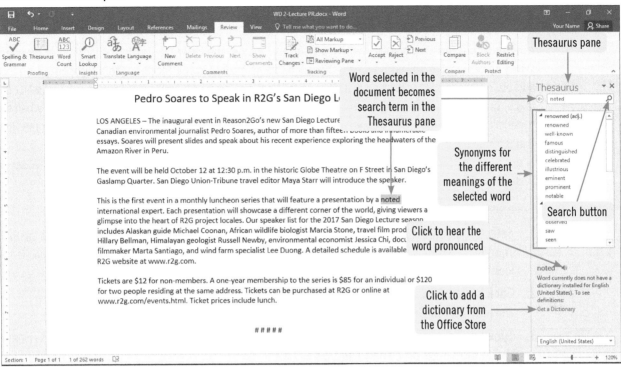

FIGURE 2-11: **Word Count dialog box**

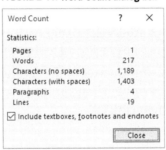

Using a dictionary and other add-ins for Word

Instead of a built-in dictionary, Word includes the ability to install a free dictionary add-in from the Office Store that you can use to see definitions of words. A dictionary add-in is just one of many add-ins that are available in Word. **Add-ins** are small programs embedded in Word that allow you to access information on the web without having to leave Word. For example, you can look up something on Wikipedia, insert an online map in one of your documents, or access dictionaries and other reference sources, all from within Word using an add-in. To install a free dictionary add-in from the Office Store, click the Thesaurus button In the Proofing group on the Review tab, click the Get a Dictionary link to open the Dictionaries pane, decide which dictionary you want, review the Terms & Conditions as well as the Privacy Policy associated with the add-in you want, and then click the Download button associated with the dictionary you want in order to install that dictionary. If you want to download other dictionaries or other add-ins, click the Store button in the Add-ins group on the Insert tab, find the add-in you want, and then follow the prompts to install the add-in. Some add-ins are free, and some require purchase. To use an add-in, click the My Add-ins button in the Add-ins group to see your list of add-ins, and then click the add-in you want to use.

Add Hyperlinks

Learning Outcomes
• Insert a hyperlink
• Test hyperlinks
• E-mail a document from Word

A **hyperlink** is text or a graphic that, when clicked, "jumps" the viewer to a different location or program. When a document is viewed on screen, hyperlinks allow readers to link (or jump) to a webpage, an e-mail address, a file, or a specific location in a document. When you create a hyperlink in a document, you select the text or graphic you want to use as a hyperlink and then you specify the location you want to jump to when the hyperlink is clicked. You create a hyperlink using the Hyperlink button in the Links group on the Insert tab. Text that is formatted as a hyperlink appears as colored, underlined text. **CASE** *Hundreds of people on your lists of press and client contacts will receive the press release by e-mail or view it on your website. To make it easier for these people to access additional information about the series, you add several hyperlinks to the press release.*

STEPS

QUICK TIP
By default, Word automatically creates a hyperlink to an e-mail address or URL when you type an e-mail address or a URL in a document.

1. **Select** your name, **click the** Insert tab, **then click the** Hyperlink button **in the Links group**

   The Insert Hyperlink dialog box opens, as shown in FIGURE 2-12. You use this dialog box to specify the location you want to jump to when the hyperlink—in this case, your name—is clicked.

2. **Click** E-mail Address **in the Link to section**

   The Insert Hyperlink dialog box changes so you can create a hyperlink to your e-mail address.

3. **Type your e-mail address in the E-mail address text box, type** San Diego Lecture Series **in the Subject text box, then click** OK

   As you type, Word automatically adds mailto: in front of your e-mail address. After you close the dialog box, the hyperlink text—your name—is formatted in blue and underlined.

TROUBLE
If an e-mail message does not open, close the window that opens and continue with step 6.

4. **Press and hold** [Ctrl]**, then click the** your name hyperlink

   An e-mail message addressed to you with the subject "San Diego Lecture Series" opens in the default e-mail program. People can use this hyperlink to send you an e-mail message.

5. **Close the e-mail message window, clicking** No **if you are prompted to save**

   The hyperlink text changes to purple, indicating the hyperlink has been followed.

QUICK TIP
To remove a hyperlink, right-click it, then click Remove Hyperlink. Removing a hyperlink removes the link, but the text remains.

6. **Scroll down, select** Gaslamp Quarter **in the second paragraph, click the** Hyperlink button, **click** Existing File or Web Page **in the Link to section, type** www.gaslamp.org **in the Address text box, then click** OK

   As you type the web address, Word automatically adds "http://" in front of "www." The text "Gaslamp Quarter" is formatted as a hyperlink to the Gaslamp Quarter Association home page at www.gaslamp.org. When clicked, the hyperlink will open the webpage in the default browser window. If you point to a hyperlink in Word, the link to location appears in a ScreenTip. You can edit ScreenTip text to make it more descriptive.

QUICK TIP
You can also edit the hyperlink destination or the hyperlink text.

7. **Right-click** Quarter **in the Gaslamp Quarter hyperlink, click** Edit Hyperlink, **click** ScreenTip **in the Edit Hyperlink dialog box, type** Map, parking, and other information about the Gaslamp Quarter **in the ScreenTip text box, click** OK, **click** OK, **save your changes, then point to the** Gaslamp Quarter hyperlink **in the document**

   The ScreenTip you created appears above the Gaslamp Quarter hyperlink, as shown in FIGURE 2-13.

TROUBLE
If you are not working with an active Internet connection, skip this step.

8. **Press** [Ctrl]**, click the** Gaslamp Quarter hyperlink, **verify the link opened in your browser, then click the** Word icon [W] **on the taskbar to return to the press release**

   Before distributing a document, it's important to test each hyperlink to verify it works as you intended.

FIGURE 2-12: **Insert Hyperlink dialog box**

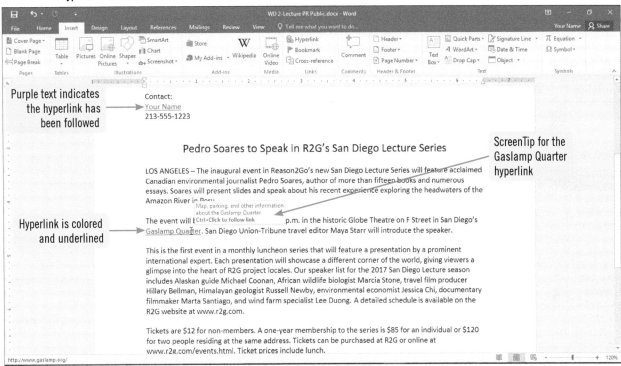

Create a hyperlink to a webpage or file

Create a hyperlink to a location in the current file

Create a hyperlink to a new blank document

Create a hyperlink to an e-mail address

Text selected to be formatted as a hyperlink

Files in the current drive or folder (yours might differ)

FIGURE 2-13: **Hyperlinks in the document**

Purple text indicates the hyperlink has been followed

Hyperlink is colored and underlined

ScreenTip for the Gaslamp Quarter hyperlink

Word 2016

Sharing documents directly from Word, including e-mailing

Word includes several options for distributing and sharing documents over the Internet directly from within Word, including saving a document to OneDrive for others to view and edit, e-mailing a document, presenting a document online so others can view it in a web browser, sending it by Instant Message, and posting a document to a blog. To share a document, open the file in Word, click the File tab, click Share, and then click one of the Share options. You can also use the Share button on the title bar to save a document to an online location.

When you e-mail a document from within Word, the document is sent as an attachment to an e-mail message using your default e-mail program. You can choose to attach the document as a Word file, a .pdf file, or an .xps file, or to send it as an Internet fax. When you click an option, a message window opens that includes the filename of the current file as the message subject and the file as an attachment. Type the e-mail address(es) of the recipient(s) in the To and Cc text boxes, any message you want in the message window, and then click Send to send the message. The default e-mail program sends a copy of the document to each recipient. Note that faxing a document directly from Word requires registration with a third-party Internet fax service.

Work with Document Properties

Before you distribute a document electronically to people outside your organization, it's wise to make sure the file does not include embedded private or confidential information. The Info screen in Backstage view includes tools for stripping a document of sensitive information, for securing its authenticity, and for guarding it from unwanted changes once it is distributed to the public. One of these tools, the Document Inspector, detects and removes unwanted private or confidential information from a document. **CASE** *Before sending the press release to the public, you remove all identifying information from the file.*

STEPS

1. **Press [Ctrl][Home], then click the File tab**

   Backstage view opens with the Info screen displayed. The left side of the Info screen includes options related to stripping the file of private information. See TABLE 2-1. The right side of the Info screen displays basic information about the document. Notice that the file contains document properties. You want to remove these before you distribute the press release to the public.

2. **Click the Show All Properties link at the bottom of the Info screen**

   The Properties section expands on the Info screen. It shows the document properties for the press release. **Document properties** are user-defined details about a file that describe its contents and origin, including the name of the author, the title of the document, and keywords that you can assign to help organize and search your files. You decide to remove this information from the file before you distribute it electronically.

3. **Click the Check for Issues button on the Info screen, then click Inspect Document, clicking Yes if prompted to save changes**

   The Document Inspector dialog box opens. You use this dialog box to indicate which private or identifying information you want to search for and remove from the document.

4. **Make sure all the check boxes are selected, then click Inspect**

   After a moment, the Document Inspector dialog box indicates the file contains document properties, as shown in FIGURE 2-14.

5. **Click Remove All next to Document Properties and Personal Information, then click Close**

   The document property information is removed from the press release document, but the change will not be reflected on the Info screen until you close the document and reopen it.

6. **Click Save on the Info screen, close the document, open the document again in Word, then click the File tab**

   The Info screen shows the document properties have been removed from the file.

7. **Save the document, submit it to your instructor, close the file, then exit Word**

   The completed press release is shown in FIGURE 2-15.

TABLE 2-1: Options on the Info screen

option	use to
Protect Document	Mark a document as final so that it is read-only and cannot be edited; encrypt a document so that a password is required to open it; restrict what kinds of changes can be made to a document and by whom; restrict access to editing, copying, and printing a document and add a digital signature to a document to verify its integrity
Check for Issues	Detect and remove unwanted information from a document, including document properties and comments; check for content that people with disabilities might find difficult to read; and check the document for features that are not supported by previous versions of Microsoft Word
Manage Document	Browse and recover draft versions of unsaved files

FIGURE 2-14: **Results after inspecting a document**

> Removes document property information from the file

FIGURE 2-15: **Completed press release for electronic distribution**

Viewing and modifying advanced document properties

The Properties section of the Info screen includes summary information about the document that you enter. To view more detailed document properties, click the Properties button on the Info screen, and then click Advanced Properties to open the Properties dialog box. The General, Statistics, and Contents tabs of the Properties dialog box display information about the file that is automatically created and updated by Word. The General tab shows the file type, location, size, and date and time the file was created and last modified; the Statistics tab displays information about revisions to the document along with the number of pages, words, lines, paragraphs, and characters in the file; and the Contents tab shows the title of the document.

You can define other document properties using the Summary and Custom tabs in the Properties dialog box. The Summary tab shows information similar to the information shown on the Info screen. The Custom tab allows you to create new document properties, such as client, project, or date completed. To create a custom property, select a property name in the Name list box on the Custom tab, use the Type list arrow to select the type of data you want for the property, type the identifying detail (such as a project name) in the Value text box, and then click Add. When you are finished viewing or modifying the document properties, click OK to close the Properties dialog box.

Practice

Concepts Review

Label the elements of the Word program window shown in FIGURE 2-16.

FIGURE 2-16

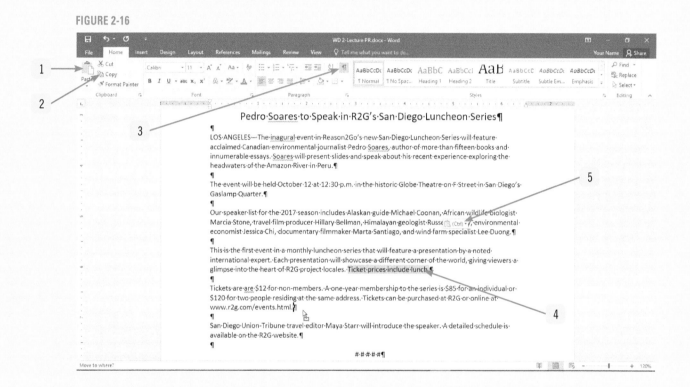

Match each term with the statement that best describes it.

6. Office Clipboard
7. Paste
8. Hyperlink
9. Thesaurus
10. Shortcut Key
11. Smart Lookup
12. Cut
13. System clipboard
14. Document properties

a. Command used to insert text stored on the Clipboard into a document
b. Temporary storage area for up to 24 items collected from Office files
c. Temporary storage area for only the last item cut or copied from a document
d. A function key or a combination of keys that perform a command when pressed
e. Text or a graphic that jumps the reader to a different location or program when clicked
f. A program that accesses information on the web from within Word
g. User-defined details about a file that describe its contents and origin
h. Feature used to suggest synonyms for words
i. Command used to remove text from a document and place it on the Clipboard

Select the best answer from the list of choices.

15. **What is the keyboard shortcut for the Cut command?**
    a. [Ctrl][V]
    b. [Ctrl][C]
    c. [Ctrl][P]
    d. [Ctrl][X]

16. **Which command is used to display a document in two panes in the document window?**
    a. Split
    b. New Window
    c. Arrange All
    d. Two pages

17. **Which of the following statements is *not* true?**
    a. You can view the contents of the Office Clipboard.
    b. The last item cut or copied from a document is stored on the system clipboard.
    c. The Office Clipboard can hold more than one item.
    d. When you move text by dragging it, a copy of the text you move is stored on the system clipboard.

18. **To locate and select all instances of a word in a document, which command do you use?**
    a. Highlight
    b. Show/Hide
    c. Find
    d. Search

19. **Which of the following is an example of a document property?**
    a. URL
    b. Keyword
    c. Permission
    d. Language

20. **A hyperlink *cannot* be linked to which of the following?**
    a. Document
    b. E-mail address
    c. ScreenTip
    d. Webpage

Skills Review

1. **Cut and paste text.**
   a. Start Word, click the Open Other Documents link, open the file WD 2-2.docx from the location where you store your Data File, then save the document with the filename **WD 2-MATOS 2017 PR**.
   b. Select **Your Name** and replace it with your name.
   c. Display paragraph and other formatting marks in your document if they are not already displayed.
   d. Use the Cut and Paste buttons to switch the order of the two sentences in the fourth body paragraph (which begins New group shows…).
   e. Use the drag-and-drop method to switch the order of the second and third paragraphs.
   f. Adjust the spacing if necessary so that there is one blank line between paragraphs, then save your changes.

2. **Copy and paste text.**
   a. Use the Copy and Paste buttons to copy **MATOS 2015** from the headline and paste it before the word **map** in the third paragraph.
   b. Change the formatting of the pasted text to match the formatting of the third paragraph, then insert a space between **2015** and **map** if necessary.
   c. Use the drag-and-drop method to copy **MATOS** from the third paragraph and paste it before the word **group** in the second sentence of the fourth paragraph, then save your changes.

3. **Use the Office Clipboard.**
   a. Use the launcher in the Clipboard group to open the Clipboard pane.
   b. Scroll so that the first body paragraph is displayed at the top of the document window.
   c. Select the fifth paragraph (which begins Studio location maps…) and cut it to the Clipboard.
   d. Select the third paragraph (which begins Manchester is easily accessible…) and cut it to the Clipboard.
   e. Use the Clipboard to paste the Studio location maps… item as the new fourth paragraph.
   f. Use the Clipboard to paste the Manchester is easily accessible… item as the new fifth paragraph.
   g. Adjust the spacing if necessary so there is one blank line between each of the six body paragraphs.
   h. Turn off the display of formatting marks, clear and close the Clipboard pane, then save your changes.

Skills Review (continued)

4. Find and replace text.

   a. Using the Replace command, replace all instances of **2015** with **2017**.

   b. Replace all instances of **tenth** with **twelfth**.

   c. Replace all instances of the abbreviation **st** with **street**, taking care to replace whole words only when you perform the replace. (*Hint*: Deselect Match case if it is selected.)

   d. Click the Find tab, deselect the Find whole words only check box, click the Reading Highlight button, click Highlight All, close the dialog box, then view all instances of **st** in the document to make sure no errors occurred when you replaced st with street.

   e. Click the Find button to open the Navigation pane, notice the results and the highlighted text, close the Navigation pane, then save your changes to the press release. (*Note: You can see the highlighted results using either the Reading Highlight button in the Find and Replace dialog box or the Navigation pane.*)

5. Check spelling and grammar and research information.

   a. Switch to the Review tab.

   b. Move the insertion point to the top of the document, then use the Spelling & Grammar command to search for and correct any spelling and grammar errors in the press release.

   c. Use the Thesaurus to replace **thriving** in the second paragraph with a different suitable word, then close the Thesaurus pane.

   d. Check the word count of the press release.

   e. Proofread your press release, correct any errors, then save your changes.

6. Add hyperlinks.

   a. Save the document as **WD 2-MATOS 2017 PR Public**, then switch to the Insert tab.

   b. Select your name, then open the Insert Hyperlink dialog box.

   c. Create a hyperlink to your e-mail address with the subject **MATOS 2017**.

   d. Test the your name hyperlink, then close the message window that opens and click No if a message window opens. (*Hint*: Press [Ctrl], then click the hyperlink.)

   e. Select **NEA** in the last paragraph of the press release, then create a hyperlink to the webpage with the URL **www.nea.gov**.

   f. Right-click the NEA hyperlink, then edit the hyperlink ScreenTip to become **Information on the National Endowment for the Arts**.

   g. Point to the NEA hyperlink to view the new ScreenTip, then save your changes.

   h. If you are working with an active Internet connection, press [Ctrl], click the NEA hyperlink, view the NEA home page in the browser window, then close the browser window and return to Word. The finished press release is shown in FIGURE 2-17.

FIGURE 2-17

PRESS RELEASE

FOR IMMEDIATE RELEASE
September 7, 2017

Contact:
Your Name
910-555-2938

MATOS 2017
Manchester Artists Open Their Studios to the Public

MANCHESTER, NH -- The fall 2017 Open Studios season kicks off with Manchester Art/Tech Open Studios (MATOS) on Saturday and Sunday, October 13 and 14, from 11 a.m. to 6 p.m. More than 60 Manchester artists will open their studios and homes to the public for this annual event, now in its twelfth year.

Manchester is a historic and diverse city, long home to a flourishing community of artists. Quiet residential streets lined with charming Victorians edge a vibrant commercial and industrial zone, all peppered with the studios of printmakers, sculptors, painters, glass and jewelry makers, illustrators, potters, photographers, watercolorists, and other artists working in a wide range of digital mediums.

Internationally celebrated sculptor Mara Currier will display her new work in the rotunda of City Library. New MATOS group shows will open at the Art 5 Gallery and at the Fisher Café, both on Hanover Street.

Studio location maps will be available prior to the opening at businesses and public libraries, and on the days of the event in Victory Park. Victory Park is located at the junction of Amherst Street and Chestnut Street in downtown Manchester.

Manchester is easily accessible from all points in New England by car or bus, and from other cities by air. On Saturday, non-Manchester residents may park in permit-only areas provided they display a copy of the MATOS 2017 map on the dashboard. There are no parking restrictions on Sundays in Manchester.

MATOS 2017 receives funds from participating artists and from the Manchester Arts Council, the North Hampshire Cultural Council, and the NEA, with valuable support from local universities and businesses.

#####

7. Work with document properties.

 a. Click the File tab, click the Properties button on the Info screen, then click Advanced Properties to open the Properties dialog box and view the document properties for the press release on the Summary tab.

 b. Close the Properties dialog box, then use the Check for Issues command to run the Document Inspector.

 c. Remove the document property and personal information data, close the Document Inspector, save your changes, then close the file.

 d. Open the file WD 2-MATOS 2017 PR Public, then verify that the document propertes have been removed both on the Info screen and in the Properties dialog box. Save the document, submit it to your instructor, close the file, then exit Word.

Independent Challenge 1

Because of your success in revitalizing a historic theatre in Auckland, New Zealand, you were hired as the director of The Adelaide Opera House in Adelaide, Australia, to breathe life into its revitalization efforts. After a year on the job, you are launching your first major fund-raising drive. You'll create a fund-raising letter for The Adelaide Opera House by modifying a letter you wrote for the Lyric Theatre in Auckland.

 a. Start Word, open the file WD 2-3.docx from the location where you store your Data Files, then save it as **WD 2-Fundraising Letter**.

 b. Replace the theatre name and address, the date, the inside address, and the salutation with the text shown in **FIGURE 2-18**.

 c. Use the Replace command to replace all instances of **Auckland** with **Adelaide**.

 d. Use the Replace command to replace all instances of **Lyric Theatre** with **Opera House**.

 e. Use the Replace command to replace all instances of **New Zealanders** with **Australians**.

 f. Use the Find command to locate the word **considerable**, then use the Thesaurus to replace the word with a synonym.

FIGURE 2-18

The Adelaide Opera House
32 King William Street, Adelaide SA 5001, Australia

March 12, 2017

Ms. Georgina Fuller
12-34 Wattle Street
Adelaide SA 5006

Dear Ms. Fuller:

 g. Move the fourth body paragraph so that it becomes the second body paragraph.

 h. Create an AutoCorrect entry that inserts **Executive Director** whenever you type **exd**.

 i. Replace Your Name with your name in the signature block, select Title, then type **exd** followed by a space.

 j. Use the Spelling and Grammar command to check for and correct spelling and grammar errors.

 k. Delete the AutoCorrect entry you created for exd. (*Hint:* Open the AutoCorrect dialog box, select the AutoCorrect entry you created, then click [Delete].)

 l. Open the Properties dialog box, add your name as the author, change the title to **Adelaide Opera House**, add the keyword **fund-raising**, then add the comment **Letter for the capital campaign**.

 m. Review the paragraph, line, word, and character count on the Statistics tab.

 n. On the Custom tab, add a property named **Project** with the value **Capital Campaign**, then close the dialog box.

 o. Proofread the letter, correct any errors, save your changes, submit a copy to your instructor, close the document, then exit Word.

Independent Challenge 2

An advertisement for job openings in Chicago caught your eye and you have decided to apply. The ad, shown in FIGURE 2-19, was printed in last weekend's edition of your local newspaper. Instead of writing a cover letter from scratch, you revise a draft of a cover letter you wrote several years ago for a summer internship position.

FIGURE 2-19

ThinkPoint Technologies

Career Opportunities in Detroit

ThinkPoint Technologies, an established software development firm with offices in North America, Asia, and Europe, is seeking candidates for the following positions in its Detroit facility:

Instructor
Responsible for delivering software training to our expanding Midwestern customer base. Duties include delivering hands-on training, keeping up-to-date with product development, and working with the Director of Training to ensure the high quality of course materials. Successful candidate will have excellent presentation skills and be proficient in Microsoft PowerPoint and Microsoft Word. Position B12C6

Administrative Assistant
Proficiency with Microsoft Word a must! Administrative office duties include making travel arrangements, scheduling meetings, taking notes and publishing meeting minutes, handling correspondence, and ordering office supplies. Must have superb multitasking abilities, excellent communication, organizational, and interpersonal skills, and be comfortable working with e-mail and the Internet. Position B16F5

Copywriter
The ideal candidate will have marketing or advertising writing experience in a high tech environment, including collateral, newsletters, and direct mail. Experience writing for the Web, broadcast, and multimedia is a plus. Fluency with Microsoft Word required. Position C13D4

Positions offer salary, excellent benefits, and career opportunities.

Send resume and cover letter referencing position code to:

Selena Torres
Director of Recruiting
ThinkPoint Technologies
700 Woodward Ave.
Detroit, MI 48226

a. Read the ad shown in FIGURE 2-19 and decide which position to apply for. Choose the position that most closely matches your qualifications.

b. Start Word, open WD 2-4.docx from the location where you store your Data Files, then save it as **WD 2-ThinkPoint Cover Letter**.

c. Replace the name, address, telephone number, and e-mail address in the letterhead with your own information.

d. Remove the hyperlink from the e-mail address.

e. Replace the date with today's date, then replace the inside address and the salutation with the information shown in FIGURE 2-19.

f. Read the draft cover letter to get a feel for its contents.

g. Rework the text in the body of the letter to address your qualifications for the job you have chosen to apply for in the following ways:

- Delete the third paragraph.
- Adjust the first sentence of the first paragraph as follows: specify the job you are applying for, including the position code, and indicate where you saw the position advertised.
- Move the first sentence in the last paragraph, which briefly states your qualifications and interest in the position, to the end of the first paragraph, then rework the sentence to describe your current qualifications.
- Adjust the second paragraph as follows: describe your work experience and skills. Be sure to relate your experience and qualifications to the position requirements listed in the advertisement. Add a third paragraph if your qualifications are extensive.
- Adjust the final paragraph as follows: politely request an interview for the position and provide your phone number and e-mail address.

h. Include your name in the signature block.

i. When you are finished revising the letter, check it for spelling and grammar errors, and correct any mistakes. Make sure to remove any hyperlinks.

j. Save your changes to the letter, submit the file to your instructor, close the document, then exit Word.

Independent Challenge 3

As administrative director of continuing education, you drafted a memo to instructors asking them to help you finalize the course schedule for next semester. Today, you'll examine the draft and make revisions before distributing it as an e-mail attachment.

a. Start Word, open the file WD 2-5.docx from the drive and folder where you store your Data Files, then save it as **WD 2-Business Courses Memo**.

Independent Challenge 3 (continued)

b. Replace Your Name with your name in the From line, then scroll until the first body paragraph is at the top of the screen.

c. Use the Split command on the View tab to split the window under the first body paragraph, then scroll until the last paragraph of the memo is displayed in the bottom pane.

d. Use the Cut and Paste buttons to move the sentence **If you are planning to teach...** from the first body paragraph to become the first sentence in the last paragraph of the memo.

e. Double-click the split bar to restore the window to a single pane.

f. Use the [Delete] key to merge the first two paragraphs into one paragraph.

g. Use the Clipboard to reorganize the list of twelve-week courses so that the courses are listed in alphabetical order, then clear and close the Clipboard.

h. Use drag-and-drop to reorganize the list of one-day seminars so they are in alphabetical order.

i. Select the phrase "website" in the first paragraph, then create a hyperlink to the URL **www.course.com** with the ScreenTip **Spring 2018 Business Courses**.

j. Select "e-mail me" in the last paragraph, then create a hyperlink to your e-mail address with the subject **Final Business Course Schedule**.

k. Use the Spelling and Grammar command to check for and correct spelling and grammar errors.

l. Use the Document Inspector to strip the document of document property information, ignore any other content that is flagged by the Document Inspector, then close the Document Inspector.

m. Proofread the memo, correct any errors, save your changes, submit a copy to your instructor, close the document, then exit Word.

Independent Challenge 4: Explore

Reference sources—dictionaries, thesauri, style and grammar guides, and guides to business etiquette and procedure—are essential for day-to-day use in the workplace. Much of this reference information is available on the World Wide Web. In this independent challenge, you will locate reference sources that might be useful to you, including the Office Add-ins resources that are available for Word. Your goal is to familiarize yourself with online reference sources and Office Add-ins for Word so you can use them later in your work. You will insert a screenshot of an Office Add-in webpage in your document.

a. Start Word, open the file WD 2-6.docx from the location where you store your Data Files, then save it as **WD 2-References**. This document contains the questions you will answer about the web reference sources you find and Office Add-ins. You will type your answers to the questions in the document.

b. Replace the placeholder text at the top of the WD 2-References document with your name and the date.

c. Use your favorite search engine to search the web for grammar and style guides, dictionaries, and thesauri. Use the keywords **grammar**, **usage**, **dictionary**, **glossary**, or **thesaurus** to conduct your search.

d. Complete question 1 of the WD 2-References document, making sure to format each website name as a hyperlink to that website.

e. Read question 2 of the WD 2-References document, then move the insertion point under question 2.

f. Click the Store button in the Add-ins group on the Insert tab. Explore the add-ins available through the Office Add-ins window, click one add-in to select it, then click the hyperlink for that add-in to open it in a new browser window. (*Hint:* The hyperlink for an add-in is located under the icon for the add-in.)

g. Switch to the WD 2-References document in Word. Close the Office Add-ins window if it is still open.

h. With the insertion point below question 2, click the Screenshot button in the Illustrations group on the Insert tab. The Available Windows gallery opens.

i. Read the ScreenTip for each thumbnail in the gallery, find the Add-in browser window thumbnail in the gallery, click it, then click Yes in the dialog box that opens. A screenshot of the Add-in you selected is inserted in the WD 2-References document.

j. Save the document, submit a copy to your instructor, close the document, then exit Word.

Visual Workshop

Open WD 2-7.docx from the drive and folder where you store your Data Files, then save the document as **WD 2-Visa Letter**. Replace the placeholders for the date, letterhead, inside address, salutation, and closing with the information shown in FIGURE 2-20, then use the Office Clipboard to reorganize the sentences to match FIGURE 2-20. Correct spelling and grammar errors, remove the document property information from the file, then submit a copy to your instructor.

FIGURE 2-20

Your Name

863 East 18th Street, Apt. 4, New York, NY 20211; Tel: 212-555-9384

1/12/2017

Embassy of the Republic of Korea
2320 Massachusetts Avenue NW
Washington, DC 20008

Dear Sir or Madam:

I am applying for a long-stay tourist visa to South Korea, valid for four years. I am scheduled to depart for Seoul on March 9, 2017, returning to Chicago on September 22, 2017.

During my stay in South Korea, I will be interviewing musicians and recording footage for a film I am making on contemporary Korean music. I would like a multiple entry visa valid for four years so I can return to South Korea after this trip to follow up on my initial research. I will be based in Seoul, but I will be traveling frequently to record performances and to meet with musicians and producers.

Included with this letter are my completed visa application form, my passport, a passport photo, a copy of my return air ticket, and the visa fee. Please contact me if you need further information.

Sincerely,

Your Name

Enc: 5

Formatting Text and Paragraphs

CASE ▶ You have finished drafting the text for a two-page flyer advertising last minute specials for R2G October projects. Now, you need to format the flyer so it is attractive and highlights the significant information.

Module Objectives

After completing this module, you will be able to:

- Format with fonts
- Use the Format Painter
- Change line and paragraph spacing
- Align paragraphs
- Work with tabs

- Work with indents
- Add bullets and numbering
- Add borders and shading
- Insert online pictures

Files You Will Need

WD 3-1.docx	WD 3-4.docx
WD 3-2.docx	WD 3-5.docx
WD 3-3.docx	WD 3-6.docx

Format with Fonts

Formatting text with fonts is a quick and powerful way to enhance the appearance of a document. A **font** is a complete set of characters with the same typeface or design. Arial, Times New Roman, Courier, Tahoma, and Calibri are some of the more common fonts, but there are hundreds of others, each with a specific design and feel. Another way to change the appearance of text is to increase or decrease its **font size**. Font size is measured in points. A **point** is 1/72 of an inch. **CASE** ➤ *You change the font and font size of the body text, title, and headings in the flyer. You select fonts and font sizes that enhance the positive tone of the document and help to structure the flyer visually for readers.*

STEPS

1. **Start Word, open the file** WD 3-1.docx **from the location where you store your Data Files, save it as** WD 3-October Projects, **then change the zoom level to 120%**

   Notice that the name of the font used in the document, Calibri, is displayed in the Font list box in the Font group. The word "(Body)" in the Font list box indicates Calibri is the font used for body text in the current theme, the default theme. A **theme** is a related set of fonts, colors, styles, and effects that is applied to an entire document to give it a cohesive appearance. The font size, 11, appears in the Font Size list box in the Font group.

2. **Scroll the document to get a feel for its contents, press** [Ctrl][Home], **press** [Ctrl][A] **to select the entire document, then click the** Font list arrow **in the Font group**

   The Font list, which shows the fonts available on your computer, opens as shown in FIGURE 3-1. The font names are formatted in the font. Font names can appear in more than one location on the Font list.

3. **Drag the pointer slowly down the font names in the Font list, drag the scroll box to scroll down the Font list, then click** Garamond

   As you drag the pointer over a font name, a preview of the font is applied to the selected text. Clicking a font name applies the font. The font of the flyer changes to Garamond.

4. **Click the** Font Size list arrow **in the Font group, drag the pointer slowly up and down the Font Size list, then click** 12

   As you drag the pointer over a font size, a preview of the font size is applied to the selected text. Clicking 12 increases the font size of the selected text to 12 points.

5. **Select the title** Reason2Go October Projects, **click the** Font list arrow, **scroll to and click** Trebuchet MS, **click the** Font Size list arrow, **click** 22, **then click the** Bold button B **in the Font group**

   The title is formatted in 22-point Trebuchet MS bold.

6. **Click the** Font Color list arrow A · **in the Font group**

   A gallery of colors opens. It includes the set of theme colors in a range of tints and shades as well as a set of standard colors. You can point to a color in the gallery to preview it applied to the selected text.

7. **Click the** Green, Accent 6 **color as shown in** FIGURE 3-2, **then deselect the text**

   The color of the title text changes to green. The active color on the Font Color button also changes to green.

8. **Scroll down, select the heading** Animal Care Rajasthan, **then, using the Mini toolbar, click the** Font list arrow, **click** Trebuchet MS, **click the** Font Size list arrow, **click** 14, **click** B, **click** A, **then deselect the text**

   The heading is formatted in 14-point Trebuchet MS bold with a green color.

9. **Press** [Ctrl][Home], **then click the** Save button **on the Quick Access toolbar**

   Compare your document to FIGURE 3-3.

FIGURE 3-1: **Font list**

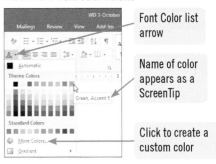

FIGURE 3-2: **Font Color Palette**

Fonts used in the default theme

List of recently used fonts (your list may differ)

Alphabetical list of all fonts on your computer (your list may differ)

Font Size list arrow

Font list arrow

Font Color list arrow

Name of color appears as a ScreenTip

Click to create a custom color

FIGURE 3-3: **Document formatted with fonts**

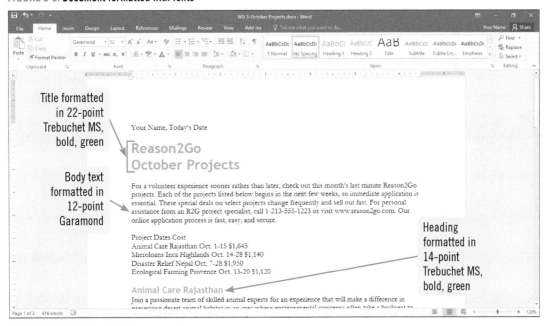

Title formatted in 22-point Trebuchet MS, bold, green

Body text formatted in 12-point Garamond

Heading formatted in 14-point Trebuchet MS, bold, green

Adding a drop cap

A fun way to illustrate a document with fonts is to add a drop cap to a paragraph. A **drop cap** is a large initial capital letter, often used to set off the first paragraph of an article. To create a drop cap, place the insertion point in the paragraph you want to format, click the Insert tab, and then click the Drop Cap button in the Text group to open a menu of Drop cap options. Preview and select one of the options on the menu, or click Drop Cap Options to open the Drop Cap dialog box, shown in FIGURE 3-4. In the Drop Cap dialog box, select the position, font, number of lines to drop, and the distance you want the drop cap to be from the paragraph text, and then click OK. The drop cap is added to the paragraph as a graphic object.

Once a drop cap is inserted in a paragraph, you can modify it by selecting it and then changing the settings in the Drop Cap dialog box. For even more interesting effects, you can enhance a drop cap with font color, font styles, or font effects. You can also fill the graphic object with shading or add a border around it. To enhance a drop cap, first select it, and then experiment with the formatting options available in the Font dialog box and in the Borders and Shading dialog box.

FIGURE 3-4: **Drop Cap dialog box**

Use the Format Painter

Learning
Outcomes
• Apply font styles
  and effects
• Add a shadow to
  text
• Change character
  spacing

You can dramatically change the appearance of text by applying different font styles, font effects, and character-spacing effects. For example, you can use the buttons in the Font group to make text darker by applying **bold** or to make text slanted by applying *italic*. When you are satisfied with the formatting of certain text, you can quickly apply the same formats to other text using the Format Painter. The **Format Painter** is a powerful Word feature that allows you to copy all the format settings applied to selected text to other text that you want to format the same way. **CASE** ▶ *You spice up the appearance of the text in the document by applying different font styles and text effects.*

STEPS

1. **Select** immediate application is essential **in the first body paragraph, click the** Bold **button** B **on the Mini toolbar, select the entire** paragraph, **then click the** Italic button I

   The phrase "immediate application is essential" is bold, and the entire paragraph is italic.

2. **Select** October Projects, **then click the launcher** ⌐ **in the Font group**

   The Font dialog box opens, as shown in FIGURE 3-5. You can use the options on the Font tab to change the font, font style, size, and color of text, and to add an underline and apply font effects to text.

3. **Scroll down the Size list, click** 48, **click the** Font color list arrow, **click the** Orange, Accent 2 **color in the Theme Colors, then click the** Text Effects button

   The Format Text Effects dialog box opens with the options for Text Fill & Outline active. You can also use this dialog box to apply text effects, such as shadow, reflection, and 3-D effects to selected text.

4. **Click the white** Text Effects icon **in the dialog box, click** Shadow, **click the** Presets list arrow, **click** Offset Diagonal Bottom Right **in the Outer section, click** OK, **click** OK, **then deselect the text**

   The text is larger, orange, and has a shadow effect.

5. **Select** October Projects, **right-click, click** Font **on the menu that opens, click the** Advanced tab, **click the** Scale list arrow, **click** 80%, **click** OK, **then deselect the text**

   You use the Advanced tab in the Font dialog box to change the scale, or width, of the selected characters, to alter the spacing between characters, or to raise or lower the characters. Decreasing the scale of the characters makes them narrower and gives the text a tall, thin appearance, as shown in FIGURE 3-6.

6. **Scroll down, select the subheading** Wildlife Refuge, **then, using the Mini toolbar, click the** Font list arrow, **click** Trebuchet MS, **click** B, **click** I, **click the** Font Color list arrow A ▾, **click the** Orange, Accent 2 **color in the Theme Colors, then deselect the text**

   The subheading is formatted in Trebuchet MS, bold, italic, and orange.

7. **Select** Wildlife Refuge, **then click the** Format Painter button **in the Clipboard group**

   The pointer changes to ▲I.

8. **Scroll down, select** Animal Shelter **with the** ▲I **pointer, then deselect the text**

   The subheading is formatted in Trebuchet MS, bold, italic, and orange, as shown in FIGURE 3-7.

9. **Scroll up, select** Animal Care Rajasthan, **then double-click the** Format Painter button

   Double-clicking the Format Painter button allows the Format Painter to remain active until you turn it off. By keeping the Format Painter active, you can apply formatting to multiple items.

10. **Scroll down, select the headings** Microloans Inca Highlands, Disaster Relief Nepal, **and** Ecological Farming Provence **with the pointer, click the** Format Painter **button to turn off the Format Painter, then save your changes**

    The headings are formatted in 14-point Trebuchet MS bold with a green font color.

FIGURE 3-5: Font tab in Font dialog box

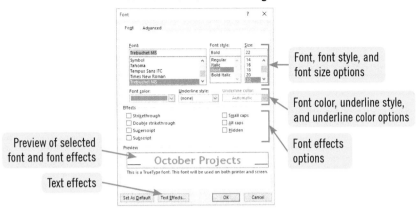

Font, font style, and font size options

Font color, underline style, and underline color options

Font effects options

Preview of selected font and font effects

Text effects

FIGURE 3-6: Font and character spacing effects applied to text

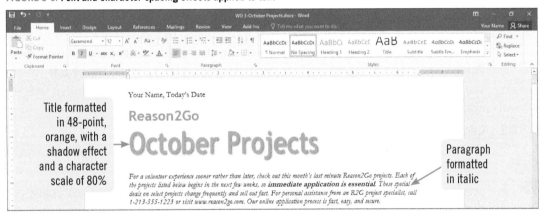

Title formatted in 48-point, orange, with a shadow effect and a character scale of 80%

Paragraph formatted in italic

FIGURE 3-7: Formats copied and applied using the Format Painter

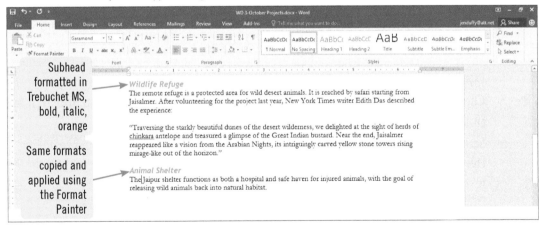

Subhead formatted in Trebuchet MS, bold, italic, orange

Same formats copied and applied using the Format Painter

Underlining text

Another creative way to call attention to text and to jazz up the appearance of a document is to apply an underline style to words you want to highlight. The Underline list arrow in the Font group displays straight, dotted, wavy, dashed, and mixed underline styles, along with a gallery of colors to choose from. To apply an underline to text, simply select it, click the Underline list arrow, and then select an underline style from the list. For a wider variety of underline styles, click More Underlines in the list, and then select an underline style in the Font dialog box. You can change the color of an underline at any time by selecting the underlined text, clicking the Underline list arrow, pointing to Underline Color, and then choosing from the options in the color gallery. If you want to remove an underline from text, select the underlined text, and then click the Underline button.

Change Line and Paragraph Spacing

Learning
Outcomes
- Add spacing under paragraphs
- Change line spacing in paragraphs
- Apply styles to text

Increasing the amount of space between lines adds more white space to a document and can make it easier to read. Adding space before and after paragraphs can also open up a document and improve its appearance. You use the Line and Paragraph Spacing list arrow in the Paragraph group on the Home tab to quickly change line spacing. To change paragraph spacing, you use the Spacing options in the Paragraph group on the Layout tab. Both line and paragraph spacing are measured in points. **CASE** *You increase the line spacing of several paragraphs and add extra space under each heading to give the flyer a more open feel. You work with formatting marks turned on, so you can see the paragraph marks (¶).*

STEPS

1. **Press [Ctrl][Home], click the** Show/Hide ¶ button 🔳 **in the Paragraph group, place the insertion point in the italicized paragraph under the title, then click the** Line and Paragraph Spacing list arrow 🔳 **in the Paragraph group on the Home tab**

   The Line Spacing list opens. This list includes options for increasing the space between lines. The check mark on the Line Spacing list indicates the current line spacing.

2. **Click** 1.15

   The space between the lines in the paragraph increases to 1.15 lines. Notice that you do not need to select an entire paragraph to change its paragraph formatting; simply place the insertion point in the paragraph.

QUICK TIP
Word recognizes any string of text that ends with a paragraph mark as a paragraph, including titles, headings, and single lines in a list.

3. **Scroll down, select the** five-line list **that begins with "Project Dates Cost", click** 🔳, **then click** 1.5

   The line spacing between the selected paragraphs changes to 1.5. To change the paragraph-formatting features of more than one paragraph, you must select the paragraphs.

4. **Scroll down, place the insertion point in the heading** Animal Care Rajasthan, **then click the** Layout tab

   The paragraph spacing settings for the active paragraph are shown in the Before and After text boxes in the Paragraph group on the Layout tab.

QUICK TIP
You can also type a number in the Before and After text boxes.

5. **Click the** After up arrow **in the Spacing section in the Paragraph group until 6 pt appears**

   Six points of space are added after the Animal Care Rajasthan heading paragraph.

TROUBLE
If your [F4] key does not work, use the After up arrow to apply 6 pts of space to the headings listed in Steps 6 and 7, then continue with Step 8.

6. **Scroll down, place the insertion point in** Microloans Inca Highlands, **then press** [F4]

   Pressing [F4] repeats the last action you took. In this case, six points of space are added after the Microloans Inca Highlands heading. Note that using [F4] is not the same as using the Format Painter. Pressing [F4] repeats only the last action you took, and using the Format Painter applies multiple format settings at the same time.

7. **Scroll down, select** Disaster Relief Nepal, **press and hold** [Ctrl], **select** Ecological Farming Provence, **release** [Ctrl], **then press** [F4]

   When you press [Ctrl] as you select items, you can select and format multiple items at once. Six points of space are added after each heading.

QUICK TIP
Adjusting the space between paragraphs is a more precise way to add white space to a document than inserting blank lines.

8. **Press [Ctrl][Home], place the insertion point in** October Projects, **then click the** Before up arrow **in the Spacing section in the Paragraph group twice so that 12 pt appears**

   The second line of the title has 12 points of space before it, as shown in FIGURE 3-8.

9. **Click the** Home tab, **click** 🔳, **then save your changes**

FIGURE 3-8: Line and paragraph spacing applied to document

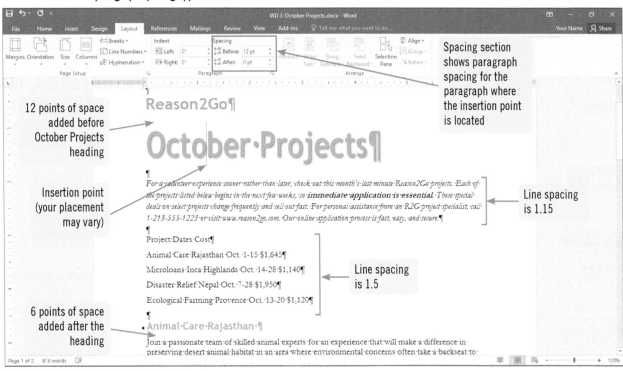

12 points of space added before October Projects heading

Insertion point (your placement may vary)

6 points of space added after the heading

Spacing section shows paragraph spacing for the paragraph where the insertion point is located

Line spacing is 1.15

Line spacing is 1.5

Formatting with Quick Styles

You can also apply multiple format settings to text in one step by applying a style. A **style** is a set of formats, such as font, font size, and paragraph alignment, that is named and stored together. Formatting a document with styles is a quick and easy way to give it a professional appearance. To make it even easier, Word includes sets of styles, called **Quick Styles**, that are designed to be used together in a document to make it attractive and readable. A Quick Style set includes styles for a title, several heading levels, body text, quotes, and lists. The styles in a Quick Style set use common fonts, colors, and formats so that using the styles together in a document gives the document a cohesive look.

To view the active set of Quick Styles, click the More button in the Styles group on the Home tab to expand the Quick Styles gallery, shown in FIGURE 3-9. As you move the pointer over each style in the gallery, a preview of the style is applied to the selected text. To apply a style to the selected text, you simply click the style in the Quick Styles gallery. To remove a style from

FIGURE 3-9: Quick Styles gallery

AaBbCcDc ¶ Normal	AaBbCcDc No Spacing	AaBbC(Heading 1	AaBbCcD Heading 2	AaB Title	AaBbCcD Subtitle	AaBbCcD Subtle Em...	AaBbCcD Emphasis
AaBbCcD Intense E...	AaBbCcDc Strong	AaBbCcDc Quote	AaBbCcD Intense Q...	AABBCCD Subtle Ref...	AABBCCD Intense R...	AaBbCcD Book Title	AaBbCcDc ¶ List Para...

Create a Style
Clear Formatting
Apply Styles...

selected text, you click the Clear All Formatting button in the Font group or the Clear Formatting command in the Quick Styles gallery.

If you want to change the active set of Quick Styles to a Quick Style set with a different design, click the Design tab, click the More button in the Document Formatting group, and then select the Quick Style set that best suits your document's content, tone, and audience. When you change the Quick Style set, a complete set of new fonts and colors is applied to the entire document. You can also change the color scheme or font used in the active Quick Style set by clicking the Colors or Fonts buttons, and then selecting from the available color schemes or font options.

Align Paragraphs

Changing paragraph alignment is another way to enhance a document's appearance. Paragraphs are aligned relative to the left and right margins in a document. By default, text is **left-aligned**, which means it is flush with the left margin and has a ragged right edge. Using the alignment buttons in the Paragraph group, you can **right-align** a paragraph—make it flush with the right margin—or **center** a paragraph so that it is positioned evenly between the left and right margins. You can also **justify** a paragraph so that both the left and right edges of the paragraph are flush with the left and right margins. **CASE** ▶ *You change the alignment of several paragraphs at the beginning of the flyer to make it more visually interesting.*

STEPS

1. **Replace** Your Name, Today's Date **with your name, a comma, and the date**

2. **Select your name, the comma, and the date, then click the** Align Right button ☰ **in the Paragraph group**

   The text is aligned with the right margin. In Page Layout view, the place where the white and shaded sections on the horizontal ruler meet shows the left and right margins.

3. **Place the insertion point between your name and the comma, press** [Delete] **to delete the comma, then press** [Enter]

   The new paragraph containing the date is also right-aligned. Pressing [Enter] in the middle of a paragraph creates a new paragraph with the same text and paragraph formatting as the original paragraph.

4. **Select the** two-line title, **then click the** Center button ☰ **in the Paragraph group**

   The two paragraphs that make up the title are centered between the left and right margins.

5. **Scroll down as needed, place the insertion point in the** Animal Care Rajasthan **heading, then click** ☰

   The Animal Care Rajasthan heading is centered.

6. **Place the insertion point in the italicized paragraph under the title, then click the** Justify button ☰ **in the Paragraph group**

   The paragraph is aligned with both the left and right margins, as shown in FIGURE 3-10. When you justify a paragraph, Word adjusts the spacing between words so that each line in the paragraph is flush with the left and the right margins.

7. **Scroll down, place the insertion point in** Animal Care Rajasthan, **then click the** launcher ⌐⌐ **in the Paragraph group**

   The Paragraph dialog box opens, as shown in FIGURE 3-11. The Indents and Spacing tab shows the paragraph format settings for the paragraph where the insertion point is located. You can check or change paragraph format settings using this dialog box.

8. **Click the** Alignment list arrow, **click** Left, **click** OK, **then save your changes**

   The Animal Care Rajasthan heading is left-aligned.

FIGURE 3-10: Modified paragraph alignment

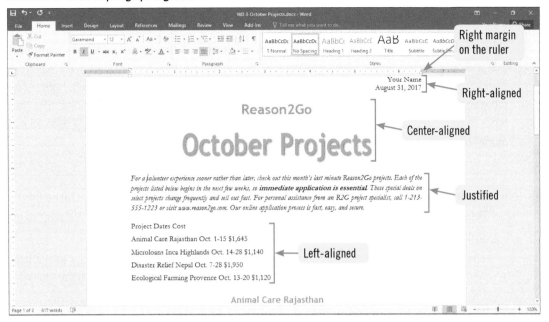

FIGURE 3-11: Indents and Spacing tab in the Paragraph dialog box

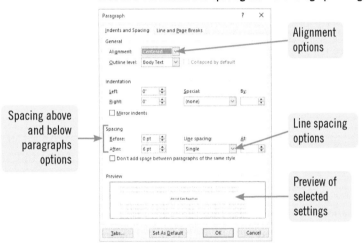

Formatting a document using themes

Changing the theme applied to a document is another powerful and efficient way to tailor a document's look and feel, particularly when a document is formatted with a Quick Style set. By default, all documents created in Word are formatted with the default Office theme—which uses Calibri as the font for the body text—but you can change the theme at any time to fit the content, tone, and purpose of a document. When you change the theme for a document, a complete set of new theme colors, fonts, and effects is applied to the whole document.

To preview how various themes look when applied to the current document, click the Themes button in the Document Formatting group on the Design tab, and then move the pointer over each theme in the gallery and notice how the document changes. When you click the theme you like, all document content that uses theme colors, all text that is formatted with a style,

including default body text, and all table styles and graphic effects change to the colors, fonts, and effects used by the theme. In addition, the gallery of colors changes to display the set of theme colors, and the active Quick Style set changes to employ the theme colors and fonts. Note that changing the theme does not change the non-theme-based font formatting that has already been applied. For example, if you changed the font of text, applied bold to text, or changed the font color of text to a standard or custom color, that formatting remains in place.

If you want to tweak the document design further, you can modify it by applying a different set of theme colors, heading and body text fonts, or graphic effects. To do this, simply click the Colors, Fonts, or Effects button in the Document Formatting group, move the pointer over each option in the gallery to preview it in the document, and then click the option you like best.

Work with Tabs

Learning
Outcomes
• Set tab stops and
  tab leaders
• Modify tabs
• Use tabs to align
  text

Tabs allow you to align text at a specific location in a document. A **tab stop** is a point on the horizontal ruler that indicates the location at which to align text. By default, tab stops are located every 1/2" from the left margin, but you can also set custom tab stops. Using tabs, you can align text to the left, right, or center of a tab stop, or you can align text at a decimal point or insert a bar character. TABLE 3-1 describes the different types of tab stops. You set tabs using the horizontal ruler or the Tabs dialog box. **CASE** ▶ *You use tabs to format the summary information on last minute projects so it is easy to read.*

STEPS

QUICK TIP
To remove a tab
stop, drag it off the
ruler.

1. **Scroll as needed, then select the** five-line list **beginning with "Project Dates Cost"**
   Before you set tab stops for existing text, you must select the paragraphs for which you want to set tabs.

2. **Point to the** tab indicator ⌊ **at the left end of the horizontal ruler**
   The icon that appears in the tab indicator indicates the active type of tab; pointing to the tab indicator displays a ScreenTip with the name of the active tab type. By default, left tab is the active tab type. Clicking the tab indicator scrolls through the types of tabs and indents.

3. **Click the** tab indicator **to see each of the available tab and indent types, make** Left Tab ⌊ **the active tab type, click the** 1" mark **on the horizontal ruler, then click the** 3½" mark **on the horizontal ruler**
   A left tab stop is inserted at the 1" mark and the 3½" mark on the horizontal ruler. Clicking the horizontal ruler inserts a tab stop of the active type for the selected paragraph or paragraphs.

4. **Click the** tab indicator **twice so the** Right Tab icon ⌐ **is active, then click the** 5" mark **on the horizontal ruler**
   A right tab stop is inserted at the 5" mark on the horizontal ruler, as shown in FIGURE 3-12.

5. **Place the insertion point before** Project **in the first line in the list, press** [Tab], **place the insertion point before** Dates, **press** [Tab], **place the insertion point before** Cost, **then press** [Tab]
   Inserting a tab before "Project" left-aligns the text at the 1" mark, inserting a tab before "Dates" left-aligns the text at the 3½" mark, and inserting a tab before "Cost" right-aligns "Cost" at the 5" mark.

6. **Insert a tab at the beginning of each remaining line in the list**
   The paragraphs left-align at the 1" mark.

QUICK TIP
Place the insertion
point in a paragraph
to see the tab stops
for that paragraph
on the horizontal
ruler.

7. **Insert a tab before each** Oct. **in the list, then insert a tab before each** $ **in the list**
   The dates left-align at the 3½" mark. The prices right-align at the 5" mark.

8. **Select the** five lines of tabbed text, **drag the right tab stop to the** 5½" mark **on the horizontal ruler, then deselect the text**
   Dragging the tab stop moves it to a new location. The prices right-align at the 5½" mark.

QUICK TIP
Double-click a tab
stop on the ruler
to open the Tabs
dialog box.

9. **Select the last** four lines **of tabbed text, click the** launcher ⌐ **in the Paragraph group, then click the** Tabs button **at the bottom of the Paragraph dialog box**
   The Tabs dialog box opens, as shown in FIGURE 3-13. You can use the Tabs dialog box to set tab stops, change the position or alignment of existing tab stops, clear tab stops, and apply tab leaders to tabs. **Tab leaders** are lines that appear in front of tabbed text.

10. **Click** 3.5" **in the Tab stop position list box, click the** 2 option button **in the Leader section, click** Set, **click** 5.5" **in the Tab stop position list box, click the** 2 option button **in the Leader section, click** Set, **click** OK, **deselect the text, then save your changes**
    A dotted tab leader is added before each 3.5" and 5.5" tab stop in the last four lines of tabbed text, as shown in FIGURE 3-14.

Formatting Text and Paragraphs

FIGURE 3-12: Left and right tab stops on the horizontal ruler

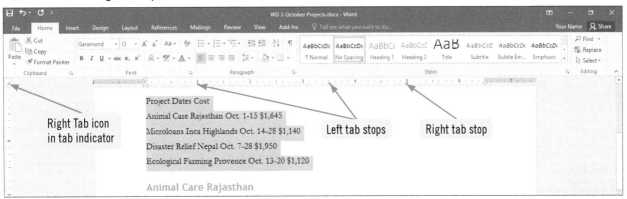

Right Tab icon
in tab indicator

Left tab stops

Right tab stop

FIGURE 3-13: Tabs dialog box

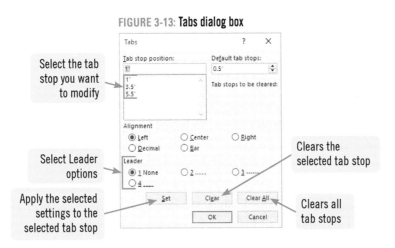

Select the tab
stop you want
to modify

Select Leader
options

Apply the selected
settings to the
selected tab stop

Clears the
selected tab stop

Clears all
tab stops

FIGURE 3-14: Tab leaders

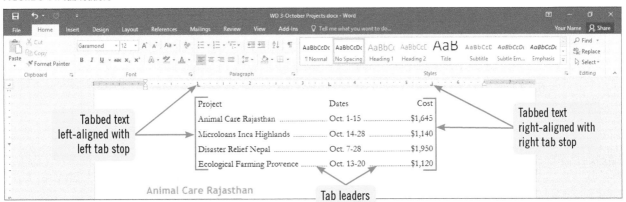

Tabbed text
left-aligned with
left tab stop

Tabbed text
right-aligned with
right tab stop

Tab leaders

TABLE 3-1: Types of tabs

tab	use to
Left tab	Set the start position of text so that text runs to the right of the tab stop as you type
Center tab	Set the center align position of text so that text stays centered on the tab stop as you type
Right tab	Set the right or end position of text so that text moves to the left of the tab stop as you type
Decimal tab	Set the position of the decimal point so that numbers align around the decimal point as you type
Bar tab	Insert a vertical bar at the tab position

Work with Indents

Learning Outcomes
• Indent a paragraph
• Indent the first line of a paragraph

When you **indent** a paragraph, you move its edge in from the left or right margin. You can indent the entire left or right edge of a paragraph, just the first line, or all lines except the first line. The **indent markers** on the horizontal ruler indicate the indent settings for the paragraph in which the insertion point is located. Dragging an indent marker to a new location on the ruler is one way to change the indentation of a paragraph; changing the indent settings in the Paragraph group on the Layout tab is another; and using the indent buttons in the Paragraph group on the Home tab is a third. TABLE 3-2 describes different types of indents and some of the methods for creating each. **CASE** ▶ *You indent several paragraphs in the flyer.*

STEPS

1. **Press [Ctrl][Home], place the insertion point in the italicized paragraph under the title, then click the** Increase Indent button 🔳 **in the Paragraph group on the Home tab**

   The entire paragraph is indented ½" from the left margin, as shown in FIGURE 3-15. The indent marker also moves to the ½" mark on the horizontal ruler. Each time you click the Increase Indent button, the left edge of a paragraph moves another ½" to the right.

2. **Click the** Decrease Indent button 🔳 **in the Paragraph group**

   The left edge of the paragraph moves ½" to the left, and the indent marker moves back to the left margin.

3. **Drag the** First Line Indent marker ▽ **to the ¼" mark on the horizontal ruler**

   FIGURE 3-16 shows the First Line Indent marker being dragged. The first line of the paragraph is indented ¼". Dragging the First Line Indent marker indents only the first line of a paragraph.

4. **Scroll to the bottom of page 1, place the insertion point in the quotation, click the** Layout tab, **click the** Indent Left text box **in the Paragraph group, type** .5, **click the** Indent Right text box, **type** .5, **then press** [Enter]

   The left and right edges of the paragraph are indented ½" from the margins, as shown in FIGURE 3-17.

5. **Press [Ctrl][Home], place the insertion point in the italicized paragraph, then click the** launcher 🔳 **in the Paragraph group**

   The Paragraph dialog box opens. You can use the Indents and Spacing tab to check or change the alignment, indentation, and paragraph and line spacing settings applied to a paragraph.

6. **Click the** Special list arrow, **click** (none), **click** OK, **then save your changes**

   The first line indent is removed from the paragraph.

Applying text effects and clearing formatting

The Word Text Effects and Typography feature allows you to add visual appeal to your documents by adding special text effects to text, including outlines, shadows, reflections, and glows. The feature also includes a gallery of preformatted combined text effect styles, called **WordArt**, that you can apply to your text to format it quickly and easily. To apply a WordArt style or a text effect to text, simply select the text, click the Text Effects and Typography button in the Font group on the Home tab, and select a WordArt style from the gallery or point to a type of text effect, such as reflection or shadow, to open a gallery of styles related to that type of text effect. Experiment with combining text effect styles to give your text a striking appearance.

If you are unhappy with the way text is formatted, you can use the Clear All Formatting command to return the text to the default format settings. The default format includes font and paragraph formatting: text is formatted in 11-point Calibri, and paragraphs are left-aligned with 1.08 point line spacing, 8 points of space after, and no indents. To clear formatting from text and return it to the default format, select the text you want to clear, and then click the Clear All Formatting button in the Font group on the Home tab. If you prefer to return the text to the default font and remove all paragraph formatting, making the text 11-point Calibri, left-aligned, single spaced, with no paragraph spacing or indents, select the text and then simply click the No Spacing button in the Styles group on the Home tab.

FIGURE 3-15: Indented paragraph

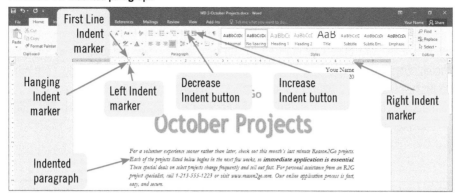

FIGURE 3-16: Dragging the First Line Indent marker

FIGURE 3-17: Paragraph indented from the left and right

TABLE 3-2: Types of indents

indent type: description	to create
Left indent: The left edge of a paragraph is moved in from the left margin	Drag the Left Indent marker ▢ on the ruler to the right to the position where you want the left edge of the paragraph to align; when you drag the left indent marker, all the indent markers move as one
Right indent: The right edge of a paragraph is moved in from the right margin	Drag the Right Indent marker △ on the ruler to the left to the position where you want the right edge of the paragraph to align
First line indent: The first line of a paragraph is indented more than the subsequent lines	Drag the First Line Indent marker ▽ on the ruler to the right to the position where you want the first line of the paragraph to begin; or activate the First Line Indent marker ▽ in the tab indicator, and then click the ruler at the position where you want the first line of the paragraph to begin
Hanging indent: The subsequent lines of a paragraph are indented more than the first line	Drag the Hanging Indent marker △ on the ruler to the right to the position where you want the hanging indent to begin; or activate the Hanging Indent marker △ in the tab indicator, and then click the ruler at the position where you want the second and remaining lines of the paragraph to begin; when you drag the hanging indent marker, the left indent marker moves with it
Negative indent (or Outdent): The left edge of a paragraph is moved to the left of the left margin	Drag the Left Indent marker ▢ on the ruler left to the position where you want the negative indent to begin; when you drag the left indent marker, all markers move as one

Add Bullets and Numbering

**Learning
Outcomes**
- Apply bullets or
numbering to lists
- Renumber a list
- Change bullet or
numbering styles

Formatting a list with bullets or numbering can help to organize the ideas in a document. A **bullet** is a character, often a small circle, that appears before the items in a list to add emphasis. Formatting a list as a numbered list helps illustrate sequences and priorities. You can quickly format a list with bullets or numbering by using the Bullets and Numbering buttons in the Paragraph group on the Home tab. **CASE** ▸ *You format the lists in your flyer with numbers and bullets.*

STEPS

1. **Scroll until the** Disaster Relief Nepal heading **is at the top of your screen**

2. **Select the** three-line list **of 3-day add-ons, click the** Home tab**, then click the** Numbering
list arrow ▦ ▾ **in the Paragraph group**

   The Numbering Library opens, as shown in FIGURE 3-18. You use this list to choose or change the numbering style applied to a list. You can drag the pointer over the numbering styles to preview how the selected text will look if the numbering style is applied.

3. **Click the numbering style called out in** FIGURE 3-18

   The paragraphs are formatted as a numbered list.

4. **Place the insertion point after** Pokhara — Valley of Lakes**, press** [Enter]**, then type**
Temples of Janakpur

   Pressing [Enter] in the middle of the numbered list creates a new numbered paragraph and automatically renumbers the remainder of the list. Similarly, if you delete a paragraph from a numbered list, Word automatically renumbers the remaining paragraphs.

5. **Click** 1 **in the list**

   Clicking a number in a list selects all the numbers, as shown in FIGURE 3-19.

6. **Click the** Bold button B **in the Font group**

   The numbers are all formatted in bold. Notice that the formatting of the items in the list does not change when you change the formatting of the numbers. You can also use this technique to change the formatting of bullets in a bulleted list.

7. **Select the list of items under "Last minute participants in the Disaster Relief Nepal
project...", then click the** Bullets button ▦ **in the Paragraph group**

   The four paragraphs are formatted as a bulleted list using the most recently used bullet style.

8. **Click a** bullet **in the list to select all the bullets, click the** Bullets list arrow ▦ ▾ **in the
Paragraph group, click the** check mark bullet style**, click the** document **to deselect the
text, then save your changes**

   The bullet character changes to a check mark, as shown in FIGURE 3-20.

Creating multilevel lists

You can create lists with hierarchical structures by applying a multilevel list style to a list. To create a **multilevel list**, also called an outline, begin by applying a multilevel list style using the Multilevel List list arrow ▦▾ in the Paragraph group on the Home tab, then type your outline, pressing [Enter] after each item. To demote items to a lower level of importance in the outline, place the insertion point in the item, then click the Increase Indent button ▦ in the Paragraph group on the

Home tab. Each time you indent a paragraph, the item is demoted to a lower level in the outline. Similarly, you can use the Decrease Indent button ▦ to promote an item to a higher level in the outline. You can also create a hierarchical structure in any bulleted or numbered list by using ▦ and ▦ to demote and promote items in the list. To change the multilevel list style applied to a list, select the list, click ▦▾ and then select a new style.

FIGURE 3-18: Numbering Library

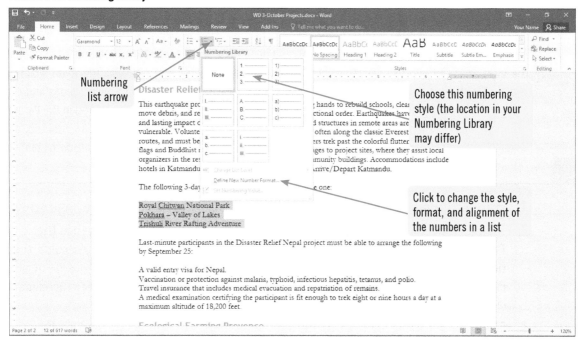

Numbering list arrow

Choose this numbering style (the location in your Numbering Library may differ)

Click to change the style, format, and alignment of the numbers in a list

FIGURE 3-19: Numbered list

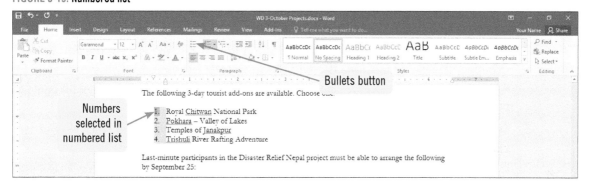

Bullets button

Numbers selected in numbered list

FIGURE 3-20: Check mark bullets applied to list

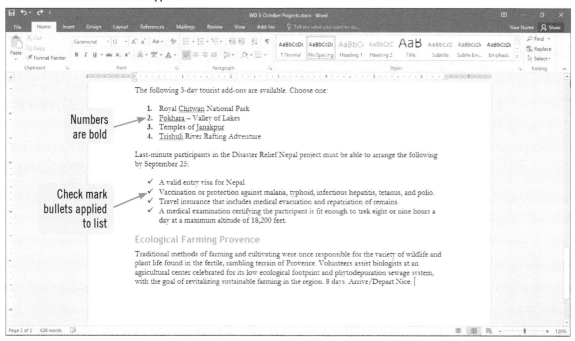

Numbers are bold

Check mark bullets applied to list

Add Borders and Shading

Learning Outcomes
- Apply shading to text
- Apply borders to text
- Highlight text

Borders and shading can add color and splash to a document. **Borders** are lines you add above, below, to the side, or around words or paragraphs. You can format borders using different line styles, colors, and widths. **Shading** is a color or pattern you apply behind words or paragraphs to make them stand out on a page. You apply borders and shading using the Borders button and the Shading button in the Paragraph group on the Home tab. **CASE** *You enhance the tabbed text of the last minute projects schedule by adding shading to it. You also apply a border around the tabbed text to set it off from the rest of the document.*

STEPS

1. **Press [Ctrl][Home], then scroll down until the tabbed text is at the top of your screen**

2. **Select the five paragraphs of tabbed text, click the Shading list arrow ⬛ ▾ in the Paragraph group on the Home tab, click the Green, Accent 6, Lighter 60% color, then deselect the text**

   Light green shading is applied to the five paragraphs. Notice that the shading is applied to the entire width of the paragraphs, despite the tab settings.

3. **Select the five paragraphs, drag the Left Indent marker ⬜ to the ¾" mark on the horizontal ruler, drag the Right Indent marker △ to the 5¾" mark, then deselect the text**

   The shading for the paragraphs is indented from the left and right, which makes it look more attractive, as shown in FIGURE 3-21.

4. **Select the five paragraphs, click the Bottom Border list arrow ⊞ ▾ in the Paragraph group, click Outside Borders, then deselect the text**

   A black outside border is added around the selected text. The style of the border added is the most recently used border style, in this case the default, a thin black line.

5. **Select the five paragraphs, click the Outside Borders list arrow ⊞ ▾, click No Border, click the No Border list arrow ⊞ ▾, then click Borders and Shading**

   The Borders and Shading dialog box opens, as shown in FIGURE 3-22. You use the Borders tab to change the border style, color, and width, and to add boxes and lines to words or paragraphs.

6. **Click the Box icon in the Setting section, scroll down the Style list, click the double-line style, click the Color list arrow, click the Green, Accent 6, Darker 25% color, click the Width list arrow, click 1½ pt, click OK, then deselect the text**

   A 1½-point dark green double-line border is added around the tabbed text.

7. **Select the five paragraphs, click the Bold button B in the Font group, click the Font Color list arrow A ▾ in the Font group, click the Green, Accent 6, Darker 25% color, then deselect the text**

   The text changes to bold dark green.

8. **Select the first line in the tabbed text, click the launcher ⌟ in the Font group, click the Font tab if it is not the active tab, scroll and click 14 in the Size list, click the Font color list arrow, click the Orange, Accent 2, Darker 25% color, click the Small caps check box in the Effects section, click OK, deselect the text, then save your changes**

   The text in the first line of the tabbed text is enlarged and changed to orange small caps, as shown in FIGURE 3-23. When you change text to small caps, the lowercase letters are changed to uppercase letters in a smaller font size.

FIGURE 3-21: Shading applied to the tabbed text

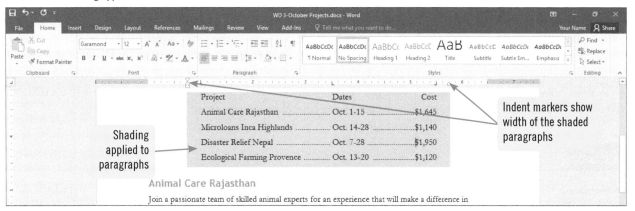

Shading applied to paragraphs

Indent markers show width of the shaded paragraphs

FIGURE 3-22: Borders tab in Borders and Shading dialog box

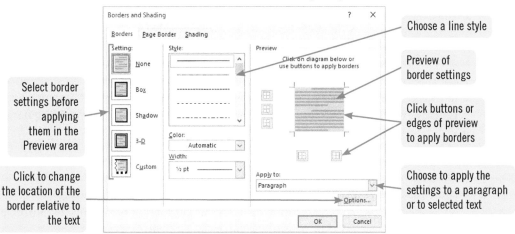

Select border settings before applying them in the Preview area

Click to change the location of the border relative to the text

Choose a line style

Preview of border settings

Click buttons or edges of preview to apply borders

Choose to apply the settings to a paragraph or to selected text

FIGURE 3-23: Borders and shading applied to the document

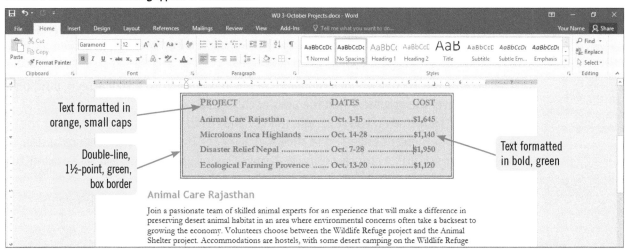

Text formatted in orange, small caps

Double-line, 1½-point, green, box border

Text formatted in bold, green

Highlighting text in a document

The Highlight tool allows you to mark and find important text in a document. **Highlighting** is transparent color that is applied to text using the Highlight pointer. To highlight text, click the Text Highlight Color list arrow in the Font group on the Home tab, select a color, then use the I-beam part of the pointer to select the text you want to highlight. Click to turn off the Highlight pointer. To remove highlighting, select the highlighted text, click then click No Color. Highlighting prints, but it is used most effectively when a document is viewed on screen.

Insert Online Pictures

Learning Outcomes
- Insert images
- Resize images
- Wrap text and position images

Clip art is a collection of graphic images that you can insert into a document. Bing Image Search clip art images are images that you can add to a document using the Online Pictures command on the Insert tab. Once you insert a clip art image, you can wrap text around it, resize it, enhance it, and move it to a different location. **CASE** ▶ *You illustrate the second page of the document with an online clip art image.*

STEPS

QUICK TIP
To complete these steps, your computer must be connected to the Internet.

1. **Scroll to the top of page 2, place the insertion point before** Microloans Inca Highlands, **click the** Insert tab, **then click the** Online Pictures button **in the Illustrations group**
   The Insert Pictures window opens. You can use this to search for images related to a keyword.

2. **Type** Inca **in the Bing Image Search text box, then press** [Enter]
   Images that have the keyword "Inca" associated with them appear in the Bing Image Search window.

TROUBLE
Select a different clip if the clip shown in FIGURE 3-24 is not available to you. You can also click the Show all web results button to see more clip art options.

3. **Scroll down the gallery of images, click the clip called out in** FIGURE 3-24, **then click** Insert
   The clip is inserted at the location of the insertion point. When a graphic is selected, the active tab changes to the Picture Tools Format tab. This tab contains commands used to adjust, enhance, arrange, and size graphics. The white circles that appear on the square edges of the graphic are the **sizing handles**.

4. **Type** 1.8 **in the Shape Height text box in the Size group on the Picture Tools Format tab, then press** [Enter]
   The size of the graphic is reduced. When you decreased the height of the graphic, the width decreased proportionally. You can also resize a graphic proportionally by dragging a corner sizing handle. Until you apply text wrapping to a graphic, it is part of the line of text in which it was inserted (an **inline graphic**). To move a graphic independently of text, you must make it a **floating graphic**.

QUICK TIP
To position a graphic using precise measurements, click the Position button, click More Layout Options, then adjust the settings on the Position tab in the Layout dialog box.

5. **Click the** Position button **in the Arrange group, then click** Position in Middle Center with Square Text Wrapping
   The graphic is moved to the middle of the page and the text wraps around it. Applying text wrapping to the graphic made it a floating graphic. A floating graphic can be moved anywhere on a page. You can also wrap text around a graphic using the Layout Options button.

6. **Scroll up until the Microloans Inca Highlands heading is at the top of your screen, position the pointer over the graphic, when the pointer changes to** ⭷, **drag the graphic up and to the right so its edges align with the right margin and the top of the paragraph under the Microloans Inca Highlands heading as shown in** FIGURE 3-25, **then release the mouse button**
   The graphic is moved to the upper-right corner of the page. Green alignment guides may appear to help you align the image with the margins.

7. **Click the** Position button **in the Arrange group, then click** Position in Top Left with Square Text Wrapping
   The graphic is moved to the upper-left corner of the page.

TROUBLE
If your document is longer than two pages, reduce the size of the graphic by dragging the lower-right corner sizing handle up and to the left.

8. **Click the** Picture Effects button **in the Picture Styles group, point to** Shadow, **point to each style to see a preview of the style applied to the graphic, then click** Offset Left
   A shadow effect is applied to the graphic.

9. **Press** [Ctrl][Home], **click the** View tab, **then click the** Multiple Pages button **in the Zoom group to view the completed document as shown in** FIGURE 3-26.

10. **Save your changes, submit the document to your instructor, then close the document and exit Word**

Formatting Text and Paragraphs

FIGURE 3-24: Insert Pictures window

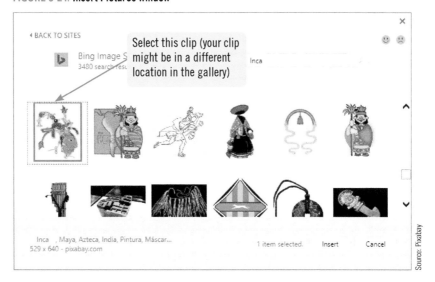

Source: Pixabay

FIGURE 3-25: Graphic being moved to a new location

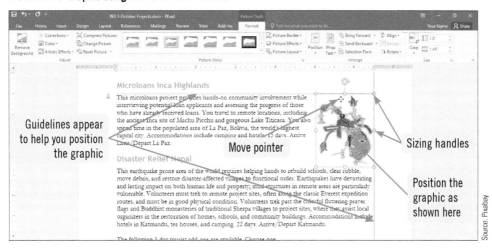

Source: Pixabay

FIGURE 3-26: Completed Document

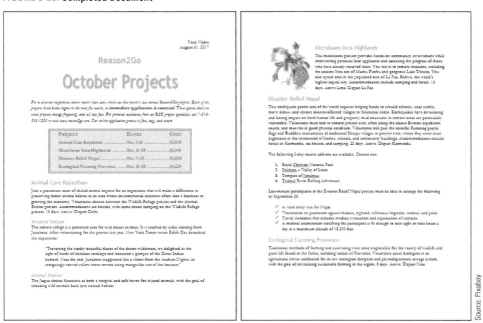

Source: Pixabay

Practice

Concepts Review

Label each element of the Word program window shown in FIGURE 3-27.

FIGURE 3-27

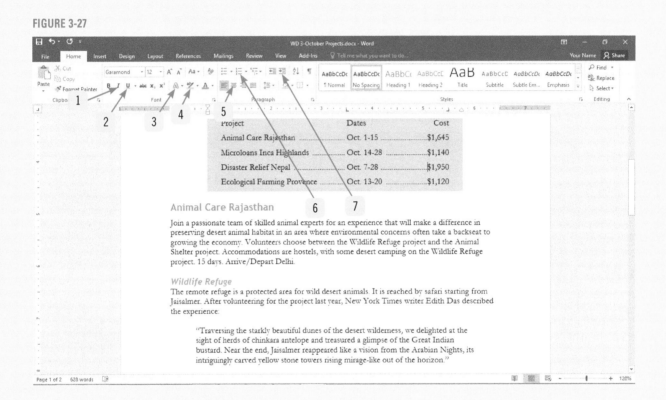

Match each term with the statement that best describes it.

8. **Inline graphic**

9. **Style**

10. **Shading**

11. **Border**

12. **Floating graphic**

13. **Highlight**

14. **Point**

15. **Bullet**

a. A graphic symbol that appears at the beginning of a paragraph in a list

b. Transparent color that is applied to text to mark it in a document

c. A set of format settings

d. An image that text wrapping has been applied to

e. An image that is inserted as part of a line of text

f. A line that can be applied above, below, or to the sides of a paragraph

g. A unit of measurement equal to $\frac{1}{72}$ of an inch

h. Color or pattern that is applied behind text to make it look attractive

Select the best answer from the list of choices.

16. **Which dialog box is used to change the scale of characters?**
    a. Paragraph
    b. Font
    c. Tabs
    d. Borders and Shading

17. **What is Calibri?**
    a. A font
    b. A style
    c. A text effect
    d. A character format

18. **What is the most precise way to increase the amount of white space between two paragraphs?**
    a. Indent the paragraphs
    b. Change the line spacing of the paragraphs
    c. Change the before spacing for the second paragraph
    d. Change the font size

19. **Which type of indent results in subsequent lines of a paragraph being indented more than the first line?**
    a. Right indent
    b. First line indent
    c. Negative indent
    d. Hanging indent

20. **Which command is used to add a reflection or an outline to text?**
    a. Underline
    b. Text Effects and Typography
    c. Strikethrough
    d. Change Case

Skills Review

1. **Format with fonts.**
   a. Start Word, open the file WD 3-2.docx from the location where you store your Data Files, save it as **WD 3-Manchester EDA Report**, then scroll through the document to get a feel for its contents.
   b. Press [Ctrl][A], then format the text in 12-point Californian FB. Choose a different serif font if Californian FB is not available to you.
   c. Press [Ctrl][Home], format the report title **City of Manchester** in 28-point Berlin Sans FB Demi. Choose a different sans serif font if Berlin Sans FB Demi is not available to you.
   d. Change the font color of the report title to Blue, Accent 5, Darker 25%.
   e. Format the subtitle **Economic Development Authority Report Executive Summary** in 16-point Berlin Sans FB Demi, then press [Enter] before Executive in the subtitle.
   f. Format the heading **Mission Statement** in 14-point Berlin Sans FB Demi with a Gold, Accent 4, Darker 25% font color.
   g. Press [Ctrl][Home], then save your changes to the report.

2. **Copy formats using the Format Painter.**
   a. Use the Format Painter to copy the format of the Mission Statement heading to the following headings: **Guiding Principles**, **Issues**, **Proposed Actions**.
   b. Show formatting marks, then format the paragraph under the Mission Statement heading in italic.
   c. Format **Years Population Growth**, the first line in the four-line list under the Issues heading, in bold, small caps, with a Blue, Accent 5, Darker 25% font color.
   d. Change the font color of the next two lines under Years Population Growth to Blue, Accent 5, Darker 25%.
   e. Format the line **Source: Office of State Planning** in italic, then save your changes.

3. **Change line and paragraph spacing.**
   a. Change the line spacing of the three-line list under the first body paragraph to 1.5 lines.
   b. Add 6 points of space after the title City of Manchester. Add 18 points of space before and 6 points of space after the Executive Summary line in the subtitle.
   c. Add 12 points of space after the Mission Statement heading, then add 12 points of space after each additional heading in the report (Guiding Principles, Issues, Proposed Actions).

   d. Add 6 points of space after each paragraph in the list under the Guiding Principles heading.

   e. Change the line spacing of the four-line list under the Issues heading that begins with Years Population Growth to 1.15.

   f. Add 6 points of space after each paragraph under the Proposed Actions heading.

   g. Press [Ctrl][Home], then save your changes to the report.

4. Align paragraphs.

   a. Press [Ctrl][A] to select the entire document, then justify all the paragraphs.

   b. Center the three-line report title.

   c. Press [Ctrl][End], press [Enter], type your name, press [Enter], type the current date, then right-align your name and the date.

   d. Save your changes to the report.

5. Work with tabs.

   a. Scroll up and select the four-line list of population information under the Issues heading.

   b. Set left tab stops at the 2" mark and the 3¾" mark.

   c. Insert a tab at the beginning of each line in the list.

   d. In the first line, insert a tab before Population. In the second line, insert a tab before 4.5%. In the third line, insert a tab before 53%.

   e. Select the first three lines, then drag the second tab stop to the 3" mark on the horizontal ruler.

   f. Press [Ctrl][Home], then save your changes to the report.

6. Work with indents.

   a. Indent the first line of the paragraph under the Mission Statement heading ½".

   b. Indent the first line of the paragraph under the Guiding Principles heading ½".

   c. Indent the first line of each of the three body paragraphs under the Issues heading ½".

   d. Press [Ctrl][Home], then save your changes to the report.

7. Add bullets and numbering.

   a. Apply bullets to the three-line list under the first body paragraph. Change the bullet style to small black circles if that is not the current bullet symbol.

   b. Change the font color of the bullets to Blue, Accent 5, Darker 25%.

   c. Scroll down until the Guiding Principles heading is at the top of your screen.

   d. Format the six-paragraph list under Guiding Principles as a numbered list.

   e. Format the numbers in 14-point Berlin Sans FB Demi, then change the font color to Blue, Accent 5, Darker 25%.

   f. Scroll down until the Proposed Actions heading is at the top of your screen, then format the paragraphs under the heading as a bulleted list using check marks as the bullet style.

   g. Change the font color of the bullets to Blue, Accent 5, Darker 25%, press [Ctrl][Home], then save your changes to the report.

8. Add borders and shading.

   a. Add a 1-point Blue, Accent 5, Darker 25% bottom border below the Mission Statement heading.

   b. Use the Format Painter or the [F4] keys to add the same border to the other headings in the report (Guiding Principles, Issues, Proposed Actions).

   c. Under the Issues heading, select the first three lines of tabbed text, which are formatted in blue, then apply Gold, Accent 4, Lighter 60% shading to the paragraphs.

   d. Select the first three lines of tabbed text again if necessary, then add a 1½ -point Blue, Accent 5, Darker 25% single line box border around the paragraphs.

   e. Indent the shading and border around the paragraphs 1¾" from the left and 1¾" from the right.

   f. Turn off formatting marks, then save your changes.

Skills Review (continued)

9. **Insert online pictures.** *(Note: To complete these steps, your computer must be connected to the Internet.)*

   a. Press [Ctrl][Home], then open the Insert Pictures window.

   b. Search using Bing Image Search to find images related to the keyword **buildings**.

   c. Insert the image shown in FIGURE 3-28. *(Note:* Select a different image if this one is not available to you. It is best to select an image that is similar in shape to the image shown in FIGURE 3-28.)

   d. Use the Shape Width text box in the Size group on the Picture Tools Format tab to change the width of the image to 1.5".

   e. Use the Position command to position the image in the top right with square text wrapping.

   f. Apply an Offset Diagonal Bottom Left shadow style to the image.

   g. View your document in two-page view and compare it to the document shown in FIGURE 3-28. Adjust the size or position of the image as needed to so that your document resembles the document shown in the figure.

   h. Save your changes to the document, submit it to your instructor, close the file, and then exit Word.

FIGURE 3-28

City of Manchester
Economic Development Authority Report
Executive Summary

The City of Manchester Economic Development Authority (EDA) has written an economic policy plan for the city of Manchester. The plan is intended to advance dynamic and interactive discussion. It will be used to continuously assess and foster decision-making about the following in the city of Manchester:

- Development
- Infrastructure
- Quality of life

Mission Statement

The purpose of the EDA is to foster a sustainable economy consistent with the city's planning objectives. The mix of industry, commerce, open space, residential development, and the arts in Manchester results in the city's vitality and an excellent quality of life for its citizens. Maintaining this balance is important.

Guiding Principles

Six basic principles guide Manchester's economic policy. These principles seek to safeguard the special features that give the city its character while embracing appropriate economic opportunities.

1. Manchester should remain a major economic center of the region.
2. Economic activity must respect Manchester's natural, cultural, and historic heritage.
3. A pedestrian-friendly commercial center is essential.
4. Sustained economic prosperity requires a balance between residential development, industrial/commercial development, and open space.
5. Open space in the rural district must be preserved.
6. Investing in the infrastructure is necessary to maintain and expand the existing tax and job base.

Issues

Of Manchester's approximately 64,000 acres of land, 12% is zoned for business, commercial, or industrial use, and 88% for residential development. Historically the city has relied upon business and industry to provide 35%-40% of the tax base, as well as employment opportunities. Non-residential development has traditionally been the backbone of the Manchester economy. Today, however, Manchester does not have a great deal of non-residential development potential.

The population of Manchester is expected to rise dramatically over the next few decades. The following chart shows the expected change:

Years	Population Growth
2020-2040	4.5%
2040-2060	53% (projected)

Source: Office of State Planning

At issue is the city's ability to continue to support increasing public costs (most importantly, education) with a tax base shifting toward residential taxpayers. The EDA believes Manchester should remain the market center of the region and avoid becoming a bedroom community. Manchester has maintained a sense of community in part because more than 50% of working residents are able to earn a living within the city. Jobs must be continuously created to sustain the percentage of residents who live and work in Manchester.

Proposed Actions

✓ Implement a business retention program that focuses on the growth and expansion of businesses already operating in Manchester.
✓ Build a consortium of technical and skill development resources to assist companies with educational and training needs.
✓ Sponsor a green business workshop.
✓ Allocate funds for expanded downtown parking.
✓ Develop a strategic open space plan.

Your Name

Today's Date

Source: Pixabay

Independent Challenge 1

You are an estimator for Sustainable Life Design | Build in Jackson, Illinois. You have drafted an estimate for a home renovation job and you need to format it. It's important that your estimate have a clean, striking design, and reflect your company's professionalism.

a. Start Word, open the file WD 3-3.docx from the drive and folder where you store your Data Files, save it as

FIGURE 3-29

SustainableLIFE Design | Build

482 North Street, Jackson, IL 62705; Tel: 217-555-3202; www.sustainablelifedesignbuild.com

WD 3-Chou Birch Estimate, then read the document to get a feel for its contents. FIGURE 3-29 shows how you will format the letterhead.

b. Select the entire document, change the style to No Spacing, then change the font to 11-point Calibri Light.

c. In the first line of the letterhead, format **Sustainable Life** in 30-point Arial Black, then apply all caps to Life. Format **Sustainable** with the Green, Accent 6, Darker 25% font color, format **LIFE** with the Green, Accent 6 font color, then delete the space between the two words. Format **Design | Build** in 30-point Arial with a Green, Accent 6, Darker 25% font color. (*Hint*: Type 30 in the Font Size text box, then press [Enter].)

d. Format the next line in 10-point Arial with a Green, Accent 6, Darker 25% font color.

e. Center the two-line letterhead.

f. Add a 2¼-point dotted Green, Accent 6, Darker 25% border below the address line paragraph.

g. With the insertion point in the address line, open the Borders and Shading dialog box, click Options to open the Border and Shading Options dialog box, change the Bottom setting to **5** points, then click OK twice to close the dialog boxes and to adjust the location of the border relative to the line of text.

h. Format the title **Proposal of Renovation** in 14-point Arial, then center the title.

i. Format the following headings (including the colons) in 11-point Arial: **Date**, **Work to be performed for and at**, **Scope of work**, **Payment schedule**, and **Agreement**.

j. Select the 14-line list under **Scope of work** that begins with **Demo of all...**, then change the paragraph spacing to add 4 points of space after each paragraph in the list. (*Hint*: Select 0 pt in the After text box, type 4, then press Enter.)

k. With the list selected, set a right tab stop at the 6¼" mark, insert tabs before every price in the list, then apply dotted line tab leaders.

l. Format the list as a numbered list, then apply bold to the numbers.

m. Apply bold and italic to the two lines, **Total estimated job cost...** and **Approximate job time...** below the list.

n. Replace Your Name with your name in the signature block, select the signature block (Respectfully submitted through your name), set a left tab stop at the 3¼" mark, then indent the signature block using tabs.

o. Examine the document carefully for formatting errors, and make any necessary adjustments.

p. Save the document, submit it to your instructor, then close the file and exit Word.

Independent Challenge 2

Your employer, the Mission Center for Contemporary Arts in Guelph, Ontario, is launching a membership drive. Your boss has written the text for a flyer advertising Mission membership, and asks you to format it so that it is eye catching and attractive.

a. Open the file WD 3-4.docx from the drive and folder where you store your Data Files, save it as **WD 3-Mission 2017**, then read the document. FIGURE 3-30 shows how you will format the first several paragraphs of the flyer.

b. Select the entire document, change the style to No Spacing, then change the font to 10-point Calibri Light.

FIGURE 3-30

c. Center the first line, **MEMBERSHIP DRIVE**, and apply shading to the paragraph. Choose a dark custom shading color of your choice for the shading color. (*Hint*: Click More Colors, then select a color from the Standard or Custom tab.) Format the text in 24-point Calibri Light, bold, with a white font color. Expand the character spacing by 10 points. (*Hint*: Use the Advanced tab in the Font dialog box. Set the Spacing to Expanded, and then type **10** in the By text box.)

d. Format the second line, **2017**, in 48-point Broadway, bold. Apply the Fill - White, Outline - Accent 2, Hard Shadow - Accent 2 text effect style to the text. (*Hint*: Use the Text Effects and Typography button.) Expand the character spacing by 10 points, and change the character scale to 250%. Center the line.

e. Format each **What we do for...** heading in 11-point Calibri Light, bold. Change the font color to the same custom color used for shading the title. (*Note*: The color now appears in the Recent Colors section of the Font Color gallery.) Add a single-line ½-point black border under each heading.

f. Format each subheading (**Gallery, Lectures, Library, All members...**, and **Membership Levels**) in 10-point Calibri Light, bold. Add 3 points of spacing before each paragraph. (*Hint*: Select 0 in the Before text box, type 3, then press Enter.)

g. Indent each body paragraph ¼", except for the lines under the **What we do for YOU** heading.

h. Format the four lines under the **All members...** subheading as a bulleted list. Use a bullet symbol of your choice, and format the bullets in the custom font color.

i. Indent the five lines under the **Membership Levels** heading ¼". For these five lines, set left tab stops at the 1¼" mark and the 2¼" mark on the horizontal ruler. Insert tabs before the price and before the word All in each of the five lines.

j. Format the name of each membership level (**Artistic, Conceptual**, etc.) in 10-point Calibri Light, bold, italic, with the custom font color.

k. Format the **For more information...** heading in 14-point Calibri Light, bold, with the custom font color, then center the heading.

l. Center the last two lines, replace Your Name with your name, then apply bold to your name.

m. Examine the document carefully for formatting errors, and make any necessary adjustments.

n. Save the flyer, submit it to your instructor, then close the file and exit Word.

Independent Challenge 3

One of your responsibilities as program coordinator at Alpine Vistas Resort is to develop a program of winter outdoor learning and adventure workshops. You have drafted a memo to your boss to update her on your progress. You need to format the memo so it is professional looking and easy to read.

a. Start Word, open the file WD 3-5.docx from the drive and folder where you store your Data Files, then save it as **WD 3-Alpine Vistas Memo**.

b. Select the **Alpine Vistas Resort Memorandum** heading, apply the Quick Style Title to it, then center the heading. (*Hint*: Open the Quick Style gallery, then click the Title style.)

c. In the memo header, replace Today's Date and Your Name with the current date and your name.

d. Select the four-line memo header, set a left tab stop at the ¾" mark, then insert tabs before the date, the recipient's name, your name, and the subject of the memo.

e. Apply the Quick Style Strong to **Date:**, **To:**, **From:**, and **Re:**.

f. Apply the Quick Style Heading 2 to the headings **Overview**, **Workshops**, **Accommodations**, **Fees**, and **Proposed winter programming**.

g. Under the Fees heading, apply the Quick Style Emphasis to the words **Workshop fees** and **Accommodations fees**.

h. On the second page of the document, format the list under the **Proposed winter programming** heading as a multilevel list. FIGURE 3-31 shows the hierarchical structure of the outline. (*Hints*: The list is on pages 2 and 3 so be sure to select the entire list before applying the multilevel style. Apply a multilevel list style, then use the Increase Indent and Decrease Indent buttons to change the level of importance of each item.)

i. Change the outline numbering style to the bullet numbering style shown in FIGURE 3-31 if a different style is used in your outline.

j. Change the font color of each bullet level in the list to a theme font color of your choice. (*Hint*: Select one bullet of each level to select all the bullets at that level, then apply a font color.)

k. Zoom out on the memo so that two pages are displayed in the document window, then, using the Change Case button, change the title Alpine Vistas Resort Memorandum so that only the initial letter of each word is capitalized.

l. Using the Fonts button on the Design tab, change the fonts to a font set of your choice. Choose fonts that allow the document to fit on two pages.

m. Using the Colors button on the Design tab, change the colors to a color palette of your choice.

n. Apply different styles and adjust other formatting elements as necessary to make the memo attractive, eye catching, and readable. The finished memo should fit on two pages.

o. Save the document, submit it to your instructor, then close the file and exit Word.

FIGURE 3-31

Proposed winter programming
- ❖ Skiing, Snowboarding, and Snowshoeing
  - ➢ Skiing and Snowboarding
    - ▪ Cross-country skiing
      - • Cross-country skiing for beginners
      - • Intermediate cross-country skiing
      - • Inn-to-inn ski touring
      - • Moonlight cross-country skiing
    - ▪ Telemarking
      - • Basic telemark skiing
      - • Introduction to backcountry skiing
      - • Exploring on skis
    - ▪ Snowboarding
      - • Backcountry snowboarding
  - ➢ Snowshoeing
    - ▪ Beginner
      - • Snowshoeing for beginners
      - • Snowshoeing and winter ecology
    - ▪ Intermediate and Advanced
      - • Intermediate snowshoeing
      - • Guided snowshoe trek
      - • Above tree line snowshoeing
- ❖ Winter Hiking, Camping, and Survival
  - ➢ Hiking
    - ▪ Beginner
      - • Long-distance hiking
      - • Winter summits
      - • Hiking for women
  - ➢ Winter camping and survival
    - ▪ Beginner
      - • Introduction to winter camping
      - • Basic winter mountain skills
      - • Building snow shelters
    - ▪ Intermediate
      - • Basic winter mountain skills II
      - • Ice climbing
      - • Avalanche awareness and rescue

Independent Challenge 4: Explore

The fonts you choose for a document can have a major effect on the document's tone. Not all fonts are appropriate for use in a business document, and some fonts, especially those with a definite theme, are appropriate only for specific purposes. In this Independent Challenge, you will use font formatting and other formatting features to design a letterhead and a fax coversheet for yourself or your business. The letterhead and coversheet should not only look professional and attract interest, but also say something about the character of your business or your personality. FIGURE 3-32 shows an example of a business letterhead.

a. Start Word, and save a new blank document as **WD 3-Personal Letterhead** to the drive and folder where you store your Data Files.

b. Type your name or the name of your business, your address, your phone number, your fax number, and your website or e-mail address.

c. Format your name or the name of your business in a font that expresses your personality or says something about the nature of your business. Use fonts, font colors, text effects and typography, borders, shading, paragraph formatting, and other formatting features to design a letterhead that is appealing and professional.

d. Save your changes, submit the document to your instructor, then close the file.

e. Open a new blank document, and save it as **WD 3-Personal Fax Coversheet**. Type FAX, your name or the name of your business, your address, your phone number, your fax number, and your website or e-mail address at the top of the document.

f. Type a fax header that includes the following: Date:, To:, From:, Re:, Pages:, and Comments:.

g. Format the information in the fax coversheet using fonts, font effects, borders, paragraph formatting, and other formatting features. Since a fax coversheet is designed to be faxed, all fonts and other formatting elements should be black or grey.

h. Save your changes, submit the document to your instructor, close the file, then exit Word.

FIGURE 3-32

Rebecca Valerino Interior Design

443 Sanchez Street, 6th floor, Santa Fe, NM 87501 Tel: 505-555-9767 Fax: 505-555-2992 www.valerino.com

Visual Workshop

Open the file WD 3-6.docx from the drive and folder where you store your Data Files. Create the menu shown in FIGURE 3-33. (*Hints*: Use the sizing handles to resize the graphic to be approximately 1.4" tall and 6.5" wide. Use Californian FB or a similar font for the text. Add color, bold, and italic as shown in the figure. Change the font size of the café name to 28 points, the font size of Today's Specials to 14 points, the font size of the menu to 12 points, and the font size of the italicized text at the bottom to 10 points. Format the prices using tabs and leader lines. Use paragraph spacing to adjust the spacing between paragraphs so that all the text fits on one page. Make other adjustments as needed so your menu is similar to the one shown in FIGURE 3-33.) Save the menu as **WD 3-Todays Specials**, then submit a copy to your instructor.

FIGURE 3-33

City Beach Café

Today's Specials

Strawberry Summer Salad

Arugula and baby spinach topped with sliced strawberries, goat cheese, sunflower seeds, and croutons, served with a strawberry vinaigrette. Add shrimp or lobster. $9.00

Shrimp and Avocado Salad

Shrimp and avocado salad over mixed greens with sliced tomatoes, cucumbers, and corn salsa, served with cilantro lime vinaigrette. $12.00

Lobster Tacos

Generous chunks of lobster over ginger slaw with chipotle crema and pickled onions. Served with cilantro lime rice and beans. $15.00

Coconut Encrusted Haddock

Filet of haddock lighted breaded with panko and coconut. Oven baked and served with cilantro lime rice and beans and corn on the cob. $16.00

Tropical Grilled Swordfish

Seasoned swordfish grilled and finished with citrus pineapple salsa. Served with cilantro lime rice and beans, and ginger slaw. $18.00

Shrimp Burrito

Tender grilled shrimp served with cilantro rice, black beans, romaine lettuce, cheese, salsa verde, pico de gallo, and corn on the cob. $11.00

Scallop Kebob

Ginger lime drenched scallops grilled and served with tropical macaroni salad, citrus pineapple salsa, and corn on the cob. $15.00

We serve only fresh, local, sustainably farmed and harvested ingredients.

Chef: Your Name

Formatting Documents

CASE You have written and formatted the text for an informational report for Reason2Go volunteers about staying healthy while traveling. You are now ready to format the pages. You plan to organize the text in columns, to illustrate the report with a table, and to add footnotes and a bibliography.

Module Objectives

After completing this module, you will be able to:

- Set document margins
- Create sections and columns
- Insert page breaks
- Insert page numbers
- Add headers and footers

- Insert a table
- Add footnotes and endnotes
- Insert citations
- Manage sources and create a bibliography

Files You Will Need

WD 4-1.docx   WD 4-5.docx

WD 4-2.docx   WD 4-6.docx

WD 4-3.docx   WD 4-7.docx

WD 4-4.docx

Set Document Margins

Learning Outcomes
• Set custom margins
• Change paper size
• Change page orientation

Changing a document's margins is one way to change the appearance of a document and control the amount of text that fits on a page. The **margins** of a document are the blank areas between the edge of the text and the edge of the page. When you create a document in Word, the default margins are 1" at the top, bottom, left, and right sides of the page. You can adjust the size of a document's margins using the Margins command on the Layout tab or using the rulers. **CASE** *The report should be a four-page document when finished. You begin by reducing the size of the document margins so that more text fits on each page.*

STEPS

TROUBLE
Click the Ruler check box in the Show group on the View tab to display the rulers if they are not already displayed.

1. **Start Word, open the file** WD 4-1.docx **from the location where you store your Data Files, then save it as** WD 4-Travel Health 2Go

   The report opens in Print Layout view.

2. **Scroll through the report to get a feel for its contents, then press** [Ctrl][Home]

   The report is currently five pages long. Notice that the status bar indicates the page where the insertion point is located and the total number of pages in the document.

3. **Click the** Layout tab, **then click the** Margins button **in the Page Setup group**

   The Margins menu opens. You can select predefined margin settings from this menu, or you can click Custom Margins to create different margin settings.

QUICK TIP
You can also click the launcher [⊡] in the Page Setup group to open the Page Setup dialog box.

4. **Click** Custom Margins

   The Page Setup dialog box opens with the Margins tab displayed, as shown in FIGURE 4-1. You can use the Margins tab to change the top, bottom, left, or right document margin, to change the orientation of the pages from portrait to landscape, and to alter other page layout settings. **Portrait orientation** means a page is taller than it is wide; **landscape orientation** means a page is wider than it is tall. This report uses portrait orientation. You can also use the Orientation button in the Page Setup group on the Layout tab to change the orientation of a document.

QUICK TIP
The minimum allowable margin settings depend on your printer and the size of the paper you are using. Word displays a warning message if you set margins that are too narrow for your printer.

5. **Click the** Top down arrow **three times until** 0.7" **appears, then click the** Bottom down arrow **until** 0.7" **appears**

   The top and bottom margins of the report will be .7".

6. **Press** [Tab], **type** .7 **in the Left text box, press** [Tab], **then type** .7 **in the Right text box**

   The left and right margins of the report will also be .7". You can change the margin settings by using the arrows or by typing a value in the appropriate text box.

7. **Click** OK

   The document margins change to .7", as shown in FIGURE 4-2. The location of each margin (right, left, top, and bottom) is shown on the horizontal and vertical rulers at the intersection of the white and shaded areas. You can also change a margin setting by using the ⤢ pointer to drag the intersection to a new location on the ruler.

TROUBLE
The number of pages you see depends on the computer you are using.

8. **Click the** View tab, **then click the** Multiple Pages button **in the Zoom group**

   The first three pages of the document appear in the document window.

9. **Scroll down to view all five pages of the report, press** [Ctrl][Home], **click the** 100% button **in the Zoom group, then save your changes**

FIGURE 4-1: Margins tab in Page Setup dialog box

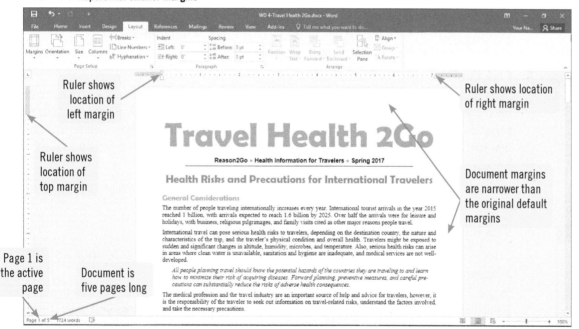

Default margin settings →

Set gutter margin →

Select page orientation →

Select gutter position

Set mirror margins and other page layout options

Preview of margin settings

Select part of document to apply settings to

FIGURE 4-2: **Report with smaller margins**

Ruler shows location of left margin

Ruler shows location of top margin

Ruler shows location of right margin

Document margins are narrower than the original default margins

Page 1 is the active page

Document is five pages long

Word 2016

Changing orientation, margin settings, and paper size

By default, the documents you create in Word use an 8½" x 11" paper size in portrait orientation with the default margin settings. You can change the orientation, margin settings, and paper size to common settings using the Orientation, Margins, and Size buttons in the Page Setup group on the Layout tab. You can also adjust these settings and others in the Page Setup dialog box. For example, to change the layout of multiple pages, use the Multiple pages list arrow on the Margins tab to create pages that use mirror margins, that include two pages per sheet of paper, or that are formatted using a book fold. **Mirror margins** are used in a document with facing pages, such as a magazine, where the

margins on the left page of the document are a mirror image of the margins on the right page. Documents with mirror margins have inside and outside margins, rather than right and left margins. Another type of margin is a gutter margin, which is used in documents that are bound, such as books. A **gutter** adds extra space to the left, top, or inside margin to allow for the binding. Add a gutter to a document by adjusting the setting in the Gutter position text box on the Margins tab. To change the size of the paper used, use the Paper size list arrow on the Paper tab to select a standard paper size, or enter custom measurements in the Width and Height text boxes.

Create Sections and Columns

Learning Outcomes
• Customize the status bar
• Insert section breaks
• Format text in columns

Dividing a document into sections allows you to format each section of the document with different page layout settings. A **section** is a portion of a document that is separated from the rest of the document by section breaks. **Section breaks** are formatting marks that you insert in a document to show the end of a section. Once you have divided a document into sections, you can format each section with different column, margin, page orientation, header and footer, and other page layout settings. By default, a document is formatted as a single section, but you can divide a document into as many sections as you like. **CASE** ➤ *You insert a section break to divide the document into two sections, and then format the text in the second section in two columns. First, you customize the status bar to display section information.*

STEPS

1. **Right-click the status bar, click Section on the Customize Status Bar menu that opens (if it is not already checked), then click the document to close the menu**

   The status bar indicates the insertion point is located in section 1 of the document.

2. **Click the Home tab, then click the Show/Hide ¶ button ¶ in the Paragraph group**

   Turning on formatting marks allows you to see the section breaks you insert in a document.

3. **Place the insertion point before the heading General Considerations, click the Layout tab, then click the Breaks button in the Page Setup group**

   The Breaks menu opens. You use this menu to insert different types of section breaks. See TABLE 4-1.

4. **Click Continuous**

   Word inserts a continuous section break, shown as a dotted double line, above the heading. When you insert a section break at the beginning of a paragraph, Word inserts the break at the end of the previous paragraph. The section break stores the formatting information for the previous section. The document now has two sections. Notice that the status bar indicates the insertion point is in section 2.

5. **Click the Columns button in the Page Setup group**

   The columns menu opens. You use this menu to format text using preset column formats or to create custom columns.

6. **Click More Columns to open the Columns dialog box**

7. **Select Two in the Presets section, click the Spacing down arrow twice until 0.3" appears as shown in FIGURE 4-3, then click OK**

   Section 2 is formatted in two columns of equal width with .3" of spacing between, as shown in FIGURE 4-4. Formatting text in columns is another way to increase the amount of text that fits on a page.

8. **Click the View tab, click the Multiple Pages button in the Zoom group, scroll down to examine all four pages of the document, press [Ctrl][Home], then save the document**

   The text in section 2—all the text below the continuous section break—is formatted in two columns. Text in columns flows automatically from the bottom of one column to the top of the next column.

TABLE 4-1: Types of section breaks

section	function
Next page	Begins a new section and moves the text following the break to the top of the next page
Continuous	Begins a new section on the same page
Even page	Begins a new section and moves the text following the break to the top of the next even-numbered page
Odd page	Begins a new section and moves the text following the break to the top of the next odd-numbered page

FIGURE 4-3: Columns dialog box

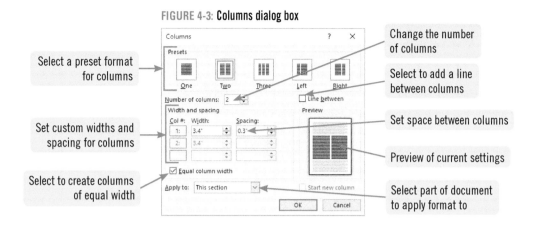

Select a preset format for columns

Change the number of columns

Select to add a line between columns

Set custom widths and spacing for columns

Set space between columns

Preview of current settings

Select to create columns of equal width

Select part of document to apply format to

FIGURE 4-4: Continuous section break and columns

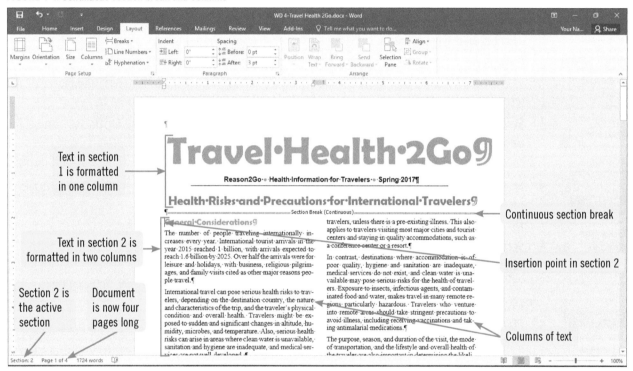

Text in section 1 is formatted in one column

Text in section 2 is formatted in two columns

Section 2 is the active section

Document is now four pages long

Continuous section break

Insertion point in section 2

Columns of text

Changing page layout settings for a section

Dividing a document into sections allows you to vary the layout of a document. In addition to applying different column settings to sections, you can apply different margins, page orientation, paper size, vertical alignment, header and footer, page numbering, footnotes, endnotes, and other page layout settings. For example, if you are formatting a report that includes a table with many columns, you might want to change the table's page orientation to landscape so that it is easier to read. To do this, you would insert a section break before and after the table to create a section that contains only the table, and then you would change the page orientation of the section that contains the table to landscape. If the table does not fill the page, you could also change the vertical alignment of the table so that it is centered

vertically on the page. To do this, use the Vertical alignment list arrow on the Layout tab of the Page Setup dialog box.

To check or change the page layout settings for an individual section, place the insertion point in the section, then open the Page Setup dialog box. Select any options you want to change, click the Apply to list arrow, click This section, then click OK. When you select This section in the Apply to list box, the settings are applied to the current section only. When you select This point forward, the settings are applied to the current section and all sections that follow it. If you select Whole document in the Apply to list box, the settings are applied to all the sections in the document. Use the Apply to list arrow in the Columns dialog box or the Footnote and Endnote dialog box to change those settings for a section.

Insert Page Breaks

Learning Outcomes
• Insert and delete page breaks
• Insert a column break
• Balance columns

As you type text in a document, Word inserts an **automatic page break** (also called a soft page break) when you reach the bottom of a page, allowing you to continue typing on the next page. You can also force text onto the next page of a document by using the Breaks command to insert a **manual page break** (also called a hard page break). Another way to control the flow of text is to apply pagination settings using the Line and Page Breaks tab in the Paragraph dialog box. **CASE** ▶ *You insert manual page breaks where you know you want to begin each new page of the report.*

STEPS

1. **Click the** 100% button, **scroll to the bottom of page 1, place the insertion point before the heading** Malaria: A Serious…, **click the** Layout tab, **then click the** Breaks button **in the Page Setup group**

   The Breaks menu opens. You also use this menu to insert page, column, and text-wrapping breaks. TABLE 4-2 describes these types of breaks.

2. **Click** Page

   Word inserts a manual page break before "Malaria: A Serious Health Risk for Travelers" and moves all the text following the page break to the beginning of the next page, as shown in FIGURE 4-5.

3. **Scroll down, place the insertion point before the heading** Preventive Options… **on page 2, press and hold** [Ctrl], **then press** [Enter]

   Pressing [Ctrl][Enter] is a fast way to insert a manual page break. The heading is forced to the top of the third page.

4. **Scroll to the bottom of page 3, place the insertion point before the heading** Insurance for Travelers **on page 3, then press** [Ctrl][Enter]

   The heading is forced to the top of the fourth page.

5. **Scroll up, click to the left of the page break on page 2 with the selection pointer** ⤢ **to select the page break, then press** [Delete]

   The manual page break is deleted and the text from pages 2 and 3 flows together. You can also use the selection pointer to click to the left of a section or a column break to select it.

6. **Place the insertion point before the heading** Medical Kit… **on page 2, then press** [Ctrl] [Enter]

   The heading is forced to the top of the third page.

7. **Click the** View tab, **click the** Multiple Pages button **in the Zoom group, scroll to view all four pages of the document, then save your changes**

   Pages 1, 2, and 3 are shown in FIGURE 4-6. Your screen might show a different number of pages.

Controlling automatic pagination

Another way to control the flow of text between pages (or between columns) is to apply pagination settings to specify where Word positions automatic page breaks. To apply automatic pagination settings, simply select the paragraphs(s) or line(s) you want to control, click the launcher in the Paragraph group on the Home or Layout tab, click the Line and Page Breaks tab in the Paragraph dialog box, and then select one or more of the following settings in the Pagination section before clicking OK.

• Keep with next: Apply to any paragraph you want to appear together with the next paragraph in order to prevent the page or column from breaking between the paragraphs.

• Keep lines together: Apply to selected paragraph or lines to prevent a page or column from breaking in the middle of a paragraph or between certain lines.

• Page break before: Apply to add an automatic page break before a specific paragraph.

• Widow/Orphan control: Turned on by default; ensures at least two lines of a paragraph appear at the top and bottom of every page or column by preventing a page or column from beginning with only the last line of a paragraph (a **widow**), or ending with only the first line of a new paragraph (an **orphan**).

FIGURE 4-5: Manual page break in document

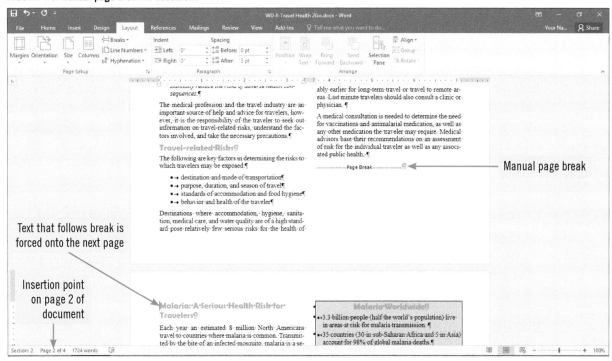

Manual page break (label pointing to Page Break marker in document)

Text that follows break is forced onto the next page

Insertion point on page 2 of document

FIGURE 4-6: Pages 1, 2, and 3

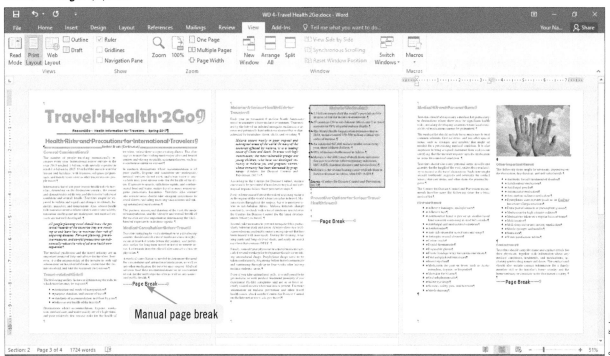

Manual page break

Source: Pixabay

TABLE 4-2: Types of breaks

break	function
Page	Forces the text following the break to begin at the top of the next page
Column	Forces the text following the break to begin at the top of the next column
Text Wrapping	Forces the text following the break to begin at the beginning of the next line

Insert Page Numbers

If you want to number the pages of a multiple-page document, you can insert a page number field to add a page number to each page. A **field** is a code that serves as a placeholder for data that changes in a document, such as a page number or the current date. When you use the Page Number button on the Insert tab to add page numbers to a document, you insert the page number field at the top, bottom, or side of any page, and Word automatically numbers all the pages in the document for you. **CASE** *You insert a page number field so that page numbers will appear centered between the margins at the bottom of each page in the document.*

STEPS

1. **Press [Ctrl][Home], click the 100% button in the Zoom group on the View tab, click the Insert tab, then click the Page Number button in the Header & Footer group**

   The Page Number menu opens. You use this menu to select the position for the page numbers. If you choose to add a page number field to the top, bottom, or side of a document, a page number will appear on every page in the document. If you choose to insert it in the document at the location of the insertion point, the field will appear on that page only.

2. **Point to Bottom of Page**

   A gallery of formatting and alignment options for page numbers to be inserted at the bottom of a page opens, as shown in FIGURE 4-7.

3. **Scroll down the gallery to view the options, scroll to the top of the gallery, then click Plain Number 2 in the Simple section**

   A page number field containing the number 1 is centered in the Footer area at the bottom of page 1 of the document, as shown in FIGURE 4-8. The document text is gray, or dimmed, because the Footer area is open. Text that is inserted in a Footer area appears at the bottom of every page in a document.

4. **Double-click the document text**

   Double-clicking the document text closes the Footer area. The page number is now dimmed because it is located in the Footer area, which is no longer the active area. When the document is printed, the page numbers appear as normal text. You will learn more about working with the Footer area in the next lesson.

5. **Scroll down the document to see the page number at the bottom of each page**

   Word numbered each page of the report automatically, and each page number is centered at the bottom of the page. If you want to change the numbering format or start page numbering with a different number, you can simply click the Page Number button, click Format Page Numbers, and then choose from the options in the Page Number Format dialog box.

6. **Press [Ctrl][Home], click the View tab, click the Page Width button in the Zoom group, then save the document**

Moving around in a long document

Rather than scrolling to move to a different place in a long document, you can use the Navigation pane to move the insertion point to the top of a specific page. To open the Navigation pane, click the Find button in the Editing group on the Home tab, and then click Pages to display a thumbnail of each page in the document in the Navigation pane. Use the scroll box in the Navigation pane to scroll through the thumbnails. Click a thumbnail in the Navigation pane to move the insertion point to the top of that page in the document window.

FIGURE 4-7: **Page Number gallery**

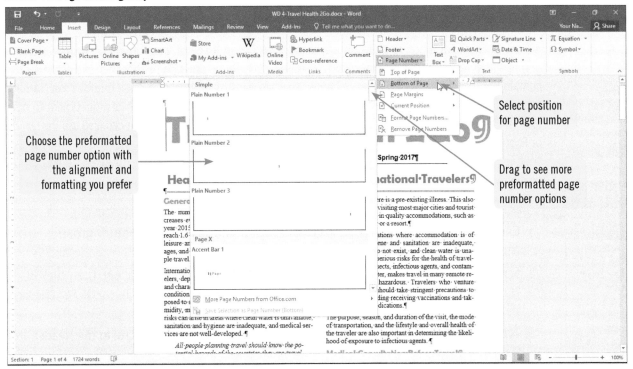

Choose the preformatted page number option with the alignment and formatting you prefer

Select position for page number

Drag to see more preformatted page number options

FIGURE 4-8: **Page number in document**

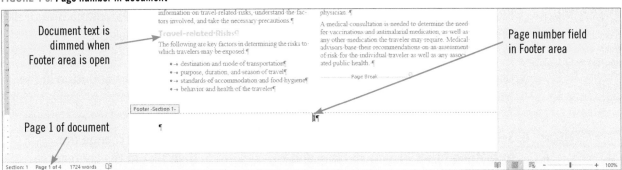

Document text is dimmed when Footer area is open

Page number field in Footer area

Page 1 of document

Inserting Quick Parts

The Word Quick Parts feature makes it easy to insert reusable pieces of content into a document quickly. The **Quick Parts** items you can insert include fields, such as for the current date or the total number of pages in a document; document property information, such as the author and title of a document; and building blocks, which are customized content that you create, format, and save for future use.

To insert a Quick Part into a document at the location of the insertion point, click the Quick Parts button in the Text group on the Insert tab (or, if headers and footers are open, click the Quick Parts button in the Insert group on the Header & Footer Tools Design tab), and then select the type of Quick Part you want to insert. To insert a field into a document, click Field on the Quick Parts menu that opens, click the name of the field you want to insert in the Field dialog box, and then click OK. Field information is updated automatically each time the document is opened or saved.

To insert a document property, point to Document Property on the Quick Parts menu, and then click the property you want to insert. The property is added to the document as a content control and contains the document property information shown in the Properties dialog box. If you did not assign a document property, the content control contains a placeholder, which you can replace with your own text. Once you replace the placeholder text—or edit the document property information that appears in the content control—this text replaces the property information in the Properties dialog box.

To insert a building block, click Building Blocks Organizer on the Quick Parts menu, select the building block you want, and then click Insert. You will learn more about working with building blocks in later lessons.

Add Headers and Footers

Learning Outcomes
- Create and format headers and footers
- Create a different first page header or footer

A **header** is text or graphics that appears at the top of every page of a document. A **footer** is text or graphics that appears at the bottom of every page. In longer documents, headers and footers often contain the title of the publication or chapter, the name of the author, or a page number. You can add headers and footers to a document by double-clicking the top or bottom margin of a document to open the Header and Footer areas, and then inserting text and graphics into them. You can also use the Header or Footer command on the Insert tab to insert predesigned headers and footers that you can modify with your information. When the header and footer areas are open, the document text is dimmed and cannot be edited. **CASE** *You create a header that includes the name of the report.*

STEPS

QUICK TIP

Unless you set different headers and footers for different sections, the information you insert in any Header or Footer area appears on every page in the document.

1. **Click the** Insert tab, **then click the** Header button **in the Header & Footer group**
   A gallery of built-in header designs opens.

2. **Scroll down the gallery to view the header designs, scroll up the gallery, then click** Blank
   The Header & Footer Tools Design tab opens and is the active tab, as shown in FIGURE 4-9. This tab is available whenever the Header and Footer areas are open.

3. **Type** Reason2Go Health Information for Travelers **in the content control in the Header area**
   This text will appear at the top of every page in the document.

QUICK TIP

You can also use the Insert Alignment Tab button in the Position group to left-, center-, and right-align text in the Header and Footer areas.

4. **Select the header text (but not the paragraph mark below it), click the** Home tab, **click the** Font list arrow **in the Font group, click** Berlin Sans FB Demi, **click the** Font Color list arrow **A ·, click** Blue, Accent 5, **click the** Center button **in the Paragraph group, click the** Bottom Border button **, then click in the Header area to deselect the text**
   The text is formatted in blue Berlin Sans FB Demi and centered in the Header area with a bottom border.

5. **Click the** Header & Footer Tools Design tab, **then click the** Go to Footer button **in the Navigation group**
   The insertion point moves to the Footer area, where a page number field is centered in the Footer area.

QUICK TIP

To change the distance between the header and footer and the edge of the page, change the Header from Top and Footer from Bottom settings in the Position group.

6. **Select the** page number field **in the footer, use the Mini toolbar to change the formatting to** Berlin Sans FB Demi **and** Blue, Accent 5, **then click in the Footer area to deselect the text and field**
   The footer text is formatted in blue Berlin Sans FB Demi.

7. **Click the** Close Header and Footer button **in the Close group, then scroll down until the bottom of page 1 and the top of page 2 appear in the document window**
   The Header and Footer areas close, and the header and footer text is dimmed, as shown in FIGURE 4-10.

8. **Press** [Ctrl][Home]
   The report already includes the company information at the top of the first page, making the header information redundant. You can modify headers and footers so that the header and footer text does not appear on the first page of a document.

9. **Position the pointer over the header text at the top of page 1, then double-click**
   The Header and Footer areas open. The Options group on the Header & Footer Tools Design tab includes options for creating a different header and footer for the first page of a document, and for creating different headers and footers for odd- and even-numbered pages.

QUICK TIP

To remove headers or footers from a document, click the Header or Footer button, and then click Remove Header or Remove Footer.

10. **Click the** Different First Page check box **to select it, click the** Close Header and Footer button, **scroll to see the header and footer on pages 2, 3, and 4, then save the document**
    The header and footer text is removed from the Header and Footer areas on the first page.

FIGURE 4-9: **Header area**

Header area is open

[Type here]¶

Content control

Header & Footer Tools Design tab active

Tab stops for the header are set for the default document margins

Travel·Health·2Go

Reason2Go·■·Health·Information·for·Travelers·■·Spring·2017¶

Document text is dimmed

Health·Risks·and·Precautions·for·International·Travelers

General·Considerations

The· number· of· people· traveling· internationally· increases·every·year.·International·tourist·arrivals·in·the· year·2015·reached·1·billion,·with·arrivals·expected·to·

Destinations· where· accommodation,· hygiene,· sanitation,·medical·care,·and·water·quality·are·of·a·high·standard·pose·relatively·few·serious·risks·for·the·health·of· travelers,·unless·there·is·a·pre-existing·illness.·This·also· applies·to·travelers·visiting·most·major·cities·and·tourist·

FIGURE 4-10: **Header and footer in document**

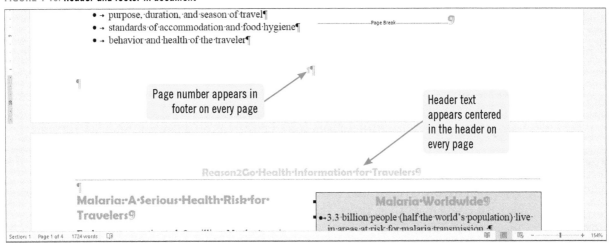

- → purpose,·duration,·and·season·of·travel¶
- → standards·of·accommodation·and·food·hygiene¶
- → behavior·and·health·of·the·traveler¶

Page number appears in footer on every page

Header text appears centered in the header on every page

Reason2Go·Health·Information·for·Travelers

Malaria:·A·Serious·Health·Risk·for· Travelers

Malaria·Worldwide
- •·3.3·billion·people·(half·the·world's·population)·live· in·areas·at·risk·for·malaria·transmission·

Adding a custom header or footer to the gallery

When you design a header that you want to use again in other documents, you can add it to the Header gallery by saving it as a building block. **Building blocks** are reusable pieces of formatted content or document parts, including headers and footers, page numbers, and text boxes, that are stored in galleries. Building blocks include predesigned content that comes with Word, as well as content that you create and save for future use. For example, you might create a custom header that contains your company name and logo and is formatted using the fonts, border, and colors you use in all company documents.

To add a custom header to the Header gallery, select all the text in the header, including the last paragraph mark, click the Header button, and then click Save Selection to Header Gallery.

In the Create New Building Block dialog box that opens, type a unique name for the header in the Name text box, click the Gallery list arrow and select the appropriate gallery, verify that the Category is General, and then type a brief description of the new header design in the Description text box. This description appears in a ScreenTip when you point to the custom header in the gallery. When you are finished, click OK. The new header appears in the Header gallery under the General category.

To remove a custom header from the Header gallery, right-click it, click Organize and Delete, make sure the appropriate building block is selected in the Building Blocks Organizer that opens, click Delete, click Yes, and then click Close. You can follow the same process to add or remove a custom footer to the Footer gallery.

Insert a Table

Learning Outcomes
• Create a table
• Delete a table
• Apply a table style

Adding a table to a document is a useful way to illustrate information that is intended for quick reference and analysis. A **table** is a grid of columns and rows that you can fill with text and graphics. A **cell** is the box formed by the intersection of a column and a row. The lines that divide the columns and rows of a table and help you see the grid-like structure of the table are called **borders**. A simple way to insert a table into a document is to use the Insert Table command on the Insert tab. **CASE** *You add a table to page 2 showing the preventive options for serious travel health diseases.*

STEPS

1. **Scroll until the heading** Preventive Options… **is at the top of your document window**

TROUBLE
If the final line in the blue shaded box on your screen wraps differently than that shown in the figure, click the References tab, click the Style list arrow in the Citations & Bibliography group, then click MLA Seventh Edition.

2. **Select the heading** Preventive Options… **and the two paragraph marks below it, click the** Layout tab, **click the** Columns button **in the Page Setup group, click** One, **click the** heading **to deselect the text, then scroll down to see the bottom half of page 2**
   A continuous section break is inserted before the heading and after the second paragraph mark, creating a new section, section 3, as shown in FIGURE 4-11. The document now includes four sections, with the heading Preventive Options… in Section 3. Section 3 is formatted as a single column.

3. **Place the insertion point before the first paragraph mark below the heading, click the** Insert tab, **click the** Table button **in the Tables group, then click** Insert Table
   The Insert Table dialog box opens. You use this dialog box to create a blank table.

QUICK TIP
To delete a table, click in the table, click the Table Tools Layout tab, click the Delete button in the Rows & Columns group, then click Delete Table.

4. **Type** 5 **in the Number of columns text box, press [Tab], type** 6 **in the Number of rows text box, make sure the** Fixed column width option button **is selected, then click** OK
   A blank table with five columns and six rows is inserted in the document. The insertion point is in the upper-left cell of the table, and the Table Tools Design tab becomes the active tab.

5. **Click the** Home tab, **click the** Show/Hide ¶ button ¶ **in the Paragraph group, type** Disease **in the first cell in the first row, press [Tab], type** Vaccine, **press [Tab], type** Prophylaxis Drug, **press [Tab], type** Eat and Drink Safely, **press [Tab], type** Avoid Insects, **then press [Tab]**
   Don't be concerned if the text wraps to the next line in a cell as you type. Pressing [Tab] moves the insertion point to the next cell in the row or to the first cell in the next row.

QUICK TIP
You can also click in a cell to move the insertion point to it.

6. **Type** Malaria, **press [Tab][Tab], click the** Bullets list arrow ⌄ **in the Paragraph group, click the** check mark style, **press [Tab][Tab], then click the** Bullets button
   The active bullet style, a check mark, is added to a cell when you click the Bullets button.

TROUBLE
If you pressed [Tab] after the last row, click the Undo button ↶ on the Quick Access toolbar to remove the blank row.

7. **Type the text shown in** FIGURE 4-12 **in the table cells**

8. **Click the** Table Tools Layout tab, **click the** AutoFit button **in the Cell Size group, click** AutoFit Contents, **click the** AutoFit button **again, then click** AutoFit Window
   The width of the table columns is adjusted to fit the text and then the window.

QUICK TIP
You can also format table text using the buttons on the Mini toolbar or the Home tab.

9. **Click the** Select button **in the Table group, click** Select Table, **click the** Align Center button **in the Alignment group, click** Disease **in the table, click the** Select button, **click** Select Column, **click the** Align Center Left button , **then click in the table to deselect the column**
   The text in the table is centered in each cell, and then the text in the first column is left-aligned.

10. **Click the** Table Tools Design tab, **click the** More button ⌄ **in the Table Styles group, scroll down, click the** List Table 3 – Accent 5 style, **then save your changes**
    The List Table 3 - Accent 5 table style is applied to the table, as shown in FIGURE 4-13. A **table style** includes format settings for the text, borders, and shading in a table.

FIGURE 4-11: **New section**

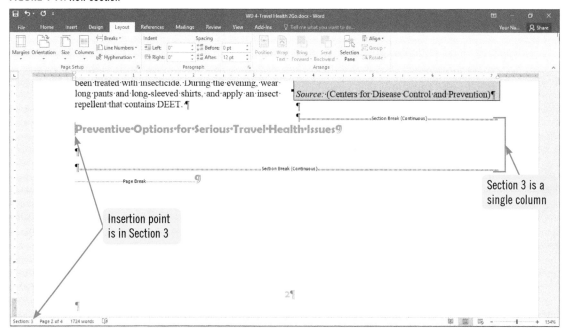

FIGURE 4-12: **Text in table**

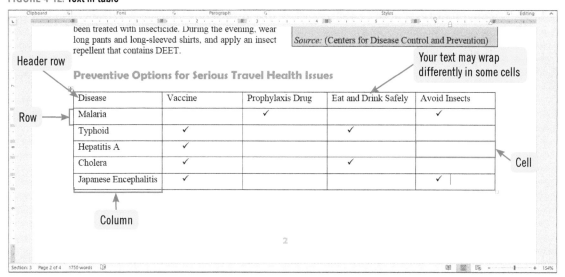

FIGURE 4-13: **Completed table**

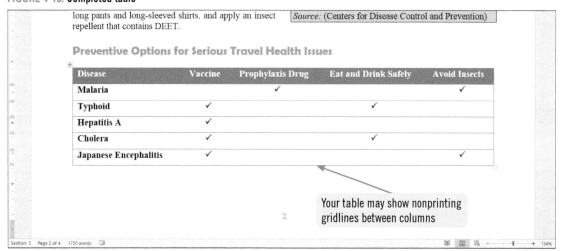

Add Footnotes and Endnotes

Learning Outcomes
• Insert and delete a footnote
• Modify note reference marks
• Convert footnotes to endnotes

Footnotes and endnotes are used in documents to provide further information, explanatory text, or references for text in a document. A **footnote** or **endnote** is an explanatory note that consists of two linked parts: the **note reference mark** that appears next to text to indicate that additional information is offered in a footnote or endnote, and the corresponding footnote or endnote text. Word places footnotes at the end of each page and endnotes at the end of the document. You insert and manage footnotes and endnotes using the tools in the Footnotes group on the References tab. **CASE** *You add several footnotes to the report.*

STEPS

1. **Press [Ctrl][Home], place the insertion point at the end of the first body paragraph in the second column of text (after "resort."), click the** References tab, **then click the** Insert Footnote button **in the Footnotes group**

   A note reference mark, in this case a superscript 1, appears after "resort.", and the insertion point moves below a separator line at the bottom of the page. A note reference mark can be a number, a symbol, a character, or a combination of characters.

2. **Type** Behavior is a critical factor. For example, going outdoors in a malaria-endemic area could result in becoming infected., **place the insertion point at the end of the second column of text (after "health."), click the** Insert Footnote button, **then type** It is best to consult a travel medicine specialist.

   The footnote text appears below the separator line at the bottom of page 1, as shown in FIGURE 4-14.

3. **Scroll down until the bottom half of page 3 appears in the document window, place the insertion point at the end of "Medications taken on a regular basis at home" in the second column, click the** Insert Footnote button, **then type** All medications should be stored in carry-on luggage, in their original containers and labeled clearly.

   The footnote text for the third footnote appears at the bottom of the first column on page 3.

4. **Place the insertion point at the end of "Sunscreen" in the bulleted list in the second column, click the** Insert Footnote button, **then type** SPF 15 or greater.

   The footnote text for the fourth footnote appears at the bottom of page 3.

5. **Place the insertion point after "Disposable gloves" in the first column, click the** Insert Footnote button, **type** At least two pairs., **place the insertion point after "Scissors, safety pins, and tweezers" in the first column, click the** Insert Footnote button, **then type** Pack these items in checked luggage.

   Notice that when you inserted new footnotes between existing footnotes, Word automatically renumbered the footnotes and wrapped the footnote text to the next column. The new footnotes appear at the bottom of the first column on page 3, as shown in FIGURE 4-15.

6. **Press [Ctrl][Home], then click the** Next Footnote button **in the Footnotes group**

   The insertion point moves to the first reference mark in the document.

7. **Click the** Next Footnote button **twice, press [Delete] to select the number 3 reference mark, then press [Delete] again**

   The third reference mark and associated footnote are deleted from the document and the footnotes are renumbered automatically. You must select a reference mark to delete a footnote; you can not simply delete the footnote text itself.

8. **Press [Ctrl][Home], then save your changes**

FIGURE 4-14: **Footnotes in the document**

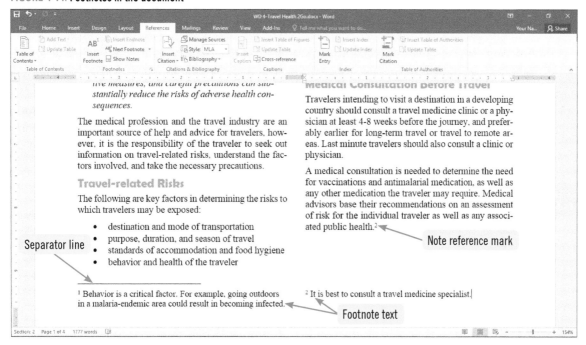

FIGURE 4-15: **Renumbered footnotes in the document**

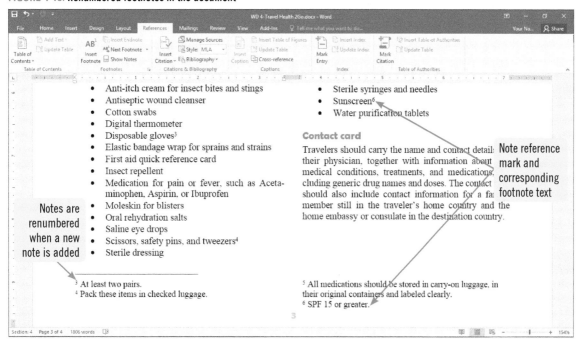

Customizing the layout and formatting of footnotes and endnotes

You can change the location, formatting, and numbering options for footnotes and endnotes in a document using the Footnote and Endnote dialog box. To open the dialog box, click the launcher in the Footnotes group on the References tab. Use the list arrows in the Location section of the dialog box to locate footnotes at the bottom of the page (the default) or directly below the text on a page, and to locate endnotes at the end of a document or at the end of a section. Use the Columns list arrow in the Footnote layout section to format footnote text in one or more columns, or to match section layout (the default). Use the options in the Format section of the dialog box to change the number format of the note reference marks, to use a symbol instead of a character, and to change the numbering of footnotes and endnotes. You can choose to apply the settings to a section or to the document as a whole. When you are finished, click Apply.

Insert Citations

Learning Outcomes
- Add a source to a document
- Insert a citation
- Edit a citation

The Word References feature allows you to keep track of the reference sources you consult when writing research papers, reports, and other documents, and makes it easy to insert a citation in a document. A **citation** is a parenthetical reference in the document text that gives credit to the source for a quotation or other information used in a document. Citations usually include the name of the author and, for print sources, a page number. When you insert a citation you can use an existing source or create a new source. Each time you create a new source, the source information is saved on your computer so that it is available for use in any document. **CASE** ▸ *The report already includes two citations. You add several more citations to the report.*

STEPS

1. **Scroll down, place the insertion point after "people travel" but before the period at the end of the first paragraph in the first column of text, click the Style list arrow in the Citations & Bibliography group, then click MLA Seventh Edition**
   You will format the sources and citations in the report using the style recommended by the Modern Language Association (MLA).

QUICK TIP
When you create a new source for a document, it appears automatically in the bibliography when you generate it.

2. **Click the Insert Citation button in the Citations & Bibliography group**
   A list of the sources already used in the document opens. You can choose to cite one of these sources, create a new source, or add a placeholder for a source. When you add a new citation to a document, the source is added to the list of master sources that is stored on the computer. The new source is also associated with the document.

QUICK TIP
Only sources that you associate with a document stay with the document when you move it to another computer. The master list of sources remains on the computer where it was created.

3. ▸ **Click Add New Source, click the Type of Source list arrow in the Create Source dialog box, scroll down to view the available source types, click Report, then click the Corporate Author check box**
   You select the type of source and enter the source information in the Create Source dialog box. The fields available in the dialog box change, depending on the type of source selected.

4. ▸ **Enter the data shown in FIGURE 4-16 in the Create Source dialog box, then click OK**
   The citation (World Tourism Organization) appears at the end of the paragraph. Because the source is a print publication, it needs to include a page number.

5. **Click the citation to select it, click the Citation Options list arrow on the right side of the citation, then click Edit Citation**
   The Edit Citation dialog box opens, as shown in FIGURE 4-17.

QUICK TIP
You can also choose to add or remove the author, year, or title from a citation.

6. ▸ **Type 19 in the Pages text box, then click OK**
   The page number 19 is added to the citation.

7. **Scroll down, place the insertion point at the end of the quotation (after ...consequences.), click the Insert Citation button, click Add New Source, enter the information shown in FIGURE 4-18, then click OK**
   A citation for the Web publication that the quotation was taken from is added to the report. No page number is used in this citation because the source is a Web site.

8. **Scroll to the bottom of page 2, click under the table, type Source:, italicize Source:, click after Source:, click the Insert Citation button, then click Johnson, Margaret in the list of sources**
   The citation (Johnson) appears under the table.

9. **Click the citation, click the Citation Options list arrow, click Edit Citation, type 55 in the Pages text box, click OK, then save your changes**
   The page number 55 is added to the citation.

FIGURE 4-16: Adding a Report source

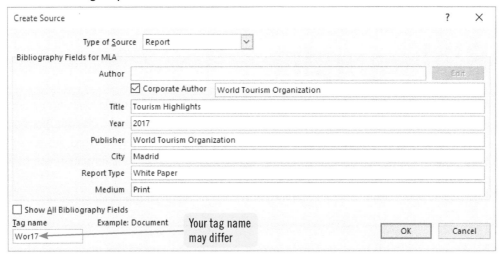

FIGURE 4-17: Edit Citation dialog box

FIGURE 4-18: Adding a Web publication source

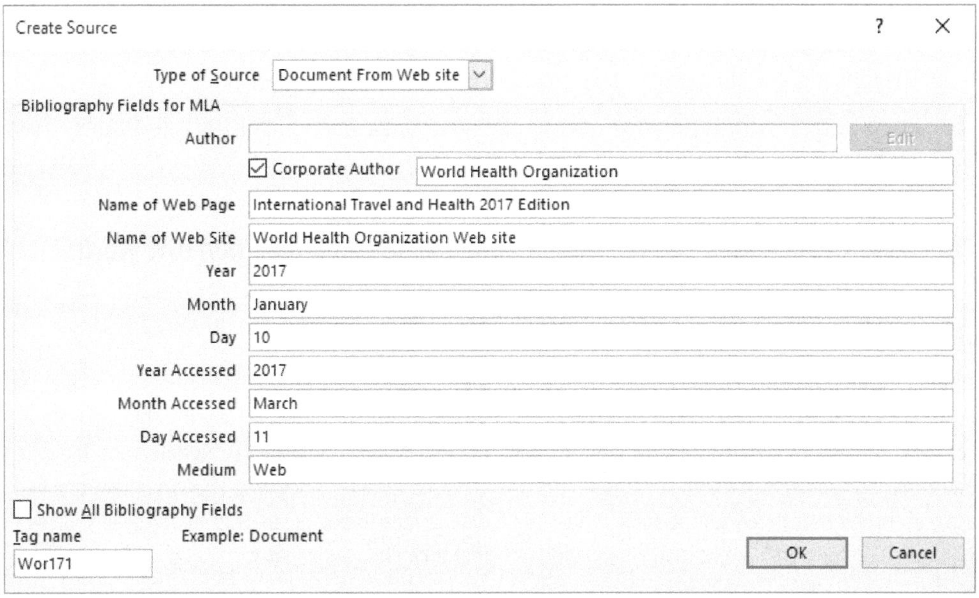

Learning
Outcomes
• Add and delete
  sources
• Edit a source
• Insert a
  bibliography field

Manage Sources and Create a Bibliography

Many documents require a **bibliography**, a list of sources that you used in creating the document. The list of sources can include only the works cited in your document (a **works cited** list) or both the works cited and the works consulted (a bibliography). The Bibliography feature in Word allows you to generate a works cited list or a bibliography automatically based on the source information you provide for the document. The Source Manager dialog box helps you to organize your sources. **CASE** ➤ *You add a bibliography to the report. The bibliography is inserted as a field and it can be formatted any way you choose.*

STEPS

QUICK TIP
You must copy
sources from the
Master List to the
Current List for the
sources to be avail-
able when you open
the document on
another computer.

1. **Press [Ctrl][End] to move the insertion point to the end of the document, then click the Manage Sources button in the Citations & Bibliography group**

   The Source Manager dialog box opens, as shown in FIGURE 4-19. The Master List shows the two sources you added and any other sources available on your computer. The Current List shows the sources available in the current document. A check mark next to a source indicates the source is cited in the document. You use the tools in the Source Manager dialog box to add, edit, and delete sources from the lists, and to copy sources between the Master and Current Lists. The sources that appear in the Current List will appear in the bibliography.

2. **Click the Baker, Mary source in the Current List**

   A preview of the citation and bibliographical entry for the source in MLA style appears in the Preview box. You do not want this source to be included in your bibliography for the report.

3. **Click Delete**

   The source is removed from the Current List but remains on the Master List on the computer where it originated.

4. **Click Close, click the Bibliography button in the Citations & Bibliography group, click References, then scroll up to see the heading References at the top of the field**

   A Bibliography field labeled "References" is added at the location of the insertion point. The bibliography includes all the sources associated with the document, formatted in the MLA style for bibliographies. The text in the Bibliography field is formatted with the default styles.

TROUBLE
Don't be concerned if
the list of sources
becomes gray
when you select the
heading Bibliography.
This simply indicates
the Bibliography field
is active. Text that
is selected is high-
lighted in dark gray.

5. **Select References; apply the following formats: Berlin Sans FB Demi and the Green, Accent 6 font color; drag down the list of sources to select the entire list and change the font size to 11; then click outside the bibliography field to deselect it**

   The format of the bibliography text now matches the rest of the report.

6. **Press [Ctrl][End], type your name, click the View tab, click Multiple Pages, then scroll up and down to view each page in the report**

   The completed report is shown in FIGURE 4-20.

7. **Save your changes, submit your document, close the file, then exit Word**

Working with Web sources

Publications found on the Web can be challenging to document. Many Web sites can be accessed under multiple domains, URLs change, and electronic publications are often updated frequently, making each visit to a Web site potentially unique. For these reasons, it's best to rely on the author, title, and publication information for a Web publication when citing it as a source in a research document. If possible, you can include a URL as supplementary information only, along with the date the Web site was last updated and the date you accessed the site. Since Web sites are often removed, it's also a good idea to download or print any Web source you use so that it can be verified later.

FIGURE 4-19: Source Manager dialog box

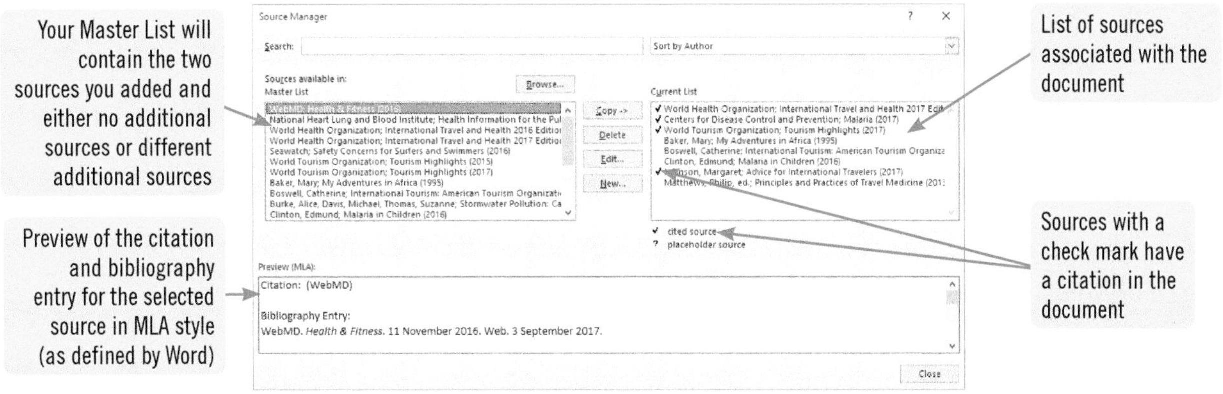

Your Master List will contain the two sources you added and either no additional sources or different additional sources

Preview of the citation and bibliography entry for the selected source in MLA style (as defined by Word)

List of sources associated with the document

Sources with a check mark have a citation in the document

FIGURE 4-20: Completed report

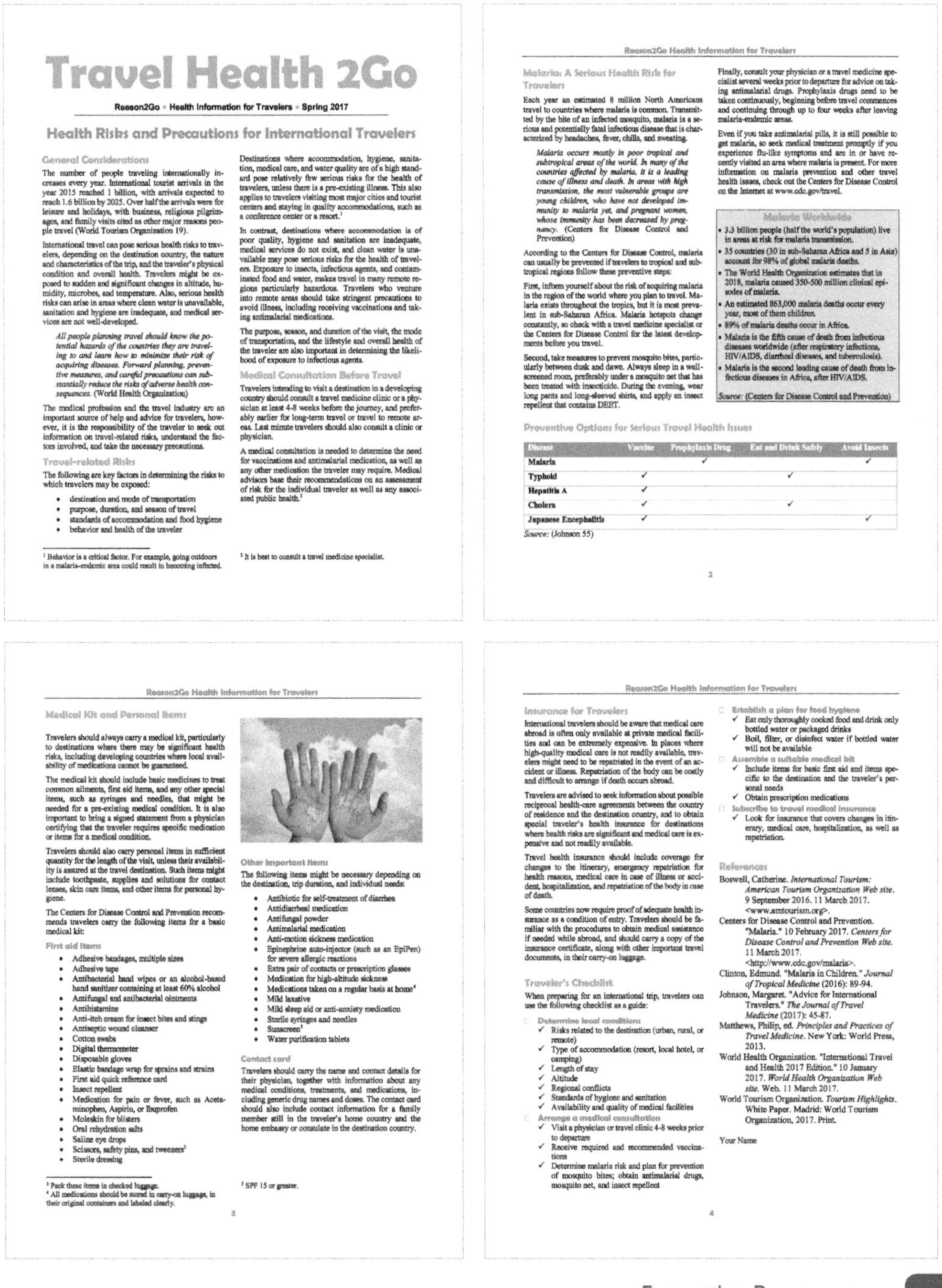

Source: Pixabay

Practice

Concepts Review

Label each element shown in FIGURE 4-21.

FIGURE 4-21

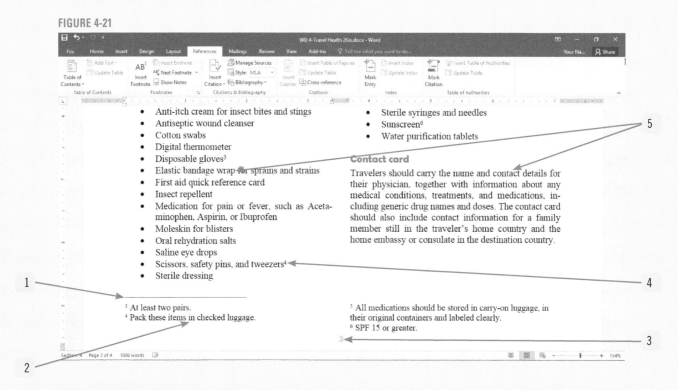

Match each term with the statement that best describes it.

6. **Bibliography**

7. **Header**

8. **Margin**

9. **Table**

10. **Citation**

11. **Manual page break**

12. **Field**

13. **Footer**

14. **Section break**

a. A grid of columns and rows that you can fill with text and graphics

b. A list of the sources used to create a document

c. Text or graphics that appear at the top of every page in a document

d. A formatting mark that forces the text following the mark to begin at the top of the next page

e. Text or graphics that appear at the bottom of every page in a document

f. A placeholder for information that changes

g. A formatting mark that divides a document into parts that can be formatted differently

h. The blank area between the edge of the text and the edge of the page

i. A parenthetical reference in the document text that gives credit to a source

Select the best answer from the list of choices.

15. Which type of break can you insert if you want to force text to begin on the next page?

  a. Column break

  b. Continuous section break

  c. Next page section break

  d. Text wrapping break

16. Which type of break do you insert if you want to balance the columns in a section?

  a. Text wrapping break

  b. Manual page break

  c. Column break

  d. Continuous section break

17. Which of the following do documents with mirror margins always have?

  a. Inside and outside margins

  b. Sections

  c. Portrait orientation

  d. Different first page headers and footers

18. Which of the following cannot be inserted using the Quick Parts command?

  a. AutoText building block

  b. Page number field

  c. Page break

  d. Document property

19. Which appears at the end of a document?

  a. Endnote

  b. Citation

  c. Page break

  d. Footnote

20. What name describes formatted pieces of content that are stored in galleries?

  a. Field

  b. Endnote

  c. Property

  d. Building Block

Skills Review

1. Set document margins.

  a. Start Word, open the file WD 4-2.docx from the location where you store your Data Files, then save it as **WD 4-Seaside Fitness**.

  b. Change the top and bottom margin settings to Moderate: 1" top and bottom, and .75" left and right.

  c. Save your changes to the document.

2. Create sections and columns.

  a. Turn on the display of formatting marks, then customize the status bar to display sections if they are not displayed already.

  b. Insert a continuous section break before the **Welcome to the Seaside Fitness Center** heading.

  c. Format the text in section 2 in two columns, then save your changes to the document.

3. Insert page breaks.

  a. Scroll to page 3, then insert a manual page break before the heading **Facilities and Services**. (*Hint*: The page break will appear at the bottom of page 2.)

  b. Scroll down and insert a manual page break before the heading **Membership**, then press [Ctrl][Home].

  c. On page 1, select the heading **Welcome to the Seaside Fitness Center** and the paragraph mark below it, use the Columns button to format the selected text as one column, then center the heading on the page.

  d. Follow the direction in step c to format the heading **Facilities and Services** and the paragraph mark below it on page 3, and the heading **Membership** and the paragraph mark below it on page 4, as one column, with centered text, then save your changes to the document.

4. Insert page numbers.

  a. Insert page numbers in the document at the bottom of the page. Select the Plain Number 2 page number style from the gallery.

  b. Close the Footer area, scroll through the document to view the page number on each page, then save your changes to the document.

Skills Review (continued)

5. Add headers and footers.

   a. Double-click the margin at the top of a page to open the Header and Footer areas.

   b. With the insertion point in the Header area, click the Quick Parts button in the Insert Group on the Header & Footer Tools Design tab, point to Document Property, then click Author.

   c. Replace the text in the Author content control with your name, press [End] to move the insertion point out of the content control, then press [Spacebar]. (*Note*: If your name does not appear in the header, right-click the Author content control, click Remove Content Control, then type your name in the header.)

   d. Click the Insert Alignment Tab button in the Position group, select the Right option button and keep the alignment relative to the margin, then click OK in the dialog box to close the dialog box and move the insertion point to the right margin.

   e. Use the Insert Date and Time command in the Insert group to insert the current date using a format of your choice as static text. (*Hint*: Be sure the Update automatically check box is not checked.)

   f. Apply italic to the text in the header.

   g. Move the insertion point to the Footer area.

   h. Double-click the page number to select it, then format the page number in bold and italic.

   i. Move the insertion point to the header on page 1, use the Header & Footer Tools Design tab to create a different header and footer for the first page of the document, type your name in the First Page Header area, then apply italic to your name.

   j. Close headers and footers, scroll to view the header and footer on each page, then save your changes to the document.

6. Insert a table.

   a. On page 4, double-click the word **Table** at the end of the Membership Rates section to select it, press [Delete], open the Insert Table dialog box, then create a table with two columns and five rows.

   b. Apply the List Table 2 table style to the table.

   c. Press [Tab] to leave the first cell in the header row blank, then type **Rate**.

   d. Press [Tab], then type the following text in the table, pressing [Tab] to move from cell to cell.

Enrollment/Individual	**$100**
Enrollment/Couple	**$150**
Monthly membership/Individual	**$125**
Monthly membership/Couple	**$200**

   e. Select the table, use the AutoFit command on the Table Tools Layout tab to select the AutoFit to Contents option, and then select the AutoFit to Window option. (*Note*: In this case, AutoFit to Window fits the table to the width of the column of text.)

   f. Save your changes to the document.

7. Add footnotes and endnotes.

   a. Press [Ctrl][Home], scroll down, place the insertion point at the end of the first body paragraph, insert a footnote, then type **People who are active live longer and feel better.**

   b. Place the insertion point at the end of the first paragraph under the Benefits of Exercise heading, insert a footnote, then type **There are 1,440 minutes in every day. Schedule 30 of them for physical activity.**

   c. Place the insertion point at the end of the first paragraph under the Tips for Staying Motivated heading, insert a footnote, type **Always consult your physician before beginning an exercise program.**, then save your changes.

8. Insert citations.

   a. Place the insertion point at the end of the second paragraph under the Benefits of Exercise heading (after "down from 52% in 2015" but before the period), then be sure the style for citations and bibliography is set to MLA Seventh Edition.

Skills Review (continued)

b. Insert a citation, add a new source, enter the source information shown in the Create Source dialog box in FIGURE 4-22, then click OK.

c. Place the insertion point at the end of the italicized quotation in the second column of text, insert a citation, then select Jason, Laura from the list of sources.

d. Edit the citation to include the page number **25**.

e. Scroll to page 2, place the insertion point at the end of the "Be a morning exerciser" paragraph but before the ending period, insert a citation for WebMD, then save your changes.

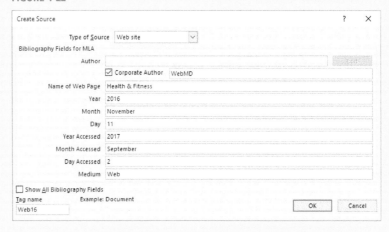

FIGURE 4-22

9. **Manage sources and create a bibliography.**

a. Press [Ctrl][End], then open the Source Manager dialog box.

b. Select the source Health, National Institute of: … in the Current List, click Edit, click the Corporate Author check box, edit the entry so it reads **National Institute of Health**, click OK, then click Close.

c. Insert a bibliography labeled References.

d. Select References, then change the font to 14-point Tahoma with a black font color. Pages 1 and 4 of the formatted document are shown in FIGURE 4-23.

e. Save your changes to the document, submit it to your instructor, then close the document and exit Word.

FIGURE 4-23

Word 2016

Independent Challenge 1

You are the owner of a small business called Lone Tree Catering. You have begun work on the text for a brochure advertising your business and you are now ready to lay out the pages and prepare the final copy. The brochure will be printed on both sides of an 8½" x 11" sheet of paper, and folded in thirds.

a. Start Word, open the file WD 4-3.docx from the location where you store your Data Files, then save it as **WD 4-Lone Tree Catering**. Read the document to get a feel for its contents.

b. Change the page orientation to landscape, and change all four margins to .6".

c. Format the document in three columns of equal width.

d. Insert a next page section break before the heading **Catering Services**.

e. On page 1, insert column breaks before the headings **Sample Tuscan Banquet Menu** and **Sample Indian Banquet Menu**.

f. Change the column spacing in section 1 (which is the first page) to .4", add lines between the columns on the first page, then select the text in the columns in section 1 and center it.

g. Double-click the bottom margin to open the footer area, create a different header and footer for the first page, then type **Call for custom menus designed to your taste and budget.** in the First Page Footer -Section 1- area.

FIGURE 4-24

h. Center the text in the footer area, format it in 20-point Papyrus, bold, with a Green, Accent 6 font color, then close headers and footers.

i. On page 2, insert a column break before Your Name, then press [Enter] 22 times to move the contact information to the bottom of the second column.

j. Replace Your Name with your name, then center the contact information in the column.

k. Press [Ctrl][End], insert a column break at the bottom of the second column. Type the text shown in FIGURE 4-24 in the third column, then apply the No Spacing style to the text. Refer to the figure as you follow the instructions for formatting the text in the third column.

l. Format Lone Tree Catering in 28-point Papyrus, bold, with a Green, Accent 6 font color.

m. Format the remaining text in 12-point Papyrus with a Green, Accent 6 font color. Center the text in the third column.

n. Insert an online picture of a tree, similar to the tree shown in FIGURE 4-24. Do not be concerned if the image you select is not the same tree image as that shown in the figure. Do not wrap text around the graphic.

o. Resize the graphic and add or remove blank paragraphs in the third column of your brochure so that the spacing between elements roughly matches the spacing shown in FIGURE 4-24.

p. Save your changes, then submit a copy to your instructor. If possible, you can print the brochure with the two pages back to back so that the brochure can be folded in thirds.

q. Close the document and exit Word.

Complete catering services available for all types of events. Menus and estimates provided upon request.

Source: Openclipart.org

Independent Challenge 2

You work in the Campus Safety Department at Valley State College. You have written the text for an informational flyer about parking regulations on campus, and now you need to format the flyer so it is attractive and readable.

    a. Start Word, open the file WD 4-4.docx from the drive and folder where you store your Data Files, then save it as **WD 4-Valley Parking**. Read the document to get a feel for its contents.

    b. Change all four margins to .7".

    c. Insert a continuous section break before **1. May I bring a car to school?** (*Hint*: Place the insertion point before the word May.)

    d. Scroll down and insert a next page section break before **Sample Parking Permit**.

    e. Format the text in section 2 in three columns of equal width with .3" of space between the columns.

    f. Hyphenate the document using the automatic hyphenation feature. (*Hint*: Use the Hyphenation button in the Page Setup group on the Layout tab.)

    g. Add a 3-point dotted-line bottom border to the blank paragraph under Valley State College Department of Campus Safety. (*Hint*: Place the insertion point before the paragraph mark under Valley State College...)

    h. Open the Header area, and type your name in the header. Right-align your name, and format it in 10-point Arial.

    i. Add the following text to the footer, inserting symbols between words as indicated: **Parking and Shuttle Service Office • 54 Buckley Street • Valley State College • 942-555-2227**. (*Hint*: Click the Symbol command in the Symbols group on the Insert tab to insert a symbol. To find a small circle symbol, be sure the font is set to (normal text) and the subset is set to General Punctuation.)

    j. Format the footer text in 9-point Arial Black, and center it in the footer.

    k. Apply a 3-point dotted-line border above the footer text. Make sure to apply the border to the paragraph.

    l. Add a continuous section break at the end of section 2 to balance the columns in section 2.

    m. Place the insertion point on page 2 (which is section 4). Change the left and right margins in section 4 to 1". Also change the page orientation of section 4 to landscape.

    n. Change the vertical alignment of section 4 to center. (*Hint*: Use the Vertical Alignment list arrow on the Layout tab in the Page Setup dialog box.)

    o. Apply an appropriate table style to the table, such as the style shown in FIGURE 4-25. (*Hint*: Check and uncheck the options in the Table Style Options group on the Table Tools Design tab to customize the style so it enhances the table data.)

    p. Save your changes, submit your work, close the document, then exit Word.

Word 2016

FIGURE 4-25

Sample Parking Permit

Valley State College
Office of Parking and Shuttle Service

2017-18 Student Parking Permit

License number:	VT 623 487
Make:	Subaru
Model:	Forester
Year:	2013
Color:	Silver
Permit Issue Date:	September 6, 2017
Permit Expiration Date:	June 4, 2018

Restrictions:
Parking is permitted in the Valley State College Greene Street lot 24 hours a day, 7 days a week. Shuttle service is available from the Greene Street lot to campus from 7 a.m. to 7 p.m. Monday through Friday. Parking is also permitted in any on-campus lot from 4:30 p.m. Friday to midnight Sunday.

Independent Challenge 3

A book publisher would like to publish an article you wrote on stormwater pollution in Australia as a chapter in a forthcoming book called *Environmental Issues for the New Millennium*. The publisher has requested that you format your article like a book chapter before submitting it for publication, and has provided you with a style sheet. According to the style sheet, the citations and bibliography should be formatted in Chicago style. You have already created the sources for the chapter, but you need to insert the citations.

FIGURE 4-26

a. Start Word, open the file WD 4-5.docx from the location where you store your Data Files, then save it as **WD 4-Chapter 8**. You will format the first page as shown in FIGURE 4-26.

b. Change the font of the entire document to 10-point Book Antigua. If this font is not available to you, select a different font suitable for the pages of a book. Change the alignment to justified.

c. Use the Page Setup dialog box to change the paper size to a custom setting of 6" x 9".

d. Create mirror margins. (*Hint*: Use the Multiple pages list arrow.) Change the top and bottom margins to .8", change the inside margin to .4", change the outside margin to .6", and create a .3" gutter to allow room for the book's binding.

e. Change the Zoom level to Page Width, open the Header and Footer areas, then apply the setting to create different headers and footers for odd- and even-numbered pages.

f. In the odd-page header, type **Chapter 8**, insert a symbol of your choice, type **The Silver Creek Catchment and Stormwater Pollution**, then format the header text in 9-point Book Antigua italic and right-align the text.

g. In the even-page header, type your name, then format the header text in 9-point Book Antigua italic. (*Note*: The even-page header should be left-aligned.)

h. Insert a left-aligned page number field in the even-page footer area, format it in 10-point Book Antigua, insert a right-aligned page number field in the odd-page footer area, then format it in 10-point Book Antigua.

i. Format the page numbers so that the first page of your chapter, which is Chapter 8 in the book, begins on page 167. (*Hint*: Select a page number field, click the Page Number button, then click Format Page Numbers.)

j. Go to the beginning of the document, press [Enter] 10 times, type **Chapter 8: The Silver Creek Catchment and Stormwater Pollution**, press [Enter] twice, type your name, then press [Enter] twice.

k. Format the chapter title in 16-point Book Antigua bold, format your name in 14-point Book Antigua, then left-align the title text and your name.

l. Click the References tab, make sure the citations and bibliography style is set to Chicago Sixteenth Edition, place the insertion point at the end of the first body paragraph on page 1 but before the ending period, insert a citation for Alice Burke, et. al., then add the page number **40** to the citation.

m. Add the citations listed in TABLE 4-3 to the document using the sources already associated with the document.

TABLE 4-3

page	location for citation	source	page number
2	End of the first complete paragraph (after ...WCSMP, but before the period)	City of Weston	3
3	End of the first complete paragraph (after ...pollution, but before the colon)	Jensen	135
4	End of first paragraph (after ...health effects, but before the period)	City of Weston	5
4	End of fourth bulleted list item (after 1 month.)	Seawatch	None
5	End of second paragraph (after ...problem arises, but before the period)	Burke, et. al.	55
6	End of paragraph before Conclusion (after ...stormwater system, but before the period)	City of Weston	7
6	End of first paragraph under Conclusion (after ...include, but before the colon)	Jensen	142

Independent Challenge 3 (continued)

n. Press [Ctrl][End], insert a Works Cited list, format the Works Cited heading in 11-point Book Antigua, black font color, bold, then format the list of works cited in 10-point Book Antigua.

o. Scroll to page 4 in the document, place the insertion point at the end of the paragraph above the Potential health effects... heading, press [Enter] twice, type **Table 1: Total annual pollutant loads per year in the Silver Creek Catchment**, press [Enter] twice, then format the text you just typed as bold if it is not bold.

p. Insert a table with four columns and four rows.

q. Type the text shown in FIGURE 4-27 in the table. Do not be concerned when the text wraps to the next line in a cell.

FIGURE 4-27

Area	Nitrogen	Phosphorus	Suspended solids
Silver Creek	9.3 tonnes	1.2 tonnes	756.4 tonnes
Durras Arm	6.2 tonnes	.9 tonnes	348.2 tonnes
Cabbage Tree Creek	9.8 tonnes	2.3 tonnes	485.7 tonnes

r. Apply the Grid Table 1 Light table style. Make sure the text in the header row is bold, then remove any bold formatting from the text in the remaining rows.

s. Use AutoFit to make the table fit the contents, then use AutoFit to make the table fit the window.

t. Save your changes, submit your work, then close the document and exit Word.

Independent Challenge 4: Explore

One of the most common opportunities to use the page layout features of Word is when formatting a research paper. The format recommended by the *MLA Handbook for Writers of Research Papers*, a style guide that includes information on preparing, writing, and formatting research papers, is the standard format used by many schools, colleges, and universities. In this independent challenge, you will research the MLA guidelines for formatting a research paper and use the guidelines you find to format the pages of a sample research report.

a. Use your favorite search engine to search the Web for information on the MLA guidelines for formatting a research report. Use the keywords **MLA Style** and **research paper format** to conduct your search.

b. Look for information on the proper formatting for the following aspects of a research paper: paper size, margins, title page or first page of the report, line spacing, paragraph indentation, and page numbers. Also find information on proper formatting for citations and a works cited page. Print the information you find.

c. Start Word, open the file WD 4-6.docx from the drive and folder where you store your Data Files, then save it as **WD 4-Research Paper**. Using the information you learned, format this document as a research report.

d. Adjust the margins, set the line spacing, and add page numbers to the document in the format recommended by the MLA. Use **The Maori History of New Zealand** as the title for your sample report, use your name as the author name, and use the name of the course you are enrolled in currently as well as the instructor's name for that course. Make sure to format the title page exactly as the MLA style dictates.

e. Format the remaining text as the body of the research report. Indent the first line of each paragraph rather than use quadruple spacing between paragraphs.

f. Create three sources, insert three citations in the document—a book, a journal article, and a Web site—and create a works cited page, following MLA style. If necessary, edit the format of the citations and works cited page to conform to MLA format. (*Note*: For this practice document, you are allowed to make up sources. Never make up sources for real research papers.)

g. Save the document, submit a copy to your instructor, close the document, then exit Word.

Visual Workshop

Open the file WD 4-7.docx from the location where you store your Data Files, then modify it to create the article shown in FIGURE 4-28. (*Hint*: Change all four margins to .6". Add the footnotes as shown in the figure.) Save the document with the filename **WD 4-Garden**, then print a copy.

FIGURE 4-28

GARDENER'S NOTEBOOK

Preparing a Perennial Garden for Winter

By Your Name

A sense of peace descends when a perennial garden is put to bed for the season. The plants are safely tucked in against the elements, and the garden is ready to welcome the winter. When the work is done, you can sit back and anticipate the bright blooms of spring. Many gardeners are uncertain about how to close a perennial garden. This week's column demystifies the process.

Clean up

Garden clean up can be a gradual process—plants will deteriorate at different rates, allowing you to do a little bit each week.

- Edge beds and borders and remove stakes, trellises, and other plant supports.
- Dig and divide irises, daylilies, and other early bloomers.
- Cut back plants when foliage starts to deteriorate, then rake all debris out of the garden and pull any weeds that remain.

Plant perennials

Fall is the perfect time to plant perennials.[1] The warm, sunny days and cool nights provide optimal conditions for new root growth, without the stress of summer heat.

- Dig deeply and enhance soil with organic matter.
- Use a good starter fertilizer to speed up new root growth and establish a healthy base.
- Untangle the roots of new plants before planting.

- Water after planting as the weather dictates, and keep plants moist for several days.

Add compost

Organic matter is the key ingredient to healthy garden soil. Composting adds nutrients to the soil, helps the soil retain water and nutrients, and keeps the soil well aerated. If you take care of the soil, your plants will become strong and disease resistant.[2]

Before adding compost, use an iron rake to loosen the top few inches of soil. Spread a one to two inch layer of compost over the entire garden—the best compost is made up of yard waste and kitchen scraps—and then refrain from stepping on the area and compacting the soil.

Winter mulch

Winter protection for perennial beds can only help plants survive the winter. Winter mulch prevents the freezing and thawing cycles, which cause plants to heave and eventually die. Here's what works and what doesn't:

- Always apply mulch after the ground is frozen.
- Never apply generic hay because it contains billions of weed seeds. Also, whole leaves and bark mulch hold too much moisture.[3]
- Use a loose material to allow air filtration. Straw and salt marsh hay are excellent choices for mulch.
- Remove the winter mulch in the spring as soon as new growth begins.

---

[1] Fall is also an excellent time to plant shrubs and trees.
[2] You can buy good compost, but it is easy and useful to make it at home. Composting kitchen scraps reduces household garbage by about one-third.

[3] If using leaves, use only stiff leaves, such as Oak or Beech. Soft leaves, such as Maple, make it difficult for air and water to filtrate.

Source: StockSnap

Develop Multipage Documents

CASE As an assistant to Mary Watson, the VP of Sales & Marketing at Reason2Go (R2G), you have been asked to edit and format a set of guidelines to help R2G managers sponsor events to promote volunteer experiences to prospective customers. You start by working in Outline view to revise the structure for the guidelines, and then you use several advanced Word features to format the document for publication.

Module Objectives

After completing this module, you will be able to:

- Build a document in Outline view
- Work in Outline view
- Navigate a document
- Insert a table of contents
- Mark text for an index
- Generate an index
- Insert footers in multiple sections
- Insert headers in multiple sections
- Finalize a multipage document

Files You Will Need

WD 9-1.docx	WD 9-6.docx
WD 9-2.docx	WD 9-7.docx
WD 9-3.docx	WD 9-8.docx
WD 9-4.docx	WD 9-9.docx
WD 9-5.docx	WD 9-10.docx

Learning
Outcomes
• Open Outline view
• Demote and
  promote headings

Build a Document in Outline View

You work in Outline view to organize the headings and subheadings that identify topics and subtopics in multipage documents. In Outline view, each heading is assigned a level from 1 to 9, with Level 1 being the highest level and Level 9 being the lowest level. In addition, you can assign the Body Text level to each paragraph of text that appears below a document heading. Each level is formatted with one of Word's predefined styles. For example, Level 1 is formatted with the Heading 1 style, and the Body Text level is formatted with the Normal style. **CASE** *You work in Outline view to develop the structure of the Promotional Event Guidelines.*

STEPS

1. **Start Word, create a new blank document, click the** View tab, **then click the** Outline button **in the Views group**

   The document appears in Outline view. Notice that the Outlining tab is now active. TABLE 9-1 describes the buttons on the Outlining tab.

TROUBLE
If the headings do not appear blue and bold, click the Show Text Formatting check box in the Outline Tools group to select it.

2. **Type** R2G Promotional Events

   FIGURE 9-1 shows the text in Outline view. By default, the text appears at the left margin, is designated as Level 1 and is formatted with the Heading 1 style. You will work more with styles in the next module.

3. **Press** [Enter], **click the** Demote button ➡ **in the Outline Tools group to move to Level 2, then type** Event Requirements

   The text is indented, designated as Level 2, and formatted with the Heading 2 style.

4. **Press** [Enter], **then click the** Demote to Body Text button ➡➡ **in the Outline Tools group**

5. **Type the following text:** Three activities relate to the organization of an R2G promotional event: gather personnel, advertise the event, and arrange the physical space.

   The text is indented, designated as Body Text level, and formatted with the Normal style. Notice that both the Level 1 and Level 2 text are preceded by a plus symbol ⊕. This symbol indicates that the heading includes subtext, which could be another subheading or a paragraph of body text.

6. **Press** [Enter], **then click the** Promote to Heading 1 button ⬅ **in the Outline Tools group**

   The insertion point returns to the left margin and the Level 1 position.

7. **Type** Personnel, **press** [Enter], **then save the document as** WD 9-Promotional Event Outline **to the location where you store your Data Files**

   When you create a long document, you often enter all the headings and subheadings first to establish the overall structure of your document.

QUICK TIP
You can press [Tab] to move from a higher level to a lower level, and you can press [Shift][Tab] to move from a lower level to a higher level.

8. **Use the** Promote ⬅, Demote ➡, **and** Promote to Heading 1 ⬅ **buttons to complete the outline shown in** FIGURE 9-2

9. **Place the insertion point after R2G Promotional Events at the top of the page, press** [Enter], **click** ➡➡, **type** Prepared by **followed by your name, save the document, submit it to your instructor, then close it**

FIGURE 9-1: **Text in Outline view**

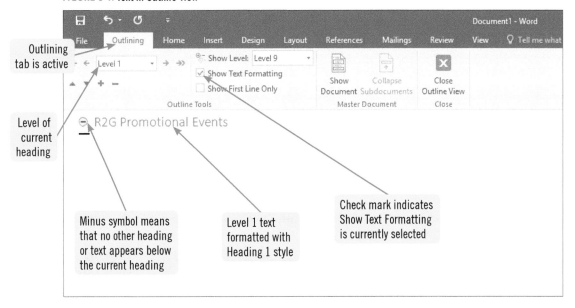

FIGURE 9-2: **Completed outline**

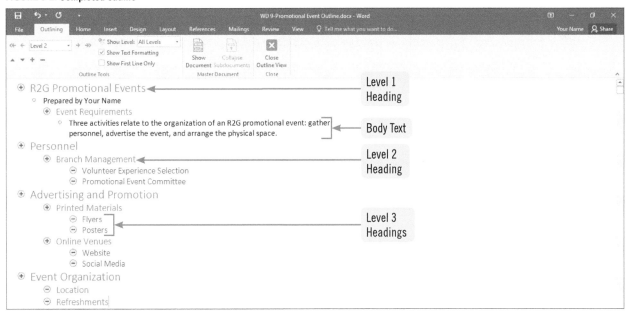

TABLE 9-1: **Frequently used outlining buttons in the Outline Tools group on the Outlining tab**

button	use to	button	use to
⇐	Promote text to Heading 1	▲	Move a heading and its text up one line
←	Promote text one level	▼	Move a heading and its text down one line
→	Demote text one level	⊕	Expand text
⇒	Demote to body text	⊖	Collapse text

Work in Outline View

Learning
Outcomes
• Collapse/expand
  headings in
  Outline view
• Move headings
• Show levels

In Outline view, you can promote and demote headings and subheadings and move or delete whole blocks of text. When you move a heading in Outline view, all of the text and subheadings under that heading move with the heading. You also can use the Collapse, Expand, and Show Level commands on the Outlining tab to view all or just some of the headings and subheadings. For example, you can choose to view just the headings assigned to Level 1 so that you can quickly evaluate the main topics of your document. **CASE** *You work in Outline view to develop a draft of the guidelines for running a promotional event. In Outline view, each heading is formatted with a heading style based on its corresponding level.*

STEPS

1. **Open the file** WD 9-1.docx **from the location where you store your Data Files, save the document as** WD 9-Promotional Event Guidelines, **scroll through the document to get a sense of its content, click the** View tab, **then click** Outline **in the Views group**

   The document changes to Outline view, and the Outlining tab opens. The chart at the end of the document is not visible in Outline view.

2. **Click the** Show Level list arrow **in the Outline Tools group, then click** Level 1

   Only the headings assigned to Level 1 appear. All the headings assigned to Level 1 are formatted with the Heading 1 style. Notice that the title of the document Promotional Event Guidelines does not appear because the title text is not formatted as Level 1.

3. **Click the** plus sign ⊕ **to the left of Printed Materials**

   The heading and all its subtext (which is hidden because the topic is collapsed) are selected.

QUICK TIP
You can use [Ctrl] to select multiple non-adjacent headings.

4. **Press and hold** [Shift], **click the heading** Online Venues, **release** [Shift], **then click the** Demote button ➔ **in the Outline Tools group**

   You use [Shift] to select several adjacent headings at once. The headings are demoted one level to Level 2, as shown in FIGURE 9-3.

5. **Press** [Ctrl][A] **to select all the headings, then click the** Expand button ➕ **in the Outline Tools group**

   The outline expands to show all the subheadings and body text associated with each of the selected headings along with the document title. You can also expand a single heading by selecting only that heading and then clicking the Expand button.

6. **Click the** plus sign ⊕ **next to Advertising and Promotion, click the** Collapse button ➖ **in the Outline Tools group two times to collapse all the subheadings and text associated with each subheading, then double-click** ⊕ **next to Personnel to collapse it**

   You can double-click headings to expand or collapse them, or you can use the Expand or Collapse buttons.

QUICK TIP
You can also use the mouse pointer to drag a heading up or down to a new location in the outline. A horizontal line appears as you drag to indicate the placement.

7. **Click the** Move Up button ▲ **in the Outline Tools group once, then double-click** ⊕ **next to Personnel**

   When you move a heading in Outline view, all subheadings and their associated text also move.

8. **Click the** Show Level list arrow, **select** Level 3, **double-click** ⊕ **next to Printed Materials under the Advertising and Promotion heading, click** ⊕ **next to Counter Items, then press** [Delete]

   The Counter Items heading and its associated subtext are deleted from the document. The revised outline is shown in FIGURE 9-4.

9. **Click the** Close Outline View button **in the Close group, then save the document**

FIGURE 9-3: Headings demoted to Level 2

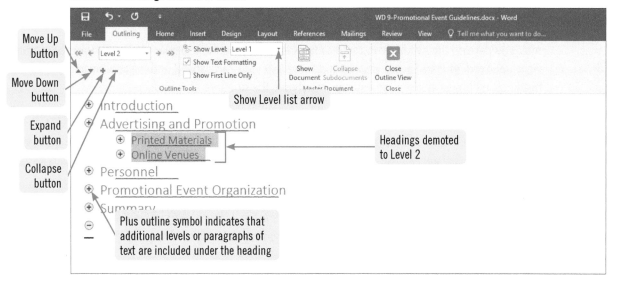

FIGURE 9-4: Revised outline

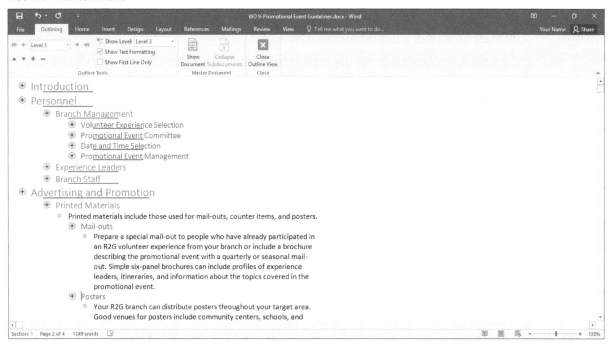

Navigate a Document

After you develop the headings and subheadings that make up the structure of your document in Outline view, you work in Print Layout view to add more text. You can expand and collapse headings and subheadings in Print Layout view so you can quickly see the structure of your document. You can also make adjustments to the document structure in the Navigation pane, which you open from Print Layout view. The **Navigation pane** shows all the headings and subheadings in the document. You can click a heading in the Navigation pane to move directly to it, and you can drag and drop headings to change their order just like you do in Outline view. You can also view thumbnails of the document pages in the Navigation pane. In addition to using the Navigation pane to navigate a document, you can create cross-references in your document. A **cross-reference** is text that electronically refers the reader to another part of the document, such as a numbered paragraph, a heading, or a figure. **CASE** ▶ *You expand and collapse headings in Print Layout view, work in the Navigation pane to make further changes to the document, and then add a cross-reference to a heading.*

STEPS

1. **Press [Ctrl][Home], click Introduction, move the mouse slightly to the left to show the Collapse icon ◢, then click ◢**

   The paragraph under the Introduction heading is hidden. You can click the Expand icon ▷ to expand the heading again so you can read the text associated with that heading.

2. **Right-click Introduction, point to Expand/Collapse, then click Collapse All Headings**

   Only Level 1 headings are visible.

3. **Right-click Introduction, point to Expand/Collapse, then click Expand All Headings**

   All headings and their associated text are visible again.

4. **Click the View tab if it is not the active tab, click the Navigation Pane check box in the Show group, then click Branch Staff in the Navigation pane**

   The Branch Staff subheading is selected in the Navigation pane, and the insertion point moves to the Branch Staff subheading in the document.

5. **In the Navigation pane, drag Branch Staff up so that it appears above Experience Leaders as shown in FIGURE 9-5**

   The order of the headings in the Navigation pane and in the document changes. From the Navigation pane, you can also right-click a heading and perform actions such as promoting, demoting, expanding, and collapsing headings, as well as deleting headings and the text associated with them.

6. **Click Pages at the top of the Navigation pane, scroll up and click the page 1 thumbnail, then, in the document text, select the word summary in paragraph 2 of the Introduction**

7. **Click the Insert tab, click Cross-reference in the Links group, click the Reference type list arrow, then click Heading**

8. **Scroll to and click Summary as shown in FIGURE 9-6**

   In the Cross-reference dialog box, you can also create a cross-reference to a numbered item, a bookmark, a footnote or an endnote, an equation, and a table, as well as a figure such as a chart, a picture, or a diagram.

9. **Click Insert, click Close, then insert a space after Summary if necessary**

   The word "Summary" is now a hyperlink to the Summary heading at the end of the document.

10. **Move the pointer over Summary to show the Click message, press and hold [Ctrl] to show 🖑, click Summary to move directly to the Summary heading, click ✕ to close the Navigation pane, then save the document**

FIGURE 9-5: Changing the order of a subheading in the Navigation pane

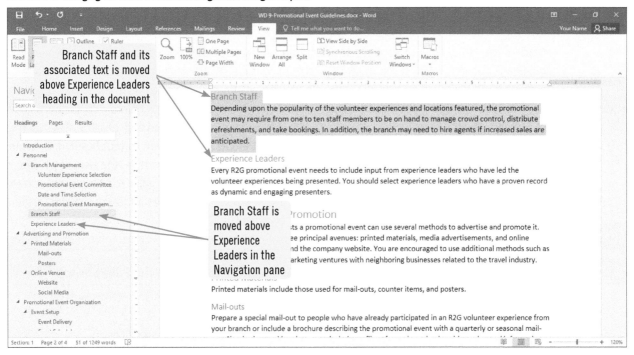

FIGURE 9-6: Cross-reference dialog box

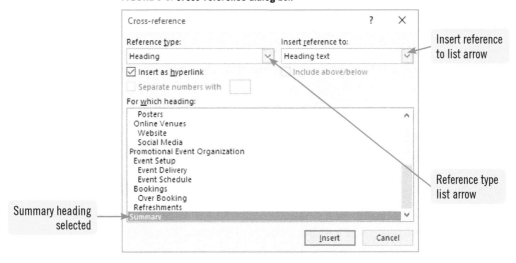

Using bookmarks

A **bookmark** identifies a location or a selection of text in a document. To create a bookmark, you first move the insertion point to the location in the text that you want to reference. This location can be a word, the beginning of a paragraph, or a heading. Click the Insert tab, then click Bookmark in the Links group to open the Bookmark dialog box. In this dialog box, you type a name (which cannot contain spaces) for the bookmark, then click Add. To find a bookmark, press [Ctrl][G] to open the Find and Replace dialog box with the Go To tab active, click Bookmark in the Go to what list box, click the Enter bookmark name list arrow to see the list of bookmarks in the document, select the bookmark you want to go to, click Go To, then close the Find and Replace dialog box. To delete a bookmark you no longer need, click Bookmark in the Links group, click the bookmark you want to remove, then click Delete in the Bookmark dialog box.

Insert a Table of Contents

Learning Outcomes
- Insert a table of contents
- Update a table of contents

Readers refer to a table of contents to obtain an overview of the topics and subtopics covered in a multipage document. When you generate a table of contents, Word searches for headings, sorts them by heading levels, and then displays the completed table of contents in the document. By default, a table of contents lists the top three heading levels in a document. Consequently, before you create a table of contents, you must ensure that all headings and subheadings are formatted with heading styles such as Heading 1, Heading 2, and Heading 3. When you work in Outline view, the correct heading styles are assigned automatically to text based on the outline level of the text. For example, the Heading 1 style is applied to Level 1 text, the Heading 2 style to Level 2 text, and so on. **CASE** *You are pleased with the content of the document and are now ready to create a new page that includes a table of contents. You use commands on the References tab to generate a table of contents.*

STEPS

1. **Press [Ctrl][Home], click the** Insert tab, **then click** Blank Page **in the Pages group**

2. **Press [Ctrl][Home], click the** Home tab, **then click the** Clear All Formatting button 🖺 **in the Font group**
   The insertion point is positioned at the left margin where the table of contents will begin.

3. **Click the** References tab, **then click the** Table of Contents button **in the Table of Contents group**
   A gallery of predefined styles for a table of contents opens.

4. **Click** Automatic Table 2 **as shown in** FIGURE 9-7, **then scroll up to see the table of contents**
   A table of contents that includes all the Level 1, 2, and 3 headings is inserted on page 1.

5. **Click the** Table of Contents button **in the Table of Contents group, click** Custom Table of Contents **to open the Table of Contents dialog box, click the** Formats list arrow, **then click** Formal
   The Formats setting is modified in the Table of Contents dialog box, as shown in FIGURE 9-8.

6. **Click** OK, **click** Yes, **click the** View tab, **click the** Navigation Pane check box **in the Show group to open the Navigation pane, then click** Headings **at the top of the Navigation pane**
   In the Navigation pane, you can move quickly to a section of the document and delete it.

7. **Right-click the** Promotional Event Management subheading **below the Branch Management subheading in the Personnel section, then click** Delete
   The Promotional Event Management subheading and its related subtext are deleted from the document but the heading is not yet deleted from the table of contents.

8. **Scroll to the top of the table of contents, click** Update Table, **then click** OK **if prompted**
   The table of contents is updated. The Promotional Event Management subheading is no longer listed in the table of contents.

9. **Move the pointer over the heading** Online Venues **in the Table of Contents, press [Ctrl], then click** Online Venues
   The insertion point moves to the Online Venues heading in the document. The Navigation pane remains open.

10. **Save the document**

FIGURE 9-7: Inserting an automatic table of contents

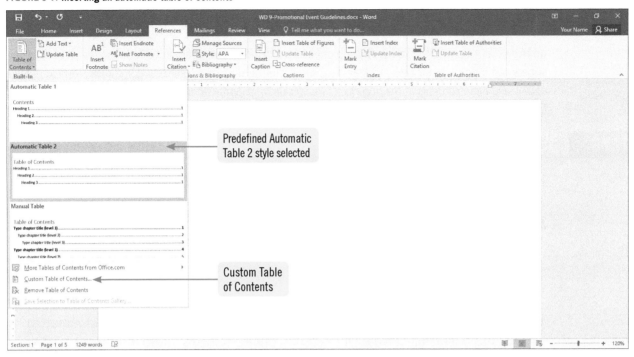

FIGURE 9-8: Table of Contents dialog box

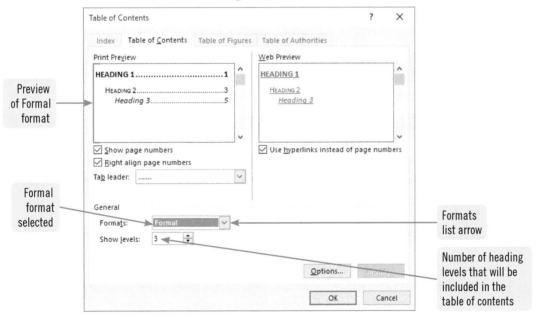

Mark Text for an Index

Learning
Outcomes
• Mark index entries
• Search for text to
index

An **index** lists many of the terms and topics included in a document, along with the pages on which they appear. An index can include main entries, subentries, and cross-references. **CASE** ▶ *To help readers quickly find main concepts in the document, you decide to generate an index. You get started by marking the terms that you want to include as main entries in the index.*

STEPS

1. **Press [Ctrl][Home], press [Ctrl], then click** Introduction **in the table of contents**
   The insertion point moves to the Introduction heading in the document.

2. **Click** Personnel **in the Navigation pane, select** branch staff **in the second line under the Personnel heading in the document, click the** References tab, **then click the** Mark Entry button **in the Index group**
   The Mark Index Entry dialog box opens. By default, the selected text is entered in the Main entry text box and is treated as a main entry in the index.

3. **Click** Mark All, **click the** Mark Index Entry dialog box title bar, **then use your mouse to drag the dialog box down so you can see "branch staff" as shown in** FIGURE 9-9
   Notice the term "branch staff" is marked with the XE field code. **XE** stands for **Index Entry**. When you mark an entry for the index, the paragraph marks are turned on automatically so that you can see hidden codes such as paragraph marks, field codes, page breaks, and section breaks. These codes do not appear in the printed document. The Mark Index Entry dialog box remains open so that you can continue to mark text for inclusion in the index.

4. **Click anywhere in the document to deselect the current index entry, click** Results **at the top of the Navigation pane, then type** branch manager **in the Search document text box in the Navigation pane**
   Each occurrence of the term "branch manager" is shown in context and in bold in the Navigation pane, and each occurrence is highlighted in the document.

5. **Click the first instance of** branch manager **in the Navigation pane, then click the** title bar **of the Mark Index Entry dialog box**
   The text "branch manager" appears in the Main entry text box in the Mark Index Entry dialog box.

6. **Click** Mark All
   All instances of "branch manager" in the document are marked for inclusion in the index.

7. **Click anywhere in the document to deselect "branch manager", type** theme **in the Search document text box, click the result in the Navigation pane, click the** title bar **of the Mark Index Entry dialog box, then click** Mark All

8. **Follow the procedure in Step 7 to find and mark all instances of the following main entries:** brochures, target market, Mary Watson, **and** shopping cart

9. **Click** ⊠ **to close the Mark Index Entry dialog box, scroll up until you see the document title (Promotional Event Guidelines), then save the document**
   You see two entries marked for the index, as shown in FIGURE 9-10. The other entries you marked are further down the document.

FIGURE 9-9: Selected text in the Mark Index Entry dialog box

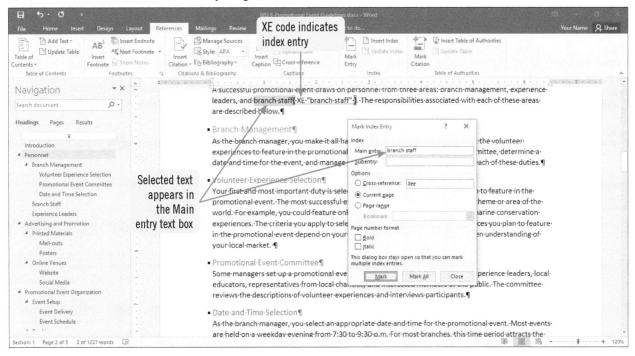

FIGURE 9-10: Index entries on the first page of the document

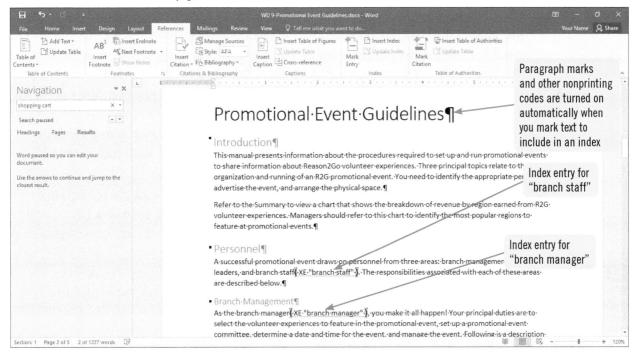

Generate an Index

Learning Outcomes
• Mark index subentries
• Insert a cross-reference in an index
• Generate an index

In addition to main entries, an index often includes subentries and cross-references. A **subentry** is text included under a main entry. For example, you could mark the text "shopping cart" as a subentry to appear under the main entry "website." A **cross-reference** in an index refers the reader to another entry in the index. For example, a cross-reference in an index might read "lecture. *See* events." Once you have marked all the index entries, you select a design for the index, and then you generate it. If you make changes to the document, you can update the index just like you can update a table of contents. **CASE** *You mark one subentry and one cross-reference for the index, create a new last page in the document, and then generate the index. You add one new main entry, and then update the index to reflect this change.*

STEPS

1. **Type charities in the Search document text box in the Navigation pane, click the entry that appears in the Navigation pane, then click Mark Entry in the Index group on the References tab to open the Mark Index Entry dialog box**

   The search term "charities" is already entered into the Mark Index Entry dialog box.

2. **Type Event Committee in the Main entry text box, click in the Subentry text box, type charities in the Subentry text box as shown in FIGURE 9-11, then click Mark**

   The first and only instance of the text "charities" is marked as a subentry that will appear following the Main entry, Event Committee.

3. **Click anywhere in the document, type laptops in the Search document text box, click the Cross-reference option button in the Mark Index Entry dialog box, click after See, type bookings as shown in FIGURE 9-12, then click Mark**

   You also need to mark "bookings" so the Index lists the page number for "bookings."

TROUBLE
Drag the Mark Index Entry dialog box out of the way as needed to see the selected phrase.

4. **Click anywhere in the document, type bookings in the Search document text box, click the entry in the Navigation pane that contains the phrase "bookings on the spot", select bookings in the phrase "bookings on the spot" in the document, click the Mark Index Entry dialog box, click Mark, then click Close**

   The term "laptops" is cross-referenced to the term "bookings" in the same paragraph. Now that you have marked entries for the index, you can generate the index at the end of the document.

5. **Press [Ctrl][End], press [Ctrl][Enter], type Index, press [Enter], select Index, click the Home tab, apply 18 pt, bold, and center alignment formatting, then click at the left margin below Index**

6. **Click the References tab, click Insert Index in the Index group, click the Formats list arrow in the Index dialog box, scroll down the list, click Formal, then click OK**

   Word has collected all the index entries, sorted them alphabetically, included the appropriate page numbers, and removed duplicate entries.

QUICK TIP
The refreshments entry that appears in the table of contents is not included because it appears before the entry you selected.

7. **Search for refreshments, click the second instance of "refreshments" (below Refreshments 4) in the search results in the Navigation pane, click the Mark Entry button in the Index Group, then click Mark All**

   The index now includes each instance of refreshments from the selected text to the end of the document.

8. **Close the dialog box and Navigation pane, scroll to the end of the document, right-click the index, click Update Field, click Index to deselect the index, then save the document**

   The updated index is shown in FIGURE 9-13.

FIGURE 9-11: **Subentry in the Mark Index Entry dialog box**

FIGURE 9-12: **Cross-reference in the Mark Index Entry dialog box**

FIGURE 9-13: **Completed index**

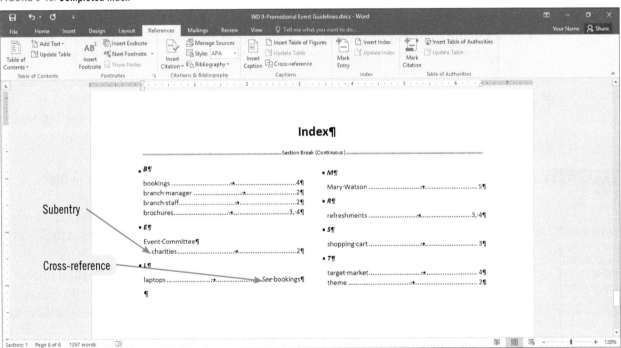

Insert Footers in Multiple Sections

Multipage documents often consist of two or more sections that you can format differently. For example, you can include different text in the footer for each section, and you can change how page numbers are formatted from section to section. **CASE** *You want to divide the report into two sections, and then format the headers and footers differently in each section. The diagram in* FIGURE 9-14 *explains how the footer should appear on each of the first three pages in the document.*

STEPS

1. **Press [Ctrl][Home] to move to the top of the document, right-click the status bar, click Section if it does not have a check mark next to it, scroll to the page break, click to the left of it, click the Layout tab, then click Breaks in the Page Setup group**

   You can see the page break because the paragraph marks were turned on when you marked entries for inclusion in the index. When you work with sections, you should leave paragraph marks showing so you can see the codes that Word inserts for section breaks and page breaks.

2. **Click Next Page under Section Breaks, press [Delete] to remove the original page break, then press [Delete] to remove the extra blank line**

   The document is divided into two sections. Section 1 contains the Table of Contents and section 2 contains the rest of the document. Section 2 appears on the status bar.

3. **Press [Ctrl][Home], click the Insert tab, click the Footer button in the Header & Footer group, then click Blank (Three Columns)**

   The footer area opens showing the Blank (Three Columns) format.

4. **Click to the left of the placeholder text to select all three items, press [Delete], press [Tab] once, type Page, press [Spacebar], click the Page Number button in the Header & Footer group, point to Current Position, then click Plain Number (the top selection)**

   The current footer for the entire document contains the word Page and a page number.

5. **Click the Page Number button, click Format Page Numbers, click the Number format list arrow, click i, ii, iii, then click OK**

   The page number in the footer area of the table of contents page is formatted as i.

QUICK TIP
Clicking Next
moved the insertion
point to the next
footer, which in this
case is also the next
section, as indicated
by the section
number in the status
bar and on the
Footer tab.

6. **Click Next in the Navigation group, then click the Link to Previous button in the Navigation group to deselect it**

   You deselect the Link to Previous button to make sure that the text you type into the footer appears only in the footer in section 2. You must deselect the Link to Previous button each time you want the header or footer in a section to be unique.

7. **Type your name, then press [Tab] once to move the phrase Page 2 to the right margin**

   By default, Word continues numbering the pages in section 2 based on the page numbers in section 1. The footer in section 2 starts with Page 2 because section 1 contains just one page. You want section 2 to start with Page 1 because the first page in section 2 is the first page of the report. Note also that the i, ii, iii format is not applied to the page number in section 2. Changes to page number formatting apply only to the section in which the change is made originally (in this case, section 1).

8. **Click the Page Number button, click Format Page Numbers, click the Start at option button, verify that 1 appears, click OK, then compare the footer to** FIGURE 9-15

9. **Click the Close Header and Footer button, then save the document**

FIGURE 9-14: Diagram of section formatting for footers

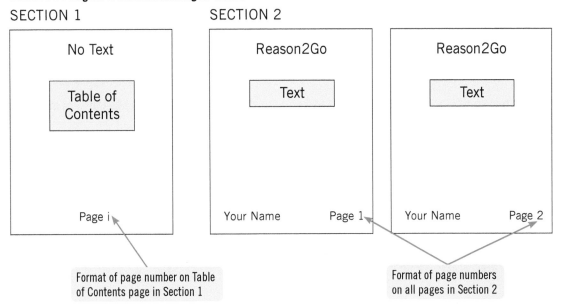

SECTION 1

No Text

Table of Contents

Page i

Format of page number on Table of Contents page in Section 1

SECTION 2

Reason2Go

Text

Your Name   Page 1

Reason2Go

Text

Your Name   Page 2

Format of page numbers on all pages in Section 2

FIGURE 9-15: Completed footer

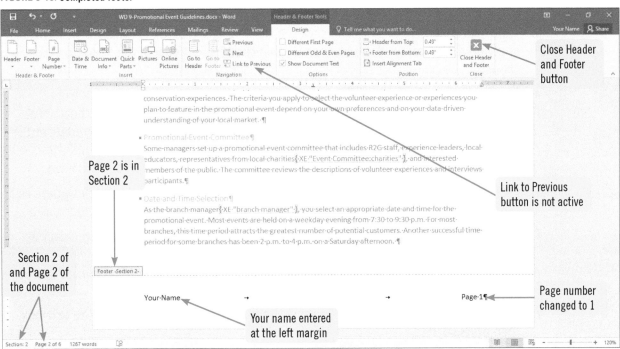

Using text flow options

You adjust text flow options to control how text in a multipage document breaks across pages. To change text flow options, you use the Paragraph dialog box. To open the Paragraph dialog box, click the launcher in the Paragraph group on the Home tab, and then select the Line and Page Breaks tab. In the Pagination section, you can choose to select or deselect four text flow options.

For example, you select the Widow/Orphan control option to prevent the last line of a paragraph from printing at the top of a page (a widow) or the first line of a paragraph from printing at the bottom of a page (an orphan). By default, Widow/Orphan control is active. You can also select the Keep lines together check box to keep a paragraph from breaking across two pages.

Insert Headers in Multiple Sections

Learning
Outcomes
• Insert headers in
  sections
• Add a cover page

When you divide your document into sections, you can modify the header to be different in each section. As you learned in the previous lesson, you must deselect the Link to Previous button when you want the text of a header (or footer) in a new section to be different from the header (or footer) in the previous section. **CASE** *The diagram in FIGURE 9-16 shows that text will appear in the header on every page in section 2. You do not want any text to appear in the header on the table of contents page (section 1). You modify the headers in the two sections of the document and then add a cover page.*

STEPS

1. **Press [Ctrl][Home] to move to the top of the document, then double-click in the blank area above Table of Contents**

   The header area opens. The Header -Section 1- identifier appears along with the Header & Footer Tools Design tab. Refer to FIGURE 9-16. Notice that you do not want text in the header in section 1.

2. **Click Next in the Navigation group, then click the Link to Previous button to deselect it**

   The identifier Header -Section 2- appears. You want text to appear on all the pages of section 2. You deselect the Link to Previous button so that the text you type appears only on this page and on subsequent pages.

3. **Type Reason2Go, select the text, click the Home tab, increase the font size to 14 pt, apply bold, and center the text, then double-click Promotional in the heading text**

   The header area closes.

4. **Scroll up to see the Table of Contents and notice that the page number for the Introduction in the table of contents is page 2, click the Table of Contents head, click Update Table to open the Update Table of Contents dialog box, click the Update entire table option button, then click OK**

   The page numbers in the table of contents are updated.

5. **Press [Ctrl][End] to move to the Index page, right-click the index, then click Update Field**

   The page numbers in the index are updated.

6. **Press [Ctrl][Home], click the Insert tab, click Cover Page in the Pages group, scroll to view the selections, then select the Facet style**

   Several placeholders called content controls are included on the cover page. Before you add text to the content controls you want to keep, you delete the ones you don't need.

7. **Scroll to Abstract, click Abstract to show the text box, click the border of the text box, then press [Delete]**

   Text on a cover page can be enclosed in a text box or displayed in a content control.

QUICK TIP
When you select a content control, the handle turns blue gray and the text in the control is shaded with light blue.

8. **Click [Email address] to show the Email content control handle, click the content control handle to select it, then press [Delete]**

   You delete individual content controls that you do not plan to use.

9. **Enter text as shown in FIGURE 9-17, then save the document**

FIGURE 9-16: **Diagram of section formatting for headers**

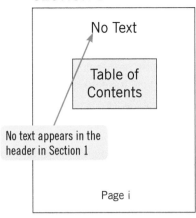

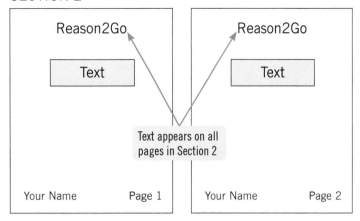

FIGURE 9-16: **Diagram of section formatting for headers**

FIGURE 9-17: **Text to type in cover page**

PROMOTIONAL·EVENT·
GUIDELINES¶

R2G·Branch·Management¶

Your·Name¶
¶

Understanding headers, footers, and sections

One reason you divide a document into sections is so that you can modify the page layout and the headers and footers differently in different sections. You can even modify the header and footer within a section because each section consists of two parts. The first part of a section is the first page, and the second part of the section is the remaining pages in the section. This section structure allows you to omit the header and footer on the first page of section 2, and then include the header and footer on all subsequent pages in section 2. To do this, place the insertion point in the section you want to modify, then click the Different First Page check box in the Options group to specify that you wish to include a different header and/or footer (or no header and footer at all) on the first page of a section. In addition, you can also choose to format odd and even pages in a document in different ways by clicking the Different Odd & Even Pages check box in the Options group. For example, you can choose to right-align the document title on odd-numbered pages and left-align the chapter indicator on even-numbered pages.

Finalize a Multipage Document

The Resume Reading feature takes you to the last location you were working on before you saved and closed a document. You can customize the table of contents so that readers can identify the document structure. By default, a table of contents shows only headings formatted with the Heading 1, Heading 2, or Heading 3 styles (Levels 1, 2, and 3 in Outline view). You can also include headings formatted with other styles, such as the Title style or a style you create. **CASE** ▸ *You use the Resume Reading feature, modify the headers and footers, and then customize the table of contents.*

STEPS

QUICK TIP
Including the cover page and table of contents page, the document contains seven physical pages with the text starting on page 3 (designated Page 1).

1. **Make sure you've saved the document, press** [Ctrl][G], **be sure** Page **in the Go to what area is selected, type** 5, **click** Go To, **click** Close, **close the document, open the document, then click the** Welcome back! notice **to go directly to page 5**

   The Resume Reading feature returns you to where you were working before saving and closing the document.

2. **Scroll up to view the page break below the chart, select the** page break, **click the** Layout tab, **click** Breaks, **then click** Next Page **in the Section Breaks area**

3. **Open** WD 9-2.docx, **press** [Ctrl][A] **to select all the text, press** [Ctrl][C] **to copy all the text, switch to the WD 9-Promotional Event Guidelines document, press** [Ctrl][V], **click the** File tab, **click** Save As, **then save the document as** WD 9-Event Guidelines

   The three pages of the Information Session Guidelines document appear in their own section.

4. **Scroll up to the Table of Contents page, double-click in the** header area **for section 1, click** Next, **select** Reason2Go, **type** Promotional Event Guidelines, **click** Next, **click the** Link to Previous button **in the Navigation group to deselect it, change the header text to** Information Session Guidelines, **then close the header**

5. **Scroll to the Index page, insert a** Next Page section break **to the left of Index, double-click in the header area, click the** Link to Previous button, **delete the header text, then close the header**

   The document now contains four sections, and you have modified the header text in sections 2, 3, and 4.

QUICK TIP
The title of each document is not included in the table of contents so you cannot easily see which headings belong to which documents.

6. **Scroll up to the table of contents page and click the** table of contents, **click** Update Table, **click the** Update entire table option button, **then click** OK

7. **Click the** References tab, **click the** Table of Contents button, **click** Custom Table of Contents, **click** Options, **select** 1 **in the TOC level text box next to Heading 1 and type** 2, **type** 3 **next to Heading 2, type** 4 **next to Heading 3 as shown in** FIGURE 9-18, **scroll down to** Title, **type** 1, **click** OK **until you are returned to the document, then click** OK **to replace this table of contents**

   The Information Session document starts at page 1 and you want page numbering to be consecutive.

8. **Press** [Ctrl], **click** Information Session Guidelines **in the table of contents, scroll to the footer (you'll see Page 1), double-click in the footer, click the** Page Number button **in the Header & Footer group, click** Format Page Numbers, **click the** Continue from previous section option button, **then click** OK

QUICK TIP
Submit files to your instructor as directed.

9. **Click** Next **in the Navigation group, click the** Page Number button, **click** Format Page Numbers, **click the** Continue from previous section option button, **click** OK, **exit the footer area, update the table of contents for page numbers only, reduce the zoom to** 80% **and hide the paragraph marks, compare the revised table of contents to** FIGURE 9-19, **then save and close all documents and exit Word**

FIGURE 9-18: Table of Contents Options dialog box

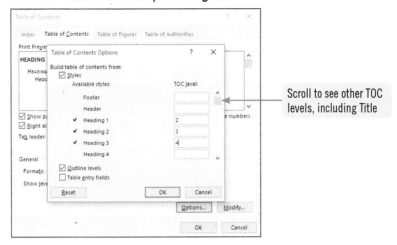

Scroll to see other TOC levels, including Title

FIGURE 9-19: Revised table of contents

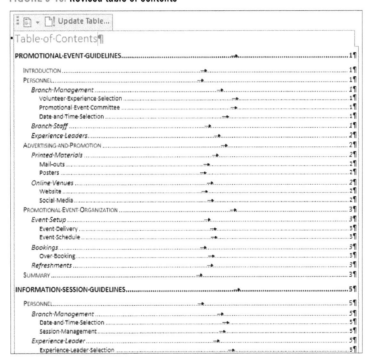

Using Advanced Print Options

With Word 2016, you can scale a document to fit a different paper size and you can choose to print pages from specific sections or a series of sections, even when the page numbering restarts in each section. To scale a document, click the File tab, click Print, click the 1 Page Per Sheet list arrow, then click Scale to Paper Size and view the list of paper sizes available. You can also choose to print a multiple-page document on fewer sheets; for example, you can print the document on two pages per sheet up to 16 pages per sheet. In the Print dialog box, you can also specify how to print the pages of a multiple-section document that uses different page numbering in each section. You need to enter both the page number and the section number for the range of pages you wish to print. The syntax required is: PageNumberSectionNumber-PageNumberSectionNumber which is shortened to p#s#-p#s#. For example, if you want to print from page 1 of section one to page 4 of section three, you enter p1s1-p4s3 in the Pages text box in the Settings area, and then click Print.

Practice

Concepts Review

Label the numbered items on the Outlining tab shown in FIGURE 9-20.

FIGURE 9-20

Match each term with the statement that best describes it.

6. **Demote button**
7. **Table of Contents**
8. **Resume Reading**
9. **Footer**
10. **Cross-reference**
11. **Link to Previous button**
12. **Mark All**

a. Feature that allows you to return to the last place you were working in a document before you saved and closed it
b. Text that electronically refers the reader to another part of the document
c. Text that appears at the bottom of every page in a document or section
d. Click to designate each instance of a specific term for inclusion in an index
e. Deselect to create a header or footer in one section that is different from the header or footer in a previous section
f. List of topics and subtopics usually with page numbers, and shown at the beginning of a document
g. Used to enter a lower-level heading in Outline view

Select the best answer from the list of choices.

13. **On the Outlining tab, which button do you click to move to Body Text from any other level?**
    a. ⇒
    b. ⇐
    c. →
    d. ▼

14. **Which symbol in Outline view indicates that a heading does not include subtext such as subheadings or paragraphs of text?**
    a. ⊕
    b. «
    c. ▲
    d. ⊖

15. **Which of the following options do you select when you want to search for text from the Navigation pane?**
    a. Headings
    b. Results
    c. Find Text
    d. Search

16. **Which index entry appears subordinate to a main entry?**
    a. Cross-reference
    b. Subentry
    c. Mark place
    d. Next Entry

17. **Which tab contains the commands used to create an index?**
    a. References
    b. Insert
    c. Layout
    d. Review

Skills Review

1. Build a document in Outline view.

a. Start Word, create a new blank document, then switch to Outline view using the View tab.

b. Type **Introduction** followed by your name as a Level 1 heading, press [Enter], type **Partnership Conditions** as another Level 1 heading, then press [Enter].

c. Type the text shown in FIGURE 9-21 as body text under the Partnership Conditions heading.

d. Type **Background**, then use the Promote and Demote buttons to promote the body text to Level 1 and then demote it to a Level 2 heading.

e. Complete the outline, as shown in FIGURE 9-21.

f. Save the document as **WD 9-Partnership Outline** to the location where you store your Data Files, then close the document.

FIGURE 9-21

⊖ Introduction by Your Name
⊕ Partnership Conditions
  ○ This section provides background information about Creston Training and discusses how the partnership could benefit both Redfern Communications and Creston Training.
  ⊖ Background
  ⊖ Benefits
  ⊖ Partnership Need
⊕ Products and Services
  ⊖ Creston Training Services
  ⊖ Redfern Communications
  ⊖ Package Opportunities
⊕ Financial Considerations
  ⊖ Projected Revenues
  ⊖ Financing Required
⊖ Conclusion

2. Work in Outline view.

a. Open the file WD 9-3.docx from the location where you store your Data Files, save it as **WD 9-Partnership Proposal**, switch to Outline view, then show all Level 1 headings.

b. Move the heading Products and Services above Financial Considerations.

c. Select the Partnership Conditions heading, expand the heading to show all subheadings and their corresponding body text, collapse Benefits, collapse Partnership Need, then move Benefits and its subtext below Partnership Need and its subtext.

d. Show all levels of the outline, close Outline view, then save the document.

3. Navigate a document.

a. In Print Layout view, collapse the Introduction heading.

b. Open the Navigation pane, navigate to Financing Required, then change "six months" to **two years** in the last line of the paragraph below the Financing Required heading.

c. Right-click the Package Opportunities heading in the Navigation pane, then delete the heading and its subtext.

d. View the thumbnails of the document pages in the Navigation pane, click the first page, close the Navigation pane, scroll to the Benefits heading, then select the text "Projected Revenues" at the end of the paragraph.

e. Create a cross-reference from the text Projected Revenues to the PROJECTED REVENUES heading.

f. Test the cross-reference, then save the document.

4. Insert a table of contents.

a. Go to the top of the document.

b. Insert a page break, then return to the top of the document.

c. Insert a table of contents using the Automatic Table 2 predefined style.

d. Replace the table of contents with a custom table of contents using the Distinctive format.

e. Use [Ctrl][click] to navigate to Partnership Need in the document, open the Navigation pane, view the document headings, then right-click and delete the Partnership Need heading from the Navigation pane.

f. Update the table of contents, then save the document.

Skills Review (continued)

5. Mark text for an index.

   a. Show the Results section of the Navigation pane, find the words **computer labs**, then mark all occurrences for inclusion in the index.

   b. Find and mark only the first instance of each of the following main entries: **website design, networking, software training**, and **PowerPoint**. (*Hint*: Click Mark instead of Mark All.)

   c. Save the document.

6. Generate an index.

   a. Find **social media**, click in the Mark Index Entry dialog box, select social media in the Main entry text box, type **Redfern Communications Products** as the Main entry and **social media** as the Subentry, then click Mark All.

   b. Repeat the process to insert **business writing seminars** as a subentry of Creston Training.

   c. Find the text **courses**, then create a cross-reference in the Mark Index Entry dialog box to **software training**. Note that you already have an index entry for software training.

   d. Close the Mark Index Entry dialog box and the Navigation pane.

   e. Insert a new page at the end of the document, type **Index** at the top of the page, and format it with bold and 18 pt and center alignment.

   f. Double-click below the index, clear any formatting so the insertion point appears at the left margin, then insert an index using the Modern format.

   g. Find and mark all instances of **Los Angeles**, close the Mark Index Entry dialog box and the Navigation pane, scroll to the index page, update the index so it includes the new entry, then save the document.

7. Insert footers in multiple sections.

   a. At the top of the document, select the page break below the Table of Contents, replace it with a Next Page section break, then remove the page break and the extra blank line.

   b. On the table of contents page, insert a footer using the Blank (Three Columns) format.

   c. Delete the placeholders, type your name, press [Tab] twice, type **Page**, press [Spacebar], then insert a page number at the current position using the Plain Number format.

   d. Change the format of the page number to i, ii, iii.

   e. Go to the next section, then deselect the Link to Previous button.

   f. Format the page number to start at 1.

   g. Exit the footer area, scroll through the document to verify that the pages are numbered correctly, scroll to and update the page numbers in the table of contents, then save the document.

8. Insert headers in multiple sections.

   a. Move to the top of the document, then double-click to position the insertion point in the header area.

   b. Go to the next section, then deselect the Link to Previous button.

   c. Type **Redfern Communications**, then apply bold and italic.

   d. Exit the header area, then scroll through the document to verify that the header text does not appear on the table of contents and that it does appear on all subsequent pages.

   e. Insert a cover page using the Semaphore style, then delete the Date content control.

   f. Enter **Partnership Agreement Proposal** as the Document title, **Redfern Communications** as the Document subtitle, and your name where indicated.

   g. Delete the Company name and Company address content controls.

   h. Save the document.

9. Finalize a multipage document.

   a. Go to the Index page, then save and close the document.

   b. Open the document, then use the Resume Reading feature to return to the last page of the document.

Skills Review (continued)

c. Scroll up to the Page Break after the Conclusion text, then insert a Next Page section break, then delete the page break and paragraph mark following the page break. The insertion point should move to the left of the word Index.

d. Open the file WD 9-4.docx from the drive and folder where you store your Data Files, copy all the text, paste it into the Partnership Agreement Proposal document at the location of the insertion point, insert a Next Page section break, then save the document as **WD 9-Partnership Agreements**.

e. From the table of contents page, access the Header area, move to section 2, replace Redfern Communications with **Creston Training**, move to section 3, deselect the Link to Previous button, replace Creston Training with **Smart Talk Presenters**, move to section 4 (the index page), then deselect the Link to Previous button and remove the header from the index page.

f. Check that the correct headers appear in each of the four sections, then update the table of contents page (select the Update entire table option).

g. Modify the table of contents options so that Heading 1 corresponds to TOC level 2 text, Heading 2 corresponds to TOC level 3 text, Heading 3 corresponds to TOC level 4 text, and Title text corresponds to TOC level 1 text.

h. Modify the footers in sections 3 and 4 so that the page numbering is continuous. You should see page 6 on the index page.

i. Update the index and table of contents pages, compare your document to the pages from the completed document shown in FIGURE 9-22, save the document, submit all files to your instructor, close it, then exit Word.

FIGURE 9-22

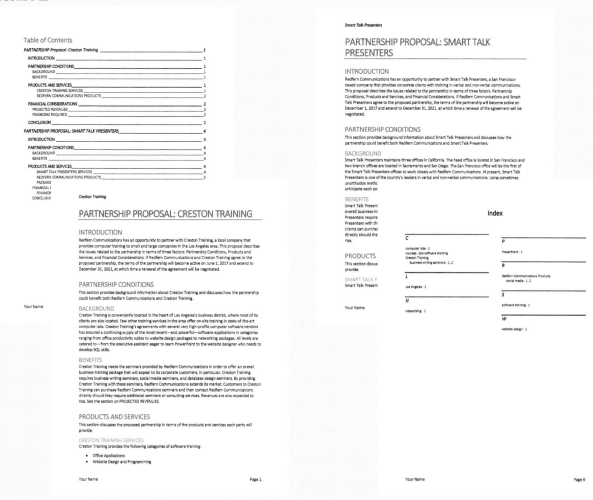

Independent Challenge 1

You work in the Finance Department of Fitness Forever. Recently, the owners began selling franchises. Your supervisor asks you to format a report that details the development of these franchise operations.

a. Start Word, open the file WD 9-5.docx from the drive and folder where you store your Data Files, then save it as **WD 9-Fitness Forever Franchises**.

b. In Outline view, organize the document as shown in the following table, starting with Introduction, followed by Scope of the Report, and then moving column by column. Text that you designate as headings will be formatted with the blue font color.

heading	level	heading	level	heading	level
Introduction	1	Gary Gleeson	2	Phoenix Clientele	3
Scope of the Report	2	Franchise Locations	1	Houston	2
Owner Information	1	Dallas	2	Houston Clientele	3
Marilyn Janzen	2	Dallas Clientele	3	Opening Schedules	2
Teresa Sanchez	2	Phoenix	2		

c. Show level 3, then switch the order of Houston and its subtext so it follows Dallas and its subtext.

d. In Print Layout view, collapse all the headings to show only Level 1 headings, then expand the headings again.

e. Show the Navigation pane, then move the Opening Schedules heading so it appears just below Franchise Locations.

f. Starting from the top of the document, find the text listed in column 1, and mark all instances of that text as Main entry or subentry for an index, based on the information in columns 2 and 3.

find this text	main entry	subentry
Dallas	Location	Dallas
Houston	Location	Houston
Phoenix	Location	Phoenix
Marilyn Janzen	Owner	Marilyn Janzen
Teresa Sanchez	Owner	Teresa Sanchez
Gary Gleeson	Owner	Gary Gleeson
marketing vice president	marketing vice president	
mall	mall	

g. Find Finest Fitness, then make it a main entry with a cross-reference to **Marilyn Janzen**.

h. Insert a new page at the end of the document, type **Index** as the page title, format it with bold, a larger font size, and center alignment, then generate an index using the Fancy format.

i. At the top of the document, insert a Next Page section break, then on the new first page, insert an automatic table of contents using the Automatic Table 1 style.

j. Add and format a header and footer so that the completed document appears as follows:

location	contents
Table of Contents page (section 1)	Footer containing your name at the left margin and Page i at the right margin
Page 1 and the following pages of the report (section 2)	Footer containing your name at the left margin and Page 1 at the right margin
Page 1 and the following pages of the report (section 2)	Header containing the text Fitness Forever Franchises, centered, and bold

k. Scroll through the document to ensure the headers and footers are correct, click the Index heading when you get to the Index page, update the index, then save and close the document.

l. Open the document and click the Resume Reading message to return to the Index page, then scroll up and update the table of contents page and then change the format to Fancy.

m. Save the document, submit your file to your instructor, then close the document.

Independent Challenge 2

As the program assistant at Marchand College in Vermont, you are responsible for creating and formatting reports about programs at the college. You work in Outline view to create a report for a college program of your choice.

a. Start Word, create a new blank document, then save it as **WD 9-Program Information Report**.

b. In Outline view, enter the headings and subheadings for the report as shown in the table starting with **Program Overview**, followed by **Career Opportunities**. You need to substitute appropriate course names for Course 1, Course 2, and so on. For example, courses in the first term of a business studies program could be **Introduction to Business, Accounting Basics**, and so on. You choose the program and courses you want to include in the report.

heading	level	heading	level
Program Overview	1	[Enter name for Course 1]	3
Career Opportunities	2	[Enter name for Course 2]	3
Admission Requirements	2	Second Term	2
Program Content	1	[Enter name for Course 1]	3
First Term	2	[Enter name for Course 2]	3

c. Enter one paragraph of appropriate body text for the following headings: Program Overview, Career Opportunities, and Admission Requirements, then enter short course descriptions for each of the four courses included in the document. For ideas, refer to college websites and catalogs. Collapse all the headings to Level 1.

d. In Print Layout view, add a cover page using the style of your choice. Include the name of the program as the title (for example, **Business Program**), the name of the college (**Marchand College, Vermont**) as the subtitle, and your name where indicated. Remove all other content controls. If the cover page style you choose does not include a content control for a subtitle, enter the information as text and format it attractively.

e. Insert a Next Page section break following the cover page, then insert a page break in the body of the report to spread the report over two pages if it does not already flow to two pages.

f. Format the cover page (section 1) with no header and no footer.

g. Go to the section 2 header and deselect the Different First Page check box in the Options group so that you see Header - Section 2 in the tab below the header area, not First Page Header - Section 2. Format the section 2 header with a right-aligned page number starting with Page 1 using the 1, 2, 3 format. Make sure you deselect Link to Previous.

h. Format the section 2 footer with the name of the program left-aligned in the footer and your name right-aligned. Make sure you deselect Link to Previous.

i. Insert a Next Page section break above the Program Overview heading.

j. Scroll up to the new blank page, then insert an automatic table of contents in either the Automatic Table 1 or Automatic Table 2 format. Replace the table of contents with a custom table of contents that uses the format of your choice (for example, Classic, Fancy, etc.).

k. Customize the table of contents so that it includes only Heading 1 at TOC level 1 and Heading 3 at TOC level 2. None of the Heading 2 headings should appear in the revised table of contents.

l. Double click in the header area on the table of contents page, then delete Page 1.

m. Go to the next section (Section 3), click the Link to Previous button to deselect it, then insert Page 1 right-aligned. Be sure the page number starts at 1. Verify that the header appears on both pages of the section 3 header and that the footer appears on all pages except the cover page.

n. Update the table of contents, save the document, close it, then submit your file to your instructor.

Independent Challenge 3

Many businesses post job opportunities on their websites. You can learn a great deal about opportunities in a wide range of fields just by checking out the job postings on these websites. You decide to create a document that describes a selection of jobs available on an employment website of your choice.

a. Use your favorite search engine and the search phrase **job search** to find websites that post jobs online. Popular sites include glassdoor.com, workopolis.com, and monster.com.

b. On the website you chose, identify two job categories (e.g., Social Media and Online Marketing, or Accounting and Communications) and then find two jobs that appeal to you and that you may even wish to apply for. You can choose to search for jobs in your home town or in another location.

c. Create a new document in Word, then save it as **WD 9-Online Job Opportunities**.

d. In Outline view, set up the document starting with the name of the employment website (e.g., monster.com) and followed by Job Category 1 as shown in the table. (*Note*: You need to enter specific text for headings such as **Marketing** for Job Category 1 and **Marketing Assistant** for Job Posting.)

heading	level
Name of website	1
Job Category 1	2
Job Name	3
Summary of Job Posting	Body Text
Job Category 2	2
Job Name	3
Summary of Job Posting	Body Text

e. Complete the Word document with information you find on the website. Include a short description of each job you select, and list some of the job duties. You do not need to include the entire job posting. If you copy selected text from a website, make sure you clear the formatting so that the text in the document is formatted only with the Normal style. Edit any copied text so that only the most important information is included.

f. Divide the document into two pages so that each job category posting appears on one page.

g. Above the first job posting, enter the following text: **Following is a description of two jobs that interest me. The first job is a[n] [name of job] and the second job is a[n] [name of job]. Information in this report was copied from the [website name or URL] website on [date].** Make sure you substitute the job titles you've identified for [name of job], the name of the website name or its URL for the [website name or URL], and the date you created the report for [date].

h. Make each job title a cross-reference to the appropriate heading in your outline, then test the cross-references.

i. Insert a header that starts on page 1 and includes the text **Online Job Opportunities for** followed by your name, then include a page number on each page of the document in the footer.

j. Save the document and submit the file to your instructor, then close the document.

Independent Challenge 4: Explore

You work for an author who has just written a series of vignettes about her travels in Europe. The author plans to publish the vignettes and accompanying illustrations in a book called *Creative Journeys*. She has written a short proposal to present to publishers. As her assistant, your job is to create a proposal that includes three of the vignettes, each with a unique header. You will further explore the features available in Outline view by using some of the tools available in the Master Document group.

a. Start Word, open WD 9-6.docx, then save it as **WD 9-Creative Journeys Proposal**. Keep the document open.

b. Open WD 9-7.docx, save it as **WD 9-Creative Journeys Venice**, then close it.

c. Open WD 9-8.docx, save it as **WD 9-Creative Journeys Seville Flamenco**, then close it.

d. Open WD 9-9.docx, save it as **WD 9-Creative Journeys Roman Rain**, then close it.

e. From the WD 9-Creative Journeys Proposal document, switch to Outline view, then promote the Creative Journeys Overview heading to Level 1.

f. Click at the end of the outline on the first blank line after the last sentence.

g. Click the Show Document button in the Master Document group.

h. Click the Insert button in the Master Document group, navigate to the location where you saved the files for this challenge, double-click WD 9-Creative Journeys Venice, then click No if prompted.

i. Repeat step h to insert WD 9-Creative Journeys Seville Flamenco as a subdocument, then repeat step h once more to insert WD 9-Creative Journeys Roman Rain as a subdocument. The master document now consists of introductory text and three subdocuments.

j. Click the Collapse Subdocuments button in the Master Document group, then click OK in response to the message. Scroll down as needed to verify that each document is now a hyperlink.

k. Press the [Ctrl] key and click the hyperlink to the Creative Journeys Venice document. View the document, then close it.

l. Click the Expand Subdocuments button, then close Outline view.

m. At the top of the document, add a Next Page section break, then at the top of the new blank page, insert one of an automatic table of contents using the style of your choice.

n. Replace the table of contents with a custom table of contents that uses the Formal format.

o. Insert a footer at the bottom of the table of contents page that includes your name at the left margin and the page number formatted in lower case Roman numerals (i) at the right margin.

p. Go to section 2, deselect Link to Previous, then format the page numbers so they start at 1.

q. Create a header for each section as shown in the table below. Make sure you deselect Link to Previous each time you go to a new section. Enter the text for each header at the left margin and format it with italic. The document contains a total of eight sections and five pages. Note that extra sections are inserted when you insert subdocuments to ensure that each subdocument starts on its own page.

section	contains	header text
1	Table of Contents	no header
2	Overview	Creative Journeys Overview
3	Venice	Venice
5	Seville Flamenco	Seville Flamenco
7	Roman Rain	Roman Rain

r. Update the table of contents, save the document, submit a copy of all four documents to your instructor, then close the document. Note that when you open the document again, the three subdocuments will appear as hyperlinks.

Visual Workshop

Open the file WD 9-10.docx from the drive and folder where you store your Data Files, then save it as **WD 9-Book Marketing Plan**. Modify the outline so that it appears as shown in FIGURE 9-23. You need to change the order of some sections. In Print Layout view, insert a Next Page section break at the beginning of the document, then generate a table of contents using the Automatic Table 2 format and the custom Distinctive format with four levels showing. *Hint*: Click the Show levels list arrow in the Table of Contents dialog box, then click 4. Insert a page break before Promotion in the text, then create a footer in section 2 (remember to deselect Link to Previous) with your name at the left margin and a page number that starts with 1 at the right margin. Make sure no text appears in the footer in section 1. Update the table of contents so that it appears as shown in FIGURE 9-24. Save and close the document, then submit the file to your instructor.

FIGURE 9-23

⊕ Introduction
    ⊕ Product Description
        ⊖ Target Audience
    ⊕ Marketing Goals
        ⊖ Promotion Goals
        ⊖ Distribution Goals
⊕ Pricing and Distribution
    ⊖ E-Book Pricing
    ⊖ Paperback Pricing
    ⊕ Sales Outlets
        ⊕ Bookstores
            ⊖ *Chain Bookstores*
            ⊖ *Independent Bookstores*
        ⊖ Libraries
        ⊖ Direct Sales
⊕ Promotion
    ⊖ Advertising
    ⊖ Author Platform
    ⊖ Contests and Giveaways
—

FIGURE 9-24

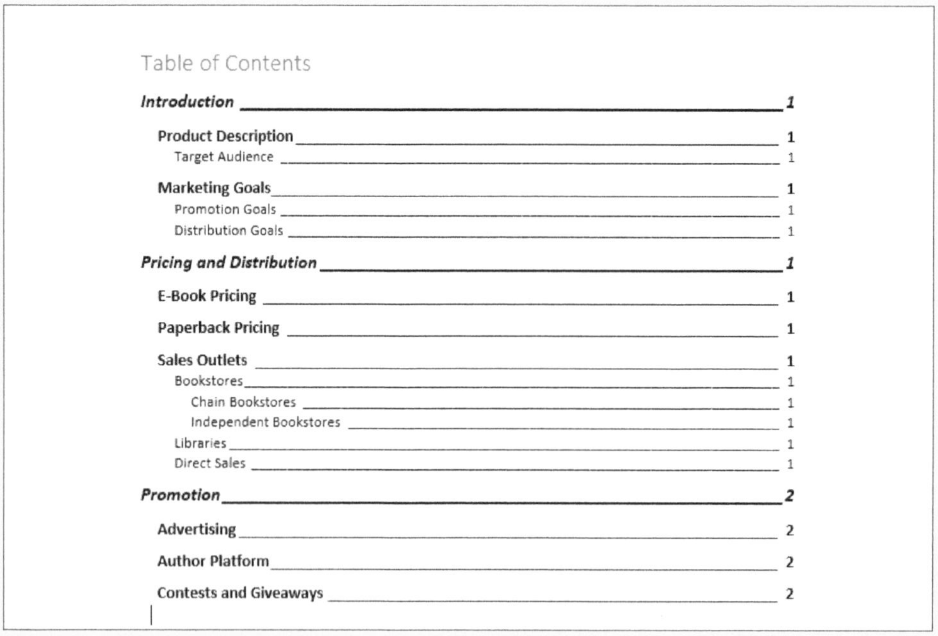

Table of Contents

Introduction	*1*
Product Description	1
Target Audience	1
Marketing Goals	1
Promotion Goals	1
Distribution Goals	1
Pricing and Distribution	*1*
E-Book Pricing	1
Paperback Pricing	1
Sales Outlets	1
Bookstores	1
Chain Bookstores	1
Independent Bookstores	1
Libraries	1
Direct Sales	1
Promotion	*2*
Advertising	2
Author Platform	2
Contests and Giveaways	2

Working with Styles and Templates

> **CASE** As a special projects assistant at Reason2Go, you've been asked to produce profiles of the top R2G experience leaders for distribution at the company's annual meeting. To save time, you modify styles in an existing profile, create new styles, and then develop a template on which to base the profile for each experience leader.

Module Objectives

After completing this module, you will be able to:

- Explore styles and templates
- Modify built-in styles
- Create paragraph styles
- Create character and linked styles
- Create list styles
- Create table styles
- Create a Style Set
- Manage styles
- Create and attach a template

Files You Will Need

WD 10-1.docx	WD 10-8.docx
WD 10-2.docx	WD 10-9.docx
WD 10-3.docx	WD 10-10.docx
WD 10-4.docx	WD 10-11.docx
WD 10-5.docx	WD 10-12.docx
WD 10-6.docx	WD 10-13.docx
WD 10-7.docx	

Explore Styles and Templates

Learning Outcomes
- Define why to use styles
- Identify style types
- Define why to use templates

You use styles and templates to automate document-formatting tasks and to ensure consistency among related documents. A **style** consists of formats such as font, font size, and alignment that you name and then save as one set. For example, the settings for a style called Main Head could be Arial font, 14-pt font size, bold, and a bottom border. Each time you apply the Main Head style to selected text, all format settings included in the style are applied. A **template** is a file that contains the basic structure of a document, such as the page layout, headers and footers, styles, graphic elements, and boilerplate text. **CASE** ➤ *You plan to use styles to format an experience leader profile and then create a template for a series of experience leader profiles. You start by familiarizing yourself with styles and templates.*

DETAILS

Information about how you can use styles and templates to help you format documents quickly and efficiently follows:

About Styles

- You apply styles to selected text from the Styles gallery on the Home tab. Using styles helps you save time in two ways. First, when you apply a style, you apply a set of formats all at once. Second, if you modify a style by changing one or more of the formats associated with that style, all text formatted with that style is updated automatically. For example, suppose you apply a style named "Section Head" to each section head in a document. If you then modify the formatting associated with the Section Head style, Word automatically updates all the text formatted with the Section Head style. As discussed in Module 9, default heading styles are applied automatically to headings and subheadings when you work in Outline view to create the structure of a document. For example, the Heading 1 style is applied to text associated with Level 1, the Heading 2 style is applied to text associated with Level 2, and so on. You can modify a default heading style or you can create a new heading style.

- In Word, you can choose from 17 built-in Style Sets on the Design tab or you can create your own Style Set. Each **Style Set** contains **styles** for text elements such as headings, titles, subtitles, and lists. All of the styles associated with a Style Set are stored in the **Styles gallery** on the Home tab.

- Word includes five major style categories. A **paragraph style** includes font formats, such as font and font size, and paragraph formats, such as line spacing or tabs. You use a paragraph style when you want to format all of the text in a paragraph at once. A **character style** includes character formats only, such as font, font size, and font color. You use a character style to apply character format settings only to selected text within a paragraph. A **linked style** contains both a character style and a paragraph style. Either the character style or the paragraph style is applied depending on whether you click in a paragraph to select the entire paragraph or you select specific text. A **table style** specifies how you want both the table grid and the text in a table to appear. A **list style** allows you to format a series of lines with numbers or bullets and with selected font and paragraph formats. FIGURE 10-1 shows a document formatted with the five style types. These styles have been saved in a new Style Set called R2G Profiles.

About Templates

- Every document you create in Word is based on a template. Most of the time, this template is the **Normal template** because the Normal template is loaded automatically when you start a new document. The styles assigned to the Normal template, such as Normal, Title, Heading 1, Heading 2, and so on, are the styles you see in the Styles gallery on the Home tab when you open a new document.

- Word includes a number of built-in templates. In addition, you can access a variety of templates online. You can also create a template, and then attach that template to an existing document. Once the template is attached to a document, the styles associated with that template become available, which means you can apply the styles included with the template to text in the document.

FIGURE 10-1: A document formatted with five style types

A **paragraph** style applies formatting to a paragraph, which might be one or more lines of text

A **Linked** style applies formatting to text within a paragraph or to an entire paragraph depending on how text is selected

A **List** style adds bullets or numbers to a series of paragraphs

A **Character** style applies formatting to text within a paragraph; this character style includes blue and italic

A **Table** style applies formatting to a table grid and table text

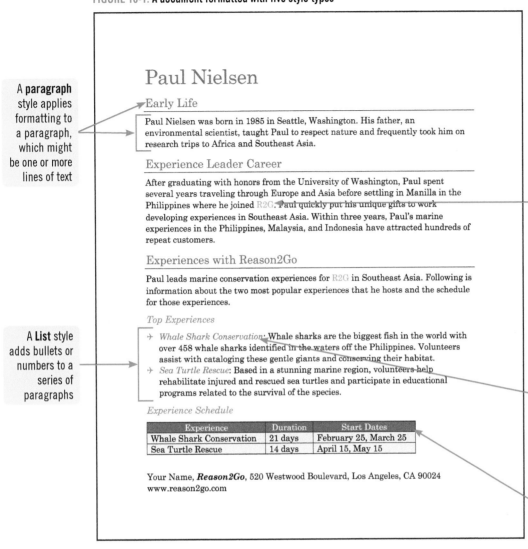

Paul Nielsen

Early Life

Paul Nielsen was born in 1985 in Seattle, Washington. His father, an environmental scientist, taught Paul to respect nature and frequently took him on research trips to Africa and Southeast Asia.

Experience Leader Career

After graduating with honors from the University of Washington, Paul spent several years traveling through Europe and Asia before settling in Manilla in the Philippines where he joined R2G. Paul quickly put his unique gifts to work developing experiences in Southeast Asia. Within three years, Paul's marine experiences in the Philippines, Malaysia, and Indonesia have attracted hundreds of repeat customers.

Experiences with Reason2Go

Paul leads marine conservation experiences for R2G in Southeast Asia. Following is information about the two most popular experiences that he hosts and the schedule for those experiences.

Top Experiences

→ *Whale Shark Conservation*: Whale sharks are the biggest fish in the world with over 458 whale sharks identified in the waters off the Philippines. Volunteers assist with cataloging these gentle giants and conserving their habitat.
→ *Sea Turtle Rescue*: Based in a stunning marine region, volunteers help rehabilitate injured and rescued sea turtles and participate in educational programs related to the survival of the species.

Experience Schedule

Experience	Duration	Start Dates
Whale Shark Conservation	21 days	February 25, March 25
Sea Turtle Rescue	14 days	April 15, May 15

Your Name, **Reason2Go**, 520 Westwood Boulevard, Los Angeles, CA 90024
www.reason2go.com

Understanding Themes, Style Sets, and the Normal style

Style Sets are not the same as themes, but they work with themes to provide you with an almost unlimited range of formatting options. A theme is a set of unified design elements including theme colors, theme fonts for body text and headings, and theme effects for graphics. When you apply a theme to a document, you can further modify the appearance of the text, colors, and graphics in the document by applying one of the 17 built-in Style Sets. You can then modify the appearance even further by changing the settings of the styles associated with the Style Set.

Text that you type into a blank document is formatted with the Normal style from the default Style Set associated with the Office 2016 theme until you specify otherwise. By default, text formatted with the Normal style uses the 11-point Calibri font and is left-aligned, with a line spacing of 1.08 within a paragraph and 8 pt After Paragraph spacing. When you select a new Style Set, the styles associated with that Style Set are applied to the document.

Modify Built-in Styles

Learning Outcomes
• Modify a style
• Update a style

Word includes built-in styles, such as the Normal, Title, Heading 1, and Heading 2 styles, for each built-in Style Set. The styles associated with the active Style Set are displayed in the Styles gallery on the Home tab. These styles along with other, less frequently used styles, can also be accessed from the Styles task pane. You can personalize documents by modifying any style. **CASE** *You modify the Normal style currently applied to all body text in a profile of Paul Nielsen, an experience leader based in the Philippines. You also modify the Heading 1 style and the Title style.*

STEPS

1. **Start Word, open the file** WD 10-1.docx **from the location where you store your Data Files, save the file as** WD 10-Profile of Paul Nielsen, **click in the paragraph below "Early Life," right-click** Normal **in the Styles gallery on the Home tab, then click** Modify

   The Modify Style dialog box opens, as shown in FIGURE 10-2.

2. **Click the** Font list arrow **in the Formatting area, scroll to and select** Century Schoolbook, **click the** Font Size list arrow, **click** 12, **then click** OK

   The Modify Style dialog box closes, and all body text in the document is modified automatically to match the new settings for the Normal style.

3. **Select the** Early Life **heading, then use the commands in the Font group to change the font to** Century Schoolbook **and the font color to** Orange, Accent 2, Darker 50%

   You made changes to the character formatting for the selected text.

4. **Be sure the Early Life heading is still selected, click the** Borders list arrow ⊞ ▾ **in the Paragraph group, click the** Bottom Border button, **click the** Layout tab, **click the** Spacing Before text box **in the Paragraph group, type** 10, **click the** Spacing After text box, **type** 6, **then press [Enter]**

   You made changes to the paragraph formatting for the selected text.

5. **Click the** Home tab, **right-click** Heading 1 **in the Styles gallery to open the menu shown in** FIGURE 10-3, **then click** Update Heading 1 to Match Selection

   The Heading 1 style is updated to match both the character and the paragraph formatting options you applied to the Early Life heading. All headings in the text that are formatted with the Heading 1 style are updated to match the new Heading 1 style. Notice that the Heading 1 style in the Styles gallery shows a preview of the formatting associated with the Heading 1 style.

6. **Click the launcher** 🗔 **in the Styles group to open the Styles task pane**

   By default, the **Styles task pane** lists a selection of the styles available in the active Style Set. The Styles task pane also includes options for creating new styles, using the Style Inspector, and managing styles.

7. **Select** Paul Nielsen **at the top of the page, point to** Title **in the Styles task pane, click the list arrow that appears, then click** Modify

8. **Change the font to** Century Schoolbook, **click the** Font Color list arrow **(currently shows Automatic as the color), select the** Orange, Accent 2, Darker 50% **color box, then click** OK

   The selected text in the document and the preview of the Title style in the Styles gallery changes to show the new settings.

9. **Save the document**

   You have used three methods to modify the formatting attached to a style. You can modify the style using the Modify Styles dialog box, you can make changes to text associated with a style and then update the style to match the selected text, or you can modify a style from the Styles task pane. You generally use this last method when you need to modify a style that does not appear in the Styles gallery.

FIGURE 10-2: Modify Style dialog box

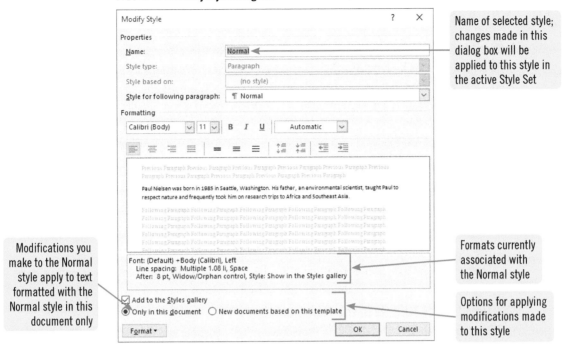

Name of selected style; changes made in this dialog box will be applied to this style in the active Style Set

Modifications you make to the Normal style apply to text formatted with the Normal style in this document only

Formats currently associated with the Normal style

Options for applying modifications made to this style

FIGURE 10-3: Updating the Heading 1 style with new formats

Heading 1 text with new formatting applied

Update Heading 1 to Match Selection

Heading 1 text before Heading 1 style updated to match selection above

Create Paragraph Styles

Learning
Outcomes
• Create a
  paragraph style
• Apply a paragraph
  style

Instead of using the built-in styles, you can create your own styles. You can base a new style on an existing style or you can base it on no style. When you base a style on an existing style, both the formatting associated with the existing style and any new formatting you apply are associated with the new style. One type of style you can create is a paragraph style. A paragraph style is a combination of character and paragraph formats that you name and store as a set. You can create a paragraph style and then apply it to any paragraph. Any line of text followed by a hard return is considered a paragraph, even if the line consists of only one or two words. **CASE** ▶ *You create a new paragraph style called Leader Subtitle and apply it to two headings in the document.*

STEPS

1. **Scroll to and select the heading** Top Experiences, **then click the** New Style button 🔲 **at the bottom of the Styles task pane**

   The Create New Style from Formatting dialog box opens. You use this dialog box to enter a name for the new style, select a style type, and select the formatting options you want associated with the new style.

2. **Type** Leader Subtitle **in the Name text box**

   The Leader Subtitle style is based on the Normal style because the selected text is formatted with the Normal style. When you create a new style, you can base it on the style applied to the selected text if a style has been applied to that text, another style by selecting a style in the Style based on list box, or no preset style. You want the new style to also include the formatting associated with the Normal style so you leave Normal as the Style based on setting.

3. **Click** 12 **in the Font Size text box, type** 13, **click the** Italic button, **click the** Font Color list arrow, **click the** Orange, Accent 2, Darker 25% color box, **then click** OK

4. **Select the heading** Experience Schedule **(you may need to scroll down), then click** Leader Subtitle **in the Styles task pane**

   The new Leader Subtitle style is applied to two headings in the document.

5. **Click the** Show Preview check box **at the bottom of the Styles task pane to select it if it is not already selected**

   With the Show Preview option active, you can quickly see the formatting associated with each of the predefined styles and the new style you created.

6. **Move your mouse over** Leader Subtitle **in the Styles task pane to show the settings associated with the Leader Subtitle style**

   The Styles task pane and the document are shown in FIGURE 10-4.

7. **Click** Options **at the bottom of the Styles task pane, then click the** Select styles to show list arrow

   The Style Pane Options dialog box appears as shown in FIGURE 10-5. You can choose to show recommended styles (the default setting), all the styles associated with the Style Set, or just the styles currently in use.

8. **Click** In use, **then click** OK

   Only the styles currently applied to the document are displayed in the Styles task pane.

9. **Save the document**

FIGURE 10-4: Formatting associated with Leader Subtitle style

FIGURE 10-5: Style Pane Options dialog box

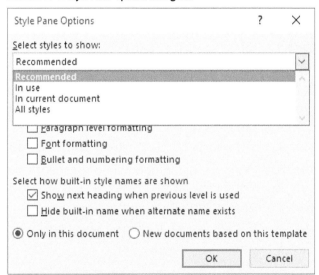

Identifying style formatting

Word includes two ways to quickly determine exactly what styles and formatting are applied to selected text. These methods are useful when you apply a style to text and not all the formatting changes you expect to be made are made. To find out why, use the Style Inspector or the Reveal Formatting task pane. To open the Style Inspector, click the text formatted with the style, then click the Style Inspector button at the bottom of the Styles task pane. The **Style Inspector** lists the styles applied to the selected text and indicates if any extra formats were applied that are not included in the style. For example, another user could apply formatting such as bold and italic that is not included in the style. You can clear these formats by clicking one of the four buttons along the right side of the Style Inspector or by clicking Clear All to remove all extra formats. If you need to investigate even further, you can click the Reveal Formatting button at the bottom of the Style Inspector to open the Reveal Formatting task pane. The **Reveal Formatting task pane** lists exactly which formats are applied to the character, paragraph, and section of the selected text.

Create Character and Linked Styles

Learning Outcomes
• Create a character style
• Create a linked style

A character style includes character format settings—such as font, font size, bold, and italic—that you name and save as a style. You apply a character style to selected text within a paragraph. Any text in the paragraph that is not formatted with the character style is formatted with the currently applied paragraph style. A linked style includes both character formats and paragraph formats, just like a paragraph style. The difference is that you can apply the paragraph style associated with a linked style to an entire paragraph or you can apply the character style associated with the linked style to selected text within a paragraph. Linked styles are therefore very versatile. **CASE** ➤ *You create a character style called Experiences to apply to each Experience name and a linked style called R2G to apply to each instance of R2G.*

STEPS

QUICK TIP
You use [Ctrl] to select all the text you wish to format with a new style.

1. **Select the text** Whale Shark Conservation **in the section below Top Experiences, press and hold [Ctrl], then select the text** Sea Turtle Rescue **at the beginning of the next paragraph**

2. **Click the** New Style button 🔲 **at the bottom of the Styles task pane, type** Experiences **in the Name text box, click the** Style type list arrow, **then click** Character

QUICK TIP
You can modify an existing character style in the same way you modify a paragraph style.

3. **Select these character formatting settings: the** Century Schoolbook font, 12 pt, Italic, **and the** Orange, Accent 2, Darker 25% font color, **click** OK, **then click away from the text to deselect it**
   The text you selected is formatted with the Experiences character style.

4. **Select** Whale Shark Conservation, **change the font color to** Blue, Accent 5, Darker 25%, **right-click** Experiences **in the Styles task pane to open the menu shown in** FIGURE 10-6, **then click** Update Experiences to Match Selection
   Both of the phrases formatted with the Experiences character style are updated.

QUICK TIP
Mouse over the options in the Text Effects gallery, then use the ScreenTips to help you make the correct selection.

5. **Scroll up and select** R2G **in the paragraph below Experience Leader Career, click the** Text Effects and Typography list arrow 🅰️ **in the Font group, then select the** Fill – Blue, Accent 1, Shadow **(first row, second column)**

6. **Right-click the selected text, click** Styles **on the Mini toolbar, then click** Create a Style
   The Create New Style from Formatting dialog box opens.

7. **Type** R2G **as the style name, click** Modify, **then click the** Center button
   In the Create New Style from Formatting dialog box, you see that the Linked (paragraph and character) style type is automatically assigned when you create a new style from selected text. The style you created includes character formatting (the text effect format) and paragraph formatting (center alignment).

TROUBLE
Drag the dialog box up as needed until you see the OK button.

8. **Click** OK, **click anywhere in the paragraph under Early Life, then click** R2G **in the Styles task pane**
   The entire paragraph is formatted with the R2G style, as shown in FIGURE 10-7. Both the character formatting and the paragraph formatting associated with the R2G linked style are applied to the paragraph, but only the character formatting associated with the R2G linked style is applied to the R2G text in the next paragraph.

9. **Click the** Undo button 🔄 **on the Quick Access toolbar, scroll to the paragraph below the Experiences with Reason2Go heading, select** R2G **in the paragraph, click** R2G **in the Styles task pane, then save the document**

FIGURE 10-6: Updating the Experiences character style

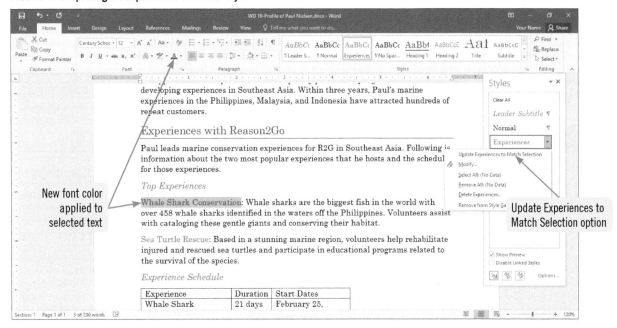

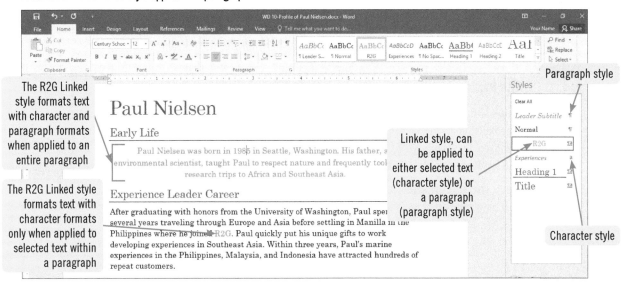

Identifying paragraph, character, and linked styles

Style types are identified in the Styles task pane by different symbols. Each paragraph style is marked with a paragraph symbol: ¶. You can apply a paragraph style just by clicking in any paragraph or line of text and selecting the style. The most commonly used predefined paragraph style is the Normal style. Each character style is marked with a character symbol: a. You apply a character style by clicking anywhere in a word or by selecting a phrase within a paragraph.

Built-in character styles include Emphasis, Strong, and Book Title. Each linked style is marked with both a paragraph symbol and a character symbol: ¶a. You can click anywhere in a paragraph to apply the linked style to the entire paragraph, or you can select text and then apply only the character formats associated with the linked style to the selected text. Predefined linked styles include Heading 1, Title, and Quote.

Create List Styles

Learning Outcomes
• Create a list style
• Modify a list style

A list style includes settings that format a series of paragraphs so they appear related in some way. For example, you can create a list style that adds bullet characters to paragraphs or sequential numbers to a list of items. **CASE** ▸ *You create a list style called Experience List that includes a special bullet character.*

STEPS

1. **Click to the left of** Whale Shark Conservation **in the Top Experiences section, then click the** New Style button ⊞ **at the bottom of the Styles task pane**

2. **Type** Experience List **as the style name, click the** Style type list arrow, **then click** List
   You can also click the Multilevel List button ⊞ in the Paragraph group on the Home tab, and then click Define New List Style to open the Define New List Style dialog box and create a new style.

3. **Click the** Bullets button ⊟, **then click the** Symbol button ⊠
   The symbol dialog box opens. You use this dialog box to insert symbols.

4. **Click the** Font list arrow, **scroll down and click** Wingdings **if it is not already selected, double-click the number in the** Character code text box, **type** 81, **then click** OK

5. **Click the** Font Color list arrow, **then click** Blue, Accent 5
   The Create New Style from Formatting dialog box appears as shown in FIGURE 10-8.

6. **Click** OK
   The paragraph is formatted with the Experience List list style. As part of the Experience List list style, a blue plane has been added as the bullet symbol at the beginning of the list item.

QUICK TIP
List styles are stored in the List Styles area of the Multilevel List gallery in the document, not in the Styles task pane.

7. **Click** Sea **in the phrase "Sea Turtle Rescue", then click the** Multilevel List button ⊞ **in the Paragraph group**

8. **Click the** Experience List **style in the List Styles area**
   The bullet character of a blue plane is added, the text is indented, and the spacing above the paragraph is removed. By default, Word removes spacing between paragraphs formatted with a list style, which is part of the List Paragraph style. When you create a list style, the List style type is based on the List Paragraph style.

9. **Save the document**
   The formatted list appears as shown in FIGURE 10-9.

FIGURE 10-8: List style formatting selections

FIGURE 10-8: **List style formatting selections**

Wingdings font selected

Bullets button

List formatting applied to 1st level only; symbol used for bullet

Description of formats applied to Experience List style

Color list arrow

Symbol button

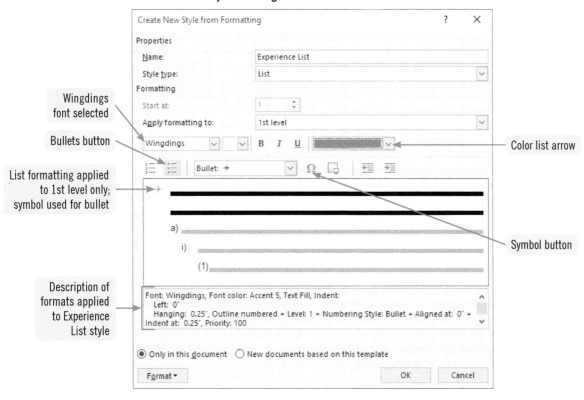

FIGURE 10-9: **Paragraphs formatted with the Experience List style**

Styles pane includes all character, paragraph, and linked styles, but not list styles

Multilevel List list arrow; click to see the Multilevel List gallery, including new list styles

Experience List list style

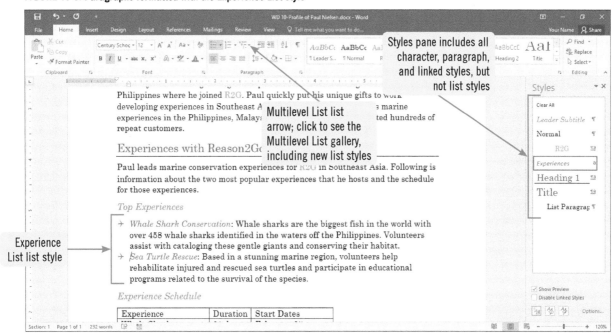

Create Table Styles

Learning Outcomes
• Create a table style
• Modify a table style

You use tables to clarify information in a visually appealing way. A table style includes formatting settings for the table grid and table text. When you have a document containing several tables, you can create a consistent look by applying the same table style to each table. **CASE** ▸ *You create a table style called Experience Schedule.*

STEPS

1. **Scroll down and click in the table, then click the** table move handle ⊞ **at the upper-left corner of the table to select the table**

2. **Click the** New Style button ▦ **, then type** Experience Schedule **in the Name text box**

3. **Click the** Style type list arrow, **then click** Table
    The Create New Style from Formatting dialog box changes to show formatting options for a table.

4. **Refer to** FIGURE 10-10**: select the** Century Schoolbook font, 12 pt font size, **a** 1 pt border width, **and** Blue, Accent 5, Lighter 80% fill color, **then click the** All Borders button

5. **Click the** Apply formatting to list arrow, **then click** Header row

6. **Change the font color to** White, Background 1 **and the fill color to** Blue, Accent 5, Darker 50%, **click the** Align list arrow, **click the** Align Center button, **then click** OK
    The table is formatted with the new Experience Schedule table style, which includes a modified header row.

7. **Double-click one of the** column dividers **in the table so all text in each row fits on one line**

8. **Click the** Table Tools Design tab, **right-click the currently selected table style (far-left selection), click** Modify Table Style, **click the** Apply formatting to list arrow, **click** Header row, **change the fill color to** Orange, Accent 2, Darker 50%, **then click** OK
    The table is modified, as shown in FIGURE 10-11.

9. **Save the document**

FIGURE 10-10: **Table style formatting selections**

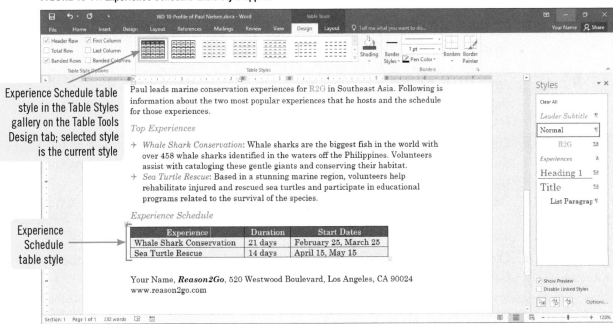

Table text font size

Table text font

Border style

Border weight

Border color

All Borders button

Apply Formatting to list arrow

Fill Color

Alignment list arrow

FIGURE 10-11: **Experience Schedule table style applied**

Experience Schedule table style in the Table Styles gallery on the Table Tools Design tab; selected style is the current style

Experience Schedule table style

Paul leads marine conservation experiences for R2G in Southeast Asia. Following is information about the two most popular experiences that he hosts and the schedule for those experiences.

Top Experiences

→ *Whale Shark Conservation*: Whale sharks are the biggest fish in the world with over 458 whale sharks identified in the waters off the Philippines. Volunteers assist with cataloging these gentle giants and conserving their habitat.
→ *Sea Turtle Rescue*: Based in a stunning marine region, volunteers help rehabilitate injured and rescued sea turtles and participate in educational programs related to the survival of the species.

Experience Schedule

Experience	Duration	Start Dates
Whale Shark Conservation	21 days	February 25, March 25
Sea Turtle Rescue	14 days	April 15, May 15

Your Name, **Reason2Go**, 520 Westwood Boulevard, Los Angeles, CA 90024
www.reason2go.com

Create a Style Set

Once you have formatted a document with a selection of styles that includes both new and existing styles, you can save all the styles as a new Style Set. You can then apply the Style Set to format other documents. **CASE** ▶ *You create a new Style Set called R2G Profiles, and then apply it to another profile.*

STEPS

1. **Press [Ctrl][Home] to move to the top of the document, click the Design tab, then click the More button ⟱ in the Document Formatting group to open the gallery of Style Sets**

2. **Click Save as a New Style Set**
   The Save as a New Style Set dialog box opens to the default location where Style Sets are saved. The Save as type is set to Word Templates (*.dotx), which is the default format for a Word template.

3. **Type R2G Profiles in the File name text box, then click Save**

4. **Click the More button ⟱ in the Document Formatting group again, move your mouse over the Style Set thumbnail that appears under Custom to show the name of the Style Set as shown in FIGURE 10-12, then click a word in the document to close the gallery**
   The R2G Profiles Style Set is now one of the Style Sets you can use to format other documents.

5. **Click the Colors button in the Document Formatting group, move the mouse over the various color schemes to see how the document changes, scroll to and click Red Violet, then save the document**
   The color scheme for the document has changed.

6. **Open the file WD 10-2.docx from the location where you store your Data Files, save it as WD 10-Profile of Jane Chow, click the Home tab, then click the More button ⟱ in the Styles group**
   Jane Chow's profile is currently formatted with one of the 17 built-in Style Sets. The styles associated with that Style Set are shown in the Styles pane. For example, the Title style is applied to "Jane Chow", and the Heading 1 style is applied to the "Early Life", "Experience Leader Career", and "Experiences with Reason2Go" headings.

7. **Click the Design tab, click the More button ⟱ in the Document Formatting group to show the gallery of Style Sets, then click the R2G Profiles Style Set thumbnail under Custom**
   The R2G Profiles Style Set is now available in Jane Chow's profile, and all the new styles you created in previous lessons, except the Experience List list style and the Experience Schedule table style, are available in the Styles gallery and the Styles task pane.

8. **Click the Home tab, apply the Leader Subtitle and Experiences styles from the Styles Gallery to the text as shown in FIGURE 10-13**
   You applied styles associated with the R2G Profiles Style Set to document text. Notice that the Red Violet color scheme you applied to Paul Nielsen's profile is not applied. Color schemes are not saved with a Style Set. You must reapply the color scheme.

9. **Click the Design tab, click the Colors button in the Document Formatting group, click Red Violet, then save the document**
   You will learn more about managing styles and applying the R2G style, the Experience List style, and the Experience Schedule style in the next lesson.

FIGURE 10-12: R2G Profiles Style Set

FIGURE 10-13: Applying styles from the R2G Profiles Style Set

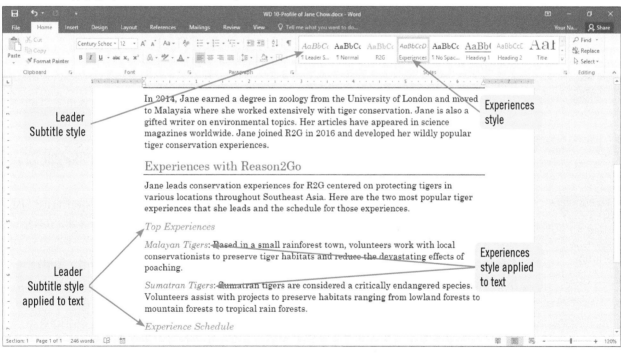

Manage Styles

Learning
Outcomes
• Find and replace
styles
• Copy styles
between
documents

You can manage styles in many ways. For example, you can rename and delete styles, find and replace styles, and copy styles from one document to another document. After you create list and table styles, you must copy them from the source file (the document where you created the styles) to the target file (the document where you want to use the styles). **CASE** *You use Find and Replace to find each instance of R2G and replace it with the same text formatted with the R2G style, then copy the Experience List and the Experience Schedule styles from Paul Nielsen's profile (source file) to Jane Chow's profile (target file).*

STEPS

1. Press [Ctrl][Home], click the Home tab, click Replace in the Editing group, type R2G in the Find what text box, press [Tab], then type R2G in the Replace with text box

2. Click More, click Format, click Style, click R2G Char, click OK, click Replace All, click OK, then click Close

   R2G is formatted with the R2G Char version of the R2G linked style. Notice that only the character formats associated with the R2G style were applied to R2G.

3. Click the launcher 🔲 in the Styles group to open the Styles task pane, click the Manage Styles button 🖋 at the bottom of the Styles task pane to open the Manage Styles dialog box, then click Import/Export to open the Organizer dialog box

   You copy styles from the document shown in the left side of the Organizer dialog box (the source file) to a new document that you open in the right side of the Organizer dialog box (the target file). By default, the target file is the Normal template. To copy between files you create, the source and destination files must be stored in the same folder for the copy function to work.

4. Click Close File under the list box on the left, click Open File, then navigate to the location where you store your files

5. Click the All Word Templates list arrow, select All Word Documents as shown in FIGURE 10-14, click WD 10-Profile of Paul Nielsen.docx, then click Open

   The styles assigned to Paul Nielsen's appear in the list box on the left side. This document contains the Experience List and Experience Schedule styles.

6. Click Close File under the list box on the right, click Open File, navigate to the location where you store your files, show all Word documents, click WD 10-Profile of Jane Chow.docx, then click Open

7. Scroll the list of styles on the left side of the Organizer dialog box, click Experience List, press and hold [Ctrl], click Experience Schedule to select both styles (see FIGURE 10-15), click Copy, then click Close

8. Select the two Experience descriptions (from the heading Malayan Tigers through the heading Sumatran Tigers), click the Multilevel List button ⸬▾ in the Paragraph group, then click the Experience List style shown under List Styles

9. Select the table, click the Table Tools Design tab, click the Experience Schedule table style, adjust column widths as needed so no lines wrap, enter your name where indicated, then save and close the document

   The file WD 10-Profile of Paul Nielsen is again the active document.

FIGURE 10-14: **Selecting All Word Documents as the file type**

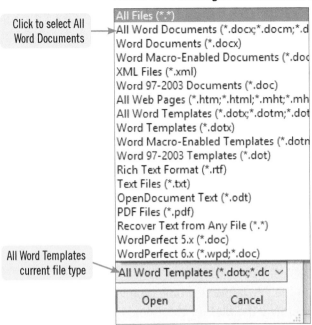

Click to select All Word Documents

All Word Templates current file type

FIGURE 10-15: **Managing styles using the Organizer dialog box**

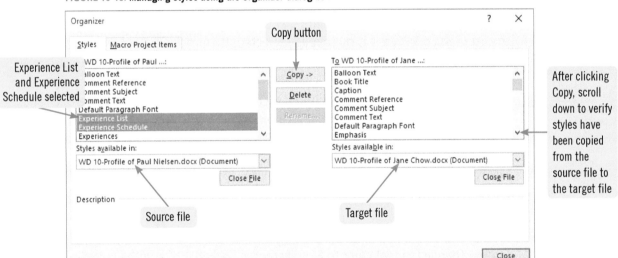

Experience List and Experience Schedule selected

Copy button

Source file

Target file

After clicking Copy, scroll down to verify styles have been copied from the source file to the target file

More ways to manage styles

To rename a style, right-click it in the Styles task pane, click Modify, type a new name, then press [Enter]. To delete a style, right-click the style, then click Delete [Style name]. The style is deleted from the Styles task pane, but it is not deleted from your computer. Click the Manage Styles button 🖉 at the bottom of the Styles task pane, select the style to delete, click Delete, then click OK to close the Manage Styles dialog box.

Create and Attach a Template

Learning Outcomes
• Create a template
• Attach a template
• Modify a template

A quick way to use all the styles contained in a document, including list and table styles, is to create a template. A template contains the basic structure of a document, including all the paragraph, character, linked, list, and table styles. You can create a template from an existing document, or you can create a template from scratch. Once you have created a template, you can attach it to a document. The Style Set and all the styles, including the List and Table styles, are then available to format the document to which the template is attached. **CASE** ▶ *You save the Paul Nielsen profile as a template, modify the template, and then attach the template to another leader profile, which you then format using the styles in the attached template.*

STEPS

1. **Click the File tab, click Save As, click This PC in the list of Save As locations, click Browse, click the Save as type list arrow, then click Word Template (*.dotx)**
   When you select Word Template, the save location automatically changes to the Custom Office Templates folder in the My Documents folder on your computer.

2. **Select the filename in the File name text box, type WD 10-Profile Template, navigate to the location where you save the files for this book, click Save, then close the template but do not exit Word**
   The file is saved as WD 10-Profile Template.dotx. The .dotx identifies this file as a template file.

3. **Open the file WD 10-3.docx from the location where you store your Data Files, save the file as WD 10-Profile of Annie Jonson, click the Design tab, then change the color scheme to Red Violet**
   You will see the new color scheme when you apply styles to the text in the document.

4. **Click the File tab, click Options, click Customize Ribbon, click the Developer check box in the list of Main Tabs if it is not already selected, then click OK**
   You use the Developer tab to work with advanced features such as attaching the Profile Template to Annie's profile and applying all the new styles you created to the document.

5. **Click the Developer tab on the Ribbon, click Document Template in the Templates group, click Attach, navigate to the location where you store your files, click WD 10-Profile Template.dotx, click Open, click the Automatically update document styles check box, then click OK**
   Now you can apply the styles associated with the WD 10-Profile Template to Annie's profile.

6. **Click the Home tab, apply styles as shown in FIGURE 10-16, then save and close the document**

7. **Click the File tab, click Open, navigate to the location where you saved the template, click WD-Profile Template.dotx, click Open, right-click Heading 1 in the Styles gallery, click Modify, change the font color to Blue, Accent 4, Darker 25% and the font size to 18 pt, click OK, then save and close the template**

8. **Open WD 10-Profile of Annie Jonson, verify that the font color of the Heading 1 text is now blue and 18 pt, add your name where indicated, then save and close the document**
   The heading style updates automatically because the document is attached to the WD 10-Profile Template that you just modified.

9. **Create a new blank document, click the Design tab, click the More button in the ▼ Document Formatting group, right-click the thumbnail under Custom, click Delete, click Yes, click the File tab, click Options, click Customize Ribbon, click the Developer check box to deselect it, click OK, exit Word, then submit all your files to your instructor**
   You delete the R2G Profiles Style Set from the list of Style Sets so only the default Style Sets appear for the next user of your computer system.

FIGURE 10-16: **Annie Jonson's profile formatted with styles**

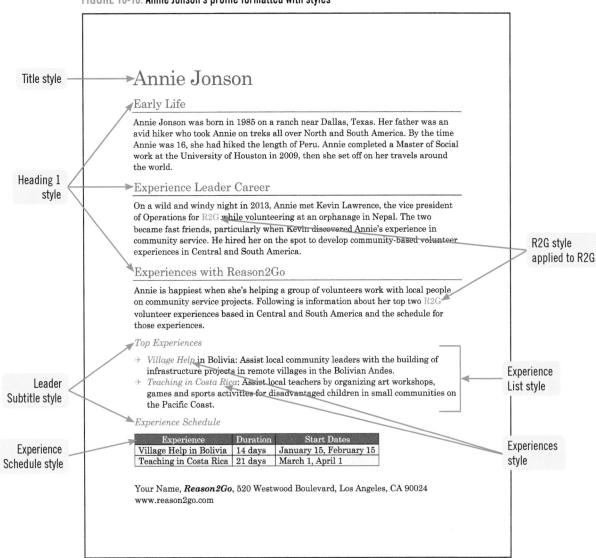

Title style → **Annie Jonson**

Early Life

Annie Jonson was born in 1985 on a ranch near Dallas, Texas. Her father was an avid hiker who took Annie on treks all over North and South America. By the time Annie was 16, she had hiked the length of Peru. Annie completed a Master of Social work at the University of Houston in 2009, then she set off on her travels around the world.

Heading 1 style

Experience Leader Career

On a wild and windy night in 2013, Annie met Kevin Lawrence, the vice president of Operations for R2G while volunteering at an orphanage in Nepal. The two became fast friends, particularly when Kevin discovered Annie's experience in community service. He hired her on the spot to develop community-based volunteer experiences in Central and South America.

R2G style applied to R2G

Experiences with Reason2Go

Annie is happiest when she's helping a group of volunteers work with local people on community service projects. Following is information about her top two R2G volunteer experiences based in Central and South America and the schedule for those experiences.

Top Experiences

Leader Subtitle style

↟ *Village Help* in Bolivia: Assist local community leaders with the building of infrastructure projects in remote villages in the Bolivian Andes.
↟ *Teaching in Costa Rica*: Assist local teachers by organizing art workshops, games and sports activities for disadvantaged children in small communities on the Pacific Coast.

Experience List style

Experience Schedule

Experience	Duration	Start Dates
Village Help in Bolivia	14 days	January 15, February 15
Teaching in Costa Rica	21 days	March 1, April 1

Experience Schedule style

Experiences style

Your Name, **Reason2Go**, 520 Westwood Boulevard, Los Angeles, CA 90024
www.reason2go.com

Using Find and Replace to Format Text

You work in the Find and Replace dialog box to replace text formatted with one set of character formats such as bold and italic and replace it with the same or different text formatted with different formatting. Click More, enter the text to find, click Format and specify the formats attached to the text (for example, Font, Bold), click the Replace tab, enter the text to replace and click Format to specify the new formats, then click Replace All.

Practice

Concepts Review

Identify each of the items in FIGURE 10-17.

FIGURE 10-17

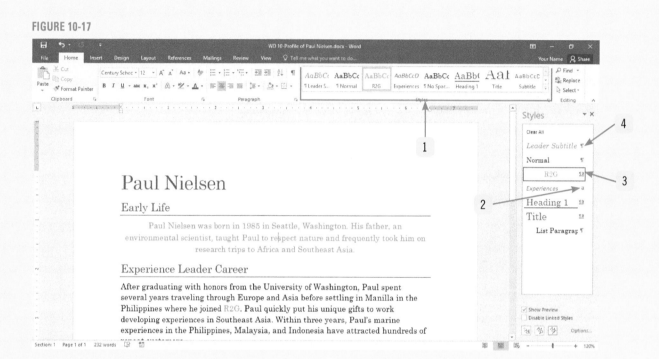

Match each term with the statement that best describes it.

5. **Template**

6. **Organizer dialog box**

7. **Style set**

8. **Character style**

9. **Style**

a. Character formats that you name and store as a set

b. A file that contains the basic structure of a document in addition to selected styles; can be custom made

c. A collection of character, paragraph, and linked styles that is named and available to all documents

d. Used to copy styles from a source document to a target document

e. A collection of saved formats that is used to provide consistent formatting to related items, such as all Heading 1 text

Select the best answer from the list of choices.

10. What is available in the Style Set gallery?

  a. Themes associated with the current Style Set

  b. The Developer tab

  c. Styles associated with the current style set

  d. Colors associated with the current Style Set

11. How do you modify a style?

  a. Right-click the style in the Styles gallery, then click Modify.

  b. Right-click the style in the Styles gallery, then click Revise.

  c. Double-click the style in the Styles task pane.

  d. Click the style in the Styles task pane, then click New Style.

12. Which of the following definitions best describes a paragraph style?

  a. Format settings applied only to selected text within a paragraph

  b. Format settings applied to a table grid

  c. Format settings applied to all text in a paragraph

  d. Format settings applied to the structure of a document

13. Which of the following style types is not saved with a Style Set?

  a. Paragraph style

  b. List style

  c. Linked style

  d. Character style

14. Which dialog box do you use to copy styles from one document to another?

  a. Reveal Formatting dialog box

  b. Styles dialog box

  c. Organizer dialog box

  d. Modify Styles dialog box

15. What is the filename extension for a template?

  a. .dotx

  b. .rtf

  c. .dotc

  d. .dotm

16. Which tab do you use to attach a template to a document?

  a. Insert

  b. References

  c. Page

  d. Developer

Skills Review

1. Modify built-in styles.

  a. Start Word, open the file WD 10-4.docx from the location where you store your Data Files, save it as **WD 10-Jigsaw Puzzles_Shaped**, then open the Styles task pane.

  b. Modify the Normal style by changing the font to Times New Roman and the font size to 12 pt.

  c. Select the Animal Jigsaw Puzzles heading, then change the font to Bookman Old Style, the font size to 18 pt, and the font color to Green, Accent 6, Darker 50%.

  d. Add a border line below the text.

  e. From the Layout tab, change the Before spacing to 6 pt and the After spacing to 6 pt.

  f. Update the Heading 1 style so that it uses the new formats.

  g. Modify the Title style by changing the font to Bookman Old Style and the color to Green, Accent 6, Darker 50%, then save the document.

2. Create paragraph styles.

  a. Scroll to and select the heading "Marketing Plan," then create a new paragraph style called **Operations** that uses the Bookman Old Style font, 14 pt, and italic, and changes the font color to Gold, Accent 4, Darker 25%.

  b. Apply the Operations style to "Summary of New Products."

  c. From the Styles task pane, show only the styles currently in use in the document and make sure the Show Preview check box is selected.

  d. Save the document.

Skills Review (continued)

3. **Create character and linked styles.**

   a. Select "Moose" under Animal Jigsaw Puzzles, then create a new character style named **Jigsaw Puzzle Theme** that uses the Bookman Old Style font, 12 pt, Italic, and the Green, Accent 6, Darker 25% font color.

   b. Apply the Jigsaw Puzzle Theme style to "Orca," "Canada," and "France."

   c. Select "Puzzle Charm" in the first paragraph, apply the Fill - Gold, Accent 4, Soft Bevel text effect, open the Create New Style from Formatting dialog box, name the style **Company**, and select the Linked style type, then select the option to right-align the paragraph.

   d. Apply the Company style to the Moose paragraph, undo the application, then apply the Company style just to the text "Puzzle Charm" in the paragraph above the table.

   e. Save the document.

4. **Create list styles.**

   a. Click to the left of "Moose" under Animal Jigsaw Puzzles, then define a new list style called **Jigsaw Puzzle List**. (*Hint:* Click the Multilevel List button in the Paragraph group on the Home tab, then click Define New List Style.)

   b. Change the list style to Bullet, open the Symbol dialog box, verify the Wingdings character set is active, type **216** in the Character code text box, then change the symbol color to Green, Accent 6, Darker 50%.

   c. Apply the Jigsaw Puzzle List style to each paragraph that describes a jigsaw puzzle: Orca, Canada, and France. (*Hint:* You access the Jigsaw Puzzle List style by clicking the Multilevel List button.)

   d. Save the document.

5. **Create a table styles.**

   a. Select the table at the bottom of the document, then create a new table style called **Jigsaw Puzzle Table**.

   b. Select Gold, Accent 4, Lighter 80% for the fill color, change the border style to 1/2 pt, verify the border color is set to Automatic, then apply All Borders to the table.

   c. Format the header row with bold, the White font color, the Gold, Accent 4, Darker 50% fill color, and Center alignment, then close the Create New Style from Formatting dialog box to apply the new table style to your table.

   d. From the Table Tools Design tab, modify the style by changing the fill color for the Header row to Green, Accent 6, Darker 50%, then save the document.

6. **Create a Style Set.**

   a. From the Design tab, save the current Style Set as **Puzzles**, then view the Puzzles Style Set in the Custom section of the Style Sets gallery.

   b. Change the color scheme to Green, then save the document.

   c. Open the file WD 10-5.docx from the location where you store your Data Files, then save it as **WD 10-Jigsaw Puzzles_3D**.

   d. Apply the Puzzles Style Set to the document, then apply the Green color scheme.

   e. Apply the Jigsaw Puzzle Theme style to the four jigsaw titles (e.g., Tulips, Palm Trees, and so on).

   f. Apply the Operations style to "Marketing Plan," and "Summary of New Products," then save the document.

7. **Manage styles.**

   a. Position the insertion point at the beginning of the document, open the Replace dialog box, enter **Puzzle Charm** in the Find what text box, then enter **Puzzle Charm** in the Replace with text box.

   b. Open the More options area, select the Style option on the Format menu, select the Company Char style, then replace both instances of Puzzle Charm with Puzzle Charm formatted with the Company Char style. (*Hint:* If formatting has been previously assigned to either the Find or Replace text, remove the formatting.)

   c. Open the Manage Styles dialog box from the Styles task pane, then click Import/Export to open the Organizer dialog box.

   d. Close the file in the left pane of the Organizer dialog box, then open the file WD 10-Jigsaw Puzzles_Shaped.docx. Remember to navigate to the location where you save files and to change the Files of type to Word documents.

   e. Close the file in the right pane of the Organizer dialog box, then open the file WD 10-Jigsaw Puzzles_3D.docx.

Skills Review (continued)

f. Copy the Jigsaw Puzzle List and Jigsaw Puzzle Table styles from the WD 10-Jigsaw Puzzles_Shaped document to the WD 10-Jigsaw Puzzles_3D document, then close the Organizer dialog box and return to the document.

g. In the file WD 10-Jigsaw Puzzles_3D.docx, apply the Jigsaw Puzzle List style to each of the four jigsaw puzzle descriptions.

h. Select the table, use the Table Tools Design tab to apply the Jigsaw Puzzle Table style to the table, type your name where indicated at the end of the document, save the document, then close it.

8. Create and attach a template.

a. Save the current document (which should be WD 10-Jigsaw Puzzles_Shaped) as a template called **WD 10-Jigsaw Puzzle Template.dotx** to the location where you save files for this book, then close it.

b. Open the file WD 10-6.docx from the location where your Data Files are located, save the file as **WD 10-Jigsaw Puzzles_Landscape**. (*Hint:* Verify that Word document is selected as the file type.) Then, from the Design tab, select the Green color scheme.

c. Show the Developer tab on the Ribbon, open the Templates and Add-ins dialog box, attach the WD 10-Jigsaw Puzzle Template.dotx template, click the Automatically update document styles check box, then click OK.

d. Apply styles from the Jigsaw Puzzles Style Set that are associated with the WD 10-Jigsaw Puzzle Template so that the WD 10-Jigsaw Puzzle_ Landscape document resembles the other documents you have formatted for this Skills Review. (*Hint:* Remember to apply the Title, Jigsaw Puzzle Theme, Operations, Jigsaw Puzzle List, and Jigsaw Puzzle Table styles, and to apply the Company style to all three instances of "Puzzle Charm.")

e. Enter your name where indicated, then save and close the document.

f. Open WD 10-Jigsaw Puzzle Template, then modify the Title style so that the font is Century Gothic and the font color is Dark Red in the Standard Colors area. Make sure you update the Title style. Save and close the template.

g. Open WD 10-Jigsaw Puzzles_Landscape, verify that the Title style is updated, compare the document to FIGURE 10-18, then close the document.

FIGURE 10-18

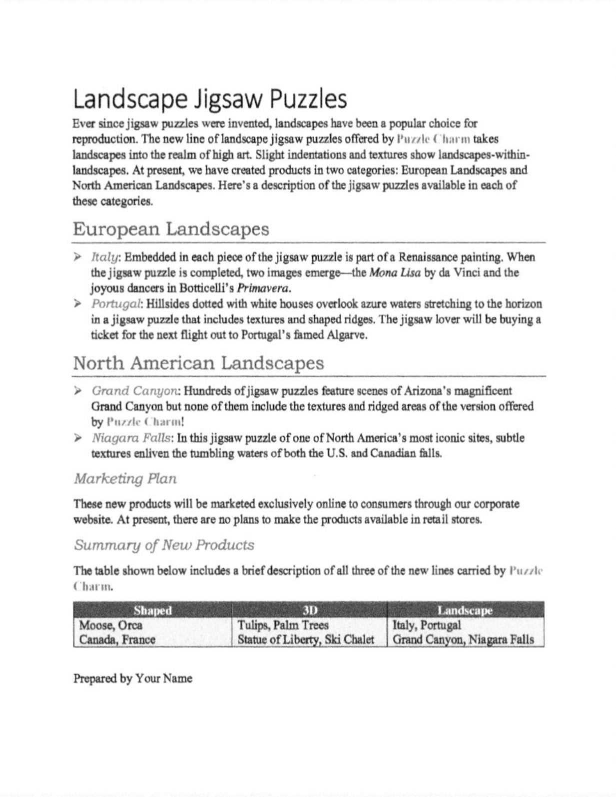

Landscape Jigsaw Puzzles

Ever since jigsaw puzzles were invented, landscapes have been a popular choice for reproduction. The new line of landscape jigsaw puzzles offered by Puzzle Charm takes landscapes into the realm of high art. Slight indentations and textures show landscapes-within-landscapes. At present, we have created products in two categories: European Landscapes and North American Landscapes. Here's a description of the jigsaw puzzles available in each of these categories.

European Landscapes

➢ *Italy:* Embedded in each piece of the jigsaw puzzle is part of a Renaissance painting. When the jigsaw puzzle is completed, two images emerge—the *Mona Lisa* by da Vinci and the joyous dancers in Botticelli's *Primavera*.
➢ *Portugal:* Hillsides dotted with white houses overlook azure waters stretching to the horizon in a jigsaw puzzle that includes textures and shaped ridges. The jigsaw lover will be buying a ticket for the next flight out to Portugal's famed Algarve.

North American Landscapes

➢ *Grand Canyon:* Hundreds of jigsaw puzzles feature scenes of Arizona's magnificent Grand Canyon but none of them include the textures and ridged areas of the version offered by Puzzle Charm!
➢ *Niagara Falls:* In this jigsaw puzzle of one of North America's most iconic sites, subtle textures enliven the tumbling waters of both the U.S. and Canadian falls.

Marketing Plan

These new products will be marketed exclusively online to consumers through our corporate website. At present, there are no plans to make the products available in retail stores.

Summary of New Products

The table shown below includes a brief description of all three of the new lines carried by Puzzle Charm.

Shaped	3D	Landscape
Moose, Orca	Tulips, Palm Trees	Italy, Portugal
Canada, France	Statue of Liberty, Ski Chalet	Grand Canyon, Niagara Falls

Prepared by Your Name

h. In a new blank document in Word, from the Design tab, delete the Jigsaw Puzzles Style Set, then remove the Developer tab from the Ribbon and exit Word.

i. Submit your files to your instructor.

Independent Challenge 1

You are the office manager of Green Times, a company that creates educational materials for courses and workshops in environmental studies. The annual company fitness day is coming soon, and you need to inform the employees about the date and time. You have already typed the text of the staff notice and included some formatting. Now you need to modify some of the styles, create new styles, create a new Style Set and copy a style to a new document, and then use the Style Set to format another staff notice about a different event.

Independent Challenge 1 (continued)

a. Start Word, open the file WD 10-7.docx from the location where you store your Data Files, then save it as **WD 10-Staff Notice of Picnic**.

TABLE 10-1

style name	changes
Title	Arial Black font; 22-pt font size; Blue, Accent 5, Darker 50%
Heading 1	Arial Black font; 14-pt font size; Blue, Accent 5, Darker 25%

b. Modify and update styles as shown in TABLE 10-1.

c. Apply the Heading 1 style to the three headings shown in ALL CAPS in the document.

d. Create a new paragraph style called **Event** that uses the Arial font, 20-pt font size, italic, and Blue, Accent 5, Darker 25%, then apply it to "Company Picnic."

e. Create a new character style called **Green** that uses the Arial font, 14-pt font size, italic, and Green, Accent 6, Darker 25%.

f. Find every instance of "Green Times" and replace it with Green Times formatted with the Green style.

TABLE 10-2

table area	changes
whole table	Fill - Green, Accent 6, Lighter 80%; all borders; 1/2 pt border lines
header row	Fill - Green, Accent 6, Darker 50%; White font color and bold

g. Modify the Green style by changing the font size to 12 pt.

h. Create a table style called **Activities** using formats as shown in TABLE 10-2, then apply the table style to the table in the document.

i. Save the Style Set as **Staff Events**, change the color scheme to Blue Green, type your name where indicated, then save the document (and keep it open).

j. Open the file WD 10-8.docx, save the document as **WD 10-Staff Notice of Holiday Party**, apply the Staff Events Style Set, then change the color scheme to Blue Green.

k. Save the file, then open the Organizer dialog box from the Manage Styles dialog box. (*Hint:* Click Import/Export.)

l. In the Organizer dialog box, make WD 10-Staff Notice of Picnic the source file and WD 10-Staff Notice of Holiday Party the target file. Remember to select All Word Documents as the file type when opening the files.

m. Copy the Activities table style from the file WD 10-Staff Notice of Picnic file to the WD 10-Staff Notice of Holiday Party file, then close the Organizer dialog box.

n. Apply styles to selected headings and text in WD 10-Staff Notice of Holiday Party to match the Staff Notice of Picnic document. (*Hint:* You need to apply the Event, Heading 1, and Green styles, as well as the Activities table style. Note that you can use Find and Replace to find every instance of "Green Times" and replace it with Green Times formatted with the Green character style.)

o. Type your name where indicated, then save the document.

p. Remove the Staff Events Style Set from the list of Style Sets, then submit the files to your instructor.

Independent Challenge 2

As the owner of the Pacific Sands Bistro, a vegetarian café in Carmel, California, you need to create two menus—one for spring and one for fall. You have already created unformatted versions of both the spring menu and the fall menu. Now you need to format text in the spring menu with styles, save the styles in a new Style Set called Menus, then use the Menus Style Set to format text in the fall version of the menu. You also need to work in the Organizer dialog box to copy the list and table styles you created for the spring menu to the fall version of the menu.

a. Start Word, open the file WD 10-9.docx from the location where you store your Data Files, then save it as **WD 10-Pacific Sands Bistro Spring Menu**. Apply the Slipstream color scheme.

Independent Challenge 2 (continued)

b. Select the title (Pacific Sands Bistro Spring Menu), apply these formats: Berlin Sans FB, 18 pt, a font color of Green, Accent 3, Darker 50%, and Center alignment, then create a new linked style called **Menu Title** based on these formats. (*Hint:* Right-click the formatted text, click the Styles button on the Mini toolbar, click Create a Style, type Menu Title, then click OK. You can verify that the style is a linked style by clicking Modify in the Create New Style from Formatting dialog box.)

c. Select Appetizers, apply the formats Berlin Sans FB, 14 pt, italic, a font color of Green, Accent 3, Darker 25%, then create a new linked style from the selection called **Menu Category**.

d. Apply the Menu Category style to each of the remaining main headings: Soups and Salads, Entrees, Desserts, and Opening Times.

e. Click to the left of Brie cheese (the first appetizer), then create a new list style called **Bistro Menu Item** that includes a bullet character from Wingdings symbol 123 (a stylized flower) that is colored Green, Accent 3, Darker 50%.

f. Click the Multilevel List button, right-click the new Bistro Menu Item style in the List Styles area, click Modify, then in the Modify Style dialog box, click Format (bottom left), click Numbering, click More (bottom left), click the Add tab stop at: check box, select the contents of the text box, type **5.5**, click OK, then click OK.

g. Apply the Bistro Menu Item list style (remember to click the Multilevel List button) to all the menu items in each category.

h. Save the styles in a Style Set called **Menus**.

i. Click anywhere in the table, then create a new table style called **Bistro Times** that fills the table cells with Green, Accent 3, Lighter 80% and includes border lines, and then format the header row with the corresponding dark green fill color and the white font color, bold, and centering.

j. Type your name where indicated at the bottom of the document, then save the document and keep it open.

k. Open the file WD 10-10.docx, save it as **WD 10-Pacific Sands Bistro Fall Menu**, then apply the Menus Style Set.

l. Format the appropriate headings with the Menu Title and Menu Category styles. Note that the Bistro Menu Items list style and the Bistro Times table styles are not saved with the Menus Style Set. You copy them separately in a later step.

m. Change the color scheme to the Red Orange color scheme.

n. Save the file, then open the Organizer dialog box from the Manage Styles dialog box.

o. In the Organizer dialog box, make WD 10-Pacific Sands Bistro Spring Menu the source file and WD 10-Pacific Sands Bistro Fall Menu the target file. Remember to select All Word Documents as the file type when opening the files.

p. Copy the Bistro Menu Item list style and the Bistro Times table style from the file WD 10-Pacific Sands Bistro Spring Menu file to the WD 10-Pacific Sands Bistro Fall Menu file, then close the Organizer dialog box.

q. In the Fall menu document, apply the Bistro Menu Item list style to the first appetizer (Old cheddar cheeses).

r. Click the Multilevel List button, right-click the Bistro Menu Item style, click Modify, then change the bullet symbol for the Menu Item style to Wingdings 124 (a dark flower symbol).

s. Apply the updated Bistro Menu Item list style to all the menu items, apply the Bistro Times table style to the table, type your name where indicated, then remove the Menus style from the list of Style Sets.

t. Save the documents, submit all files to your instructor, then close all files.

Independent Challenge 3

As a student in the marketing program at your local community college, you have volunteered to create a design for a class newsletter and another classmate has volunteered to write text for the first newsletter, which is to be distributed in December. First, you create a template for the newsletter, then you apply the template to the document containing the newsletter text.

a. Open the file WD 10-11.docx, then save it as a template called **WD 10-Newsletter Template.dotx** to the location where you save files for this book.

Independent Challenge 3 (continued)

b. Enter text and create styles as shown in FIGURE 10-19. (*Hint:* Use the text in bold for the style names.)

FIGURE 10-19

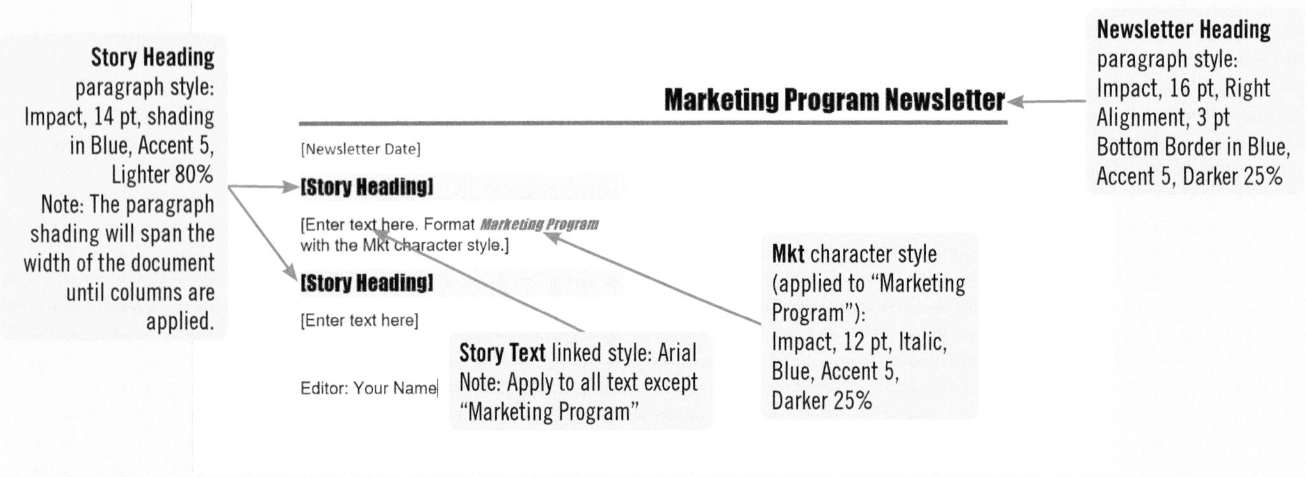

Story Heading paragraph style: Impact, 14 pt, shading in Blue, Accent 5, Lighter 80% Note: The paragraph shading will span the width of the document until columns are applied.

Newsletter Heading paragraph style: Impact, 16 pt, Right Alignment, 3 pt Bottom Border in Blue, Accent 5, Darker 25%

Marketing Program Newsletter

[Newsletter Date]

[Story Heading]

[Enter text here. Format *Marketing Program* with the Mkt character style.]

[Story Heading]

[Enter text here]

Editor: Your Name|

Story Text linked style: Arial Note: Apply to all text except "Marketing Program"

Mkt character style (applied to "Marketing Program"): Impact, 12 pt, Italic, Blue, Accent 5, Darker 25%

c. Click to the left of the first [Story Heading], then create two columns from this point forward. (*Hint:* Click the Layout tab, click the Columns button in the Page Setup group, click More Columns, then in the Columns dialog box, click Two in the Presets section, click the Apply to list arrow, select This point forward, then click OK.)

d. Type your name where indicated, then save and close the template.

e. Open the file WD 10-12.docx, save it as a Word document called **WD 10-Newsletter_December**, show the Developer tab on the Ribbon, attach the WD 10-Newsletter Template.dotx to the document, verify that styles will update automatically, then apply styles and formatting as follows: apply the Newsletter Heading style to the newsletter title, the Story Heading style to all four headings, the Story Text style to all paragraphs of text that are not headings, and the Mkt style to Marketing Program (*Hint:* Use the Find Next, not Replace All, Replace feature to replace three instances of Marketing Program in the story text (but do not replace Marketing Program in the Newsletter Heading.)

f. Apply the two-column format starting at the Class Projects heading. (*Note:* You need to apply the two-column format because options related to the structure of a document that are saved with a template are lost when you attach the template to an existing document.)

g. Click at the end of the document (following your name), click the Layout tab, click Breaks, then click Continuous to balance the columns in the newsletter.

h. Save and close the document.

i. Open the file WD 10-Newsletter Template.dotx (*Hint:* Be sure to open the template using the File menu. Do not double-click it.)

j. Modify the Newsletter Heading style so the font size is 20 pt, modify the Mkt character style so the font size is 11 pt and the color is Orange, Accent 2, then save and close the template.

k. Open WD 10-Newsletter_December, verify the changes to the Newsletter Heading and Mtk styles, then close the document.

l. Remove the Developer tab from the Ribbon, then submit all files to your instructor.

Independent Challenge 4: Explore

From Microsoft Word, you can access templates that you can use to create and then customize hundreds of different types of documents from calendars to business proposals to trip itineraries. You use keywords to search for a template, select and create it in Word, and then modify it for your own purposes. You also explore more options in the Styles task pane. *(Note: To complete these steps your computer must be connected to the Internet.)*

a. Start Word, open a new blank document, click the File tab, click New, click in the Search text box, type **itinerary**, then press [Enter].

b. Select the template Business trip itinerary, click Create, then save the document as **WD 10-Business Trip Itinerary.docx.**

c. Enter your name where indicated above the itinerary table.

d. Select and then delete the Phone number and Travel time columns in the itinerary table, then widen the Comments column so its right edge is even with the border line above the itinerary title.

e. Complete the itinerary table with the information shown in FIGURE 10-20.

FIGURE 10-20

Business Trip Itinerary | Your Name

Date	Depart from	Depart time	Destination	Arrival time	Destination address	Comments
June 10	New York, NY	20:00	London, UK	07:00 (June 11)	Hyde Park Hotel	Meet with Jane Harrison for lunch
June 15	London, UK	10:00	Paris, France	14:40	Hotel LeRiche	Train arrives at the Gare du Nord
June 20	Paris, France	9:00	Rome, Italy	11:00	Hotel da Vinci	Fly from Orly airport

f. Open the Styles task pane, then click the Style Inspector button at the bottom of the task pane.

g. Click to the left of Business Trip Itinerary and notice that the Style Inspector lists the Title style as the current paragraph formatting.

h. Click Date and notice that the Style Inspector lists the Normal style with the addition of Bold and the Background 1 color. You can use the Style Inspector to determine exactly what formatting is applied to selected text and then clear the formatting if you wish.

i. Click the Reveal Formatting button at the bottom of the Style Inspector and if necessary, move the Styles task pane so you can see the Reveal Formatting task pane that opens to the right of your screen. The Reveal Formatting task pane lists all the formatting applied to the document.

j. Scroll down the Reveal Formatting task pane to view all the settings. You can click the arrow to the left of any heading to see additional settings.

k. Click TABLE STYLE once under the Table heading to open the Table AutoFormat dialog box. In this dialog box you can quickly select a new built-in table style for the table.

l. Click Grid Table 4 - Accent 2 (orange), then click OK.

m. Close the Reveal Formatting, Styles, and Style Inspector task panes.

n. Select the Orange Red color scheme, save and close the document, exit Word, then submit the file to your instructor.

Visual Workshop

Create a new document, then type the text and create the tables shown in FIGURE 10-21. Save the file as **WD 10-Price List_Flowers Forever**. Do not include any formatting. Select the Green Yellow color scheme, apply the Title style to the title, then modify the Title style so that it appears as shown in FIGURE 10-21. Note that all the colors are variations of the Green Yellow color scheme, Green, Accent 3, and the font style for the title and headings is Comic Sans MS font (or a similar font). Apply the Heading 1 style to the names of the price lists, then modify the Heading 1 style so that it appears as shown in FIGURE 10-21. Create a new Style Set called **Prices**. Create a table style called **Price List** that formats each table as shown in FIGURE 10-21, then modify the column widths as shown. Save the document. Open WD 10-13.docx, save it as **WD 10-Price List_Bundles of Bouquets**, apply the Prices Style Set, copy the Price List table style from WD 10-Price List_Flowers Forever to WD 10-Price List_Bundles of Bouquets, then apply styles and modify column widths so the document resembles the document shown in FIGURE 10-21. Apply the Green Yellow color scheme. Save and close the documents, then submit both files to your instructor.

FIGURE 10-21

Flowers Forever

Gift Basket Price List

Product #	Gift Basket	Price
3300	Thanksgiving Celebration	$65.00
3500	Spring Awakening	$75.00
4000	My Special Valentine	$90.00
4500	New Baby	$60.00

Potted Plants Price List

Product #	Potted Plant	Price
5000	Pink Orchid	$30.00
7780	Mini Peppers	$25.00
7790	Fig Tree	$50.00
7792	Rubber Plant	$40.00
7795	Areca Palm	$30.00

Prepared by Your Name

Getting Started with Excel 2016

CASE You have been hired as an assistant at Reason2Go (R2G), a company that allows travelers to make a difference in the global community through voluntourism, while having a memorable vacation experience. You report to Yolanda Lee, the vice president of finance. As Yolanda's assistant, you create worksheets to analyze data from various divisions of the company, so you can help her make sound decisions on company expansion, investments, and new voluntourism opportunities.

Module Objectives

After completing this module, you will be able to:

- Understand spreadsheet software
- Identify Excel 2016 window components
- Understand formulas
- Enter labels and values and use the AutoSum button
- Edit cell entries
- Enter and edit a simple formula
- Switch worksheet views
- Choose print options

Files You Will Need

Learning
Outcomes
• Describe the
uses of Excel
• Define key spread-
sheet terms

Understand Spreadsheet Software

Microsoft Excel is the electronic spreadsheet program within the Microsoft Office suite. An **electronic spreadsheet** is an app you use to perform numeric calculations and to analyze and present numeric data. One advantage of a spreadsheet program over pencil and paper is that your calculations are updated automatically, so you can change entries without having to manually recalculate. TABLE 1-1 shows some of the common business tasks people accomplish using Excel. In Excel, the electronic spreadsheet you work in is called a **worksheet**, and it is contained in a file called a **workbook**, which has the file extension .xlsx. **CASE** > *At R2G, you use Excel extensively to track finances and manage corporate data.*

DETAILS

When you use Excel, you have the ability to:

QUICK TIP
You can also use the
**Quick Analysis
tool** to easily create
charts and other
elements that help
you visualize how
data is distributed.

• **Enter data quickly and accurately**

With Excel, you can enter information faster and more accurately than with pencil and paper. FIGURE 1-1 shows a payroll worksheet created using pencil and paper. FIGURE 1-2 shows the same worksheet created using Excel. Equations were added to calculate the hours and pay. You can use Excel to recreate this information for each week by copying the worksheet's structure and the information that doesn't change from week to week, then entering unique data and formulas for each week.

• **Recalculate data easily**

Fixing typing errors or updating data is easy in Excel. In the payroll example, if you receive updated hours for an employee, you just enter the new hours and Excel recalculates the pay.

QUICK TIP
Power users can
perform more
complex analysis
using **Business
Intelligence tools**
such as Power Query
and new forecasting
functions.

• **Perform what-if analysis**

The ability to change data and quickly view the recalculated results gives you the power to make informed business decisions. For instance, if you're considering raising the hourly rate for an entry-level tour guide from $12.50 to $15.00, you can enter the new value in the worksheet and immediately see the impact on the overall payroll as well as on the individual employee. Any time you use a worksheet to ask the question "What if?" you are performing **what-if analysis**. Excel also includes a Scenario Manager where you can name and save different what-if versions of your worksheet.

• **Change the appearance of information**

Excel provides powerful features, such as the Quick Analysis tool, for making information visually appealing and easier to understand. Format text and numbers in different fonts, colors, and styles to make it stand out.

• **Create charts**

Excel makes it easy to create charts based on worksheet information. Charts are updated automatically in Excel whenever data changes. The worksheet in FIGURE 1-2 includes a 3-D pie chart.

• **Share information**

It's easy for everyone at R2G to collaborate in Excel using the company intranet, the Internet, or a network storage device. For example, you can complete the weekly payroll that your boss, Yolanda Lee, started creating. You can also take advantage of collaboration tools such as shared workbooks so that multiple people can edit a workbook simultaneously.

QUICK TIP
The **flash fill** feature
makes it easy to fill a
range of text based
on examples that are
already in your work-
sheet. Simply type
[Ctrl][E] if Excel
correctly matches the
information you want,
and it will be entered
in a cell for you.

• **Build on previous work**

Instead of creating a new worksheet for every project, it's easy to modify an existing Excel worksheet. When you are ready to create next week's payroll, you can open the file for last week's payroll, save it with a new filename, and modify the information as necessary. You can also use predesigned, formatted files called **templates** to create new worksheets quickly. Excel comes with many templates that you can customize.

FIGURE 1-1: Traditional paper worksheet

Reason2Go
Project Leader Divison Payroll Calculator

Name	Hours	O/T Hrs	Hrly Rate	Reg Pay	O/T Pay	Gross Pay
Brucker, Pieter	40	4	16.75	670	134	804
Cucci, Lucia	35	0	12	420	0	420
Klimt, Gustave	40	2	13.25	530	53	583
Lafontaine, Jeanne	29	0	15.25	442.25	0	442.25
Martinez, Juan	37	0	13.2	488.4	0	488.4
Mioshi, Keiko	39	0	21	819	0	819
Shernwood, Burt	40	0	16.75	670	0	670
Strano, Riccardo	40	8	16.25	650	260	910
Wadsworth, Alice	40	5	13.25	530	132.5	662.5
Yamamoto, Johji	38	0	15.5	589	0	589

FIGURE 1-2: Excel worksheet

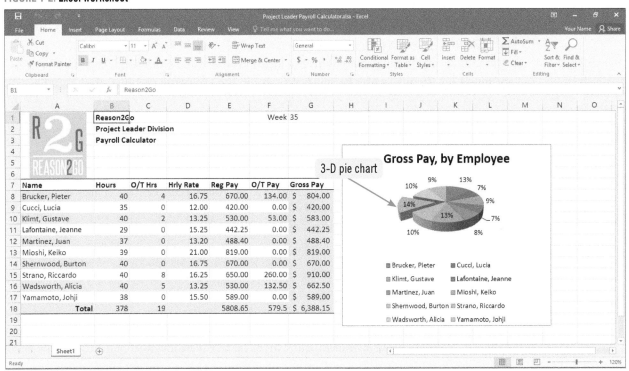

TABLE 1-1: Business tasks you can accomplish using Excel

you can use spreadsheets to	by
Perform calculations	Adding formulas and functions to worksheet data; for example, adding a list of sales results or calculating a car payment
Represent values graphically	Creating charts based on worksheet data; for example, creating a chart that displays expenses
Generate reports	Creating workbooks that combine information from multiple worksheets, such as summarized sales information from multiple stores
Organize data	Sorting data in ascending or descending order; for example, alphabetizing a list of products or customer names, or prioritizing orders by date
Analyze data	Creating data summaries and short lists using PivotTables or AutoFilters; for example, making a list of the top 10 customers based on spending habits
Create what-if data scenarios	Using variable values to investigate and sample different outcomes, such as changing the interest rate or payment schedule on a loan

Identify Excel 2016 Window Components

Learning Outcomes
- Open and save an Excel file
- Identify Excel window elements

To start Excel, Microsoft Windows must be running. Similar to starting any app in Office, you can use the Start button on the Windows taskbar, the Start button on your keyboard, or you may have a shortcut on your desktop you prefer to use. If you need additional assistance, ask your instructor or technical support person. **CASE** ▶ *You decide to start Excel and familiarize yourself with the worksheet window.*

STEPS

1. **Start Excel, click** Open Other Workbooks **on the navigation bar, click** This PC, **then click** Browse **to open the Open dialog box**

2. **In the Open dialog box, navigate to the location where you store your Data Files, click** EX 1-1.xlsx, **then click** Open

   The file opens in the Excel window.

3. **Click the** File tab, **click** Save As **on the navigation bar, then click** Browse **to open the Save As dialog box**

4. **In the Save As dialog box, navigate to the location where you store your Data Files if necessary, type** EX 1-Project Leader Payroll Calculator **in the File name text box, then click** Save

   Using FIGURE 1-3 as a guide, identify the following items:

   - The **Name box** displays the active cell address. "A1" appears in the Name box.
   - The **formula bar** allows you to enter or edit data in the worksheet.
   - The **worksheet window** contains a grid of columns and rows. Columns are labeled alphabetically and rows are labeled numerically. The worksheet window can contain a total of 1,048,576 rows and 16,384 columns. The intersection of a column and a row is called a **cell**. Cells can contain text, numbers, formulas, or a combination of all three. Every cell has its own unique location or **cell address**, which is identified by the coordinates of the intersecting column and row. The column and row indicators are shaded to make identifying the cell address easy.
   - The **cell pointer** is a dark rectangle that outlines the cell you are working in. This cell is called the **active cell**. In FIGURE 1-3, the cell pointer outlines cell A1, so A1 is the active cell. The column and row headings for the active cell are highlighted, making it easier to locate.
   - **Sheet tabs** below the worksheet grid let you switch from sheet to sheet in a workbook. By default, a workbook file contains one worksheet—but you can have as many sheets as your computer's memory allows, in a workbook. The New sheet button to the right of Sheet 1 allows you to add worksheets to a workbook. **Sheet tab scrolling buttons** let you navigate to additional sheet tabs when available.
   - You can use the **scroll bars** to move around in a worksheet that is too large to fit on the screen at once.
   - The **status bar** is located at the bottom of the Excel window. It provides a brief description of the active command or task in progress. **The mode indicator** in the lower-left corner of the status bar provides additional information about certain tasks.

5. **Click cell** A4

   Cell A4 becomes the active cell. To activate a different cell, you can click the cell or press the arrow keys on your keyboard to move to it.

6. **Click cell** B5, **press and hold the mouse button, drag ✛ to cell** B14, **then release the mouse button**

   You selected a group of cells and they are highlighted, as shown in FIGURE 1-4. A selection of two or more cells such as B5:B14 is called a **range**; you select a range when you want to perform an action on a group of cells at once, such as moving them or formatting them. When you select a range, the status bar displays the average, count (or number of items selected), and sum of the selected cells as a quick reference.

FIGURE 1-3: Open workbook

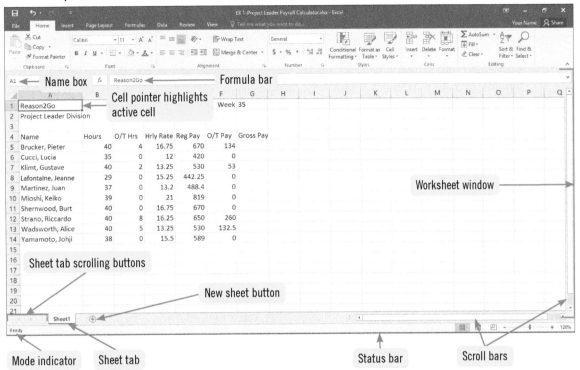

FIGURE 1-4: Selected range

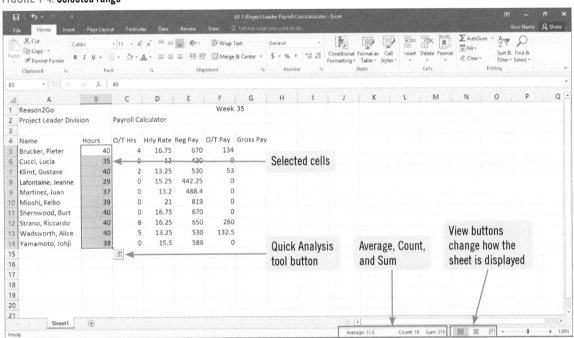

Using OneDrive and Office Online

If you have a Microsoft account, you can save your Excel files and photos in OneDrive, a cloud-based service from Microsoft. When you save files in OneDrive, you can access them on other devices—such as a tablet or smartphone. OneDrive is available as an app on smartphones and tablets, making access simple. You can open files to view them on any device, and you can even make edits to them using **Office Online**, which includes simplified versions of the apps found in the Office 2016 suite. Because Office Online is web-based, the apps take up no computer disk space and you can use them on any Internet-connected device.

Understand Formulas

Learning
Outcomes
• Explain how a
  formula works
• Identify Excel
  arithmetic operators

Excel is a truly powerful program because users at every level of mathematical expertise can make calculations with accuracy. To do so, you use formulas. A **formula** is an equation in a worksheet. You use formulas to make calculations as simple as adding a column of numbers, or as complex as creating profit-and-loss projections for a global corporation. To tap into the power of Excel, you should understand how formulas work. **CASE** *Managers at R2G use the Project Leader Payroll Calculator workbook to keep track of employee hours prior to submitting them to the Payroll Department. You'll be using this workbook regularly, so you need to understand the formulas it contains and how Excel calculates the results.*

STEPS

1. Click cell E5

The active cell contains a formula, which appears on the formula bar. All Excel formulas begin with the equal sign (=). If you want a cell to show the result of adding 4 plus 2, the formula in the cell would look like this: =4+2. If you want a cell to show the result of multiplying two values in your worksheet, such as the values in cells B5 and D5, the formula would look like this: =B5*D5, as shown in FIGURE 1-5. While you're entering a formula in a cell, the cell references and arithmetic operators appear on the formula bar. See TABLE 1-2 for a list of commonly used arithmetic operators. When you're finished entering the formula, you can either click the Enter button on the formula bar or press [Enter].

2. Click cell F5

This cell contains an example of a more complex formula, which calculates overtime pay. At R2G, overtime pay is calculated at twice the regular hourly rate times the number of overtime hours. The formula used to calculate overtime pay for the employee in row 5 is:

O/T Hrs times (2 times Hrly Rate)

In the worksheet cell, you would enter: =C5*(2*D5), as shown in FIGURE 1-6. The use of parentheses creates groups within the formula and indicates which calculations to complete first—an important consideration in complex formulas. In this formula, first the hourly rate is multiplied by 2, because that calculation is within the parentheses. Next, that value is multiplied by the number of overtime hours. Because overtime is calculated at twice the hourly rate, managers are aware that they need to closely watch this expense.

DETAILS

In creating calculations in Excel, it is important to:

- **Know where the formulas should be**

  An Excel formula is created in the cell where the formula's results should appear. This means that the formula calculating Gross Pay for the employee in row 5 will be entered in cell G5.

- **Know exactly what cells and arithmetic operations are needed**

  Don't guess; make sure you know exactly what cells are involved before creating a formula.

- **Create formulas with care**

  Make sure you know exactly what you want a formula to accomplish before it is created. An inaccurate formula may have far-reaching effects if the formula or its results are referenced by other formulas, as shown in the payroll example in FIGURE 1-6.

- **Use cell references rather than values**

  The beauty of Excel is that whenever you change a value in a cell, any formula containing a reference to that cell is automatically updated. For this reason, it's important that you use cell references in formulas, rather than actual values, whenever possible.

- **Determine what calculations will be needed**

  Sometimes it's difficult to predict what data will be needed within a worksheet, but you should try to anticipate what statistical information may be required. For example, if there are columns of numbers, chances are good that both column and row totals should be present.

FIGURE 1-5: Viewing a formula

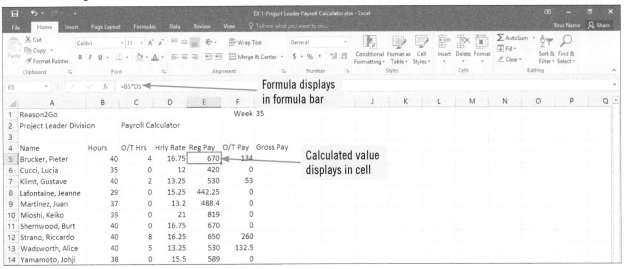

Formula displays in formula bar

Calculated value displays in cell

FIGURE 1-6: Formula with multiple operators

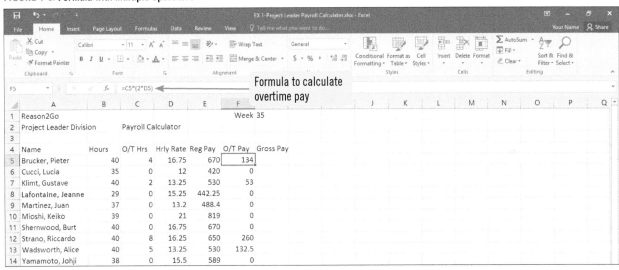

Formula to calculate overtime pay

TABLE 1-2: Excel arithmetic operators

operator	purpose	example
+	Addition	=A5+A7
-	Subtraction or negation	=A5-10
*	Multiplication	=A5*A7
/	Division	=A5/A7
%	Percent	=35%
^ (caret)	Exponent	=6^2 (same as 6^2)

Enter Labels and Values and Use the AutoSum Button

Learning
Outcomes
• Build formulas with
  the AutoSum
  button
• Copy formulas
  with the fill handle

To enter content in a cell, you can type in the formula bar or directly in the cell itself. When entering content in a worksheet, you should start by entering all the labels first. **Labels** are entries that contain text and numerical information not used in calculations, such as "2019 Sales" or "Travel Expenses". Labels help you identify data in worksheet rows and columns, making your worksheet easier to understand. **Values** are numbers, formulas, and functions that can be used in calculations. To enter a calculation, you type an equal sign (=) plus the formula for the calculation; some examples of an Excel calculation are "=2+2" and "=C5+C6". Functions are built-in formulas; you learn more about them in the next module. **CASE** ▶ *You want to enter some information in the Project Leader Payroll Calculator workbook and use a very simple function to total a range of cells.*

STEPS

1. **Click cell A15, then click in the formula bar**

   Notice that the **mode indicator** on the status bar now reads "Edit," indicating you are in Edit mode. You are in Edit mode any time you are entering or changing the contents of a cell.

2. **Type Totals, then click the Enter button ✓ on the formula bar**

   Clicking the Enter button accepts the entry. The new text is left-aligned in the cell. Labels are left-aligned by default, and values are right-aligned by default. Excel recognizes an entry as a value if it is a number or it begins with one of these symbols: +, -, =, @, #, or $. When a cell contains both text and numbers, Excel recognizes it as a label.

3. **Click cell B15**

   You want this cell to total the hours worked by all the trip advisors. You might think you need to create a formula that looks like this: =B5+B6+B7+B8+B9+B10+B11+B12+B13+B14. However, there's an easier way to achieve this result.

4. **Click the AutoSum button Σ in the Editing group on the Home tab on the Ribbon**

   The SUM function is inserted in the cell, and a suggested range appears in parentheses, as shown in FIGURE 1-7. A **function** is a built-in formula; it includes the **arguments** (the information necessary to calculate an answer) as well as cell references and other unique information. Clicking the AutoSum button sums the adjacent range (that is, the cells next to the active cell) above or to the left, although you can adjust the range if necessary by selecting a different range before accepting the cell entry. Using the SUM function is quicker than entering a formula, and using the range B5:B14 is more efficient than entering individual cell references.

5. **Click ✓ on the formula bar**

   Excel calculates the total contained in cells B5:B14 and displays the result, 378, in cell B15. The cell actually contains the formula =SUM(B5:B14), and the result is displayed.

6. **Click cell C13, type 6, then press [Enter]**

   The number 6 replaces the cell's contents, the cell pointer moves to cell C14, and the value in cell F13 changes.

7. **Click cell C18, type Average Gross Pay, then press [Enter]**

   The new label is entered in cell C18. The contents appear to spill into the empty cells to the right.

8. **Click cell B15, position the pointer on the lower-right corner of the cell (the fill handle) so that the pointer changes to ＋, drag ＋ to cell G15, then release the mouse button**

   Dragging the fill handle across a range of cells copies the contents of the first cell into the other cells in the range. In the range B15:G15, each filled cell now contains a function that sums the range of cells above, as shown in FIGURE 1-8.

9. **Save your work**

FIGURE 1-7: Creating a formula using the AutoSum button

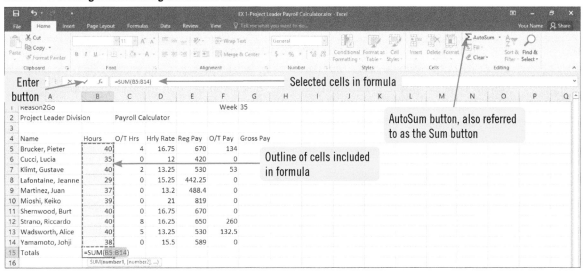

FIGURE 1-8: Results of copied SUM functions

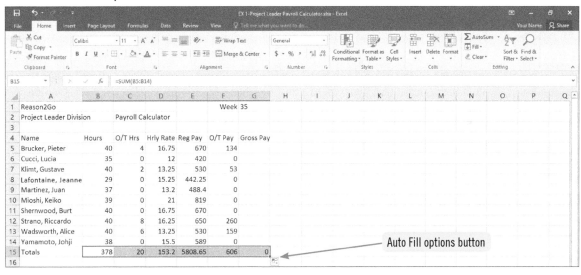

Navigating a worksheet

With over a million cells available in a worksheet, it is important to know how to move around in, or **navigate**, a worksheet. You can use the arrow keys on the keyboard ↑, ↓, →, or ← to move one cell at a time, or press [Page Up] or [Page Down] to move one screen at a time. To move one screen to the left, press [Alt][Page Up]; to move one screen to the right, press

[Alt][Page Down]. You can also use the mouse pointer to click the desired cell. If the desired cell is not visible in the worksheet window, use the scroll bars or use the Go To command by clicking the Find & Select button in the Editing group on the Home tab on the Ribbon. To quickly jump to the first cell in a worksheet, press [Ctrl][Home]; to jump to the last cell, press [Ctrl][End].

Edit Cell Entries

Learning
Outcomes
• Edit cell entries in
the formula bar
• Edit cell entries in
the cell

You can change, or **edit**, the contents of an active cell at any time. To do so, double-click the cell, and then click in the formula bar or just start typing. Excel switches to Edit mode when you are making cell entries. Different pointers, shown in TABLE 1-3, guide you through the editing process. **CASE** *You noticed some errors in the worksheet and want to make corrections. The first error is in cell A5, which contains a misspelled name.*

STEPS

1. **Click cell A5, then click to the right of P in the formula bar**

   As soon as you click in the formula bar, a blinking vertical line called the **insertion point** appears on the formula bar at the location where new text will be inserted. See FIGURE 1-9. The mouse pointer changes to I when you point anywhere in the formula bar.

2. **Press [Delete], then click the Enter button ✓ on the formula bar**

   Clicking the Enter button accepts the edit, and the spelling of the employee's first name is corrected. You can also press [Enter] or [Tab] to accept an edit. Pressing [Enter] to accept an edit moves the cell pointer down one cell, and pressing [Tab] to accept an edit moves the cell pointer one cell to the right.

   > **QUICK TIP**
   > On some keyboards, you might need to press an [F-Lock] key to enable the function keys.

3. **Click cell B6, then press [F2]**

   Excel switches to Edit mode, and the insertion point blinks in the cell. Pressing [F2] activates the cell for editing directly in the cell instead of the formula bar. Whether you edit in the cell or the formula bar is simply a matter of preference; the results in the worksheet are the same.

   > **QUICK TIP**
   > The Undo button allows you to reverse up to 100 previous actions, one at a time.

4. **Press [Backspace], type 8, then press [Enter]**

   The value in the cell changes from 35 to 38, and cell B7 becomes the active cell. Did you notice that the calculations in cells B15 and E15 also changed? That's because those cells contain formulas that include cell B6 in their calculations. If you make a mistake when editing, you can click the Cancel button ✕ on the formula bar *before* pressing [Enter] to confirm the cell entry. The Enter and Cancel buttons appear only when you're in Edit mode. If you notice the mistake *after* you have confirmed the cell entry, click the Undo button ↺ ▾ on the Quick Access toolbar.

   > **QUICK TIP**
   > You can use the keyboard to select all cell contents by clicking to the right of the cell contents in the cell or formula bar, pressing and holding [Shift], then pressing [Home].

5. **Click cell A9, then double-click the word Juan in the formula bar**

   Double-clicking a word in a cell selects it. When you selected the word, the Mini toolbar automatically displayed.

6. **Type Javier, then press [Enter]**

   When text is selected, typing deletes it and replaces it with the new text.

7. **Double-click cell C12, press [Delete], type 4, then click ✓**

   Double-clicking a cell activates it for editing directly in the cell. Compare your screen to FIGURE 1-10.

8. **Save your work**

Recovering unsaved changes to a workbook file

You can use Excel's AutoRecover feature to automatically save (Autosave) your work as often as you want. This means that if you suddenly lose power or if Excel closes unexpectedly while you're working, you can recover all or some of the changes you made since you saved it last. (Of course, this is no substitute for regularly saving your work: this is just added insurance.) To customize the AutoRecover settings, click the File tab, click Options, then click

Save. AutoRecover lets you decide how often and into which location it should Autosave files. When you restart Excel after losing power, a Document Recovery pane opens and provides access to the saved and Autosaved versions of the files that were open when Excel closed. You can also click the File tab, click Open on the navigation bar, then click any file in the Recover Unsaved Workbooks list to open Autosaved workbooks.

FIGURE 1-9: Worksheet in Edit mode

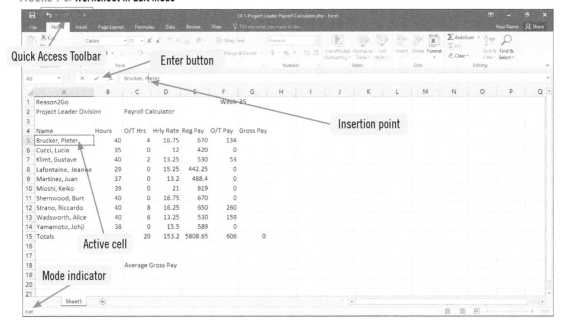

Quick Access Toolbar

Enter button

Insertion point

Active cell

Mode indicator

FIGURE 1-10: Edited worksheet

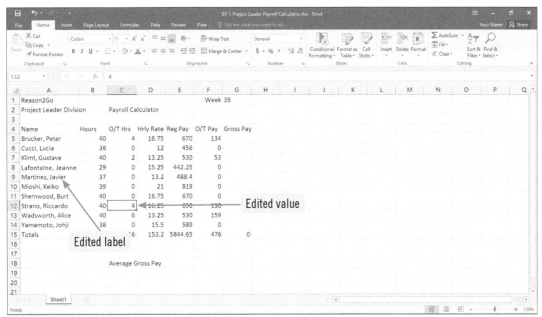

Edited value

Edited label

TABLE 1-3: Common pointers in Excel

name	pointer	use to	visible over the
Normal		Select a cell or range; indicates Ready mode	Active worksheet
Fill handle		Copy cell contents to adjacent cells	Lower right corner of the active cell or range
I-beam	I	Edit cell contents in active cell or formula bar	Active cell in Edit mode or over the formula bar
Move		Change the location of the selected cell(s)	Perimeter of the active cell(s)
Copy		Create a duplicate of the selected cell(s)	Perimeter of the active cell(s) when [Ctrl] is pressed
Column resize		Change the width of a column	Border between column heading indicators

Excel 2016

Enter and Edit a Simple Formula

Learning Outcomes
- Enter a formula
- Use cell references to create a formula

You use formulas in Excel to perform calculations such as adding, multiplying, and averaging. Formulas in an Excel worksheet start with the equal sign (=), also called the **formula prefix**, followed by cell addresses, range names, values, and **calculation operators**. Calculation operators indicate what type of calculation you want to perform on the cells, ranges, or values. They can include **arithmetic operators**, which perform mathematical calculations (see TABLE 1-2 in the "Understand Formulas" lesson); **comparison operators**, which compare values for the purpose of true/false results; **text concatenation operators**, which join strings of text in different cells; and **reference operators**, which enable you to use ranges in calculations. **CASE** *You want to create a formula in the worksheet that calculates gross pay for each employee.*

STEPS

1. **Click cell G5**

   This is the first cell where you want to insert the formula. To calculate gross pay, you need to add regular pay and overtime pay. For employee Peter Brucker, regular pay appears in cell E5 and overtime pay appears in cell F5.

2. **Type =, click cell E5, type +, then click cell F5**

   Compare your formula bar to FIGURE 1-11. The blue and red cell references in cell G5 correspond to the colored cell outlines. When entering a formula, it's a good idea to use cell references instead of values whenever you can. That way, if you later change a value in a cell (if, for example, Peter's regular pay changes to 690), any formula that includes this information reflects accurate, up-to-date results.

3. **Click the Enter button ✓ on the formula bar**

   The result of the formula =E5+F5, 804, appears in cell G5. This same value appears in cell G15 because cell G15 contains a formula that totals the values in cells G5:G14, and there are no other values at this time.

4. **Click cell F5**

   The formula in this cell calculates overtime pay by multiplying overtime hours (C5) times twice the regular hourly rate (2*D5). You want to edit this formula to reflect a new overtime pay rate.

5. **Click to the right of 2 in the formula bar, then type .5 as shown in FIGURE 1-12**

   The formula that calculates overtime pay has been edited.

6. **Click ✓ on the formula bar**

   Compare your screen to FIGURE 1-13. Notice that the calculated values in cells G5, F15, and G15 have all changed to reflect your edits to cell F5.

7. **Save your work**

Understanding named ranges

It can be difficult to remember the cell locations of critical information in a worksheet, but using cell names can make this task much easier. You can name a single cell or range of contiguous, or touching, cells. For example, you might name a cell that contains data on average gross pay "AVG_GP" instead of trying to remember the cell address C18. A named range must begin with a letter or an underscore. It cannot contain any spaces or be the same as a built-in name, such as a function or another object (such as a different named range) in the workbook. To name a range, select the cell(s) you want to name, click the Name box in the formula bar, type the name you want to use, then press [Enter]. You can also name a range by clicking the Formulas tab, then clicking the Define Name button in the Defined Names group. Type the new range name in the Name text box in the New Name dialog box, verify the selected range, then click OK. When you use a named range in a formula, the named range appears instead of the cell address. You can also create a named range using the contents of a cell already in the range. Select the range containing the text you want to use as a name, then click the Create from Selection button in the Defined Names group. The Create Names from Selection dialog box opens. Choose the location of the name you want to use, then click OK.

FIGURE 1-11: Simple formula in a worksheet

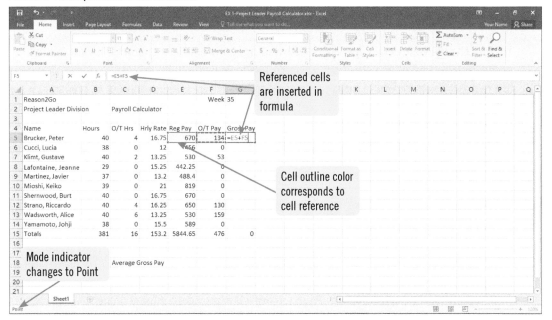

Referenced cells are inserted in formula

Cell outline color corresponds to cell reference

Mode indicator changes to Point

FIGURE 1-12: Edited formula in a worksheet

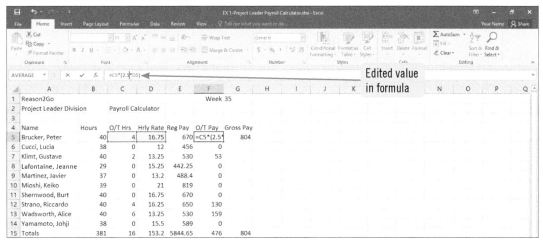

Edited value in formula

FIGURE 1-13: Edited formula with changes

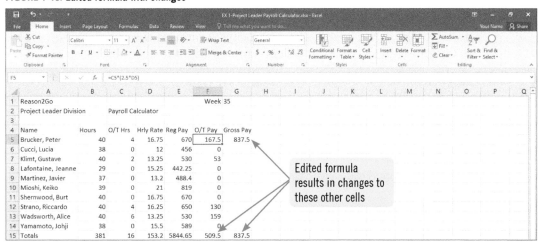

Edited formula results in changes to these other cells

Switch Worksheet Views

You can change your view of the worksheet window at any time, using either the View tab on the Ribbon or the View buttons on the status bar. Changing your view does not affect the contents of a worksheet; it just makes it easier for you to focus on different tasks, such as entering content or preparing a worksheet for printing. The View tab includes a variety of viewing options, such as View buttons, zoom controls, and the ability to show or hide worksheet elements such as gridlines. The status bar offers fewer View options but can be more convenient to use. **CASE** *You want to make some final adjustments to your worksheet, including adding a header so the document looks more polished.*

STEPS

1. **Click the View tab on the Ribbon, then click the Page Layout button in the Workbook Views group**

   The view switches from the default view, Normal, to Page Layout view. **Normal view** shows the worksheet without including certain details like headers and footers, or tools like rulers and a page number indicator; it's great for creating and editing a worksheet, but may not be detailed enough when you want to put the finishing touches on a document. **Page Layout view** provides a more accurate view of how a worksheet will look when printed, as shown in FIGURE 1-14. The margins of the page are displayed, along with a text box for the header. A footer text box appears at the bottom of the page, but your screen may not be large enough to view it without scrolling. Above and to the left of the page are rulers. Part of an additional page appears to the right of this page, but it is dimmed, indicating that it does not contain any data. A page number indicator on the status bar tells you the current page and the total number of pages in this worksheet.

2. **Move the pointer over the header *without clicking***

   The header is made up of three text boxes: left, center, and right. Each text box is outlined in green as you pass over it with the pointer.

3. **Click the left header text box, type Reason2Go, click the center header text box, type Project Leader Payroll Calculator, click the right header text box, then type Week 35**

   The new text appears in the text boxes, as shown in FIGURE 1-15. You can also press the [Tab] key to advance from one header box to the next.

4. **Select the range A1:G2, then press [Delete]**

   The duplicate information you just entered in the header is deleted from cells in the worksheet.

5. **Click the View tab if necessary, click the Ruler check box in the Show group, then click the Gridlines check box in the Show group**

   The rulers and the gridlines are hidden. By default, gridlines in a worksheet do not print, so hiding them gives you a more accurate image of your final document.

6. **Click the Page Break Preview button on the status bar**

   Your view changes to Page Break Preview, which displays a reduced view of each page of your worksheet, along with page break indicators that you can drag to include more or less information on a page.

7. **Drag the pointer from the bottom page break indicator to the bottom of row 20**

   See FIGURE 1-16. When you're working on a large worksheet with multiple pages, sometimes you need to adjust where pages break; in this worksheet, however, the information all fits comfortably on one page.

8. **Click the Page Layout button in the Workbook Views group, click the Ruler check box in the Show group, then click the Gridlines check box in the Show group**

   The rulers and gridlines are no longer hidden. You can show or hide View tab items in any view.

9. **Save your work**

FIGURE 1-14: **Page Layout view**

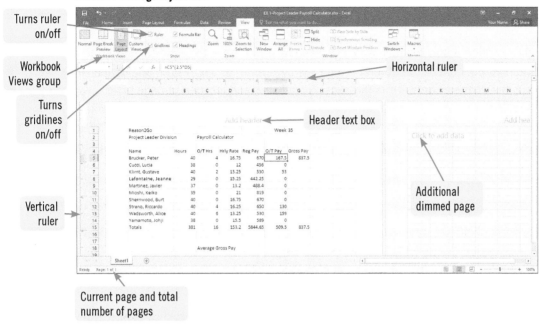

FIGURE 1-15: **Header text entered**

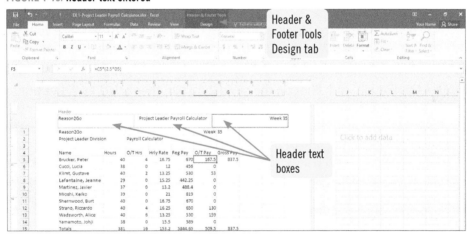

FIGURE 1-16: **Page Break Preview**

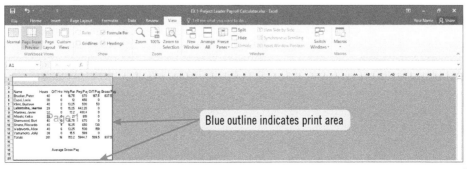

Choose Print Options

Learning
Outcomes
• Change the page
  orientation
• Hide/view gridlines
  when printing
• Preview and print
  a worksheet

Before printing a document, you may want to review it using the Page Layout tab to fine-tune your printed output. You can use tools on the Page Layout tab to adjust print orientation (the direction in which the content prints across the page), paper size, and location of page breaks. You can also use the Scale to Fit options on the Page Layout tab to fit a large amount of data on a single page without making changes to individual margins, and to turn gridlines and column/row headings on and off. When you are ready to print, you can set print options such as the number of copies to print and the correct printer, and you can preview your document in Backstage view using the File tab. You can also adjust page layout settings from within Backstage view and immediately see the results in the document preview. **CASE** ▶ *You are ready to prepare your worksheet for printing.*

STEPS

1. **Click cell A20, type your name, then click** ☑

2. **Click the Page Layout tab on the Ribbon**
   Compare your screen to FIGURE 1-17. The solid outline indicates the default **print area**, the area to be printed.

> **QUICK TIP**
> You can use the Zoom slider on the status bar at any time to enlarge your view of specific areas of your worksheet.

3. **Click the Orientation button in the Page Setup group, then click Landscape**
   The paper orientation changes to **landscape**, so the contents will print across the length of the page instead of across the width. Notice how the margins of the worksheet adjust.

4. **Click the Orientation button in the Page Setup group, then click Portrait**
   The orientation returns to **portrait**, so the contents will print across the width of the page.

5. **Click the Gridlines View check box in the Sheet Options group on the Page Layout tab, click the Gridlines Print check box to select it if necessary, then save your work**
   Printing gridlines makes the data easier to read, but the gridlines will not print unless the Gridlines Print check box is checked.

> **QUICK TIP**
> To change the active printer, click the current printer in the Printer section in Backstage view, then choose a different printer.

6. **Click the File tab, click Print on the navigation bar, then select an active printer if necessary**
   The Print tab in Backstage view displays a preview of your worksheet exactly as it will look when it is printed. To the left of the worksheet preview, you can also change a number of document settings and print options. To open the Page Setup dialog box and adjust page layout options, click the Page Setup link in the Settings section. Compare your preview screen to FIGURE 1-18. You can print from this view by clicking the Print button, or return to the worksheet without printing by clicking the Back button ⬅. You can also print an entire workbook from the Backstage view by clicking the Print button in the Settings section, then selecting the active sheet or entire workbook.

> **QUICK TIP**
> If the Quick Print button 🖨 appears on the Quick Access Toolbar, you can click it to print a worksheet using the default settings.

7. **Compare your settings to FIGURE 1-18, then click the Print button**
   One copy of the worksheet prints.

8. **Submit your work to your instructor as directed, then exit Excel**

Printing worksheet formulas

Sometimes you need to keep a record of all the formulas in a worksheet. You might want to do this to see exactly how you came up with a complex calculation, so you can explain it to others. To prepare a worksheet to show formulas rather than results when printed, open the workbook containing the formulas you want to print. Click the Formulas tab, then click the Show Formulas button in the Formula Auditing group to select it. When the Show Formulas button is selected, formulas rather than resulting values are displayed in the worksheet on screen and when printed. (The Show Formulas button is a toggle: click it again to hide the formulas.)

FIGURE 1-17: Worksheet with Portrait orientation

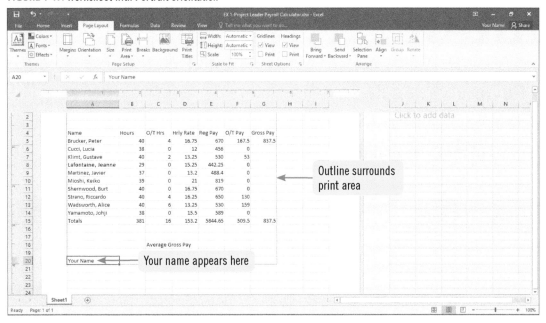

Outline surrounds print area

Your name appears here

FIGURE 1-18: Worksheet in Backstage view

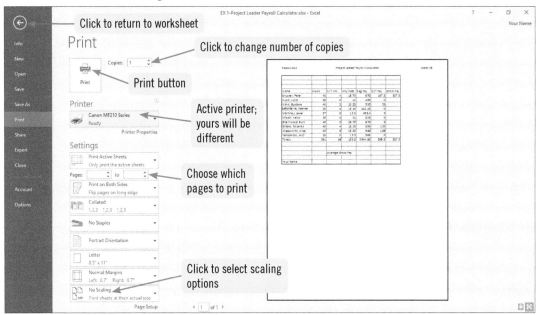

Click to return to worksheet

Click to change number of copies

Print button

Active printer; yours will be different

Choose which pages to print

Click to select scaling options

Scaling to fit

If you have a large amount of data that you want to fit to a single sheet of paper, but you don't want to spend a lot of time trying to adjust the margins and other settings, you have several options. You can easily print your work on a single sheet by clicking the No Scaling list arrow in the Settings section on the Print place in Backstage view, then clicking Fit Sheet in One Page. Another method for fitting worksheet content onto one page is to click the Page Layout tab, then change the Width and Height settings in the Scale to Fit group each to 1 Page. You can also use the Fit to option in the Page Setup dialog box to fit a worksheet on one page. To open the Page Setup dialog box, click the dialog box launcher in the Scale to Fit group on the Page Layout tab, or click the Page Setup link in the Print place in Backstage view. Make sure the Page tab is selected in the Page Setup dialog box, then click the Fit to option button.

Practice

Concepts Review

Label the elements of the Excel worksheet window shown in FIGURE 1-19.

FIGURE 1-19

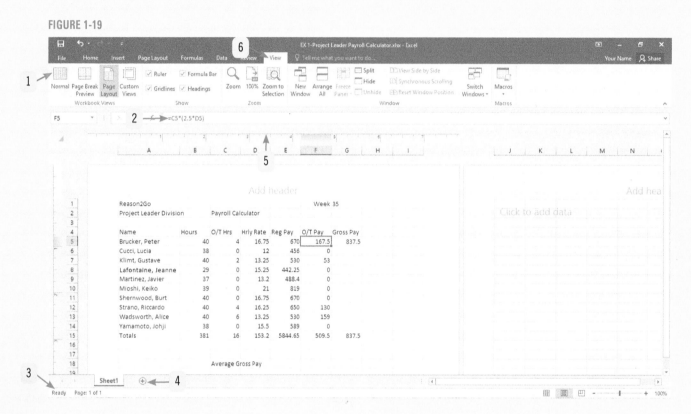

Match each term with the statement that best describes it.

7. **Name box**
8. **Workbook**
9. **Formula prefix**
10. **Orientation**
11. **Cell**
12. **Normal view**

a. Part of the Excel program window that displays the active cell address
b. Default view in Excel
c. Direction in which contents of page will print
d. Equal sign preceding a formula
e. File consisting of one or more worksheets
f. Intersection of a column and a row

Select the best answer from the list of choices.

13. **Which feature could be used to print a very long worksheet on a single sheet of paper?**
    a. Show Formulas
    b. Scale to Fit
    c. Page Break Preview
    d. Named Ranges

14. **In which area can you see a preview of your worksheet?**
    a. Page Setup
    b. Backstage view
    c. Printer Setup
    d. View tab

15. **A selection of multiple cells is called a:**
    a. Group.
    b. Range.
    c. Reference.
    d. Package.

16. **Using a cell address in a formula is known as:**
    a. Formularizing.
    b. Prefixing.
    c. Cell referencing.
    d. Cell mathematics.

17. **Which worksheet view shows how your worksheet will look when printed?**
    a. Page Layout
    b. Data
    c. Review
    d. View

18. **Which key can you press to switch to Edit mode?**
    a. [F1]
    b. [F2]
    c. [F4]
    d. [F6]

19. **In which view can you see the header and footer areas of a worksheet?**
    a. Normal view
    b. Page Layout view
    c. Page Break Preview
    d. Header/Footer view

20. **Which view shows you a reduced view of each page of your worksheet?**
    a. Normal
    b. Page Layout
    c. Thumbnail
    d. Page Break Preview

21. **The maximum number of worksheets you can include in a workbook is:**
    a. 3.
    b. 250.
    c. 255.
    d. Unlimited.

Skills Review

1. **Understand spreadsheet software.**
   a. What is the difference between a workbook and a worksheet?
   b. Identify five common business uses for electronic spreadsheets.
   c. What is what-if analysis?

2. **Identify Excel 2016 window components.**
   a. Start Excel.
   b. Open EX 1-2.xlsx from the location where you store your Data Files, then save it as **EX 1-Weather Data**.
   c. Locate the formula bar, the Sheet tabs, the mode indicator, and the cell pointer.

3. **Understand formulas.**
   a. What is the average high temperature of the listed cities? (*Hint*: Select the range B5:G5 and use the status bar.)
   b. What formula would you create to calculate the difference in altitude between Atlanta and Dallas? Enter your answer (as an equation) in cell D13.

Skills Review (continued)

4. Enter labels and values and use the AutoSum button.

  a. Click cell H8, then use the AutoSum button to calculate the total snowfall.

  b. Click cell H7, then use the AutoSum button to calculate the total rainfall.

  c. Save your changes to the file.

5. Edit cell entries.

  a. Use [F2] to correct the spelling of SanteFe in cell G3 (the correct spelling is Santa Fe).

  b. Click cell A17, then type your name.

  c. Save your changes.

6. Enter and edit a simple formula.

  a. Change the value 41 in cell C8 to **52**.

  b. Change the value 37 in cell D6 to **35.4**.

  c. Select cell J4, then use the fill handle to copy the formula in cell J4 to cells J5:J8.

  d. Save your changes.

7. Switch worksheet views.

  a. Click the View tab on the Ribbon, then switch to Page Layout view.

  b. Add the header **Average Annual Weather Data** to the center header text box.

  c. Add your name to the right header box.

  d. Delete the contents of cell A17.

  e. Delete the contents of cell A1.

  f. Save your changes.

8. Choose print options.

  a. Use the Page Layout tab to change the orientation to Portrait.

  b. Turn off gridlines by deselecting both the Gridlines View and Gridlines Print check boxes (if necessary) in the Sheet Options group.

  c. Scale the worksheet so all the information fits on one page. If necessary, scale the worksheet so all the information fits on one page. (*Hint*: Click the Width list arrow in the Scale to Fit group, click 1 page, click the Height list arrow in the Scale to Fit group, then click 1 page.) Compare your screen to FIGURE 1-20.

  d. Preview the worksheet in Backstage view, then print the worksheet.

  e. Save your changes, submit your work to your instructor as directed, then close the workbook and exit Excel.

FIGURE 1-20

Average Annual Weather Data — Your Name

	Atlanta	Boston	Dallas	Orlando	Phoenix	Santa Fe	Total		Average
Altitude	1050	20	430	91	1110	7000			1616.83
High Temp	89	69	96	82	86	70			82
Low Temp	33.5	44	35.4	62	59	43			46.15
Rain (in.)	50.19	42.53	21.32	47.7	7.3	14	183.04		30.5067
Snow (in.)	0	52	6	0	0	32	90		15

Alt. Diff. ->	Atlanta & Dallas		620

Click

Independent Challenge 1

A real estate development company has hired you to help them make the transition to using Excel in their office. They would like to list properties they are interested in acquiring in a workbook. You've started a worksheet for this project that contains labels but no data.

a. Open the file EX 1-3.xlsx from the location where you store your Data Files, then save it as **EX 1-Real Estate Acquisitions**.

b. Enter the data shown in TABLE 1-4 in columns A, C, D, and E (the property address information should spill into column B).

TABLE 1-4

Property Address	Price	Bedrooms	Bathrooms	Area
1507 Pinon Lane	575000	4	2.5	NE
32 Zanzibar Way	429000	3	4	SE
60 Pottery Lane	526500	2	2	NE
902 Excelsior Drive	315000	4	3	NW

c. Use Page Layout view to create a header with the following components: the title **Real Estate Acquisitions** in the center and your name on the right.

d. Create formulas for totals in cells C6:E6.

e. Save your changes, then compare your worksheet to FIGURE 1-21.

f. Submit your work to your instructor as directed.

g. Close the worksheet and exit Excel.

FIGURE 1-21

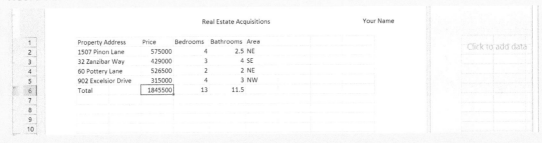

Independent Challenge 2

You are the general manager for Luxury Motors, a high-end auto reseller. Although the company is just five years old, it is expanding rapidly, and you are continually looking for ways to save time. You recently began using Excel to manage and maintain data on inventory and sales, which has greatly helped you to track information accurately and efficiently.

a. Start Excel.

b. Save a new workbook as **EX 1-Luxury Motors** in the location where you store your Data Files.

c. Switch to an appropriate view, then add a header that contains your name in the left header text box and the title **Luxury Motors** in the center header text box.

Independent Challenge 2 (continued)

d. Using FIGURE 1-22 as a guide, create labels for at least seven car manufacturers and sales for three months. Include other labels as appropriate. The car make should be in column A and the months should be in columns B, C, and D. A Total row should be beneath the data, and a Total column should be in column E.

FIGURE 1-22

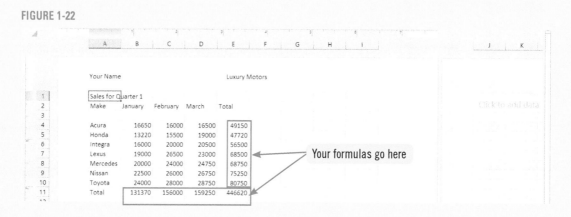

e. Enter values of your choice for the monthly sales for each make.

f. Add formulas in the Total column to calculate total quarterly sales for each make. Add formulas at the bottom of each column of values to calculate the total for that column. Remember that you can use the AutoSum button and the fill handle to save time.

g. Save your changes, preview the worksheet in Backstage view, then submit your work to your instructor as directed.

h. Close the workbook and exit Excel.

Independent Challenge 3

This Independent Challenge requires an Internet connection.

Your company, which is headquartered in Paris, is planning to open an office in New York City. You think it would be helpful to create a worksheet that can be used to convert Celsius temperatures to Fahrenheit, to help employees who are unfamiliar with this type of temperature measurement.

a. Start Excel, then save a blank workbook as **EX 1-Temperature Conversions** in the location where you store your Data Files.

b. Create column headings using FIGURE 1-23 as a guide. (*Hint*: You can widen column B by clicking cell B1, clicking the Format button in the Cells group on the Home tab, then clicking AutoFit Column Width.)

FIGURE 1-23

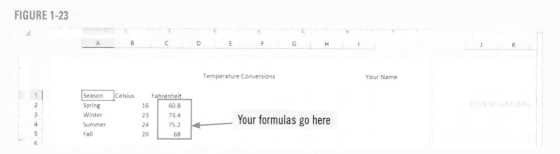

c. Create row labels for each of the seasons.

d. In the appropriate cells, enter what you determine to be a reasonable indoor temperature for each season.

e. Use your web browser to find out the conversion rate for Fahrenheit to Celsius. (*Hint*: Use your favorite search engine to search on a term such as **temperature conversion formula**.)

Independent Challenge 3 (continued)

f. In the appropriate cells, create a formula that calculates the conversion of the Fahrenheit temperature you entered into a Celsius temperature.

g. In Page Layout View, add your name and the title **Temperature Conversions** to the header.

h. Save your work, then submit your work to your instructor as directed.

i. Close the file, then exit Excel.

Independent Challenge 4: Explore

You've been asked to take over a project started by a co-worker whose Excel skills are not as good as your own. The assignment was to create a sample invoice for an existing client. The invoice will include personnel hours, supplies, and sales tax. Your predecessor started the project, including layout and initial calculations, but she has not made good use of Excel features and has made errors in her calculations. Complete the worksheet by correcting the errors and improving the design. Be prepared to discuss what is wrong with each of the items in the worksheet that you change.

a. Start Excel, open the file EX 1-4.xlsx from the location where you store your Data Files, then save it as **EX 1-Improved Invoice**.

b. There is an error in cell E5: please use the Help feature to find out what is wrong. If you need additional assistance, search Help on *overview of formulas*.

c. Correct the error in the formula in cell E5, then copy the corrected formula into cells E6:E7.

d. Correct the error in the formula in cell E11, then copy the corrected formula into cells E12 and E13.

e. Cells E8 and E14 also contain incorrect formulas. Cell E8 should contain a formula that calculates the total personnel expense, and cell E14 should calculate the total supplies used.

f. Cell G17 should contain a formula that adds the Invoice subtotal (total personnel and total supplies).

g. Cell G18 should calculate the sales tax by multiplying the Subtotal (G17) and the sales tax (cell G18).

h. The Invoice Total (cell G19) should contain a formula that adds the Invoice subtotal (cell G17) and Sales tax (cell G18).

i. Add the following to cell A21: **Terms**, then add the following to cell B21: **Net 10**.

j. Switch to Page Layout view and make the following changes to the Header: Improved Invoice for Week 22 (in the left header box), Client ABC (in the center header box), and your name (in the right header box).

k. Delete the contents of A1:A2, switch to Normal view, then compare your worksheet to FIGURE 1-24.

l. Save your work.

FIGURE 1-24

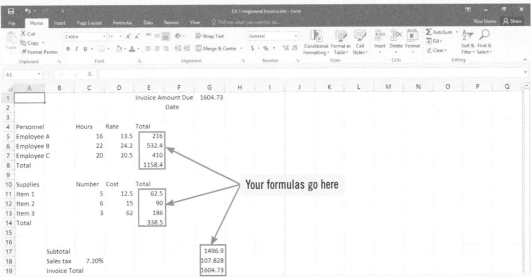

Excel 2016

Visual Workshop

Open the file EX 1-5.xlsx from the location where you store your Data Files, then save it as **EX 1-Project Tools**. Using the skills you learned in this module, modify your worksheet so it matches FIGURE 1-25. Enter formulas in cells D4 through D13 and in cells B14 and C14. Use the AutoSum button and fill handle to make entering your formulas easier. Add your name in the left header text box, then print one copy of the worksheet with the formulas displayed.

FIGURE 1-25

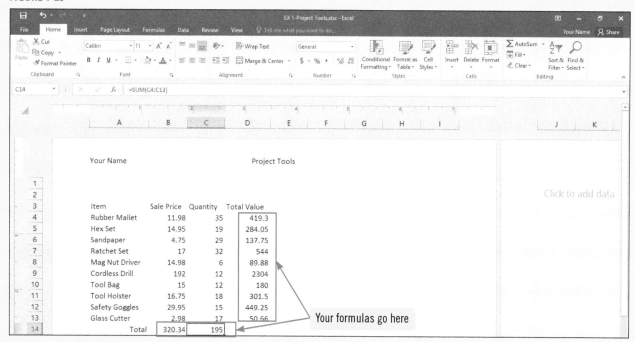

Working with Formulas and Functions

CASE Yolanda Lee, the vice president of finance at Reason2Go, needs to analyze tour expenses for the current year. She has asked you to prepare a worksheet that summarizes this expense data and includes some statistical analysis. She would also like you to perform some what-if analysis, to see what quarterly expenses would look like with various projected increases.

Module Objectives

After completing this module, you will be able to:

- Create a complex formula
- Insert a function
- Type a function
- Copy and move cell entries
- Understand relative and absolute cell references

- Copy formulas with relative cell references
- Copy formulas with absolute cell references
- Round a value with a function

Files You Will Need

EX 2-1.xlsx   EX 2-3.xlsx

EX 2-2.xlsx   EX 2-4.xlsx

Create a Complex Formula

Learning
Outcomes:
• Create a complex
  formula by
  pointing
• Use the fill handle
  and Auto Fill

A **complex formula** is one that uses more than one arithmetic operator. You might, for example, need to create a formula that uses addition and multiplication. In formulas containing more than one arithmetic operator, Excel uses the standard **order of precedence** rules to determine which operation to perform first. You can change the order of precedence in a formula by using parentheses around the part you want to calculate first. For example, the formula =4+2*5 equals 14, because the order of precedence dictates that multiplication is performed before addition. However, the formula =(4+2)*5 equals 30, because the parentheses cause 4+2 to be calculated first. **CASE** *You want to create a formula that calculates a 20% increase in tour expenses.*

STEPS

1. **Start Excel, open the file** EX 2-1.xlsx **from the location where you store your Data Files, then save it as** EX 2-R2G Tour Expense Analysis

2. **Select the range** B4:B11, **click the** Quick Analysis tool 🗔 **that appears below the selection, then click the** Totals tab

   The Totals tab in the Quick Analysis tool displays commonly used functions, as seen in FIGURE 2-1.

3. **Click the** AutoSum button ∑ **in the Quick Analysis tool**

   The newly calculated value displays in cell B12 and has bold formatting automatically applied, helping to set it off as a sum. This shading is temporary, and will not appear after you click a cell.

4. **Click cell** B12, **then drag the** fill handle **to cell** E12

   The formula in cell B12, as well as the bold formatting, is copied to cells C12:E12.

QUICK TIP

When the mode
indicator on the
status bar says
"Point," cells you
click are added to
the formula.

5. **Click cell** B14, **type** =, **click cell** B12, **then type** +

   In this first part of the formula, you are inserting a reference to the cell that contains total expenses for Quarter 1.

6. **Click cell** B12, **then type** *.2

   The second part of this formula adds a 20% increase (B12*.2) to the original value of the cell (the total expenses for Quarter 1).

7. **Click the** Enter button ✓ **on the formula bar**

   The result, 42749.58, appears in cell B14.

8. **Press [Tab], type** =, **click cell** C12, **type** +, **click cell** C12, **type** *.2, **then click** ✓

   The result, 42323.712, appears in cell C14.

QUICK TIP

You can also copy
the formulas by
selecting the range
C14:E14, clicking the
Fill button 🔽 in the
Editing group on the
Home tab, then
clicking Right.

9. **Drag the fill handle from cell** C14 **to cell** E14, **then save your work**

   The calculated values appear in the selected range, as shown in FIGURE 2-2. Dragging the fill handle on a cell copies the cell's contents or continues a series of data (such as Quarter 1, Quarter 2, etc.) into adjacent cells. This option is called **Auto Fill**.

Using Add-ins to improve worksheet functionality

Excel has more functionality than simple and complex math computations. Using the My Add-ins feature (found in the Add-ins group in the Insert tab), you can insert an add-in into your worksheet that accesses the web and adds functionality. Many of the add-ins are free or available for a small fee and can be used to create an email, appointment, meeting, contact, or task, or be a reference source, such as the Mini Calendar or Date Picker. When you click the My Add-ins button list arrow, you'll see

any Recently Used Add-ins. Click See All to display the featured Add-ins for Office and to go to the Store to view available add-ins. When you find one you want, make sure you're logged in to Office.com, click the add-in, click Trust It, and the add-in will be installed. Click the My Add-ins button and your add-in should display under Recently Used Add-ins. Click it, then click Insert. The add-in will display in the Recently Used Add-ins pane when you click the My Add-ins button.

FIGURE 2-1: **Totals tab in the Quick Analysis tool**

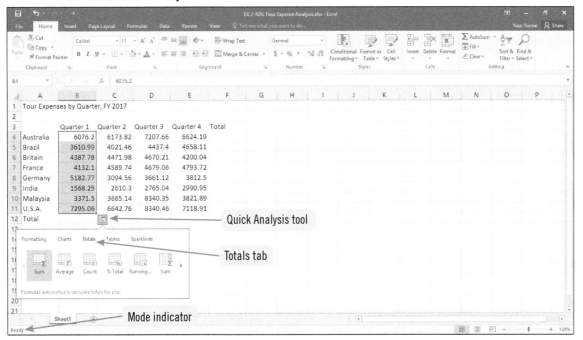

Quick Analysis tool

Totals tab

Mode indicator

FIGURE 2-2: **Results of copied formulas**

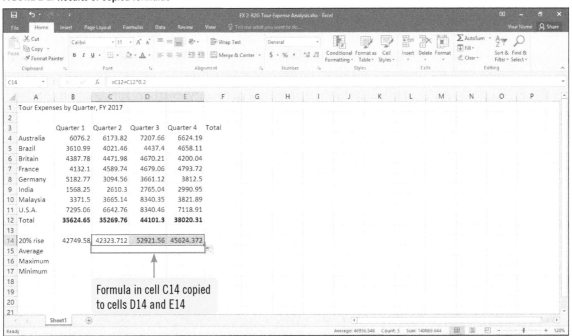

Formula in cell C14 copied
to cells D14 and E14

Reviewing the order of precedence

When you work with formulas that contain more than one operator, the order of precedence is very important because it affects the final value. If a formula contains two or more operators, such as 4+.55/4000*25, Excel performs the calculations in a particular sequence based on the following rules: Operations inside parentheses are calculated before any other operations. Reference operators (such as ranges) are calculated first. Exponents are calculated next, then any multiplication and division—progressing from left to right. Finally, addition and subtraction are calculated from left to right. In the example 4+.55/4000*25, Excel performs the arithmetic operations by first dividing .55 by 4000, then multiplying the result by 25, then adding 4. You can change the order of calculations by using parentheses. For example, in the formula (4+.55)/4000*25, Excel would first add 4 and .55, then divide that amount by 4000, then finally multiply by 25.

Insert a Function

Learning Outcomes
- Use the Insert Function button
- Select a range for use in a function
- Select a function from the AutoSum list arrow

Functions are predefined worksheet formulas that enable you to perform complex calculations easily. You can use the Insert Function button on the formula bar to choose a function from a dialog box. You can quickly insert the SUM function using the AutoSum button on the Ribbon, or you can click the AutoSum list arrow to enter other frequently used functions, such as **AVERAGE**. You can also use the Quick Analysis tool to calculate commonly used functions. Functions are organized into categories, such as Financial, Date & Time, and Statistical, based on their purposes. You can insert a function on its own or as part of another formula. For example, you have used the SUM function on its own to add a range of cells. You could also use the SUM function within a formula that adds a range of cells and then multiplies the total by a decimal. If you use a function alone, it always begins with an equal sign (=) as the formula prefix. **CASE** *You need to calculate the average expenses for the first quarter of the year and decide to use a function to do so.*

STEPS

QUICK TIP

When using the Insert Function button or the AutoSum list arrow, it is not necessary to type the equal sign (=); Excel adds it as necessary.

1. **Click cell B15**

   This is the cell where you want to enter a calculation that averages expenses per country for the first quarter.

2. **Click the** Insert Function button f_x **on the formula bar**

   An equal sign (=) is inserted in the active cell and in the formula bar, and the Insert Function dialog box opens, as shown in FIGURE 2-3. In this dialog box, you specify the function you want to use by clicking it in the Select a function list. The Select a function list initially displays recently used functions. If you don't see the function you want, you can click the Or select a category list arrow to choose the desired category. If you're not sure which category to choose, you can type the function name or a description in the Search for a function field. The AVERAGE function is a statistical function, but you don't need to open the Statistical category because this function already appears in the Most Recently Used category.

QUICK TIP

To learn about a function, click it in the Select a function list. The arguments and format required for the function appear below the list.

3. **Click AVERAGE in the Select a function list if necessary, read the information that appears under the list, then click OK**

   The Function Arguments dialog box opens, in which you define the range of cells you want to average.

QUICK TIP

When selecting a range, remember to select all the cells between and including the two references in the range.

4. **Click the** Collapse button **in the Number1 field of the Function Arguments dialog box, select the range B4:B11 in the worksheet, then click the** Expand button **in the Function Arguments dialog box**

   Clicking the Collapse button minimizes the dialog box so that you can select cells in the worksheet. When you click the Expand button, the dialog box is restored, as shown in FIGURE 2-4. You can also begin dragging in the worksheet to automatically minimize the dialog box; after you select the desired range, the dialog box is restored.

5. **Click OK**

   The Function Arguments dialog box closes, and the calculated value is displayed in cell B15. The average expenses per country for Quarter 1 is 4453.0813.

6. **Click cell C15, click the** AutoSum list arrow Σ **in the Editing group on the Home tab, then click** Average

   A ScreenTip beneath cell C15 displays the arguments needed to complete the function. The text "number1" is in boldface, telling you that the next step is to supply the first cell in the group you want to average.

7. **Select the range C4:C11 in the worksheet, then click the** Enter button ✓ **on the formula bar**

   The average expenses per country for the second quarter appear in cell C15.

8. **Drag the fill handle from cell C15 to cell E15**

   The formula in cell C15 is copied to the rest of the selected range, as shown in FIGURE 2-5.

9. **Save your work**

FIGURE 2-3: **Insert Function dialog box**

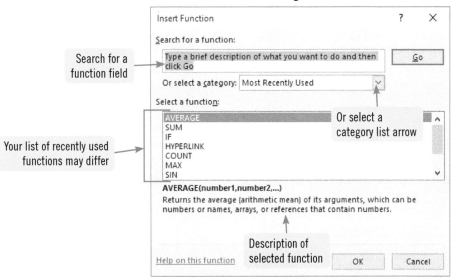

Search for a function field

Your list of recently used functions may differ

Or select a category list arrow

FIGURE 2-4: **Expanded Function Arguments dialog box**

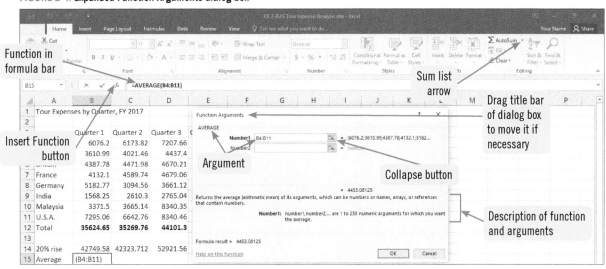

Function in formula bar

Insert Function button

Argument

Sum list arrow

Drag title bar of dialog box to move it if necessary

Collapse button

Description of function and arguments

FIGURE 2-5: **Average functions used in worksheet**

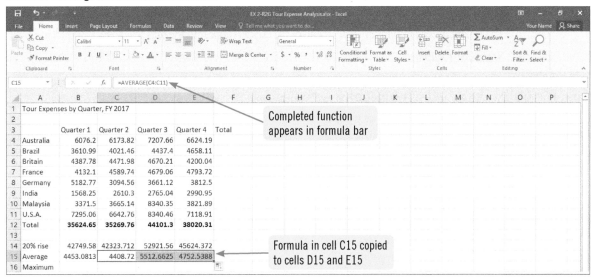

Completed function appears in formula bar

Formula in cell C15 copied to cells D15 and E15

Working with Formulas and Functions

Type a Function

Learning Outcomes
- Select a function by typing
- Use AutoComplete to copy formulas

In addition to using the Insert Function dialog box, the AutoSum button, or the AutoSum list arrow on the Ribbon to enter a function, you can manually type the function into a cell and then complete the arguments needed. This method requires that you know the name and initial characters of the function, but it can be faster than opening several dialog boxes. Experienced Excel users often prefer this method, but it is only an alternative, not better or more correct than any other method. The Excel **Formula AutoComplete** feature makes it easier to enter function names by typing, because it suggests functions depending on the first letters you type. **CASE** *You want to calculate the maximum and minimum quarterly expenses in your worksheet, and you decide to manually enter these statistical functions.*

STEPS

1. **Click cell B16, type =, then type m**

   Because you are manually typing this function, it is necessary to begin with the equal sign (=). The Formula AutoComplete feature displays a list of function names beginning with "M" beneath cell B16. Once you type an equal sign in a cell, each letter you type acts as a trigger to activate the Formula AutoComplete feature. This feature minimizes the amount of typing you need to do to enter a function and reduces typing and syntax errors.

2. **Click MAX in the list**

   Clicking any function in the Formula AutoComplete list opens a ScreenTip next to the list that describes the function.

   QUICK TIP
   When you select the function, a ScreenTip automatically displays more detailed information about the function.

3. **Double-click MAX**

   The function is inserted in the cell, and a ScreenTip appears beneath the cell to help you complete the formula. See FIGURE 2-6.

4. **Select the range B4:B11, as shown in FIGURE 2-7, then click the Enter button ✓ on the formula bar**

   The result, 7295.06, appears in cell B16. When you completed the entry, the closing parenthesis was automatically added to the formula.

5. **Click cell B17, type =, type m, then double-click MIN in the list of function names**

   The MIN function appears in the cell.

6. **Select the range B4:B11, then press [Enter]**

   The result, 1568.25, appears in cell B17.

7. **Select the range B16:B17, then drag the fill handle from cell B17 to cell E17**

   The maximum and minimum values for all of the quarters appear in the selected range, as shown in FIGURE 2-8.

8. **Save your work**

Using the COUNT and COUNTA functions

When you select a range, a count of cells in the range that are not blank appears in the status bar. You can use this information to determine things such as how many team members entered project hours in a worksheet. For example, if you select the range A1:A5 and only cells A1, A4, and A5 contain data, the status bar displays "Count: 3." To count nonblank cells more precisely, or to incorporate these calculations in a worksheet, you can use the COUNT and COUNTA functions. The COUNT function returns the number of cells in a range that contain numeric data, including numbers, dates, and formulas. The COUNTA function returns the number of cells in a range that contain any data at all, including numeric data, labels, and even a blank space. For example, the formula =COUNT(A1:A5) returns the number of cells in the range that contain numeric data, and the formula =COUNTA(A1:A5) returns the number of cells in the range that are not empty. If you use the COUNT functions in the Quick Analysis tool, the calculation is entered in the cell immediately beneath the selected range.

FIGURE 2-6: **MAX function in progress**

13					
14	20% rise	42749.58	42323.712	52921.56	45624.372
15	Average	4453.0813	4408.72	5512.6625	4752.5388
16	Maximum	=MAX(			
17	Minimum	MAX(**number1**, [number2], ...)			

FIGURE 2-7: **Completing the MAX function**

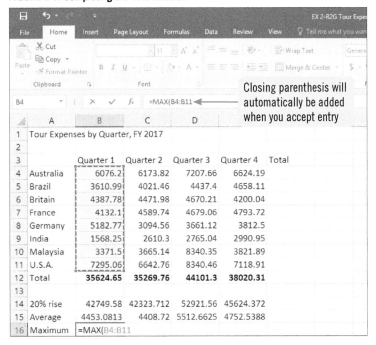

FIGURE 2-8: **Completed MAX and MIN functions**

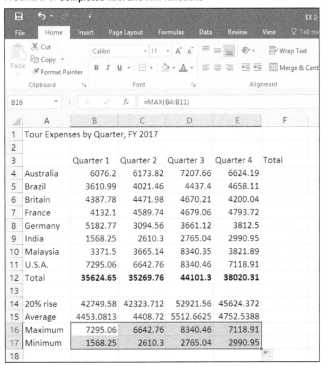

Working with Formulas and Functions

Copy and Move Cell Entries

Learning Outcomes
- Copy a range to the Clipboard
- Paste a Clipboard entry
- Empty cell contents
- Copy cell contents

There are three ways you can copy or move cells and ranges (or the contents within them) from one location to another: the Cut, Copy, and Paste buttons on the Home tab on the Ribbon; the fill handle in the lower-right corner of the active cell or range; or the drag-and-drop feature. When you copy cells, the original data remains in the original location; when you cut or move cells, the original data is deleted from its original location. You can also cut, copy, and paste cells or ranges from one worksheet to another. **CASE** ➤ *In addition to the 20% rise in tour expenses, you also want to show a 30% rise. Rather than retype this information, you copy and move selected cells.*

STEPS

1. **Select the range B3:E3, then click the Copy button 📋 in the Clipboard group on the Home tab**

   The selected range (B3:E3) is copied to the **Clipboard**, a temporary Windows storage area that holds the selections you copy or cut. A moving border surrounds the selected range until you press [Esc] or copy an additional item to the Clipboard.

2. **Click the launcher 🔲 in the Clipboard group**

   The Office Clipboard opens in the Clipboard task pane, as shown in FIGURE 2-9. When you copy or cut an item, it is cut or copied both to the Clipboard provided by Windows and to the Office Clipboard. Unlike the Windows Clipboard, which holds just one item at a time, the Office Clipboard contains up to 24 of the most recently cut or copied items from any Office program. Your Clipboard task pane may contain more items than shown in the figure.

3. **Click cell B19, then click the Paste button in the Clipboard group**

   A copy of the contents of range B3:E3 is pasted into the range B19:E19. When pasting an item from the Office Clipboard or Clipboard into a worksheet, you only need to specify the upper left cell of the range where you want to paste the selection. Notice that the information you copied remains in the original range B3:E3; if you had cut instead of copied, the information would have been deleted from its original location once it was pasted.

4. **Press [Delete]**

   The selected cells are empty. You have decided to paste the cells in a different row. You can repeatedly paste an item from the Office Clipboard as many times as you like, as long as the item remains in the Office Clipboard.

5. **Click cell B20, click the first item in the Office Clipboard, then click the Close button ✖ on the Clipboard task pane**

   Cells B20:E20 contain the copied labels.

6. **Click cell A14, press and hold [Ctrl], point to any edge of the cell until the pointer changes to ⟋, drag cell A14 to cell A21, release the mouse button, then release [Ctrl]**

   The copy pointer ⟋ continues to appear as you drag, as shown in FIGURE 2-10. When you release the mouse button, the contents of cell A14 are copied to cell A21.

7. **Click to the right of 2 in the formula bar, press [Backspace], type 3, then click the Enter button ✓**

8. **Click cell B21, type =, click cell B12, type *1.3, click ✓ on the formula bar, then save your work**

   This new formula calculates a 30% increase of the expenses for Quarter 1, though using a different method from what you previously used. Anything you multiply by 1.3 returns an amount that is 130% of the original amount, or a 30% increase. Compare your screen to FIGURE 2-11.

FIGURE 2-9: Copied data in Office Clipboard

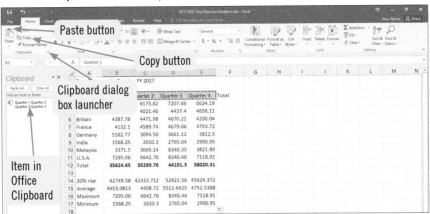

FIGURE 2-10: Copying cell contents with drag-and-drop

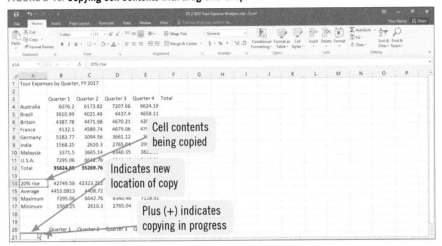

FIGURE 2-11: Formula entered to calculate a 30% increase

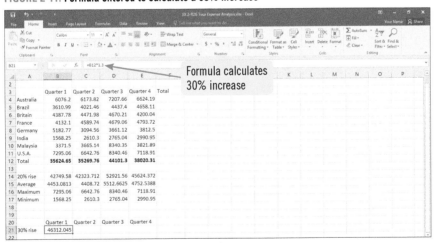

Inserting and deleting selected cells

As you add formulas to your workbook, you may need to insert or delete cells. When you do this, Excel automatically adjusts cell references to reflect their new locations. To insert cells, click the Insert list arrow in the Cells group on the Home tab, then click Insert Cells. The Insert dialog box opens, asking if you want to insert a cell and move the current active cell down or to the right of the new one. To delete one or more selected cells, click the Delete list arrow in the Cells group, click Delete Cells, and in the Delete dialog box, indicate which way you want to move the adjacent cells. When using this option, be careful not to disturb row or column alignment that may be necessary to maintain the accuracy of cell references in the worksheet. Click the Insert button or Delete button in the Cells group to insert or delete a single cell.

Understand Relative and Absolute Cell References

As you work in Excel, you may want to reuse formulas in different parts of a worksheet to reduce the amount of data you have to retype. For example, you might want to include a what-if analysis in one part of a worksheet showing a set of sales projections if sales increase by 10%. To include another analysis in another part of the worksheet showing projections if sales increase by 50%, you can copy the formulas from one section to another and simply change the "1" to a "5". But when you copy formulas, it is important to make sure that they refer to the correct cells. To do this, you need to understand the difference between relative and absolute cell references. **CASE** *You plan to reuse formulas in different parts of your worksheets, so you want to understand relative and absolute cell references.*

DETAILS

Consider the following when using relative and absolute cell references:

• **Use relative references when you want to preserve the relationship to the formula location**

When you create a formula that references another cell, Excel normally does not "record" the exact cell address for the cell being referenced in the formula. Instead, it looks at the relationship that cell has to the cell containing the formula. For example, in FIGURE 2-12, cell F5 contains the formula: =SUM(B5:E5). When Excel retrieves values to calculate the formula in cell F5, it actually looks for "the four cells to the left of the formula," which in this case is cells B5:E5. This way, if you copy the cell to a new location, such as cell F6, the results will reflect the new formula location and will automatically retrieve the values in cells B6, C6, D6, and E6. These are **relative cell references**, because Excel is recording the input cells *in relation to* or *relative to* the formula cell.

In most cases, you want to use relative cell references when copying or moving, so this is the Excel default. In FIGURE 2-12, the formulas in cells F5:F12 and cells B13:F13 contain relative cell references. They total the "four cells to the left of" or the "eight cells above" the formulas.

• **Use absolute cell references when you want to preserve the exact cell address in a formula**

There are times when you want Excel to retrieve formula information from a specific cell, and you don't want the cell address in the formula to change when you copy it to a new location. For example, you might have a price in a specific cell that you want to use in all formulas, regardless of their location. If you use relative cell referencing, the formula results would be incorrect, because the formula would reference a different cell every time you copy it. Therefore, you need to use an **absolute cell reference**, which is a reference that does not change when you copy the formula.

You create an absolute cell reference by placing a $ (dollar sign) in front of both the column letter and the row number of the cell address. You can either type the dollar sign when typing the cell address in a formula (for example, "=C12*$B$16") or you can select a cell address on the formula bar and then press [F4], and the dollar signs are added automatically. FIGURE 2-13 shows formulas containing both absolute and relative references. The formulas in cells B19 to E26 use absolute cell references to refer to a potential sales increase of 50%, shown in cell B16.

FIGURE 2-12: Formulas containing relative references

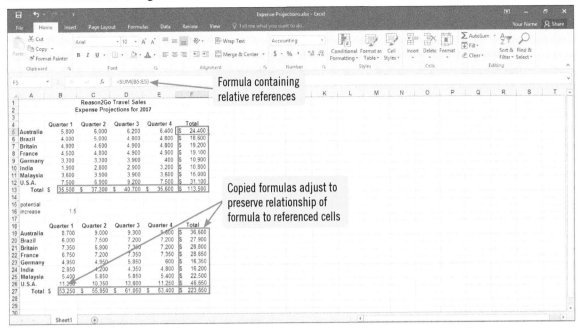

Formula containing relative references

Copied formulas adjust to preserve relationship of formula to referenced cells

FIGURE 2-13: Formulas containing absolute and relative references

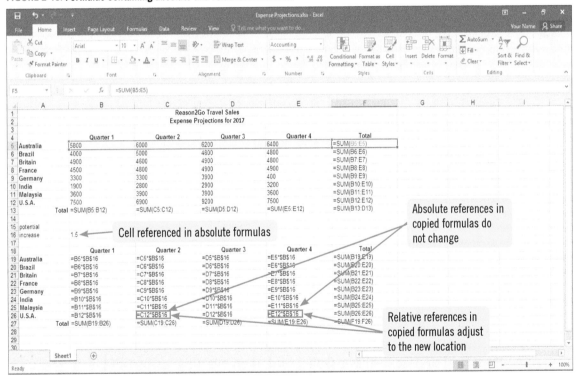

Absolute references in copied formulas do not change

Cell referenced in absolute formulas

Relative references in copied formulas adjust to the new location

Using a mixed reference

Sometimes when you copy a formula, you want to change the row reference, but keep the column reference the same. This type of cell referencing combines elements of both absolute and relative referencing and is called a **mixed reference**. For example, when copied, a formula containing the mixed reference C$14 would change the column letter relative to its new location, but not the row number. In the mixed reference $C14, the column letter would not change, but the row number would be updated relative to its location. Like an absolute reference, a mixed reference can be created by pressing the [F4] function key with the cell reference selected. With each press of the [F4] key, you cycle through all the possible combinations of relative, absolute, and mixed references (C14, $C$14, C$14, and $C14).

Copy Formulas with Relative Cell References

Learning
Outcomes
• Copy and Paste
  formulas with
  relative cell
  references
• Examine Auto Fill
  and Paste Options
• Use the Fill button

Copying and moving a cell allow you to reuse a formula you've already created. Copying cells is usually faster than retyping the formulas in them and helps to prevent typing errors. If the cells you are copying contain relative cell references and you want to maintain the relative referencing, you don't need to make any changes to the cells before copying them. **CASE** *You want to copy the formula in cell B21, which calculates the 30% increase in quarterly expenses for Quarter 1, to cells C21 through E21. You also want to create formulas to calculate total expenses for each tour country.*

STEPS

1. **Click cell B21 if necessary, then click the Copy button 📋 in the Clipboard group on the Home tab**

   The formula for calculating the 30% expense increase during Quarter 1 is copied to the Clipboard. Notice that the formula =B12*1.3 appears in the formula bar, and a moving border surrounds the active cell.

2. **Click cell C21, then click the Paste button 📋 (not the list arrow) in the Clipboard group**

   The formula from cell B21 is copied into cell C21, where the new result of 45850.688 appears. Notice in the formula bar that the cell references have changed so that cell C12 is referenced instead of B12. This formula contains a relative cell reference, which tells Excel to substitute new cell references within the copied formulas as necessary. This maintains the same relationship between the new cell containing the formula and the cell references within the formula. In this case, Excel adjusted the formula so that cell C12—the cell reference nine rows above C21—replaced cell B12, the cell reference nine rows above B21.

3. **Drag the fill handle from cell C21 to cell E21**

   A formula similar to the one in cell C21 now appears in cells D21 and E21. After you use the fill handle to copy cell contents, the **Auto Fill Options button** appears, as shown in FIGURE 2-14. You can use the Auto Fill Options button to fill the cells with only specific elements of the copied cell if you wish.

4. **Click cell F4, click the AutoSum button Σ in the Editing group, then click the Enter button ✓ on the formula bar**

5. **Click 📋 in the Clipboard group, select the range F5:F6, then click 📋**

   See FIGURE 2-15. After you click the Paste button, the **Paste Options button** appears.

6. **Click the Paste Options button 📋 (Ctrl)▾ adjacent to the selected range**

   You can use the Paste options list to paste only specific elements of the copied selection if you wish. The formula for calculating total expenses for tours in Britain appears in the formula bar. You would like totals to appear in cells F7:F11. The Fill button in the Editing group can be used to copy the formula into the remaining cells.

7. **Press [Esc] to close the Paste Options list, then select the range F6:F11**

8. **Click the Fill button ⬇ in the Editing group, then click Down**

   The formulas containing relative references are copied to each cell. Compare your worksheet to FIGURE 2-16.

9. **Save your work**

FIGURE 2-14: Formula copied using the fill handle

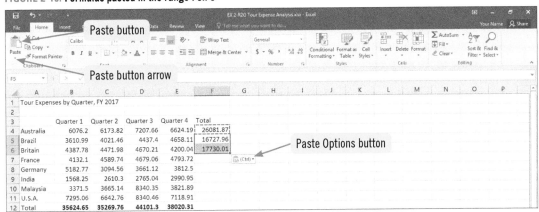

FIGURE 2-15: Formulas pasted in the range F5:F6

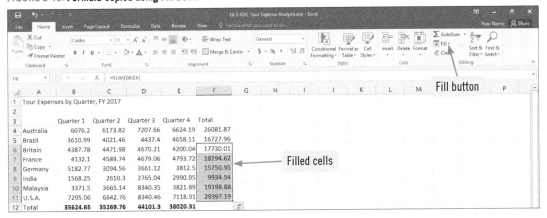

FIGURE 2-16: Formula copied using Fill Down

Using Paste Preview

You can selectively copy formulas, values, or other choices using the Paste list arrow, and you can see how the pasted contents will look using the Paste Preview feature. When you click the Paste list arrow, a gallery of paste option icons opens. When you point to an icon, a preview of how the content will be pasted using that option is shown in the worksheet. Options include pasting values only, pasting values with number formatting, pasting formulas only, pasting formatting only, pasting transposed data so that column data appears in rows and row data appears in columns, and pasting with no borders (to remove any borders around pasted cells).

Copy Formulas with Absolute Cell References

Learning
Outcomes
• Create an absolute
  cell reference
• Use the fill handle
  to copy absolute
  cell references

When copying cells, you might want one or more cell references in a formula to remain unchanged. In such an instance, you need to apply an absolute cell reference before copying the formula to preserve the specific cell address when the formula is copied. You create an absolute reference by placing a dollar sign ($) before the column letter and row number of the address (for example, $A$1). **CASE** *You need to do some what-if analysis to see how various percentage increases might affect total expenses. You decide to add a column that calculates a possible increase in the total tour expenses, and then change the percentage to see various potential results.*

STEPS

1. **Click cell G1, type Change, then press [Enter]**

2. **Type 1.1, then press [Enter]**

   You store the increase factor that will be used in the what-if analysis in this cell (G2). The value 1.1 can be used to calculate a 10% increase: anything you multiply by 1.1 returns an amount that is 110% of the original amount.

3. **Click cell H3, type What if?, then press [Enter]**

4. **In cell H4, type =, click cell F4, type *, click cell G2, then click the Enter button ✓ on the formula bar**

   The result, 28690.1, appears in cell H4. This value represents the total annual expenses for Australia if there is a 10% increase. You want to perform a what-if analysis for all the tour countries.

QUICK TIP

Before you copy or move a formula, always check to see if you need to use an absolute cell reference.

5. **Drag the fill handle from cell H4 to cell H11**

   The resulting values in the range H5:H11 are all zeros, which is not the result you wanted. Because you used relative cell addressing in cell H4, the copied formula adjusted so that the formula in cell H5 is =F5*G3; because there is no value in cell G3, the result is 0, an error. You need to use an absolute reference in the formula to keep the formula from adjusting itself. That way, it will always reference cell G2.

QUICK TIP

When changing a cell reference to an absolute reference, make sure the reference is selected or the insertion point is next to it in the cell before pressing [F4].

6. **Click cell H4, press [F2] to change to Edit mode, then press [F4]**

   When you press [F2], the range finder outlines the arguments of the equation in blue and red. The insertion point appears next to the G2 cell reference in cell H4. When you press [F4], dollar signs are inserted in the G2 cell reference, making it an absolute reference. See FIGURE 2-17.

7. **Click ✓, then drag the fill handle from cell H4 to cell H11**

   Because the formula correctly contains an absolute cell reference, the correct values for a 10% increase appear in cells H4:H11. You now want to see what a 20% increase in expenses looks like.

8. **Click cell G2, type 1.2, then click ✓**

   The values in the range H4:H11 change to reflect the 20% increase. Compare your worksheet to FIGURE 2-18.

9. **Save your work**

FIGURE 2-17: Absolute reference created in formula

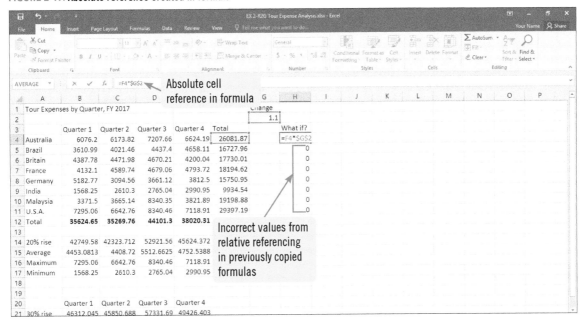

Absolute cell reference in formula

Incorrect values from relative referencing in previously copied formulas

FIGURE 2-18: What-if analysis with modified change factor

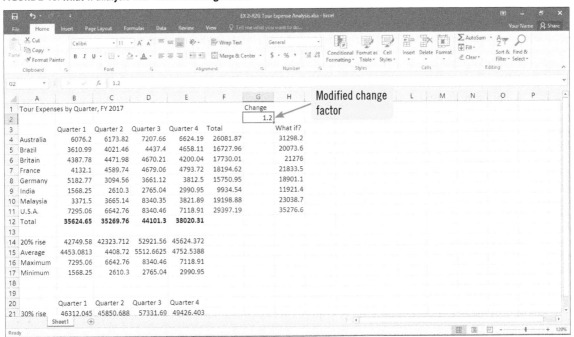

Modified change factor

Using the fill handle for sequential text or values

Often, you need to fill cells with sequential text: months of the year, days of the week, years, or text plus a number (Quarter 1, Quarter 2,...). For example, you might want to create a worksheet that calculates data for every month of the year. Using the fill handle, you can quickly and easily create labels for the months of the year just by typing "January" in a cell. Drag the fill handle from the cell containing "January" until you have all the monthly labels you need. You can also easily fill cells with a date sequence by dragging the fill handle on a single cell containing a date. You can

fill cells with a number sequence (such as 1, 2, 3,...) by dragging the fill handle on a selection of two or more cells that contain the sequence. To create a number sequence using the value in a single cell, press and hold [Ctrl] as you drag the fill handle of the cell. As you drag the fill handle, Excel automatically extends the existing sequence into the additional cells. (The content of the last filled cell appears in the ScreenTip.) To choose from all the fill series options for the current selection, click the Fill button in the Editing group on the Home tab, then click Series to open the Series dialog box.

Round a Value with a Function

Learning Outcomes
- Use Formula AutoComplete to insert a function
- Copy an edited formula

The more you explore features and tools in Excel, the more ways you'll find to simplify your work and convey information more efficiently. For example, cells containing financial data are often easier to read if they contain fewer decimal places than those that appear by default. You can round a value or formula result to a specific number of decimal places by using the ROUND function. **CASE** *In your worksheet, you'd like to round the cells showing the 20% rise in expenses to show fewer digits; after all, it's not important to show cents in the projections, only whole dollars. You want Excel to round the calculated value to the nearest integer. You decide to edit cell B14 so it includes the ROUND function, and then copy the edited formula into the other formulas in this row.*

STEPS

1. **Click cell B14, then click to the right of = in the formula bar**

   You want to position the function at the beginning of the formula, before any values or arguments.

2. **Type RO**

   Formula AutoComplete displays a list of functions beginning with RO beneath the formula bar.

3. **Double-click ROUND in the functions list**

   The new function and an opening parenthesis are added to the formula, as shown in FIGURE 2-19. A few additional modifications are needed to complete your edit of the formula. You need to indicate the number of decimal places to which the function should round numbers, and you also need to add a closing parenthesis around the set of arguments that comes after the ROUND function.

4. **Press [END], type ,0), then click the Enter button ✓ on the formula bar**

   The comma separates the arguments within the formula, and 0 indicates that you don't want any decimal places to appear in the calculated value. When you complete the edit, the parentheses at either end of the formula briefly become bold, indicating that the formula has the correct number of open and closed parentheses and is balanced.

5. **Drag the fill handle from cell B14 to cell E14**

   The formula in cell B14 is copied to the range C14:E14. All the values are rounded to display no decimal places. Compare your worksheet to FIGURE 2-20.

6. **Scroll down so row 25 is visible, click cell A25, type your name, then click ✓**

7. **Save your work, preview the worksheet in the Print place in Backstage view, then submit your work to your Instructor as directed**

8. **Exit Excel**

Using Auto Fill options

When you use the fill handle to copy cells, the Auto Fill Options button appears. Auto Fill options differ depending on what you are copying. If you had selected cells containing a series (such as "Monday" and "Tuesday") and then used the fill handle, you would see options for continuing the series (such as "Wednesday" and "Thursday") or for simply pasting the copied cells. Clicking the Auto Fill Options button opens a list that lets you choose from the following options: Copy Cells, Fill Series (if applicable), Fill Formatting Only, Fill Without Formatting, or Flash Fill. Choosing Copy Cells means that the cell's contents and its formatting will be copied. The Fill Formatting Only option copies only the formatting attributes, but not cell contents. The Fill Without Formatting option copies the cell contents, but no formatting attributes. Copy Cells is the default option when using the fill handle to copy a cell, so if you want to copy the cell's contents and its formatting, you can ignore the Auto Fill Options button. The Flash Fill option allows you to create customized fill ranges on the fly, such as 2, 4, 6, 8, 10, by entering at least two values in a pattern: Excel automatically senses the pattern.

FIGURE 2-19: **ROUND function added to an existing formula**

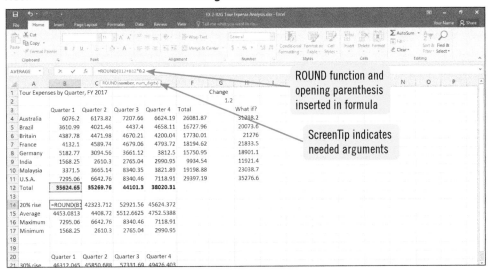

ROUND function and opening parenthesis inserted in formula

ScreenTip indicates needed arguments

FIGURE 2-20: **Completed worksheet**

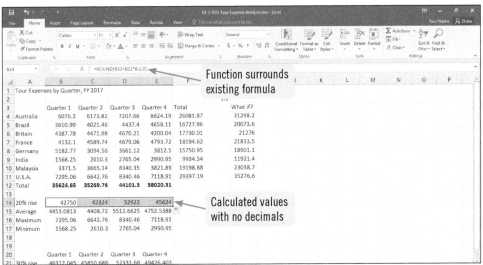

Function surrounds existing formula

Calculated values with no decimals

Creating a new workbook using a template

Excel **templates** are predesigned workbook files intended to save time when you create common documents such as balance sheets, budgets, or time cards. Templates contain labels, values, formulas, and formatting, so all you have to do is customize them with your own information. Excel comes with many templates, and you can also create your own or find additional templates on the web. Unlike a typical workbook, which has the file extension .xlsx, a template has the extension .xltx. To create a workbook using a template, click the File tab, then click New on the navigation bar. The New place in Backstage view displays thumbnails of some of the many templates available. The Blank workbook template is selected by default and is used to create a blank workbook with no content or special formatting. To select a different template, click one of the selections in the New place, view the preview, then click Create. FIGURE 2-21 shows an example. (Your available templates may differ.) When you click

Create, a new workbook is created based on the template; when you save the new file in the default format, it has the regular .xlsx extension. To save a workbook of your own as a template, open the Save As dialog box, click the Save as type list arrow, then change the file type to Excel Template.

FIGURE 2-21: **Previewing the Budget Planner template**

Practice

Concepts Review

Label each element of the Excel worksheet window shown in FIGURE 2-22.

FIGURE 2-22

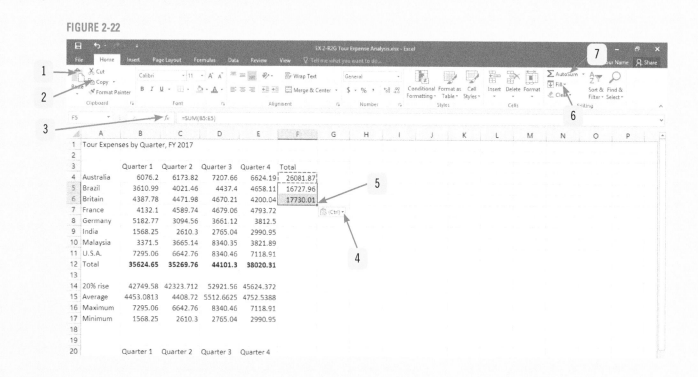

Match each term or button with the statement that best describes it.

8. Launcher

9. Fill handle

10. Drag-and-drop method

11. Formula
    AutoComplete

12. [Delete] key

a. Clears the contents of selected cells

b. Item on the Ribbon that opens a dialog box or task pane

c. Lets you move or copy data from one cell to another without using
   the Clipboard

d. Displays an alphabetical list of functions from which you can choose

e. Lets you copy cell contents or continue a series of data into a range of
   selected cells

Select the best answer from the list of choices.

13. You can use any of the following features to enter a new function *except*:

a. Insert Function button.

b. Formula AutoComplete.

c. AutoSum list arrow.

d. Clipboard.

14. Which key do you press and hold to copy while dragging and dropping selected cells?

a. [Alt]

b. [Ctrl]

c. [F2]

d. [Tab]

15. What type of cell reference is C$19?

a. Relative

b. Absolute

c. Mixed

d. Certain

16. Which key do you press to convert a relative cell reference to an absolute cell reference?

a. [F2]

b. [F4]

c. [F5]

d. [F6]

17. What type of cell reference changes when it is copied?

a. Circular

b. Absolute

c. Relative

d. Specified

Skills Review

1. Create a complex formula.

a. Open EX 2-2.xlsx from the location where you store your Data Files, then save it as **EX 2-Construction Supply Company Inventory**.

b. Select the range B4:B8, click the Totals tab in the Quick Analysis tool, then click the AutoSum button.

c. Use the fill handle to copy the formula in cell B9 to cells C9:E9.

d. In cell B11, create a complex formula that calculates a 30% decrease in the total number of cases of pylons.

e. Use the fill handle to copy this formula into cell C11 through cell E11.

f. Save your work.

2. Insert a function.

a. Use the AutoSum list arrow to create a formula in cell B13 that averages the number of cases of pylons in each storage area.

b. Use the Insert Function button to create a formula in cell B14 that calculates the maximum number of cases of pylons in a storage area.

c. Use the AutoSum list arrow to create a formula in cell B15 that calculates the minimum number of cases of pylons in a storage area.

d. Save your work.

Skills Review (continued)

3. Type a function.

    a. In cell C13, type a formula that includes a function to average the number of cases of bricks in each storage area. (*Hint*: Use Formula AutoComplete to enter the function.)

    b. In cell C14, type a formula that includes a function to calculate the maximum number of cases of bricks in a storage area.

    c. In cell C15, type a formula that includes a function to calculate the minimum number of cases of bricks in a storage area.

    d. Save your work.

4. Copy and move cell entries.

    a. Select the range B3:F3.

    b. Copy the selection to the Clipboard.

    c. Open the Clipboard task pane, then paste the selection into cell B17.

    d. Close the Clipboard task pane, then select the range A4:A9.

    e. Use the drag-and-drop method to copy the selection to cell A18. (*Hint*: The results should fill the range A18:A23.)

    f. Save your work.

5. Understand relative and absolute cell references.

    a. Write a brief description of the difference between relative and absolute references.

    b. List at least three situations in which you think a business might use an absolute reference in its calculations. Examples can include calculations for different types of worksheets, such as time cards, invoices, and budgets.

6. Copy formulas with relative cell references.

    a. Calculate the total in cell F4.

    b. Use the Fill button to copy the formula in cell F4 down to cells F5:F8.

    c. Select the range C13:C15.

    d. Use the fill handle to copy these cells to the range D13:F15.

    e. Save your work.

7. Copy formulas with absolute cell references.

    a. In cell H1, change the existing value to **1.575**.

    b. In cell H4, create a formula that multiplies F4 and an absolute reference to cell H1.

    c. Use the fill handle to copy the formula in cell H4 to cells H5 and H6.

    d. Use the Copy and Paste buttons to copy the formula in cell H4 to cells H7 and H8.

    e. Change the amount in cell H1 to **2.5**.

    f. Save your work.

Skills Review (continued)

8. **Round a value with a function.**

   a. Click cell H4.

   b. Edit this formula to include the ROUND function showing zero decimal places.

   c. Use the fill handle to copy the formula in cell H4 to the range H5:H8.

   d. Enter your name in cell A25, then compare your work to FIGURE 2-23.

   e. Save your work, preview the worksheet in Backstage view, then submit your work to your instructor as directed.

   f. Close the workbook, then exit Excel.

FIGURE 2-23

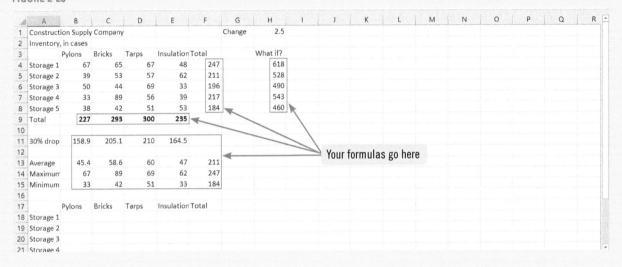

Independent Challenge 1

You are thinking of starting a small coffee shop where locals can gather. Before you begin, you need to evaluate what you think your monthly expenses will be. You've started a workbook, but need to complete the entries and add formulas.

a. Open EX 2-3.xlsx from the location where you store your Data Files, then save it as **EX 2-Coffee Shop Expenses**.

b. Make up your own expense data, and enter it in cells B4:B10. (Monthly sales are already included in the worksheet.)

c. Create a formula in cell C4 that calculates the annual rent.

d. Copy the formula in cell C4 to the range C5:C10.

e. Move the label in cell A15 to cell A14.

f. Create formulas in cells B11 and C11 that total the monthly and annual expenses.

g. Create a formula in cell C13 that calculates annual sales.

h. Create a formula in cell B14 that determines whether you will make a profit or loss, then copy the formula into cell C14.

i. Copy the labels in cells B3:C3 to cells E3:F3.

j. Type **Projected Increase** in cell G1, then type **.2** in cell H2.

k. Create a formula in cell E4 that calculates an increase in the monthly rent by the amount in cell H2. You will be copying this formula to other cells, so you'll need to use an absolute reference.

l. Create a formula in cell F4 that calculates the increased annual rent expense based on the calculation in cell E4.

m. Copy the formulas in cells E4:F4 into cells E5:F10 to calculate the remaining monthly and annual expenses.

n. Create a formula in cell E11 that calculates the total monthly expenses, then copy that formula to cell F11.

o. Copy the contents of cells B13:C13 into cells E13:F13.

p. Create formulas in cells E14 and F14 that calculate profit/loss based on the projected increase in monthly and annual expenses.

q. Change the projected increase to **.17**, then compare your work to the sample in FIGURE 2-24.

r. Enter your name in a cell in the worksheet.

s. Save your work, preview the worksheet in Backstage view, submit your work to your instructor as directed, close the workbook, and exit Excel.

FIGURE 2-24

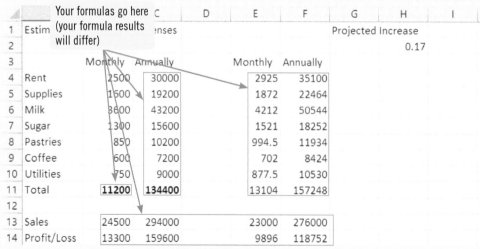

Independent Challenge 2

The Office Specialists Center is a small, growing business that rents small companies space and provides limited business services. They have hired you to organize their accounting records using Excel. The owners want you to track the company's expenses. Before you were hired, one of the bookkeepers began entering last year's expenses in a workbook, but the analysis was never completed.

a. Start Excel, open EX 2-4.xlsx from the location where you store your Data Files, then save it as **EX 2-Office Specialists Center Finances**. The worksheet includes labels for functions such as the average, maximum, and minimum amounts of each of the expenses in the worksheet.

b. Think about what information would be important for the bookkeeping staff to know.

c. Using the Quick Analysis tool, create a formula in the Quarter 1 column that uses the SUM function, then copy that formula into the Total row for the remaining quarters.

d. Use the SUM function to create formulas for each expense in the Total column.

e. Create formulas for each expense and each quarter in the Average, Maximum, and Minimum columns and rows using the method of your choice.

f. Compare your worksheet to the sample shown in FIGURE 2-25.

g. Enter your name in cell A25, then save your work.

h. Preview the worksheet, then submit your work to your instructor as directed.

i. Close the workbook and exit Excel.

FIGURE 2-25

	A	B	C	D	E	F	G	H	I	J
1	Office Specialists Center									
2										
3	Operating Expenses for 2017									
4										
5	Expense	Quarter 1	Quarter 2	Quarter 3	Quarter 4	Total	Average	Maximum	Minimum	
6	Rent	10240	10240	10240	10240	40960	10240	10240	10240	
7	Utilities	9500	8482	7929	8596	34507	8626.75	9500	7929	
8	Payroll	24456	27922	26876	30415	109669	27417.3	30415	24456	
9	Insurance	9000	8594	8472	8523	34589	8647.25	9000	8472	
10	Education	4000	4081	7552	5006	20639	5159.75	7552	4000	
11	Inventory	15986	14115	14641	15465	60207	15051.8	15986	14115	
12	Total	**73182**	**73434**	**75710**	**78245**					
13										
14	Average	12197	12239	12618.3	13040.8		Your formulas go here			
15	Maximum	24456	27922	26876	30415					
16	Minimum	4000	4081	7552	5006					

Independent Challenge 3

As the accounting manager of a locally owned food co-op with multiple locations, it is your responsibility to calculate accrued sales tax payments on a monthly basis and then submit the payments to the state government. You've decided to use an Excel workbook to make these calculations.

a. Start Excel, then save a new, blank workbook to the drive and folder where you store your Data Files as **EX 2-Food Co-op Sales Tax Calculations**.

b. Decide on the layout for all columns and rows. The worksheet will contain data for six stores, which you can name by store number, neighborhood, or another method of your choice. For each store, you will calculate total sales tax based on the local sales tax rate. You'll also calculate total tax owed for all six locations.

c. Make up sales data for all six stores.

d. Enter the rate to be used to calculate the sales tax, using your own local rate.

e. Create formulas to calculate the sales tax owed for each location. If you don't know the local tax rate, use **6.5%**.

f. Create a formula to total all the accrued sales tax.

g. Use the ROUND function to eliminate any decimal places in the sales tax figures for each location and in the total due.

h. Add your name to the header, then compare your work to the sample shown in FIGURE 2-26.

i. Save your work, preview the worksheet, and submit your work to your instructor as directed.

j. Close the workbook and exit Excel.

FIGURE 2-26

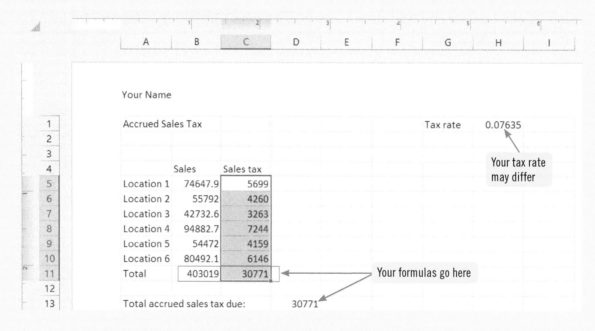

Independent Challenge 4: Explore

So many friends have come to you for help in understanding the various fees associated with purchasing a home that you've decided to create a business that specializes in helping first-time home-buyers. Your first task is to create a worksheet that clearly shows all the information a home buyer will need. Some fees are based on a percentage of the purchase price, and others are a flat fee; overall, they seem to represent a substantial amount above the purchase prices you see listed. A client has seen five houses so far that interest her; one is easily affordable, and the remaining four are all nice, but increasingly more expensive. You decide to create an Excel workbook to help her figure out the real cost of each home.

a. Find out the typical cost or percentage rate of at least three fees that are usually charged when buying a home and taking out a mortgage. (*Hint*: If you have access to the Internet, you can research the topic of home buying on the web, or you can ask friends about standard rates or percentages for items such as title insurance, credit reports, and inspection fees.)

b. Start Excel, then save a new, blank workbook to the location where you store your Data Files as **EX 2-Home Purchase Fees Worksheet**.

c. Create labels and enter data for at least five homes. If you enter this information across the columns in your worksheet, you should have one column for each house, with the purchase price in the cell below each label. Be sure to enter a different purchase price for each house.

d. Create labels for the Fees column and for an Amount or Rate column. Enter the information for each of the fees you have researched.

e. In each house column, enter formulas that calculate the fee for each item. The formulas (and use of absolute or relative referencing) will vary depending on whether the charges are a flat fee or based on a percentage of the purchase price. Make sure that the formulas for items that are based on a percentage of the purchase price (such as the fees for the Title Insurance Policy, Loan Origination, and Underwriter) contain absolute references. A sample of what your workbook might look like is shown in FIGURE 2-27.

f. Total the fees for each house, then create formulas that add the total fees to the purchase price.

g. Enter a title for the worksheet and include your client's name (or use Client 1) in the header.

h. Enter your name in the header, save your work, preview the worksheet, then submit your work to your instructor as directed.

i. Close the file and exit Excel.

FIGURE 2-27

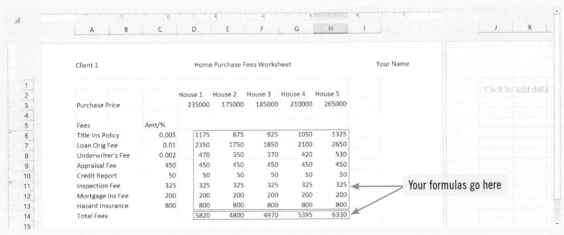

Excel 2016

Visual Workshop

Create the worksheet shown in FIGURE 2-28 using the skills you learned in this module. Save the workbook as **EX 2-Monthly Expenses** to the location where you store your Data Files. Enter your name and worksheet title in the header as shown, hide the gridlines, preview the worksheet, and then submit your work to your instructor as directed. (*Hint:* Change the Zoom factor to 90% by using the Zoom out button.)

FIGURE 2-28

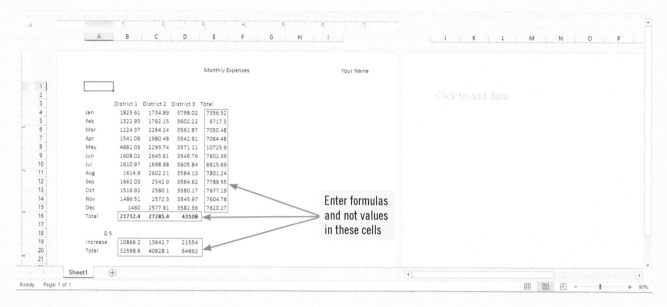

Formatting a Worksheet

CASE ▶ The marketing managers at Reason2Go have requested data from all R2G locations for advertising expenses incurred during the first quarter of this year. Mary Watson has created a worksheet listing this information. She asks you to format the worksheet to make it easier to read and to call attention to important data.

Module Objectives

After completing this module, you will be able to:

- Format values
- Change font and font size
- Change font styles and alignment
- Adjust column width
- Insert and delete rows and columns

- Apply colors, patterns, and borders
- Apply conditional formatting
- Rename and move a worksheet
- Check spelling

Files You Will Need

EX 3-1.xlsx	EX 3-4.xlsx
EX 3-2.xlsx	EX 3-5.xlsx
EX 3-3.xlsx	

Format Values

The **format** of a cell determines how the labels and values look—for example, whether the contents appear boldfaced, italicized, or with dollar signs and commas. Formatting changes only the appearance of a value or label; it does not alter the actual data in any way. To format a cell or range, first you select it, then you apply the formatting using the Ribbon, Mini toolbar, or a keyboard shortcut. You can apply formatting before or after you enter data in a cell or range. **CASE** *Mary has provided you with a worksheet that details advertising expenses, and you're ready to improve its appearance and readability. You start by formatting some of the values so they are displayed as currency, percentages, and dates.*

STEPS

1. **Start Excel, open the file** EX 3-1.xlsx **from the location where you store your Data Files, then save it as** EX 3-R2G Advertising Expenses

   This worksheet is difficult to interpret because all the information is crowded and looks the same. In some columns, the contents appear cut off because there is too much data to fit given the current column width. You decide not to widen the columns yet, because the other changes you plan to make might affect column width and row height. The first thing you want to do is format the data showing the cost of each ad.

2. **Select the range** D4:D32, **then click the** Accounting Number Format button $ **in the Number group on the Home tab**

   The default Accounting **number format** adds dollar signs and two decimal places to the data, as shown in FIGURE 3-1. Formatting this data in Accounting format makes it clear that its values are monetary values. Excel automatically resizes the column to display the new formatting. The Accounting and Currency number formats are both used for monetary values, but the Accounting format aligns currency symbols and decimal points of numbers in a column.

3. **Select the range** F4:H32, **then click the** Comma Style button ' **in the Number group**

   The values in columns F, G, and H display the Comma Style format, which does not include a dollar sign but can be useful for some types of accounting data.

4. **Select the range** J4:J32, **click the** Number Format list arrow, **click** Percentage, **then click the** Increase Decimal button **in the Number group**

   The data in the % of Total column is now formatted with a percent sign (%) and three decimal places. The Number Format list arrow lets you choose from popular number formats and shows an example of what the selected cell or cells would look like in each format (when multiple cells are selected, the example is based on the first cell in the range). Each time you click the Increase Decimal button, you add one decimal place; clicking the button twice would add two decimal places.

5. **Click the** Decrease Decimal button **in the Number group** twice

   Two decimal places are removed from the percentage values in column J.

6. **Select the range** B4:B31, **then click the** launcher **in the Number group**

   The Format Cells dialog box opens with the Date category already selected on the Number tab.

7. **Select the first** 14-Mar-12 format **in the Type list box as shown in** FIGURE 3-2, **then click** OK

   The dates in column B appear in the 14-Mar-12 format. The second 14-Mar-12 format in the list (visible if you scroll down the list) displays all days in two digits (it adds a leading zero if the day is only a single-digit number), while the one you chose displays single-digit days without a leading zero.

8. **Select the range** C4:C31, **right-click the** range, **click** Format Cells **on the shortcut menu, click** 14-Mar **in the Type list box in the Format Cells dialog box, then click** OK

   Compare your worksheet to FIGURE 3-3.

9. **Press** [Ctrl][Home], **then save your work**

FIGURE 3-1: **Accounting number format applied to range**

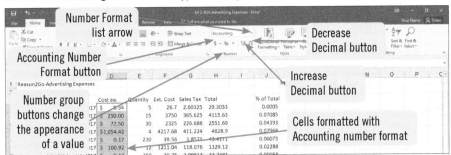

FIGURE 3-2: **Format Cells dialog box**

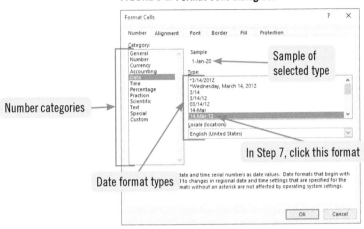

FIGURE 3-3: **Worksheet with formatted values**

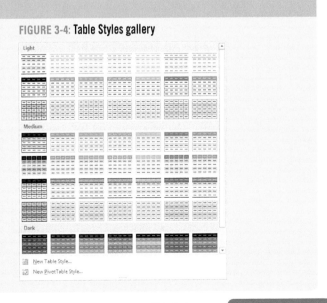

Formatting as a table

Excel includes 60 predefined **table styles** to make it easy to format selected worksheet cells as a table. You can apply table styles to any range of cells that you want to format quickly, or even to an entire worksheet, but they're especially useful for those ranges with labels in the left column and top row, and totals in the bottom row or right column. To apply a table style, select the data to be formatted or click anywhere within the intended range (Excel can automatically detect a range of cells filled with data), click the Format as Table button in the Styles group on the Home tab, then click a style in the gallery, as shown in **FIGURE 3-4**. Table styles are organized in three categories: Light, Medium, and Dark. Once you click a style, Excel asks you to confirm the range selection, then applies the style. Once you have formatted a range as a table, you can use Live Preview to preview the table in other styles by pointing to any style in the Table Styles gallery.

FIGURE 3-4: **Table Styles gallery**

Change Font and Font Size

Learning Outcomes
• Change a font
• Change a font size
• Use the Mini toolbar

A **font** is the name for a collection of characters (letters, numbers, symbols, and punctuation marks) with a similar, specific design. The **font size** is the physical size of the text, measured in units called points. A **point** is equal to 1/72 of an inch. The default font and font size in Excel is 11-point Calibri. TABLE 3-1 shows several fonts in different font sizes. You can change the font and font size of any cell or range using the Font and Font Size list arrows. The Font and Font Size list arrows appear on the Home tab on the Ribbon and on the Mini toolbar, which opens when you right-click a cell or range. **CASE** *You want to change the font and font size of the labels and the worksheet title so that they stand out more from the data.*

STEPS

QUICK TIP
When you point to an option in the Font or Font Size list, Live Preview shows the selected cells with the option temporarily applied.

1. **Click the** Font list arrow **in the Font group on the Home tab, scroll down in the Font list to see an alphabetical listing of the fonts available on your computer, then click** Times New Roman, **as shown in** FIGURE 3-5

   The font in cell A1 changes to Times New Roman. Notice that the font names on the list are displayed in the font they represent.

QUICK TIP
You can format an entire row by clicking the row indicator button to select the row before formatting (or select an entire column by clicking the column indicator button before formatting).

2. **Click the** Font Size list arrow **in the Font group, then click** 20

   The worksheet title appears in 20-point Times New Roman, and the Font and Font Size list boxes on the Home tab display the new font and font size information.

3. **Click the** Increase Font Size button A^ **in the Font group twice**

   The font size of the title increases to 24 point.

4. **Select the range** A3:J3, **right-click, then click the** Font list arrow **on the Mini toolbar**

   The Mini toolbar includes the most commonly used formatting tools, so it's great for making quick formatting changes.

QUICK TIP
To quickly move to a font in the Font list, type the first few characters of its name.

5. **Scroll down in the Font list and click** Times New Roman, **click the** Font Size list arrow **on the Mini toolbar, then click** 14

   The Mini toolbar closes when you move the pointer away from the selection. Compare your worksheet to FIGURE 3-6. Notice that some of the column labels are now too wide to appear fully in the column. Excel does not automatically adjust column widths to accommodate cell formatting; you have to adjust column widths manually. You'll learn to do this in a later lesson.

6. **Save your work**

TABLE 3-1: Examples of fonts and font sizes

font	12 point	24 point
Calibri	Excel	Excel
Playbill	Excel	Excel
Comic Sans MS	Excel	Excel
Times New Roman	Excel	Excel

FIGURE 3-5: Font list

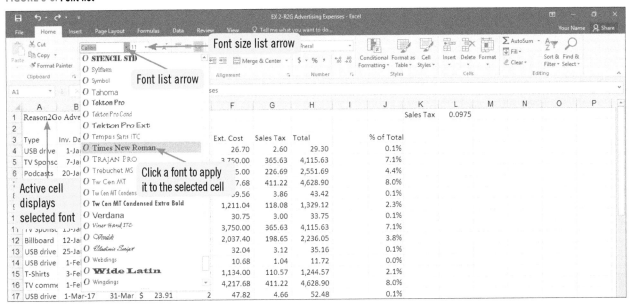

FIGURE 3-6: Worksheet with formatted title and column labels

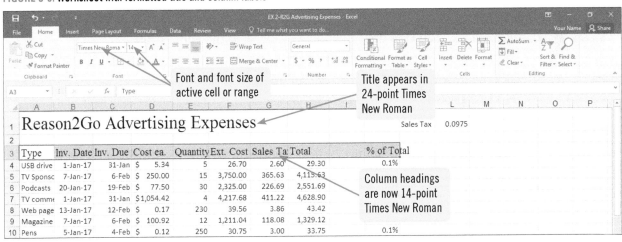

Inserting and adjusting online pictures and other images

You can illustrate your worksheets using online pictures and other images. Office.com makes many photos and animations available for your use. To add a picture to a worksheet, click the Online Pictures button in the Illustrations group on the Insert tab. The Insert Pictures window opens. Here you can search for online pictures (or Clip Art) from a variety of popular sources such as Facebook and Flickr, through the Bing search engine, or on OneDrive. To search, type one or more **keywords** (words related to your subject) in the appropriate Search text box, then press [Enter]. For example, pictures that relate to the keyword house in a search of Office.com appear in the Office.com window, as shown in FIGURE 3-7. When you double-click the image you want in the window, the image is inserted at the location of the active cell. To add images on your computer (or computers on your network) to a worksheet, click the Insert tab on the Ribbon, then click the Pictures button in the Illustrations group. Navigate to

the file you want, then click Insert. To resize an image, drag any corner sizing handle. To move an image, point inside the clip until the pointer changes to ⊹, then drag it to a new location.

FIGURE 3-7: Results of Online Picture search

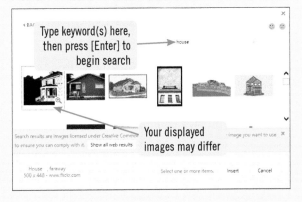

Change Font Styles and Alignment

Learning
Outcomes
• Apply formatting
• Use the Format
  Painter
• Change cell
  alignment

Font styles are formats such as bold, italic, and underlining that you can apply to affect the way text and numbers look in a worksheet. You can also change the **alignment** of labels and values in cells to position them in relation to the cells' edges—such as left-aligned, right-aligned, or centered. You can apply font styles and alignment options using the Home tab, the Format Cells dialog box, or the Mini toolbar. See TABLE 3-2 for a description of common font style and alignment buttons that are available on the Home tab and the Mini toolbar. Once you have formatted a cell the way you want it, you can "paint" or copy the cell's formats into other cells by using the Format Painter button in the Clipboard group on the Home tab. This is similar to using copy and paste, but instead of copying cell contents, it copies only the cell's formatting. **CASE** *You want to further enhance the worksheet's appearance by adding bold and underline formatting and centering some of the labels.*

STEPS

QUICK TIP
You can use the
following keyboard
shortcuts to format a
selected cell or
range: [Ctrl][B] to
bold, [Ctrl][I] to
italicize, and [Ctrl][U]
to underline.

1. **Press [Ctrl][Home], then click the** Bold button B **in the Font group on the Home tab**
   The title in cell A1 appears in bold.

2. **Click cell** A3, **then click the** Underline button U **in the Font group**
   The column label is now underlined.

3. **Click the** Italic button I **in the Font group, then click** B
   The heading now appears in boldface, underlined, italic type. Notice that the Bold, Italic, and Underline buttons in the Font group are all selected.

QUICK TIP
Overuse of any font
style and random
formatting can make
a workbook difficult
to read. Be consistent
and add the same
formatting to similar
items throughout a
worksheet or in
related worksheets.

4. **Click the** Italic button I **to deselect it**
   The italic font style is removed from cell A3, but the bold and underline font styles remain.

5. **Click the** Format Painter button **in the Clipboard group, then select the range** B3:J3
   The formatting in cell A3 is copied to the rest of the column labels. To paint the formats on more than one selection, double-click the Format Painter button to keep it activated until you turn it off. You can turn off the Format Painter by pressing [Esc] or by clicking . You decide the title would look better if it were centered over the data columns.

6. **Select the range** A1:H1, **then click the** Merge & Center button **in the Alignment group**
   The Merge & Center button creates one cell out of the eight cells across the row, then centers the text in that newly created, merged cell. The title "Reason2Go Advertising Expenses" is centered across the eight columns you selected. To split a merged cell into its original components, select the merged cell, then click the Merge & Center button to deselect it. Occasionally, you may find that you want cell contents to wrap within a cell. You can do this by selecting the cells containing the text you want to wrap, then clicking the Wrap Text button in the Alignment group on the Home tab on the Ribbon.

QUICK TIP
To clear all format-
ting from a selected
range, click the
Clear button in
the Editing group
on the Home tab,
then click Clear
Formats.

7. **Select the range** A3:J3, **right-click, then click the** Center button **on the Mini toolbar**
   Compare your screen to FIGURE 3-8. Although they may be difficult to read, notice that all the headings are centered within their cells.

8. **Save your work**

FIGURE 3-8: Worksheet with font styles and alignment applied

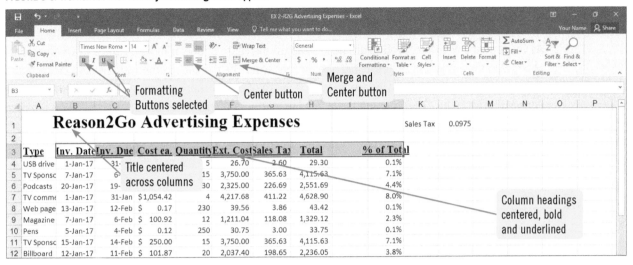

TABLE 3-2: Common font style and alignment buttons

button	description
B	Bolds text
I	Italicizes text
U	Underlines text
	Centers text across columns, and combines two or more selected, adjacent cells into one cell
	Aligns text at the left edge of the cell
	Centers text horizontally within the cell
	Aligns text at the right edge of the cell
	Wraps long text into multiple lines

Rotating and indenting cell entries

In addition to applying fonts and font styles, you can rotate or indent data within a cell to further change its appearance. You can rotate text within a cell by altering its alignment. Click the Home tab, select the cells you want to modify, then click the launcher in the Alignment group to open the Alignment tab of the Format Cells dialog box. Click a position in the Orientation box or type a number in the Degrees text box to rotate text from its default horizontal orientation, then click OK. You can indent cell contents using the Increase Indent button in the Alignment group, which moves cell contents to the right one space, or the Decrease Indent button, which moves cell contents to the left one space.

Adjust Column Width

As you format a worksheet, you might need to adjust the width of one or more columns to accommodate changes in the amount of text, the font size, or font style. The default column width is 8.43 characters, a little less than 1". With Excel, you can adjust the width of one or more columns by using the mouse, the Format button in the Cells group on the Home tab, or the shortcut menu. Using the mouse, you can drag or double-click the right edge of a column heading. The Format button and shortcut menu include commands for making more precise width adjustments. TABLE 3-3 describes common column formatting commands. **CASE** *You have noticed that some of the labels in columns A through J don't fit in the cells. You want to adjust the widths of the columns so that the labels appear in their entirety.*

STEPS

1. **Position the mouse pointer on the line between the column A and column B headings until it changes to ++**

   See FIGURE 3-9. The **column heading** is the box at the top of each column containing a letter. Before you can adjust column width using the mouse, you need to position the pointer on the right edge of the column heading for the column you want to adjust. The cell entry "TV commercials" is the widest in the column.

2. **Click and drag the ++ to the right until the column displays the "TV commercials" cell entries fully (approximately 15.29 characters, 1.23", or 112 pixels)**

   As you change the column width, a ScreenTip is displayed listing the column width. In Normal view, the ScreenTip lists the width in characters and pixels; in Page Layout view, the ScreenTip lists the width in inches and pixels.

3. **Position the pointer on the line between columns B and C until it changes to ++, then double-click**

   Double-clicking the right edge of a column heading activates the **AutoFit** feature, which automatically resizes the column to accommodate the widest entry in the column. Column B automatically widens to fit the widest entry, which is the column label "Inv. Date".

4. **Use AutoFit to resize columns C, D, and J**

5. **Select the range E5:H5**

   You can change the width of multiple columns at once, by first selecting either the column headings or at least one cell in each column.

6. **Click the Format button in the Cells group, then click Column Width**

   The Column Width dialog box opens. Column width measurement is based on the number of characters that will fit in the column when formatted in the Normal font and font size (in this case, 11-point Calibri).

7. **Drag the dialog box by its title bar if its placement obscures your view of the worksheet, type 11 in the Column width text box, then click OK**

   The widths of columns E, F, G, and H change to reflect the new setting. See FIGURE 3-10.

8. **Save your work**

TABLE 3-3: Common column formatting commands

command	description	available using
Column Width	Sets the width to a specific number of characters	Format button; shortcut menu
AutoFit Column Width	Fits to the widest entry in a column	Format button; mouse
Hide & Unhide	Hides or displays hidden column(s)	Format button; shortcut menu
Default Width	Resets column to worksheet's default column width	Format button

FIGURE 3-9: Preparing to change the column width

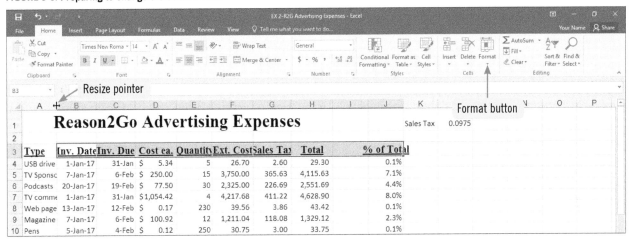

FIGURE 3-10: Worksheet with column widths adjusted

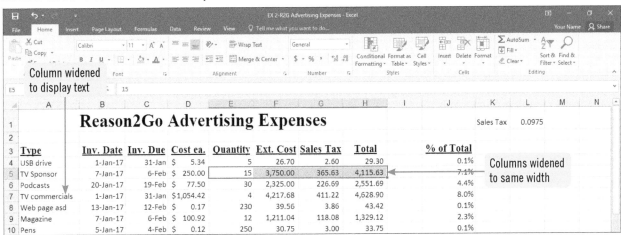

Changing row height

Changing row height is as easy as changing column width. Row height is calculated in points, the same units of measure used for fonts. The row height must exceed the size of the font you are using. Normally, you don't need to adjust row heights manually, because row heights adjust automatically to accommodate font size changes. If you format something in a row to be a larger point size, Excel adjusts the row to fit the largest point size in the row. However, you have just as many options for changing row height as you do column width. Using the mouse, you can place the ✛ pointer on the line dividing a row heading from the heading below, and then drag to the desired height; double-clicking the line AutoFits the row height where necessary. You can also select one or more rows, then use the Row Height command on the shortcut menu, or click the Format button on the Home tab and click the Row Height or AutoFit Row Height command.

Insert and Delete Rows and Columns

Learning Outcomes
- Use the Insert dialog box
- Use column and row heading buttons to insert and delete

As you modify a worksheet, you might find it necessary to insert or delete rows and columns to keep your worksheet current. For example, you might need to insert rows to accommodate new inventory products or remove a column of yearly totals that are no longer necessary. When you insert a new row, the row is inserted above the cell pointer and the contents of the worksheet shift down from the newly inserted row. When you insert a new column, the column is inserted to the left of the cell pointer and the contents of the worksheet shift to the right of the new column. To insert multiple rows, select the same number of row headings as you want to insert before using the Insert command. **CASE** *You want to improve the overall appearance of the worksheet by inserting a row between the last row of data and the totals. Also, you have learned that row 27 and column J need to be deleted from the worksheet.*

STEPS

1. **Right-click cell A32, then click Insert on the shortcut menu**

    The Insert dialog box opens. See FIGURE 3-11. You can choose to insert a column or a row; insert a single cell and shift the cells in the active column to the right; or insert a single cell and shift the cells in the active row down. An additional row between the last row of data and the totals will visually separate the totals.

2. **Click the Entire row option button, then click OK**

    A blank row appears between the Billboard data and the totals, and the formula result in cell E33 has not changed. The Insert Options button 🖋 appears beside cell A33. Pointing to the button displays a list arrow, which you can click and then choose from the following options: Format Same As Above (the default setting, already selected), Format Same As Below, or Clear Formatting.

3. **Click the row 27 heading**

    All of row 27 is selected, as shown in FIGURE 3-12.

4. **Click the Delete button in the Cells group; *do not click the list arrow***

    Excel deletes row 27, and all rows below it shift up one row. You must use the Delete button or the Delete command on the shortcut menu to delete a row or column; pressing [Delete] on the keyboard removes only the *contents* of a selected row or column.

5. **Click the column J heading**

    The percentage information is calculated elsewhere and is no longer necessary in this worksheet.

6. **Click the Delete button in the Cells group**

    Excel deletes column J. The remaining columns to the right shift left one column.

7. **Use AutoFit to resize columns F and H, then save your work**

Hiding and unhiding columns and rows

When you don't want data in a column or row to be visible, but you don't want to delete it, you can hide the column or row. To hide a selected column, click the Format button in the Cells group on the Home tab, point to Hide & Unhide, then click Hide Columns. A hidden column is indicated by a dark green vertical line in its original position. This green line disappears when you click elsewhere in the worksheet. You can display a hidden column by selecting the columns on either side of the hidden column, clicking the Format button in the Cells group, pointing to Hide & Unhide, and then clicking Unhide Columns. (To hide or unhide one or more rows, substitute Hide Rows and Unhide Rows for the Hide Columns and Unhide Columns commands.)

FIGURE 3-11: Insert dialog box

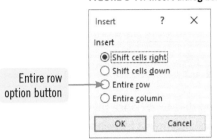

Entire row
option button

FIGURE 3-12: Worksheet with row 27 selected

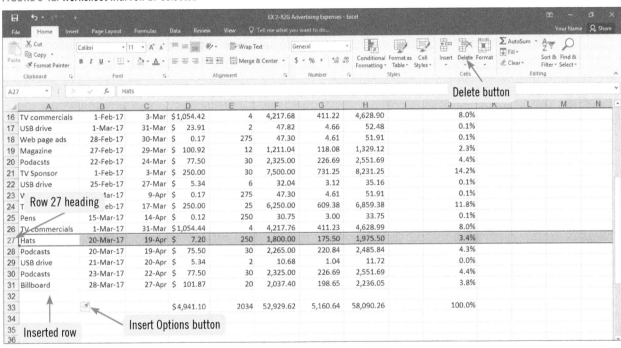

Delete button

Row 27 heading

Insert Options button

Inserted row

Adding and editing comments

Much of your work in Excel may be in collaboration with teammates with whom you share worksheets. You can share ideas with other worksheet users by adding comments within selected cells. To include a comment in a worksheet, click the cell where you want to place the comment, click the Review tab on the Ribbon, then click the New Comment button in the Comments group. You can type your comments in the resizable text box that opens containing the computer user's name. A small, red triangle appears in the upper-right corner of a cell containing a comment. If comments are not already displayed in a workbook, other users can point to the triangle to display the comment. To see all worksheet comments, as shown in FIGURE 3-13, click the Show All Comments button in the Comments group. To edit a comment, click the cell containing the comment, then click the Edit Comment button in the Comments

group. To delete a comment, click the cell containing the comment, then click the Delete button in the Comments group.

FIGURE 3-13: Comments displayed in a worksheet

21	TV Sponsor	1-Feb-16	2-Mar Food Network
22	Newspaper	25-Feb-16	26-Mar Village Reader
23	Web page ads	10-Mar-16	9-Apr Advertising Concepts
24	TV Sponsor	15-Feb-16	16-Mar Food Network
25	Pens	15-Mar-16	14-Apr Mass Appeal, Inc.
26	TV commercials	1-Mar-16	31-Mar Discovery Channel
27	Podcasts	20-Mar-16	19-Apr iPodAds
28	Newspaper	1-Apr-16	1-May University Voice
29	Podcasts	10-Apr-16	10-May iPodAds
30	Billboard	28-Mar-16	27-Apr Advertising Concepts

Harriet McDonald:
I think this will turn out to be a very good decision.

Will Moss:
Should we continue with this market, or expand to other types of publications?

Excel 2016

Apply Colors, Patterns, and Borders

Learning Outcomes
- Use Live Preview to apply color to cells
- Format cells using the shortcut menu
- Apply a border and pattern to a cell

You can use colors, patterns, and borders to enhance the overall appearance of a worksheet and make it easier to read. You can add these enhancements by using the Borders, Font Color, and Fill Color buttons in the Font group on the Home tab of the Ribbon and on the Mini toolbar, or by using the Fill tab and the Border tab in the Format Cells dialog box. You can open the Format Cells dialog box by clicking the dialog box launcher in the Font, Alignment, or Number group on the Home tab, or by right-clicking a selection, then clicking Format Cells on the shortcut menu. You can apply a color to the background of a cell or a range or to cell contents (such as letters and numbers), and you can apply a pattern to a cell or range. You can apply borders to all the cells in a worksheet or only to selected cells to call attention to selected information. To save time, you can also apply **cell styles**, predesigned combinations of formats. **CASE** *You want to add a pattern, a border, and color to the title of the worksheet to give the worksheet a more professional appearance.*

STEPS

1. **Select cell** A1, **click the** Fill Color list arrow ⬜ ⋄ **in the Font group, then hover the pointer over the** Turquoise, Accent 2 color **(first row, sixth column from the left)**

   See FIGURE 3-14. Live Preview shows you how the color will look *before* you apply it. (Remember that cell A1 spans columns A through H because the Merge & Center command was applied.)

2. **Click the** Turquoise, Accent 2 color

   The color is applied to the background (or fill) of this cell. When you change fill or font color, the color on the Fill Color or Font Color button changes to the last color you selected.

> **QUICK TIP**
> Use fill colors and patterns sparingly. Too many colors can be distracting or make it hard to see which information is important.

3. **Right-click cell** A1, **then click** Format Cells **on the shortcut menu**

   The Format Cells dialog box opens.

4. **Click the** Fill tab, **click the** Pattern Style list arrow, **click the** 6.25% Gray style **(first row, sixth column from the left), then click** OK

> **QUICK TIP**
> You can also create custom cell borders. Click the Borders list arrow in the Font group, click More Borders, then click the individual border buttons to apply the borders you want to the selected cell(s).

5. **Click the** Borders list arrow ⬜ ⋄ **in the Font group, then click** Thick Bottom Border

   Unlike underlining, which is a text-formatting tool, borders extend to the width of the cell, and can appear at the bottom of the cell, at the top, on either side, or on any combination of the four sides. It can be difficult to see a border when the cell is selected.

6. **Select the range** A3:H3, **click the** Font Color list arrow ⬜ **in the Font group, then click the** Blue, Accent 1 color **(first Theme Colors row, fifth column from the left) on the palette**

   The new color is applied to the labels in the selected range.

7. **Select the range** J1:K1, **click the** Cell Styles button **in the Styles group, click the** Neutral cell style **(first row, fourth column from the left) in the gallery, then** AutoFit column J

   The font and color change in the range, as shown in FIGURE 3-15.

8. **Save your work**

FIGURE 3-14: Live Preview of fill color

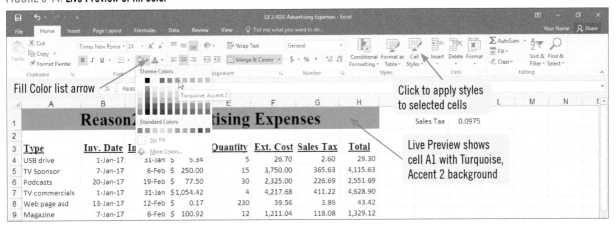

Fill Color list arrow

Click to apply styles to selected cells

Live Preview shows cell A1 with Turquoise, Accent 2 background

FIGURE 3-15: Worksheet with color, patterns, border, and style applied

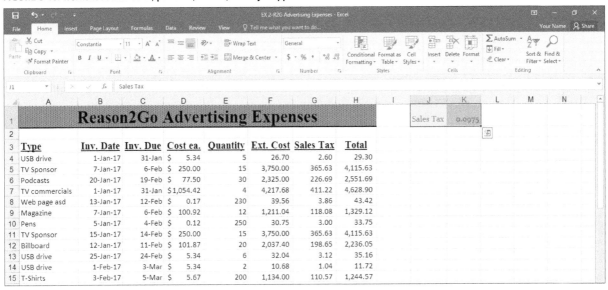

Working with themes and cell styles

Using themes and cell styles makes it easier to ensure that your worksheets are consistent. A **theme** is a predefined set of formats that gives your Excel worksheet a professional look. Formatting choices included in a theme are colors, fonts, and line and fill effects. To apply a theme, click the Themes button in the Themes group on the Page Layout tab to open the Themes gallery, as shown in FIGURE 3-16, then click a theme in the gallery. **Cell styles** are automatically updated if you change a theme. For example, if you apply the 20% - Accent1 cell style to cell A1 in a worksheet that has no theme applied, the fill color changes to light blue with no pattern, and the font changes to Calibri. If you change the theme of the worksheet to Ion Boardroom, cell A1's fill color changes to red and the font changes to Century Gothic, because these are the new theme's associated formats.

FIGURE 3-16: Themes gallery

Formatting a Worksheet

Apply Conditional Formatting

So far, you've used formatting to change the appearance of different types of data, but you can also use formatting to highlight important aspects of the data itself. For example, you can apply formatting that changes the font color to red for any cells where the value is greater than $100 and to green where the value is below $50. This is called **conditional formatting** because Excel automatically applies different formats to data if the data meets conditions you specify. The formatting is updated if you change data in the worksheet. You can also copy conditional formats the same way you copy other formats. **CASE** ➤ *Mary is concerned about advertising costs exceeding the yearly budget. You decide to use conditional formatting to highlight certain trends and patterns in the data so that it's easy to spot the most expensive advertising.*

STEPS

1. **Select the range H4:H30, click the** Conditional Formatting button **in the Styles group on the Home tab, point to** Data Bars, **then point to the** Light Blue Data Bar **(second row, second from left)**

   Data bars are colored horizontal bars that visually illustrate differences between values in a range of cells. Live Preview shows how this formatting will appear in the worksheet, as shown in FIGURE 3-17.

2. **Point to the** Green Data Bar **(first row, second from left), then click it**

3. **Select the range F4:F30, click the** Conditional Formatting button **in the Styles group, then point to** Highlight Cells Rules

   The Highlight Cells Rules submenu displays choices for creating different formatting conditions. For example, you can create a rule for values that are greater than or less than a certain amount, or between two amounts.

4. **Click** Between **on the submenu**

   The Between dialog box opens, displaying input boxes you can use to define the condition and a default format (Light Red Fill with Dark Red Text) selected for cells that meet that condition. Depending on the condition you select in the Highlight Cells Rules submenu (such as "Greater Than" or "Less Than"), this dialog box displays different input boxes. You define the condition using the input boxes and then assign the formatting you want to use for cells that meet that condition. Values used in input boxes for a condition can be constants, formulas, cell references, or dates.

5. **Type** 2000 **in the first text box, type** 4000 **in the second text box, click the** with list arrow, **click** Light Red Fill, **compare your settings to** FIGURE 3-18, **then click** OK

   All cells with values between 2000 and 4000 in column F appear with a light red fill.

6. **Click cell** E7, **type** 3, **then press** [Enter]

   When the value in cell E7 changes, the formatting also changes because the new value meets the condition you set. Compare your results to FIGURE 3-19.

7. **Press** [Ctrl][Home] **to select cell A1, then save your work**

Formatting a Worksheet

FIGURE 3-17: Previewing data bars in a range

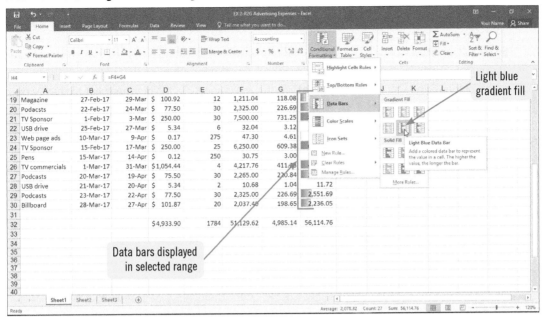

Light blue gradient fill

Data bars displayed in selected range

FIGURE 3-18: Between dialog box

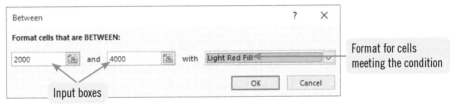

Format for cells meeting the condition

Input boxes

FIGURE 3-19: Worksheet with conditional formatting

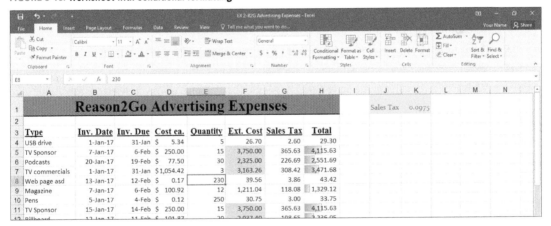

Managing conditional formatting rules

If you create a conditional formatting rule and then want to change a condition, you don't need to create a new rule; instead, you can modify the rule using the Rules Manager. Click the Conditional Formatting button in the Styles group, then click Manage Rules. The Conditional Formatting Rules Manager dialog box opens. Select the rule you want to edit, click Edit Rule, and then modify the settings in the Edit the Rule Description area in the Edit Formatting Rule dialog box. To change the formatting for

a rule, click the Format Style button in the Edit the Rule Description area, select the formatting styles you want the text to have, then click OK three times to close the Format Cells dialog box, the Edit Formatting Rule dialog box, and the Conditional Formatting Rules Manager dialog box. The rule is modified, and the new conditional formatting is applied to the selected cells. To delete a rule, select the rule in the Conditional Formatting Rules Manager dialog box, then click the Delete Rule button.

Rename and Move a Worksheet

Learning Outcomes
• Rename a sheet
• Apply color to a sheet tab
• Reorder sheets in a workbook

By default, an Excel workbook initially contains one worksheet named Sheet1, although you can add sheets at any time. Each sheet name appears on a sheet tab at the bottom of the worksheet. When you open a new workbook, the first worksheet, Sheet1, is the active sheet. To move from sheet to sheet, you can click any sheet tab at the bottom of the worksheet window. The sheet tab scrolling buttons, located to the left of the sheet tabs, are useful when a workbook contains too many sheet tabs to display at once. To make it easier to identify the sheets in a workbook, you can rename each sheet and add color to the tabs. You can also organize them in a logical way. For instance, to better track performance goals, you could name each workbook sheet for an individual salesperson, and you could move the sheets so they appear in alphabetical order. **CASE** ▶ *In the current worksheet, Sheet1 contains information about actual advertising expenses. Sheet2 contains an advertising budget, and Sheet3 contains no data. You want to rename the two sheets in the workbook to reflect their contents, add color to a sheet tab to easily distinguish one from the other, and change their order.*

STEPS

1. **Click the** Sheet2 tab

   Sheet2 becomes active, appearing in front of the Sheet1 tab; this is the worksheet that contains the budgeted advertising expenses. See FIGURE 3-20.

2. **Click the** Sheet1 tab

   Sheet1, which contains the actual advertising expenses, becomes active again.

3. **Double-click the** Sheet2 tab, **type** Budget, **then press** [Enter]

   The new name for Sheet2 automatically replaces the default name on the tab. Worksheet names can have up to 31 characters, including spaces and punctuation.

4. **Right-click the** Budget tab, **point to** Tab Color **on the shortcut menu, then click the** Bright Green, Accent 4, Lighter 40% color **(fourth row, third column from the right) as shown in** FIGURE 3-21

5. **Double-click the** Sheet1 tab, **type** Actual, **then press** [Enter]

   Notice that the color of the Budget tab changes depending on whether it is the active tab; when the Actual tab is active, the color of the Budget tab changes to the green tab color you selected. You decide to rearrange the order of the sheets so that the Budget tab is to the left of the Actual tab.

6. **Click the** Budget tab, **hold down the mouse button, drag it to the left of the** Actual tab, **as shown in** FIGURE 3-22, **then release the mouse button**

   As you drag, the pointer changes to ⬚, the sheet relocation pointer, and a small, black triangle just above the tabs shows the position the moved sheet will be in when you release the mouse button. The first sheet in the workbook is now the Budget sheet. See FIGURE 3-23. You can move multiple sheets by pressing and holding [Shift] while clicking the sheets you want to move, then dragging the sheets to their new location.

7. **Click the** Actual sheet tab, **click the** Page Layout button 🖹 **on the status bar to open Page Layout view, enter your name in the left header text box, then click anywhere in the worksheet to deselect the header**

8. **Click the** Page Layout tab **on the Ribbon, click the** Orientation button **in the Page Setup group, then click** Landscape

9. **Right-click the** Sheet3 tab, **click** Delete **on the shortcut menu, press** [Ctrl][Home], **then save your work**

FIGURE 3-20: **Sheet tabs in workbook**

Sheet1 tab   Sheet2 tab

FIGURE 3-21: **Tab Color palette**

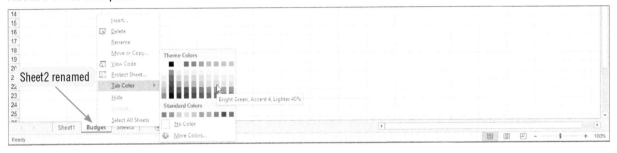

Sheet2 renamed

FIGURE 3-22: **Moving the Budget sheet**

Sheet relocation pointer

FIGURE 3-23: **Reordered sheets**

Budget sheet comes
before Actual sheet

Copying, adding, and deleting worksheets

There are times when you may want to copy a worksheet. For example, a workbook might contain a sheet with Quarter 1 expenses, and you want to use that sheet as the basis for a sheet containing Quarter 2 expenses. To copy a sheet within the same workbook, press and hold [Ctrl], drag the sheet tab to the desired tab location, release the mouse button, then release [Ctrl]. A duplicate sheet appears with the same name as the copied sheet followed by "(2)" indicating that it is a copy. You can then rename the sheet to a more meaningful name. To copy a sheet to a different workbook, both the source and destination workbooks must be open. Select the sheet to copy or move, right-click the sheet tab, then click Move or Copy in the shortcut menu. Complete the information in the Move or Copy dialog box. Be sure to click the Create a copy check box if you are copying rather than moving the worksheet. Carefully check your calculation results whenever you move or copy a worksheet. You can add multiple worksheets to a workbook by clicking the Home tab on the Ribbon, pressing and holding [Shift], then clicking the number of existing worksheet tabs that correspond with the number of sheets you want to add, clicking the Insert list arrow in the Cells group on the Home tab, then clicking Insert Sheet. You can delete multiple worksheets from a workbook by clicking the Home tab, pressing and holding [Shift], clicking the sheet tabs of the worksheets you want to delete, clicking the Delete list arrow in the Cells group on the Home tab, then clicking Delete Sheet.

Check Spelling

Learning
Outcomes
• Describe how spell
  checking works
• Change the
  spelling using
  a suggestion
• Replace a word
  using Find & Select

Excel includes a spell checker to help you ensure that the words in your worksheet are spelled correctly. The spell checker scans your worksheet, displays words it doesn't find in its built-in dictionary, and suggests replacements when they are available. To check all of the sheets in a multiple-sheet workbook, you need to display each sheet individually and run the spell checker for each one. Because the built-in dictionary cannot possibly include all the words that anyone needs, you can add words to the dictionary, such as your company name, an acronym, or an unusual technical term. Once you add a word or term, the spell checker no longer considers that word misspelled. Any words you've added to the dictionary using Word, Access, or PowerPoint are also available in Excel. **CASE** *Before you distribute this workbook to Mary, you check the spelling.*

STEPS

QUICK TIP
The Spelling dialog box lists the name of the language currently being used in its title bar.

1. **Click the** Review tab **on the Ribbon, then click the** Spelling button **in the Proofing group**
   The Spelling: English (United States) dialog box opens, as shown in FIGURE 3-24, with "asd" selected as the first misspelled word in the worksheet, and with "ads" selected in the Suggestions list as a possible replacement. For any word, you have the option to Ignore this case of the flagged word, Ignore All cases of the flagged word, Change the word to the selected suggestion, Change All instances of the flagged word to the selected suggestion, or add the flagged word to the dictionary using Add to Dictionary.

2. **Click** Change
   Next, the spell checker finds the word "Podacsts" and suggests "Podcasts" as an alternative.

3. **Verify that the word** Podcasts **is selected in the Suggestions list, then click** Change
   When no more incorrect words are found, Excel displays a message indicating that the spell check is complete.

4. **Click** OK

5. **Click the** Home tab, **click** Find & Select **in the Editing group, then click** Replace
   The Find and Replace dialog box opens. You can use this dialog box to replace a word or phrase. It might be a misspelling of a proper name that the spell checker didn't recognize as misspelled, or it could simply be a term that you want to change throughout the worksheet. Mary has just told you that each instance of "Billboard" in the worksheet should be changed to "Sign."

6. **Type** Billboard **in the Find what text box, press [Tab], then type** Sign **in the Replace with text box**
   Compare your dialog box to FIGURE 3-25.

7. **Click** Replace All, **click** OK **to close the Microsoft Excel dialog box, then click** Close **to close the Find and Replace dialog box**
   Excel has made two replacements.

8. **Click the** File tab, **click** Print **on the navigation bar, click the** No Scaling setting **in the Settings section on the Print tab, then click** Fit Sheet on One Page

9. **Click the** Return button ⊙ **to return to your worksheet, save your work, submit it to your instructor as directed, close the workbook, then exit Excel**
   The completed worksheet is shown in FIGURE 3-26.

Emailing a workbook

You can send an entire workbook from within Excel using your installed email program, such as Microsoft Outlook. To send a workbook as an email message attachment, open the workbook, click the File tab, then click Share on the navigation bar. With the Email option selected in the Share section in Backstage view, click Send as Attachment in the right pane. An email message opens in your default email program with the workbook automatically attached; the filename appears in the Attached field. Complete the To and optional Cc fields, include a message if you wish, then click Send.

FIGURE 3-24: Spelling: English (United States) dialog box

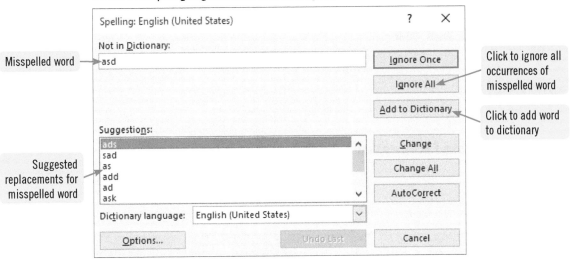

Misspelled word →

Suggested replacements for misspelled word →

Click to ignore all occurrences of misspelled word

Click to add word to dictionary

FIGURE 3-25: Find and Replace dialog box

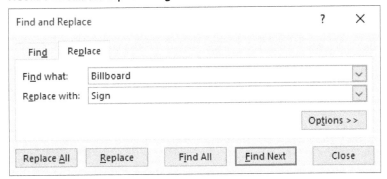

FIGURE 3-26: Completed worksheet

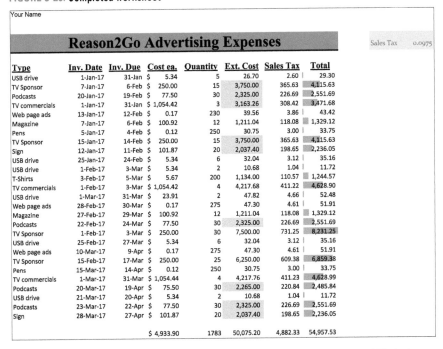

Your Name

Reason2Go Advertising Expenses

Sales Tax   0.0975

Type	Inv. Date	Inv. Due	Cost ea.	Quantity	Ext. Cost	Sales Tax	Total
USB drive	1-Jan-17	31-Jan	$ 5.34	5	26.70	2.60	29.30
TV Sponsor	7-Jan-17	6-Feb	$ 250.00	15	3,750.00	365.63	4,115.63
Podcasts	20-Jan-17	19-Feb	$ 77.50	30	2,325.00	226.69	2,551.69
TV commercials	1-Jan-17	31-Jan	$ 1,054.42	3	3,163.26	308.42	3,471.68
Web page ads	13-Jan-17	12-Feb	$ 0.17	230	39.56	3.86	43.42
Magazine	7-Jan-17	6-Feb	$ 100.92	12	1,211.04	118.08	1,329.12
Pens	5-Jan-17	4-Feb	$ 0.12	250	30.75	3.00	33.75
TV Sponsor	15-Jan-17	14-Feb	$ 250.00	15	3,750.00	365.63	4,115.63
Sign	12-Jan-17	11-Feb	$ 101.87	20	2,037.40	198.65	2,236.05
USB drive	25-Jan-17	24-Feb	$ 5.34	6	32.04	3.12	35.16
USB drive	1-Feb-17	3-Mar	$ 5.34	2	10.68	1.04	11.72
T-Shirts	3-Feb-17	5-Mar	$ 5.67	200	1,134.00	110.57	1,244.57
TV commercials	1-Feb-17	3-Mar	$ 1,054.42	4	4,217.68	411.22	4,628.90
USB drive	1-Mar-17	31-Mar	$ 23.91	2	47.82	4.66	52.48
Web page ads	28-Feb-17	30-Mar	$ 0.17	275	47.30	4.61	51.91
Magazine	27-Feb-17	29-Mar	$ 100.92	12	1,211.04	118.08	1,329.12
Podcasts	22-Feb-17	24-Mar	$ 77.50	30	2,325.00	226.69	2,551.69
TV Sponsor	1-Feb-17	3-Mar	$ 250.00	30	7,500.00	731.25	8,231.25
USB drive	25-Feb-17	27-Mar	$ 5.34	6	32.04	3.12	35.16
Web page ads	10-Mar-17	9-Apr	$ 0.17	275	47.30	4.61	51.91
TV Sponsor	15-Feb-17	17-Mar	$ 250.00	25	6,250.00	609.38	6,859.38
Pens	15-Mar-17	14-Apr	$ 0.12	250	30.75	3.00	33.75
TV commercials	1-Mar-17	31-Mar	$ 1,054.44	4	4,217.76	411.23	4,628.99
Podcasts	20-Mar-17	19-Apr	$ 75.50	30	2,265.00	220.84	2,485.84
USB drive	21-Mar-17	20-Apr	$ 5.34	2	10.68	1.04	11.72
Podcasts	23-Mar-17	22-Apr	$ 77.50	30	2,325.00	226.69	2,551.69
Sign	28-Mar-17	27-Apr	$ 101.87	20	2,037.40	198.65	2,236.05
			$ 4,933.90	1783	50,075.20	4,882.33	54,957.53

Practice

Concepts Review

Label each element of the Excel worksheet window shown in FIGURE 3-27.

FIGURE 3-27

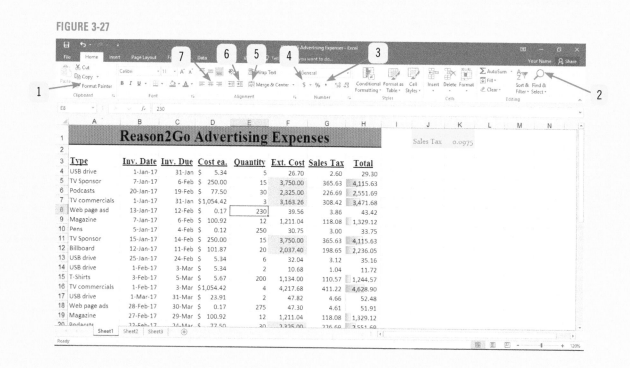

Match each command or button with the statement that best describes it.

8. Spelling button

9. $

10. [fill color button]

11. [Ctrl][Home]

12. [merge & center button]

13. Conditional formatting

a. Checks for apparent misspellings in a worksheet

b. Adds dollar signs and two decimal places to selected data

c. Displays fill color options for a cell

d. Moves cell pointer to cell A1

e. Centers cell contents across multiple cells

f. Changes formatting of a cell that meets a certain rule

Formatting a Worksheet

Select the best answer from the list of choices.

14. Which of the following is an example of Accounting number format?

- **a.** 5555
- **b.** $5,555.55
- **c.** 55.55%
- **d.** 5,555.55

15. What is the name of the feature used to resize a column to accommodate its widest entry?

- **a.** AutoFormat
- **b.** AutoFit
- **c.** AutoResize
- **d.** AutoRefit

16. Which button copies multiple formats from selected cells to other cells?

- **a.**
- **b.**
- **c.**
- **d.**

17. Which button increases the number of decimal places in selected cells?

- **a.**
- **b.**
- **c.**
- **d.**

18. Which button removes the italic font style from selected cells?

- **a.**
- **b.**
- **c.**
- **d.**

19. What feature is used to delete a conditional formatting rule?

- **a.** Rules Reminder
- **b.** Conditional Formatting Rules Manager
- **c.** Condition Manager
- **d.** Format Manager

Skills Review

1. Format values.

- **a.** Start Excel, open the file EX 3-2.xlsx from the location where you store your Data Files, then save it as **EX 3-Health Insurance Premiums**.
- **b.** Use the Sum function to enter a formula in cell B10 that totals the number of employees.
- **c.** Create a formula in cell C5 that calculates the monthly insurance premium for the accounting department. (*Hint*: Make sure you use the correct type of cell reference in the formula. To calculate the department's monthly premium, multiply the number of employees by the monthly premium in cell B14.)
- **d.** Copy the formula in cell C5 to the range C6:C10.
- **e.** Format the range C5:C10 using Accounting number format.
- **f.** Change the format of the range C6:C9 to the Comma Style.
- **g.** Reduce the number of decimals in cell B14 to 0 using a button in the Number group on the Home tab.
- **h.** Save your work.

2. Change font and font sizes.

- **a.** Select the range of cells containing the column labels (in row 4).
- **b.** Change the font of the selection to Times New Roman.
- **c.** Increase the font size of the selection to 12 points.
- **d.** Increase the font size of the label in cell A1 to 14 points.
- **e.** Save your changes.

3. Change font styles and alignment.

- **a.** Apply the bold and italic font styles to the worksheet title in cell A1.
- **b.** Use the Merge & Center button to center the Health Insurance Premiums label over columns A–C.
- **c.** Apply the italic font style to the Health Insurance Premiums label.
- **d.** Add the bold font style to the labels in row 4.
- **e.** Use the Format Painter to copy the format in cell A4 to the range A5:A10.
- **f.** Apply the format in cell C10 to cell B14.
- **g.** Change the alignment of cell A10 to Align Right using a button in the Alignment group.

Skills Review (continued)

    h. Select the range of cells containing the column labels, then center them.

    i. Remove the italic font style from the Health Insurance Premiums label, then increase the font size to 14.

    j. Move the Health Insurance Premiums label to cell A3, remove the Merge & Center format, then add the bold and underline font styles.

    k. Save your changes.

4. Adjust column width.

    a. Resize column C to a width of 10.71 characters.

    b. Use the AutoFit feature to resize columns A and B.

    c. Clear the contents of cell A13 (do not delete the cell).

    d. Change the text in cell A14 to **Monthly Premium**, then change the width of the column to 25 characters.

    e. Save your changes.

5. Insert and delete rows and columns.

    a. Insert a new row between rows 5 and 6.

    b. Add a new department, **Donations**, in the newly inserted row. Enter **6** as the number of employees in the department.

    c. Copy the formula in cell C7 to C6.

    d. Add the following comment to cell A6: **New department**. Display the comment, then drag to move it out of the way, if necessary.

    e. Add a new column between the Department and Employees columns with the title **Family Coverage**, then resize the column using AutoFit.

    f. Delete the Legal row from the worksheet.

    g. Move the value in cell C14 to cell B14.

    h. Save your changes.

6. Apply colors, patterns, and borders.

    a. Add Outside Borders around the range A4:D10.

    b. Add a Bottom Double Border to cells C9 and D9 (above the calculated employee and premium totals).

    c. Apply the Aqua, Accent 5, Lighter 80% fill color to the labels in the Department column (do not include the Total label).

    d. Apply the Orange, Accent 6, Lighter 60% fill color to the range A4:D4.

    e. Change the color of the font in the range A4:D4 to Red, Accent 2, Darker 25%.

    f. Add a 12.5% Gray pattern style to cell A1.

    g. Format the range A14:B14 with a fill color of Dark Blue, Text 2, Lighter 40%, change the font color to White, Background 1, then apply the bold font style.

    h. Save your changes.

7. Apply conditional formatting.

    a. Select the range D5:D9, then create a conditional format that changes cell contents to green fill with dark green text if the value is between 150 and 275.

    b. Select the range C5:C9, then create a conditional format that changes cell contents to red text if the number of employees exceeds 10.

    c. Apply a purple gradient-filled data bar to the range C5:C9. (*Hint*: Click Purple Data Bar in the Gradient Fill section.)

    d. Use the Rules Manager to modify the conditional format in cells C5:C9 to display values greater than 10 in bold dark red text.

    e. Save your changes.

8. Rename and move a worksheet.

    a. Name the Sheet1 tab **Insurance Data**.

    b. Add a sheet to the workbook, then name the new sheet **Employee Data**.

    c. Change the Insurance Data tab color to Red, Accent 2, Lighter 40%.

Skills Review (continued)

d. Change the Employee Data tab color to Aqua, Accent 5, Lighter 40%.

e. Move the Employee Data sheet so it comes before (to the left of) the Insurance Data sheet.

f. Make the Insurance Data sheet active, enter your name in cell A20, then save your work.

9. Check spelling.

a. Move the cell pointer to cell A1.

b. Use the Find & Select feature to replace the Accounting label with **Accounting/Legal**.

c. Check the spelling in the worksheet using the spell checker, and correct any spelling errors if necessary.

d. Save your changes, then compare your Insurance Data sheet to FIGURE 3-28.

e. Preview the Insurance Data sheet in Backstage view, submit your work to your instructor as directed, then close the workbook and exit Excel.

FIGURE 3-28

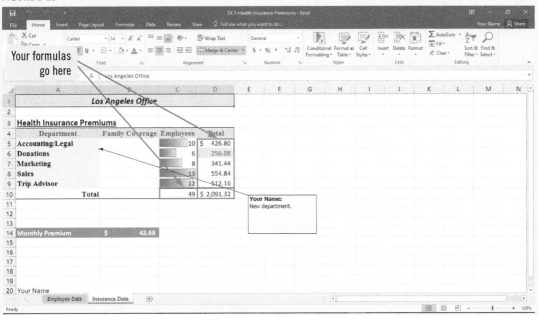

Independent Challenge 1

You run a freelance accounting business, and one of your newest clients is Fresh To You, a small local grocery store. Now that you've converted the store's accounting records to Excel, the manager would like you to work on an analysis of the inventory. Although more items will be added later, the worksheet has enough items for you to begin your modifications.

a. Start Excel, open the file EX 3-3.xlsx from the location where you store your Data Files, then save it as **EX 3-Fresh To You Inventory**.

b. Create a formula in cell E4 that calculates the value of the items in stock based on the price paid per item in cell B4. Format the cell in the Comma Style.

c. In cell F4, calculate the sale value of the items in stock using an absolute reference to the markup value shown in cell H1.

d. Copy the formulas created above into the range E5:F14; first convert any necessary cell references to absolute so that the formulas work correctly.

e. Apply bold to the column labels, and italicize the inventory items in column A.

f. Make sure that all columns are wide enough to display the data and labels.

g. Format the values in the Sale Value column as Accounting number format with two decimal places.

h. Format the values in the Price Paid column as Comma Style with two decimal places.

Independent Challenge 1 (continued)

i. Add a row under Cheddar Cheese for **Whole Wheat flour**, price paid **0.95**, sold by weight (**pound**), with **23** on hand. Copy the appropriate formulas to cells E7:F7.

j. Verify that all the data in the worksheet is visible and formulas are correct. Adjust any items as needed, and check the spelling of the entire worksheet.

k. Use conditional formatting to apply yellow fill with dark yellow text to items with a quantity of less than 25 on hand.

l. Use an icon set of your choosing in the range D4:D14 to illustrate the relative differences between values in the range.

m. Add an outside border around the data in the Item column (*do not* include the Item column label).

n. Delete the row containing the Resource Coffee - decaf entry.

o. Enter your name in an empty cell below the data, then save the file. Compare your worksheet to the sample in FIGURE 3-29.

p. Preview the worksheet in Backstage view, submit your work to your instructor as directed, close the workbook, then exit Excel.

FIGURE 3-29

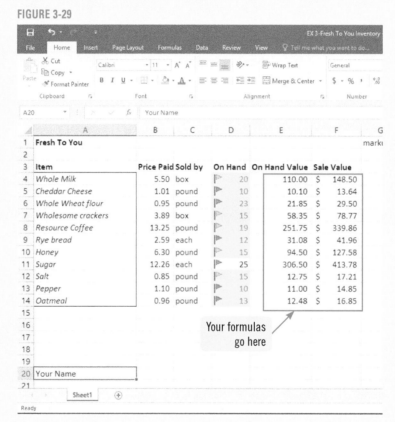

Independent Challenge 2

You volunteer several hours each week with the Assistance League of San Antonio, and you are in charge of maintaining the membership list. You're currently planning a mailing campaign to members in certain regions of the city. You also want to create renewal letters for members whose membership expires soon. You decide to format the list to enhance the appearance of the worksheet and make your upcoming tasks easier to plan.

a. Start Excel, open the file EX 3-4.xlsx from the location where you store your Data Files, then save it as **EX 3-Memphis Assistance League**.

b. Remove any blank columns.

c. Create a conditional format in the Zip Code column so that entries greater than 38249 appear in light red fill with dark red text.

d. Make all columns wide enough to fit their data and labels. (*Hint*: You can use any method to size the columns.)

e. Use formatting enhancements, such as fonts, font sizes, font styles, and fill colors, to make the worksheet more attractive.

Independent Challenge 2 (continued)

f. Center the column labels.

g. Use conditional formatting so that entries for Year of Membership Expiration that are between 2021 and 2023 appear in green fill with bold black text. (*Hint:* Create a custom format for cells that meet the condition.)

h. Adjust any items as necessary, then check the spelling.

i. Change the name of the Sheet1 tab to one that reflects the sheet's contents, then add a tab color of your choice.

j. Enter your name in an empty cell, then save your work.

k. Preview the worksheet, make any final changes you think necessary, then submit your work to your instructor as directed. Compare your work to the sample shown in FIGURE 3-30.

l. Close the workbook, then exit Excel.

FIGURE 3-30

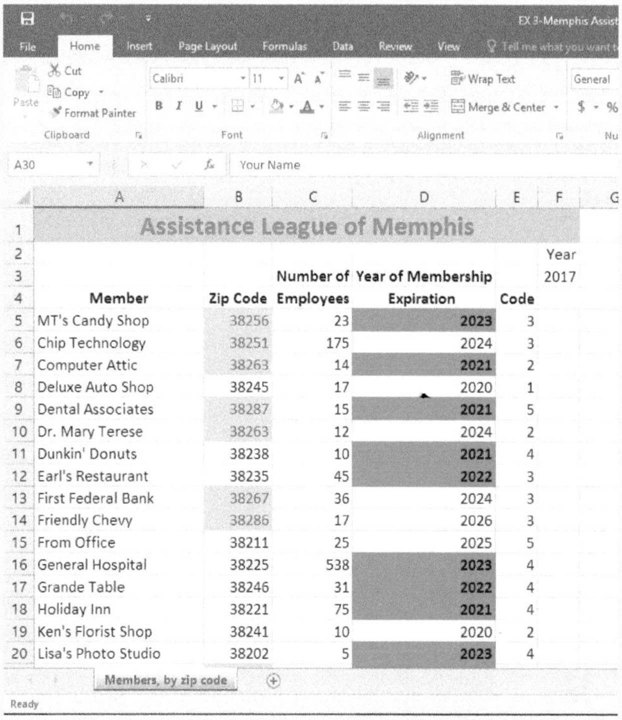

Independent Challenge 3

Advantage Calendars is a Dallas-based printer that prints and assembles calendars. As the finance manager for the company, one of your responsibilities is to analyze the monthly reports from the five district sales offices. Your boss, Joanne Bennington, has just asked you to prepare a quarterly sales report for an upcoming meeting. Because several top executives will be attending this meeting, Joanne reminds you that the report must look professional. In particular, she asks you to highlight the fact that the Northeastern district continues to outpace the other districts.

a. Plan a worksheet that shows the company's sales during the first quarter. Assume that all calendars are the same price. Make sure you include the following:
   - The number of calendars sold (units sold) and the associated revenues (total sales) for each of the five district sales offices. The five sales districts are Northeastern, Midwestern, Southeastern, Southern, and Western.
   - Calculations that show month-by-month totals for January, February, and March, and a 3-month cumulative total.
   - Calculations that show each district's share of sales (percent of Total Sales).
   - Labels that reflect the month-by-month data as well as the cumulative data.
   - Formatting enhancements such as data bars that emphasize the recent month's sales surge and the Northeastern district's sales leadership.

b. Ask yourself the following questions about the organization and formatting of the worksheet: What worksheet title and labels do you need, and where should they appear? How can you calculate the totals? What formulas can you copy to save time and keystrokes? Do any of these formulas need to use an absolute reference? How do you show dollar amounts? What information should be shown in bold? Do you need to use more than one font? Should you use more than one point size?

c. Start Excel, then save a new, blank workbook as **EX 3-Advantage Calendars** to the location where you store your Data Files.

Independent Challenge 3 (continued)

d. Build the worksheet with your own price and sales data. Enter the titles and labels first, then enter the numbers and formulas. You can use the information in TABLE 3-4 to get started.

TABLE 3-4

Advantage Calendars										
1st Quarter Sales Report										
		January		February		March		Total		
Office	Price	Units Sold	Sales	Units Sold	Sales	Units Sold	Sales	Units Sold	Sales	Total % of Sales
Northeastern										
Midwestern										
Southeastern										
Southern										
Western										

e. Add a row beneath the data containing the totals for each column.

f. Adjust the column widths as necessary.

g. Change the height of row 1 to 33 points.

h. Format labels and values to enhance the look of the worksheet, and change the font styles and alignment if necessary.

i. Resize columns and adjust the formatting as necessary.

j. Add data bars for the monthly Units Sold columns.

k. Add a column that calculates a 25% increase in total sales dollars. Use an absolute cell reference in this calculation. (*Hint*: Make sure that the current formatting is applied to the new information.)

l. Delete the contents of cells J4:K4 if necessary, then merge and center cell I4 over column I:K.

m. Add a bottom double border to cells I10:L10.

n. Enter your name in an empty cell.

o. Check the spelling in the workbook, change to a landscape orientation, save your work, then compare your work to FIGURE 3-31.

p. Preview the worksheet in Backstage view, then submit your work to your instructor as directed.

q. Close the workbook file, then exit Excel.

FIGURE 3-31

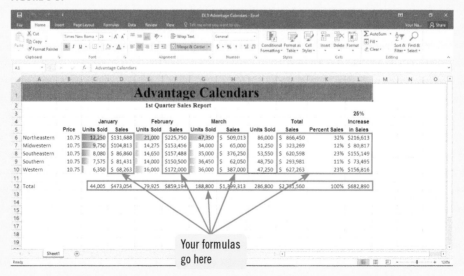

Formatting a Worksheet

Independent Challenge 4: Explore

This Independent Challenge requires an Internet connection.

Your corporate relocation company helps employees to settle quickly and easily into new cities around the world. Your latest client plans to send employees to seven different countries. All employees will receive the same weekly budget in American currency. You need to create a worksheet to help all the employees understand the currency conversion rates in the different countries so that they can plan their spending effectively.

a. Start Excel, then save a new, blank workbook as **EX 3-Foreign Currency Rates** to the location where you store your Data Files.

b. Add a title at the top of the worksheet.

c. Think of seven countries that each use a different currency, then enter column and row labels for your worksheet. (*Hint*: You may wish to include row labels for each country, plus column labels for the country, the $1 equivalent in native currency, the total amount of native currency employees will have in each country, and the name of each country's monetary unit.)

d. Decide how much money employees will bring to each country (for example, $1,000), and enter that in the worksheet.

e. Use your favorite search engine to find your own information sources on currency conversions for the countries you have listed.

f. Enter the cash equivalent to $1 in U.S. dollars for each country in your list.

g. Create an equation that calculates the amount of native currency employees will have in each country, using an absolute cell reference in the formula.

h. Format the entries in the column containing the native currency $1 equivalent as Number number format with three decimal places, and format the column containing the total native currency budget with two decimal places, using the correct currency number format for each country. (*Hint*: Use the Number tab in the Format cells dialog box; choose the appropriate currency number format from the Symbol list.)

i. Create a conditional format that changes the font style and color of the calculated amount in the $1,000 US column to light red fill with dark red text if the amount exceeds **1000** units of the local currency.

j. Merge and center the worksheet title over the column headings.

k. Add any formatting you want to the column headings, and resize the columns as necessary.

l. Add a background color to the title and change the font color if you choose.

m. Enter your name in the header of the worksheet.

n. Spell check the worksheet, save your changes, compare your work to FIGURE 3-32, then preview the worksheet, and submit your work to your instructor as directed.

o. Close the workbook and exit Excel.

FIGURE 3-32

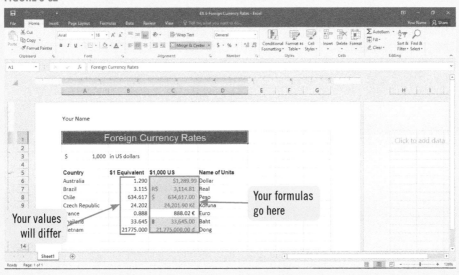

Visual Workshop

Open the file EX 3-5.xlsx from the location where you store your Data Files, then save it as **EX 3-London Employees**. Use the skills you learned in this module to format the worksheet so it looks like the one shown in FIGURE 3-33. Create a conditional format in the Level column so that entries greater than 3 appear in light red fill with dark red text. Create an additional conditional format in the Review Cycle column so that any value equal to 3 appears in black fill with white bold text. Replace the Accounting department label with **Legal**. (*Hint*: The only additional font used in this exercise is 18-point Times New Roman in row 1.) Enter your name in the upper-right part of the header, check the spelling in the worksheet, save your changes, then submit your work to your instructor as directed. (*Hint*: To match the figure exactly, remember to match the zoom level.)

FIGURE 3-33

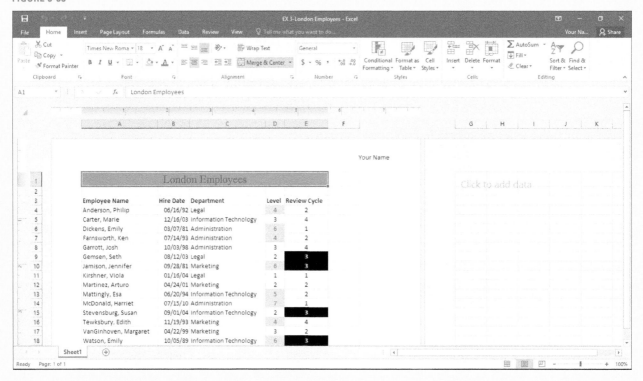

Working with Charts

CASE At the upcoming annual meeting, Yolanda Lee wants to discuss spending patterns at Reason2Go. She asks you to create a chart showing the trends in company expenses over the past four quarters.

Module Objectives

After completing this module, you will be able to:

- Plan a chart
- Create a chart
- Move and resize a chart
- Change the chart design
- Change the chart format
- Format a chart
- Annotate and draw on a chart
- Create a pie chart

Files You Will Need

EX 4-1.xlsx	EX 4-4.xlsx
EX 4-2.xlsx	EX 4-5.xlsx
EX 4-3.xlsx	EX 4-6.xlsx

Plan a Chart

Learning
Outcomes
• Prepare to create
  a chart
• Identify chart
  elements
• Explore common
  chart types

Before creating a chart, you need to plan the information you want your chart to show and how you want it to look. Planning ahead helps you decide what type of chart to create and how to organize the data. Understanding the parts of a chart makes it easier to format and change specific elements so that the chart best illustrates your data. **CASE** ▶ *In preparation for creating the chart for Yolanda's presentation, you identify your goals for the chart and plan its layout.*

DETAILS

Use the following guidelines to plan the chart:

• **Determine the purpose of the chart, and identify the data relationships you want to communicate graphically**

  You want to create a chart that shows quarterly tour expenses for each country where Reason2Go provides tours. This worksheet data is shown in FIGURE 4-1. You also want the chart to illustrate whether the quarterly expenses for each country increased or decreased from quarter to quarter.

• **Determine the results you want to see, and decide which chart type is most appropriate**

  Different chart types display data in distinctive ways. For example, a pie chart compares parts to the whole, so it's useful for showing what proportion of a budget amount was spent on tours in one country relative to what was spent on tours in other countries. A line chart, in contrast, is best for showing trends over time. To choose the best chart type for your data, you should first decide how you want your data displayed and interpreted. TABLE 4-1 describes several different types of charts you can create in Excel and their corresponding buttons on the Insert tab on the Ribbon. Because you want to compare R2G tour expenses in multiple countries over a period of four quarters, you decide to use a column chart.

• **Identify the worksheet data you want the chart to illustrate**

  Sometimes you use all the data in a worksheet to create a chart, while at other times you may need to select a range within the sheet. The worksheet from which you are creating your chart contains expense data for each of the past four quarters and the totals for the past year. You will need to use all the quarterly data except the quarterly totals.

• **Understand the elements of a chart**

  The chart shown in FIGURE 4-2 contains basic elements of a chart. In the figure, R2G tour countries are on the horizontal axis (also called the **x-axis**) and expense dollar amounts are on the vertical axis (also called the **y-axis**). The horizontal axis is also called the **category axis** because it often contains the names of data groups, such as locations, months, or years. The vertical axis is also called the **value axis** because it often contains numerical values that help you interpret the size of chart elements. (3-D charts also contain a **z-axis**, for comparing data across both categories and values.) The area inside the horizontal and vertical axes is the **plot area**. The **tick marks**, on the vertical axis, and **gridlines** (extending across the plot area) create a scale of measure for each value. Each value in a cell you select for your chart is a **data point**. In any chart, a **data marker** visually represents each data point, which in this case is a column. A collection of related data points is a **data series**. In this chart, there are four data series (Quarter 1, Quarter 2, Quarter 3, and Quarter 4). Each is made up of column data markers of a different color, so a **legend** is included to make it easy to identify them.

FIGURE 4-1: Worksheet containing expense data

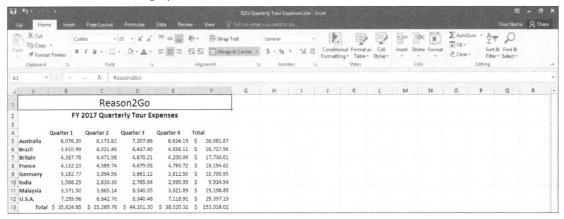

FIGURE 4-2: Chart elements

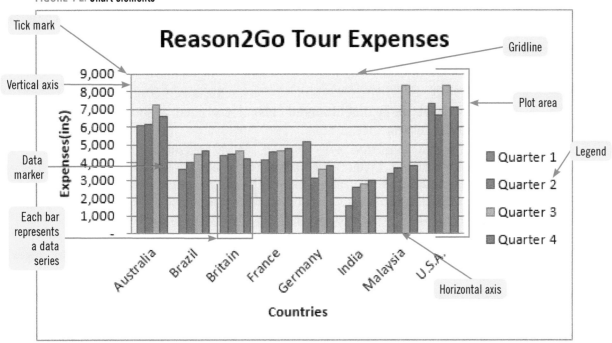

TABLE 4-1: Common chart types

type	button	description
Column		Compares data using columns; the Excel default; sometimes referred to as a bar chart in other spreadsheet programs
Line		Compares trends over even time intervals; looks similar to an area chart, but does not emphasize total
Pie		Compares sizes of pieces as part of a whole; used for a single series of numbers
Bar		Compares data using horizontal bars; sometimes referred to as a horizontal bar chart in other spreadsheet programs
Area		Shows how individual volume changes over time in relation to total volume
Scatter		Compares trends over uneven time or measurement intervals; used in scientific and engineering disciplines for trend spotting and extrapolation
Combo		Displays two or more types of data using different chart types; illustrates mixed or widely varying types of data

Create a Chart

Learning
Outcomes
• Create a chart
• Switch a chart's
  columns/rows
• Add a chart title

To create a chart in Excel, you first select the range in a worksheet containing the data you want to chart. Once you've selected a range, you can use The Quick Analysis tool or the Insert tab on the Ribbon to create a chart based on the data in the range. **CASE** *Using the worksheet containing the quarterly expense data, you create a chart that shows how the expenses in each country varied across the quarters.*

STEPS

QUICK TIP
When charting data for a particular time period, make sure that all series are for the same time period.

1. **Start Excel, open the file** EX 4-1.xlsx **from the location where you store your Data Files, then save it as** EX 4-R2G Quarterly Tour Expenses

   You want the chart to include the quarterly tour expenses values, as well as quarter and country labels. You don't include the Total column and row because the figures in these cells would skew the chart.

2. **Select the range A4:E12, click the** Quick Analysis tool 🗐 **in the lower-right corner of the range, then click** Charts

   The Charts tab on the Quick Analysis tool recommends commonly used chart types based on the range you have selected. The Charts tab also includes a More Charts button for additional chart types, such as stock charts for charting stock market data.

QUICK TIP
To base a chart on data in nonadjacent ranges, press and hold [Ctrl] while selecting each range, then use the Insert tab to create the chart.

3. **On the** Charts tab, **verify that** Clustered Column **is selected, as shown in** FIGURE 4-3, **then click** Clustered Column

   The chart is inserted in the center of the worksheet, and two contextual Chart Tools tabs appear on the Ribbon: Design and Format. On the Design tab, which is currently active, you can quickly change the chart type, chart layout, and chart style, and you can swap how the columns and rows of data in the worksheet are represented in the chart. When seen in the Normal view, three tools display to the right of the chart: these enable you to add, remove, or change chart elements ➕, set a style and color scheme 🖌, and filter the results shown in a chart 🔽. Currently, the countries are charted along the horizontal x-axis, with the quarterly expense dollar amounts charted along the y-axis. This lets you easily compare the quarterly expenses for each country.

4. **Click the** Switch Row/Column button **in the Data group on the Chart Tools Design tab**

   The quarters are now charted along the x-axis. The expense amounts per country are charted along the y-axis, as indicated by the updated legend. See FIGURE 4-4.

5. **Click the** Undo button 🔄 **on the Quick Access Toolbar**

   The chart returns to its original design.

QUICK TIP
You can also triple-click to select the chart title text.

6. **Click the** Chart Title placeholder **to show the text box, click anywhere in the** Chart Title text box, **press [Ctrl][A] to select the text, type** R2G Quarterly Tour Expenses, **then click anywhere in the chart to deselect the title**

   Adding a title helps identify the chart. The border around the chart and the **sizing handles**, the small series of dots at the corners and sides of the chart's border, indicate that the chart is selected. See FIGURE 4-5. Your chart might be in a different location on the worksheet and may look slightly different; you will move and resize it in the next lesson. Any time a chart is selected, as it is now, a blue border surrounds the worksheet data range on which the chart is based, a purple border surrounds the cells containing the category axis labels, and a red border surrounds the cells containing the data series labels. This chart is known as an **embedded chart** because it is inserted directly in the current worksheet and doesn't exist in a separate file. Embedding a chart in the current sheet is the default selection when creating a chart, but you can also embed a chart on a different sheet in the workbook, or on a newly created chart sheet. A **chart sheet** is a sheet in a workbook that contains only a chart that is linked to the workbook data.

7. **Save your work**

FIGURE 4-3: **Charts tab in Quick Analysis tool**

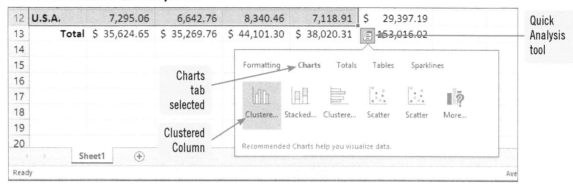

FIGURE 4-4: **Clustered Column chart with different configuration of rows and columns**

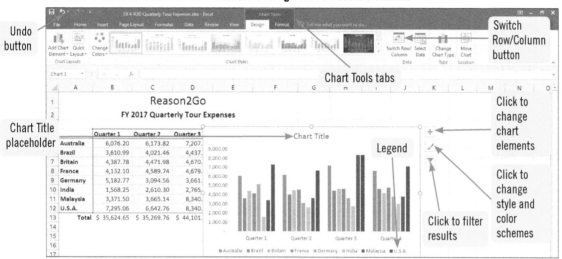

FIGURE 4-5: **Chart with original configuration restored and title added**

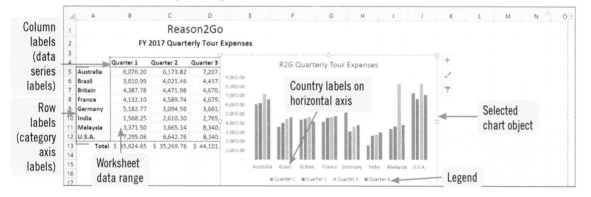

Creating sparklines

You can quickly create a miniature chart called a **sparkline** that serves as a visual indicator of data trends. You can create a sparkline by selecting a range of data, clicking the Quick Analysis tool, clicking the Sparklines tab, then clicking the type of sparkline you want. (The sparkline appears in the cell immediately adjacent to the selected range.) You can also select a range, click the Insert tab, then click the Line, Column, or Win/Loss button in the Sparklines group. In the Create Sparklines dialog box that opens, enter the cell in which you want the sparkline to appear,

then click OK. FIGURE 4-6 shows a sparkline created in a cell. Any changes to data in the range are reflected in the sparkline. To delete a selected sparkline from a cell, click the Clear button in the Group group on the Sparkline Tools Design tab.

FIGURE 4-6: **Sparklines in a cell**

Move and Resize a Chart

Learning Outcomes
• Reposition a chart
• Resize a chart
• Modify a legend
• Modify chart data

A chart is an **object**, or an independent element on a worksheet, and is not located in a specific cell or range. You can select an object by clicking it; sizing handles around the object indicate it is selected. (When a chart is selected in Excel, the Name box, which normally tells you the address of the active cell, tells you the chart number.) You can move a selected chart anywhere on a worksheet without affecting formulas or data in the worksheet. Any data changed in the worksheet is automatically updated in the chart. You can even move a chart to a different sheet in the workbook, and it will still reflect the original data. You can resize a chart to improve its appearance by dragging its sizing handles. You can reposition chart objects (such as a title or legend) to predefined locations using commands using the Chart Elements button or the Add Chart Element button on the Chart Tools Design tab, or you can freely move any chart object by dragging it or by cutting and pasting it to a new location. When you point to a chart object, the name of the object appears as a ScreenTip. **CASE** ➤ *You want to resize the chart, position it below the worksheet data, and move the legend.*

STEPS

1. **Make sure the chart is still selected, then position the pointer over the chart**

   The pointer shape ✥ indicates that you can move the chart. For a table of commonly used object pointers, refer to TABLE 4-2.

2. **Position ✥ on a blank area near the upper-left edge of the chart, press and hold the left mouse button, drag the chart until its upper-left corner is at the upper-left corner of cell A16, then release the mouse button**

   When you release the mouse button, the chart appears in the new location.

3. **Scroll down so you can see the whole chart, position the pointer on the right-middle sizing handle until it changes to ⟷, then drag the right border of the chart to the right edge of column G**

   The chart is widened. See FIGURE 4-7.

4. **Position the pointer over the upper-middle sizing handle until it changes to ↕, then drag the top border of the chart to the top edge of row 15**

5. **Position the pointer over the lower-middle sizing handle until it changes to ↕, then drag the bottom border of the chart to the bottom border of row 26**

   You can move any object on a chart. You want to align the top of the legend with the top of the plot area.

6. **Click the Quick Layout button in the Chart Layouts group of the Chart Tools Design tab, click Layout 1 (in the upper-left corner of the palette), click the legend to select it, press and hold [Shift], drag the legend up using ✥ so the dotted outline is approximately ¼″ above the top of the plot area, then release [Shift]**

   When you click the legend, sizing handles appear around it and "Legend" appears as a ScreenTip when the pointer hovers over the object. As you drag, a dotted outline of the legend border appears. Pressing and holding the [Shift] key holds the horizontal position of the legend as you move it vertically. Although the sizing handles on objects within a chart look different from the sizing handles that surround a chart, they function the same way.

7. **Click cell A12, type United States, click the Enter button ✓ on the formula bar, use AutoFit to resize column A, then save your work**

   The axis label changes to reflect the updated cell contents, as shown in FIGURE 4-8. Changing any data in the worksheet modifies corresponding text or values in the chart. Because the chart is no longer selected, the Chart Tools tabs no longer appear on the Ribbon.

FIGURE 4-7: **Moved and resized chart**

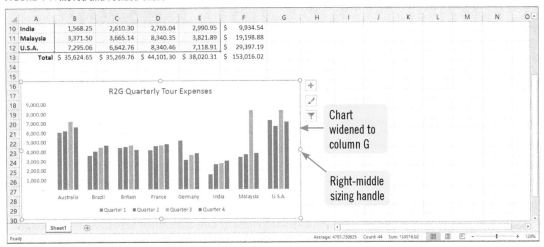

FIGURE 4-8: **Worksheet with modified legend and label**

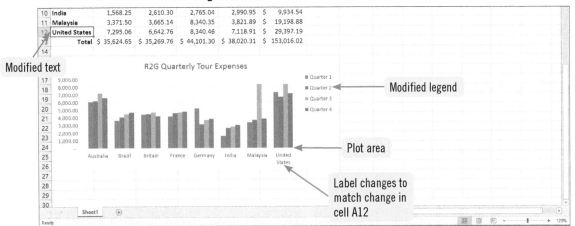

TABLE 4-2: **Common object pointers**

name	pointer	use	name	pointer	use
Diagonal resizing	⬀ or ⬂	Change chart shape from corners	I-beam	I	Edit object text
Draw	+	Draw an object	Move	⌖	Move object
Horizontal resizing	⟺	Change object width	Vertical resizing	↕	Change object height

Moving an embedded chart to a sheet

Suppose you have created an embedded chart that you decide would look better on a chart sheet or in a different worksheet. You can make this change without recreating the entire chart. To do so, first select the chart, click the Chart Tools Design tab, then click the Move Chart button in the Location group. The Move Chart dialog box opens. To move the chart to its own chart sheet, click the New sheet option button, type a name for the new sheet if desired, then click OK. If the chart is already on its own sheet or you want to move it to a different existing sheet, click the Object in option button, click the desired worksheet, then click OK.

Change the Chart Design

Learning Outcomes
- Change the chart design
- Change the chart type
- Apply a chart style

Once you've created a chart, you can change the chart type, modify the data range and column/row configuration, apply a different chart style, and change the layout of objects in the chart. The layouts in the Chart Layouts group on the Chart Tools Design tab offer arrangements of objects in your chart, such as its legend, title, or gridlines; choosing one of these layouts is an alternative to manually changing how objects are arranged in a chart. **CASE** *You discovered that the data for Malaysia and the United States in Quarter 3 is incorrect. After the correction, you want to see how the data looks using different chart layouts and types.*

STEPS

1. **Click cell D11, type** 5568.92, **press** [Enter], **type** 7107.09, **then press** [Enter]

   In the chart, the Quarter 3 data markers for Malaysia and the United States reflect the adjusted expense figures. See FIGURE 4-9.

2. **Select the** chart **by clicking a blank area within the chart border, click the** Chart Tools Design tab **on the Ribbon, click the** Quick Layout button **in the Chart Layouts group, then click** Layout 3

   The legend moves to the bottom of the chart. You prefer the original layout.

3. **Click the** Undo button ↻ ▾ **on the Quick Access Toolbar, then click the** Change Chart Type button **in the Type group**

   The Change Chart Type dialog box opens, as shown in FIGURE 4-10. The left pane of the dialog box lists the available categories, and the right pane shows the individual chart types. A pale gray border surrounds the currently selected chart type.

4. **Click** Bar **in the left pane of the Change Chart Type dialog box, confirm that the first Clustered Bar chart type is selected in the right pane, then click** OK

   The column chart changes to a clustered bar chart. See FIGURE 4-11. You decide to see how the data looks in a three-dimensional column chart.

5. **Click the** Change Chart Type button **in the Type group, click** Column **in the left pane of the Change Chart Type dialog box, click** 3-D Clustered Column **(fourth from the left in the top row) in the right pane, verify that the left-most 3-D chart is selected, then click** OK

   A three-dimensional column chart appears. You notice that the three-dimensional column format gives you a sense of volume, but it is more crowded than the two-dimensional column format.

6. **Click the** Change Chart Type button **in the Type group, click** Clustered Column **(first from the left in the top row) in the right pane of the Change Chart Type dialog box, then click** OK

7. **Click the** Style 3 chart style **in the Chart Styles group**

   The columns change to lighter shades of color. You prefer the previous chart style's color scheme.

8. **Click** ↻ ▾ **on the Quick Access Toolbar, then save your work**

Creating a combo chart

A **combo chart** presents two or more charts in one; a column chart with a line chart, for example. This type of chart is helpful when charting dissimilar but related data. For example, you can create a combo chart based on home price and home size data, showing home prices in a column chart and related home sizes in a line chart. Here a **secondary axis** (such as a vertical axis on the right side of the chart) would supply the scale for the home sizes.

To create a combo chart, select all the data you want to plot, click the Combo chart button 📊▾ in the Charts group in the Insert tab, click a suggested type or Create Custom Combo Chart, supply additional series information if necessary, then click OK. To change an existing chart to a combo chart, select the chart, click Change Chart Type in the Type group on the Chart Tools Design tab, then follow the same procedure.

FIGURE 4-9: **Worksheet with modified data**

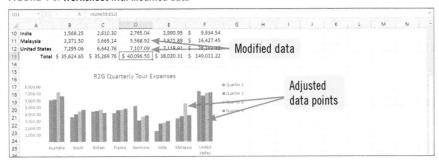

FIGURE 4-10: **Change Chart Type dialog box**

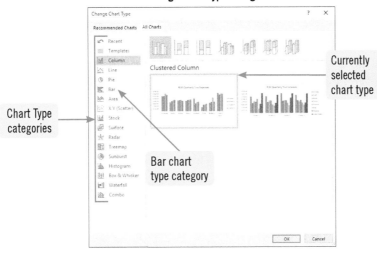

FIGURE 4-11: **Column chart changed to bar chart**

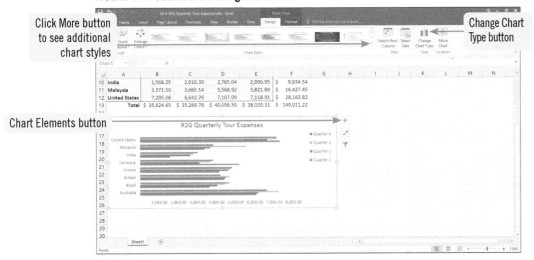

Working with a 3-D chart

Excel includes two kinds of 3-D chart types. In a true 3-D chart, a third axis, called the **z-axis**, lets you compare data points across both categories and values. The z-axis runs along the depth of the chart, so it appears to advance from the back of the chart. To create a true 3-D chart, look for chart types that begin with "3-D," such as 3-D Column. In a 3-D chart, data series can sometimes obscure other columns or bars in the same chart, but you can rotate the chart to obtain a better view. Right-click the chart, then click 3-D Rotation. The Format Chart Area pane opens with the 3-D Rotation category active. The 3-D Rotation options let you change the orientation and perspective of the chart area, plot area, walls, and floor. The 3-D Format category lets you apply three-dimensional effects to selected chart objects. (Not all 3-D Rotation and 3-D Format options are available on all charts.)

Working with Charts

Excel 87

Change the Chart Format

Learning
Outcomes
• Change the
  gridlines display
• Add axis titles
• Change the
  border color
• Add a shadow
  to an object

While the Chart Tools Design tab contains preconfigured chart layouts you can apply to a chart, the Chart Elements button makes it easy to add, remove, and modify individual chart objects such as a chart title or legend. Using options on this shortcut menu (or using the Add Chart Element button on the Chart Tools Design tab), you can also add text to a chart, add and modify labels, change the display of axes, modify the fill behind the plot area, create titles for the horizontal and vertical axes, and eliminate or change the look of gridlines. You can format the text in a chart object using the Home tab or the Mini toolbar, just as you would the text in a worksheet. **CASE** *You want to change the layout of the chart by creating titles for the horizontal and vertical axes. To improve the chart's appearance, you'll add a drop shadow to the chart title.*

STEPS

1. **With the chart still selected, click the** Add Chart Element button **in the Chart Layouts group on the Chart Tools Design tab, point to** Gridlines, **then click** Primary Major Horizontal **to deselect it**

   The gridlines that extend from the value axis tick marks across the chart's plot area are removed as shown in FIGURE 4-12.

2. **Click the** Chart Elements button ⊞ **in the upper-right corner** *outside* **the chart border, click the** Gridlines arrow, **click** Primary Major Horizontal, **click** Primary Minor Horizontal, **then click** ⊞ **to close the Chart Elements fly-out menu**

   Both major and minor gridlines now appear in the chart. **Major gridlines** represent the values at the value axis tick marks, and **minor gridlines** represent the values between the tick marks.

3. **Click** ⊞, **click the** Axis Titles checkbox **to select all the axis titles options, triple-click the vertical axis title on the chart, then type** Expenses (in $)

   Descriptive text on the category axis helps readers understand the chart.

4. **Triple-click the** horizontal axis title **on the chart, then type** Tour Countries

   The text "Tour Countries" appears on the horizontal axis, as shown in FIGURE 4-13.

5. **Right-click the** horizontal axis labels ("Australia", "Brazil", etc.), **click** Font **on the shortcut menu, click the** Latin text font list arrow **in the Font dialog box, click** Times New Roman, **click the** Size down arrow **until** 8 **is displayed, then click** OK

   The font of the horizontal axis labels changes to Times New Roman, and the font size decreases, making more of the plot area visible.

6. **Right-click the** vertical axis labels, **then click** Reset to Match

7. **Right-click the** Chart Title ("R2G Quarterly Tour Expenses"), **click** Format Chart Title **on the shortcut menu, click the** Border arrow ▶ **in the Format Chart Title pane to display the options if necessary, then click the** Solid line option button **in the pane**

   A solid border appears around the chart title with the default blue color.

8. **Click the** Effects button ⬠ **in the Format Chart Title pane, click** Shadow, **click the** Presets list arrow, **click** Offset Diagonal Bottom Right **in the Outer group (first row, first from the left), click the** Format Chart Title pane Close button ✕, **then save your work**

   A blue border with a drop shadow surrounds the title. Compare your work to FIGURE 4-14.

FIGURE 4-12: Gridlines removed from chart

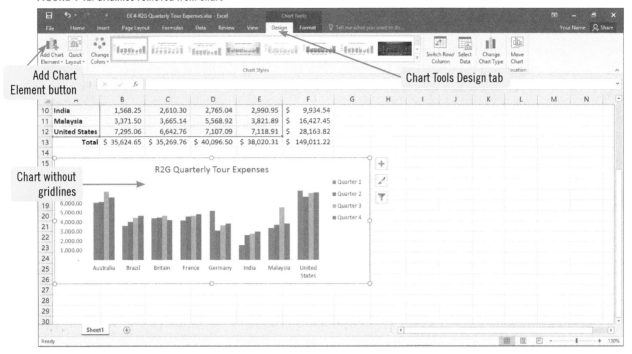

Add Chart Element button

Chart Tools Design tab

Chart without gridlines

FIGURE 4-13: Axis titles added to chart

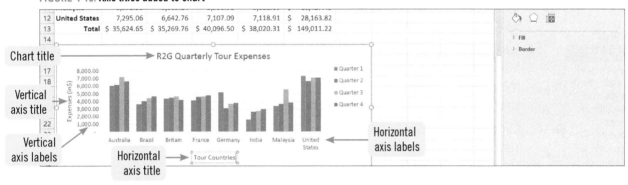

Chart title

Vertical axis title

Vertical axis labels

Horizontal axis title

Horizontal axis labels

FIGURE 4-14: Enhanced chart

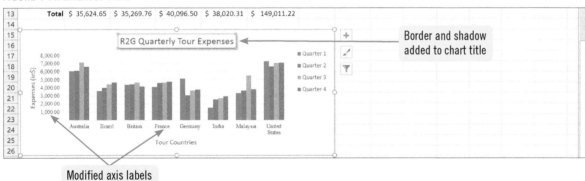

Border and shadow added to chart title

Modified axis labels

Adding data labels to a chart

There are times when your audience might benefit by seeing data labels on a chart. These labels appear next to the data markers in the chart and can indicate the series name, category name, and/or the value of one or more data points. Once your chart is selected, you can add this information to your chart by clicking the Chart Elements button in the upper-right corner outside the selected chart, clicking the Data Labels arrow, and then clicking a display option for the data labels. Once you have added the data labels, you can format them or delete individual data labels. To delete a data label, select it and then press [Delete].

Format a Chart

Formatting a chart can make it easier to read and understand. Many formatting enhancements can be made using the Chart Tools Format tab. You can change the fill color for a specific data series, or you can apply a shape style to a title or a data series using the Shape Styles group. Shape styles make it possible to apply multiple formats, such as an outline, fill color, and text color, all with a single click. You can also apply different fill colors, outlines, and effects to chart objects using arrows and buttons in the Shape Styles group. **CASE** *You want to use a different color for one data series in the chart and apply a shape style to another, to enhance the look of the chart.*

STEPS

1. **With the chart selected, click the** Chart Tools Format tab **on the Ribbon, then click any column in the** Quarter 4 data series

   Handles appear on each column in the Quarter 4 data series, indicating that the entire series is selected.

2. **Click the** Shape Fill list arrow **in the Shape Styles group on the Chart Tools Format tab**

3. **Click** Orange, Accent 6 **(first row, 10th from the left) as shown in** FIGURE 4-15

   All the columns for the series become orange, and the legend changes to match the new color. You can also change the color of selected objects by applying a shape style.

4. **Click any** column **in the** Quarter 3 data series

   Handles appear on each column in the Quarter 3 data series.

5. **Click the** More button ▾ **on the Shape Styles gallery, then** *hover the pointer* **over the** Moderate Effect – Olive Green, Accent 3 shape style **(fifth row, fourth from the left) in the gallery, as shown in** FIGURE 4-16

   Live Preview shows the data series in the chart with the shape style applied.

6. **Click the** Subtle Effect – Olive Green, Accent 3 shape style

   The style for the data series changes, as shown in FIGURE 4-17.

7. **Save your work**

Previewing a chart

To print or preview just a chart, select the chart (or make the chart sheet active), click the File tab, then click Print on the navigation bar. To reposition a chart by changing the page's margins, click the Show Margins button ⊞ in the lower-right corner of the Print tab to display the margins in the preview. You can drag the margin lines to the exact settings you want; as the margins change, the size and placement of the chart on the page change too.

FIGURE 4-15: New shape fill applied to data series

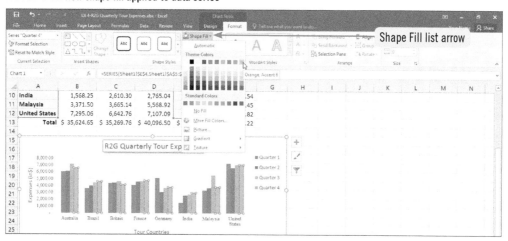

FIGURE 4-16: Live Preview of new style applied to data series

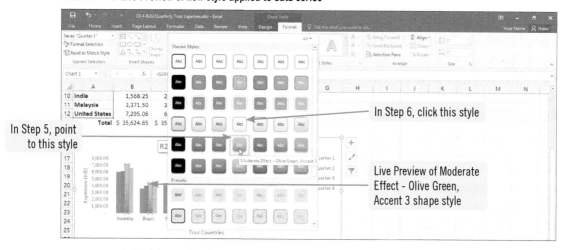

FIGURE 4-17: Style of data series changed

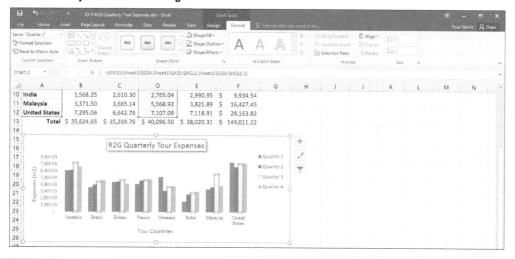

Changing alignment and angle in axis labels and titles

The buttons on the Chart Tools Design tab provide a few options for positioning axis labels and titles, but you can customize their position and rotation to exact specifications using the Format Axis pane or Format Axis Title pane. With a chart selected, right-click the axis text you want to modify, then click Format Axis or Format Axis Title on the shortcut menu. In the pane that opens, click the Size & Properties button, then select the appropriate option. You can also create a custom angle by clicking the Custom angle up and down arrows. When you have made the desired changes, close the pane.

Annotate and Draw on a Chart

Learning
Outcomes
• Type text in a text
  box
• Draw an arrow on
  a chart
• Modify a drawn
  object

You can use text annotations and graphics to point out critical information in a chart. **Text annotations** are labels that further describe your data. You can also draw lines and arrows that point to the exact locations you want to emphasize. Shapes such as arrows and boxes can be added from the Illustrations group on the Insert tab or from the Insert Shapes group on the Chart Tools Format tab on the Ribbon. The Insert group is also used to insert pictures into worksheets and charts. **CASE** *You want to call attention to the Germany tour expense decrease, so you decide to add a text annotation and an arrow to this information in the chart.*

STEPS

1. **With the chart selected and the Chart Tools Format tab active, click the Text Box button ▣ in the Insert Shapes group, then move the pointer over the worksheet**
   The pointer changes to ↓, indicating that you will insert a text box where you next click.

2. **Click to the right of the chart (anywhere *outside* the chart boundary)**
   A text box is added to the worksheet, and the Drawing Tools Format tab appears on the Ribbon so that you can format the new object. First you need to type the text.

3. **Type Great Improvement**
   The text appears in a selected text box on the worksheet, and the chart is no longer selected, as shown in FIGURE 4-18. Your text box may be in a different location; this is not important because you'll move the annotation in the next step.

4. **Point to an edge of the text box so that the pointer changes to ⁺ᵣ, drag the text box into the chart to the left of the chart title, as shown in FIGURE 4-19, then release the mouse button**
   The text box is a text annotation for the chart. You also want to add a simple arrow shape in the chart.

5. **Click the chart to select it, click the Chart Tools Format tab, click the Arrow button ◺ in the Insert Shapes group, then move the pointer over the text box on the chart**
   The pointer changes to ✚, and the status bar displays "Click and drag to insert an AutoShape." When ✚ is over the text box, black handles appear around the text in the text box. A black handle can act as an anchor for the arrow.

6. **Position ✚ on the black handle to the right of the "t" in the word "improvement" (in the text box), press and hold the left mouse button, drag the line to the Quarter 2 column for the Germany category in the chart, then release the mouse button**
   An arrow points to the Quarter 2 expense for Germany, and the Drawing Tools Format tab displays options for working with the new arrow object. You can resize, format, or delete it just like any other object in a chart.

7. **Click the Shape Outline list arrow in the Shape Styles group, click the Automatic color, click the Shape Outline list arrow again, point to Weight, then click 1½ pt**
   Compare your finished chart to FIGURE 4-20.

8. **Save your work**

FIGURE 4-18: **Text box added**

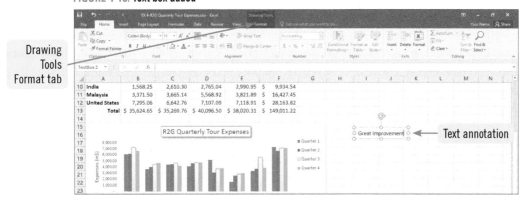

Drawing
Tools
Format tab

Text annotation

FIGURE 4-19: **Text annotation on the chart**

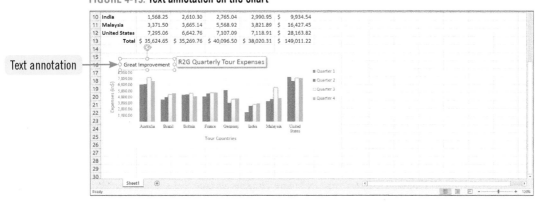

Text annotation

FIGURE 4-20: **Arrow shape added to chart**

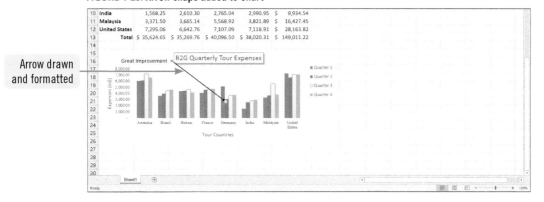

Arrow drawn
and formatted

Adding SmartArt graphics

In addition to charts, annotations, and drawn objects, you can create a variety of diagrams using SmartArt graphics. **SmartArt graphics** are available in List, Process, Cycle, Hierarchy, Relationship, Matrix, Pyramid, Picture, and Office.com categories. To insert SmartArt, click the Insert a SmartArt Graphic button in the Illustrations group on the Insert tab to open the Choose a SmartArt Graphic dialog box. Click a SmartArt category in the left pane, then click a layout for the graphic in the right pane. The right pane shows sample layouts for the selected SmartArt, as shown in FIGURE 4-21. The SmartArt graphic appears in the worksheet as an embedded object with sizing handles. Depending on the type of SmartArt graphic you selected, a text pane opens next

to the graphic; you can enter text into the graphic using the text pane or by typing directly in the shapes in the diagram.

FIGURE 4-21: **Choose a SmartArt Graphic dialog box**

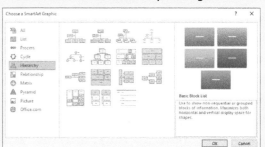

Create a Pie Chart

Learning
Outcomes
• Create a pie chart
• Explode a pie
chart slice

You can create multiple charts based on the same worksheet data. While a column chart may illustrate certain important aspects of your worksheet data, you may find that you want to create an additional chart to emphasize a different point. Depending on the type of chart you create, you have additional options for calling attention to trends and patterns. For example, if you create a pie chart, you can emphasize one data point by **exploding**, or pulling that slice away from, the pie chart. When you're ready to print a chart, you can preview it just as you do a worksheet to check the output before committing it to paper. You can print a chart by itself or as part of the worksheet. **CASE** ▶ *At an upcoming meeting, Yolanda plans to discuss the total tour expenses and which countries need improvement. You want to create a pie chart she can use to illustrate total expenses. Finally, you want to fit the worksheet and the charts onto one worksheet page.*

STEPS

1. **Select the range** A5:A12, **press and hold** [Ctrl], **select the range** F5:F12, **click the** Insert tab, **click the** Insert Pie or Doughnut Chart button **in the Charts group, then click** 3-D Pie **in the chart gallery**

   The new chart appears in the center of the worksheet. You can move the chart and quickly format it using a chart layout.

2. **Drag the** chart **so its upper-left corner is at the upper-left corner of cell** G1, **click the** Quick Layout button **in the Chart Layouts group of the Chart Tools Design tab, then click** Layout 2

   The chart is repositioned on the page, and its layout changes so that a chart title is added, the percentages display on each slice, and the legend appears just below the chart title.

3. **Select the** Chart Title text, **then type** R2G Total Expenses, by Country

4. **Click the slice for the** India data point, **click it again so it is the only slice selected, right-click it, then click** Format Data Point

   The Format Data Point pane opens, as shown in FIGURE 4-22. You can use the Point Explosion slider to control the distance a pie slice moves away from the pie, or you can type a value in the Point Explosion text box.

5. **Double-click** 0 **in the** Point Explosion text box, **type** 40, **then click the** Close button ⊠

   Compare your chart to FIGURE 4-23. You decide to preview the chart and data before you print.

6. **Click cell** A1, **switch to** Page Layout view, **type your name in the left header text box, then click cell** A1

   You decide the chart and data would fit better on the page if they were printed in landscape orientation.

7. **Click the** Page Layout tab, **click the** Orientation button **in the Page Setup group, then click** Landscape

8. **Click the** File tab, **click** Print **on the navigation bar, verify that the correct printer is selected, click the** No Scaling setting **in the Settings section on the Print tab, then click** Fit Sheet on One Page

   The data and chart are positioned horizontally on a single page, as shown in FIGURE 4-24. The printer you have selected may affect the appearance of your preview screen.

9. **Save and close the workbook, submit your work to your instructor as directed, then exit Excel**

FIGURE 4-22: **Format Data Point pane**

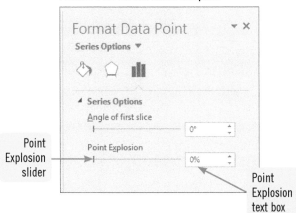

Point Explosion slider

Point Explosion text box

FIGURE 4-23: **Exploded pie slice**

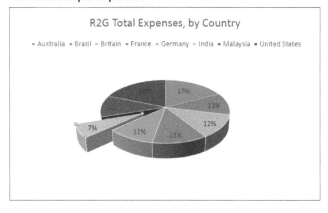

FIGURE 4-24: **Preview of worksheet with charts in Backstage view**

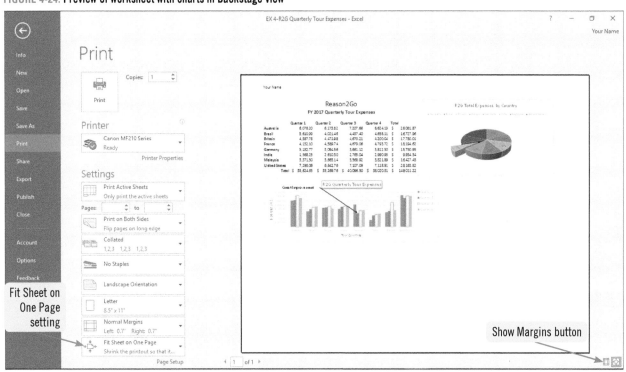

Fit Sheet on One Page setting

Show Margins button

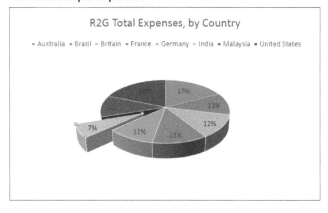

Using the Insert Chart dialog box to discover new chart types

Excel 2016 includes five new chart types. You can explore these charts by clicking the Insert tab on the Ribbon, clicking Recommended Charts, then clicking the All Charts tab in the Insert Chart dialog box. Near the bottom of the list in the left panel are the new chart types: Treemap (which has nine variations), Sunburst, Histogram, Box & Whisker, and Waterfall. If cells are selected prior to opening the Insert Chart dialog box, you will see a sample of the chart type when you click

each chart type; the sample will be magnified when you hover the mouse over the sample. The Treemap and Sunburst charts both offer visual comparisons of relative sizes. The Histogram looks like a column chart, but each column (or bin) represents a range of values. The Box & Whisker chart shows distribution details as well as the mean, quartiles, and outliers. The Waterfall chart shows results above and below an imaginary line.

Excel 2016

Practice

Concepts Review

Label each element of the Excel chart shown in FIGURE 4-25.

FIGURE 4-25

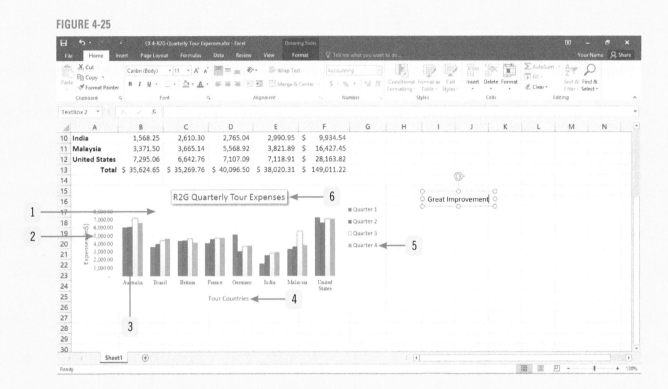

Match each chart type with the statement that best describes it.

7. **Combo**   a. Displays different chart types within one chart
8. **Pie**   b. Compares trends over even time intervals
9. **Area**   c. Compares data using columns
10. **Column**   d. Compares data as parts of a whole
11. **Line**   e. Shows how volume changes over time

Select the best answer from the list of choices.

12. Which tab on the Ribbon do you use to create a chart?
  a. Design
  b. Insert
  c. Page Layout
  d. Format

13. A collection of related data points in a chart is called a:
  a. Data series.
  b. Data tick.
  c. Cell address.
  d. Value title.

14. The object in a chart that identifies the colors used for each data series is a(n):
  a. Data marker.
  b. Data point.
  c. Organizer.
  d. Legend.

15. How do you move an embedded chart to a chart sheet?
  a. Click a button on the Chart Tools Design tab.
  b. Drag the chart to the sheet tab.
  c. Delete the chart, switch to a different sheet, then create a new chart.
  d. Use the Copy and Paste buttons on the Ribbon.

16. Which is *not* an example of a SmartArt graphic?
  a. Sparkline
  b. Basic Matrix
  c. Organization Chart
  d. Basic Pyramid

17. Which tab appears only when a chart is selected?
  a. Insert
  b. Chart Tools Format
  c. Review
  d. Page Layout

Skills Review

1. Plan a chart.
  a. Start Excel, open the Data File EX 4-2.xlsx from the location where you store your Data Files, then save it as **EX 4-Software Usage Polling Results**.
  b. Describe the type of chart you would use to plot this data.
  c. What chart type would you use to compare the number of Excel users in each type of business?

2. Create a chart.
  a. In the worksheet, select the range containing all the data and headings.
  b. Click the Quick Analysis tool.
  c. Create a Clustered Column chart, then add the chart title **Software Usage, by Business** above the chart.
  d. If necessary, click the Switch Row/Column button so the business type (Accounting, Advertising, etc.) appears as the x-axis.
  e. Save your work.

Skills Review (continued)

3. **Move and resize a chart.**
   a. Make sure the chart is still selected, and close any open panes if necessary.
   b. Move the chart beneath the worksheet data.
   c. Widen the chart so it extends to the right edge of column H.
   d. Use the Quick Layout button in the Chart Tools Design tab to move the legend to the right of the charted data. (*Hint*: Use Layout 1.)
   e. Resize the chart so its bottom edge is at the top of row 25.
   f. Save your work.

4. **Change the chart design.**
   a. Change the value in cell B3 to **8**. Observe the change in the chart.
   b. Select the chart.
   c. Use the Quick Layout button in the Chart Layouts group on the Chart Tools Design tab to apply the Layout 10 layout to the chart, then undo the change.
   d. Use the Change Chart Type button on the Chart Tools Design tab to change the chart to a Clustered Bar chart.
   e. Change the chart to a 3-D Clustered Column chart, then change it back to a Clustered Column chart.
   f. Save your work.

5. **Change the chart layout.**
   a. Use the Chart Elements button to turn off the primary major horizontal gridlines in the chart.
   b. Change the font used in the horizontal and vertical axis labels to Times New Roman.
   c. Turn on the primary major gridlines for both the horizontal and vertical axes.
   d. Change the chart title's font to Times New Roman if necessary, with a font size of 20.
   e. Insert **Business** as the primary horizontal axis title.
   f. Insert **Number of Users** as the primary vertical axis title.
   g. Change the font size of the horizontal and vertical axis titles to 10 and the font to Times New Roman, if necessary.
   h. Change "Personnel" in the worksheet column heading to **Human Resources**, then AutoFit column D, and any other columns as necessary.
   i. Change the font size of the legend to 14.
   j. Add a solid line border in the default color and a (preset) Offset Diagonal Bottom Right shadow to the chart title.
   k. Save your work.

6. **Format a chart.**
   a. Make sure the chart is selected, then select the Chart Tools Format tab, if necessary.
   b. Change the shape fill of the Excel data series to Dark Blue, Text 2.
   c. Change the shape style of the Excel data series to Subtle Effect – Orange, Accent 6.
   d. Save your work.

7. **Annotate and draw on a chart.**
   a. Make sure the chart is selected, then create the text annotation **Needs more users**.
   b. Position the text annotation so the word "Needs" is just below the word "Software" in the chart title.
   c. Select the chart, then use the Chart Tools Format tab to create a 1½ pt weight dark blue arrow that points from the bottom center of the text box to the Excel users in the Human Resources category.
   d. Deselect the chart.
   e. Save your work.

Skills Review (continued)

8. Create a pie chart.

   a. Select the range A1:F2, then create a 3-D Pie chart.

   b. Drag the 3-D pie chart beneath the existing chart.

   c. Change the chart title to **Excel Users**.

   d. Apply the Style 7 chart style to the chart, then apply Layout 6 using the Quick Layout button.

   e. Explode the Human Resources slice from the pie chart at **25%**.

   f. In Page Layout view, enter your name in the left section of the worksheet header.

   g. Preview the worksheet and charts in Backstage view, make sure all the contents fit on one page, then submit your work to your instructor as directed. When printed, the worksheet should look like FIGURE 4-26. (Note that certain elements such as the title may look slightly different when printed.)

   h. Save your work, close the workbook, then exit Excel.

FIGURE 4-26

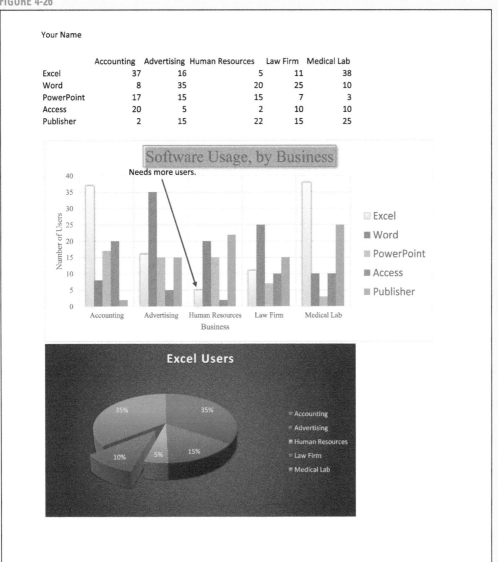

Independent Challenge 1

You are the operations manager for the Chicago Arts Alliance. Each year the group revisits the number and types of activities they support to better manage their budgets. For this year's budget, you need to create charts to document the number of events in previous years.

a. Start Excel, open the file EX 4-3.xlsx from the location where you store your Data Files, then save it as **EX 4-Chicago Arts Alliance**.

b. Take some time to plan your charts. Which type of chart or charts might best illustrate the information you need to display? What kind of chart enhancements do you want to use? Will a 3-D effect make your chart easier to understand?

c. Create a Clustered Column chart for the data.

d. Change at least one of the colors used in a data series.

e. Make the appropriate modifications to the chart to make it visually attractive and easier to read and understand. Include a legend to the right of the chart, and add chart titles and horizontal and vertical axis titles using the text shown in TABLE 4-3.

TABLE 4-3

title	text
Chart title	Chicago Arts Alliance Events
Vertical axis title	Number of Events
Horizontal axis title	Types of Events

f. Create at least two additional charts for the same data to show how different chart types display the same data. Reposition each new chart so that all charts are visible in the worksheet. One of the additional charts should be a pie chart for an appropriate data set; the other is up to you.

g. Modify each new chart as necessary to improve its appearance and effectiveness. A sample worksheet containing three charts based on the worksheet data is shown in FIGURE 4-27.

h. Enter your name in the worksheet header.

i. Save your work. Before printing, preview the worksheet in Backstage view, then adjust any settings as necessary so that all the worksheet data and charts will print on a single page.

j. Submit your work to your instructor as directed.

k. Close the workbook, then exit Excel.

FIGURE 4-27

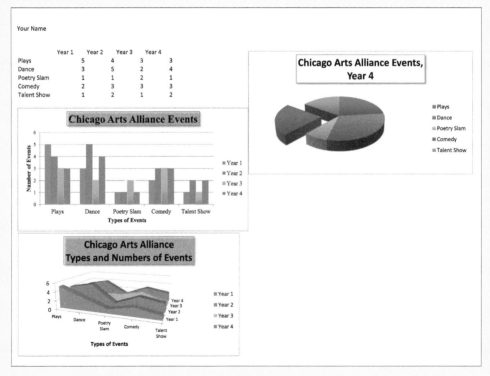

Independent Challenge 2

You work at Canine Companions, a locally owned dog obedience school. One of your responsibilities at the school is to manage the company's sales and expenses using Excel. As part of your efforts, you want to help the staff better understand and manage the school's largest sources of both expenses and sales. To do this, you've decided to create charts using current operating expenses including rent, utilities, and payroll. The manager will use these charts at the next monthly meeting.

a. Start Excel, open EX 4-4.xlsx from the location where you store your Data Files, then save it as **EX 4-Canine Companions Expense Analysis**.

b. Decide which data in the worksheet should be charted. What chart types are best suited for the information you need to show? What kinds of chart enhancements are necessary?

c. Create a 3-D Clustered Column chart in the worksheet showing the expense data for all four quarters. (*Hint*: The expense categories should appear on the x-axis. Do not include the totals.)

d. Change the vertical axis labels (Expenses data) so that no decimals are displayed. (*Hint*: Use the Number category in the Format Axis pane.)

e. Using the sales data, create two charts on this worksheet that compare the sales amounts. (*Hint*: Move each chart to a new location on the worksheet, then deselect it before creating the next one.)

f. In one chart of the sales data, add data labels, then add chart titles as you see fit.

g. Make any necessary formatting changes to make the charts look more attractive, then enter your name in a worksheet cell.

h. Save your work.

i. Preview each chart in Backstage view, and adjust any items as needed. Fit the worksheet to a single page, then submit your work to your instructor as directed. A sample of a printed worksheet is shown in FIGURE 4-28.

j. Close the workbook, then exit Excel.

FIGURE 4-28

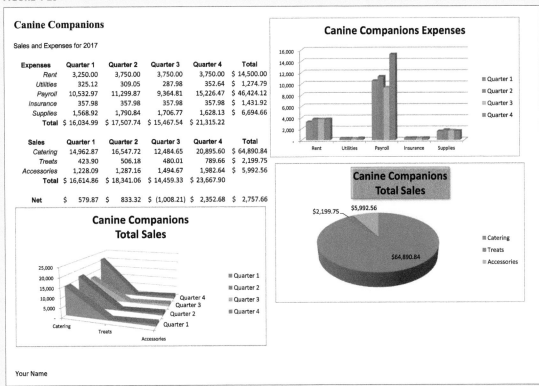

Independent Challenge 3

You are working as an account representative at a clothing store called Zanzibar. You have been examining the advertising expenses incurred recently. The CEO wants to examine expenses designed to increase sales and has asked you to prepare charts that can be used in this evaluation. In particular, you want to see how dollar amounts compare among the different expenses, and you also want to see how expenses compare with each other proportional to the total budget.

a. Start Excel, open the Data File EX 4-5.xlsx from the location where you store your Data Files, then save it as **EX 4-Zanzibar Advertising Expenses**.

b. Identify three types of charts that seem best suited to illustrate the data in the range A16:B24. What kinds of chart enhancements are necessary?

c. Create at least two different types of charts that show the distribution of advertising expenses. (*Hint*: Move each chart to a new location on the same worksheet.) One of the charts should be a 3-D pie chart.

d. In at least one of the charts, add annotated text and arrows highlighting important data, such as the largest expense.

e. Change the color of at least one data series in at least one of the charts.

f. Add chart titles and category and value axis titles where appropriate. Format the titles with a font of your choice. Apply a shadow to the chart title in at least one chart.

g. Add your name to a section of the header, then save your work.

h. Explode a slice from the 3-D pie chart.

i. Add a data label to the exploded pie slice.

j. Preview the worksheet in Backstage view. Adjust any items as needed. Be sure the charts are all visible on one page. Compare your work to the sample in FIGURE 4-29.

k. Submit your work to your instructor as directed, close the workbook, then exit Excel.

FIGURE 4-29

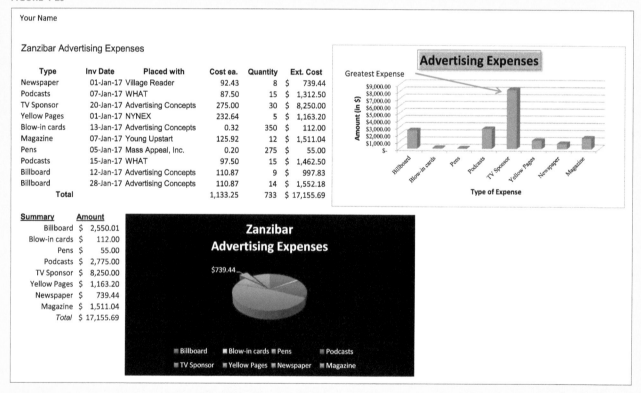

Independent Challenge 4: Explore

This Independent Challenge requires an Internet connection.

All the years of hard work and saving money have paid off, and you have decided to purchase a home. You know where you'd like to live, and you decide to use the web to find out more about houses that are currently available. A worksheet would be a great place to compare the features and prices of potential homes.

a. Start Excel, then save a new, blank workbook as **EX 4-My New House** to the location where you save your Data Files.

b. Decide on where you would like to live, and use your favorite search engine to find information sources on homes for sale in that area. (*Hint*: Try using realtor.com or other realtor-sponsored sites.)

c. Determine a price range and features within the home. Find data for at least five homes that meet your location and price requirements, and enter them in the worksheet. See TABLE 4-4 for a suggested data layout.

d. Format the data so it looks attractive and professional.

e. Create any type of column chart using only the House and Asking Price data. Place it on the same worksheet as the data. Include a descriptive title.

TABLE 4-4

suggested data layout					
Location					
Price range					
	House 1	House 2	House 3	House 4	House 5
Asking price					
Bedrooms					
Bathrooms					
Year built					
Size (in sq. ft.)					

f. Change the colors in the chart using the chart style of your choice.

g. Enter your name in a section of the header.

h. Create an additional chart: a combo chart that plots the asking price on one axis and the size of the home on the other axis. (*Hint*: Use the Tell me what you want to do text box above the Ribbon to get more guidance on creating a Combo Chart.)

i. Save the workbook. Preview the worksheet in Backstage view and make adjustments if necessary to fit all of the information on one page. See FIGURE 4-30 for an example of what your worksheet might look like.

j. Submit your work to your instructor as directed.

k. Close the workbook, then exit Excel.

FIGURE 4-30

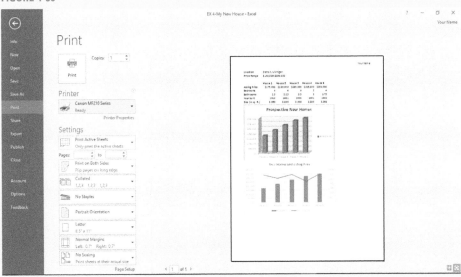

Visual Workshop

Open the Data File EX 4-6.xlsx from the location where you store your Data Files, then save it as **EX 4-Estimated Cost Center Expenses**. Format the worksheet data so it looks like FIGURE 4-31, then create and modify two charts to match the ones shown in the figure. You will need to make formatting, layout, and design changes once you create the charts. (*Hint*: The shadow used in the 3-D pie chart title is made using the Outer Offset Diagonal Top Right shadow.) Enter your name in the left text box of the header, then save and preview the worksheet. Submit your work to your instructor as directed, then close the workbook and exit Excel.

FIGURE 4-31

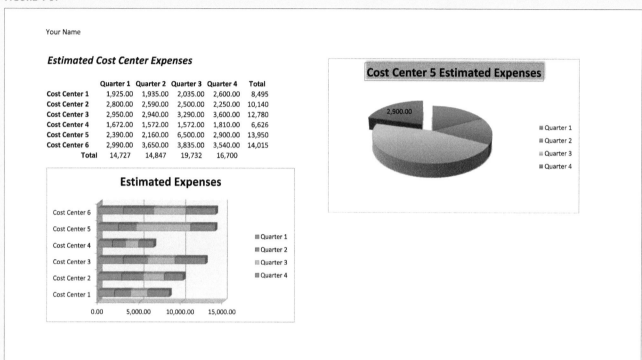

Managing Data Using Tables

> **CASE**   Reason2Go uses tables to analyze project data. The vice president of sales and marketing, Mary Watson, asks you to help her build and manage a table of information about 2017 conservation projects. You will help by planning and creating a table; adding, changing, finding, and deleting table information; sorting table data; and performing calculations with table data.

Module Objectives

After completing this module, you will be able to:

- Plan a table
- Create and format a table
- Add table data
- Find and replace table data

- Delete table data
- Sort table data
- Use formulas in a table
- Print a table

Files You Will Need

EX 7-1.xlsx	EX 7-4.xlsx
EX 7-2.xlsx	EX 7-5.xlsx
EX 7-3.xlsx	EX 7-6.xlsx

Plan a Table

Learning
Outcomes
• Plan the data
  organization for
  a table
• Plan the data
  elements for
  a table

In addition to using Excel spreadsheet features, you can analyze and manipulate data in a table structure. An Excel **table** is an organized collection of rows and columns of similarly structured worksheet data. Tables are a convenient way to understand and manage large amounts of information. When planning a table, consider what information you want your table to contain and how you want to work with the data, now and in the future. As you plan a table, you should understand its most important components. A table is organized into rows called records. A **record** is a table row that contains data about an object, person, or other items. Records are composed of fields. **Fields** are columns in the table; each field describes one element of the record, such as a customer's last name or street address. Each field has a **field name**, which is a column label, such as "Address," that describes its contents. Tables usually have a **header row** as the first row, which contains the field names. To plan your table, use the guidelines below. **CASE** *Mary asks you to compile a table of the 2017 conservation projects. Before entering the project data into an Excel worksheet, you plan the table contents.*

DETAILS

As you plan your table, use the following guidelines:

- **Identify the purpose of the table**

  The purpose of the table determines the kind of information the table should contain. You want to use the conservation projects table to find all departure dates for a particular project and to display the projects in order of departure date. You also want to quickly calculate the number of available places for a project.

- **Plan the structure of the table**

  In designing your table's structure, determine the fields (the table columns) you need to achieve the table's purpose. You have worked with the sales department to learn the type of information they need for each project. FIGURE 7-1 shows a layout sketch for the table. Each row will contain one project record. The columns represent fields that contain pieces of descriptive information you will enter for each project, such as the name, departure date, and duration.

- **Plan your row and column structure**

  You can create a table from any contiguous range of cells on your worksheet. Plan and design your table so that all rows have similar types of information in the same column. A table should not have any blank rows or columns. Instead of using blank rows to separate table headings from data, use a table style, which will use formatting to make column labels stand out from your table data. FIGURE 7-2 shows a table, populated with data that has been formatted using a table style.

- **Document the table design**

  In addition to your table sketch, you should make a list of the field names to document the type of data and any special number formatting required for each field. Field names should be as short as possible while still accurately describing the column information. When naming fields it is important to use text rather than numbers because Excel could interpret numbers as parts of formulas. Your field names should be unique and not easily confused with cell addresses, such as the name D2. You want your table to contain eight field names, each one corresponding to the major characteristics of the 2017 conservation projects. TABLE 7-1 shows the documentation of the field names in your table.

FIGURE 7-1: **Table layout sketch**

Project	Depart Date	Number of Days	Project Capacity	Places Reserved	Price	Air Included	Insurance Included

Each project will be placed in a table row

Header row will contain field names

FIGURE 7-2: **Formatted table with data**

Header row contains field names

Records for each project, organized by field name

	Project	Depart Date	Number of Days	Project Capacity	Places Reserved	Price	Air Included	Insurance Included
2	Elephant	12/20/2017	12	10	0	$ 4,100	Yes	Yes
3	Dolphin	1/28/2017	14	10	0	$ 3,200	Yes	Yes
4	Coral Reef	7/25/2017	18	10	0	$ 3,100	Yes	No
5	Dolphin	8/11/2017	14	10	1	$ 4,600	Yes	No
6	Dolphin	9/14/2017	14	10	1	$ 2,105	No	No
7	Sumatran Orangutan	5/27/2017	17	10	1	$ 1,890	No	No
8	Sumatran Orangutan	12/18/2017	17	8	1	$ 2,204	No	Yes
9	Elephant	12/31/2017	12	10	2	$ 2,100	No	No
10	Great White Shark	8/20/2017	14	8	2	$ 3,922	Yes	Yes
11	Cheetah	7/12/2017	15	9	2	$ 2,100	No	No
12	Cheetah	9/20/2017	15	9	2	$ 3,902	Yes	Yes
13	Rhino	12/18/2017	15	8	2	$ 2,204	No	Yes
14	African Wild Dog	7/27/2017	18	10	2	$ 1,890	No	No
15	Elephant	9/23/2017	12	9	3	$ 2,110	No	No
16	Dolphin	6/9/2017	14	8	3	$ 4,200	Yes	Yes
17	Sumatran Orangutan	8/12/2017	17	10	3	$ 1,970	No	Yes
18	Great White Shark	5/20/2017	14	9	4	$ 2,663	No	Yes
19	Rhino	5/23/2017	15	9	4	$ 4,635	Yes	No

Practice | 2017 Projects

Ready

TABLE 7-1: **Table documentation**

field name	type of data	description of data
Project	Text	Name of project
Depart Date	Date	Date project departs
Number of Days	Number with 0 decimal places	Duration of the project
Project Capacity	Number with 0 decimal places	Maximum number of people the project can accommodate
Places Reserved	Number with 0 decimal places	Number of reservations for the project
Price	Accounting with 0 decimal places and $ symbol	Project price (This price is not guaranteed until a 30% deposit is received)
Air Included	Text	Yes: Airfare is included in the price No: Airfare is not included in the price
Insurance Included	Text	Yes: Insurance is included in the price No: Insurance is not included in the price

Create and Format a Table

Learning
Outcomes
• Create a table
• Format a table

Once you have planned the table structure, the sequence of fields, and appropriate data types, you are ready to create the table in Excel. After you create a table, a Table Tools Design tab appears, containing a gallery of table styles. **Table styles** allow you to easily add formatting to your table by using preset formatting combinations of fill color, borders, type style, and type color. **CASE** Mary asks you to build a table with the 2017 conservation project data. You begin by entering the field names. Then you enter the project data that corresponds to each field name, create the table, and format the data using a table style.

STEPS

1. **Start Excel, open** EX 7-1.xlsx **from the location where you store your Data Files, then save it as** EX 7-Conservation Projects

2. **Beginning in cell** A1 **of the** Practice **sheet, enter each field name in a separate column, as shown in the first row of** FIGURE 7-3
   Field names are usually in the first row of the table.

3. **Enter the information shown in** FIGURE 7-3 **in the rows immediately below the field names, leaving no blank rows**
   The data appears in columns organized by field name.

4. **Select the range** A1:H4, **click the** Format button **in the Cells group, click** AutoFit Column Width, **then click cell** A1
   Resizing the column widths this way is faster than double-clicking the column divider lines.

5. **With cell A1 selected, click the** Insert tab, **click the** Table button **in the Tables group, in the Create Table dialog box verify that your table data is in the range** $A$1:$H$4, **make sure** My table has headers **is checked as shown in** FIGURE 7-4, **then click** OK
   The data range is now defined as a table. **Filter list arrows**, which let you display portions of your data, now appear next to each column header. When you create a table, Excel automatically applies a table style. The default table style has a dark blue header row and alternating light and dark blue data rows. The Table Tools Design tab appears, and the Table Styles group displays a gallery of table formatting options. You decide to choose a different table style from the gallery.

6. **Click the** Table Styles More button ▼, **scroll to view all of the table styles, then move the mouse pointer over several styles without clicking**
   The Table Styles gallery on the Table Tools Design tab has three style categories: Light, Medium, and Dark. Each category has numerous design types; for example, in some of the designs, the header row and total row are darker and the rows alternate colors. The available table designs use the current workbook theme colors so the table coordinates with your existing workbook content. If you select a different workbook theme and color scheme in the Themes group on the Page Layout tab, the Table Styles gallery uses those colors. As you point to each table style, Live Preview shows you what your table will look like with the style applied. However, you only see a preview of each style; you need to click a style to apply it.

7. **Click** Table Style Medium 23 **to apply it to your table, then click cell** A1
   Compare your table to FIGURE 7-5.

FIGURE 7-3: **Field names and three records entered in worksheet**

	A	B	C	D	E	F	G	H
1	Project	Depart Date	Number of Days	Project Capacity	Places Reserved	Price	Air Included	Insurance Included
2	Elephant	42747	12	10	5	4255	Yes	No
3	Rhino	42748	15	8	8	1984	No	No
4	Cheetah	42754	15	10	8	1966	No	Yes
5								

FIGURE 7-4: **Create Table dialog box**

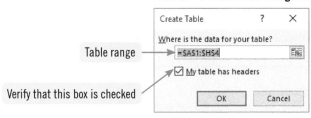

Create Table   ?   ✕

Where is the data for your table?

Table range → =$A$1:$H$4

Verify that this box is checked → ☑ My table has headers

OK   Cancel

FIGURE 7-5: **Formatted table with three records**

	A	B	C	D	E	F	G	H
1	Project	Depart Date	Number of Days	Project Capacity	Places Reserved	Price	Air Included	Insurance Included
2	Elephant	1/12/2017	12	10	5	4255	Yes	No
3	Rhino	1/13/2017	15	8	8	1984	No	No
4	Cheetah	1/19/2017	15	10	8	1966	No	Yes

Changing table style options

You can change a table's appearance by using the check boxes in the Table Style Options group on the Table Tools Design tab, shown in FIGURE 7-6. For example, you can turn on or turn off the following options: Header Row, which displays or hides the header row; Total Row, which calculates totals for each column; **banding**, which creates different formatting for adjacent rows and columns; and special formatting for first and last columns. Use these options to modify a table's appearance either before or after applying a table style.

You can also create your own table style by clicking the Table Styles More button, then at the bottom of the Table Styles Gallery, clicking New Table Style. In the New Table Style dialog box, name the style in the Name text box, click a table element, then format selected table elements by clicking Format. You can also set a custom style as the default style for your tables by checking the Set as default table quick style for this document check box. You can click Clear at the bottom of the Table Styles gallery if you want to delete a table style from the currently selected table.

FIGURE 7-6: **Table Style Options**

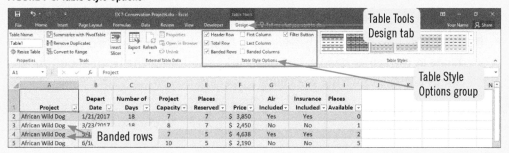

Add Table Data

Learning Outcomes
- Add fields to a table
- Add records to a table

You can add records to a table by typing data directly below the last row of the table. After you press [Enter], the new row becomes part of the table and the table formatting extends to the new data. When the active cell is the last cell of a table, you can add a new row by pressing [Tab]. You can also insert rows in any table location. If you decide you need additional data fields, you can add new columns to a table. You can also expand a table by dragging the sizing handle in a table's lower-right corner; drag down to add rows and drag to the right to add columns. **CASE** ▸ *After entering all of the 2017 project data, Mary decides to offer two additional projects. She also wants the table to display the number of available places for each project and whether visas are required for the destination.*

STEPS

1. **Click the** 2017 Projects sheet tab
   The 2017 sheet containing the 2017 project data becomes active.

2. **Scroll down to the last table row, click cell** A65, **enter the data for the new Coral Reef project, as shown below, then press** [Enter]

Coral Reef	7/25/2017	18	10	0	$ 3,100	Yes	No

   As you scroll down, notice that the table headers are visible at the top of the table as long as the active cell is inside the table. The new Coral Reef project is now part of the table. You want to enter a record about a new January project above row 6.

3. **Scroll up to and click the** inside left edge of cell A6 **to select the table row data as shown in** FIGURE 7-7, **click the** Insert list arrow **in the Cells group, then click** Insert Table Rows Above
   Clicking the left edge of the first cell in a table row selects the entire table row, rather than the entire worksheet row. A new blank row 6 is available for the new record.

4. **Click cell** A6, **then enter the Dolphin record shown below**

Dolphin	1/28/2017	14	10	0	$ 3,200	Yes	Yes

   The new Dolphin project is part of the table. You want to add a new field that displays the number of available places for each project.

5. **Click cell** I1, **type the field name** Places Available, **then press** [Enter]
   The new field becomes part of the table, and the header formatting extends to the new field, as shown in FIGURE 7-8. The AutoCorrect menu allows you to undo or stop the automatic table expansion, but in this case you decide to leave this feature on. You want to add another new field to the table to display projects that require visas, but this time you will add the new field by resizing the table.

QUICK TIP
You can also resize a table by clicking the Table Tools Design tab, clicking the Resize Table button in the Properties group, selecting the new data range for the table, then clicking OK.

6. **Scroll down until cell** I66 **is visible, then drag the** sizing handle **in the table's lower-right corner one column to the right to add column J to the table, as shown in** FIGURE 7-9
   The table range is now A1:J66, and the new field name is Column1.

7. **Scroll up to and click cell** J1, **type** Visa Required, **then press** [Enter]

8. **Click the** Insert tab, **click the** Header & Footer button **in the Text group, enter your name in the center header text box, click cell** A1, **click the** Normal button ▦ **on the status bar, then save the workbook**

FIGURE 7-7: Table row 6 selected

	A	B	C	D	E	F	G	H
1	Project	Depart Date	Number of Days	Project Capacity	Places Reserved	Price	Air Included	Insurance Included
2	Elephant	1/12/2017	12	10	5	$ 4,255	Yes	No
3	Rhino	1/13/2017	15	8	8	$ 1,984	No	No
4	Cheetah	1/19/2017	15	10	8	$ 1,966	No	Yes
5	African Wild Dog	1/21/2017	18	7	7	$ 3,850	Yes	Yes
6	Dolphin	2/22/2017	14	10	10	$ 2,134	No	No
7	Orangutan	2/28/2017	17	8	4	$ 4,812	Yes	No
8	Great White Shark	3/13/2017	14	10	5	$ 4,350	Yes	No
9	Coral Reef	3/19/2017	18	6	5	$ 2,110	No	Yes
10	Orangutan	3/20/2017	17	10	8	$ 1,755	No	Yes
11	African Wild Dog	3/23/2017	18	8	7	$ 2,450	No	No
12	Rhino	4/8/2017	15	10	10	$ 3,115	Yes	Yes
13	Elephant	4/11/2017	12	10	5	$ 4,255	Yes	No

Clicking here selects the entire worksheet row

Clicking here selects the table row

Row 6 of table selected

FIGURE 7-8: New table column

	A	B	C	D	E	F	G	H	I	J
1	Project	Depart Date	Number of Days	Project Capacity	Places Reserved	Price	Air Included	Insurance Included	Places Available	
2	Elephant	1/12/2017	12	10	5	$ 4,255	Yes	No		
3	Rhino	1/13/2017	15	8	8	$ 1,984	No	No		
4	Cheetah	1/19/2017	15	10	8	$ 1,966	No	Yes		
5	African Wild Dog	1/21/2017	18	7	7	$ 3,850	Yes	Yes		
6	Dolphin	1/28/2017	14	10	0	$ 3,200	Yes	Yes		
7	Dolphin	2/22/2017	14	10	10	$ 2,134	No	No		
8	Orangutan	2/28/2017	17	8	4	$ 4,812	Yes	No		
9	Great White Shark	3/13/2017	14	10	5	$ 4,350	Yes	No		
10	Coral Reef	3/19/2017	18	6	5	$ 2,110	No	Yes		

New table column will show available places for each project

New record in row 6

FIGURE 7-9: Resizing a table using the resizing handle

	Project	Depart Dat	Number of	Project Cap	Places Reser	Price	Air Include	Insurance In	Places Avai	J	K	L
55	African Wild Dog	10/29/2017	18	10	6	$ 4,200	Yes	Yes				
56	Great White Shark	10/31/2017	14	9	8	$ 1,900	No	No				
57	African Wild Dog	10/31/2017	18	9	5	$ 3,908	Yes	No				
58	Great White Shark	11/18/2017	14	10	5	$ 2,200	No	Yes				
59	Rhino	12/18/2017	15	8	2	$ 2,204	No	Yes				
60	Orangutan	12/18/2017	17	8	1	$ 2,204	No	Yes				
61	Elephant	12/20/2017	12	10	0	$ 4,100	Yes	Yes				
62	Dolphin	12/20/2017	14	10	5	$ 2,100	No	Yes				
63	African Wild Dog	12/21/2017	18	9	8	$ 2,105	No	No				
64	Cheetah	12/30/2017	15	9	5	$ 3,922	Yes	Yes				
65	Elephant	12/31/2017	12	10	2	$ 2,100	No	No				
66	Coral Reef	7/25/2017	18	10	0	$ 3,100	Yes	No				
67												
68												

Drag sizing handle to add column J

Selecting table elements

When working with tables you often need to select rows, columns, and even the entire table. Clicking to the right of a row number, inside column A, selects the entire table row. You can select a table column by clicking the top edge of the header. Be careful not to click a column letter or row number, however, because this selects the entire worksheet row or column. You can select the table data by clicking the upper-left corner of the first table cell. When selecting a column or a table, the first click selects only the data in the column or table. If you click a second time, you add the headers to the selection.

Find and Replace Table Data

Learning
Outcomes
• Find data in a
  table
• Replace data in a
  table

From time to time, you need to locate specific records in your table. You can use the Excel Find feature to search your table for the information you need. You can also use the Replace feature to locate and replace existing entries or portions of entries with information you specify. If you don't know the exact spelling of the text you are searching for, you can use wildcards to help locate the records. **Wildcards** are special symbols that substitute for unknown characters. **CASE** *Because the Sumatran Orangutans are critically endangered, Mary wants you to replace "Orangutan" with "Sumatran Orangutan" to avoid confusion with last year's Borneo projects. She also wants to know how many Cheetah projects are scheduled for the year. You begin by searching for records with the text "Cheetah".*

STEPS

1. **Click cell A1 if necessary, click the Home tab, click the Find & Select button in the Editing group, then click Find**

   The Find and Replace dialog box opens, as shown in FIGURE 7-10. In the Find what text box, you enter criteria that specify the records you want to find. You want to search for records whose Project field contains the label "Cheetah".

2. **Type Cheetah in the Find what text box, then click Find Next**

   A4 is the active cell because it is the first instance of Cheetah in the table.

3. **Click Find Next and examine the record for each Cheetah project found until no more matching cells are found in the table and the active cell is A4 again, then click Close**

   There are seven Cheetah projects.

4. **Return to cell A1, click the Find & Select button in the Editing group, then click Replace**

   The Find and Replace dialog box opens with the Replace tab selected and "Cheetah" in the Find what text box, as shown in FIGURE 7-11. You will search for entries containing "Orangutan" and replace them with "Sumatran Orangutan". To save time, you will use the asterisk (*) wildcard to help you locate the records containing Orangutan.

QUICK TIP
You can also use the question mark (?) wildcard to represent any single character. For example, using "to?" as your search text would only find 3-letter words beginning with "to", such as "top" and "tot"; it would not find "tone" or "topography".

5. **Delete the text in the Find what text box, type Or* in the Find what text box, click the Replace with text box, then type Sumatran Orangutan**

   The asterisk (*) wildcard stands for one or more characters, meaning that the search text "Or*" will find words such as "orange", "cord", and "for". Because you notice that there are other table entries containing the text "or" with a lowercase "o" (Coral Reef), you need to make sure that only capitalized instances of the letter "O" are replaced.

6. **Click Options >>, click the Match case check box to select it, click Options <<, then click Find Next**

   Excel moves the cell pointer to the cell containing the first occurrence of "Orangutan".

7. **Click Replace All, click OK, then click Close**

   The dialog box closes. Excel made ten replacements. The Coral Reef projects remain unchanged because the "or" in "Coral" is lowercase.

8. **Save the workbook**

FIGURE 7-10: **Find and Replace dialog box**

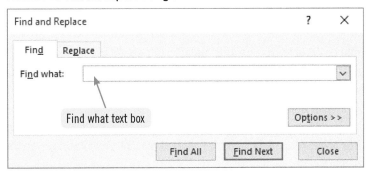

FIGURE 7-11: **The Replace tab in the Find and Replace dialog box**

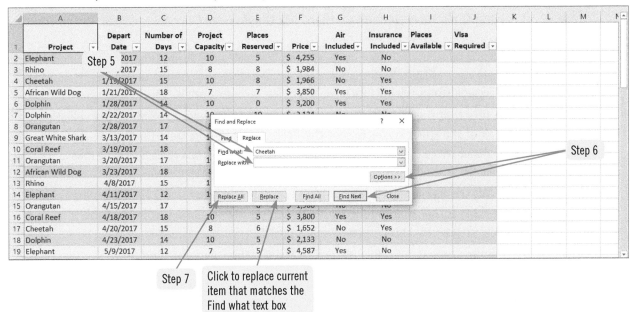

Using Find and Select features

You can also use the Find feature to navigate to a specific place in a workbook by clicking the Find & Select button in the Editing group on the Home tab, clicking Go To, typing a cell address, then clicking OK. Clicking the Find & Select button also allows you to find comments and conditional formatting in a worksheet. You can use the Go to Special dialog box to select cells that contain different types of formulas or objects. Some Go to Special commands also appear on the Find & Select menu. Using this menu, you can also change the mouse pointer shape to the Select Objects pointer ⬚ so you can quickly select drawing objects when necessary. To return to the standard Excel pointer ✚, press [Esc].

Delete Table Data

Learning
Outcomes
• Delete a table field
• Delete a table row
• Remove duplicate
  data from a table

To keep a table up to date, you need to be able to periodically remove records. You may even need to remove fields if the information stored in a field becomes unnecessary. You can delete table data using the Delete button in the Cells group or by dragging the sizing handle at the table's lower-right corner. You can also easily delete duplicate records from a table. **CASE** *Mary is canceling the Rhino project that departs on 1/13/2017 and asks you to delete the record from the table. You will also remove any duplicate records from the table. Because the visa requirements are difficult to keep up with, Mary asks you to delete the field with visa information.*

STEPS

1. **Click the inside** left edge of cell A3 **to select the table row, click the** Delete list arrow **in the Cells group, then click** Delete Table Rows

    The Rhino project is deleted, and the Cheetah project moves up to row 3, as shown in FIGURE 7-12. You can also delete a table row or a column using the Resize Table button in the Properties group of the Table Tools Design tab, or by right-clicking the row or column, pointing to Delete on the shortcut menu, then clicking Table Columns or Table Rows. You decide to check the table for duplicate records.

QUICK TIP
You can also remove
duplicates from
worksheet data by
clicking the Data tab,
then clicking the
Remove Duplicates
button in the Data
Tools group.

2. **Click the** Table Tools Design tab, **then click the** Remove Duplicates button **in the Tools group**

    The Remove Duplicates dialog box opens, as shown in FIGURE 7-13. You need to select the columns that will be used to evaluate duplicates. Because you don't want to delete projects with the same destination but different departure dates, you will look for duplicate data in those columns.

3. **Make sure that the** My data has headers **check box is checked, remove the selection from all of the check boxes except the Project and Depart Date fields, then click** OK

    One duplicate record is found and removed, leaving 63 records of data and a total of 64 rows in the table, including the header row. You want to remove the last column, which contains space for visa information.

4. **Click** OK, **scroll down until cell** J64 **is visible, then drag the** sizing handle **of the table's lower-right corner one column to the left to remove column J from the table**

    The table range is now A1:I64, and the Visa Required field no longer appears in the table.

5. **Delete the contents of cell** J1, **return to cell** A1, **then save the workbook**

FIGURE 7-12: Table with row deleted

	Project	Depart Date	Number of Days	Project Capacity	Places Reserved	Price	Air Included	Insurance Included	Places Available	Visa Required
2	Elephant	1/12/2017	12	10	5	$ 4,255	Yes	No		
3	Cheetah	1/19/2017	15	10	8	$ 1,966	No	Yes		
4	African Wild Dog	1/21/2017	18	7	7	$ 3,850	Yes	Yes		
5	Dolphin	1/28/2017	14	10	0	$ 3,200	Yes	Yes		
6	Dolphin	2/22/2017	14	10	10	$ 2,134	No	No		
7	Sumatran Orangutan	2/28/2017	17	8	4	$ 4,812	Yes	No		
8	Great White Shark	3/13/2017	14	10	5	$ 4,350	Yes	No		
9	Coral Reef	3/19/2017	18	6	5	$ 2,110	No	Yes		
10	Sumatran Orangutan	3/20/2017	17	10	8	$ 1,755	No	Yes		
11	African Wild Dog	3/23/2017	18	8	7	$ 2,450	No	No		
12	Rhino	4/8/2017	15	10	10	$ 3,115	Yes	Yes		
13	Elephant	4/11/2017	12	10	5	$ 4,255	Yes	No		
14	Sumatran Orangutan	4/15/2017	17	9	8	$ 1,900	No	No		
15	Coral Reef	4/18/2017	18	10	5	$ 3,800	Yes	Yes		
16	Cheetah	4/20/2017	15	8	6	$ 1,652	No	Yes		
17	Dolphin	4/23/2017	14	10	5	$ 2,133	No	No		
18		/2017	12	7	5	$ 4,587	Yes	No		

Row is deleted and rows below move up by one

FIGURE 7-13: Remove Duplicates dialog box

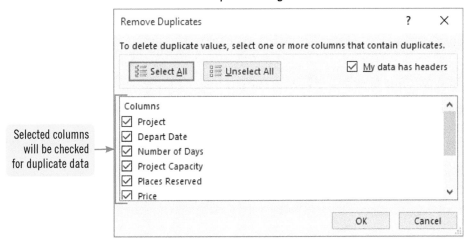

Selected columns will be checked for duplicate data

Sort Table Data

Learning Outcomes
- Sort a table in ascending order
- Sort a table in descending order
- Sort a table using custom sort options

Usually, you enter table records in the order in which you receive information, rather than in alphabetical or numerical order. When you add records to a table, you usually enter them at the end of the table. You can change the order of the records any time using the Excel **sort** feature. Because the data is structured as a table, Excel changes the order of the records while keeping each record, or row of information, together. You can sort a table in ascending or descending order on one field using the filter list arrows next to the field name. In **ascending order**, the lowest value (the beginning of the alphabet or the earliest date) appears at the top of the table. In a field containing labels and numbers, numbers appear first in the sorted list. In **descending order**, the highest value (the end of the alphabet or the latest date) appears at the top of the table. In a field containing labels and numbers, labels appear first. TABLE 7-2 provides examples of ascending and descending sorts. **CASE** *Mary wants the project data sorted by departure date, displaying projects that depart the soonest at the top of the table.*

STEPS

1. **Click the** Depart Date filter list arrow, **then click** Sort Oldest to Newest

   Excel rearranges the records in ascending order by departure date, as shown in FIGURE 7-14. The Depart Date filter list arrow has an upward pointing arrow indicating the ascending sort in the field. You can also sort the table on one field using the Sort & Filter button.

2. **Click the** Home tab, **click any cell in the** Price column, **click the** Sort & Filter button **in the Editing group, then click** Sort Largest to Smallest

   Excel sorts the table, placing records with higher prices at the top. The Price filter list arrow now has a downward pointing arrow next to the filter list arrow, indicating the descending sort order. You can also rearrange the table data using a **multilevel sort**. This type of sort rearranges the table data using more than one field, where each field is a different level, based on its importance in the sort. If you use two sort levels, the data is sorted by the first field, and the second field is sorted within each grouping of the first field. Since you have many groups of projects with different departure dates, you want to use a multilevel sort to arrange the table data first by projects and then by departure dates within each project.

3. **Click the** Sort & Filter button **in the Editing group, then click** Custom Sort

   The Sort dialog box opens, as shown in FIGURE 7-15.

4. **Click the** Sort by list arrow, **click** Project, **click the** Order list arrow, **click** A to Z, **click** Add Level, **click the** Then by list arrow, **click** Depart Date, **click the second** Order list arrow, **click** Oldest to Newest **if necessary, then click** OK

   FIGURE 7-16 shows the table sorted alphabetically in ascending order (A–Z) by Project and, within each project grouping, in ascending order by the Depart Date.

5. **Save the workbook**

Sorting conditionally formatted data

If conditional formats have been applied to a table, you can sort the table using conditional formatting to arrange the rows. For example, if cells are conditionally formatted with color, you can sort a field on Cell Color, using the color with the order of On Top or On Bottom in the Sort dialog box. If the data is not in a table, you can select a cell in the column of conditionally formatted data you want to sort by, or select the range of cells to be sorted, right-click the selection, point to Sort, then select the font color, highlighted color, or icon that you want to appear on top.

FIGURE 7-14: Table sorted by departure date

Records are sorted by departure date in ascending order →

Up arrow indicates ascending sort in the field

	Project	Depart Date	Number of Days	Project Capacity	Places Reserved	Price	Air Included	Insurance Included	Places Available
2	Elephant	1/12/2017	12	10		4,255	Yes	No	
3	Cheetah	1/19/2017	15	10		,966	No	Yes	
4	African Wild Dog	1/21/2017	18	7		,850	Yes	Yes	
5	Dolphin	1/28/2017	14	10		,200	Yes	Yes	
6	Dolphin	2/22/2017	14	10		,134	No	No	
	tran Orangutan	2/28/2017	17	8	4	$ 4,812	Yes	No	
	White Shark	3/13/2017	14	10	5	$ 4,350	Yes	No	
	Reef	3/19/2017	18	6	5	$ 2,110	No	Yes	
	tran Orangutan	3/20/2017	17	10	8	$ 1,755	No	Yes	
	an Wild Dog	3/23/2017	18	8	7	$ 2,450	No	No	
12	Rhino	4/8/2017	15	10	10	$ 3,115	Yes	Yes	
13	Elephant	4/11/2017	12	10	5	$ 4,255	Yes	No	
14	Sumatran Orangutan	4/15/2017	17	9	8	$ 1,900	No	No	
15	Coral Reef	4/18/2017	18	10	5	$ 3,800	Yes	Yes	
16	Cheetah	4/20/2017	15	8	6	$ 1,652	No	Yes	
17	Dolphin	4/23/2017	14	10	5	$ 2,133	No	No	
18	Elephant	5/9/2017	12	7	5	$ 4,587	Yes	No	

FIGURE 7-15: Sort dialog box

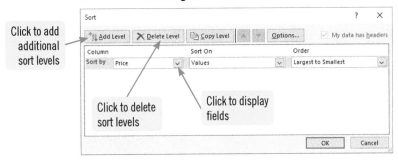

Click to add additional sort levels

Click to delete sort levels

Click to display fields

FIGURE 7-16: Table sorted using two levels

First-level sort on project arranges records by project name

Second-level sort arranges records by departure date within each project grouping

	Project	Depart Date	Number of Days	Project Capacity	Places Reserved	Price	Air Included	Insurance Included	Places Available
2	African Wild Dog	1/21/2017	18	7	7	$ 3,850	Yes	Yes	
3	African Wild Dog	3/23/2017	18	8	7	$ 2,450	No	No	
4	African Wild Dog	5/18/2017	18	7	5	$ 4,638	Yes	Yes	
5	African Wild Dog	6/10/2017	18	10	5	$ 2,190	No	No	
6	African Wild Dog	6/27/2017	18	10	7	$ 1,944	No	No	
7	African Wild Dog	7/27/2017	18	10	2	$ 1,890	No	No	
8	African Wild Dog	8/23/2017	18	7			No	No	
9	African Wild Dog	9/18/2017	18	10			Yes	Yes	
10	African Wild Dog	10/29/2017	18	10			Yes	Yes	
11	African Wild Dog	10/31/2017	18	9			Yes	No	
12	African Wild Dog	12/21/2017	18	9			No	No	
13	Cheetah	1/19/2017	15	10	8	$ 1,966	No	Yes	
14	Cheetah				6	$ 1,652	No	Yes	
15	Cheetah				8	$ 4,600	Yes	No	
16	Cheetah				2	$ 2,100	No	No	
17	Cheetah	9/20/2017	15	9	2	$ 3,902	Yes	Yes	

TABLE 7-2: Sort order options and examples

option	alphabetic	numeric	date	alphanumeric
Ascending	A, B, C	7, 8, 9	1/1, 2/1, 3/1	12A, 99B, DX8, QT7
Descending	C, B, A	9, 8, 7	3/1, 2/1, 1/1	QT7, DX8, 99B, 12A

Specifying a custom sort order

You can identify a custom sort order for the field selected in the Sort by box. Click the Order list arrow in the Sort dialog box, click Custom List, then click the desired custom order. Commonly used custom sort orders are days of the week (Sun, Mon, Tues, Wed, etc.) and months (Jan, Feb, Mar, etc.); alphabetic sorts do not sort these items properly.

Use Formulas in a Table

Many tables are large, making it difficult to know from viewing them the "story" the table tells. The Excel table calculation features help you summarize table data so you can see important patterns and trends. After you enter a single formula into a table cell, the **calculated columns** feature fills in the remaining cells with the formula's results. The column continues to fill with the formula results as you enter rows in the table. This makes it easy to update your formulas because you only need to edit the formula once, and the change will fill in to the other column cells. The **structured reference** feature allows your formulas to refer to table columns by names that are automatically generated when you create the table. These names adjust as you add or delete table fields. An example of a table reference is =[Sales]–[Costs], where Sales and Costs are field names in the table. Tables also have a specific area at the bottom called the **table total row** for calculations using the data in the table columns. The cells in this row contain a dropdown list of functions that can be used for the column calculation. The table total row adapts to any changes in the table size. **CASE** ► *Mary asks you to calculate the number of available places for each project. You will also add summary information to the end of the table.*

STEPS

1. **Click cell I2, then type =[**

   A list of the table field names appears, as shown in FIGURE 7-17. Structured referencing allows you to use the names that Excel created when you defined your table to reference fields in a formula. You can choose a field by clicking it and pressing [Tab] or by double-clicking the field name.

2. **Click [Project Capacity], press [Tab], then type]**

   Excel begins the formula, placing [Project Capacity] in the cell in blue and framing the Project Capacity data in a blue border.

3. **Type -[, double-click [Places Reserved], then type]**

   Excel places [Places Reserved] in the cell in red and outlines the Places Reserved data in a red border.

4. **Press [Enter]**

   The formula result, 0, is displayed in cell I2. The table column also fills with the formula, displaying the number of available places for each project.

5. **Click the AutoCorrect Options list arrow 🔲▾ to view options for the column**

   Because the calculated columns option saves time, you decide to leave the feature on. You want to display the total number of available places on all of the projects.

6. **Press [Esc] to close the menu, click the Table Tools Design tab, then click the Total Row check box in the Table Style Options group to select it**

   A total row appears at the bottom of the table, and the sum of the available places, 268, is displayed in cell I65. You can include other formulas in the total row.

7. **Click cell C65 (the Number of Days column), then click the cell list arrow on the right side of the cell**

   The list of available functions appears, as shown in FIGURE 7-18. You want to find the average project length.

8. **Click Average, then save your workbook**

   The average project length, 15 days, appears in cell C65.

FIGURE 7-17: Table field names

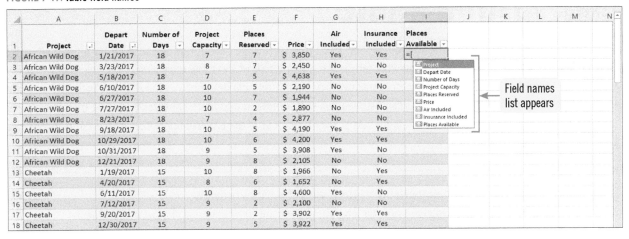

FIGURE 7-18: Functions in the Total row

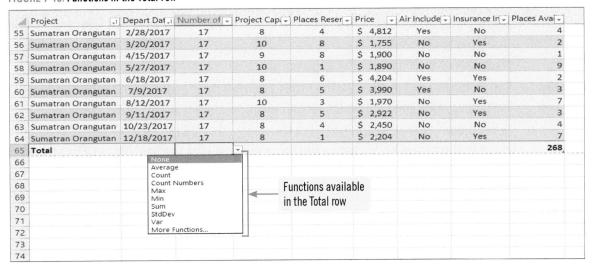

Print a Table

Learning
Outcomes
• Preview a table
• Add print titles
  to a table

You can determine the way a table will print using the Page Layout tab. Because tables often have more rows than can fit on a page, you can define the first row of the table (containing the field names) as the **print title**, which prints at the top of every page. If your table does not include any descriptive information above the field names, you can use headers and footers to add identifying text, such as the table title or the report date. **CASE** ▶ *Mary asks you for a printout of the project information. You begin by previewing the table.*

STEPS

1. **Click the File tab, click Print, then view the table preview**

   Below the table you see 1 of 2, which indicates you are viewing page 1 of a 2-page document.

2. **In the Preview window, click the Next Page button ▶ in the Preview area to view the second page**

   All of the field names in the table fit across the width of page 1. Because the records on page 2 appear without column headings, you want to set up the first row of the table, which contains the field names, as a print title.

3. **Return to the worksheet, click the Page Layout tab, click the Print Titles button in the Page Setup group, click inside the Rows to repeat at top text box under Print titles, in the worksheet scroll up to row 1 if necessary, click any cell in row 1 on the table, then compare your Page Setup dialog box to FIGURE 7-19**

   When you select row 1 as a print title, Excel automatically inserts an absolute reference to the row that will repeat at the top of each page.

4. **Click the Print Preview button in the Page Setup dialog box, then click ▶ in the preview window to view the second page**

   Setting up a print title to repeat row 1 causes the field names to appear at the top of each printed page. The printout would be more informative with a header to identify the table information.

5. **Return to the worksheet, click the Insert tab, click the Header & Footer button in the Text group, click the left header section text box, then type 2017 Conservation Projects**

6. **Select the left header section text, click the Home tab, click the Increase Font Size button Aˆ in the Font group twice to change the font size to 14, click the Bold button B in the Font group, click any cell in the table, then click the Normal button in the status bar**

7. **Save the table, preview it, close the workbook, exit Excel, then submit the workbook to your instructor**

   Compare your printed table with FIGURE 7-20.

FIGURE 7-19: **Page Setup dialog box**

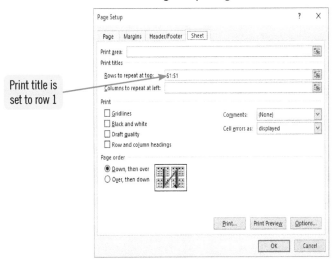

Print title is set to row 1

FIGURE 7-20: **Printed table**

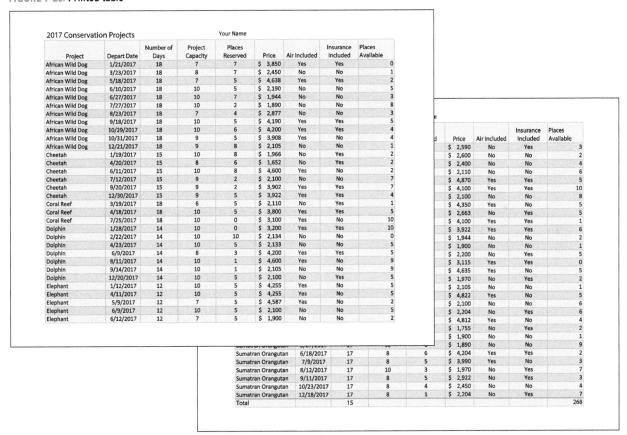

Setting a print area

Sometimes you will want to print only part of a worksheet. To do this, select any worksheet range, click the File tab, click Print, click the Print Active Sheets list arrow, then click Print Selection. If you want to print a selected area repeatedly, it's best to define a **print area**, the area of the worksheet that previews and prints when you use the Print command in Backstage view. To set a print area, select the range of data on the worksheet that you want to print, click the Page Layout tab, click the Print Area button in the Page Setup group, then click Set Print Area. You can add to the print area by selecting a range, clicking the Print Area button, then clicking Add to Print Area. A print area can consist of one contiguous range of cells, or multiple areas in different parts of a worksheet.

Practice

Concepts Review

FIGURE 7-21

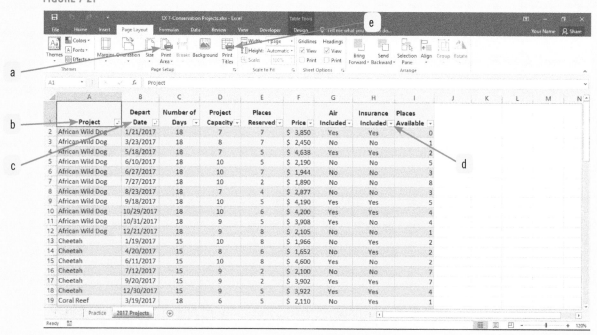

1. Which element do you click to set a range in a table that will print using the Print command?
2. Which element do you click to print field names at the top of every page?
3. Which element do you click to sort field data on a worksheet?
4. Which element points to a second-level sort field?
5. Which element points to a top-level sort field?

Match each term with the statement that best describes it.

6. Sort
7. Field
8. Table
9. Record
10. Header row

    a. Organized collection of related information in Excel
    b. Arrange records in a particular sequence
    c. Column in an Excel table
    d. First row of a table containing field names
    e. Row in an Excel table

Select the best answer from the list of choices.

11. Which of the following series appears in descending order?
    a. 8, 6, 4, C, B, A
    b. 4, 5, 6, A, B, C
    c. 8, 7, 6, 5, 6, 7
    d. C, B, A, 6, 5, 4

12. Which of the following Excel options do you use to sort a table of employee names in order from Z to A?

a. Ascending   **c.** Alphabetic

b. Absolute   **d.** Descending

13. When printing a table on multiple pages, you can define a print title to:

a. Include the sheet name in table reports.

b. Include field names at the top of each printed page.

c. Exclude from the printout all rows under the first row.

d. Include gridlines in the printout.

14. You can easily add formatting to a table by using:

a. Table styles.   **c.** Print areas.

b. Print titles.   **d.** Calculated columns.

Skills Review

1. Create and format a table.

a. Start Excel, open EX 7-2.xlsx from the location where you store your Data Files, then save it as **EX 7-Employees**.

b. Using the Practice sheet, enter the field names in the first row and the first two records in rows two and three, as shown in the table below, adjusting column widths as necessary to fit the text entries.

Last Name	First Name	Years Employed	Department	Full/Part Time	Training Completed
Diamond	Irene	4	Support	P	Y
Mendez	Darryl	3	Sales	F	N

c. Define the data you entered as a table, then add a table style of Medium 9.

d. On the Staff sheet, define the cells containing data as a table with a header row. Adjust the column widths, if necessary, to display the field names. Enter your name in the center section of the worksheet footer, return to Normal view if necessary, then save the workbook.

e. Apply a table style of Light 19 to the table.

f. Enter your name in the center section of the worksheet footer, return to Normal view if necessary, then save the workbook.

2. Add table data.

a. Add a new record in row seven for **Holly Wallace**, a 5-year employee in the Support department. Holly works part time and has completed training. Adjust the height of the new row to match the other table rows.

b. Insert a table row above Julie Kosby's record, and add a new record for **Sally Alden**. Sally works full time, has worked at the company for 2 years in Sales, and has not completed training. Adjust the table formatting if necessary.

c. Insert a new data field in cell G1 with a label **Weeks Vacation**. Wrap the label in the cell to display the field name with **Weeks** above **Vacation**, and then widen the column as necessary to see both words. (*Hint*: Use the Wrap Text button in the Alignment group on the Home tab.)

d. Add a new column to the table by dragging the table's sizing handle, and give the new field a label of **Employee #**. Widen the column to fit the label.

e. Save the file.

3. Find and replace table data.

a. Return to cell A1.

b. Open the Find and Replace dialog box and, then if necessary uncheck the Match case option. Find the first record that contains the text **Support**.

c. Find the second and third records that contain the text **Support**.

d. Replace all **Support** text in the table with **Service**, then save the file.

Skills Review (continued)

4. Delete table data.

a. Go to cell A1.

b. Delete the record for Irene Diamond.

c. Use the Remove Duplicates button to confirm that the table does not have any duplicate records.

d. Delete the Employee # table column, then delete its column header, if necessary.

e. Save the file.

5. Sort table data.

a. Sort the table by Years Employed in largest to smallest order.

b. Sort the table by Last Name in A to Z order.

c. Perform a multilevel sort: Sort the table first by Full/Part Time in A to Z order and then by Last Name in A to Z order.

d. Check the table to make sure the records appear in the correct order.

e. Save the file.

6. Use formulas in a table.

a. In cell G2, enter the formula that calculates an employee's vacation time; base the formula on the company policy that employees working at the company less than 4 years have 2 weeks of vacation. At 4 years of employment and longer, an employee has 3 weeks of vacation time. Use the table's field names where appropriate. (*Hint*: The formula is: **=IF([Years Employed]<4,2,3).**)

b. Check the table to make sure the formula filled into the cells in column G and that the correct vacation time is calculated for all cells in the column.

c. Add a Total Row to display the total number of vacation weeks.

d. Change the function in the Total Row to display the maximum number of vacation weeks. Change the entry in cell A8 from Total to **Maximum**.

e. Compare your table to FIGURE 7-22, then save the workbook.

FIGURE 7-22

	A	B	C	D	E	F	G
1	Last Name	First Name	Years Employed	Department	Full/Part Time	Training Completed	Weeks Vacation
2	Alden	Sally	2	Sales	F	N	2
3	Green	Jane	1	Service	F	N	2
4	Kosby	Julie	4	Sales	F	Y	3
5	Mendez	Darryl	3	Sales	F	N	2
6	Ropes	Mark	1	Sales	P	Y	2
7	Wallace	Holly	5	Service	P	Y	3
8	Maximum						3

7. Print a table.

a. Add a header that reads **Employees** in the left section, then format the header in bold with a font size of **16**.

b. Add column A as a print title that repeats at the left of each printed page.

c. Preview your table to check that the last names appear on both pages.

d. Change the page orientation to landscape, preview the worksheet, then save the workbook.

e. Submit your workbook to your instructor. Close the workbook, then exit Excel.

Independent Challenge 1

You are the clinical coordinator for an acupuncture clinic. Your administrative assistant created an Excel worksheet with client data including the results of a survey. You will create a table using the client data, and analyze the survey results to help focus the clinic's expenses in the most successful areas.

a. Start Excel, open EX 7-3.xlsx from the location where you store your Data Files, then save it as **EX 7-Clients**.

b. Create a table from the worksheet data, and apply Table Style Light 10.

Independent Challenge 1 (continued)

c. Add the two records shown in the table below:

Last Name	First Name	Street Address	City	State	Zip	Area Code	Ad Source
Ross	Kim	4 Ridge Rd.	San Francisco	CA	94177	415	Health Center
Jones	Kathy	512 17th St.	Seattle	WA	98001	206	Radio

d. Find the record for Mike Rondo, then delete it.

e. Click cell A1 and replace all instances of **TV** with **Social Media**.

f. Remove duplicate records where all fields are identical.

g. Sort the list by Last Name in A to Z order.

h. Sort the list again by Area Code in Smallest to Largest order.

i. Sort the table first by Survey Source in A to Z order, then by State in A to Z order. Compare your table to FIGURE 7-23.

FIGURE 7-23

	A	B	C	D	E	F	G	H	I
1	Last Name	First Name	Street Address	City	State	Zip	Area Code	Survey Source	
2	Graham	Shelley	989 26th St.	Chicago	IL	60611	773	Education Website	
3	Hogan	Andy	32 William St.	Concord	MA	01742	508	Education Website	
4	Kelly	Shawn	22 Kendall St.	Cambridge	MA	02138	617	Education Website	
5	Masters	Latrice	88 Las Puntas Rd.	Boston	MA	02205	617	Education Website	
6	Nelson	Michael	229 Rally Rd.	Kansas City	MO	64105	816	Education Website	
7	Dickenson	Tonia	883 E. 34th St.	New York	NY	10044	212	Education Website	
8	Gonzales	Fred	5532 West St.	Houston	TX	77098	281	Education Website	
9	Chelly	Yvonne	900 Sola St.	San Diego	CA	92106	619	Health Center	
10	Worthen	Sally	2120 Central St.	San Francisco	CA	93772	415	Health Center	
11	Malone	Kris	1 South St.	San Francisco	CA	94177	415	Health Center	
12	Ross	Kim	4 Ridge Rd.	San Francisco	CA	94177	415	Health Center	
13	Roberts	Bob	56 Water St.	Chicago	IL	60618	771	Health Center	
14	Kim	Janie	9 First St.	San Francisco	CA	94177	415	Health Website	
15	Oren	Scott	72 Yankee St.	Brookfield	CT	06830	203	Health Website	
16	Duran	Maria	Galvin St.	Chicago	IL	60614	773	Health Website	
17	Smith	Carolyn	921 Lopez St.	San Diego	CA	92104	619	Newspaper	
18	Herbert	Greg	1192 Dome St.	San Diego	CA	93303	619	Newspaper	
19	Kelly	Janie	9 First St.	San Francisco	CA	94177	415	Newspaper	
20	Roberts	Bob	56 Water St.	Chicago	IL	60614	312	Newspaper	
21	Miller	Hope	111 Stratton St.	Chicago	IL	60614	773	Newspaper	
22	Warner	Salvatore	100 Westside St.	Chicago	IL	60620	312	Newspaper	

j. Enter your name in the center section of the worksheet footer.

k. Add a centered header that reads **Client Survey** in bold with a font size of 16.

l. Add print titles to repeat the first row at the top of each printed page.

m. Save the workbook, preview it, then submit the workbook to your instructor.

n. Close the workbook, then exit Excel.

Independent Challenge 2

You manage Illuminate, a store that sells LED bulbs in bulk online. Your customers purchase items in quantities of 10 or more. You decide to plan and build a table that tracks recent sales, and includes customer information and transaction details.

a. Prepare a plan for a table that includes details about sales transactions, including the customer's name and what they purchased.

b. Sketch a sample table on a piece of paper, indicating how the table should be built. Create a table documenting the table design including the field names, type of data, and description of the data. Some examples of items are 60W Soft White, 65W Soft White, 60W Daylight, 65W Daylight, and 100W Daylight.

Independent Challenge 2 (continued)

c. Start Excel, create a new workbook, then save it as **EX 7-LED** in the location where you store your Data Files. Enter the field names shown in the table below in the designated cells:

cell	field name
A1	Customer Last
B1	Customer First
C1	Item
D1	Quantity
E1	Cost

d. Enter eight data records using your own data.
e. Define the data as a table using the data in the range A1:E9. Adjust the column widths as necessary.
f. Apply the Table Style Light 7 to the table.
g. Add a field named **Total** in cell F1.
h. Enter a formula in cell F2 that calculates the total by multiplying the Quantity field by the Cost field. Check that the formula was filled down in the column.
i. Format the Cost and Total columns using the Accounting number format. Adjust the column widths as necessary.
j. Add a new record to your table in row 10. Add another record above row 4.
k. Sort the table in ascending order by Cost.
l. Enter your name in the worksheet footer, then save the workbook.
m. Preview the worksheet, then submit your workbook to your instructor.
n. Close the workbook, then exit Excel.

Independent Challenge 3

You are a sales manager at a consulting firm. You are managing your accounts using an Excel worksheet and have decided that a table will provide additional features to help you keep track of the accounts. You will use the table sorting features and table formulas to analyze your account data.

a. Start Excel, open EX 7-4.xlsx from the location where you store your Data Files, then save it as **EX 7-Accounts**.
b. Create a table with the worksheet data, and apply a table style of your choice. Adjust the column widths as necessary.
c. Sort the table on the Budget field using the Smallest to Largest order.
d. Sort the table using two fields, first by Contact in A to Z order, then by Budget in Smallest to Largest order.
e. Add the new field label **Balance** in cell G1, and adjust the column width as necessary.
f. Enter a formula in cell G2 that uses structured references to table fields to calculate the balance on an account as the Budget minus the Expenses.
g. Add a new record with an account number of **4113** with a type of **Inside**, a code of **I5**, a budget of **$550,000**, expenses of **$400,000**, and a contact of **Maureen Smith**.
h. Verify that the formula accurately calculated the balance for the new record.
i. Replace all of the Maureen Smith data with **Maureen Lang**.
j. Find the record for the 2188 account number and delete it.
k. Delete the Type and code fields from the table.

Independent Challenge 3 (continued)

l. Add a total row to the table and display the totals for appropriate columns. Adjust the column widths as necessary. Compare your table to FIGURE 7-24. (Your table style may differ.)

FIGURE 7-24

	A	B	C	D	E
1	Account Number	Budget	Expenses	Contact	Balance
2	1084	$ 275,000	$ 215,000	Cindy Boil	$ 60,000
3	5431	$ 375,000	$ 250,000	Cindy Boil	$ 125,000
4	9624	$ 650,000	$ 550,000	Cindy Boil	$ 100,000
5	2117	$ 550,000	$ 525,000	Kathy Jenkins	$ 25,000
6	5647	$ 750,000	$ 600,000	Kathy Jenkins	$ 150,000
7	6671	$ 175,000	$ 150,000	Maureen Lang	$ 25,000
8	1097	$ 250,000	$ 210,000	Maureen Lang	$ 40,000
9	4301	$ 350,000	$ 210,000	Maureen Lang	$ 140,000
10	7814	$ 410,000	$ 320,000	Maureen Lang	$ 90,000
11	4113	$ 550,000	$ 400,000	Maureen Lang	$ 150,000
12	Total	$ 4,335,000	$ 3,430,000		$ 905,000
13					
14					

m. Enter your name in the center section of the worksheet footer, add a center section header of **Accounts** using formatting of your choice, change the page orientation to landscape, then save the workbook.

n. Preview your workbook, submit the workbook to your instructor, close the workbook, then exit Excel.

Independent Challenge 4: Explore

As the sales manager at a environmental supply firm, you track the sales data of the associates in the department using a table in Excel. You decide to highlight associates that have met the annual sales targets for the annual meeting.

a. Start Excel, open EX 7-5.xlsx from the location where you store your Data Files, then save it as **EX 7-Sales**.

b. Create a table that includes all the worksheet data, and apply the table style of your choice. Adjust the column widths as necessary.

c. Sort the table on the Balance field using the Largest to Smallest order.

d. Use conditional formatting to format the cells of the table containing positive balances with a light red fill.

e. Sort the table using the Balance field using the order of No Fill on top.

f. Format the table to emphasize the Balance column, and turn off the banded rows. (*Hint*: Use the Table Style Options on the Table Tools Design tab.)

g. Research how to print nonadjacent areas on a single page. (Excel prints nonadjacent areas of a worksheet on separate pages by default.) Add a new sheet to the workbook, then enter the result of your research on Sheet2 of the workbook.

h. Return to Sheet1 and create a print area that prints only the Employee Number, Associate, and Balance columns of the table on one page.

i. Compare your table with FIGURE 7-25. Save the workbook.

j. Preview your print area to make sure it will print on a single page.

k. Enter your name in the worksheet footer, then save the workbook.

l. Submit the workbook to your instructor, close the workbook, then exit Excel.

FIGURE 7-25

	A	B	E
1	Employee Number	Associate	Balance
2	6547	Larry Makay	$ (5,000)
3	2984	George Well	$ (10,000)
4	4874	George Well	$ (73,126)
5	6647	Kris Lowe	$ (95,000)
6	5512	Nancy Alden	$ 108,357
7	3004	Lou Colby	$ 95,000
8	4257	Bob Allen	$ 50,000
9	9821	Joe Wood	$ 45,000
10	8624	Judy Smith	$ 25,000
11	1005	Janet Casey	$ 17,790

Visual Workshop

Start Excel, open EX 7-6.xlsx from the location where you store your Data Files, then save it as **EX 7-Technicians**. Create a table and sort the data as shown in FIGURE 7-26. (*Hint*: The table is formatted using Table Style Medium 13.) Add a worksheet header with the sheet name in the center section that is formatted in bold with a size of 14. Enter your name in the center section of the worksheet footer. Save the workbook, preview the table, close the workbook, submit the workbook to your instructor, then exit Excel.

FIGURE 7-26

	Job Number	Employee Number	Amount Billed	Location	Technician Name
1	Job Number	Employee Number	Amount Billed	Location	Technician Name
2	2257	69741	$ 109.88	Main	Eric Mallon
3	1032	65418	$ 158.32	Satellite	Eric Mallon
4	1587	10057	$ 986.34	Main	Jerry Thomas
5	1533	66997	$ 112.98	Satellite	Jerry Thomas
6	2187	58814	$ 521.77	Satellite	Jerry Thomas
7	2588	69784	$ 630.55	Main	Joan Rand
8	2001	48779	$ 478.24	Satellite	Joan Rand
9	1251	69847	$ 324.87	Main	Kathy Green
10	2113	36697	$ 163.88	Main	Kathy Green
11	2357	10087	$ 268.24	Main	Mark Eaton
12	1111	13987	$ 658.30	Satellite	Mark Eaton
13					

Analyzing Table Data

CASE The vice president of sales and marketing, Mary Watson, asks you to display information from a table of scheduled projects to help the sales representatives with customer inquiries. She also asks you to summarize the project sales for a presentation at the international sales meeting. You will prepare these using various filters, subtotals, and Excel functions.

Module Objectives

After completing this module, you will be able to:

- Filter a table
- Create a custom filter
- Filter a table with the Advanced Filter
- Extract table data
- Look up values in a table
- Summarize table data
- Validate table data
- Create subtotals

Files You Will Need

EX 8-1.xlsx   EX 8-5.xlsx

EX 8-2.xlsx   EX 8-6.xlsx

EX 8-3.xlsx   EX 8-7.xlsx

EX 8-4.xlsx

Filter a Table

Learning
Outcomes
• Filter records using
AutoFilter
• Filter records using
search criteria

An Excel table lets you easily manipulate large amounts of data to view only the data you want, using a feature called **AutoFilter**. When you create a table, arrows automatically appear next to each column header. These arrows are called **filter list arrows**, **AutoFilter list arrows**, or **list arrows**, and you can use them to **filter** a table to display only the records that meet criteria you specify, temporarily hiding records that do not meet those criteria. For example, you can use the filter list arrow next to the Project field header to display only records that contain Cheetah in the Project field. Once you filter data, you can copy, chart, and print the displayed records. You can easily clear a filter to redisplay all the records. **CASE** *Mary asks you to display only the records for the Cheetah projects. She also asks for information about the projects that have the most reservations and the projects that depart in March.*

STEPS

1. **Start Excel, open** EX 8-1.xlsx **from where you store your Data Files, then save it as** EX 8-Projects

2. **Click the** Project list arrow

   Sort options appear at the top of the menu, advanced filtering options appear in the middle, and at the bottom is a list of the project data from column A, as shown in FIGURE 8-1. Because you want to display data for only the Cheetah projects, your **search criterion** (the text you are searching for) is Cheetah. You can select one of the Project data options in the menu, which acts as your search criterion.

QUICK TIP
You can also filter the table to display only the Cheetah project information by clicking the Project list arrow, entering "Cheetah" in the Search text box on the menu below Text Filters, then clicking OK.

3. **In the list of projects for the Project field, click** Select All **to clear the check marks from the projects, scroll down the list of projects, click** Cheetah, **then click** OK

   Only those records containing "Cheetah" in the Project field appear, as shown in FIGURE 8-2. The row numbers for the matching records change to blue, and the list arrow for the filtered field has a filter icon ⧨. Both indicate that there is a filter in effect and that some of the records are temporarily hidden.

4. **Move the pointer over the** Project list arrow

   The ScreenTip Project: Equals "Cheetah" describes the filter for the field, meaning that only the Cheetah records appear. You decide to remove the filter to redisplay all of the table data.

5. **Click the** Project list arrow, **then click** Clear Filter From "Project"

   You have cleared the Cheetah filter, and all the records reappear. You want to display the most popular projects, those that are in the top five percent of seats reserved.

QUICK TIP
You can also filter or sort a table by the color of the cells if conditional formatting has been applied.

6. **Click the** Places Reserved list arrow, **point to** Number Filters, **click** Top 10, **select** 10 in **the middle box, type** 5, **click the** Items list arrow, **click** Percent, **then click** OK

   Excel displays the records for the top five percent in the number of Places Reserved field, as shown in FIGURE 8-3. You decide to clear the filter to redisplay all the records.

7. **On the Home tab, click the** Sort & Filter button **in the Editing group, then click** Clear

   You have cleared the filter and all the records reappear. You can clear a filter using either the AutoFilter menu command or the Sort & Filter button on the Home tab. The Sort & Filter button is convenient for clearing multiple filters at once. You want to find all of the projects that depart in March.

8. **Click the** Depart Date list arrow, **point to** Date Filters, **point to** All Dates in the Period, **then click** March

   Excel displays the records for only the projects that leave in March. You decide to clear the filter and display all of the records.

QUICK TIP
You can also clear a filter by clicking the Clear button in the Sort & Filter group on the Data tab.

9. **Click the** Sort & Filter button **in the Editing group, click** Clear, **then save the workbook**

FIGURE 8-1: Worksheet showing AutoFilter options

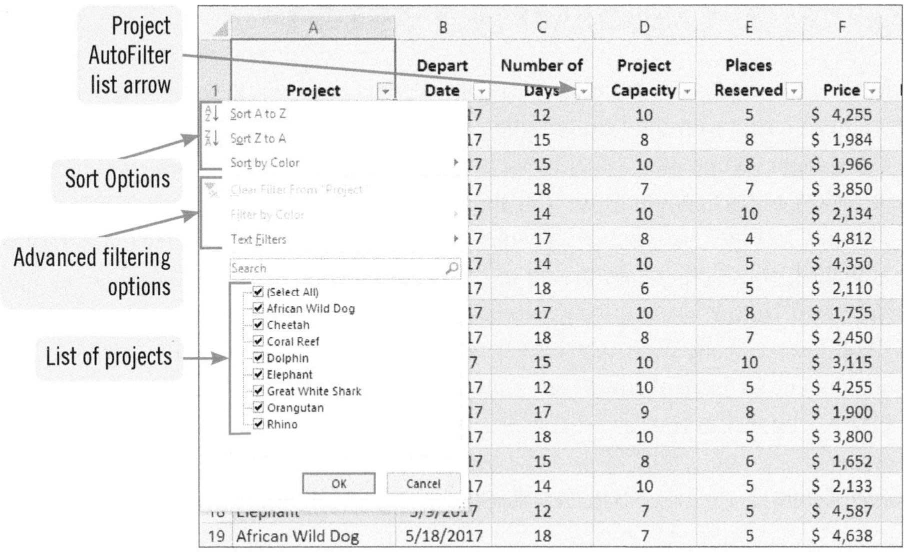

Project AutoFilter list arrow

Sort Options

Advanced filtering options

List of projects

	A	B	C	D	E	F
1	Project	Depart Date	Number of Days	Project Capacity	Places Reserved	Price
	Sort A to Z	17	12	10	5	$ 4,255
	Sort Z to A	17	15	8	8	$ 1,984
	Sort by Color ▸	17	15	10	8	$ 1,966
	Clear Filter From "Project"	17	18	7	7	$ 3,850
	Filter by Color ▸	17	14	10	10	$ 2,134
	Text Filters ▸	17	17	8	4	$ 4,812
	Search 🔍	17	14	10	5	$ 4,350
	☑ (Select All)	17	18	6	5	$ 2,110
	☑ African Wild Dog	17	17	10	8	$ 1,755
	☑ Cheetah	17	18	8	7	$ 2,450
	☑ Coral Reef	7	15	10	10	$ 3,115
	☑ Dolphin	17	12	10	5	$ 4,255
	☑ Elephant	17	17	9	8	$ 1,900
	☑ Great White Shark	17	18	10	5	$ 3,800
	☑ Orangutan	17	15	8	6	$ 1,652
	☑ Rhino	17	14	10	5	$ 2,133
	OK Cancel					
18	Elephant	5/9/2017	12	7	5	$ 4,587
19	African Wild Dog	5/18/2017	18	7	5	$ 4,638

FIGURE 8-2: Table filtered to show Cheetah projects

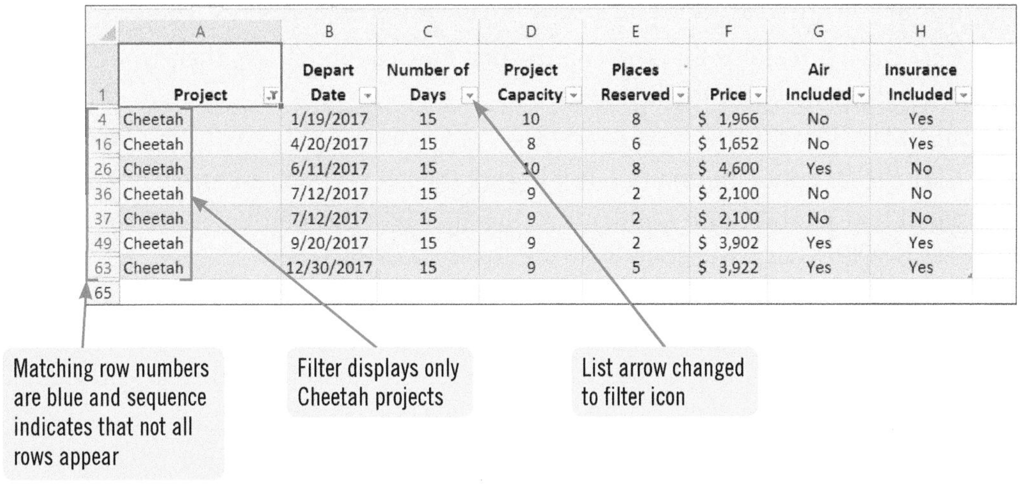

	A	B	C	D	E	F	G	H
1	Project	Depart Date	Number of Days	Project Capacity	Places Reserved	Price	Air Included	Insurance Included
4	Cheetah	1/19/2017	15	10	8	$ 1,966	No	Yes
16	Cheetah	4/20/2017	15	8	6	$ 1,652	No	Yes
26	Cheetah	6/11/2017	15	10	8	$ 4,600	Yes	No
36	Cheetah	7/12/2017	15	9	2	$ 2,100	No	No
37	Cheetah	7/12/2017	15	9	2	$ 2,100	No	No
49	Cheetah	9/20/2017	15	9	2	$ 3,902	Yes	Yes
63	Cheetah	12/30/2017	15	9	5	$ 3,922	Yes	Yes
65								

Matching row numbers are blue and sequence indicates that not all rows appear

Filter displays only Cheetah projects

List arrow changed to filter icon

FIGURE 8-3: Table filtered with top 5% of Places Reserved

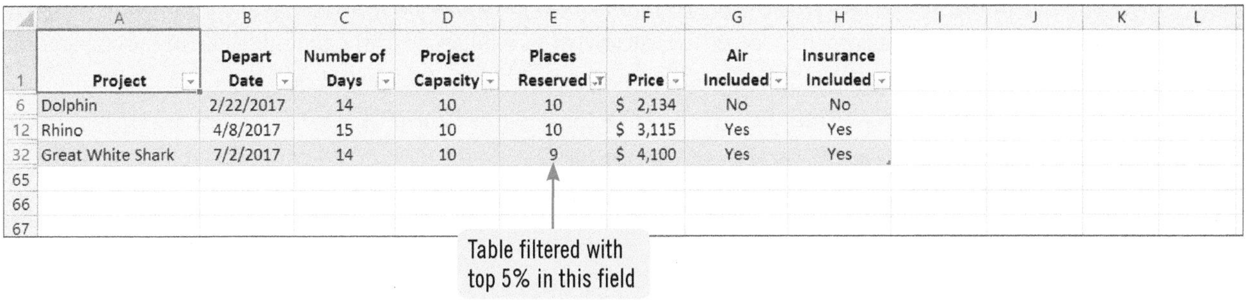

	A	B	C	D	E	F	G	H	I	J	K	L
1	Project	Depart Date	Number of Days	Project Capacity	Places Reserved	Price	Air Included	Insurance Included				
6	Dolphin	2/22/2017	14	10	10	$ 2,134	No	No				
12	Rhino	4/8/2017	15	10	10	$ 3,115	Yes	Yes				
32	Great White Shark	7/2/2017	14	10	9	$ 4,100	Yes	Yes				
65												
66												
67												

Table filtered with top 5% in this field

Create a Custom Filter

While AutoFilter lists can display records that are equal to certain amounts, you often need more detailed filters, which you can create with the help of options in the Custom AutoFilter dialog box. For example, your criteria can contain comparison operators such as "greater than" or "less than" that let you display values above or below a certain amount. You can also use **logical conditions** like And and Or to narrow a search even further. You can have Excel display records that meet a criterion in a field *and* another criterion in that same field. This is often used to find records between two values. For example, by specifying an **And logical condition**, you can display records for customers with incomes that are above $40,000 *and* below $70,000. You can also have Excel display records that meet either criterion in a field by specifying an Or condition. The **Or logical condition** is used to find records that satisfy either of two values. For example, in a table of book data you can use the Or condition to find records that contain either Beginning or Introduction in the title name. **CASE** *Mary wants to locate projects for customers who want to participate in the winter months. She also wants to find projects that depart between February 15, 2017 and April 15, 2017. She asks you to create custom filters to find the projects satisfying these criteria.*

STEPS

1. **Click the** Depart Date list arrow, **point to** Date Filters, **then click** Custom Filter

   The Custom AutoFilter dialog box opens. You enter your criteria in the text boxes. The left text box on the first line currently displays "equals." Because you want to find all projects that occur in the winter months, you decide to search for tours starting before March 1 and after December 1.

2. **Click the** left text box list arrow **on the first line, click** is before, **then type** 3/1/2017 **in the right text box on the first line**

   To complete the custom filter, you need to add a condition for projects starting after December 1.

3. **Click the** Or option button **to select it, click the** left text box list arrow **on the second line, select** is after, **then type** 12/1/2017 **in the right text box on the second line**

   Your completed Custom AutoFilter dialog box should match FIGURE 8-4.

4. **Click** OK

   The dialog box closes, and only those records having departing before 3/1 or after 12/1 appear in the worksheet. You want to find all projects that depart between February 15, 2017 and April 15, 2017.

5. **Click the** Depart Date list arrow, **click** Clear Filter From "Depart Date", **click the** Depart Date list arrow, **point to** Date Filters, **then click** Custom Filter

   You want to find the departure dates that are between February 15, 2017 and April 15, 2017 (that is, after February 15 *and* before April 15).

6. **Click the** left text box list arrow **on the first line, click** is after, **then type** 2/15/2017 **in the right text box on the first line**

   The And condition is selected, which is correct.

7. **Click the** left text box list arrow **on the second line, select** is before, **type** 4/15/2017 **in the right text box on the second line, then click** OK

   The records displayed have departure dates between February 15, 2017 and April 15, 2017. Compare your records to those shown in FIGURE 8-5.

8. **Click the** Depart Date list arrow, **click** Clear Filter From "Depart Date", **then add your name to the center section of the footer**

   You have cleared the filter, and all the project records reappear.

FIGURE 8-4: Custom AutoFilter dialog box

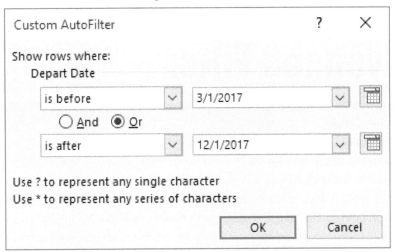

FIGURE 8-5: Results of custom filter

	Project	Depart Date	Number of Days	Project Capacity	Places Reserved	Price	Air Included	Insurance Included	I	J	K	L	M
6	Dolphin	2/22/2017	14	10	10	$ 2,134	No	No					
7	Orangutan	2/28/2017	17	8	4	$ 4,812	Yes	No					
8	Great White Shark	3/13/2017	14	10	5	$ 4,350	Yes	No					
9	Coral Reef	3/19/2017	18	6	5	$ 2,110	No	Yes					
10	Orangutan	3/20/2017	17	10	8	$ 1,755	No	Yes					
11	African Wild Dog	3/23/2017	18	8	7	$ 2,450	No	No					
12	Rhino	4/8/2017	15	10	10	$ 3,115	Yes	Yes					
13	Elephant	4/11/2017	12	10	5	$ 4,255	Yes	No					
65													
66													

Departure dates are between 2/15 and 4/15

Using more than one rule when conditionally formatting data

You can apply conditional formatting to table cells in the same way that you can format a range of worksheet data. You can add multiple rules by clicking the Home tab, clicking the Conditional Formatting button in the Styles group, then clicking New Rule for each additional rule that you want to apply. You can also add rules using the Conditional Formatting Rules Manager, which displays all of the rules for a data range. To use the Rules Manager, click the Home tab, click the Conditional Formatting button in the Styles group, click Manage Rules, then click New Rule for each rule that you want to apply to the data range. You can also use a function to conditionally format cells. For example, if you have a column of invoice dates and you want to format the dates that are overdue, open the Rules Manager, click Use a formula in the Select a Rule Type section, and then edit the rule description add a formula such as "<TODAY()."

Filter a Table with the Advanced Filter

When you want to see table data that meets a detailed set of conditions, you can use the Advanced Filter feature. This feature lets you specify data that you want to display from the table using And and Or conditions. Rather than entering the criteria in a dialog box, you enter the criteria in a criteria range on your worksheet. A **criteria range** is a cell range containing one row of labels (usually a copy of the column labels) and at least one additional row underneath the row of labels that contains the criteria you want to match. Placing the criteria in the same row indicates that the records you are searching for must match both criteria; that is, it specifies an **And condition**. Placing the criteria in the different rows indicates that the records you are searching for must match only one of the criterion; that is, it specifies an **Or condition**. With the criteria range on the worksheet, you can easily see the criteria by which your table is sorted. Another advantage of the Advanced Filter is that you can move filtered table data to a different area of the worksheet or to a new worksheet, as you will see in the next lesson. **CASE** *Mary wants to identify projects that depart after 6/1/2017 and that cost less than $2,000. She asks you to use the Advanced Filter to retrieve these records. You begin by defining the criteria range.*

STEPS

1. **Select** table rows 1 through 6, **then click the** Insert list arrow **in the Cells group**
    Six blank rows are added above the table.

2. **Click** Insert Sheet Rows; **click cell** A1, **type** Criteria Range, **then click the** Enter button ☑️ **on the formula bar**
    Excel does not require the label "Criteria Range", but it is useful to see the column labels as you organize the worksheet and use filters.

3. **Select the range** A7:H7, **click the** Copy button **in the Clipboard group, click cell** A2, **click the** Paste button **in the Clipboard group, then press** [Esc]
    Next, you want to insert criteria that will display records for only those projects that depart after June 1, 2017 and that cost under $2,000.

4. **Click cell** B3, **type** >6/1/2017, **click cell** F3, **type** <2000, **then click** ☑️
    You have entered the criteria in the cells directly beneath the Criteria Range labels, as shown in FIGURE 8-6.

5. **Click any cell in the table, click the** Data tab, **then click the** Advanced button **in the Sort & Filter group**
    The Advanced Filter dialog box opens, with the table (list) range already entered. The default setting under Action is to filter the table in its current location ("in-place") rather than copy it to another location.

6. **Click the** Criteria range text box, **select the range** A2:H3 **in the worksheet, then click** OK
    You have specified the criteria range and used the filter. The filtered table contains seven records that match both criteria—the departure date is after 6/1/2017 and the price is less than $2,000, as shown in FIGURE 8-7. You'll filter this table even further in the next lesson.

FIGURE 8-6: Criteria in the same row indicating an and condition

	Project	Depart Date	Number of Days	Project Capacity	Places Reserved	Price	Air Included	Insurance Included
1	Criteria Range							
2								
3		>6/1/2017				<2000		
4								
5								
6								
7	Project	Date	Days	Capacity	Reserved	Price	Included	Included
8	Elephant	1/12/2017	12	10	5	$ 4,255	Yes	No
9	Rhino	1/13/2017	15	8	8	$ 1,984	No	No

Filtered records will match these criteria

FIGURE 8-7: Filtered table

	Project	Depart Date	Number of Days	Project Capacity	Places Reserved	Price	Air Included	Insurance Included
1	Criteria Range							
2								
3		>6/1/2017				<2000		
4								
5								
6								
7	Project	Depart Date	Number of Days	Project Capacity	Places Reserved	Price	Air Included	Insurance Included
33	Elephant	6/12/2017	12	7	5	$ 1,900	No	No
34	Rhino	6/12/2017	15	8	6	$ 1,970	No	Yes
37	African Wild Dog	6/27/2017	18	10	7	$ 1,944	No	No
44	African Wild Dog	7/27/2017	18	10	2	$ 1,890	No	No
46	Orangutan	8/12/2017	17	10	3	$ 1,970	No	Yes
49	Great White Shark	8/27/2017	14	10	8	$ 1,944	No	No
61	Great White Shark	10/31/2017	14	9	8	$ 1,900	No	No
71								
72								

Depart dates are after 6/1/2017

Prices are less than $2000

Saving time with conditional formatting

You can emphasize top- or bottom-ranked values in a field using conditional formatting. To highlight the top or bottom values in a field, select the field data, click the Conditional Formatting button in the Styles group on the Home tab, point to Top/Bottom Rules, select a Top or Bottom rule, if necessary enter the percentage or number of cells in the selected range that you want to format, select the format for the cells that meet the top or bottom criteria, then click OK. You can also format your worksheet or table data using icon sets and color scales based on the cell values. A **color scale** uses a set of two, three, or four fill colors to convey relative values. For example, red could fill cells to indicate they have higher values and green could signify lower values. To add a color scale, select a data range, click the Home tab, click the Conditional Formatting button in the Styles group, then point to Color Scales. On the submenu, you can select preformatted color sets or click More Rules to create your own color sets. **Icon sets** let you visually communicate relative cell values by adding icons to cells based on the values they contain. An upward-pointing green arrow might represent the highest values, and downward-pointing red arrows could represent lower values. To add an icon set to a data range, select a data range, click the Conditional Formatting button in the Styles group, then point to Icon Sets. You can customize the values that are used as thresholds for color scales and icon sets by clicking the Conditional Formatting button in the Styles group, clicking Manage Rules, clicking the rule in the Conditional Formatting Rules Manager dialog box, then clicking Edit Rule.

Extract Table Data

Learning Outcomes
• Extract filtered records to another worksheet location
• Clear filtered records

Whenever you take the time to specify a complicated set of search criteria, it's a good idea to extract the matching records, rather than filtering it in place. When you **extract** data, you place a copy of a filtered table in a range that you specify in the Advanced Filter dialog box. This way, you won't accidentally clear the filter or lose track of the records you spent time compiling. To extract data, you use an Advanced Filter and enter the criteria beneath the copied field names, as you did in the previous lesson. You then specify the location where you want the extracted data to appear. **CASE** *Mary needs to filter the table one step further to reflect only African Wild Dog or Great White Shark projects in the current filtered table. She asks you to complete this filter by specifying an Or condition, which you will do by entering two sets of criteria in two separate rows. You decide to save the filtered records by extracting them to a different location in the worksheet.*

STEPS

1. **In cell A3 enter African Wild Dog, then in cell A4 enter Great White Shark**

   The new sets of criteria need to appear in two separate rows, so you need to copy the previous filter criteria to the second row.

2. **Copy the criteria in cells B3:F3 to B4:F4**

   The criteria are shown in FIGURE 8-8. When you use the Advanced Filter this time, you indicate that you want to copy the filtered table to a range beginning in cell A75, so that Mary can easily refer to the data, even if you use more filters later.

3. **If necessary, click the Data tab, then click Advanced in the Sort & Filter group**

4. **Under Action, click the Copy to another location option button to select it, click the Copy to text box, then type A75**

   The last time you filtered the table, the criteria range included only rows 2 and 3. Now you have criteria in row 4, so you need to adjust the criteria range.

QUICK TIP
Make sure the criteria range in the Advanced Filter dialog box includes the field names and the number of rows underneath the names that contain criteria. If you leave a blank row in the criteria range, Excel filters nothing and shows all records.

5. **Edit the contents of the Criteria range text box to show the range $A$2:$H$4, click OK, then if necessary scroll down until row 75 is visible**

   The matching records appear in the range beginning in cell A75, as shown in FIGURE 8-9. The original table, starting in cell A7, contains the records filtered in the previous lesson.

6. **Press [Ctrl][Home], then click the Clear button in the Sort & Filter group**

   The original table is displayed starting in cell A7, and the extracted table remains in A75:H79.

7. **Save the workbook**

FIGURE 8-8: Criteria in separate rows

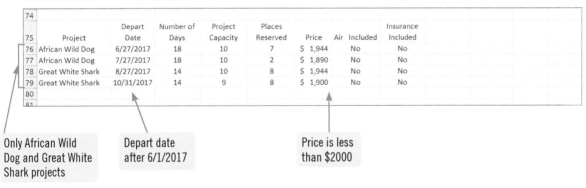

	A	B	C	D	E	F	G	H	I	J	K
1	Criteria Range										
2	Project	Depart Date	Number of Days	Project Capacity	Places Reserved	Price	Air Included	Insurance Included			
3	African Wild Dog	>6/1/2017				<2000					
4	Great White Shark	>6/1/2017				<2000					

Criteria on two lines indicates an OR condition

FIGURE 8-9: Extracted data records

74								
75	Project	Depart Date	Number of Days	Project Capacity	Places Reserved	Price	Air Included	Insurance Included
76	African Wild Dog	6/27/2017	18	10	7	$ 1,944	No	No
77	African Wild Dog	7/27/2017	18	10	2	$ 1,890	No	No
78	Great White Shark	8/27/2017	14	10	8	$ 1,944	No	No
79	Great White Shark	10/31/2017	14	9	8	$ 1,900	No	No
80								
81								

Only African Wild Dog and Great White Shark projects

Depart date after 6/1/2017

Price is less than $2000

Understanding the criteria range and the copy-to location

When you define the criteria range and the copy-to location in the Advanced Filter dialog box, Excel automatically creates the range names Criteria and Extract for these ranges in the worksheet. The Criteria range includes the field names and any criteria rows underneath them. The Extract range includes just the field names above the extracted table. You can select these ranges by clicking the Name box list arrow, then clicking the range name. If you click the Name Manager button in the Defined Names group on the Formulas tab, you will see these new names and the ranges associated with each one.

Look Up Values in a Table

The Excel VLOOKUP function helps you locate specific values in a table. VLOOKUP searches vertically (V) down the far left column of a table, then reads across the row to find the value in the column you specify, much as you might look up a number in a name and address list: You locate a person's name, then read across the row to find the phone number you want. **CASE** ▶ *Mary wants to be able to find a project by entering the project code. You will use the VLOOKUP function to accomplish this task. You begin by viewing the table name so you can refer to it in a lookup function.*

STEPS

1. **Click the** Lookup sheet tab, **click the** Formulas tab **in the Ribbon, then click the** Name Manager button **in the Defined Names group**

   The named ranges for the workbook appear in the Name Manager dialog box, as shown in FIGURE 8-10. The Criteria and Extract ranges appear at the top of the range name list. At the bottom of the list is information about the three tables in the workbook. Table1 refers to the table on the 2017 Projects sheet, Table2 refers to the table on the Lookup sheet, and Table3 refers to the table on the Subtotals worksheet. The Excel structured reference feature automatically created these table names when the tables were created.

2. **Click** Close

   You want to find the project represented by the code 754Q. The VLOOKUP function lets you find the project name for any project code. You will enter a project code in cell M1 and a VLOOKUP function in cell M2.

3. **Click cell** M1, **enter** 754Q, **click cell** M2, **click the** Lookup & Reference button **in the Function Library group, then click** VLOOKUP

   The Function Arguments dialog box opens, with boxes for each of the VLOOKUP arguments. Because the value you want to find is in cell M1, M1 is the Lookup_value. The table you want to search is the table on the Lookup sheet, so its assigned name, Table2, is the Table_array.

4. **With the insertion point in the Lookup_value text box, click cell** M1, **click the** Table_array text box, **then type** Table2

   The column containing the information that you want to find and display in cell M2 is the second column from the left in the table range, so the Col_index_num is 2. Because you want to find an exact match for the value in cell M1, the Range_lookup argument is FALSE.

5. **Click the** Col_index_num **text box, type** 2, **click the** Range_lookup **text box, then enter** FALSE

   Your completed Function Arguments dialog box should match FIGURE 8-11.

6. **Click** OK

   Excel searches down the far-left column of the table until it finds a project code that matches the one in cell M1. It then looks in column 2 of the table range and finds the project for that record, Dolphin, and displays it in cell M2. You use this function to determine the project for one other project code.

7. **Click cell** M1, **type** 335P, **then click the** Enter button ☑ **on the formula bar**

   The VLOOKUP function returns the value of Elephant in cell M2.

8. **Press** [Ctrl][Home], **then save the workbook**

FIGURE 8-10: **Named ranges in the workbook**

Created by Advanced Filter

Tables in the workbook

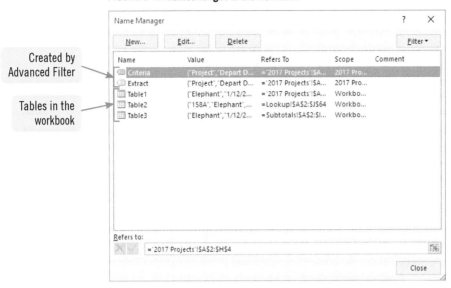

FIGURE 8-11: **Completed Function Arguments dialog box for VLOOKUP**

Range name of table to search

Location of value you want to search for

Search the second column

Finds exact match

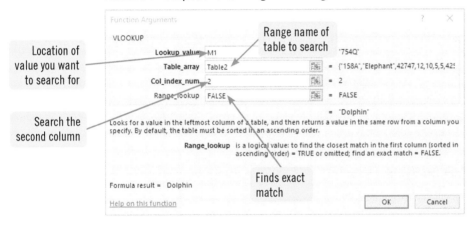

Using other LOOKUP functions

When your data is arranged horizontally in rows instead of vertically in columns, use the HLOOKUP (Horizontal Lookup) function. HLOOKUP searches horizontally across the upper row of a table until it finds the matching value, then looks down the number of rows you specify. The arguments are identical to those for the VLOOKUP function, except that instead of a Col_index_number, HLOOKUP uses a Row_index_number, which indicates the location of the row you want to search. You can use the MATCH function when you want the position of an item in a range. The MATCH function uses the syntax: MATCH (lookup_value,lookup_array,match_ type) where the lookup_value is the value you want to match in the lookup_ array range. The match_type can be 0 for an exact match,

1 for matching the largest value that is less than or equal to lookup_value, or –1 for matching the smallest value that is greater than or equal to the lookup_value. The Transpose function is a LOOKUP function that can be used to rearrange a range of cells, which is also called an array. For example, a vertical range of cells will be arranged horizontally or vice versa. The Transpose array function is entered using the syntax: =TRANSPOSE(range array).

The LOOKUP function is used to locate information in a table. The syntax for the LOOKUP formula is LOOKUP(lookup_value, array). The lookup_value is the value that will be used in the search, the array is the range of cells that will be searched for the lookup_value.

Summarize Table Data

Learning Outcomes
- Summarize table data using DSUM
- Summarize table data using DCOUNT or DCOUNTA

Because a table acts much like a database, database functions allow you to summarize table data in a variety of ways. When working with a sales activity table, for example, you can use Excel to count the number of client contacts by sales representative or to total the amount sold to specific accounts by month. **TABLE 8-1** lists database functions commonly used to summarize table data. **CASE** ▶ *Mary is considering adding projects for the 2017 schedule. She needs your help in evaluating the number of places available for scheduled projects.*

STEPS

1. **Review the criteria range for the Rhino project in the range** L5:L6

   The criteria range in L5:L6 tells Excel to summarize records with the entry "Rhino" in the Project column. The functions will be in cells M8 and M9. You use this criteria range in a DSUM function to sum the places available for only the Rhino projects.

2. **Click cell M8, click the** Insert Function button **in the Function Library group, in the Search for a function text box type** database, **click** Go, **scroll to and click** DSUM **under Select a function, then click** OK

   The first argument of the DSUM function is the table, or database.

QUICK TIP
Because the DSUM formula uses the column headings to locate and sum the table data, you need to include the header row in the database range.

3. **In the Function Arguments dialog box, with the insertion point in the Database text box, move the pointer over the upper-left corner of cell** A1 **until the pointer changes to** ↘, **click once, then click again**

   The first click selects the table's data range, and the second click selects the entire table, including the header row. The second argument of the DSUM function is the label for the column that you want to sum. You want to total the number of available places. The last argument for the DSUM function is the criteria that will be used to determine which values to total.

QUICK TIP
You can move the Function Arguments dialog box if it overlaps a cell or range that you need to click. You can also click the Collapse Dialog Box button [icon], select the cell or range, then click the Expand Dialog Box button [icon] to return to the Function Arguments dialog box.

4. **Click the** Field text box, **then click cell** G1, **Places Available; click the** Criteria text box **and select the range** L5:L6

   Your completed Function Arguments dialog box should match **FIGURE 8-12**.

5. **Click** OK

   The result in cell M8 is 25. Excel totaled the information in the Places Available column for those records that meet the criterion of Project equals Rhino. The DCOUNT and the DCOUNTA functions can help you determine the number of records meeting specified criteria in a database field. DCOUNTA counts the number of nonblank cells. You will use DCOUNTA to determine the number of projects scheduled.

6. **Click cell M9, click the** Insert Function button [icon] **on the formula bar, in the Search for a function text box type** database, **click** Go, **then double-click** DCOUNTA **in the Select a function list**

7. **With the insertion point in the Database text box, move the pointer over the upper-left corner of cell** A1 **until the pointer changes to** ↘, **click once, click again to include the header row, click the** Field text box, **click cell** B1, **click the** Criteria text box **and select the range** L5:L6, **then click** OK

   The result in cell M9 is 8, and it indicates that there are eight Rhino projects scheduled for the year. You also want to display the number of places available for the Dolphin projects.

8. **Click cell** L6, **type** Dolphin, **then click the** Enter button [icon] **on the formula bar**

   The formulas in cells M8 and M9 are updated to reflect the new criteria. **FIGURE 8-13** shows that 33 places are available in the six scheduled Dolphin projects.

FIGURE 8-12: Completed Function Arguments dialog box for DSUM

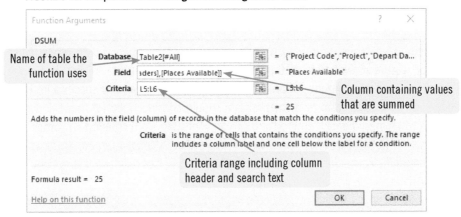

FIGURE 8-13: Result generated by database functions

	E	F	G	H	I	J	K	L	M
1	Project Capacity	Places Reserved	Places Available	Price	Air Included	Insurance Included		Project Code	335P
2	10	5	5	$ 4,255	Yes	No		Project	Elephant
3	8	8	0	$ 1,984	No	No		*Project Information*	
4	10	8	2	$ 1,966	No	Yes			
5	7	7	0	$ 3,850	Yes	Yes		Project	
6	10	10	0	$ 2,134	No	No		Dolphin	
7	8	4	4	$ 4,812	Yes	No			
8	10	5	5	$ 4,350	Yes	No		Places Available	33
9	6	5	1	$ 2,110	No	Yes		Number of projects scheduled	6
10	10	8	2	$ 1,755	No	Yes			
11	8	7	1	$ 2,450	No	No			
12	10	10	0	$ 3,115	Yes	Yes			
13	10	5	5	$ 4,255	Yes	No			
14	9	8	1	$ 1,900	No	No			

Information for Dolphin projects

TABLE 8-1: Common database functions

function	result
DGET	Extracts a single record from a table that matches criteria you specify
DSUM	Totals numbers in a given table column that match criteria you specify
DAVERAGE	Averages numbers in a given table column that match criteria you specify
DCOUNT	Counts the cells that contain numbers in a given table column that match criteria you specify
DCOUNTA	Counts the cells that contain nonblank data in a given table column that match criteria you specify

Validate Table Data

When setting up tables, you want to help ensure accuracy when you or others enter data. The Data Validation feature allows you to do this by specifying what data users can enter in a range of cells. You can restrict data to whole numbers, decimal numbers, or text. You can also specify a list of acceptable entries. Once you've specified what data the program should consider valid for that cell, Excel displays an error message when invalid data is entered and can prevent users from entering any other data that it considers to be invalid. **CASE** *Mary wants to make sure that information in the Air Included column is entered consistently in the future. She asks you to restrict the entries in that column to two options: Yes and No. First, you select the table column you want to restrict.*

STEPS

1. **Click the top edge of the** Air Included **column header**

   The column data is selected.

2. **Click the** Data tab**, click the** Data Validation button **in the Data Tools group, in the Data Validation dialog box click the** Settings tab **if necessary, click the** Allow list arrow**, then click** List

   Selecting the List option lets you type a list of specific options.

3. **Click the** Source text box**, then type** Yes, No

   You have entered the list of acceptable entries, separated by commas, as shown in FIGURE 8-14. You want the data entry person to be able to select a valid entry from a drop-down list.

4. **Verify that the** In-cell dropdown check box **contains a check mark, then click** OK

   The dialog box closes, and you return to the worksheet.

5. **Click the** Home tab**, click any cell in the last table row, click the** Insert list arrow **in the Cells group, click** Insert Table Row Below**, click the** Air Included cell **in this row, then click its** list arrow

   A list of valid list entries opens, as shown in FIGURE 8-15. You could click an item in the list to enter in the cell, but you want to test the data restriction by entering an invalid entry.

6. **Click the** list arrow **to close the list, type** Maybe**, then press** [Enter]

   A warning dialog box appears and prevents you from entering the invalid data, as shown in FIGURE 8-16.

7. **Click** Cancel**, click the** list arrow**, then click** Yes

   The cell accepts the valid entry. The data restriction ensures that records contain only one of the two correct entries in the Air Included column. The table is ready for future data entry.

8. **Delete the last table row, add your name to the center section of the footer, then save the workbook**

Restricting cell values and data length

In addition to providing an in-cell drop-down list for data entry, you can use data validation to restrict the values that are entered into cells. For example, you might want to restrict cells in a selected range to values less than a certain number, date, or time. To do so, click the Data tab, click the Data Validation button in the Data Tools group, on the Settings tab click the Allow list arrow, select Whole number, Decimal, Date, or Time, click the Data list arrow, select less than, then in the bottom text box, enter the maximum value. You can also limit the length of data entered into cells by choosing Text length in the Allow list, clicking the Data list arrow and selecting less than, then entering the maximum length in the Maximum text box.

FIGURE 8-14: **Creating data restrictions**

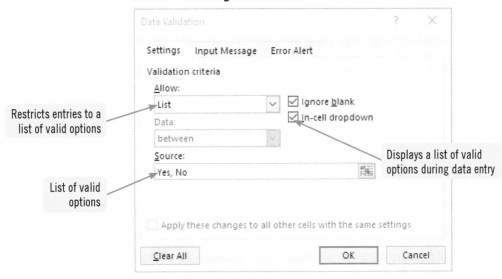

Restricts entries to a list of valid options →

List of valid options →

Displays a list of valid options during data entry

FIGURE 8-15: **Entering data in restricted cells**

59	621R	Orangutan	12/18/2017	17	8	1	7	$ 2,204	No	Yes
60	592D	Elephant	12/20/2017	12	10	0	10	$ 4,100	Yes	Yes
61	793T	Dolphin	12/20/2017	14	10	5	5	$ 2,100	No	Yes
62	307R	African Wild Dog	12/21/2017	18	9	8	1	$ 2,105	No	No
63	927F	Cheetah	12/30/2017	15	9	5	4	$ 3,922	Yes	Yes
64	448G	Elephant	12/31/2017	12	10	2	8	$ 2,100	No	No
65							0			
66										
67										
68										

Dropdown list →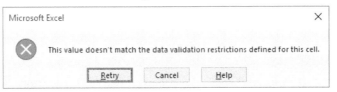
Yes
No

FIGURE 8-16: **Invalid data warning**

Microsoft Excel ✕

❌ This value doesn't match the data validation restrictions defined for this cell.

[Retry] [Cancel] [Help]

Adding input messages and error alerts

You can customize the way data validation works by using the two other tabs in the Data Validation dialog box: Input Message and Error Alert. The Input Message tab lets you set a message that appears when the user selects that cell. For example, the message might contain instructions about what type of data to enter. On the Input Message tab, enter a message title and message, then click OK. The Error Alert tab lets you set one of three alert styles if a user enters invalid data. The Information style displays your message with the information icon but allows the user to proceed with data entry. The Warning style displays your information with the warning icon and gives the user the option to proceed with data entry or not. The Stop style, which you used in this lesson, is the default; it displays your message and only lets the user retry or cancel data entry for that cell.

Create Subtotals

Learning
Outcomes
• Summarize
  worksheet data
  using subtotals
• Use outline symbols
• Convert a table to
  a range

In a large range of data, you often need to perform calculations that summarize groups within a set of data. For example, you might need to subtotal the sales for several sales reps listed in a table. The Excel Subtotals feature provides a quick, easy way to group and summarize a range of data. It lets you create not only subtotals using the SUM function, but other statistics as well, including COUNT, AVERAGE, MAX, and MIN. However, these statistical functions can only be used with ranges, not with tables, so before using one you need to convert your table to a range. In order to get meaningful statistics, data must be sorted on the field on which you will group. **CASE** *Mary wants you to group data by projects, with subtotals for the number of places available and the number of places reserved. You begin by first sorting the table and then converting the table to a range.*

STEPS

1. **Click the** Subtotals **sheet tab, click the** Data tab, **click the** Sort button **in the Sort & Filter group, in the Sort dialog box click the** Sort by list arrow, **click** Project, **click the** Add Level button, **click the** Then by list arrow, **click** Depart Date, **verify that the order is** Oldest to Newest, **then click** OK

   You have sorted the table in ascending order, first by project, then by departure date within each project grouping.

2. **Click any cell in the table, click the** Table Tools Design tab, **click the** Convert to Range button **in the Tools group, then click** Yes

   The filter list arrows and the Table Tools Design tab no longer appear.

3. **Click the** Data tab **if necessary, click any cell in the data range if necessary, then click the** Subtotal button **in the Outline group**

   The Subtotal dialog box opens. Here you specify the items you want subtotaled, the function you want to apply to the values, and the fields you want to summarize.

4. **Click the** At each change in list arrow, **click** Project **if necessary, click the** Use function list arrow, **click** Sum; **in the "Add subtotal to" list click the** Places Reserved **and** Places Available check boxes **to select them if necessary, then click the** Insurance Included check box **to deselect it**

5. **If necessary, click the** Replace current subtotals **and** Summary below data check boxes **to select them**

   Your completed Subtotal dialog box should match FIGURE 8-17.

QUICK TIP
You can click the
[−] button to hide
or the [+] button to
show a group of
records in the
subtotaled structure.

6. **Click** OK, **then scroll down so you can see row 73**

   The subtotaled data appears after each project grouping, showing the calculated subtotals and grand total in columns E and F. Excel displays an outline to the left of the worksheet, with outline buttons to control the level of detail that appears. The button number corresponds to the detail level that is displayed. You want to show the second level of detail, the subtotals and the grand total.

7. **Click the** outline symbol [2]

   Only the subtotals and the grand total appear. Your subtotals and grand total should match FIGURE 8-18.

QUICK TIP
You can remove sub-
totals in a worksheet
by clicking the
Subtotal button and
clicking Remove All.
The subtotals no
longer appear, and
the Outline feature
is turned off
automatically.

8. **Add your name to the center section of the footer, preview the worksheet, then save the workbook**

9. **Close the workbook, exit Excel, then submit the workbook to your instructor**

FIGURE 8-17: Completed Subtotal dialog box

Field to use in grouping data →

Function to apply to groups →

Subtotal these fields →

Confirm these check boxes are selected →

FIGURE 8-18: Data with subtotals and grand total

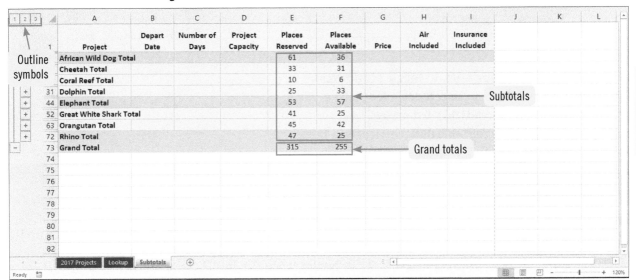

Practice

Concepts Review

FIGURE 8-19

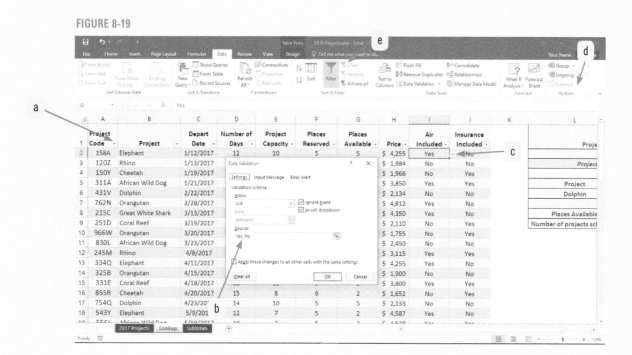

1. Which element would you click to toggle off a filter?
2. Which element points to an in-cell drop-down list arrow?
3. Which element points to a field's list arrow?
4. Where do you specify acceptable data entries for a table?
5. Which element do you click to group and summarize data?

Match each term with the statement that best describes it.

6. Extracted table
7. Table_array
8. Criteria range
9. Data validation
10. DSUM

a. Cell range when Advanced Filter results are copied to another location
b. Range in which search conditions are set
c. Restricts table entries to specified entries or types of entries
d. Name of the table searched in a VLOOKUP function
e. Function used to total table values that meet specified criteria

Select the best answer from the list of choices.

11. What does it mean when you select the Or option when creating a custom filter?
    a. Both criteria must be true to find a match.
    b. Neither criterion has to be 100% true.
    c. Either criterion can be true to find a match.
    d. A custom filter requires a criteria range.

12. The _____ logical condition finds records matching both listed criteria.
    a. True
    b. Or
    c. And
    d. False

13. Which function finds the position of an item in a table?

   a. VLOOKUP   **c.** DGET

   b. MATCH   **d.** HLOOKUP

14. What must a data range have before subtotals can be inserted?

   a. Enough records to show multiple subtotals   **c.** Formatted cells

   b. Sorted data   **d.** Grand totals

Skills Review

1. Filter a table.

   a. Start Excel, open EX 8-2.xlsx from where you store your Data Files, then save it as **EX 8-HR**.

   b. With the Compensation sheet active, filter the table to list only records for employees in the Dallas branch.

   c. Clear the filter, then add a filter that displays the records for employees in the Dallas and LA branches.

   d. Redisplay all employees, then use a filter to show the three employees with the highest annual salary.

   e. Redisplay all the records.

2. Create a custom filter.

   a. Create a custom filter showing employees hired before 1/1/2015 or after 12/31/2016.

   b. Create a custom filter showing employees hired between 1/1/2014 and 12/31/2015.

   c. Enter your name in the worksheet footer, then preview the filtered worksheet.

   d. Redisplay all records.

   e. Save the workbook.

3. Filter and extract a table with the Advanced Filter.

   a. Retrieve a list of employees who were hired before 1/1/2017 and who have an annual salary of more than $75,000 a year. Define a criteria range by inserting six new rows above the table on the worksheet and copying the field names into the first row.

   b. In cell D2, enter the criterion **<1/1/2017**, then in cell G2 enter **>75000**.

   c. Click any cell in the table.

   d. Open the Advanced Filter dialog box.

   e. Indicate that you want to copy to another location, enter the criteria range **A1:J2**, verify that the List range is $A$7:$J$17, then indicate that you want to place the extracted list in the range starting at cell **A20**.

   f. Confirm that the retrieved list meets the criteria as shown in FIGURE 8-20.

   g. Save the workbook, then preview the worksheet.

FIGURE 8-20

	A	B	C	D	E	F	G	H	I	J	K
1	Employee Number	First Name	Last Name	Hire Date	Branch	Monthly Salary	Annual Salary	Annual Bonus	Benefits Dollars	Annual Compensation	
2				<1/1/2017			>75000				
3											
4											
5											
6											
7	Employee Number	First Name	Last Name	Hire Date	Branch	Monthly Salary	Annual Salary	Annual Bonus	Benefits Dollars	Annual Compensation	
8	1005	Molly	Lake	2/12/2015	LA	$ 4,850	$ 58,200	$ 1,470	$ 13,386	$ 73,056	
9	1778	Lynn	Waters	4/1/2016	Chicago	$ 5,170	$ 62,040	$ 5,125	$ 14,269	$ 81,434	
10	1469	Donna	Davie	5/6/2016	Dallas	$ 6,550	$ 78,600	$ 6,725	$ 18,078	$ 103,403	
11	1734	Martha	Mele	12/10/2016	Dallas	$ 7,450	$ 89,400	$ 5,550	$ 20,562	$ 115,512	
12	1578	Hank	Gole	2/15/2014	Chicago	$ 4,950	$ 59,400	$ 1,680	$ 13,662	$ 74,742	
13	1499	Peter	East	3/25/2015	LA	$ 1,750	$ 21,000	$ 1,630	$ 4,830	$ 27,460	
14	1080	Emily	Malone	6/23/2014	Chicago	$ 4,225	$ 50,700	$ 2,320	$ 11,661	$ 64,681	
15	1998	Mike	Magee	8/3/2017	Chicago	$ 5,750	$ 69,000	$ 5,900	$ 15,870	$ 90,770	
16	1662	Ted	Reily	9/29/2016	LA	$ 7,500	$ 90,000	$ 3,002	$ 20,700	$ 113,702	
17	1322	Jason	Round	5/12/2016	Dallas	$ 4,750	$ 57,000	$ 995	$ 13,110	$ 71,105	
18											
19											
20	Employee Number	First Name	Last Name	Hire Date	Branch	Monthly Salary	Annual Salary	Annual Bonus	Benefits Dollars	Annual Compensation	
21	1469	Donna	Davie	5/6/2016	Dallas	$ 6,550	$ 78,600	$ 6,725	$ 18,078	$ 103,403	
22	1734	Martha	Mele	12/10/2016	Dallas	$ 7,450	$ 89,400	$ 5,550	$ 20,562	$ 115,512	
23	1662	Ted	Reily	9/29/2016	LA	$ 7,500	$ 90,000	$ 3,002	$ 20,700	$ 113,702	
24											

Skills Review (continued)

4. Look up values in a table.

   a. Click the Summary sheet tab. Use the Name Manager to view the table names in the workbook, then close the dialog box.

   b. Prepare to use a lookup function to locate an employee's annual compensation; enter the Employee Number **1578** in cell A18.

   c. In cell B18, use the VLOOKUP function and enter **A18** as the Lookup_value, **Table2** as the Table_array, **10** as the Col_index_num, and **FALSE** as the Range_lookup; observe the compensation displayed for that employee number, then check it against the table to make sure it is correct.

   d. Replace the existing Employee Number in cell A18 with **1998**, and view the annual compensation for that employee.

   e. Format cell B18 with the Accounting format with the $ symbol and no decimal places.

   f. Save the workbook.

5. Summarize table data.

   a. Prepare to enter a database function to average the annual salaries by branch, using the LA branch as the initial criterion. In cell E18, use the DAVERAGE function, and click the upper-left corner of cell A1 twice to select the table and its header row as the Database, select cell G1 for the Field, and select the range D17:D18 for the Criteria. Verify that the average LA salary is 56400.

   b. Test the function further by entering the text **Dallas** in cell D18. When the criterion is entered, cell E18 should display 75000.

   c. Format cell E18 in Accounting format with the $ symbol and no decimal places.

   d. Save the workbook.

6. Validate table data.

   a. Select the data in column E of the table, and set a validation criterion specifying that you want to allow a list of valid options.

   b. Enter a list of valid options that restricts the entries to **LA**, **Chicago**, and **Dallas**. Remember to use a comma between each item in the list.

   c. Indicate that you want the options to appear in an in-cell drop-down list, then close the dialog box.

   d. Add a row to the table. Go to cell E12, then select Chicago in the drop-down list.

   e. Complete the new record by adding an Employee Number of **1119**, a First Name of **Cate**, a Last Name of **Smith**, a Hire Date of **10/1/2017**, a monthly salary of **$5000**, and an Annual Bonus of **$5000**. Format the range F12:J12 as Accounting with no decimal places and using the $ symbol. Compare your screen to FIGURE 8-21.

   f. Add your name to the center section of the footer, save the worksheet, then preview the worksheet.

FIGURE 8-21

	A	B	C	D	E	F	G	H	I	J	K
1	Employee Number	First Name	Last Name	Hire Date	Branch	Monthly Salary	Annual Salary	Annual Bonus	Benefits Dollars	Annual Compensation	
2	1005	Molly	Lake	2/12/2015	LA	$ 4,850	$ 58,200	$ 1,470	$ 13,386	$ 73,056	
3	1778	Lynn	Waters	4/1/2016	Chicago	$ 5,170	$ 62,040	$ 5,125	$ 14,269	$ 81,434	
4	1469	Donna	Davie	5/6/2016	Dallas	$ 6,550	$ 78,600	$ 6,725	$ 18,078	$ 103,403	
5	1734	Martha	Mele	12/10/2016	Dallas	$ 7,450	$ 89,400	$ 5,550	$ 20,562	$ 115,512	
6	1578	Hank	Gole	2/15/2014	Chicago	$ 4,950	$ 59,400	$ 1,680	$ 13,662	$ 74,742	
7	1499	Peter	East	3/25/2015	LA	$ 1,750	$ 21,000	$ 1,630	$ 4,830	$ 27,460	
8	1080	Emily	Malone	6/23/2014	Chicago	$ 4,225	$ 50,700	$ 2,320	$ 11,661	$ 64,681	
9	1998	Mike	Magee	8/3/2017	Chicago	$ 5,750	$ 69,000	$ 5,900	$ 15,870	$ 90,770	
10	1662	Ted	Reily	9/29/2016	LA	$ 7,500	$ 90,000	$ 3,002	$ 20,700	$ 113,702	
11	1322	Jason	Round	5/12/2016	Dallas	$ 4,750	$ 57,000	$ 995	$ 13,110	$ 71,105	
12	1119	Cate	Smith	10/1/2017	Chicago	$ 5,000	$ 60,000	$ 5,000	$ 13,800	$ 78,800	
13											
14											
15											
16											
17	Employee Number	Annual Compensation			Branch	Average Annual Salary					
18	1998	$ 90,770			Dallas	$ 75,000					
19											
20											

Skills Review (continued)

7. Create subtotals.

a. Click the Subtotals sheet tab.

b. Use the Branch field list arrow to sort the table in ascending order by branch.

c. Convert the table to a range.

d. Group and create subtotals of the Annual Compensation data by branch, using the SUM function.

e. Click the 2 outline button on the outline to display only the subtotals and the grand total. Compare your screen to FIGURE 8-22.

f. Enter your name in the worksheet footer, save the workbook, then preview the worksheet.

g. Save the workbook, close the workbook, exit Excel, then submit your workbook to your instructor.

FIGURE 8-22

	A	B	C	D	E	F	G	H	I	J
1	Employee Number	First Name	Last Name	Hire Date	Branch	Monthly Salary	Annual Salary	Annual Bonus	Benefits Dollars	Annual Compensation
6					Chicago Total					$ 311,627
10					Dallas Total					$ 290,020
14					LA Total					$ 214,218
15					Grand Total					$ 815,865
16										
17										
18										

Independent Challenge 1

As the manager of Tampa Medical, a diagnostic supply company, you spend a lot of time managing your inventory. To help with this task, you have created an Excel table that you can extract information from using filters. You also need to add data validation and summary information to the table.

a. Start Excel, open EX 8-3.xlsx from where you store your Data Files, then save it as **EX 8-Diagnostic**.

b. Using the table data on the Inventory sheet, create a filter to display information about only the pulse monitors. Clear the filter.

c. Use a Custom Filter to generate a list of products with a quantity greater than 15. Clear the filter.

d. Copy the labels in cells A1:E1 into A16:E16. Type **Stethoscope** in cell A17, and type <**$275.00** in cell C17. Use the Advanced Filter with a criteria range of A16:E17 to extract a table of stethoscopes priced less than $275.00 to the range of cells beginning in cell A20. Enter your name in the worksheet footer, save the workbook, then preview the worksheet.

e. On the Summary sheet, select the table data in column B. Open the Data Validation dialog box, then indicate you want to use a validation list with the acceptable entries of **Lee**, **Rand**, **Barry**. Make sure the In-cell dropdown check box is selected.

f. Test the data validation by trying to change any cell in column B of the table to **Lane**.

g. Using FIGURE 8-23 as a guide, enter a function in cell E18 that calculates the total quantity of Stethoscopes available in your inventory. Enter your name in the worksheet footer, preview the worksheet, then save the workbook.

h. On the Subtotals sheet, sort the table in ascending order by product. Convert the table to a range. Insert subtotals by product using the Sum function, then select Quantity in the "Add Subtotal to" box. Remove the check box for the Total field, if necessary. Use the appropriate button on the outline to display only the subtotals and grand total. Save the workbook, then preview the worksheet.

i. Submit the workbook to your instructor. Close the workbook, then exit Excel.

FIGURE 8-23

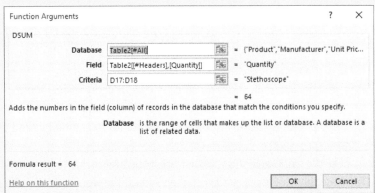

Independent Challenge 2

As the senior accountant at Miami Plumbing Supply, you are adding new features to the company's accounts receivables workbook. The business supplies both residential and commercial plumbers. You have put together an invoice table to track sales for the month of June. Now that you have this table, you would like to manipulate it in several ways. First, you want to filter the table to show only invoices over a certain amount with certain order dates. You also want to subtotal the total column by residential and commercial supplies. To prevent data entry errors you will restrict entries in the Order Date column. Finally, you would like to add database and lookup functions to your worksheet to efficiently retrieve data from the table.

   a. Start Excel, open EX 8-4.xlsx from where you store your Data Files, then save it as **EX 8-Invoices**.
   b. Use the Advanced Filter to show invoices with amounts more than $300.00 ordered before 6/15/2017, using cells A27:B28 to enter your criteria and extracting the results to cell A33. (*Hint*: You don't need to specify an entire row as the criteria range.) Enter your name in the worksheet footer.
   c. Use the Data Validation dialog box to restrict entries to those with order dates between 6/1/2017 and 6/30/2017. Test the data restrictions by attempting to enter an invalid date in cell B25.
   d. Enter **23706** in cell G28. Enter a VLOOKUP function in cell H28 to retrieve the total based on the invoice number entered in cell G28. Make sure you have an exact match with the invoice number. Test the function with the invoice number 23699.
   e. Enter the date **6/1/2017** in cell J28. Use the database function, DCOUNT, in cell K28 to count the number of invoices for the date in cell J28. Save the workbook, then preview the worksheet.
   f. On the Subtotals worksheet, sort the table in ascending order by Type, then convert the table to a range. Create subtotals showing the totals for commercial and residential invoices. Display only the subtotals for the commercial and residential accounts, along with the grand total.
   g. Save the workbook, preview the worksheet, close the workbook, then exit Excel. Submit the workbook to your instructor.

Independent Challenge 3

You are the manager of Fitness Now, a service company for fitness equipment. You have created an Excel table that contains your invoice data, along with the totals for each invoice. You would like to manipulate this table to display service categories and invoices meeting specific criteria. You would also like to add subtotals to the table and add database functions to total categories of invoices. Finally, you want to restrict entries in the Category column.

   a. Start Excel, open EX 8-5.xlsx from where you store your Data Files, then save it as **EX 8-Equipment**.
   b. On the Invoice sheet, use the headings in row 37 to create an advanced filter that extracts records with the following criteria to cell A42: totals greater than $1500 having dates either before 9/10/2017 or after 9/19/2017. (*Hint*: Recall that when you want records to meet one criterion or another, you need to place the criteria on separate lines.)
   c. Use the DSUM function in cell G2 to let worksheet users find the total amount for the category entered in cell F2. Format the cell containing the total using the Accounting format with the $ symbol and no decimals. Verify the warranty category total is $8,228. Preview the worksheet.
   d. Use data validation to create an in-cell drop-down list that restricts category entries to "Preventative Maintenance", "Warranty", and "Service". Use the Error Alert tab of the Data Validation dialog box to set the alert style to the Warning style with the message "Data is not valid." Test the validation in the table with valid and invalid entries. Save the workbook, enter your name in the worksheet footer, then preview the worksheet.
   e. Using the Subtotals sheet, sort the table by category in ascending order. Convert the table to a range, and add Subtotals to the totals by category. Widen the columns, if necessary.
   f. Use the outline to display only category names with subtotals and the grand total. Enter your name in the worksheet footer.
   g. Save the workbook, then preview the worksheet.
   h. Close the workbook, exit Excel, then submit the workbook to your instructor.

Independent Challenge 4: Explore

You are an inventory manager at East Coast Medical, a medical equipment distributor. You track your inventory of equipment in an Excel worksheet. You would like to use conditional formatting in your worksheet to help track the products that need to be reordered as well as your inventory expenses. You would also like to prevent data entry errors. Finally, you would like to add an area to quickly look up prices and quantities for customers.

a. Start Excel, open EX 8-6.xlsx from where you store your Data Files, then save it as **EX 8-East Coast Medical**.

b. Using FIGURE 8-24 as a guide, use conditional formatting to add icons to the quantity column using the following criteria: format quantities greater than or equal to 300 with a green circle, quantities greater than or equal to 100 but less than 300 with a yellow circle, and quantities less than 100 with a red circle. (*Hint*: You may need to click in the top Value text box for the correct value to display for the red circle.)

FIGURE 8-24

c. Conditionally format the Total data using Top/Bottom Rules to emphasize the cells containing the top 30 percent with red text.

d. Add another rule to format the bottom 20 percent in the Total column with purple text from the standard colors palette.

e. Restrict the Wholesale Price field entries to decimal values between 0 and 10000. Add an input message of **Prices must be less than $10,000**. Add an Information level error message of **Please check price**. Test the validation entering a price of $10,100 in cell C3 and allow the new price to be entered.

f. Below the table, create a product lookup area with the following labels in adjacent cells: **Product Number, Wholesale Price, Quantity**. Right align these labels in the cells.

g. Using the Table Tools Design tab, name the table "Inventory".

h. Enter 1445 under the label Product Number in your products lookup area.

i. In the product lookup area, enter lookup functions to locate the wholesale price and quantity information for the product number that you entered in the previous step. Use the assigned table name of Inventory and make sure you match the product number exactly. Format the wholesale price with the Accounting format and two decimal places.

j. Enter your name in the center section of the worksheet header, save the workbook, then preview the worksheet comparing it to FIGURE 8-25.

k. Close the workbook, exit Excel, then submit the workbook to your instructor.

FIGURE 8-25

Your Name

East Coast Medical

Product Number	Category	Wholesale Price		Quantity	Total
1122	Hospital	$10,100.00		310	$3,131,000.00
1132	Surgery Center	$1,005.34		250	$251,335.00
1184	Lab	$18.21		24	$437.04
1197	Physician Office	$32.22		350	$11,277.00
1225	Home Health	$33.99		47	$1,597.53
1267	Home Health	$34.19		101	$3,453.19
1298	Lab	$21.97		375	$8,238.75
1345	Lab	$652.01		105	$68,461.05
1367	Lab	$17.18		168	$2,886.24
1398	Physician Office	$3,657.21		97	$354,749.37
1422	Surgery Center	$259.36		157	$40,719.52
1436	Surgery Center	$598.36		81	$48,467.16
1445	Surgery Center	$45.20		150	$6,780.00
1456	Hospital	$82.33		377	$31,038.41
1498	Hospital	$1,968.21		51	$100,378.71
1521	Hospital	$7,418.21		87	$645,384.27
1531	Lab	$40.34		197	$7,946.98
1544	Home Health	$236.98		472	$111,854.56
1556	Home Health	$459.24		12	$5,510.88
1569	Physician Office	$1,263.25		178	$224,858.50
1578	Surgery Center	$368.34		35	$12,891.90
1622	Physician Office	$25.33		874	$22,138.42
1634	Surgery Center	$18.47		501	$9,253.47
1657	Surgery Center	$362.51		10	$3,625.10
1688	Lab	$1,287.63		73	$93,996.99
1723	Hospital	$257.01		534	$137,243.34
1736	Home Health	$25.66		15	$384.90
1798	Hospital	$32.78		640	$20,979.20
1822	Lab	$179.21		86	$15,412.06

Product Number	Wholesale Price		Quantity	
1445	$	45.20	150	

Visual Workshop

Open EX 8-7.xlsx from where you store your Data Files, then save it as **EX 8-Therapy**. Complete the worksheet as shown in FIGURE 8-26. An in-cell drop-down list has been added to the data entered in the Pool field. The range A18:F21 is extracted from the table using the criteria in cells A15:A16. Add your name to the worksheet footer, save the workbook, preview the worksheet, then submit the workbook to your instructor.

FIGURE 8-26

	A	B	C	D	E	F
1			Aquatic Therapy Schedule			
2						
3	Code	Group	Time	Day	Pool	Instructor
4	AQA100	Baby	10:30 AM	Thursday	Teaching Pool	Malone
5	AQA101	Child	8:00 AM	Tuesday	Teaching Pool	Grey
6	AQA102	Adult	9:00 AM	Wednesday	Lap Pool	Malone
7	AQA103	Senior	10:00 AM	Monday	Lap Pool	Brent
8	AQA104	Senior	11:00 AM	Friday	Lap Pool	Paulson
9	AQA105	Adult	12:00 PM	Saturday	Lap Pool	Grey
10	AQA106	Child	12:00 PM	Tuesday	Teaching Pool	Rand
11	AQA107	Senior	2:00 PM	Monday	Lap Pool	Walton
12	AQA108	Adult	4:00 PM	Tuesday	Lap Pool	Malone
13						
14					Please select Teaching Pool or Lap Pool.	
15	Group					
16	Senior					
17						
18	Code	Group	Time	Day	Pool	Instructor
19	AQA103	Senior	10:00 AM	Monday	Lap Pool	Brent
20	AQA104	Senior	11:00 AM	Friday	Lap Pool	Paulson
21	AQA107	Senior	2:00 PM	Monday	Lap Pool	Walton
22						

Automating Worksheet Tasks

CASE ▶ Jo Katz, director of operations for Africa at Reason2Go, asks you to help automate tasks so that staff at the Cape Town headquarters can work more efficiently. You start by creating a macro that will save people time when working in Excel. The macro will automatically insert text that identifies the worksheet as a Cape Town headquarters document.

Module Objectives

After completing this module, you will be able to:

- Plan a macro
- Enable a macro
- Record a macro
- Run a macro
- Edit a macro
- Assign keyboard shortcuts to macros
- Use the Personal Macro Workbook
- Assign a macro to a button

Files You Will Need

EX 9-1.xlsx
EX 9-2.xlsx
EX 9-3.xlsx

Plan a Macro

Learning
Outcomes
• Plan a macro
• Determine the
  storage location
  for a macro

A **macro** is a named set of instructions you can create that performs tasks automatically, in an order you specify. You create macros to automate Excel tasks that you perform frequently. For example, you can create a macro to enter and format text or to save and print a worksheet. To create a macro, you record the series of actions using the macro recorder built in to Excel, or you write the instructions in a special programming language. Because the sequence of actions in a macro is important, you need to plan the macro carefully before you record it. **CASE** *Jo likes your idea to create a macro for the Africa headquarters to place the location of the office in the upper-left corner of any worksheet. You work with Jo to plan the macro.*

DETAILS

To plan a macro, use the following guidelines:

• **Assign the macro a descriptive name**

  The first character of a macro name must be a letter; the remaining characters can be letters, numbers, or underscores. Letters can be uppercase or lowercase. Spaces are not allowed in macro names; use underscores in place of spaces. Press [Shift][-] to enter an underscore character. You decide to name the macro "HQStamp". See TABLE 9-1 for a list of macros that could be created to automate other tasks at Reason2Go.

• **Write out the steps the macro will perform**

  This planning helps eliminate careless errors. After discussion with Jo, you write down a description of the new HQStamp macro, as shown in FIGURE 9-1.

• **Decide how you will perform the actions you want to record**

  You can use the mouse, the keyboard, or a combination of the two. For the new HQStamp macro, you want to use both the mouse and the keyboard.

• **Practice the steps you want Excel to record, and write them down**

  During your meeting with Jo, you write down the sequence of actions to include in the macro.

• **Decide where to store the description of the macro and the macro itself**

  Macros can be stored in an active workbook, in a new workbook, or in the **Personal Macro Workbook**, a special workbook used only for macro storage. You decide to store the macro in a new workbook.

FIGURE 9-1: Handwritten description of planned macro

> ## Macro to create stamp with the Headquarters location
>
> Name: HQStamp
>
> Description: Adds a stamp to the top left of the worksheet, identifying it as a
>   Cape Town office worksheet
>
> Steps: 1. Position the cell pointer in cell A1.
>   2. Type Cape Town, then click the Enter button.
>   3. Click the Format button, then click Format Cells.
>   4. Click the Font tab, under Font style, click Bold; under Underline, click
>   Single; under Color, click Blue; then click OK.

TABLE 9-1: Possible macros and their descriptive names

description of macro	descriptive name for macro
Enter a frequently used proper name, such as "Jo Katz"	JoKatz
Enter a frequently used company name, such as Reason2Go	Company_Name
Print the active worksheet on a single page, in landscape orientation	FitToLand
Add a footer to a worksheet	FooterStamp
Add totals to a worksheet	AddTotals

Using a macro to filter table data

You can create a macro using the Advanced Filter feature to automate the filtering process for table data that you filter frequently. To create a filtering macro, create a criteria range on the worksheet and determine the sheet location where the filtered records will be displayed. Then, record the macro by creating an advanced filter that uses the criteria range, the list range (table range), and the location where the filtered results will be displayed. As long as you keep the same ranges on the worksheet, you can change the data in either the criteria or table ranges and then run the macro to filter the table for that new data.

Enable a Macro

Learning Outcomes
- Create a macro-enabled workbook
- Enable macros by changing a workbook's security level

Because a macro may contain a **virus**—destructive software that can damage your computer files—the default security setting in Excel disables macros from running. Although a workbook containing a macro will open, if macros are disabled they will not function. You can manually change the Excel security setting to allow macros to run if you know a macro came from a trusted source. When saving a workbook with a macro, you need to save it as a macro-enabled workbook with the extension .xlsm. **CASE** *Jo asks you to change the security level to enable all macros. As a courtesy to others who are sharing your computer in a classroom or lab, you will change the security level back to the default setting after you create and run your macros.*

STEPS

1. **Start Excel, open a blank workbook, click the** Save button 💾 **on the Quick Access Toolbar, navigate to where you store your Data Files, in the Save As dialog box click the** Save as type list arrow, **click** Excel Macro-Enabled Workbook (*.xlsm), **in the File name text box type** EX 9-Macro Workbook, **then click** Save

   The security settings that enable macros are available on the Developer tab. The Developer tab does not appear by default, but you can display it by customizing the Ribbon.

   QUICK TIP
   If the Developer tab is displayed on your Ribbon, skip steps 2 and 3.

2. **Click the** File tab, **click** Options, **then click** Customize Ribbon **in the category list**

   The Customize the Ribbon options open in the Excel Options dialog box, as shown in FIGURE 9-2.

3. **Click the** Developer check box, **if necessary, in the Main Tabs area on the right side of the screen to select it, then click** OK

   The Developer tab appears on the Ribbon. You are ready to change the security settings.

4. **Click the** Developer tab, **then click the** Macro Security button **in the Code group**

   The Trust Center dialog box opens.

   QUICK TIP
   For increased security, you can click the security setting "Disable all macros with notification" instead. Using that setting, you will need to click Enable Content to run macros in a .xlsm file.

5. **Click** Macro Settings **if necessary, click the** Enable all macros (not recommended; potentially dangerous code can run) option button **to select it, as shown in** FIGURE 9-3, **then click** OK

   The dialog box closes. Macros will remain enabled until you disable them by deselecting the Enable all macros option. As you work with Excel, you should disable macros when you are not working with them.

FIGURE 9-2: Excel Options dialog box

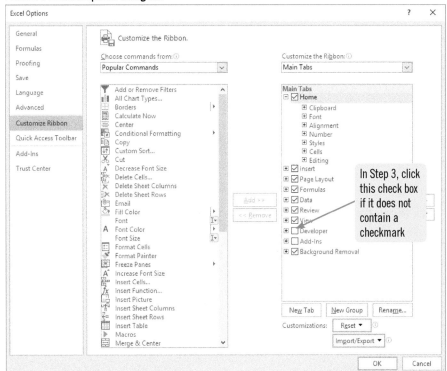

FIGURE 9-3: Trust Center dialog box

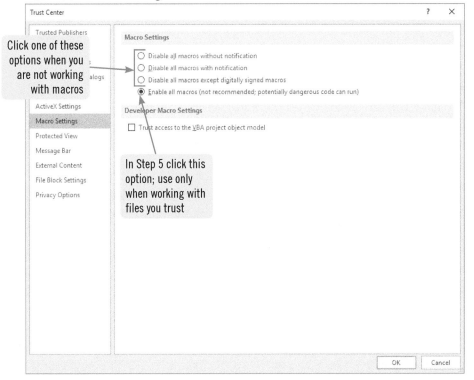

Disabling macros

To prevent viruses from running on your computer, you should disable all macros when you are not working with them. To disable macros, click the Developer tab then click the Macro Security button in the Code group. Clicking any of the first three options disables macros. The first option disables all macros without notifying you. The second option notifies you when macros are disabled, and the third option allows only digitally signed macros to run.

Record a Macro

Learning
Outcomes
• Choose a macro
storage location
• Create a macro by
recording steps

The easiest way to create a macro is to record it using the Excel Macro Recorder. You turn the Macro Recorder on, name the macro, enter the keystrokes and select the commands you want the macro to perform, then stop the recorder. As you record the macro, Excel automatically translates each action into program code that you can later view and modify. You can take as long as you want to record the macro; a recorded macro contains only your actions, not the amount of time you took to record them. **CASE** *You are ready to create a macro that enters a headquarters location "stamp" in cell A1 of the active worksheet. You create this macro by recording your actions.*

STEPS

1. **Click the Record Macro button** 📇 **on the left side of the status bar**

   The Record Macro dialog box opens, as shown in FIGURE 9-4. The default name Macro1 is selected. You can either assign this name or enter a new name. This dialog box also lets you assign a shortcut key for running the macro and assign a storage location for the macro.

2. **Type HQStamp in the Macro name text box**

   It is important to check where the macro will be stored because the default choice is the last location that was selected.

3. **If the Store macro in list box does not display "This Workbook", click the list arrow, then click This Workbook**

4. **Type your name in the Description text box, then click OK**

   The dialog box closes, and the Record Macro button on the status bar is replaced with a Stop Recording button 🔳. Take your time performing the steps below. Excel records every keystroke, menu selection, and mouse action that you make.

5. **Press [Ctrl][Home]**

   When you begin an Excel session, macros record absolute cell references. By beginning the recording with a command to move to cell A1, you ensure that the macro includes the instruction to select cell A1 as the first step, in cases where A1 is not already selected.

6. **Type Cape Town in cell A1, then click the Enter button** ✅ **on the formula bar**

7. **Click the Home tab, click the Format button in the Cells group, then click Format Cells**

8. **Click the Font tab, in the Font style list box click Bold, click the Underline list arrow and click Single, click the Color list arrow and click the Blue color in the Standard Colors row, then compare your dialog box to** FIGURE 9-5

9. **Click OK, click the Format button in the Cells group, click AutoFit Column Width, click the Stop Recording button** 🔳 **on the left side of the status bar, click cell D1 to deselect cell A1, then save the workbook**

   FIGURE 9-6 shows the result of the actions you took while recording the macro.

FIGURE 9-4: **Record Macro dialog box**

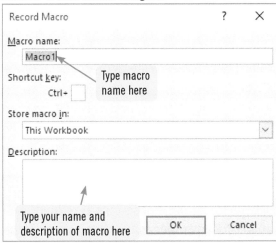

FIGURE 9-5: **Font tab of the Format Cells dialog box**

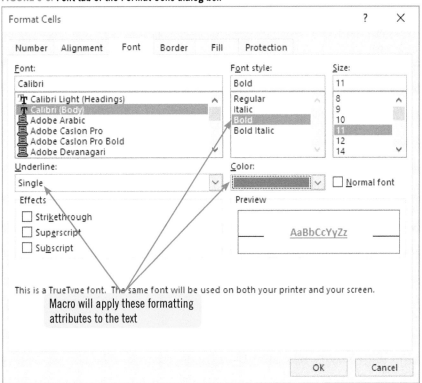

FIGURE 9-6: **Headquarters stamp**

Run a Macro

Learning
Outcomes
• Display selected
macros
• Run a macro
using the Macro
dialog box

Once you record a macro, you should test it to make sure that the actions it performs are correct. To test a macro, you **run** (play) it. You can run a macro using the Macros button in the Code group of the Developer tab. **CASE** *In order to test the HQStamp macro, you clear the contents of cell A1. After completing this test, you want to test the macro from a different, newly opened workbook.*

STEPS

1. **Click cell A1, click the Home tab if necessary, click the Clear button in the Editing group, click Clear All, then click any other cell to deselect cell A1**

   When you delete only the contents of a cell, any formatting still remains in the cell. By using the Clear All option you can be sure that the cell is free of contents and formatting.

2. **Click the Developer tab, click the Macros button in the Code group, click the Macros in list arrow, then click This Workbook**

   The Macro dialog box, shown in FIGURE 9-7, lists all the macros contained in the workbook.

3. **Click HQStamp in the Macro name list if necessary, as you watch cell A1 click Run, then deselect cell A1**

   The macro quickly plays back the steps you recorded in the previous lesson. When the macro is finished, your screen should look like FIGURE 9-8. As long as the workbook containing the macro remains open, you can run the macro in any open workbook.

4. **Click the File tab, click New, then click Blank workbook**

   Because the EX 9-Macro Workbook.xlsm is still open, you can use its macros.

5. **Deselect cell A1, click the Developer tab, click the Macros button in the Code group, click the Macros in list arrow, then click All Open Workbooks, click 'EX 9-Macro Workbook. xlsm'!HQStamp, click Run, then deselect cell A1**

   When multiple workbooks are open, the macro name in the Macro dialog box includes the workbook name between single quotation marks, followed by an exclamation point which is an **external reference indicator**, indicating that the macro is outside the active workbook. Because you only used this workbook to test the macro, you don't need to save it.

6. **Close Book2 without saving changes**

   The EX 9-Macro Workbook.xlsm workbook remains open.

FIGURE 9-7: **Macro dialog box**

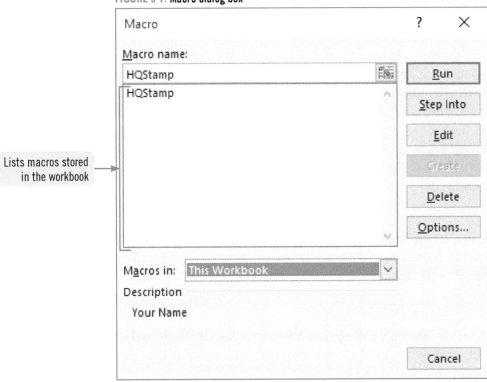

Lists macros stored in the workbook →

Macro name: HQStamp

HQStamp

Macros in: This Workbook
Description
    Your Name

[Run] [Step Into] [Edit] [Create] [Delete] [Options...] [Cancel]

FIGURE 9-8: **Result of running HQStamp macro**

Formatted text inserted into cell A1 →

	A	B
1	Cape Town	
2		
3		

Running a macro automatically

You can create a macro that automatically performs certain tasks when the workbook in which it is saved is opened. This is useful for actions you want to do every time you open a workbook. For example, you may import data from an external data source into the workbook or format the worksheet data in a certain way. To create a macro that will automatically run when the workbook is opened, you need to name the macro Auto_Open and save it in that workbook.

Edit a Macro

Learning
Outcomes
• Edit a macro using
VBA
• Add comments to
Visual Basic Code

When you use the Macro Recorder to create a macro, the program instructions, called **program code**, are recorded automatically in the **Visual Basic for Applications (VBA)** programming language. Each macro is stored as a **module**, or program code container, attached to the workbook. After you record a macro, you might need to change it. If you have a lot of changes to make, it might be best to record the macro again. But if you need to make only minor adjustments, you can edit the macro code directly using the **Visual Basic Editor**, a program that lets you display and edit your macro code. **CASE** *Jo wants the HQStamp macro to display the department stamp in a slightly larger font size. This is a small change you can easily make by editing the macro code.*

STEPS

QUICK TIP
You can also open the Editor by clicking the Developer tab, then clicking the Visual Basic button in the Code group.

1. **Make sure the EX 9-Macro Workbook.xlsm workbook is open, click the** Macros button **in the Code group, make sure** HQStamp **is selected, click** Edit**, then maximize the Code window, if necessary**

   The Visual Basic Editor starts, showing three windows: the Project Explorer window, the Properties window, and the Code window, as shown in FIGURE 9-9.

TROUBLE
If the Properties window does not appear in the lower-left portion of your screen, click the Properties Window button 🔲 on the Visual Basic Standard toolbar, then resize it as shown in the figure if necessary.

2. **Click** Module 1 **in the VBAProject (EX 9-Macro Workbook.xlsm) within the Project Explorer window if it's not already selected, then examine the steps in the macro, comparing your screen to** FIGURE 9-9

   The name of the macro and your name appear at the top of the Code window. Below this area, Excel has translated your keystrokes and commands into macro code. When you open and make selections in a dialog box during macro recording, Excel automatically stores all the dialog box settings in the macro code. For example, the line .FontStyle = "Bold" was generated when you clicked Bold in the Format Cells dialog box. You also see lines of code that you didn't generate directly while recording the HQStamp macro, for example, .Name = "Calibri".

3. **In the line .Size = 11, double-click** 11 **to select it, then type** 12

   Because Module1 is attached to the workbook and not stored as a separate file, any changes to the module are saved automatically when you save the workbook.

4. **Review the code in the Code window**

QUICK TIP
You can return to Excel without closing the module by clicking the View Microsoft Excel button 🔲 on the Visual Basic Editor toolbar.

5. **Click** File **on the menu bar, then click** Close and Return to Microsoft Excel

   You want to rerun the HQStamp macro to make sure the macro reflects the change you made using the Visual Basic Editor. You begin by clearing the headquarters location from cell A1.

6. **Click cell** A1**, click the** Home tab**, click the** Clear button **in the Editing group, then click** Clear All

7. **Click any other cell to deselect cell A1, click the** Developer tab**, click the** Macros button **in the Code group, make sure** HQStamp **is selected, click** Run**, then deselect cell** A1

   The headquarters stamp is now in 12-point type, as shown in FIGURE 9-10.

8. **Save the workbook**

FIGURE 9-9: Visual Basic Editor showing Module1

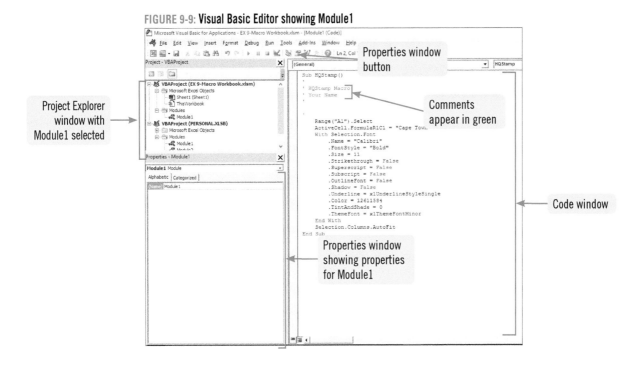

FIGURE 9-10: Result of running edited HQStamp macro

◢	A	B	C	D
1	Cape Town			
2				
3				

Font size is enlarged to 12-point

Adding comments to Visual Basic code

With practice, you will be able to interpret the lines of macro code. Others who use your macro, however, might want to review the code to, for example, learn the function of a particular line. You can explain the code by adding comments to the macro. **Comments** are explanatory text added to the lines of code. When you enter a comment, you must type an apostrophe (') before the comment text. Otherwise, the program tries to interpret it as a command. On the screen, comments appear in green after you press [Enter], as shown in FIGURE 9-9. You can also insert blank lines as comments in the macro code to make the code more readable. To do this, type an apostrophe, then press [Enter].

Assign Keyboard Shortcuts to Macros

For macros that you run frequently, you can run them by using shortcut key combinations instead of the Macro dialog box. You can assign a shortcut key combination to any macro. Using shortcut keys saves you time by reducing the number of actions you need to take to run a macro. You assign shortcut key combinations in the Record Macro dialog box. **CASE** ▶ *Jo also wants you to create a macro called Region to enter the headquarters region into a worksheet. You assign a shortcut key combination to run the macro.*

STEPS

1. **Click cell B2**

   You want to record the macro in cell B2, but you want the macro to enter the region of Africa anywhere in a worksheet. Therefore, you will not begin the macro with an instruction to position the cell pointer, as you did in the HQStamp macro.

2. **Click the Record Macro button 🖩 on the status bar**

   The Record Macro dialog box opens.

3. **With the default macro name selected, type Region in the Macro name text box**

   Notice the option Shortcut key: Ctrl+ followed by a text box. You can type a letter (A–Z) in the Shortcut key text box to assign the key combination of [Ctrl] plus that letter to run the macro. Because some common Excel shortcuts use the [Ctrl][*letter*] combination, such as [Ctrl][C] for Copy, you decide to use the key combination [Ctrl][Shift] plus a letter to avoid overriding any of these shortcut key combinations.

4. **Click the Shortcut key text box, press and hold [Shift], type R, then in the Description box type your name**

   You have assigned the shortcut key combination [Ctrl][Shift][R] to the Region macro. After you create the macro, you will use this shortcut key combination to run it. Compare your screen with FIGURE 9-11. You are ready to record the Region macro.

5. **Click OK to close the dialog box**

6. **Type Africa in cell B2, click the Enter button ✓ on the formula bar, press [Ctrl][I] to italicize the text, click the Stop Recording button ▦ on the status bar, then deselect cell B2**

   Africa appears in italics in cell B2. You are ready to run the macro in cell A5 using the shortcut key combination.

7. **Click cell A5, press and hold [Ctrl][Shift], type R, then deselect the cell**

   The region appears in cell A5, as shown in FIGURE 9-12. The macro played back in the selected cell (A5) instead of the cell where it was recorded (B2) because you did not click cell B2 after you began recording the macro.

FIGURE 9-11: **Record Macro dialog box with shortcut key assigned**

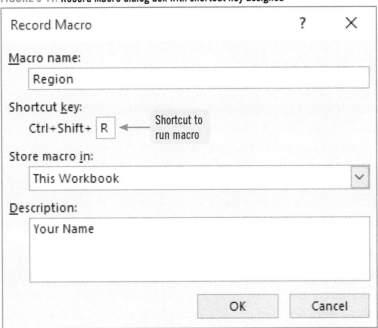

FIGURE 9-12: **Result of running the Region macro**

	A	B	C	D	E	F	G	H
1	Cape Town							
2		*Africa*	Result of recording macro in cell B2					
3								
4								
5	*Africa*		Result of running macro in cell A5					
6								
7								
8								

Using relative referencing when creating a macro

By default, Excel records absolute cell references in macros. You can record a macro's actions based on the relative position of the active cell by clicking the Use Relative References button in the Code group prior to recording the action. For example, when you create a macro using the default setting of absolute referencing, bolding the range A1:D1 will always bold that range when the macro is run. However, if you click the Use Relative References button when recording the macro before bolding the range, then running the macro will not necessarily result in bolding the range A1:D1. The range that will be bolded will depend on the location of the active cell when the macro is run. If the active cell is A4,

then the range A4:D4 will be bolded. Selecting the Use Relative References button highlights the button name, indicating it is active, as shown in FIGURE 9-13. The button remains active until you click it again to deselect it. This is called a toggle, meaning that it acts like an off/on switch: it retains the relative reference setting until you click it again to turn it off or you exit Excel.

FIGURE 9-13: **Use Relative References button selected**

Use the Personal Macro Workbook

Learning
Outcomes
- Determine when to use the Personal Macro Workbook
- Save a macro in the Personal Macro Workbook

When you create a macro, it is automatically stored in the workbook in which you created it. But if you wanted to use that macro in another workbook, you would have to copy the macro to that workbook. Instead, it's easier to store commonly used macros in the Personal Macro Workbook. The **Personal Macro Workbook** is an Excel file that is always available, unless you specify otherwise, and gives you access to all the macros it contains, regardless of which workbooks are open. The Personal Macro Workbook file is automatically created the first time you choose to store a macro in it, and is named PERSONAL.XLSB. You can add additional macros to the Personal Macro Workbook by saving them in the workbook. By default, the PERSONAL.XLSB workbook opens each time you start Excel, but you don't see it because Excel designates it as a hidden file. When you exit Excel at the end of this module, you will not save any changes that you make to the Personal Macro Workbook in this lesson. **CASE** *You often print worksheets in landscape orientation with 1" left, right, top, and bottom margins. You decide to create a macro that automatically formats a worksheet for printing this way. Because you plan to use this macro in future workbooks, you will store the macro in the Personal Macro Workbook.*

STEPS

1. **Click the** Record Macro button 🖩 **on the status bar**
   The Record Macro dialog box opens.

2. **Type** FormatPrint **in the Macro name text box, click the** Shortcut key text box, **press and hold** [Shift], **type** F, **then click the** Store macro in list arrow
   You have named the macro FormatPrint and assigned it the shortcut combination [Ctrl][Shift][F]. The "This Workbook" storage option is selected by default, indicating that Excel automatically stores macros in the active workbook, as shown in FIGURE 9-14. You can also choose to store the macro in a new workbook or in the Personal Macro Workbook.

TROUBLE
If a dialog box appears saying that a macro is already assigned to this shortcut combination, choose another letter for a keyboard shortcut. If a dialog box appears with the message that a macro named FormatPrint already exists, click Yes to replace it.

3. **Click** Personal Macro Workbook, **in the Description text box enter your name, then click** OK
   The recorder is on, and you are ready to record the macro keystrokes.

4. **Click the** Page Layout tab, **click the** Orientation button **in the Page Setup group, click** Landscape, **click the** Margins button **in the Page Setup group, click** Custom Margins, **then enter** 1 **in the Top, Left, Bottom, and Right text boxes**
   Compare your margin settings to FIGURE 9-15.

5. **Click** OK, **then click the** Stop Recording button ▥ **on the status bar**
   You want to test the macro.

TROUBLE
You may have to wait a few moments for the macro to finish. If you are using a different letter for the shortcut key combination, type that letter instead of the letter F.

6. **Add a new worksheet, in cell A1 type** Macro Test, **press** [Enter], **press and hold** [Ctrl][Shift], **then type** F
   The FormatPrint macro plays back the sequence of commands.

7. **Preview Sheet2 in Backstage view and verify in the Settings that the orientation is landscape and the Last Custom Margins are 1" on the left, right, top, and bottom**

8. **Click the** Back button ⬅, **then save the workbook**

FIGURE 9-14: **Record Macro dialog box showing macro storage options**

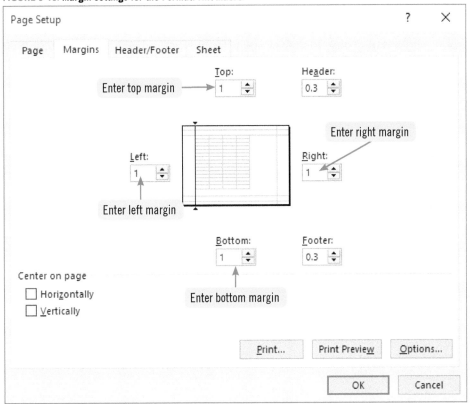

FIGURE 9-15: **Margin settings for the FormatPrint macro**

Working with the Personal Macro Workbook

Once you use the Personal Macro Workbook, it opens automatically each time you start Excel so you can add macros to it. By default, the Personal Macro Workbook is hidden in Excel as a precautionary measure so you don't accidentally delete anything from it. If you need to delete a macro from the Personal Macro Workbook, click the View tab click Unhide in the Window group, click PERSONAL.XLSB, then click OK. To hide the Personal Macro Workbook, make it the active workbook, click the View tab then click Hide in the Window group. If you should see a message that Excel is unable to record to your Personal Macro Workbook, check to make sure it is enabled: Click the File tab, click Options, click Add-ins, click the Manage list arrow, click Disabled Items, then click Go. If your Personal Macro Workbook is listed in the Disabled items dialog box, click its name, then click Enable.

Assign a Macro to a Button

Learning
Outcomes
• Create a button
shape in a
worksheet
• Assign a macro to
a button

When you create macros for others who will use your workbook, you might want to make the macros more visible so they're easier to use. In addition to using shortcut keys, you can run a macro by assigning it to a button on your worksheet. Then when you click the button the macro will run. **CASE** ▶ *To make it easier for people in the sales division to run the HQStamp macro, you decide to assign it to a button on the workbook. You begin by creating the button.*

STEPS

1. **Add a new worksheet to the workbook, click the** Insert tab**, click the** Shapes button ⊡ **in the Illustrations group, then click the** first rectangle **in the Rectangles group**
   The mouse pointer changes to a + symbol.

QUICK TIP
To format a macro
button using 3-D
effects, clip art,
photographs, fills,
and shadows,
right-click it, select
Format Shape
from the shortcut
menu, then select
the desired options
in the Format
Shape pane.

2. **Click at the top-left corner of cell** A8**, then drag** ┿ **to the lower-right corner of cell B9**
   Compare your screen to FIGURE 9-16.

3. **Type** HQ Macro **to label the button, click the** Home tab**, click the** Center button ☰ **in the Alignment group, then click the** Middle Align button ☰ **in the Alignment group**
   Now that you have created the button, you are ready to assign the macro to it.

4. **Right-click the** new button**, then on the shortcut menu click** Assign Macro
   The Assign Macro dialog box opens.

5. **Click** HQStamp **under Macro name, then click** OK
   You have assigned the HQStamp macro to the button.

6. **Click any cell to deselect the button, then click the button**
   The HQStamp macro plays, and the text Cape Town appears in cell A1, as shown in FIGURE 9-17.

7. **Save the workbook, preview Sheet3 in Backstage view, then close the workbook**

8. **Click the** Developer tab**, click the** Macro Security button **in the Code group, click** Macro Settings **if necessary, click the** Disable all macros with notification option button **to select it, then click** OK

9. **Exit Excel, clicking** Don't Save **when asked to save changes to the Personal Macro Workbook, then submit the workbook to your instructor**

FIGURE 9-16: **Button shape**

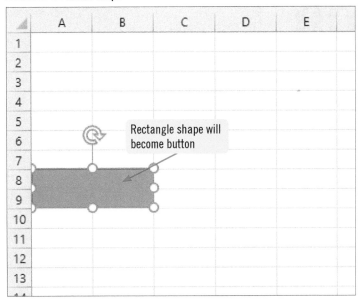

FIGURE 9-17: **Sheet3 with the headquarters location text**

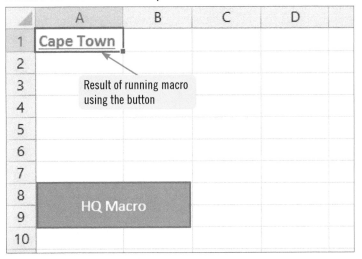

Creating and formatting a form control

You can add an object called a **form control** to an Excel worksheet to make it easier for users to enter or select data. Click the Developer tab on the Ribbon, click the Insert button in the Controls group, click the desired control in the Form Controls area of the Insert gallery, then draw the shape on the worksheet. After adding a control to a worksheet, you need to link it to a cell or cells in the worksheet. To do this, right-click it, select Format Control, then click the Control tab if necessary. For example, if you add a list box form control, the input range is the location of the list box selections and the cell link is the cell with the numeric value for the current position of the list control. To edit the form control's positioning properties (such as moving, sizing, and printing) right-click the form control, select Format Control, then click the Properties tab. See FIGURE 9-18.

FIGURE 9-18: **Properties tab of the Format Control dialog box**

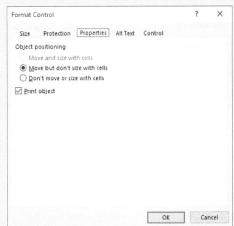

Practice

Concepts Review

FIGURE 9-19

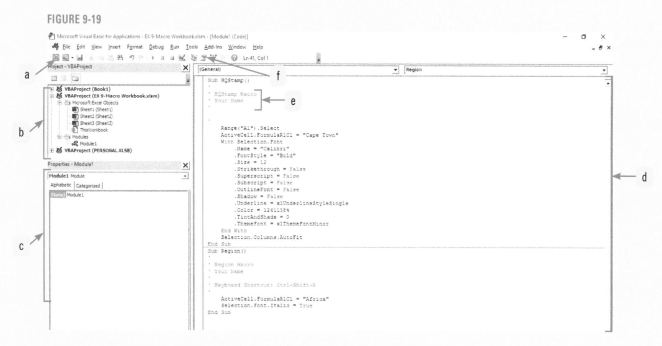

1. **Which element do you click to return to Excel without closing the module?**
2. **Which element points to comments?**
3. **Which element points to the Properties Window button?**
4. **Which element points to the Code window?**
5. **Which element points to the Properties window?**
6. **Which element points to the Project Explorer window?**

Match each term or button with the statement that best describes it.

7. **Virus**
8. **Macro**
9. **Comments**
10. **Visual Basic Editor**
11. **Personal Macro Workbook**

a. Set of instructions that performs a task in a specified order
b. Statements that appear in green explaining the macro
c. Destructive software that can damage computer files
d. Used to make changes to macro code
e. Used to store frequently used macros

Select the best answer from the list of choices.

12. **You can open the Visual Basic Editor by clicking the _____ button in the Macro dialog box.**
   a. Edit
   b. Programs
   c. Modules
   d. Visual Basic Editor
13. **Which of the following is the best candidate for a macro?**
   a. An often-used sequence of commands or actions
   b. A nonsequential task
   c. A seldom-used command or task
   d. A one-button or one-keystroke command

14. Which of the following is *not* true about editing a macro?

  a. You edit macros using the Visual Basic Editor.

  b. A macro cannot be edited and must be recorded again.

  c. You can type changes directly in the existing program code.

  d. You can make more than one editing change in a macro.

15. A macro named _____ will automatically run when the workbook it is saved in opens.

  a. Default   **c.** Macro1

  b. Auto_Open   **d.** Open_Macro

16. Macros are recorded with relative references:

  a. Only if the Use Relative References button is selected.   **c.** By default.

  b. In all cases.   **d.** Only if the Use Absolute References button is not selected.

17. Why is it important to plan a macro?

  a. Macros can't be deleted.

  b. Planning helps prevent careless errors from being introduced into the macro.

  c. It is impossible to edit a macro.

  d. Macros won't be stored if they contain errors.

18. Macro security settings can be changed using the _____ tab.

  a. Home   **c.** Security

  b. Developer   **d.** Review

19. You can run macros:

  a. From the Macro dialog box.   **c.** From a button on the worksheet.

  b. From shortcut key combinations.   **d.** Using all of the above.

Skills Review

1. Plan and enable a macro.

  a. You need to plan a macro that enters and formats your name and department in a worksheet, in the range A1:A2.

  b. Write out the steps the macro will perform.

  c. Write out how the macro could be used in a workbook.

  d. Start Excel, open a new workbook, then save it as a Macro-Enabled workbook named **EX 9-Macros** in the location where you store your Data Files. (*Hint*: The file will have the file extension .xlsm.)

  e. Use the Excel Options feature to display the Developer tab if it is not showing in the Ribbon.

  f. Using the Trust Center dialog box, enable all macros.

2. Record a macro.

  a. Open the Record Macro dialog box.

  b. Name the new macro **MyDept**, store it in the current workbook, and enter your name in the Description text box as the person who recorded the macro.

  c. Record the macro, entering your name in cell A1 and **Sales Department** in cell A2. (*Hint*: You need to press [Ctrl][Home] first to ensure cell A1 will be selected when the macro runs.)

  d. Resize column A to fit the information entirely in that column.

  e. Format the font using Purple from Standard Colors.

  f. Add bold formatting to the text in the range A1:A2.

  g. Stop the recorder, then save the workbook.

Skills Review (continued)

3. Run a macro.

    a. Clear cell entries and formats in the range affected by the macro, resize the width of column A to 8.43, then select cell B3.

    b. Run the MyDept macro. Confirm that your name and your sales department are entered in the range A1:A2.

    c. On the worksheet, clear all the cell entries and formats generated by running the MyDept macro. Resize the width of column A to 8.43.

    d. Save the workbook.

4. Edit a macro.

    a. Open the MyDept macro in the Visual Basic Editor.

    b. Change the line of code above the last line from Selection.Font.Bold = True to **Selection.Font.Bold = False**.

    c. Use the Close and Return to Microsoft Excel command on the File menu to return to Excel.

    d. Test the macro on Sheet1, click outside the range A1:A2, then compare your worksheet to FIGURE 9-20, verifying that the text is not bold.

    e. Save the workbook.

FIGURE 9-20

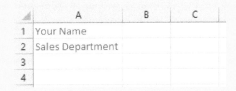

5. Assign keyboard shortcuts to macros.

    a. Create a macro named **DeptStamp** in the current workbook, assign your macro the shortcut key combination [Ctrl][Shift][D], enter your name in the description. (*Hint:* If you get an error when trying to use [Ctrl][Shift][D], select another key combination.)

    b. Begin recording, starting in the current cell of the worksheet. Type **Sales Department**, format it in bold, italic, and with a font color of green, without underlining. Stop recording.

    c. Clear the contents and formats from the cell containing the sales department text that you used to record the macro.

    d. Use the shortcut key combination to run the DeptStamp macro in a cell other than the one in which it was recorded. Compare your macro result to FIGURE 9-21. The Sales Department text may appear in a different cell.

    e. Save the workbook.

FIGURE 9-21

6. Use the Personal Macro Workbook.

    a. Using Sheet1, record a new macro called **FitToLand** and store it in the Personal Macro Workbook with your name in the Description text box. If you already have a macro named FitToLand, replace that macro. The macro should set the print orientation to landscape.

    b. After you record the macro, add a new worksheet, and enter **Test data for FitToLand macro** in cell A1.

    c. Preview Sheet2 in Backstage view to verify the orientation is set to portrait.

    d. Run the FitToLand macro. (You may have to wait a few moments.)

    e. Add your name to the Sheet2 footer, then preview Sheet2 to verify that it is now in Landscape.

    f. Save the workbook.

7. Assign a macro to a button.

    a. Add a new worksheet, then enter **Landscape Button Test** in cell A1.

    b. Using the rectangle shape, draw a rectangle in the range A7:B8.

    c. Label the button with the text **Landscape Macro**, then center and middle align the text. Compare your worksheet to FIGURE 9-22.

    d. Assign the macro PERSONAL.XLSB!FitToLand to the button.

    e. Verify that the orientation of Sheet3 is set to portrait.

    f. Run the FitToLand macro using the button.

Skills Review (continued)

g. Preview the worksheet, and verify that it is in Landscape.

h. Add your name to the Sheet3 footer, then save the workbook.

i. Click the Developer tab, click the Macro Security button in the Code group, click Macro Settings if necessary, click the Disable all macros with notification option button to select it, then click OK.

j. Close the workbook, exit Excel without saving the FitToLand macro in the Personal Macro Workbook, then submit your workbook to your instructor.

FIGURE 9-22

Independent Challenge 1

As the office manager of Cape Engineering, you need to develop ways to help your fellow employees work more efficiently. Employees have asked for Excel macros that can do the following:

- Adjust the column widths to display all column data in a worksheet.
- Place the company name of Cape Engineering in the header of a worksheet.

(Note: Remember to enable macros before beginning this independent challenge, and to disable them when you are finished.)

a. Plan and write the steps necessary for each macro.

b. Start Excel, open EX 9-1.xlsx from where you store your Data Files, then save it as a macro-enabled workbook called **EX 9-Engineering**.

c. Check your macro security on the Developer tab to be sure that macros are enabled.

d. Create a macro named **ColumnFit**, save it in the EX 9-Engineering.xlsm workbook, assign the ColumnFit macro a shortcut key combination of [Ctrl][Shift][F] (if this shortcut is already in use, choose a different keyboard combination), and add your name in the description area for the macro. Record the macro using the following instructions:

- Adjust a worksheet's column widths to display all data. (*Hint*: Select the entire sheet, click the Home tab, click the Format button in the Cells group, select AutoFit Column Width, then click cell A1 to deselect the worksheet.)
- End the macro recording.

e. Format the widths of columns A through G to 8.43, then test the ColumnFit macro with the shortcut key combination [Ctrl][Shift][F].

f. Create a macro named **CompanyName**, and save it in the EX 9-Engineering.xlsm workbook. Assign the macro a shortcut key combination of [Ctrl][Shift][N] (or a different keyboard combination if necessary), and add your name in the description area for the macro.

g. Record the CompanyName macro. The macro should place the company name of Cape Engineering in the center section of the worksheet header.

h. Enter **Cape Engineering Header test data** in cell A1 of Sheet2 and test the CompanyName macro using the shortcut key combination you set in Step f. Preview Sheet2 to view the header.

i. Edit the CompanyName macro in the Visual Basic Editor to change the company name from Cape Engineering to **Shore Engineering**. Close the Visual Basic Editor and return to Excel.

j. Add a rectangle button to Sheet3 in the range A6:D7. Label the button with the text **Company Name Header Macro**. Center and middle align the button text on the button.

k. Assign the CompanyName macro to the button.

Independent Challenge 1 (continued)

l. Enter **Shore Engineering header test data** in cell A1. Compare your screen to FIGURE 9-23. Use the button to run the CompanyName macro. Preview the worksheet, checking the header to be sure it is displaying the new company name.

m. Enter your name in the footers of all three worksheets. Save the workbook, close the workbook, then submit the workbook to your instructor and exit Excel.

FIGURE 9-23

Independent Challenge 2

You are an assistant to the VP of Sales at Green Horizons, a landscape distributor. As part of your work, you create spreadsheets with sales projections for different regions of the company. You frequently have to change the print settings so that workbooks print in landscape orientation with custom margins of 1" on the top and bottom. You also add a header with the company name on every worksheet. You have decided that it's time to create a macro to streamline this process. (*Note: Remember to enable macros before beginning this independent challenge, and to disable them when you are finished.*)

a. Plan and write the steps necessary to create a macro that performs all of the tasks described above.

b. Check your macro security settings to confirm that macros are enabled.

c. Start Excel, create a new workbook, then save it as a macro-enabled file named **EX 9-Sales Macro** in the location where you store your Data Files.

d. Create a macro that changes the page orientation to landscape, adds custom margins of 1" at the top and bottom of the page, adds a header of **Green Horizons** in the center section, formatted in bold with a font size of 12 points. Name the macro **Format**, add your name in the description, assign it the shortcut key combination [Ctrl][Shift][F] (or a different combination if necessary), and store it in the current workbook.

e. Add a new worksheet and enter the text **Format Macro Test** in cell A1. Test the macro using the shortcut key combination you set in Step d. Preview Sheet2 to check the page orientation, margins, and header.

f. Add a new worksheet, enter the text **Format Worksheet Button Test** in cell A1, add a rectangular button with the text **Format Worksheet** that runs the Format macro, then test the macro using the button.

g. Preview the Visual Basic code for the macro.

h. Save the workbook, close the workbook, exit Excel, then submit the workbook to your instructor.

Independent Challenge 3

You are the Southeast regional sales manager of Atlantic Consulting, a technology consulting firm. You manage the Southeast operations and frequently create workbooks with data from three office locations. It's tedious to change the tab names and colors every time you open a new workbook, so you decide to create a macro that will add the office locations and colors to the three office location worksheet tabs, as shown in FIGURE 9-24. (*Note: Remember to enable macros before beginning this independent challenge, and to disable them when you are finished.*)

FIGURE 9-24

a. Plan and write the steps to create the macro described above.

b. Start Excel and open a new workbook.

c. Create the macro using the plan you created in Step a, name it **WBFormat**, assign it the shortcut key combination [Ctrl][Shift][W] (or a different combination if necessary), store it in the Personal Macro Workbook, and add your name in the description area. (*Hint*: The tab colors are red, green, and blue from the Standard Colors.)

d. After recording the macro, close the workbook without saving it. Save the changes to the Personal Macro workbook.

Independent Challenge 3 (continued)

e. Open a new workbook, then save it as a macro-enabled workbook named **EX 9-Atlantic Test** in the location where you store your Data Files. Use the shortcut key combination you created in Step c to test the macro in the new workbook.

f. Unhide the PERSONAL.XLSB workbook. (*Hint*: Click the View tab click the Unhide button in the Window group, click PERSONAL.XLSB, then click OK. You will hide PERSONAL.XLSB at the end of this exercise.)

g. Edit the WBFormat macro using FIGURE 9-25 as a guide, changing the Charlotte sheet name to Durham. (*Hint*: There are two instances of Charlotte that need to be changed.)

h. Open a new workbook, then save it as a macro-enabled workbook named **EX 9-Atlantic** in the location where you store your Data Files. Test the edited macro using the shortcut key combination you set in Step c.

i. Add a new sheet in the workbook, and name it **Code**. Copy the WBFormat macro code from the Personal Macro Workbook, and paste it in the Code sheet beginning in cell A1 (be careful to select only the code for this macro). Save the workbook, close the workbook, hide the Personal Macro Workbook, then submit EX 9-Atlantic to your instructor.

j. Hide the PERSONAL.XLSB workbook. (*Hint*: With the PERSONAL.XLSB workbook active, click the View tab, then click the Hide button in the Window group.)

k. Close the workbook without saving changes to the PERSONAL.XLSB workbook, then exit Excel.

FIGURE 9-25

```
Sub WBFormat()
'
' WBFormat Macro
' Your Name
'
' Keyboard Shortcut: Ctrl+Shift+W
'
    Sheets.Add After:=ActiveSheet
    Sheets.Add After:=ActiveSheet
    Sheets("Sheet1").Select
    Sheets("Sheet1").Name = "Miami"
    Sheets("Sheet2").Select
    Sheets("Sheet2").Name = "Atlanta"
    Sheets("Sheet3").Select
    Sheets("Sheet3").Name = "Durham"
    Sheets("Miami").Select
    With ActiveWorkbook.Sheets("Miami").Tab
        .Color = 255
        .TintAndShade = 0
    End With
    Sheets("Atlanta").Select
    With ActiveWorkbook.Sheets("Atlanta").Tab
        .Color = 5287936
        .TintAndShade = 0
    End With
    Sheets("Durham").Select
    With ActiveWorkbook.Sheets("Durham").Tab
        .Color = 12611584
        .TintAndShade = 0
    End With
End Sub
```

Independent Challenge 4: Explore

As the business manager for a hospital, you work with confidential information in a patient information workbook. To make sure your office colleagues understand the confidential nature of this workbook, you need to create a macro that provides a confidentiality message when this workbook is opened. (*Note: Remember to enable macros before beginning this independent challenge, and to disable them when you are finished.*)

a. Start Excel, open EX 9-2.xlsx from where you store your Data Files, then save it as a Macro-Enabled workbook named **EX 9-Patient Information**.

b. Create a new macro with the name Auto_Open, store it in the Patient Information workbook, and add your name in the description area.

c. Stop the macro recording before completing any steps.

d. Open the Auto_Open macro in the Visual Basic Editor.

e. Use FIGURE 9-26 as a guide to add a message box to the Auto_Open macro.

f. Return to Excel and save the workbook.

g. Close, then reopen, the workbook.

h. Close the message box.

i. Enter your name in the footer. Save the workbook, close the workbook, then submit the workbook to your instructor and exit Excel.

FIGURE 9-26

```
Sub Auto_Open()
'
' Auto_Open Macro
' Your Name
'
MsgBox "Confidential"
'
End Sub
```

Visual Workshop

Start Excel, open EX 9-3.xlsx from the location where you store your Data Files, then save it as a macro-enabled workbook called **EX 9-Accounts**. Create a macro with the name **TotalAccounts**, save the macro in the EX 9-Accounts workbook that does the following:

- Totals the weekly accounts for each employee by totaling the accounts for the first employee and copying that formula for the other employees
- Adds a row at the top of the worksheet and inserts a label of **Accounts** in a font size of 14 point, in bold font, centered across all columns
- Adds your name in the worksheet footer

Test the TotalAccounts macro by reopening EX 9-3.xlsx and running the macro. Compare your macro results to FIGURE 9-27. Close the Data File EX 9-3 without saving it, then save the EX 9-Accounts workbook. Submit the EX 9-Accounts workbook to your instructor. *(Note: Remember to enable macros before beginning this visual workshop, and to disable them when you are finished.)*

FIGURE 9-27

	A	B	C	D	E	F	G	H	I
1	Accounts								
2		Monday	Tuesday	Wednesday	Thursday	Friday	Saturday	Sunday	Total
3	John Smith	5	6	8	2	1	0	0	22
4	Paula Jones	6	8	8	7	7	6	2	44
5	Linda Kristol	4	3	7	6	3	5	0	28
6	Al Meng	7	6	6	5	5	1	0	30
7	Robert Delgado	7	6	5	8	7	7	0	40
8	Harry Degual	7	6	5	5	7	8	0	38
9	Jody Williams	8	6	2	6	8	5	3	38
10	Mary Abbott	7	8	8	6	7	2	0	38
11	Ken Yang	6	8	4	4	4	4	1	31
12	Cathy Martin	7	8	2	8	8	1	0	34
13									
14									
15									

Analyzing Data with PivotTables

CASE Reason2Go uses PivotTables to analyze sales data. Dawn Parsons is preparing for the annual directors' meeting and asks you to analyze sales in Reason2Go's North American branches over the past year. You will create a PivotTable to summarize last year's sales data by quarter, product, and branch, and illustrate the information using a PivotChart.

Module Objectives

After completing this module, you will be able to:

- Plan and design a PivotTable report
- Create a PivotTable report
- Change a PivotTable's summary function and design
- Filter and sort PivotTable data
- Update a PivotTable report
- Explore PivotTable Data Relationships
- Create a PivotChart report
- Use the GETPIVOTDATA function

Files You Will Need

EX 12-1.xlsx   EX 12-5.xlsx
EX 12-2.xlsx   EX 12-6.xlsx
EX 12-3.xlsx   EX 12-7.xlsx
EX 12-4.xlsx

Plan and Design a PivotTable Report

Learning
Outcomes
• Develop guidelines
  for a PivotTable
• Develop an
  understanding of
  PivotTable
  vocabulary

The Excel **PivotTable Report** feature lets you summarize large amounts of columnar worksheet data in a compact table format. Then you can freely rearrange, or "pivot", PivotTable rows and columns to explore the relationships within your data by category. Creating a PivotTable report (often called a PivotTable) involves only a few steps. Before you begin, however, you need to review the data and consider how a PivotTable can best summarize it. **CASE** ▶ *Dawn asks you to design a PivotTable to display Reason2Go's sales information for its branches in North America. You begin by reviewing guidelines for creating PivotTables.*

DETAILS

Before you create a PivotTable, think about the following guidelines:

- **Review the source data**

  Before you can effectively summarize data in a PivotTable, you need to understand the source data's scope and structure. The source data does not have to be defined as a table, but should be in a table-like format. That is, it should have column headings, should not have any blank rows or columns, and should have the same type of data in each column. To create a meaningful PivotTable, make sure that one or more of the fields have repeated information so that the PivotTable can effectively group it. Also be sure to include numeric data that the PivotTable can total for each group. The data columns represent categories of data, which are called **fields**, just as in a table. You are working with sales information that Dawn received from Reason2Go's North American branch managers, shown in FIGURE 12-1. Information is repeated in the Product ID, Category, Branch, and Quarter columns, and numeric information is displayed in the Sales column, so you will be able to summarize this data effectively in a PivotTable.

- **Determine the purpose of the PivotTable and write the names of the fields you want to include**

  The purpose of your PivotTable is to summarize sales information by quarter across various branches. You want your PivotTable to summarize the data in the Product ID, Category, Branch, Quarter, and Sales columns, so you need to include those fields in your PivotTable.

- **Determine which field contains the data you want to summarize and which summary function you want to use**

  The components of a Reason2Go project are organized into products, such as Insurance, Transportation, and Experience. You want to summarize sales information by summing the Sales field for each product in a branch by quarter. You'll do this by using the Excel SUM function.

- **Decide how you want to arrange the data**

  The PivotTable layout you choose is crucial to delivering the message you intend. Product ID values will appear in the PivotTable columns, Branch and Quarter numbers will appear in rows, and the PivotTable will summarize Sales figures, as shown in FIGURE 12-2.

- **Determine the location of the PivotTable**

  You can place a PivotTable in any worksheet of any workbook. Placing a PivotTable on a separate worksheet makes it easier to locate and prevents you from accidentally overwriting parts of an existing sheet. You decide to create the PivotTable as a new worksheet in the current workbook.

FIGURE 12-1: **Sales worksheet**

	A	B	C	D	E	F	G
1			Sales				
2	Product ID	Category	Branch	Quarter	Sales		
3	240	Transportation	Los Angeles	1	$ 1,115.33		
4	240	Transportation	Los Angeles	2	$ 1,974.21		
5	240	Transportation	Los Angeles	3	$ 822.87		
6	240	Transportation	Los Angeles	4	$ 1,089.24		
7	110	Insurance	Los Angeles	1	$ 975.50		
8	110	Insurance	Los Angeles	2	$ 2,566.41		
9	110	Insurance	Los Angeles	3	$ 2,355.78		
10	110	Insurance	Los Angeles	4	$ 3,117.22		
11	340	Experience	Los Angeles	1	$ 7,772.31		
12	340	Experience	Los Angeles	2	$ 7,655.21		
13	340	Experience	Los Angeles	3	$ 8,100.34		
14	340	Experience	Los Angeles	4	$ 8,566.14		
15	780	Transportation	Los Angeles	1	$ 1,027.25		
16	780	Transportation	Los Angeles	2	$ 2,231.47		
17	780	Transportation	Los Angeles	3	$ 2,136.11		
18	780	Transportation	Los Angeles	4	$ 1,117.36		
19	640	Insurance	Los Angeles	1	$ 1,499.31		
20	640	Insurance	Los Angeles	2	$ 6,321.22		
21	640	Insurance	Los Angeles	3	$ 6,002.11		
22	640	Insurance	Los Angeles	4	$ 6,211.87		
23	510	Experience	Los Angeles	1	$ 877.41		
24	510	Experience	Los Angeles	2	$ 1,889.35		
25	510	Experience	Los Angeles	3	$ 2,122.54		
26	510	Experience	Los Angeles	4	$ 2,556.74		
27	240	Transportation	New York	1	$ 1,897.51		
28	240	Transportation	New York	2	$ 2,374.32		
29	240	Transportation	New York	3	$ 1,032.57		
30	240	Transportation	New York	4	$ 1,230.41		
31	110	Insurance	New York	1	$ 4,921.45		
32	110	Insurance	New York	2	$ 3,319.92		

North America ⊕

Data with repeated information

Numeric data

FIGURE 12-2: **PivotTable report based on Sales worksheet**

Product ID values are column labels

	A	B	C	D	E	F	G	H	I	J	K
1											
2											
3	Sum of Sales	Column Labels ▼									
4	Row Labels ▼	110	240	340	510	640	780	Grand Total			
5	⊟ Los Angeles	9014.91	5001.65	32094	7446.04	20034.51	6512.19	80103.3			
6	1	975.5	1115.33	7772.31	877.41	1499.31	1027.25	13267.11			
7	2	2566.41	1974.21	7655.21	1889.35	6321.22	2231.47	22637.87			
8	3	2355.78	822.87	8100.34	2122.54	6002.11	2136.11	21539.75			
9	4	3117.22	1089.24	8566.14	2556.74	6211.87	1117.36	22658.57			
10	⊟ New York	15057.69	6534.81	29818.65	20039.58	8856.97	5056.28	85363.98			
11	1	4921.45	1897.51	6258.21	2987.14	1305.47	1522.14	18891.92			
12	2	3319.92	2374.32	7628.78	3880.78	2183.98	208.64	19596.42			
13	3	4176.89	1032.57	8198.9	6728.9	2577.98	1324.14	24039.38			
14	4	2639.43	1230.41	7732.76	6442.76	2789.54	2001.36	22836.26			
15	⊟ Toronto	31883.87	3237.62	32350.46	9567.18	10106.56	4008.7	91154.39			
16	1	6634.43	895.65	7790.34	2310.34	1376.34	781.14	19788.24			
17	2	8100.14	921.32	6700.15	2524.87	3394.21	968.24	22608.93			
18	3	8324.65	398.77	8883.54	2183.54	2412.58	1002.21	23205.29			
19	4	8824.65	1021.88	8976.43	2548.43	2923.43	1257.11	25551.93			
20	Grand Total	55956.47	14774.08	94263.11	37052.8	38998.04	15577.17	256621.67			
21											
22											
23											

PivotTable summarizes sales figures by product ID, branch, and quarter

Branches and quarters are row labels

Create a PivotTable Report

Learning Outcomes
- Create a PivotTable
- Move PivotTable fields to rearrange data

Once you've planned and designed your PivotTable report, you can create it. After you create the PivotTable, you **populate** it by adding fields to areas in the PivotTable. A PivotTable has four areas: the Report Filter, which is the field by which you want to filter the PivotTable; the Row Labels, which contain the fields whose labels will describe the values in the rows; the Column Labels, which appear above the PivotTable values and describe the columns; and the Values, which summarize the numeric data. **CASE ▶** *With the planning and design stage complete, you are ready to create a PivotTable that summarizes sales information.*

STEPS

1. **Start Excel, open** EX 12-1.xlsx **from the location where you store your Data Files, then save it as** EX 12-NA Sales

    This worksheet contains last year's sales information for R2G's North American branches, including Product ID, Category, Branch, Quarter, and Sales. The records are sorted by branch. You first want to see what PivotTables Excel recommends for your data.

2. **Click the** Insert tab, **click the** Recommended PivotTables button **in the Tables group, then click each of the recommended** layouts **in the left side of the Recommended PivotTables dialog box, scrolling as necessary**

    The Recommended PivotTables dialog box displays recommended PivotTable layouts that summarize your data, as shown in FIGURE 12-3. You decide to create your own PivotTable.

    > **QUICK TIP**
    > To create your own PivotTable without reviewing recommended ones, click the PivotTable button in the Tables group, verify your data range or enter an external data source such as a database, specify a PivotTable location, then click OK.

3. **Click** Blank PivotTable **at the bottom of the dialog box**

    A new, blank PivotTable appears on the left side of the worksheet and the PivotTable Fields List appears in a pane on the right, as shown in FIGURE 12-4. You populate the PivotTable by clicking field check boxes in the PivotTable Fields List pane, often simply called the Field List. The diagram area at the bottom of the pane represents the main PivotTable areas and helps you track field locations as you populate the PivotTable. You can also drag fields among the diagram areas to change the PivotTable layout.

4. **Click the** Branch field check box **in the Field List**

    Because the Branch field is a text, rather than a numeric, field, Excel adds branch names to the rows area of the PivotTable, and adds the Branch field name to the ROWS area in the PivotTable Fields pane.

    > **QUICK TIP**
    > To remove a field from a PivotTable, click its check box to remove the check mark.

5. **Click the** Product ID check box **in the Field List**

    The Product ID information is automatically added to the PivotTable, and "Sum of Product ID" appears in the VALUES area in the diagram area. But because the data type of the Product ID field is numeric, the field is added to the VALUES area of the PivotTable and the Product ID values are summed, which is not meaningful. Instead, you want the Product IDs as column headers in the PivotTable.

6. **Click the** Sum of Product ID list arrow **in the VALUES area at the bottom of the PivotTable Fields List pane, then choose** Move to Column Labels

    The Product ID field becomes a column label, causing the Product ID values to appear in the PivotTable as column headers.

    > **QUICK TIP**
    > PivotTables containing a data field can be filtered by date: Click the PivotTable Tools Analyze tab, then click the Insert Timeline button in the Filter group.

7. **Drag the** Quarter field **from the PivotTable Fields List pane and drop it below the Branch field in the** ROWS **area, select the** Sales field check box **in the PivotTable Fields List pane, then save the workbook**

    You have created a PivotTable that totals North American sales, with the Product IDs as column headers and Branches and Quarters as row labels. SUM is the Excel default function for data fields containing numbers, so Excel automatically calculates the sum of the sales in the PivotTable. The PivotTable tells you that Toronto sales of Product #110 (Insurance) were twice the New York sales level and more than three times the Los Angeles level. Product #340 (Experience) was the best selling product overall, as shown in the Grand Total row. See FIGURE 12-5.

FIGURE 12-3: **Recommended PivotTables dialog box**

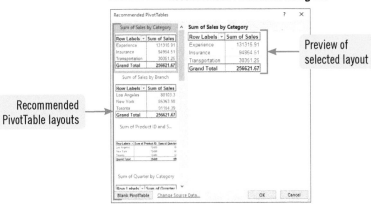

Recommended PivotTable layouts →

Preview of selected layout

FIGURE 12-4: **Empty PivotTable ready to receive field data**

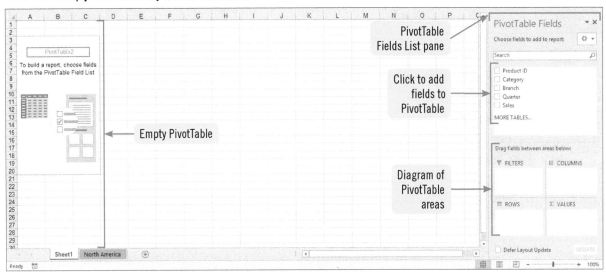

PivotTable Fields List pane

Click to add fields to PivotTable

Diagram of PivotTable areas

Empty PivotTable

FIGURE 12-5: **New PivotTable with fields in place**

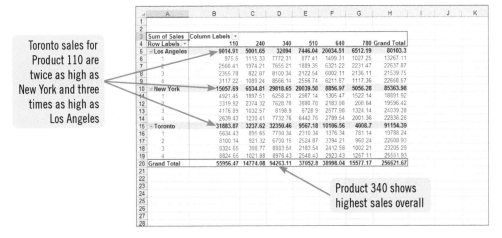

Toronto sales for Product 110 are twice as high as New York and three times as high as Los Angeles

Product 340 shows highest sales overall

Changing the PivotTable layout

The default layout for PivotTables is the compact form; the row labels are displayed in a single column, and the second-level field items (such as the quarters in the R2G example) are indented for readability. You can change the layout of your PivotTable by clicking the PivotTable Tools Design tab, clicking the Report Layout button in the Layout group, then clicking either Show in Outline Form or Show in Tabular Form. The tabular form and the outline form show each row label in its own column. The tabular and outline layouts take up more space on a worksheet than the compact layout.

Change a PivotTable's Summary Function and Design

A PivotTable's **summary function** controls what calculation Excel uses to summarize the table data. Unless you specify otherwise, Excel applies the SUM function to numeric data and the COUNT function to data fields containing text. However, you can easily change the default summary functions to different ones. **CASE** *Dawn wants you to calculate the average sales for the North American branches using the AVERAGE function and to improve the appearance of the PivotTable for her presentation.*

STEPS

1. **Right-click cell** A3, **then point to** Summarize Values By **in the shortcut menu**

   The shortcut menu shows that the Sum function is selected by default, as shown in FIGURE 12-6.

2. **Click** Average

   The data area of the PivotTable shows the average sales for each product by branch and quarter, and cell A3 now contains "Average of Sales". You want to view the PivotTable data without the subtotals.

3. **Click the** PivotTable Tools Design tab, **click the** Subtotals button **in the Layout group, then click** Do Not Show Subtotals

   After reviewing the data, you decide that it would be more useful to sum the sales information than to average it. You also want to redisplay the subtotals.

4. **Right-click cell** A3, **point to** Summarize Values By **in the shortcut menu, then click** Sum

   Excel recalculates the PivotTable—in this case, summing the sales data instead of averaging it.

5. **Click the** Subtotals button **in the Layout group, then click** Show all Subtotals at Top of Group

   Just as Excel tables have styles that let you quickly format them, PivotTables have a gallery of styles to choose from. You decide to add a PivotTable style to the PivotTable to improve its appearance.

6. **Click the** More button ⏷ **in the PivotTable Styles gallery, then click** Pivot Style Light 16

   To further improve the appearance of the PivotTable, you decide to remove the unnecessary headers "Column Labels" and "Row Labels" and format the sales values as currency.

7. **Click the** PivotTable Tools Analyze tab, **then click the** Field Headers button **in the Show group to deselect it**

8. **Click any sales value in the PivotTable, click the** Field Settings button **in the Active Field group, click** Number Format **in the Value Field Settings dialog box, click** Currency **in the Category list, make sure Decimal places is** 2 **and Symbol is** $, **click** OK, **click** OK **again, then compare your PivotTable to** FIGURE 12-7

   You decide to give the PivotTable sheet a more descriptive name. When you name a PivotTable sheet, it is best to avoid using spaces in the name. If a PivotTable name contains a space, you must put single quotes around the name if you refer to it in a function.

9. **Rename Sheet1** PivotTable, **add your name to the worksheet footer, save the workbook, then preview the sheet**

FIGURE 12-6: Shortcut menu showing Sum function selected

FIGURE 12-6: Shortcut menu showing Sum function selected

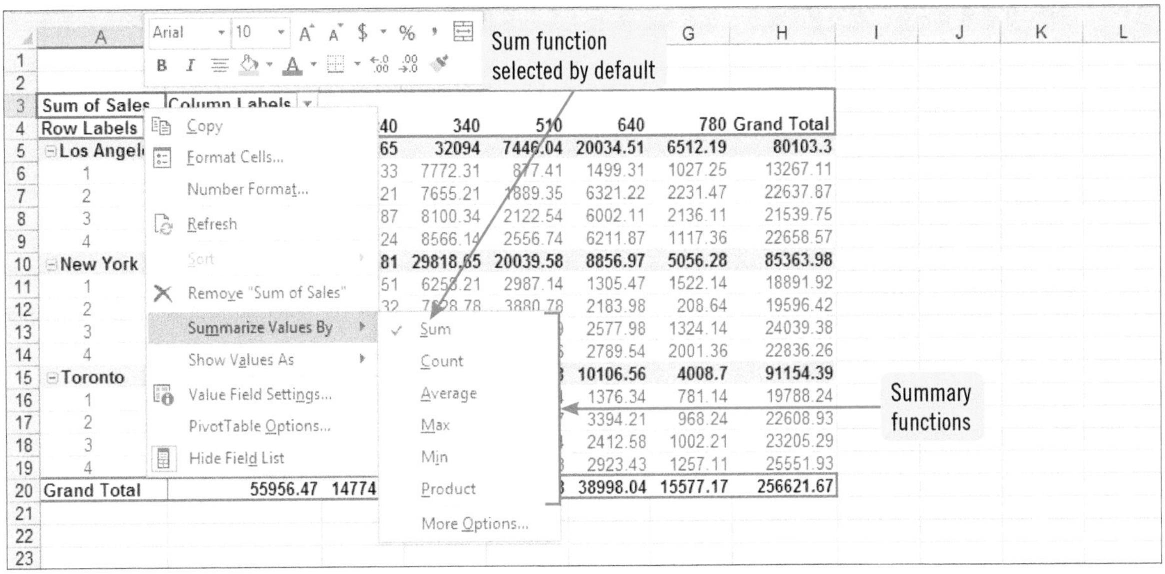

FIGURE 12-7: Formatted PivotTable

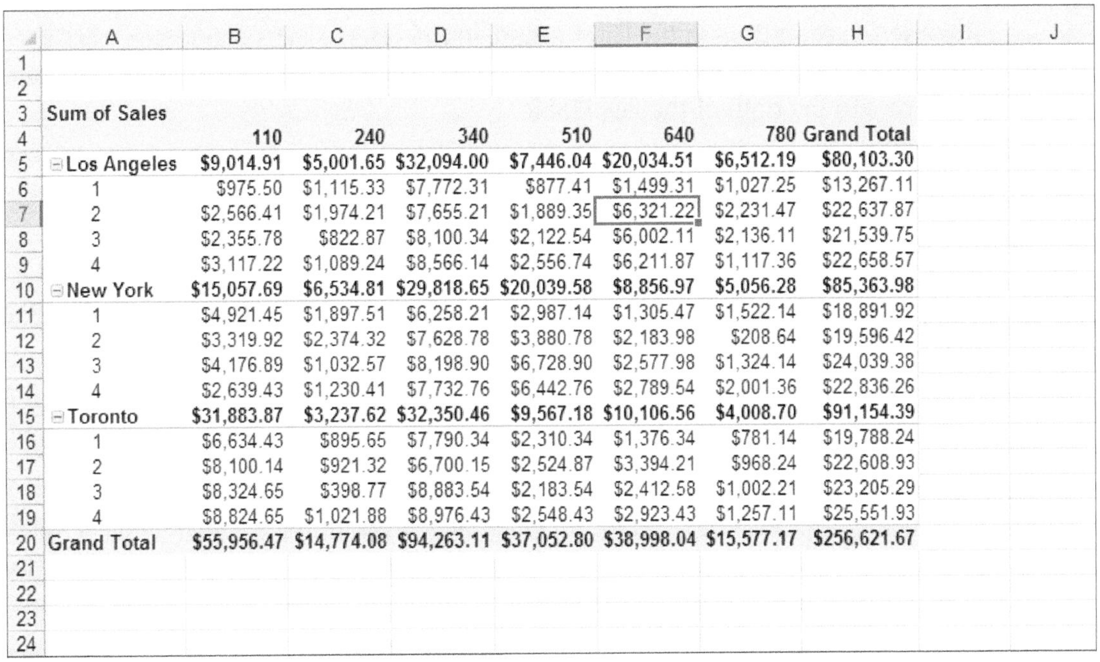

	110	240	340	510	640	780 Grand Total
Sum of Sales						
⊟Los Angeles	$9,014.91	$5,001.65	$32,094.00	$7,446.04	$20,034.51	$6,512.19 $80,103.30
1	$975.50	$1,115.33	$7,772.31	$877.41	$1,499.31	$1,027.25 $13,267.11
2	$2,566.41	$1,974.21	$7,655.21	$1,889.35	$6,321.22	$2,231.47 $22,637.87
3	$2,355.78	$822.87	$8,100.34	$2,122.54	$6,002.11	$2,136.11 $21,539.75
4	$3,117.22	$1,089.24	$8,566.14	$2,556.74	$6,211.87	$1,117.36 $22,658.57
⊟New York	$15,057.69	$6,534.81	$29,818.65	$20,039.58	$8,856.97	$5,056.28 $85,363.98
1	$4,921.45	$1,897.51	$6,258.21	$2,987.14	$1,305.47	$1,522.14 $18,891.92
2	$3,319.92	$2,374.32	$7,628.78	$3,880.78	$2,183.98	$208.64 $19,596.42
3	$4,176.89	$1,032.57	$8,198.90	$6,728.90	$2,577.98	$1,324.14 $24,039.38
4	$2,639.43	$1,230.41	$7,732.76	$6,442.76	$2,789.54	$2,001.36 $22,836.26
⊟Toronto	$31,883.87	$3,237.62	$32,350.46	$9,567.18	$10,106.56	$4,008.70 $91,154.39
1	$6,634.43	$895.65	$7,790.34	$2,310.34	$1,376.34	$781.14 $19,788.24
2	$8,100.14	$921.32	$6,700.15	$2,524.87	$3,394.21	$968.24 $22,608.93
3	$8,324.65	$398.77	$8,883.54	$2,183.54	$2,412.58	$1,002.21 $23,205.29
4	$8,824.65	$1,021.88	$8,976.43	$2,548.43	$2,923.43	$1,257.11 $25,551.93
Grand Total	$55,956.47	$14,774.08	$94,263.11	$37,052.80	$38,998.04	$15,577.17 $256,621.67

Using the Show buttons

To display and hide PivotTable elements, you can use the buttons in the Show group on the PivotTable Tools Analyze tab. For example, the Field List button will hide or display the PivotTable Fields List pane. The +/– buttons button will hide or display the Expand and Collapse Outline buttons, and the Field Headers button will hide or display the Row and Column Label headers on the PivotTable.

Filter and Sort PivotTable Data

You can restrict the display of PivotTable data using slicers and report filters. A **slicer** is a graphic object with a set of buttons that let you easily filter PivotTable data to show only the data you need. For example, you can use slicer buttons to show only data about a specific product. You can also filter a PivotTable using a **report filter**, which lets you filter the data using a list arrow to show data for one or more field values. For example, if you add a Month field to the FILTERS area, you can filter a PivotTable so that only January sales data appears in the PivotTable. You can also sort PivotTable data on any field in ascending or descending order. **CASE** *Dawn wants to see sales data about specific products for specific branches and quarters.*

STEPS

1. **Right-click cell H5, point to** Sort **in the shortcut menu, then click** More Sort Options
   The Sort By Value dialog box opens. As you select options in the dialog box, the Summary information at the bottom of the dialog box changes to describe the sort results using your field names.

2. **Click the** Largest to Smallest option button **to select it under Sort options, make sure the** Top to Bottom option button **is selected under Sort direction, review the sort description under Summary, then click** OK
   The branches appear in the PivotTable in decreasing order of total sales from top to bottom. You want to easily display the sales for specific product IDs at certain branches.

3. **Click any cell in the PivotTable, click the** PivotTable Tools Analyze tab **if necessary, click the** Insert Slicer button **in the Filter group, in the Insert Slicers dialog box, click the** Product ID check box **and the** Branch check box **to select both fields, click** OK, **then drag the** slicers **to the right of the PivotTable**
   The slicers contain buttons representing the Product ID numbers and Branch names, as shown in FIGURE 12-8. You want to filter the data to show only Product IDs 110 and 510 in the New York and Toronto branches.

4. **Click the** 110 button **in the Product ID slicer, press** [CTRL], **click the** 510 button **in the Product ID slicer, release** [CTRL], **click the** New York button **in the Branch slicer, press** [CTRL], **click the** Toronto button **in the Branch slicer, then release** [CTRL]
   The PivotTable displays only the data for Product IDs 110 and 510 in New York and Toronto, as shown in FIGURE 12-9. In the slicers, the Filter symbol changes, indicating the PivotTable is filtered to display the selected fields. You decide to clear the filter and remove the slicers.

5. **Click the** Clear Filter button 🖫 **in the Product ID slicer, click** 🖫 **in the Branch slicer, click the top of the** Branch slicer, **press** [CTRL], **click the top of the** Product ID slicer, **release** [CTRL], **right-click the** Product ID slicer, **then click** Remove Slicers **on the shortcut menu**
   You want to display the PivotTable data by quarter using a Report Filter.

6. **In the PivotTable Fields List pane, click the** Quarter field list arrow **in the ROWS area, then select** Move to Report Filter **in the list that opens**
   The Quarter field moves to cell A1, and a list arrow and the word "(All)" appear in cell B1. The list arrow lets you filter the data in the PivotTable by Quarter. "(All)" indicates that the PivotTable currently shows data for all quarters. You decide to filter the data to show only data for the fourth quarter.

7. **Click the** cell B1 list arrow, **click** 4, **click** OK, **then save your work**
   The PivotTable filters the sales data to display the fourth quarter only, as shown in FIGURE 12-10. The Quarter field list arrow changes to a filter symbol. A filter symbol also appears to the right of the Quarter field in the PivotTable Fields List pane, indicating that the PivotTable is filtered and summarizes only a portion of the PivotTable data.

FIGURE 12-8: Slicers for Product ID and Branch fields

FIGURE 12-9: PivotTable filtered by Product ID and Branch

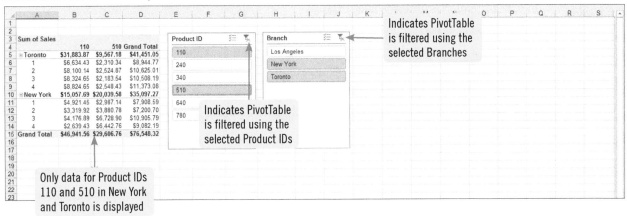

FIGURE 12-10: PivotTable filtered by fourth quarter

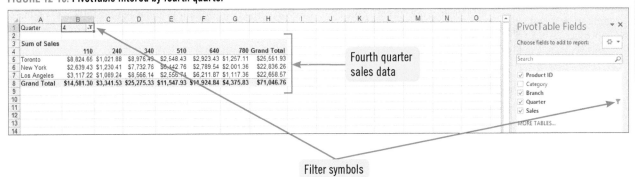

Filtering PivotTables using multiple values

You can select multiple values when filtering a PivotTable report using a report filter. After clicking a field's report filter list arrow in the top section of the PivotTable Fields List pane or in cell B1 on the PivotTable itself, click the Select Multiple Items check box at the bottom of the filter selections. This lets you select multiple values for the filter. For example, selecting 1 and 2 as the report filter in a

PivotTable with quarters would display all of the data for the first two quarters. You can also select multiple values for the row and column labels by clicking the PivotTable Tools Analyze tab, clicking the Field Headers button in the Show group, clicking the Row Labels list arrow or the Column Labels list arrow in cells A4 and B3 on the PivotTable, and selecting the data items that you want to display.

Update a PivotTable Report

The data in a PivotTable report looks like typical worksheet data. However, because the PivotTable data is linked to a **data source** (the data you used to create the PivotTable), the results it displays are read-only. That means you cannot move or modify a part of a PivotTable by inserting or deleting rows, editing results, or moving cells. To change PivotTable data, you must edit the items directly in the data source, then update, or **refresh**, the PivotTable to reflect the changes. **CASE** *Dawn just learned that sales information for a custom group experience sold in New York during the fourth quarter was never entered into the Sales worksheet. Dawn asks you to add information about this experience to the data source and PivotTable. You start by inserting a row for the new information in the North America worksheet.*

STEPS

QUICK TIP

If you want to change the PivotTable's source data range, click the PivotTable Tools Analyze tab, then click the Change Data Source button in the Data group.

1. **Click the** North America sheet tab

    By inserting the new row in the correct position by branch, you avoid having to sort the data again.

2. **Scroll to and right-click the** row 47 heading, **then click** Insert **on the shortcut menu**

    A blank row appears as the new row 47, and the data in the old row 47, moves down to row 48. You now have room for the experience data.

3. **Enter the data for the new experience in row** 47 **using the following information**

    Product ID 450

    Category Experience

    Branch New York

    Quarter 4

    Sales 3015.05

    The PivotTable does not yet reflect the additional data.

QUICK TIP

If you want Excel to refresh a PivotTable report automatically when you open a workbook, click the Options button in the PivotTable group, click the Data tab in the PivotTable Options dialog box, click the Refresh data when opening the file check box, then click OK.

4. **Click the** PivotTable sheet tab, **then verify that the** Quarter 4 **data appears**

    The PivotTable does not currently include the new experience information, and the grand total is $71,046.76. Before you refresh the PivotTable data, you need to make sure that the cell pointer is located within the PivotTable range.

5. **Click anywhere within the PivotTable if necessary, click the** PivotTable Tools Analyze tab, **then click the** Refresh button **in the Data group**

    The PivotTable now contains a column for the new product ID, which includes the new experience information, in column H, and the grand total has increased by the amount of the experience's sales ($3015.05) to $74,061.81, as shown in FIGURE 12-11.

6. **Save the workbook**

Grouping PivotTable data

You can group PivotTable data to analyze specific values in a field as a unit. For example, you may want to group sales data for quarters one and two to analyze sales for the first half of the year. To group PivotTable data, first select the rows and columns that you want to group, click the PivotTable Tools Analyze tab, then click the Group Selection button in the Group group. To summarize grouped data, click the Field Settings button in the Active Field group, click the Custom option button in the Field Settings dialog box, select the function that you want to use to summarize the data, then click OK. To collapse the group and show the function results, click the Collapse Outline button ▬ next to the group name. You can click the Expand Outline button ➕ next to the group name to display the rows or columns in the group. To ungroup data, select the Group name in the PivotTable, then click the Ungroup button in the Group group. If you add data with dates or times to a Pivot Table Time groups are automatically created that can be expanded and collapsed.

FIGURE 12-11: Updated PivotTable report

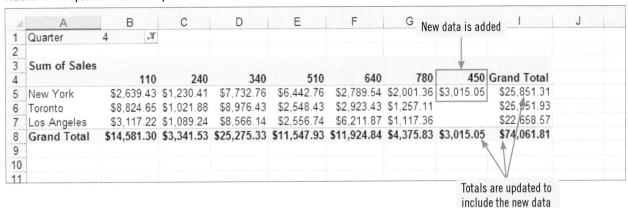

New data is added

Totals are updated to
include the new data

Adding a calculated field to a PivotTable

You can use formulas to analyze PivotTable data in a field by adding a calculated field. A calculated field appears in the Field List and can be manipulated like other PivotTable fields. To add a calculated field, click any cell in the PivotTable, click the PivotTable Tools Analyze tab, click the Fields, Items, & Sets button in the Calculations group, then click Calculated Field. The Insert Calculated Field dialog box opens. Enter the field name in the Name text box, click in the Formula text box, click a field name in the

Field list that you want to use in the formula, and click Insert Field. Use standard arithmetic operators to enter the formula you want to use. For example, FIGURE 12-12 shows a formula to increase the Sales data by 20 percent. After entering the formula in the Insert Calculated Field dialog box, click Add, then click OK. The new field with the formula results appears in the PivotTable, and the field is added to the PivotTable Fields List pane, as shown in FIGURE 12-13.

FIGURE 12-12: Insert Calculated Field dialog box

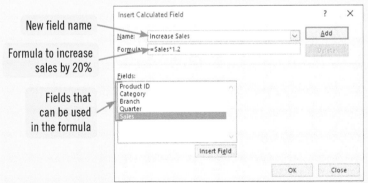

New field name

Formula to increase
sales by 20%

Fields that
can be used
in the formula

FIGURE 12-13: PivotTable with calculated field

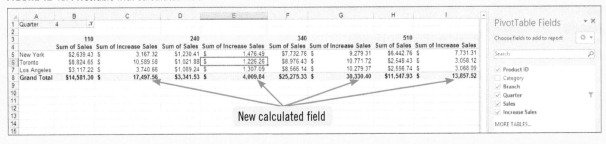

New calculated field

Explore PivotTable Data Relationships

What makes a PivotTable such a powerful analysis tool is the ability to change the way data is organized in the report. By moving fields to different positions in the report, you can explore relationships and trends that you might not see in the original report structure. **CASE** ▶ *Dawn asks you to include category information in the sales report. She is also interested in viewing the PivotTable in different arrangements to find the best organization of data for her presentation.*

STEPS

1. **Make sure that the** PivotTable sheet **is active, that the active cell is located anywhere inside the PivotTable, and that the PivotTable Fields List pane is visible**

2. **Click the** Category check box **in the Field List**
   The category data is added to the ROWS area below the corresponding branch data. As you learned earlier, you can move fields within an area of a PivotTable by dragging and dropping them to the desired location.

3. **In ROWS area of the PivotTable Fields List pane, drag the** Category field **up and drop it above the Branch field**
   As you drag, a green bar shows where the field will be inserted. The Category field is now the outer or upper field, and the Branch field is the inner or lower field. The PivotTable is restructured to display the sales data first by category and then by branch. The subtotals now reflect the sum of the categories, as shown in FIGURE 12-14. You can also move fields to different areas in the PivotTable.

4. **Drag the** Category field **from the ROWS area to anywhere in the COLUMNS area, then drag the** Product ID field **from the COLUMNS area to the ROWS area below the Branch field**
   The PivotTable now displays the sales data with the category values in the columns and then the product IDs grouped by branches in the rows. The product ID values are indented below the branches because the Product ID field is the inner row label.

5. **Drag the** Category field **from the COLUMNS area to the** FILTERS **area above the Quarter field, then drag the** Product ID field **from the ROWS area to the COLUMNS area**
   The PivotTable now has two report filters. The upper report filter, Category, summarizes data using all of the categories. Dawn asks you to display the experience sales information for all quarters.

6. **Click the** cell B1 list arrow **of the PivotTable, click** Experience, **click** OK, **click the** cell B2 list arrow, **click** All, **then click** OK
   The PivotTable displays sales totals for the Experience category for all quarters. Dawn asks you to provide the sales information for all categories.

7. **Click the** cell B1 list arrow, **click** All, **then click** OK
   The completed PivotTable appears as shown in FIGURE 12-15.

8. **Save the workbook, change the page orientation of the PivotTable sheet to** Landscape, **then preview the PivotTable**

FIGURE 12-14: PivotTable structured by branches within categories

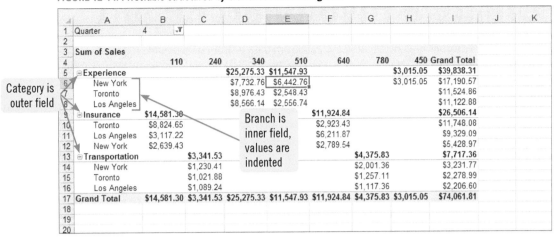

Category is outer field

Branch is inner field, values are indented

	110	240	340	510	640	780	450	Grand Total
Quarter 4								
Sum of Sales								
⊟Experience			$25,275.33	$11,547.93			$3,015.05	$39,838.31
New York			$7,732.76	$6,442.76			$3,015.05	$17,190.57
Toronto			$8,976.43	$2,548.43				$11,524.86
Los Angeles			$8,566.14	$2,556.74				$11,122.88
⊟Insurance	$14,581.30				$11,924.84			$26,506.14
Toronto	$8,824.65				$2,923.43			$11,748.08
Los Angeles	$3,117.22				$6,211.87			$9,329.09
New York	$2,639.43				$2,789.54			$5,428.97
⊟Transportation		$3,341.53				$4,375.83		$7,717.36
New York		$1,230.41				$2,001.36		$3,231.77
Toronto		$1,021.88				$1,257.11		$2,278.99
Los Angeles		$1,089.24				$1,117.36		$2,206.60
Grand Total	$14,581.30	$3,341.53	$25,275.33	$11,547.93	$11,924.84	$4,375.83	$3,015.05	$74,061.81

FIGURE 12-15: Completed PivotTable report

	110	240	340	510	640	780	450	Grand Total
Category (All)								
Quarter (All)								
Sum of Sales								
Toronto	$31,883.87	$3,237.62	$32,350.46	$9,567.18	$10,106.56	$4,008.70		$91,154.39
New York	$15,057.69	$6,534.81	$29,818.65	$20,039.58	$8,856.97	$5,056.28	$3,015.05	$88,379.03
Los Angeles	$9,014.91	$5,001.65	$32,094.00	$7,446.04	$20,034.51	$6,512.19		$80,103.30
Grand Total	$55,956.47	$14,774.08	$94,263.11	$37,052.80	$38,998.04	$15,577.17	$3,015.05	$259,636.72

Creating relationships with Power Pivot

Power Pivot is a data analysis tool included in most versions of Excel 2016. To make sure the Data Analysis add-ins are enabled, click the File tab, click Options, click Advanced, scroll to the bottom of the Advanced options, then click if necessary to add a checkmark to the Enable Data Analysis add-ins: Power Pivot, Power View, and Power Map checkbox. Power Pivot can be used to import data into Excel. For example, to use Power Pivot to import Access table data, click the Power Pivot tab on the Ribbon, click the Manage button in the Data Model group, click the Home tab in the Power Pivot for Excel window, click the Get External Data button, click From Database, click From Access, click Browse in the Table Import Wizard, navigate to the Access file, click Next, click Next again, select the table(s) for import, click Finish, then click Close after the import is completed. The imported table names are displayed at the bottom of the Power Pivot window along with the table data. You can expand the types of information you have access to by creating relationships between fields with similar data types in different data sources. This allows you to pull together columns from multiple tables in different sources into your PivotTable. To create a relationship in Power Pivot, click the Power Pivot tab if necessary, click the Manage button in the Data Model group, click the Design tab, in the Power Pivot for Excel window, click the

Create Relationship in the Relationships group, in the Create Relationship dialog box, select the Tables and Columns between which you want to create relationships, then click Create. FIGURE 12-16 shows a relationship defined between fields in the Schedule and Employee tables of an Access database. A PivotTable can be created to display information about an employee from the Employee table and the number of hours worked from the Schedule table. Note that some versions of Excel, including Office 365 Home and Office 365 Personal, do not include Power Pivot. For more information, visit the Microsoft website.

FIGURE 12-16: Relationship between the Schedule and Employee tables

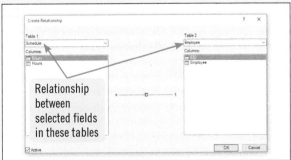

Relationship between selected fields in these tables

Create a PivotChart Report

Learning
Outcomes
• Create a PivotChart
• Format a PivotChart

A **PivotChart report** is a chart that you create from data or from a PivotTable report. TABLE 12-1 describes how the elements in a PivotTable report correspond to the elements in a PivotChart report. When you create a PivotChart directly from data, Excel automatically creates a corresponding PivotTable report. If you change a PivotChart report by filtering or sorting the charted elements, Excel updates the corresponding PivotTable report to show the new data values. You can move the fields of a PivotChart using the PivotTable Fields List window; the new layout will be reflected in the PivotTable. **CASE** *Dawn wants you to chart the fourth quarter experience sales and the yearly experience sales average for her presentation. You create the PivotChart report from the PivotTable data.*

STEPS

1. **Click the** cell B1 list arrow, **click** Experience, **click** OK, **click the** Quarter list arrow, **click** 4, **then click** OK

   The fourth quarter experience sales information appears in the PivotTable. You want to create the PivotChart from the PivotTable information you have displayed.

2. **Click any cell in the PivotTable, click the** PivotTable Tools Analyze tab, **then click the** PivotChart button **in the Tools group**

   The Insert Chart dialog box opens and shows a gallery of chart types.

3. **Click the** Clustered Column chart **if necessary, then click** OK

   The PivotChart appears on the worksheet as shown in FIGURE 12-17. The chart has Field buttons that let you filter and sort a PivotChart in the same way you do a PivotTable. It will be easier to view the PivotChart if it is on its own sheet.

QUICK TIP

You can add a chart style to a PivotChart by clicking a style In the Chart Styles group on the PivotChart Tools Design tab.

4. **Click the** PivotChart Tools Design tab, **click the** Move Chart button **in the Location group, click the** New sheet option button, **type** PivotChart **in the text box, then click** OK

   The chart represents the fourth quarter experience sales. Dawn asks you to change the chart to show the average sales for all quarters.

5. **Click the** Quarter field button **at the top of the PivotChart, click** All, **then click** OK

   The chart now represents the sum of experience sales for the year as shown in FIGURE 12-18. You can change a PivotChart's summary function to display averages instead of totals.

QUICK TIP

If you have grouped data in a PivotTable, it will be grouped in the corresponding PivotChart. You can expand and collapse a group by selecting it, clicking the PivotChart Tools Analyze tab, and then using the Expand Field and Collapse Field buttons in the Active Field group. Also, you can use the Drill Up and Drill Down buttons in that group to work with the different levels of data.

6. **Click the** Sum of Sales list arrow **in the VALUES area of the PivotTable Fields List pane, click** Value Field Settings, **click** Average **In the Value Field Settings dialog box, then click** OK

   The PivotChart report recalculates to display averages. The chart would be easier to understand if it had a title.

7. **Click the** PivotChart Tools Design tab, **click the** Add Chart Element button **in the Chart Layouts group, point to** Chart Title, **click** Above Chart, **type** Average Experience Sales, **press** [Enter], **then drag the** chart title border **to center the title over the columns**

   You are finished filtering the chart data and decide to remove the field buttons.

8. **Click the** PivotChart Tools Analyze tab, **then click the** Field Buttons button **in the Show/Hide group**

9. **Enter your name in the PivotChart sheet footer, save the workbook, then preview the PivotChart report**

   The final PivotChart report displaying the average experience sales for the year is shown in FIGURE 12-19.

FIGURE 12-17: **PivotChart with fourth quarter experience sales**

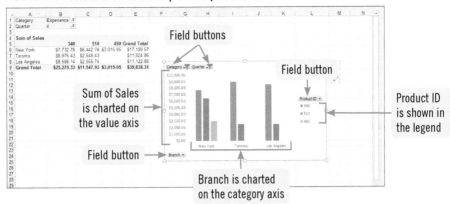

FIGURE 12-18: **PivotChart displaying experience sales for the year**

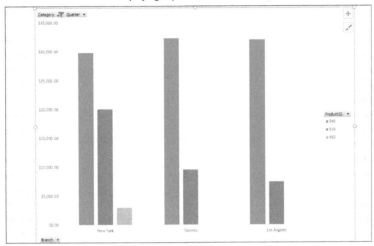

FIGURE 12-19: **Completed PivotChart report**

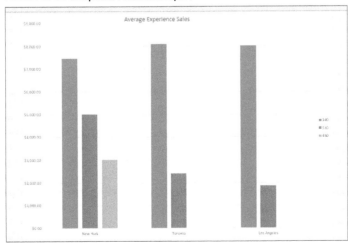

TABLE 12-1: **PivotTable and PivotChart elements**

PivotTable items	PivotChart items
Row labels	Axis fields
Column labels	Legend fields
Report filters	Report filters

Use the GETPIVOTDATA Function

Learning Outcomes
• Analyze the GETPIVOTDATA function
• Retrieve information from a PivotTable using the GETPIVOTDATA function

Because you can rearrange a PivotTable so easily, you can't use an ordinary cell reference when you want to reference a PivotTable cell in another worksheet. The reason is that if you change the way data is displayed in a PivotTable, the data moves, making an ordinary cell reference incorrect. Instead, to retrieve summary data from a PivotTable, you need to use the Excel GETPIVOTDATA function. See FIGURE 12-20 for the GETPIVOTDATA function format. **CASE** *Dawn wants to include the yearly sales total for the Los Angeles branch in the North America sheet. She asks you to retrieve this information from the PivotTable and place it in the North America sheet. You use the GETPIVOTDATA function to retrieve this information.*

STEPS

1. **Click the** PivotTable sheet tab

   The sales figures in the PivotTable are average values for experiences. You decide to show sales information for all categories and change the summary information back to Sum.

2. **Click the** Category filter arrow **in cell B1, click** All, **then click** OK

   The PivotChart report displays sales information for all categories.

3. **Right-click cell** A4 **on the PivotTable, point to** Summarize Values By **on the shortcut menu, then click** Sum

   The PivotChart report recalculates to display sales totals. Next, you want to include the total for sales for the Los Angeles branch in the North America sheet by retrieving it from the PivotTable.

4. **Click the** North America sheet tab, **click cell** G1, **type** Total Los Angeles Sales, **click the** Enter button ✓ **on the formula bar, click the** Home tab, **click the** Align Right button ≡ **in the Alignment group, click the** Bold button B **in the Font group, then adjust the width of column G to display the new label**

   You want the GETPIVOTDATA function to retrieve the total Los Angeles sales from the PivotTable. Cell I8 on the PivotTable contains the data you want to display on the North America sheet.

5. **Click cell** G2, **type** =, **click the** PivotTable sheet tab, **click cell** I8 **on the PivotTable, then click** ✓

   The GETPIVOTDATA function, along with its arguments, is inserted into cell G2 of the North America sheet as shown in FIGURE 12-21. You want to format the sales total.

6. **Click the** Accounting Number Format button $ **in the Number group**

   The current sales total for the Los Angeles branch is $80,103.30. This is the same value displayed in cell I8 of the PivotTable.

7. **Enter your name in the North America sheet footer, save the workbook, then preview the North America worksheet**

8. **Close the file, exit Excel, then submit the workbook to your instructor**

   The North America worksheet is shown in FIGURE 12-22.

FIGURE 12-20: Format of GETPIVOTDATA function

=GETPIVOTDATA("Sales",PivotTable!$A$4,"Branch","Los Angeles")
Field where data is extracted from
PivotTable name and cell in the report that contains the data you want to retrieve
Field and value pair that describe the data you want to retrieve

FIGURE 12-21: GETPIVOTDATA function in the North America sheet

G2
=GETPIVOTDATA("Sales",PivotTable!$A$4,"Branch","Los Angeles")
Sales
Product ID Category Branch Quarter Sales
Total Los Angeles Sales
80103.3
Function is entered into the formula bar and result appears in the cell

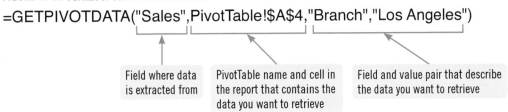

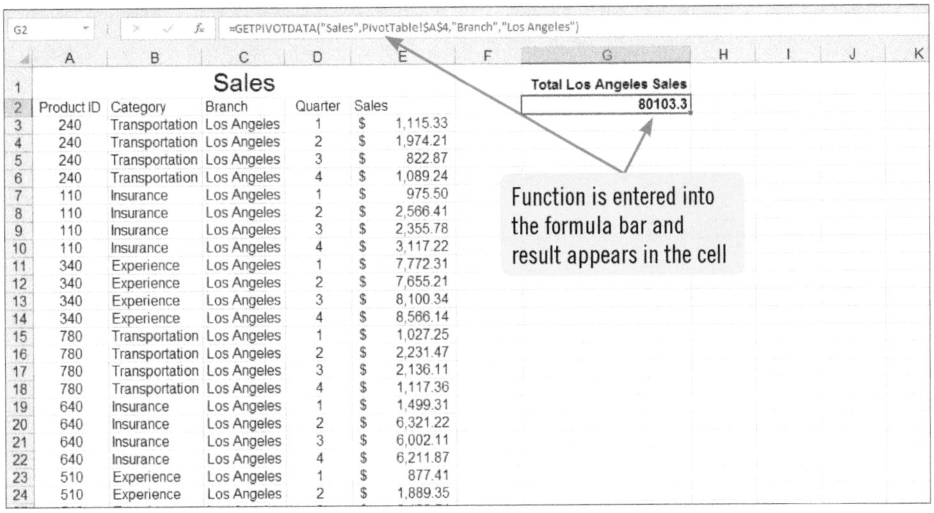

FIGURE 12-22: Completed North America worksheet showing total Los Angeles sales

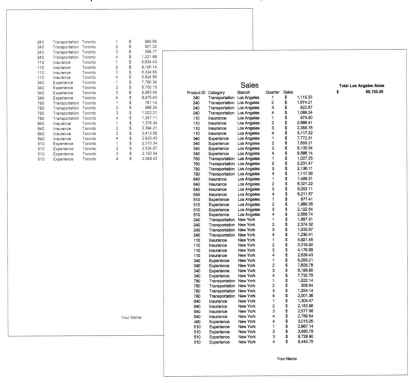

Practice

Concepts Review

FIGURE 12-23

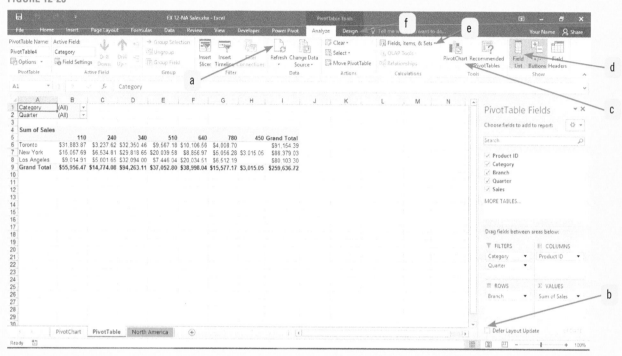

1. Which element do you click to create a chart based on the data in a PivotTable?
2. Which element do you click to create a calculated field in a PivotTable?
3. Which element do you click to control when PivotTable changes will occur?
4. Which element do you click to display a gallery of PivotTable Styles?
5. Which element do you click to update a PivotTable?
6. Which element do you click to display or hide the PivotTable Fields List pane?

Match each term with the statement that best describes it.

7. Slicer
8. PivotTable Row Label
9. Summary function
10. Compact form
11. GETPIVOTDATA function

a. Retrieves information from a PivotTable
b. Default layout for a PivotTable
c. PivotTable filtering tool
d. PivotChart axis field
e. Determines if data is summed or averaged

Select the best answer from the list of choices.

12. Which PivotTable report area allows you to display only certain data using a list arrow?
    - **a.** Values
    - **b.** Column Labels
    - **c.** Report Filter
    - **d.** Row Labels

13. When a numeric field is added to a PivotTable, it is placed in the _____ area.
    - **a.** VALUES
    - **b.** ROWS
    - **c.** COLUMNS
    - **d.** FILTERS

14. When a nonnumeric field is added to a PivotTable, it is placed in the _____ area.
    - **a.** VALUES
    - **b.** Report Filter
    - **c.** ROWS
    - **d.** COLUMNS

15. To make changes to PivotTable data, you must:
    - **a.** Drag a column header to the column area.
    - **b.** Create a page field.
    - **c.** Edit cells in the PivotTable, then refresh the source list.
    - **d.** Edit cells in the source list, then refresh the PivotTable.

Skills Review

1. **Plan and design a PivotTable report.**
   - **a.** Start Excel, open EX 12-2.xlsx from the location where you store your Data Files, then save it as **EX 12-US Sales**.
   - **b.** Review the fields and data values in the worksheet.
   - **c.** Verify that the worksheet data contains repeated values in one or more fields.
   - **d.** Verify that there are not any blank rows or columns in the range A1:E25.
   - **e.** Verify that the worksheet data contains a field that can be summed in a PivotTable.

2. **Create a PivotTable report.**
   - **a.** Create a blank PivotTable report on a new worksheet using the January Sales worksheet data in the range A1:E25.
   - **b.** Add the UPC field in the PivotTable Fields List pane to the COLUMNS area.
   - **c.** Add the Sales field in the PivotTable Fields List pane to the VALUES area.
   - **d.** Add the Store field in the PivotTable Fields List pane to the ROWS area.
   - **e.** Add the Sales Rep field in the PivotTable Fields List pane to the ROWS area below the Store field.

3. **Change a PivotTable's summary function and design.**
   - **a.** Change the PivotTable summary function to Average.
   - **b.** Rename the new sheet **Jan Sales PT**.
   - **c.** Change the PivotTable Style to Pivot Style Light 18. Format the sales values in the PivotTable as Currency with a $ symbol and two decimal places.
   - **d.** Enter your name in the center section of the PivotTable report footer, then save the workbook.
   - **e.** Change the Summary function back to Sum. Remove the headers "Row Labels" and "Column Labels."

4. **Filter and sort PivotTable data.**
   - **a.** Sort the stores in ascending order by total sales.
   - **b.** Use slicers to filter the PivotTable to display sales for the UPC 101548792461 in the Atlanta and Miami stores.
   - **c.** Clear the filters and delete the slicers.
   - **d.** Add the Region field to the FILTERS area in the PivotTable Fields List pane. Use the FILTERS list arrow to display sales for only the East region. Display sales for all regions.
   - **e.** Save the workbook.

5. **Update a PivotTable report.**
   - **a.** With the Jan Sales PT sheet active, note the Seattle total for UPC 101548792461.
   - **b.** Activate the January Sales sheet, and change L. Bartlet's sales of UPC 101548792461 in cell D8 to **$2,000**.
   - **c.** Refresh the PivotTable so it reflects the new sales figure.
   - **d.** Verify the Seattle total for UPC 101548792461 increased to $2,699. Save the workbook.

Skills Review (continued)

6. **Explore PivotTable Data Relationships.**

   a. In the PivotTable Fields List pane, drag the UPC field from the COLUMNS area to the ROWS area below the Sales Rep field. Drag the Sales Rep field from the ROWS area to the COLUMNS area.

   b. Drag the Store field from the ROWS area to the FILTERS area below the Region field. Drag the UPC field back to the COLUMNS area.

   c. Drag the Store field back to the ROWS area.

   d. Remove the Sales Rep field from the PivotTable.

   e. Compare your completed PivotTable to FIGURE 12-24, save the workbook.

7. **Create a PivotChart report.**

   a. Use the existing PivotTable data to create a Clustered Column PivotChart report.

   b. Move the PivotChart to a new worksheet, and name the sheet **PivotChart**.

   c. Add the title **Total Sales** above the chart.

   d. Filter the chart to display only sales data for the east region. Display the sales data for all regions. Hide all of the Field Buttons.

   e. Add your name to the center section of the PivotChart sheet footer. Compare your PivotChart with FIGURE 12-25, and save the workbook.

8. **Use the GETPIVOTDATA function.**

   a. In cell D27 of the January Sales sheet type =, click the Jan Sales PT sheet, click the cell that contains the grand total for Miami, then press [Enter].

   b. Review the GETPIVOTDATA function that was entered in cell D27.

   c. Enter your name in the January Sales sheet footer, compare your January Sales sheet to FIGURE 12-26, save the workbook, then preview the January Sales worksheet.

   d. Close the workbook and exit Excel. Submit the workbook to your instructor.

Independent Challenge 1

You are the accountant for the Service Department of an electrical services company. The Service Department employs three technicians that service business and residential accounts. Until recently, the owner had been tracking the technicians' hours manually in a log. You have created an Excel worksheet to track the following basic information: service date, technician name, job #, job category, hours, and billing information. The owner has asked you to analyze the data to provide information about the number of hours being spent on the various job categories. He also wants to find out how much of the technicians' work is on residential or business sites. You will create a PivotTable that sums the hours by category and technician. Once the table is completed, you will create a column chart representing the billing information.

   a. Start Excel, open EX 12-3.xlsx from the location where you store your Data Files, then save it as **EX 12-Service**.

   b. Create a PivotTable on a separate worksheet that sums hours by technician and category. Use FIGURE 12-27 as a guide.

   c. Name the new sheet **PivotTable**, and apply the Pivot Style Light 20.

   d. Add slicers to filter the PivotTable using the category and technician data. Display only service data for Ryan's category Level 1 jobs. Remove the filters, and remove the slicers.

FIGURE 12-24

FIGURE 12-25

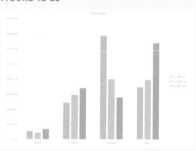

FIGURE 12-26

FIGURE 12-27

Independent Challenge 1 (continued)

e. Add the Billing field to the FILTERS area of the PivotTable. Display only the PivotTable data for residential jobs.

f. Remove the headers of "Column Labels" and "Row Labels" from the PivotTable.

g. Create a clustered column PivotChart that shows the residential hours. Move the PivotChart to a new sheet named **PivotChart**.

h. Add the title **Residential Hours** above the chart.

i. Change the PivotChart filter to display hours for business sites. Edit the chart title to read **Business Hours**.

j. Hide the field buttons on the chart.

k. Add your name to the center section of the PivotTable and PivotChart footers, then save the workbook. Preview the PivotTable and the PivotChart. Close the workbook and exit Excel. Submit the workbook to your instructor.

Independent Challenge 2

You are the director of marketing for a fitness equipment company. The company sells new and used equipment as well as multi-year leases at stores as well as online. You also take orders by phone from your catalog customers. You have been using Excel to maintain a sales summary for the second quarter sales of the different categories of products sold by the company. You want to create a PivotTable to analyze and graph the sales in each product category by month and type of order.

a. Start Excel, open EX 12-4.xlsx from the location where you store your Data Files, then save it as **EX 12-Fitness Equipment**.

b. Create a PivotTable on a new worksheet named **PivotTable** that sums the sales amount for each category across the rows and each type of sale down the columns. Add the month field as an inner row label. Use FIGURE 12-28 as a guide.

c. Move the month field to the FILTERS area. Display the sum of sales data for the month of April.

FIGURE 12-28

d. Turn off the grand totals for the columns. (*Hint*: Use the Grand Totals button in the Layout group on the PivotTable Tools Design tab and choose On for Rows Only.)

e. Change the summary function in the PivotTable to Average.

f. Format the sales values using the Currency format with two decimal places and the $ symbol. Widen the columns as necessary to display the sales data.

g. On the Sales worksheet, change the April online used sales in cell D3 to $32,000. Update the PivotTable to reflect this increase in sales.

h. Sort the average sales of categories from smallest to largest using the grand total of sales.

i. Create a stacked column PivotChart report for the average April sales data for all three types of sales.

j. Change the PivotChart to display the June sales data.

k. Move the PivotChart to a new sheet, and name the chart sheet **PivotChart**.

l. Add the title **Average June Sales** above your chart.

m. On the PivotTable, move the Month field from the FILTERS area to the ROWS area of the PivotTable below the Category field.

n. Add a slicer to filter the PivotTable by month. Use the slicer to display the average sales in May and June.

o. Check the PivotChart to be sure that the filtered data is displayed.

p. Change the chart title to **Average Sales May and June** to describe the charted sales.

q. Add your name to the center section of the PivotTable and PivotChart worksheet footers, save the workbook, then preview the PivotTable and the PivotChart. Close the workbook and exit Excel. Submit the workbook to your instructor.

Excel 2016

Independent Challenge 3

You are the North American sales manager for a medical equipment company with sales offices in the United States and Canada. You use Excel to keep track of the staff in the U.S. and Canadian offices. Management asks you to provide a summary table showing information on your sales staff, including their locations, status, and titles. You will create a PivotTable and PivotChart summarizing this information.

a. Start Excel, open EX 12-5.xlsx from the location where you store your Data Files, then save it as **EX 12-Sales Employees**.

b. Create a PivotTable on a new worksheet that shows the number of employees in each city, with the names of the cities listed across the columns, the titles listed down the rows, and the status indented below the titles. (*Hint*: Remember that the default summary function for cells containing text is Count.) Use FIGURE 12-29 as a guide. Rename the new sheet **PivotTable**.

FIGURE 12-29

3	Count of Last Name	Column Labels								
4	Row Labels	Boston	Los Angeles	Miami	Montreal	San Francisco	St. Louis	Toronto	Vancouver	Grand Total
5	⊟ Sales Manager	1	1	2	3	3	2	3	1	16
6	Junior	1				1	1	1		4
7	Senior		1	2	3	2	1	2	1	12
8	⊟ Sales Representative	4	5	7	6	7	2	3	3	37
9	Junior	1	1	2	2	2	1	1	1	11
10	Senior	3	4	5	4	5	1	2	2	26
11	Grand Total	5	6	9	9	10	4	6	4	53
12										
13										

c. Change the structure of the PivotTable to display the data as shown in FIGURE 12-30.

d. Add a report filter using the Region field. Display only the U.S. employees.

e. Create a clustered column PivotChart from the PivotTable and move the chart to its own sheet named PivotChart. Rearrange the fields to create the PivotChart shown in FIGURE 12-31.

f. Add the title **U.S. Sales Staff** above the chart.

g. Add the Pivot Style Light 12 style to the PivotTable.

h. Insert a new row in the Employees worksheet above row 7. In the new row, add information reflecting the recent hiring of Cathy Olsen, a senior sales manager at the Boston office. Update the PivotTable to display the new employee information.

i. Add the label **Total Miami Staff** in cell G1 of the Employees sheet. Widen column G to fit the label.

j. Enter a function in cell H1 that retrieves the total number of employees located in Miami from the PivotTable. Change the page orientation of the Employees sheet to landscape.

k. Use a slicer to filter the PivotTable to display only the data for the cities of Boston, Miami, and Los Angeles.

l. Add another slicer for the Status field to display only the senior staff members.

m. Verify that the number of Miami staff in cell H1 of the Employees sheet is now 7.

FIGURE 12-30

3	Count of Last Name	Column Labels		
4	Row Labels	Junior	Senior	Grand Total
5	⊟ Sales Manager	4	12	16
6	Boston	1		1
7	Los Angeles		1	1
8	Miami		2	2
9	Montreal		3	3
10	San Francisco	1	2	3
11	St. Louis	1	1	2
12	Toronto	1	2	3
13	Vancouver		1	1
14	⊟ Sales Representative	11	26	37
15	Boston	1	3	4
16	Los Angeles	1	4	5
17	Miami	2	5	7
18	Montreal	2	4	6
19	San Francisco	2	5	7
20	St. Louis	1	1	2
21	Toronto	1	2	3
22	Vancouver	1	2	3
23	Grand Total	15	38	53
24				
25				

FIGURE 12-31

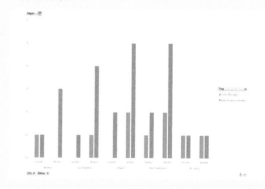

Independent Challenge 3 (continued)

n. Remove the slicers, but do not remove the filters.

o. Add your name to the center section of all three worksheet footers, save the workbook, then preview the PivotTable, the first page of the Employees worksheet, and the PivotChart.

p. Close the workbook and exit Excel. Submit the workbook to your instructor.

Independent Challenge 4: Explore

You are the Regional sales manager for a Massachusetts plumbing supplies company with offices in Boston, Worcester, and Springfield. You use Excel to keep track of the revenue generated by sales contracts in these offices. The CEO asks you to provide a summary table showing information on your offices' revenue over the past two years.

a. Start Excel, open EX 12-6.xlsx, then save it as **EX 12-Plumbing Revenue** in the location where you save your Data Files.

b. Create a PivotTable on a separate worksheet that sums revenue by office, year, and month. Use FIGURE 12-32 as a guide.

c. Name the new sheet **Summary**, and apply the Pivot Style Light 19.

d. Add slicers to filter the PivotTable using the Quarter and Office fields. Display only revenue data for Boston and Worcester for quarters 3 and 4. Remove the filters, but do not remove the slicers.

e. Format the Office slicer using the Slicer Style Light 5 in the Slicer Styles gallery on the Slicer Tools Options tab.

f. Change the Office slicer caption from Office to **Sales Office**. (*Hint*: Use the Slicer Caption text box in the Slicer group of the Slicer Tools Options tab.)

g. Change the Quarter slicer buttons to appear in two columns, with a button height of .3" and a button width of .56". (*Hint*: Use the options in the Buttons group of the Slicer Tools Options tab.)

h. Change the Quarter slicer shape to a height of 1.2" and width of 1.33". (*Hint*: Use the options in the Size group of the Slicer Tools Options tab.) Shorten the Sales Office slicer shape by dragging the lower slicer edge up to just below the bottom button.

i. Add a calculated field named **Average Sale** to the PivotTable to calculate the average sale using the formula =Revenue/Number of Contracts. Change the labels in cells C5, E5, and G5 to **Average** and format all of the Average labels as right justified.

j. Add the Quarter field to the PivotTable as a Report Filter.

k. Copy each quarter's data to a separate sheet. (*Hint*: Select the Quarter field in cell A1, click the Options list arrow in the PivotTable group of the PivotTable Tools Analyze tab, then select Show Report Filter Pages.) View the sheet for each quarter.

l. Remove the field headers, Group all of the worksheets, add your name to the center section of the footer for the worksheets, save the workbook, then preview the worksheets.

m. Close the workbook and exit Excel. Submit the workbook to your instructor.

FIGURE 12-32

Visual Workshop

Open EX 12-7.xlsx from the location where you store your Data Files, then save it as **EX 12-Quarterly Sales**. Using the data in the workbook, create the PivotTable shown in FIGURE 12-33 on a worksheet named PivotTable, then generate a PivotChart on a new sheet named PivotChart as shown in FIGURE 12-34. (*Hint*: The PivotTable has been formatted using the Pivot Style Light 19. Note that the PivotChart has been filtered. The filtered data will be reflected in your PivotTable, which will no longer match FIGURE 12-33.) Add your name to the PivotTable and the PivotChart footers, then preview the PivotTable and the PivotChart. Save the workbook, close the workbook, exit Excel, then submit the workbook to your instructor.

FIGURE 12-33

◢	A	B	C	D	E	F	G
1							
2							
3	**Sum of Sales**						
4		**1**	**2**	**3**	**4**	**Grand Total**	
5	⊟Commercial	80774626	81505385	123475318	33314800	319070129	
6	Dallas	4715847	9489557	81027452	3250500	98483356	
7	LA	40015554	16505384	3942221	10018800	70481959	
8	NY	36043225	55510444	38505645	20045500	150104814	
9	⊟Residential	75533481	80665842	177575141	126661103	460435567	
10	Dallas	37515814	45048442	81020776	70504845	234089877	
11	LA	8015222	6605700	18045854	41025800	73692576	
12	NY	30002445	29011700	78508511	15130458	152653114	
13	**Grand Total**	156308107	162171227	301050459	159975903	779505696	
14							

FIGURE 12-34

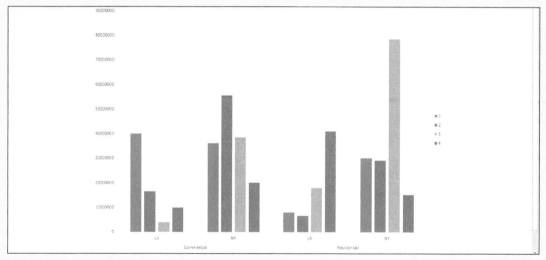

Exchanging Data with Other Programs

CASE Reason2Go's upper management has asked Mary Watson, the vice president of sales and marketing, to research the possible purchase of Service Adventures, a small company specializing in combining travel with volunteer work for corporate employees. Mary is reviewing the organization's files and developing a presentation on the feasibility of acquiring the company. She asks you to help set up the data exchange between Excel and other programs.

Module Objectives

After completing this module, you will be able to:

- Plan a data exchange
- Import a text file
- Import a database table
- Insert a graphic file in a worksheet
- Embed a workbook in a Word document
- Link a workbook to a Word document
- Link an Excel chart to a PowerPoint slide
- Import a table into Access

Files You Will Need

EX 13-1.txt	EX 13-12.xlsx
EX 13-2.accdb	EX 13-13.pptx
EX 13-3.jpg	EX 13-14.xlsx
EX 13-4.docx	EX 13-15.xlsx
EX 13-5.xlsx	EX 13-16.pptx
EX 13-6.pptx	EX 13-17.txt
EX 13-7.xlsx	EX 13-18.docx
EX 13-8.xlsx	EX 13-19.xlsx
EX 13-9.txt	EX 13-20.docx
EX 13-10.accdb	EX 13-21.xlsx
EX 13-11.jpg	EX 13-22.accdb

Plan a Data Exchange

Learning
Outcomes
• Plan a data
exchange between
Office programs
• Develop an
understanding of
data exchange
vocabulary

Because the tools available in Microsoft Office apps are designed to be compatible, exchanging data between Excel and other programs is easy. The first step involves planning what you want to accomplish with each data exchange. **CASE** *Mary asks you to use the following guidelines to plan data exchanges between Excel and other apps in order to complete the business analysis project.*

DETAILS

To plan an exchange of data:

- **Identify the data you want to exchange, its file type, and, if possible, the app used to create it**

  Whether the data you want to exchange is a graphics file, a database file, a worksheet, or consists only of text, it is important to identify the data's **source program** (the app used to create it) and file type. Once you identify the source program, you can determine options for exchanging the data with Excel. Mary needs to analyze a text file containing the Service Adventures sales data. Although she does not know the source program, Mary knows that the file contains unformatted text. A file that consists of text but no formatting is sometimes called an **ASCII** or **text** file. Because ASCII is a universally accepted file format, you can easily import an ASCII file into Excel. See TABLE 13-1 for a partial list of other file formats that Excel can import.

- **Determine the app with which you want to exchange data**

  Besides knowing which program created the data you want to exchange, you must also identify which app will receive the data, called the **destination program**. This determines the procedure you use to perform the exchange. You might want to insert a graphic object into an Excel worksheet or add a spreadsheet to a Word document. Mary received a database table of Service Adventures' corporate customers created with the Access database app. After determining that Excel can import Access tables and reviewing the import procedure, you will import the database file into Excel so Mary can analyze it using Excel tools.

- **Determine the goal of your data exchange**

  Windows offers two ways to transfer data within and between apps that allow you to retain some connection with the source program. These data transfer methods use a Windows feature known as **object linking and embedding**, or **OLE**. The data to be exchanged, called an **object**, may consist of text, a worksheet, or any other type of data. You use **embedding** to insert a copy of the original object into the destination document and, if necessary, to then edit this data separately from the source document. This process is illustrated in FIGURE 13-1. You use **linking** when you want the information you inserted to be updated automatically if the data in the source document changes. This process is illustrated in FIGURE 13-2. You learn more about embedding and linking later in this module. Mary and you have determined that you need to use both object embedding and object linking for the analysis and presentation project.

- **Set up the data exchange**

  When you exchange data between two programs, it is often best to start both apps before starting the exchange. You might also want to tile the program windows on the screen either horizontally or vertically so that you can see both during the exchange. You will work with Excel, Word, Access, and PowerPoint when exchanging data for this project.

- **Execute the data exchange**

  The steps you use will vary, depending on the type of data you want to exchange. You are ready to start the data exchanges for the business analysis of Service Adventures.

FIGURE 13-1: Embedded object

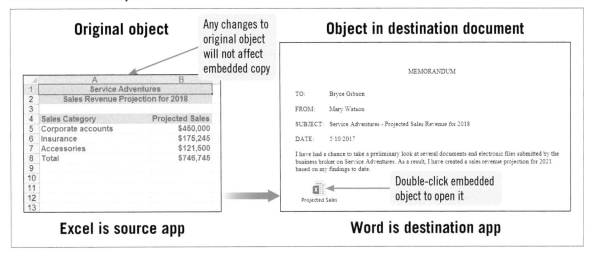

FIGURE 13-2: Linked object

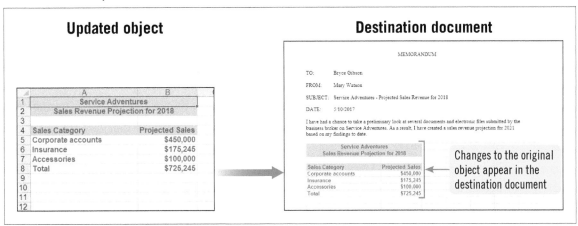

TABLE 13-1: File formats Excel can import

file format	file extension(s)	file format	file extension(s)
Access	.mdb, .accdb	All Data Sources	.odc, .udl, .dsn
Text	.txt, .prn, .csv, .dif, .sylk	OpenDocument Spreadsheet	.ods
Query	.iqy, .dqy, .oqy, .rqy	XML	.xml
Web page	.htm, .html, .mht, .mhtml	dBASE	.dbf

Import a Text File

Learning Outcomes
• Import a text file into an Excel workbook
• Format text data

You can import text data into Excel and save the imported data in Excel format. Text files use a tab or space as the **delimiter**, or column separator, to separate columns of data. When you import a text file into Excel, the Text Import Wizard automatically opens and describes how text is separated in the imported file. **CASE** ▶ *Now that you have planned the data exchange, you are ready to import a tab-delimited text file containing branch and profit data from Service Adventures.*

STEPS

1. **Start Excel, open a new blank workbook, click the** Data tab, **click** From Text **in the Get External Data group, then navigate to where you store your Data Files**

   The Import Text File dialog box shows only text files.

QUICK TIP
The data in the text file was separated, or delimited, by tabs, which is the default setting in the Text Import Wizard.

2. **Click** EX 13-1.txt, **then click** Import

   Step 1 of the Text Import Wizard dialog box opens, as shown in FIGURE 13-3. Under Original data type, the Delimited option button is selected. In the Preview of file box, line 1 indicates that the file contains two columns of data: Branch and Profit. No changes are necessary in this dialog box.

3. **Click** Next

   Step 2 of the Text Import Wizard dialog box opens. Under Delimiters, Tab is selected as the delimiter, indicating that tabs separate the columns of incoming data. The Data preview box contains a line showing where the tab delimiters divide the data into columns.

4. **Click** Next

   Step 3 of the Text Import Wizard dialog box opens, with options for formatting the two columns of data. Under Column data format, the General option button is selected. The Data preview area shows that both columns will be formatted with the General format. This is the best formatting option for text mixed with numbers.

5. **Click** Finish, **then click** OK **to put the data into cell** $A$1 **of the existing worksheet**

   Excel imports the text file into the blank workbook starting in cell A1 of the worksheet as two columns of data: Branch and Profit.

6. **Click the** File tab, **click** Save, **navigate to where you store your Data Files, change the filename to** EX 13-Branch Profit, **then click** Save

   The information is saved as an Excel workbook. It would be easier to read if it were formatted and if it showed the total profit for all branches.

7. **Click cell** A8, **type** Total Profit, **click cell** B8, **click the** Home tab, **click the** AutoSum **button in the Editing group, then click the** Enter button ✓ **on the formula bar**

8. **Rename the sheet tab** Profit, **center the column labels, apply bold formatting to them, format the data in column** B **using the Currency style with the $ symbol and no decimal places, then click cell** A1

   FIGURE 13-4 shows the completed worksheet, which analyzes the text file data you imported into Excel.

9. **Add your name to the** center section **of the worksheet footer, save the workbook, preview the worksheet, close the workbook, then submit the workbook to your instructor**

FIGURE 13-3: First Text Import Wizard dialog box

Original data is delimited

Two column headings

Preview of data

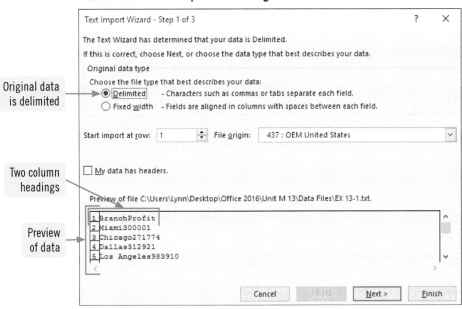

FIGURE 13-4: Completed worksheet with imported text file

Total profit added after importing data

Columns from text file

Importing text files using other methods

Another way to open the Text Import Wizard to import a text file into Excel is to click the File tab, click Open, then navigate to the location where you store your Data Files. In the Open dialog box you will see only files that match the file types listed in the Files of type box—usually Microsoft Excel files. To import a text file, you need to change the file type: click All Excel Files (or the list arrow on the box to the right of the File name text box), click Text Files (*.prn; *.txt; *.csv), click the text file name, then click Open; the Text Import Wizard opens so you can complete the import. You can also drag the icon representing a text file on the Windows desktop into a blank worksheet window. Excel will create a worksheet from the data without opening the wizard.

Import a Database Table

Learning Outcomes
- Import Access data into an Excel workbook
- Format imported data

In addition to text files, you can also import data from database tables into Excel. A **database table** is a set of data organized using columns and rows that is created in a database program. A **database program** is an application, such as Microsoft Access, that lets you manage large amounts of data organized in tables. FIGURE 13-5 shows a table in Access. To import data from an Access table into Excel, you can copy the table in Access and paste it into an Excel worksheet. This method places a copy of the Access data into Excel; if you change the data in the Access file, the data will not change in the Excel copy. If you want the data in Excel to update when you edit the Access source file, you create a connection, or a **link**, to the database. This lets you work with current data in Excel without recopying the data from Access whenever the Access data changes. **CASE** ▶ *Mary received a database table containing Service Adventures' corporate customer information, which was created with Access. She asks you to import this table into an Excel workbook. She would also like you to format, sort, and total the data.*

STEPS

1. **Click the** File Tab, **click** New, **then click** Blank workbook

   A new workbook opens, displaying a blank worksheet for you to use to import the Access data.

2. **Click the** Data tab, **click the** From Access button **in the Get External Data group, then navigate to where you store your Data Files**

3. **Click** EX 13-2.accdb, **then click** Open

   The Import Data dialog box opens, so that you can select how you want the data to be used, and where you want to place it.

QUICK TIP

You can import data as a PivotTable Report or PivotChart using those option buttons in this dialog box. If the imported data is part of a larger data set in your workbook, you can place the imported data on a new worksheet or in a specified location on a worksheet.

4. **Verify that the** Table option button **and the** Existing worksheet button **are selected in the Import Data dialog box, then click** OK

   Excel inserts the Access data into the worksheet as a table with the default Table Style Medium 2 format applied, as shown in FIGURE 13-6.

5. **Rename the sheet tab** Customer Information, **then format the data in columns** F **and** G **with the Currency format with the $ symbol and no decimal places**

   You are ready to sort the data using the values in column G.

6. **Click any cell in the table if necessary, click the cell** G1 **list arrow, then click** Sort Smallest to Largest

   The records are reorganized in ascending order according to the amount of the 2017 sales.

7. **Click the** Table Tools Design tab **if necessary, click the** Total Row check box **in the Table Style Options group to select it, click cell** F19, **click the cell** F19 **list arrow, click** Sum **in the drop-down function list, then click cell** A1

   Your completed worksheet should match FIGURE 13-7.

8. **Add your name to the center section of the worksheet footer, change the worksheet orientation to** Landscape, **save the workbook as** EX 13-Customer Information, **then preview the worksheet**

FIGURE 13-5: Access Table

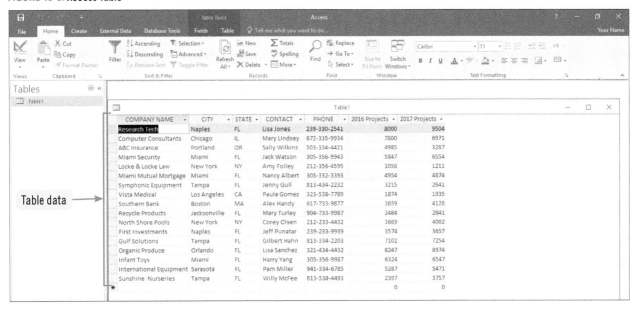

Table data →

FIGURE 13-6: Access table imported to Excel

COMPANY NAME	CITY	STATE	CONTACT	PHONE	2016 Projects	2017 Projects
Research Tech	Naples	FL	Lisa Jones	239-330-2541	8000	9504
Computer Consultants	Chicago	IL	Mary Lindsey	872-335-9934	7800	6971
ABC Insurance	Portland	OR	Sally Wilkins	503-334-4421	4985	3287
Miami Security	Miami	FL	Jack Watson	305-356-9943	5847	6554
Locke & Locke Law	New York	NY	Amy Folley	212-356-4595	1058	1211
Miami Mutual Mortgage	Miami	FL	Nancy Albert	305-332-3393	4954	4874
Symphonic Equipment	Tampa	FL	Jenny Gull	813-434-2232	3215	2641
Vista Medical	Los Angeles	CA	Paula Gomez	323-538-7789	1874	1935
Southern Bank	Boston	MA	Alex Handy	617-733-9877	3659	4128
Recycle Products	Jacksonville	FL	Mary Turley	904-733-9987	2484	2841
North Shore Pools	New York	NY	Corey Olsen	212-233-4432	3669	4002
First Investments	Naples	FL	Jeff Punatar	239-233-9939	3574	3657
Gulf Solutions	Tampa	FL	Gilbert Hahn	813-334-2203	7102	7254
Organic Produce	Orlando	FL	Lisa Sanchez	321-434-4432	8247	8974
Infant Toys	Miami	FL	Harry Yang	305-356-9987	6324	6547
International Equipment	Sarasota	FL	Pam Miller	941-334-6785	5287	5471
Sunshine Nurseries	Tampa	FL	Willy McFee	813-538-4493	2397	3757

FIGURE 13-7: Completed worksheet containing imported data

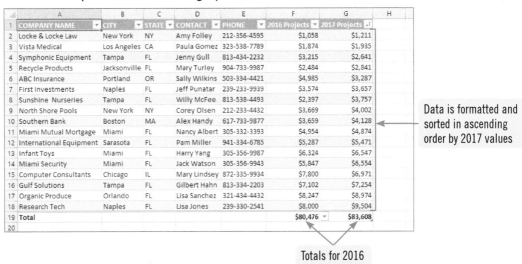

COMPANY NAME	CITY	STATE	CONTACT	PHONE	2016 Projects	2017 Projects
Locke & Locke Law	New York	NY	Amy Folley	212-356-4595	$1,058	$1,211
Vista Medical	Los Angeles	CA	Paula Gomez	323-538-7789	$1,874	$1,935
Symphonic Equipment	Tampa	FL	Jenny Gull	813-434-2232	$3,215	$2,641
Recycle Products	Jacksonville	FL	Mary Turley	904-733-9987	$2,484	$2,841
ABC Insurance	Portland	OR	Sally Wilkins	503-334-4421	$4,985	$3,287
First Investments	Naples	FL	Jeff Punatar	239-233-9939	$3,574	$3,657
Sunshine Nurseries	Tampa	FL	Willy McFee	813-538-4493	$2,397	$3,757
North Shore Pools	New York	NY	Corey Olsen	212-233-4432	$3,669	$4,002
Southern Bank	Boston	MA	Alex Handy	617-733-9877	$3,659	$4,128
Miami Mutual Mortgage	Miami	FL	Nancy Albert	305-332-3393	$4,954	$4,874
International Equipment	Sarasota	FL	Pam Miller	941-334-6785	$5,287	$5,471
Infant Toys	Miami	FL	Harry Yang	305-356-9987	$6,324	$6,547
Miami Security	Miami	FL	Jack Watson	305-356-9943	$5,847	$6,554
Computer Consultants	Chicago	IL	Mary Lindsey	872-335-9934	$7,800	$6,971
Gulf Solutions	Tampa	FL	Gilbert Hahn	813-334-2203	$7,102	$7,254
Organic Produce	Orlando	FL	Lisa Sanchez	321-434-4432	$8,247	$8,974
Research Tech	Naples	FL	Lisa Jones	239-330-2541	$8,000	$9,504
Total					$80,476	$83,608

Data is formatted and sorted in ascending order by 2017 values →

Totals for 2016 and 2017 sales

Insert a Graphic File in a Worksheet

Learning
Outcomes
• Insert an image into an Excel worksheet
• Add a style to an image

A graphic object, such as a drawing, logo, or photograph, can greatly enhance your worksheet's visual impact. You can insert a graphic image into a worksheet and then format it using the options on the Format tab. **CASE** ▸ *Mary wants you to insert the R2G logo at the top of the customer worksheet. The company's graphic designer created the image and saved it in JPG (commonly pronounced "jay-peg") format. You insert and format the image on the worksheet. You start by creating a space for the logo on the worksheet.*

STEPS

1. **Select rows 1 through 5, click the Home tab, then click the Insert button in the Cells group**
   Five blank rows appear above the header row, leaving space to insert the picture.

2. **Click cell A1, click the Insert tab, then click the Pictures button in the Illustrations group**
   The Insert Picture dialog box opens. Because you specified that you want to insert a picture, the dialog box displays only files that contain graphics file extensions, just as .jpg.

3. **Navigate to where you store your Data Files if necessary, click EX 13-3.jpg, then click Insert**
   Excel inserts the image and displays the Picture Tools Format tab. The small circles around the picture's border are sizing handles. Sizing handles appear when a picture is selected; you use them to change the size of a picture.

4. **Position the pointer over the sizing handle in the logo's lower-right corner until the pointer becomes ⤡, then drag the sizing handle up and to the left so that the logo's outline fits within rows 1 through 5**
   Compare your screen to FIGURE 13-8. You decide the logo will be more visually interesting with a frame and a border color.

5. **With the image selected, click the More button ⤓ in the Picture Styles group, point to several styles and observe the effect on the graphic, click the Bevel Rectangle style (the last in the third row), click the Picture Border list arrow in the Picture Styles group, then click Blue, Accent 1, Lighter 40% in the Theme Colors group**
   You decide to add a glow to the image.

6. **Click the Picture Effects button in the Picture Styles group, point to Glow, point to More Glow Colors, click Blue, Accent 1, Lighter 80% in the Theme Colors group, resize the logo again to fit it in rows 1 through 5, then drag it above column D**
   Compare your worksheet to FIGURE 13-9.

7. **Save the workbook, preview the worksheet, close the workbook, exit Excel, then submit the workbook to your instructor**

FIGURE 13-8: **Resized logo**

In Step 4, drag this sizing handle

FIGURE 13-9: **Worksheet with formatted picture**

Formatted image

Formatting SmartArt graphics

SmartArt graphics provide another way to visually communicate information on a worksheet. Each SmartArt type communicates a kind of information or relationship, such as a list, process, or hierarchy. Each type has various layouts you can choose. To insert a SmartArt graphic into a worksheet, click the Insert tab, then click the Insert a SmartArt Graphic button in the Illustrations group. In the Choose a SmartArt Graphic dialog box, choose from eight SmartArt types: List, Process, Cycle, Hierarchy, Relationship, Matrix, Pyramid, and Picture. There is also a link for SmartArt available on Office.com. The dialog box describes the type of information that is appropriate for each selected layout. After you choose a layout and click OK, a SmartArt object appears on your worksheet. As you enter text in the text entry areas, the font automatically resizes to fit the graphic. The SmartArt Tools Design tab lets you choose color schemes and styles for your SmartArt. You can add shape styles, fills, outlines and other shape effects to SmartArt graphics using choices on the SmartArt Tools

Format tab. You can also add fills, outlines and other effects to text using this tab. FIGURE 13-10 shows examples of SmartArt graphics. You can create a SmartArt graphic from an existing image by clicking the image, clicking the Picture Layout button in the Picture Styles group of the Picture Tools Format tab, then selecting the SmartArt type.

FIGURE 13-10: **Examples of SmartArt graphics**

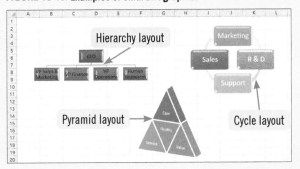

Embed a Workbook in a Word Document

Learning Outcomes
- Embed Excel data in a Word document
- Edit an embedded file icon caption

Microsoft Office programs work together to make it easy to copy an object (such as text, data, or a graphic) in a source program and then insert it into a document in a different program (the destination program). If you insert copied Excel data using a simple Paste command, however, you retain no connection to the source program. That's why it is often more useful to embed objects rather than simply paste them. Embedding allows you to edit an Excel workbook from within the source program using that program's commands and tools. If you send a Word document with an embedded workbook to another person, you do not need to send a separate Excel file with it. All the necessary information is embedded in the Word document. When you embed information, you can either display the data itself or an icon representing the data; users double-click the icon to view the embedded data. An icon is often used rather than the data when the worksheet data is too large to fit well on a Word document. **CASE** *Mary wants to update Bryce Gibson, the CEO of Reason2Go, on the project status. She asks you to prepare a Word memo that includes the projected sales workbook embedded as an icon. You begin by starting Word and opening the memo.*

STEPS

1. **Open a File Explorer window, navigate to the location where you store your Data Files, then double-click EX 13-4.docx to open the file in Word**

   The memo opens in Word.

2. **Click the File tab, click Save As, navigate to the location where you store your Data Files, change the file name to EX 13-Service Adventures Memo, then click Save**

   You want to embed the workbook below the last line of the document.

3. **Press [Ctrl][End], click the Insert tab, click the Object button in the Text group, then click the Create from File tab**

   FIGURE 13-11 shows the Create from File tab in the Object dialog box. You need to indicate the file you want to embed.

   QUICK TIP
   To display a different icon to represent the file, click the Change Icon button in the Object dialog box, scroll down the icon list in the Change Icon dialog box, and select any icon. You can also click Browse and choose an .ico file located on your computer.

4. **Click Browse, navigate to the location where you store your Data Files, click EX 13-5.xlsx, click Insert, then select the Display as icon check box**

   You will change the icon caption to a more descriptive name.

5. **Click Change Icon, select the text in the Caption text box, type Projected Sales, click OK twice, then click anywhere in the Word document**

   The memo contains an embedded copy of the sales projection data, displayed as an icon, as shown in FIGURE 13-12.

   TROUBLE
   If the Excel program window does not come to the front automatically, click the Excel icon in the taskbar.

6. **Double-click the Projected Sales icon on the Word memo, if the Open Package Contents dialog box opens click Open, then maximize the Excel window and the worksheet window if necessary**

   The Excel program starts and displays the embedded worksheet, with its location displayed in the title bar, as shown in FIGURE 13-13. Any changes you make to the embedded object using Excel tools are not reflected in the source document. Similarly, if you open the source document in the source program, changes you make are not reflected in the embedded copy.

7. **Click the File tab, click Close, exit Excel, click the Word File tab, then click Save**

   Your changes to the memo are saved, and the memo remains open.

FIGURE 13-11: **Object dialog box**

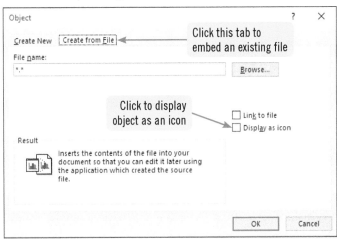

FIGURE 13-12: **Memo with embedded worksheet displayed as an icon**

FIGURE 13-13: **Embedded worksheet open in Excel**

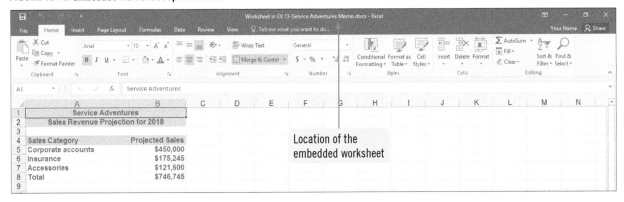

Link a Workbook to a Word Document

Learning
Outcomes
• Link data from an
Excel worksheet to
a Word document
• Update links in a
Word document

Linking a workbook to another file retains a connection with the original document as well as the original program. When you link a workbook to another program, the link contains a connection to the source document so that, when you double-click it, the source document opens for editing. In addition, any changes you make to the original workbook (the source document) are reflected in the linked object. **CASE** ▶ *Mary has just told you she may need to edit the workbook she embedded in the memo to Bryce. To ensure that these changes will be reflected in the memo, you decide to use linking instead of embedding. You need to delete the embedded worksheet icon and replace it with a linked version of the same workbook.*

STEPS

1. **With the Word memo still open, click the** Projected Sales Worksheet icon **to select it if necessary, then press** [Delete]

   The workbook is no longer embedded in the memo. The process of linking a file is similar to embedding, with a few important differences.

2. **Make sure the insertion point is below the last line of the memo, click the** Insert tab **if necessary, click the** Object button **in the Text group, then click the** Create from File tab **in the Object dialog box**

3. **Click** Browse, **navigate to the location where you store your Data Files, click** EX 13-5.xlsx, **click** Insert, **select the** Link to file check box, **then click** OK

   You didn't select the Display as icon check box so the memo now displays a linked copy of the sales projection data rather than an icon, as shown in FIGURE 13-14. In the future, any changes made to the source file, EX 13-5, will also be made to the linked copy in the Word memo. You verify this by making a change to the source file and viewing its effect on the memo.

4. **Click the** File tab, **click** Save, **close the Word memo, then exit Word**

5. **Start Excel, open** EX 13-5.xlsx **from where you store your Data Files, click cell B7, type 100000, then press** [Enter]

   You want to verify that the same change was made automatically to the linked copy of the workbook.

6. **Start Word, open the** EX 13-Service Adventures Memo.docx **file from where you store your Data Files, then click** Yes **if asked if you want to update the document's links**

   The memo displays the new value for Accessories, and the total has been updated as shown in FIGURE 13-15.

7. **Click the** Insert tab, **click the** Header button **in the Header & Footer group, click** Edit Header, **type your name in the Header area, then click the** Close Header and Footer button **in the Close group**

8. **Save the Word memo, preview it, close the file, exit Word, then submit the file to your instructor**

9. **In the Excel window, click** File **on the Ribbon, click** Close, **click** Don't Save **in the dialog box, then exit Excel**

FIGURE 13-14: **Memo with linked worksheet**

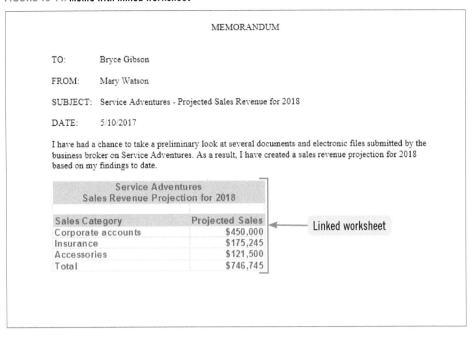

FIGURE 13-15: **Memo with updated values**

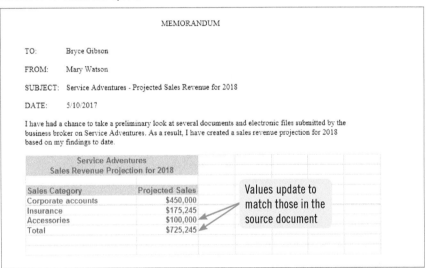

Managing links

When you open a document containing linked data, you are asked if you want to update the linked data. You can manage the updating of links by clicking the File tab, and clicking Edit Links to Files in the right pane. The Links dialog box opens, allowing you to change a link's update from the default setting of automatic to manual. The Links dialog box also allows you to change the link source, permanently break a link, open the source file, and manually update a link. If you send your linked files to another user, the links will be broken because the linked file path references the local machine where you inserted the links. Because the file path will not be valid on the recipient user's machine, the links will no longer be updated when the user opens the destination document. To correct this, recipients who have both the destination and source documents can use the Links dialog box to change the link's source in the destination document to their own machines. Then the links will be automatically updated when they open the destination document in the future.

Link an Excel Chart to a PowerPoint Slide

Microsoft PowerPoint is a **presentation graphics** program that you can use to create slide show presentations. PowerPoint slides can include a mix of text, data, and graphics. Adding an Excel chart to a slide can help to illustrate data and give your presentation more visual appeal. **CASE** ▶ *Mary asks you to add an Excel chart to one of the PowerPoint slides, illustrating the 2018 sales projection data. She wants you to link the chart in the PowerPoint file.*

STEPS

1. **Start PowerPoint, open** EX 13-6.pptx **from where you store your Data Files, then save it as** EX 13-Management Presentation

   The presentation appears in Normal view and contains three panes, as shown in FIGURE 13-16. You need to open the Excel file and copy the chart that you will paste in the PowerPoint presentation.

2. **Start Excel, open** EX 13-7.xlsx **from where you store your Data Files, right-click the** Chart Area **on the Sales Categories sheet, click** Copy **on the shortcut menu, then click the** PowerPoint program button **on the taskbar to display the presentation**

   To add the copied chart, you first need to select the slide on which it will appear.

3. **Click** Slide 2 **in the Thumbnails pane, right-click** Slide 2 **in the Slide pane, then click the** Use Destination Theme & Link Data button 📋 **in the Paste Options group**

   A pie chart illustrating the 2018 sales projections appears in the slide. The chart matches the colors and fonts in the presentation, which is the destination document. You decide to edit the link so it will update automatically if the data source changes.

4. **Click the** File tab, **click** Edit Links to Files **at the bottom of the right pane, in the Links dialog box click the** Automatic Update check box **to select it, then click** Close

5. **Click the** Back button ⬅ **at the top of the pane to return to the presentation, click the** Save button 💾 **on the Quick Access Toolbar, then close the file**

   Mary has learned that the sales projection for the Accessories category has increased.

6. **Switch to Excel, click the** Sales sheet tab, **change the Accessories value in cell** B7 **to** 125,000, **then press** [Enter]

   You decide to reopen the PowerPoint presentation to check the chart data.

7. **Switch to PowerPoint, open** EX 13-Management Presentation.pptx, **click** Update Links, **click** Slide 2 **in the Thumbnails pane, then point to the** Accessories pie slice

   The ScreenTip shows that the chart has updated to display the revised Accessories value, $125,000, you entered in the Excel workbook.

8. **Click the** Slide Show button 🖵 **on the status bar**

   Slide Show view shows the slide full screen, the way the audience will see it, as shown in FIGURE 13-17.

9. **Press** [Esc] **to return to Normal view; with Slide 2 selected click the** Insert tab, **click the** Header & Footer button **in the Text group, select the** Footer check box, **type your name in the Footer text box, click** Apply to All, **save and close the presentation, close the Excel file without saving it, exit PowerPoint and Excel, then submit the file to your instructor**

FIGURE 13-16: Presentation in Normal view

Thumbnails pane

Slide pane

Slide 2

Notes pane

FIGURE 13-17: Completed Sales Projections slide in Slide Show view

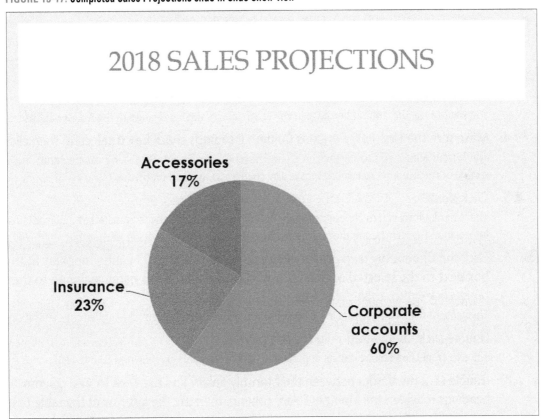

Import a Table into Access

If you need to analyze Excel data using the more extensive tools of a database, you can import it into Microsoft Access. When you import Excel table data into Access, the data becomes an Access table using the same field names as the Excel table. In the process of importing an Excel table, Access specifies a primary key for the new table. A **primary key** is the field that contains unique information for each record (row) of information. **CASE** ▸ *Mary has just received a workbook containing salary information for the managers at Service Adventures, organized in a table. She asks you to convert the Excel table to a Microsoft Access table.*

STEPS

1. **Start Access, click the** Blank desktop database button, **change the filename in the File Name text box to** EX 13-SA Management, **click the** Browse button 🗔 **next to the filename, navigate to where you store your Data Files, click OK, click** Create, **then click the** Close Table1 button ✖ **on the right side of the Table1 pane (Do not close Access)**

   The empty table that opens in the EX 13-SA Management database is removed. You are ready to import the Excel table data.

2. **Click the** External Data tab, **then click the** Excel button **in the Import & Link group**

   The Get External Data - Excel Spreadsheet dialog box opens, as shown in FIGURE 13-18. This dialog box allows you to specify how you want the data to be stored in Access.

3. **Click** Browse, **navigate to where you store your Data Files, click** EX 13-8.xlsx, **click** Open, **if necessary click the** Import the source data into a new table in the current database **option button, then click** OK

   The first Import Spreadsheet Wizard dialog box opens, with a sample of the sheet data in the lower section. You want to use the column headings in the Excel table as the field names in the Access database.

4. **Make sure the** First Row Contains Column Headings check box **is selected, then click** Next

   The Wizard allows you to review and change the field properties by clicking each column in the lower section of the window. You will not make any changes to the field properties.

5. **Click** Next

   The Wizard allows you to choose a primary key for the table. The table's primary key field contains unique information for each record; the ID Number field is unique for each person in the table.

6. **Click the** Choose my own primary key option, **make sure** ID Number **appears in the text box next to the selected option button, click** Next, **note the name assigned to the new table, click** Finish, **then click** Close

   The name of the new Access table ("Compensation") appears in the left pane, called the Navigation pane.

7. **Double-click** Compensation **in the left pane**

   The data from the Excel worksheet appears in a new Access table, as shown in FIGURE 13-19.

8. **Double-click the** border **between the** Monthly Salary **and the** Click to Add column headings to widen the Monthly Salary column, **then use the last row of the table to enter your name in the** First Name **and** Last Name columns and enter 0 for the ID Number

9. **Click the** Save button 🖫 **on the Quick Access Toolbar, close the file, then exit Access**

FIGURE 13-18: **Get External Data - Excel Spreadsheet dialog box**

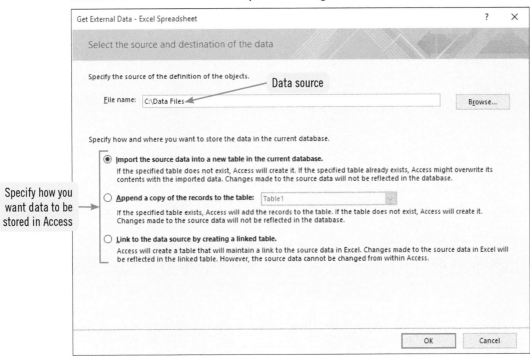

FIGURE 13-19: **Completed Access table with data imported from Excel**

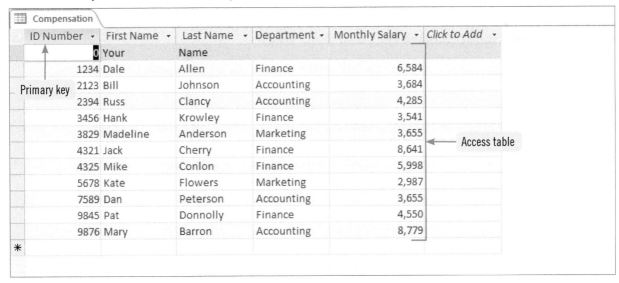

Practice

Concepts Review

FIGURE 13-20

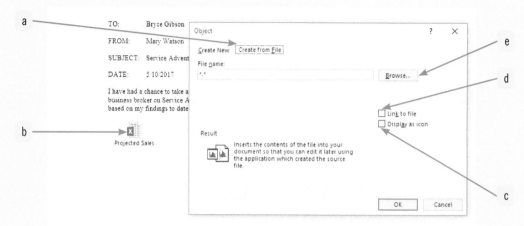

1. Which element do you click to insert an existing object into a Word document rather than creating a new file?
2. Which element do you click to embed information that can be viewed by double-clicking an icon?
3. Which element do you double-click to display an embedded Excel workbook?
4. Which element do you click to find a file to be embedded or linked?
5. Which element do you click to insert an object that maintains a connection to the source document?

Match each term with the statement that best describes it.

6. **Embedding**
7. **Source document**
8. **Destination document**
9. **Presentation graphics program**
10. **Linking**
11. **OLE**

a. File from which the object to be embedded or linked originates
b. Copies an object and retains a connection with the source program and source document
c. Document receiving the object to be embedded or linked
d. Data transfer method used in Windows programs
e. Copies an object and retains a connection with the source program only
f. Used to create slide shows

Select the best answer from the list of choices.

12. An object can consist of:
   a. Text, a worksheet, or any other type of data.
   b. A worksheet only.
   c. Text only.
   d. Database data only.
13. An ASCII file:
   a. Contains formatting but no text.
   b. Contains text but no formatting.
   c. Contains a PowerPoint presentation.
   d. Contains an unformatted worksheet.

14. To view a workbook that has been embedded as an icon in a Word document, you need to:

a. Double-click the icon.

b. Drag the icon.

c. Click View, then click Worksheet.

d. Click File, then click Open.

15. A column separator in a text file is called a(n):

a. Object.

b. Link.

c. Primary key.

d. Delimiter.

16. A field that contains unique information for each record in a database table is called a(n):

a. Primary key.

b. ID Key.

c. First key.

d. Header key.

Skills Review

1. Import a text file.

a. Start Excel, open a new blank workbook, import the tab-delimited text file EX 13-9.txt from where you store your Data Files, accepting the defaults in the Text Import Wizard, then save it as a Microsoft Office Excel workbook with the name **EX 13-Coffee Corner**.

b. Format the data in columns B and C using the Currency style with two decimal places.

c. Widen the columns if necessary so that all the data is visible.

d. Center the column labels and apply bold formatting, as shown in FIGURE 13-21.

e. Add your name to the center section of the worksheet footer, save the workbook, preview the worksheet, close the workbook, then submit the workbook to your instructor.

FIGURE 13-21

	A	B	C
1	Item	Cost	Price
2	Small	$0.59	$1.59
3	Medium	$0.80	$1.89
4	Large	$1.15	$2.09
5	X-Large	$1.30	$2.29
6	Latte, small	$1.50	$2.69
7	Latte, medium	$1.75	$3.19
8	Latte, large	$2.15	$3.69
9	Iced, small	$1.10	$1.99
10	Iced, medium	$1.70	$2.49
11	Iced, large	$2.10	$2.79
12			

2. Import a database table.

a. Open a blank workbook in Excel, use the From Access button in the Get External Data group on the Data tab to import the Access Data File EX 13-10.accdb from where you store your Data Files, then save it as a Microsoft Excel workbook named **EX 13-May Budget**.

b. Rename the sheet with the imported data **Budget**.

c. Delete the first data record in row 2.

d. Add a total row to the table to display the sum of the budgeted amounts in cell D25 (the Amount column).

e. Apply the Light 20 Table Style. Format range D2:D25 using the Currency style, the $ symbol, and two decimal places.

f. Save the workbook, and compare your screen to FIGURE 13-22.

FIGURE 13-22

	A	B	C	D	E
1	Category	Item	Month	Amount	
2	Compensation	Bonuses	May	$40,000.00	
3	Compensation	Commissions	May	$35,000.00	
4	Compensation	Conferences	May	$42,000.00	
5	Compensation	Promotions	May	$65,048.00	
6	Compensation	Payroll Taxes	May	$18,954.00	
7	Compensation	Salaries	May	$63,514.00	
8	Compensation	Training	May	$8,544.00	
9	Facility	Lease	May	$42,184.00	
10	Facility	Maintenance	May	$63,214.00	
11	Facility	Other	May	$11,478.00	
12	Facility	Rent	May	$80,214.00	
13	Facility	Telephone	May	$62,584.00	
14	Facility	Utilities	May	$57,964.00	
15	Supplies	Food	May	$61,775.00	
16	Supplies	Computer	May	$43,217.00	
17	Supplies	General Office	May	$47,854.00	
18	Supplies	Other	May	$56,741.00	
19	Supplies	Outside Services	May	$41,874.00	
20	Equipment	Computer	May	$49,874.00	
21	Equipment	Other	May	$43,547.00	
22	Equipment	Cash Registers	May	$55,987.00	
23	Equipment	Software	May	$63,147.00	
24	Equipment	Telecommunications	May	$58,779.00	
25	Total			$1,113,493.00	
26					
27					

3. Insert a graphic file in a worksheet.

a. Add four rows above row 1 to create space for an image.

b. In rows 1 through 4, insert the picture file EX 13-11.jpg from the location where you store your Data Files.

c. Resize and reposition the picture as necessary to make it fit in rows 1 through 4.

d. Apply the Beveled Matte, White Picture Style, and change the picture border color to Blue, Accent 5, Lighter 60%. Resize the picture to fit the image and the border in the first four rows. Move the picture to the center of the range A1:D4.

e. Compare your worksheet to FIGURE 13-23, add your name to the center section of the worksheet footer, preview the workbook, save and close the workbook, then submit the workbook to your instructor.

FIGURE 13-23

	A	B	C	D	E
1					
2					
3					
4					
5	Category	Item	Month	Amount	
6	Compensation	Bonuses	May	$40,000.00	
7	Compensation	Commissions	May	$35,000.00	
8	Compensation	Conferences	May	$42,000.00	
9	Compensation	Promotions	May	$65,048.00	
10	Compensation	Payroll Taxes	May	$18,954.00	
11	Compensation	Salaries	May	$63,514.00	
12	Compensation	Training	May	$8,544.00	
13	Facility	Lease	May	$42,184.00	
14	Facility	Maintenance	May	$63,214.00	
15	Facility	Other	May	$11,478.00	
16	Facility	Rent	May	$80,214.00	
17	Facility	Telephone	May	$62,584.00	
18	Facility	Utilities	May	$57,964.00	
19	Supplies	Food	May	$61,775.00	
20	Supplies	Computer	May	$43,217.00	
21	Supplies	General Office	May	$47,854.00	
22	Supplies	Other	May	$56,741.00	
23	Supplies	Outside Services	May	$41,874.00	
24	Equipment	Computer	May	$49,874.00	
25	Equipment	Other	May	$43,547.00	
26	Equipment	Cash Registers	May	$55,987.00	
27	Equipment	Software	May	$63,147.00	

Skills Review (continued)

4. Embed a workbook in a Word document.

a. Start Word, type a memo addressed to your instructor, enter your name in the From line, enter **May Salaries** as the subject, and enter the current date in the Date line.

b. In the memo body, enter **The May salaries are provided in the worksheet below**:

c. At the bottom of the memo body, use the Object dialog box to embed the workbook EX 13-12.xlsx from where you store your Data Files, displaying it as an icon with the caption **Salary Details**.

d. Save the document as **EX 13-May Salaries** in the location where you store your Data Files, then double-click the icon to verify that the workbook opens. (*Hint*: If the workbook does not appear after you double-click it, click the Excel icon on the taskbar.)

e. Close the workbook and return to Word.

f. Compare your memo to FIGURE 13-24.

FIGURE 13-24

To: Your Instructor

From: Your Name

Subject: May Salaries

Date: 11/1/2017

The May salaries are provided in the worksheet below:

Salary Details

5. Link a workbook to a Word document.

a. Delete the icon in the memo body.

b. In the memo body, link the workbook EX 13-12.xlsx, displaying the data, not an icon.

c. Save the document, then note that Mark Glory's salary is $7000. Close the document.

d. Open the EX 13-12.xlsx workbook in Excel, and change Mark Glory's salary to **$7500**.

e. Open the **EX 13-May Salaries** document in Word, update the links, and verify that Mark Glory's salary has changed to $7,500 and that the new total salaries amount is $43,725, as shown in FIGURE 13-25. (*Hint*: If the dialog box does not open, giving you the opportunity to update the link, then right-click the worksheet object and click Update Link.)

f. Save the **EX 13-May Salaries** document, preview the memo, close the document, exit Word, then submit the document to your instructor.

g. Close the EX 13-12 workbook without saving changes, then exit Excel.

FIGURE 13-25

To: Your Instructor

From: Your Name

Subject: May Salaries

Date: 11/1/2017

The May salaries are provided in the worksheet below:

Coffee Corner Salary Summary				
First Name	Last Name	Position	Salary	
Mark	Glory	Manager	$	7,500
John	Crowley	Manager	$	6,500
Melissa	Donolly	Manager	$	5,954
Cathy	Wallace	Sales Associate	$	6,325
Sandra	Jung	Custodian	$	5,635
Karen	Aloitz	Sales Associate	$	5,847
Gerry	Stimpson	Sales Associate	$	5,964
		Total	$	43,725

6. Link an Excel chart to a PowerPoint slide.

a. Start PowerPoint.

b. Open the PowerPoint file EX 13-13.pptx from where you store your Data Files, then save it as **EX 13-Budget Meeting**.

c. Display Slide 2, May Expenditures.

d. Start Excel, open EX 13-14 from where you store your data files, copy the chart, switch to PowerPoint, then link the chart on Slide 2, using the theme of the destination file. Edit the link to be updated automatically. Save and close the EX 13-Budget Meeting file.

e. Change the Equipment amount on Sheet1 of EX 13-14 to $200,000, open the EX 13-Budget Meeting file, updating the links, and verify the Equipment percentage changed to 21% on Slide 2.

f. View the slide in Slide Show view.

g. Press [Esc] to return to Normal view. Resize and reposition the chart. Compare your slide to FIGURE 13-26.

FIGURE 13-26

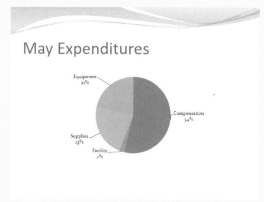

May Expenditures

Skills Review (continued)

h. Add a footer to all of the slides with your name.

i. Save the presentation, exit PowerPoint, close EX 13-14 without saving it, then submit the presentation to your instructor.

7. Import a table into Access.

a. Start Access.

b. Create a blank desktop database named **EX 13-Budget** in the location where you store your Data Files. Close Table1.

c. Use the External Data tab to import the Excel table in EX 13-15.xlsx from the location where you store your Data Files. Store the data in a new table, use the first row as column headings, let Access add the primary key, and use the default table name May Budget.

d. Open the May Budget table in Access, and widen the columns as necessary to fully display the field names and field information. Adjust the width of the Month column if necessary to more closely fit the May month data.

e. Enter your name in the Category column of row 24 in the table, save the database file, compare your screen to FIGURE 13-27, exit Access, then submit the database file to your instructor.

FIGURE 13-27

ID	Category	Item	Month	Amount	Click to Add
1	Compensation	Bonuses	May	$40,000.00	
2	Compensation	Commissions	May	$35,000.00	
3	Compensation	Conferences	May	$42,000.00	
4	Compensation	Promotions	May	$65,048.00	
5	Compensation	Payroll Taxes	May	$18,954.00	
6	Compensation	Salaries	May	$63,514.00	
7	Compensation	Training	May	$8,544.00	
8	Facility	Lease	May	$42,184.00	
9	Facility	Maintenance	May	$63,214.00	
10	Facility	Other	May	$11,478.00	
11	Facility	Rent	May	$80,214.00	
12	Facility	Telephone	May	$62,584.00	
13	Facility	Utilities	May	$57,964.00	
14	Supplies	Food	May	$61,775.00	
15	Supplies	Computer	May	$43,217.00	
16	Supplies	General Office	May	$47,854.00	
17	Supplies	Other	May	$56,741.00	
18	Supplies	Outside Services	May	$41,874.00	
19	Equipment	Computer	May	$49,874.00	
20	Equipment	Other	May	$43,547.00	
21	Equipment	Cash Registers	May	$55,987.00	
22	Equipment	Software	May	$63,147.00	
23	Equipment	Telecommunications	May	$58,779.00	
24	Your Name				

Independent Challenge 1

You are an agent for the LA office of West Coast Insurance. You have been asked to give a presentation to the regional manager about your sales in the past year. To illustrate your sales data, you will add an Excel chart to one of your slides, showing the different categories of insurance sales and the sales amounts for each category.

a. Start Excel, create a new workbook, then save it as **EX 13-Insurance Sales** in the location where you store your Data Files.

b. Starting in cell A1, enter the categories and the corresponding sales amounts shown below into the EX 13-Insurance Sales workbook. Name the sheet **Sales**.

Category	Sales
Homeowners	$10,500,000
Auto	$15,200,000
Umbrella	$7,000,000

c. Create a 3-D pie chart from the sales data. Format it using Chart Style 2.

d. Copy the chart to the Clipboard.

e. Start PowerPoint, open EX 13-16.pptx from where you store your Data Files, then save it as **EX 13-Sales Presentation**.

f. Link the Excel chart to Slide 2 using the destination theme. Use the sizing handles to change the size if necessary, and drag the edge of the chart to position it in the center of the slide if necessary.

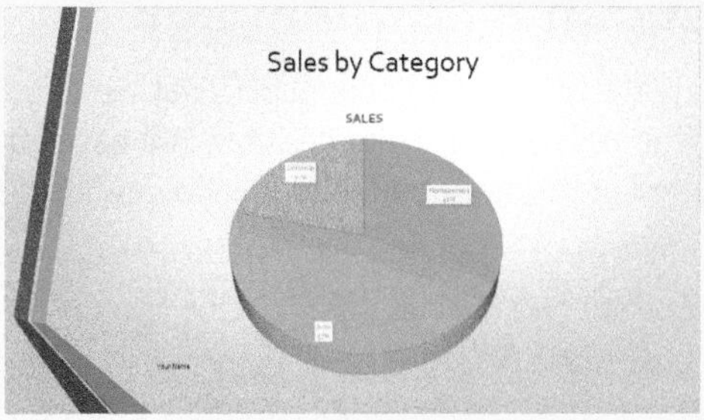

g. View the slide in Slide Show view, then press [Esc] to end the show.

h. Add a footer to the slides with your name, then save the presentation. Slide 2 should look like FIGURE 13-28.

i. Change the status of links in the PowerPoint file to update automatically.

j. Close the presentation, exit PowerPoint, then submit the PowerPoint file to your instructor.

k. Save the workbook, then close the workbook, and exit Excel.

FIGURE 13-28

Sales by Category

SALES

Independent Challenge 2

You are opening a new physical therapy clinic in Santa Barbara, California. The owner of a clinic in the area is retiring and has agreed to sell you a text file containing his list of supplier information. You need to import this text file into Excel so that you can manipulate the data. Later, you will convert the Excel file to an Access table so that you can give it to your business partner who is building a supplier database.

a. Start Excel, import EX 13-17.txt from where you store your Data Files, then save it as an Excel file named **EX 13-PT Suppliers**. (*Hint*: This is a tab-delimited text file, and the data has headers.)

b. Adjust the column widths as necessary. Rename the worksheet **Suppliers**.

c. Sort the worksheet data in ascending order by Supplier.

d. Add your name to the center section of the worksheet footer, save and close the workbook, then exit Excel.

e. Start Access, then create a new blank desktop database in the location where you store your Data Files. Name the new database **EX 13-Suppliers**. Close Table1.

f. Use the External Data tab to import the Excel file EX 13-PT Suppliers from where you store your Data Files. Store the data in a new table, use the column labels as the field names, let Access add the primary key, and accept the default table name.

g. Open the Suppliers table, then AutoFit the columns.

h. Enter your name in the Supplier column in row 13, then compare your database file to FIGURE 13-29.

i. Save and close the table, then exit Access.

j. Submit the database file to your instructor.

FIGURE 13-29

ID	Supplier	Address	City	State	Zip	Phone	Contact	Click to Add
1	Ace Equipment	45 Main St	Oakland	CA	94611	510-422-9923	R. Juan	
2	All Equipment	1157 East Rd	Daly City	CA	94623	415-465-7855	M. Lyons	
3	Elite Equipment	PO Box 1587	Milpitas	CA	94698	408-345-9343	P. Volez	
4	Equipment Plus	33 Jackson St	Fresno	CA	96899	608-332-8790	J. Jerry	
5	Holly Medial	44 West St	Brisbane	CA	94453	415-223-9912	H. Tran	
6	Jackson Equipment	394 19th Ave	San Francisco	CA	94554	415-444-9932	L. Solade	
7	Medical Pro	998 Little St	San Francisco	CA	94622	415-665-7342	W. Kitter	
8	Rehab Pro	223 Main St	Ventura	CA	93143	213-332-5568	A. Blume	
9	Rehab Unlimited	77 Sunrise St	Malibu	CA	93102	213-223-5432	J. Walsh	
10	West Coast Equipment	343 Upham St	Los Angeles	CA	93111	213-887-4456	P. Newhall	
11	West Coast Fitness	8 High St	San Jose	CA	94671	408-332-9981	K. McGuire	
12	West Medical	102 Lake Dr	San Diego	CA	93112	212-223-9934	S. Werthen	
13	Your Name							
*	(New)							

Independent Challenge 3

You are the newly hired sales manager at West Food Supplies. You would like to promote one of the account representatives, Caroline Walker, to a senior position. You have examined the sales of the other account representatives in the company and will present this information to the vice president of Human Resources, requesting permission to grant Caroline a promotion.

a. Start Word, open the Word file EX 13-18.docx from where you store your Data Files, then save it as **EX 13-Promotion**.

b. Add your name to the From line of the memo, and change the date to the current date.

c. At the end of the memo, embed the workbook EX 13-19.xlsx as an icon from the location where you store your Data Files. Change the caption for the icon to **Sales**. Double-click the icon to verify that the workbook opens.

d. Close the workbook, return to Word, delete the Sales icon, and link the workbook EX 13-19 to the memo, displaying the data, not an icon.

e. Save the EX 13-Promotion memo, then close the file.

f. Open the EX 13-19.xlsx workbook in Excel, then change Caroline Walker's sales to 800,000.

Independent Challenge 3 (continued)

g. Open the EX 13-Promotion memo, update the links, then make sure Caroline Walker's sales amount is updated.

h. Save and close the memo. Exit Word and submit the memo to your instructor.

i. Close EX 13-19 without saving the changes to Caroline Walker's information, then exit Excel.

Independent Challenge 4: Explore

You work as an account representative for a financial analyst. Each week you are required to submit your travel expenses to your supervisor in a Word document. You prefer to use Excel to track your expenses so you will link your worksheet to a Word document for your supervisor.

a. Open EX 13-20.docx from the location where you store your Data Files, then save it as **EX 13-Mileage**.

b. Replace the text "Your Name" in the FROM line with your own name.

c. Open EX 13-21.xlsx from where you store your Data Files, then copy the range A1:C6 to the Clipboard.

d. Return to the EX 13-Mileage document, then use the Paste Special command in the Paste Options to paste the copied range as a linked worksheet object with the destination style. (*Hint*: Using FIGURE 13-30 as a guide, right-click below the line "My travel expenses for this week are shown below.", then click the Link & Use Destination Styles option in the Paste Options group. It is the 4th option from the left.) Save and close the memo.

FIGURE 13-30

e. In the EX 13-21 workbook, change Monday's mileage to 80.

f. Return to Word, open the EX 13-Mileage memo, update links, then verify that Monday's reimbursement amount is now $46.00. Save and close the memo, then exit Word. Close the EX 13-21 workbook without saving the file, then exit Excel.

g. Using Access, create a new blank desktop database named **EX 13-Reimbursement** in the location where you store your Data Files. Open EX 13-21 and save it as EX 13-Report. Link the Excel data in the EX 13-Report.xlsx file to the EX 13-Reimbursement database file using FIGURE 13-31 as a guide. View the data in the linked Mileage table by double-clicking the object's name.

h. Save and close the database file, open the EX 13-Report.xlsx file, then change the mileage for Friday to 10. Save and close the Excel file.

i. Open the EX 13-Reimbursement database, then verify that the mileage figure for Friday was updated in the linked Mileage table. Enter your name in the Description column of the Design View (*Hint*: Click the View button in the Views group, enter your name, then click the View button again to return to the Datasheet View, saving the table.). Close the database and exit Access.

j. Submit the EX 13-Mileage Word document, the EX 13-Report Excel file, and the EX 13-Reimbursement Access file to your instructor.

FIGURE 13-31

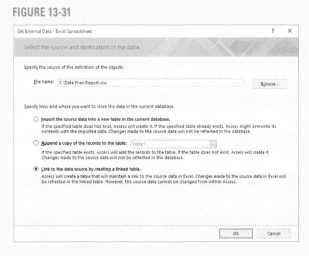

Visual Workshop

Create the worksheet shown in FIGURE 13-32 by opening a blank workbook, importing the Access data in file EX 13-22.accdb, sorting the data in Excel, and formatting the price data. The image is EX 13-11.jpg and the picture border is the standard color blue. Add your name to the center section of the worksheet. Save the workbook as **EX 13-Prices**, close the workbook, then exit Excel. Submit the file to your instructor.

FIGURE 13-32

	A	B	C	D
1				
2				
3				
4				
5				
6	**Item Code** ▾	**Product** ▾	**Price** ▾↑	
7	A43	Cup, small	$8.55	
8	A53	Cup, medium	$9.45	
9	A37	Cup, large	$10.55	
10	A10	Mug, small	$10.75	
11	B98	Water bottle	$10.85	
12	B21	Cold cups	$11.75	
13	A51	Mug, medium	$11.95	
14	A67	Mug, large	$12.55	
15	B54	Tea infuser	$14.55	
16	B76	Travel mug	$18.55	
17	A41	Teapot	$22.75	
18	B11	Tea kettle	$38.75	
19				
20				

Topseller/shutterstock.com

Programming with Excel

CASE ▶ Reason2Go's vice president of sales and marketing, Mary Watson, would like to automate some of the time-consuming tasks for the sales group. She asks you to create macros, using the Visual Basic for Applications (VBA) programming language, that format worksheet data, calculate sales totals, evaluate whether sales quotas are met, and insert user information in a worksheet footer.

Module Objectives

After completing this module, you will be able to:

- View VBA code
- Analyze VBA code
- Write VBA code
- Add a conditional statement
- Prompt the user for data
- Debug a macro
- Create a main procedure
- Run a main procedure

Files You Will Need

EX 16-1.xlsm	EX 16-5.xlsm
EX 16-2.xlsx	EX 16-6.xlsm
EX 16-3.xlsm	EX 16-7.xlsm
EX 16-4.xlsm	EX 16-8.xlsm

View VBA Code

As you learned in Module 9, you can create macros using the Excel macro recorder, which automatically writes Visual Basic for Applications (VBA) instructions for you as you perform actions. For additional flexibility, you can also create entire Excel macros by typing VBA program code. To enter and edit VBA code, you work in the **Visual Basic Editor**, a tool you can start from within Excel. A common method of learning any programming language is to view existing code. In VBA macro code, a sequence of VBA statements is called a **procedure**. The first line of a procedure, called the **procedure header**, defines the procedure's type, name, and arguments. **Arguments** are variables used by other procedures that the main procedure might run. **CASE** *Each month, Mary receives text files containing sales information from the Reason2Go branches. Mary has already imported the text file for the Toronto January sales into a worksheet, but it still needs to be formatted. She asks you to work on a macro to automate the process of formatting the imported information.*

STEPS

1. **Start Excel if necessary, open a blank workbook, click the** Developer tab, **then click the** Macro Security button **in the Code group**

   The Trust Center dialog box opens, as shown in FIGURE 16-1. You know the Reason2Go branch files are from a trusted source, so you decide to allow macros to run in the workbook.

2. **Click the** Enable all macros option button **if necessary, then click** OK

   You are ready to open a file and view its VBA code. A macro-enabled workbook has the extension .xlsm. Although a workbook containing a macro will open if macros are disabled, they will not function.

3. **Open** EX 16-1.xlsm **from the location where you store your Data Files, save it as** EX 16-Monthly Sales, **click the** Developer tab **then click the** Macros button **in the Code group**

   The Macro dialog box opens, showing the FormatFile macro procedure in the list box. If you have any macros saved in your Personal Macro workbook, they are also listed in the Macro dialog box.

4. **If it is not already selected click the** FormatFile **macro, then click** Edit

   The Microsoft Visual Basic for Applications window opens, containing three windows, shown in FIGURE 16-2. See TABLE 16-1 to make sure your screen matches the ones shown in this module. You may need to select the Format module in the Project Explorer window. See also the yellow box on the next page for more information about the VBA window.

5. **Make sure both the Visual Basic window and the Code window are maximized to match** FIGURE 16-2

   In the Code window, the different parts of the FormatFile procedure appear in various colors. Comments explaining the code are displayed in green.

6. **Examine the top three lines of code, which contain comments, and the first line of code beginning with** Sub FormatFile( )

   The first two comment lines give the procedure name and tell what the procedure does. The third comment line explains that the keyboard shortcut for this macro procedure is Ctrl+Shift+F. Items that appear in blue are **keywords**, which are words Excel recognizes as part of the VBA programming language. The keyword Sub in the procedure header indicates that this is a **Sub procedure**, or a series of Visual Basic statements that perform an action but do not return (create and display) a value. An empty set of parentheses after the procedure name means the procedure doesn't have any arguments. In the next lesson, you analyze the procedure code to see what each line does.

FIGURE 16-1: **Macro settings in the Trust Center dialog box**

Select to allow
macros to run

FIGURE 16-2: **Procedure displayed in the Visual Basic Editor**

Procedure
header

Project
Explorer
window

Format
module

Properties
window

Comments in green

Keywords in blue

Code
window

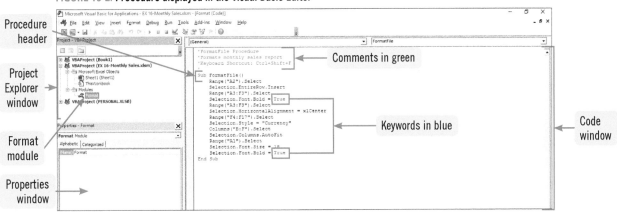

TABLE 16-1: **Matching your screen to the module figures**

if...	do this...
The Properties window is not displayed	Click the Properties Window button 📑 on the toolbar
The Project Explorer window is not displayed	Click the Project Explorer button 📑 on the toolbar
You see only the Code window	Click Tools on the menu bar, click Options, click the Docking tab, then make sure the Project Explorer and Properties Window options are selected
You do not see folders in the Explorer window	Click the Toggle Folders button 📁 on the Project Explorer window Project toolbar

Understanding the Visual Basic Editor

In Excel, a **module** is the Visual Basic equivalent of a worksheet. In it, you store macro procedures, just as you store data in worksheets. Modules, in turn, are stored in workbooks (or projects), along with worksheets. A **project** is the collection of all procedures in a workbook. You view and edit modules in the Visual Basic Editor, which is made up of the Project Explorer window (also called the Project window), the Code window, and the Properties window. **Project Explorer** displays a list of all open projects (or workbooks) and the worksheets and modules they contain. To view the procedures stored in a module, you must first select the module in Project Explorer (just as you would select a file in Windows Explorer). The **Code window** then displays the selected module's procedures. The **Properties window** displays a list of characteristics (or properties) associated with the module. A newly inserted module has only one property, its name.

Analyze VBA Code

Learning
Outcomes
• Examine the struc-
  ture of VBA code
• Run a procedure

You can learn a lot about the VBA language simply by analyzing the code generated by the Excel macro recorder. The more VBA code you analyze, the easier it is for you to write your own programming code. **CASE** ▶ *Before writing any new procedures, you analyze a previously written procedure that applies formatting to a worksheet. Then you open a worksheet that you want to format and run the macro.*

STEPS

1. **With the FormatFile procedure still displayed in the Code window, examine the next four lines of code, beginning with** Range("A2"). Select

   Refer to FIGURE 16-3 as you analyze the code in this lesson. Every Excel element, including a range, is considered an **object**. A **range object** represents a cell or a range of cells. The statement Range("A2").Select selects the range object cell A2. Notice that several times in the procedure, a line of code (or **statement**) selects a range, and then subsequent lines act on that selection. The next statement, Selection.EntireRow. Insert, inserts a row above the selection, which is currently cell A2. The next two lines of code select range A3:F3 and apply bold formatting to that selection. In VBA terminology, bold formatting is a value of an object's Bold property. A **property** is an attribute of an object that defines one of the object's characteristics (such as size) or an aspect of its behavior (such as whether it is enabled). To change the characteristics of an object, you change the values of its properties. For example, to apply bold formatting to a selected range, you assign the value True to the range's Bold property. To remove bold formatting, assign the value False.

2. **Examine the remaining lines of code, beginning with the second occurrence of the line** Range("A3:F3"). Select

   The next two statements select the range object A3:F3 and center its contents, then the following two statements select the F4:F17 range object and format it as currency. Column objects B through F are then selected, and their widths set to AutoFit. Finally, the range object cell A1 is selected, its font size is changed to 20, and its Bold property is set to True. The last line, End Sub, indicates the end of the Sub procedure and is also referred to as the **procedure footer**.

3. **Click the** View Microsoft Excel button ⊠ **on the Visual Basic Editor toolbar to return to Excel**

   Because the macro is stored in the EX 16-Monthly Sales workbook, you can open this workbook and repeatedly use the macro stored there each month after you receive that month's sales data. You want to open the workbook containing data for Toronto's January sales and run the macro to format the data. You must leave the EX 16-Monthly Sales workbook open to use the macro stored there.

4. **Open** EX 16-2.xlsx **from the location where you store your Data Files, then save it as** EX 16-January Sales

   This is the workbook containing the data you want to format.

5. **Press** [Ctrl][Shift][F] **to run the procedure**

   The FormatFile procedure formats the text, as shown in FIGURE 16-4.

6. **Save the workbook**

   Now that you've successfully viewed and analyzed VBA code and run the macro, you will learn how to write your own code.

FIGURE 16-3: VBA code for the FormatFile procedure

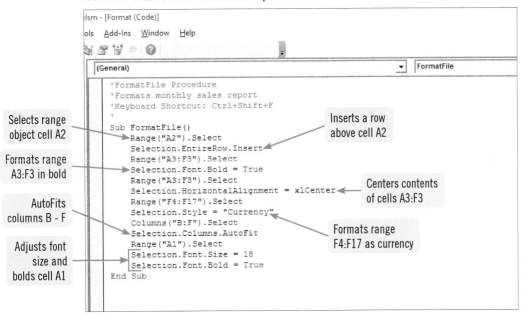

Selects range object cell A2

Formats range A3:F3 in bold

AutoFits columns B - F

Adjusts font size and bolds cell A1

Inserts a row above cell A2

Centers contents of cells A3:F3

Formats range F4:F17 as currency

FIGURE 16-4: Worksheet formatted using the FormatFile procedure

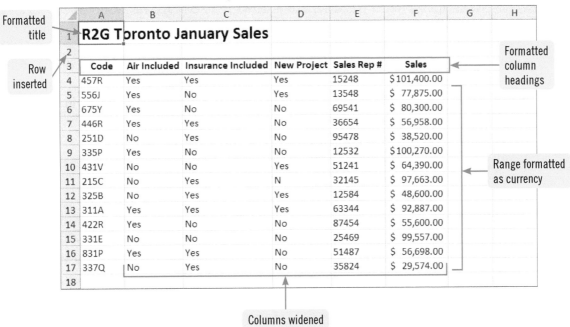

Formatted title

Row inserted

Formatted column headings

Range formatted as currency

Columns widened

Write VBA Code

To write your own code, you first need to open the Visual Basic Editor and add a module to the workbook. You can then begin entering the procedure code. In the first few lines, you typically include comments indicating the name of the procedure, a brief description, and shortcut keys, if applicable. When entering code, you must follow the formatting rules, or **syntax**, of the VBA programming language. A misspelled keyword or variable name causes a procedure to fail. **CASE** ▸ *Mary would like to total the monthly sales. You help her by writing a procedure that automates this routine task.*

STEPS

1. **With the January Sales worksheet still displayed, click the** Developer tab, **then click the** Visual Basic button **in the Code group**

   Two projects are displayed in the Project Explorer window, EX 16-Monthly Sales.xlsm (which contains the FormatFile macro) and EX 16-January Sales.xlsx (which contains the monthly data). The FormatFile procedure is again displayed in the Visual Basic Editor. You may have other projects in the Project Explorer window.

2. **Click the** Modules folder **in the EX 16-Monthly Sales.xlsm project**

   You need to store all of the procedures in the EX 16-Monthly Sales.xlsm project, which is in the EX 16-Monthly Sales.xlsm workbook. By clicking the Modules folder, you have activated the workbook, and the title bar changes from EX 16-January Sales to EX 16-Monthly Sales.

3. **Click** Insert **on the Visual Basic Editor menu bar, then click** Module

   A new, blank module with the default name Module1 appears in the EX 16-Monthly Sales.xlsm project, under the Format module. You think the property name of the module could be more descriptive.

4. **Click** (Name) **in the Properties window, type** Total, **then press** [ENTER]

   The module name is Total. The module name should not be the same as the procedure name (which will be AddTotal). In the code shown in FIGURE 16-5, comments begin with an apostrophe, and the lines of code under Sub AddTotal( ) have been indented using the Tab key. When you enter the code in the next step, after you type the procedure header Sub AddTotal( ) and press [Enter], the Visual Basic Editor automatically enters End Sub (the procedure footer) in the Code window.

5. **Click in the** Code window, **then type the procedure code exactly as shown in** FIGURE 16-5, **entering your name in the second line, and pressing** [Tab] **to indent text and** [Shift][Tab] **to move the insertion point to the left**

   The lines that begin with ActiveCell.Formula insert the information enclosed in quotation marks into the active cell. For example, ActiveCell.Formula = "Total Sales:" inserts the words "Total Sales:" into cell E18, the active cell. As you type each line, Excel adjusts the spacing.

6. **Compare the code you entered in the Code window with** FIGURE 16-5, **make any corrections if necessary, then click the** Save button 🖫 **on the Visual Basic Editor toolbar**

7. **Click the** View Microsoft Excel button 🔀 **on the toolbar, click** EX 16-January Sales.xlsx **on the taskbar to activate the workbook if necessary, with the January worksheet displayed click the** Developer tab **if necessary, then click the** Macros button **in the Code group**

   Macro names have two parts. The first part ('EX 16-Monthly Sales.xlsm'!) indicates the workbook where the macro is stored. The second part (AddTotal or FormatFile) is the name of the procedure, taken from the procedure header.

8. **Click** 'EX 16-MonthlySales.xlsm'!AddTotal **to select it if necessary, then click** Run

   The AddTotal procedure inserts and formats the total sales in cell F18, as shown in FIGURE 16-6.

9. **Save the workbook**

FIGURE 16-5: **VBA code for the AddTotal procedure**

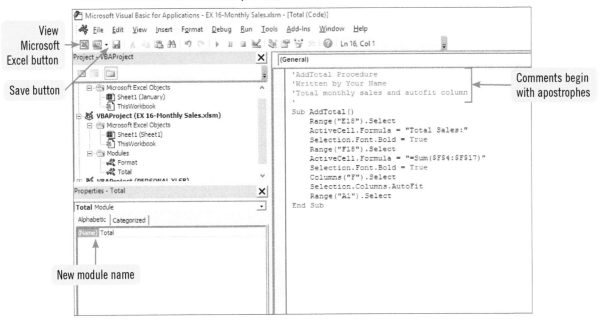

Microsoft Visual Basic for Applications - EX 16-Monthly Sales.xlsm - [Total (Code)]

File Edit View Insert Format Debug Run Tools Add-Ins Window Help

View Microsoft Excel button

Save button

Ln 16, Col 1

Project - VBAProject

Microsoft Excel Objects
  Sheet1 (January)
  ThisWorkbook
VBAProject (EX 16-Monthly Sales.xlsm)
  Microsoft Excel Objects
    Sheet1 (Sheet1)
    ThisWorkbook
  Modules
    Format
    Total
VBAProject (PERSONAL.XLSB)

Properties - Total

Total Module

Alphabetic Categorized

(Name) Total

New module name

(General)

```
'AddTotal Procedure
'Written by Your Name
'Total monthly sales and autofit column
'
Sub AddTotal()
    Range("E18").Select
    ActiveCell.Formula = "Total Sales:"
    Selection.Font.Bold = True
    Range("F18").Select
    ActiveCell.Formula = "=Sum($F$4:$F$17)"
    Selection.Font.Bold = True
    Columns("F").Select
    Selection.Columns.AutoFit
    Range("A1").Select
End Sub
```

Comments begin with apostrophes

FIGURE 16-6: **Worksheet after running the AddTotal procedure**

	A	B	C	D	E	F	G
1	R2G Toronto January Sales						
2							
3	Code	Air Included	Insurance Included	New Project	Sales Rep #	Sales	
4	457R	Yes	Yes	Yes	15248	$ 101,400.00	
5	556J	Yes	No	Yes	13548	$ 77,875.00	
6	675Y	Yes	No	No	69541	$ 80,300.00	
7	446R	Yes	Yes	No	36654	$ 56,958.00	
8	251D	No	Yes	No	95478	$ 38,520.00	
9	335P	Yes	No	No	12532	$ 100,270.00	
10	431V	No	No	Yes	51241	$ 64,390.00	
11	215C	No	Yes	N	32145	$ 97,663.00	
12	325B	No	Yes	Yes	12584	$ 48,600.00	
13	311A	Yes	Yes	Yes	63344	$ 92,887.00	
14	422R	Yes	No	No	87454	$ 55,600.00	
15	331E	No	No	No	25469	$ 99,557.00	
16	831P	Yes	Yes	No	51487	$ 56,698.00	
17	337Q	No	Yes	No	35824	$ 29,574.00	
18					Total Sales:	$ 1,000,292.00	

Result of AddTotal procedure

Entering code using AutoComplete

To assist you in entering the VBA code, the Editor uses **AutoComplete**, a list of words that can be used in the macro statement and match what you type. The list usually appears after you press [.] (period). To include a word from the list in the macro statement, select the word in the list, then double-click it or press [Tab]. For example, to enter the Range("E12").Select instruction, type Range("E12"), then press [.] (period). Type s to bring up the words beginning with the letter "s", select the Select command in the list, then press [Tab] to enter the word "Select" in the macro statement.

Add a Conditional Statement

Learning Outcomes

- Enter a VBA conditional statement
- Run a VBA conditional statement

The formatting macros you entered in the previous lesson could have been created using the macro recorder. However, there are some situations where you cannot use the recorder and must type the VBA macro code, such as when you want a procedure to take an action based on a certain condition or set of conditions. One way of adding this type of conditional statement in Visual Basic is to use an **If...Then...Else statement**. For example, *if* a salesperson's performance rating is a 5 (top rating), *then* calculate a 10% bonus; otherwise (*else*), there is no bonus. The syntax for this statement is: "If *condition* Then *statements* Else [*else statements*]." The brackets indicate that the Else part of the statement is optional. **CASE** *Mary wants the worksheet to indicate if the total sales figure meets or misses the $1,000,000 monthly quota. You use Excel to add a conditional statement that indicates this information. You start by returning to the Visual Basic Editor and inserting a new module in the Monthly Sales project.*

STEPS

1. **With the January worksheet still displayed click the Developer tab if necessary, then click the Visual Basic button in the Code group**

2. **Verify that the Total module in the Modules folder of the EX 16-Monthly Sales VBAProject is selected in the Project Explorer window, click Insert on the Visual Basic Editor menu bar, then click Module**

   A new, blank module named Module1 is inserted in the EX 16-Monthly Sales workbook.

3. **In the Properties window click (Name), then type Sales**

   There is no need to press [Enter] after typing "Sales" because the new name will be entered once you click in the Code window.

   > **QUICK TIP**
   > The If...Then...Else statement is similar to the Excel IF function.

4. **Click in the Code window, then type the code exactly as shown in FIGURE 16-7, entering your name in the second line**

   Notice the green comment lines in the middle of the code. These lines help explain the procedure.

5. **Compare the procedure you entered with FIGURE 16-7, make any corrections if necessary, click the Save button 🔲 on the Visual Basic Editor toolbar, then click the View Microsoft Excel button 🔳 on the Visual Basic Editor toolbar**

   > **TROUBLE**
   > If you get an error message check your code for errors, correct the errors, save your macro, click the Reset button 🔲 on the Visual Basic Editor toolbar, then rerun the macro.

6. **If necessary, click EX 16-January Sales.xlsx on the taskbar to display it, click the Macros button in the Code group, in the Macro dialog box click 'EX 16-Monthly Sales.xlsm'!SalesStatus, then click Run**

   The SalesStatus procedure indicates the status "Met Quota", as shown in FIGURE 16-8.

7. **Save the EX 16-January Sales workbook, then save the EX 16-Monthly Sales.xlsm workbook**

FIGURE 16-7: VBA code for the SalesStatus procedure

```
'SalesStatus Procedure
'Written by Your Name
'Tests whether total sales meet the monthly quota
'
Sub SalesStatus()
    Range("E20").Select
    ActiveCell.Formula = "Sales Status:"
    Selection.Font.Bold = True
    'If the total is less than 1000000 then
    'insert "Missed Quota" in cell F20
    If Range("F18") <= 1000000 Then
        Range("F20").Select
        ActiveCell.Formula = "Missed Quota"
    'otherwise, insert "Met Quota" in cell F20
    Else
        Range("F20").Select
        ActiveCell.Formula = "Met Quota"
    End If
    Range("A1").Select
End Sub
```

If ... Then ... Else statement →

FIGURE 16-8: Result of running the SalesStatus procedure

	A	B	C	D	E	F	G
1	**R2G Toronto January Sales**						
2							
3	**Code**	**Air Included**	**Insurance Included**	**New Project**	**Sales Rep #**	**Sales**	
4	457R	Yes	Yes	Yes	15248	$ 101,400.00	
5	556J	Yes	No	Yes	13548	$ 77,875.00	
6	675Y	Yes	No	No	69541	$ 80,300.00	
7	446R	Yes	Yes	No	36654	$ 56,958.00	
8	251D	No	Yes	No	95478	$ 38,520.00	
9	335P	Yes	No	No	12532	$ 100,270.00	
10	431V	No	No	Yes	51241	$ 64,390.00	
11	215C	No	Yes	N	32145	$ 97,663.00	
12	325B	No	Yes	Yes	12584	$ 48,600.00	
13	311A	Yes	Yes	Yes	63344	$ 92,887.00	
14	422R	Yes	No	No	87454	$ 55,600.00	
15	331E	No	No	No	25469	$ 99,557.00	
16	831P	Yes	Yes	No	51487	$ 56,698.00	
17	337Q	No	Yes	No	35824	$ 29,574.00	
18					**Total Sales:**	**$ 1,000,292.00**	
19							
20				Indicates status of monthly total →	**Sales Status** Met Quota		
21							
22							

Prompt the User for Data

Learning
Outcome
• Enter a VBA
  function

Another situation where you must type, not record, VBA code is when you need to pause a macro to allow user input. You use the VBA InputBox function to display a dialog box that prompts the user for information. A **function** is a predefined procedure that returns (creates and displays) a value; in this case the value returned is the information the user enters. The required elements of an InputBox function are as follows: *object*.InputBox("*prompt*"), where "*prompt*" is the message that appears in the dialog box. For a detailed description of the InputBox function, use the Visual Basic Editor's Help menu. **CASE** *You decide to create a procedure that will insert the user's name in the left footer area of the worksheet. You use the InputBox function to display a dialog box in which the user can enter his or her name. You also type an intentional error into the procedure code, which you will correct in the next lesson.*

STEPS

1. **With the January worksheet displayed click the** Developer tab **if necessary, click the** Visual Basic button **in the Code group, verify that the** Sales **module is selected in the EX 16-Monthly Sales VBAProject Modules folder, click** Insert **on the Visual Basic Editor menu bar, then click** Module

   A new, blank module named Module1 is inserted in the EX 16-Monthly Sales workbook.

2. **In the Properties window click** (Name), **then type** Footer

3. **Click in the Code window, then type the procedure code exactly as shown in** FIGURE 16-9, **entering your name in the second line**

   Like the SalesStatus procedure, this procedure also contains comments that explain the code. The first part of the code, Dim LeftFooterText As String, **declares**, or defines, LeftFooterText as a text string variable. In Visual Basic, a **variable** is a location in memory in which you can temporarily store one item of information. Dim statements are used to declare variables and must be entered in the following format: Dim *variablename* As *datatype*. The datatype here is "string." In this case, you plan to store the information received from the input box in the temporary memory location called LeftFooterText. Then you can place this text in the left footer area. The remaining statements in the procedure are explained in the comment line directly above each statement. Notice the comment pointing out the error in the procedure code. You will correct this in the next lesson.

4. **Review your code, make any necessary changes, click the** Save button 🖫 **on the Visual Basic Editor toolbar, then click the** View Microsoft Excel button 🖾 **on the Visual Basic Editor toolbar**

5. **With the January worksheet displayed, click the** Macros button **in the Code group, in the Macro dialog box click** 'EX 16-Monthly Sales.xlsm'!FooterInput, **then click** Run

   The procedure begins, and a dialog box generated by the InputBox function opens, prompting you to enter your name, as shown in FIGURE 16-10.

TROUBLE
If your macro doesn't prompt you for your name, it may contain an error. Return to the Visual Basic Editor, click the Reset button ⬛ correct the error by referring to FIGURE 16-9, then repeat Steps 4 and 5. You learn more about how to correct errors in the next lesson.

6. **With the cursor in the text box, type your name, then click** OK

7. **Click the** File tab, **click** Print, **then view the worksheet preview**

   Although the customized footer with the date is inserted on the sheet, because of the error your name does *not* appear in the left section of the footer. In the next lesson, you will learn how to step through a procedure's code line by line. This will help you locate the error in the FooterInput procedure.

8. **Click the** Back button 🗘, **save the EX 16-January Sales workbook, then save the EX 16-Monthly Sales.xlsm workbook**

FIGURE 16-9: VBA code for the FooterInput procedure

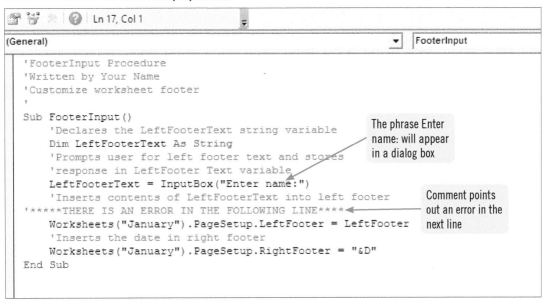

```
                        Ln 17, Col 1

(General)                                          FooterInput

    'FooterInput Procedure
    'Written by Your Name
    'Customize worksheet footer
    '
    Sub FooterInput()
        'Declares the LeftFooterText string variable
        Dim LeftFooterText As String
        'Prompts user for left footer text and stores
        'response in LeftFooter Text variable
        LeftFooterText = InputBox("Enter name:")
        'Inserts contents of LeftFooterText into left footer
    '*****THERE IS AN ERROR IN THE FOLLOWING LINE****
        Worksheets("January").PageSetup.LeftFooter = LeftFooter
        'Inserts the date in right footer
        Worksheets("January").PageSetup.RightFooter = "&D"
    End Sub
```

The phrase Enter name: will appear in a dialog box

Comment points out an error in the next line

FIGURE 16-10: InputBox function's dialog box

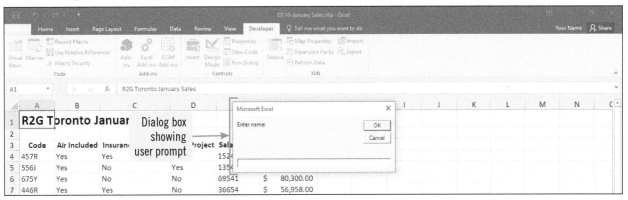

Dialog box showing user prompt

Naming variables

Variable names in VBA must begin with a letter. Letters can be uppercase or lowercase. Variable names cannot include periods or spaces, and they can be up to 255 characters long. Each variable name in a procedure must be unique. Examples of valid and invalid variable names are shown in TABLE 16-2.

TABLE 16-2: Variable names

valid	invalid
Sales_Department	Sales Department
SalesDepartment	Sales Department
Quarter1	1stQuarter

Debug a Macro

Learning
Outcomes
• Locate VBA errors
• Correct VBA errors

When a macro procedure does not run properly, it can be due to an error, referred to as a **bug**, in the code. To help you find the bug(s) in a procedure, the Visual Basic Editor lets you step through the procedure's code, one line at a time. When you locate the error, you can then correct, or **debug**, it. **CASE** *You decide to debug the macro procedure to find out why it failed to insert your name in the worksheet footer.*

STEPS

QUICK TIP

A common mistake is to confuse the module name with the procedure name. remember that the module is the container that holds the procedure. To run a macro, always use the procedure name, not the module name.

1. **Activate the January worksheet click the** Developer tab **if necessary, click the** Macros **button in the Code group, in the Macro dialog box click** 'EX 16-Monthly Sales. xlsm'!FooterInput, **then click** Step Into

   The Visual Basic Editor opens with the yellow statement selector positioned on the first statement of the procedure, as shown in FIGURE 16-11.

2. **Press [F8] to step to the next statement**

   The statement selector skips over the comments and the line of code beginning with Dim. The Dim statement indicates that the procedure will store your name in a variable named LeftFooterText. Because Dim is a declaration of a variable and not a procedure statement, the statement selector skips it and moves to the line containing the InputBox function.

3. **Press [F8] again, with the cursor in the text box in the Microsoft Excel dialog box type your name, then click** OK

   The Visual Basic Editor opens. The statement selector is now positioned on the statement that reads Worksheets("January").PageSetup.LeftFooter = LeftFooter. This statement should insert your name (which you just typed in the text box) in the left section of the footer. This is the instruction that does not appear to be working correctly.

4. **If necessary scroll right until the end of the LeftFooter instruction is visible, then point to** LeftFooter

   The value of the LeftFooter variable is displayed as shown in FIGURE 16-12. Rather than containing your name, the variable LeftFooter at the end of this line is empty. This is because the InputBox function assigned your name to the LeftFooterText variable, not to the LeftFooter variable. Before you can correct this bug, you need to turn off the Step Into feature.

5. **Click the** Reset button ▦ **on the Visual Basic Editor toolbar to turn off the Step Into feature, click at the end of the statement containing the error, then replace the variable LeftFooter with** LeftFooterText

   The revised statement now reads Worksheets("January").PageSetup.LeftFooter = LeftFooterText.

6. **Delete the comment line pointing out the error, then click the** Save button 🖫 **on the Visual Basic Editor toolbar, then click the** View Microsoft Excel button 🖾 **on the Visual Basic Editor toolbar**

7. **With the January worksheet displayed click the** Macros button **in the Code group, in the Macro dialog box click** 'EX 16-Monthly Sales.xlsm'!FooterInput, **click** Run **to rerun the procedure, when prompted type your name, then click** OK

8. **Click the** File tab, **click** Print, **then view the worksheet preview**

   Your name now appears in the left section of the footer.

9. **Click the** Back button ⬅, **save the EX 16-January Sales workbook, then save the EX 16-Monthly Sales.xlsm workbook**

FIGURE 16-11: **Statement selector positioned on first procedure statement**

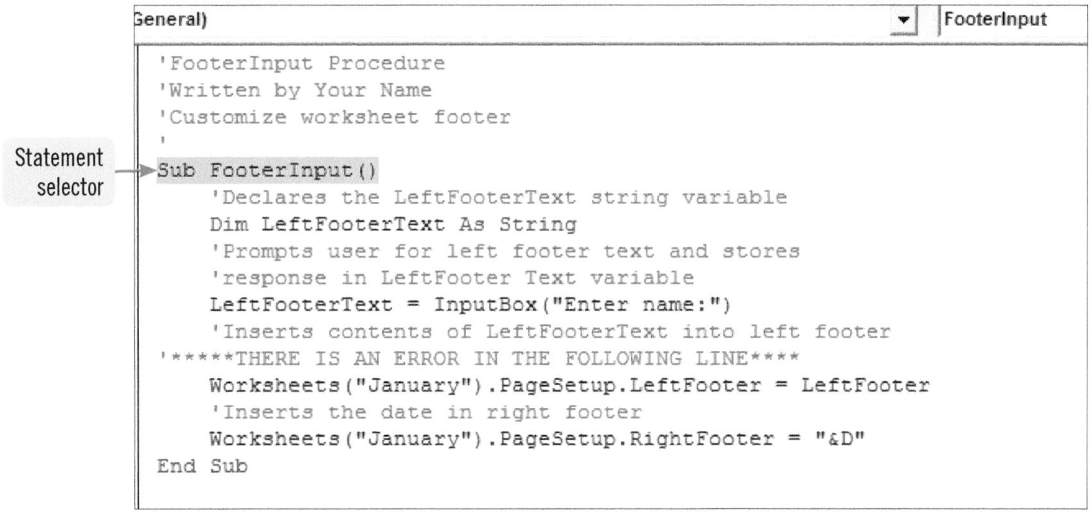

```
General)                                                    ▼    FooterInput

    'FooterInput Procedure
    'Written by Your Name
    'Customize worksheet footer
    '
Sub FooterInput()
        'Declares the LeftFooterText string variable
        Dim LeftFooterText As String
        'Prompts user for left footer text and stores
        'response in LeftFooter Text variable
        LeftFooterText = InputBox("Enter name:")
        'Inserts contents of LeftFooterText into left footer
    '*****THERE IS AN ERROR IN THE FOLLOWING LINE****
        Worksheets("January").PageSetup.LeftFooter = LeftFooter
        'Inserts the date in right footer
        Worksheets("January").PageSetup.RightFooter = "&D"
End Sub
```

Statement selector

FIGURE 16-12: **Value contained in LeftFooter variable**

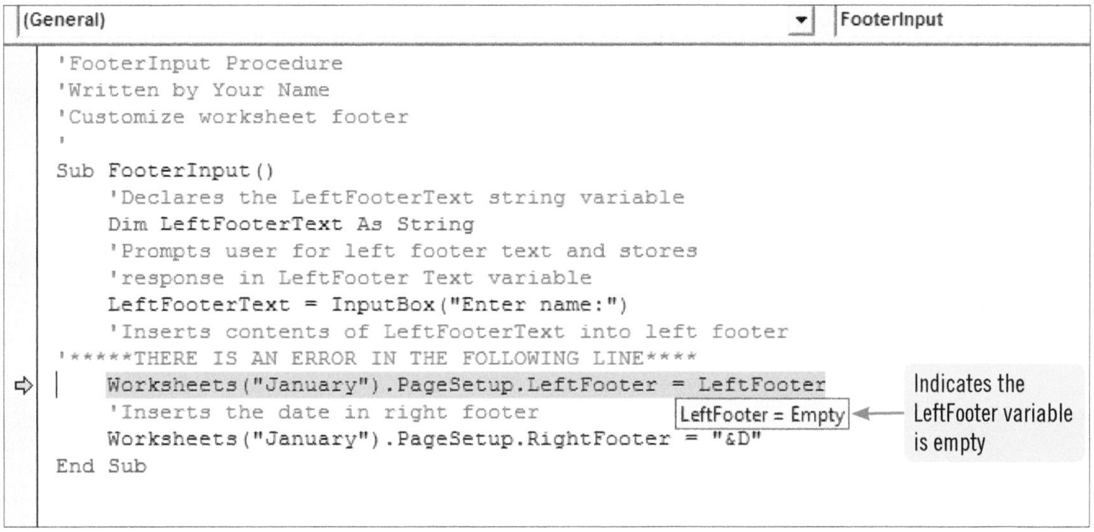

```
(General)                                                  ▼    FooterInput

    'FooterInput Procedure
    'Written by Your Name
    'Customize worksheet footer
    '
Sub FooterInput()
        'Declares the LeftFooterText string variable
        Dim LeftFooterText As String
        'Prompts user for left footer text and stores
        'response in LeftFooter Text variable
        LeftFooterText = InputBox("Enter name:")
        'Inserts contents of LeftFooterText into left footer
    '*****THERE IS AN ERROR IN THE FOLLOWING LINE****
⇨ |     Worksheets("January").PageSetup.LeftFooter = LeftFooter     LeftFooter = Empty
        'Inserts the date in right footer
        Worksheets("January").PageSetup.RightFooter = "&D"
End Sub
```

Indicates the LeftFooter variable is empty

Excel 2016

Adding security to your macro projects

To add security to your projects, you can add a digital signature to the project. A **digital signature** guarantees the project hasn't been altered since it was signed. Sign macros only after you have tested them and are ready to distribute them. If the code in a digitally signed macro project is changed in any way, its digital signature is removed. To add a digital signature to a Visual Basic project, select the project that you want to sign in the Visual Basic Project Explorer window, click the Tools menu in the Visual Basic Editor, click Digital Signature, click Choose, select the certificate, then click OK twice. When you add a digital signature to a project, the macro project is automatically re-signed whenever it is saved on your computer. You can get a digital certificate from your administrator. There are also third-party certification authorities that issue certificates that are trusted by Microsoft.

Create a Main Procedure

When you routinely need to run several macros one after another, you can save time by combining them into one procedure. The resulting procedure, which processes (or calls) multiple procedures in sequence, is referred to as the **main procedure**. To create a main procedure, you type a **Call statement** for each procedure you want to run. The syntax of the Call statement is Call *procedurename*, where *procedurename* is the name of the procedure you want to run. **CASE** *To avoid having to run each of the macros you've created, one after another, every month, you want to create a main procedure that will call each of them in sequence in the EX 16-Monthly Sales workbook.*

STEPS

1. **With the January worksheet displayed, click the** Developer tab **if necessary, then click the** Visual Basic button **in the Code group**

2. **Verify that EX 16-Monthly Sales is the active project, click** Insert **on the menu bar, then click** Module

   A new, blank module named Module1 is inserted in the EX 16-Monthly Sales workbook.

3. **In the Properties window click** (Name), **then type** MainProc

4. **In the Code window enter the procedure code exactly as shown in** FIGURE 16-13, **entering your name in the second line**

5. **Compare your main procedure code with** FIGURE 16-13, **correct any errors if necessary, then click the** Save button 💾 **on the Visual Basic Editor toolbar**

   To test the new main procedure, you need an unformatted version of the EX 16-January Sales worksheet.

6. **Click the** View Microsoft Excel button ☒ **on the toolbar, save the EX 16-Monthly Sales.xlsm workbook, then save and close the EX 16-January Sales workbook**

   The EX 16-Monthly Sales workbook remains open.

7. **Open** EX 16-2.xlsx **from the location where you store your Data Files, then save it as** EX 16-January Sales 2

   In the next lesson, you'll run the main procedure.

Copying a macro to another workbook

If you would like to use a macro in another workbook, you can copy the module to that workbook using the Visual Basic Editor. Open both the source and destination Excel workbooks, then open the Visual Basic Editor and verify that macros are enabled. In Project Explorer, drag the module that will be copied from the source workbook to the destination workbook.

FIGURE 16-13: **VBA code for the MainProcedure procedure**

```
(General)

    'MainProcedure Procedure
    'Written by Your Name
    'Calls sub procedures in sequence
    '
    Sub MainProcedure()
        Call FormatFile
        Call AddTotal
        Call SalesStatus
        Call FooterInput
    End Sub
```

MainProcedure calls each procedure in the order shown

Writing and documenting VBA code

When you write VBA code in the Visual Basic Editor, you want to make it as readable as possible. This makes it easier for you or your coworkers to edit the code when changes need to be made. The procedure statements should be indented, leaving the procedure name and its End statement easy to spot in the code. This is helpful when a module contains many procedures. It is also good practice to add comments at the beginning of each procedure that describe its purpose and any assumptions made in the procedure, such as the quota amounts. You should also explain each code statement with a comment. You have seen comments inserted into VBA code by beginning the statement with an apostrophe. You can also add comments to the end of a line of VBA code by placing an apostrophe before the comment, as shown in FIGURE 16-14.

FIGURE 16-14: **VBA code with comments at the end of statements**

```
(General)                                          ▼   MainProcedure

    'MainProcedure Procedure
    'Written by Your Name
    'Calls sub procedures in sequence
    '
    Sub MainProcedure()
        Call FormatFile 'Run FormatFile procedure
        Call AddTotal  'Run AddTotal procedure
        Call SalesStatus  'Run SalesStatus procedure
        Call FooterInput  'Run FooterInput procedure
    End Sub
```

Comments at the end of the statements in green

Excel 2016

Run a Main Procedure

Running a main procedure allows you to run several macros in sequence. You can run a main procedure just as you would any other macro procedure. **CASE** ▸ *You have finished creating a main procedure, and you are ready to run it. If the main procedure works correctly, it should format the worksheet, insert the sales total, insert a sales status message, and add your name and the date to the worksheet footer.*

STEPS

1. **In the January Sales 2 workbook click the** Developer tab, **click the** Macros button **in the Code group, in the Macro dialog box click** 'EX 16-Monthly Sales.xlsm'!MainProcedure, **click** Run, **when prompted type your name, then click** OK

   The MainProcedure runs the FormatFile, AddTotal, SalesStatus, and FooterInput procedures in sequence. You can see the results of the FormatFile, AddTotal, and SalesStatus procedures in the worksheet window, as shown in FIGURE 16-16. To view the results of the FooterInput procedure, you need to preview the worksheet.

2. **Click the** File tab, **click** Print, **view the worksheet preview and verify that your name appears in the left footer area and the date appears in the right footer area, click the Back button** ⬅, **then click the** Developer tab **if necessary**

3. **Click the** Visual Basic button **in the Code group**

   You need to add your name to the Format module.

4. **In the Project Explorer window, double-click the** Format module, **add a comment line after the procedure name that reads** Written by [Your Name], **then click the** Save button 💾

   You want to see the options for printing VBA code.

5. **Click** File **on the Visual Basic Editor menu bar, then click** Print

   The Print - VBAProject dialog box opens, as shown in FIGURE 16-17. The Current Module is selected which will print each procedure separately. It is faster to print all the procedures in the workbook at one time by clicking the Current Project option button to select it. You can also create a file of the VBA code by selecting the Print to File check box. You do not want to print the modules at this time.

6. **Click** Cancel **in the Print - VBAProject dialog box**

7. **Click the** View Microsoft Excel button 🅧 **on the toolbar**

8. **Save the** EX 16-Monthly Sales.xlsm **workbook, save the** EX 16-January Sales 2 workbook, **then preview the worksheet**

   Compare your formatted worksheet to FIGURE 16-18.

9. **Close the** EX 16-January Sales 2 workbook, **close the** EX 16-Monthly Sales workbook, **exit Excel, then submit the EX 16-January Sales 2 workbook to your instructor**

Running a macro using a button

You can run a macro by assigning it to a button on your worksheet. Create a button by clicking the Insert tab, clicking the Shapes button 📐 ▾ in the Illustrations group, choosing a shape, then drawing the shape on the worksheet. After you create the button, right-click it, click Assign Macro, then click the macro the button will run and click OK. It is a good idea to label the button with descriptive text; select it and begin typing. You can also format macro buttons using clip art, photographs, fills, and shadows. You format a button using the buttons on the Drawing Tools Format tab. To add a fill to the button, click the Shape Fill list arrow and select a fill color, picture, texture, or gradient.

To add a shape effect, click the Shape Effects button and select an effect. You can also use the WordArt styles in the WordArt Styles group. FIGURE 16-15 shows a button formatted with a gradient, bevel and WordArt.

FIGURE 16-15: Formatted macro button

FIGURE 16-16: **Result of running MainProcedure procedure**

Formatted title

Row inserted

Total sales calculated

Sales status message inserted

FIGURE 16-17: **Printing options for macro procedures**

Current Project option button

Print to File check box

FIGURE 16-18: **Formatted January worksheet**

R2G Toronto January Sales

Code	Air Included	Insurance Included	New Project	Sales Rep #	Sales
457R	Yes	Yes	Yes	15248	$ 101,400.00
556J	Yes	No	Yes	13548	$ 77,875.00
675Y	Yes	No	No	69541	$ 80,300.00
446R	Yes	Yes	No	36654	$ 56,958.00
251D	No	Yes	No	95478	$ 38,520.00
335P	Yes	No	No	12532	$ 100,270.00
431V	No	No	Yes	51241	$ 64,390.00
215C	No	Yes	N	32145	$ 97,663.00
325B	No	Yes	Yes	12584	$ 48,600.00
311A	Yes	Yes	Yes	63344	$ 92,887.00
422R	Yes	No	No	87454	$ 55,600.00
331E	No	No	No	25469	$ 99,557.00
831P	Yes	Yes	No	51487	$ 56,698.00
337Q	No	Yes	No	35824	$ 29,574.00
				Total Sales:	$ 1,000,292.00

Sales Status: Met Quota

Your Name 11/7/2017

Practice

Concepts Review

1. Which element points to the Project Explorer window?
2. Which element do you click to return to Excel from the Visual Basic Editor?
3. Which element do you click to turn off the Step Into feature?
4. Which element points to the Code window?
5. Which element points to comments in the VBA code?

FIGURE 16-19

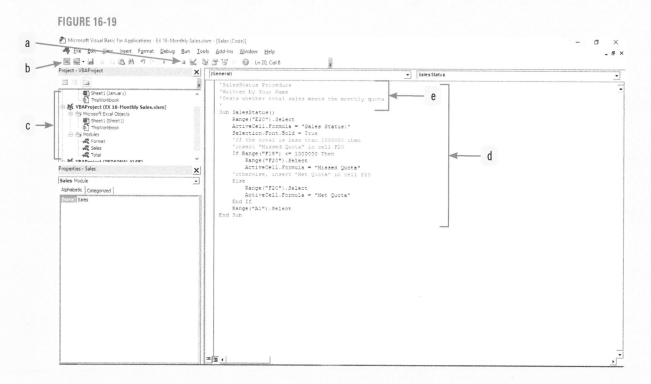

Match each term with the statement that best describes it.

6. Function
7. Sub procedure
8. Procedure
9. Keywords
10. Comments

a. Another term for a macro in Visual Basic for Applications (VBA)
b. A procedure that returns a value
c. Words that are recognized as part of the programming language
d. A series of statements that perform an action but don't return a value
e. Descriptive text used to explain parts of a procedure

Select the best answer from the list of choices.

11. You enter the statements of a macro in:
    a. The Macro dialog box.
    b. Any blank worksheet.
    c. The Properties window of the Visual Basic Editor.
    d. The Code window of the Visual Basic Editor.

12. A location in memory where you can temporarily store information is a:
    a. Variable.
    b. Procedure.
    c. Sub procedure.
    d. Function.

13. Comments are displayed in _____ in VBA code.

   a. Black

   b. Blue

   c. Red

   d. Green

14. If your macro doesn't run correctly, you should:

   a. Select the macro in the Macro dialog box, click Step Into, then debug the macro.

   b. Create an If...Then...Else statement.

   c. Click the Project Explorer button.

   d. Click the Properties button.

15. Keywords are displayed in _____ in VBA code.

   a. Black

   b. Blue

   c. Green

   d. Red

Skills Review

1. View and analyze VBA code.

   a. Start Excel, open EX 16-3.xlsm from the location where you store your Data Files, enable macros, then save it as **EX 16-HVAC**.

   b. Review the unformatted December worksheet.

   c. Open the Visual Basic Editor.

   d. Select the DataFormat module, and review the Format procedure.

   e. Insert comments in the procedure code describing what action you think each line of code will perform. (*Hint:* One of the statements will sort the list by Store #.) Add comment lines to the top of the procedure to describe the purpose of the macro and to enter your name.

   f. Save the macro, return to the worksheet, then run the Format macro.

   g. Compare the results with the code and your comments.

   h. Save the workbook.

2. Write VBA code.

   a. Open the Visual Basic Editor, and insert a new module named **Total** in the EX 16-HVAC project.

   b. Enter the code for the SalesTotal procedure exactly as shown in FIGURE 16-20. Enter your name in the second line.

   c. Save the macro, return to the December worksheet, then run the SalesTotal macro.

   d. Save the workbook.

3. Add a conditional statement.

   a. Open the Visual Basic Editor, and insert a new module named **Goal** in the EX 16-HVAC project.

   b. Enter the SalesGoal procedure exactly as shown in FIGURE 16-21. Enter your name on the second line.

   c. Save the macro, return to the December worksheet, and run the SalesGoal macro. The procedure should enter the message **Missed goal** in cell E18. Save the workbook.

FIGURE 16-20

```
'SalesTotal Procedure
'Written by Your Name
'Totals December sales
Sub SalesTotal()
    Range("E17").Select
    ActiveCell.Formula = "=SUM($E$3:$E$16)"
    Selection.Font.Bold = True
    With Selection.Borders(xlTop)
        .LineStyle = xlSingle
    End With
    Columns("E").Select
    Selection.Columns.AutoFit
    Range("A1").Select
End Sub
```

FIGURE 16-21

```
'SalesGoal Procedure
'Written by Your Name
'Tests whether sales goal was met
Sub SalesGoal()
    'If the total is >=100000, then insert "Met Goal"
    'in cell E18
    If Range("E17") >= 100000 Then
        Range("E18").Select
        ActiveCell.Formula = "Met goal"
    'otherwise, insert "Missed goal" in cell E18
    Else
        Range("E18").Select
        ActiveCell.Formula = "Missed goal"
    End If
    Range("A1").Select
End Sub
```

Skills Review (continued)

4. Prompt the user for data.

a. Open the Visual Basic Editor, and insert a new module named **Header** in the EX 16-HVAC project.

b. Enter the HeaderFooter procedure exactly as shown in FIGURE 16-22. You are entering an error in the procedure that will be corrected in Step 5.

c. Save the macro, then return to the December worksheet, and run the HeaderFooter macro.

d. Preview the December worksheet. Your name should be missing from the left section of the footer.

e. Save the workbook.

FIGURE 16-22

```
(General)                                                    ▼    HeaderFooter

'HeaderFooter Procedure
'Written by Your Name
'Procedure to customize the header and footer
Sub HeaderFooter()
    'Inserts the filename in the header
    Worksheets("December").PageSetup.CenterHeader = "&F"
    'Declares the variable FooterText as a string
    Dim FooterText As String
    'Prompts user for footer text
    Footer = InputBox("Enter your full name:")
    'Inserts response into left footer
    Worksheets("December").PageSetup.LeftFooter = FooterText
    'Inserts the date into right footer
    Worksheets("December").PageSetup.RightFooter = "&D"
End Sub
```

5. Debug a macro.

a. Return to the Visual Basic Editor and use the Step Into feature to locate where the error occurred in the HeaderFooter procedure. Use the Reset button to turn off the debugger.

b. Edit the procedure in the Visual Basic Editor to correct the error. (*Hint*: The error occurs on the line: Footer = InputBox("Enter your full name:"). The variable that will input the response text into the worksheet footer is FooterText. The line should be: FooterText = InputBox("Enter your full name:").)

c. Save the macro, return to the December worksheet, then run the HeaderFooter macro again.

d. Verify that your name now appears in the left section of the footer, then save the file.

6. Create and run a main procedure.

a. Return to the Visual Basic Editor, insert a new module, then name it **MainProc**.

b. Begin the main procedure by entering comments in the code window that provide the procedure's name (MainProcedure) and explain that its purpose is to run the Format, SalesTotal, SalesGoal, and HeaderFooter procedures. Enter your name in a comment.

c. Enter the procedure header **Sub MainProcedure()**.

d. Enter four Call statements that will run the Format, SalesTotal, SalesGoal, and HeaderFooter procedures in sequence.

e. Save the procedure and return to Excel.

f. Open EX 16-3.xlsm, then save it as **EX 16-HVAC 2**.

g. Run the MainProcedure macro, entering your name when prompted. (*Hint*: In the Macro dialog box, the macro procedures you created will now have EX 16-HVAC.xlsm! as part of their names. This is because the macros are stored in the EX 16-HVAC workbook, not in the EX 16-HVAC 2 workbook.)

h. Verify that the macro ran successfully by comparing your worksheet to FIGURE 16-23.

i. Save the EX 16-HVAC 2 workbook, preview the December worksheet to check the header and footer, then close the EX 16-HVAC 2 workbook.

j. Save the EX 16-HVAC workbook, close the workbook, exit Excel, then submit the EX 16-HVAC workbook to your instructor.

FIGURE 16-23

	A	B	C	D	E	F
1	Texas HVAC					
2	Store #	City	State	Manager	Sales	
3	157	Lubbock	TX	Golly	$ 5,534.34	
4	241	Beaumont	TX	Lin	$ 4,643.93	
5	312	Dallas	TX	Hall	$ 7,225.22	
6	336	Galveston	TX	Holland	$ 7,715.68	
7	367	Midland	TX	Nason	$ 7,654.32	
8	457	Corpus Christi	TX	Mores	$ 5,987.36	
9	527	San Antonio	TX	Dally	$ 8,228.33	
10	547	Arlington	TX	Pearcy	$ 5,251.22	
11	627	Houston	TX	Early	$ 8,583.66	
12	634	Austin	TX	Ebson	$ 6,594.22	
13	641	Alpine	TX	Hornsby	$ 8,001.34	
14	756	El Paso	TX	Carnes	$ 6,645.93	
15	963	Waco	TX	Cleaver	$ 8,656.83	
16	998	Fort Worth	TX	Dover	$ 4,442.90	
17					$95,165.28	
18					Missed goal	
19						

Independent Challenge 1

You are the sales manager for a plumbing supply company with offices in Miami, Boston, and Chicago. You have been given a macro written by the previous sales manager that you need to document and test. You will first run the macro procedure to see what it does, then add comments to the VBA code to document it. You will also enter data to verify that the formulas in the macro work correctly.

a. Start Excel, open EX 16-4.xlsm from the location where you store your Data Files, then save it as **EX 16-First Quarter**.

b. Run the First macro, noting anything that you think should be mentioned in your documentation.

c. Review the First procedure in the Visual Basic Editor. It is stored in the FirstQtr module.

FIGURE 16-24

d. Document the procedure by adding comments to the code, indicating the actions the procedure performs.

e. Enter your name in a comment line, then save the procedure.

f. Return to the Jan-Mar worksheet, and use FIGURE 16-24 as a guide to enter data in cells B4:D6. The totals will appear as you enter the income data.

	A	B	C	D
1		January	February	March
2	Sales			
3				
4	Miami	$ 5,000	$ 4,000	$ 7,000
5	Boston	$ 6,000	$ 5,000	$ 8,000
6	Chicago	$ 7,000	$ 6,000	$ 9,000
7				
8	Total Sales	$ 18,000	$ 15,000	$ 24,000
9				

g. Format the range B4:D8 using the Accounting Number format with no decimal places, as shown in FIGURE 16-24.

h. Check the total income calculations in row 8 to verify that the macro is working correctly.

i. Save the workbook, then preview the worksheet.

j. Close the workbook, exit Excel, then submit the workbook to your instructor.

Independent Challenge 2

You manage a car dealership that sells Volvos, Toyotas, and Subarus. Each month you are required to produce a report stating whether sales quotas were met for the three models of automobiles. The quotas for each month are as follows: Volvo 15, Toyota 12, and Subaru 10. You decide to create a procedure to automate your monthly task of determining the sales quota status for the three models. You would like your assistant to take this task over when you go on vacation next month. Because he has little experience with Excel, you decide to create a second procedure that prompts a user with input boxes to enter the actual placement results for the month.

a. Start Excel, open EX 16-5.xlsm from the location where you store your Data Files, then save it as **EX 16-Car Sales**.

b. Use the Visual Basic Editor to insert a new module named **Quotas** in the EX 16-Car Sales workbook. Create a procedure in the new module named **SalesQuota** that determines the quota status for each category and enters Yes or No in the Status column. The VBA code is shown in FIGURE 16-25.

c. Add comments to the SalesQuota procedure, including the procedure name, your name, and the purpose of the procedure.

FIGURE 16-25

```
Sub SalesQuota()

    If Range("C4") >= 15 Then
        Range("D4").Select
        ActiveCell.Formula = "Yes"
    Else
        Range("D4").Select
        ActiveCell.Formula = "No"
    End If


    If Range("C5") >= 12 Then
        Range("D5").Select
        ActiveCell.Formula = "Yes"
    Else
        Range("D5").Select
        ActiveCell.Formula = "No"
    End If


    If Range("C6") >= 10 Then
        Range("D6").Select
        ActiveCell.Formula = "Yes"
    Else
        Range("D6").Select
        ActiveCell.Formula = "No"
    End If

End Sub
```

Independent Challenge 2 (continued)

d. Insert a new module named **MonthlySales**. Create a second procedure named **Sales** that prompts a user for placement data for each car model, enters the input data in the appropriate cells, then calls the SalesQuota procedure. The VBA code is shown in FIGURE 16-26. (*Hint*: The procedure's blank lines group the macro code in related modules. These blank lines are optional and their purpose is to make the procedure easier to understand.)

e. Add a comment noting the procedure name on the first line. Add a comment with your name on the second line. Add a third comment line at the top of the procedure describing its purpose. Enter comments in the code to document the macro actions.

f. Run the Sales macro, and enter **13** for Volvo sales, **14** for Toyota sales, and **11** for Subaru sales. Correct any errors in the VBA code.

g. Return to the worksheet, save the workbook, then preview the worksheet. Close the workbook, exit Excel, then submit your workbook to·your instructor.

FIGURE 16-26

```
Sub Sales()

    Dim Volvo As String
    Volvo = InputBox("Enter Number of Volvos Sold")
    Range("C4").Select
    Selection = Volvo

    Dim Toyota As String
    Toyota = InputBox("Enter Number of Toyotas Sold")
    Range("C5").Select
    Selection = Toyota

    Dim Subaru As String
    Subaru = InputBox("Enter Number of Subarus sold")
    Range("C6").Select
    Selection = Subaru

    Call SalesQuota

End Sub
```

Independent Challenge 3

You are the business manager for Boston Pilates. Every month you prepare a report showing the income by studio. You decide to create a macro that will format the monthly reports. You add the same footers on every report, so you will create another macro that adds a footer to a document. Finally, you will create a main procedure that calls the macros to format the report and adds a footer, and then run it. You begin by opening a workbook with the January data. You will save the macros you create in this workbook.

a. Start Excel, open EX 16-6.xlsm from the location where you store your Data Files, then save it as **EX 16-Pilates**.

b. Insert a module named **Format**, then create a procedure named **Formatting** that:

- Selects cells A1 and A2, and formats that range in bold font and 14 pt font size.
- Selects the range containing fee data in column C, and formats it as currency.
- Selects cell A1 before ending.

c. Save the Formatting procedure.

d. Insert a module named **Foot**, then create a procedure named **Footer** that:

- Declares a string variable for text that will be placed in the left footer.
- Uses an input box to prompt the user for his or her name, and places the name in the left footer.
- Places the date in the right footer.

e. Save the Footer procedure.

f. Insert a module named **Main**, then create a procedure named **MainProc** that calls the Footer procedure and the Formatting procedure.

Independent Challenge 3 (continued)

g. Save the procedure, return to the January worksheet, then run the MainProc procedure. Debug each procedure as necessary. Your worksheet should look like FIGURE 16-27.

h. Document each procedure by inserting a comment line with the procedure name, your name, and a description of the procedure.

i. Preview the January worksheet, save the workbook, close the workbook, exit Excel, then submit the workbook to your instructor.

FIGURE 16-27

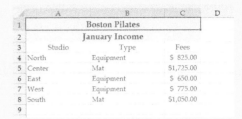

Independent Challenge 4: Explore

As the business manager of a florist shop, you decide to create a log of your non-payroll monthly expenses in an effort to budget the shop's expenses. You have a workbook with a macro that tracks the major expenses for the first three months of the year. You want to expand this macro to track six months of expenses.

a. Start Excel, open EX 16-7.xlsm from the location where you store your Data Files, then save it as **EX 16-Expenses**.

b. Run the MonthExpenses macro and enter expense numbers of your choosing to verify the macro is working properly.

c. Edit the MonthExpenses procedure to add the abbreviated month entries of Apr, May, and Jun in cells E1, F1, and G1, and the totals for these months in cells E8, F8, and G8.

d. Run the macro and debug the procedure as necessary. Enter expense numbers to verify the macro is working properly. Widen columns where necessary.

e. Save your work.

f. Verify that the totals are correct for each month.

g. Enter your name as a comment in the second line of the procedure.

h. Insert a module named **Format** with a procedure named **Formatting** that formats cells B2:G8 as currency, formats the total label and totals in cells A8:G8 in bold, widens the width of columns A through G to AutoFit the formatted data, and then selects cell A1. The VBA code is shown in FIGURE 16-28.

i. Save the macro, return to the worksheet, then without running the macro, assign the macro Formatting to a button on the worksheet. (*Hint:* Use the Rectangle tool to create the button, label the button **Format**, then right-click the button to assign the macro.)

j. Format the button and its label with styles and attributes of your choice.

k. Test the button and debug the Formatting macro if necessary.

l. Save the workbook, close the workbook, exit Excel, then submit the workbook to your instructor.

FIGURE 16-28

```
'Formatting Procedure
'Your Name
'Formats Expenses
'
Sub Formatting()
    Range("B2:G8").Select
    Selection.Style = "Currency"
    Range("A8:G8").Select
    Selection.Font.Bold = True
    Range("A1").Select
    Columns("A:G").Select
    Selection.Columns.AutoFit
End Sub
```

Excel 2016

Visual Workshop

Open EX 16-8.xlsm from the location where you store your Data Files, then save it as **EX 16-Events**. Create a macro procedure named **Format** in a module named **FormatTotal** that will format the worksheet as shown in FIGURE 16-29. (*Hints*: The font size of the first two rows is 14 pt and the other rows are 12 pt. Notice that a total row has been added.) Run the macro and debug it as necessary to make the worksheet match FIGURE 16-29. Insert your name in a comment line under the procedure name, then preview the worksheet. Submit the workbook to your instructor.

FIGURE 16-29

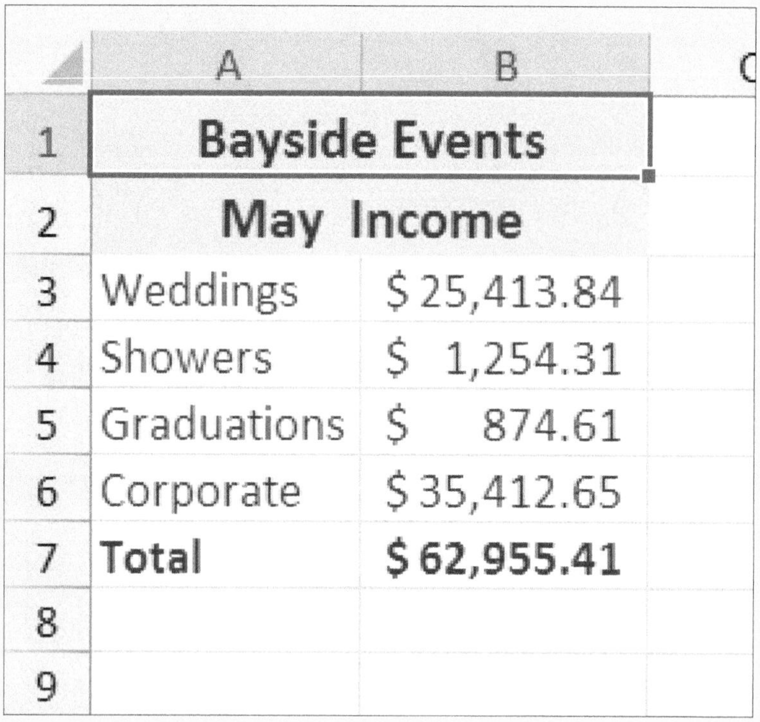

	A	B
1	**Bayside Events**	
2	**May Income**	
3	Weddings	$ 25,413.84
4	Showers	$ 1,254.31
5	Graduations	$ 874.61
6	Corporate	$ 35,412.65
7	**Total**	**$ 62,955.41**
8		
9		

Getting Started with Access 2016

CASE ▶ Julia Rice is the developer for a new initiative at Reason 2 Go (R2G), a specialized type of travel company that combines volunteer opportunities and tourism into meaningful experiences for its customers. Julia has been asked to create products to meet a market demand for shorter experiences in the United States. Julia uses Microsoft Access 2016 to store, maintain, and analyze customer and trip information.

Module Objectives

After completing this module, you will be able to:

- Understand relational databases
- Explore a database
- Create a database
- Create a table

- Create primary keys
- Relate two tables
- Enter data
- Edit data

Files You Will Need

R2G-1.accdb
LakeHomes-1.accdb
Salvage-1.accdb

Contacts-1.accdb
Basketball-1.accdb

Access 2016
Module 1

Learning
Outcomes
• Describe relational
database concepts
• Explain when to
use a database
• Compare a
relational database
to a spreadsheet

Understand Relational Databases

Microsoft Access 2016 is relational database software that runs on the Windows operating system. You use **relational database software** to manage data that is organized into lists, such as information about customers, products, vendors, employees, projects, or sales. Many small companies track customer, inventory, and sales information in a spreadsheet program such as Microsoft Excel. Although Excel offers some list management features, Access provides many more tools and advantages for managing data. Some advantages are due to Access using a relational database model whereas Excel manages data as a single list. TABLE 1-1 compares the two programs. **CASE** *You and Julia review the advantages of database software over spreadsheets for managing lists of information.*

DETAILS

The advantages of using Access for database management include the following:

- **Duplicate data is minimized**

  FIGURES 1-1 and 1-2 compare how you might store sales data in a single Excel spreadsheet list versus three related Access tables. With Access, you do not have to reenter information such as a customer's name and address or trip name every time a sale is made, because lists can be linked, or "related," in relational database software.

- **Information is more accurate, reliable, and consistent because duplicate data is minimized**

  The relational nature of data stored in an Access database allows you to minimize duplicate data entry, which creates more accurate, reliable, and consistent information. For example, customer data in a Customers table is entered only once, not every time a customer makes a purchase.

- **Data entry is faster and easier using Access forms**

  Data entry forms (screen layouts) make data entry faster, easier, and more accurate than entering data in a spreadsheet.

- **Information can be viewed and sorted in many ways using Access queries, forms, and reports**

  In Access, you can save multiple queries (questions about the data), data entry forms, and reports, allowing you to use them over and over without performing extra work to re-create a particular view of the data.

- **Information is more secure using Access passwords and security features**

  Access databases can be encrypted and password protected.

- **Several users can share and edit information at the same time**

  Unlike spreadsheets or word-processing documents, more than one person can enter, update, and analyze data in an Access database at the same time.

FIGURE 1-1: Using a spreadsheet to organize sales data

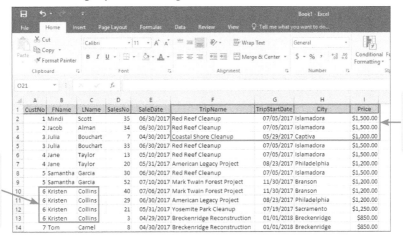

Customer information is duplicated when the same customer purchases multiple trips

Trip information is duplicated when the same trip is purchased by multiple customers

FIGURE 1-2: Using a relational database to organize sales data

Customers table

CustNo	FName	LName	Street	City	State	Zip	Phone
1	Mindi	Scott	52411 Oakmont Rd	Kansas City	MO	64144	(555) 444-1234
2	Jacob	Alman	2505 McGee St	Des Moines	IA	50288	(555) 111-6931
3	Julia	Bouchart	5200 Main St	Kansas City	MO	64105	(555) 111-3081

Sales table

CustNo	TripNo	SaleDate	SalesNo
1	2	7/1/17	35
2	2	7/1/17	34
3	2	7/1/17	33

Trips table

TripNo	TripName	TripStartDate	Duration	City	Price
1	Stanley Bay Cleanup	07/06/2017	3	Captiva	$750.00
2	Red Reef Cleanup	07/06/2017	3	Islamadora	$1,500.00
3	Breckenridge Recon	01/02/2018	7	Breckenridge	$850.00

TABLE 1-1: Comparing Excel with Access

feature	Excel	Access
Layout	Provides only a tabular spreadsheet layout	Provides tabular layouts as well as the ability to create customized data entry screens called forms
Storage	Restricted to a file's limitations	Virtually unlimited when coupled with the ability to use Microsoft SQL Server to store data
Linked tables	Manages single lists of information—no relational database capabilities	Relates lists of information to reduce data redundancy and create a powerful relational database
Reporting	Limited	Provides the ability to create an unlimited number of reports
Security	Limited to file security options such as marking the file "read-only" or protecting a range of cells	When used with SQL Server, provides extensive security down to the user and data level
Multiuser capabilities	Not allowed	Allows multiple users to simultaneously enter and update data
Data entry	Provides only one spreadsheet layout	Provides the ability to create an unlimited number of data entry forms

Explore a Database

Learning Outcomes
- Start Access and open a database
- Open and define Access objects

You can start Access in many ways. If you double-click an existing Access database icon or shortcut, that specific database opens directly within Access. This is the fastest way to open an existing Access database. If you start Access on its own, however, you see a window that requires you to make a choice between opening a database and creating a new database. **CASE** *Julia Rice has developed a database called R2G-1, which contains trip information. She asks you to start Access 2016 and review this database.*

STEPS

1. **Start Access**

   Access starts, as shown in FIGURE 1-3. This window allows you to open an existing database, create a new database from a template, or create a new blank database.

   TROUBLE
   If a yellow Security Warning bar appears below the Ribbon, click Enable Content.

2. **Click the Open Other Files link, navigate to the location where you store your Data Files, click the R2G-1.accdb database, click Open, then click the Maximize button ▣ if the Access window is not already maximized**

   The R2G-1.accdb Access database application contains five tables of data named Categories, Customers, Sales, States, and Trips. It also includes five queries, six forms, and four reports. Each of these items (table, query, form, and report) is a different type of **object** in an Access database application and is displayed in the **Navigation Pane**. The purpose of each object is defined in TABLE 1-2. To learn about an Access database application, you explore its objects.

   TROUBLE
   If the Navigation Pane is not open, click the Shutter Bar Open/Close Button ≫ to open it and view the database objects.

3. **In the Navigation Pane, double-click the Trips table to open it, then double-click the Customers table to open it**

   The Trips and Customers tables open in Datasheet View to display the data they store. A **table** is the fundamental building block of a relational database because it stores all of the data.

4. **In the Navigation Pane, double-click the TripSales query to open it, double-click any occurrence of Heritage in "American Heritage Tour," type Legacy, then click any other row**

   A **query** selects a subset of data from one or more tables. In this case, the TripSales query selects data from the Trips, Sales, and Customers tables. Entering or editing data in one object changes that information in every other object of the database, because all objects build on the same data stored only in the tables.

5. **Double-click the CustomerRoster form to open it, double-click Tour in "American Legacy Tour," type Project, then click any name in the middle part of the window**

   An Access **form** is a data entry screen. Users prefer forms for data entry (rather than editing and entering data in tables and queries) because forms can present information in any layout and include command buttons to make common tasks easy to perform.

6. **Double-click the TripSales report to open it**

   An Access **report** is a professional printout that can be distributed electronically or on paper. As shown in FIGURE 1-4, the edits made to the American Legacy Project name have carried through to the report, demonstrating the power and productivity of a relational database.

7. **Click the Close button ⊠ in the upper-right corner of the window**

   Clicking the Close button in the upper-right corner of the window closes Access as well as the database on which you are working. Changes to data, such as the edits you made to the American Legacy Project record, are automatically saved as you work. Access will prompt you to save design changes to objects before it closes.

FIGURE 1-3: Opening the Microsoft Access 2016 window

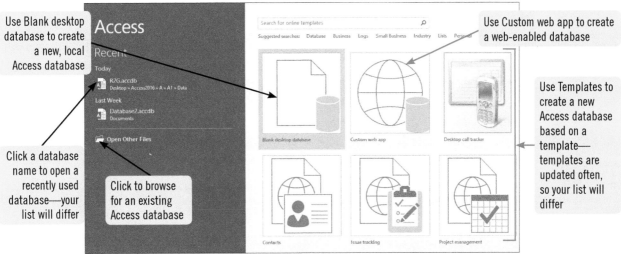

Use Blank desktop database to create a new, local Access database

Click a database name to open a recently used database—your list will differ

Click to browse for an existing Access database

Use Custom web app to create a web-enabled database

Use Templates to create a new Access database based on a template— templates are updated often, so your list will differ

FIGURE 1-4: Objects in the R2G-1 database

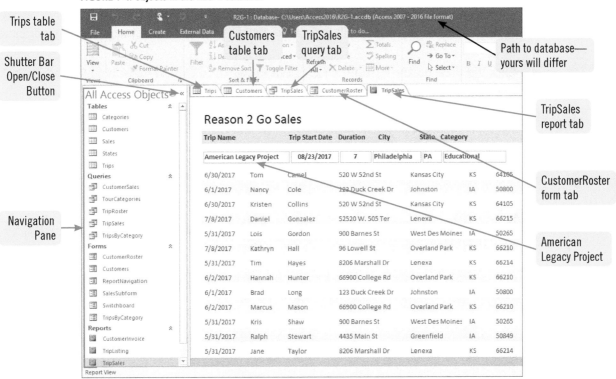

Trips table tab

Shutter Bar Open/Close Button

Navigation Pane

Customers table tab

TripSales query tab

Path to database— yours will differ

TripSales report tab

CustomerRoster form tab

American Legacy Project

TABLE 1-2: Access objects and their purpose

object	icon	purpose
Table		Contains all of the data within the database in a spreadsheet-like view called Datasheet View; tables are linked with a common field to create a relational database, which minimizes redundant data
Query		Allows you to select a subset of fields or records from one or more tables; create a query when you have a question about the data
Form		Provides an easy-to-use data entry screen
Report		Provides a professional presentation of data with headers, footers, graphics, and calculations on groups of records

Create a Database

Learning
Outcomes
• Create a database
• Create a table
• Define key
  database terms

You can create a database using an Access **template**, a sample database provided within the Microsoft Access program, or you can start with a blank database to create a database from scratch. Your decision depends on whether Access has a template that closely resembles the type of data you plan to manage. If it does, building your own database from a template might be faster than creating the database from scratch. Regardless of which method you use, you can always modify the database later, tailoring it to meet your specific needs. **CASE** *Julia Rice reasons that the best way for you to learn Access is to start a new database from scratch, so she asks you to create a new database that will track customer communication.*

STEPS

1. **Start Access**

2. **Click the** Blank desktop database icon, **click the** Browse button 📁**, navigate to the location where you store your Data Files, type** R2G **in the File name box, click** OK**, then click the** Create button

   A new database file with a single table named Table1 is created, as shown in FIGURE 1-5. Although you might be tempted to start entering data into the table, a better way to build a table is to first define the columns, or **fields**, of data that the table will store. **Table Design View** provides the most options for defining fields.

3. **Click the** View button 📐 **on the Fields tab to switch to Design View, type** Customers **in the Save As dialog box as the new table name, then click** OK

   The table name changes from Table1 to Customers, and you are positioned in Table Design View, a window you use to name and define the fields of a table. Access automatically created a field named ID with an AutoNumber data type. The **data type** is a significant characteristic of a field because it determines what type of data the field can store such as text, dates, or numbers. See TABLE 1-3 for more information about data types.

4. **Type** CustID **to rename ID to CustID, press [▼] to move to the first blank Field Name cell, type** FirstName, **press [▼], type** LastName, **press [▼], type** Phone, **press [▼], type** Birthday, **then press [▼]**

   Be sure to always separate a person's first and last names into two fields so that you can easily sort, find, and filter on either part of the name later. The Birthday field will only contain dates, so you should change its data type from Short Text (the default data type) to Date/Time.

5. **Click** Short Text **in the Birthday row, click the** list arrow, **then click** Date/Time

   With these five fields properly defined for the new Customers table, as shown in FIGURE 1-6, you're ready to enter data. You switch back to Datasheet View to enter or edit data. **Datasheet View** is a spreadsheet-like view of the data in a table. A **datasheet** is a grid that displays fields as columns and records as rows. The new **field names** you just defined are listed at the top of each column.

6. **Click the** View button ▦ **to switch to Datasheet View, click** Yes **when prompted to save the table, press [Tab] to move to the FirstName field, type** *your* first name, **press [Tab] to move to the LastName field, type** *your* last name, **press [Tab] to move to the Phone field, type** 555-666-7777, **press [Tab], type** 1/32/1990, **then press [Tab]**

   Because 1/32/1990 is not a valid date, Access does not allow you to make that entry and displays an error message, as shown in FIGURE 1-7. This shows that selecting the best data type for each field in Table Design View before entering data in Datasheet View helps prevent data entry errors.

TROUBLE
Tab through the
CustID field rather
than typing a value.
The CustID value
automatically
increments to the
next number.

7. **Press [Esc], edit the Birthday entry for the first record to** 1/31/1990, **press [Tab], enter two more sample records using realistic data, right-click the** Customers **table tab, then click** Close **to close the Customers table**

FIGURE 1-5: Creating a database with a new table

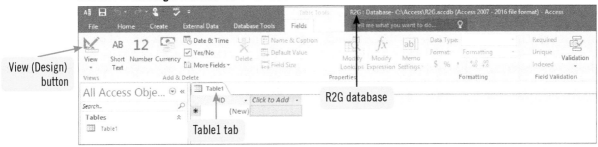

FIGURE 1-6: Defining field names and data types for the Customers table in Table Design View

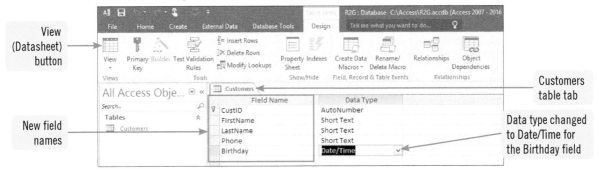

FIGURE 1-7: Entering your first record in the Customers table

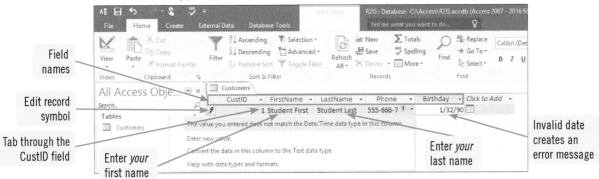

TABLE 1-3: Data types

data type	description of data
Short Text	Text or numbers not used in calculations such as a name, zip code, or phone number less than 255 characters
Long Text	Lengthy text greater than 255 characters, such as comments or notes
Number	Numeric data that can be used in calculations, such as quantities
Date/Time	Dates and times
Currency	Monetary values
AutoNumber	Sequential integers controlled by Access
Yes/No	Only two values: Yes or No
OLE Object	OLE (Object Linking and Embedding) objects such as an Excel spreadsheet or Word document
Hyperlink	Web and email addresses or links to local files
Attachment	Files such as .jpg images, spreadsheets, and documents
Calculated	Result of a calculation based on other fields in the table
Lookup Wizard	The Lookup Wizard helps you set Lookup properties, which display a drop-down list of values for the field; after using the Lookup Wizard, the final data type for the field is either Short Text or Number depending on the values in the drop-down list

Create a Table

Learning
Outcomes
• Create a table in
  Table Design View
• Set appropriate
  data types for fields

After creating your database and first table, you need to create new, related tables to build a relational database. Creating a table consists of these essential tasks: defining the fields in the table, selecting an appropriate data type for each field, naming the table, and determining how the table will participate in the relational database. **CASE** *Julia Rice asks you to create another table to store customer comments. The new table will eventually be connected to the Customers table so each customer record in the Customers table may be related to many records in the Comments table.*

STEPS

1. **Click the Create tab on the Ribbon, then click the Table Design button in the Tables group**

   You create and manipulate the structure of an object in **Design View**.

2. **Enter the field names and data types, as shown in FIGURE 1-8**

   The Comments table will contain four fields. CommentID is set with an AutoNumber data type so each record is automatically numbered by Access. The CommentText field has a Long Text data type so a long comment can be recorded. CommentDate is a Date/Time field to identify the date of the comment. CustID has a Number data type and will be used to link the Comments table to the Customers table later.

TROUBLE
To rename an object,
close it, right-click it
in the Navigation
Pane, and then click
Rename.

3. **Click the View button [icon] to switch to Datasheet View, click Yes when prompted to save the table, type Comments as the table name, click OK, then click No when prompted to create a primary key**

   A **primary key field** contains unique data for each record. You'll identify a primary key field for the Comments table later. For now, you'll enter the first record in the Comments table in Datasheet View. A **record** is a row of data in a table. Refer to TABLE 1-4 for a summary of important database terminology.

4. **Press [Tab] to move to the CommentText field, type Wants to help with the Rose Bowl Parade, press [Tab], type 1/7/17 in the CommentDate field, press [Tab], then type 1 in the CustID field**

   You entered 1 in the CustID field to connect this comment with the customer in the Customers table that has a CustID value of 1. Knowing which CustID value to enter for each comment is difficult. After you relate the tables properly (a task you have not yet performed), Access can make it easier to link each comment to the correct customer.

TROUBLE
The CommentID field
is an AutoNumber
field, which will auto-
matically increment
to provide a unique
value. If the number
has already incre-
mented beyond 1 for
the first record,
AutoNumber still
works as intended.

5. **Point to the divider line between the CommentText and CommentDate field names, and then double-click the ⬌ pointer to widen the CommentText field to read the entire comment, as shown in FIGURE 1-9**

6. **Right-click the Comments table tab, click Close, then click Yes if prompted to save the table**

Creating a table in Datasheet View

You can also create a new table in Datasheet View using the commands on the Fields tab of the Ribbon. However, if you use Design View to design your table before entering data, you will probably avoid some common data entry errors. Design View helps you focus on the appropriate data type for each field.

Selecting the best data type for each field before entering any data into that field helps prevent incorrect data and unintended typos. For example, if a field has a Number, Currency, or Date/Time data type, you will not be able to enter text into that field by mistake.

FIGURE 1-8: Creating the Comments table

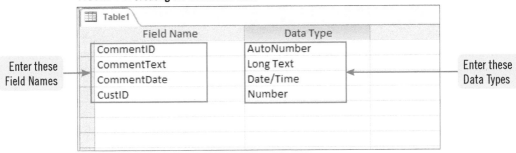

Enter these Field Names →

Enter these Data Types →

FIGURE 1-9: Entering a record in the Comments table

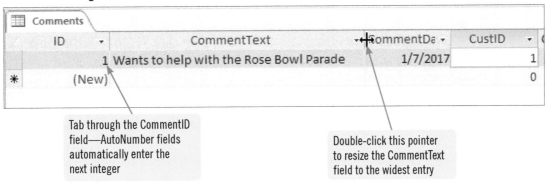

Tab through the CommentID field—AutoNumber fields automatically enter the next integer

Double-click this pointer to resize the CommentText field to the widest entry

TABLE 1-4: Important database terminology

term	description
Field	A specific piece or category of data such as a first name, last name, city, state, or phone number
Record	A group of related fields that describes a person, place, thing, or transaction such as a customer, location, product, or sale
Key field	A field that contains unique information for each record, such as a customer number for a customer
Table	A collection of records for a single subject such as Customers, Products, or Sales
Relational database	Multiple tables that are linked together to address a business process such as managing trips, sales, and customers at Reason 2 Go
Objects	The parts of an Access database that help you view, edit, manage, and analyze the data: tables, queries, forms, reports, macros, and modules

Create Primary Keys

Learning Outcomes
- Set the primary key field
- Define one-to-many relationships

The **primary key field** of a table serves two important purposes. First, it contains data that uniquely identifies each record. No two records can have the exact same entry in the field designated as the primary key field. Second, the primary key field helps relate one table to another in a **one-to-many relationship**, where one record from one table may be related to many records in the second table. For example, one record in the Customers table may be related to many records in the Comments table. (One customer may have many comments.) The primary key field is always on the "one" side of a one-to-many relationship between two tables. **CASE** *Julia Rice asks you to check that a primary key field has been appropriately identified for each table in the new R2G database.*

STEPS

1. **Right-click the** Comments table **in the Navigation Pane, then click** Design View

   Table Design View for the Comments table opens. The field with the AutoNumber data type is generally the best candidate for the primary key field in a table because it automatically contains a unique number for each record.

TROUBLE
Make sure the Design tab is selected on the Ribbon.

2. **Click the** CommentID field **if it is not already selected, then click the** Primary Key button **in the Tools group on the Design tab**

   The CommentID field is now set as the primary key field for the Comments table, as shown in FIGURE 1-10.

QUICK TIP
You can also click the Save button 💾 on the Quick Access Toolbar to save a table.

3. **Right-click the** Comments table tab, **click** Close, **then click** Yes **to save the table**

   Any time you must save design changes to an Access object such as a table, Access displays a dialog box to remind you to save the object.

4. **Right-click the** Customers table **in the Navigation Pane, then click** Design View

   Access has already set CustID as the primary key field for the Customers table, as shown in FIGURE 1-11.

5. **Right-click the** Customers table tab, **then click** Close

   You were not prompted to save the Customers table because you did not make any design changes. Now that you're sure that each table in the R2G database has an appropriate primary key field, you're ready to link the tables. The primary key field plays a critical role in this relationship.

Object views

Each object has a number of **views** that allow you to complete different tasks. For example, to enter and edit data into the database, use **Datasheet View** for tables and queries and **Form View** for forms. To change the structure of an object, you most often work in **Design View**. Use **Print Preview** to see how a report will appear on a physical piece of paper. Click the arrow at the bottom of the View button on the Design tab of the Ribbon to see all of the available views for an object.

Learning about field properties

Properties are the characteristics that define the field. Two properties are required for every field: Field Name and Data Type. Many other properties, such as Field Size, Format, Caption, and Default Value, are defined in the Field Properties pane in the lower half of a table's Design View. As you add more property entries, you are generally restricting the amount or type of data that can be entered in the field, which increases data entry accuracy. For example, you might change the Field Size property for a State field to 2 to eliminate an incorrect entry such as FLL. Field properties change depending on the data type of the selected field. For example, date fields do not have a Field Size property because Access controls the size of fields with a Date/Time data type.

FIGURE 1-10: Creating a primary key field for the Comments table

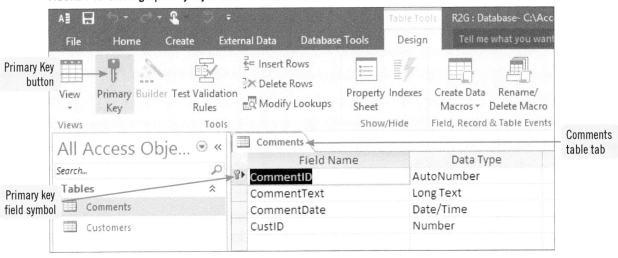

FIGURE 1-11: Confirming the primary key field for the Customers table

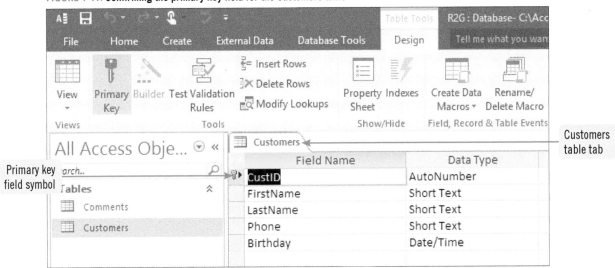

Relate Two Tables

Learning Outcomes
- Define foreign key field
- Create one-to-many relationships
- Set referential integrity

After you create tables and set primary key fields, you must connect the tables in one-to-many relationships to enjoy the benefits of a relational database. A one-to-many relationship between two tables means that one record from the first table is related to many records in the second table. You use a common field to make this connection. The common field is always the primary key field in the table on the "one" side of the relationship. **CASE** ▶ *Julia Rice explains that she has new comments to enter into the R2G database. To identify which customer is related to each comment, you define a one-to-many relationship between the Customers and Comments tables.*

STEPS

1. **Click the Database Tools tab on the Ribbon, then click the Relationships button**

2. **In the Show Table dialog box, double-click Customers, double-click Comments, then click Close**

   Each table is represented by a small **field list** window that displays the table's field names. A **key symbol** identifies the primary key field in each table. To relate the two tables in a one-to-many relationship, you connect them using a common field, which is always the primary key field on the "one" side of the relationship.

3. **Drag CustID in the Customers field list to the CustID field in the Comments field list**

   The Edit Relationships dialog box opens, as shown in FIGURE 1-12. **Referential integrity**, a set of Access rules that governs data entry, helps ensure data accuracy.

4. **Click the Enforce Referential Integrity check box in the Edit Relationships dialog box, then click Create**

   The **one-to-many line** shows the link between the CustID field of the Customers table (the "one" side) and the CustID field of the Comments table (the "many" side, indicated by the **infinity symbol**), as shown in FIGURE 1-13. The linking field on the "many" side is called the **foreign key field**. Now that these tables are related, it is much easier to enter comments for the correct customer.

5. **Right-click the Relationships tab, click Close, click Yes to save changes, then double-click the Customers table in the Navigation Pane to open it in Datasheet View**

   When you relate two tables in a one-to-many relationship, expand buttons appear to the left of each record in the table on the "one" side of the relationship. In this case, the Customers table is on the "one" side of the relationship.

6. **Click the expand button ⊞ to the left of the first record**

   A **subdatasheet** shows the related comment records for each customer. In other words, the subdatasheet shows the records on the "many" side of a one-to-many relationship. The expand button ⊞ also changed to the collapse button ⊟ for the first customer. Widening the CommentText field allows you to see the entire entry in the Comments subdatasheet. Now the task of entering comments for the correct customer is much more straightforward.

7. **Enter two more comments, as shown in** FIGURE 1-14

   Interestingly, the CustID field in the Comments table (the foreign key field) is not displayed in the subdatasheet. Behind the scenes, Access is entering the correct CustID value in the Comments table, which is the glue that ties each comment to the correct customer.

8. **Close the Customers table, then click Yes if prompted to save changes**

FIGURE 1-12: Edit Relationships dialog box

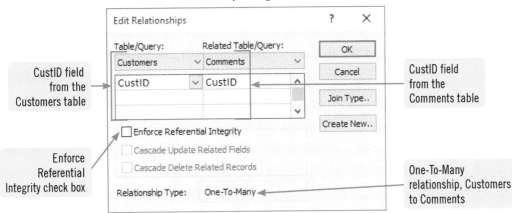

FIGURE 1-13: Linking the Customers and Comments tables

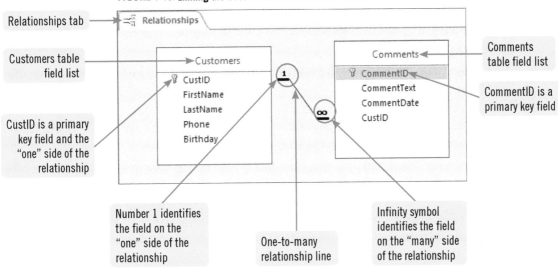

FIGURE 1-14: Entering comments using the subdatasheet

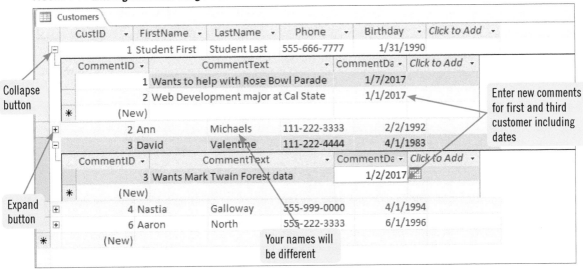

Enter Data

Learning Outcomes
- Navigate records in a datasheet
- Enter records in a datasheet

Your skill in navigating and entering new records is a key to your success with a relational database. You can use many techniques to navigate through the records in the table's datasheet. **CASE** ▶ *Even though you have already successfully entered some records, Julia Rice asks you to master this essential skill by entering several more customers in the R2G database.*

STEPS

1. **Double-click the Customers table in the Navigation Pane to open it, press [Tab] three times, then press [Enter] three times**

   The Customers table reopens. The Comments subdatasheets are collapsed. Both the [Tab] and [Enter] keys move the focus to the next field. The **focus** refers to which data you would edit if you started typing. When you navigate to the last field of the record, pressing [Tab] or [Enter] advances the focus to the first field of the next record. You can also use the Next record ▶ and Previous record ◀ **navigation buttons** on the navigation bar in the lower-left corner of the datasheet to navigate through the records. The **Current record** text box on the navigation bar tells you the number of the current record as well as the total number of records in the datasheet.

QUICK TIP
Press [Tab] in the CustID AutoNumber field.

2. **Click the FirstName field of the fourth record to position the insertion point to enter a new record**

   You can also use the New (blank) record button ▶* on the navigation bar to move to a new record. You enter new records at the end of the datasheet. You learn how to sort and reorder records later. A complete list of navigation keystrokes is shown in TABLE 1-5.

QUICK TIP
Access databases are multiuser with one important limitation: Two users cannot edit the same record at the same time. In that case, a message explains that the second user must wait until the first user moves to a different record.

3. **At the end of the datasheet, enter the last three records shown in FIGURE 1-15**

   The **edit record symbol** 🖉 appears to the left of the record you are currently editing. When you move to a different record, Access saves the data. Therefore, Access never prompts you to save data because it performs that task automatically. Saving data automatically allows Access databases to be **multiuser** databases, which means that more than one person can enter and edit data in the same database at the same time.

   Your CustID values might differ from those in FIGURE 1-15. Because the CustID field is an **AutoNumber** field, Access automatically enters the next consecutive number into the field as it creates the record. If you delete a record or are interrupted when entering a record, Access discards the value in the AutoNumber field and does not reuse it. Therefore, AutoNumber values do not represent the number of records in your table. Instead, they provide a unique value per record, similar to check numbers.

Changing from Navigation mode to Edit mode

If you navigate to another area of the datasheet by clicking with the mouse pointer instead of pressing [Tab] or [Enter], you change from **Navigation mode** to Edit mode. In **Edit mode**, Access assumes that you are trying to make changes to the current field value, so keystrokes such as [Ctrl][End], [Ctrl][Home], [←], and [→] move the insertion point within the field. To return to Navigation mode, press [Tab] or [Enter] (thus moving the focus to the next field), or press [↑] or [↓] (thus moving the focus to a different record).

FIGURE 1-15: **New records in the Customers table**

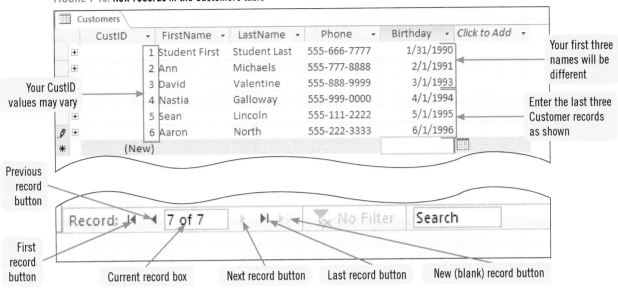

TABLE 1-5: **Navigation mode keyboard shortcuts**

shortcut key	moves to the
[Tab], [Enter], or [→]	Next field of the current record
[Shift][Tab] or [←]	Previous field of the current record
[Home]	First field of the current record
[End]	Last field of the current record
[Ctrl][Home] or [F5]	First field of the first record
[Ctrl][End]	Last field of the last record
[↑]	Current field of the previous record
[↓]	Current field of the next record

Cloud computing

Using **OneDrive**, a free service from Microsoft, you can store files in the "cloud" and retrieve them anytime you are connected to the Internet. Saving your files to the OneDrive is one example of cloud computing. **Cloud computing** means you are using an Internet resource to complete your work.

Edit Data

Learning Outcomes
- Edit data in a datasheet
- Delete records in a datasheet
- Preview and print a datasheet

Updating existing data in a database is another critical database task. To change the contents of an existing record, navigate to the field you want to change and type the new information. You can delete unwanted data by clicking the field and using [Backspace] or [Delete] to delete text to the left or right of the insertion point. Other data entry keystrokes are summarized in TABLE 1-6. **CASE** *Julia Rice asks you to correct two records in the Customers table.*

STEPS

1. **Select the phone number in the Phone field of the second record, type 111-222-3333, press [Enter], type 2/2/92, then press [Enter]**

   You changed the telephone number and birth date of the second customer. When you entered the last two digits of the year value, Access inserted the first two digits after you pressed [Enter]. You'll also update the third customer.

   QUICK TIP
   The ScreenTip for the Undo button displays the action you can undo.

2. **Press [Enter] enough times to move to the Phone field of the third record, type 111-222-4444, then press [Esc]**

   Pressing [Esc] once removes the current field's editing changes, so the Phone value changes back to the previous entry. Pressing [Esc] twice removes all changes to the current record. When you move to another record, Access saves your edits, so you can no longer use [Esc] to remove editing changes to the current record. You can, however, click the Undo button on the Quick Access Toolbar to undo changes to a previous record.

3. **Retype 111-222-4444, press [Enter], type 3/1/83 in the Birthday field, press [Enter], click the 3/1/83 date you just entered, click the Calendar icon , then click April 1, 1983, as shown in FIGURE 1-16**

   When you are working in the Birthday field, which has a Date/Time data type, you can enter a date from the keyboard or use the **Calendar Picker**, a pop-up calendar, to find and select a date.

4. **Click the record selector for the fifth record (Sean Lincoln), click the Delete button in the Records group on the Home tab, then click Yes**

   A message warns that you cannot undo a record deletion. The Undo button is dimmed, indicating that you cannot use it. The Customers table now has five records, as shown in FIGURE 1-17. Keep in mind that your CustID values might differ from those in the figure because they are controlled by Access.

   QUICK TIP
   If requested to print the Customers datasheet by your instructor, click the Print button, then click OK.

5. **Click the File tab, click Print, then click Print Preview to review the printout of the Customers table before printing**

6. **Click the Close Print Preview button, then click the Close button in the upper-right corner of the window to close the R2G.accdb database and Access 2016**

FIGURE 1-16: **Editing customer records**

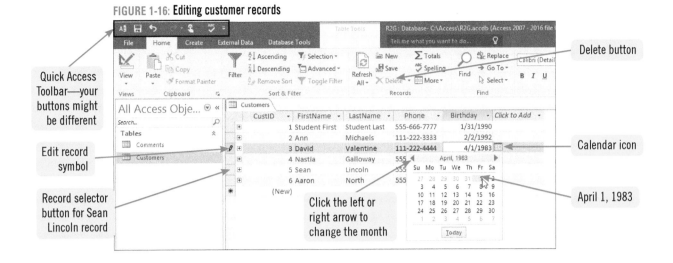

Quick Access Toolbar—your buttons might be different

Edit record symbol

Record selector button for Sean Lincoln record

Click the left or right arrow to change the month

Delete button

Calendar icon

April 1, 1983

FIGURE 1-17: **Final Customers datasheet**

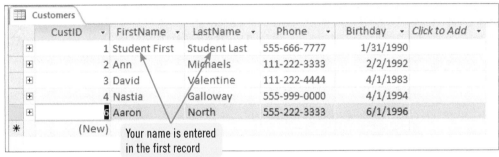

Your name is entered in the first record

TABLE 1-6: **Edit mode keyboard shortcuts**

editing keystroke	action
[Backspace]	Deletes one character to the left of the insertion point
[Delete]	Deletes one character to the right of the insertion point
[F2]	Switches between Edit and Navigation mode
[Esc]	Undoes the change to the current field
[Esc][Esc]	Undoes all changes to the current record
[F7]	Starts the spell-check feature
[Ctrl][']	Inserts the value from the same field in the previous record into the current field
[Ctrl][;]	Inserts the current date in a Date field

Resizing and moving datasheet columns

You can resize the width of a field in a datasheet by dragging the column separator, the thin line that separates the field names to the left or right. The pointer changes to ✛ as you make the field wider or narrower. Release the mouse button when you have resized the field. To adjust the column width to accommodate the widest entry in the field, double-click the column separator. To move a column, click the field name to select the entire column, then drag the field name left or right.

Practice

Concepts Review

Label each element of the Access window shown in FIGURE 1-18.

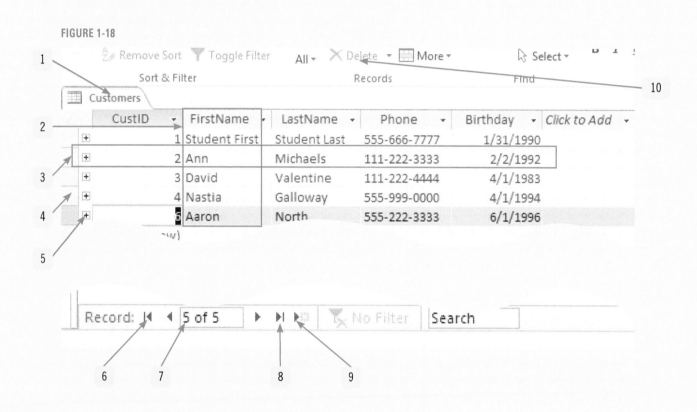

FIGURE 1-18

Match each term with the statement that best describes it.

11. Field	**a.** A subset of data from one or more tables
12. Record	**b.** A collection of records for a single subject, such as all the customer records
13. Table	**c.** A professional printout of database information
14. Datasheet	**d.** A spreadsheet-like grid that displays fields as columns and records as rows
15. Query	**e.** A group of related fields for one item, such as all of the information for one customer
16. Form	**f.** A category of information in a table, such as a company name, city, or state
17. Report	**g.** An easy-to-use data entry screen

Select the best answer from the list of choices.

18. **When you create a new database, which object is created first?**
    a. Module
    b. Query
    c. Table
    d. Form

19. **Which of the following is *not* a typical benefit of relational databases?**
    a. Minimized duplicate data entry
    b. More accurate data
    c. Tables automatically create needed relationships
    d. More consistent data

20. **Which of the following is *not* an advantage of managing data with relational database software such as Access versus spreadsheet software such as Excel?**
    a. Allows multiple users to enter data simultaneously
    b. Uses a single table to store all data
    c. Provides data entry forms
    d. Reduces duplicate data entry

Skills Review

1. **Understand relational databases.**
   a. Write down five advantages of managing database information in Access versus using a spreadsheet.
   b. Write a sentence to explain how the terms field, record, table, and relational database relate to one another.

2. **Explore a database.**
   a. Start Access.
   b. Open the LakeHomes-1.accdb database from the location where you store your Data Files. Click Enable Content if a yellow Security Warning message appears.
   c. Open each of the four tables to study the data they contain. Complete the following table:

table name	number of records	number of fields

   d. Double-click the ListingsByRealtor query in the Navigation Pane to open it. Change any occurrence of Gordon Bono to *your* name. Move to another record to save your changes.
   e. Double-click the RealtorsMainForm in the Navigation Pane to open it. Use the navigation buttons to navigate through the 13 realtors to observe each realtor's listings.
   f. Double-click the RealtorListingReport in the Navigation Pane to open it. The records are listed in ascending order by realtor last name. Scroll through the report to make sure your name is positioned correctly.
   g. Close the LakeHomes-1 database, then close Access 2016.

3. **Create a database.**
   a. Start Access, click the Blank desktop database icon, use the Browse button to navigate to the location where you store your Data Files, type **LakeHomeMarketing** as the filename, click OK, and then click Create to create a new database named LakeHomeMarketing.accdb.

Skills Review (continued)

b. Switch to Table Design View, name the table **Prospects**, then enter the following fields and data types:

field name	data type
ProspectID	AutoNumber
ProspectFirst	Short Text
ProspectLast	Short Text
Phone	Short Text
Email	Hyperlink
Street	Short Text
City	Short Text
State	Short Text
Zip	Short Text

c. Save the table, switch to Datasheet View, and enter two records using your name in the first record and your instructor's name in the second. Tab through the ProspectID field, an AutoNumber field.

d. Enter **TN** (Tennessee) as the value in the State field for both records. Use school or fictitious (rather than personal) data for all other field data, and be sure to fill out each record completely.

e. Widen each column in the Prospects table so that all data is visible, then save and close the Prospects table.

4. **Create a table.**

a. Click the Create tab on the Ribbon, click the Table Design button in the Tables group, then create a new table with the following two fields and data types:

field name	data type
State2	Short Text
StateName	Short Text

b. Save the table with the name **States**. Click No when asked if you want Access to create the primary key field.

5. **Create primary keys.**

a. In Table Design View of the States table, set the State2 field as the primary key field.

b. Save the States table and open it in Datasheet View.

c. Enter one state record, using **TN** for the State2 value and **Tennessee** for the StateName value to match the State value of TN that you entered for both records in the Prospects table.

d. Close the States table.

6. **Relate two tables.**

a. From the Database Tools tab, open the Relationships window.

b. Add the States, then the Prospects table to the Relationships window.

c. Drag the bottom edge of the Prospects table to expand the field list to display all of the fields.

FIGURE 1-19

d. Drag the State2 field from the States table to the State field of the Prospects table.

e. In the Edit Relationships dialog box, click the Enforce Referential Integrity check box, then click Create. Your Relationships window should look like FIGURE 1-19. If you connect the wrong fields by mistake, right-click the line connecting the two fields, click Delete, then try again.

f. Close the Relationships window, and save changes when prompted.

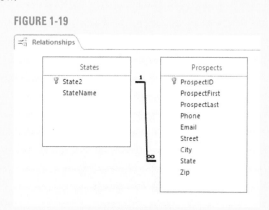

Skills Review (continued)

7. Enter data.

a. Open the States table and enter the following records:

State2 field	StateName field
CO	Colorado
IA	Iowa
KS	Kansas
MO	Missouri
NE	Nebraska
OK	Oklahoma
WI	Wisconsin
TX	Texas

b. Add three more state records of your choice for a total of 12 records in the States table using the correct two-character abbreviation for the state and the correctly spelled state name.

c. Close and reopen the States table. Notice that Access automatically sorts the records by the values in the primary key field, the State2 field.

8. Edit data.

a. Click the Expand button for the TN record to see the two related records from the Prospects table.

b. Enter two more prospects in the TN subdatasheet using any fictitious but realistic data, as shown in FIGURE 1-20. Notice that you are not required to enter a value for the State field, the foreign key field in the subdatasheet.

c. If required by your instructor, print the States datasheet and the Prospects datasheet.

d. Click the Close button in the upper-right corner of the Access window to close all open objects as well as the LakeHomeMarketing.accdb database and Access 2016. If prompted to save any design changes, click Yes.

FIGURE 1-20

Independent Challenge 1

Consider the following twelve subject areas:

- Telephone directory
- Islands of the Caribbean
- Members of the U.S. House of Representatives
- College course offerings

- Physical activities
- Ancient wonders of the world
- Restaurant menu
- Shopping catalog items

- Vehicles
- Conventions
- Party guest list
- Movie listings

a. For each subject, build a Word table with 4–7 columns and three rows. In the first row, enter field names that you would expect to see in a table used to manage that subject.

b. In the second and third rows of each table, enter two realistic records. The first table, Telephone Directory, is completed as an example to follow.

TABLE: **Telephone Directory**

FirstName	LastName	Street	Zip	Phone
Marco	Lopez	100 Main Street	88715	555-612-3312
Christopher	Stafford	253 Maple Lane	77824	555-612-1179

c. Consider the following guidelines as you build the table:

Make sure each record represents one item in that table. For example, in the Restaurant Menu table, the following table is a random list of categories of food. The records do not represent one item in a restaurant menu.

Beverage	Appetizer	Meat	Vegetable	Dessert
Milk	Chicken wings	Steak	Carrots	Chocolate cake
Tea	Onion rings	Salmon	Potato	Cheesecake

A better example of records that describe an item in the restaurant menu would be the following:

Category	Description	Price	Calories	Spicy
Appetizer	Chicken wings	$10	800	Yes
Beverage	Milk	$2	250	No

Do not put first and last names in the same field. This prevents you from easily sorting, filtering, or searching on either part of the name later.

For the same reasons, break street, city, state, zip, and country data into separate fields as well.

Do not put values and units of measure such as 5 minutes, 4 lbs, or 6 sq. miles in the same field. This also prevents you from sorting and calculating on the numeric part of the information. Make your field names descriptive such as TimeInMinutes or AreaInSquareMiles so that each record's entries are consistent.

Do not put these tables in one Access database. Putting all of these tables in one Access database would be analogous to putting a letter to your Congressman, a creative poem, and a cover letter to a future employer all in the same Word file. Just as that wouldn't make organizational sense, these tables do not belong together in the same Access database either. Create your sample tables in a Word document to stay focused on proper field and record construction versus the task of building Access tables.

Independent Challenge 2

You are working with several civic groups to coordinate a community-wide recycling effort. You have started a database called Salvage-1, which tracks the clubs, their recyclable material deposits, and the collection centers that are participating.

a. Start Access, then open the Salvage-1.accdb database from the location where you store your Data Files. Enable content if prompted.

b. Open each table's datasheet to study the number of fields and records per table. Notice that there are no expand buttons to the left of any records because relationships have not yet been established between these tables.

c. In a Word document, re-create the following table and fill in the blanks:

table name	number of records	number of fields

d. Close all table datasheets, then open the Relationships window and create the following one-to-many relationships. Drag the tables from the Navigation Pane to the Relationships window, and drag the title bars and borders of the field lists to position them as shown in FIGURE 1-21.

field on the "one" side of the relationship	field on the "many" side of the relationship
ClubNumber in Clubs table	ClubNumber in Deposits table
CenterNumber in Centers table	CenterNumber in Deposits table

e. Be sure to enforce referential integrity on all relationships. If you create an incorrect relationship, right-click the line linking the fields, click Delete, and try again. Your final Relationships window should look like FIGURE 1-21.

f. Click the Relationship Report button on the Design tab, and if required by your instructor, click Print to print a copy of the Relationships for Salvage-1 report. To close the report, right-click the Relationships for Salvage-1 tab and click Close. Click Yes when prompted to save changes to the report with the name **Relationships for Salvage-1**. Save and close the Relationships window.

g. Open the Clubs table and add a new record with fictitious but realistic data in all of the fields. Enter **8** as the ClubNumber value and your name in the FName (first name) and LName (last name) fields.

h. Expand the subdatasheets for each record in the Clubs table to see the related records from the Deposits table. Which club made the most deposits? Be ready to answer in class. Close the Clubs table.

i. Open the Centers table and add a new record with fictitious but realistic data in all of the fields. Enter your first and last names in the CenterName field and enter **5** as the CenterNumber.

j. Expand the subdatasheets for each record in the Centers table to see the related records from the Deposits table. Which center made the most deposits? Be ready to answer in class. Close the Centers table.

k. Close the Salvage-1.accdb database, then exit Access 2016.

FIGURE 1-21

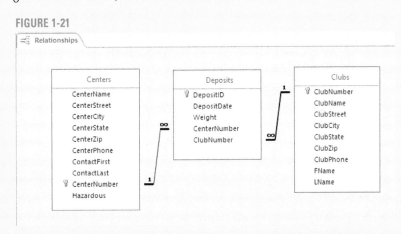

Independent Challenge 3

You are working for an advertising agency that provides social media consulting for small and large businesses in the midwestern United States. You have started a database called Contacts-1, which tracks your company's customers. (*Note*: To complete this Independent Challenge, make sure you are connected to the Internet.)

a. Start Access and open the Contacts-1.accdb database from the location where you store your Data Files. Enable content if prompted.

b. Add a new record to the Customers table, using any local business name, your first and last names, **$10,500** in the YTDSales field, and fictitious but reasonable entries for the rest of the fields.

c. Edit the Sprint Systems record (ID 1). Change the Company name to **A1 Cellular**, and change the Street value to **4455 Mastin St**.

d. Delete the record for EBC (ID 18), then close the Customers table.

e. Create a new table with two fields, **State2** and **StateName**. Assign both fields a Short Text data type. The State2 field will contain the two-letter abbreviation for state names. The StateName field will contain the Set the State2 field as the primary key field, then save the table as **States**.

f. Enter at least three records into the States table, making sure that all of the states used in the Customers datasheet are entered in the States table. This includes **KS Kansas**, **MO Missouri**, and any other state you entered in Step b when you added a new record to the Customers table.

g. Close all open tables. Open the Relationships window, add both the States and Customers field lists to the window, then expand the size of the Customers field list so that all fields are visible. (*Hint*: The field list will not show a vertical scroll bar when all fields in the list are visible.)

h. Build a one-to-many relationship between the States and Customers tables by dragging the State2 field from the States table to the State field of the Customers table to create a one-to-many relationship between the two tables. Enforce referential integrity on the relationship. If you are unable to enforce referential integrity, it means that a value in the State field of the Customers table doesn't have a perfect match in the State2 field of the States table. Open both table datasheets, making sure every state in the State field of the Customers table is also represented in the State2 field of the States table, close all datasheets, then reestablish the one-to-many relationship between the two tables with referential integrity.

i. Click the Relationship Report button on the Design tab, then if requested by your instructor, click Print to print the report.

j. Right-click the Relationships for Contacts-1 tab, then click Close. Click Yes when prompted to save the report with the name **Relationships for Contacts-1**.

k. Close the Relationships window, saving changes as prompted.

l. Close the Contacts-1.accdb database, then exit Access 2016.

Independent Challenge 4: Explore

Now that you've learned about Microsoft Access and relational databases, brainstorm how you might use an Access database in your daily life or career. Start by visiting the Microsoft website, and explore what's new in Access 2016.

(*Note*: To complete this Independent Challenge, make sure you are connected to the Internet.)

a. Using your favorite search engine, look up the keywords *benefits of a relational database* or *benefits of Microsoft Access* to find articles that discuss the benefits of organizing data in a relational database.

b. Read several articles about the benefits of organizing data in a relational database such as Access, identifying three distinct benefits. Use a Word document to record those three benefits. Also, copy and paste the website address of the article you are referencing for each benefit you have identified.

c. In addition, as you read the articles that describe relational database benefits, list any terminology unfamiliar to you, identifying at least five new terms.

d. Using a search engine or a website that provides a computer glossary such as www.whatis.com or www.webopedia.com, look up the definition of the new terms, and enter both the term and the definition of the term in your document as well as the website address where your definition was found.

e. Finally, based on your research and growing understanding of Access 2016, list three ways you could use an Access database to organize, enhance, or support the activities and responsibilities of your daily life or career. Type your name at the top of the document, and submit it to your instructor as requested.

Visual Workshop

Open the Basketball-1.accdb database from the location where you store your Data Files, then enable content if prompted. Open the Offense query datasheet, which lists offensive statistics by player by game. Modify any of the Matthew Douglas records to contain your first and last names, then move to a different record, observing the power of a relational database to modify every occurrence of that name throughout the database. Close the Offense query, then open the Players table. Note that there are no expand buttons to the left of the records, indicating that this table does not participate on the "one" side of a one-to-many relationship. Close the Players table and open the Relationships window. Drag the tables from the Navigation Pane and create the relationships with referential integrity, as shown in FIGURE 1-22. Note the one-to-many relationship between the Players and Stats table. Print the Relationships report if requested by your instructor and save it with the name **Relationships for Basketball-1**. Close the report and close and save the Relationships window. Now reopen the Players table noting the expand buttons to the left of each record. Expand the subdatasheet for your name and for several other players to observe the "many" records from the Stats table that are now related to each record in the Players table.

FIGURE 1-22

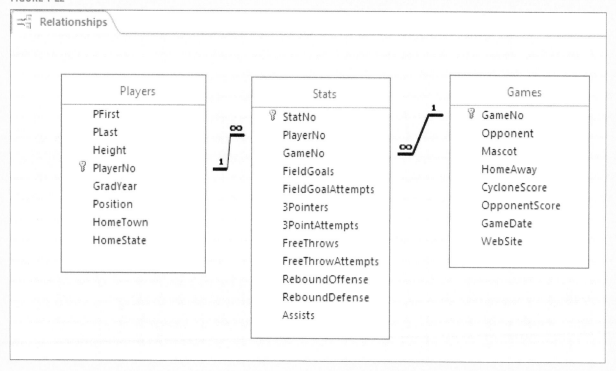

Building and Using Queries

CASE Julia Rice, trip developer for U.S. group travel at Reason 2 Go, has several questions about the customer and trip information in the R2G database. You'll develop queries to provide Julia with up-to-date answers.

Module Objectives

After completing this module, you will be able to:

- Use the Query Wizard
- Work with data in a query
- Use Query Design View
- Sort and find data

- Filter data
- Apply AND criteria
- Apply OR criteria
- Format a datasheet

Files You Will Need

R2G-2.accdb	HouseOfReps-2.accdb
Salvage-2.accdb	VetClinic-2.accdb
Service-2.accdb	Baseball-2.accdb

Use the Query Wizard

Learning
Outcomes
• Describe the
  purpose for a
  query
• Create a query
  with the Simple
  Query Wizard

A **query** answers a question about the information in the database. A query allows you to select a subset of fields and records from one or more tables and then present the selected data as a single datasheet. A major benefit of working with data through a query is that you can focus on only the specific information you need, rather than navigating through all the fields and records from one or more large tables. You can enter, edit, and navigate data in a query datasheet just like a table datasheet. However, keep in mind that Access data is physically stored only in tables, even though you can select, view, and edit it through other Access objects such as queries and forms. Because a query doesn't physically store the data, a query datasheet is sometimes called a **logical view** of the data. A query stores a set of **SQL (Structured Query Language)** instructions, but because you can use Access query tools such as Query Design View to create and modify the query, you are not required to write SQL statements to build or use Access queries. Access provides several tools to create a new query, one of which is the Simple Query Wizard. **CASE** *Julia Rice suggests that you use the Simple Query Wizard to create a query that displays fields from the Trips and Customers tables in one datasheet.*

STEPS

1. **Start Access, open the** R2G-2.accdb database, **enable content if prompted, then maximize the window**

   Access provides several tools to create a new query. One way is to use the **Simple Query Wizard**, which prompts you for the information it needs to create the query.

2. **Click the** Create tab on the Ribbon, click the Query Wizard button **in the Queries group, then click** OK **to start the Simple Query Wizard**

   The first Simple Query Wizard dialog box opens, prompting you to select the fields you want to view in the new query. You can select fields from one or more existing tables or queries.

3. **Click the** Tables/Queries list arrow, click Table: Trips, double-click TripName, double-click City, double-click Category, **then double-click** Price

   So far, you've selected four fields from the Trips table to display basic trip information in this query. You also want to add the first and last name information from the Customers table so you know which customers purchased each trip.

4. **Click the** Tables/Queries list arrow, click Table: Customers, double-click FName, **then double-click** LName

   You've selected four fields from the Trips table and two from the Customers table for your new query, as shown in FIGURE 2-1.

5. **Click** Next, click Next to select Detail, select Trips Query **in the title text box, type** TripCustomerList **as the name of the query, then click** Finish

   The TripCustomerList datasheet opens, displaying four fields from the Trips table and two from the Customers table, as shown in FIGURE 2-2. The query can show which customers have purchased which Trips because of the one-to-many table relationships established in the Relationships window.

Simple Query Wizard

The **Simple Query Wizard** is a series of dialog boxes that prompt you for the information needed to create a Select query. A **Select query** selects fields from one or more tables in your database and is by far the most common type of query. The other query wizards—Crosstab, Find Duplicates, and Find Unmatched—are used to create queries that do specialized types of data analysis and are covered in Module 10 on advanced queries.

FIGURE 2-1: Selecting fields using the Simple Query Wizard

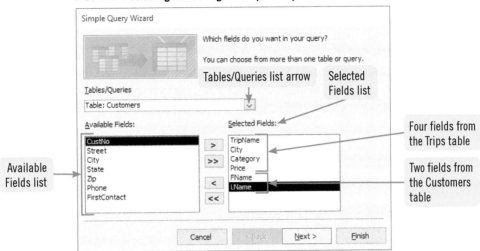

Simple Query Wizard

Which fields do you want in your query?

You can choose from more than one table or query.

Tables/Queries list arrow   Selected Fields list

Tables/Queries

Table: Customers

Available Fields: Selected Fields:

CustNo   TripName
Street   City   Four fields from
City   Category   the Trips table
State   Price
Zip   FName   Two fields from
Phone   LName   the Customers
FirstContact   table

Available Fields list

Cancel   < Back   Next >   Finish

FIGURE 2-2: TripCustomerList datasheet

TripCustomerList   TripCustomerList query

TripName	City	Category	Price	FName	LName
Stanley Bay Cleanup	Captiva	Eco	$750	Ralph	Stewart
Stanley Bay Cleanup	Captiva	Eco	$750	Lisa	Gomez
Breckenridge Reconstruction	Breckenridge	Eco	$850	Kristen	Collins
Stanley Bay Cleanup	Captiva	Eco	$750	Kris	Shaw
Stanley Bay Cleanup	Captiva	Eco	$750	Lois	Gordon
Stanley Bay Cleanup	Captiva	Eco	$750	Naresh	Blackwell
Coastal Shore Cleanup	Captiva	Family	$1,000	Julia	Bouchart
Breckenridge Reconstruction	Breckenridge	Eco	$850	Tom	Camel
Golden Hands Venture	Orlando	Family	$900	Shirley	Cruz
Golden Hands Venture	Orlando	Family	$900	Zohra	Bell
Golden Hands Venture	Orlando	Family	$900	Kathryn	Hall
Golden Hands Venture	Orlando	Family	$900	Jose	Edwards
Red Reef Cleanup	Islamadora	Eco	$1,500	Jane	Taylor
Stanley Bay Cleanup	Captiva	Eco	$750	Kori	James
American Heritage Tour	Philadelphia	Educational	$1,200	Sharol	Wood
American Heritage Tour	Philadelphia	Educational	$1,200	Lois	Gordon
American Heritage Tour	Philadelphia	Educational	$1,200	Tim	Hayes
American Heritage Tour	Philadelphia	Educational	$1,200	Frank	Torres
Yosemite Park Cleanup	Sacramento	Eco	$1,250	Tom	Camel
American Heritage Tour	Philadelphia	Educational	$1,200	Jane	Taylor
Yosemite Park Cleanup	Sacramento	Eco	$1,250	Kristen	Collins
American Heritage Tour	Philadelphia	Educational	$1,200	Kris	Shaw
American Heritage Tour	Philadelphia	Educational	$1,200	Ralph	Stewart
American Heritage Tour	Philadelphia	Educational	$1,200	Nancy	Cole
American Heritage Tour	Philadelphia	Educational	$1,200	Brad	Long

Four fields from Trips table   Two fields from Customers table

Record: 14   1 of 106   ▶ ▶I ▶▦   No Filter   Search

106 records

Work with Data in a Query

Learning
Outcomes
• Edit records in
  a query
• Delete records in
  a query

You enter and edit data in a query datasheet the same way you do in a table datasheet. Because all data is stored in tables, any edits you make to data in a query datasheet are actually stored in the underlying tables and are automatically updated in all views of the data in other queries, forms, and reports. **CASE** *Julia Rice wants to change the name of one trip and update a city name. You can use the TripCustomerList query datasheet to make these edits.*

STEPS

TROUBLE
Be sure the final TripName is *Captiva Bay Cleanup*, not just *Captiva*.

1. **Double-click** Stanley **in the TripName field of the first or second record, type** Captiva, **then click any other record**

   All occurrences of Stanley Bay Cleanup automatically update to Captiva Bay Cleanup because this TripName field value is stored only once in the Trips table. See FIGURE 2-3. The TripName is selected from the Trips table and displayed in the TripCustomerList query for each customer who purchased this trip.

2. **Double-click** Orlando **in the City field of any record for the Golden Hands Venture trip, type** College Park, **then click any other record**

   All occurrences of Orlando automatically update to College Park for the Golden Hands Venture trip because this value is stored only once in the City field of the Trips table for the Golden Hands Venture record. The Golden Hands Venture trip is displayed in the TripCustomerList query for each customer who purchased that trip.

3. **Click the** record selector button **to the left of the first record, click the** Home tab, **click the** Delete button **in the Records group, then click** Yes

   You can delete records from a query datasheet the same way you delete them from a table datasheet. Notice that the navigation bar now indicates you have 105 records in the datasheet, as shown in FIGURE 2-4.

4. **Right-click the** TripCustomerList query tab, **then click** Close

   Each time a query is opened, it shows a current view of the data. This means that as new trips, customers, or sales are recorded in the database, the next time you open this query, the information will include all updates.

Hiding and unhiding fields in a datasheet

To hide a field in a datasheet, right-click the field name at the top of the datasheet and click the Hide Fields option on the shortcut menu. To unhide a field, right-click any field name, click Unhide

Fields, and check the hidden field's check box in the Unhide Columns dialog box.

Freezing and unfreezing fields in a datasheet

In large datasheets, you may want to freeze certain fields so that they remain on the screen at all times. To freeze a field, right-click its

field name in the datasheet, and then click Freeze Fields. To unfreeze a field, right-click any field name and click Unfreeze All Fields.

FIGURE 2-3: Working with data in a query datasheet

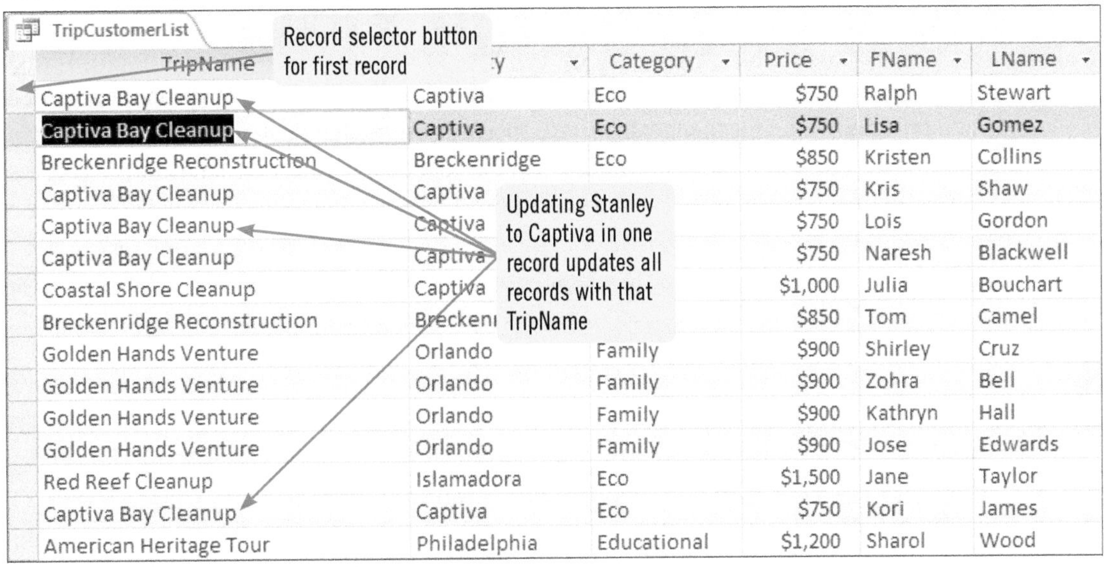

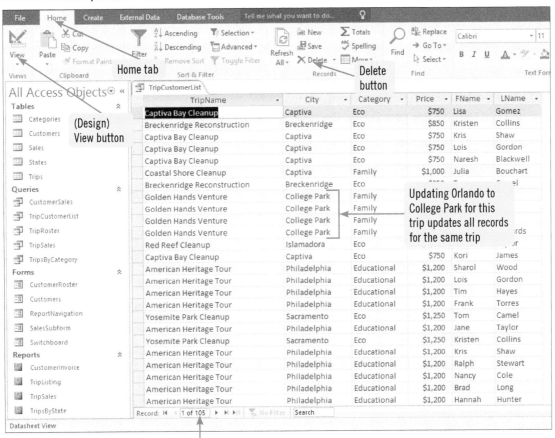

FIGURE 2-4: Final TripCustomerList datasheet

Use Query Design View

Learning
Outcomes
• Work in Query
  Design View
• Add criteria to a
  query

You use **Query Design View** to add, delete, or move the fields in an existing query; to specify sort orders; or to add **criteria** to limit the number of records shown in the resulting datasheet. You can also use Query Design View to create a new query from scratch. In the upper pane, Query Design View presents the fields you can use for that query in small windows called **field lists**. If you use the fields of two or more related tables in the query, the relationship between two tables is displayed with a **join line** (also called a **link line**) identifying which fields are used to establish the relationship. **CASE** *Julia Rice asks you to produce a list of trips in California. You use Query Design View to modify the existing TripsByState query to meet her request.*

STEPS

1. **Double-click the** TripsByState query **in the Navigation Pane to review the datasheet, then click the** View button ☑ **on the Home tab to switch to Query Design View**

   The TripsByState query contains the StateName field from the States table and the TripName, TripStartDate, and Price fields from the Trips table. This query contains two ascending sort orders: StateName and TripName. All records in California, for example, are further sorted by the TripName value.

QUICK TIP
Drag the lower edge of the field list to resize it to view all fields.

2. **Click the** File tab, **click** Save As, **click** Save Object As, **click the** Save As button, **type** CATrips **to replace Copy of TripsByState, then click** OK

   If you want to build a new query starting from an existing query, use the Save As command and give the new query a new name before you start working on it. This will prevent you from accidentally changing the original query.

   In Access, the **Save As command** on the File tab allows you to save the *entire database* (the entire database includes all objects within it) or just the *current object* with a new name. Recall that Access saves *data* automatically as you move from record to record.

   Query Design View displays the tables used in the upper pane of the window. The link line shows that one record in the States table may be related to many records in the Trips table. The lower pane of the window, called the **query design grid** (or **query grid** for short), displays the field names, sort orders, and criteria used within the query.

QUICK TIP
Query criteria are not case sensitive, so "California" equals "CALIFORNIA" equals "california".

3. **Click the** first Criteria cell **for the StateName field, type** California, **then click any other cell in the query grid as shown in** FIGURE 2-5

   Criteria are limiting conditions you set in the query design grid. In this case, the condition limits the selected records to only those with "California" in the StateName field. Criteria for a field with a Short Text data type are surrounded by "quotation marks" though you do not need to type the quotation marks. Access automatically adds them for you.

4. **Click the** View button ▦ **in the Results group to switch to Datasheet View**

   Now only 15 records are selected, because only 15 of the trips have "California" in the StateName field, as shown in FIGURE 2-6.

5. **Right-click the** CATrips query tab, **click** Close, **then click** Yes **when prompted to save changes**

Adding or deleting a table in a query

You might want to add a table's field list to the upper pane of Query Design View to select fields from that table for the query. To add a new table to Query Design View, drag it from the Navigation Pane to Query Design View, or click the Show Table button on the Design tab, then add the desired table(s). To delete an unneeded table from Query Design View, click its title bar, then press [Delete].

FIGURE 2-5: CATrips query in Design View

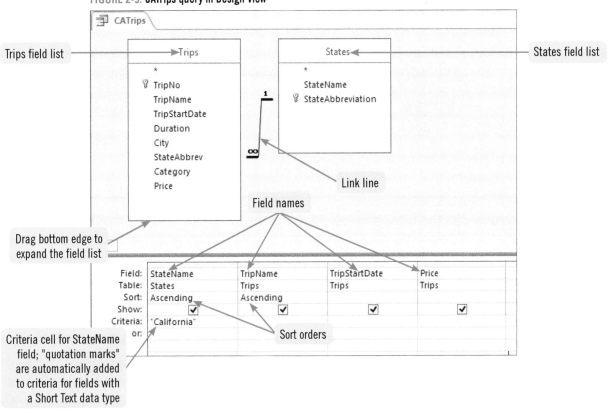

Trips field list

States field list

Trips field list →

States field list

Link line

Field names

Drag bottom edge to expand the field list

Criteria cell for StateName field; "quotation marks" are automatically added to criteria for fields with a Short Text data type

Sort orders

FIGURE 2-6: CATrips query with California criterion

TripName values are in ascending order

Only 15 California records are selected

Sort and Find Data

Learning
Outcomes
• Apply sort orders to
  a query
• Add fields to a query
• Find and replace
  data
• Undo edits

The Access sort and find features are handy tools that help you quickly organize and find data in a table or query datasheet. TABLE 2-1 describes the Sort and Find buttons on the Home tab. Besides using these buttons, you can also click the list arrow on the field name in a datasheet, and then click a sorting option. **CASE** ▶ *Julia asks you to provide a list of trips sorted by Category, and then by Price. You'll modify the TripsByCategory query to answer this request.*

STEPS

1. **Double-click the** TripsByCategory query **in the Navigation Pane to open its datasheet**

   The TripsByCategory query currently sorts Trips by Category, then by TripName. You'll add the Duration field to this query, then change the sort order for the records.

2. **Click the** View button ⊠ **in the Views group to switch to Design View, then double-click the** Duration field **in the Trips field list**

   When you double-click a field in a field list, Access inserts it in the next available column in the query grid. You can also drag a field from a field list to a specific column of the query grid. To select a field in the query grid, you click its field selector. The **field selector** is the thin gray bar above each field in the query grid. To delete a field from a query, click its field selector, then press [Delete]. Deleting a field from a query does not delete it from the underlying table; the field is only deleted from the query.

   Currently, the TripsByCategory query is sorted by Category and then by TripName. Access evaluates sort orders from left to right. You want to change the sort order so that the records sort first by Category then by Price.

3. **Click** Ascending **in the TripName Sort cell, click the** list arrow, **click** (not sorted), **double-click the** Price Sort cell, **click the** list arrow, **then click** Descending

   The records are now set to be sorted in ascending order by Category, and within each Category, in a descending order by the Price field, as shown in FIGURE 2-7. Because sort orders always work from left to right, you might need to rearrange the fields before applying a sort order that uses more than one field. To move a field in the query design grid, click its field selector, then drag it left or right.

4. **Click the** View button ▦ **in the Results group to switch to Datasheet View**

   The new datasheet shows the Duration field in the fifth column. The records are now sorted in ascending order by the Category field, but for records in the same Category, they are further sorted in descending order by Price. Your next task is to replace all occurrences of "Tour" with "Trip" in the TripName field.

5. **Click in any** TripName field, **click the** Replace button **on the Home tab, type** Tour **in the Find What box, click in the** Replace With box, **type** Trip, **click the** Match arrow button, **then click** Any Part of Field

   The Find and Replace dialog box is shown in FIGURE 2-8.

6. **Click the** Replace All button **in the Find and Replace dialog box, click** Yes **to continue, then click** Cancel **to close the Find and Replace dialog box**

   Access replaced both occurrences of "Tour" with "Trip" in the TripName field, as shown in FIGURE 2-9.

7. **Right-click the** TripsByCategory query tab, **click** Close, **then click** Yes **if prompted to save changes**

FIGURE 2-7: **Changing sort orders for the TripsByCategory query**

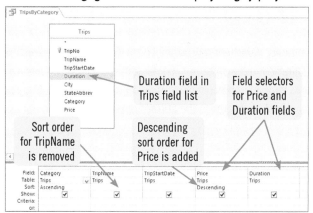

Duration field in Trips field list

Field selectors for Price and Duration fields

Sort order for TripName is removed

Descending sort order for Price is added

Field:	Category	TripName	TripStartDate	Price	Duration
Table:	Trips	Trips	Trips	Trips	Trips
Sort:	Ascending			Descending	
Show:	✓	✓	✓	✓	✓
Criteria:					
or:					

FIGURE 2-8: **Find and Replace dialog box**

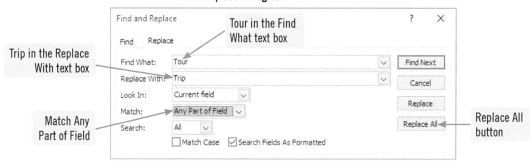

Tour in the Find What text box

Trip in the Replace With text box

Match Any Part of Field

Replace All button

FIGURE 2-9: **Final TripsByCategory datasheet with new sort orders**

Trip replaces Tour in the TripName field

Records with the same Category are further sorted in descending order by the Price field

TABLE 2-1: **Sort and Find buttons**

name	button	purpose
Ascending		Sorts records based on the selected field in ascending order (0 to 9, A to Z)
Descending		Sorts records based on the selected field in descending order (Z to A, 9 to 0)
Remove Sort		Removes the current sort order
Find		Opens the Find and Replace dialog box to find data
Replace		Opens the Find and Replace dialog box to find and replace data
Go To		Helps you navigate to the first, previous, next, last, or new record
Select		Helps you select a single record or all records in a datasheet

Filter Data

Learning
Outcomes
• Apply and remove
filters in a query
• Use wildcards in
criteria

Filtering a table or query datasheet temporarily displays only those records that match given criteria. Recall that criteria are limiting conditions you set. For example, you might want to show only trips in the state of Missouri, or only trips with a duration of fewer than 14 days. Although filters provide a quick and easy way to display a temporary subset of records in the current datasheet, they are not as powerful or flexible as queries. Most important, a query is a saved object within the database, whereas filters are temporary. Access removes all filters when you close the datasheet. TABLE 2-2 compares filters and queries. **CASE** *Julia asks you to find all Family trips offered in the month of August. You can filter the Trips table datasheet to provide this information.*

STEPS

1. **Double-click the Trips table to open it, click any occurrence of Family in the Category field, click the Selection button in the Sort & Filter group on the Home tab, then click Equals "Family"**

   Six records are selected as shown in FIGURE 2-10. A filter icon appears to the right of the Category field. Filtering by the selected field value, called **Filter By Selection**, is a fast and easy way to filter the records for an exact match. To filter for comparative data (for example, where TripStartDate is equal to or greater than 7/1/2017), you must use the **Filter By Form** feature. Filter buttons are summarized in TABLE 2-3.

2. **Click the Advanced button in the Sort & Filter group, then click Filter By Form**

   The Filter by Form window opens. The previous Filter By Selection criterion, "Family" in the Category field, is still in the grid. Access places "quotation marks" around text criteria.

3. **Click the TripStartDate cell, then type 8/*/2017 as shown in FIGURE 2-11**

   Filter By Form also allows you to apply two or more criteria at the same time. An asterisk (*) in the day position of the date criterion works as a wildcard, selecting any date in the month of August in the year 2017.

4. **Click the Toggle Filter button in the Sort & Filter group**

   The datasheet selects one record that matches both filter criteria, as shown in FIGURE 2-12. Note that filter icons appear next to the TripStartDate and Category field names as both fields are involved in the filter.

5. **Close the Trips datasheet, then click Yes when prompted to save the changes**

   Saving changes to the datasheet saves the last sort order and column width changes. *Filters are not saved.*

Using wildcard characters

To search for a pattern, you can use a **wildcard** character to represent any character in the condition entry. Use a question mark (?) to search for any single character and an asterisk (*) to search for any number of characters. Wildcard characters are often used with the **Like** operator. For example, the criterion Like "12/*/17" would find all dates in December of 2017, and the criterion Like "F*" would find all entries that start with the letter F.

FIGURE 2-10: Filtering the Trips table

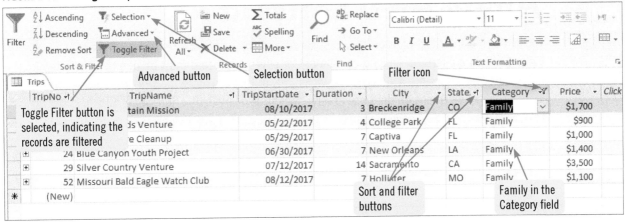

Toggle Filter button is selected, indicating the records are filtered

TripNo	TripName	TripStartDate	Duration	City	State	Category	Price	Click
	tain Mission	08/10/2017	3	Breckenridge	CO	Family	$1,700	
	ds Venture	05/22/2017	4	College Park	FL	Family	$900	
	e Cleanup	05/29/2017	7	Captiva	FL	Family	$1,000	
24	Blue Canyon Youth Project	06/30/2017	7	New Orleans	LA	Family	$1,400	
29	Silver Country Venture	07/12/2017	14	Sacramento	CA	Family	$3,500	
52	Missouri Bald Eagle Watch Club	08/12/2017	7	Hollister	MO	Family	$1,100	
(New)								

Sort and filter buttons

Family in the Category field

FIGURE 2-11: Filtering by Form criteria

TripNo	TripName	TripStartDate	Duration	City	StateAb	Category	Price
		8/*/2017				"Family"	

TripStartDate criterion   Category criterion

FIGURE 2-12: Results of filtering by form

Filter icons

TripNo	TripName	TripStartDate	Duration	City	State	Category	Price
6	Rocky Mountain Mission	08/10/2017	3	Breckenridge	CO	Family	$1,700
(New)							

TripStartDate value is in August 2017

Category is equal to Family

TABLE 2-2: Filters vs. queries

characteristics	filters	queries
Are saved as an object in the database		•
Can be used to select a subset of records in a datasheet	•	•
Can be used to select a subset of fields in a datasheet		•
Resulting datasheet used to enter and edit data	•	•
Resulting datasheet used to sort, filter, and find records	•	•
Commonly used as the source of data for a form or report		•
Can calculate sums, averages, counts, and other types of summary statistics across records		•
Can be used to create calculated fields		•

TABLE 2-3: Filter buttons

name	button	purpose
Filter		Provides a list of values in the selected field that can be used to customize a filter
Selection		Filters records that equal, do not equal, or are otherwise compared with the current value
Advanced		Provides advanced filter features such as Filter By Form, Save As Query, and Clear All Filters
Toggle Filter		Applies or removes the current filter

Apply AND Criteria

You can limit the number of records that appear on a query datasheet by entering criteria in Query Design View. **Criteria** are tests, or limiting conditions, for which the record must be true to be selected for the query datasheet. To create **AND criteria**, which means that *all* criteria must be true to select the record, enter two or more criteria on the *same* Criteria row of the query design grid. **CASE** ▶ *Julia Rice asks you to provide a list of all Eco (ecological) trips in the state of Colorado with a duration of seven days or more. Use Query Design View to create the query with AND criteria to meet her request.*

STEPS

1. **Click the** Create tab **on the Ribbon, click the** Query Design button, **double-click** Trips, **then click** Close **in the Show Table dialog box**

   You want four fields from the Trips table in this query.

2. **Drag the** bottom edge of the Trips field list **down to display all of the fields, double-click** TripName, **double-click** Duration, **double-click** StateAbbrev, **then double-click** Category **to add these fields to the query grid**

   First add criteria to select only those records in Colorado. Because you are using the StateAbbrev field, you need to use the two-letter state abbreviation for Colorado, CO, as the Criteria entry.

3. **Click the** first Criteria cell **for the StateAbbrev field, type** CO, **then click the** View button 🖽 **to display the results**

   Querying for only those trips in the state of Colorado selects seven records. Next, you add criteria to select only the trips in the Eco category.

4. **Click the** View button 🖾, **click the** first Criteria cell for the Category field, **type** Eco, **then click the** View button 🖽 **in the Results group**

   Criteria added to the same line of the query design grid are AND criteria. When entered on the same line, each criterion must be true for the record to appear in the resulting datasheet. Querying for both CO and Eco trips narrows the selection to three records. Every time you add AND criteria, you narrow the number of records that are selected because the record must be true for all criteria.

5. **Click the** View button 🖾, **click the** first Criteria cell for the Duration field, **then type** >=7, **as shown in** FIGURE 2-13

   Access assists you with **criteria syntax**, rules that specify how to enter criteria. Access automatically adds "quotation marks" around text criteria in Short Text and Long Text fields ("CO" and "Eco") and pound signs (#) around date criteria in Date/Time fields. The criteria in the Number, Currency, and Yes/No fields are not surrounded by any characters. See TABLE 2-4 for more information about comparison operators such as >= (greater than or equal to).

6. **Click the** View button 🖽 **in the Results group**

   The third AND criterion further narrows the number of records selected to two, as shown in FIGURE 2-14.

7. **Click the** Save button 🖫 **on the Quick Access Toolbar, type** EcoCO7 **as the query name, click** OK, **then close the query**

   The query is saved with the new name, EcoCO7, as a new object in the R2G-2 database. Criteria entered in Query Design View are permanently saved with the query (as compared to filters in the previous lesson, which are temporary and not saved with the object).

FIGURE 2-13: Query Design View with AND criteria

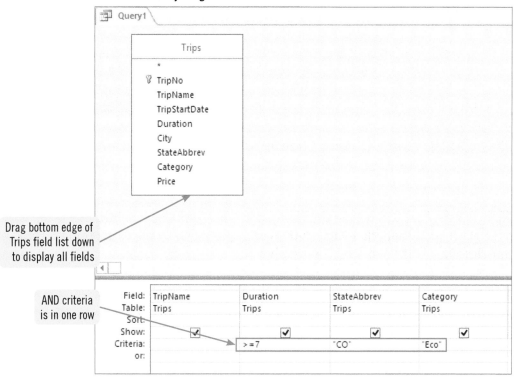

Drag bottom edge of Trips field list down to display all fields

AND criteria is in one row

FIGURE 2-14: Final datasheet of EcoCO7 query

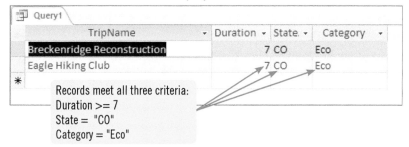

Records meet all three criteria:
Duration >= 7
State = "CO"
Category = "Eco"

TABLE 2-4: Comparison operators

operator	description	expression	meaning
>	Greater than	>500	Numbers greater than 500
>=	Greater than or equal to	>=500	Numbers greater than or equal to 500
<	Less than	<"Elder"	Names from A to Elder, but not Elder
<=	Less than or equal to	<="Buehler"	Names from A through Buehler, inclusive
<>	Not equal to	<>"Bridgewater"	Any name except for Bridgewater

Searching for blank fields

Is Null and Is Not Null are two other types of common criteria. The **Is Null** criterion finds all records where no entry has been made in the field. **Is Not Null** finds all records where there is any entry in the field, even if the entry is 0. Primary key fields cannot have a null entry.

Apply OR Criteria

Learning Outcomes
- Enter OR criteria in a query
- Rename a query

You use **OR criteria** when *any one criterion* must be true in order for the record to be selected. Enter OR criteria on *different* Criteria rows of the query design grid. As you add rows of OR criteria to the query design grid, you increase the number of records selected for the resulting datasheet because the record needs to match only one of the Criteria rows to be selected for the datasheet. **CASE** *Julia Rice asks you to add criteria to the previous query. She wants to include Adventure trips in the state of Colorado that are greater than or equal to seven days in duration. To do this, you make a copy of the EcoCO7 query to modify with OR criteria to add the new records for the Adventure trips.*

STEPS

1. **Right-click the** EcoCO7 **query in the Navigation Pane, click** Copy**, right-click a** blank spot **in the Navigation Pane, click** Paste**, type** EcoAdventureCO7 **in the Paste As dialog box, then click** OK

   By copying the EcoCO7 query before starting your modifications, you avoid changing the EcoCO7 query by mistake.

2. **Right-click the** EcoAdventureCO7 **query in the Navigation Pane, click** Design View**, click the** second Criteria cell **in the Category field, type** Adventure**, then click the View button** 🔲 **to display the query datasheet**

   The query selected 11 records including all of the trips with Adventure in the Category field. Note that some of the Duration values are less than seven and some of the StateAbbrev values are not CO. Because each row of the query grid is evaluated separately, *all* Adventure trips are selected regardless of criteria in any other row. In other words, the criteria in one row have no effect on the criteria of other rows. To make sure that the Adventure trips are also in Colorado and have a duration of greater than or equal to seven days, you need to modify the second row of the query grid (the "or" row) to add that criteria.

QUICK TIP

Datasheet View 🔳, Design View 📝, and other view buttons are also located in the lower-right corner of the Access window.

3. **Click the View button** 📝**, click the** second Criteria cell **in the Duration field, type** >=7**, click the** second Criteria cell **in the StateAbbrev field, type** CO**, then click in any other cell of the grid**

   Query Design View should look like FIGURE 2-15.

4. **Click the View button** 🔲

   Three records are selected that meet all three criteria as entered in row one or row two of the query grid, as shown in FIGURE 2-16.

5. **Right-click the** EcoAdventureCO7 **query tab, click** Close**, then click** Yes **to save and close the query datasheet**

FIGURE 2-15: Query Design View with OR criteria

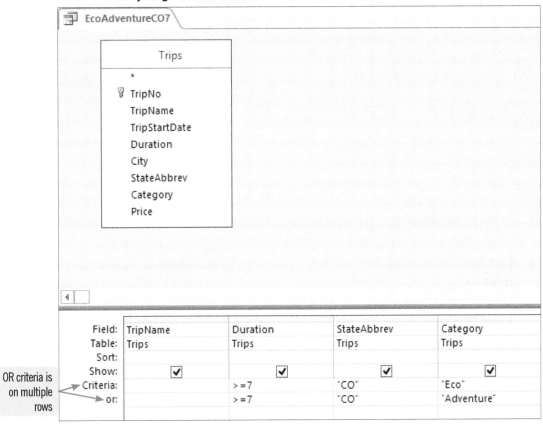

OR criteria is
on multiple
rows

FIGURE 2-16: Final datasheet of EcoAdventureCO7 query

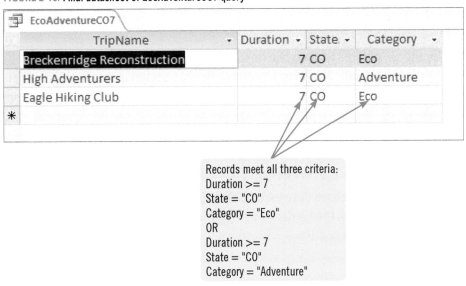

Records meet all three criteria:
Duration >= 7
State = "CO"
Category = "Eco"
OR
Duration >= 7
State = "CO"
Category = "Adventure"

Format a Datasheet

Learning Outcomes
• Zoom in print preview
• Format a datasheet
• Change page orientation

A report is the primary Access tool to create a professional printout, but you can print a datasheet as well. A datasheet allows you to apply some basic formatting modifications such as changing the font size, font face, colors, and gridlines. All formatting changes apply to the entire datasheet. **CASE** *Julia Rice asks you to print a list of customers. You decide to format the Customers table datasheet before printing it for her.*

STEPS

1. **In the Navigation Pane, double-click the** Customers table **to open it in Datasheet View**
   Before applying new formatting enhancements, you preview the default printout.

2. **Click the** File tab, **click** Print, **click** Print Preview, **then click the** header **of the printout to zoom in**
   The preview window displays the layout of the printout, as shown in FIGURE 2-17. By default, the printout of a datasheet contains the object name and current date in the header. The page number is in the footer.

3. **Click the** Next Page button ▶ **in the navigation bar to move to the next page of the printout**
   The last two fields, Phone and FirstContact, print on the second page because the first is not wide enough to accommodate them. You decide to switch the report to landscape orientation so that all of the fields print on one page, and then increase the size of the font before printing to make the text easier to read.

4. **Click the** Landscape button **on the Print Preview tab to switch the report to landscape orientation, then click the** Close Print Preview button
   You return to Datasheet View where you can make font face, font size, font color, gridline color, and background color choices.

5. **Click the** Font list arrow [Calibri (Detail) ▾] **in the Text Formatting group, click** Arial Narrow, **click the** Font Size list arrow [11 ▾], **then click** 12
   You decide to widen the Street column.

6. **Use the** ↔ **pointer to drag the** field separator **between the Street and City field names slightly to the right to widen the Street field as shown in** FIGURE 2-18
   Double-clicking the field separators widens the columns as needed to display every entry in those fields.

QUICK TIP
If you need a printout of this datasheet, add your name as a new record to the Customers table, then print it.

7. **Click the** File tab, **click** Print, **click** Print Preview, **then click the preview to zoom in and out to review the information**
   All of the fields now fit across a page in landscape orientation. The preview of the printout is two pages, and in landscape orientation, it is easier to read.

8. **Right-click the** Customers table tab, **click** Close, **click** Yes **when prompted to save changes, then click the** Close button ☒ **on the title bar to close the R2G-2.accdb database and Access 2016**

FIGURE 2-17: **Preview of Customers datasheet**

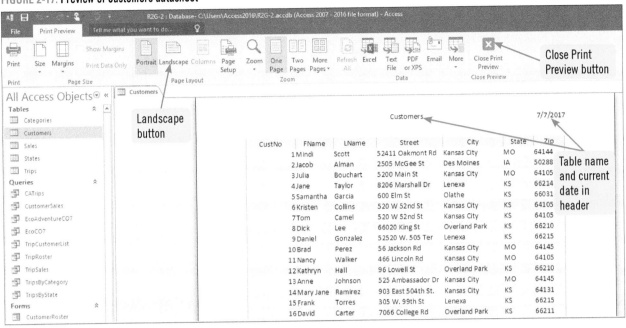

FIGURE 2-18: **Formatting the Customers datasheet**

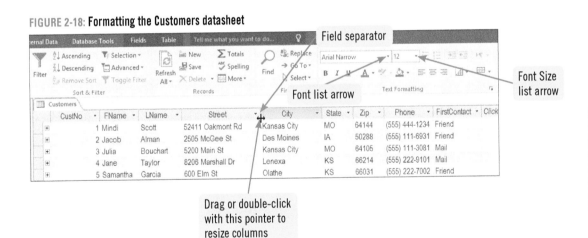

Practice

Concepts Review

Label each element of the Access window shown in FIGURE 2-19.

FIGURE 2-19

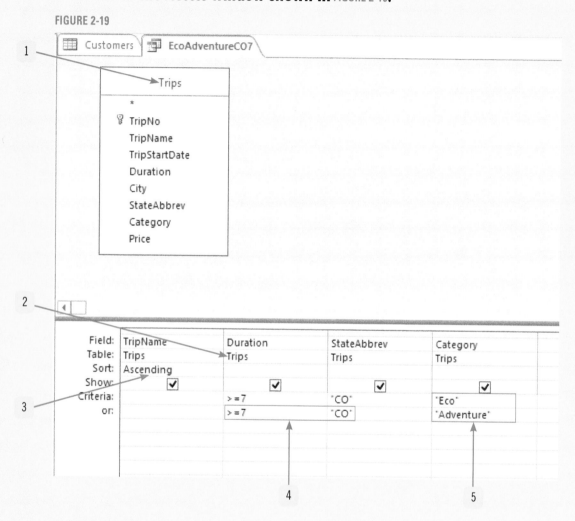

Match each term with the statement that best describes it.

6. **Query grid**

7. **Field selector**

8. **Filter**

9. **Filter By Selection**

10. **Field lists**

11. **Sorting**

12. **Join line**

13. **Criteria**

14. **Syntax**

15. **Wildcard**

a. Putting records in ascending or descending order based on the values of a field

b. Limiting conditions used to restrict the number of records that are selected in a query

c. The thin gray bar above each field in the query grid

d. Creates a temporary subset of records

e. Small windows that display field names

f. Rules that determine how criteria are entered

g. Used to search for a pattern of characters

h. The lower pane in Query Design View

i. Identifies which fields are used to establish a relationship between two tables

j. A fast and easy way to filter the records for an exact match

Select the best answer from the list of choices.

16. **AND criteria:**
    a. determine sort orders.
    b. must all be true for the record to be selected.
    c. determine fields selected for a query.
    d. help set link lines between tables in a query.

17. **SQL stands for which of the following?**
    a. Structured Query Language
    b. Standard Query Language
    c. Special Query Listing
    d. Simple Query Listing

18. **A query is sometimes called a logical view of data because:**
    a. you can create queries with the Logical Query Wizard.
    b. queries contain logical criteria.
    c. query naming conventions are logical.
    d. queries do not store data—they only display a view of data.

19. **Which of the following describes OR criteria?**
    a. Selecting a subset of fields and/or records to view as a datasheet from one or more tables
    b. Using two or more rows of the query grid to select only those records that meet given criteria
    c. Reorganizing the records in either ascending or descending order based on the contents of one or more fields
    d. Using multiple fields in the query design grid

20. **Which of the following is *not* true about a query?**
    a. A query is the same thing as a filter.
    b. A query can select fields from one or more tables in a relational database.
    c. A query can be created using different tools.
    d. An existing query can be modified in Query Design View.

Skills Review

1. Use the Query Wizard.

a. Open the Salvage-2.accdb database from the location where you store your Data Files. Enable content if prompted.

b. Create a new query using the Simple Query Wizard. Select the CenterName field from the Centers table, the DepositDate and Weight fields from the Deposits table, and the ClubName field from the Clubs table. Select Detail, and enter **CenterDeposits** as the name of the query.

c. Open the query in Datasheet View, then change any record with the Johnson Recycling value to a center name that includes your last name.

2. Work with data in a query.

a. Delete the first record (A1 Salvage Center with a DepositDate value of 2/4/2014).

b. Change any occurrence of JavaScript KC in the ClubName field to **Bootstrap Club**.

c. Click any value in the DepositDate field, then click the Descending button on the Home tab to sort the records in descending order on the DepositDate field.

d. Use the Calendar Picker to choose the date of **1/30/17** for the first record.

e. Save and close the CenterDeposits query.

3. Use Query Design View.

a. Click the Create tab, click the Query Design button, double-click Clubs, double-click Deposits, and then click Close to add the Clubs and Deposits tables to Query Design View.

b. Drag the bottom edge of both field lists down as needed to display all of the field names in both tables.

c. Add the following fields from the Clubs table to the query design grid in the following order: FName, LName, ClubName. Add the following fields from the Deposits table in the following order: DepositDate, Weight. View the results in Datasheet View, observing the number of records that are selected in the record navigation bar at the bottom of the datasheet.

d. In Design View, enter criteria to display only those records with a Weight value of **>=100**, then observe the number of records that are selected in Datasheet View.

e. Save the query with the name **100PlusDeposits**.

4. Sort and find data.

a. In Query Design View of the 100PlusDeposits query, choose an ascending sort order for the ClubName field and a descending sort order for the Weight field.

b. Display the query in Datasheet View, noting how the records have been resorted.

c. In the ClubName field, change any occurrence of Boy Scout Troop 324 to Boy Scout Troop **6**.

d. In the FName field, change any occurrence of Trey to *your* initials and save the query.

5. Filter data.

a. Filter the 100PlusDeposits datasheet for only those records where the ClubName equals **Access Users Group**.

b. Apply an advanced Filter By Form and use the >= operator to further narrow the records so that only the deposits with a DepositDate value on or after 1/1/2015 are selected.

c. Apply the filter to see the datasheet and, if requested by your instructor, print the filtered 100PlusDeposits datasheet.

d. Save and close the 100PlusDeposits query. Reopen the 100PlusDeposits query to confirm that filters are temporary (not saved), and then close the 100PlusDeposits query again.

Skills Review (continued)

6. Apply AND criteria.

a. Right-click the 100PlusDeposits query, copy it, and then paste it as **100PlusDeposits2016**.

b. Open the 100PlusDeposits2016 query in Query Design View.

c. Modify the criteria to select all of the records with a DepositDate in **2016** and a Weight value **greater than or equal to 100**. (*Hint*: To select all records with a DepositDate in 2016, use a wildcard character for the month and day positions of the date criterion.)

d. Display the results in Datasheet View. If requested by your instructor, print the 100PlusDeposits2016 datasheet, then save and close it.

7. Apply OR criteria.

a. Right-click the 100PlusDeposits query, copy it, then paste it as **100PlusDeposits2Clubs**.

b. Open the 100PlusDeposits2Clubs query in Design View, then add criteria to select the records with a ClubName of **Social Media Club** and a Weight value **greater than or equal to 100**.

c. Add criteria to also include the records with a ClubName of **Access Users Group** with a Weight value **greater than or equal to 100**. FIGURE 2-20 shows the results.

d. If requested by your instructor, print the 100PlusDeposits2Clubs datasheet, then save and close it.

FIGURE 2-20

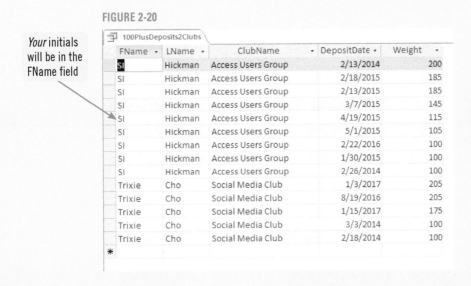

Your initials will be in the FName field

8. Format a datasheet.

a. In the Centers table datasheet, apply the Times New Roman font and a 14-point font size.

b. Resize all columns so that all data and field names are visible.

c. Display the Centers datasheet in Print Preview, switch the orientation to landscape, click the Margins button in the Page Size group, then click Narrow.

d. If requested by your instructor, print the Centers datasheet.

e. Save and close the Centers table, then close Access 2016.

Independent Challenge 1

You have built an Access database to track membership in a community service club. The database tracks member names and addresses as well as their community service hours.

a. Open the Service-2.accdb database from the location where you store your Data Files, enable content if prompted, then open the Activities, Members, and Zips tables to review their datasheets.

b. In the Zips table, click the expand button to the left of the 64111, Kansas City, MO record to display the two members linked to that zip code. Click the expand button to the left of the Jeremiah Hopper record to display the three activity records linked to Jeremiah.

c. Close all three datasheets, click the Database Tools tab, then click the Relationships button. The Relationships window shows you that one record in the Zips table is related to many records in the Members table through the common ZipCode field, and that one record in the Members table is related to many records in the Activities table through the common MemberNo field.

d. Click the Relationship Report button, then if requested by your instructor, print the Relationship report. Close and save the report with the default name **Relationships for Service-2**. Close the Relationships window.

e. Using Query Design View, build a query with the following fields: FirstName and LastName from the Members table and ActivityDate and HoursWorked from the Activities table.

f. View the datasheet, observe the number of records selected, then return to Query Design View.

g. Add criteria to select only those records where the ActivityDate is in March of 2017.

h. In Query Design View, apply an ascending sort order to the LastName and a descending sort order to the ActivityDate field, then view the datasheet.

i. Change the name Quentin Garden to your name, widen all columns so that all data and field names are visible, and save the query with the name **March2017**, as shown in FIGURE 2-21.

j. If requested by your instructor, print the March2017 datasheet, then close the March2017 query and close Access 2016.

FIGURE 2-21

FirstName	LastName	ActivityDate	HoursWorked
Rhea	Alman	3/23/2017	4
Micah	Ati	3/23/2017	4
Evan	Bouchart	3/24/2017	8
Forrest	Browning	3/23/2017	5
Patch	Bullock	3/21/2017	4
Angela	Cabriella	3/23/2017	5
Andrea	Collins	3/25/2017	8
Student First	Student Last	3/25/2017	8
Student First	Student Last	3/23/2017	4
Gabriel	Hammer	3/23/2017	5
Jeremiah	Hopper	3/21/2017	4
Heidi	Kalvert	3/23/2017	4
Karla	Larson	3/23/2017	5
Katrina	Margolis	3/23/2017	4
Jose	Martin	3/24/2017	8
Jon	Maxim	3/24/2017	4
Harvey	McCord	3/24/2017	4
Mallory	Olson	3/25/2017	8
Jana	Pence	3/24/2017	10
Allie	Pitt	3/23/2017	4
Su	Vogue	3/24/2017	8
Taney	Wilson	3/24/2017	8

Record: 23 of 23 — No Filter — Search

Independent Challenge 2

You work for a nonprofit agency that tracks voting patterns. You have developed an Access database with contact information for members of the House of Representatives. The director of the agency has asked you to create several state lists of representatives. You will use queries to extract this information.

a. Open the HouseOfReps-2.accdb database from the location where you store your Data Files, then enable content if prompted.

b. Open the Representatives and the States tables. Notice that one state is related to many representatives as evidenced by the expand buttons to the left of the records in the States tables.

c. Close both datasheets, then using Query Design View, create a query with the StateAbbrev, StateName, and Capital fields from the States table (in that order) as well as the FName and LName fields from the Representatives table.

d. Sort the records in ascending order on the StateName field, then in ascending order on the LName field.

e. Add criteria to select the representatives from Ohio or Pennsylvania. Use the StateAbbrev field to enter your criteria, using the two-character state abbreviations of **OH** and **PA**.

f. Save the query with the name **OhioAndPenn**, view the results, shown in FIGURE 2-22, then change the last name of Butterfield in the second record to *your* last name. Resize the columns as needed to view all the data and field names.

g. Print the OhioAndPenn datasheet if requested by your instructor, then close it and exit Access 2016.

FIGURE 2-22

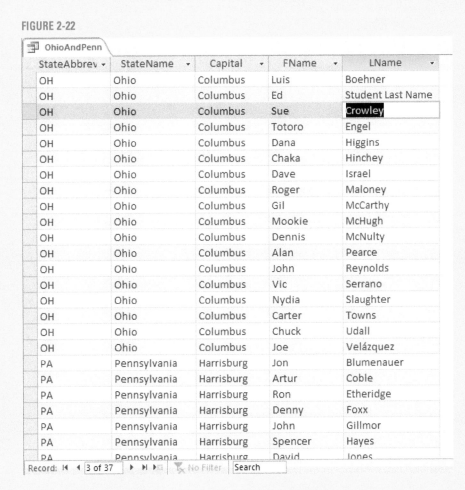

Independent Challenge 3

You have built an Access database to track the veterinarian clinics in your area.

a. Open the VetClinic-2.accdb database from the location where you store your Data Files, then enable content if prompted.

b. Open the Vets table and then the Clinics table to review the data in both datasheets.

c. Click the expand button next to the Animal Haven record in the Clinics table, then add your name as a new record to the Vets subdatasheet.

d. Close both datasheets.

e. Using the Simple Query Wizard, select the VetLast and VetFirst fields from the Vets table, and select the ClinicName and Phone fields from the Clinics table. Title the query **ClinicVetListing**, then view the datasheet.

f. Update any occurrence of Animal Haven in the ClinicName field to **Animal Emergency Shelter**.

g. In Query Design View, add criteria to select only **Animal Emergency Shelter** or **Veterinary Specialists** in the ClinicName field, then view the datasheet.

h. In Query Design View, move the ClinicName field to the first column, then add an ascending sort order on the ClinicName and VetLast fields.

i. Display the ClinicVetListing query in Datasheet View, resize the fields as shown in FIGURE 2-23, then print the datasheet if requested by your instructor.

j. Save and close the ClinicVetListing datasheet, then exit Access 2016.

FIGURE 2-23

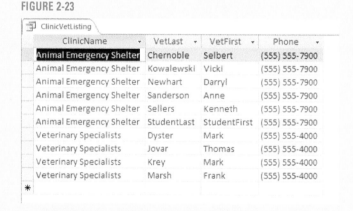

Independent Challenge 4: Explore

An Access database is an excellent tool to help record and track job opportunities. For this exercise, you'll create a database from scratch that you can use to enter, edit, and query data in pursuit of a new job or career.

a. Create a new desktop database named **Jobs.accdb**.

b. Create a table named **Positions** with the following field names, data types, and descriptions:

Field name	Data type	Description
PositionID	AutoNumber	Primary key field
Title	Short Text	Title of position such as Accountant, Assistant Court Clerk, or Web Developer
CareerArea	Short Text	Area of the career field such as Accounting, Government, or Information Systems
AnnualSalary	Currency	Annual salary
Desirability	Number	Desirability rating of 1 = low to 5 = high to show how desirable the position is to you
EmployerID	Number	Foreign key field to the Employers table

c. Create a table named **Employers** with the following field names, data types, and descriptions:

Field name	Data type	Description
EmployerID	AutoNumber	Primary key field
CompanyName	Short Text	Company name of the employer
EmpStreet	Short Text	Employer's street address
EmpCity	Short Text	Employer's city
EmpState	Short Text	Employer's state
EmpZip	Short Text	Employer's zip code
EmpPhone	Short Text	Employer's phone, such as 111-222-3333

d. Be sure to set EmployerID as the primary key field in the Employers table and the PositionID as the primary key field in the Positions table.

e. Link the Employers and Positions tables together in a one-to-many relationship using the common EmployerID field. One employer record will be linked to many position records. Be sure to enforce referential integrity.

f. Using any valid source of potential employer data, enter five records into the Employers table.

g. Using any valid source of job information, enter five records into the Positions table by using the subdatasheets from within the Employers datasheet.

Because one employer may have many positions, all five of your Positions records may be linked to the same employer, you may have one position record per employer, or any other combination.

h. Build a query that selects CompanyName from the Employers table, and the Title, CareerArea, AnnualSalary, and Desirability fields from the Positions table. Sort the records in descending order based on Desirability. Save the query as **JobList**, and print it if requested by your instructor.

i. Close the JobList datasheet, then exit Access 2016.

Visual Workshop

Open the Baseball-2.accdb database from the location where you store your Data Files, and enable content if prompted. Create a query in Query Design View based on the Players and Teams tables, as shown in FIGURE 2-24. Add criteria to select only those records where the PlayerPosition field values are equal to 1 or 2 (representing pitchers and catchers). In Query Design View, set an ascending sort order on the TeamName and PlayerPosition fields. In the results, change the name of Aaron Campanella to your name. Save the query with the name **PitchersAndCatchers**, then compare the results with FIGURE 2-24, making changes and widening columns to display all of the data. Print the datasheet if requested by your instructor. Save and close the query and the Baseball-2.accdb database, then exit Access 2016.

FIGURE 2-24

TeamName	PlayerFirst	PlayerLast	Positic
Brooklyn Beetles	Student First	Student Last	1
Brooklyn Beetles	Cy	Young	2
Mayfair Monarchs	Luis	Durocher	1
Mayfair Monarchs	Carl	Mathewson	2
Rocky's Rockets	Andrew	Spalding	1
Rocky's Rockets	Sanford	Koufax	2
Snapping Turtles	Charles	Ford	1
Snapping Turtles	Greg	Perry	2

Using Forms

CASE Julia Rice, a trip developer at Reason 2 Go, asks you to create forms to make trip information easier to access, enter, and update.

Module Objectives

After completing this module, you will be able to:

- Use the Form Wizard
- Create a split form
- Use Form Layout View
- Add fields to a form

- Modify form controls
- Create calculations
- Modify tab order
- Insert an image

Files You Will Need

R2G-3.accdb
R2GLogo.jpg
LakeHomes-3.accdb
LakeHome.jpg
Scuba-3.accdb

Service-3.accdb
Salvage-3.accdb
Jobs-3.accdb
Baseball-3.accdb

Use the Form Wizard

Learning
Outcomes
• Create a form with
  the Form Wizard
• Sort data in a form
• Describe form
  terminology and
  views

A **form** is an easy-to-use data entry and navigation screen. A form allows you to arrange the fields of a record in any layout so a database **user** can quickly and easily find, enter, edit, and analyze data. The database **designer** or **application developer** is the person responsible for building and maintaining tables, queries, forms, and reports for all of the users. **CASE** ▶ *Julia Rice asks you to build a form to enter and maintain trip information.*

STEPS

1. **Start Access, open the** R2G-3.accdb database **from the location where you store your Data Files, then enable content if prompted**

   You can use many methods to create a new form, but the Form Wizard is a fast and popular tool that helps you get started. The **Form Wizard** prompts you for information it needs to create a form, such as the fields, layout, and title for the form.

2. **Click the** Create tab **on the Ribbon, then click the** Form Wizard button **in the Forms group**

   The Form Wizard starts, prompting you to select the fields for this form. You want to create a form to enter and update data in the Trips table.

3. **Click the** Tables/Queries list arrow, **click** Table: Trips, **then click the** Select All Fields button >>

   You could now select fields from other tables, if necessary, but in this case, you have all of the fields you need.

4. **Click** Next, **click the** Columnar option button, **click** Next, **type** Trips Entry Form **as the title, then click** Finish

   The Trips Entry Form opens in **Form View**, as shown in FIGURE 3-1. Access provides three different views of forms, as summarized in TABLE 3-1. Each item on the form is called a **control**. A **label control** is used to describe the data shown in other controls such as text boxes. A label is also used for the title of the form, Trips Entry Form. A **text box** is used to display the data as well as enter, edit, find, sort, and filter the data. A **combo box** is a combination of two controls: a text box and a list. The Category data is displayed in a combo box control. You click the arrow button on a combo box control to display a list of values, or you can edit data directly in the combo box itself.

   QUICK TIP
   Click in the text box of the field you want to sort before clicking a sort button.

5. **Click** Stanley Bay Cleanup **in the TripName text box, click the** Ascending button **in the Sort & Filter group, then click the** Next record button ▶ **in the navigation bar to move to the second record**

   The Bass Habitat Project trip is the second record when the records are sorted in ascending order on the TripName data. Information about the current record number and total number of records appears in the navigation bar, just as it does in a datasheet.

6. **Click the** Previous record button ◀ **in the navigation bar to move back to the first record, click the** TripName text box, **then change American Legacy Project to American Heritage Project**

   Your screen should look like FIGURE 3-2. Forms displayed in Form View are the primary tool for database users to enter, edit, and delete data in an Access database.

7. **Right-click the** Trips Entry Form tab, **then click** Close

   When a form is closed, Access automatically saves any edits made to the current record.

FIGURE 3-1: **Trips Entry Form in Form View**

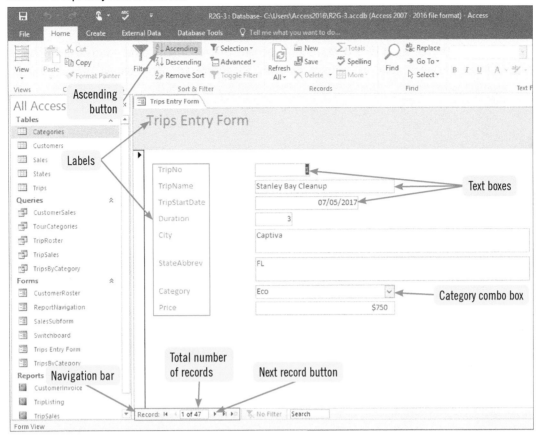

FIGURE 3-2: **Editing data in Form View**

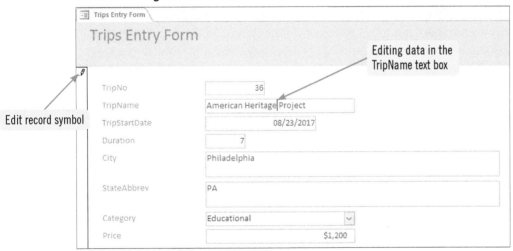

TABLE 3-1: **Form views**

view	primary purpose
Form	To find, sort, enter, and edit data
Layout	To modify the size, position, or formatting of controls; shows data as you modify the form, making it the tool of choice when you want to change the appearance and usability of the form while viewing data
Design	To modify the Form Header, Detail, and Footer section, or to access the complete range of controls and form properties; Design View does not display data

Create a Split Form

In addition to the Form Wizard, you should be familiar with several other form creation tools. TABLE 3-2 identifies those tools and the purpose for each. **CASE** *Julia Rice asks you to create another form to manage customer data. You'll work with the Split Form tool for this task.*

Learning Outcomes
• Create a split form
• Enter and edit data in a form

STEPS

QUICK TIP
Layout View allows you to view and filter the data, but not edit it.

1. **Click the** Customers table **in the Navigation Pane, click the** Create tab, **click the** More Forms button, **click** Split Form, **then click the** Add Existing Fields button **in the Tools group on the Design tab to close the Field List if it opens**

   The Customers data appears in a split form with the top half in **Layout View**. The benefit of a **split form** is that the upper pane allows you to display the fields of one record in any arrangement, and the lower pane maintains a datasheet view of the first few records. If you edit, sort, or filter records in the upper pane, the lower pane is automatically updated, and vice versa.

2. **Click** MO **in the State text box in the upper pane, click the** Home tab, **click the** Selection button **in the Sort & Filter group, then click** Does Not Equal "MO"

   Thirty-seven records are filtered where the State field is not equal to MO. You also need to change a value in the Jacob Alman record.

TROUBLE
Make sure you edit the record in the datasheet in the lower pane.

3. **In the lower pane, select** Des Moines **in the City field of the first record, edit the entry to read** Waukee, **then press [Enter]**

   Note that "Waukee" is now the entry in the City field in both the upper and lower panes, as shown in FIGURE 3-3.

4. **Click the** record selector **for the Kristen Collins record in the lower pane as shown in** FIGURE 3-4, **then click the** Delete button **in the Records group on the Home tab**

   You cannot delete this record because it contains related records in the Sales table. This is a benefit of referential integrity on the one-to-many relationship between the Customers and Sales tables. Referential integrity prevents the creation of **orphan records**, records on the many side of a relationship that do not have a match on the one side.

5. **Click** OK, **right-click the** Customers form tab, **click** Close, **click** Yes **when prompted to save changes, then click** OK **to save the form with Customers as the name**

TABLE 3-2: Form creation tools

tool	icon	creates a form
Form		with one click based on the selected table or query
Form Design		from scratch in Form Design View
Blank Form		from scratch in Form Layout View
Form Wizard		by answering a series of questions provided by the Form Wizard dialog boxes
Navigation		used to navigate or move between different areas of the database
More Forms		based on Multiple Items, Datasheet, Split Form, or Modal Dialog arrangements
Split Form		with two panes, the upper showing one record at a time and the lower displaying a datasheet of many records

FIGURE 3-3: Customers table in a split form

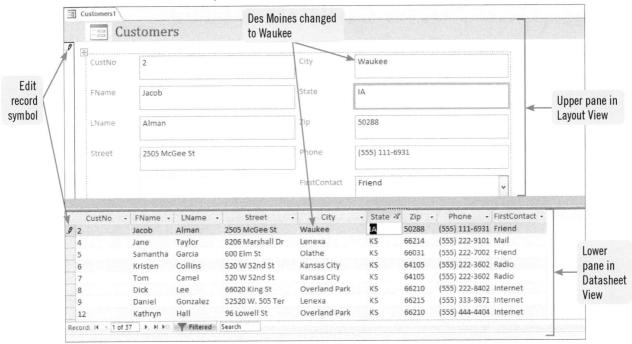

Edit record symbol

Des Moines changed to Waukee

Upper pane in Layout View

Lower pane in Datasheet View

FIGURE 3-4: Editing data in a split form

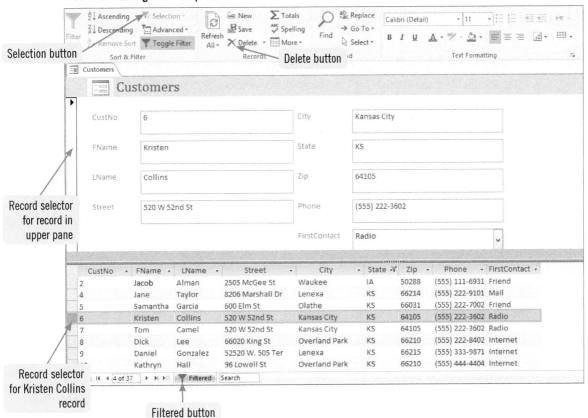

Selection button

Delete button

Record selector for record in upper pane

Record selector for Kristen Collins record

Filtered button

Use Form Layout View

Learning
Outcomes
• Resize controls in
Layout View
• Format controls in
Layout View

Layout View lets you make some design changes to a form while you are browsing the data. For example, you can move and resize controls, add or delete a field on the form, filter and sort data, or change formatting characteristics, such as fonts and colors. TABLE 3-4 lists several of the most popular formatting commands found on the Format tab when you are working in Layout or Form Design View. **CASE** *Julia Rice asks you to make several design changes to the Trips Entry Form. You can make these changes in Layout View.*

STEPS

1. **Right-click** Trips Entry Form **in the Navigation Pane, then click** Layout View

   In Layout View, you can move through the records, but you cannot enter or edit the data as you can in Form View.

TROUBLE
If your third record is not Bear Valley Adventures, sort the records in ascending order on the TripName field.

2. **Click the** Next record button ▶ **in the navigation bar twice to move to the third record, Bear Valley Adventures**

   You often use Layout View to make minor design changes, such as editing labels and changing formatting characteristics.

3. **Click the** TripNo label **to select it if it is not already selected, click between the words Trip and No, then press** [Spacebar]

   You also want to edit a few more labels.

TROUBLE
Be sure to modify the labels in the left column instead of the text boxes on the right.

4. **Continue editing the labels, as shown in** FIGURE 3-5

   You also want to change the text color of the labels to black to make them more noticeable.

5. **Click the** Trip No label, **press and hold** [Shift] **while clicking all of the other labels in the first column to select them together, release** [Shift], **click the** Format tab, **click the** Font Color list arrow **in the Font group, then click** Automatic **at the top of the list**

   You also decide to narrow the City and StateAbbrev text boxes.

TROUBLE
Be sure to modify the text boxes in the right column instead of the labels on the left.

6. **Click** Sacramento **in the City text box, press and hold** [Shift], **click** CA **in the StateAbbrev text box to select the two text boxes at the same time, release** [Shift], **then use the ↔ pointer to drag the** right edge of the selection **to the left to make the text boxes approximately half as wide**

   Layout View for the Trips Entry Form should look like FIGURE 3-5. Mouse pointers in Form Layout and Form Design View are very important as they indicate what happens when you drag the mouse. Mouse pointers are described in TABLE 3-3.

TABLE 3-3: Mouse pointer shapes

shape	when does this shape appear?	action
⬚	When you point to any unselected control on the form (the default mouse pointer)	Single-clicking with this mouse pointer selects a control
✛	When you point to the upper-left corner or edge of a selected control in Form Design View or the middle of the control in Form Layout View	Dragging with this mouse pointer moves the selected control(s)
↕ ↔ ⤢ ⤢	When you point to any sizing handle (except the larger one in the upper-left corner in Form Design View)	Dragging with one of these mouse pointers resizes the control

FIGURE 3-5: Using Layout View to modify controls on the Trips Entry Form

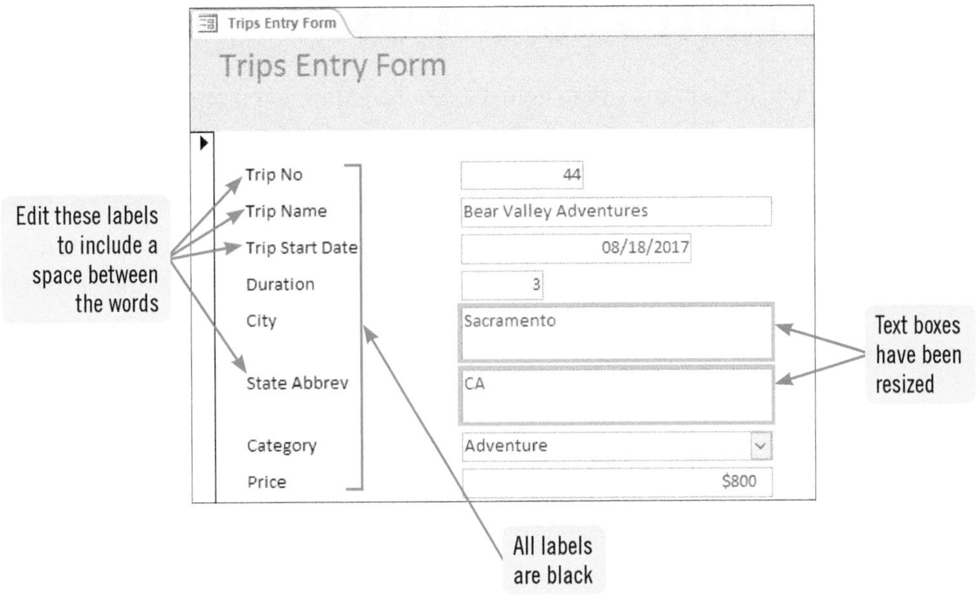

TABLE 3-4: Useful formatting commands

button	button name	description
B	Bold	Toggles bold on or off for the selected control(s)
I	Italic	Toggles italic on or off for the selected control(s)
U	Underline	Toggles underline on or off for the selected control(s)
A	Font Color	Changes the text color of the selected control(s)
	Background Color or Shape Fill	Changes the background color of the selected control(s)
	Align Left	Left-aligns the selected control(s) within its own border
	Center	Centers the selected control(s) within its own border
	Align Right	Right-aligns the selected control(s) within its own border
	Alternate Row Color	Changes the background color of alternate records in the selected section
	Shape Outline	Changes the border color, thickness, or style of the selected control(s)
	Shape Effects	Changes the special visual effect of the selected control(s)

Table layouts

Layouts provide a way to group several controls together on a form or report to more quickly add, delete, rearrange, resize, or align controls. To insert a layout into a form or report, select the controls you want to group together, then choose the Stacked or Tabular button on the Arrange tab in Layout View. Each option applies a table layout to the controls so that you can insert, delete, merge, or split the cells in the layout to quickly rearrange or edit the controls in the layout. To remove a layout, use the Remove Layout button on the Arrange tab in Form Design View.

Access 2016

Add Fields to a Form

Learning Outcomes
• Add fields to a form
• Define bound and unbound controls

Adding and deleting fields in an existing form is a common activity. You can add or delete fields in a form in either Layout View or Design View using the Field List. The **Field List** lists the database tables and the fields they contain. To add a field to the form, drag it from the Field List to the desired location on the form. To delete a field on a form, click the field to select it, then press the [Delete] key. Deleting a field from a form does not delete it from the underlying table or have any effect on the data contained in the field. You can toggle the Field List on and off using the Add Existing Fields button on the Design tab in Layout or Design View. **CASE** ▶ *Julia Rice asks you to add the Trip description from the Categories table to the Trips Entry Form. You can use Layout View and the Field List to accomplish this goal.*

STEPS

1. **Click the** Design tab **on the Ribbon, click the** Add Existing Fields button **in the Tools group, then click the** Show all tables link **in the Field List**

   The Field List opens in Layout View, as shown in FIGURE 3-6. Notice that the Field List is divided into sections. The upper section shows the tables currently used by the form, the middle section shows directly related tables, and the lower section shows other tables in the database. The expand/collapse button to the left of the table names allows you to expand (show) the fields within the table or collapse (hide) them. The Description field is in the Categories table in the middle section.

   To move the Field List, drag its title bar. Double-click the title bar of the Field List to dock it to the right.

2. **Click the** expand button ⊞ **to the left of the Categories table, drag the** Description field **to the form, then use the** ▚ **pointer to drag the new Description combo box and label below the Price text box**

   When you add a new field to a form, two controls are usually created: a label and a text box. The label contains the field name and the text box displays the data in the field. The Categories table moved from the middle to the top section of the Field List. You also want to align and format the new controls with others already on the form.

3. **Click the** Description label, **click the** Format tab **on the Ribbon, then click the** Font color **button** 🇦 ▾ **to change the text color from gray to black**

   With the new controls in position and formatted, you want to enter a new record. You must switch to Form View to edit, enter, or delete data.

4. **Click the** Home tab, **click the** View button 🖺 **to switch to Form View, click the** New (blank) record button ▶* **in the navigation bar, click the** TripName text box, **then enter a new record in the updated form, as shown in** FIGURE 3-7

   Be sure to enter the correct value for each field and note that when you select a value in the Category combo box, the Description is automatically updated. This is due to the one-to-many relationship between the Categories and Trips tables in the Relationships window.

FIGURE 3-6: Field List in Form Layout View

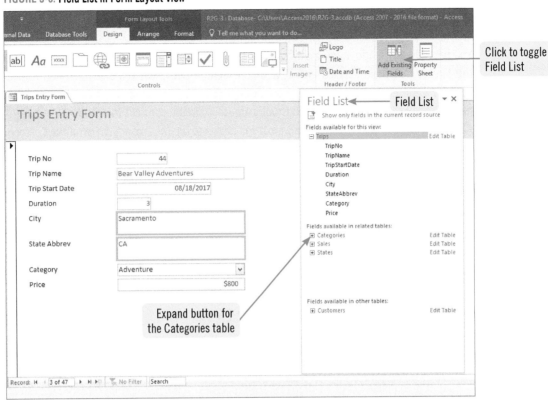

FIGURE 3-7: Entering a record in the updated Trips Entry Form in Form View

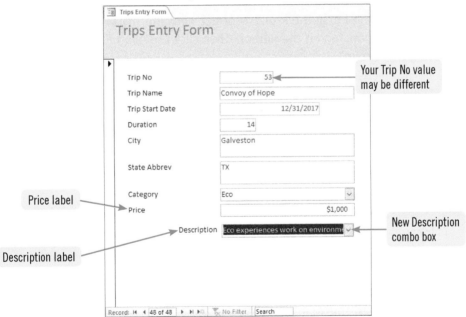

Bound versus unbound controls

Controls are either bound or unbound. **Bound controls** display values from a field such as text boxes and combo boxes. **Unbound controls** do not display data; unbound controls describe data or enhance the appearance of the form. Labels are the most common type of unbound control, but other types include lines, images, tabs, and command buttons. Another way to distinguish bound from unbound controls is to observe the form as you move from record to record. Because bound controls display data, their contents change as you move through the records, displaying data from the field of the current record. Unbound controls such as labels and lines do not change as you move through the records in a form.

Modify Form Controls

You have already made many modifications to form controls, such as changing the font color of labels and the size of text boxes. Labels and text boxes are the two most popular form controls. Other common controls are listed in TABLE 3-5. When you modify controls, you change their **properties** (characteristics). All of the control characteristics you can modify are stored in the control's **Property Sheet.** **CASE** *Because R2G is now focused on Eco (ecological) trips, you decide to use the Property Sheet of the Category field to modify the default value to be "Eco." Julia asks you to use the Property Sheet to make other control modifications to better size and align the controls.*

STEPS

1. **Right-click the** Trips Entry Form tab, **click** Layout View, **then click the** Property Sheet button **in the Tools group**

   The Property Sheet opens, replacing the Field List and showing you all of the properties for the selected item. Drag the title bar of the Property Sheet to move it. Double-click the title bar to dock it to the right.

2. **Click the** Category combo box on the form, **click the** Data tab in the Property Sheet **(if it is not already selected), click the** Default Value box, **type** Eco, **then press** [Enter]

   The Property Sheet should look like FIGURE 3-8. Access often helps you with the **syntax** (rules) of entering property values. In this case, Access added quotation marks around "Eco" to indicate that the default entry is text. Properties are categorized in the Property Sheet with the Format, Data, Event, and Other tabs. The All tab is a complete list of all the control's properties. You can use the Property Sheet to make all control modifications, although you'll probably find that some changes are easier to make using the Ribbon. The property values change in the Property Sheet as you modify a control using the Ribbon and vice versa.

   TROUBLE
   Be sure to click the Trip No label on the left, not the TripNo text box on the right.

3. **Click the** Format tab in the Property Sheet, **click the** Trip No label in the form to select it, **click the** Home tab on the Ribbon, **then click the** Align Right button ≡ **in the Text Formatting group**

   Notice that the **Text Align property** on the Format tab in the Property Sheet is automatically updated from Left to Right even though you changed the property using the Ribbon instead of the Property Sheet.

4. **Click the** Trip Name label, **press and hold** [Shift], **then click** each other label **in the first column on the form**

   With all the labels selected, you can modify their Text Align property at the same time.

   TROUBLE
   You may need to click ≡ twice.

5. **Click** ≡ **in the Text Formatting group**

   Don't be overwhelmed by the number of properties available for each control on the form or the number of ways to modify each property. Over time, you will learn about most of these properties. At this point, it's only important to know the purpose of the Property Sheet and understand that properties are modified in various ways.

   TROUBLE
   Your Trip No value might not match FIGURE 3-9. It is an AutoNumber value, controlled by Access.

6. **Click the** Save button 🖫 **on the Quick Access Toolbar, click the** Form View button ▭ **to switch to Form View, click the** New (blank) record button ▶※ **in the navigation bar, then enter the record shown in** FIGURE 3-9

   For new records, "Eco" is provided as the default value for the Category combo box, but you can change it by typing a new value or selecting one from the list. With the labels right-aligned, they are much closer to the data in the text boxes that they describe.

FIGURE 3-8: Using the Property Sheet

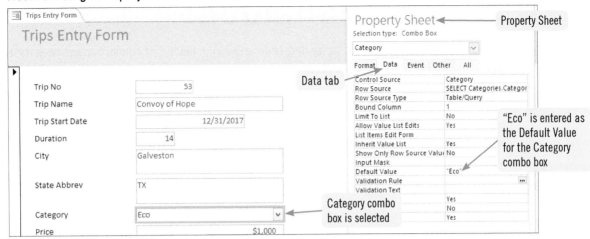

FIGURE 3-8: Using the Property Sheet

FIGURE 3-9: Modified Trips Entry Form

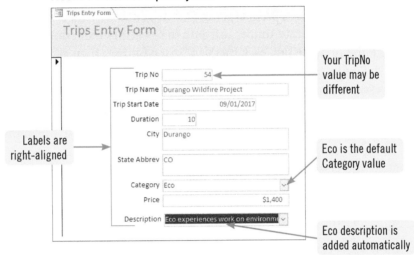

TABLE 3-5: Common form controls

name	used to	bound	unbound
Label	Provide consistent descriptive text as you navigate from record to record; the label is the most common type of unbound control and can also be used as a hyperlink to another database object, external file, or webpage		•
Text box	Display, edit, or enter data for each record from an underlying record source; the text box is the most common type of bound control	•	
List box	Display a list of possible data entries	•	
Combo box	Display a list of possible data entries for a field, and provide a text box for an entry from the keyboard; combines the list box and text box controls	•	
Tab control	Create a three-dimensional aspect on a form		•
Check box	Display "yes" or "no" answers for a field; if the box is checked, it means "yes"	•	
Toggle button	Display "yes" or "no" answers for a field; if the button is pressed, it means "yes"	•	
Option button	Display a choice for a field	•	
Option group	Display and organize choices (usually presented as option buttons) for a field	•	
Line and Rectangle	Draw lines and rectangles on the form		•
Command button	Provide an easy way to initiate a command or run a macro		•

Create Calculations

Learning Outcomes
• Build calculations on a form
• Move controls on a form

Text boxes are generally used to display data from underlying fields. The connection between the text box and field is defined by the **Control Source property** on the Data tab of the Property Sheet for that text box. A text box control can also display a calculation. To create a calculation in a text box, you enter an expression instead of a field name in the Control Source property. An **expression** is a combination of field names, operators (such as +, −, /, and *), and functions (such as Sum, Count, or Avg) that results in a single value. Sample expressions are shown in TABLE 3-6. **CASE** ▶ *Julia Rice asks you to add a text box to the Trips Entry Form to calculate the trip end date. You can add a text box in Form Design View to accomplish this.*

STEPS

1. **Right-click the** Trips Entry Form tab, **then click** Design View
   You want to add the trip end date calculation just below the Duration text box. First, you'll resize the City and State Abbrev fields.

2. **Click the** City label, **press and hold** [Shift], **click the** City text box, **click the** State Abbrev label, **click the** StateAbbrev text box **to select the four controls together, release** [Shift], **click the** Arrange tab, **click the** Size/Space button, **then click** To Shortest
   With the City and StateAbbrev fields resized, you're ready to move them to make room for the new control to calculate the tour end date.

   QUICK TIP
   You can also press an arrow key to move a selected control.

3. **Click a** blank spot **on the form to deselect the four controls, click the** StateAbbrev text box, **use the** ⟲ **pointer to move it down, click the** City text box, **then use the** ⟲ **pointer to move it down**
   To add the calculation to determine the trip end date (the trip start date plus the duration), start by adding a new text box to the form between the Duration and City text boxes.

   TROUBLE
   If you position the new text box incorrectly, click ↩ on the Quick Access Toolbar and try again.

4. **Click the** Design tab, **click the** Text Box button 🔲 **in the Controls group, then click between the Duration and City text boxes to insert the new text box**
   Adding a new text box automatically adds a new label to the left of the text box.

   TROUBLE
   The number such as Text23 or Text25 in a new label is based on previous work done to the form, so it might vary.

5. **Double-click** Text23, **type** Trip End Date, **click the** Home tab, **click the** Font Color **button** ⬛ ▾, **then press** [Enter]
   With the label updated to correctly identify the text box to the right, you're ready to enter the expression to calculate the tour end date.

   QUICK TIP
   Move the Property Sheet by dragging its title bar.

6. **Click the** new text box **to select it, click the** Data tab **in the Property Sheet, click the** Control Source property, **type** =[TripStartDate]+[Duration], **then press** [Enter] **to update the form as shown in** FIGURE 3-10
   All expressions entered in a control must start with an equal sign (=). When referencing a field name within an expression, [square brackets]—(not parentheses) and not {curly braces}—surround the field name. In an expression, you must type the field name exactly as it was created in Table Design View, but you do not need to match the capitalization.

7. **Click the** View button 🔲 **to switch to Form View, tab three times to the Duration field, type** 5, **then press** [Enter]
   Note that the trip end date, calculated by an expression, automatically changed to five days after the trip start date to reflect the new duration value. The updated Trips Entry Form with the trip end date calculation for the Bikers for Ecology is shown in FIGURE 3-11.

FIGURE 3-10: **Adding a text box to calculate a value**

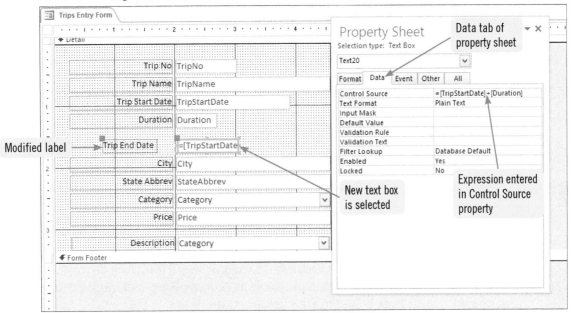

FIGURE 3-11: **Displaying the results of a calculation in Form View**

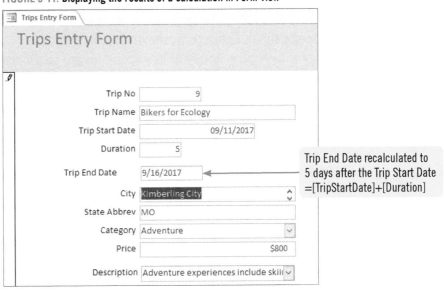

TABLE 3-6: **Sample expressions**

sample expression	description
=Sum([Salary])	Uses the **Sum** function to add the values in the Salary field
=[Price] * 1.05	Multiplies the Price field by 1.05 (adds 5% to the Price field)
=[Subtotal] + [Shipping]	Adds the value of the Subtotal field to the value of the Shipping field
=Avg([Freight])	Uses the **Avg** function to display an average of the values in the Freight field
=Date()	Uses the **Date** function to display the current date in the form of mm-dd-yy
="Page " &[Page]	Displays the word Page, a space, and the result of the [Page] field, an Access field that contains the current page number
=[FirstName]& " " &[LastName]	Displays the value of the FirstName and LastName fields in one control, separated by a space
=Left([ProductNumber],2)	Uses the **Left** function to display the first two characters in the ProductNumber field

Modify Tab Order

Learning
Outcomes
• Modify tab order
  properties

After positioning all of the controls on the form, you should check the tab order and tab stops. **Tab order** is the order the focus moves as you press [Tab] in Form View. A **tab stop** refers to whether a control can receive the focus in the first place. By default, the Tab Stop property for all text boxes and combo boxes is set to Yes, but some text boxes, such as those that contain expressions, will not be used for data entry. Therefore, the Tab Stop property for a text box that contains a calculation should be set to No. Unbound controls such as labels and lines do not have a Tab Stop property because they cannot be used to enter or edit data. **CASE** *Julia suggests that you check the tab order of the Trips Entry Form, then change tab stops and tab order as necessary.*

STEPS

1. **Press [Tab] enough times to move through several records, watching the focus move through the bound controls of the form**

   Because the Trip End Date text box is a calculated field, you don't want it to receive the focus. To prevent the Trip End Date text box from receiving the focus, you set its Tab Stop property to No using its Property Sheet. You can work with the Property Sheet in either Layout or Design View.

QUICK TIP

You can also switch between views using the View buttons in the lower-right corner of the window.

2. **Right-click the** Trips Entry Form tab, **click** Design View, **click the** text box **with the Trip End Date calculation if it is not already selected, click the** Other tab **in the Property Sheet, double-click the** Tab Stop property **to toggle it from Yes to** No, **then change the Name property to** TripEndDate, **as shown in** FIGURE 3-12

   The Other tab of the Property Sheet contains the properties you need to change the tab stop and tab order. The **Tab Stop property** determines whether the field accepts focus, and the **Tab Index property** indicates the numeric tab order for all controls on the form that have the Tab Stop property set to Yes. The **Name property** on the Other tab is also important as it identifies the name of the control, which is used in other areas of the database. To review your tab stop changes, return to Form View.

QUICK TIP

In Form Design View, press [Ctrl][.] to switch to Form View. In Form View, press [Ctrl][,] to switch to Form Design View.

3. **Click the** View button [icon] **to switch to Form View, then press [Tab] nine times to move to the next record**

   Now that the tab stop has been removed from the TripEndDate text box, the tab order flows correctly from the top to the bottom of the form, skipping the calculated field. To review the tab order for the entire form in one dialog box, you must switch to Form Design View.

4. **Right-click the** Trips Entry Form tab, **click** Design View, **then click the** Tab Order button **in the Tools group to open the Tab Order dialog box**

   The Tab Order dialog box allows you to view and change the tab order by dragging fields up or down using the **field selector** to the left of the field name. Moving fields up and down in this list also renumbers the Tab Index property for the controls in their respective Property Sheets. If you want Access to create a top-to-bottom and left-to-right tab order, click **Auto Order**.

TROUBLE

If the order of your fields does not match those in FIGURE 3-13, move a field by clicking the field selector and then dragging the field up or down.

5. **Click the** Auto Order button **to make sure your tab order goes top to bottom as shown in** FIGURE 3-13, **click** OK **to close the Tab Order dialog box, click the** Property Sheet button **to toggle it off, click the** Save button [icon] **on the Quick Access Toolbar to save your work, then click a** blank spot on the form **to deselect the text box**

FIGURE 3-12: Using the Property Sheet to set tab properties

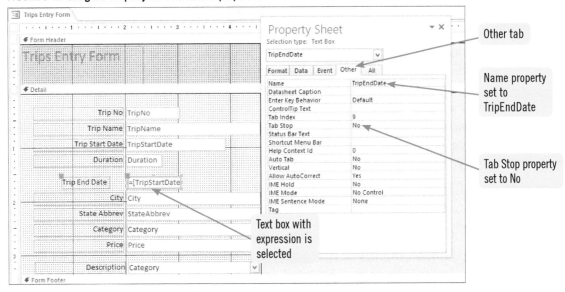

FIGURE 3-13: Tab Order dialog box

Form layouts

A **layout** helps you keep the controls on a form organized as a group. You can apply a stacked or tabular layout to the controls on your form by clicking the Stacked or Tabular buttons on the Arrange tab in Form Design View. Remove a layout by clicking the Remove Layout button. You can also modify a layout by modifying the margins, padding, and anchoring options of the layout using buttons found in the Position group on the Arrange tab in Form Design View. **Margin** refers to the space between the outer edge of the control and the data displayed inside the control. **Padding** is the space between the controls. **Anchoring** allows you to tie controls together so you can work with them as a group. Some of the Form Wizards automatically apply a layout to the controls that you can modify or remove as needed.

Insert an Image

Graphic images, such as pictures, logos, or clip art, can add style and professionalism to a form. The form section in which you place the images is significant. **Form sections** determine where controls are displayed and printed; they are described in TABLE 3-7. For example, if you add a company logo to the Form Header section, the image appears at the top of the form in Form View as well as at the top of a printout. If you add the same image to the Detail section, it prints next to each record in the printout because the Detail section is printed for every record. **CASE** *Julia Rice suggests that you add the R2G logo to the top of the Trips Entry Form. You can add the control in either Layout or Design View, but if you want to place it in the Form Header section, you have to work in Design View.*

STEPS

1. **Click the** Insert Image button **in the Controls group, click** Browse, **then navigate to the location where you store your Data Files**

   The Insert Picture dialog box opens, prompting you for the location of the image.

2. **Click the** Web-Ready Image Files button, **click** All Files, **double-click** R2GLogo.jpg, **then click at the top of the Form Header section at about the 3" mark on the ruler**

   The R2GLogo image is added to the right side of the Form Header section. When an image or control is selected in Design View, you can use **sizing handles,** which are small squares at the corners of the selection box. Drag a handle to resize the image or control. You use the ⁺↖ pointer to move a control.

3. **Use the** ⁺↖ **pointer to move the logo to the top edge of the Form Header section, then drag the** top edge **of the** Detail section **up using the** ✛ **pointer**

   You also want to align the Trip End Date label with the other labels in the first column.

4. **Click the** Trip End Date label, **click the** Home tab **on the Ribbon, click the** Align Right **button** ☰, **press and hold [Shift], click the** Duration label, **click the** Arrange tab **on the Ribbon, click the** Align button, **then click** Right **as shown in** FIGURE 3-14

   With the form completed, you open it in Form View to observe the changes.

5. **Click the** Save button ☐ **on the Quick Access Toolbar, click the** Home tab, **then click the** View button ☐ **to switch to Form View**

   You decide to add one more record with your final Trips Entry Form.

6. **Click the** New (blank) record button ▸ **in the navigation bar, then enter the new record shown in** FIGURE 3-15, **using your last name in the Trip Name field**

   Now print only this single new record.

7. **Click the** File tab, **click** Print **in the navigation bar, click** Print, **click the** Selected Record(s) **option button, then click** OK

8. **Close the Trips Entry Form, click** Yes **if prompted to save it, close the R2G-3.accdb database, then exit Access 2016**

FIGURE 3-14: **Adding an image to the Form Header section**

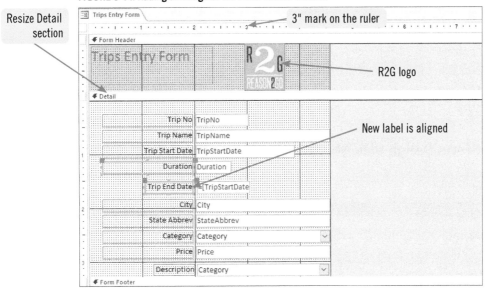

FIGURE 3-15: **Final Trips Entry Form with new record**

TABLE 3-7: **Form sections**

section	controls placed in this section print
Form Header	Only once at the top of the first page of the printout
Detail	Once for every record
Form Footer	Only once at the end of the last page of the printout

Applying a background image

A **background image** is an image that fills the entire form or report, appearing "behind" the other controls. A background image is sometimes called a watermark image. To add a background image, use the Picture property for the form or report to browse for the image that you want to use in the background.

Practice

Concepts Review

Label each element of Form Design View shown in FIGURE 3-16.

FIGURE 3-16

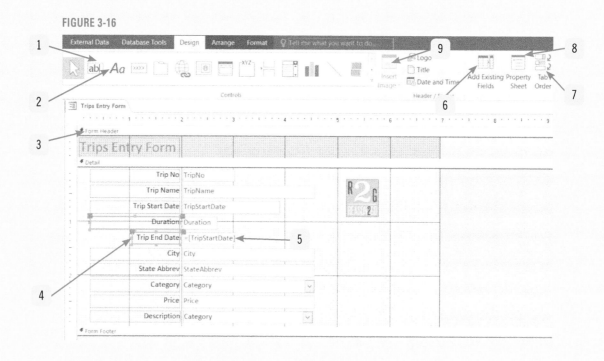

Match each term with the statement that best describes it.

10. **Tab order**
11. **Calculated control**
12. **Detail section**
13. **Form Footer section**
14. **Bound control**
15. **Database designer**

a. Created by entering an expression in a text box
b. Controls placed here print once for every record in the underlying record source
c. Used on a form to display data from a field
d. Controls placed here print only once at the end of the printout
e. The way the focus moves from one bound control to the next in Form View
f. Responsible for building and maintaining tables, queries, forms, and reports

Select the best answer from the list of choices.

16. **Every element on a form is called a(n):**
    a. property.
    b. item.
    c. control.
    d. tool.

17. **Which of the following is probably *not* a graphic image?**
    a. Logo
    b. Clip art
    c. Calculation
    d. Picture

18. **The most common bound control is the:**
    a. combo box.
    b. label.
    c. list box.
    d. text box.

19. **The most common unbound control is the:**
    a. text box.
    b. combo box.
    c. label.
    d. command button.

20. **Which form view cannot be used to view data?**
    a. Layout
    b. Design
    c. Datasheet
    d. Preview

Skills Review

1. **Use the Form Wizard.**
   a. Start Access and open the LakeHomes-3.accdb database from the location where you store your Data Files. Enable content if prompted.
   b. Click the Create tab, then use the Form Wizard to create a form based on all of the fields in the Realtors table. Use a Columnar layout and type **Realtor Entry Form** to title the form.
   c. Add a *new record* with your name in the RFirst and RLast text boxes. Note that the RealtorNo field is an AutoNumber field that is automatically incremented as you enter your first and last names. Enter your school's telephone number for the RPhone field value, and enter **4** as the AgencyNo field value.
   d. Save and close the Realtor Entry Form.

2. **Create a split form.**
   a. Click the Agencies table in the Navigation Pane, click the Create tab, click the More Forms button, then click Split Form.
   b. Close the Property Sheet if it opens then switch to Form View.
   c. Click the record selector in the lower pane for AgencyNo 3, Green Mountain Realty, then click the Delete button in the Records group to delete this realtor. Click OK when prompted that you cannot delete this record because there are related records in the Realtors table.
   d. Navigate to the AgencyNo 4 record, Shepherd of the Hills Realtors, in either the upper or lower pane of the split form. Change 7744 Pokeberry Lane to **800 Lake Shore Drive**.
   e. Right-click the Agencies form tab, click Close, click Yes when prompted to save changes, type **Agencies Split Form** as the name of the form, then click OK.

3. **Use Form Layout View.**
   a. Open the Realtor Entry Form in Layout View.
   b. Modify the labels on the left to read: **Realtor Number**, **Realtor First Name**, **Realtor Last Name**, **Realtor Cell**, **Agency Number**.
   c. Modify the text color of the labels to be black.
   d. Resize all of the text boxes on the right to be the same width as the RealtorNo text box.
   e. Save the Realtor Entry Form.

4. **Add fields to a form.**
   a. Open the Field List, show all the tables, then expand the Agencies table to display its fields.
   b. Drag the AgencyName field to the form, then move the AgencyName label and combo box below the Agency Number controls.
   c. Modify the AgencyName label to read **Agency Name**.
   d. Modify the text color of the Agency Name label to black.
   e. Close the Field List and save and close the Realtor Entry Form.

Skills Review (continued)

5. Modify form controls.

a. Reopen the Realtor Entry Form in Layout View, then select all of the labels in the left column and use the Align Right button on the Home tab to right-align them.

b. Save the form, switch to Form View, navigate to Realtor No 5 (Jane Ann Welch), then use the Agency Name combo box to change the Agency Name to **Big Cedar Realtors**.

c. In Layout View, resize and align all controls so that the labels are lined up on the left and the text boxes are lined up on the right, as shown in FIGURE 3-17.

FIGURE 3-17

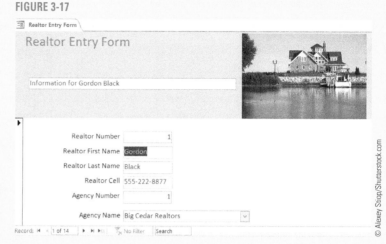

6. Create calculations.

a. Switch to Form Design View, expand the size of the Form Header section by dragging the top edge of the Detail section down about 0.5", then add a text box at about the 1" mark below the Realtor Entry Form label in the Form Header section.

b. Delete the Text14 label that is created when you add a new text box. The number in your label is based on previous work done to the form, so it might vary.

c. Widen the text box to be almost as wide as the entire form, then enter the following expression into the text box, which will add the words *Information for* to the realtor's first name, a space, and then the realtor's last name.
="**Information for** "&[**RFirst**]&" "&[**RLast**]

d. Save the form, then view it in Form View. Be sure the new text box correctly displays a space before and after the realtor's first name. If #Name? appears, which indicates that the expression was entered incorrectly, return to Design View to correct the expression.

e. In Form View, change the Realtor Last Name for Realtor Number 1 from Bono to **Black**. Tab to the RPhone text box to observe how the expression in the Form Header automatically updates.

f. Tab through several records, observing the expression in the Form Header section.

7. Modify tab order.

a. Switch to Form Design View, then open the Property Sheet.

b. Select the new text box with the expression in the Form Header section, then change the Tab Stop property from Yes to **No**.

c. Select the RealtorNo text box in the Detail section, then change the Tab Stop property from Yes to **No**. (AutoNumber fields cannot be edited, so they do not need to have a tab stop.)

d. Close the Property Sheet.

e. Open the Tab Order dialog box and click the Auto Order button to make sure the focus moves from top to bottom through the form.

f. Save the form and view it in Form View. Tab through the form to make sure that the tab order is sequential and skips the expression in the Form Header as well as the Realtor Number text box. Use the Tab Order button on the Design tab in Form Design View to modify the tab order, if necessary.

Skills Review (continued)

8. Insert an image.

  a. Switch to Design View, then click the Form Header section bar.

  b. Add the LakeHome.jpg image to the right side of the Form Header, then resize the image to be about 2.5" × 1.5". Remember to search for All files.

  c. Remove the extra blank space in the Form Header section by dragging the top edge of the Detail section up as far as possible.

  d. Drag the right edge of the form as far as possible to the left.

  e. Save the form, then switch to Form View as shown in FIGURE 3-17. Move through the records, observing the calculated field from record to record to make sure it is calculating correctly.

  f. Find the record with your name, and if requested by your instructor, print only that record.

  g. Close the Realtor Entry Form, close the LakeHomes-3.accdb database, then exit Access.

Independent Challenge 1

As a volunteer for a scuba divers' club, you have developed a database to help manage scuba dives. In this exercise, you'll create a data entry form to manage the dive trips.

  a. Start Access, then open the Scuba-3.accdb database from the location where you store your Data Files. Enable content if prompted.

  b. Using the Form Wizard, create a form that includes all the fields in the DiveTrips table and uses the Columnar layout, then type **Dive Trip Entry** as the title of the form.

  c. Switch to Layout View, then delete the ID text box and label.

  d. Using Form Design View, use the [Shift] key to select all of the text boxes except the last one for TripReport, then resize them to the shortest size using the To Shortest option on the Size/Space button on the Arrange tab.

  e. Using Form Design View, resize the Location, City, State/Province, Country, and Lodging text boxes to be no wider than the Rating text box.

  f. Using Form Design View, move and resize the controls, as shown in FIGURE 3-18. This will require several steps. Once the controls are resized, drag the top of the Form Footer section up to remove the extra blank space in the Detail section.

  g. Using Form Layout View, modify the labels and alignment of the labels, as shown in FIGURE 3-18. Note that there are spaces between the words in the labels, the labels are right-aligned, and the text boxes are left-aligned.

  h. In Form View, sort the records in ascending order on the Dive Master ID field, which will order the Great Barrier Reef tour as the first record. Edit the Certification Diving and Trip Report fields, as shown in FIGURE 3-18 for the TripReport field using your name.

  i. Save the form, then if requested by your instructor, print only the record with your name.

  j. Close the Dive Trip Entry form, close the Scuba-3.accdb database, then exit Access 2016.

FIGURE 3-18

Independent Challenge 2

You have built an Access database to track membership in a community service club. The database tracks member names and addresses as well as their status in the club.

a. Start Access, then open the Service-3.accdb database from the location where you store your Data Files. Enable content if prompted.

b. Using the Form Wizard, create a form based on all of the fields of the Members table and the DuesOwed field in the Status table.

c. View the data by Members, use a Columnar layout, then enter **Member Information** as the title of the form.

d. Enter a new record with your name and the school name, and address of your school for the Company and address fields. Give yourself a StatusNo entry of **1**. In the DuesPaid field, enter **50**. The DuesOwed field automatically displays 100 because that value is pulled from the Status table and is based on the entry in the StatusNo field, which links the Members table to the Status table.

e. In Layout View, add a text box to the form and move it below the DuesOwed text box.

f. Open the Property Sheet for the new text box, display the Data tab, and in the Control Source property of the new text box, enter **=[DuesOwed]-[DuesPaid]**, the expression that calculates the balance between DuesOwed and DuesPaid.

g. Open the Property Sheet for the new label, and change the Caption property on the Format tab for the new label to **Balance**. Resize the label to be as wide as the labels above it.

h. Right-align all of the labels in the first column.

i. Set the Tab Stop property for the text box that contains the calculated Balance to **No**.

j. In Layout or Design View, resize DuesPaid and DuesOwed text boxes to be the same width as the new Balance text box, then right-align all data within the three text boxes because numbers are clearer when they align on the decimal point.

k. Make sure that the Format property on the Format tab is Currency for the DuesPaid, DuesOwed, and Balance expression text boxes. Close the Property Sheet.

l. In Form Design View, make sure that the right edge of the form is at or less than the 7" mark on the horizontal ruler. The horizontal ruler is located just above the Form Header section.

m. Save the form, find the record with your name, change the DuesPaid value to **60**, then move and resize controls as necessary to match **FIGURE 3-19**.

n. If requested by your instructor, print only the record with your name.

o. Save and close the Member Information form, then close the Service-3.accdb database and exit Access 2016.

FIGURE 3-19

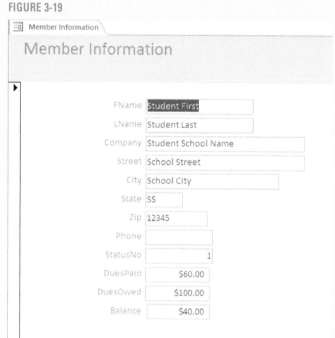

Independent Challenge 3

You have built an Access database to organize the deposits at a salvage and recycling center. Various clubs regularly deposit recyclable material, which is measured in pounds when the deposits are made.

a. Open the Salvage-3.accdb database from the location where you store your Data Files. Enable content if prompted.

b. Using the Form Wizard, create a form based on all of the fields in the CenterDeposits query. View the data by Deposits, use the Columnar layout, and title the form **Deposit Listing**.

c. Switch to Layout View, then make each label bold.

d. Modify the labels so that CenterName is **Center Name**, DepositDate is **Deposit Date**, and ClubName is **Club Name**.

e. Switch to Form Design View and resize the CenterName and ClubName text boxes so they are the same height and width as the Weight text box, as shown in FIGURE 3-20.

f. Switch to Form View, find and change any entry of A1 Salvage Center to *your* last name, then print one record with your name if requested by your instructor.

g. Using Form View of the Deposit Listing form, filter for all records with your last name in the CenterName field.

h. Using Form View of the Deposit Listing form, sort the filtered records in descending order on the DepositDate field.

i. In Form Design View, narrow the form by dragging the right edge as far left as possible.

j. Preview the first record, as shown in FIGURE 3-20. If requested by your instructor, print the first record.

k. Save and close the Deposit Listing form, close the Salvage-3.accdb database, then exit Access.

FIGURE 3-20

Independent Challenge 4: Explore

One way you can use an Access database on your own is to record and track your job search efforts. In this exercise, you will develop a form to help you enter data into your job-tracking database.

a. Start Access and open the Jobs-3.accdb database from the location where you store your Data Files. Enable content if prompted.

b. Click the Create tab, then use the Form Wizard to create a new form based on all the fields of both the Employers and Positions tables.

c. View the data by Employers, use a Datasheet layout for the subform, accept the default names for the form and subform, then open the form to view information.

d. Use Layout View and Design View to modify the form labels, text box positions, alignment, and sizes, as shown in FIGURE 3-21. Also note that the columns within the subform have been resized to display all of the data in the subform.

FIGURE 3-21

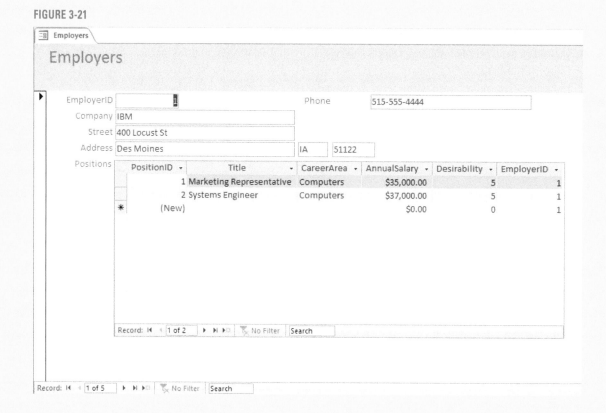

Independent Challenge 4: Explore (continued)

e. Change the CompanyName of IBM in the first record to *Your* **Last Name Software**, and if instructed to create a printout, print only that record. Close the Employers form.

f. Click the Employers table in the Navigation Pane, then use the Split Form option on the More Forms button of the Create tab to create a split form on the Employers table. Close and save the split form with the name **Employers Split Form**.

g. Open the Employers Split Form in Form View, change the address and phone number information for EmployerID 1 to your school's address and phone information, as shown in FIGURE 3-22.

h. Navigate through all five records, then back to EmployerID 1, observing both the upper and lower panes of the split form as you move from record to record.

i. Open the Employers form and navigate forward and backward through all five records to study the difference between the Employers form, which uses a form/subform versus the Employers Split Form. Even though both the Employers form and Employers Split Form show datasheets in the bottom halves of the forms, they are fundamentally very different. The split form is displaying the records of only the Employers table, whereas the Employers form is using a subform to display related records from the Positions table in the lower datasheet. You will learn more about forms and subforms in later modules.

j. Close the Jobs-3.accdb database, then exit Access.

FIGURE 3-22

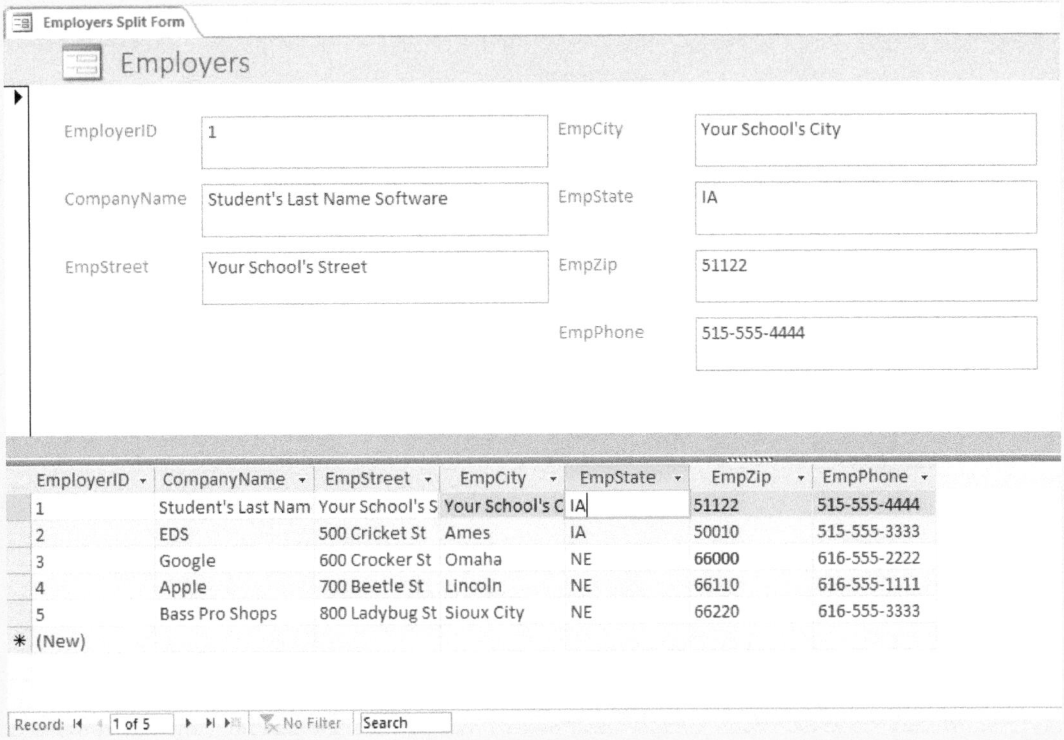

Visual Workshop

Open the Baseball-3.accdb database, enable content if prompted, then use the Split Form tool to create a form named **Players**, as shown in FIGURE 3-23, based on the Players table. Switch to Form Design View, remove the layout, and resize the controls as shown. Modify the labels as shown and note that they are all right-aligned. View the data in Form View, and sort the records in ascending order by last name. Change the first, last, and nickname of the John Bench record in the first record to your name, and if instructed to create a printout, print only that record. Save and close the Players form, close the Baseball-3.accdb database, then exit Access.

FIGURE 3-23

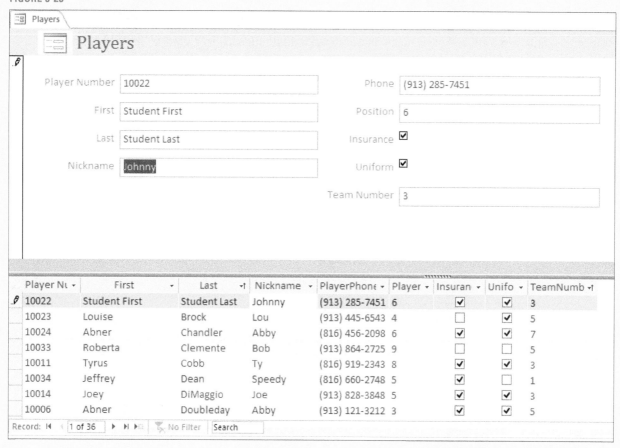

Using Reports

CASE Julia Rice, a trip developer at Reason 2 Go, asks you to produce some reports to help her share and analyze data. A report is an Access object that creates a professional-looking printout.

Module Objectives

After completing this module, you will be able to:

- Use the Report Wizard
- Use Report Layout View
- Review report sections
- Apply group and sort orders
- Add subtotals and counts
- Resize and align controls
- Format a report
- Create mailing labels

Files You Will Need

R2G-4.accdb
LakeHomes-4.accdb
Conventions-4.accdb
Service-4.accdb

Salvage-4.accdb
JobSearch-4.accdb
Basketball-4.accdb

Use the Report Wizard

Learning
Outcomes
• Create a report
  with the Report
  Wizard
• Change page
  orientation

A **report** is the primary object you use to print database content because it provides the most formatting, layout, and summary options. A report may include various fonts and colors, clip art and lines, and multiple headers and footers. A report can also calculate subtotals, averages, counts, and other statistics for groups of records. You can create reports in Access by using the **Report Wizard**, a tool that asks questions to guide you through the initial development of the report. Your responses to the Report Wizard determine the record source, style, and layout of the report. The **record source** is the table or query that defines the fields and records displayed on the report. The Report Wizard also helps you sort, group, and analyze the records. **CASE** *Julia Rice asks you to use the Report Wizard to create a report to display the trips within each state.*

STEPS

1. **Start Access, open the** R2G-4.accdb database, **enable content if prompted, click the** Create tab **on the Ribbon, then click the** Report Wizard button **in the Reports group**

   The Report Wizard starts, prompting you to select the fields you want on the report. You can select fields from one or more tables or queries.

2. **Click the** Tables/Queries list arrow, **click** Table: States, **double-click the** StateName field, **click the** Tables/Queries list arrow, **click** Table: Trips, **click the** Select All Fields button >> , **click** StateAbbrev **in the Selected Fields list, then click the** Remove Field button <

   By selecting the StateName field from the States table, and all fields from the Trips table except the StateAbbrev field, you have all of the fields you need for the report, as shown in FIGURE 4-1.

3. **Click** Next, **then click** by States **if it is not already selected**

   Choosing "by States" groups the records for each state. In addition to record-grouping options, the Report Wizard later asks if you want to sort the records within each group. You can use the Report Wizard to specify up to four fields to sort in either ascending or descending order.

4. **Click** Next, **click** Next **again to include no additional grouping levels, click the** first sort list arrow, **click** TripName, **then click** Next

   The last questions in the Report Wizard deal with report appearance and the report title.

5. **Click the** Stepped option button, **click the** Landscape option button, **click** Next, **type** State Trips **for the report title, then click** Finish

   The State Trips report opens in **Print Preview**, which displays the report as it appears when printed, as shown in FIGURE 4-2. The records are grouped by state, the first state being California, and then sorted in ascending order by the TripName field within each state. Reports are **read-only** objects, meaning you can use them to read and display data but not to change (write to) data. As you change data using tables, queries, or forms, reports constantly display those up-to-date edits just like all of the other Access objects.

6. **Scroll down to see the second grouping section on the report for the state of Colorado, then click the** Next Page button ▶ **in the navigation bar to see the second page of the report**

   Even in **landscape orientation** (11" wide by 8.5" tall as opposed to **portrait orientation**, which is 8.5" wide by 11" tall), the fields on the State Trips report may not fit on one sheet of paper. The labels in the column headings and the data in the columns need to be resized to improve the layout. Depending on your monitor, you might need to scroll to the right to display all the fields on this page.

FIGURE 4-1: **Selecting fields for a report using the Report Wizard**

Report Wizard

Which fields do you want on your report?

You can choose from more than one table or query.

Tables/Queries

Table: Trips

Tables/Queries list arrow

Available Fields:

StateAbbrev

Select All fields button

Remove Field button

Selected Fields:

StateName
TripNo
TripName
TripStartDate
Duration
City
Category
Price

Selected fields

Cancel   < Back   Next >   Finish

FIGURE 4-2: **State Trips report in Print Preview**

State Trips

Some information is cut off and needs to be resized

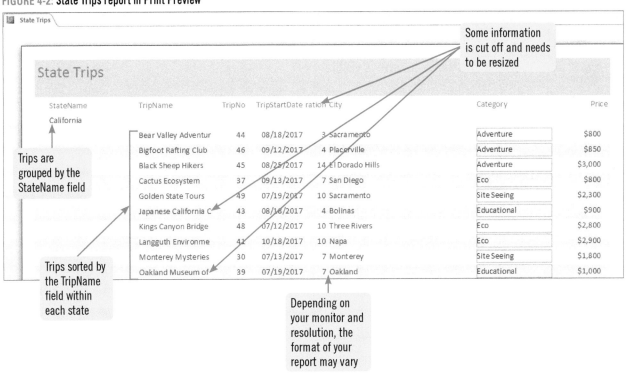

State Trips

StateName	TripName	TripNo	TripStartDate	ration	City	Category	Price
California							
	Bear Valley Adventur	44	08/18/2017	3	Sacramento	Adventure	$800
	Bigfoot Rafting Club	46	09/12/2017	4	Placerville	Adventure	$850
	Black Sheep Hikers	45	08/25/2017	14	El Dorado Hills	Adventure	$3,000
	Cactus Ecosystem	37	09/13/2017	7	San Diego	Eco	$800
	Golden State Tours	49	07/19/2017	10	Sacramento	Site Seeing	$2,300
	Japanese California C	43	08/18/2017	4	Bolinas	Educational	$900
	Kings Canyon Bridge	48	07/12/2017	10	Three Rivers	Eco	$2,800
	Langguth Environme	41	10/18/2017	10	Napa	Eco	$2,900
	Monterey Mysteries	30	07/13/2017	7	Monterey	Site Seeing	$1,800
	Oakland Museum of	39	07/19/2017	7	Oakland	Educational	$1,000

Trips are grouped by the StateName field

Trips sorted by the TripName field within each state

Depending on your monitor and resolution, the format of your report may vary

Changing page orientation

To change page orientation from Portrait (8.5" wide by 11" tall) to Landscape (11" wide by 8.5" tall) and vice versa, click the Portrait or Landscape button on the Print Preview tab when viewing the report in Print Preview. To switch to Print Preview, right-click the report in the Navigation Pane, and then choose Print Preview on the shortcut menu.

Use Report Layout View

Learning Outcomes
- Move and resize controls in Layout View
- Modify labels

Reports have multiple views that you use for various report-building and report-viewing activities. Although some tasks can be accomplished in more than one view, each view has a primary purpose to make your work with reports as easy and efficient as possible. The different report views are summarized in TABLE 4-1. **CASE** *Julia Rice asks you to modify the State Trips report so that all of the fields fit comfortably across one sheet of paper in landscape orientation.*

STEPS

TROUBLE
If the Field List or Property Sheet window opens, close it.

1. **Right-click the** State Trips report tab, **then click** Layout View
   Layout View opens and applies a grid to the report that helps you resize, move, and position controls. You decide to narrow the City column to make room for the Price data.

2. **Click** Sacramento **(or any value in the City column), then use the ↔ pointer to drag the left edge of the City column to the right to narrow it to about half of its current size, as shown in** FIGURE 4-3
   By narrowing the City column, you create extra space in the report.

QUICK TIP
If you select the entire row, just click again directly on the label to select it.

3. **Click the** City label, **then use ↔ to drag the left edge to the right to position it above the column of City data**
   You use the extra room to better display the data on the report.

QUICK TIP
You can use the Undo button ↶ to undo multiple actions in Layout View.

4. **Continue to use ↔ to resize the columns of data and labels so that the entire trip name in the TripName column is visible**
   The TripName column now has more space to completely display the trip names.

5. **Click the** StateName label, **click between the words** State **and** Name, **press the** [Spacebar] **so that the label reads** State Name, **then modify the** TripName, TripNo, **and** TripStartDate **labels to contain spaces as well**

6. **Click the** StateName label, **press and hold** [Shift], **click each of the other seven labels to select them as a group, release** [Shift], **click the** Format tab, **click the** Font Color **drop-down list arrow** [A ▾], **then click** Automatic

7. **Continue working with the columns so that all of the data is visible and your report looks like** FIGURE 4-4

Using Reports

FIGURE 4-3: Modifying the column width in Report Layout View

FIGURE 4-4: Final State Trips report in Report Layout View

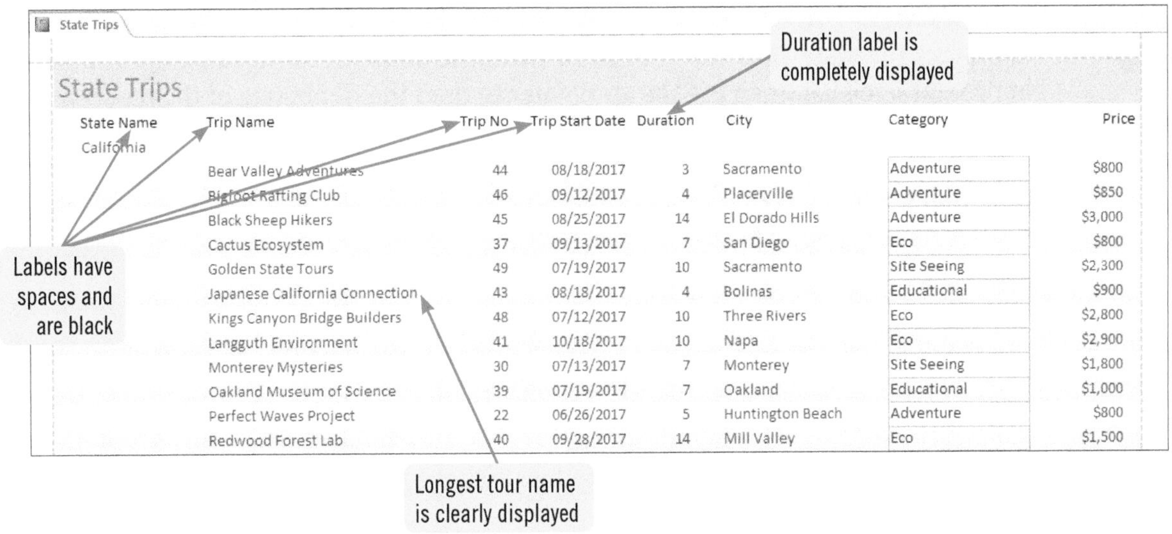

TABLE 4-1: Report views

view	primary purpose
Report View	To quickly review the report without page breaks
Print Preview	To review each page of an entire report as it will appear if printed
Layout View	To modify the size, position, or formatting of controls; shows live data as you modify the report, making it the tool of choice when you want to change the appearance and positioning of controls on a report while also reviewing live data
Design View	To work with report sections or to access the complete range of controls and report properties; Design View does not display data

Review Report Sections

Learning
Outcomes
• Navigate through
report sections
and pages
• Resize the width of
the report
• Work with error
indicators

Report **sections** determine where and how often controls in that section print in the final report. For example, controls in the Report Header section print only once at the beginning of the report, but controls in the Detail section print once for every record the report displays. TABLE 4-2 describes report sections. **CASE** You and Julia Rice preview the State Trips report to review and understand report sections.

STEPS

1. **Right-click the State Trips tab, click Print Preview, then scroll up as needed and click the light blue bar at the top of the report above the Trip Start Date label until you display the first page of the report, as shown in** FIGURE 4-5

   The first page shows four report sections: Report Header, Page Header, StateAbbreviation Header, and Detail.

2. **Click the Next Page button ▶ on the navigation bar to move to the second page of the report**

   If the second page of the report does not contain data, it means that the report may be too wide to fit on a single sheet of paper. You fix that problem in Report Design View.

3. **Right-click the State Trips tab, click Design View, scroll to the far right using the bottom horizontal scroll bar, then use the ↔ pointer to drag the right edge of the report as far as you can to the left, as shown in** FIGURE 4-6

   In Report Design View, you can work with the report sections and make modifications to the report that you cannot make in other views, such as narrowing the width. Report Design View does not display any data, however. For your report to fit on one page in landscape orientation, you need to move all of the controls to the left of the 10.5" mark on the horizontal **ruler** using the default 0.25" left and right margins. You will practice fixing this problem by moving the page calculation in the Page Footer section.

4. **Use the ✥ pointer to drag the page calculation text box about 0.5" to the left**

   To review your modifications, show the report in Print Preview.

5. **Right-click the State Trips tab, click Print Preview, click the Last Page button ▶| to navigate to the last page of the report, then click the report to zoom in and out to examine the page, as shown in** FIGURE 4-7

   Previewing each page of the report helps you confirm that no blank pages are created and allows you to examine how the different report sections print on each page.

TABLE 4-2: **Report sections**

section	where does this section print?
Report Header	At the top of the first page
Page Header	At the top of every page (but below the Report Header on the first page)
Group Header	Before every group of records
Detail	Once for every record
Group Footer	After every group of records
Page Footer	At the bottom of every page
Report Footer	At the end of the report

FIGURE 4-5: State Trips in Print Preview

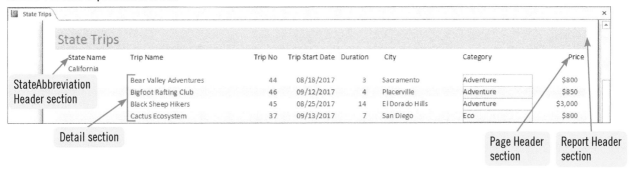

FIGURE 4-5: **State Trips in Print Preview**

FIGURE 4-6: **State Trips report in Design View**

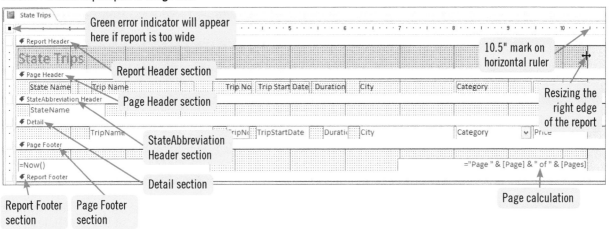

FIGURE 4-7: **Last page of State Trips report in Print Preview**

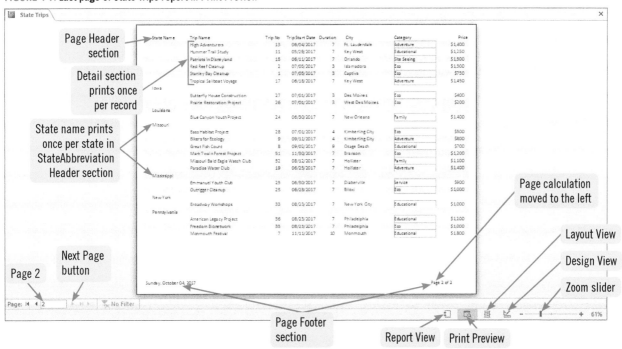

Using Reports

Access 85

Apply Group and Sort Orders

Learning
Outcomes
• Group and sort
  records in a report
• Cut and paste
  controls

Grouping means to sort records by a particular field plus provide a header and/or footer section before or after each group of sorted records. For example, if you group records by the StateAbbreviation field, the Group Header is called the StateAbbreviation Header and the Group Footer is called the StateAbbreviation Footer. The StateAbbreviation Header section appears once for each state in the report, immediately before the records in that state. The StateAbbreviation Footer section also appears once for each state in the report, immediately after the records for that state. **CASE** ▸ *The records in the State Trips report are currently grouped by the StateAbbreviation field. Julia Rice asks you to further group the records by the Category field (Adventure, Eco, Educational, and Family, for example) within each state.*

STEPS

1. **Click the** Close Print Preview button **to return to Report Design View, then click the** Group & Sort button **in the Grouping & Totals group to open the Group, Sort, and Total pane**

   Currently, the records are grouped by the StateAbbreviation field and further sorted by the TripName field. To add the Category field as a grouping field within each state, you work with the Group, Sort, and Total pane in Report Design View.

2. **Click the** Add a group button **in the Group, Sort, and Total pane, click** Category, **then click the** Move up button ⊕ **on the right side of the Group, Sort, and Total pane so that Category is positioned between StateAbbreviation and TripName**

   A Category Header section is added to Report Design View just below the StateAbbreviation Header section. You move the Category control from the Detail section to the Category Header section so it prints only once for each new Category instead of once for each record in the Detail section.

TROUBLE
Use the Move up
⊕ and Move
down ⊽ buttons
as needed to make
sure your Group,
Sort, and Total pane
looks exactly like
FIGURE 4-8.

3. **Right-click the** Category combo box **in the Detail section, click** Cut **on the shortcut menu, right-click the** Category Header section, **click** Paste, **then use the** ⁺ₖ **pointer to drag the** Category combo box **to the right to position it as shown in** FIGURE 4-8

   Now that you've moved the Category combo box to the Category Header, it will print only once per category within each state. You no longer need the Category label in the Page Header section.

4. **Click the** Category label **in the Page Header section, press** [Delete], **then switch to Print Preview and zoom to** 100%

   The State Trips report should look like FIGURE 4-9. Notice that the records are now grouped by category within state. Detail records are further sorted in ascending order by the TripName field value.

FIGURE 4-8: Group, Sort, and Total pane and new Category Header section

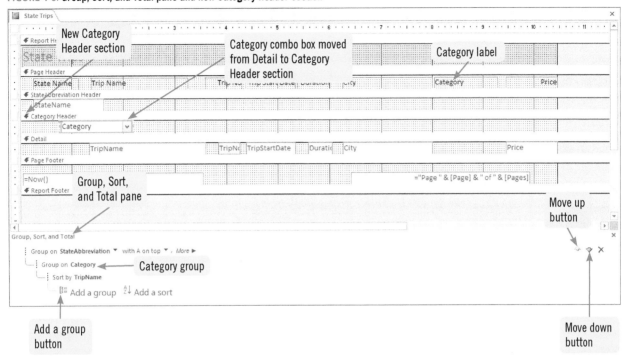

FIGURE 4-9: State Trips report grouped by category within state

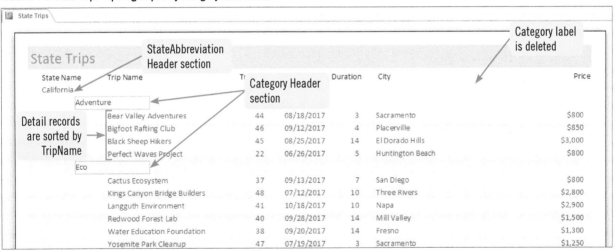

Record Source Property

The **Record Source property** of a report or form determines what fields and records that report or form will display. It is the first property on the Data tab of the Property Sheet for a report or form. The value of the Record Source property may be the name of a table or query. The Record Source property can also be a SELECT statement, which is SQL (Structured Query Language) code. In the Property Sheet for a report, click the Record Source property, and then click the Build button [...] to enter Query Design View, where you can change the Record Source property or save it as a query object within the database.

Add Subtotals and Counts

Learning
Outcomes
- Create calculations
  to subtotal and
  count records
- Copy and paste
  controls

In a report, you create a **calculation** by entering an expression into a text box. When a report is previewed or printed, the expression is evaluated and the resulting calculation is placed on the report. An **expression** is a combination of field names, operators (such as +, −, /, and *), and functions that results in a single value. A **function** is a built-in formula, such as Sum or Count, that helps you quickly create a calculation. Notice that every expression starts with an equal sign (=), and when it uses a function, the arguments for the function are placed in (parentheses). **Arguments** are the pieces of information that the function needs to create the final answer. When an argument is a field name, the field name must be surrounded by [square brackets]. **CASE** *Julia Rice asks you to add a calculation to the State Trips report to sum the total number of trip days within each category and within each state.*

STEPS

1. **Switch to Report Design View**

   A logical place to add subtotals for each group is right after that group of records prints, in the Group Footer section. You use the Group, Sort, and Total pane to open Group Footer sections.

   TROUBLE
   Click Category in the Group, Sort, and Total pane to display the grouping options.

2. **Click the** More button **for the StateAbbreviation field in the Group, Sort, and Total pane, click the** without a footer section list arrow, **click** with a footer section, **then do the same for the** Category field, **as shown in** FIGURE 4-10

   With the StateAbbreviation Footer and Category Footer sections open, you're ready to add controls to calculate the total number of trip days within each category and within each state. You use a text box control with an expression to make this calculation.

3. **Click the** Text Box button ab| **in the Controls group, then click just below the Duration text box in the Category Footer section**

   Adding a new text box automatically adds a new label to its left. First, you modify the label to identify the information; then you modify the text box to contain the correct expression to sum the number of trip days for that category.

   TROUBLE
   Depending on your activity, you may see a different number in the Text##: label.

4. **Click the** Text20 label **to select it, double-click** Text20, **type** Total days:, **click the** Unbound text box **to select it, click** Unbound **again, type** =Sum([Duration]), **press** [Enter], **then widen the text box to view the entire expression**

   The expression =Sum([Duration]) uses the Sum function to add the days in the Duration field. Because the expression is entered in the Category Footer section, it will sum all Duration values for that category within that state. To sum the Duration values for each state, the expression also needs to be inserted in the StateAbbreviation Footer.

   QUICK TIP
   An expression in the Report Footer section would subtotal values for the entire report.

5. **Right-click the** =Sum([Duration]) text box, **click** Copy, **right-click the** StateAbbreviation Footer section, **click** Paste, **then press** [→] **enough times to position the controls in the StateAbbreviation Footer section just below those in the Category Footer section, as shown in** FIGURE 4-11

   With the expression copied to the StateAbbreviation Footer section, you're ready to preview your work.

   TROUBLE
   If your pages are different, it's probably due to extra white space. In Design View, drag the top edge of all section bars up to eliminate extra blank space.

6. **Switch to Print Preview, navigate to the last page of the report, then click to zoom so you can see all of the Pennsylvania trips**

   As shown in FIGURE 4-12, seven trip days are totaled for the Eco category, and 17 for the Educational category, which is a total of 24 trip days for the state of Pennsylvania. The summary data would look better if it were aligned more directly under the trip Duration values. You resize and align controls in the next lesson.

FIGURE 4-10: **Opening group footer sections**

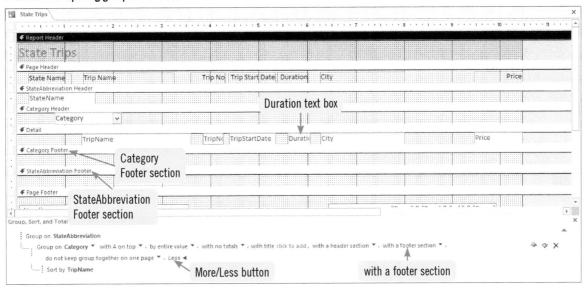

FIGURE 4-11: **Adding subtotals to group footer sections**

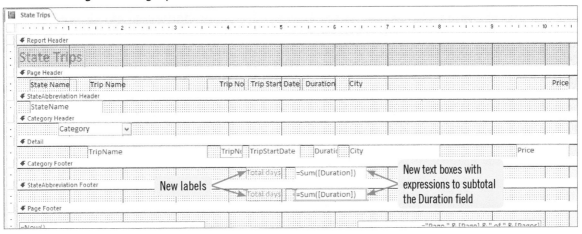

FIGURE 4-12: **Previewing the new group footer calculations**

Resize and Align Controls

Learning
Outcomes
• Align data within a control
• Align the borders of controls

After you add information to the appropriate section of a report, you might also want to align the data in precise columns and rows to make the information easier to read. To do so, you can use two different types of **alignment** commands. You can left-, right-, or center-align a control within its own border using the Align Left ▤, Center ▤, and Align Right ▤ buttons on the Home tab. You can also align the edges of controls with respect to one another using the Left, Right, Top, and Bottom commands on the Align button of the Arrange tab in Report Design View. **CASE** ▶ *You decide to resize and align several controls to improve the readability of the State Trips report. Layout View is a good choice for these tasks.*

STEPS

1. **Switch to Layout View, click the** Design tab **on the Ribbon, then click the** Group & Sort **button to toggle off the Group, Sort, and Total pane**

   You decide to align the expressions that subtotal the number of trip days for each category within the Duration column to make the report easier to read and more professional.

2. **Click the** Total days text box **in the Category Footer, then use the ↔ pointer to resize the text box so that the data is aligned in the Duration column, as shown in** FIGURE 4-13

   If the value in your Total days text box is not right-aligned, click the Align Right button (shown in FIGURE 4-13). With the calculation formatted as desired in the Category Footer, you can quickly apply those modifications to the calculation in the StateAbbreviation Footer as well.

3. **Scroll down the report far enough to find and then click the** Total days text box **in the StateAbbreviation Footer, then use the ↔ pointer to resize the text box so that it is the same width as the text box in the Category Footer section**

   With both expressions resized so they line up under the Duration values in the Detail section, they are easier to read on the report.

4. **Scroll the report so you can see all of the Colorado trips, as shown in** FIGURE 4-14

   You can apply resize, alignment, or formatting commands to more than one control at a time. TABLE 4-3 provides techniques for selecting more than one control at a time in Report Design View.

Precisely moving and resizing controls

You can move and resize controls using the mouse or other pointing device, but you can move controls more precisely using the keyboard. Pressing the arrow keys while holding [Ctrl] moves selected controls one **pixel** (picture element) at a time in the direction of the arrow. Pressing the arrow keys while holding [Shift] resizes selected controls one pixel at a time.

FIGURE 4-13: **Resizing controls in Layout View**

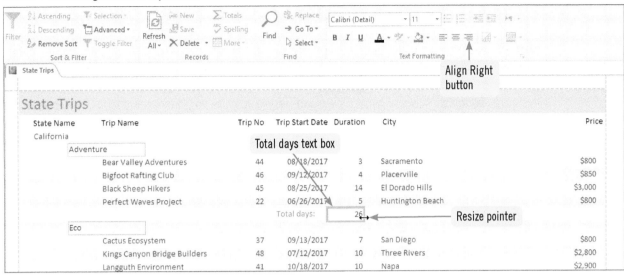

FIGURE 4-14: **Reviewing the aligned and resized controls**

TABLE 4-3: **Selecting more than one control at a time in Report Design View**

technique	description
Click, [Shift]+click	Click a control, and then press and hold [Shift] while clicking other controls; each one is selected
Drag a selection box	Drag a selection box (an outline box you create by dragging the pointer in Report Design View); every control that is in or is touched by the edges of the box is selected
Click in the ruler	Click in either the horizontal or vertical ruler to select all controls that intersect the selection line
Drag in the ruler	Drag through either the horizontal or vertical ruler to select all controls that intersect the selection line as it is dragged through the ruler

Format a Report

Formatting refers to enhancing the appearance of the information. Although the Report Wizard automatically applies many formatting embellishments, you often want to change the appearance of the report to fit your particular needs. **CASE** *When reviewing the State Trips report with Julia, you decide to change the background color of some of the report sections to make the data easier to read. The Report Wizard applied alternating formats, which you want to change. You want to shade each Category Header and Category Footer section using the same color. To make changes to entire report sections, you work in Report Design View.*

STEPS

1. **Switch to Design View, click the** Category Header section bar, **click the** Format tab **on the Ribbon, click the** Alternate Row Color button arrow, **click the** Maroon 2 color square **as shown in** FIGURE 4-15, **click the** Shape Fill button, **then click the** Maroon 2 color square

   Make a similar modification by applying a different fill color to the Category Footer section.

2. **Click the** Category Footer section bar, **click the** Alternate Row Color button arrow, **click the** Maroon 1 color square **(just above Maroon 2 in the Standard Colors section), click the** Shape Fill button, **then click the** Maroon 1 color square

   When you use the Alternate Row Color and Shape Fill buttons, you're actually modifying the **Back Color** and **Alternate Back Color** properties in the Property Sheet of the section or control you selected. Background shades can help differentiate parts of the report, but be careful with dark colors, as they may print as solid black on some printers and fax machines.

3. **Switch to Layout View to review your modifications**

   The category sections are clearer, but you decide to make one more modification to emphasize the report title.

4. **Click the** State Trips label **in the Report Header section, click the** Home tab, **then click the** Bold button B **in the Text Formatting group**

   The report in Layout View should look like FIGURE 4-16. You also want to add a label to the Report Footer section to identify yourself.

5. **Switch to Report Design View, drag the** bottom edge of the Report Footer **down about 0.5", click the** Label button Aa **in the Controls group, click at the** 1" mark in the Report Footer, **type** Created by *your* name, **press [Enter], click the** Home tab, **then click** B **in the Text Formatting group**

6. **Save and preview the State Trips report**

7. **If required by your instructor, print the report, and then close it**

FIGURE 4-15: Formatting section backgrounds

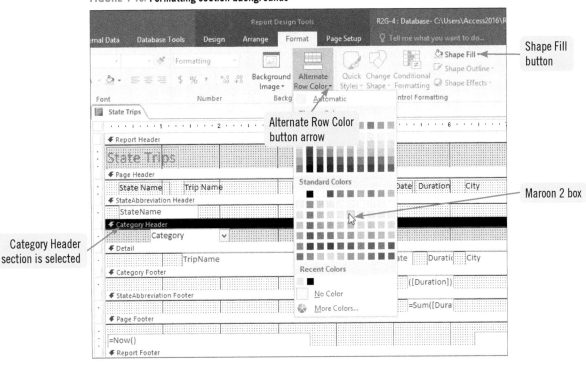

Shape Fill button

Alternate Row Color button arrow

Maroon 2 box

Category Header section is selected

FIGURE 4-16: Final formatted State Trips report

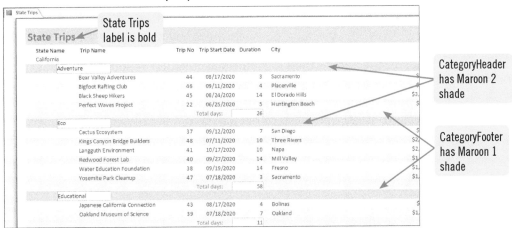

State Trips label is bold

CategoryHeader has Maroon 2 shade

CategoryFooter has Maroon 1 shade

Create Mailing Labels

Learning Outcomes
- Create a report of labels
- Print specific pages of a report

Mailing labels are often created to apply to envelopes, postcards, or letters when assembling a mass mailing. They have many other business purposes too, such as labels for paper file folders or name tags. Any data in your Access database can be converted into labels using the **Label Wizard**, a special report wizard that precisely positions and sizes information for hundreds of standard business labels. **CASE** ➤ *Julia Rice asks you to create mailing labels for all of the addresses in the Customers table. You use the Label Wizard to handle this request.*

STEPS

1. **Click the** Customers table **in the Navigation Pane, click the** Create tab, **then click the** Labels button **in the Reports group**

   The first Label Wizard dialog box opens. The Filter by manufacturer list box provides over 30 manufacturers of labels. Avery is the default choice. With the manufacturer selected, your next task is to choose the product number of the labels you will feed through the printer. The cover on the box of labels you are using provides this information. In this case, you'll be using Avery 5160 labels, a common type of sheet labels used for mailings and other purposes.

2. **Scroll through the Product number list, then click** 5160 **as shown in** FIGURE 4-17

   Note that by selecting a product number, you also specify the dimensions of the label and number of columns.

3. **Click** Next, **then click** Next **again to accept the default font and color choices**

   The third question of the Label Wizard asks how you want to construct your label. You'll add the fields from the Customers table with spaces and line breaks to pattern a standard mailing format.

4. **Double-click** FName, **press** [Spacebar], **double-click** LName, **press** [Enter], **double-click** Street, **press** [Enter], **double-click** City, **type a** comma (,) **and press** [Spacebar], **double-click** State, **press** [Spacebar], **then double-click** Zip

   If your prototype label doesn't look exactly like FIGURE 4-18, delete the fields in the Prototype label box and try again. Be careful to put a space between the FName and LName fields in the first row, a comma and a space between the City and State fields, and a space between the State and Zip fields.

5. **Click** Next, **double-click** LName **to select it as a sorting field, click** Next, **click** Finish **to accept the name** Labels Customers **for the new report, then click** OK **if prompted that some data may not be displayed**

   A portion of the new report is shown in FIGURE 4-19. It is generally a good idea to print the first page of the report on standard paper to make sure everything is aligned correctly before printing on labels.

6. **If requested by your instructor, click the** Print button **on the Print Preview tab, click the** From box, **type** 1, **click the** To box, **type** 1, **then click** OK **to print the first page of the report**

7. **Close the Labels Customers report, close the R2G-4.accdb database, then exit Access 2016**

FIGURE 4-17: **Label Wizard dialog box**

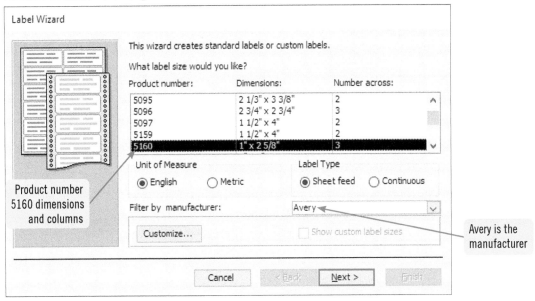

FIGURE 4-18: **Building a prototype label**

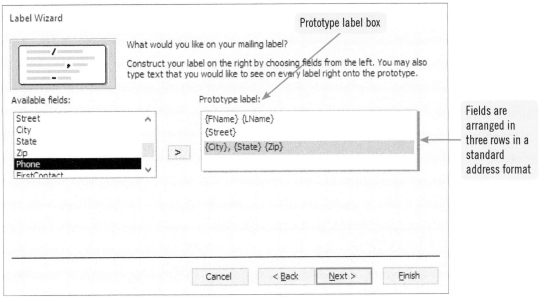

FIGURE 4-19: **Labels Customers report**

Practice

Concepts Review

Label each element of the Report Design View window shown in FIGURE 4-20.

FIGURE 4-20

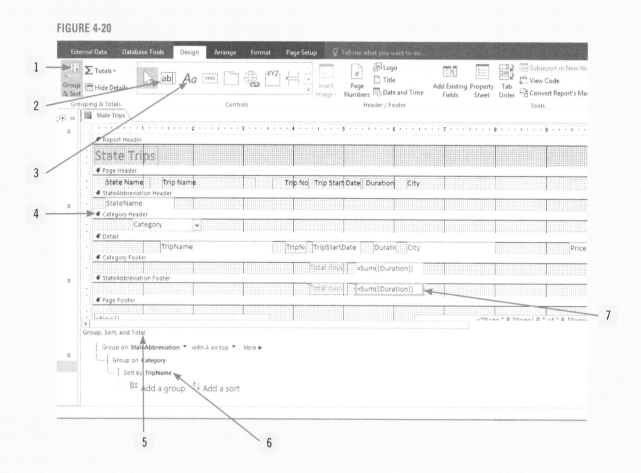

Match each term with the statement that best describes it.

8. Record source
9. Alignment
10. Detail section
11. Expression
12. Grouping
13. Section
14. Formatting

a. Left, center, or right are common choices
b. Prints once for every record
c. Used to identify which fields and records are passed to the report
d. Sorting records *plus* providing a header or footer section
e. Determines how controls are positioned on the report
f. A combination of field names, operators, and functions that results in a single value
g. Enhancing the appearance of information displayed in the report

Select the best answer from the list of choices.

15. **Which type of control is most commonly placed in the Detail section?**
    a. Image
    b. Line
    c. Text box
    d. Label

16. **Which of the following is not a valid report view?**
    a. Print Preview
    b. Section View
    c. Layout View
    d. Design View

17. **A title for a report would most commonly be placed in which report section?**
    a. Group Footer
    b. Detail
    c. Report Header
    d. Report Footer

18. **A calculated expression that presents page numbering information would probably be placed in which report section?**
    a. Report Header
    b. Detail
    c. Group Footer
    d. Page Footer

19. **To align the edges of several controls with each other, you use the alignment commands on the:**
    a. Formatting tab.
    b. Design tab.
    c. Print Preview tab.
    d. Arrange tab.

20. **Which of the following expressions counts the number of records using the FirstName field?**
    a. =Count([FirstName])
    b. =Count[FirstName]
    c. =Count((FirstName))
    d. =Count{FirstName}

21. **What is the difference between grouping and sorting in a report?**
    a. Grouping allows you to add a Group Header and/or Group Footer section to a report.
    b. Grouping means to sort in ascending order.
    c. Grouping means to sort by more than one field.
    d. You can have more than one grouping field, but you can only have one sorting field.

Skills Review

1. **Use the Report Wizard.**
   a. Start Access and open the LakeHomes-4.accdb database from the location where you store your Data Files. Enable content if prompted.
   b. Use the Report Wizard to create a report based on the RLast and RPhone fields from the Realtors table and the Type, SqFt, BR, Bath, and Asking fields from the Listings table. (*Hint*: Make sure your fields are added in the order listed.)
   c. View the data by Realtors, do not add any more grouping levels, and sort the records in descending order by the Asking field. (*Hint*: Click the Ascending button to toggle it to Descending.)
   d. Use a Stepped layout and a Landscape orientation. Title the report **Listings by Realtor**.
   e. Preview the first and second pages of the new report.

2. **Use Report Layout View.**
   a. Switch to Layout View and close the Field List and Property Sheet if they are open.
   b. Drag the right edge of the Asking column and label to the left to provide a little more space between the Asking column and Type column.
   c. Modify the RLast label to read **Realtor**, the RPhone label to read **Cell**, the SqFt label to read **Square Ft**, the BR label to read **Bedrooms**, and the Bath label to read **Baths**.
   d. Switch to Print Preview to review your changes.

Skills Review (continued)

3. Review report sections.

   a. Switch to Report Design View.

   b. Drag the text box that contains the Page calculation in the lower-right corner of the Page Footer section to the left so that it is to the left of the 9" mark on the horizontal ruler.

   c. Drag the right edge of the entire report to the left as far as possible.

   d. Preview the report and make sure there are no blank pages between printed pages. You may need to move or narrow more controls and narrow the report again in order to accomplish this.

4. Apply group and sort orders.

   a. Open the Group, Sort, and Total pane.

   b. Add the Type field as a grouping field between the RealtorNo grouping field and Asking sort field. Make sure the sort order on the Asking field is in descending order (from largest to smallest). (*Hint*: Use the Move up button to move the Type field between the RealtorNo and Asking fields in the Group, Sort, and Total pane.)

   c. Cut and paste the Type combo box from its current position in the Detail section to the Type Header section.

   d. Move the Type combo box in the Type Header section so its left edge is at about the 1" mark on the horizontal ruler.

   e. Delete the Type label in the Page Header section.

   f. Switch to Layout View, and resize the Asking, Square Ft, Bedrooms, and Baths columns as needed so they are more evenly spaced across the page.

5. Add subtotals and counts.

   a. Switch to Report Design View, then open the RealtorNo Footer section. (*Hint*: Use the More button on the RealtorNo field in the Group, Sort, and Total pane.)

   b. Add a text box control to the RealtorNo Footer section, just below the Asking text box in the Detail section. Change the label to read **Subtotal:**, and enter the expression **=Sum([Asking])** in the text box.

   c. Drag the bottom edge of the Report Footer section down about 0.25" to add space to the Report Footer.

   d. Copy and paste the new expression in the RealtorNo Footer section to the Report Footer section. Position the new controls in the Report Footer section directly below the controls in the RealtorNo Footer section.

   e. Modify the Subtotal: label in the Report Footer section to read **Grand Total:**.

   f. Preview the last page of the report to view the new subtotals in the RealtorNo Footer and Report Footer sections.

6. Resize and align controls.

   a. Switch to Design View, then click the Group & Sort button on the Design tab to close the Group, Sort, and Total pane if it is open.

   b. Click the Asking text box in the Detail section, press and hold [Shift], and then click the expression in the RealtorNo Footer as well as the Report Footer sections to select the three text boxes at the same time. Click the Arrange tab on the Ribbon, click the Align button, then click Right to right-align the edges of the three text boxes.

   c. With all three text boxes still selected, click the Format tab on the Ribbon, click the Apply Comma Number Format button, and click the Decrease Decimals button twice so that the values appear as whole dollar amounts without cents.

   d. Preview the report to view the alignment and format on the Asking data and subtotals.

7. Format a report.

   a. In Report Design View, change the Alternate Row Color of the Detail section to No Color.

   b. Change the Alternate Row Color of the Type Header, the RealtorNo Header, and the RealtorNo Footer sections to No Color.

   c. Change the Shape Fill color of the RealtorNo Header section to Green 2. (*Hint*: The Shape Fill button will change the Back Color property in the Property Sheet.)

Skills Review (continued)

d. Select the RLast and RPhone text boxes in the RealtorNo Header section, and change the Shape Fill color to Green 2 to match the RealtorNo Header section.

e. Bold the title of the report, which is the **Listings by Realtor** label in the Report Header, and resize it to make it a little wider to accommodate the bold text.

f. Change the font color of each label in the Page Header section to Automatic (black).

g. Save and preview the report in Print Preview. It should look like FIGURE 4-21. The report should fit on three pages, and the grand total for all Asking values should be 7,957,993. If there are blank pages between printed pages, return to Report Design View and drag the right edge of the report to the left.

FIGURE 4-21

h. In Report Design View, add a label to the left side of the Report Footer section with your name. Be sure to add a label and not a text box control. Make sure that your name is displayed clearly on the last page only in Print Preview.

i. Print the report if requested by your instructor, then save and close the Listings by Realtor report.

8. Create mailing labels.

a. Click the Agencies table in the Navigation Pane, then start the Label Wizard.

b. Choose Avery 5160 labels and the default text appearance choices.

c. Build a prototype label with the AgencyName on the first line, Street on the second line, and City, State, and Zip on the third line with a comma and space between City and State, and a space between State and Zip.

d. Sort by AgencyName, and name the report **Labels Agencies**.

e. Preview then save and close the report. Click OK if a warning dialog box appears regarding horizontal space. The data in your label report does not exceed the dimensions of the labels.

f. Open the Agencies table and change the name of Big Cedar Realtors to *Your Last Name* **Realtors**. Close the Agencies table, reopen the Labels Agencies report, then print it if requested by your instructor.

g. Close the Labels Agencies report, close the LakeHomes-4.accdb database, then exit Access 2016.

Independent Challenge 1

As the office manager of an international convention planning company, you have created a database to track convention, enrollment, and company data. Your goal is to create a report of up-to-date attendee enrollments.

a. Start Access, then open the Conventions-4.accdb database from the location where you store your Data Files. Enable content if prompted.

b. Use the Report Wizard to create a report with the AttendeeLast and AttendeeFirst fields from the Attendees table, the CompanyName field from the Companies table, and the ConventionName and CountryName from the Conventions table. Add the fields in the order listed.

c. View your data by Conventions, add the CompanyName as a second grouping field, then sort in ascending order by AttendeeLast.

d. Use the Block layout and Portrait orientation, then name the report **Convention Attendees**.

e. In Layout View, change the labels in the Page Header section from ConventionName to **Convention** and CompanyName to **Company**. Delete the CountryName, AttendeeLast, and AttendeeFirst labels in the Page Header section.

f. In Report Design View, open the Group, Sort, and Total pane, then open the ConventionNo Footer section.

g. In Report Design View, add a text box to the ConventionNo Footer section just below the AttendeeLast text box in the Detail section. The purpose of the text box is to count the number of people enrolled for each convention. The label should read **Count of Attendees:**, and the expression in the text box should be **=Count([AttendeeLast])**.

h. Resize the new label and text box as needed to make their contents clearly visible.

i. Copy and paste the new label and expression to the Report Footer section. Move and align the controls so they are at the same horizontal position on the page.

j. Change the text color of all labels to Automatic (black). (*Hint*: There are labels in the Report Header, Page Header, ConventionNo Footer, and Report Footer sections.)

k. Preview the report and make sure there are no blank pages between pages. Resize controls in Layout View and narrow the report in Report Design view as needed to remove blank pages.

l. Preview the last page of the report to make sure the subtotal count for each convention and grand total count for the report are aligned as shown in FIGURE 4-22.

m. Add a label with your name to the left side of the Report Footer section, change the text color to Automatic (black), and then print the last page if required by your instructor.

n. Save and close the Convention Attendees report, close the Conventions-4.accdb database, then exit Access 2016.

FIGURE 4-22

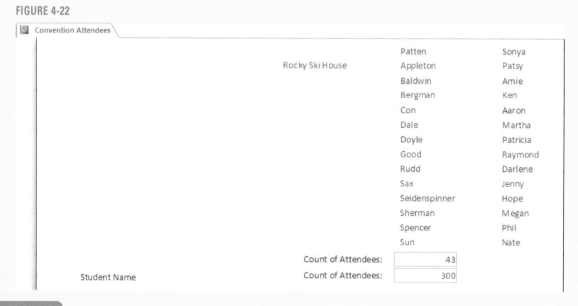

Independent Challenge 2

You have built an Access database to track membership in a community service club. The database tracks member names and addresses as well as their status and rank in the club and their hours of service to the community.

a. Start Access and open the Service-4.accdb database from the location where you store your Data Files. Enable content if prompted.

b. Open the Members table, find and change the name of Micah Ati to *your* name, then close the Members table.

c. Use the Report Wizard to create a report using the FirstName, LastName, and Dues fields from the Members table and the ActivityDate and HoursWorked fields from the Activities table, all in that order.

d. View the data by Members. Do not add any more grouping fields, and sort the records in ascending order by ActivityDate.

e. Use a Stepped layout and Portrait orientation, title the report **Activity Log**, then preview the report.

f. Use Report Layout View to resize the controls to fit the available space and display all data clearly.

g. Change the FirstName label to **First Name**. Change the LastName label to **Last Name**. Change the ActivityDate label to **Date**. Change the HoursWorked label to **Hours**.

h. Switch to Report Design View, then use the Group, Sort, and Total pane to open the MemberNo Footer section.

i. Add a text box to the MemberNo Footer section, just below the HoursWorked text box in the Detail section. Change the label to **Total:** and the expression in the text box to =**Sum([HoursWorked])**.

j. Open the Report Footer section, then copy and paste the =**Sum([HoursWorked])** text box to the Report Footer section. Change the label in the Report Footer section to read **Grand Total:**.

k. Align the HoursWorked text box in the Detail section and the two expressions in the MemberNo Footer and Report Footer sections so that the numbers are perfectly aligned. Be sure to preview the last page of the report to make sure all three controls are aligned as shown in FIGURE 4-23.

l. Add a label to the left edge of the Report Footer section with your name.

m. Preview each page of the report to make sure there are no blank pages. If there are, narrow the controls and the right edge of the report in Report Design View to fix this problem.

n. Print the last page of the report if requested to do so by your instructor.

o. Close the Activity Log report, close the Service-4.accdb database, then exit Access.

FIGURE 4-23

Total:	13
Grand Total:	476

Independent Challenge 3

You have built an Access database to organize the deposits at a salvage center. Various clubs regularly deposit material, which is measured in pounds when the deposits are made.

   a. Start Access and open the Salvage-4.accdb database from the location where you store your Data Files. Enable content if prompted.

   b. Open the Centers table, change **A1 Salvage Center** to **Your Last Name Salvage**, then close the table.

   c. Use the Report Wizard to create a report with the CenterName field from the Centers table, the DepositDate and Weight fields from the Deposits table, and the ClubName field from the Clubs table.

   d. View the data by Centers, do not add any more grouping levels, and sort the records in ascending order by DepositDate.

   e. Use a Stepped layout and a Portrait orientation, then title the report **Deposit Log**.

   f. In Layout View, resize the Weight label and Weight data to better position the data across the report. Rename the DepositDate label to **Date**.

   g. Add spaces to the labels so that CenterName becomes **Center Name**, and ClubName becomes **Club Name**.

   h. In Report Design View, open the Group, Sort, and Total pane and then open the CenterNumber Footer section.

   i. Add a text box to the CenterNumber Footer section just below the Weight text box with the expression **=Sum([Weight])**.

   j. Rename the new label to be **Subtotal:**.

   k. Copy the new text box and paste it back to the CenterNumber Footer section. Change the new label to **Count:** and the expression to **=Count([Weight])**. Align the new controls directly below the Subtotal and =Sum([Weight]) expression.

   l. Paste the controls a second time to the CenterNumber Footer section, and change the new label to **Average:** and the expression to **=Avg([Weight])**.

   m. Change the Format property of the =Avg([Weight]) expression to **Standard**, and change the Decimal Places property to **0**. (*Hint*: Open the Property Sheet for the text box and click the Format tab to find the Format and Decimal Places properties.)

   n. Expand the Report Footer section, then copy and paste the three text boxes from the CenterNumber Footer section to the Report Footer section.

   o. Move and align the text boxes in the CenterNumber Footer and Report Footer sections to be positioned directly under the Weight text box in the Detail section. (*Hint*: You may need to both right-align the text boxes as well as align the right edges of the text boxes.)

   p. Change the Subtotal label in the Report Footer section to **Total Sum:**. Change the Count label in the Report Footer section to **Total Count:** and also left-align the labels in the CenterNumber Footer and Report Footer sections.

   q. Add a label to the left edge of the Report Footer section with your name and preview the last page of the report, a portion of which is shown in FIGURE 4-24. Your numbers should match.

   r. Continue to improve the report as needed to align all numbers and labels and to remove any extra blank space in the report by making your sections as vertically short as possible in Report Design View.

   s. Save and close the Deposit Log report, close the Salvage-4.accdb database, then exit Access.

FIGURE 4-24

1/16/2017	85	Access Users Group
1/21/2017	150	Boy Scout Troop 324
Subtotal:	3315	
Count:	36	
Average:	92	
Total Sum:	11360	
Total Count:	118	
Average:	96	

Student Name

Independent Challenge 4: Explore

One way you can use an Access database on your own is to record and track your job search efforts. In this exercise, you create a report to help read and analyze data in your job-tracking database.

a. Start Access and open the JobSearch-4.accdb database from the location where you store your Data Files. Enable content if prompted.

b. Open the Employers table, and enter five more records to identify five more potential employers.

c. Use subdatasheets in the Employers table to enter five more potential jobs. You may enter all five jobs for one employer, one job for five different employers, or any combination thereof. Be sure to check the spelling of all data entered. For the Desirability field, enter a value from **1** to **5**, 1 being the least desirable and 5 being the most desirable. Close the Employers table.

d. Use the Report Wizard to create a report that lists the CompanyName, EmpCity, and EmpState fields from the Employers table, and the Title, AnnualSalary, and Desirability fields from the Positions table.

e. View the data by Employers, do not add any more grouping levels, and sort the records in descending order by Desirability.

f. Use an Outline layout and a Portrait orientation, then title the report **Jobs**.

g. In Design View, revise the labels in the EmployerID Header section from CompanyName to **Company**, EmpCity to **City**, EmpState to **State**, and AnnualSalary to **Salary**.

h. Right-align the text within the Company, City, and State labels so they are closer to the text boxes they describe.

i. In Report Layout View, resize the Desirability, Title, and Salary labels and text boxes to space the controls evenly across the report.

j. Preview the report, then switch to Report Design View to remove any extra space in the report sections. This will involve moving the controls in the EmployerID Header section as far to the top of that section as possible, then dragging the top edge of the Detail section up.

k. Preview the report, making sure all controls fit within the width of portrait orientation. If not, switch to Report Design View and fix this problem.

l. Print the first page if requested by your instructor.

m. Close the Jobs report, close the JobSearch-4.accdb database, then exit Access 2016.

Visual Workshop

Open the Basketball-4.accdb database from the location where you store your Data Files and enable content if prompted. Open the Players table, change the name of Matthew Douglas to *your* name, then close the table. Your goal is to create the report shown in FIGURE 4-25. Use the Report Wizard, and select the PFirst, PLast, HomeTown, and HomeState fields from the Players table. Select the FieldGoals, 3Pointers, and FreeThrows fields from the Stats table. View the data by Players, do not add any more grouping levels, and do not add any more sorting levels. Use a Block layout and a Portrait orientation, then title the report **Scoring Report**. In Layout View, resize all of the columns so that they fit on a single piece of portrait paper, and change the labels in the Page Header section as shown. In Design View, open the PlayerNo Footer section and add text boxes with expressions to sum the FieldGoals, 3Pointers, and FreeThrows fields and bold those controls. Drag the top edge of the Page Footer section down a little to add a little space between the subtotals in the PlayerNo Footer section and the next set of records for the next player. Move, modify, align, and resize all controls as needed to match FIGURE 4-25. (*Hint*: Change the Shape Outline of the text boxes in the PlayerNo Footer section to Transparent to remove the outline.) Be sure to print preview the report to make sure that it fits within the width of one sheet of paper. Modify the report to narrow it in Report Design View if needed.

FIGURE 4-25

Player Name		Home Town	State	Field Goals	3 Pointers	Free Throws
Student First	Student Last	Linden	IA	4	1	3
				5	2	2
				5	3	3
				6	3	5
				4	1	1
				4	2	2
				3	2	1
				4	2	3
				4	2	3
				3	2	1
				42	**20**	**24**
Deonte	Cook	Osseo	MN	6	0	4
				4	1	3
				4	0	4

Improving Queries

CASE The Reason 2 Go database has been updated to contain more customers, trips, and sales. You help Julia Rice, an R2G trip developer for U.S. travel, create queries to analyze this information.

Module Objectives

After completing this module, you will be able to:

- Create multitable queries
- Apply sorts and view SQL
- Develop AND criteria
- Develop OR criteria
- Create calculated fields
- Build summary queries
- Build crosstab queries
- Create a report on a query

Files You Will Need

R2G-6.accdb
Service-6.accdb
Music-6.accdb
LakeHomes-6.accdb
Scholarships-6.accdb
Training-6.accdb

Create Multitable Queries

Learning Outcomes
• Create a multitable query in Query Design View
• Add and delete fields in Query Design View

A **select query**, the most common type of query, selects fields from related tables and displays records in a datasheet where you can view, enter, edit, or delete data. You can create select queries by using the Simple Query Wizard, or you can start from scratch in Query Design View. **Query Design View** gives you more options for selecting and presenting information. When you open (or **run**) a query, the fields and records that you selected for the query are presented in **Query Datasheet View**, also called a **logical view** of the data. **CASE** ▶ *Julia Rice asks you to create a query to analyze customer payments. You select fields from the Customers, Trips, Sales, and Payments tables to complete this analysis.*

STEPS

1. **Start Access, open the** R2G-6.accdb database **from the location where you store your Data Files, then enable content if prompted**

2. **Click the** Create tab **on the Ribbon, then click the** Query Design button **in the Queries group**

   The Show Table dialog box opens and lists all the tables in the database.

3. **Double-click** Customers, **double-click** Sales, **double-click** Trips, **double-click** Payments, **then click** Close

   Recall that the upper pane of Query Design View displays the fields for each of the selected tables in field lists. The name of the table is shown in the field list title bar. Primary key fields are identified with a small key icon. Relationships between tables are displayed with **one-to-many join lines** that connect the linking fields. You select the fields you want by adding them to the query design grid.

4. **Double-click the** FName field **in the Customers table field list to add this field to the first column of the query design grid, double-click** LName, **double-click** TripName **in the Trips field list, scroll then double-click** Price **in the Trips field list, double-click** PaymentDate **in the Payments field list, then double-click** PaymentAmt, **as shown in** FIGURE 6-1

   When you double-click a field in a field list, it is automatically added as the next field in the query grid. When you drag a field to the query design grid, any existing fields move to the right to accommodate the new field.

5. **Click the** View button ▦ **in the Results group to run the query and display the query datasheet**

   The resulting datasheet looks like FIGURE 6-2. The datasheet shows the six fields selected in Query Design View: FName and LName from the Customers table, TripName and Price from the Trips table, and PaymentDate and PaymentAmt from the Payments table. The datasheet displays 78 records because 78 different payments have been made. Some of the payments are from the same customer. For example, Kristen Collins has made payments on multiple trips (records 2 and 20). Kristen's last name has changed to Lang.

6. **Double-click** Collins **in the LName field of the second record, type** Lang, **then click any other record**

   Because Kristen's data is physically stored in only one record in the Customers table (but selected multiple times in this query because Kristen has made more than one payment), changing any occurrence of her last name updates all other selections of that data in this query and throughout all other queries, forms, and reports in the database, too. Note that Kristen's name has been updated to Kristen Lang in record 20, as shown in FIGURE 6-2.

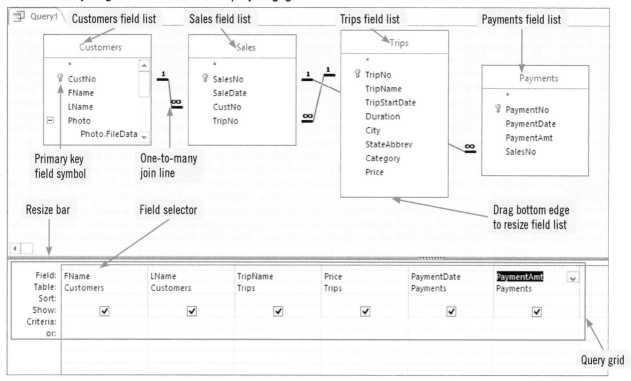

FIGURE 6-2: **Query datasheet**

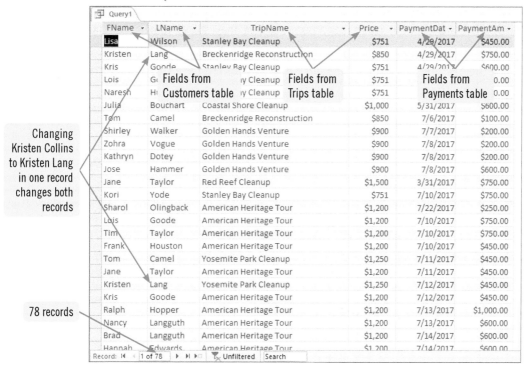

Deleting a field from the query grid

If you add the wrong field to the query design grid, you can delete it by clicking the **field selector**, the thin gray bar above each field name, then pressing [Delete]. Deleting a field from the query design grid removes it from the logical view of this query's datasheet, but does not delete the field from the database. A field is defined and the field's contents are stored in a table object only.

Access 2016

Apply Sorts and View SQL

Learning
Outcomes
• Apply sort orders
  in Query Design
  View
• View Structured
  Query Language
• Define SQL
  keywords

Sorting refers to reordering records in either ascending or descending order based on the values in a field. You can specify more than one sort field in Query Design View. Sort orders are evaluated from left to right, meaning that the sort field on the far left is the primary sort field. Sort orders defined in Query Design View are saved with the query object. **CASE** ▶ *Julia Rice wants to list the records in alphabetical order based on the customer's last name. If the customer has made more than one payment, Julia asks you to further sort the records by the payment date.*

STEPS

1. **Click the** View button ⊠ **on the Home tab to return to Query Design View**

   To sort the records by last name then by payment date, the LName field must be the primary sort field, and the PaymentDate field must be the secondary sort field.

2. **Click the** LName field Sort cell **in the query design grid, click the** Sort list arrow, **click** Ascending, **click the** PaymentDate field Sort cell **in the query design grid, click the** Sort list arrow, **then click** Ascending

   The resulting query design grid should look like FIGURE 6-3.

QUICK TIP

You can resize the columns of a datasheet by pointing to the right column border that separates the field names, then dragging left or right to resize the columns. Double-click to adjust the column width to fit the widest entry.

3. **Click the** View button ▦ **in the Results group to display the query datasheet**

   The records of the datasheet are now listed in ascending order based on the values in the LName field. When the same value appears in the LName field, the records are further sorted by the secondary sort field, PaymentDate, as shown in FIGURE 6-4. Jacob Alman made two payments, one on 7/25/2017 and the next on 8/31/2017. Julia Bouchart made many payments and they are all listed in ascending order on the PaymentDate field.

4. **Click the** Save button 🖫 **on the Quick Access Toolbar, type** CustPayments **in the Save As dialog box, then click** OK

   When you save a query, you save a logical view of the data, a selection of fields and records from underlying tables. Technically, when you save a query, you are saving a set of instructions written in **Structured Query Language (SQL)**. You can view the SQL code for any query by switching to **SQL View**.

QUICK TIP

SQL keywords such as SELECT, FROM, or ORDER BY should not be used as field names.

5. **Click the** View button list arrow, **click** SQL View, **then click in the** lower part of the SQL window **to deselect the code**

   The SQL statements shown in FIGURE 6-5 start with the **SELECT** keyword. Field names follow SELECT, and how the tables are joined follow the **FROM** keyword. The **ORDER BY** keyword determines how records are sorted. Fortunately, you do not have to write or understand SQL to use Access or select data from multiple tables. The easy-to-use Query Design View gives you a way to select and sort data from underlying tables without being an SQL programmer.

6. **Close the CustPayments query**

FIGURE 6-3: Specifying multiple sort orders in Query Design View

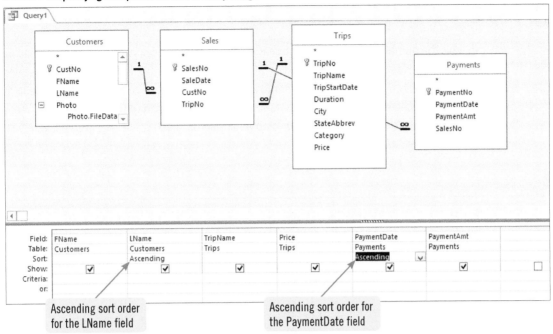

Ascending sort order for the LName field

Ascending sort order for the PaymentDate field

FIGURE 6-4: Records sorted by LName, then by PaymentDate

FName	LName	TripName	Price	PaymentDat	PaymentAm
Jacob	Alman	Red Reef Cleanup	$1,500	7/25/2017	$300.00
Jacob	Alman	Red Reef Cleanup	$1,500	8/31/2017	$100.00
Julia	Bouchart	Coastal Shore Cleanup	$1,000	5/31/2017	$600.00
Julia	Bouchart	Coastal Shore Cleanup	$1,000	6/30/2017	$200.00
Julia	Bouchart	Red Reef Cleanup	$1,500	7/21/2017	$300.00
Julia	Bouchart	anup	$1,000	7/31/2017	$200.00
Julia	Bouchart	ꞏꞏꞏ	$1,500	8/20/2017	$100.00
Julia	Bouchart	Coastal Shore Cleanup	$1,000	8/31/2017	$200.00

Secondary sort order

Primary sort order

FIGURE 6-5: SQL View

SELECT keyword

SELECT Customers.FName, Customers.LName, Trips.TripName, Trips.Price, Payments.PaymentDate, Payments.PaymentAmt
FROM (Trips INNER JOIN (Customers INNER JOIN Sales ON Customers.CustNo = Sales.CustNo) ON Trips.TripNo = Sales.TripNo) INNER JOIN Payments ON Sales.SalesNo = Payments.SalesNo
ORDER BY Customers.LName, Payments.PaymentDate;

FROM keyword

ORDER BY keyword

Specifying a sort order different from the field order in the datasheet

If your database has several customers with the same last name, you can include a secondary sort on the first name field to distinguish the customers. If you want to display the fields in a different order from which they are sorted, you can use the solution shown in FIGURE 6-6. Add a field to the query design grid twice, once to select for the datasheet, and once to use as a sort order. Use the Show check box to deselect the field used as a sort order.

FIGURE 6-6: Sorting on a field that is not displayed

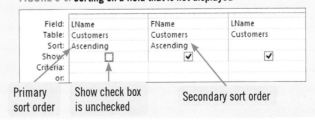

Field:	LName	FName	LName
Table:	Customers	Customers	Customers
Sort:	Ascending	Ascending	
Show:	☐	✓	✓
Criteria:			
or:			

Primary sort order

Show check box is unchecked

Secondary sort order

Develop AND Criteria

You can limit the number of records that appear on the resulting datasheet by entering criteria in Query Design View. **Criteria** are tests, or limiting conditions, that must be true for the record to be selected for a datasheet. To create **AND criteria**, which means the query selects a record only if all criteria are true, enter two or more criteria on the same Criteria row of the query design grid. **CASE** *Julia Rice predicts strong sales for ecological (Eco) trips that start on or after August 1, 2018. She asks you to create a list of the existing trips that meet those criteria.*

STEPS

1. **Click the** Create tab, **click the** Query Design button, **double-click** Trips, **then click** Close **in the Show Table dialog box**
   To query for ecological trips, you need to add the Category field to the query grid. In addition, you want to know the trip name and start date.

2. **Drag the** bottom edge of the Trips field list **down to resize it to display all fields, double-click the** TripName field, **double-click the** TripStartDate field, **then double-click the** Category field
   To find trips in the Eco category, you need to add a criterion for the Category field in the query grid.

3. **Click the** first Criteria cell for the Category field, **then type** Eco
   To find all trips that start on or after August 1st, use the >= (greater than or equal to) operator.

4. **Click the** first Criteria cell **for the TripStartDate field, type** >=8/1/2018, **then press [↓]**
   As shown in FIGURE 6-7, Access assists you with criteria syntax, rules by which criteria need to be entered. Access automatically adds quotation marks around text criteria in Short Text fields, such as "Eco" in the Category field, and pound signs around date criteria in Date/Time fields, such as #8/1/2018# in the TripStartDate field. The criteria in Number, Currency, and Yes/No fields are not surrounded by any characters. See TABLE 6-1 for more information on common Access comparison operators and criteria syntax.

5. **Click the** Save button 🖫 **on the Quick Access Toolbar, type** EcoAugust2018 **in the Save As dialog box, click** OK, **then click the** View button 🖽 **to view the query results**
   The query results are shown in FIGURE 6-8.

6. **Close the EcoAugust2018 datasheet**

FIGURE 6-7: Entering AND criteria on the same row

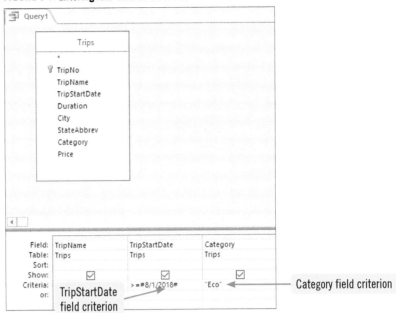

TripStartDate field criterion

Category field criterion

FIGURE 6-8: Datasheet for EcoAugust2018 records

TripName	TripStartDate	Category
Breckenridge Reconstruction	01/01/2019	Eco
Cactus Ecosystem	09/13/2018	Eco
Water Education Foundation	09/20/2018	Eco
Redwood Forest Lab	09/28/2018	Eco
Langguth Environment	10/18/2018	Eco
Mark Twain Forest Project	11/30/2018	Eco

All records have TripStartDate on or after 8/1/2018 AND are in the Eco Category

TABLE 6-1: Common comparison operators

operator	description	example	result
>	Greater than	>500	Value exceeds 500
>=	Greater than or equal to	>=500	Value is 500 or greater
<	Less than	<500	Value is less than 500
<=	Less than or equal to	<=500	Value is 500 or less
<>	Not equal to	<>500	Value is any number other than 500
Between...And	Finds values between two numbers or dates	Between #2/2/2017# And #2/2/2020#	Dates between 2/2/2017 and 2/2/2020, inclusive
In	Finds a value that is one of a list	In ("NC","SC","TN")	Value equals NC or SC or TN
Null	Finds records that have no entry in a particular field	Null	No value has been entered in a field
Is Not Null	Finds records that have any entry in a particular field	Is Not Null	Any value has been entered in a field
Like	Finds records that match the criterion, used with the * (asterisk) wildcard character	Like "C*"	Value starts with C
Not	Finds records that do not match the criterion	Not 100	Numbers other than 100

Develop OR Criteria

Learning Outcomes
• Use AND and OR criteria in the same query
• Define advanced wildcard characters

As you experienced in the previous lesson, AND criteria narrow the number of records in the datasheet by requiring that a record be true for multiple criteria. You also learned that AND criteria are entered on the same row. OR criteria work in the opposite way. **OR criteria** expand the number of records in the datasheet because a record needs to be true for only one of the criteria. You enter OR criteria in the query design grid on different criteria rows.   **CASE**   *Julia Rice asks you to modify the EcoAugust2018 query to expand the number of records to include trips in the Service category that start on or after 8/1/2018 as well.*

STEPS

1. **Right-click the** EcoAugust2018 query **in the Navigation Pane, click** Copy, **right-click a blank spot in the** Navigation Pane, **click** Paste, **type** EcoServiceAugust2018 **in the Paste As dialog box, then click** OK

   By making a copy of the EcoAugust2018 query before modifying it, you won't change the EcoAugust2018 query by mistake. To add OR criteria, you enter criteria in the next available "or" row of the query design grid. By default, the query grid displays eight rows for additional OR criteria, but you can add even more rows using the Insert Rows button on the Design tab.

2. **Right-click the** EcoServiceAugust2018 query, **click** Design View, **type** Service **in the next row (the "or" row) of the Category column, then click the** View button ▦ **to display the datasheet**

   The datasheet expands from 6 to 10 records because four trips with a Category of Service were added to the datasheet. But notice that two of the TripStartDate values for the Service records are prior to 8/1/2018. To select only those Service trips with a TripStartDate on or after 8/1/2018, you need to add more criteria to Query Design View.

QUICK TIP
The criterion >7/31/2018 would work the same as >=8/1/2018.

3. **Click the** View button ▦ **to return to Query Design View, click the next** TripStartDate Criteria cell, **type** >=8/1/2018, **then click elsewhere in the grid, as shown in** FIGURE 6-9

   Criteria in one row do not affect criteria in another row. Therefore, to select only those trips that start on or after 8/1/2018, you must put the same TripStartDate criterion in both rows of the query design grid.

4. **Click** ▦ **to return to Datasheet View**

   The resulting datasheet selects 8 records, as shown in FIGURE 6-10. When no sort order is applied, the records are sorted by the primary key field of the first table in the query (in this case, TripNo, which is not selected for this query). All of the records have a Category of Eco or Service and a TripStartDate value greater than or equal to 8/1/2018.

5. **Save and close the EcoServiceAugust2018 query**

   The R2G-6.accdb Navigation Pane displays the three queries you created plus the RevByState query that was already in the database.

FIGURE 6-9: Entering OR criteria on different rows

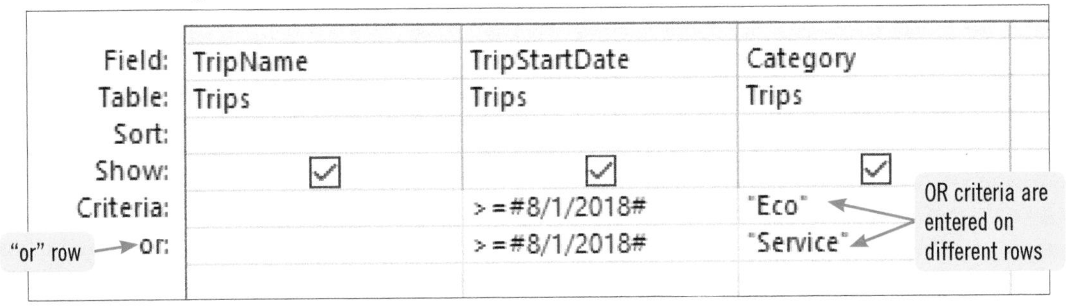

Field:	TripName	TripStartDate	Category	
Table:	Trips	Trips	Trips	
Sort:				
Show:	☑	☑	☑	
Criteria:		>=#8/1/2018#	"Eco"	
or:		>=#8/1/2018#	"Service"	

"or" row → or:

OR criteria are entered on different rows

FIGURE 6-10: Datasheet for EcoServiceAugust2018 query

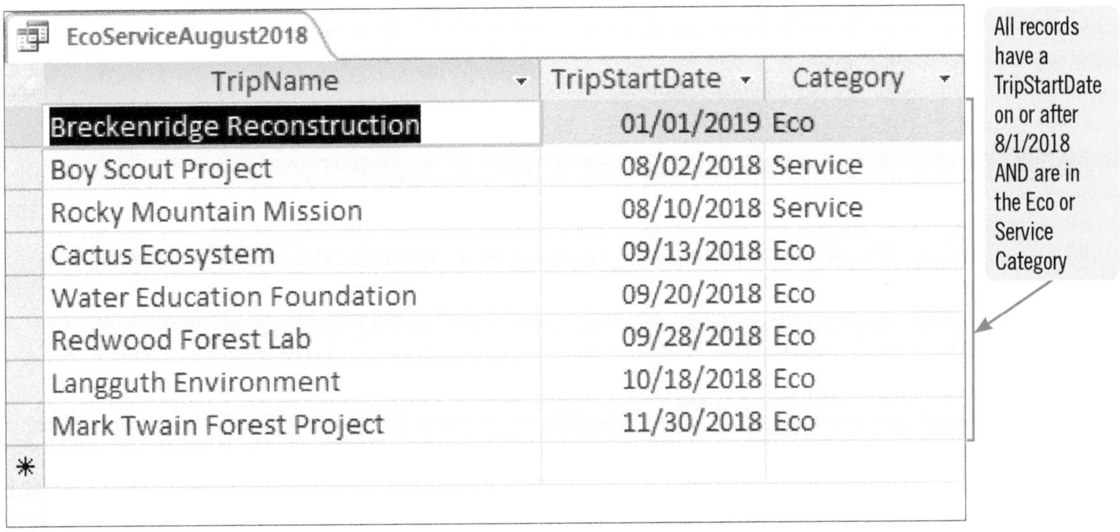

EcoServiceAugust2018		
TripName ▾	TripStartDate ▾	Category ▾
Breckenridge Reconstruction	01/01/2019	Eco
Boy Scout Project	08/02/2018	Service
Rocky Mountain Mission	08/10/2018	Service
Cactus Ecosystem	09/13/2018	Eco
Water Education Foundation	09/20/2018	Eco
Redwood Forest Lab	09/28/2018	Eco
Langguth Environment	10/18/2018	Eco
Mark Twain Forest Project	11/30/2018	Eco
*		

All records have a TripStartDate on or after 8/1/2018 AND are in the Eco or Service Category

Using wildcard characters in query criteria

To search for a pattern, use a **wildcard character** to represent any character in the criteria entry. Use a **question mark (?)** to search for any single character, and an **asterisk (*)** to search for any number of characters. Wildcard characters are often used with the Like operator. For example, the criterion Like "10/*/2017" finds all dates in October of 2017, and the criterion Like "F*" finds all entries that start with the letter F.

Create Calculated Fields

Learning
Outcomes
• Create calculated
  fields in queries
• Define functions
  and expressions

A **calculated field** is a field of data that can be created based on the values of other fields. For example, you can calculate the value for a discount, commission, or tax amount by multiplying the value of the Sales field by a percentage. To create a calculated field, define it in Query Design View using an expression that describes the calculation. An **expression** is a combination of field names, operators (such as +, –, /, and *), and functions that result in a single value. A **function** is a predefined formula that returns a value such as a subtotal, count, average, or the current date. See TABLE 6-2 for more information on arithmetic operators and TABLE 6-3 for more information on functions. **CASE** *Julia Rice asks you to find the number of days between the sale date and the trip start date. To determine this information, you create a calculated field called DaysToTrip that subtracts the SaleDate from the TripStartDate. You create another calculated field to determine the down payment amount for each trip sale.*

STEPS

1. **Click the** Create tab **on the Ribbon, click the** Query Design button, **double-click** Trips, **double-click** Sales, **then click** Close **in the Show Table dialog box**

   First, you add the fields to the grid that you want to display in the query.

2. **Double-click the** TripName field, **double-click the** TripStartDate field, **double-click the** Price field, **then double-click the** SaleDate field

   You create a calculated field in the Field cell of the design grid by entering a new descriptive field name followed by a colon, followed by an expression. Field names used in an expression must be surrounded by square brackets.

3. **Click the blank Field cell in the fifth column, type** DaysToTrip:[TripStartDate]-[SaleDate], **then drag the ↔ pointer on the right edge of the fifth column selector to the right to display the entire entry**

   You create another calculated field to determine the down payment for each sale, which is calculated as 10% of the Price field.

4. **Click the blank Field cell in the sixth column, type** DownPayment:[Price]*0.1, **then widen the column, as shown in** FIGURE 6-11

   You view the datasheet to see the resulting calculated fields.

5. **Click the** View button ▦, **press** [Tab], **type** 7/20/18 **in the TripStartDate field for the first record, press** [Tab], **type** 1000 **in the Price field for the first record, then press** [↓]

   A portion of the resulting datasheet, with two calculated fields, is shown in FIGURE 6-12. The DaysToTrip field is automatically recalculated, showing the number of days between the SaleDate and the TripStartDate. The DownPayment field is also automatically recalculated, multiplying the Price value by 10%.

6. **Click the** Save button 🖫 **on the Quick Access Toolbar, type** TripCalculations **in the Save As dialog box, click** OK, **then close the datasheet**

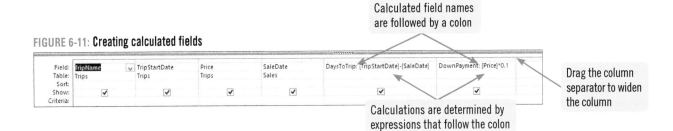

FIGURE 6-11: **Creating calculated fields**

Calculated field names are followed by a colon

Calculations are determined by expressions that follow the colon

Drag the column separator to widen the column

FIGURE 6-12: **Viewing and testing calculated fields**

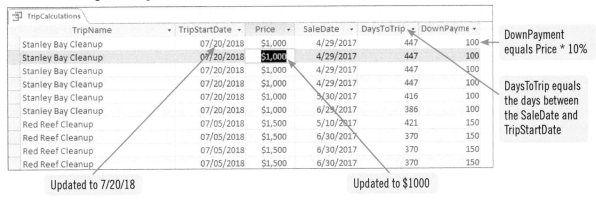

DownPayment equals Price * 10%

DaysToTrip equals the days between the SaleDate and TripStartDate

Updated to 7/20/18

Updated to $1000

TABLE 6-2: **Arithmetic operators**

operator	description
+	Addition
−	Subtraction
*	Multiplication
/	Division
^	Exponentiation

TABLE 6-3: **Common functions**

function	sample expression and description
DATE	DATE()-[BirthDate] Calculates the number of days between today and the date in the BirthDate field; Access expressions are not case sensitive, so DATE()-[BirthDate] is equivalent to date()-[birthdate] and DATE()-[BIRTHDATE]; therefore, use capitalization in expressions in any way that makes the expression easier to read
PMT	PMT([Rate],[Term],[Loan]) Calculates the monthly payment on a loan where the Rate field contains the monthly interest rate, the Term field contains the number of monthly payments, and the Loan field contains the total amount financed
LEFT	LEFT([LastName],2) Returns the first two characters of the entry in the LastName field
RIGHT	RIGHT([PartNo],3) Returns the last three characters of the entry in the PartNo field
LEN	LEN([Description]) Returns the number of characters in the Description field

Build Summary Queries

Learning
Outcomes
• Create a summary
query
• Define aggregate
functions

A **summary query** calculates statistics for groups of records. To create a summary query, you add the **Total row** to the query design grid to specify how you want to group and calculate the records using aggregate functions. **Aggregate functions** calculate a statistic such as a subtotal, count, or average on a field in a group of records. Some aggregate functions, such as Sum or Avg (Average), work only on fields with Number or Currency data types. Other functions, such as Min (Minimum), Max (Maximum), or Count, also work on Short Text fields. TABLE 6-4 provides more information on aggregate functions. A key difference between the statistics displayed by a summary query and those displayed by calculated fields is that summary queries provide calculations that describe a group of records, whereas calculated fields provide a new field of information for each record. **CASE** ▶ *Julia Rice asks you to calculate total sales for each trip category. You build a summary query to provide this information.*

STEPS

QUICK TIP
In Query Design
View, drag a table
from the Navigation
Pane to add it to
the query.

1. **Click the** Create tab **on the Ribbon, click the** Query Design button, **double-click** Sales, **double-click** Trips, **then click** Close **in the Show Table dialog box**

   It doesn't matter in what order you add the field lists to Query Design View, but it's important to move and resize the field lists as necessary to clearly see all field names and relationships.

2. **Double-click the** Category field **in the Trips field list, double-click the** Price field **in the Trips field list, double-click the** SalesNo field **in the Sales field list, then click the** View button 🔳 **to view the datasheet**

   One hundred and one records are displayed, representing all 101 records in the Sales table. You can add a Total row to any datasheet to calculate grand total statistics for that datasheet.

3. **Click the** Totals button **in the Records group, click the** Total cell **below the Price field, click the** Total list arrow, **click** Sum, **then use** ✛ **to widen the Price column to display the entire total**

   The Total row is added to the bottom of the datasheet and displays the sum total of the Price field, $129,550. Other Total row statistics you can select include Average, Count, Maximum, Minimum, Standard Deviation, and Variance. To create subtotals per Category, you need to modify the query in Query Design View.

4. **Click the** View button 🔳 **to return to Query Design View, click the** Totals button **in the Show/Hide group, click** Group By **in the Price column, click the** list arrow, **click** Sum, **click** Group By **in the SalesNo column, click the** list arrow, **then click** Count

   The Total row is added to the query grid below the Table row. To calculate summary statistics for each category, the Category field is the Group By field, as shown in FIGURE 6-13. With the records grouped together by Category, you subtotal the Price field using the Sum operator to calculate a subtotal of revenue for each Category of trip sales and count the SalesNo field using the Count operator to calculate the number of sales in each category.

5. **Click** 🔳 **to display the datasheet, widen each column as necessary to view all field names, click in the** Total row **for the SumOfPrice field, click the** list arrow, **click** Sum, **then click another row in the datasheet to remove the selection**

   The Eco category leads all others with a count of 42 sales totaling $47,450. The total revenue for all sales is still $129,550, as shown in FIGURE 6-14, but now each record represents a subtotal for each Category instead of an individual sale.

TROUBLE
To delete or rename
any object, close it,
then right-click it in
the Navigation Pane
and click Delete or
Rename on the
shortcut menu.

6. **Click the** Save button 🔳 **on the Quick Access Toolbar, type** CategorySales, **click** OK, **then close the datasheet**

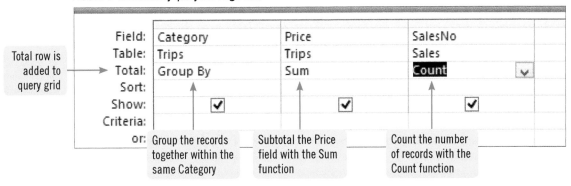

FIGURE 6-13: Summary query in Design View

Total row is added to query grid →

Field:	Category	Price	SalesNo	
Table:	Trips	Trips	Sales	
Total:	Group By	Sum	Count	⌄
Sort:				
Show:	☑	☑	☑	
Criteria:				
or:	Group the records together within the same Category	Subtotal the Price field with the Sum function	Count the number of records with the Count function	

FIGURE 6-14: Summary query datasheet

Group By the Category field →

Count the SalesNo field

Sum the Price field

Category	SumOfPrice	CountOfSalesNo
Adventure	$12,500.00	10
Cultural	$12,600.00	7
Eco	$47,450.00	42
Educational	$36,800.00	27
Family	$1,000.00	1
Service	$19,200.00	14
Total	$129,550.00	

Grand total for the Price field

TABLE 6-4: Aggregate functions

aggregate function	used to find the
Sum	Total of values in a field
Avg	Average of values in a field
Min	Minimum value in a field
Max	Maximum value in a field
Count	Number of values in a field (not counting null values)
StDev	Standard deviation of values in a field
Var	Variance of values in a field
First	Field value from the first record in a table or query
Last	Field value from the last record in a table or query

Build Crosstab Queries

A **crosstab query** subtotals one field by grouping records using two other fields that are placed in the column heading and row heading positions. You can use the **Crosstab Query Wizard** to guide you through the steps of creating a crosstab query, or you can build the crosstab query from scratch using Query Design View. **CASE** *Julia Rice asks you to continue your analysis of prices per category by summarizing the price values for each trip within each category. A crosstab query works well for this request because you want to subtotal the Price field as summarized by two other fields, TripName and Category.*

STEPS

1. **Click the** Create tab **on the Ribbon, click the** Query Design button, **double-click** Trips, **double-click** Sales, **then click** Close **in the Show Table dialog box**

   The fields you need for your crosstab query come from the Trips table, but you also need to include the Sales table in this query to select trip information for each record (sale) in the Sales table.

2. **Double-click the** TripName field, **double-click the** Category field, **then double-click the** Price field

   The first step in creating a crosstab query is to create a select query with the three fields you want to use in the crosstabular report.

3. **Click the** View button █ **to review the unsummarized datasheet of 101 records, then click the** View button █ **to return to Query Design View**

   To summarize these 101 records in a crosstabular report, you need to change the current select query into a crosstab query.

4. **Click the** Crosstab button **in the Query Type group**

   Note that two new rows are added to the query grid—the Total row and the Crosstab row. The **Total row** helps you determine which fields group or summarize the records, and the **Crosstab row** identifies which of the three positions each field takes in the crosstab report: Row Heading, Column Heading, or Value. The **Value field** is typically a numeric field, such as Price, that can be summed or averaged.

5. **Click the** Crosstab cell **for the TripName field, click the** list arrow, **click** Row Heading, **click the** Crosstab cell **for the Category field, click the** list arrow, **click** Column Heading, **click the** Crosstab cell **for the Price field, click the** list arrow, **click** Value, **click** Group By **in the Total cell of the Price field, click the** list arrow, **then click** Sum

   The completed Query Design View should look like FIGURE 6-15. Note the choices made in both the Total and Crosstab rows of the query grid.

6. **Click** █ **to review the crosstab datasheet**

   The final crosstab datasheet is shown in FIGURE 6-16. The datasheet summarizes all 101 sales records by the Category field used as the column headings and by the TripName field used in the row heading position. Although you can switch the row and column heading fields without changing the numeric information on the crosstab datasheet, you should generally place the field with the most entries (in this case, TripName has more values than Category) in the row heading position so that the printout is taller than it is wide.

7. **Click the** Save button █ **on the Quick Access Toolbar, type** TripCrosstab **as the query name, click** OK, **then close the datasheet**

   Crosstab queries appear with a crosstab icon to the left of the query name in the Navigation Pane.

FIGURE 6-15: Query Design View of crosstab query

FIGURE 6-15: Query Design View of crosstab query

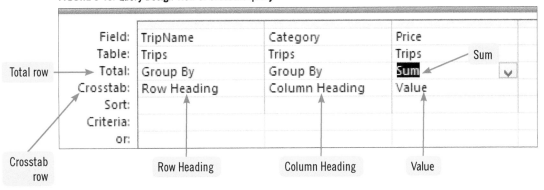

FIGURE 6-16: Crosstab query datasheet

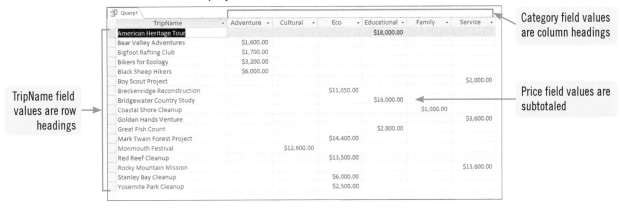

Using query wizards

Four query wizards are available to help you build queries including the Simple (which creates a select query), Crosstab, Find Duplicates, and Find Unmatched Query Wizards. Use the **Find Duplicates Query Wizard** to determine whether a table contains duplicate values in one or more fields. Use the **Find Unmatched Query Wizard** to find records in one table that do not have related records in another table. To use the query wizards, click the Query Wizard button on the Create tab.

Create a Report on a Query

Learning Outcomes
- Create a report on a query
- Modify a report's Record Source property

When you want a more professional printout of the information than can be provided by a query data-sheet, you use a report object. By first selecting the fields and records you want in a query and then basing the report on that query, you can easily add new fields and calculations to the report by adding them to the underlying query. When you base a report on a query, the query name is identified in the **Record Source** property of the report. **CASE** ▶ *Julia Rice asks you to create a report to subtotal the revenue for each trip.*

STEPS

1. **Double-click the** RevByState query **in the Navigation Pane to open its datasheet**

   The RevByState query contains the customer state, trip name, and price of each trip sold. Analyzing which trips are the most popular in various states will help focus marketing expenses. Creating a query to select the fields and records needed on a report is the first step in creating a report that can be easily modified later.

2. **Close the** RevByState query, **click the** Create tab **on the Ribbon, click the** Report Wizard **button, click the** Select All button >> **to select all fields in the RevByState query, then click** Next

   The Report Wizard wants to group the records by the State field. This is also how you want to analyze the data.

QUICK TIP
You may want to name a query and the report based on that query the same to organize your objects.

3. **Click** Next, **click** TripName, **then click the** Select Field button > **to add the TripName field as a second grouping level, click** Next, **click** Next **to not choose any sort orders, click** Next **to accept a Stepped layout and Portrait orientation, type** Revenue by State **as the title for the report, then click** Finish

   The report lists each trip sold within each state as many times as it has been sold. You decide to add the name of the customers who have purchased these trips to the report. First, you will need to add them to the RevByState query. Given that the Revenue by State report is based on the RevByState query, you can access the RevByState query from Report Design View of the Revenue by State report.

QUICK TIP
You can also double-click the report selector button to open the Property Sheet for the report.

4. **Right-click the** Revenue by State tab, **click** Design View, **close the Field List if it is open, then click the** Property Sheet button **in the Tools group on the Design tab**

   The Property Sheet for the Revenue by State report opens.

TROUBLE
If the RevByState query opens in SQL View, right-click the RevByState tab and click Design View.

5. **Click the** Data tab **in the Property Sheet, click** RevByState **in the Record Source property, then click the** Build button ... , **as shown in** FIGURE 6-17

   The RevByState query opens in Query Design View.

6. **Double-click the** FName field, **double-click the** LName field, **click the** Close button **on the Design tab, then click** Yes **when prompted to save the changes**

   Now that the FName and LName fields have been added to the RevByState query, they are available to the report.

TROUBLE
Close the query Property Sheet if it remains open.

7. **Click the** Design tab **on the Ribbon, click the** Text Box button abl, **click to the left of the Price text box in the Detail section, click the** Text13 label, **press** [Delete], **click** Unbound **in the text box, type** =[FName] &" "&[LName], **then press** [Enter]

   You could have added the FName and LName fields directly to the report but the information looks more professional as the result of one expression that calculates the entire name.

TROUBLE
The number in the default caption of the label such as Text13 varies based on previous activity in the report.

8. **Switch to Layout View, resize the new text box as shown in** FIGURE 6-18 **to see the entire name, save and close the Revenue by State report, close the R2G-6.accdb database, then exit Access**

FIGURE 6-17: Modifying a query from the Record Source property

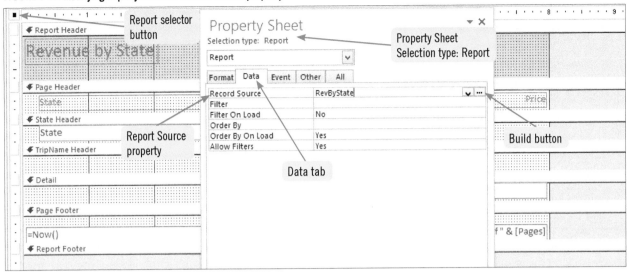

FIGURE 6-18: Final State Revenue Report

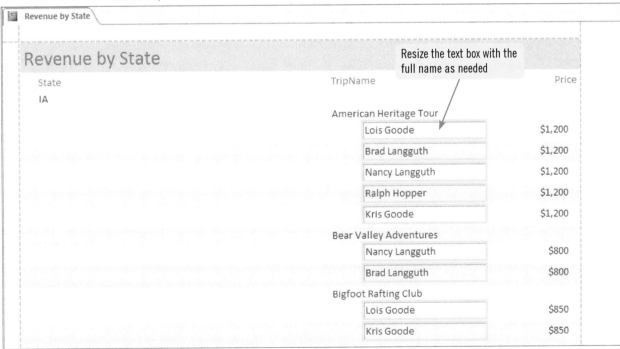

Practice

Concepts Review

Identify each element of Query Design View shown in FIGURE 6-19.

FIGURE 6-19

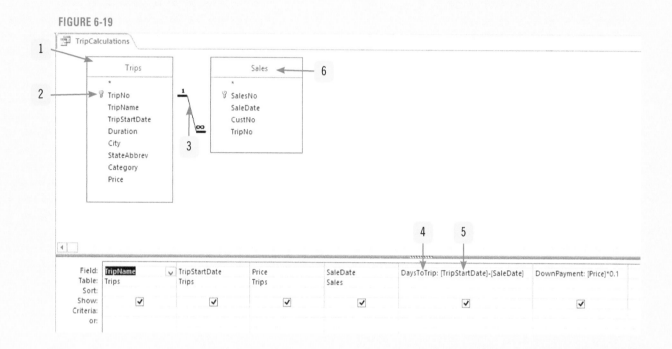

Match each term with the statement that best describes it.

7. **AND criteria**
8. **OR criteria**
9. **Record Source**
10. **Select query**
11. **Wildcard character**
12. **Sorting**

a. Placing the records of a datasheet in a certain order
b. Entered on more than one row of the query design grid
c. Report property that determines what fields and records the report will display
d. Asterisk (*) or question mark (?) used in query criteria
e. Retrieves fields from related tables and displays records in a datasheet
f. Entered on one row of the query design grid

Select the best answer from the list of choices.

13. The query datasheet can best be described as a:
   a. Logical view of the selected data from underlying tables.
   b. Duplication of the data in the underlying table's datasheet.
   c. Separate file of data.
   d. Second copy of the data in the underlying tables.

14. Queries may not be used to:
   a. Calculate new fields of data.
   b. Enter or update data.
   c. Set the primary key field for a table.
   d. Sort records.

15. When you update data in a table that is also selected in a query:
   a. You must relink the query to the table to refresh the data.
   b. The updated data is automatically displayed in the query.
   c. You must also update the data in the query datasheet.
   d. You can choose whether to update the data in the query.

16. Which of the following is *not* an aggregate function available to a summary query?
   a. Avg
   b. Count
   c. Subtotal
   d. Max

17. The order in which records in a query are sorted is determined by:
   a. The order in which the fields are defined in the underlying table.
   b. The importance of the information in the field.
   c. The alphabetic order of the field names.
   d. The left-to-right position of the fields in the query design grid that contain a sort order choice.

18. A crosstab query is generally constructed with how many fields?
   a. 1
   b. 2
   c. 3
   d. More than 5

19. In a crosstab query, which field is the most likely candidate for the Value position?
   a. FName
   b. Cost
   c. Department
   d. Country

20. Which property determines the fields and records available to a report?
   a. Field List
   b. Underlying Query
   c. Data
   d. Record Source

Skills Review

1. Create multitable queries.

a. Start Access and open the Service-6.accdb database from the location where you store your Data Files, then enable content if prompted.

b. Create a new select query in Query Design View using the Names and Zips tables.

c. Add the following fields to the query design grid in this order:
- FirstName and LastName from the Names table
- City, State, and Zip from the Zips table

d. In Datasheet View, replace the LastName value in the Martha Robison record with your last name.

e. Save the query as **MemberList**, print the datasheet if requested by your instructor, then close the query.

2. Apply sorts and view SQL.

a. Open the MemberList query in Query Design View.

b. Drag the FirstName field from the Names field list to the third column in the query design grid to make the first three fields in the query design grid FirstName, LastName, and FirstName.

c. Add an ascending sort to the *second* and *third* fields in the query design grid, and uncheck the Show check box in the *third* column. The query is now sorted in ascending order by LastName, then by FirstName, though the order of the fields in the resulting datasheet still appears as FirstName, LastName.

d. Click the File tab, click Save As, then use Save Object As to save the query as **SortedMemberList**. View the datasheet, print the datasheet if requested by your instructor, then close the SortedMemberList query.

3. Develop AND criteria.

a. Right-click the SortedMemberList query in the Navigation Pane, click Copy, right-click a blank spot in the Navigation Pane, click Paste, then type **KansasB** as the name for the new query.

b. Open the KansasB query in Design View, then type **B*** (the asterisk is a wildcard) in the LastName field Criteria cell to choose all people whose last name starts with B. Access assists you with the syntax for this type of criterion and enters Like "B*" in the cell when you click elsewhere in the query design grid.

c. Enter **KS** as the AND criterion for the State field. Be sure to enter the criterion on the same line in the query design grid as the Like "B*" criterion.

d. View the datasheet. It should select only those people from Kansas with a last name that starts with the letter B.

e. Enter your hometown in the City field of the first record to uniquely identify the printout.

f. Save the KansasB query, print the datasheet if requested by your instructor, then close the KansasB query.

4. Develop OR criteria.

a. Right-click the KansasB query in the Navigation Pane, click Copy, right-click a blank spot in the Navigation Pane, click Paste, then type **KansasBC** as the name for the new query.

b. Open the KansasBC query in Design View, then enter **C*** in the second Criteria row (the or row) of the LastName field.

c. Enter **KS** as the criterion in the second Criteria row (the or row) of the State field so that those people from KS with a last name that starts with the letter C are added to this query.

d. View the datasheet. It should select only those people from Kansas with a last name that starts with the letter B or C. Print the datasheet if requested by your instructor, then save and close the query.

5. Create calculated fields.

a. Create a new select query in Query Design View using only the Names table.

b. Add the following fields to the query design grid in this order: FirstName, LastName, Birthday.

c. Create a calculated field called Age in the fourth column of the query design grid by entering the expression: **Age: Int((Now()-[Birthday])/365)** to determine the age of each person in years based on the information in the Birthday field. The Now() function returns today's date. Now()-[Birthday] determines the number of days a person has lived. Dividing that value by 365 determines the number of years a person has lived. The Int() function is used to return the integer portion of the answer. So if a person has lived 23.5 years, Int(23.5) = 23.

Skills Review (continued)

   d. Sort the query in descending order on the calculated Age field.

   e. Save the query with the name **AgeCalc**, view the datasheet, print the datasheet if requested by your instructor, then close the query.

6. Build summary queries.

   a. Create a new select query in Query Design View using the Names and Activities tables.

   b. Add the following fields: FirstName and LastName from the Names table, and Hours from the Activities table.

   c. Add the Total row to the query design grid, then change the aggregate function for the Hours field from Group By to Sum.

   d. Sort in descending order by Hours.

   e. Save the query as **HoursSum**, view the datasheet, widen all columns so that all data is clearly visible, print the datasheet if requested by your instructor, then save and close the query.

7. Build crosstab queries.

   a. Use Query Design View to create a select query with the City and State fields from the Zips table and the Dues field from the Names table. Save the query as **DuesCrosstab**, then view the datasheet.

   b. Return to Query Design View, then click the Crosstab button to add the Total and Crosstab rows to the query design grid.

   c. Specify City as the crosstab row heading, State as the crosstab column heading, and Dues as the summed value field within the crosstab datasheet.

   d. View the datasheet as shown in FIGURE 6-20, print the datasheet if requested by your instructor, then save and close the DuesCrosstab query.

FIGURE 6-20

City	IA	KS	MO
Blue Springs			$50.00
Bridgewater	$50.00		
Buehler		$50.00	
Clear Water		$100.00	
Des Moines	$25.00		
Dripping Springs		$25.00	
Flat Hills		$50.00	
Fontanelle	$50.00		
Greenfield	$50.00		
Kansas City		$50.00	$100.00
Langguth		$25.00	
Leawood			$50.00
Lee's Summit			$75.00
Lenexa		$25.00	
Manawatta		$25.00	
Manhattan		$25.00	
Overland Park		$100.00	
Red Bridge		$425.00	
Running Deer			$25.00
Student Hometown		$200.00	

Skills Review (continued)

8. Create a report on a query.

a. Use the Report Wizard to create a report on all of the fields of the SortedMemberList query. View the data by Names, add State as a grouping level, add LastName then FirstName as the ascending sort orders, use a Stepped layout and Landscape orientation, then title the report **Members by State**.

b. In Design View, open the Property Sheet for the report, then open the SortedMemberList query in Design View using the Build button on the Record Source property.

c. Add the Birthday field to the SortedMemberList query then close the query.

d. To the left of the LastName field in the Detail section, add a text box bound to the Birthday field. (*Hint*: Type **Birthday** in place of Unbound or modify the text box's Control Source property to be Birthday.) Delete the label that is automatically created to the left of the text box.

e. In Layout View, resize the City and Zip columns so that all data is clearly visible, as shown in FIGURE 6-21. Be sure to preview the report to make sure it fits on the paper.

f. If requested by your instructor, print the first page of the Members by State report, save and close it, close the Service-6.accdb database, then exit Access.

FIGURE 6-21

Independent Challenge 1

As the manager of a music store's instrument rental program, you have created a database to track rentals to elementary through high school students. Now that several rentals have been made, you want to query the database and produce different datasheet printouts to analyze school information.

a. Start Access and open the Music-6.accdb database from the location where you store your Data Files, then enable content if prompted.

b. In Query Design View, create a query with the following fields in the following order:
- SchoolName field from the Schools table
- RentalDate field from the Rentals table
- Description field from the Instruments table

(*Hint*: Although you don't use any fields from the Students table, you need to add the Students table to this query to make the connection between the Schools table and the Rentals table.)

c. Sort in ascending order by SchoolName, then in ascending order by RentalDate.

d. Save the query as **SchoolActivity**, view the datasheet, replace Lincoln Elementary with your elementary school name, print the datasheet if requested by your instructor, then close the datasheet.

e. Copy and paste the SchoolActivity query as **SchoolSummary**, then open the SchoolSummary query in Query Design View.

Independent Challenge 1 (continued)

f. Modify the SchoolSummary query by deleting the Description field. Use the Totals button to group the records by SchoolName and to count the RentalDate field. Print the datasheet if requested by your instructor, then save and close the SchoolSummary query.

g. Create a crosstab query named **SchoolCrosstab** based on the SchoolActivity query. (*Hint*: Select the SchoolActivity query in the Show Table dialog box.) Use Description as the column heading position and SchoolName in the row heading position. Count the RentalDate field.

h. View the SchoolCrosstab query in Datasheet View. Resize each column to best fit the data in that column, then print the datasheet if requested by your instructor. Save and close the SchoolCrosstab query.

i. Copy and paste the SchoolActivity query as **HSRentals**. Modify the HSRentals query in Query Design View so that only those schools with the words **"High School"** in the SchoolName field are displayed. (*Hint*: You have to use wildcard characters in the criteria.)

j. View the HSRentals query in Datasheet View, print it if requested by your instructor, then save and close the datasheet.

k. Close the Music-6.accdb database, then exit Access.

Independent Challenge 2

As the manager of a music store's instrument rental program, you have created a database to track rentals to elementary through high school students. You can use queries to analyze customer and rental information.

a. Start Access and open the Music-6.accdb database from the location where you store your Data Files, then enable content if prompted.

b. In Query Design View, create a query with the following fields in the following order:
  • Description and MonthlyFee fields from the Instruments table
  • LastName, Zip, and City fields from the Students table
  (*Hint*: Although you don't need any fields from the Rentals table in this query's datasheet, you need to add the Rentals table to this query to make the connection between the Customers table and the Instruments table.)

c. Add the Zip field to the first column of the query grid, and specify an ascending sort order for this field. Uncheck the Show check box for the first Zip field so that it does not appear in the datasheet.

d. Add an ascending sort order to the Description field.

e. Save the query as **RentalsByZipCode**.

f. View the datasheet, replace Johnson with your last name in the LastName field, print the datasheet if requested by your instructor, then save and close the datasheet. (*Note*: If you later view this query in Design View, note that Access changes the way the sort orders are specified but in a way that gives you the same results in the datasheet.)

g. In Query Design View, create a query with the following fields in the following order:
  • Description and MonthlyFee fields from the Instruments table
  • LastName, Zip, and City fields from the Students table
  (*Hint*: You'll need to add the Rentals table.)

h. Add criteria to find the records where the Description is equal to **cello**. Sort in ascending order based on the Zip then City fields. Save the query as **Cellos**, view the datasheet, print it if requested by your instructor, then close the datasheet.

i. Copy and paste the Cellos query as **CellosAndAnkeny**, then modify the CellosAndAnkeny query with AND criteria to further specify that the City must be **Ankeny**. View the datasheet, print it if requested by your instructor, then save and close the datasheet.

Independent Challenge 2 (continued)

j. Copy and paste the CellosAndAnkeny query as **CellosOrAnkeny**, then modify the CellosOrAnkeny query so that all records with a Description equal to Cello *or* a City value of **Ankeny** are selected. View the datasheet, print it if requested by your instructor, then save and close the datasheet.

k. Close the MusicStore-6.accdb database, then exit Access.

Independent Challenge 3

As a real estate agent, you use an Access database to track residential real estate listings in your area. You can use queries to answer questions about the real estate properties and to analyze home values.

a. Start Access and open the LakeHomes-6.accdb database from the location where you store your Data Files, then enable content if prompted.

b. In Query Design View, create a query with the following fields in the following order:
   - AgencyName from the Agencies table
   - RFirst and RLast from the Realtors table
   - SqFt and Asking from the Listings table

c. Sort the records in descending order by the SqFt field.

d. Save the query as **BySqFt**, view the datasheet, enter your last name instead of Schwartz for the listing with the largest SqFt value, then print the datasheet if requested by your instructor.

e. In Query Design View, modify the BySqFt query by creating a calculated field that determines price per square foot. The new calculated field's name should be **PerSqFt**, and the expression should be the asking price divided by the square foot field, or **[Asking]/[SqFt]**.

f. Remove any former sort orders, sort the records in descending order based on the PerSqFt calculated field, and view the datasheet. Save and close the BySqFt query. ###### means the data is too wide to display in the column. You can make the data narrower and also align it by applying a Currency format.

g. Reopen the BySqFt query in Query Design View, right-click the calculated PerSqFt field, click Properties, then change the Format property to Currency. View the datasheet, print it if requested by your instructor, then save and close the BySqFt query.

h. Copy and paste the BySqFt query as **CostSummary**.

i. In Design View of the CostSummary query, delete the RFirst, RLast, and SqFt fields.

j. View the datasheet, then change the Big Cedar Realtors agency name to *your last name* followed by **Realtors**.

k. In Design View, add the Total row, then sum the Asking field and use the Avg (Average) aggregate function for the PerSqFt calculated field.

l. In Datasheet View, add the Total row and display the sum of the SumOfAsking field. Widen all columns as needed, as shown in FIGURE 6-22.

m. If requested by your instructor, print the CostSummary query, then save and close it.

n. Close the LakeHomes-6.accdb database, then exit Access.

FIGURE 6-22

AgencyName	SumOfAsking	PerSqFt
Sunset Cove Realtors	$2,628,840.00	$113.87
Student Last Name Realtors	$3,835,214.40	$113.51
Green Mountain Realty	$1,493,940.00	$83.12
Total	$7,957,994.40	

Independent Challenge 4: Explore

You're working with the local high school guidance counselor to help her with an Access database used to manage college scholarship opportunities. You help her with the database by creating several queries. (*Note*: To complete this Independent Challenge, make sure you are connected to the Internet.)

a. Start Access, open the Scholarships-6.accdb database from the location where you store your Data Files, then enable content if prompted.

b. Conduct research on the Internet or at your school to find at least five new scholarships relevant to your major, and enter them into the Scholarships table.

c. Conduct research on the Internet or at your school to find at least one new scholarship relevant to a Computer Science major, and enter the two records into the Scholarships table. Enter **Computer Science** in the Major field.

d. Create a query called **ComputerScience** that displays all fields from the Scholarships table and selects all records with a **Computer Science** major. If requested by your instructor, print the ComputerScience query then save and close it.

e. Copy and paste the ComputerScience query as **BusinessOrCS**. Add OR criteria to the BusinessOrCS query to add all scholarships in the **Business** major to the existing scholarships in the Computer Science major. If requested by your instructor, print the BusinessOrCS query then save and close it.

f. Create a new query that selects the ScholarshipName, DueDate, and Amount from the Scholarships table, and sorts the records in ascending order by DueDate, then descending order by Amount. Name the query **AllScholarshipsByDueDate**. If requested by your instructor, print the AllScholarshipsByDueDate query then save and close it.

g. Use the Report Wizard to create a report on the AllScholarshipsByDueDate query, do not add any grouping levels or additional sort orders, use a Tabular layout and a Portrait orientation, and title the report **All Scholarships by Due Date**.

h. In Design View of the All Scholarships by Due Date report, open the Property Sheet, and use the Record Source Build button to open the AllScholarshipsByDueDate query in Design View. Add the Major field to the query, save and close it.

i. In Report Design View, open the Group, Sort, and Total pane, add the Major field as a grouping field. Add DueDate as a sort order from newest to oldest, then add Amount as a sort field from largest to smallest.

j. Add a text box to the Major Header section, and bind it to the Major field. (*Hint*: Type **Major** in place of Unbound or modify the text box's Control Source property to be Major.) Delete the label that is automatically created to the left of the text box. Preview the report, modify the ScholarshipName and DueDate labels in the Page Header section to show spaces between the words, and move and resize any controls as needed to match FIGURE 6-23. Print the report if requested by your instructor.

k. Save and close the All Scholarships by Due Date report, close the Scholarships-6.accdb database, then exit Access.

FIGURE 6-23

Visual Workshop

Open the Training-6.accdb database from the location where you store your Data Files, then enable content if prompted. In Query Design View, create a new select query with the DeptName field from the Departments table, the CourseCost field from the Courses table, and the Description field from the Courses table. (*Hint*: You will also have to add the Employees and Enrollments tables to Query Design View to build relationships from the Departments table to the Courses table.) Save the query with the name **DeptCrosstab**, then display it as a crosstab query, as shown in FIGURE 6-24. Print the DeptCrosstab query if requested by your instructor, save and close it, then close the Training-6.accdb database.

FIGURE 6-24

Description	Accounting	Book	Human Resc	Information	Marketing	Operations	Shipping	Training	Warehouse
Access Case Problems	$400.00	$600.00			$200.00	$200.00		$200.00	$400.00
Computer Fundamentals	$200.00	$800.00	$400.00	$200.00	$600.00		$400.00	$400.00	$800.00
Dynamite Customer Service Skills		$100.00	$100.00	$100.00	$200.00				$200.00
Employee Benefits Made Clear		$150.00	$100.00	$50.00	$150.00	$50.00	$100.00	$50.00	$200.00
Excel Case Problems	$200.00		$200.00			$400.00	$400.00	$200.00	$400.00
Intermediate Access	$800.00	$1,200.00			$400.00	$400.00		$400.00	$800.00
Intermediate Excel	$400.00	$200.00	$200.00			$400.00	$400.00	$200.00	$400.00
Intermediate Internet Explorer	$400.00	$800.00	$400.00	$200.00	$400.00	$200.00	$200.00	$400.00	$600.00
Intermediate Phone Skils	$300.00	$300.00				$300.00		$150.00	$300.00
Intermediate PowerPoint	$400.00	$600.00	$200.00		$200.00	$200.00	$200.00	$400.00	$600.00
Intermediate Tax Planning	$100.00	$50.00	$50.00	$50.00		$50.00	$100.00	$50.00	$200.00
Intermediate Windows		$200.00	$400.00	$200.00	$400.00		$400.00	$200.00	$600.00
Intermediate Word		$200.00	$200.00	$200.00	$400.00				$400.00
Internet Fundamentals		$600.00	$400.00	$200.00	$600.00		$400.00	$400.00	$800.00
Introduction to Access	$400.00	$600.00	$200.00		$400.00	$200.00		$200.00	$400.00
Introduction to Excel	$400.00	$200.00	$200.00			$400.00	$400.00	$200.00	$800.00
Introduction to Insurance Planning	$150.00	$225.00	$75.00		$75.00	$75.00	$150.00	$150.00	$225.00
Introduction to Internet Explorer	$400.00	$800.00	$400.00	$200.00	$600.00	$200.00	$200.00	$400.00	$1,000.00
Introduction to Networking		$400.00	$400.00	$200.00	$600.00		$400.00	$200.00	$800.00
Introduction to Outlook	$400.00	$600.00	$400.00		$400.00	$400.00	$400.00	$400.00	$400.00
Introduction to Phone Skills	$300.00	$450.00			$150.00	$300.00	$150.00	$150.00	$450.00
Introduction to PowerPoint	$400.00	$800.00	$400.00	$200.00	$600.00	$200.00	$200.00	$400.00	$600.00
Introduction to Project	$1,200.00	$2,000.00	$400.00		$1,600.00	$1,600.00	$1,600.00	$1,200.00	$3,200.00
Introduction to Tax Planning	$100.00	$100.00	$50.00	$50.00	$50.00	$50.00	$100.00	$50.00	$200.00
Introduction to Windows		$600.00	$400.00	$200.00	$600.00	$200.00	$400.00	$400.00	$800.00

Record: 1 of 31   No Filter   Search

Creating Macros

> **CASE** Aaron Scout, the network administrator at Reason 2 Go, has identified several Access tasks that are repeated on a regular basis. He has asked you to help him automate these processes with macros.

Module Objectives

After completing this module, you will be able to:

- Understand macros
- Create a macro
- Modify actions and arguments
- Assign a macro to a command button
- Use If statements
- Work with events
- Create a data macro
- Troubleshoot macros

Files You Will Need

Equipment-12.accdb   Patients-12.accdb
Basketball-12.accdb   Candy-12.accdb

Understand Macros

Learning
Outcomes
• Describe the
benefits of macros
• Define macro
terminology
• Describe Macro
Design View
components

A **macro** is a database object that stores actions to complete Access tasks. Repetitive Access tasks such as printing several reports or opening and maximizing a form are good candidates for a macro. Automating routine tasks by using macros builds efficiency, accuracy, and flexibility into your database. **CASE** ▸ *Aaron Scout encourages you to study the major benefits of using macros, macro terminology, and the components of the Macro Design View before building your first macro.*

DETAILS

The major benefits of using macros include the following:

- Saving time by automating routine tasks
- Increasing accuracy by ensuring that tasks are executed consistently
- Improving the functionality and ease of use of forms by using macros connected to command buttons
- Ensuring data accuracy in forms by using macros to respond to data entry errors
- Automating data transfers such as collecting data from Excel
- Helping users by responding to their interactions within a form

Macro terminology:

- A **macro** is an Access object that stores a series of actions to perform one or more tasks.
- **Macro Design View** is the window in which you create a macro. FIGURE 12-1 shows Macro Design View with an OpenForm action. See TABLE 12-1 for a description of the Macro Design View components.
- Each task that you want the macro to perform is called an **action**. A macro may contain one or more actions.
- **Arguments** are properties of an action that provide additional information on how the action should execute.
- A **conditional expression** is an expression resulting in either a true or false answer that determines whether a macro action will execute. Conditional expressions are used in If statements.
- An **event** is something that happens to a form, window, toolbar, or control—such as the click of a command button or an entry in a field—that can be used to initiate the execution of a macro.
- A **submacro** is a collection of actions within a macro object that allows you to name and create multiple, separate macros within a single macro object.

FIGURE 12-1: **Macro Design View with OpenForm action**

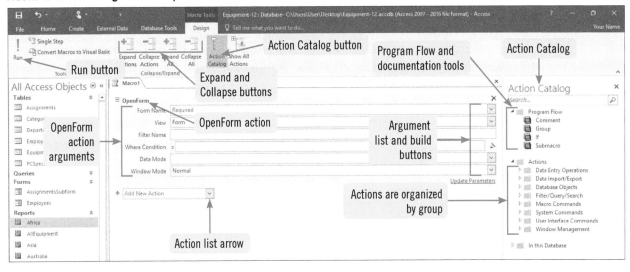

TABLE 12-1: **Macro Design View components**

component	description
Action Catalog	Lists all available macro actions organized by category. Use the Search box to narrow the number of macro actions to a particular subject.
If statement	Contains conditional expressions that are evaluated as either true or false. If true, the macro action is executed. If false, the macro action is skipped. If statements in Access 2016 may contain Else If and Else clauses.
Comment	Allows you to document the macro with explanatory text.
Arguments	Lists required and optional arguments for the selected action.
Run button	Runs the selected macro.
Expand and Collapse buttons	Allows you to expand or collapse the macro actions to show or hide their arguments.

Create a Macro

Learning Outcomes
• Create a macro
• Describe macro actions

In Access, you create a macro by choosing a series of actions in Macro Design View that accomplishes the job you want to automate. Therefore, to become proficient with Access macros, you must be comfortable with macro actions. Some of the most common actions are listed in TABLE 12-2. When you create a macro in other Microsoft Office products such as Word or Excel, you create Visual Basic for Applications (VBA) statements. In Access, macros do not create VBA code, although after creating a macro, you can convert it to VBA if desired. **CASE** *Aaron Scout observes that users want to open the AllEquipment report from the Employees form, so he asks you to create a macro to help automate this task.*

STEPS

> **TROUBLE**
> If you do not enable content, your macros will not run.

1. **Start Access, open the Equipment-12.accdb database from the where you store your Data Files, enable content if prompted, click the Create tab, then click the Macro button**

   Macro Design View opens, ready for you to choose your first action.

> **TROUBLE**
> If you choose the wrong macro action, click the Delete button ✕ in the upper-right corner of the macro action block and try again.

2. **Click the Action list arrow, type op to quickly scroll to the actions that start with the letters op, then scroll and click OpenReport**

   The OpenReport action is now the first action in the macro, and the arguments that further define the OpenReport action appear in the action block. The **action block** organizes all of the arguments for a current action and is visually highlighted with a rectangle and gray background. You can expand or collapse the action block to view or hide details by clicking the Collapse/Expand button to the left of the action name or the Expand and Collapse buttons on the Design tab in Macro Design View.

   The **OpenReport action** has three required arguments: Report Name, View, and Window Mode. View and Window Mode have default values, and if you start working with the OpenReport action's arguments but do not select a Report Name, the word "Required" is shown, indicating that you must select a choice. The Filter Name and Where Condition arguments are optional as indicated by their blank boxes.

> **QUICK TIP**
> Hover over any macro action or argument to see a ScreenTip of information about that item.

3. **Click the Report Name argument list arrow, then click AllEquipment**

   All of the report objects in the Equipment-12.accdb database appear in the Report Name argument list, making it easy to choose the report you want.

4. **Click the View argument list arrow, then click Print Preview**

   Your screen should look like FIGURE 12-2. Macros can contain one or many actions. In this case, the macro has only one action.

5. **Click the Save button 🖫 on the Quick Access Toolbar, type PreviewAllReport in the Macro Name text box, click OK, right-click the PreviewAllReport macro tab, then click Close**

   The Navigation Pane lists the PreviewAllReport object in the Macros group.

> **QUICK TIP**
> To print Macro Design View, click the File tab, click Print, click the Print button, then click OK.

6. **Double-click the PreviewAllReport macro in the Navigation Pane to run the macro**

   The AllEquipment report opens in Print Preview.

7. **Close the AllEquipment report**

FIGURE 12-2: Macro Design View with OpenReport action

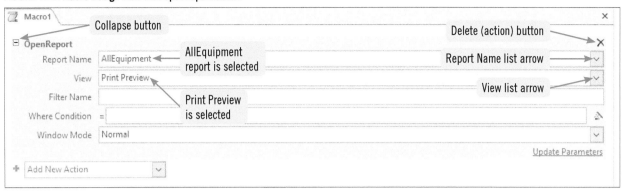

TABLE 12-2: Common macro actions

subject area	macro action	description
Data Entry Operations	DeleteRecord	Deletes the current record
	SaveRecord	Saves the current record
Data Import/Export	ImportExportSpreadsheet*	Imports or exports the spreadsheet you specify
	ImportExportText*	Imports or exports the text file you specify
	EMailDatabaseObject	Sends the specified database object through Outlook with specified email settings
Database Objects	GoToControl	Moves the focus (where you are currently typing or clicking) to a specific field or control
	GoToRecord	Makes a specified record the current record
	OpenForm	Opens a form in Form View, Design View, Print Preview, or Datasheet View
	OpenReport	Opens a report in Design View or Print Preview, or prints the report
	OpenTable	Opens a table in Datasheet View, Design View, or Print Preview
	SetValue*	Sets the value of a field, control, or property
Filter/Query/Search	ApplyFilter	Restricts the number of records that appear in the resulting form or report by applying limiting criteria
	FindRecord	Finds the first record that meets the criteria
	OpenQuery	Opens a select or crosstab query; runs an action query
Macro Commands	RunCode	Runs a Visual Basic function (a series of programming statements that does a calculation or comparison and returns a value)
	RunMacro	Runs a macro or attaches a macro to a custom menu command
	StopMacro	Stops the currently running macro
System Commands	Beep	Sounds a beep tone through the computer's speaker
	PrintOut*	Prints the active object, such as a datasheet, report, form, or module
	SendKeys*	Sends keystrokes directly to Microsoft Access or to an active Windows application
User Interface Commands	MessageBox	Displays a message box containing a warning or an informational message
	ShowToolbar*	Displays or hides a given toolbar
Window Management	CloseWindow	Closes a window
	MaximizeWindow	Enlarges the active window to fill the Access window

*Must click Show All Actions button on Ribbon for these actions to appear.

Modify Actions and Arguments

Learning
Outcomes
• Modify macro
  actions
• Modify macro
  arguments

Macros can contain as many actions as necessary to complete the process that you want to automate. Each action is evaluated in the order in which it appears in Macro Design View, starting at the top. Whereas some macro actions open, close, preview, or export data or objects, others are used only to make the database easier to use. **MessageBox** is a useful macro action because it displays an informational message to the user. **CASE** *Aaron Scout wants you to add a MessageBox action to the PreviewAllReport macro to display a descriptive message in a dialog box.*

STEPS

1. **Right-click the** PreviewAllReport macro **in the Navigation Pane, then click** Design View **on the shortcut menu**

   The PreviewAllReport macro opens in Macro Design View.

2. **Click the** Add New Action list arrow, **type** me **to quickly scroll to the actions that start with the letters me, then click** MessageBox

   Each action has its own arguments that further clarify what the action does.

3. **Click the** Message argument text box **in the action block, then type** Click the Print button to print this report

   The Message argument determines what text appears in the message box. By default, the Beep argument is set to "Yes" and the Type argument is set to "None."

4. **Click the** Type argument list arrow **in the action block, then click** Information

   The Type argument determines which icon appears in the dialog box that is created by the MessageBox action.

5. **Click the** Title argument text box **in the action block, then type** To print this report...

   Your screen should look like FIGURE 12-3. The Title argument specifies what text is displayed in the title bar of the resulting dialog box. If you leave the Title argument empty, the title bar of the resulting dialog box displays "Microsoft Access."

6. **Save the macro, then click the** Run button **in the Tools group**

   If your speakers are turned on, you should hear a beep, then the message box appears, as shown in FIGURE 12-4.

7. **Click** OK **in the dialog box, close the AllEquipment report, then save and close Macro Design View**

FIGURE 12-3: Adding the MessageBox action

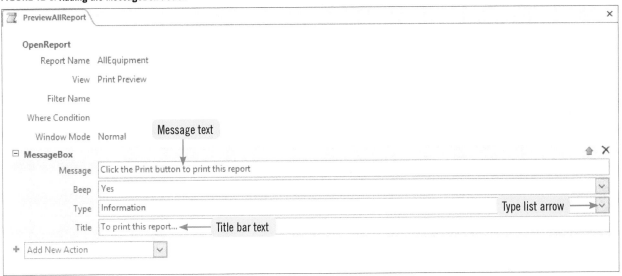

FIGURE 12-4: Dialog box created by MessageBox action

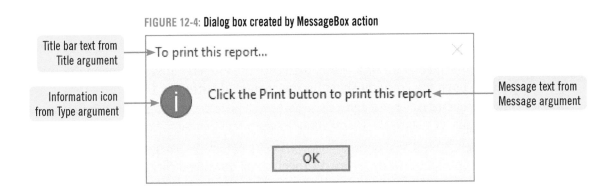

Assigning a macro to a key combination

You can assign a key combination such as [Shift][Ctrl][L] to a macro by creating a macro with the name **AutoKeys**. Enter the key combination as the submacro name. Use + for Shift, % for Alt, and ^ for Ctrl. Enclose special keys such as F3 in {curly braces}. For example, to assign a macro to [Shift][Ctrl][L], use +^L as the submacro name. To assign a macro to [Shift][F3], use +{F3} as the submacro name. Any key combination assignments you make in the AutoKeys macro override those that Access has already specified. Therefore, check the Keyboard Shortcuts information in the Microsoft Access Help system to make sure that the AutoKey assignment that you are creating doesn't override an existing Access quick keystroke that may be used for another purpose.

Assign a Macro to a Command Button

Learning Outcomes
- Tie a command button to a macro
- Describe trusted folders and files

Access provides many ways to run a macro: clicking the Run button in Macro Design View, assigning the macro to a command button, or assigning the macro to a Ribbon or shortcut menu command. Assigning a macro to a command button on a form provides a very intuitive way for the user to access the macro's functionality. **CASE** *You and Aaron decide to modify the Employees form to include a command button that runs the PreviewAllReport macro.*

STEPS

QUICK TIP

Be sure the Use Control Wizards button is selected. To find it, click the More button in the Controls group on the Design tab.

1. **Right-click the** Employees form **in the Navigation Pane, click** Design View, **use ⬍ to expand the** Form Footer **about 0.5", click the** Button button **in the Controls group, then click the** left side of the Form Footer section

   The **Command Button Wizard** starts, presenting you with 28 actions on the right organized within 6 categories on the left. For example, if you want the command button to open a report, you choose the OpenReport action in the Report Operations category. In this case, you want to run the PreviewAllReport macro, which not only opens a report, but also presents a message. The Miscellaneous category contains an action that allows you to run an existing macro.

2. **Click** Miscellaneous **in the Categories list, click** Run Macro **in the Actions list as shown in** FIGURE 12-5, **click** Next, **click** PreviewAllReport, **click** Next, **click the** Text option button, **select** Run Macro, **type** All Equipment Report, **then click** Next

   The Command Button Wizard asks you to give the button a meaningful name. When assigning names, a common three-character prefix for command buttons is **cmd**.

3. **Type** cmdAllEquipment, **click** Finish, **then click the** Property Sheet button **in the Tools group to open the Property Sheet for the command button**

   The new command button that runs a macro has been added to the Employees form in Form Design View. You work with the Property Sheet to change the text color to differentiate it from the button color as well as to examine how the macro was attached to the command button.

4. **Click the** Format tab **in the Property Sheet, scroll down and click the** Fore Color list arrow, **click** Text Dark, **then click the** Event tab **in the Property Sheet, noting that the On Click property contains [Embedded Macro]**

   The PreviewAllReport macro was attached to the **On Click property** of this command button. In other words, the macro is run when the user clicks the command button. To make sure that the new command button works as intended, you view the form in Form View and test the command button.

5. **Close the Property Sheet, click the** View button **to switch to Form View, click the** All Equipment Report command button **in the Form Footer section, click** OK **in the message box, then close the AllEquipment report**

   The Employees form with the new command button should look like FIGURE 12-6. It's common to put command buttons in the Form Footer so that users have a consistent location to find them.

6. **Save and close the Employees form**

FIGURE 12-5: Adding a command button to run a macro

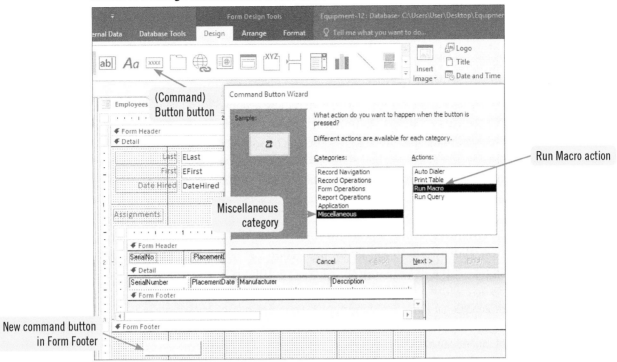

FIGURE 12-6: Employees form with new command button

Using a trusted database and setting up a trusted folder

A **trusted database** allows you to run macros and Visual Basic for Applications code (VBA). By default, a database is not trusted. To trust a database, click the Enable Content button on the Security Warning bar each time you open a database. To permanently trust a database, store the database in a **trusted folder**. To create a trusted folder, open the Options dialog box from the File tab, click the Trust Center, click the Trust Center Settings button, click the Trusted Locations option, click the Add new location button, then browse to and choose the folder you want to trust.

Use If Statements

Learning Outcomes
- Apply If statements to macros
- Enter conditional expressions

An **If statement** allows you to run macro actions based on the result of a conditional expression. A **conditional expression** is an expression such as [Price]>100 or [StateName]="MO" that results in a true or false value. If the condition evaluates true, the actions that follow the If statement are executed. If the condition evaluates false, the macro skips those actions. When building a conditional expression that refers to a value in a control on a form or report, use the following syntax: [Forms]![formname]![controlname], which is called **bang notation**. **CASE** *At R2G, everyone who has been with the company longer than five years is eligible to take their old PC equipment home as soon as it has been replaced. Aaron asks you to use a conditional macro to help evaluate and present this information in a form.*

STEPS

1. **Click the Create tab, click the Macro button, click the Action Catalog button in the Show/Hide group to toggle on the Action Catalog window if it is not already visible, double-click If in the Program Flow area, then type the following in the If box:**
   [Forms]![Employees]![DateHired]<Date()-(5*365)

   The conditional expression shown in FIGURE 12-7 says, "Check the value in the DateHired control on the Employees form and evaluate true if the value is earlier than 5 years from today. Evaluate false if the value is not earlier than 5 years ago."

2. **Click the Add New Action list arrow in the If block, then scroll and click SetProperty**
   The **SetProperty** action has three arguments—Control Name, Property, and Value.

3. **Click the Control Name argument text box in the Action Arguments pane, type LabelPCProgram, click the Property argument list arrow, click Visible, click the Value Property argument, then type True**

   Your screen should look like FIGURE 12-8. The **Control Name** argument must match the **Name property** in the Property Sheet of the label that will be modified. The **Property argument** determines what property is being modified. The **Value argument** determines the value of the **Visible property**. For properties such as the Visible property that have only two choices in the Property Sheet, Yes or No, you enter a value of False for No and True for Yes.

4. **Save the macro with the name 5Years, then close Macro Design View**
   Test the macro using the Employees form.

5. **Double-click the Employees form to open it, then navigate to the second record**
   The record for Ron Dawson, hired 2/15/2000, appears. Given that Ron has worked at R2G much longer than 5 years, you anticipate that the macro will display the label when it is run.

6. **Click the Database Tools tab, click the Run Macro button, verify that 5Years is in the Macro Name text box, then click OK**
   After evaluating the DateHired field of this record and determining that this employee has been working at R2G longer than five years, the LabelPCProgram label's Visible property was set to Yes, as shown in FIGURE 12-9. The LabelPCProgram label's **Caption property** is "Eligible for PC Program!"

7. **Navigate through several records and note that the label remains visible for each employee even though the hire date may not be longer than 5 years ago**
   Because the macro only ran once, the label's Visible property remains Yes regardless of the current data in the DateHired field. You need a way to rerun or trigger the macro to evaluate the data in the DateHired field for each employee.

8. **Close the Employees form**

FIGURE 12-7: Using an If statement to set a control's Visible property

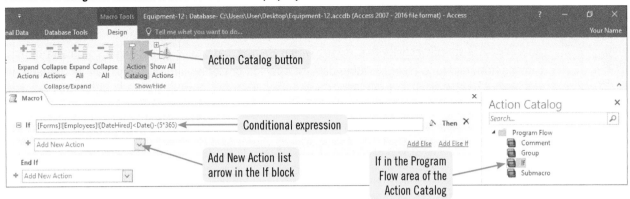

FIGURE 12-8: Entering arguments for the SetProperty action

FIGURE 12-9: Running the 5Years macro

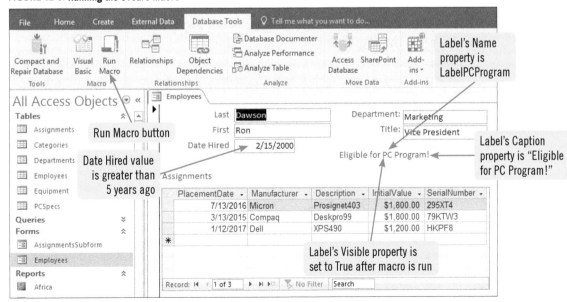

Work with Events

An **event** is a specific activity that occurs within the database, such as clicking a command button, moving from record to record, editing data, or opening or closing a form. Events can be triggered by the user or by the database itself. By assigning a macro to an appropriate event rather than running the macro from the Database Tools tab or command button, you further automate and improve your database. **CASE** ▶ *Aaron Scout asks you to modify the 5Years macro so that it evaluates the DateHired field to display or hide the label as you move from record to record.*

STEPS

1. **Right-click the** 5Years macro **in the Navigation Pane, click** Design View **on the shortcut menu, click anywhere in the** If block **to activate it, then click the** Add Else link **in the lower-right corner of the If block**

   The **Else** portion of an If statement allows you to run a different set of macro actions if the conditional expression evaluates False. In this case, you want to set the Value of the Visible property to False if the conditional expression evaluates False (if the DateHired is less than five years from today's date) so that the label does not appear if the employee is not eligible for the PC program.

2. **Add the same** SetProperty action **to the Else block, but enter** False **for the Value argument as shown in** FIGURE 12-10

   With the second action edited, the macro will now turn the label's Visible property to True (Yes) or False (No), depending on DateHired value. To make the macro run each time you move to a new employee record, you attach the macro to the event that is triggered as you move from record to record.

3. **Save and close the** 5Years macro, **right-click the** Employees form **in the Navigation Pane, click** Design View, **then click the** Property Sheet button

   All objects, sections, and controls have a variety of events to which macros can be attached. Most event names are self-explanatory, such as the **On Click event** (which occurs when that item is clicked).

4. **Click the** Event tab **in the Property Sheet, click the** On Current list arrow, **then click** 5Years

   Your Property Sheet should look like FIGURE 12-11. Because the **On Current event** occurs when focus moves from one record to another, the 5Years macro will automatically run each time you move from record to record in the form. Test your new macro by moving through several records in Form View.

5. **Close the** Property Sheet, **click the** View button **to switch to Form View, then click the** Next record button ▶ **in the navigation bar for the main form several times while observing the Eligible for PC Program! label**

   For every DateHired value that is earlier than five years before today's date, the Eligible for PC Program! label is visible. If the DateHired is less than five years before today's date, the label is hidden.

6. **Save and close the Employees form**

FIGURE 12-10: **Adding an Else portion to an If block**

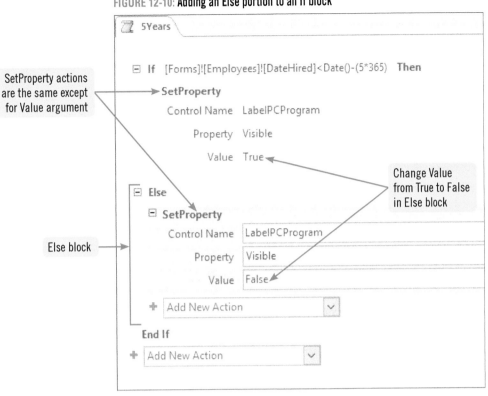

SetProperty actions are the same except for Value argument →

☐ If   [Forms]![Employees]![DateHired]<Date()-(5*365)   **Then**

→ **SetProperty**

Control Name   LabelPCProgram

Property   Visible

Value   True ←

Change Value from True to False in Else block

Else block →

☐ **Else**

☐ **SetProperty**

Control Name   LabelPCProgram

Property   Visible

Value   False

✚ Add New Action

End If

✚ Add New Action

FIGURE 12-11: **Attaching a macro to the On Current event of the form**

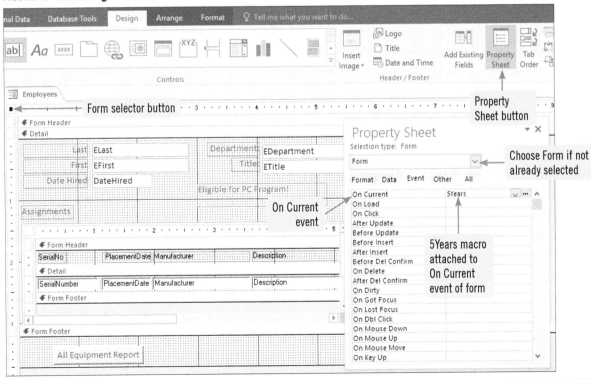

Form selector button

Property Sheet button

Choose Form if not already selected

On Current event

5Years macro attached to On Current event of form

Create a Data Macro

Learning
Outcomes
• Describe the use
of data macros
• Create a data
macro

A data macro allows you to embed macro capabilities directly in a table to add, change, or delete data based on conditions you specify. Data macros are managed directly from within tables and do not appear in the Macros group in the Navigation Pane. You most often run a data macro based on a table event, such as modifying data or deleting a record, but you can run a data macro separately as well, similar to how you run a regular macro. **CASE** *R2G grants 10 days of regular vacation to all employees except for those in the Africa and Asia departments, who receive 15 days due to the extra travel requirements of their positions. Aaron asks you to figure out an automatic way to assign each employee the correct number of vacation days based on his or her department. A data macro will work well for this task.*

STEPS

1. **Double-click the Employees table in the Navigation Pane, then observe the Vacation field throughout the datasheet**

   Currently, the Vacation field contains the value of 10 for each record, or each employee.

2. **Right-click the Employees table tab, click Design View on the shortcut menu, click the Create Data Macros button in the Field, Record & Table Events group, click After Insert, then click the Action Catalog button in the Show/Hide group if the Action Catalog window is not already open**

   In this case, you chose the After Insert event, which is run after a new record is entered. See TABLE 12-3 for more information on table events. Creating a data macro is very similar to creating a regular macro. You add the logic and macro actions needed to complete the task at hand.

3. **Double-click the ForEachRecord data block in the Action Catalog to add a For Each Record In block, click the For Each Record In list arrow, click Employees in the list, click the Where Condition text box, type [EDepartment]="Africa" or [EDepartment]="Asia", double-click the EditRecord data block in the Action Catalog, double-click the SetField data action in the Action Catalog, click the Name box in the SetField block, type Vacation, click the Value box in the SetField block, then type 15, as shown in** FIGURE 12-12

   Test the new data macro by adding a new record.

4. **Click the Close button, click Yes when prompted to save changes, click the View button to display the datasheet, click Yes when prompted to save changes, click the New button in the Records group, enter the new record as shown in** FIGURE 12-13 **except do not enter a Vacation value, then press [Tab] to move to a new record**

   The macro is triggered by the After Insert event of the record, and the Vacation field is automatically updated to 15 for the new record and all other records with Asia or Africa in the Department field, as shown in FIGURE 12-13.

5. **Right-click the Employees table tab, then click Close on the shortcut menu**

   Data is automatically saved when you move from record to record or close a database object.

FIGURE 12-12: **Creating a data macro**

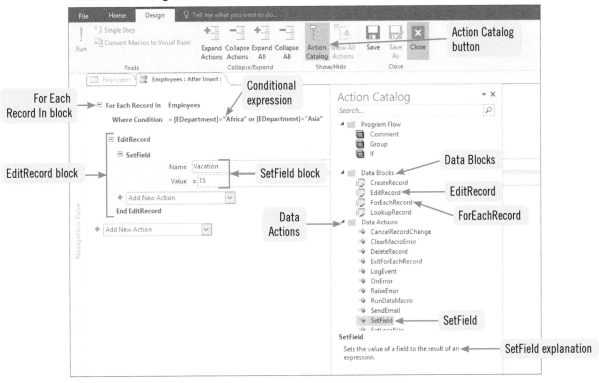

FIGURE 12-13: **Running a data macro**

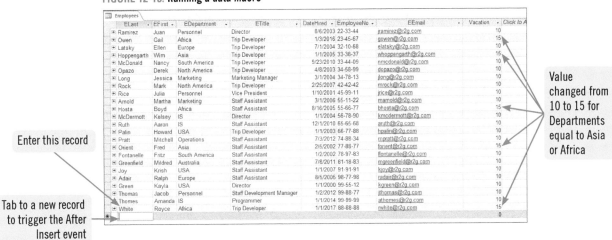

TABLE 12-3: **Table events**

table event	runs...
After Insert	...after a new record has been inserted into the table
After Update	...after an existing record has been changed
After Delete	...after an existing record has been deleted
Before Delete	...before a record is deleted, to help the user validate or cancel the deletion
Before Change	...before a record is changed, to help the user validate or cancel the edits

Troubleshoot Macros

Learning
Outcomes
• Single step a
  macro
• Describe debug-
  ging techniques

When macros don't run properly, Access supplies several tools to debug them. **Debugging** means determining why the macro doesn't run correctly. It usually involves breaking down a dysfunctional macro into smaller pieces that can be individually tested. For example, you can **single step** a macro, which means to run it one action at a time to observe the effect of each specific action in the Macro Single Step dialog box. **CASE** ▶ *Aaron suggests that you use the PreviewAllReport macro to learn debugging techniques.*

STEPS

1. **Right-click the** PreviewAllReport macro, **click** Design View **on the shortcut menu, click the** Single Step button **in the Tools group, then click the** Run button

   The screen should look like FIGURE 12-14, with the Macro Single Step dialog box open. This dialog box displays information including the macro's name, the action's name, and the action's arguments. From the Macro Single Step dialog box, you can step into the next macro action, halt execution of the macro, or continue running the macro without single stepping.

2. **Click** Step **in the Macro Single Step dialog box**

   Stepping into the second action lets the first action run and pauses the macro at the second action. The Macro Single Step dialog box now displays information about the second action.

3. **Click** Step

   The second action, the MessageBox action, is executed, which displays the message box.

4. **Click** OK, **then close the AllEquipment report**

5. **Click the** Design tab, **then click the** Single Step button **to toggle it off**

   Another technique to help troubleshoot macros is to use the built-in prompts and Help system provided by Microsoft Access. For example, you may have questions about how to use the optional Filter Name argument for the OpenReport macro action.

6. **Click the** OpenReport action block, **then point to the** Where Condition argument **to view the ScreenTip that supplies information about that argument, as shown in** FIGURE 12-15

   The Access 2016 Macro Design View window has been improved with interactive prompts.

7. **Save and close the PreviewAllReport macro, close the Equipment-12.accdb database, then exit Access**

FIGURE 12-14: **Single stepping through a macro**

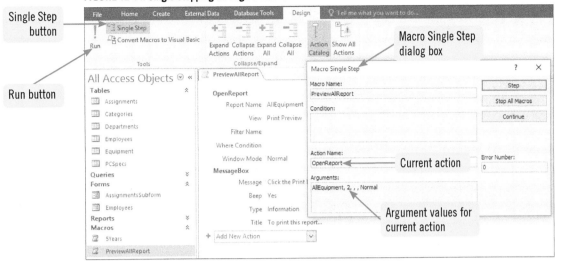

Single Step button

Run button

Macro Single Step dialog box

Current action

Argument values for current action

FIGURE 12-15: **Viewing automatic prompts**

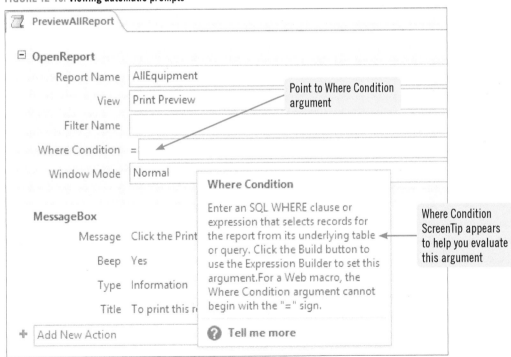

Point to Where Condition argument

Where Condition

Enter an SQL WHERE clause or expression that selects records for the report from its underlying table or query. Click the Build button to use the Expression Builder to set this argument. For a Web macro, the Where Condition argument cannot begin with the "=" sign.

❓ Tell me more

Where Condition ScreenTip appears to help you evaluate this argument

Practice

Concepts Review

Identify each element of Macro Design View shown in FIGURE 12-16.

FIGURE 12-16

Match each term with the statement that best describes its function.

8. Macro
9. Debugging
10. Action
11. Argument
12. Event
13. Conditional expression

a. Specific action that occurs within the database, such as clicking a button or opening a form
b. Part of an If statement that evaluates as either true or false
c. Individual step that you want the Access macro to perform
d. Access object that stores one or more actions that perform one or more tasks
e. Provides additional information to define how an Access action will perform
f. Determines why a macro doesn't run properly

Select the best answer from the list of choices.

14. Which of the following is not a major benefit of using a macro?
    a. To save time by automating routine tasks
    b. To make the database more flexible or easy to use
    c. To ensure consistency in executing routine or complex tasks
    d. To redesign the relationships among the tables of the database

15. Which of the following best describes the process of creating an Access macro?
    a. Open Macro Design View and add actions, arguments, and If statements to accomplish the desired task.
    b. Use the Macro Wizard to determine which tasks are done most frequently.
    c. Use the single step recorder to record clicks and keystrokes as you complete a task.
    d. Use the macro recorder to record clicks and keystrokes as you complete a task.

16. Which of the following would not be a way to run a macro?
    a. Click the Run Macro button on the Database Tools tab.
    b. Double-click a macro action within the Macro Design View window.
    c. Assign the macro to a command button on a form.
    d. Assign the macro to an event of a control on a form.

17. **Which of the following is not a reason to run a macro in single step mode?**
    a. You want to observe the effect of each macro action individually.
    b. You want to run only a few of the actions of a macro.
    c. You want to change the arguments of a macro while it runs.
    d. You want to debug a macro that isn't working properly.

18. **Which of the following is not true of conditional expressions in If statements in macros?**
    a. Conditional expressions allow you to skip over actions when the expression evaluates as false.
    b. Macro If statements provide for Else and Else If clauses.
    c. More macro actions are available when you are also using conditional expressions.
    d. Conditional expressions give the macro more power and flexibility.

19. **Which example illustrates the proper syntax to refer to a specific control on a form?**
    a. [Forms] ! [formname] ! [controlname]
    b. {Forms} ! {formname} ! (controlname)
    c. Forms ! formname. controlname
    d. (Forms) ! (formname) ! (controlname)

20. **Which event is executed every time you move from record to record in a form?**
    a. On Move
    b. Next Record
    c. New Record
    d. On Current

Skills Review

1. **Understand macros.**
    a. Start Access, then open the Basketball-12.accdb database from the location where you store your Data Files. Enable content if prompted.
    b. Open the PrintMacroGroup macro in Macro Design View, then record your answers to the following questions on a sheet of paper:
       • What is the name of the first submacro?
       • How many macro actions are in the first submacro?
       • What arguments does the first action in the first submacro contain?
       • What values were chosen for these arguments?
       • Close Macro Design View for the PrintMacroGroup object.

2. **Create a macro.**
    a. Start a new macro in Macro Design View.
    b. Add the OpenQuery action.
    c. Select PlayerStats as the value for the Query Name argument.
    d. Select Datasheet for the View argument.
    e. Select Edit for the Data Mode argument.
    f. Save the macro with the name **ViewPlayerStats**.
    g. Run the macro to make sure it works, close the PlayerStats query, then close the ViewPlayerStats macro.

3. **Modify actions and arguments.**
    a. Open the ViewPlayerStats macro in Macro Design View.
    b. Add a MessageBox action as the second action of the query.
    c. Type **What a great season!** for the Message argument.
    d. Select Yes for the Beep argument.
    e. Select Warning! for the Type argument.
    f. Type **Iowa State Cyclones** for the Title argument.
    g. Save the macro, then run it to make sure the MessageBox action works as intended.
    h. Click OK in the dialog box created by the MessageBox action, close the PlayerStats query, then close the ViewPlayerStats macro.

Skills Review (continued)

    i. Open the PrintMacroGroup macro object in Design View.

    j. Modify the View argument for the OpenReport object of the PlayerStatistics submacro from Print to **Print Preview**.

    k. Modify the Message argument for the MessageBox object of the PlayerStatistics submacro to read **Click the Print button to send this report to the printer.**

    l. Save and close the PrintMacroGroup macro.

4. Assign a macro to a command button.

    a. In Design View of the Player Information Form, use the Command Button Wizard to the right of the FirstName text box. The new button should run the PlayerStatistics submacro in the PrintMacroGroup macro (PrintMacroGroup.PlayerStatistics).

    b. The text on the button should read **View Player Statistics**.

    c. The meaningful name for the button should be **cmdPlayerStatistics**.

    d. Test the command button in Form View, click OK in the message box, then close the PlayerStats report.

    e. Save and close the Player Information Form.

5. Use If statements.

    a. Start a new macro in Macro Design View, and open the Action Catalog window if it is not already open.

    b. Double-click If in the Action Catalog window to add an If block to the macro.

    c. Enter the following condition in the If box: **[Forms]![GameInfo]![CycloneScore]>[OpponentScore]**.

    d. Add the SetProperty action to the If block.

    e. Type **VictoryLabel** in the Control Name box for the SetProperty action.

    f. Select Visible for the Property argument for the SetProperty action.

    g. Enter **True** for the Value argument for the SetProperty action to indicate Yes.

    h. Click the Add Else link in the lower-right corner of the If block.

    i. Enter the same SetProperty action from the If statement under the Else clause.

    j. Use the same argument values for the second SetProperty action, but modify the Value property from True to **False** for the second SetProperty action.

    k. Save the macro with the name **VictoryCalculator**, compare it with FIGURE 12-17, make any necessary adjustments, then close Macro Design View.

6. Work with events.

    a. Open the GameInfo form in Form Design View.

    b. Open the Property Sheet for the form.

    c. Assign the VictoryCalculator macro to the On Current event of the form.

    d. Close the Property Sheet, save the form, then open the GameInfo form in Form View.

    e. Navigate through the first four records. The Victory label should be visible for the first three records, but not the fourth.

    f. Add your name as a label in the Form Footer section to identify your printouts, print the third and fourth records if requested by your instructor, then save and close the GameInfo form.

FIGURE 12-17

7. Create a data macro.

    a. Open the Games table in Table Design View.

    b. Add a field named **RoadWin** with a Yes/No data type and the following Description: **Enter Yes if the Home-Away field is Away and the CycloneScore is greater than the OpponentScore.**

    c. Save the Games table and switch to Datasheet View to note that the RoadWin check box is empty (No) for every record.

    d. Switch back to Table Design View, then create a data macro based on the After Insert event.

Skills Review (continued)

e. Insert a ForEachRecord data block, and specify **Games** for the For Each Record In argument.

f. The Where Condition should be **[Home-Away]="A" and [CycloneScore]>[OpponentScore]**.

g. Add an EditRecord data block in the For Each Record In block, and a SetField data action. Be careful to add the EditRecord block within the For Each Record Block.

h. Enter **RoadWin** in the Name argument and **Yes** in the Value argument, as shown in FIGURE 12-18.

i. Save and close the data macro, save the Games table, switch to Datasheet View, then test the new data macro by entering a new record in the Games table as follows:

Opponent: **Johnson College**
Mascot: **Cavaliers**
Home-Away: **A**
CycloneScore: **100**
OpponentScore: **50**
GameDate: **3/2/2018**

FIGURE 12-18

j. Tab to a new record. Six records where the Home-Away field is set to "A" and the CycloneScore is greater than the OpponentScore should be checked. Close the Games table.

8. Troubleshoot macros.

a. Open the PrintMacroGroup in Macro Design View.

b. Click the Single Step button, then click the Run button.

c. Click Step twice to step through the two actions of the submacro PlayerStatistics, then click OK in the resulting message box.

d. Close the PlayerStats report.

e. Return to Macro Design View of the PrintMacroGroup macro and click the Single Step button on the Design tab to toggle off this feature.

f. Save and close the PrintMacroGroup macro, close the Basketball-12.accdb database, then exit Access.

Independent Challenge 1

As the manager of a doctor's clinic, you have created an Access database called Patients-12.accdb to track insurance claim reimbursements. You use macros to help automate the database.

a. Start Access, then open the database Patients-12.accdb from the location where you store your Data Files. Enable content if prompted.

b. Open Macro Design View of the CPT Form Open macro. (CPT stands for Current Procedural Terminology, which is a code that describes a medical procedure.) If the Single Step button is toggled on, toggle it off.

c. On a separate sheet of paper, identify the macro actions, arguments for each action, and values for each argument.

d. In two or three sentences, explain in your own words what tasks this macro automates.

e. Close the CPT Form Open macro.

f. Open the Claim Entry Form in Form Design View.

g. The Form Footer of the Claim Entry Form contains several command buttons. Open the Property Sheet of the Add CPT Code button, then click the Event tab.

h. On your paper, write the event to which the CPT Form Open macro is assigned.

i. Open the Claim Entry Form in Form View, then click the Add CPT Code button in the Form Footer.

j. On your paper, write the current record number that is displayed for you.

k. Close the Patients-12.accdb database, then exit Access.

Independent Challenge 2

As the manager of a doctor's clinic, you have created an Access database called Patients-12.accdb to track insurance claim reimbursements. You use macros to help automate the database.

a. Start Access, then open the database Patients-12.accdb from the location where you store your Data Files. Enable content if prompted.

b. Start a new macro in Macro Design View, and open the Action Catalog window if it is not already open.

c. Double-click the Submacro entry in the Program Flow folder to add a submacro block.

d. Type **Preview Monthly Brown Report** as the first submacro name, then add the OpenReport macro action.

e. Select Monthly Brown for the Report Name argument, then select Print Preview for the View argument of the OpenReport action.

f. Double-click the Submacro entry in the Program Flow folder to add another submacro block.

g. Type **Preview Monthly Katera Report** as a new submacro name, then add the OpenReport macro action.

h. Select Monthly Katera for the ReportName argument, then select Print Preview for the View argument of the second OpenReport action.

i. Save the macro with the name **Preview Group**, then close Macro Design View.

j. Using the Run Macro button on the Database Tools tab, run the Preview Group.Preview Monthly Brown Report macro to test it, then close Print Preview.

k. Using the Run Macro button on the Database Tools tab, run the Preview Group.Preview Monthly Katera Report macro to test it, then close Print Preview.

l. Open the Preview Group macro in Macro Design View, then click the Collapse buttons to the left of the submacro statements to collapse the two submacro blocks.

m. Create one more submacro that previews the Monthly Winters report. Name the submacro **Preview Monthly Winters Report** as shown in FIGURE 12-19.

n. Save and close the Preview Group macro.

o. In Design View of the Claim Line Items Subform, add three separate command buttons to the Form Footer to run the three submacros in the Preview Group macro. Use the captions and meaningful names of **Brown** and **cmdBrown**, **Katera** and **cmdKatera**, **Winters** and **cmdWinters** to correspond with the three submacros in the Preview Group macro.

p. Change the font color on the new command buttons to black.

q. Select all three new command buttons and use the Size/Space and Align commands on the Arrange tab to precisely size, align, and space the buttons equally in the Form Footer section.

r. Save and close the Claim Line Items Subform, then open the Claim Entry Form in Form View, as shown in FIGURE 12-20. Test each of the new command buttons to make sure it opens the correct report.

s. Close the Claim Entry Form, close the Patients-12.accdb database, then exit Access

FIGURE 12-19

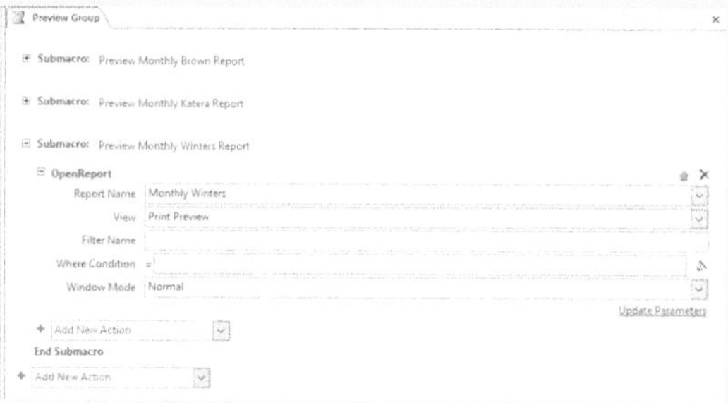

FIGURE 12-20

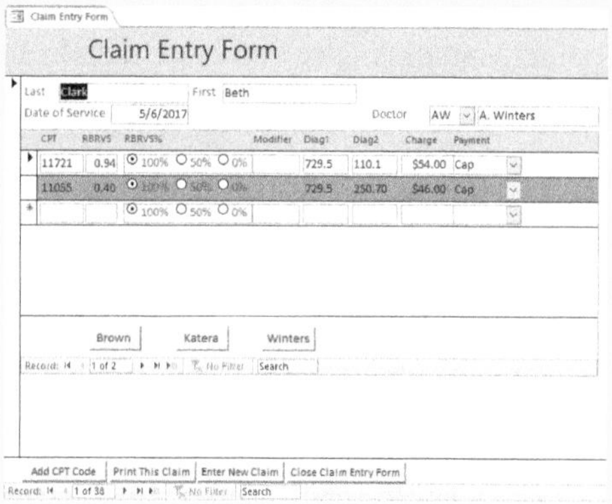

Independent Challenge 3

As the manager of a doctor's clinic, you have created an Access database called Patients-12.accdb to track insurance claim reimbursements. You use macros to help automate the database.

a. Start Access, then open the Patients-12.accdb database from the location where you store your Data Files. Enable content if prompted.

Independent Challenge 3 (continued)

b. Start a new macro in Macro Design View, then add an If statement.

c. Enter the following in the If box: **[Forms]![CPT Form]![RBRVS]=0**.

d. Select the SetProperty action for the first action in the If block.

e. Enter the following arguments for the SetProperty action: Control Name: **ResearchLabel**, Property: **Visible**, and Value: **True**.

f. Click the Add Else link, then select the SetProperty action for the first action of the Else clause.

g. Enter the following arguments for the SetProperty action: Control Name: **ResearchLabel**, Property: **Visible**, and Value: **False**.

h. Save the macro with the name **Research**, then close Macro Design View.

i. Open the CPT Form in Form Design View, then open the Property Sheet for the form.

j. Click the Research! label in the Detail section, and enter **ResearchLabel** as the Name property in the Property Sheet. (*Hint*: The Name property is on the Other tab in the Property Sheet.)

k. Assign the Research macro to the On Current event of the form.

l. Close the Property Sheet, save the form, then open the CPT Form in Form View.

m. Use the Next record button to move quickly through all 64 records in the form. Notice that the macro displays Research! only when the RBRVS value is equal to zero.

n. Save and close the CPT Form, then close the Patients-12.accdb database.

Independent Challenge 4: Explore

You are collecting information on international candy and chocolate factories, museums, and stores in an Access database. You tie the forms together with macros attached to command buttons.

a. Open the Candy-12.accdb database from the location where you store your Data Files, enable content if prompted, then open the Countries form in Form View. The database option to show overlapping windows versus tabbed documents has been set. Overlapping windows allows you to restore and size windows.

b. Click the New (blank) record button for the main form, then type **Poland** in the Country text box.

c. In the subform for the Poland record, enter **Cadbury-Wedel Polska** in the Name field, **F** in the Type field (F for factory), **Praga** in the City field, and **Lodz** in the StateProvince field. Close the Countries form. To maximize the windows of this database when they open, attach a macro to the On Load event of the form.

d. Open Macro Design View for a new macro, then add the MaximizeWindow action. Save the macro with the name **Maximize**, then close it. The Maximize macro helps you maximize windows if a database option is set to Overlapping Windows. To see this setting, click the File tab, click Options, click Current Database, and then view the Document Window Options section. When Tabbed Documents is selected, the windows are maximized and provide tabs for navigation. When Overlapping Windows is selected, windows can be any size.

e. Open the Countries form in Design View, add the Maximize macro to the On Load event of the Countries form, then open the Countries form in Form View to test it.

f. Save the Countries form and return to Design View.

g. In the Property Sheet for the form, click the On Load event, delete the Maximize macro entry, click the Build button, click Macro Builder, then click OK.

h. Add the MaximizeWindow action to the macro design window, then save and close it. Note that the Property Sheet now shows [Embedded Macro] for the On Load event vs. the Maximize macro.

i. Save the Countries form, open it in Form View, and resize it to something less than maximized. Close and reopen the form in Form View to test the embedded macro.

j. The Countries form should open maximized with either the embedded macro or the Maximize macro attached to the On Load event. Close the Candy-12.accdb database, then exit Access.

Visual Workshop

As the manager of a doctor's clinic, you have created an Access database called Patients-12.accdb to track insurance claim reimbursements. Develop a new macro called **Query Group** with the actions and argument values shown in FIGURE 12-21. Run both macros to test them by using the Run Macro button on the Database Tools tab, and debug the macros if necessary.

FIGURE 12-21

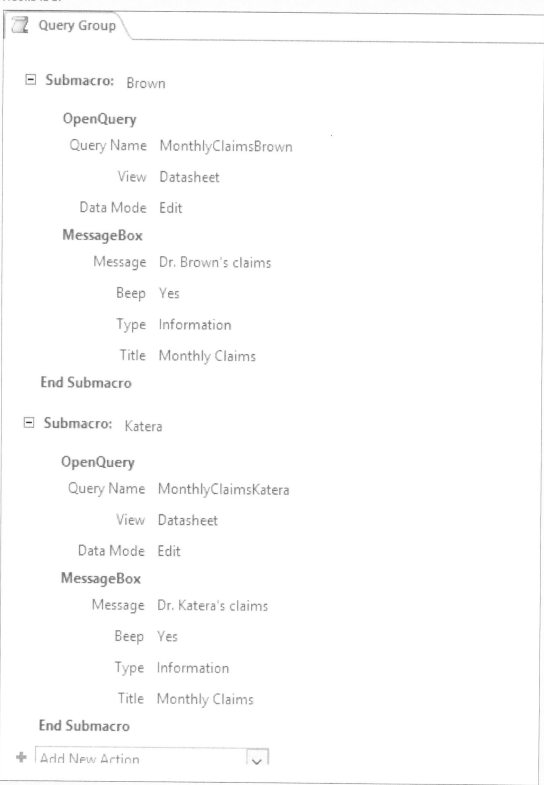

Creating Modules and VBA

CASE You and Aaron Scout, the network administrator at Reason 2 Go, want to learn about VBA and create modules to enhance the capabilities of the Equipment-13 database for Reason 2 Go.

Module Objectives

After completing this module, you will be able to:

- Understand modules and VBA
- Compare macros and modules
- Create functions
- Use If statements

- Document procedures
- Build class modules
- Modify sub procedures
- Troubleshoot modules

Files You Will Need

Equipment-13.accdb   Insurance-13.accdb

Baseball-13.accdb   Basketball-13.accdb

Understand Modules and VBA

Learning
Outcomes
• Define VBA terms
• Describe Visual
  Basic Editor
  components

Access is a robust and easy-to-use relational database program. Access provides user-friendly tools, such as wizards and Design Views, to help users quickly create reports and forms that previously took programmers hours to build. You may, however, want to automate a task or create a new function that goes beyond the capabilities of the built-in Access tools. Within each program of the Microsoft Office suite, a programming language called **Visual Basic for Applications (VBA)** is provided to help you extend the program's capabilities. In Access, VBA is stored within modules. A **module** is an Access object that stores Visual Basic for Applications (VBA) programming code. VBA is written in the **Visual Basic Editor (VBE)**, shown in FIGURE 13-1. The components and text colors of the VBE are described in TABLE 13-1. An Access database has two kinds of modules. **Standard modules** contain global code that can be executed from anywhere in the database. Standard modules are displayed as module objects in the Navigation Pane. **Class modules** are stored within the form or report object itself. Class modules contain VBA code used only within that particular form or report. **CASE** ▶ *Before working with modules, you ask some questions about VBA.*

DETAILS

The following questions and answers introduce the basics of Access modules:

- **What does a module contain?**

  A module contains VBA programming code organized in procedures. A procedure contains several lines of code, each of which is called a **statement**. Modules can also contain **comments**, text that helps explain and document the code.

- **What is a procedure?**

  A **procedure** is a series of VBA statements that performs an operation or calculates an answer. VBA has two types of procedures: functions and subs. **Declaration statements** precede procedure statements and help set rules for how the statements in the module are processed.

- **What is a function?**

  A **function** is a procedure that returns a value. Access supplies many built-in functions, such as Sum, Count, Pmt, and Now, that can be used in an expression in a query, form, or report to calculate a value. You might want to create a new function, however, to help perform calculations unique to your database. For example, you might create a new function called Commission to calculate a sales commission using a formula unique to your business.

- **What is a sub?**

  A **sub** (also called **sub procedure**) performs a series of VBA statements to manipulate controls and objects. Subs are generally executed when an event occurs, such as when a command button is clicked or a form is opened.

- **What are arguments?**

  Arguments are constants, variables, or expressions passed to a procedure that the procedure needs in order to execute. For example, the full syntax for the Sum function is Sum(*expr*), where *expr* represents the argument for the Sum function, the field that is being summed. In VBA, arguments are declared in the first line of the procedure. They are specified immediately after a procedure's name and are enclosed in parentheses. Multiple arguments are separated by commas.

- **What is an object?**

  In VBA, an **object** is any item that can be used or manipulated, including the traditional Access objects (table, query, form, report, macro, and module), as well as form controls and sections, existing procedures, and built-in VBA objects that provide functionality to your code.

- **What is a method?**

  A **method** is an action that an object can perform. Procedures are often written to invoke methods in response to user actions. For example, you could invoke the GoToControl method to move the focus to a specific control on a form in response to the user clicking a command button.

FIGURE 13-1: Visual Basic Editor (VBE) window for a standard module

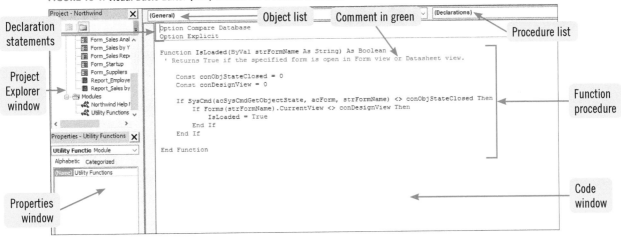

TABLE 13-1: Components and text colors for the Visual Basic Editor window

component or color	description
Visual Basic Editor, VBE	Comprises the entire Microsoft Visual Basic program window that contains smaller windows, including the Code window and Project Explorer window
Code window	Contains the VBA for the project selected in the Project Explorer window
Project Explorer window	Displays a hierarchical list of the projects in the database; a project can be a module object or a form or report object that contains a class module
Declaration statements	Includes statements that apply to every procedure in the module, such as declarations for variables, constants, user-defined data types, and external procedures in a dynamic-link library
Object list	In a class module, lists the objects associated with the current form or report
Procedure list	In a standard module, lists the procedures in the module; in a class module, lists events (such as Click or Dblclick)
Blue	Indicates a VBA keyword; blue words are reserved by VBA and are already assigned specific meanings
Black	Indicates normal text; black text is the unique VBA code created by the developer
Red	Indicates syntax error text; a red statement indicates that it will not execute correctly because of a syntax error (perhaps a missing parenthesis or a spelling error)
Green	Indicates comment text; any text after an apostrophe is considered documentation, or a comment, and is therefore ignored in the execution of the procedure

Access 2016

Compare Macros and Modules

Both macros and modules help run your database more efficiently and effectively. Creating a macro or a module requires some understanding of programming concepts, an ability to follow a process through its steps, and patience. Some tasks can be accomplished by using an Access macro or by writing VBA. Guidelines can help you determine which tool is best for the task. **CASE** ▶ *You compare Access macros and modules by asking more questions.*

DETAILS

The following questions and answers provide guidelines for using macros and modules:

- **For what types of tasks are macros best suited?**

  Macros are an easy way to handle common, repetitive, and simple tasks such as opening and closing forms, positioning a form to enter a new record, and printing reports.

- **Which is easier to create, a macro or a module, and why?**

  Macros are generally easier to create because Macro Design View is more structured than the VBE. The hardest part of creating a macro is choosing the correct macro action. But once the action is selected, the arguments associated with that macro action are displayed, eliminating the need to learn any special programming syntax. To create a module, however, you must know a robust programming language, VBA, as well as the correct **syntax** (rules) for each VBA statement. In a nutshell, macros are simpler to create, but VBA is more powerful.

- **When must I use a macro?**

  You must use macros to make global, shortcut key assignments. **AutoExec** is a special macro name that automatically executes when the database first opens.

- **When must I use a module?**

  1. You must use modules to create unique functions. For instance, you might want to create a function called Commission that calculates the appropriate commission on a sale using your company's unique commission formula.

  2. Access error messages can be confusing to the user. However, by using VBA procedures, you can detect the error when it occurs and display your own message.

  3. Although Access macros have recently been enhanced to include more powerful If-Then logic, VBA is still more robust in the area of programming flow statements with tools such as nested If statements, Case statements, and multiple looping structures. Some of the most common VBA keywords, including If...Then, are shown in TABLE 13-2. VBA keywords appear blue in the VBE code window.

  4. VBA code may declare **variables**, which are used to store data that can be used, modified, or displayed during the execution of the procedure.

  5. VBA may be used in conjunction with SQL (Structured Query Language) to select, update, append, and delete data.

  Like macros, modules can be accessed through the Navigation Pane or embedded directly within a form or report. When embedded in a form or report object, the module is called a **class module**, like the one shown in FIGURE 13-2. If you develop forms and reports in one database and copy them to another, the class modules automatically travel with the object that stores it. Use class modules for code that is unique to that form or report. Use standard modules (also called **global modules**) to store code that will be reused in many places in the database application.

FIGURE 13-2: Visual Basic Editor window for a class module

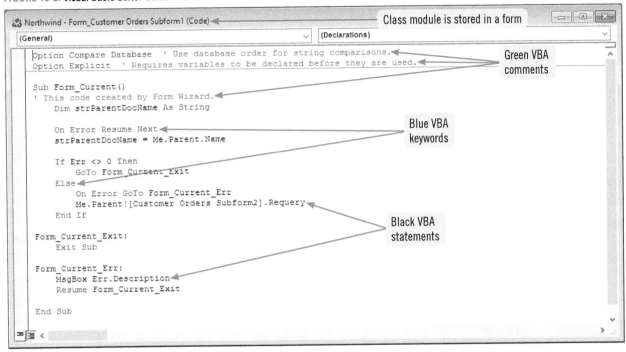

TABLE 13-2: Common VBA keywords

statement	explanation
Function	Declares the name and arguments that create a new function procedure
End Function	When defining a new function, the End Function statement is required as the last statement to mark the end of the VBA code that defines the function
Sub	Declares the name for a new Sub procedure; **Private Sub** indicates that the Sub is accessible only to other procedures in the module where it is declared
End Sub	When defining a new sub, the End Sub statement is required as the last statement to mark the end of the VBA code that defines the sub
If...Then	Executes code (the code follows the Then statement) when the value of an expression is true (the expression follows the If statement)
End If	When creating an If...Then...Else clause, the End If statement is required as the last statement
Const	Declares the name and value of a **constant**, an item that retains a constant value throughout the execution of the code
Option Compare Database	A declaration statement that determines the way string values (text) will be sorted
Option Explicit	A declaration statement that specifies that you must explicitly declare all variables used in all procedures; if you attempt to use an undeclared variable name, an error occurs at **compile time**, the period during which source code is translated to executable code
Dim	Declares a **variable**, a named storage location that contains data that can be modified during program execution
On Error GoTo	Upon an error in the execution of a procedure, specifies the location (the statement) where the procedure should continue
Select Case	Executes one of several groups of statements called a **Case** depending on the value of an expression; using the Select Case statement is an alternative to using **ElseIf** in **If...Then...Else** statements when comparing one expression with several different values
End Select	When defining a new Select Case group of statements, the End Select statement is required as the last statement to mark the end of the VBA code

Create Functions

Learning Outcomes
- Create a custom function
- Use a custom function

Access and VBA supply hundreds of built-in functions such as Sum, Count, IIf, First, Last, Date, and Hour. However, you might want to create a new function to calculate a value based on your company's unique business rules. You generally create new functions in a standard or global module so that it can be used in any query, form, or report throughout the database. **CASE** ▶ *Reason 2 Go allows employees to purchase computer equipment when it is replaced. Equipment that is less than a year old will be sold to employees at 75 percent of its initial value, and equipment that is more than a year old will be sold at 50 percent of its initial value. Aaron Scout, network administrator, asks you to create a new function called EPrice that determines the employee purchase price of replaced computer equipment.*

STEPS

TROUBLE
If you do not enable content, your VBA will not run.

1. **Start Access, open the** Equipment-13.accdb database **from the location where you store your Data Files, enable content if prompted, click the** Create tab, **then click the** Module button **in the Macros & Code group**

   Access automatically inserts the Option Compare Database declaration statement in the Code window. You will create the new EPrice function one step at a time.

QUICK TIP
The Option Explicit statement appears if the Require Variable Declaration option is checked in the VBA Options dialog box. To view the default settings, click Options on the VBA Tools menu.

2. **Type** function EPrice(StartValue), **then press** [Enter]

   This statement creates a new function named EPrice, which uses one argument, StartValue. The VBE automatically capitalized Function and added the **End Function** statement, a required statement to mark the end of the function. VBA keywords are blue.

3. **Press [Tab], type** EPrice = StartValue * 0.5, **then press [Enter]**

   Your screen should look like FIGURE 13-3. The EPrice= statement explains how the EPrice function will calculate. The function will return a value that is calculated by multiplying the StartValue by 0.5. It is not necessary to indent statements, but indenting code between matching Function/End Function, Sub/End Sub, or If/End If statements enhances the program's readability. When you press [Enter] at the end of a VBA statement, the VBE automatically adds spaces as appropriate to enhance the readability of the statement.

4. **Click the** Save button ⊞ **on the Standard toolbar, type** basFunctions **in the Save As dialog box, click** OK, **then click the upper** Close button ⊠ **in the upper-right corner of the VBE window to close the Visual Basic Editor**

   It is common for VBA programmers to use three-character prefixes to name objects and controls. This makes it easier to identify that object or control in expressions and modules. The prefix **bas** is short for Basic and applies to standard (global) modules. Naming conventions for other objects and controls are listed in TABLE 13-3 and are used throughout the Equipment-13.accdb database. You can use the new function, EPrice, in a query, form, or report.

5. **Right-click the** qryEmpPricing query **in the Navigation Pane, then click** Design View **on the shortcut menu**

   You use the new EPrice function in the query to determine the employee purchase price of replaced computer equipment.

QUICK TIP
Field names used in expressions are not case sensitive, but they must exactly match the spelling of the field name as defined in Table Design View.

6. **Click the** blank Field cell **to the right of the** InitialValue field, **type** Price:EPrice ([InitialValue]), **then click the** View button ▦ **to switch to Datasheet View**

   Your screen should look like FIGURE 13-4. In this query, you created a new field called Price that uses the EPrice function. The value in the InitialValue field is used for the StartValue argument of the new EPrice function. The InitialValue field is multiplied by 0.5 to create the new Price field.

7. **Save and then close the** qryEmpPricing query

FIGURE 13-3: Creating the EPrice function

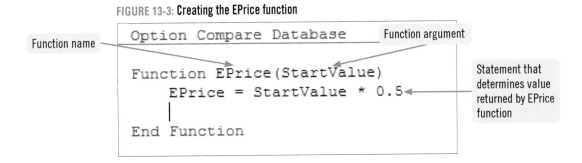

Function name → Function argument →

```
Option Compare Database

Function EPrice(StartValue)
     EPrice = StartValue * 0.5 ←
     |

End Function
```

Statement that determines value returned by EPrice function

FIGURE 13-4: Using the EPrice function in a query

ELast	Manufacture	Description	PlacementDat	InitialValue	Price
Dawson	Compaq	Deskpro99	3/13/2015	$1,800.00	900
Dawson	Micron	Prosignet403	7/13/2016	$1,800.00	900
Dawson	Dell	XPS490	1/12/2017	$1,200.00	600
Lane	Micron	Transtrek4000	8/29/2016	$1,900.00	950
Lane	HP	Deskjet 900XJ2	1/12/2017	$500.00	250
Wong	Compaq	Deskpro2099	5/7/2016	$1,700.00	850
Wong	Dell	Inspiron809	6/2/2017	$2,400.00	1200
Ramirez	Dell	XPS490	1/2/2012	$1,200.00	600
Latsky	Compaq	Deskpro99	4/12/2016	$2,000.00	1000
Latsky	Micron	Transtrek4000	8/29/2017	$1,800.00	900
Hoppengarth	Compaq	Deskpro99	4/12/2016	$1,800.00	900
Hoppengarth	Micron	Transtrek4000	8/29/2016	$1,800.00	900

qryEmpPricing

Calculated field, Price, uses EPrice custom function to multiply the InitialValue by 0.5

TABLE 13-3: Three-character prefix naming conventions

object or control type	prefix	example
Table	tbl	tblProducts
Query	qry	qrySalesByRegion
Form	frm	frmProducts
Report	rpt	rptSalesByCategory
Macro	mcr	mcrCloseInventory
Module	bas	basRetirement
Label	lbl	lblFullName
Text Box	txt	txtLastName
Combo box	cbo	cboStates
Command button	cmd	cmdPrint

Use If Statements

Learning
Outcomes
• Use VBA If Then
  Else logic
• Use the Zoom
  feature

If...Then...Else logic allows you to test logical conditions and execute statements only if the conditions are true. If...Then...Else code can be composed of one or several statements, depending on how many conditions you want to test, how many possible answers you want to provide, and what you want the code to do based on the results of the tests. **CASE** ➤ *Aaron notes that you need to add an If statement to the EPrice function to test the age of the equipment and then calculate the answer based on that age. You want to modify the EPrice function so that if the equipment is less than one year old, the StartValue is multiplied by 75% (0.75) rather than by 50% (0.5).*

STEPS

1. **Scroll down the Navigation Pane, right-click the** basFunctions module, **then click** Design View

   To determine the age of the equipment, the EPrice function needs another argument: the purchase date of the equipment.

2. **Click just before the right parenthesis in the Function statement, type** , (a comma), **press** [Spacebar], **type** DateValue, **then press** [↓]

   Now that you established another argument, you can work with the argument in the definition of the function.

3. **Click to the** right of the right parenthesis in the Function statement, **press** [Enter], **press** [Tab], **then type** If (Now() – DateValue) > 365 Then

   The expression compares whether today's date, represented by the Access function **Now( )**, minus the DateValue argument value is greater than 365 days (1 year). If true, this indicates that the equipment is older than one year.

4. **Indent and type the rest of the statements exactly as shown in** FIGURE 13-5

   The **Else** statement is executed only if the expression is false (if the equipment is less than 365 days old). The **End If** statement is needed to mark the end of the If block of code.

5. **Click the** Save button 🖫 **on the Standard toolbar, close the Visual Basic window, right-click the** qryEmpPricing query **in the Navigation Pane, then click** Design View **on the shortcut menu**

   Now that you've modified the EPrice function to include two arguments, you need to modify the calculated Price field expression, too.

6. **Right-click the** Price field **in the query design grid, click** Zoom **on the shortcut menu, click** between the right square bracket and right parenthesis, **then type** ,[PlacementDate]

   Your Zoom dialog box should look like FIGURE 13-6. Both of the arguments used to define the EPrice function in the VBA code are replaced with actual field names that contain the data to be analyzed. Field names must be typed exactly as shown and surrounded by square brackets. Commas separate multiple arguments in the function.

7. **Click** OK **in the Zoom dialog box, then click the** View button 🗔 **to display the datasheet**

8. **Click any entry in the** PlacementDate field, **then click the** Ascending button **in the Sort & Filter group, as shown in** FIGURE 13-7

   The EPrice function now calculates one of two different results, depending on the age of the equipment determined by the date in the PlacementDate field.

9. **Save and then close the** qryEmpPricing query

FIGURE 13-5: Using an If…Then…Else structure

```
                             Function EPrice(StartValue, DateValue)  ← Second argument
If ————————————→ If (Now() - DateValue) > 365 Then ←———— Then
                                EPrice = StartValue * 0.5
Else ———————————→ Else
                                EPrice = StartValue * 0.75
End If ——————————→ End If
                             End Function
```

FIGURE 13-6: Using the Zoom dialog box for long expressions

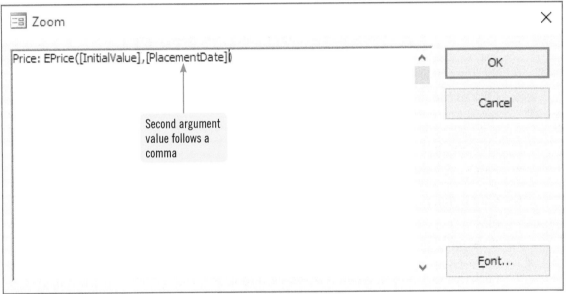

Price: EPrice([InitialValue],[PlacementDate])

OK

Cancel

Second argument
value follows a
comma

Font...

FIGURE 13-7: Price field is calculated at 50% or 75% based on the age of equipment

qryEmpPricing					
ELast ▾	Manufacture ▾	Description ▾	PlacementDat ◂	InitialValue ◂	Sort in ascending order on PlacementDate
Ramirez	Dell	XPS490	1/2/2012	$1,200.00	600
Dawson	Compaq	Deskpro99	3/13/2015	$1,800.00	1350
Greenfield	Compaq	Deskpro89	4/8/2015	$2,200.00	1650
Rock	Compaq	Deskpro2099	5/8/2015	$1,700.00	1275
Joy	Dell	Inspiron609	6/8/2015	$3,200.00	2400
Adair	Micron	Transtrek4000	12/30/2015	$1,900.00	1425
Rice	Micron	Prosignet403	1/8/2016	$1,700.00	1275
Arnold	Lexmark	Optra2000	1/13/2016	$2,000.00	1500
Orient	Lexmark	Optra2000	1/13/2016	$2,000.00	1500

InitialValue * 50%

InitialValue * 75%

Document Procedures

Learning
Outcomes
• Add VBA
  comments
• Use the VBE
  toolbar

Comment lines are statements in the code that document the code; they do not affect how the code runs. At any time, if you want to read or modify existing code, you can write the modifications much more quickly if the code is properly documented. Comment lines start with an apostrophe and are green in the VBE. **CASE** *Aaron asks you to document the EPrice function in the basFunctions module with descriptive comments. This will make it easier for you and others to follow the purpose and logic of the function later.*

STEPS

QUICK TIP
You can also create comments by starting the statement with the rem statement (for remark).

1. **Right-click the** basFunctions module **in the Navigation Pane, then click** Design View
   The VBE window for the basFunctions module opens.

2. **Click the** blank line between the Option Compare Database and Function statements, **press [Enter], type** 'This function is called EPrice and has two arguments, **then press [Enter]**
   As soon as you move to another line, the comment statement becomes green.

TROUBLE
Be sure to use an ' (apostrophe) and not a " (quotation mark) to begin the comment line.

3. **Type** 'Created by Your Name on Today's Date, **then press [Enter]**
   You can also place comments at the end of a line by entering an apostrophe to mark that the next part of the statement is a comment.

4. **Click to the** right of Then at the end of the If statement, **press [Spacebar], type** 'Now( ) returns today's date, **then press [↓]**
   This comment explains that the Now() function returns today's date. All comments are green, regardless of whether they are on their own line or at the end of an existing line.

5. **Click to the** right of 0.5, **press [Spacebar]** three times, **then type** 'If > 1 year, multiply by 50%

6. **Click to the** right of 0.75, **press [Spacebar]** twice, **type** 'If < 1 year, multiply by 75%, **then press [↓]**
   Your screen should look like FIGURE 13-8. Each comment will turn green as soon as you move to a new statement.

7. **Click the** Save button ⊟ **on the Standard toolbar, click** File **on the menu bar, click** Print **if requested by your instructor, then click** OK
   TABLE 13-4 provides more information about the Standard toolbar buttons in the VBE window.

8. **Click** File **on the menu bar, then click** Close and Return to Microsoft Access

FIGURE 13-8: Adding comments to a module

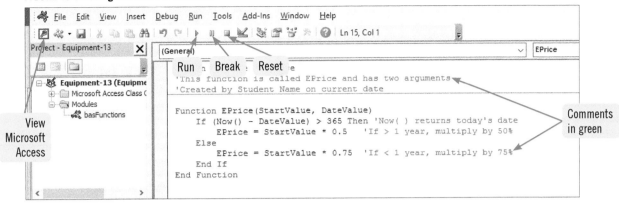

TABLE 13-4: Standard toolbar buttons in the Visual Basic window

button name	button	description
View Microsoft Access		Switches from the active Visual Basic window to the Access window
Insert Module		Opens a new module or class module Code window, or inserts a new procedure in the current Code window
Run Sub/UserForm		Runs the current procedure if the insertion point is in a procedure, or runs the UserForm if it is active
Break		Stops the execution of a program while it's running and switches to Break mode, which is the temporary suspension of program execution in which you can examine, debug, reset, step through, or continue program execution
Reset		Resets the procedure
Project Explorer		Displays the Project Explorer, which displays a hierarchical list of the currently open projects (set of modules) and their contents
Object Browser		Displays the Object Browser, which lists the defined modules and procedures as well as available methods, properties, events, constants, and other items that you can use in the code

Using comments for debugging

You can use comments to "comment out" or temporarily hide statements that you want to leave in your module but do not want to execute. "Commenting out" statements that do not work (versus editing the same broken statement(s) over and over) keeps a trail of every line of code that you have written.

This process makes development, debugging, and sharing your thought processes with other developers much more productive. When the code is working as intended, extra lines that have been "commented out" are no longer needed and can be deleted.

Build Class Modules

Learning Outcome
• Build event handlers

Class modules are contained and executed within specific forms and reports. Class modules most commonly run in response to an **event**, a specific action that occurs as the result of a user action. Common events include clicking a command button, editing data, and closing a form. **CASE** ➤ *Aaron wants you to examine an existing class module and create sub procedures connected to events that occur on the form.*

STEPS

1. **Double-click the** frmEmployees form **in the Navigation Pane to open it in Form View, then click the** Branch of Service combo box list arrow **to review the choices**

   A choice in the Branch of Service combo box only makes sense if an employee was a veteran. You'll set the Visible property for the Branch of Service combo box to True if the Veteran check box is checked and False if the Veteran check box is not checked.

   TROUBLE
   If the first line of your procedure is not Private Sub chkVeteran_AfterUpdate( ), delete the stub, close the VBE, and repeat Step 2.

2. **Right-click the** Employees form tab, **click** Design View **on the shortcut menu, double-click the** edge of the Veteran check box **to open its Property Sheet, click the** Event tab **in the Property Sheet, click the** After Update property, **click the** Build button **[…], then click** Code Builder **and click** OK **if the Choose Builder dialog box opens**

   The class module for the frmEmployees form opens. Because you opened the VBE window from a specific event of a control on the form, the **stub**, the first and last lines of the sub procedure, were automatically created. The procedure's name in the first line, chkVeteran_AfterUpdate, contains the name of the control, chkVeteran, and the name of the event, AfterUpdate, that triggers this procedure. (The **Name property** of a control is on the Other tab in the control's property sheet. The **After Update property** is on the Event tab.) A sub procedure triggered by an event is often called an **event handler**.

   QUICK TIP
   Write your VBA code in lowercase. The VBE will automatically correct the case if your code is correct.

3. **Enter the statements shown in** FIGURE 13-9

   The name of the sub procedure shows that it runs on the AfterUpdate event of the chkVeteran control. (The sub runs when the Veteran check box is checked or unchecked.) The If structure contains VBA that makes the cboBranchOfService control visible or not visible based on the value of the chkVeteran control.

   QUICK TIP
   The **On Current** event of the form is triggered when you navigate through records.

4. **Save the changes and close the VBE window, click the** View button **[ ], click the** Veteran check box **for the first record several times, then navigate through several records**

   Clicking the Veteran check box triggers the procedure that responds to the After Update event. However, you also want the procedure to run every time you move from record to record.

   TROUBLE
   If the Code window appears with a yellow line, it means the code cannot be run successfully. Click the Reset button [ ] on the toolbar, then compare your VBA with FIGURE 13-10.

5. **Right-click the** Employees form tab, **click** Design View **on the shortcut menu, click the** Form Selector button **[■], click the** Event tab **in the Property Sheet, click the** On Current event property **in the Property Sheet, click the** Build button **[…], click** Code Builder **and click** OK **if the Choose Builder dialog box opens, then copy or retype the If structure from the chkVeteran_AfterUpdate sub to the Form_Current sub, as shown in** FIGURE 13-10

   By copying the If structure to a second sub procedure, you create a second event handler. Now, the cboBranchOfService combo box will be visible or not based on updating the chkVeteran check box or moving from record to record. To test the new sub procedure, switch to Form View.

6. **Save the changes and close the VBE window, click [ ] to switch to Form View, then navigate through several records to test the new procedures**

   Now, as you move from record to record, the Branch of Service combo box should be visible for those employees with the Veteran check box selected and not visible if the Veteran check box is not selected.

7. **Return to the first record for David Fox, click the** Veteran check box **(if it is not already selected), click the** Branch of Service combo box list arrow, **click** Army as shown in FIGURE 13-11, **then save and close the frmEmployees form**

FIGURE 13-9: **Creating an event handler procedure**

Three-character prefixes in sub and control names enhance the meaning of the VBA

```vba
Private Sub chkVeteran_AfterUpdate()
    If chkVeteran.Value = True Then
        cboBranchOfService.Visible = True
    Else
        cboBranchOfService.Visible = False
    End If
End Sub
```

FIGURE 13-10: **Copying the If structure to a new event handler procedure**

Copy If structure from chkVeteran_ AfterUpate sub to Form_Current sub

```vba
Private Sub chkVeteran_AfterUpdate()
    If chkVeteran.Value = True Then
        cboBranchOfService.Visible = True
    Else
        cboBranchOfService.Visible = False
    End If
End Sub

Private Sub Form_Current()
    If chkVeteran.Value = True Then
        cboBranchOfService.Visible = True
    Else
        cboBranchOfService.Visible = False
    End If
End Sub
```

FIGURE 13-11: **Branch of Service combo box is visible when Veteran box is checked**

David Fox record

Employees	
Last: Fox	Department: USA
First: David	Title: Director
Date Hired: 1/1/2011	Veteran: ☑
Assignments	Branch of Service: Army

Veteran check box is selected

Army is selected in Branch of Service combo box

Serial No	Placement Date	Manufacturer	Description	Initial Value
▶				

Modify Sub Procedures

Learning Outcomes
• Attach procedures to events
• Use IntelliSense technology

Sub procedures can be triggered on any event in the Property Sheet such as **On Got Focus** (when the control gets the focus), **After Update** (after a field is updated), or **On Dbl Click** (when the control is double-clicked). Not all items have the same set of event properties. For example, a text box control has both a Before Update and After Update event property, but neither of these events exists for a label or command button because those controls are not used to update data. **CASE** *Aaron Scout asks if there is a way to require a choice in the Branch of Service combo box if the Veteran check box is checked. You use VBA sub procedures to handle this request.*

STEPS

QUICK TIP
If you select the Always use event procedures check box in the Object Designers section of the Access Options dialog box, you bypass the Choose Builder dialog box and go directly to the VBE.

1. **Right-click the** frmEmployees form, **click** Design View **on the shortcut menu, click the** Before Update property **in the Property Sheet, click the** Build button ⸱⸱⸱ , **click** Code Builder **and click** OK **if the Choose Builder dialog box opens, then enter the code in** FIGURE 13-12 **into the Form_BeforeUpdate stub**

   Test the procedure.

2. **Close the VBE window, click the** View button 📰 **to switch to Form View, click the** Last record button ▶︎ **to navigate to the last record, click the** Veteran check box **to select it, then navigate to the previous record**

   Because the chkVeteran control is selected but the cboBranchOfService combo box is null, the MsgBox statement produces the message shown in FIGURE 13-13.

3. **Click** OK, **navigate back to the last record, then click the** Veteran check box **to uncheck it**

   The code produces the correct message, but you want the code to place the focus in the cboBranchOfService combo box to force the user to choose a branch of service when this condition occurs.

   DoCmd is a VBA object that supports many methods to run common Access commands, such as closing windows, opening forms, previewing reports, navigating records, setting focus, and setting the value of controls. As you write a VBA statement, visual aids that are part of **IntelliSense technology** help you complete it. For example, when you type the period (.) after the DoCmd object, a list of available methods appears. Watching the VBA window carefully and taking advantage of all IntelliSense clues as you complete a statement can greatly improve your accuracy and productivity in writing VBA.

TROUBLE
Be sure to type a period (.) after DoCmd.

4. **Right-click the** Employees form tab, **click** Design View, **click the** View Code button **in the Tools group, click** after the MsgBox statement, **press [Enter], then type** docmd. **(including the period)**

   Your sub procedure should look like FIGURE 13-14.

5. **Type** gotocontrol, **press [Spacebar] noting the additional IntelliSense prompt, type** "cboBranchOfService", **then press [↓] as shown in** FIGURE 13-15

   IntelliSense helps you fill out each statement, indicating the order of arguments needed for the method to execute. If IntelliSense displays more than one argument, the current argument is listed in bold. Optional arguments are listed in [square brackets]. The VBE also capitalizes the VBA it recognizes, such as DoCmd. GoToControl. Test the new procedure.

6. **Close the VBE window, click the** View button 📰 **to switch to Form View, navigate to the last record for Amanda Thomes, click the** Veteran check box, **then navigate to the previous record**

7. **Click** OK **to respond to the message box, choose** Navy **from the Branch of Service combo box, navigate to the previous record, then save and close the Employees form**

   VBA is a robust and powerful programming language. With only modest programming skills, however, you can create basic sub procedures that greatly help users work more efficiently and effectively in forms.

FIGURE 13-12: Form_BeforeUpdate sub

```
Private Sub Form_BeforeUpdate(Cancel As Integer)
    If chkVeteran = True Then
        If IsNull(cboBranchOfService.Value) Then         Form_BeforeUpdate sub
            MsgBox "Please select a branch of service"
        End If
    End If
End Sub
```

FIGURE 13-13: Message produced by MsgBox statement

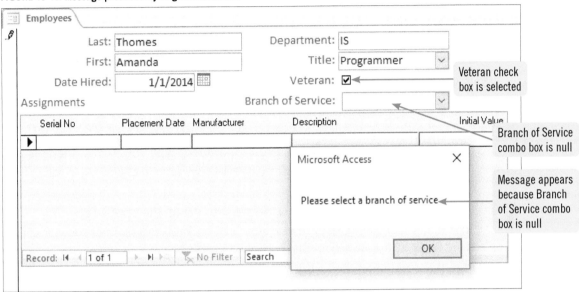

FIGURE 13-14: IntelliSense technology prompts you as you write VBA statements

```
Private Sub Form_BeforeUpdate(Cancel As Integer)
    If chkVeteran = True Then
        If IsNull(cboBranchOfService.Value) Then
            MsgBox "Please select a branch of service"
            docmd.|
        End If      AddMenu
    End If           ApplyFilter
End Sub               Beep
                      BrowseTo
Private Sub Forr      CancelEvent         IntelliSense list
    If chkVetera      ClearMacroError
        cboBranc      Close
    Else
```

FIGURE 13-15: New DoCmd statement

```
Private Sub Form_BeforeUpdate(Cancel As Integer)
    If chkVeteran = True Then
        If IsNull(cboBranchOfService.Value) Then
            MsgBox "Please select a branch of service"
            DoCmd.GoToControl "cboBranchOfService"      New DoCmd
        End If                                           statement
    End If
End Sub
```

Troubleshoot Modules

Learning Outcomes
• Set breakpoints
• Use the Immediate window

Access provides several techniques to help you **debug** (find and resolve) different types of VBA errors. A **syntax error** occurs immediately as you are writing a VBA statement that cannot be read by the Visual Basic Editor. This is the easiest type of error to identify because your code turns red when the syntax error occurs. **Compile-time errors** occur as a result of incorrectly constructed code and are detected as soon as you run your code or select the Compile option on the Debug menu. For example, you may have forgotten to insert an End If statement to finish an If structure. **Run-time errors** occur as incorrectly constructed code runs and include attempting an illegal operation such as dividing by zero or moving focus to a control that doesn't exist. When you encounter a run-time error, VBA will stop executing your procedure at the statement in which the error occurred and highlight the line with a yellow background in the Visual Basic Editor. **Logic errors** are the most difficult to troubleshoot because they occur when the code runs without obvious problems, but the procedure still doesn't produce the desired result. **CASE** *You study debugging techniques using the basFunctions module.*

STEPS

1. **Right-click the** basFunctions module **in the Navigation Pane, click** Design View, **click to the** right of the End If statement, **press [Spacebar], type** your name, **then press [↓]**

   Because the End If your name statement cannot be resolved by the Visual Basic Editor, the statement immediately turns red and an error message box appears.

2. **Click** OK **in the error message box, delete** your name, **then press [↓]**

   Another VBA debugging tool is to set a **breakpoint**, a bookmark that suspends execution of the procedure at that statement to allow you to examine what is happening.

   > **QUICK TIP**
   > Click the gray bar to the left of a statement to toggle a breakpoint on and off.

3. **Click the** If statement line, **click** Debug **on the menu bar, then click** Toggle Breakpoint

   Your screen should look like FIGURE 13-16.

4. **Click the** View Microsoft Access button 🔑 **on the Standard toolbar, then double-click the** qryEmpPricing query **in the Navigation Pane**

   When the qryEmpPricing query opens, it immediately runs the EPrice function. Because you set a breakpoint at the If statement, the statement is highlighted, indicating that the code has been suspended at that point.

   > **QUICK TIP**
   > Pointing to an argument in the Code window displays a ScreenTip with the argument's current value.

5. **Click** View **on the menu bar, click** Immediate Window, **type** ? StartValue, **then press [Enter]**

   Your screen should look like FIGURE 13-17. The **Immediate window** is an area where you can determine the value of any argument at the breakpoint. Note that the first record's InitialValue is 1200 when the records are sorted in ascending order by PlacementDate.

6. **Click** Debug **on the menu bar, click** Clear All Breakpoints, **click the** Continue button ▶ **on the Standard toolbar to execute the remainder of the function, then save and close the basFunctions module**

   The qryEmpPricing query's datasheet should be visible.

7. **Close the qryEmpPricing datasheet, close the Equipment-13.accdb database, then exit Access**

FIGURE 13-16: **Setting a breakpoint**

```
Option Compare Database
'This function is called EPrice and has two arguments
'Created by Student Name on 2/1/2019

Function EPrice(StartValue, DateValue)
    If (Now() - DateValue) > 365 Then 'Now( ) returns today's date
        EPrice = StartValue * 0.5    'If > 1 year, multiply by 50%
    Else
        EPrice = StartValue * 0.75   'If < 1 year, multiply by 75%
    End If
End Function
```

Breakpoint →

FIGURE 13-17: **Stopping execution at a breakpoint**

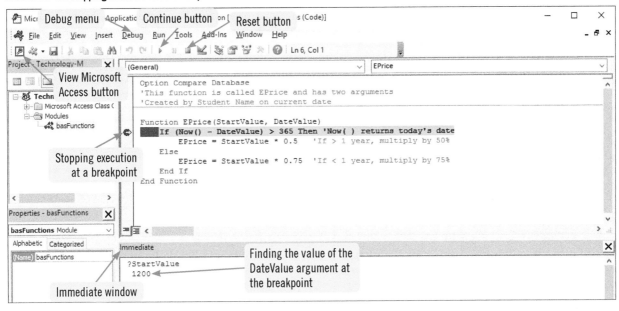

Debugging

Debugging is the process of finding and resolving bugs or problems in code. The term is generally attributed to Grace Hopper, a computer pioneer. Wikipedia (https://en.wikipedia.org/wiki/Debugging) states that while Grace was working at Harvard University in the 1940s, a moth was found in a relay component of the computer, which impeded operations. After the moth was removed, Grace remarked that they were "debugging" the system.

Practice

Concepts Review

Identify each element of the Visual Basic window shown in FIGURE 13-18.

FIGURE 13-18

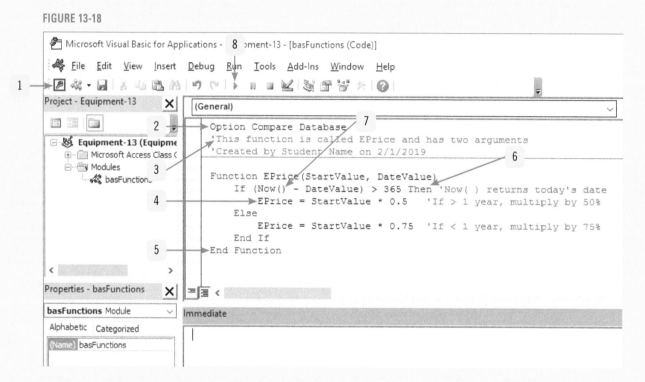

Match each term with the statement that best describes its function.

9. **Visual Basic for Applications (VBA)**

10. **Module**

11. **Debugging**

12. **If...Then...Else statement**

13. **Procedure**

14. **Class modules**

15. **Breakpoint**

16. **Arguments**

17. **Function**

a. Allows you to test a logical condition and execute commands only if the condition is true

b. The programming language used in Access modules

c. A line of code that automatically suspends execution of the procedure

d. A process to find and resolve programming errors

e. A procedure that returns a value

f. Constants, variables, or expressions passed to a procedure to further define how it should execute

g. Stored as part of the form or report object in which they are created

h. The Access object where VBA code is stored

i. A series of VBA statements that performs an operation or calculates a value

Skills Review

1. **Understand modules and VBA.**

   a. Start Access, then open the Baseball-13.accdb (not Basketball-13.accdb) database from the location where you store your Data Files. Enable content if prompted.

   b. Open the VBE window for the basFunctions module.

Skills Review (continued)

   c. Record your answers to the following questions about this module:

- What are the names of the functions?
- What are the names of the arguments for each function?
- What is the purpose of the End Function statements?
- Why are the End Function statements in blue?
- Why are some of the lines indented?

2. Compare macros and modules.

   a. If not already opened, open the VBE window for the basFunctions module.

   b. Record your answers to the following questions on a sheet of paper:

- Why was a module rather than a macro used to create these procedures?
- Why is VBA generally more difficult to create than a macro?
- Identify each of the VBA keywords or keyword phrases, and explain the purpose for each.

3. Create functions.

   a. If not already opened, open the VBE window for the basFunctions module.

   b. Create a function called **TotalBases** below the End Function statement of the Slugging function by typing the VBA statements shown in FIGURE 13-19.

FIGURE 13-19

```
Function TotalBases(Base1, Base2, Base3, Base4)
    TotalBases = Base1 + (2 * Base2) + (3 * Base3) + (4 * Base4)
End Function
```

In baseball, total bases is a popular statistic because it accounts for the power of each hit. In the TotalBases function, each hit is multiplied by the number of bases earned (1 for single, 2 for double, 3 for triple, and 4 for home run).

   c. Save the basFunctions module, then close the VBE window.

   d. Use Query Design View to create a new query using the PlayerFName and PlayerLName fields from the tblPlayers table and the AtBats field from the tblPlayerStats table.

   e. Create a calculated field named **Batting** in the next available column by carefully typing the expression as follows: **Batting: BattingAverage([1Base],[2Base],[3Base],[4Base],[AtBats])**. (*Hint*: Use the Zoom dialog box to enter long expressions.)

   f. Create a second calculated field named **Slugger** in the next available column by carefully typing the expression as follows: **Slugger: Slugging([1Base],[2Base],[3Base],[4Base],[AtBats])**. (*Hint*: Use the Zoom dialog box to enter long expressions.)

   g. Create a third calculated field named **Bases** in the next available column by carefully typing the expression: **Bases: TotalBases([1Base],[2Base],[3Base],[4Base])**. (*Hint*: Use the Zoom dialog box.)

   h. View the datasheet, change Doug Schaller to *your* first and last name, save the query as **qryStats**, then close it.

4. Use If statements.

   a. Open the VBE window for the basFunctions module, then modify the BattingAverage and Slugging functions to add the If structure shown in FIGURE 13-20. The If structure

FIGURE 13-20

```
Function BattingAverage(SingleValue, DoubleValue, TripleValue, HRValue, AtBatsValue)
    If AtBatsValue = 0 Then
        BattingAverage = 0
    Else
        BattingAverage = (SingleValue + DoubleValue + TripleValue + HRValue) / AtBatsValue
    End If
End Function

Function Slugging(Base1, Base2, Base3, Base4, AtBats)
    If AtBats = 0 Then
        Slugging = 0
    Else
        Slugging = (Base1 + (2 * Base2) + (3 * Base3) + (4 * Base4)) / AtBats
    End If
End Function
```

prevents the error caused by attempting to divide by zero. The If structure checks to see if the AtBatsValue argument is equal to 0. If so, the BattingAverage function is set to 0. Otherwise, the BattingAverage function is calculated.

Skills Review (continued)

b. Save the basFunctions module, then close the VBE window.

c. Open the qryStats datasheet, then change the AtBats field value to **0** for the first record and press [Tab] to test the If statement. The Batting and Slugger calculated fields should equal 0.

d. Close the datasheet.

5. Document procedures.

a. Open the VBE window for the basFunctions module, and add the two statements above the End Function statement for the BattingAverage and Slugging functions, as shown in FIGURE 13-21. The statements use the Format function to format the calculation as a number with three digits to the right of the decimal point. The comments help clarify the statement.

b. Add a comment at the beginning of the VBA code that identifies *your name* and today's date, as shown in FIGURE 13-21.

FIGURE 13-21

```
Option Compare Database
'Created by Your Name on <insert today's date>
Function BattingAverage(SingleValue, DoubleValue, TripleValue, HRValue, AtBatsValue)
    If AtBatsValue = 0 Then
        BattingAverage = 0
    Else
        BattingAverage = (SingleValue + DoubleValue + TripleValue + HRValue) / AtBatsValue
    End If
    'Format as a number with three digits to the right of the decimal point
    BattingAverage = Format(BattingAverage, "0.000")
End Function

Function Slugging(Base1, Base2, Base3, Base4, AtBats)
    If AtBats = 0 Then
        Slugging = 0
    Else
        Slugging = (Base1 + (2 * Base2) + (3 * Base3) + (4 * Base4)) / AtBats
    End If
    'Format as a number with three digits to the right of the decimal point
    Slugging = Format(Slugging, "0.000")
End Function
```

c. Save the changes to the basFunctions module, print the module if requested by your instructor, then close the VBE window.

d. Open the qryStats query datasheet to observe how the values in the Batting and Slugger calculated fields are formatted with three digits to the right of the decimal point.

e. Print the qryStats datasheet if requested by your instructor, then close it.

6. Build class modules.

a. Open frmPlayerEntry in Form View, then move through several records to observe the data.

b. Switch to Design View, and on the right side of the form, select the Print Current Record button.

c. Open the Property Sheet for the button, click the Event tab, click the On Click property, then click the Build button to open the class module.

d. Add a statement using the MsgBox command after the DoCmd statement to send the following message to the user: "Printout sent to printer!"

e. Add a comment to the top of the module to show *your name* and the current date. Save the module, print it if requested by your instructor, then close the VBE window.

f. Test the code by switching to Form View and clicking the Print Current Record button on the form. (This action will send the current record in this form to the default printer.)

7. Modify sub procedures.

a. Open the frmPlayerEntry form in Form View, move through a couple of records to observe the txtSalary text box (currently blank), then switch to Design View.

b. The base starting salary in this league is $45,000. You will add a command button with VBA to help enter the correct salary for each player. Use the Button button to add a command button below the txtSalary text box, then cancel the Command Button Wizard if it starts.

Skills Review (continued)

    c. Open the Property Sheet for the new command button, then change the Caption property on the Format tab to **Base Salary**. Change the Name property on the Other tab to **cmdBaseSalary**.

    d. On the Event tab of the Property Sheet, click the On Click property, click the Build button, then click Code Builder if prompted. The stub for the new cmdBaseSalary_Click sub is automatically created for you.

    e. Enter the following statement between the Sub and End Sub statements:

    txtSalary.Value = 45000

    f. Save the changes, then close the VBE window.

    g. Close the Property Sheet, then save and open the frmPlayerEntry form in Form View.

    h. Click the Base Salary command button for the first player, move to the second record, then click the Base Salary command button for the second player.

    i. Save, then close the frmPlayerEntry form.

8. Troubleshoot modules.

    a. Open the VBE window for the basFunctions module.

    b. Click anywhere in the If AtBatsValue = 0 Then statement in the BattingAverage function.

    c. Click Debug on the menu bar, then click Toggle Breakpoint to set a breakpoint at this statement.

    d. Save the changes, then close the VBE window and return to Microsoft Access.

    e. Open the qryStats query datasheet. This action attempts to use the BattingAverage function to calculate the value for the Batting field, which stops and highlights the statement in the VBE window where you set a breakpoint.

    f. Click View on the menu bar, click Immediate Window (if not already visible), delete any previous entries in the Immediate window, type **?AtBatsValue**, then press [Enter]. At this point in the execution of the VBA, the AtBatsValue should be 0, the value you entered for the first record.

    g. Type **?SingleValue**, then press [Enter]. At this point in the execution of the VBA code, the SingleValue should be 1, the value for the first record. (*Hint*: You can resize the Immediate window by dragging the top edge.)

    h. Click Debug on the menu bar, click Clear All Breakpoints, then click the Continue button on the Standard toolbar. Close the VBE window.

    i. Return to and close the qryStats query, close the Baseball-13.accdb database, then exit Access.

Independent Challenge 1

As the manager of a doctor's clinic, you have created an Access database called Insurance-13.accdb to track insurance claim reimbursements and general patient health. You want to modify an existing function within this database.

    a. Start Access, then open the Insurance-13.accdb database from the location where you store your Data Files. Enable content if prompted.

    b. Open the basBodyMassIndex module in Design View, and enter the **Option Explicit** declaration statement just below the existing Option Compare Database statement.

    c. Record your answers to the following questions on a sheet of paper:

      • What is the name of the function in the module?

      • What are the function arguments?

      • What is the purpose of the Option Explicit declaration statement?

    d. Edit the BMI function by adding a comment as the first line of code with *your name* and today's date.

    e. Edit the BMI function by adding a comment above the Function statement with the following information: **'A healthy BMI is in the range of 21-24.**

Independent Challenge 1 (continued)

f. Edit the BMI function by adding an If clause that checks to make sure the height argument is not equal to 0. The final BMI function code should look like FIGURE 13-22.

g. Save the module, print it if requested by your instructor, then close the VBE window.

h. Create a new query that includes the following fields from the tblPatients table: **PtLastName, PtFirstName, PtHeight, PtWeight**.

FIGURE 13-22

```
'Student name and current date
Option Compare Database
Option Explicit

'A healthy BMI is in the range of 21-24.
Function BMI(weight, height)
    If height = 0 Then
        BMI = 0
    Else
        BMI = (weight * 0.4536) / (height * 0.0254) ^ 2
    End If
End Function
```

i. Create a calculated field with the following field name and expression: **BodyMassIndex: BMI([PtWeight], [PtHeight])**. (*Hint*: Use the Zoom dialog box for long expressions.)

j. Save the query as **qryPatientBMI**, view the qryPatientBMI query datasheet, then test the If statement by entering **0** in the PtHeight field for the first record. Press [Tab] to move to the BodyMassIndex field, which should recalculate to 0.

k. Edit the first record to contain *your* last and first names, print the datasheet if requested by your instructor, then close the qryPatientBMI query.

l. Close the Insurance-13.accdb database, then exit Access.

Independent Challenge 2

As the manager of a doctor's clinic, you have created an Access database called Insurance-13.accdb to track insurance claim reimbursements. You want to study the existing sub procedures stored as class modules in the Claim Entry Form.

a. Start Access, then open the Insurance-13.accdb database from the location where you store your Data Files. Enable content if prompted.

b. Open frmClaimEntryForm in Form View, then switch to Design View.

c. Open the VBE window to view this class module, then record your answers to the following questions on a sheet of paper:
- What are the names of the sub procedures in this class module? (*Hint*: Be sure to scroll the window to see the complete contents.)
- What Access functions are used in the PtFirstName_AfterUpdate sub?
- How many arguments do the functions in the PtFirstName_AfterUpdate sub have?
- What do the functions in the PtFirstName_AfterUpdate sub do? (*Hint*: You may have to use the Visual Basic Help system if you are not familiar with the functions.)
- What is the purpose of the On Error command in the cmdEnterNewClaim_Click sub? (*Hint*: Use the Visual Basic Help system if you are not familiar with this command.)

d. Use the Property Sheet of the form to create an event-handler procedure based on the On Load property. Enter one statement using the Maximize method of the DoCmd object, which will maximize the form each time it is loaded.

e. Save the changes, close the VBE window and the Claim Entry Form, then open frmClaimEntryForm in Form View to test the new sub, which should automatically maximize the form in Form View.

f. Close frmClaimEntryForm, close the Insurance-13.accdb database, then exit Access.

Independent Challenge 3

As the manager of a doctor's clinic, you have created an Access database called Insurance-13.accdb to track insurance claim reimbursements that are fixed (paid at a predetermined fixed rate) or denied (not paid by the insurance company). You want to enhance the database with a class module.

a. Start Access, then open the Insurance-13.accdb database from the location where you store your Data Files. Enable content if prompted.

b. Open frmCPT in Form Design View.

c. Use the Command Button Wizard to add a command button in the Form Header section. Choose the Add New Record action from the Record Operations category.

d. Accept **Add Record** as the text on the button, then name the button **cmdAddRecord**.

e. Use the Command Button Wizard to add a command button in the Form Header section to the right of the existing Add Record button. (*Hint*: Move and resize controls as necessary to put two command buttons in the Form Header section.)

f. Choose the Delete Record action from the Record Operations category.

g. Accept **Delete Record** as the text on the button, and name the button **cmdDeleteRecord**.

h. Size the two buttons to be the same height and width, and align their top edges. Move them as needed so that they do not overlap.

i. Save and view frmCPT in Form View, then click the Add Record command button.

j. Add a new record (it will be record number 65) with a CPTCode value of **999** and an RBRVS value of **1.5**.

k. To make sure that the Delete Record button works, click the record selector for the new record you just entered, click the Delete Record command button, then click Yes to confirm the deletion. Close frmCPT.

l. In Design View of the frmCPT form, open the Property Sheet for the Delete Record command button, click the Event tab, then click the Build button beside [Embedded Macro]. The Command Button Wizard created the embedded macro that deletes the current record. You can convert macro objects to VBA code to learn more about VBA. To convert an embedded macro to VBA, you must first copy and paste the embedded macro actions to a new macro object. (*Hint*: You can widen the property sheet by dragging the left edge.)

m. Press [Ctrl][A] to select all macro actions, then press [Ctrl][C] to copy all macro actions to the Clipboard.

n. Close the macro window, then save and close frmCPT.

o. On the Create tab, open Macro Design View, then press [Ctrl][V] to paste the macro actions to the window.

p. Click the Convert Macros to Visual Basic button, click Yes when prompted to save the macro, click Convert, then click OK when a dialog box indicates that the conversion is finished.

q. Save and close all open windows with default names. Open the Converted Macro-Macro1 VBE window. Add a comment as the first line of code in the Code window with *your* name and the current date, save the module, print it if requested by your instructor, then close the VBE window.

r. Close the Insurance-13.accdb database, then exit Access.

Independent Challenge 4: Explore

(*Note*: To complete this Independent Challenge, make sure you are connected to the Internet.)

Learning a programming language is sometimes compared with learning a foreign language. Imagine how it would feel to learn a new programming language if English wasn't your primary language or if you had another type of accessibility challenge. Advances in technology are helping to break down many barriers to those with vision, hearing, mobility, cognitive, and language issues. In this challenge, you explore the Microsoft website for resources to address these issues.

a. Go to www.microsoft.com/enable, then print that page. Explore the website.

b. After exploring the website for products, demos, tutorials, guides, and articles, describe five types of accessibility solutions that might make a positive impact on someone. Identify both the problem and the solution.

c. Use bold headings for the five types of accessibility solutions to make those sections of your paper easy to find and read. Be sure to spell and grammar check your paper.

Visual Workshop

As the manager of a college basketball team, you are helping the coach build meaningful statistics to compare the relative value of the players in each game. The coach has stated that one offensive rebound is worth as much to the team as two defensive rebounds, and she would like you to use this rule to develop a "rebounding impact statistic" for each game. Open the Basketball-13.accdb (not Baseball-13.accdb) database, enable content if prompted, and use FIGURE 13-23 to develop a new function in a standard module. Name the new function **ReboundImpact** in a new module called **basFunctions** to calculate this statistic. Include *your* name and the current date as a comment in the first row of the function.

FIGURE 13-23

```
Function ReboundImpact(OffenseVal As Integer, DefenseVal As Integer) As Integer
    ReboundImpact = (OffenseVal * 2) + DefenseVal
End Function
```

Create a query called **qryRebounds** with the fields shown in FIGURE 13-24. Note that the records are sorted in ascending order on GameNo and LastName. The **ReboundPower** field is created using the following expression: **ReboundImpact([Reb-O],[Reb-D])**. Enter *your* first and last name instead of Kristen Czyenski, and print the datasheet if requested by your instructor.

FIGURE 13-24

GameN ▾	FirstName ▾	LastName ▾	Reb-O ▾	Reb-D ▾	ReboundPower ▾
1	Student First	Student Last	2	2	6
1	Denise	Franco	2	3	7
1	Theresa	Grant	1	3	5
1	Megan	Hile	1	2	4
1	Amy	Hodel	5	3	13
1	Ellyse	Howard	1	2	4
1	Jamie	Johnson	0	1	1
1	Lindsey	Swift	1	2	4
1	Morgan	Tyler	4	6	14
2	Student First	Student Last	3	2	8
2	Denise	Franco	5	3	13
2	Sydney	Freesen	2	3	7
2	Theresa	Grant	3	3	9
2	Megan	Hile	1	5	7
2	Amy	Hodel	1	4	6
2	Ellyse	Howard	3	3	9
2	Sandy	Robins	0	1	1
2	Lindsey	Swift	2	2	6
2	Morgan	Tyler	3	6	12
2	Abbey	Walker	2	4	8

Creating a Presentation in PowerPoint 2016

CASE Reason2Go (R2G) is a voluntourism company that provides customers a unique experience of traveling to different countries and performing volunteer work. As a marketing representative for R2G, one of your responsibilities is to develop materials that describe the company vision, philosophy, and services. You have been asked to create a presentation using PowerPoint 2016 that describes projects R2G is currently developing in Kenya Africa.

Module Objectives

After completing this module, you will be able to:

- Define presentation software
- Plan an effective presentation
- Examine the PowerPoint window
- Enter slide text

- Add a new slide
- Apply a design theme
- Compare presentation views
- Print a PowerPoint presentation

Files You Will Need

No files needed.

Define Presentation Software

Presentation software (also called presentation graphics software) is a computer program you use to organize and present information to others. Presentations are typically in the form of a slide show. Whether you are explaining a new product or moderating a meeting, presentation software can help you effectively communicate your ideas. You can use PowerPoint to create informational slides that you print or display on a monitor, share in real time on the web, or save as a video for others to watch. **CASE** *You need to start working on your Kenya presentation. Because you are only somewhat familiar with PowerPoint, you get to work exploring its capabilities.* FIGURE 1-1 *shows how a presentation looks printed as handouts.* FIGURE 1-2 *shows how the same presentation might look shared on the Internet with others.*

DETAILS

You can easily complete the following tasks using PowerPoint:

*   **Enter and edit text easily**
    Text editing and formatting commands in PowerPoint are organized by the task you are performing at the time, so you can enter, edit, and format text information simply and efficiently to produce the best results in the least amount of time.

*   **Change the appearance of information**
    PowerPoint has many effects that can transform the way text, graphics, and slides appear. By exploring some of these capabilities, you discover how easy it is to change the appearance of your presentation.

*   **Organize and arrange information**
    Once you start using PowerPoint, you won't have to spend much time making sure your information is correct and in the right order. With PowerPoint, you can quickly and easily rearrange and modify text, graphics, and slides in your presentation.

*   **Include information from other sources**
    Often, when you create presentations, you use information from a variety of sources. With PowerPoint, you can import text, photographs, videos, numerical data, and other information from files created in programs such as Adobe Photoshop, Microsoft Word, Microsoft Excel, and Microsoft Access. You can also import information from other PowerPoint presentations as well as graphic images from a variety of sources such as the Internet, other computers, a digital camera, or other graphics programs. Always be sure you have permission to use any work that you did not create yourself.

*   **Present information in a variety of ways**
    With PowerPoint, you can present information using a variety of methods. For example, you can print handout pages or an outline of your presentation for audience members. You can display your presentation as an on-screen slide show using your computer, or if you are presenting to a large group, you can use a video projector and a large screen. If you want to reach an even wider audience, you can broadcast the presentation or upload it as a video to the Internet so people anywhere in the world can use a web browser to view your presentation.

*   **Collaborate with others on a presentation**
    PowerPoint makes it easy to collaborate or share a presentation with colleagues and coworkers using the Internet. You can use your email program to send a presentation as an attachment to a colleague for feedback. If you have a number of people that need to work together on a presentation, you can save the presentation to a shared workspace such as a network drive or OneDrive so authorized users in your group with an Internet connection can access the presentation.

FIGURE 1-1: PowerPoint handout

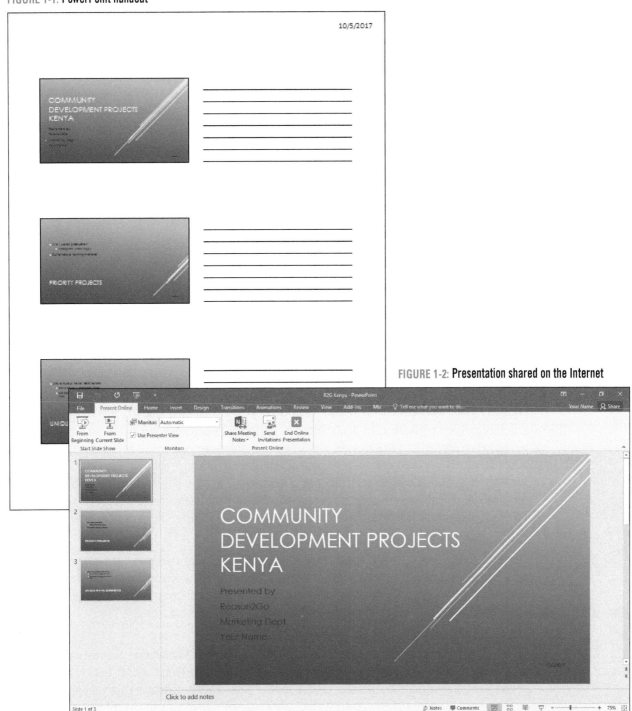

FIGURE 1-2: Presentation shared on the Internet

Using PowerPoint on a touch screen

You can use PowerPoint 2016 on a Windows computer with a touch-enabled monitor or any other compatible touch screen, such as a tablet computer. Using your fingers, you can use typical touch gestures to create, modify, and navigate presentations. To enable touch mode capabilities in PowerPoint, you need to add the Touch Mode button 👆 to the Quick Access toolbar. Click the Customize Quick Access Toolbar button, click Touch/Mouse Mode, click the 👆 on the Quick Access toolbar then click Touch. In Touch mode, additional space is added around all of the buttons and icons in the Ribbon and the status bar to make them easier to touch. Common gestures that you can use in PowerPoint include double-tapping text to edit it and tapping a slide then dragging it to rearrange it in the presentation.

Plan an Effective Presentation

Learning
Outcomes
• Determine
presentation
content and
design

Before you create a presentation, you need to have a general idea of the information you want to communicate. PowerPoint is a powerful and flexible program that gives you the ability to start a presentation simply by entering the text of your message. If you have a specific design in mind that you want to use, you can start the presentation by working on the design. In most cases you'll probably enter the text of your presentation into PowerPoint first and then tailor the design to the message and audience. When preparing your presentation, you need to keep in mind not only who you are giving it to, but also how you are presenting it. For example, if you are giving a presentation using a projector, you need to know what other equipment you will need, such as a sound system and a projector. **CASE** *Use the planning guidelines below to help plan an effective presentation.* FIGURE 1-3 *illustrates a storyboard for a well-planned presentation.*

DETAILS

In planning a presentation, it is important to:

• **Determine and outline the message you want to communicate**

The more time you take developing the message and outline of your presentation, the better your presentation will be in the end. A presentation with a clear message that reads like a story and is illustrated with appropriate visual aids will have the greatest impact on your audience. Start the presentation by providing a general description of the Kenyan projects currently being developed. See FIGURE 1-3.

• **Identify your audience and where and how you are giving the presentation**

Audience and delivery location are major factors in the type of presentation you create. For example, a presentation you develop for a staff meeting that is held in a conference room would not necessarily need to be as sophisticated or detailed as a presentation that you develop for a large audience held in an auditorium. Room lighting, natural light, screen position, and room layout all affect how the audience responds to your presentation. You might also broadcast your presentation over the Internet to several people who view the presentation on their computers in real time. This presentation will be broadcast over the Internet.

• **Determine the type of output**

Output choices for a presentation include black-and-white or color handouts for audience members, on-screen slide show, a video, or an online broadcast. Consider the time demands and computer equipment availability as you decide which output types to produce. Because this presentation will be broadcast over the Internet, the default output settings work just fine.

• **Determine the design**

Visual appeal, graphics, and presentation design work together to communicate your message. You can choose one of the professionally designed themes that come with PowerPoint, modify one of these themes, or create one of your own. You decide to choose one of PowerPoint's design themes for your presentation.

FIGURE 1-3: **Storyboard of the presentation**

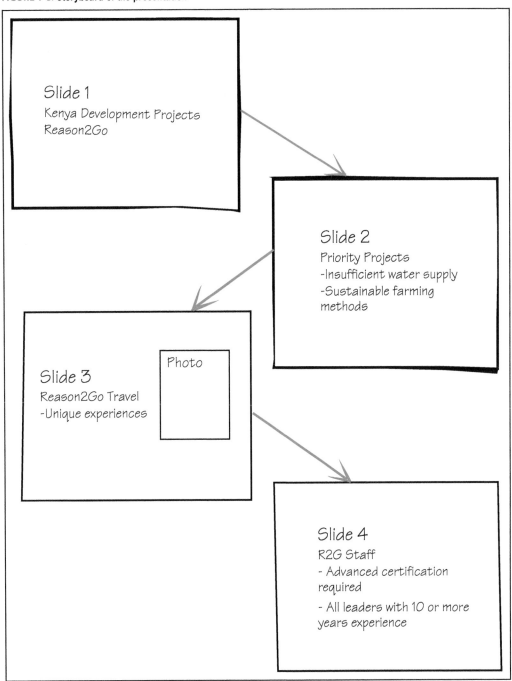

Slide 1
Kenya Development Projects
Reason2Go

Slide 2
Priority Projects
-Insufficient water supply
-Sustainable farming
methods

Slide 3
Reason2Go Travel
-Unique experiences

Photo

Slide 4
R2G Staff
- Advanced certification
required
- All leaders with 10 or more
years experience

Understanding copyright

Intellectual property is any idea or creation of the human mind. Copyright law is a type of intellectual property law that protects works of authorship, including books, webpages, computer games, music, artwork, and photographs. Copyright protects the expression of an idea, but not the underlying facts or concepts. In other words, the general subject matter is not protected, but how you express it is, such as when several people photograph the same sunset. Copyright attaches to any original work of authorship as soon as it is created, you do not have to register it with the Copyright Office or display the copyright symbol, ©. Fair use is an exception to copyright and permits the public to use copyrighted material for certain purposes without obtaining prior consent from the owner. Determining whether fair use applies to a work depends on its purpose, the nature of the work, how much of the work you want to copy, and the effect on the work's value. Unauthorized use of protected work (such as downloading a photo or a song from the web) is known as copyright infringement and can lead to legal action.

Examine the PowerPoint Window

When you first start PowerPoint, you have the ability to choose what kind of presentation you want to use to start—a blank one, or one with a preformatted design. You can also open and work on an existing presentation. PowerPoint has different **views** that allow you to see your presentation in different forms. By default, the PowerPoint window opens in **Normal view**, which is the primary view that you use to write, edit, and design your presentation. Normal view is divided into areas called **panes**: the pane on the left, called the **Slides tab**, displays the slides of your presentation as small images, called **slide thumbnails**. The large pane is the Slide pane where you do most of your work on the slide. **CASE** The PowerPoint window and the specific parts of Normal view are described below.

STEPS

1. **Start** PowerPoint 2016

   PowerPoint starts and the PowerPoint start screen opens, as shown in FIGURE 1-4.

2. **Click the** Blank Presentation slide thumbnail

   The PowerPoint window opens in Normal view, as shown in FIGURE 1-5.

DETAILS

TROUBLE
If you are unsure
how to start
PowerPoint, refer to
the "Getting Started
with Office 2016"
Module in this book
for specific instruc-
tions on how to start
the application.

Using Figure 1-5 as a guide, examine the elements of the PowerPoint window, then find and compare the elements described below:

• The **Ribbon** is a wide band spanning the top of the PowerPoint window that organizes all of PowerPoint's primary commands. Each set of primary commands is identified by a **tab**; for example, the Home tab is selected by default, as shown in FIGURE 1-5. Commands are further arranged into **groups** on the Ribbon based on their function. So, for example, text formatting commands such as Bold, Underline, and Italic are located on the Home tab, in the Font group.

• The **Slides tab** is to the left. You can navigate through the slides in your presentation by clicking the slide thumbnails. You can also add, delete, or rearrange slides using this pane.

• The **Slide pane** displays the current slide in your presentation.

• The **Quick Access toolbar** provides access to common commands such as Save, Undo, Redo, and Start From Beginning. The Quick Access toolbar is always visible no matter which Ribbon tab you select. Click the Customize Quick Access Toolbar button to add or remove buttons.

• The **View Shortcuts** buttons on the status bar allow you to switch quickly between PowerPoint views.

• The **Notes button** on the status bar opens the Notes pane and is used to enter text that references a slide's content. You can print these notes and refer to them when you make a presentation or use them as audience handouts. The Notes pane is not visible in Slide Show view.

• The **Comments button** on the status bar opens the Comments pane. In the Comments pane you can create, edit, select, and delete comments.

• The **status bar**, located at the bottom of the PowerPoint window, shows messages about what you are doing and seeing in PowerPoint, including which slide you are viewing and the total number of slides. In addition, the status bar displays the Zoom slider controls, the Fit slide to current window button ⊞, and other functionality information.

• The **Zoom slider** on the lower-right corner of the status bar is used to zoom the slide in and out.

FIGURE 1-4: PowerPoint start screen

Recent presentations that have been opened

PowerPoint themes and templates

FIGURE 1-5: PowerPoint window in Normal view

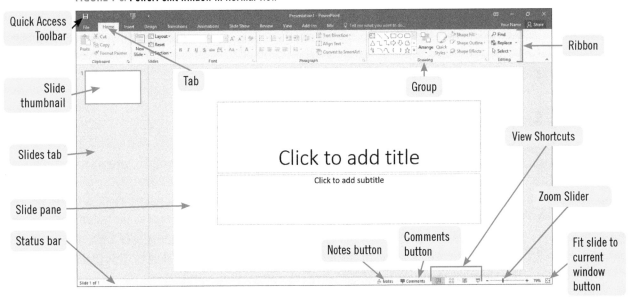

Quick Access Toolbar

Slide thumbnail

Tab

Group

Ribbon

View Shortcuts

Slides tab

Zoom Slider

Slide pane

Status bar

Notes button

Comments button

Fit slide to current window button

Viewing your presentation in gray scale or black and white

Viewing your presentation in gray scale (using shades of gray) or pure black and white is very useful when you are printing a presentation on a black-and-white printer and you want to make sure your presentation prints correctly. To see how your color presentation looks in gray scale or black and white, click the View tab, then click either the Grayscale or Black and White button in the Color/Grayscale group. Depending on which button you select, the Grayscale or the Black and White tab appears, and the Ribbon displays different settings that you can customize. If you don't like the way an individual object looks in black and white or gray scale, you can change its color. Click the object while still in Grayscale or Black and White view, then choose an option in the Change Selected Object group on the Ribbon.

Enter Slide Text

Learning Outcomes
- Enter slide text
- Change slide text

When you start a blank PowerPoint presentation, an empty title slide appears in Normal view. The title slide has two **text placeholders**—boxes with dotted borders—where you enter text. The top text placeholder on the title slide is the **title placeholder**, labeled "Click to add title". The bottom text placeholder on the title slide is the **subtitle text placeholder**, labeled "Click to add subtitle". To enter text in a placeholder, click the placeholder and then type your text. After you enter text in a placeholder, the placeholder becomes a text object. An **object** is any item on a slide that can be modified. Objects are the building blocks that make up a presentation slide. **CASE** ▶ *Begin working on your presentation by entering text on the title slide.*

STEPS

1. **Move the pointer ⬉ over the title placeholder labeled** Click to add title **in the Slide pane**
   The pointer changes to Ⅰ when you move the pointer over the placeholder. In PowerPoint, the pointer often changes shape, depending on the task you are trying to accomplish.

2. **Click the** title placeholder **in the Slide pane**
   The **insertion point**, a blinking vertical line, indicates where your text appears when you type in the placeholder. A **selection box** with a dashed line border and **sizing handles** appears around the placeholder, indicating that it is selected and ready to accept text. When a placeholder or object is selected, you can change its shape or size by dragging one of the sizing handles. See FIGURE 1-6.

3. **Type** Community Development Projects Kenya
   PowerPoint wraps the text to a second line and then center-aligns the title text within the title placeholder, which is now a text object. Notice the text also appears on the slide thumbnail on the Slides tab.

4. **Click the** subtitle text placeholder **in the Slide pane**
   The subtitle text placeholder is ready to accept text.

5. **Type** Presented by, **then press** [Enter]
   The insertion point moves to the next line in the text object.

6. **Type** Community Health Education, **press** [Enter], **type** Reason2Go, **press** [Enter], **type** Marketing Dept., **press** [Enter], **then type** your name
   Notice the AutoFit Options button ⊞ appears near the text object. The AutoFit Options button on your screen indicates that PowerPoint has automatically decreased the font size of all the text in the text object so it fits inside the text object.

7. **Click the** AutoFit Options button ⊞, **then click** Stop Fitting Text to This Placeholder **on the shortcut menu**
   The text in the text object changes back to its original size and no longer fits inside the text object.

8. **In the subtitle text object, position** Ⅰ **to the right of** Education, **drag left to select the entire line of text, press** [Backspace], **then click outside the text object in a blank area of the slide**
   The Community Health Education line of text is deleted and the AutoFit Options button menu closes, as shown in FIGURE 1-7. Clicking a blank area of the slide deselects all selected objects on the slide.

9. **Click the** Save button 🖫 **on the Quick Access toolbar to open Backstage view, then save the presentation as** PPT 1-R2G **in the location where you store your Data Files**
   In Backstage view, you have the option of saving your presentation to your computer or OneDrive. Notice that PowerPoint automatically entered the title of the presentation as the filename in the Save As dialog box.

FIGURE 1-6: **Title text placeholder selected**

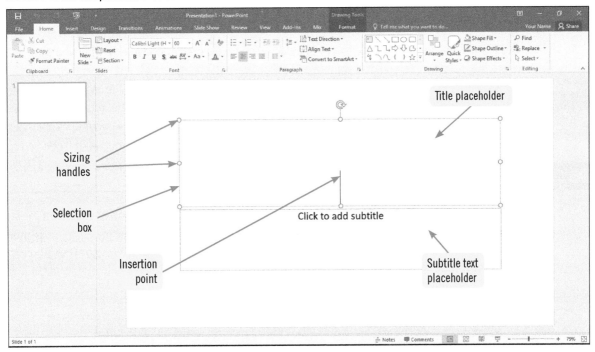

FIGURE 1-7: **Text on title slide**

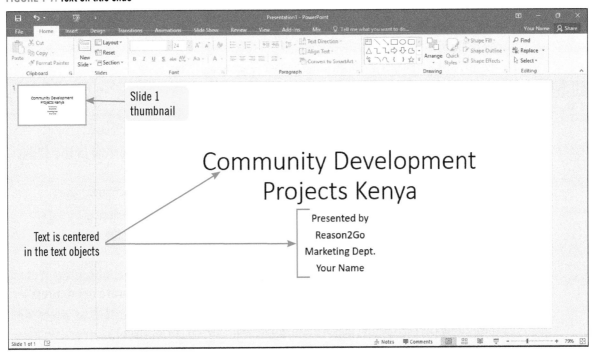

Inking a slide

In Slide View, you can add freehand pen and highlighter marks, also known as **inking**, to the slides of your presentation to emphasize information. To begin inking, go to the slide you want mark up, click the Review tab, then click the Start Inking button in the Ink group. The Pens tab appears on the Ribbon and the Pen tool appears on the slide ready for you to draw using your mouse. To customize your pen, select a different pen color, style, or thickness from options in the Pens group. Click the Highlighter button in the Write group to insert highlighter strokes on your slide. To erase inking on the slide, click the Eraser button in the Write group.

Add a New Slide

Learning Outcomes
- Add a new slide
- Indent text levels
- Modify slide layout

Usually when you add a new slide to a presentation, you have a pretty good idea of what you want the slide to look like. For example, you may want to add a slide that has a title over bulleted text and a picture. To help you add a slide like this quickly and easily, PowerPoint provides many standard slide layouts. A **slide layout** contains text and object placeholders that are arranged in a specific way on the slide. You have already worked with the Title Slide layout in the previous lesson. In the event that a standard slide layout does not meet your needs, you can modify an existing slide layout or create a new, custom slide layout. **CASE** *To continue developing the presentation, you create a slide that explains the needs in Kenya.*

STEPS

1. **Click the** New Slide button **in the Slides group on the Home tab on the Ribbon**

   A new blank slide (now the current slide) appears as the second slide in your presentation, as shown in FIGURE 1-8. The new slide contains a title placeholder and a content placeholder. A **content placeholder** can be used to insert text or objects such as tables, charts, videos, or pictures. Notice the status bar indicates Slide 2 of 2 and the Slides tab now contains two slide thumbnails.

2. **Type** Priority Projects, **then click the** bottom content placeholder

   The text you typed appears in the title placeholder, and the insertion point is now at the top of the bottom content placeholder.

3. **Type** Well water production, **then press** [Enter]

   The insertion point appears directly below the text when you press [Enter], and a new first-level bullet automatically appears.

4. **Press** [Tab]

   The new first-level bullet is indented and becomes a second-level bullet.

QUICK TIP
You can also press [Shift][Tab] to decrease the indent level.

5. **Type** Inadequate water supply, **press** [Enter], **then click the** Decrease List Level button ◧ **in the Paragraph group**

   The Decrease List Level button changes the second-level bullet into a first-level bullet.

6. **Type** Sustainable farming methods, **then click the** New Slide list arrow **in the Slides group**

   The Office Theme layout gallery opens. Each slide layout is identified by a descriptive name.

7. **Click the** Two Content slide layout, **then type** Unique Travel Experience

   A new slide with a title placeholder and two content placeholders appears as the third slide. The text you typed is the title text for the slide.

8. **Click the left content placeholder, type** Adventurous travel destinations, **press** [Enter], **click the** Increase List Level button ◨, **type** Serve others in desperate need, **press** [Enter], **then type** Satisfaction of helping your fellow man

   The Increase List Level button moves the insertion point one level to the right.

9. **Click a blank area of the slide, then click the** Save button 🖫 **on the Quick Access toolbar**

   The Save button saves all of the changes to the file. Compare your screen with FIGURE 1-9.

FIGURE 1-8: **New blank slide in Normal view**

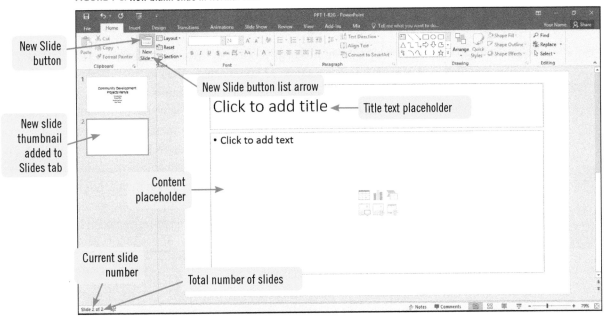

New Slide button

New Slide button list arrow

New slide thumbnail added to Slides tab

Title text placeholder

Content placeholder

Current slide number

Total number of slides

FIGURE 1-9: **New slide with Two Content slide layout**

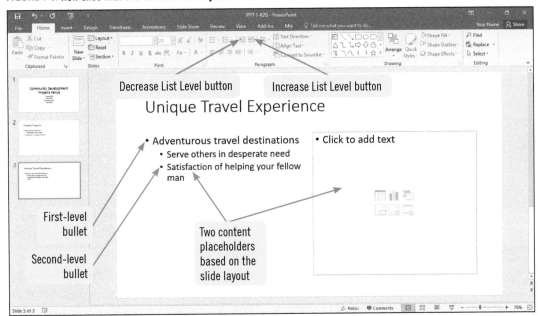

Decrease List Level button

Increase List Level button

First-level bullet

Second-level bullet

Two content placeholders based on the slide layout

Entering and printing notes

You can add notes to your slides when there are certain facts you want to remember during a presentation or when there is additional information you want to hand out to your audience. Notes do not appear on the slides when you run a slide show. Use the Notes pane in Normal view or Notes Page view to enter notes for your slides. To open or close the Notes pane, click the Notes button on the status bar. To enter text notes on a slide, click in the Notes pane, then type. If you want to insert graphics as notes, you must use Notes Page view. To open Notes Page view, click the View tab on the Ribbon, then click the Notes Page button in the Presentation Views group. You can print your notes by clicking the File tab on the Ribbon to open Backstage view. Click Print, click the Full Page Slides list arrow in the Settings group (this button retains the last setting for what was printed previously so it might differ) to open the gallery, and then click Notes Pages. Once you verify your print settings, click the Print button. If you don't enter any notes in the Notes pane, and print the notes pages, the slides print as large thumbnails with blank space below the thumbnails to hand write notes.

Apply a Design Theme

PowerPoint provides many design themes to help you quickly create a professional and contemporary looking presentation. A **theme** includes a set of 12 coordinated colors for text, fill, line, and shadow, called **theme colors**; a set of fonts for titles and other text, called **theme fonts**; and a set of effects for lines and fills, called **theme effects** to create a cohesive look. Each theme has at least four custom coordinated variants that provides you with additional color options. In most cases, you would apply one theme to an entire presentation; you can, however, apply multiple themes to the same presentation. You can use a design theme as is, or you can alter individual elements of the theme as needed. Unless you need to use a specific design theme, such as a company theme or product design theme, it is faster and easier to use one of the themes supplied with PowerPoint. If you design a custom theme, you can save it to use in the future. **CASE** *You decide to change the default design theme in the presentation to a new one.*

STEPS

1. **Click the** Slide 1 thumbnail **on the Slides tab**

   Slide 1, the title slide, appears in the Slide pane.

2. **Click the** Design tab **on the Ribbon, then point to the** Integral theme **in the Themes group, as shown in** FIGURE 1-10

   The Design tab appears, and a Live Preview of the Integral theme is displayed on the selected slide. A **Live Preview** allows you to see how your changes affect the slides before actually making the change. The Live Preview lasts about 1 minute, and then your slide reverts back to its original state. The first (far left) theme thumbnail identifies the current theme applied to the presentation, in this case, the default design theme called the Office Theme. The number of themes you can see in the Themes group depends on your monitor resolution and screen size.

3. **Slowly move your pointer** 🔖 **over the other design themes, then click the** Themes group down scroll arrow

   A Live Preview of the theme appears on the slide each time you pass your pointer over the theme thumbnails, and a ScreenTip identifies the theme names.

4. **Move** 🔖 **over the** design themes, **then click the** Wisp theme

   The Wisp design theme is applied to all the slides in the presentation. Notice the new slide background color, graphic elements, fonts, and text color. You decide this theme isn't right for this presentation.

5. **Click the** More button 🔽 **in the Themes group**

   The Themes gallery window opens. At the top of the gallery window in the This Presentation section is the current theme applied to the presentation. Notice that just the Wisp theme is listed here because when you changed the theme in the last step, you replaced the default theme with the Wisp theme. The Office section identifies all of the standard themes that come with PowerPoint.

6. **Right-click the** Slice theme **in the Office section, then click** Apply to Selected Slides

   The Slice theme is applied only to Slide 1. You like the Slice theme better, and decide to apply it to all slides.

7. **Right-click the** Slice theme **in the Themes group, then click** Apply to All Slides

   The Slice theme is applied to all three slides. Preview the next slides in the presentation to see how it looks.

8. **Click the** Next Slide button ⬇ **at the bottom of the vertical scroll bar**

   Compare your screen to FIGURE 1-11.

9. **Click the** Previous Slide button ⬆ **at the bottom of the vertical scroll bar, then save your changes**

FIGURE 1-10: Slide showing a different design theme

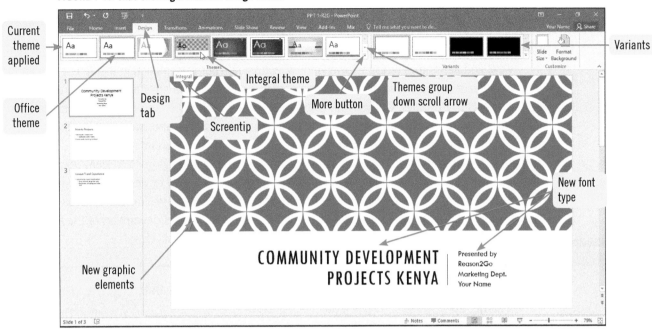

FIGURE 1-11: Presentation with Slice theme applied

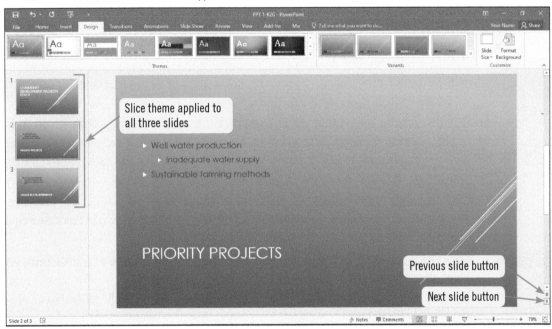

Customizing themes

You are not limited to using the standard themes PowerPoint provides; you can also modify a theme to create your own custom theme. For example, you might want to incorporate your school's or company's colors on the slide background of the presentation or be able to type using fonts your company uses for brand recognition. To change an existing theme, click the View tab on the Ribbon, then click one of the Master buttons in the Master Views group. Click the Theme Colors button, the Theme Fonts button, or the Theme Effects button in the Background group to make changes to the theme, save this new theme for future use by clicking the Themes button in the Edit Themes group, then click Save Current Theme. You also have the ability to create a new font theme or color theme from scratch by clicking the Theme Fonts button or the Theme Colors button and then clicking Customize Fonts or Customize Colors. You work in the Create New Theme Fonts or Create New Theme Colors dialog box to define the custom theme fonts or colors.

Compare Presentation Views

PowerPoint has six primary views: Normal view, Outline view, Slide Sorter view, Notes Page view, Slide Show view, and Reading view. Each PowerPoint view displays your presentation in a different way and is used for different purposes. Normal view is the primary editing view where you add text, graphics, and other elements to the slides. Outline view is the view you use to focus on the text of your presentation. Slide Sorter view is primarily used to rearrange slides; however, you can also add slide effects and design themes in this view. You use Notes Page view to type notes that are important for each slide. Slide Show view displays your presentation over the whole computer screen and is designed to show your presentation to an audience. Similar to Slide Show view, Reading view is designed to view your presentation on a computer screen. To move easily among the PowerPoint views, use the View Shortcuts buttons located on the status bar and the View tab on the Ribbon. TABLE 1-1 provides a brief description of the PowerPoint views. **CASE** ▶ *Examine each of the PowerPoint views, starting with Normal view.*

STEPS

1. **Click the View tab on the Ribbon, then click the Outline View button in the Presentation Views group**

   The presentation text is in the Outline pane on the left side of the window, as shown in FIGURE 1-12. Notice the status bar identifies the number of the slide you are viewing and the total number of slides in the presentation.

2. **Click the small slide icon ⬜ next to Slide 2 in the Outline pane, then click the Slide Sorter button 🔠 on the status bar**

   Slide Sorter View opens to display a thumbnail of each slide in the presentation in the window. You can examine the flow of your slides and drag any slide or group of slides to rearrange the order of the slides in the presentation.

3. **Double-click the Slide 1 thumbnail, then click the Reading View button 📖 on the status bar**

   The first slide fills the screen, as shown in FIGURE 1-13. Use Reading view to review your presentation or to show your presentation to someone directly on your computer. The status bar controls at the bottom of the window make it easy to move between slides in this view.

4. **Click the Slide Show button 🖵 on the status bar**

   The first slide fills the entire screen now without the title bar and status bar. In this view, you can practice running through your slides as they would appear in a slide show.

5. **Click the left mouse button to advance through the slides one at a time until you see a black slide, then click once more to return to Outline view**

   The black slide at the end of the slide show indicates the slide show is finished. At the end of a slide show, you return to the slide and PowerPoint view you were in before you ran the slide show, in this case, Slide 1 in Outline view.

6. **Click the Notes Page button in the Presentation Views group**

   Notes Page view appears, showing a reduced image of the current slide above a large text placeholder. You can enter text in this placeholder and then print the notes page for your own use.

7. **Click the Normal button in the Presentation Views group, then click the Home tab on the Ribbon**

FIGURE 1-12: **Outline view**

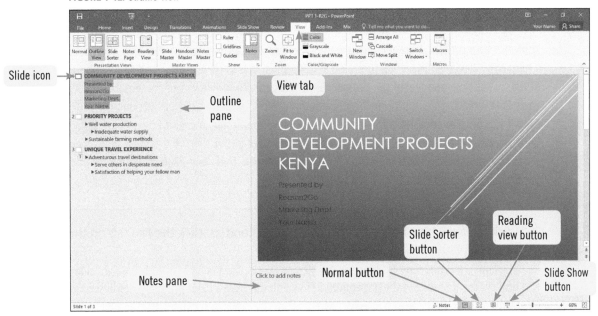

FIGURE 1-13: **Reading view**

TABLE 1-1: **PowerPoint views**

view name	button	button name	displays
Normal	▣	Normal	The Slide pane and the Slides tab at the same time
Outline View	(no View Shortcuts button)		An outline of the presentation and the Slide pane at the same time
Slide Sorter	▦	Slide Sorter	Thumbnails of all slides
Slide Show	▭	Slide Show	Your presentation on the whole computer screen
Reading View	▥	Reading View	Your presentation in a large window on your computer screen
Notes Page	(no View Shortcuts button)		A reduced image of the current slide above a large text box

Print a PowerPoint Presentation

You print your presentation when you want to review your work or when you have completed it and want a hard copy. Reviewing your presentation at different stages of development gives you a better perspective of the overall flow and feel of the presentation. You can also preview your presentation to see exactly how each slide looks before you print the presentation. When you are finished working on your presentation, even if it is not yet complete, you can close the presentation file and exit PowerPoint. **CASE** *You are done working on the Kenya presentation for now. You save and preview the presentation, then you print the slides and notes pages of the presentation so you can review them later. Before leaving for the day, you close the file and exit PowerPoint.*

STEPS

1. **Click the Save button 🖫 on the Quick Access toolbar, click the File tab on the Ribbon, then click Print**

   The Print window opens, as shown in FIGURE 1-14. Notice the preview pane on the right side of the window displays the first slide of the presentation. If you do not have a color printer, you will see a grayscale image of the slide.

2. **Click the Next Page button ▶ at the bottom of the Preview pane, then click ▶ again**

   Each slide in the presentation appears in the preview pane.

3. **Click the Print button**

   Each slide in the presentation prints.

4. **Click the File tab on the Ribbon, click Print, then click the Full Page Slides button in the Settings group**

   The Print Layout gallery opens. In this gallery you can specify what you want to print (slides, handouts, notes pages, or outline), as well as other print options. To save paper when you are reviewing your slides, you can print in handout format, which lets you print up to nine slides per page. The options you choose in the Print window remain there until you change them or close the presentation.

5. **Click 3 Slides, click the Color button in the Settings group, then click Pure Black and White**

   PowerPoint removes the color and displays the slides as thumbnails next to blank lines, as shown in FIGURE 1-15. Using the Handouts with three slides per page printing option is a great way to print your presentation when you want to provide a way for audience members to take notes. Printing pure black-and-white prints without any gray tones can save printer toner.

6. **Click the Print button**

   The presentation prints one page showing all the slides of the presentation as thumbnails next to blank lines.

7. **Click the File tab on the Ribbon, then click Close**

   If you have made changes to your presentation, a Microsoft PowerPoint alert box opens asking you if you want to save changes you have made to your presentation file.

8. **Click Save, if necessary, to close the alert box**

   Your presentation closes.

9. **Click the Close button ☒ in the Title bar**

   The PowerPoint program closes, and you return to the Windows desktop.

FIGURE 1-14: Print window

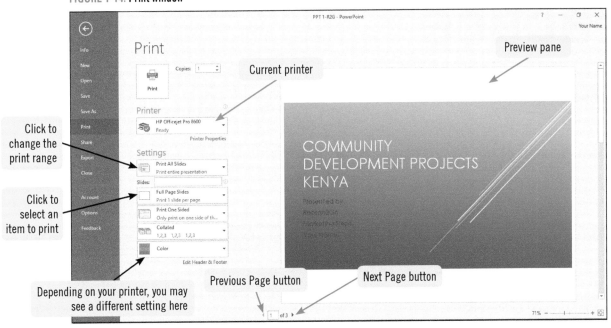

FIGURE 1-15: Print window with changed settings

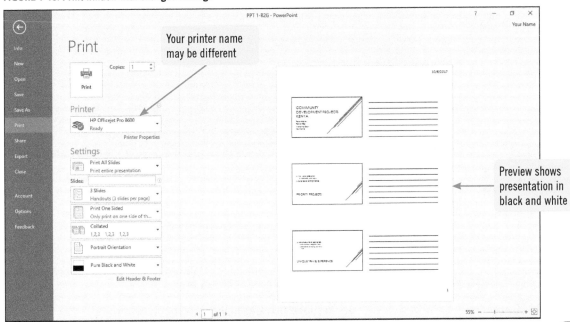

Microsoft Office Online Apps

Some Office programs, PowerPoint for example, include the capability to incorporate feedback—called online collaboration—across the Internet or a company network. Using **cloud computing** (work done in a virtual environment), you can take advantage of web programs called Microsoft Office Online Apps, which are simplified versions of the programs found in the Microsoft Office 2016 suite. Because these programs are online,

they take up no computer disk space and are accessed using Microsoft OneDrive, a free service from Microsoft. Using Microsoft OneDrive, you and your colleagues can create and store documents in the "cloud" and make the documents available to whomever you grant access. To use Microsoft OneDrive, you need to create a free Microsoft account, which you obtain at the Microsoft website.

Practice

Concepts Review

Label each element of the PowerPoint window shown in FIGURE 1-16.

FIGURE 1-16

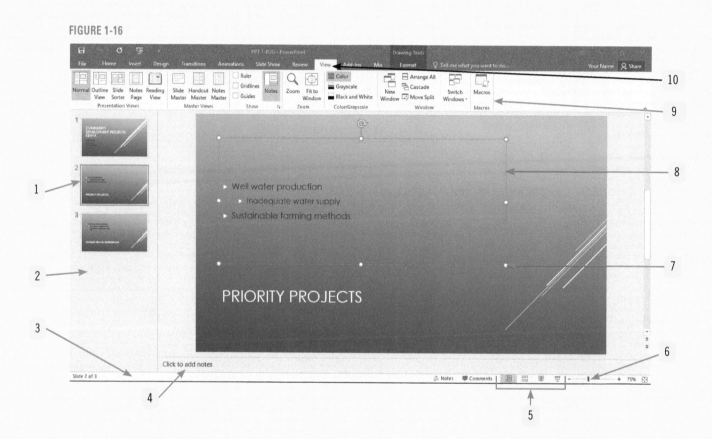

Match each term with the statement that best describes it.

11. **Slide Show view**
12. **Slide Layout**
13. **Inking**
14. **Theme**
15. **Zoom slider**
16. **Text placeholder**

a. Freehand pen and highlighter marks on a slide
b. A view that displays a presentation to show to an audience
c. Allows you to change the size of the slide in the window
d. Set of coordinated colors, fonts, and effects
e. Placeholders arranged in a specific way on the slide
f. Box with dotted border where you enter text

Select the best answer from the list of choices.

17. The view that fills the entire computer screen with each slide in the presentation is called:
    a. Outline view.
    c. Slide Show view.
    b. Normal view.
    d. Fit to window view.

18. You can enter slide text in the Slide Pane and in the _____.
    a. Reading pane
    c. Outline view
    b. Notes Page view
    d. Slides tab

19. What is the function of the slide layout?
    a. Defines how all the elements on a slide are arranged.
    b. Enables you to apply a template to the presentation.
    c. Puts all your slides in order.
    d. Shows you which themes you can apply.

20. Which of the following is not included in a design theme?
    a. Pictures
    c. Fonts
    b. Normal view
    d. Colors

21. Which button indents the insertion point to the right?
    a. Right Indent Level
    c. Decrease Indent Level
    b. Increase List Level
    d. Move Margin

22. Which status bar feature allows you to quickly switch between views?
    a. Zoom Slider
    c. Fit slide to current window button
    b. View Shortcuts
    d. Switch view button

23. What can you drag to adjust the size of an object?
    a. Rotate handle
    c. Sizing handle
    b. Object border point
    d. Selection box

24. What are the basic building blocks of any presentation?
    a. Placeholders
    c. Slides
    b. Objects
    d. Graphics

Skills Review

1. **Examine the PowerPoint window.**
   a. Start PowerPoint, if necessary then open a new blank presentation.
   b. Identify as many elements of the PowerPoint window as you can without referring to the lessons in this module.
   c. Be able to describe the purpose or function of each element.
   d. For any elements you cannot identify, refer to the lessons in this module.

2. **Enter slide text.**
   a. In the Slide pane in Normal view, enter the text **Nelsonville** in the title placeholder.
   b. In the subtitle text placeholder, enter **Wyoming Ghost Town Preservation Society**.
   c. On the next line of the placeholder, enter your name.
   d. Deselect the text object.
   e. Save the presentation using the filename **PPT 1-Nelsonville** to location where you store your Data Files.

Skills Review (continued)

3. Add a new slide.

a. Create a new slide.

b. Using FIGURE 1-17, enter text on the slide.

c. Create another new slide.

d. Using FIGURE 1-18, enter text on the slide.

e. Save your changes.

4. Apply a design theme.

a. Click the Design tab.

b. Click the Themes group More button, then point to all of the themes.

c. Locate the Ion Boardroom theme, then apply it to the selected slide.

d. Select Slide 1.

e. Locate the Wisp theme, then apply it to Slide 1.

f. Apply the Wisp theme to all of the slides in the presentation.

g. Use the Next Slide button to move to Slide 3, then save your changes.

5. Compare presentation views.

a. Click the View tab, then click the Outline View button in the Presentation Views group.

b. Click the Slide Sorter button in the Presentation Views group.

c. Click the Notes Page button in the Presentation Views group, then click the Previous Slide button twice.

d. Click the Reading View button in the Presentation Views group, then click the Next button on the status bar.

e. Click the Normal button on the status bar, then click the Slide Show button.

f. Advance the slides until a black screen appears, then click to end the presentation.

g. Save your changes.

6. Print a PowerPoint presentation.

a. Print all the slides as handouts, 3 Slides, in color.

b. Print the presentation outline.

c. Close the file, saving your changes.

d. Exit PowerPoint.

FIGURE 1-17

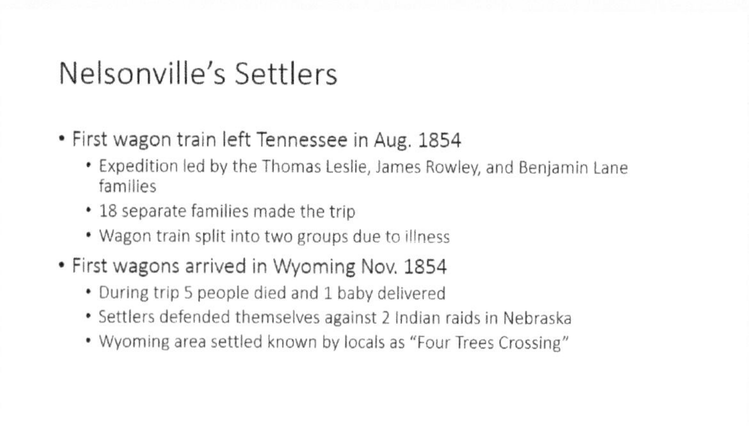

Nelsonville's Settlers

- First wagon train left Tennessee in Aug. 1854
  - Expedition led by the Thomas Leslie, James Rowley, and Benjamin Lane families
  - 18 separate families made the trip
  - Wagon train split into two groups due to illness
- First wagons arrived in Wyoming Nov. 1854
  - During trip 5 people died and 1 baby delivered
  - Settlers defended themselves against 2 Indian raids in Nebraska
  - Wyoming area settled known by locals as "Four Trees Crossing"

FIGURE 1-18

Nelsonville Hotel & Bar History

- Built by John Nelson in 1868
  - Constructed from local lodgepole and ponderosa pine
  - Sold cattle and land for construction capital
- Continuously operated from 1870 to 1929
  - Featured 14 double rooms and 1 bridal suite
  - Restaurant, bath house, and barber shop eventually added to property
  - Featured gambling tables until 1911

Independent Challenge 1

You work for RuraLink Systems, a business that offers rural broadband Internet service and network server management. One of your jobs at the company is to present the company's services to local government and community meetings. Your boss has asked you to create a company profile presentation that describes company goals and services.

a. Start PowerPoint then open a new blank presentation.

b. In the title placeholder on Slide 1, type **RuraLink Systems**.

c. In the subtitle placeholder, type your name, press [Enter], then type today's date.

d. Apply the Ion Boardroom design theme to the presentation.

e. Save your presentation with the filename **PPT 1-RuraLink** to the location where you store your Data Files.

f. Use FIGURE 1-19 and FIGURE 1-20 to add two more slides to your presentation. (*Hint*: Slide 3 uses the Comparison layout.)

g. Use the buttons on the View tab to switch between all of PowerPoint's views.

h. Print the presentation using handouts, 3 Slides, in black and white.

i. Save and close the file, then exit PowerPoint.

FIGURE 1-19

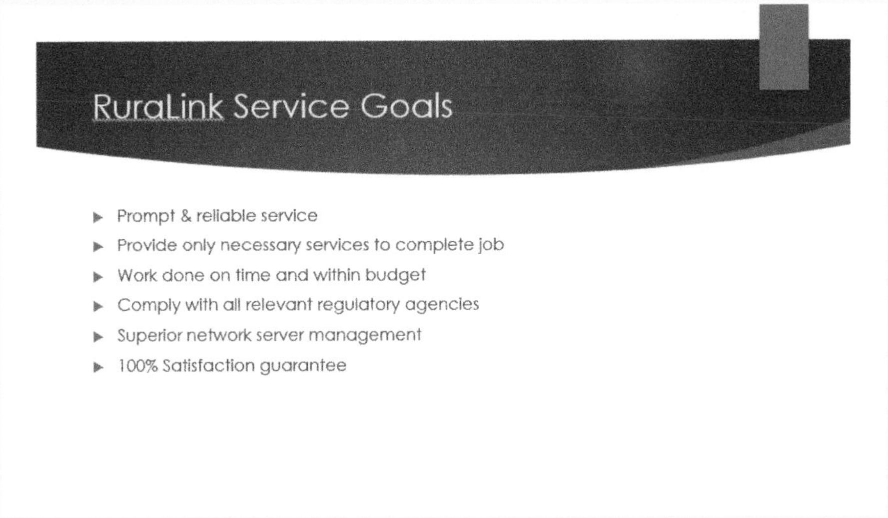

FIGURE 1-20

Independent Challenge 2

You have recently been promoted to sales manager at General Hardwood Industries, which sells and distributes specialty hardwood products used in flooring, cabinets, and furniture. Part of your job is to present company sales figures at a yearly sales meeting. Use the following information as the basis for units of wood sold nationally in your presentation: 501 units cherry, 429 units birch, 95 units hickory, 742 units mahogany, 182 units Brazilian walnut, 401 units American walnut, and 269 units pine. Assume that General Hardwood has five sales regions throughout the country: Pacific Northwest, West, South, Midwest, and Northeast. Also, assume the sales in each region rose between 1.2% and 3.6% over last year, and gross sales reached $31 million. The presentation should have at least five slides.

a. Spend some time planning the slides of your presentation. What is the best way to show the information provided? What other information could you add that might be useful for this presentation?

b. Start PowerPoint.

c. Give the presentation an appropriate title on the title slide, and enter today's date and your name in the subtitle placeholder.

d. Add slides and enter appropriate slide text.

e. On the last slide of the presentation, include the following information:
   General Hardwood Industries
   "Your specialty hardwood store"

f. Apply a design theme. A typical slide might look like the one shown in FIGURE 1-21.

g. Switch views. Run through the slide show at least once.

h. Save your presentation with the filename **PPT 1-General** where you store your Data Files.

i. Close the presentation and exit PowerPoint.

FIGURE 1-21

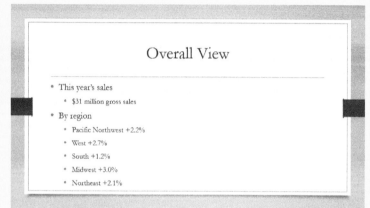

Independent Challenge 3

You work for Janic Corporation, an international trade company that distributes products made in the Midwest. The marketing manager has asked you to plan and create a PowerPoint presentation that describes the primary products Janic exports and the top 3 importing countries; Saudi Arabia, Mexico, and Japan. Describe the top exports, which include tractors, fresh and frozen pork meat, soybeans, corn, and aircraft engine parts. Use the Internet, if possible, to research information that will help you formulate your ideas. The presentation should have at least five slides.

a. Spend some time planning the slides of your presentation.

b. Start PowerPoint then open a new blank presentation.

c. Give the presentation an appropriate title on the title slide, and enter today's date and your name in the subtitle placeholder.

d. Add slides and enter appropriate slide text.

e. On the last slide of the presentation, type the following information:
   Janic Corp.
   Est. 1948
   Headquarters: Independence, MO

f. Apply a design theme.

g. Switch views. Run through the slide show at least once.

h. Save your presentation with the filename **PPT 1-Janic** to the location where you store your Data Files.

i. Close the presentation and exit PowerPoint.

Independent Challenge 4: Explore

You are a member of the Chattanooga Service Organization (CSO), a non profit organization in Chattanooga, TN. This organization raises money throughout the year to support community needs such as schools, youth organizations, and other worthy causes. This year CSO has decided to support the Penhale Youth Center by hosting a regional barbeque cook-off, called the Ultimate BBQ Cook-Off. The competition includes over 20 cooking teams from a five-state region. Create a presentation that describes the event.

a. Spend some time planning the slides of your presentation. Assume the following: the competition is a 2-day event; event advertising will be multistate wide; musical groups will be invited; there will be events and games for kids; the event will be held at the county fairgrounds. Use the Internet, if possible, to research information that will help you formulate your ideas.

b. Start PowerPoint then open a new blank presentation.

c. Give the presentation an appropriate title on the title slide, and enter your name and today's date in the subtitle placeholder.

d. Add slides and enter appropriate slide text. You must create at least three slides.

e. Apply a Design Theme. Typical slides might look like the ones shown in FIGURE 1-22 and FIGURE 1-23.

f. View the presentation.

g. Save your presentation with the filename **PPT 1-CSO** to the location where you store your Data Files.

h. Close the presentation and exit PowerPoint.

FIGURE 1-22

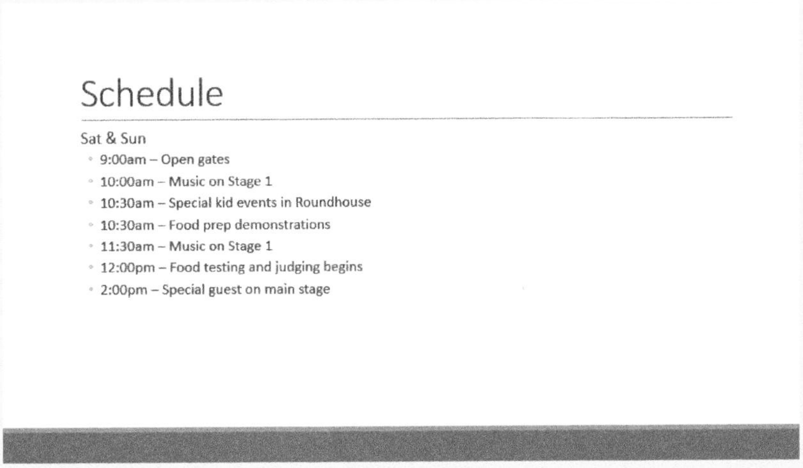

Schedule

Sat & Sun
- 9:00am – Open gates
- 10:00am – Music on Stage 1
- 10:30am – Special kid events in Roundhouse
- 10:30am – Food prep demonstrations
- 11:30am – Music on Stage 1
- 12:00pm – Food testing and judging begins
- 2:00pm – Special guest on main stage

FIGURE 1-23

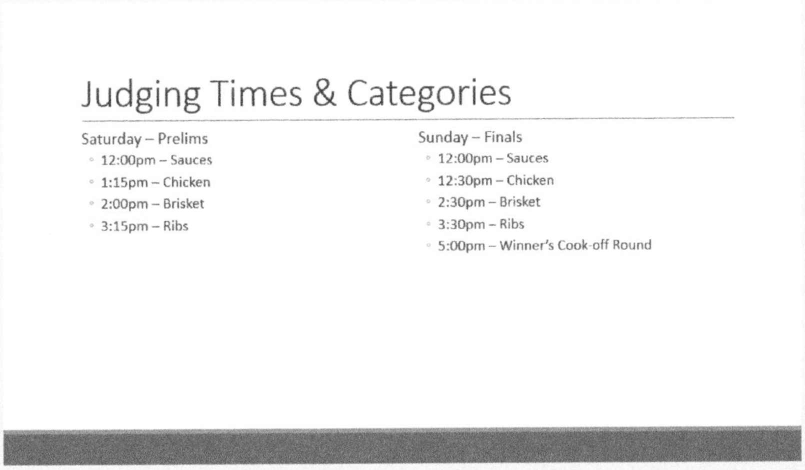

Judging Times & Categories

Saturday – Prelims
- 12:00pm – Sauces
- 1:15pm – Chicken
- 2:00pm – Brisket
- 3:15pm – Ribs

Sunday – Finals
- 12:00pm – Sauces
- 12:30pm – Chicken
- 2:30pm – Brisket
- 3:30pm – Ribs
- 5:00pm – Winner's Cook-off Round

Visual Workshop

Create the presentation shown in FIGURE 1-24 and FIGURE 1-25. Make sure you include your name on the title slide. Save the presentation as **PPT 1-Neptune** to the location where you store your Data Files. Print the slides.

FIGURE 1-24

NEPTUNE INDUSTRIES

Your Name
Senior Project Manager

FIGURE 1-25

PRODUCT OVERVIEW

Product designation: Genford XDS-2000
- Turf reduction device
- Primary guidance system: global positioning system

Systems tested
- Integrated on-board computer system
- Engine and hydraulics
- Turf reduction components
- Obstacle detection system

Modifying a Presentation

CASE You continue working on your Kenya Africa projects presentation. In this module, you'll enter text using Outline view, then you'll format text, create a SmartArt graphic, draw and modify objects, and add slide footer information in the presentation.

Module Objectives

After completing this module, you will be able to:

- Enter text in Outline view
- Format text
- Convert text to SmartArt
- Insert and modify shapes
- Rearrange and merge shapes
- Edit and duplicate shapes
- Align and group objects
- Add slide footers

Files You Will Need

PPT 2-1.pptx   PPT 2-4.pptx

PPT 2-2.pptx   PPT 2-5.pptx

PPT 2-3.pptx

Enter Text in Outline View

Learning
Outcomes
• Enter text in
  Outline view
• Create a new slide

You can enter presentation text by typing directly on the slide in the Slide pane, or, if you need to focus on the text of the presentation, you can enter text in Outline view. Text in Outline view is organized so the headings, or slide titles, appear at the top of the outline. Each subpoint, or each line of bulleted text, appears as one or more indented lines under the title. Each indent in the outline creates another level of bulleted text on the slide. **CASE** *You switch to Outline view to enter text for two more slides for your presentation.*

STEPS

QUICK TIP

To open a PowerPoint 97-2007 presentation in PowerPoint 2016, open the presentation, click the File tab, click the Convert button, name the file in the Save As dialog box, then click Save.

1. **Start PowerPoint, open the presentation** PPT 2-1.pptx **from the location where you store your Data Files, then save it as** PPT 2-R2G.pptx

   A presentation with the new name appears in the PowerPoint window.

2. **Click the** Slide 2 thumbnail **in the Slides tab, click the** New Slide button list arrow **in the Slides group, then click** Title and Content

   A new slide, Slide 3, with the Title and Content layout appears as the current slide below Slide 2.

3. **Click the** View tab **on the Ribbon, then click the** Outline View button **in the Presentation Views group**

   The text of the presentation appears in the Outline pane next to the Slide pane. The slide icon and the insertion point for Slide 3 are highlighted, indicating it is selected and ready to accept text. Text that you enter next to a slide icon becomes the title for that slide.

4. **Type** Water: The Strategic Commodity, **press [Enter], then press [Tab]**

   When you pressed [Enter] after typing the slide title, you created a new slide. However, because you want to enter bulleted text on Slide 3, you then pressed [Tab] so the text you type will be entered as bullet text on Slide 3. See FIGURE 2-1.

5. **Type** Economic efficiency, **press [Enter], type** Social fairness, **press [Enter], type** Sustainability, **press [Enter], type** Population demands, **then press [Enter]**

   Each time you press [Enter], the insertion point moves down one line.

6. **Press [Shift][Tab]**

   Because you are working in Outline view, a new slide with the same layout, Slide 4, is created when you press [Shift][Tab].

QUICK TIP

Press [Ctrl][Enter] while the cursor is in the text object to create a new slide with the same layout as the previous slide.

7. **Type** Water: Developmental Essentials, **press [Ctrl][Enter], type** Household water safety, **press [Enter], type** Catchment area, **press [Enter], type** Water quality, **press [Enter], then type** Conflict resolution

   Pressing [Ctrl][Enter] while the insertion point is in the title text object moves the cursor into the content placeholder.

8. **Position the pointer on the** Slide 3 icon ☐ **in the Outline pane**

   The pointer changes to ✥. The Water: The Strategic Commodity slide, Slide 3, is out of order.

9. **Drag** ☐ **down until a horizontal indicator line appears above the Slide 5 icon, then release the mouse button**

   The third slide moves down and switches places with the fourth slide, as shown in FIGURE 2-2.

10. **Click the** Normal button ▣ **on the status bar, then save your work**

    The Outline pane closes, and the Slides tab is now visible in the window.

FIGURE 2-1: Outline view showing new slide

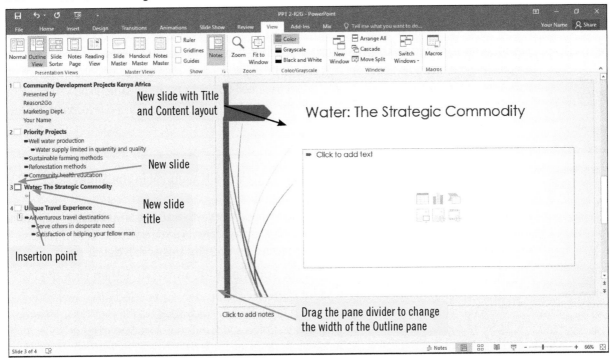

FIGURE 2-2: Outline view showing moved slide

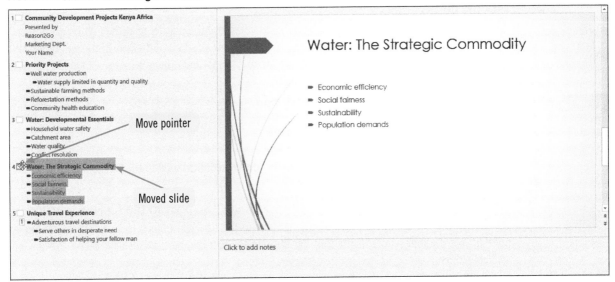

Using proofing tools for other languages

If you have a presentation in another language, how would you check the spelling and grammar of that presentation? Every version of PowerPoint contains a language pack with a primary language, such as English, Italian, or Arabic. Each language pack includes additional languages other than the primary language. For example, the English language pack also includes French and Spanish. So, let's say you have an English version of PowerPoint and you want to check the spelling of a presentation that is written in French. To check the spelling of a French presentation, click a text object on a slide, click the Review tab on the Ribbon, click the Language button in the Language group, then click Set Proofing Language to open the Language dialog box. Click one of the French options from the list, then click OK. Only languages in the list with a spelling symbol are available to use for checking spelling and grammar. Now when you check the spelling, PowerPoint will do so in French. If your version of PowerPoint does not have the language you want to use, you can purchase additional language packs from Microsoft.

Format Text

Learning
Outcomes
• Modify text
  characteristics

Once you have entered and edited the text in your presentation, you can modify the way the text looks to emphasize your message. Important text should be highlighted in some way to distinguish it from other text or objects on the slide. For example, if you have two text objects on the same slide, you could draw attention to one text object by changing its color, font, or size. **CASE** *You decide to format the text on Slide 5 of the presentation.*

STEPS

QUICK TIP

To show or hide the Mini toolbar, click the File tab on the Ribbon, click Options, then click the Show Mini Toolbar on selection check box.

1. **Click the** Home tab **on the Ribbon, click the** Slide 5 thumbnail **in the Slides tab, then double-click** Travel **in the title text object**

   The word "Travel" is selected, and a Mini toolbar appears above the text. The **Mini toolbar** contains basic text-formatting commands, such as bold and italic, and appears when you select text using the mouse. This toolbar makes it quick and easy to format text, especially when the Home tab is closed.

2. **Move** 🗘 **over the** Mini toolbar, **click the** Font Color list arrow 🅰 ▾**, then click the** Dark Red color box **in the Standard Colors row**

   The text changes color to dark red, as shown in FIGURE 2-3. When you click the Font Color list arrow, the Font Color gallery appears showing the Theme Colors and Standard Colors. ScreenTips help identify font colors. Notice that the Font Color button on the Mini toolbar and the Font Color button in the Font group on the Home tab change color to reflect the new color choice, which is now the active color.

QUICK TIP

To select an unselected text object, press [Shift], click the text object, then release [Shift].

3. **Move the pointer over the** title text object border **until the pointer changes to** 🛇**, then click the** border

   The border changes from a dashed to a solid line as you move the pointer over the text object border. The entire title text object is selected, and changes you make now affect all of the text in the text object. When the whole text object is selected, you can change its size, shape, and other attributes. Changing the color of the text helps emphasize it.

QUICK TIP

For more text formatting options, right-click a text object, then click Format Text Effects to open the Format Shape - Text Options pane.

4. **Click the** Font Color button 🅰 ▾ **in the Font group**

   All of the text in the title text object changes to the current active color, dark red.

5. **Click the** Font list arrow **in the Font group**

   A list of available fonts opens with Century Gothic, the current font used in the title text object, selected at the top of the list in the Theme Fonts section.

6. **Scroll down the alphabetical list, then click** Goudy Old Style **in the All Fonts section**

   The Goudy Old Style font replaces the original font in the title text object. Notice that as you move the pointer over the font names in the font list the selected text on the slide displays a Live Preview of the available fonts.

7. **Click the** Underline button 🅄 **in the Font group, then click the** Increase Font Size button 🄰 **in the Font group**

   All of the text now displays an underline and increases in size to 40.

8. **Click the** Character Spacing button 🄰⌄ ▾ **in the Font group, then click** Tight

   The spacing between the letters in the title decreases. Compare your screen to FIGURE 2-4.

9. **Click a blank area of the slide outside the text object to deselect it, then save your work**

   Clicking a blank area of the slide deselects all objects that are selected.

FIGURE 2-3: Selected word with Mini toolbar open

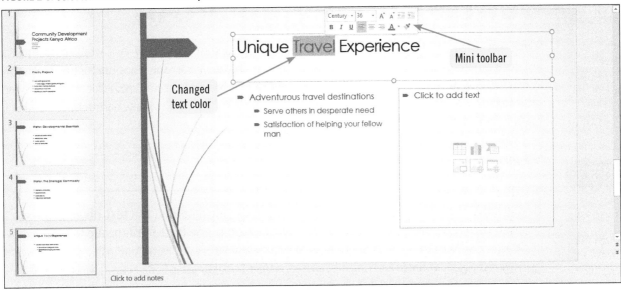

FIGURE 2-4: Formatted text

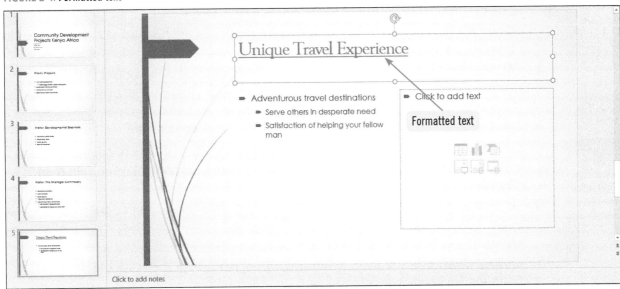

Replacing text and fonts

As you review your presentation, you may decide to replace certain text or fonts throughout the entire presentation using the Replace command. Text can be a word, phrase, or sentence. To replace specific text, click the Home tab on the Ribbon, then click the Replace button in the Editing group. In the Replace dialog box, enter the text you want to replace, then enter the text you want to use as its replacement. You can also use the Replace command to replace one font for another. Simply click the Replace button list arrow in the Editing group, then click Replace Fonts to open the Replace Font dialog box.

Convert Text to SmartArt

Learning Outcomes
- Create a SmartArt graphic
- Modify the SmartArt design

Sometimes when you are working with text it just doesn't capture your attention. The ability to convert text to a SmartArt graphic provides a creative way to convey a message using text and graphics. A **SmartArt** graphic is a professional-quality diagram that graphically illustrates text. For example, you can show steps in a process or timeline, show proportional relationships, or show how parts relate to a whole. You can create a SmartArt graphic from scratch or create one by converting existing text you have entered on a slide. **CASE** *You want the presentation to appear visually dynamic, so you convert the text on Slide 3 to a SmartArt graphic.*

STEPS

1. **Click the Slide 3 thumbnail in the Slides tab, click Household in the text object, then click the Convert to SmartArt Graphic button in the Paragraph group**

   A gallery of SmartArt graphic layouts opens. As with many features in PowerPoint, you can preview how your text will look prior to applying the SmartArt graphic layout by using PowerPoint's Live Preview feature. You can review each SmartArt graphic layout and see how it changes the appearance of the text.

2. **Move ⌖ over the SmartArt graphic layouts in the gallery**

   Notice how the text becomes part of the graphic and the color and font changes each time you move the pointer over a different graphic layout. SmartArt graphic names appear in ScreenTips.

3. **Click the Basic Process layout in the SmartArt graphics gallery**

   A SmartArt graphic appears on the slide in place of the text object, and the SmartArt Tools Design tab opens on the Ribbon, as shown in FIGURE 2-5. A SmartArt graphic consists of two parts: the SmartArt graphic and a Text pane where you type and edit text. This graphic also has placeholders where you can add pictures to the SmartArt graphic.

4. **Click each bullet point in the Text pane, then click the Text pane control button ⟩**

   Notice that each time you select a bullet point in the text pane, a selection box appears around the text objects in the SmartArt graphic. The Text pane control opens and closes the Text pane. You can also open and close the Text pane using the Text Pane button in the Create Graphic group.

5. **Click the More button ⥥ in the Layouts group, click More Layouts to open the Choose a SmartArt Graphic dialog box, click Matrix, click the Basic Matrix layout icon, then click OK**

   The SmartArt graphic changes to the new graphic layout. You can change how the SmartArt graphic looks by applying a SmartArt Style. A **SmartArt Style** is a preset combination of simple and 3-D formatting options that follows the presentation theme.

6. **Move ⌖ slowly over the styles in the SmartArt Styles group, then click the More button ⥥ in the SmartArt Styles group**

   A Live Preview of each style is displayed on the SmartArt graphic. The SmartArt styles are organized into sections; the top group offers suggestions for the best match for the document, and the bottom group shows you all of the possible 3-D styles that are available.

7. **Move ⌖ over the styles in the gallery, click Intense Effect in the Best Match for Document section, then click in a blank area of the slide outside the SmartArt graphic**

   Notice how this new style adds a shadow to each object to achieve a dimensional effect. Compare your screen to FIGURE 2-6.

8. **Click the Slide 4 thumbnail in the Slides tab, then save your work**

   Slide 4 appears in the Slide pane.

FIGURE 2-5: **Text converted to a SmartArt graphic**

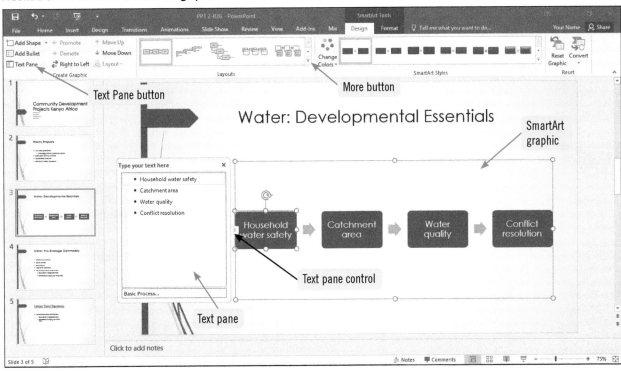

FIGURE 2-6: **Final SmartArt graphic**

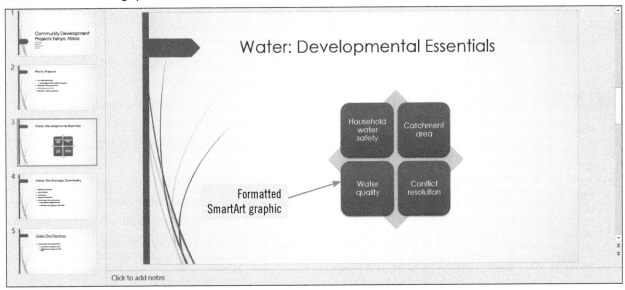

Choosing SmartArt graphics

When choosing a SmartArt graphic to use on your slide, remember that you want the SmartArt graphic to communicate the message of the text effectively; not every SmartArt graphic layout achieves that goal. You must consider the type of text you want to illustrate. For example, does the text show steps in a process, does it show a continual process, or does it show nonsequential information? The answer to this question will dictate the type of SmartArt graphic layout you should choose. Also, the amount of text you want to illustrate will have an effect on the SmartArt graphic layout you choose. Most of the time key points will be the text you use in a SmartArt graphic. Finally, some SmartArt graphic layouts are limited by the number of shapes they can accommodate, so be sure to choose a graphic layout that can illustrate your text appropriately. Experiment with the SmartArt graphic layouts until you find the right one, and have fun in the process!

Insert and Modify Shapes

Learning
Outcomes
• Create a shape
• Modify a shape's
  style

In PowerPoint you can insert many different types of shapes including lines, geometric figures, arrows, stars, callouts, and banners to enhance your presentation. You can modify many aspects of a shape including its fill color, line color, and line style, as well as add shadows and 3-D effects. A quick way to alter the appearance of a shape is to apply a Quick Style. A **Quick Style** is a set of formatting options, including line style, fill color, and effects. **CASE** ▶ *You decide to draw some shapes on Slide 4 of your presentation that identify strategies for increasing water supply.*

STEPS

1. **Click the** More button ▼ **in the Drawing group, click the** Diamond button ◇ **in the Basic Shapes section, then position** + **in the blank area of Slide 4 below the slide title**
   ScreenTips help you identify the shapes.

TROUBLE
If your shape is not
approximately the
same size as the one
shown in Figure 2-7,
press [Shift], then
drag one of the
corner sizing handles
to resize the object.

2. **Press and hold** [Shift], **drag** + **down and to the right to create the shape, as shown in** FIGURE 2-7, **release the mouse button, then release** [Shift]
   A diamond shape appears on the slide, filled with the default theme color. Pressing [Shift] while you create the object maintains the object proportions as you change its size. A **rotate handle**—circular arrow— appears on top of the shape, which you can drag to manually rotate the shape. To change the style of the shape, apply a Quick Style from the Shape Styles group.

3. **Click the** Drawing Tools Format tab **on the Ribbon, click the** ▼ **in the Shape Styles group, move** ⌖ **over the styles in the gallery to review the effects on the shape, then click** Moderate Effect - Orange, Accent 2
   An orange Quick Style with coordinated gradient fill, line, and shadow color is applied to the shape.

4. **Click the** Shape Outline list arrow **in the Shape Styles group, point to** Weight, **move** ⌖ **over the line weight options to review the effect on the shape, then click** 4½ pt
   The outline weight (or width) increases and is easier to see now.

QUICK TIP
To change the trans-
parency of a shape or
text object filled with
a color, right-click
the object, click
Format Shape, click
Fill, then move the
Transparency slider.

5. **Click the** Shape Effects button **in the Shape Styles group, point to** Preset, **move** ⌖ **over the effect options to review the effect on the shape, then click** Preset 7
   Lighting and shadow effects are added to the shape to give it a three-dimensional appearance. It is easy to change the shape to any other shape in the shapes gallery.

6. **Click the** Edit Shape button **in the Insert Shapes group, point to** Change Shape **to open the shapes gallery, then click the** Teardrop button ◯ **in the Basic Shapes section**
   The diamond shape changes to a teardrop shape and a yellow circle—called an **adjustment handle**— appears in the upper-right corner of the shape. Some shapes have an adjustment handle that can be moved to change the most prominent feature of an object, in this case the end of the teardrop. You can rotate the shape to make the shape look different.

7. **Click the** Rotate button **in the Arrange group, move** ⌖ **over the** rotation options **to review the effect on the shape, then click** Flip Horizontal
   Notice that the adjustment handle is now on the top left of the shape, indicating that the shape has flipped horizontally, or rotated 180 degrees, as shown in FIGURE 2-8. You prefer the diamond shape, and you decide the shape looks better rotated back the way it was before.

8. **Click the** Undo button list arrow ↺ ▾ **in the Quick Access Toolbar, click** Change Shape, **click a blank area of the slide, then save your work**
   The last two commands you performed are undone, and the shape changes back to a diamond and is flipped back to its original position. Clicking a blank area of the slide deselects all selected objects.

FIGURE 2-7: Diamond shape added to slide

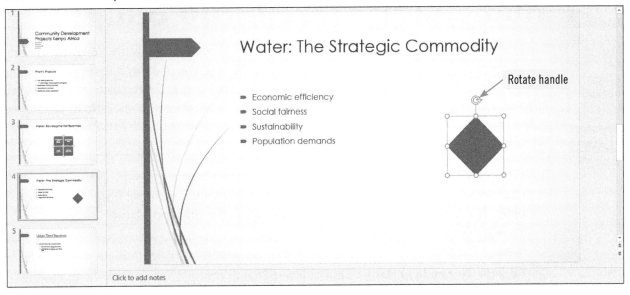

FIGURE 2-8: Rotated teardrop shape

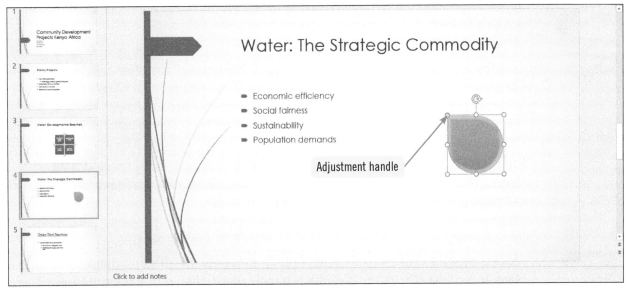

Using the Eyedropper to match colors

As you develop your presentation and work with different shapes and pictures, sometimes from other sources, there may be a certain color that is not in the theme colors of the presentation that you want to capture and apply to objects in your presentation. To capture a color on a specific slide, select any object on the slide, click any button list arrow with a color feature, such as the Shape Fill button or the Shape Outline button on the Drawing Tools Format tab, then click Eyedropper. Move the ✐ over the color you want to capture and pause, or hover. As you hover over a color, a Live Preview of the color appears and the RGB (Red Green Blue) values, called coordinates, appear in a ScreenTip. Click when you see the color you want to capture. The new color now appears in any color gallery under Recent Colors. If you decide not to capture a new color, press [Esc] to close the Eyedropper without making any change.

Rearrange and Merge Shapes

Every object on a slide is placed, or stacked, on the slide in the order it was created, like a deck of cards placed one on top of another. Each object on a slide can be moved up or down in the stack depending on how you want the objects to look on the slide. **Merging** shapes, which combines multiple shapes together, provides you the potential to create unique geometric shapes not available in the Shapes gallery. **CASE** *You create a rectangle shape on Slide 4 and then merge it with the diamond shape.*

STEPS

1. **Click Economic in the text object, position ⬚ over the right-middle sizing handle, ⬚ changes to ⬌, then drag the sizing handle to the left until the right border of the text object is under the middle of the word Strategic in the title text object**

   The width of the text object decreases. When you position ⬚ over a sizing handle, it changes to ⬌. This pointer points in different directions depending on which sizing handle it is over.

2. **Click the Rectangle button ⬚ in the Insert Shapes group, then drag down and to the right to create the shape**

   Compare your screen to FIGURE 2-9. A rectangle shape appears on the slide, filled with the default theme color. You can move shapes by dragging them on the slide.

3. **Drag the rectangle shape over the diamond shape, then use the Smart Guides that appear to position the rectangle shape in the center of the diamond shape where the guides intersect**

   Smart Guides help you position objects relative to each other and determine equal distances between objects.

4. **Click the Select button in the Editing group, click Selection Pane, then click the Send Backward button ⬇ in the Selection pane once**

   The Selection pane opens on the right side of the window showing the four objects on the slide and the order they are stacked on the slide. The Send Backward and Bring Forward buttons let you change the stacking order. The rectangle shape moves back one position in the stack behind the diamond shape.

5. **Press [SHIFT], click the diamond shape on the slide, release [SHIFT] to select both shapes, click the Drawing Tools Format tab on the Ribbon, click the Merge Shapes button in the Insert Shapes group, then point to Union**

   The two shapes appear to merge, or combine, together to form one shape. The merged shape assumes the theme and formatting style of the rectangle shape because it was selected first.

6. **Move ⬚ over the other merge shapes options to review the effect on the shape, click a blank area of the slide twice, click the rectangle shape, then click the Bring Forward button in the Arrange group on the Drawing Tools Format tab once**

   Each merge option produces a different result. The rectangle shape moves back to the top of the stack. Now, you want to see what happens when you select the diamond shape first before you merge the two shapes together.

7. **Click the diamond shape, press [SHIFT], click the rectangle shape, release [SHIFT], click the Merge Shapes button in the Insert Shapes group, then point to Union**

   The merged shape adopts the theme and formatting style of the diamond shape.

8. **Point to each of the merge shapes options, then click Subtract**

   The two shapes merge into one shape. This merge option deletes the area of all shapes from the first shape you selected, so in this case the area of the rectangle shape is deleted from the diamond shape. The merged shape is identified as Freeform 5 in the Selection pane. See FIGURE 2-10.

9. **Click the Selection Pane button in the Arrange group, click a blank area of the slide, then save your work**

FIGURE 2-9: Rectangle shape added to slide

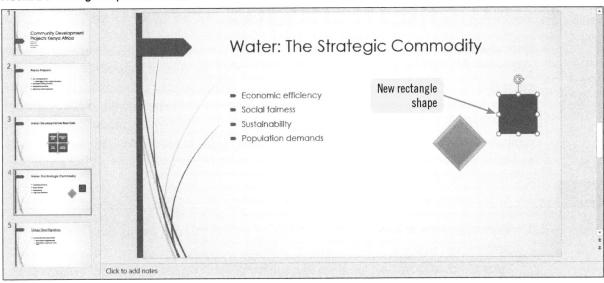

FIGURE 2-10: New Merged shape

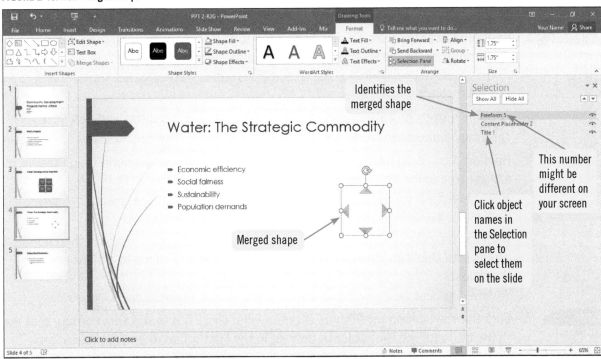

Changing the size and position of shapes

Usually when you resize a shape you can simply drag one of the sizing handles around the outside of the shape, but sometimes you may need to resize a shape more precisely. When you select a shape, the Drawing Tools Format tab appears on the Ribbon, offering you many different formatting options including some sizing commands located in the Size group. The Width and Height commands in the Size group allow you to change the width and height of a shape. You also have the option to open the Format Shape pane, which allows you to change the size of a shape, as well as the rotation, scale, and position of a shape on the slide.

Edit and Duplicate Shapes

Once you have created a shape you still have the ability to refine its basic characteristics, which helps change the size and appearance of the shape. For example, if you create a shape and it is too large, you can reduce its size by dragging any of its sizing handles. Most PowerPoint shapes can have text attached to them. All shapes can be moved and copied. To help you resize and move shapes and other objects precisely, PowerPoint has rulers you can add to the Slide pane. Rulers display the measurement system your computer uses, either inches or metric measurements. **CASE** *You want three identical diamond shapes on Slide 4. You first add the ruler to the slide to help you change the size of the diamond shape you've already created, and then you make copies of it.*

STEPS

1. **Right-click a blank area of Slide 4, click** Ruler **on the shortcut menu, then click the bottom part of the** diamond shape **to select it**

   Rulers appear on the left and top of the Slide pane. Unless the ruler has been changed to metric measurements, it is divided into inches with half-inch and eighth-inch marks. Notice the current location of the ⇧ is identified on both rulers by a small dotted red line in the ruler.

2. **Drag the** middle left sizing handle **on the diamond shape to the left approximately ½",
   then release the mouse button**

   The diamond shape is now slightly larger in diameter.

QUICK TIP
To display or hide gridlines, click the Gridlines check box in the Show group on the View tab.

3. **Position** ⇧ **over the selected** diamond shape **so that it changes to** ⇧, **then drag the** diamond shape **to the Smart Guides on the slide, as shown in** FIGURE 2-11

   PowerPoint uses a series of evenly spaced horizontal and vertical lines—called **gridlines**—to align objects, which force objects to "snap" to the grid.

4. **Position** ⇧ **over the bottom part of the** diamond shape, **then press and hold** [Ctrl]

   The pointer changes to ⇧, indicating that PowerPoint makes a copy of the shape when you drag the mouse.

5. **Holding** [Ctrl], **drag the** diamond shape **to the right until the diamond shape copy is in a blank area of the slide, release the mouse button, then release** [Ctrl]

   An identical copy of the diamond shape appears on the slide and Smart Guides appear above and below the shape as you drag the new shape to the right, which helps you align shapes.

6. **With the** second diamond shape **still selected, click the** Copy list arrow **in the Clipboard group, click** Duplicate, **then move the** duplicated diamond **shape to a blank area of the slide**

   You have duplicated the diamond shape twice and now have three identical shapes on the slide.

QUICK TIP
Press and hold [Alt] to temporarily turn the snap-to-grid feature off while dragging objects on the slide or dragging a sizing handle to make precise adjustments.

7. **Click the** View tab **on the Ribbon, click the** Ruler **check box in the Show group, click the** Home tab, **click the** Font Color button **⒜ in the Font group, then type** Rainwater Harvesting

   The ruler closes, and the text you type appears in the selected diamond shape and becomes a part of the shape. Now if you move or rotate the shape, the text moves with it. Compare your screen with FIGURE 2-12.

8. **Click the** left diamond shape, **click** ⒜, **type** Salt Removal, **click the** right diamond shape, **click** ⒜, **type** Continuous Water Use, **click in a blank area of the slide, then save your work**

   All three diamond shapes include text.

FIGURE 2-11: Merged shape moved on slide

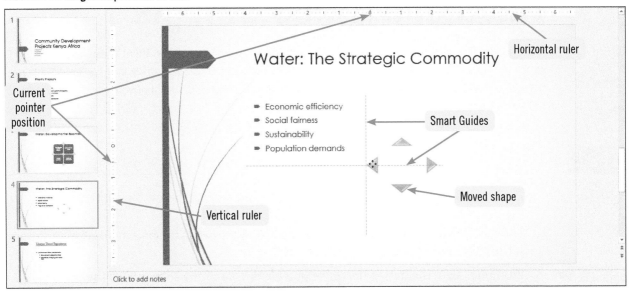

FIGURE 2-12: Duplicated shapes

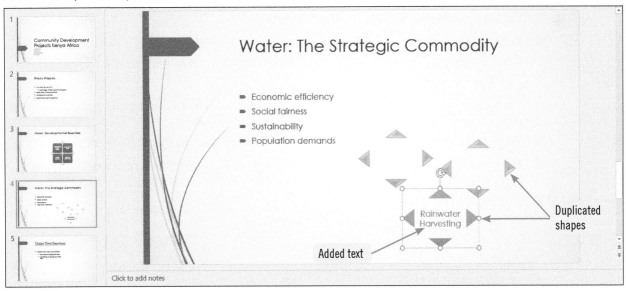

Editing points of a shape

If you want to customize the form (or outline) of any shape in the shapes gallery, you can modify its edit points. To display a shape's edit points, select the shape you want to modify, click the Drawing Tools Format tab on the Ribbon, click the Edit Shape button in the Insert Shapes group, then click Edit Points. Black edit points appear on the shape. To change the form of a shape, drag a black edit point. When you click a black edit

point, white square edit points appear on either side of the black edit point, which allow you to change the curvature of a line between two black edit points. When you are finished with your custom shape, you can save it as picture and reuse it in other presentations or other files. To save the shape as a picture, right-click the shape, then click Save as Picture.

Align and Group Objects

After you are finished creating and modifying your objects, you can position them accurately on the slide to achieve the look you want. Using the Align commands in the Arrange group, you can align objects relative to each other by snapping them to the gridlines on a slide or to guides that you manually position on the slide. The Group command groups two or more objects into one object, which secures their relative position to each other and makes it easy to edit and move them. **CASE** *You are ready to position and group the diamond shapes on Slide 4 to finish the slide.*

Learning Outcomes
- Move shapes using guides
- Align and group shapes

STEPS

1. **Right-click a blank area of the slide, point to** Grid and Guides **on the shortcut menu, then click** Guides

   The guides appear as dotted lines on the slide and usually intersect at the center of the slide. Guides help you position objects precisely on the slide.

   QUICK TIP
   To quickly add a new guide to the slide, press [Ctrl], then drag an existing guide. The original guide remains in place. Drag a guide off the slide to delete it.

2. **Position** ⬚ **over the** horizontal guide **in a blank area of the slide, notice the pointer change to** ⬚, **press and hold the mouse button until the pointer changes to a measurement guide box, then drag the** guide **up until the guide position box reads** 1.33

3. **Drag the** vertical guide **to the left until the guide position box reads** .33, **then drag the** Salt Removal shape **so that the top and left edges of the shape touch the guides, as shown in** FIGURE 2-13

   The Salt Removal shape attaches or "snaps" to the guides.

4. **Drag the** Continuous Water Use shape **to the right until it touches a vertical Smart Guide, press and hold** [Shift], **click the** Salt Removal shape, **then release** [Shift]

   Two shapes are now selected.

5. **Click the** Drawing Tools Format tab **on the Ribbon, click the** Align button **in the Arrange group, click** Align Top, **then click a blank area of the slide**

   The right diamond shape moves up and aligns with the other shape along their top edges.

6. **Drag the** Rainwater Harvesting diamond shape **in between the other two shapes, as shown in** FIGURE 2-14

   QUICK TIP
   To set the formatting of a shape as the default, right-click the shape, then click Set as Default Shape on the Shortcut menu.

7. **Press and hold** [Shift], **click the other two** diamond shapes, **release** [Shift], **click the** Group button **in the Arrange group, then click** Group

   The shapes are now grouped together to form one object without losing their individual attributes. Notice that the sizing handles and rotate handle now appear on the outer edge of the grouped object, not around each individual object.

8. **Drag the** horizontal guide **to the middle of the slide until its guide position box reads** 0.00, **then drag the** vertical guide **to the middle of the slide until its guide position box reads** 0.00

9. **Click the** View tab **on the Ribbon, click the** Guides check box **in the Show group, click a blank area of the slide, then save your work**

   The guides are no longer displayed on the slide.

FIGURE 2-13: **Repositioned shape**

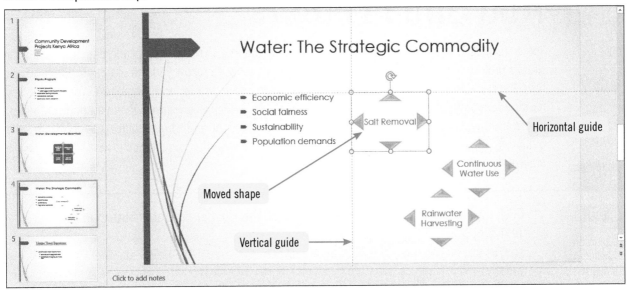

FIGURE 2-14: **Repositioned shapes**

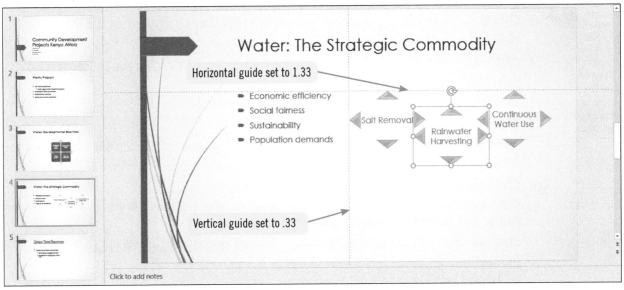

Distributing objects

There are two ways to distribute objects in PowerPoint: relative to each other and relative to the slide edge. If you choose to distribute objects relative to each other, PowerPoint evenly divides the empty space between all of the selected objects. When distributing objects in relation to the slide, PowerPoint evenly splits the empty space from slide edge to slide edge between the selected objects. To distribute objects relative to each other, click the Align button in the Arrange group on the Drawing Tools Format tab, then click Align Selected Objects. To distribute objects relative to the slide, click the Align button in the Arrange group on the Drawing Tools Format tab, then click Align to Slide.

Add Slide Footers

Footer text, such as a company, school, or product name, the slide number, or the date, can give your slides a professional look and make it easier for your audience to follow your presentation. Slides do not have headers. However, notes or handouts can include both header and footer text. You can review footer information that you apply to the slides in the PowerPoint views and when you print the slides. Notes and handouts header and footer text is visible when you print notes pages, handouts, and the outline. **CASE** *You add footer text to the slides of the Kenya Africa presentation to make it easier for the audience to follow.*

STEPS

1. **Click the** Insert tab **on the Ribbon, then click the** Header & Footer button **in the Text group**

   The Header and Footer dialog box opens, as shown in FIGURE 2-15. The Header and Footer dialog box has two tabs: a Slide tab and a Notes and Handouts tab. The Slide tab is selected. There are three types of footer text, Date and time, Slide number, and Footer. The bold rectangles in the Preview box identify the default position of the three types of footer text placeholders on the slides.

2. **Click the** Date and time check box **to select it**

   The date and time options are now available to select. The Update automatically date and time option button is selected by default. This option updates the date and time to the date and time set by your computer every time you open or print the file.

3. **Click the** Update automatically list arrow, **then click the** third option **in the list**

   The month is spelled out in this option.

4. **Click the** Slide number check box, **click the** Footer check box, **click the** Footer text box, **then type your name**

   The Preview box now shows all three footer placeholders are selected.

5. **Click the** Don't show on title slide check box

   Selecting this check box prevents the footer information you entered in the Header and Footer dialog box from appearing on the title slide.

6. **Click** Apply to All

   The dialog box closes, and the footer information is applied to all of the slides in your presentation except the title slide. Compare your screen to FIGURE 2-16.

7. **Click the** Slide 1 thumbnail **in the Slides tab, then click the** Header & Footer button **in the Text group**

   The Header and Footer dialog box opens again.

8. **Click the** Don't show on title slide check box **to deselect it, click the** Footer check box, **then select the text in the Footer text box**

9. **Type** Striving Toward a Sustainable Future, **click** Apply, **then save your work**

   Only the text in the Footer text box appears on the title slide. Clicking Apply applies this footer information to just the current slide.

10. **Submit your presentation to your instructor, then exit PowerPoint**

FIGURE 2-15: Header and Footer dialog box

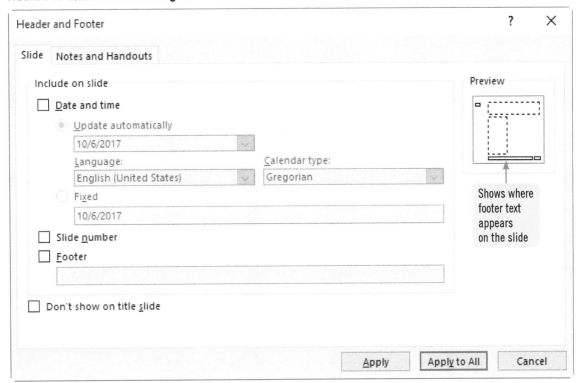

FIGURE 2-16: Footer information added to presentation

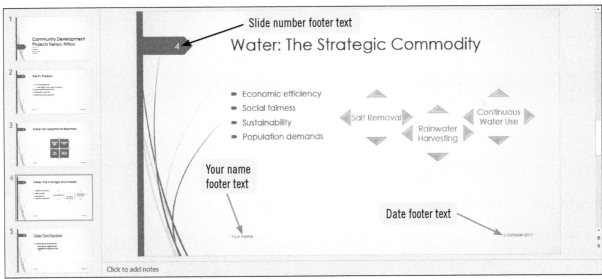

Creating superscript and subscript text

Superscript or subscript text is a number, figure, symbol, or letter that appears smaller than other text and is positioned above or below the normal line of text. A common superscript in the English language is the sign indicator next to number, such as 1st or 3rd. Other examples of superscripts are the trademark symbol^{TM} and the copyright symbol$^{©}$. To create superscript text in PowerPoint, select the text, number, or symbol, then press [CTRL] [SHIFT] [+] at the same time. Probably the most familiar subscript text are the numerals in chemical compounds and formulas, for example, H_2O and CO_2. To create subscript text, select the text, number, or symbol, then press [CTRL] [=] at the same time. To change superscript or subscript text back to normal text, select the text, then press [CTRL] [Spacebar].

Practice

Concepts Review

Label each element of the PowerPoint window shown in FIGURE 2-17.

FIGURE 2-17

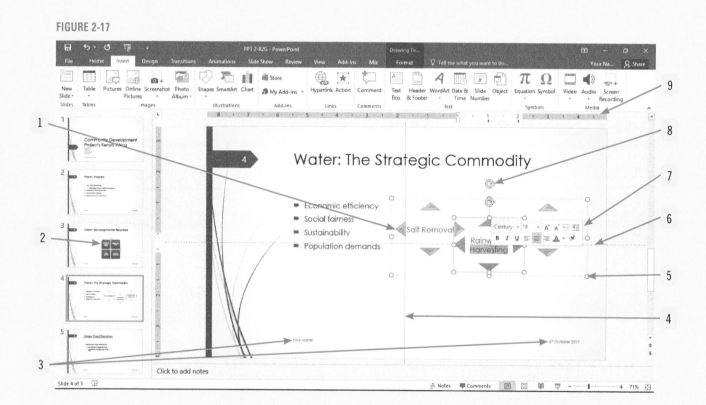

Match each term with the statement that best describes it.

10. **Adjustment handle**
11. **Quick Style**
12. **Rotate handle**
13. **Gridlines**
14. **Merge**
15. **Smart Guides**

a. Evenly spaced horizontal and vertical lines
b. A set of formatting options you apply to an object
c. Combines multiple shapes to create a unique geometric shape
d. Changes the most prominent feature of an object
e. Helps you determine equal distances between objects
f. Drag to turn an object

Select the best answer from the list of choices.

16. What is *not* true about grouped objects?

    a. Grouped objects have one rotate handle.

    b. Grouped objects act as one object but maintain their individual attributes.

    c. Sizing handles appear around the grouped object.

    d. Each object is distributed relative to the slide edges.

17. A professional-quality diagram that visually illustrates text best describes which of the following?

    a. A SmartArt Style   **c.** A subscript

    b. A merged shape   **d.** A SmartArt graphic

18. Which of the following statements is *not* true about Outline view?

    a. Pressing [Enter] moves the insertion point down one line.

    b. Text you enter next to the slide icon becomes a bullet point for that slide.

    c. Headings are the same as slide titles.

    d. Added slides use the same layout as the previous slide.

19. What do you have to drag to customize the form or outline of a shape?

    a. Anchor points   **c.** Slide edges

    b. Edit points   **d.** Shape area

20. Why would you use the Eyedropper tool?

    a. To format an object with a new style   **c.** To capture and apply a new color to an object

    b. To soften the edges of a shape   **d.** To change the fill color of an object

21. What appears just above text when it is selected?

    a. Mini toolbar   **c.** Adjustment handle

    b. QuickStyles   **d.** AutoFit Options button

22. Which of the following statements about merged shapes is *not* true?

    a. Merged shapes can be added to the shapes gallery.

    b. A merged shape assumes the theme of the shape that is selected first.

    c. The stacking order of shapes changes the way a merged shape looks.

    d. A merged shape is a combination of multiple shapes.

Skills Review

FIGURE 2-18

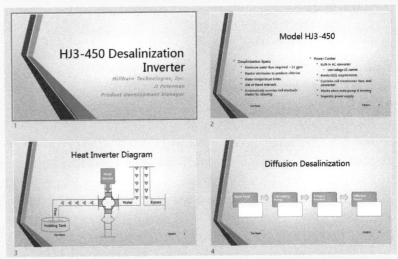

1. Enter text in Outline view.

    a. Open the presentation PPT 2-2.pptx from the location where you store your Data Files, then save it as **PPT 2-Inverter**. The completed presentation is shown in FIGURE 2-18.

    b. Create a new slide after Slide 2 with the Title and Content layout.

    c. Open Outline view, then type **Diffusion Desalinization**.

    d. Press [Enter], press [Tab], type **Main Feed**, press [Enter], type **Circulating Pump**, press [Enter], type **Primary Heaters**, press [Enter], then type **Diffusion Tower**.

Skills Review (continued)

e. Move Slide 3 below Slide 4, then switch back to Normal view.

f. Click the Home tab, then save your changes.

2. Format text.

a. Go to Slide 1, select the name JJ Peterman, then move the pointer over the Mini Toolbar.

b. Click the Font Color list arrow, then click Green under Standard Colors.

c. Select the text object, then change all of the text to the color Green.

d. Click the Font Size list arrow, click 24, then click the Italic button.

e. Click the Character Spacing button, click Loose, then save your changes.

3. Convert text to SmartArt.

a. Click the text object on Slide 4.

b. Click the Convert to SmartArt Graphic button, then apply the Basic Matrix graphic layout to the text object.

c. Click the More button in the Layouts group, click More Layouts, click Process in the Choose a SmartArt Graphic dialog box, click Accent Process, then click OK.

d. Click the More button in the SmartArt Styles group, then apply the Intense Effect style from the Best Match for Document group to the graphic.

e. Close the text pane if necessary, then click outside the SmartArt graphic in a blank part of the slide.

f. Save your changes.

4. Insert and modify shapes.

a. Go to Slide 3, then add rulers to the Slide pane.

b. Click the More button in the Drawing group to open the Shapes gallery, click the Plus button in the Equation Shapes section, press [Shift], then draw a two-inch shape in a blank area of the slide.

c. On the Drawing Tools Format tab, click the More button in the Shape Styles group, then click Colored Fill – Orange, Accent 3.

d. Click the Shape Effects button, point to Shadow, then click Offset Diagonal Bottom Left.

e. Click the Shape Outline list arrow, then click Black, Text 1, Lighter 15% in the Theme Colors section.

f. Drag the Plus shape to the small open area in the middle of the diagram, adjust the shape if needed to make it fit in the space as shown in FIGURE 2-19, then save your changes.

FIGURE 2-19

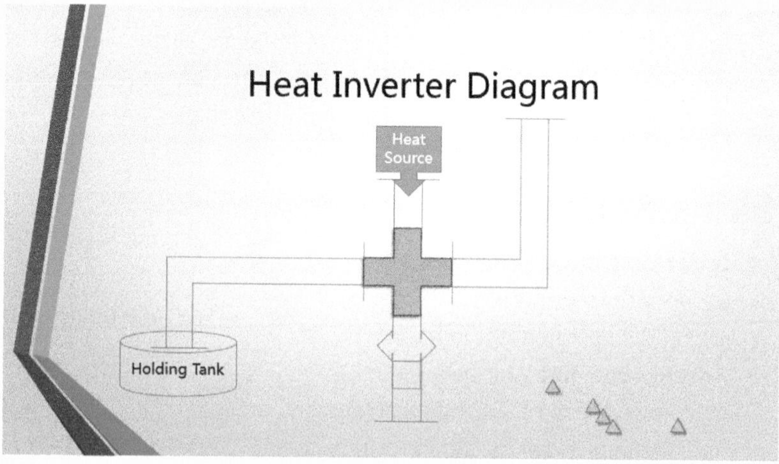

Heat Inverter Diagram

5. Rearrange and merge shapes.

a. Click the title text object on Slide 3, then drag the bottom-middle sizing handle up above the shapes.

b. Click the More button in the Insert Shapes group, click the Hexagon button in the Basic Shapes section, press and hold [Shift], then draw a 1-inch shape.

c. Drag the hexagon shape over top of the plus shape and center it, then open the Selection pane.

d. Send the hexagon shape back one level, press [Shift], click the plus shape, then click the Merge Shapes button in the Insert Shapes group on the Drawing Tools Format tab.

e. Point to each of the merge shapes options, click a blank area of the slide twice, then click the plus shape.

Skills Review (continued)

   f. Send the plus shape back one level, press [Shift], click the hexagon shape, click the Merge Shapes button, then click Combine.

   g. Close the Selection pane, then save your work.

6. Edit and duplicate shapes.

   a. Select the up-angled shape to the right of the merged shape, then using [Ctrl] make one copy of the shape.

   b. Use Smart Guides to align the new up-angled shape just to the right of the original shape.

   c. Click the Rotate button in the Arrange group, click Flip Vertical, click the Undo button, click the Rotate button, then click Flip Horizontal.

   d. Type **Bypass**, click the up-angled shape to the right of the merged shape, type **Water**, click the down-angled shape to the left of the merged shape, then type **Flow**.

   e. Click the Heat Source arrow shape above the merged shape, then drag the bottom-middle sizing handle down until the arrow touches the merged shape.

   f. Click a blank area of the slide, add the guides to the Slide pane, then save your changes.

7. Align and group objects.

   a. Move the vertical guide to the left until 3.42 appears, drag a selection box to select the five small purple triangle shapes at the bottom of the slide, then click the Drawing Tools Format tab.

   b. Click the Align button in the Arrange group, click Align Middle, click the Align button, then click Distribute Horizontally.

   c. Click the Rotate button in the Arrange group, click Rotate Left 90°, click the Group button in the Arrange group, then click Group.

   d. Move the grouped triangle shape object to the guide in the blank space on the down-angled shape to the left of the merged shape.

FIGURE 2-20

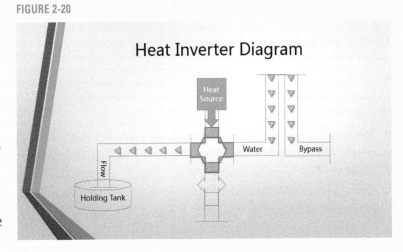

   e. Duplicate the grouped triangle shape object, then rotate the new object to the left 90°.

   f. Duplicate the rotated grouped triangle shape object, then move the two new triangle shape objects on the slide as shown in FIGURE 2-20.

   g. Set the guides back to 0.00, remove the guides from your screen, remove the rulers, then save your work.

8. Add slide footers.

   a. Open the Header and Footer dialog box.

   b. On the Slide tab, click the Date and time check box to select it, then click the Fixed option button.

   c. Add the slide number to the footer, then type your name in the Footer text box.

   d. Apply the footer to all of the slides except the title slide.

   e. Open the Header and Footer dialog box again, then click the Notes and Handouts tab.

   f. Click the Date and time check box, then type today's date in the Fixed text box.

   g. Type the name of your class in the Header text box, then click the Page number check box.

   h. Type your name in the Footer text box.

   i. Apply the header and footer information to all the notes and handouts, then save your changes.

   j. Submit your presentation to your instructor, close the presentation, then exit PowerPoint.

Independent Challenge 1

You are the director of the Center for the Arts in Rapid City, South Dakota, and one of your many duties is to raise funds to cover operation costs. One of the primary ways you do this is by speaking to businesses, community clubs, and other organizations throughout the region. Every year you speak to many organizations, where you give a short presentation detailing what the theater center plans to do for the coming season. You need to continue working on the presentation you started already.

a. Start PowerPoint, open the presentation PPT 2-3.pptx from the location where you store your Data Files, and save it as **PPT 2-Arts**.

b. Use Outline view to enter the following as bulleted text on the Commitment to Excellence slide:
   Excellence
   Testing
   Study
   Diligence

c. Apply the Ion design theme to the presentation.

d. Change the font color of each play name on Slide 3 to Gold, Accent 3.

e. Change the bulleted text on Slide 5 to the Trapezoid List SmartArt Graphic, then apply the Polished SmartArt style.

f. Add your name and slide number as a footer on the slides, then save your changes.

g. Submit your presentation to your instructor, close your presentation, then exit PowerPoint.

Independent Challenge 2

You are a manager for J Barrett Inc., a financial services company. You have been asked by your boss to develop a presentation outlining important details and aspects of the mortgage process to be used at a financial seminar.

a. Start PowerPoint, open the presentation PPT 2-4.pptx from the location where you store your Data Files, and save it as **PPT 2-Broker**.

b. Apply the Facet design theme to the presentation.

c. On Slide 3, press [Shift], select the three shapes, Banks, Mortgage Bankers, and Private Investors, release [Shift], then using the Align command align them to their left edges.

d. Select the blank shape, type **Borrower**, press [Shift], select the Mortgage Broker and Mortgage Bankers shapes, release [Shift], then using the Align command distribute them horizontally and align them to the middle.

e. Select all of the shapes, then apply Intense Effect – Orange, Accent 4 from the Shape Styles group.

f. Create a diamond shape, then merge it with the Borrower shape as shown in FIGURE 2-21. (*Hint*: Use the Fragment Merge option.)

g. Using the Arrow shape from the Shapes gallery, draw a 6-pt arrow between all of the shapes. (*Hint*: Draw one arrow shape, change the line weight using the Shape Outline list arrow, then duplicate the shape.)

FIGURE 2-21

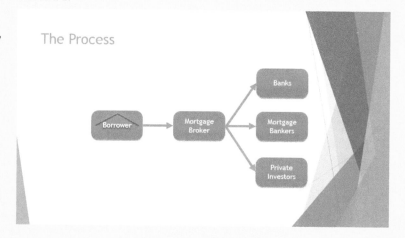

h. Group all the shapes together.

i. Add the page number and your name as a footer on the notes and handouts, then save your changes.

j. Submit your presentation to your instructor, close your presentation, then exit PowerPoint.

Independent Challenge 3

You are an independent distributor of natural foods in Birmingham, Alabama. Your business, Southern Whole Foods, has grown progressively since its inception 5 years ago, but sales have leveled off over the last 9 months. In an effort to increase your market share, you decide to purchase J&R Foods, a natural food dealer, which would allow your company to expand into surrounding states. Use PowerPoint to develop a presentation you can use to gain a financial backer for the acquisition. Create your own information for the presentation.

a. Start PowerPoint, create a new presentation, then apply the Wood Type design theme to the presentation.

b. Type **A Plan for Growth** as the main title on the title slide, and **Southern Whole Foods** as the subtitle.

c. Save the presentation as **PPT 2-Southern** to the location where you store your Data Files.

d. Add five more slides with the following titles: Slide 2, **Trends**; Slide 3, **Growth**; Slide 4, **Funding**; Slide 5, **History**; Slide 6, **Management Team**.

e. Enter appropriate text into the text placeholders of the slides. Use both the Slide pane and Outline view to enter text.

f. Convert text on one slide to a SmartArt graphic, then apply the SmartArt graphic style Inset Effect.

g. Create two shapes, format the shapes, then merge the shapes together.

h. View the presentation as a slide show, then view the slides in Slide Sorter view.

i. Add the slide number and your name as a footer on the slides, then save your changes.

j. Submit your presentation to your instructor, close your presentation, then exit PowerPoint.

Independent Challenge 4: Explore

Your computer instructor at Basset City College has been asked by the department head to convert her Computer Basics 101 course into an accelerated night course designed for adult students. Your instructor has asked you to help her create a presentation for the class that she can post on the Internet. Most of the basic text information is already on the slides, you primarily need to add a theme and other object formatting.

a. Start PowerPoint, open the presentation PPT 2-5.pptx from the location where you store your Data Files, and save it as **PPT 2-Basset**.

b. Add a new slide after the Course Facts slide with the same layout, type **Course Details** in the title text placeholder, then enter the following as bulleted text in Outline view:
Information systems
Networking
Applied methods
Technology solutions
Software design
Applications

c. Apply the Retrospect design theme to the presentation.

d. Select the title text object on Slide 1 (*Hint*: Press [Shift] to select the whole object), then change the text color to Orange.

e. Change the font of the title text object to Biondi, then decrease the font size to 48.

f. Click the subtitle text object on Slide 1, then change the character spacing to Very Loose.

g. Change the text on Slide 4 to a SmartArt graphic. Use an appropriate diagram type for a list.

h. Change the style of the SmartArt diagram using one of the SmartArt Styles, then view the presentation in Slide Show view.

i. Add the slide number and your name as a footer on the notes and handouts, then save your changes.

j. Submit your presentation to your instructor, close your presentation, then exit PowerPoint.

Visual Workshop

Create the presentation shown in FIGURE 2-22 and FIGURE 2-23. Add today's date as the date on the title slide. Save the presentation as **PPT 2-Nebraska Trade** to the location where you store your Data Files. (*Hint*: The SmartArt style used for the SmartArt is a 3D style.) Review your slides in Slide Show view, then add your name as a footer to the notes and handouts. Submit your presentation to your instructor, save your changes, close the presentation, then exit PowerPoint.

FIGURE 2-22

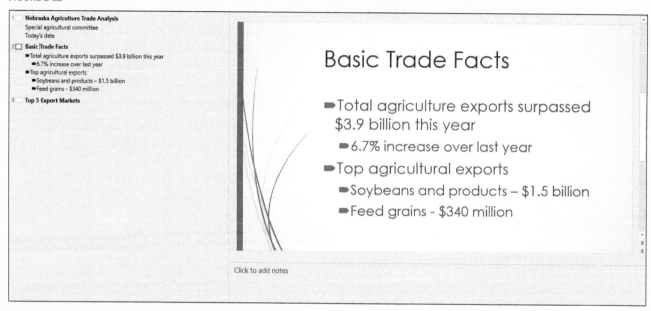

FIGURE 2-23

Inserting Objects into a Presentation

CASE In this module, you continue working on the presentation by inserting text from Microsoft Word. You also add visual elements into the presentation including a photograph, a table, and a chart. You format these objects using PowerPoint's powerful object-editing features.

Module Objectives

After completing this module, you will be able to:

- Insert text from Microsoft Word
- Insert and style a picture
- Insert a text box
- Insert a chart
- Enter and edit chart data
- Insert slides from other presentations
- Insert a table
- Insert and format WordArt

Files You Will Need

PPT 3-1.pptx	PPT 3-10.pptx
PPT 3-2.docx	PPT 3-11.pptx
PPT 3-3.jpg	PPT 3-12.jpg
PPT 3-4.pptx	PPT 3-13.pptx
PPT 3-5.pptx	PPT 3-14.docx
PPT 3-6.docx	PPT 3-15.jpg
PPT 3-7.jpg	PPT 3-16.jpg
PPT 3-8.pptx	PPT 3-17.jpg
PPT 3-9.pptx	PPT 3-18.jpg

Insert Text from Microsoft Word

It is easy to insert documents saved in Microsoft Word format (.docx), Rich Text Format (.rtf), plain text format (.txt), and HTML format (.htm) into a PowerPoint presentation. If you have an outline saved in a document file, you can import it into PowerPoint to create a new presentation or create additional slides in an existing presentation. When you import a document into a presentation, PowerPoint creates an outline structure based on the styles in the document. For example, a Heading 1 style in the Word document becomes a slide title and a Heading 2 style becomes the first level of text in a bulleted list. If you insert a plain text format document into a presentation, PowerPoint creates an outline based on the tabs at the beginning of the document's paragraphs. Paragraphs without tabs become slide titles, and paragraphs with one tab indent become first-level text in bulleted lists. **CASE** ▶ *You have a Microsoft Word document with information about the new Kenyan well project tour that you want to insert into your presentation.*

STEPS

1. **Start PowerPoint, open the presentation PPT 3-1.pptx from the location where you store your Data Files, save it as PPT 3-R2G, click the View tab on the Ribbon, then click the Outline View button in the Presentation Views group**

2. **Click the Slide 6 icon ▢ in the Outline pane, click the Home tab on the Ribbon, click the New Slide button list arrow in the Slides group, then click Slides from Outline**

   Slide 6 appears in the Slide pane. The Insert Outline dialog box opens. Before you insert an outline into a presentation, you need to determine where you want the new slides to be placed. You want the text from the Word document inserted as new slides after Slide 6.

3. **Navigate to the location where you store your Data Files, click the Word document file PPT 3-2.docx, then click Insert**

   Six new slides (7, 8, 9, 10, 11, and 12) are added to the presentation, and the new Slide 7 appears in the Slide pane. See FIGURE 3-1.

4. **Click the down scroll arrow ▾ in the Outline pane and read the text for all the new slides, then click the Normal button ▣ on the status bar**

   The information on Slides 7 and 12 refer to information not needed for this presentation.

5. **Click the Slide 7 thumbnail in the Slides tab, press [Ctrl], click the Slide 12 thumbnail, then click the Cut button in the Clipboard group**

   Slides 7 and 12 are deleted, and the next slide down (Suggested Itinerary) becomes the new Slide 10 and appears in the Slide pane.

6. **Drag the Slide 10 thumbnail in the Slides tab above Slide 8**

   Slide 10 becomes Slide 8. The inserted slides have a different slide layout and font style than the other slides. You want the text of the inserted outline to adopt the theme fonts of the presentation.

7. **Click the Slide 7 thumbnail in the Slides tab, press [Shift], click the Slide 10 thumbnail, release [Shift], click the Reset button in the Slides group, click the Layout button in the Slides group, then click the Title and Content slide layout**

   The new slides now follow the presentation design and font themes. Compare your screen to FIGURE 3-2.

8. **Click the Save button ▣ on the Quick Access toolbar**

FIGURE 3-1: Outline pane showing imported text

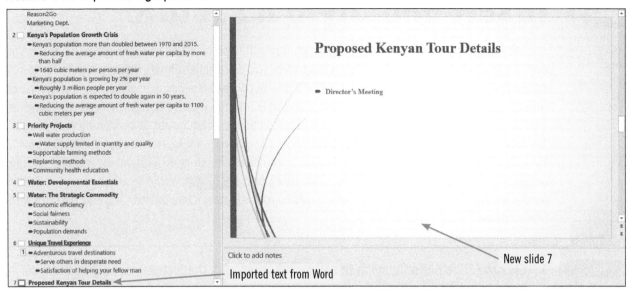

FIGURE 3-2: Slides reset to Wisp theme default settings

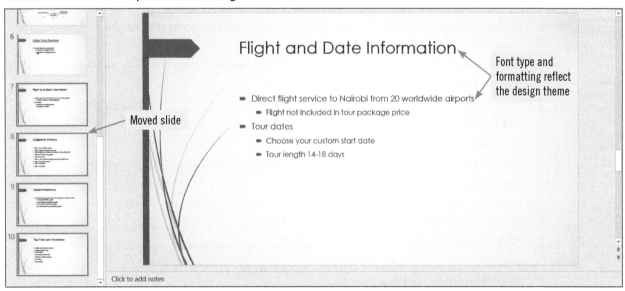

Sending a presentation using email

You can send a copy of a presentation over the Internet to a reviewer to edit and add comments. You can use Microsoft Outlook to send your presentation. Although your email program allows you to attach files, you can send a presentation using Outlook from within PowerPoint. Click the File tab, click Share, click Email in the center pane, then click Send as Attachment. Outlook opens and automatically creates an email with a copy of the presentation attached to it. You can also attach and send a PDF copy or an XPS copy of the presentation using your email program. Both of these file formats preserve document formatting, enable file sharing, and can be viewed online and printed.

Insert and Style a Picture

In PowerPoint, a **picture** is defined as a digital photograph, a piece of line art or clip art, or other artwork that is created in another program. PowerPoint gives you the ability to insert different types of pictures including JPEG File Interchange Format and BMP Windows Bitmap files into a PowerPoint presentation. As with all objects in PowerPoint, you can format and style inserted pictures to help them fit the theme of your presentation. You can also hide a portion of the picture you don't want to be seen by **cropping** it. The cropped portion of a picture is still available to you if you ever want to show that part of picture again. To reduce the size of the file you can permanently delete the cropped portion by applying picture compression settings in the Compress Pictures dialog box. **CASE** *In this lesson you insert a JPG file picture taken by an R2G staff member that is saved on your computer. Once inserted, you crop and style it to best fit the slide.*

STEPS

1. **Click the** Slide 6 thumbnail **in the Slides tab, then click the** Pictures icon 🖼 **in the content placeholder on the slide**

   The Insert Picture dialog box opens displaying the pictures available in the default Pictures folder.

2. **Navigate to location where you store your Data Files, select the picture file** PPT 3-3.jpg, **then click** Insert

   The picture fills the content placeholder on the slide, and the Picture Tools Format tab opens on the Ribbon. The picture would look better if you cropped some of the image.

3. **Click the** Crop button **in the Size group, then place the pointer over the** middle-left cropping handle **on the picture**

   The pointer changes to ⌐. When the Crop button is active, cropping handles appear next to the sizing handles on the selected object.

4. **Drag the** middle of the picture **to the right as shown in** FIGURE 3-3, **release the mouse button, then press** [Esc]

   The picture would look better on the slide if it were larger.

5. **Click the** number (3.08) **in the Width text box in the Size group to select it, type** 4, **then press** [Enter]

   The picture height and width increase proportionally. PowerPoint has a number of picture formatting options, and you decide to experiment with some of them.

6. **Click the** More button ▼ **in the Picture Styles group, move your pointer over the** style thumbnails **in the gallery to see how the different styles change the picture, then click** Bevel Rectangle **(3rd row)**

   The picture now has rounded corners and a background shadow.

7. **Click the** Corrections button **in the Adjust group, move your pointer over the** thumbnails **to see how the picture changes, then click** Sharpen: 25% **in the Sharpen/Soften section**

   The picture clarity is better.

8. **Click the** Artistic Effects button **in the Adjust group, move your pointer over the** thumbnails **to see how the picture changes, then click a blank area of the slide**

   The artistic effects are all interesting, but none of them will work well for this picture.

9. **Drag the** picture **to the center of the blank area of the slide to the right of the text object, click a blank area on the slide, then save your changes**

   Compare your screen to FIGURE 3-4.

FIGURE 3-3: Using the cropping pointer to crop a picture

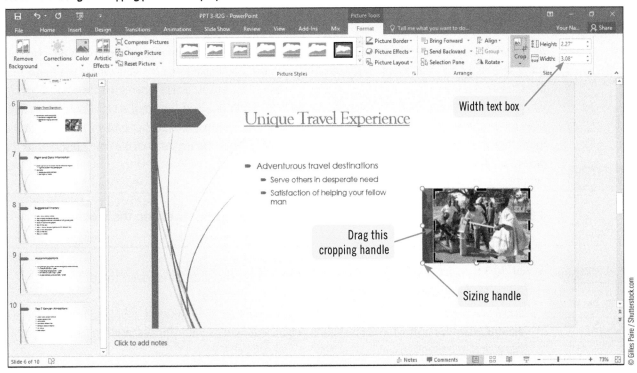

FIGURE 3-4: Cropped and styled picture

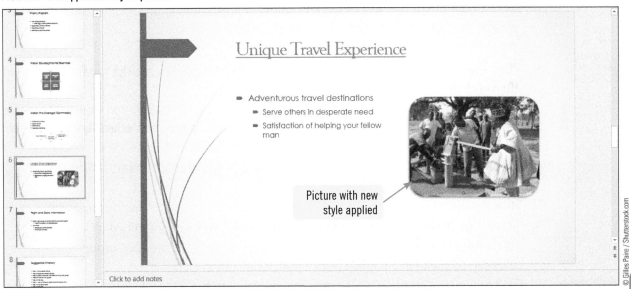

Inserting a screen recording

Using the Screen Recording button in the Media group on the Insert tab, you can record your computer screen with audio and insert the recording to a slide. For example, if you want to make a recording of an Internet video, locate and display the video on your computer screen. In PowerPoint on the slide where you want to insert the recording, click the Screen Recording button.

On the toolbar, click the Select Area button, drag a selection box around the video, click the Audio button if necessary, then click the Record button on the toolbar. Click the video play button. When finished recording, click Windows Logo+[Shift]+Q to stop recording. PowerPoint opens and the recording appears on your slide. Click the Play button to review your recording.

PowerPoint 2016

Inserting Objects into a Presentation

Insert a Text Box

Learning Outcomes
- Insert a text box
- Format text in a text box
- Resize and move a text box

As you've already learned, you enter text on a slide using a title or content placeholder that is arranged on the slide based on a slide layout. Every so often you need additional text on a slide where the traditional placeholder does not place text. There are two types of text boxes: a text label, used for a small phrase where text doesn't automatically wrap inside the boundaries of a text box, and a word-processing box, used for a sentence or paragraph where the text wraps inside a text box. Either type of text box can be formatted and edited just like any other text object. **CASE** ▶ *You decide to create a text box next to the picture on Slide 6 and then edit and format the text.*

STEPS

1. **Click the** Slide 6 thumbnail **in the Slides tab, click the** Insert tab **on the Ribbon, then click the** Text Box button **in the Text group**

   The pointer changes to ↓.

QUICK TIP
To create a text label, click the Text Box button, position the pointer on the slide, click once, then enter your text.

2. **Move ↓ to the blank area below the text object on the slide, then drag the pointer ✛ down and toward the right about 3" to create a text box**

   When you begin dragging, an outline of the text box appears, indicating the size of the text box you are drawing. After you release the mouse button, a blinking insertion point appears inside the text box, in this case a word-processing box, indicating that you can enter text.

3. **Type** Village chief in March 2017 inaugurates new hand pump

   Notice the text box increases in size as your text wraps to additional lines inside the text box. Your screen should look similar to FIGURE 3-5. After entering the text, you decide to edit the sentence.

4. **Drag I over the phrase** in March 2017 **to select it, position ↳ on top of the selected phrase, then press and hold the** left mouse button

   The pointer changes to ↳.

5. **Drag the selected words to the right of the word "pump", release the mouse button, then click outside the text box**

   A grey insertion line appears as you drag, indicating where PowerPoint places the text when you release the mouse button. The phrase "in March 2017" moves after the word "pump". Notice there is no space between the words "pump" and "in" and the spelling error is identified by a red wavy underline.

6. **Right-click the** red underlined words **in the text box, then click "pump in" on the shortcut menu**

   Space is added between the two words in the text box.

7. **Move I to the edge of the text box, which changes to ↖, click the** text box border **(it changes to a solid line), then click the** Italic button *I* **in the Font group**

   All of the text in the text box is italicized.

QUICK TIP
Click the Shape Outline list arrow in the Drawing group, then click Weight or Dashes to change the outline width or style of a text object.

8. **Click the** Shape Fill list arrow **in the Drawing group, click the** Light Green, Background 2, Darker 10% color box, **click the** Shape Outline list arrow **in the Drawing group, then click the** Dark Red, Accent 1, Lighter 40% color box

   The text object is now filled with a light green color and has a red outline.

9. **Position ↖ over the text box edge, drag the** text box **to the Smart Guide on the slide as shown in** FIGURE 3-6, **then save your changes**

FIGURE 3-5: **New text object**

FIGURE 3-6: **Formatted text object**

Changing text box defaults

You can change the default formatting characteristics of text boxes you create using the Text Box button on the Insert tab. To change the formatting defaults for text boxes, select an existing formatted text box, or create a new one and format it using any of PowerPoint's formatting commands. When you are ready to change the text box defaults of a text box that is not selected, press [Shift], right-click the formatted text box, release [Shift], then click Set as Default Text Box on the shortcut menu. Any new text boxes you create now will display the formatting characteristics of this formatted text box.

Insert a Chart

Learning Outcomes
• Insert a new chart on a slide

Frequently, the best way to communicate numerical information is with a visual aid such as a chart. A **chart** is the graphical representation of numerical data. PowerPoint uses Excel to create charts. Every chart has a corresponding **worksheet** that contains the numerical data displayed by the chart. When you insert a chart object into PowerPoint, you are embedding it. An **embedded object** is one that is a part of your presentation (just like any other object you insert into PowerPoint) except that an embedded object's data source can be opened, in this case using Excel, for editing purposes. Changes you make to an embedded object in PowerPoint using the features in PowerPoint do not affect the data source for the data. **CASE** ➤ *You insert a chart on a new slide.*

STEPS

QUICK TIP
Right-click a slide in the Slides tab, then click Duplicate Slide to create an exact copy of the slide.

1. **Click the** Slide 2 thumbnail **in the Slides tab, then press** [Enter]

   Pressing [Enter] adds a new slide to your presentation with the slide layout of the selected slide, in this case the Title and Content slide layout.

2. **Click the** Title placeholder, **type** Population Growth Comparison, **then click the Insert Chart icon** in the Content placeholder

   The Insert Chart dialog box opens as shown in FIGURE 3-7. Each chart type includes a number of 2D and 3D styles. The Clustered Column chart is the default 2D chart style. For a brief explanation of common chart types, refer to TABLE 3-1.

QUICK TIP
You can also add a chart to a slide by clicking the Chart button in the Illustrations group on the Insert tab.

3. **Click** OK

   The PowerPoint window displays a clustered column chart below a worksheet with sample data, as shown in FIGURE 3-8. The Chart Tools Design tab on the Ribbon contains commands you use in PowerPoint to work with the chart. The worksheet consists of rows and columns. The intersection of a row and a column is called a **cell**. Cells are referred to by their row and column location; for example, the cell at the intersection of column A and row 1 is called cell A1. Each column and row of data in the worksheet is called a **data series**. Cells in column A and row 1 contain **data series labels** that identify the data or values in the column and row. "Category 1" is the data series label for the data in the second row, and "Series 1" is a data series label for the data in the second column. Cells below and to the right of the data series labels, in the shaded blue portion of the worksheet, contain the data values that are represented in the chart. Cells in row 1 appear in the chart **legend** and describe the data in the series. Each data series has corresponding **data series markers** in the chart, which are graphical representations such as bars, columns, or pie wedges. The boxes with the numbers along the left side of the worksheet are **row headings**, and the boxes with the letters along the top of the worksheet are **column headings**.

4. **Move the pointer over the worksheet, then click cell** C4

   The pointer changes to ✛. Cell C4, containing the value 1.8, is the selected cell, which means it is now the **active cell**. The active cell has a thick green border around it.

5. **Click the** Close button ✕ **on the worksheet title bar, then click the** Quick Layout button **in the Chart Layouts group**

   The worksheet window closes, and the Quick Layout gallery opens.

6. **Move** ⇖ **over the layouts in the gallery, then click** Layout 1

   This new layout moves the legend to the right side of the chart and increases the size of the data series markers.

7. **Click in a blank area of the slide to deselect the chart, then save your changes**

   The Chart Tools Design tab is no longer active.

FIGURE 3-7: **Insert Chart dialog box**

FIGURE 3-8: **Worksheet open showing chart data**

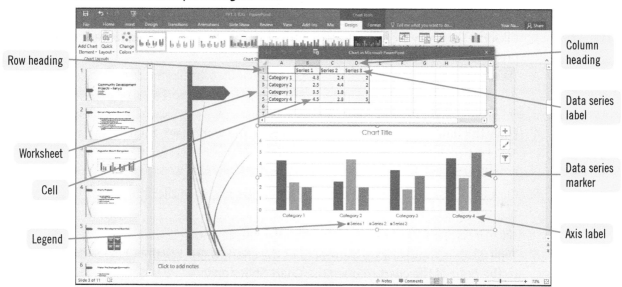

TABLE 3-1: **Chart types**

chart type	icon looks like	use to
Column		Track values over time or across categories
Line		Track values over time
Pie		Compare individual values to the whole
Bar		Compare values in categories or over time
Area		Show contribution of each data series to the total over time
X Y (Scatter)		Compare pairs of values
Stock		Show stock market information or scientific data
Surface		Show value trends across two dimensions
Radar		Show changes in values in relation to a center point
Combo		Use multiple types of data markers to compare values

Enter and Edit Chart Data

Learning Outcomes
• Change chart data values and labels
• Format a chart

After you insert a chart into your presentation, you need to replace the sample information with the correct data. If you have the data you want to chart in an Excel worksheet, you can import it from Excel; otherwise, you can type your own data into the worksheet on the slide. As you enter data and make other changes in the worksheet, the chart on the slide automatically reflects the new changes. **CASE** *You enter and format population data you have gathered comparing the growth trends of three African countries.*

STEPS

1. **Click the chart on Slide 3, click the Chart Tools Design tab on the Ribbon, then click the Edit Data button in the Data group**

   The chart is selected and the worksheet opens in a separate window. The information in the worksheet needs to be replaced with the correct data.

2. **Click the Series 1 cell, type Kenya, press [Tab], type Uganda, press [Tab], then type S. Africa**

   The data series labels you enter in the worksheet are displayed in the legend on the chart. Pressing [Tab] moves the active cell from left to right one cell at a time in a row. Pressing [Enter] in the worksheet moves the active cell down one cell at a time in a column.

3. **Click the Category 1 cell, type 1990, press [Enter], type 2000, press [Enter], type 2010, press [Enter], type 2015, then press [Enter]**

   These data series labels appear in the worksheet and along the bottom of the chart on the x-axis. The x-axis is the horizontal axis also referred to as the **category axis**, and the y-axis is the vertical axis also referred to as the **value axis**.

4. **Enter the data shown in FIGURE 3-9 to complete the worksheet, then press [Enter]**

   Notice that the height of each column in the chart, as well as the values along the y-axis, adjust to reflect the numbers you typed. You have finished entering the data in the Excel worksheet.

5. **Click the Close button** ☒ **on the worksheet title bar, then click the Chart Title text box object in the chart**

   The worksheet window closes. The Chart Title text box is selected.

6. **Type 25 Year Trend, click a blank area of the chart, then click the Chart Styles button** ☑ **to the right of the chart to open the Chart Styles gallery**

   The Chart Styles gallery opens on the left side of the chart with Style selected.

7. **Scroll down the gallery, click Style 6, click Color at the top of the Chart Styles gallery, then click the Color 3 palette in the Colorful section**

   The new chart style and color gives the column data markers a professional look as shown in FIGURE 3-10.

8. **Click a blank area on the slide, then save the presentation**

   The Chart Styles gallery closes.

FIGURE 3-9: **Worksheet data for the chart**

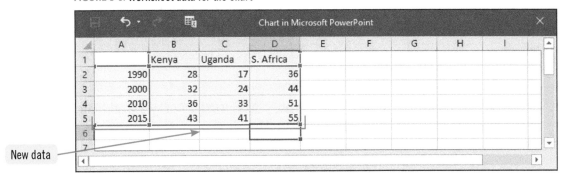

New data

FIGURE 3-10: **Formatted chart**

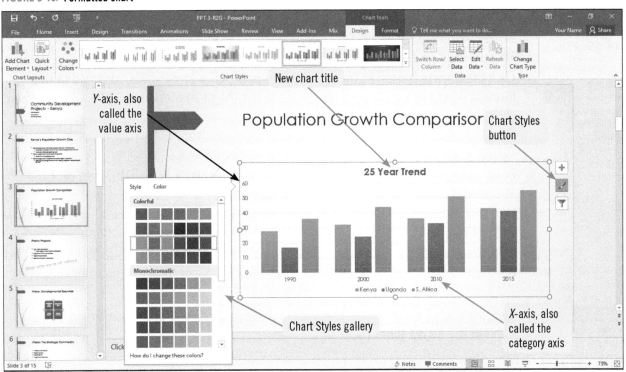

Adding a hyperlink to a chart

You can add a hyperlink to any object in PowerPoint, including a chart. Select that chart, click the Insert tab on the Ribbon, then click the Hyperlink button in the Links group. If you are linking to another file, click the Existing File or Web Page button, locate the file you want to link to the chart, then click OK. Or, if you want to link to another slide in the presentation, click the Place in This Document button, click the slide in the list, then click OK. Now, during a slide show you can click the chart to open the linked object. To remove the link, click the chart, click the Hyperlink button in the Links group, then click Remove Link.

PowerPoint 2016
Module 3

Learning
Outcomes
• Insert slides
  from another
  presentation

Insert Slides from Other Presentations

To save time and energy, you can insert one or more slides you already created in other presentations into an existing presentation or one you are currently working on. One way to share slides between presentations is to open an existing presentation, copy the slides you want to the Clipboard, and then paste them into your open presentation. However, PowerPoint offers a simpler way to transfer slides directly between presentations. By using the Reuse Slides pane, you can insert slides from another presentation or a network location called a Slide Library. A **Slide Library** is folder that you and others can access to open, modify, and review presentation slides. Newly inserted slides automatically take on the theme of the open presentation, unless you decide to use slide formatting from the original source presentation. **CASE** You decide to insert slides you created for another presentation into the Kenya presentation.

STEPS

QUICK TIP
You can also open a second presentation window and work on the same presentation in different places at the same time. Click the View tab, then click the New Window button in the Window group.

1. **Click the** Slide 6 thumbnail **in the Slides tab, click the** New Slide list arrow **in the Slides group, then click** Reuse Slides

   The Reuse Slides pane opens on the right side of the pre sentation window.

2. **Click the** Browse button **in the Reuse Slides pane, click** Browse File, **navigate to the location where you store your Data Files, select the presentation file** PPT 3-4.pptx, **then click** Open

   Five slide thumbnails are displayed in the pane with the first slide thumbnail selected as shown in FIGURE 3-11. The slide thumbnails identify the slides in the **source presentation**, PPT 3-4.pptx.

3. **Point to each slide in the Reuse Slides pane list to display a ScreenTip, then click the** Strategies for Managing Water Demand slide

   The new slide appears in the Slides tab and Slide pane as the new Slide 7. Notice the title new slide assumes the design style and formatting of your presentation, which is called the **destination presentation**.

4. **Click the** Keep source formatting check box **at the bottom of the Reuse Slides pane, click the** Water Restructuring Policies slide, **then click the** Keep source formatting check box

   This new slide keeps the design style and formatting of the source presentation.

QUICK TIP
To copy noncontiguous slides, open Slide Sorter view, click the first slide thumbnail, press and hold [Ctrl], click each additional slide thumbnail, release [Ctrl], then click the Copy button.

5. **Click the** Slide 7 thumbnail **in the Slides tab, then click each of the remaining three slides in the Reuse Slides pane**

   Three more slides are inserted into the presentation with the design style and formatting of the destination presentation. You realize that Slides 7 and 11 are not needed for this presentation.

6. **Click the** Slide 11 thumbnail **in the Slides tab, press [Ctrl], click the** Slide 7 thumbnail, **release [Ctrl], right-click the** Slide 7 thumbnail, **then click** Delete Slide **in the shortcut menu**

   Slides 7 and 11 are deleted.

7. **Click the** Reuse Slides pane Close button ☒, **click a blank area of the slide, then save the presentation**

   The Reuse Slides pane closes. Compare your screen to FIGURE 3-12.

FIGURE 3-11: Presentation window with Reuse Slides pane open

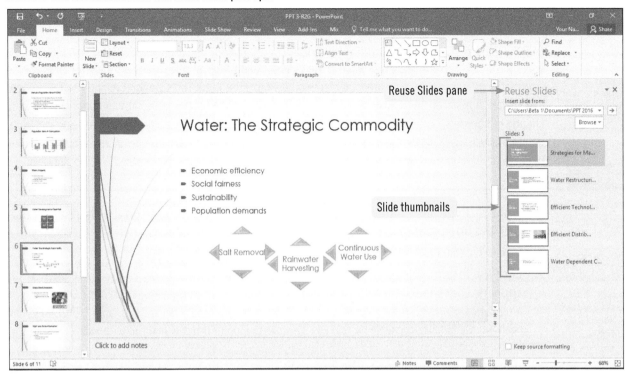

FIGURE 3-12: New slides added to presentation

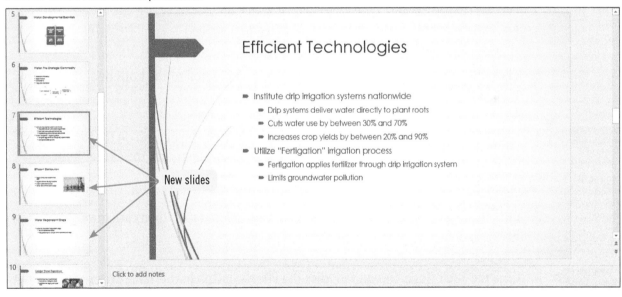

Working with multiple windows

Another way to work with information in multiple presentations is to arrange the presentation windows on your monitor so you see each window side by side. Open each presentation, click the View tab on the Ribbon in any presentation window, then click the Arrange All button in the Window group. Each presentation you have open is placed next to each other so you can easily drag, or transfer, information between the presentations.

If you are working with more than two open presentations, you can overlap the presentation windows on top of one another. Open all the presentations you want, then click the Cascade Windows button in the Window group. Now you can easily jump from one presentation to another by clicking on the presentation title bar or any part of the presentation window.

Insert a Table

Learning Outcomes
- Insert a table
- Add text to a table
- Change table size and layout

As you create your presentation, you may have some information that would look best organized in rows and columns. For example, if you want to view related data side by side, a table is ideal for this type of information. Once you have created a table, two new tabs, the Table Tools Design tab and the Table Tools Layout tab, appear on the Ribbon. You can use the commands on the table tabs to apply color styles, change cell borders, add cell effects, add rows and columns to your table, adjust the size of cells, and align text in the cells. **CASE** ▸ *You decide a table best illustrates the technology considerations for building a well in Kenya.*

STEPS

1. **Right-click the** Slide 9 thumbnail **in the Slides tab, click** New Slide **on the shortcut menu, click the** title placeholder, **then type** Technology Considerations

   A new slide with the Title and Content layout appears.

2. **Click the** Insert Table icon ⊞, **click the** Number of columns down arrow **twice until** 3 **appears, click the** Number of rows up arrow **twice until** 4 **appears, then click** OK

   A formatted table with three columns and four rows appears on the slide, and the Table Tools Design tab opens on the Ribbon. The table has 12 cells. The insertion point is in the first cell of the table and is ready to accept text.

QUICK TIP
Press [Tab] when the insertion point is in the last cell of a table to create a new row.

3. **Type** Financial, **press** [Tab], **type** Maintenance, **press** [Tab], **type** Population, **then press** [Tab]

   The text you typed appears in the top three cells of the table. Pressing [Tab] moves the insertion point to the next cell; pressing [Enter] moves the insertion point to the next line in the same cell.

4. **Enter the rest of the table information shown in** FIGURE 3-13

   The table would look better if it were formatted differently.

5. **Click the** More button ⧩ **in the Table Styles group, scroll to the bottom of the gallery, then click** Medium Style 3

   The background and text color change to reflect the table style you applied.

QUICK TIP
Change the height or width of any table cell by dragging its borders.

6. **Click the** Financial **cell in the table, click the** Table Tools Layout tab **on the Ribbon, click the** Select button **in the Table group, click** Select Row, **then click the** Center button ▤ **in the Alignment group**

   The text in the top row is centered horizontally in each cell.

7. **Click the** Select button **in the Table group, click** Select Table, **then click the** Center Vertically button ▤ **in the Alignment group**

   The text in the entire table is aligned in the center of each cell.

QUICK TIP
To change the cell color behind text, click the Shading list arrow in the Table Styles group, then choose a color.

8. **Click the** Table Tools Design tab, **click the** Effects button **in the Table Styles group, point to** Cell Bevel, **then click** Soft Round **(2nd row)**

   The 3D effect makes the cells of the table stand out. The table would look better in a different place on the slide.

9. **Place the pointer** ⌖ **over the top edge of the table, drag the table straight down so it is placed as shown in** FIGURE 3-14, **click a blank area of the slide, then save the presentation**

   The slide looks better with more space between the table and the slide title.

FIGURE 3-13: **Inserted table with data**

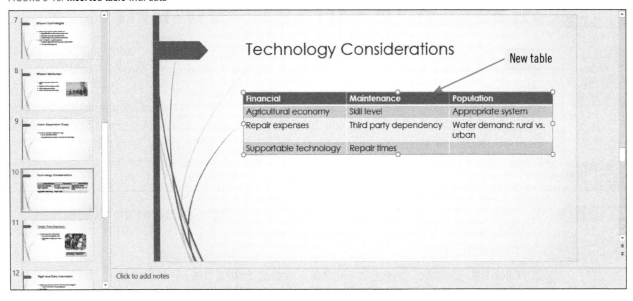

FIGURE 3-14: **Formatted table**

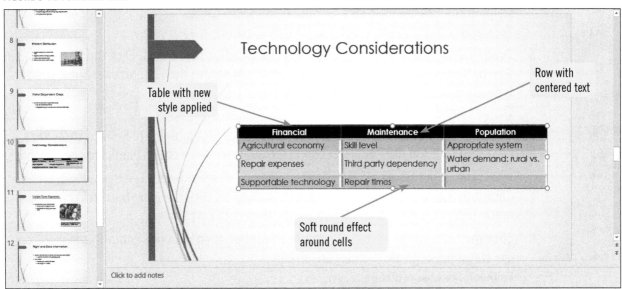

Setting permissions

In PowerPoint, you can set specific access permissions for people who review or edit your work so you have better control over your content. For example, you may want to give a user permission to edit or change your presentation but not allow them to print it. You can also restrict a user by permitting them to view the presentation without the ability to edit or print the presentation, or you can give the user full access or control of the presentation. To use this feature, you first must have access to an information rights management company. Then, to set user access permissions, click the File tab, click the Protect Presentation button, point to Restrict Access, then click an appropriate option.

Insert and Format WordArt

As you work to create an interesting presentation, your goal should include making your slides visually appealing. Sometimes plain text can come across as dull and unexciting in a presentation. **WordArt** is a set of decorative text styles, or text effects, you can apply to any text object to help direct the attention of your audience to a certain piece of information. You can use WordArt in two different ways: you can apply a WordArt text style to an existing text object that converts the text into WordArt, or you can create a new WordArt object. The WordArt text styles and effects include text shadows, reflections, glows, bevels, 3D rotations, and transformations. **CASE** ▶ *Create a new WordArt text object on Slide 4.*

STEPS

QUICK TIP
To format any text
with a WordArt style,
select the text, click
the Drawing Tools
Format tab on the
Ribbon, then click a
WordArt style option
in the WordArt
Styles group.

1. **Click the** Slide 4 thumbnail **in the Slides tab, click the** Insert tab **on the Ribbon, then click the** WordArt button **in the Text group**
   The WordArt gallery appears displaying 20 WordArt text styles.

2. **Click** Fill – Orange, Accent 2, Outline – Accent 2 **(first row)**
   A text object appears in the middle of the slide displaying sample text with the WordArt style you just selected. The Drawing Tools Format tab is open on the Ribbon.

3. **Click the edge of the** WordArt text object, **then when the pointer changes to** ⬚, **drag the text object to the blank area of the slide**

4. **Click the** More button ⯆ **in the WordArt Styles group, move** ⬚ **over all of the WordArt styles in the gallery, then click** Gradient Fill – Olive Green, Accent 1, Reflection
   The sample text in the WordArt text object changes to the new WordArt style.

5. **Drag to select the text** Your text here **in the WordArt text object, click the** Decrease Font Size button A⁻ **in the Mini toolbar so that** 48 **appears in the Font Size text box, then type** Clean water equals self-reliance
   The text is smaller.

QUICK TIP
To convert a WordArt
object to a SmartArt
object, right-click the
WordArt object,
point to Convert to
SmartArt on the
shortcut menu,
then click a
SmartArt layout.

6. **Click the** Text Effects button **in the WordArt Styles group, point to** 3-D Rotation, **click** Off Axis 1 Right **in the Parallel section (second row), then click a blank area of the slide**
   The off-axis effect is applied to the text object. Compare your screen to FIGURE 3-15.

7. **Click the** Reading View button 📖 **on the status bar, click the** Next button ⏵ **until you reach Slide 15, click the** Menu button ▤, **then click** End Show

8. **Click the** Slide Sorter button ▤▤ **on the status bar, then click the** Zoom Out icon ➖ **on the status bar until all 15 slides are visible**
   Compare your screen with FIGURE 3-16.

9. **Click the** Normal button ▣ **on the status bar, add your name, the slide number and the date as a footer to the slides, save your changes, submit your presentation to your instructor, then exit PowerPoint**

FIGURE 3-15: WordArt inserted on slide

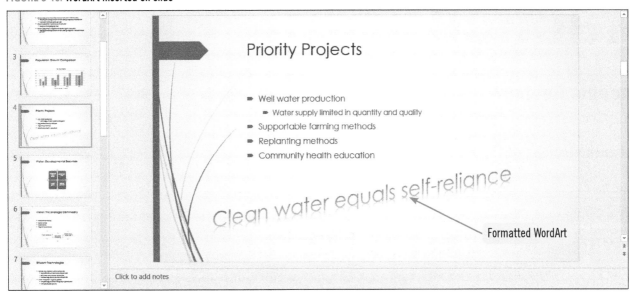

FIGURE 3-16: Completed presentation in Slide Sorter view

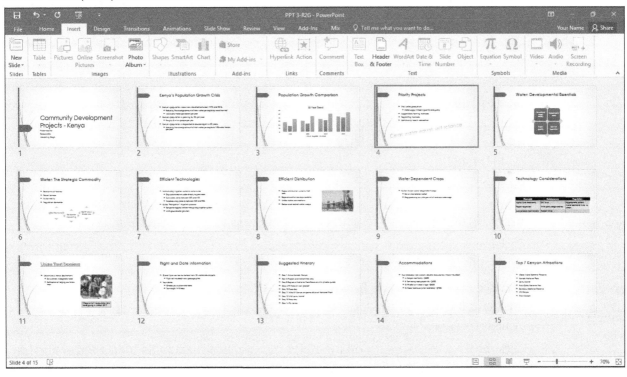

Saving a presentation as a video

You can save your PowerPoint presentation as a full-fidelity video, which incorporates all slide timings, transitions, animations, and narrations. The video can be distributed using a disc, the web, or email. Depending on how you want to display your video, you have three resolution settings from which to choose: Presentation Quality, Internet Quality, and Low Quality. The Large setting, Presentation Quality (1920 X 1080), is used for viewing on a computer monitor, projector, or other high-definition displays. The Medium setting, Internet Quality (1280 X 720), is used for uploading to the web or copying to a standard DVD. The Small setting, Low Quality (852 X 480), is used on portable media players. To save your presentation as a video, click the File tab, click Export, click Create a Video, choose your settings, then click the Create Video button.

Practice

Concepts Review

Label each element of the PowerPoint window shown in FIGURE 3-17.

FIGURE 3-17

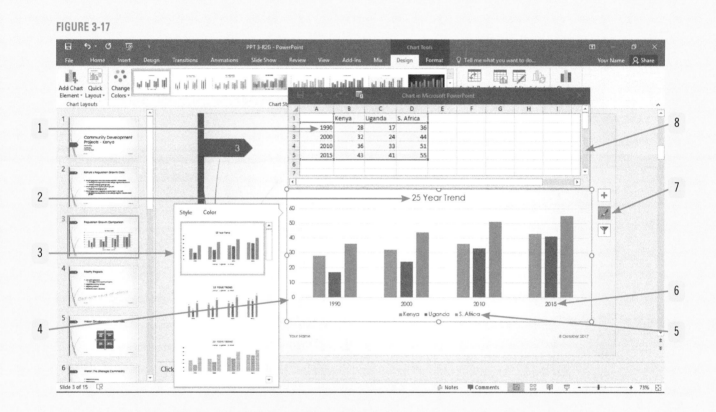

Match each term with the statement that best describes it.

9. **Category axis**
10. **Crop**
11. **Cell**
12. **Value axis**
13. **Chart**

a. The *y*-axis (vertical) in a chart
b. Intersection of a row and column in a worksheet
c. The graphical representation of numerical data
d. The *x*-axis (horizontal) in a chart
e. Hide a portion of a picture

Select the best answer from the list of choices.

14. _____ is the network folder that you can open in the Reuse Slides pane to insert slides from other presentations.
    a. Slide Library
    b. Slide Exchange
    c. Export Exchange
    d. Slide Room

15. Use a(n) _____ object to best illustrate information you want to compare side by side.
    a. WordArt
    b. Table
    c. SmartArt
    d. Equation

16. An object that has its own data source and becomes a part of your presentation after you insert it best describes which of the following?
    a. Embedded object
    b. WordArt
    c. Table
    d. Screenshot

17. Each column and row of data in a worksheet are _____.
    a. Data series labels
    b. Headings
    c. Data series
    d. Data markers

18. The slide thumbnails in the Reuse Slides pane identify the slides of the _____ presentation.
    a. destination
    b. default
    c. source
    d. open

19. _____ to permanently delete a cropped portion of a picture.
    a. Use the Crop to Fit feature
    b. Change the aspect ratio
    c. Change the picture's artistic effect
    d. Apply picture compression

20. _____ is created by inserting text from Word document that does not have tabs.
    a. A new presentation
    b. A slide title
    c. A first level text in a bulleted list
    d. A Heading 1 style

Skills Review

1. **Insert text from Microsoft Word.**
    a. Open PPT 3-5.pptx from the location where you store your Data Files, then save it as **PPT 3-Tsar Tour**. You will work to create the completed presentation as shown in FIGURE 3-18.
    b. Click Slide 2 in the Slides tab, then use the Slides from Outline command to insert the file PPT 3-6.docx from the location where you store your Data Files.
    c. In the Slides tab, drag Slide 7 above Slide 6, then delete Slide 9, "Budapest, Hungary".
    d. Select Slides 3, 4, 5, 6, 7, and 8 in the Slides tab, reset the slides to the default theme settings, then save your work.

FIGURE 3-18

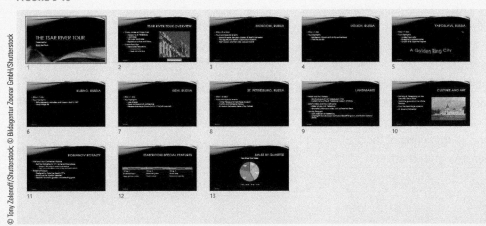

© Tony Zelenoff/Shutterstock; © Bildagentur Zoonar GmbH/Shutterstock

Skills Review (continued)

2. Insert and style a picture.

   a. Select Slide 2 in the Slides tab, then insert the picture PPT 3-7.jpg from the location where you store your Data Files.

   b. Crop the right side of the picture up to the building, then increase the size of the picture so it is 5" wide.

   c. Drag the picture to the right so it is in the center of the blank area of the slide.

   d. Click the Color button, change the color tone to Temperature: 11200 K, then save your changes.

3. Insert a text box.

   a. On Slide 2, insert a text box below the picture.

   b. Type **Catherine palace**.

   c. Select the text object, then click the More button in the Shape Styles group on the Drawing Tools Format tab.

   d. Click Moderate Effect – Orange, Accent 5, then fit the text box to the text by dragging its sizing handles.

   e. Center the text object under the picture using Smart Guides.

   f. In the main text object, type the word **on** before the word **Volga**, then move the word **cruise** before the word **on**.

4. Insert a chart.

   a. Create a new slide after Slide 8 with a Title Only layout and title it **Sales by Quarter**.

   b. On the Insert tab, click the Chart button in the Illustrations group, click Pie in the left column, then insert a Pie chart.

   c. Close the worksheet, drag the top-middle sizing handle of the chart down under the slide title, then apply the Layout 1 quick layout to the chart.

5. Enter and edit chart data.

TABLE 3-2

	Sales
1st Qtr	11
2nd Qtr	31
3rd Qtr	37
4th Qtr	21

   a. Show the worksheet, enter the data shown in TABLE 3-2 into the worksheet, then close the worksheet.

   b. Type **Tsar River Tour Sales** in the chart title text object.

   c. Click the Chart Styles button next to the chart, then change the chart style to Style 12.

   d. Click Color in the Charts Styles gallery, then change the color to Color 3 in the Colorful section.

   e. Close the Charts Styles gallery, then save your changes.

6. Insert slides from other presentations.

   a. Go to Slide 8, then open the Reuse Slides pane.

   b. Open PPT 3-8.pptx from the location where you store your Data Files.

   c. Insert the fourth slide thumbnail, insert the second slide thumbnail, and then insert the third slide thumbnail.

   d. Close the Reuse Slides pane, then save your work.

7. Insert a table.

   a. Add a new slide after Slide 11 with the Title and Content layout.

   b. Add the slide title **Stateroom Special Features**.

   c. Insert a table with three columns and four rows.

   d. Enter the information shown in TABLE 3-3, then change the table style to Light Style 2 – Accent 2.

   e. In the Table Tools Layout tab, center the text in the top row.

   f. Open the Table Tools Design tab, click the Effects button, point to Cell Bevel, then apply the Convex effect.

   g. Move the table to the center of the blank area of the slide, then save your changes.

TABLE 3-3

Deluxe Stateroom	Veranda Suite	Master Suite
160 sq. ft.	225 sq. ft.	400 sq. ft.
Private bathroom	Glass sliding door	Queen bed
Large picture window	Walk-in closet	Panoramic veranda

Skills Review (continued)

8. Insert and format WordArt.

   a. Go to Slide 5, then, insert a WordArt text object using the style Fill – Yellow, Accent 3, Sharp Bevel.

   b. Type **A Golden Ring City**, apply the Triangle Down Transform text effect (first row in the Warp section) to the text object, then move the text object to the middle of the blank area of the slide.

   c. View the presentation in Slide Show view, add your name as a footer to all the slides, then save your changes.

   d. Submit your presentation to your instructor, close your presentation, and exit PowerPoint.

Independent Challenge 1

You are a financial management consultant for Pitlock, Bryer & Mansouetti, located in Bradenton, Florida. One of your responsibilities is to create standardized presentations on different financial investments for use on the company website. As part of the presentation for this meeting, you insert a chart, add a WordArt object, and insert slides from another presentation.

   a. Open PPT 3-9.pptx from the location where you store your Data Files, then save it as **PPT 3-BIP**.

   b. Add your name as the footer on all of the slides, then apply the Frame Design Theme.

   c. Insert a clustered column chart on Slide 2, then enter the data in TABLE 3-4 into the worksheet.

   d. Close the worksheet, format the chart using Style 14, then resize and move the chart to the blank area beside the text object.

   e. Type **Annualized Return** in the chart title text object.

   f. Open the Reuse Slides pane, open PPT 3-10.pptx from the location where you store your Data Files, then insert Slides 2, 3, and 4.

TABLE 3-4

	Stocks	**Bonds**	**Mutual funds**
1 Year	5.3%	1.9%	3.8%
3 Year	4.8%	3.7%	6.7%
5 Year	3.2%	2.2%	8.3%
10 Year	2.6%	3.4%	7.2%

   g. Close the Reuse Slides pane, move Slide 5 above Slide 4, then select Slide 3.

   h. Insert a WordArt object using the Fill - Orange, Accent 4, Soft Bevel style, type **Invest early**, press [Enter], type **for**, press [Enter], then type **the long haul**.

   i. Click the Text Effects button, point to Transform, then apply the Button text effect from the Follow Path section.

   j. Move the WordArt object to a blank area of the slide, click the Text Effects button, point to Shadow, then apply an Outer shadow effect.

   k. View the presentation slide show, make any necessary changes, then save your work. See FIGURE 3-19.

   l. Submit the presentation to your instructor, then close the presentation, and exit PowerPoint.

FIGURE 3-19

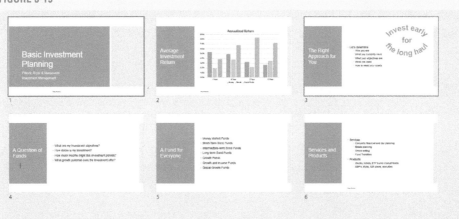

Independent Challenge 2

You work for the Boston Port Group in the commercial container division. You have been asked to enhance a marketing presentation that is going to promote the port facilities. You work on completing a presentation by inserting a picture, a text box, and a table.

a. Start PowerPoint, open PPT 3-11.pptx from the location where you store your Data Files, and save it as **PPT 3-Port**.

b. Add your name and today's date to Slide 1 in the Subtitle text box.

c. Apply the Droplet theme to the presentation.

d. On Slide 5, click the Pictures icon in the content placeholder, then insert the file PPT 3-12.jpg from the location where you store your Data Files.

e. Apply the Simple Frame, Black picture style to the picture, click the Color button, then change the color saturation to Saturation: 0%.

f. Change the size of the picture so its width is 5.2" using the Width text box in the Size group.

g. Insert a text box on the slide below the picture, type **Largest volume port on East Coast**, then format the text and text box with three formatting commands.

h. Go to Slide 2, select the picture, click the Picture Effects button, point to Soft Edges, then click 5 Point.

i. Open the Artistic Effects gallery, then apply the Cement effect to the picture.

j. Go to Slide 4, create a new table, then enter the data in TABLE 3-5. Format the table using at least two formatting commands. Be able to identify which formatting commands you applied to the table.

k. View the final presentation in Slide Show view. Make any necessary changes (refer to FIGURE 3-20).

l. Save the presentation, submit the presentation to your instructor, close the file, and exit PowerPoint.

TABLE 3-5

Total	August	September
Total containers	25,524.0	22,417.0
Loaded containers	15,283.0	14,016.0
Empty containers	10,241.0	8,401.0
Total tons	375,240	334,180

FIGURE 3-20

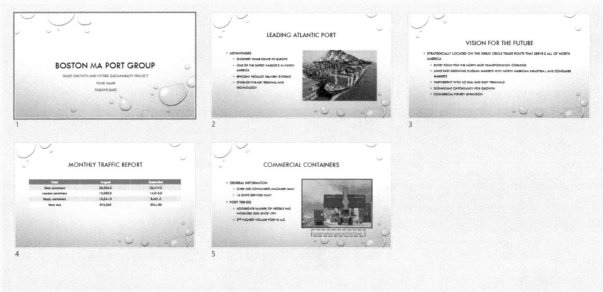

© tcly/Shutterstock; © Prasit Rodphan/Shutterstock

Independent Challenge 3

You work for World Partners Inc., a company that produces instructional software to help people learn foreign languages. Once a year, World Partners holds a meeting with their biggest client, the United States Department of Homeland Security, to brief the government on new products and to receive feedback on existing products. Your supervisor has started a presentation and has asked you to look it over and add other elements to make it look better.

a. Start PowerPoint, open PPT 3-13.pptx from the location where you store your Data Files, and save it as **PPT 3-World**.
b. Add an appropriate design theme to the presentation.
c. Insert the Word outline PPT 3-14.docx after the Product Revisions slide, then reset the new slides to the design theme.
d. Insert and format a text object and a WordArt object.
e. Insert an appropriate table on a slide of your choice. Use your own information, or use text from a bulleted list on one of the slides.
f. Add your name as footer text on the slides, then save the presentation.
g. Submit your presentation to your instructor, close the file, then exit PowerPoint.

Independent Challenge 4: Explore

As an international exchange student at your college, one of your assignments in your Intercultural Communication Studies class is to present information on a student exchange you took last semester. You need to create a pictorial presentation that highlights a trip to a different country. Create a presentation using your own pictures. If you don't have access to any appropriate pictures, use the three pictures provided in the Data Files for this unit: PPT 3-15.jpg, PPT 3-16.jpg, and PPT 3-17.jpg. (*NOTE: To complete steps below, your computer must be connected to the Internet.*)

a. Start PowerPoint, create a new blank presentation, and save it as **PPT 3-Exchange** to the location where you store your Data Files.
b. Locate and insert the pictures you want to use. Place one picture on each slide using the Content with Caption slide layout, then apply a picture style to each picture.
c. Click the Crop list arrow, and use one of the other cropping options to crop a picture.
d. Add information about each picture in the text placeholder, and enter a slide title. If you use the pictures provided, research Costa Rica, using the Internet for relevant information to place on the slides.
e. Apply an appropriate design theme, then apply an appropriate title and your name to the title slide.

FIGURE 3-21

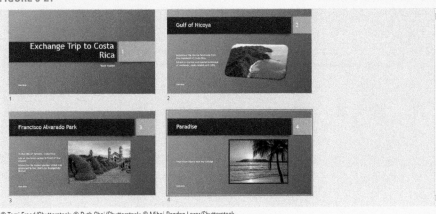

© Tami Freed/Shutterstock; © Ruth Choi/Shutterstock; © Mihai-Bogdan Lazar/Shutterstock

f. View the final presentation slide show (refer to FIGURE 3-21).
g. Add a slide number and your class name as footer text to all of the slides, save your work, then submit your presentation to your instructor.
h. Close the file, and exit PowerPoint.

Visual Workshop

Create a one-slide presentation that looks like FIGURE 3-22. The slide layout used is a specific layout designed for pictures. Insert the picture file PPT 3-18.jpg to complete this presentation. Add your name as footer text to the slide, save the presentation as **PPT 3-TCM** to the location where you store your Data Files, then submit your presentation to your instructor.

FIGURE 3-22

© tcly/Shutterstock

Finishing a Presentation

CASE ▶ You have reviewed your work and are pleased with the slides you created so far for the Reason2Go presentation. Now you are ready to add some final enhancements to the slides to make the PowerPoint presentation interesting to watch.

Module Objectives

After completing this module, you will be able to:

- Modify masters
- Customize the background and theme
- Use slide show commands
- Set slide transitions and timings
- Animate objects
- Use proofing and language tools
- Inspect a presentation
- Create an Office Mix

Files You Will Need

PPT 4-1.pptx	PPT 4-6.jpg
PPT 4-2.jpg	PPT 4-7.pptx
PPT 4-3.pptx	PPT 4-8.pptx
PPT 4-4.jpg	PPT 4-9.jpg
PPT 4-5.pptx	PPT 4-10.jpg

Modify Masters

Each presentation in PowerPoint has a set of **masters** that store information about the theme and slide layouts. Masters determine the position and size of text and content placeholders, fonts, slide background, color, and effects. There are three Master views: Slide Master view, Notes Master view, and Handout Master view. Changes made in Slide Master view are reflected on the slides in Normal view; changes made in Notes Master view are reflected in Notes Page view, and changes made in Handout Master view appear when you print your presentation using a handout printing option. The primary benefit to modifying a master is that you can make universal changes to your whole presentation instead of making individual repetitive changes to each of your slides. **CASE** ▶ *You want to add the R2G company logo to every slide in your presentation, so you open your presentation and insert the logo on the slide master.*

STEPS

1. **Start PowerPoint, open the presentation** PPT 4-1.pptx **from the location where you store your Data Files, save the presentation as** PPT 4-R2G, **then click the** View tab **on the Ribbon**

   The title slide for the presentation appears.

2. **Click the** Slide Master button **in the Master Views group, scroll to the top of the Master Thumbnails pane, then click the** Wisp Slide Master thumbnail (first thumbnail)

   The Slide Master view appears with the slide master displayed in the Slide pane as shown in FIGURE 4-1. A new tab, the Slide Master tab, appears next to the Home tab on the Ribbon. The slide master is the Wisp theme slide master. Each theme comes with its own slide master. Each master text placeholder on the slide master identifies the font size, style, color, and position of text placeholders on the slides in Normal view. For example, for the Wisp theme, the Master title placeholder positioned at the top of the slide uses a black, 36 pt, Century Gothic font. Slide titles use this font style and formatting. Each slide master comes with associated slide layouts located below the slide master in the Master Thumbnails pane. Slide layouts follow the information on the slide master, and changes you make are reflected in all of the slide layouts.

3. **Point to each of the** slide layouts **in the Master Thumbnails pane, then click the** Title and Content Layout thumbnail

   As you point to each slide layout, a ScreenTip appears identifying each slide layout by name and lists if any slides in the presentation are using the layout. Slides 2–9 and 12–15 are using the Title and Content Layout.

4. **Click the** Wisp Slide Master thumbnail, **click the** Insert tab **on the Ribbon, then click the** Pictures button **in the Images group**

   The Insert Picture dialog box opens.

5. **Select the picture file** PPT 4-2.jpg **from the location where you store your Data Files, then click** Insert

   The R2G logo picture is placed on the slide master and will now appear on all slides in the presentation. The picture is too large and would look better with a transparent background.

6. **Click** 2.45" **in the** Width text box **in the Size group, type** 1.75, **press [Enter], click the** Color button **in the Adjust group, then click** Set Transparent Color

   The pointer changes to ◌.

7. **Click the** lime green color **in the logo picture, drag the** logo **as shown in** FIGURE 4-2, **then click a blank area of the slide**

   The picture background color is now transparent.

8. **Click the** Normal button ▣ **on the status bar, then save your changes**

FIGURE 4-1: **Slide Master view**

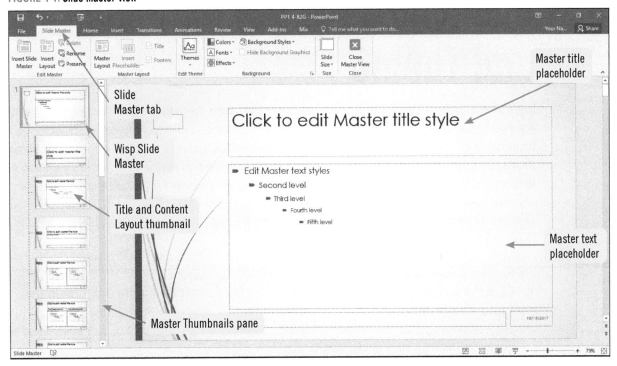

FIGURE 4-2: **Picture added to slide master**

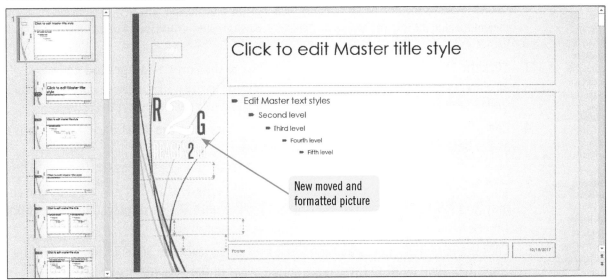

Create custom slide layouts

As you work with PowerPoint, you may find that you need to develop a customized slide layout. For example, you may need to create a presentation for a client that has a slide that displays four pictures with a caption underneath each picture. To make everyone's job easier, you can create a custom slide layout that includes only the placeholders you need. To create a custom slide layout, open Slide Master view, and then click the Insert Layout button in the Edit Master group. A new slide layout appears below the last layout for the selected master in the Master Thumbnails pane.

You can choose to add several different placeholders including Content, Text, Picture, Chart, Table, SmartArt, Media, and Online Image. Click the Insert Placeholder list arrow in the Master Layout group, click the placeholder you want to add, drag ✛ to create the placeholder, then position the placeholder on the slide. In Slide Master view, you can add or delete placeholders in any of the slide layouts. You can rename a custom slide layout by clicking the Rename button in the Edit Master group and entering a descriptive name to better identify the layout.

Customize the Background and Theme

Learning Outcomes
- Apply a slide background and change the style
- Modify presentation theme

Every slide in a PowerPoint presentation has a **background**, the area behind the text and graphics. You modify the background to enhance the slides using images and color. You can quickly change the background appearance by applying a background style, which is a set of color variations derived from the theme colors. Theme colors determine the colors for all slide elements in your presentation, including slide background, text and lines, shadows, fills, accents, and hyperlinks. Every PowerPoint theme has its own set of theme colors. See TABLE 4-1 for a description of the theme colors. **CASE** ▷ *The R2G presentation can be improved with some design enhancements. You decide to modify the background of the slides by changing the theme colors and fonts.*

STEPS

1. **Click the** Design tab **on the Ribbon, then click the** Format Background button **in the Customize group**

   The Format Background pane opens displaying the Fill options. The gradient option button is selected indicating the slide has a gradient background.

QUICK TIP

To add artistic effects, picture corrections, or picture color changes to a slide background, click the Effects or Picture icons in the Format Background pane, then click one of the options.

2. **Click the** Solid fill option button, **review the slide, click the** Pattern fill option button, **then click the** Dotted diamond **pattern (seventh row)**

   FIGURE 4-3 shows the new background on Slide 1 of the presentation. The new background style covers the slide behind the text and background graphics. **Background graphics** are objects placed on the slide master.

3. **Click the** Hide background graphics check box **in the Format Background pane**

   All of the background objects, which include the R2G logo, the red pentagon shape, and the other colored shapes, are hidden from view, and only the text objects and slide number remain visible.

4. **Click the** Hide background graphics check box, **then click the** Reset Background button **at the bottom of the Format Background pane**

   All of the background objects and the gradient fill slide background appear again as specified by the theme.

QUICK TIP

To create a custom theme, click the View tab, click the Slide Master button in the Master Views group, then click the Colors button, the Fonts button, or the Effects button in the Background group.

5. **Click the** Picture or texture fill option button, **click the** Texture button ▦, **click** Woven mat **(top row), then drag the** Transparency slider **until** 40% **is displayed in the text box**

   The new texture fills the slide background behind the background items.

6. **Click the** Format Background pane Close button ☒, **click the** Slide 3 thumbnail **in the Slides tab, then point to the** black theme variant **in the Variants group**

   The new theme variant changes the color of the shapes on the slide and the background texture. A **variant** is a custom variation of the applied theme, in this case the Wisp theme. Theme variants are similar to the original theme, but they are made up of different complementary colors, slide backgrounds, such as textures and patterns, and background elements, such as shapes and pictures.

7. **Point to the other** variants **in the Variants group, click the** second variant **from the left, then save your work**

   The new variant is applied to the slide master and to all the slides in the presentation. Compare your screen to FIGURE 4-4.

FIGURE 4-3: New background style applied

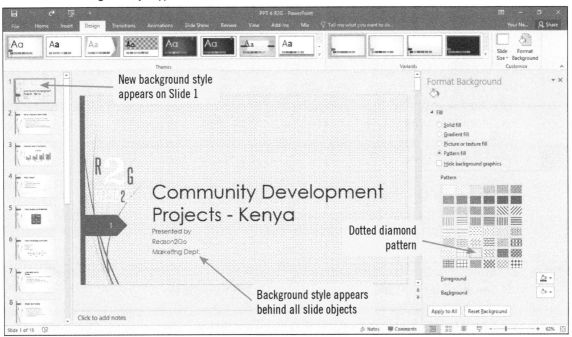

FIGURE 4-4: New theme variant

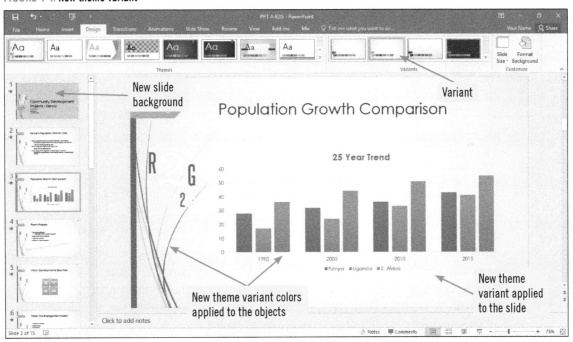

TABLE 4-1: Theme colors

color element	description
Text/Background colors	Contrasting colors for typed characters and the slide background
Accent colors	There are six accent colors used for shapes, drawn lines, and text; the shadow color for text and objects and the fill and outline color for shapes are all accent colors; all of these colors contrast appropriately with background and text colors
Hyperlink color	Colors used for hyperlinks you insert
Followed Hyperlink color	Color used for hyperlinks after they have been clicked

Use Slide Show Commands

Learning Outcomes
• Preview a slide show
• Navigate a slide show
• Use slide show tools

With PowerPoint, Slide Show view is used primarily to deliver a presentation to an audience, either over the Internet using your computer or through a projector connected to your computer. As you've seen, Slide Show view fills your computer screen with the slides of the presentation, showing them one at a time. In Slide Show view, you can draw freehand pen or highlighter strokes, also known as **ink annotations**, on the slide or jump to other slides in the presentation. **CASE** *You run the slide show of the presentation and practice using some of the custom slide show options.*

STEPS

1. **Click the** Slide Show button ⬚ **on the status bar, then press** [Spacebar]

   Slide 3 filled the screen first, and then Slide 4 appears. Pressing [Spacebar] or clicking the left mouse button is an easy way to move through a slide show. See TABLE 4-2 for other basic slide show keyboard commands. You can easily navigate to other slides in the presentation during the slide show.

2. **Move** ⬚ **to the lower-left corner of the screen to display the Slide Show toolbar, click the** See all slides button ○, **then click the** Slide 2 thumbnail

   Slide 2 appears on the screen. With the Slide Show toolbar you can emphasize points in your presentation by drawing highlighter strokes on the slide during a slide show.

3. **Click the** Pen and laser pointer tools button ⬚, **on the Slide Show toolbar, then click** Highlighter

   The pointer changes to the highlighter pointer ▌. You can use the highlighter anywhere on the slide.

4. **Drag** ▌, **to highlight** doubled between 1970 and 2015 **and** double again in 50 years **in the text object, then press** [Esc]

   Two lines of text are highlighted as shown in FIGURE 4-5. While the ▌ is visible, mouse clicks do not advance the slide show; however, you can still move to the next slide by pressing [Spacebar] or [Enter]. Pressing [Esc] or [Ctrl][A] while drawing with the highlighter or pen switches the pointer back to ⬚.

5. **Right-click anywhere on the screen, point to** Pointer Options, **click** Eraser, **the pointer changes to** ⬚, **then click the** lower highlight annotation **in the text object**

   The highlight annotation on the "double again in 50 years" text is erased.

6. **Press** [Esc], **click the** More slide show options button ○ **on the Slide Show toolbar, click** Show Presenter View, **then click the** Pause the timer button ▐▐ **above the slide as shown in** FIGURE 4-6

   Presenter view is a view that you can use when showing a presentation through two monitors; one that you see as the presenter and one that your audience sees. The current slide appears on the left of your screen (which is the only object your audience sees), the next slide in the presentation appears in the upper-right corner of the screen. Speaker notes, if you have any, appear in the lower-right corner. The timer you paused identifies how long the slide has been viewed by the audience.

7. **Click** ○, **click** Hide Presenter View, **then click the** Advance to the next slide button ⊙ **on the Slide Show toolbar**

   Slide 3 appears.

8. **Press** [Enter] **to advance through the entire slide show until you see a black slide, then press** [Spacebar]

   If there are ink annotations on your slides, you have the option of saving them when you quit the slide show. Saved ink annotations appear as drawn objects in Normal view.

9. **Click** Discard, **then save the presentation**

   The highlight ink annotation is deleted on Slide 2, and Slide 3 appears in Normal view.

FIGURE 4-5: Slide 2 in Slide Show view with highlighter drawings

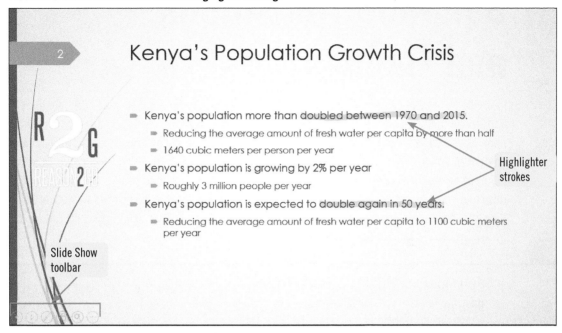

FIGURE 4-6: Slide 2 in Presenter view

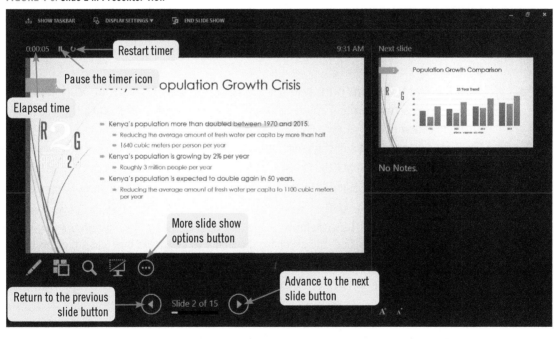

TABLE 4-2: Basic Slide Show view keyboard commands

keyboard commands	description
[Enter], [Spacebar], [PgDn], [N], [down arrow], or [right arrow]	Advances to the next slide
[E]	Erases the ink annotation drawing
[Home], [End]	Moves to the first or last slide in the slide show
[up arrow], [PgUp], or [left arrow]	Returns to the previous slide
[S]	Pauses the slide show when using automatic timings; press again to continue
[B]	Changes the screen to black; press again to return
[Esc]	Stops the slide show

Learning
Outcomes
• Apply and modify
a transition
• Modify slide
timings

Set Slide Transitions and Timings

In a slide show, you can determine how each slide advances in and out of view and how long each slide appears on the screen. **Slide transitions** are the visual and audio effects you apply to a slide that determine how each slide moves on and off the screen during the slide show. **Slide timing** refers to the amount of time a slide is visible on the screen. Typically, you set slide timings only if you want the presentation to automatically progress through the slides during a slide show. Setting the correct slide timing, in this case, is important because it determines how much time your audience has to view each slide. Each slide can have a different slide transition and different slide timing. **CASE ▶** *You decide to set slide transitions and 7-second slide timings for all the slides.*

STEPS

1. **Click the Slide 1 thumbnail in the Slides tab, then click the Transitions tab on the Ribbon**

   Transitions are organized by type into three groups: Subtle, Exciting, and Dynamic Content.

2. **Click the More button ⥥ in the Transition to This Slide group, then click Drape in the Exciting section**

   The new slide transition plays on the slide, and a transition icon ✴ appears next to the slide thumbnail in the Slides tab as shown in FIGURE 4-7. You can customize the slide transition by changing its direction and speed.

QUICK TIP
You can add a sound that plays with the transition from the Sound list arrow in the Timing group.

3. **Click the Effect Options button in the Transition to This Slide group, click Right, click the Duration up arrow in the Timing group until 3.00 appears, then click the Preview button in the Preview group**

   The Drape slide transition now plays from the right on the slide for 3.00 seconds. You can apply this transition with the custom settings to all of the slides in the presentation.

4. **Click the Apply To All button in the Timing group, then click the Slide Sorter button ⊞ on the status bar**

   All of the slides now have the customized Drape transition applied to them as identified by the transition icons located below each slide. You also have the ability to determine how slides progress during a slide show—either manually by mouse click or automatically by slide timing.

5. **Click the On Mouse Click check box under Advance Slide in the Timing group to clear the check mark**

   When this option is selected, you would have to click to manually advance slides during a slide show. Now, with this option disabled, you can set the slides to advance automatically after a specified amount of time.

QUICK TIP
Click the transition icon under any slide in Slide Sorter view to see its transition play.

6. **Click the After up arrow in the Timing group, until 00:07.00 appears in the text box, then click the Apply To All button**

   The timing between slides is 7 seconds as indicated by the time under each slide thumbnail in FIGURE 4-8. When you run the slide show, each slide will remain on the screen for 7 seconds. You can override a slide's timing and speed up the slide show by using any of the manual advance slide commands.

7. **Click the Slide Show button ⬚ on the status bar**

   The slide show advances automatically. A new slide appears every 7 seconds using the Drape transition.

8. **When you see the black slide, press [Spacebar], then save your changes**

   The slide show ends and returns to Slide Sorter view with Slide 1 selected.

FIGURE 4-7: **Applied slide transition**

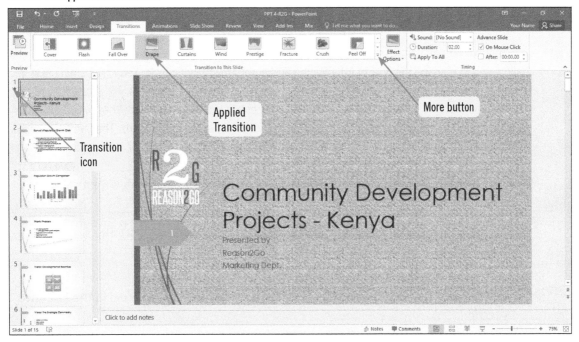

FIGURE 4-8: **Slide sorter view showing applied transition and timing**

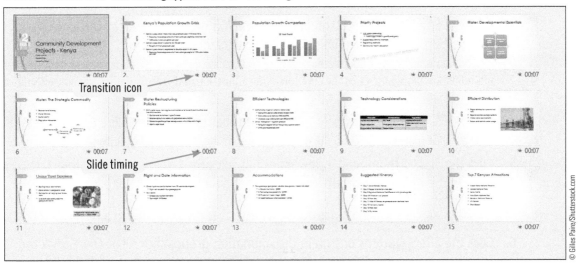

© Gilles Paire/Shutterstock.com

Rehearsing slide show timings

You can set different slide timings for each slide; for example, the title slide can appear for 20 seconds and the second slide for 1 minute. To set timings click the Rehearse Timings button in the Set Up group on the Slide Show tab. Slide Show view opens and the Recording toolbar shown in FIGURE 4-9 opens. It contains buttons to pause between slides and to advance to the next slide. After opening the Recording toolbar, you can practice giving your presentation by manually advancing each slide in the presentation. When you are finished, PowerPoint displays the total recorded time for the presentation and you have the option to save the recorded timings. The next time you run the slide show, you can use the timings you rehearsed.

FIGURE 4-9: **Recording toolbar**

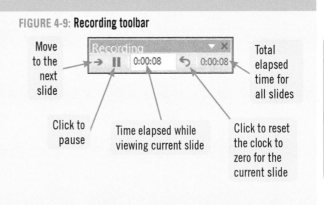

Animate Objects

Animations let you control how objects and text appear and move on the screen during a slide show and allow you to manage the flow of information and emphasize specific facts. You can animate text, pictures, sounds, hyperlinks, SmartArt diagrams, charts, and individual chart elements. For example, you can apply a Fade animation to bulleted text so each paragraph enters the slide separately from the others. Animations are organized into four categories, Entrance, Emphasis, Exit, and Motion Paths. The Entrance and Exit animations cause an object to enter or exit the slide with an effect. An Emphasis animation causes an object visible on the slide to have an effect and a Motion Path animation causes an object to move on a specified path on the slide. **CASE** ► *You animate the text and graphics of several slides in the presentation.*

STEPS

1. **Double-click the** Slide 5 thumbnail **to return to Normal view, click the** Animations tab **on the Ribbon, then click the** SmartArt object

   Text as well as other objects, such as a shape or picture, can be animated during a slide show.

2. **Click the** More button ▼ **in the Animation group, then click** Swivel **in the Entrance section**

   Animations can be serious and business-like, or humorous, so be sure to choose appropriate effects for your presentation. A small numeral 1, called an animation tag 🔲, appears near the object. **Animation tags** identify the order in which objects are animated during slide show.

3. **Click the** Effect Options button **in the Animation group, click** All at Once, **then click the** Duration up arrow **in the Timing group until** 03.00 **appears**

   Effect options are different for every animation, and some animations don't have effect options. Changing the animation timing increases the duration of the animation and gives it a more dramatic effect. Compare your screen to FIGURE 4-10.

4. **Click the** Slide Show button 🖵 **on the status bar until you see Slide 6, then press** [Esc]

   After the slide transition finishes, the shapes object spins twice for a total of three seconds.

5. **Click the** Slide 2 thumbnail **in the Slides tab, click the** bulleted list text object, **then click** Wipe **in the Animation group**

   The text object is animated with the Wipe animation. Each line of text has an animation tag with each paragraph displaying a different number. Accordingly, each paragraph is animated separately.

6. **Click the** Effect Options button **in the Animation group, click** All at Once, **click the** Duration up arrow **in the Timing group until** 02.00 **appears, then click the** Preview **button in the Preview group**

   Notice the animation tags for each line of text in the text object now have the same numeral (1), indicating that each line of text animates at the same time.

7. **Click** Population **in the title text object, click** ▼ **in the Animation group, scroll down, then click** Shapes **in the Motion Paths section**

   A motion path object appears over the shapes object and identifies the direction and shape, or path, of the animation. When needed, you can move, resize, and change the direction of the motion path. Notice the numeral 2 animation tag next to the title text object indicating that it is animated *after* the bulleted list text object. Compare your screen to FIGURE 4-11.

8. **Click the** Move Earlier button **in the Timing group, click the** Slide Show tab **on the Ribbon, then click the** From Beginning button **in the Start Slide Show group**

   The slide show begins from Slide 1. The animations make the presentation more interesting to view.

9. **When you see the black slide, press** [Enter], **then save your changes**

FIGURE 4-10: Animation applied to SmartArt object

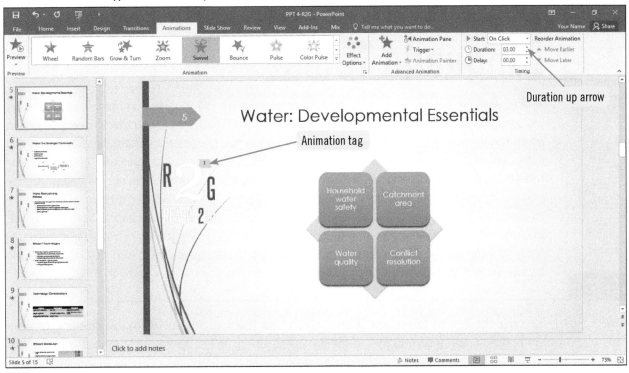

FIGURE 4-11: Motion path applied to title text object

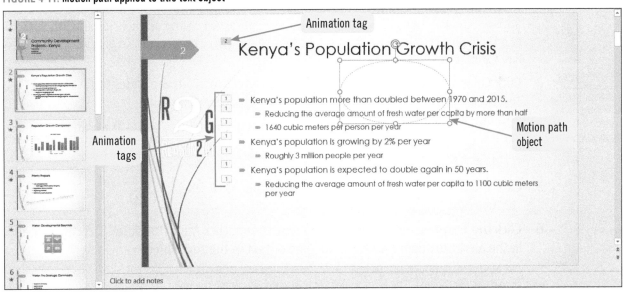

Attaching a sound to an animation

Text or objects that have animation applied can be customized further by attaching a sound for extra emphasis. First, select the animated object, then on the Animations tab, click the Animation Pane button in the Advanced Animation group. In the Animation Pane, click the animation you want to apply the sound to, click the Animation list arrow, then click Effect Options to open the animation effect's dialog box. In the Enhancements section, click the Sound list arrow, then choose a sound. Click OK when you are finished. Now, when you run the slide show, the sound you applied will play with the animation.

Use Proofing and Language Tools

Learning Outcomes
- Spell check a presentation
- Translate slide text

As your work on the presentation file nears completion, you need to review and proofread your slides thoroughly for errors. You can use the Spell Checker feature in PowerPoint to check for and correct spelling errors. This feature compares the spelling of all the words in your presentation against the words contained in the dictionary. You still must proofread your presentation for punctuation, grammar, and word-usage errors because the Spell Checker recognizes only misspelled and unknown words, not misused words. For example, the spell checker would not identify the word "last" as an error, even if you had intended to type the word "past." PowerPoint also includes language tools that translate words or phrases from your default language into another language using the Microsoft Translator. **CASE ▶** *You're finished working on the presentation for now, so it's a good time to check spelling. You then experiment with language translation because the final presentation will be translated into different languages.*

STEPS

1. **Click the** Review tab **on the Ribbon, then click the** Spelling button **in the Proofing group**
   PowerPoint begins to check the spelling in your presentation. When PowerPoint finds a misspelled word or a word that is not in its dictionary, the Spelling pane opens, as shown in FIGURE 4-12. In this case, the Spell Checker identifies a word on Slide 13, but it does not recognize that is spelled correctly and suggests some replacement words.

2. **Click** Ignore All **in the Spelling pane**
   PowerPoint ignores all instances of this word and continues to check the rest of the presentation for errors. If PowerPoint finds any other words it does not recognize, either change or ignore them. When the Spell Checker finishes checking your presentation, the Spelling pane closes, and an alert box opens with a message stating the spelling check is complete.

   > **QUICK TIP**
   > The Spell Checker does not check the text in inserted pictures or objects.

3. **Click** OK **in the Alert box, then click the** Slide 4 thumbnail **in the Slides tab**
   The alert box closes. Now you experiment with the language translation feature.

4. **Click the** Translate button **in the Language group, then click** Choose Translation Language
   The Translation Language Options dialog box opens.

5. **Click the** Translate to list arrow, **click** Czech, **then click** OK
   The Translation Language Options dialog box closes.

6. **Click the** Translate button **in the Language group, click** Mini Translator [Czech], **click** Yes **in the alert box, then select the first line of text in the text object**
   The Microsoft Translator begins to analyze the selected text, and a semitransparent Microsoft Translator box appears below the text. The Mini toolbar may also appear above the text.

   > **QUICK TIP**
   > To copy the translated text to a slide, click the Copy button at the bottom of the Microsoft Translator box, right-click the slide, then click a Paste option.

7. **Move the pointer over the** Microsoft Translator box
   A Czech translation of the text appears as shown in FIGURE 4-13. The translation language setting remains in effect until you reset it.

8. **Click the** Translate button **in the Language group, click** Choose Translation Language, **click the** Translate to list arrow, **click** English (United States), **click** OK, **click the** Translate button **again, then click** Mini Translator [English (United States)]
   The Mini Translator is turned off, and the translation language is restored to the default setting.

FIGURE 4-12: **Spelling pane**

FIGURE 4-13: **Translated text in the Microsoft Translator box**

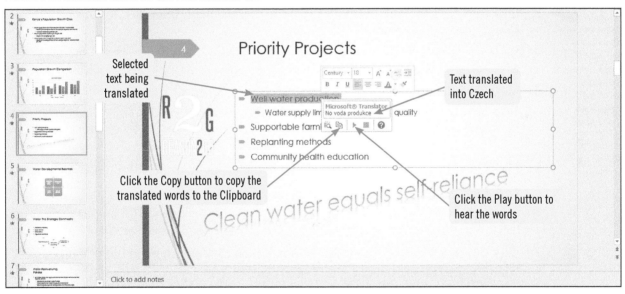

Checking spelling as you type

By default, PowerPoint checks your spelling as you type. If you type a word that is not in the dictionary, a wavy red line appears under it. To correct an error, right-click the misspelled word, then review the suggestions, which appear in the shortcut menu. You can select a suggestion, add the word you typed to your custom dictionary, or ignore it. To turn off automatic spell checking, click the File tab, then click Options to open the PowerPoint Options dialog box. Click Proofing in the left column, then click the Check spelling as you type check box to deselect it. To temporarily hide the wavy red lines, click the Hide spelling and grammar errors check box to select it. Contextual spelling in PowerPoint identifies common grammatically misused words, for example, if you type the word "their" and the correct word is "there," PowerPoint will identify the mistake and place a wavy red line under the word. To turn contextual spelling on or off, click Proofing in the PowerPoint Options dialog box, then click the Check grammar with spelling check box.

Inspect a Presentation

Learning Outcomes
- Modify document properties
- Inspect and remove unwanted data

Reviewing your presentation can be an important step. You should not only find and fix errors, but also locate and delete confidential company or personal information and document properties you do not want to share with others. If you share presentations with others, especially over the Internet, it is a good idea to inspect the presentation file using the Document Inspector. The **Document Inspector** looks for hidden data and personal information that is stored in the file itself or in the document properties. Document properties, also known as **metadata**, include specific data about the presentation, such as the author's name, subject matter, title, who saved the file last, and when the file was created. Other types of information the Document Inspector can locate and remove include presentation notes, comments, ink annotations, invisible on-slide content, off-slide content, and custom XML data. **CASE** ▶ *You decide to view and add some document properties, inspect your presentation file, and learn about the Mark as Final command.*

STEPS

1. **Click the** File tab **on the Ribbon, click the** Add a tag text box **in the Properties section, type** Kenya, water well, **then click the** Add a category text box

   This data provides some descriptive keywords for the presentation.

2. **Type** Proposal, **then click the** Show All Properties link

   The information you enter here about the presentation file can be used to identify and organize your file. The Show All Properties link displays all of the file properties and those you can change. You now use the Document Inspector to search for information you might want to delete in the presentation.

3. **Click the** Check for Issues button, **click** Inspect Document, **then click** Yes **to save the changes to the document**

   The Document Inspector dialog box opens. The Document Inspector searches the presentation file for seven different types of information that you might want removed from the presentation before sharing it.

4. **Make sure all of the check boxes have check marks, then click** Inspect

   The presentation file is reviewed, and the results are shown in FIGURE 4-14. The Document Inspector found items having to do with document properties, which you just entered, and embedded documents which are the pictures in the file. You decide to leave all the document properties alone.

5. **Click** Close, **click the** File tab **on the Ribbon, then click the** Protect Presentation button

6. **Click** Mark as Final, **then click** OK **in the alert box**

   An information alert box opens. Be sure to read the message to understand what happens to the file and how to recognize a marked-as-final presentation. You decide to complete this procedure.

7. **Click** OK, **click the** Home tab **on the Ribbon, then click anywhere in the title text object**

   When you select the title text object, the Ribbon closes automatically and an information alert box at the top of the window notes that the presentation is marked as final, making it a read-only file. Compare your screen to FIGURE 4-15. A **read-only** file is one that can't be edited or modified in any way. Anyone who has received a read-only presentation can only edit the presentation by changing its marked-as-final status. You still want to work on the presentation, so you remove the marked-as-final status.

8. **Click the** Edit Anyway button **in the information alert box, then save your changes**

   The Ribbon and all commands are active again, and the file can now be modified.

FIGURE 4-14: Document Inspector dialog box

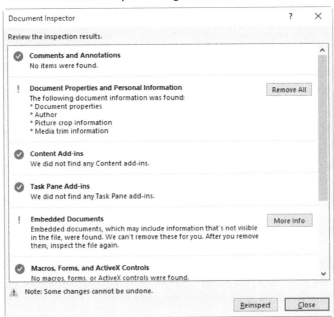

FIGURE 4-15: Marked as final presentation

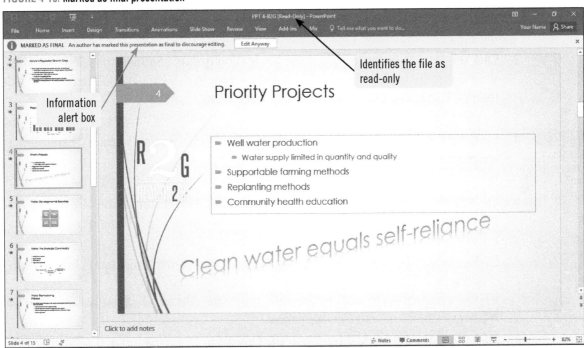

Digitally sign a presentation

What is a digital signature, and why would you want to use one in PowerPoint? A **digital signature** is similar to a handwritten signature in that it authenticates your document; however, a digital signature, unlike a handwritten signature, is created using computer cryptography and is not visible within the presentation itself. There are three primary reasons you would add a digital signature to a presentation: one, to authenticate the signer of the document; two, to ensure that the content of the presentation has not been changed since it was signed; and three, to assure the reader of the origin of the signed document. To add a digital signature, click the File tab on the Ribbon, click the Protect Presentation button, click Add a Digital Signature, then follow the dialog boxes.

Create an Office Mix

Learning Outcomes
- Create and insert an Office Mix
- Publish an Office Mix

Office Mix is a free add-in application developed by Microsoft which, once downloaded from the web, is integrated directly on the PowerPoint Ribbon with its own set of tools located on the Mix tab. Using Office Mix, you create and then insert interactive content onto the slides of your presentation. Content such as a video recording of you giving a presentation, video clips from the web, and interactive quizzes or polls are easy to create. Once you are finished creating your Office Mix, you can publish it to the Office Mix website or the cloud to be shared with others. **CASE** ➤ *You decide to create a short recording explaining the chart and introducing a priority project. You then publish the Mix to the Office Mix website. (Note: The Office Mix add-in must be installed from the Office Mix website prior to performing the steps of this lesson.)*

STEPS

> **TROUBLE**
> If you want to record audio and video in this lesson, make sure your microphone, speakers, and camera equipment are connected and working properly.

1. **Click the** Slide 3 thumbnail **in the Slides tab, click the** Mix tab **on the Ribbon, look over the commands on the Mix tab, then click the** Slide Recording button **in the Record group**
   The Screen Recording view opens as shown in FIGURE 4-16. The Screen Recording view displays the current slide with navigation, recording, and inking tools.

2. **When you are ready to begin recording, click the** Record button **in the Record group, look into your computer's camera, then speak these words into your microphone** "This chart shows the population trends for Kenya, Uganda, and South Africa"
   Your Office Mix recording begins as soon as you click the Record button. If a slide has animations, each animation must be advanced manually during the recording in order to see the animation.

3. **Click the** Next Slide button ➡ **in the Navigation group, continue speaking** "R2G has several priority projects", **drag** ✏ **under the words** Well Water Production **on the slide, then click the** Stop button **in the Navigation group**
   A small speaker appears in the upper right corner of the slide indicating there is a recording on the slide.

> **QUICK TIP**
> Click the Delete Slide Recording button in the Recording Tools group to delete slide recordings.

4. **Click the** Preview Slide Recording **button in the Recording Tools group, then listen and watch your recording**
   You can move to any slide and preview its recording using the buttons in the Navigation group.

5. **Click the window** Close button, **click the** Upload to Mix button **in the Mix group, read the information, then click the** Next button **in the Upload to Mix pane**
   The Upload to Mix pane displays sign in account methods.

> **TROUBLE**
> If you are not sure which account login option to use, check with your instructor.

6. **Click your** account button **in the Upload to Mix pane, enter your sign in information, click the** Sign in **button, then click the** Next button
   The new Office Mix is uploaded and published to the Office Mix website. There is a percentage counter showing you the upload and publishing progress.

7. **Click the** Show me my Mix button **in the Upload to Mix pane, then, if necessary, click the** Sign in button **on the webpage that appears**
   The Office Mix webpage appears with the new Office Mix you just created as shown in FIGURE 4-17. On this page you can provide a content description, a category, or a tag, as well as set permissions.

8. **Click** My Mixes **at the top of the window, click the** PPT 4-R2G Play button, **then follow the directions on the screen to watch the Office Mix**
   Each slide in the presentation, including the Office Mix recordings you made on Slide 3 and 4, appears.

9. **Click** Your Name **at the top of the window, click** sign out, **click your** web browser Close button, **click the** Close button **in the Upload to Mix pane, save your changes, submit your presentation to your instructor, then exit PowerPoint**

FIGURE 4-16: **Office Mix screen recording view**

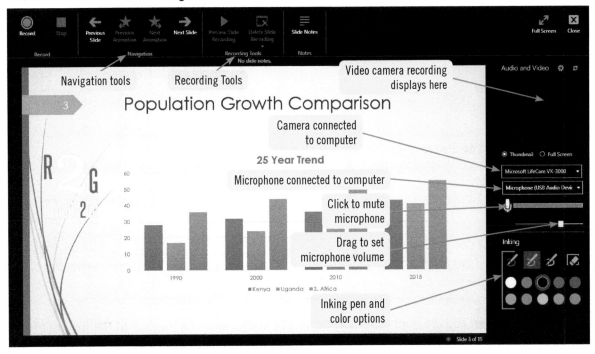

FIGURE 4-17: **Office Mix webpage**

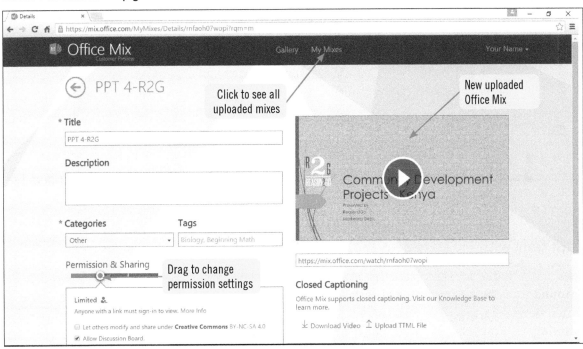

Inserting a multiple choice interactive quiz

Using the Mix tab, you can create a custom interactive quiz that can be presented in Slide Show view or uploaded to the Office Mix website to share with others. On the Mix tab, click the Quizzes Videos Apps button in the Insert group. In the Lab Office Add-ins dialog box, click Multiple Choice Quiz, then click Trust It. A multiple choice quiz object appears on your slide with blank text boxes that you fill out with a quiz question and answers. Be sure to enter the correct answer in the light green answer text box, then add as many other possible answers as you like. You can customize your question by shuffling the answer every time the question is opened, limiting the number of answer attempts, and allowing more than one right answer.

Practice

Concepts Review

Label each element of the PowerPoint window shown in FIGURE 4-18.

FIGURE 4-18

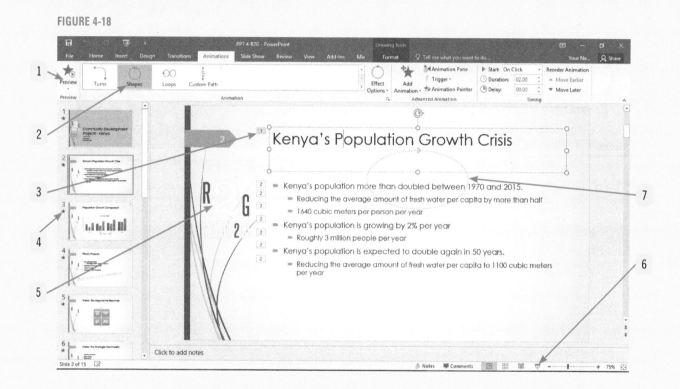

Match each term with the statement that best describes it.

8. **Masters**
9. **Background**
10. **Presenter view**
11. **Slide timing**
12. **Office Mix**
13. **Ink annotations**

a. The area behind the text and graphics
b. Drawings on slide created during slide show
c. A special view that you use when showing a presentation on two monitors
d. Add-in application you use to create interactive content
e. Determines how long slide is visible on screen
f. Slides that store theme and placeholder information

Select the best answer from the list of choices.

14. **What determines the position and size of text and content placeholders and the slide background of a presentation?**
    - **a.** Home tab
    - **b.** Background
    - **c.** Master
    - **d.** Normal view

15. **Apply this to your presentation to quickly modify the applied theme.**
    - **a.** Office Mix
    - **b.** Background
    - **c.** Animation
    - **d.** Variant

16. **Freehand pen and highlighter strokes are also known as _____.**
    - **a.** ink annotations
    - **b.** pictures
    - **c.** markings
    - **d.** scribbles

17. **A slide _____ is a special visual effect that determines how a slide moves during a slide show.**
    - **a.** annotation
    - **b.** view
    - **c.** background
    - **d.** transition

18. **Set slide _____ to make your presentation automatically progress through the slides during a slide show.**
    - **a.** animations
    - **b.** timings
    - **c.** hyperlinks
    - **d.** recordings

19. **Animation _____ identify the order in which objects are animated during a slide show.**
    - **a.** tags
    - **b.** paths
    - **c.** thumbnails
    - **d.** schemes

20. **A _____ file is one that can't be edited or modified in any way.**
    - **a.** signed
    - **b.** final
    - **c.** read-only
    - **d.** saved

Skills Review

1. **Modify masters.**
   a. Open the presentation PPT 4-3.pptx from the location where you store your Data Files, then save the presentation as **PPT 4-Dual Arm**.
   b. Open Slide Master view using the View tab, then click the Circuit Slide Master thumbnail.
   c. Insert the picture PPT 4-4.jpg, then set the background color to transparent.
   d. Resize the picture so it is 1.0" wide.
   e. Drag the picture to the upper-right corner of the slide to align with the top of the Title text object, then deselect the picture.
   f. Switch to Normal view, then save your changes.

2. **Customize the background and theme.**
   a. Click the Design tab, then click the second variant from the left.
   b. Go to Slide 4, then open the Format Background pane.
   c. Click the Solid fill option button, then click Gold, Accent 1, Darker 25%.
   d. Set the Transparency to 30%, close the Format Background pane then save your changes.

Skills Review (continued)

3. Use slide show commands.

  a. Open Slide Show view, then go to Slide 1 using the See all slides button on the Slide Show toolbar.

  b. Use the Pen ink annotation tool to circle the slide title.

  c. Go to Slide 2, then use the Highlighter to highlight four points in the bulleted text on the slide.

  d. Erase two highlight annotations on the bulleted text, then press [Esc].

  e. Open Presenter view, then stop the timer.

  f. Advance the slides to Slide 5, then click the Zoom into the slide button (now called the Zoom out button) on the Slide Show toolbar, then click in the center of the graph.

  g. Click the Zoom into the slide button, then return to Slide 1.

  h. Hide Presenter view, advance through the slide show, save your ink and highlight annotations, then save your work.

4. Set slide transitions and timings.

  a. Go to Slide Sorter view, click the Slide 1 thumbnail, then apply the Fall Over transition to the slide.

  b. Change the effect option to Right, change the duration to 2.50, then apply to all the slides.

  c. Change the slide timing to 5 seconds, then apply to all of the slides.

  d. Switch to Normal view, view the slide show, then save your work.

5. Animate objects.

  a. Go to Slide 3, click the Animations tab, then select both arrows on the slide. (*Hint:* Use SHIFT to select both arrows.)

  b. Apply the Wipe effect to the objects, click the Effect Options button, then apply the From Top effect.

  c. Select the lower two box shapes, apply the Random Bars animation, then preview the animations.

  d. Change the effect options to Vertical, then preview the animations.

  e. Select the top two box shapes, apply the Shape animation, click the Effect Options button, then click Box.

  f. Click the Move Earlier button in the Timing group until the two top box shape animation tags display 1.

  g. Preview the animations, then save your work.

6. Use proofing and language tools.

  a. Check the spelling of the document, and change any misspelled words. Ignore any words that are correctly spelled but that the spell checker doesn't recognize. There is one misspelled word in the presentation.

  b. Go to Slide 6, then set the Mini Translator language to Thai.

  c. View the Thai translation of text on Slide 6.

  d. Choose one other language (or as many as you want), translate words or phrases on the slide, reset the default language to English (United States), turn off the Mini Translator, then save your changes.

7. Inspect a presentation.

  a. On the File tab in the Properties section, type information of your choosing in the Tags and Categories text fields.

  b. Open the Document Inspector dialog box.

  c. Make sure the Off-Slide Content check box is selected, then inspect the presentation.

  d. Delete the off-slide content, then close the dialog box. Save your changes.

8. Create an Office Mix.

  a. Go to Slide 2, open the Mix tab, then click the Slide Recording button.

  b. Click the Record button, speak these words into your microphone, "Here you see the typical applications for the new R2G series dual robotic arm," use your pen to underline the slide title, then click the Stop button.

  c. Preview your slide recording, then close the window.

  d. Click the Upload to Mix button, sign in to your account, then upload your new mix to the Office Mix website.

  e. Watch the Office Mix, sign out of your account, then close the webpage window.

  f. Close the Upload to Mix pane, then save your work.

Skills Review (continued)

g. Switch to Slide Sorter view, then compare your presentation to FIGURE 4-19.

h. Submit your presentation to your instructor, then close the presentation.

FIGURE 4-19

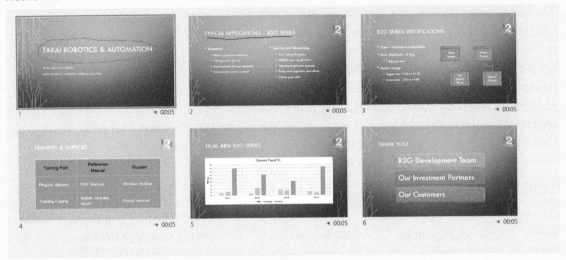

Independent Challenge 1

You work for World International Studies Program (WISP) as a study consultant. You have been working on a presentation that describes a new study program developed in Russia. You need to finish up what you have been working on by adding transitions, timings, and animation effects to the presentation.

a. Open the file PPT 4-5.pptx from the location where you store your Data Files, and save the presentation as **PPT 4-WISP**.

b. Add the slide number and your name as the footer on all slides, except the title slide.

c. Open Slide Master view, click the Celestial Slide Master thumbnail, insert the picture PPT 4-6.jpg, then resize the picture so it is 1.5" wide.

d. Click the Color button, then click the Purple, Accent color 1 Dark in the Recolor section.

e. Move the picture to the top left corner of the slide, then close Slide Master view.

f. Apply the Shape animation to the title text on each slide.

g. Apply the Float In animation to the bulleted text objects on each slide.

h. Apply the Shape animation to the picture on Slide 3, then change the effect option to Box.

i. Apply the Vortex slide transition, apply a 5-second slide timing, then apply to all of the slides.

j. Check the spelling of the presentation, save your changes, then view the presentation in Slide Show view.

k. Submit your presentation to your instructor, close the presentation, then exit PowerPoint.

Independent Challenge 2

You are a development engineer at Adtec Global Systems, Inc., a manufacturer of civilian drone technology located in Phoenix, Arizona. Adtec designs and manufactures personal drone systems largely used in the movie industry and in commercial agricultural business. You need to finish the work on a quarterly presentation that outlines the progress of the company's newest technologies by adding animations, customizing the background, and using the Document Inspector.

a. Open the file PPT 4-7.pptx from the location where you store your Data Files, and save the presentation as **PPT 4-Adtec**.

Independent Challenge 2 (continued)

b. Apply an appropriate design theme, then apply a gradient fill slide background to the title slide using the Format Background pane.

c. Apply the Airplane slide transition to all slides, apply the Shape animation to the following objects: the bulleted text on Slide 2 and the table on Slide 4, then change the Effect options on the table to a box shape with an out direction.

d. Use the Microsoft Translator to translate the bulleted text on Slide 2 using two different languages.

e. Run the Document Inspector with all options selected, identify what items the Document Inspector finds, close the Document Inspector dialog box, then review the slides to find the items.

f. Add a slide at the end of the presentation that identifies the items the Document Inspector found.

g. Run the Document Inspector again, and remove all items except the document properties.

h. View the slide show, and make ink annotations to the slides. Save the annotations at the end of the slide show.

i. Add your name as a footer to all slides, check the spelling, fix any misspellings, then save your work.

j. Submit your presentation to your instructor, then close the presentation and exit PowerPoint.

Independent Challenge 3

You work for Buffington, Genung, O'Lynn & Associates, a full-service investment and pension firm. Your manager wants you to create a presentation on pension plan options. You completed adding the information to the presentation, now you need to add a design theme, format information to highlight important facts, add animation effects, and add slide timings.

a. Open the file PPT 4-8.pptx from the location where you store your Data Files, and save the presentation as **PPT 4-Invest**.

b. Apply an appropriate design theme, then apply a theme variant.

c. Apply animation effects to the following objects: the shapes on Slide 3 and the bulleted text on Slide 4. View the slide show to evaluate the effects you added, and make adjustments as necessary.

d. Convert the text on Slide 5 to a Circle Relationship SmartArt graphic (found in the Relationship category).

e. Apply the Inset SmartArt style to the SmartArt graphic, then change its color to Dark 2 Fill.

f. Go to Slide 3, align the Sector and Quality arrow shapes to their bottoms, then align the Allocation and Maturity arrow shapes to their right edges.

g. On Slides 6 and 7, change the table style format to Themed Style 1 - Accent 2, and adjust the tables.

h. Apply a 7-second timing to Slides 3–7 and a 5-second timing to Slides 1 and 2.

i. Add your name as a footer to the slides, check the spelling, then save your work. An example of a finished presentation is shown in FIGURE 4-20.

j. Submit your presentation to your instructor, then close the presentation and exit PowerPoint.

FIGURE 4-20

Independent Challenge 4: Explore

You work for the Office of Veterans Affairs at your college. Create a basic presentation that you can publish to the Office Mix website that describes the basic services offered by the school to service members. (*Note: To complete this Independent Challenge, you may need to be connected to the Internet.*)

a. Plan and create the slide presentation that describes the veteran services provided by the college. To help create content, use your school's website or use the Internet to locate information at another college. The presentation should contain at least six slides.

b. Use an appropriate design theme then change the theme variant.

c. Add one or more photographs to the presentation, then style and customize at least one photo.

d. Save the presentation as **PPT 4-Vet** to the location where you store your Data Files.

e. Add slide transitions and animation effects to the presentation. View the slide show to evaluate the effects you added.

f. Go to Slide 5, translate the last line of text in the bulleted text box into Greek, then click the Copy button on the Microsoft Translator box.

g. Insert a new text box on Slide 5, paste the Greek text into the text box, then drag the Greek text box below the bulleted text box.

h. Change the language in the Microsoft translator back to English, then turn off the Microsoft Translator.

i. Add the slide number and your name as a footer to the slides, check the spelling, inspect the presentation, then save your work.

j. Make an Office Mix of this presentation, then upload it to the Office Mix website. Make sure to include information in your recording on at least 2 slides and use the pen to make ink annotations on your slides.

k. Submit your presentation to your instructor, then exit PowerPoint. An example of a finished presentation is shown in FIGURE 4-21.

FIGURE 4-21

Visual Workshop

Create a presentation that looks like FIGURE 4-22, and FIGURE 4-23, which shows two slides with a specific slide layout, slide background, theme, and theme variant. Insert pictures **PPT 4-9** and **PPT 4-10** to the slides, then insert the picture **PPT 4-6** to the presentation slide master. (*Hint*: the slide master picture background is transparent.) Add your name as footer text to the slide, save the presentation as **PPT 4-Corp** to the location where you store your Data Files, then submit your presentation to your instructor.

FIGURE 4-22

© Prasit Rodphan/Shutterstock.com

FIGURE 4-23

© tcly/Shutterstock.com

Glossary

3D printer Deposits multiple layers of material (typically heated plastic) onto a surface. To achieve the desired shape, the tool head may travel in a different direction as each layer is applied.

Absolute cell reference In a formula, a cell address that refers to a specific cell and does not change when you copy the formula; indicated by a dollar sign before the column letter and/or row number. *See also* Relative cell reference.

Accessories Simple Windows application programs (apps) that perform specific tasks, such as the Calculator accessory for performing calculations. Also called Windows accessories.

Account Log-on information including ISP, email address, and password for each person using Outlook; used to create folders in Outlook for contacts, email, and schedules. *See* also Personal account.

Action Center Opened by clicking the Notifications button on the right side of the taskbar; shows notifications, tips, and reminders. Contains Quick Actions buttons for commonly-used Windows settings.

Active The currently available document, program, or object; on the taskbar, when more than one program is open, the button for the active program appears slightly lighter.

Active cell The cell in which you are currently working.

Active window The window you are currently using; if multiple windows are open, the window in front of other open windows.

Add-in Software that works with an installed app to extend its features.

Add-ins Small programs available from the online Office Store that allow you to access information on the web without having to leave Word.

Address A sequence of drive and folder names that describes a folder's or file's location in the file hierarchy; the highest hierarchy level is on the left, with lower hierarchy levels separated by the ⮞ symbol to its right.

Address bar In a window, the area just below the Ribbon that shows the file hierarchy, or address of the files that appear in the file list below it; the address appears as a series of links you can click to navigate to other locations on your computer.

Address book A stored list of names and email addresses that you can access through an email program such as Outlook to address messages.

Adjustment handle A small yellow handle that changes the appearance of an object's most prominent feature.

Align To place objects' edges or centers on the same plane.

Alignment The placement of cell contents in relation to a cell's edges; for example, left-aligned, centered, or right-aligned.

Alignment command A command used in Layout or Design View for a form or report to left-, center-, or right-align a value within its control using the Align Left, Center, or Align Right buttons on the Home tab. In Design View, you can also align the top, bottom, right, or left edge of selected controls using the Align button.

Alternate Back Color property A property that determines the alternating background color of the selected section in a form or report.

Anchoring A layout positioning option that allows you to tie controls together so you can work with them as a group.

AND criteria Criteria placed in the same row of the query design grid. All criteria on the same row must be true for a record to appear on the resulting datasheet.

Animation emphasis effect In Sway, a special effect you can apply to an object to animate it.

Animation tag Identifies the order an object is animated on a slide during a slide show.

App An application program; Windows 10 apps are smaller apps available at the Windows store. Desktop apps, such as Microsoft Office, are more full-featured programs and are available from many software companies.

App window The window that opens after you start an app, showing you the tools you need to use the program and any open program documents.

Application developer The person responsible for building and maintaining tables, queries, forms, and reports for all of the database users.

Application program Any program that lets you work with files or create and edit files such as graphics, letters, financial summaries, and other useful documents, as well as view Web pages on the Internet and send and receive e-mail. Also called an app.

Appointment In the Outlook Calendar, an activity that does not involve inviting other people or scheduling resources.

Argument Information that a function uses to create the final answer. Multiple arguments are separated by commas. All of the arguments for a function are surrounded by a single set of parentheses.

Arithmetic operators In a formula, symbols that perform mathematical calculations, such as addition (+), subtraction (–), multiplication (*), division (/), or exponentiation (^).

Attachment A file, such as a picture, audio clip, video clip, document, worksheet, or presentation, that is sent in addition to the email message composed by typing in the message window.

AutoComplete A feature that automatically suggests text to insert.

AutoCorrect A feature that automatically detects and corrects typing errors, minor spelling errors, and capitalization, and inserts certain typographical symbols as you type.

AutoFill Feature activated by dragging the fill handle; copies a cell's contents or continues a series of entries into adjacent cells.

AutoFill Options button Button that appears after using the fill handle to copy cell contents; enables you to choose to fill cells with specific elements (such as formatting) of the copied cell if desired.

AutoFit A feature that automatically adjusts the width of a column or the height of a row to accommodate its widest or tallest entry.

Automatic page break A page break that is inserted automatically at the bottom of a page.

AutoNumber A field data type in which Access enters a sequential integer for each record added into the datasheet. Numbers cannot be reused even if the record is deleted.

Avg function A built-in Access function used to calculate the average of the values in a given field.

Background The area behind the text and graphics on a slide.

Background graphic An object placed on the slide master

Background image An image that fills an entire form or report, appearing "behind" the other controls; also sometimes called a watermark.

Backstage view View that appears when the File tab is clicked as shown. The navigation bar on the left side contains commands to perform actions common to most Office programs, such as opening a file, saving a file, and closing the file.

Backup A duplicate copy of a file that is stored in another location.

Backward-compatible Software feature that enables documents saved in an older version of a program to be opened in a newer version of the program.

Bibliography A list of sources that you consulted or cited while creating a document.

Blind courtesy copy (Bcc) A way to send an email message to recipients when the sender does not want to reveal who has received courtesy copies.

Blog An informal journal that is created by an individual or a group and available to the public on the Internet; short for weblog.

Blogger The person who creates and maintains a blog.

Bluetooth A type of wireless technology that uses short range radio waves. A Bluetooth device must first be "paired" with a computer so that it knows to trust that particular device.

Bold Formatting applied to text to make it thicker and darker.

Border A line that can be added above, below, or to the sides of a paragraph, text, or table cell; a line that divides the columns and rows of a table.

Bound control A control used in either a form or report to display data from the underlying field; used to edit and enter new data in a form.

Building block Reusable piece of formatted content or document part that is stored in a gallery.

Bullet A small graphic symbol used to identify an item in a list.

Business Intelligence tools Excel features for gathering and analyzing data to answer sophisticated business questions.

Button A small rectangle you can click in order to issue a command to an application program.

Calculation A new value that is created by an expression in a text box on a form or report.

Calculation operators Symbols in a formula that indicate what type of calculation to perform on the cells, ranges, or values.

Calendar In Outlook, provides a convenient way to manage appointments and events.

Calendar Picker A pop-up calendar from which you can choose dates for a date field.

Canvas In the Paint accessory, the area in the center of the app window that you use to create drawings.

Card A section for a particular type of content in a Sway presentation.

Case sensitive An application program's (app's) ability to differentiate between uppercase and lowercase letters; usually used to describe how an operating system evaluates passwords that users type to gain entry to user accounts.

Categories In Outlook, a feature used to tag items so you can track and organize them by specific criteria.

Category axis Horizontal axis in a chart, usually containing the names of data categories; in a 2-dimensional chart, also known as the x-axis.

Cell The box formed by the intersection of a table row and table column.

Cell address The location of a cell, expressed by cell coordinates; for example, the cell address of the cell in column A, row 1 is A1.

Cell pointer Dark rectangle that outlines the active cell.

Cell styles Predesigned combinations of formats based on themes that can be applied to selected cells to enhance the look of a worksheet.

Center Alignment in which an item is centered between the margins.

Character spacing Formatting that changes the width or scale of characters, expands or condenses the amount of space between characters, raises or lowers characters relative to the line of text, and adjusts kerning (the space between standard combinations of letters).

Chart A graphical representation of numerical data from a worksheet. Chart types include 2-D and 3-D column, bar, pie, area, and line charts.

Chart sheet A separate sheet in a workbook that contains only a chart, which is linked to the workbook data.

Charts Pictorial representations of worksheet data that make it easier to see patterns, trends, and relationships; *also called* graphs.

Check box A box that turns an option on when checked or off when unchecked.

Citation A parenthetical reference in the document text that gives credit to the source for a quotation or other information used in a document.

Click To quickly press and release the left button on the pointing device; also called single-click. The touch-screen equivalent is a tap on the screen.

Click and Type A feature that allows you to automatically apply the necessary paragraph formatting to a table, graphic, or text when you insert the item in a blank area of a document in Print Layout or Web Layout view.

Click and Type pointer A pointer used to move the insertion point and automatically apply the paragraph formatting necessary to insert text at that location in the document.

Clip A media file, such as a graphic, sound, animation, or movie.

Clip art A collection of graphic images that can be inserted into documents, presentations, Web pages, spreadsheets, and other Office files.

Clipboard A temporary storage area for items that are cut or copied from any Office file and are available for pasting. *See* Office Clipboard and System Clipboard.

Close button In a Windows title bar, the rightmost button; closes the open window, app, and/or document.

Cloud computing When data, applications, and resources are stored on servers accessed over the Internet or a private internal network rather than on a local computer.

Cloud storage location File storage locations on the World Wide Web, such as Windows OneDrive or Dropbox.

Column break A break that forces text following the break to begin at the top of the next column.

Column heading The box containing the column letter on top of the columns in the worksheet.

Column separator The thin line that separates field names to the left or right in a datasheet or the query design grid.

Combination chart Two charts in one, such as a column chart combined with a line chart, that together graph related but dissimilar data.

Combo box A bound control used to display a drop-down list of possible entries for a field. You can also type an entry from the keyboard into the control so it is a "combination" of the list box and text box controls.

Command An instruction to perform a task, such as opening a file or emptying the Recycle Bin.

Comments button A button on the PowerPoint status bar in Normal view allows you to open the Comments pane where you can create, edit, select, and delete comments.

Comparison operators In a formula, symbols that compare values for the purpose of true/false results.

Compatibility The ability of different programs to work together and exchange data.

Complex formula A formula that uses more than one arithmetic operator.

Computer network The hardware and software that make it possible for two or more computers to share information and resources.

Conditional formatting A type of cell formatting that changes based on the cell's value or the outcome of a formula.

Contact Group A named subset of the people in your Outlook Contacts folder, the named group includes the email addresses for all people in the group so you can send a message or invitation to everyone in the group at once. *See* also Distribution list.

Contacts In Outlook, all information related to people, such as business associates and personal friends.

Content control An interactive object that is embedded in a document you create from a template and that expedites your ability to customize the document with your own information.

Content placeholder A placeholder that is used to enter text or objects such as clip art, charts, or pictures.

Contextual tab A tab that appears only when a specific task can be performed; contextual tabs appear in an accent color and close when no longer needed.

Continuous section break A break that begins a new section on the same page.

Control Any element on a form or report such as a label, text box, line, or combo box. Controls can be bound, unbound, or calculated.

Control Source property A property of a bound control in a form or report that determines the field to which the control is connected.

Conversations Emails that discuss a common subject or thread.

Copy To make a duplicate copy of a file, folder, or other object that you want to store in another location.

Copy and paste To move text or graphics using the Copy and Paste commands.

Cortana The digital personal assistant that comes with Windows 10 and Windows phones; can search, give you reminders, alarms, directions, news, weather, and more.

Courtesy copy (Cc) In email, a way to send a message to a recipient who needs to be aware of the correspondence between the sender and the recipients but who is not the primary recipient of the message.

Creative Commons license A public copyright license that allows the free distribution of an otherwise copyrighted work.

Criteria Entries (rules and limiting conditions) that determine which records are displayed when finding or filtering records in a datasheet or form, or when building a query.

Criteria syntax Rules by which criteria need to be entered. For example, text criteria syntax requires that the criteria are surrounded by quotation marks (" "). Date criteria are surrounded by pound signs (#).

Crop To hide part of an object by using the Cropping tool or to delete a part of a picture.

Current record The record that has the focus or is being edited.

Cut To remove an item from a document and place it on the Clipboard.

Cut and paste To move text or graphics using the Cut and Paste commands.

Data marker A graphical representation of a data point in a chart, such as a bar or column.

Data point Individual piece of data plotted in a chart.

Data series The selected range in a worksheet whose related data points Excel converts into a chart.

Data series label Text in the first row and column of a worksheet that identifies data in a chart.

Data series marker A graphical representation of a data series, such as a bar or column.

Data type A required property for each field that defines the type of data that can be entered in each field. Valid data types include AutoNumber, Short Text, Long Text, Number, Currency, Yes/No, Date/Time, and Hyperlink.

Database designer The person responsible for building and maintaining tables, queries, forms, and reports.

Database user The person primarily interested in entering, editing, and analyzing the data in the database.

Datasheet A spreadsheet-like grid that displays fields as columns and records as rows.

Datasheet View A view that lists the records of an object in a datasheet. Tables, queries, and most form objects have a Datasheet View.

Date function A built-in Access function used to display the current date on a form or report; enter the Date function as Date().

Date Navigator A monthly calendar in the To-Do Bar that gives you an overview of the month.

Default In an app window or dialog box, a value that is automatically set; you can change the default to any valid value.

Delete To permanently remove an item from a document.

Deleted Items The folder that stores items when you delete or erase a message from any email folder, which means a deleted item, such as an email or contact card, is actually stored rather than being immediately and permanently deleted. *Also called* Trash folder.

Design View A view in which the structure of an object can be manipulated. Every Access object (table, query, form, report, macro, and module) has a Design View.

Desktop apps Application programs (apps), such as Microsoft Word, that are full-featured and that are often purchased, either from the Windows Store or from a software developer; also called traditional apps.

Destination file In integration, the file that receives the copied information. A Word file that contains an Excel file is the destination file.

Destination presentation The presentation you insert slides to when you reuse slides from another presentation.

Device A hardware component that is part of your computer system, such as a disk drive, a pointing device, or a touch screen device.

Dialog box A window with controls that lets you tell Windows how you want to complete an application program's (app's) command.

Dialog box launcher An icon you can click to open a dialog box or task pane from which to choose related commands.

Digital signature A way to authenticate a presentation files using computer cryptography. A digital signature is not visible in a presentation.

Distribute To evenly divide the space horizontally or vertically between objects relative to each other or the slide edges.

Distribution list A collection of contacts to whom you want to send the same messages; makes it possible for you to send a message to the same group without having to select each contact in the group. *See also* Contact Group.

Docs.com A Microsoft website designed for sharing Sway sites.

Document The electronic file you create using Word.

Document Inspector A PowerPoint feature that examines a presentation for hidden data or personal information.

Document properties Details about a file, such as author name or the date the file was created, that are used to describe, organize, and search for files.

Document window The portion of a application program's (app's) window in which you create the document; displays all or part of an open document.

Documents folder The folder on your hard drive used to store most of the files you create or receive from others; might contain subfolders to organize the files into smaller groups.

Double-click To quickly press and release or click the left button on the pointing device twice. The touch-screen equivalent is a double-tap on the screen.

Draft view A view that shows a document without margins, headers and footers, or graphics.

Drafts The folder that stores unfinished messages that you can finish writing at a later time; many email programs automatically save unsent messages at regular intervals in the Drafts folder as a safety measure.

Drag To point to an object, press and hold the left button on the pointing device, move the object to a new location, and then release the left button. Touch-screen users can press and hold a location, then move along the screen with a finger or stylus.

Drag and drop To move text or a graphic by dragging it to a new location using the mouse.

Drawing canvas In OneNote, a container for shapes and lines.

Drive A physical location on your computer where you can store files.

Drive name A name for a drive that consists of a letter followed by a colon, such as C: for the hard disk drive.

Drop cap A large dropped initial capital letter that is often used to set off the first paragraph of an article.

Dropbox A free online storage site that lets you transfer files that can be retrieved by other people you invite. *See also* Cloud storage location.

Edit To make a change to the contents of an active cell.

Edit mode The mode in which Access assumes you are trying to edit a particular field, so keystrokes such as [Ctrl][End], [Ctrl][Home], [↓], and [↑] move the insertion point within the field.

Edit record symbol A pencil-like symbol that appears in the record selector box to the left of the record that is currently being edited in either a datasheet or a form.

Electronic mail (email) The technology that makes it possible for you to send and receive messages through the Internet.

Electronic spreadsheet A computer program used to perform calculations and analyze and present numeric data.

Email message A message sent using email technology.

Email software A computer program that enables you to send and receive email messages over a network, within an intranet, and through the Internet.

Embed Placement of an object such as a text selection, value, or picture created in a source file into a destination file. An embedded object is edited by opening it in the destination file and then using the tools of the source file to make changes. These changes appear only in the embedded object in the destination file.

Embedded chart A chart displayed as an object in a worksheet.

Embedded object An object that is created in one application and inserted to another; can be edited using the original program file in which they were created.

Emoticon A symbol created by combining keyboard characters; used to communicate feelings in emails.

Endnote Text that provides additional information or acknowledges sources for text in a document and that appears at the end of a document.

Error indicator An icon that automatically appears in Design View to indicate some type of error. For example, a green error indicator appears in the upper-left corner of a text box in Form Design View if the text box Control Source property is set to a field name that doesn't exist.

Even page section break A break that begins a new section on the next even-numbered page.

Event In the Outlook Calendar, an activity that lasts 24 hours or longer.

Exploding Visually pulling a slice of a pie chart away from the whole pie chart in order to add emphasis to the pie slice.

Expression A combination of values, functions, and operators that calculates to a single value. Access expressions start with an equal sign and are placed in a text box in either Form Design View or Report Design View.

Field A code that serves as a placeholder for data that changes in a document, such as a page number.

Field list A list of the available fields in the table or query that the field list represents. Also, a pane that opens in Access and lists the database tables and the fields they contain.

Field name The name given to each field in a table.

Field selector The button to the left of a field in Table Design View that indicates the currently selected field. Also the thin gray bar above each field in the query grid.

File A collection of information stored on your computer, such as a letter, video, or app.

File Explorer A Windows app that allows you to navigate your computer's file hierarchy and manage your files and folders.

File extension A three- or four-letter sequence, preceded by a period, at the end of a filename that identifies the file as a particular type of document; for example, documents in the Rich Text Format have the file extension .rtf.

File hierarchy The tree-like structure of folders and files on your computer.

File list A section of a window that shows the contents of the folder or drive currently selected in the Navigation pane.

File management The ability to organize folders and files on your computer.

File syncing Changes to files stored in the Cloud are automatically synced to all devices.

File tab Provides access to Backstage view and the Word Options dialog box.

Filename A unique, descriptive name for a file that identifies the file's content.

Filter A way to temporarily display only those records that match given criteria.

Filter By Form A way to filter data that allows two or more criteria to be specified at the same time.

Filter By Selection A way to filter records for an exact match.

First line indent A type of indent in which the first line of a paragraph is indented more than the subsequent lines.

Flag A method of coding email messages by assigning different flags to the messages to categorize them or indicate their level of importance for follow up.

Flash Fill A feature that lets you fill a range of text based on samples existing in the current worksheet.

Floating graphic A graphic to which text wrapping has been applied, making the graphic independent of text and able to be moved anywhere on a page.

Focus The property that indicates which field would be edited if you were to start typing.

Folder An electronic container that helps you organize your computer files, like a cardboard folder on your desk; it can contain subfolders for organizing files into smaller groups.

Folder name A unique, descriptive name for a folder that helps identify the folder's contents.

Font The typeface or design of a set of characters (letters, numbers, symbols, and punctuation marks).

Font effect Font formatting that applies a special effect to text, such as small caps or superscript.

Font size The size of characters, measured in units called points.

Font style Format such as bold, italic, and underlining that can be applied to change the way characters look in a worksheet or chart.

Footer Information, such as text, a page number, or a graphic, that appears at the bottom of every page in a document or a section.

Footnote Text that provides additional information or acknowledges sources for text in a document and that appears at the bottom of the page on which the note reference mark appears.

Foreign key field In a one-to-many relationship between two tables, the foreign key field is the field in the "many" table that links the table to the primary key field in the "one" table.

Form An Access object that provides an easy-to-use data entry screen that generally shows only one record at a time.

Form section A location in a form that contains controls. The section in which a control is placed determines where and how often the control prints.

Form View View of a form object that displays data from the underlying recordset and allows you to enter and update data.

Form Wizard An Access wizard that helps you create a form.

Format The appearance of a cell and its contents, including font, font styles, font color, fill color, borders, and shading. *See also* Number format.

Format Painter A feature used to copy the format settings applied to the selected text to other text you want to format the same way.

Formatting Enhancing the appearance of information through font, size, and color changes.

Formatting marks Nonprinting characters that appear on screen to indicate the ends of paragraphs, tabs, and other formatting elements.

Formula A set of instructions used to perform one or more numeric calculations, such as adding, multiplying, or averaging, on values or cells.

Formula bar The area above the worksheet grid where you enter or edit data in the active cell.

Formula prefix An arithmetic symbol, such as the equal sign (=), used to start a formula.

Forwarding Sending an email message you have received to someone else.

Free response quiz A type of Office Mix quiz containing questions that require short answers.

Function A special, predefined formula that provides a shortcut for a commonly used or complex calculation, such as SUM (for calculating a sum) or FV (for calculating the future value of an investment).

Gallery A collection of choices you can browse through to make a selection. Often available with Live Preview.

Gesture An action you take with your finger (or fingers) directly on the screen, such as tapping or swiping.

Graphic image *See* Image.

Gridlines Evenly spaced horizontal and vertical lines on the slide that help you align objects.

Group A PowerPoint feature in which you combine multiple objects into one object.

Grouping A way to sort records in a particular order, as well as provide a section before and after each group of records.

Groups Areas of the Ribbon that arrange commands based on their function, for example, text formatting commands such as Bold, Underline, and Italic are located on the Home tab, in the Font group.

Gutter Extra space left for a binding at the top, left, or inside margin of a document.

Hanging indent A type of indent in which the second and subsequent lines of a paragraph are indented more than the first.

Hard disk A built-in, high-capacity, high-speed storage medium for all the software, folders, and files on a computer. Also called a hard drive.

Hard page break *See* Manual page break.

have not yet been sent.

Header Information, such as text, a page number, or a graphic, that appears at the top of every page in a document or a section.

Highlighted Describes the changed appearance of an item or other object, usually a change in its color, background color, and/or border; often used for an object on which you will perform an action, such as a desktop icon.

Highlighting Transparent color that can be applied to text to call attention to it.

Horizontal ruler A ruler that appears at the top of the document window in Print Layout, Draft, and Web Layout view.

Horizontal scroll bar *See* Scroll bar.

Hub A pane in Microsoft Edge that provides access to favorite websites, a reading list, browsing history, and downloaded files.

Hyperlink Text or a graphic that opens a file, Web page, or other item when clicked. *Also called* a link.

I-beam pointer The pointer used to move the insertion point and select text.

Icon A small image that represents an item, such as the Recycle Bin on your Windows desktop; you can rearrange, add, and delete desktop icons.

Image A nontextual piece of information such as a picture, piece of clip art, drawn object, or graph. Because images are graphical (andnot numbers or letters), they are sometimes referred to as graphical images.

Inactive window An open window you are not currently using; if multiple windows are open, the window(s) behind the active window.

Inbox An email folder that stores all incoming email.

Indent The space between the edge of a line of text or a paragraph and the margin.

Indent marker A marker on the horizontal ruler that shows the indent settings for the active paragraph.

Infinity symbol The symbol that indicates the "many" side of a one-to-many relationship.

Ink annotations A freehand drawing on the screen in Slide Show view made by using the pen or highlighter tool.

Ink to Math tool The OneNote tool that converts handwritten mathematical formulas to formatted equations or expressions.

Ink to Text tool The OneNote tool that converts inked handwriting to typed text.

Inked handwriting In OneNote, writing produced when using a pen tool to enter text.

Inking Freehand pen and highlighter marks you can draw on a slide in Normal view to emphasize information.

Inking toolbar In Microsoft Edge, a collection of tools for annotating a webpage.

Inline graphic A graphic that is part of a line of text.

Insertion point A blinking vertical line that appears when you click in a text box; indicates where new text will be inserted.

Integrate To incorporate a document and parts of a document created in one program into another program; for example, to incorporate an Excel chart into a PowerPoint slide, or an Access table into a Word document.

Integration Term used to describe the process of combining objects and data from two or more applications. For example, a report created in Word can include a chart copied from Excel, or a presentation created in PowerPoint can include a table copied from Access.

Interface The look and feel of a program; for example, the appearance of commands and the way they are organized in the program window.

Is Not Null A criterion that finds all records in which any entry has been made in the field.

Is Null A criterion that finds all records in which no entry has been made in the field.

Italic Formatting applied to text to make the characters slant to the right.

Join line The line identifying which fields establish the relationship between two related tables. Also called a link line.

Junk email Unwanted email that arrives from unsolicited sources. *Also called* spam. Also a default folder in Outlook for junk email.

Justify Alignment in which an item is flush with both the left and right margins.

Key symbol The symbol that identifies the primary key field in each table.

Keyboard shortcut A combination of keys or a function key that can be pressed to perform a command.

Keyword A descriptive word or phrase you enter to obtain a list of results that include that word or phrase. *Also called* shortcut key.

Label control An unbound control that displays text to describe and clarify other information on a form or report.

Label Wizard A report wizard that precisely positions and sizes information to print on a vast number of standard business label specifications.

Labels Descriptive text or other information that identifies data in rows, columns, or charts, but is not included in calculations.

Landscape Page orientation in which the contents of a page span the length of a page rather than its width, making the page wider than it is tall.

Landscape orientation Page orientation in which the page is wider than it is tall.

Launch To open or start a program on your computer.

Launcher An icon you click to open a dialog box or task pane.

Layout A way to group several controls together on a form or report to more quickly add, delete, rearrange, resize, or align controls.

Layout View An Access view that lets you make some design changes to a form or report while you are browsing the data.

Left function An Access function that returns a specified number of characters, starting with the left side of a value in a Text field.

Left indent A type of indent in which the left edge of a paragraph is moved in from the left margin.

Left-align Alignment in which the item is flush with the left margin.

Legend Text box feature in a chart that provides an explanation about the data presented in a chart.

Like operator An operator used in a query to find values in a field that match the pattern you specify.

Line spacing The amount of space between lines of text.

Link A connection created between a source file and a destination file. When an object created in a source file is inserted into or copied to a destination file, any changes made to the object in the source file also appear in the object contained in the destination file.

Link line The line identifying which fields establish the relationship between two related tables.

Linked object An object such as a text selection, value, or picture that is contained in a destination file and linked to a source file. When a change is made to the linked object in the source file, the change also occurs in the linked object in the destination file.

List box A box that displays a list of options from which you can choose (you may need to scroll and adjust your view to see additional options in the list).

Live Preview A feature that lets you point to a choice in a gallery or palette and see the results in the document or object without actually clicking the choice.

Live tile Updated, "live" content that appears on some apps' tiles on the Windows Start menu, including the Weather app and the News app.

Lock screen The screen that appears when you first start your computer, or after you leave it unattended for a period of time, before the sign-in screen.

Log in To select a user account name when a computer starts up, giving access to that user's files. Also called sign in.

Logical view The datasheet of a query is sometimes called a logical view of the data because it is not a copy of the data, but rather, a selected view of data from the underlying tables.

Macro An Access object that stores a collection of keystrokes or commands such as those for printing several reports in a row or providing a toolbar when a form opens.

Mail In Outlook, lets you manage all email.

Major gridlines In a chart, the gridlines that represent the values at the tick marks on the value axis.

Manual page break A page break inserted to force the text following the break to begin at the top of the next page.

Map It An Outlook feature on a Contact card that lets you view a contact's address on a map.

Margin The blank area between the edge of the text and the edge of a page.

Masters One of three views that stores information about the presentation theme, fonts, placeholders, and other background objects. The three master views are Slide Master view, Handout Master view, and Notes Master view.

Maximize button On the right side of a window's title bar, the center button of three buttons; used to expand a window so that it fills the entire screen. In a maximized window, this button changes to a Restore button.

Maximized window A window that fills the desktop.

Meeting In the Outlook Calendar, an activity you invite people to or reserve resources for.

Menu A list of related commands.

Merge A feature in PowerPoint used to combine multiple shapes together; provides you a way to create a variety of unique geometric shapes that are not available in the Shapes gallery.

Message body In an email message, where you write the text of your message.

Message header Contains the basic information about a message including the sender's name and email address, the names and email addresses of recipients and Cc recipients, a date and time stamp, and the subject of the message.

Message threading Allows you to navigate through a group of messages, seeing all replies and forwards from all recipients; includes all emails that discuss a common subject.

Metadata Another name for document properties that includes the author name, the document subject, the document title, and other personal information.

Microsoft account A web service that lets users sign on to one web address so they can use Windows 10 computers as well as Outlook com.

Microsoft Edge New in Windows 10, the Microsoft Web browser that is intended to replace Internet Explorer.

Microsoft OneDrive A Microsoft Web site where you can obtain free file storage space, using your own account, that you can share with others; you can access OneDrive from a laptop, tablet computer, or smartphone.

Microsoft OneNote Mobile app The lightweight version of Microsoft OneNote designed for phones, tablets, and other mobile devices.

Microsoft Store A website, accessible from the Store icon in the Windows 10 taskbar, where you can purchase and download apps, including games, productivity tools, and media software.

Microsoft Windows 10 An operating system.

Mini toolbar A small toolbar that appears next to selected text that contains basic text-formatting commands.

Minimize button On the right side of a window's title bar, the leftmost button of three buttons; use to reduce a window so that it only appears as an icon on the taskbar.

Minimized window A window that is visible only as an icon on the taskbar.

Minor gridlines In a chart, the gridlines that represent the values between the tick marks on the value axis.

Mirror margins Margins used in documents with facing pages, where the inside and outside margins are mirror images of each other.

Mixed reference Cell reference that combines both absolute and relative cell addressing.

Mode indicator An area on the left end of the status bar that indicates the program's status. For example, when you are changing the contents of a cell, the word 'Edit' appears in the mode indicator.

Module An Access object that stores Visual Basic programming code that extends the functions of automated Access processes.

Mouse pointer A small arrow or other symbol on the screen that you move by manipulating the pointing device; also called a pointer.

Move To change the location of a file, folder, or other object by physically placing it in another location.

Multilevel list A list with a hierarchical structure; an outline.

Multiuser A characteristic that means more than one person can enter and edit data in the same Access database at the same time.

Name box Box to the left of the formula bar that shows the cell reference or name of the active cell.

Name property A property that uniquely identifies each object and control on a form or report.

Navigate To move around in a worksheet; for example, you can use the arrow keys on the keyboard to navigate from cell to cell, or press [Page Up] or [Page Down] to move one screen at a time.

Navigate down To move to a lower level in your computer's file hierarchy.

Navigate up To move to a higher level in your computer's file hierarchy.

Navigation buttons Buttons in the lower-left corner of a datasheet or form that allow you to quickly navigate between the records in the underlying object as well as add a new record.

Navigation mode A mode in which Access assumes that you are trying to move between the fields and records of the datasheet (rather than edit a specific field's contents), so keystrokes such as [Ctrl][Home] and [Ctrl][End] move you to the first and last field of the datasheet.

Navigation Pane A pane in the Access program window that provides a way to move between objects (tables, queries, forms, reports, macros, and modules) in the database.

Negative indent A type of indent in which the left edge of a paragraph is moved to the left of the left margin. *Also called* outdent.

Next page section break A break that begins a new section on the next page.

Normal style The default style for text and paragraphs in Word.

Normal view Default worksheet view that shows the worksheet without features such as headers and footers; ideal for creating and editing a worksheet, but may not be detailed enough when formatting a document.

Note In OneNote, a small window that contains text or other types of information.

Note reference mark A mark (such as a letter or a number) that appears next to text to indicate that additional information is offered in a footnote or endnote.

Notebook In OneNote, the container for notes, drawings, and other content.

Notes In Outlook, the electronic version of the sticky notes you buy at your local stationery store; a convenient way to quickly jot down a reminder or an idea.

Notes button A button on the status bar in PowerPoint that opens the Notes pane.

Notes Page view A presentation view that displays a reduced image of the current slide above a large text box where you can type notes.

Notes pane The area in Normal view that shows speaker notes for the current slide; also in Notes Page view, the area below the slide image that contains speaker notes.

Notification area An area on the right side of the Windows 10 taskbar that displays the current time as well as icons representing selected information; the Notifications button displays pop-up messages when a program on your computer needs your attention. Click the Notifications button to display the Action Center. *See also* Action Center.

Number format A format applied to values to express numeric concepts, such as currency, date, and percentage.

Object A table, query, form, report, macro, or module in an Access database.

Object Linking and Embedding (OLE) The term used to refer to the technology Microsoft uses to allow the integration of data between programs. The difference between linking and embedding relates to where the object is stored and how the object is updated after placement in a document. A linked object in a destination file is an image of an object contained in a source file. Both objects share a single source, which means the object is updated only in the source file.

Odd page section break A break that begins a new section on the next odd-numbered page.

Office Clipboard A temporary storage area shared by all Office programs that can be used to cut, copy, and paste multiple items within and between Office programs. The Office Clipboard can hold up to 24 items collected from any Office program. *See also* System Clipboard.

Office Mix A free add-in application integrated to the PowerPoint Ribbon that allows you to create interactive content.

Office Online Apps Versions of the Microsoft Office applications with limited functionality that are available online from Microsoft OneDrive. Users can view documents online and then edit them in the browser using a selection of functions.

Off-site backup Duplicate storage of computer data at a remote location other than your home or office. The backup may be stored on a removable hard drive or sent over the Internet to a Cloud service.

OneDrive An online storage and file sharing service. Access to OneDrive is through a Microsoft account.

One-to-many line The line that appears in the Relationships window and shows which field is duplicated between two tables to serve as the linking field. The one-to-many line displays a "1" next to the field that serves as the "one" side of the relationship and displays an infinity symbol next to the field that serves as the "many" side of the relationship when referential integrity is specified for the relationship. Also called the one-to-many join line.

One-to-many relationship The relationship between two tables in an Access database in which a common field links the tables together. The linking field is called the primary key field in the "one" table of the relationship and the foreign key field in the "many" table of the relationship.

Online collaboration The ability to incorporate feedback or share information across the Internet or a company network or intranet.

Open To use one of the methods for opening a document to retrieve it and display it in the document window.

Operating system A program that manages the complete operation of your computer and lets you interact with it.

Option button A small circle in a dialog box that you click to select only one of two or more related options.

OR criteria Criteria placed on different rows of the query design grid. A record will be selected for the resulting datasheet if it is true for any single row.

Order of precedence Rules that determine the order in which operations are performed within a formula containing more than one arithmetic operator.

Orphan The first line of a paragraph when it appears alone at the bottom of a page.

Orphan record A record in the "many" table of a one-to-many relationship that doesn't have a matching entry in the linking field of the "one" table. Orphan records cannot be created if referential integrity is enforced on a relationship.

Outbox A temporary storage folder for email messages that have not yet been sent.

Outdent *See* Negative indent.

Outline view A view in PowerPoint where you can enter text on slides in outline form. Includes three areas. The Outline pane where you enter text, the Slide pane for the main slide, and the Notes pane where you enter notes.

Outlook Today A feature in Outlook that shows your day at a glance, like an electronic version of a daily planner book; when it is open, you can see what is happening in the Calendar, Tasks, and Messages for the day.

Padding The space between controls.

Page In OneNote, a workspace for inserting notes and other content, similar to a page in a physical notebook.

Page break *See* Automatic page break or Manual page break.

Page Break Preview A worksheet view that displays a reduced view of each page in your worksheet, along with page break indicators that you can drag to include more or less information on a page.

Page Layout view Provides an accurate view of how a worksheet will look when printed, including headers and footers.

Pane A section of a window, such as the Navigation pane in the File Explorer window.

Paragraph spacing The amount of space between paragraphs.

Password A special sequence of numbers and letters that users can employ to control who can access the files in their user account area; keeping the password private helps keep users' computer information secure.

Paste To place a copied item from the Clipboard to a location in a document.

Paste Options button Button that appears onscreen after pasting content; enables you to choose to paste only specific elements of the copied selection, such as the formatting or values, if desired.

Path An address that describes the exact location of a file in a file hierarchy; shows the folder with the highest hierarchy level on the left and steps through each hierarchy level toward the right. Locations are separated by small triangles or by backslashes.

Peek A feature in Outlook that opens a small window when you mouse over an event, task, or some activity and shows you a snapshot of the details for the item.

People In Outlook, where you manage all your business and personal contact information.

People Pane Available in several Outlook views; shows you any social media information available for the person sending the current message and included files, appointments, and notes related to that person.

Personal account In Outlook, identifies you as a user with information such as your email address and password, the type of Internet service provider (ISP) you are using, and the incoming and outgoing email server address for your ISP. *See also* Account.

Photos app A Windows 10 app that lets you view and organize your pictures.

Picture A digital photograph, piece of line art, or other graphic that is created in another program and is inserted into PowerPoint.

Pixel (picture element) One pixel is the measurement of one picture element on the screen.

Plot area In a chart, the area inside the horizontal and vertical axes.

Point A unit of measure used for font size and row height. One point is equal to 1/72nd of an inch.

Pointer *See* Mouse pointer.

Pointing device A device that lets you interact with your computer by controlling the movement of the mouse pointer on your computer screen; examples include a mouse, trackball, touchpad, pointing stick, on-screen touch pointer, or a tablet.

Pointing device action A movement you execute with your computer's pointing device to communicate with the computer; the five basic pointing device actions are point, click, double-click, drag, and right-click.

Portrait Page orientation in which the contents of a page span the width of a page, so the page is taller than it is wide.

Portrait orientation A printout that is 8.5 inches wide by 11 inches tall.

Power button The physical button on your computer that turns your computer on.

PowerPoint window A window that contains the running PowerPoint application including the Ribbon, panes, and tabs.

Presentation software A software program used to organize and present information typically as part of an electronic slide show.

Presenter view A PowerPoint view you access while in Slide Show view. Typically you use this view when showing a presentation through two monitors, one that you see as the presenter and one that the audience sees.

Preview pane A pane on the right side of a File Explorer window that shows the actual contents of a selected file without opening an app; might not work for some types of files, such as databases.

Previewing Prior to printing, seeing onscreen exactly how the printed document will look.

Primary key field A field that contains unique information for each record. A primary key field cannot contain a null entry.

primary recipient of the message.

Print area The portion of a worksheet that will be printed; can be defined by selecting a range and then using the Print Area button on the Page Layout tab.

Print Layout view A view that shows a document as it will look on a printed page.

Print Preview An Access view that shows you how a report or other object will print on a sheet of paper.

Program A set of instructions written for a computer, such as an operating system program or an application program; also called an application or an app.

Property A characteristic that further defines a field (if field properties), control (if control properties), section (if section properties), or object (if object properties).

Property Sheet A window that displays an exhaustive list of properties for the chosen control, section, or object on a form or report.

Query An Access object that provides a spreadsheet-like view of the data, similar to that in tables. It may provide the user with a subset of fields and/or records from one or more tables. Queries are created when the user has a "question" about the data in the database.

Query design grid The bottom pane of the Query Design View window in which you specify the fields, sort order, and limiting criteria for the query.

Query Design View The window in which you develop queries by specifying the fields, sort order, and limiting criteria that determine which fields and records are displayed in the resulting datasheet.

Quick Access buttons Buttons that appear at the bottom of the Windows Action Center; single-click to perform common actions such as turning WiFi on or off.

Quick Access toolbar A customizable toolbar that contains buttons you can click to perform frequently used commands.

Quick Access view A list of frequently-used folders and recently used files that appears when you first open File Explorer.

Quick Analysis tool An icon that is displayed below and to the right of a range that lets you easily create charts and other elements.

Quick Part A reusable piece of content that can be inserted into a document, including a field, document property, or a preformatted building block.

Quick Style Determines how fonts, colors, and effects of the theme are combined and which color, font, and effect is dominant. A Quick Style can be applied to shapes or text.

RAM (Random Access Memory) The storage location that is part of every computer, that temporarily stores open apps and document data while a computer is on.

Range A selection of two or more cells, such as B5:B14.

Read Mode view A document view that hides the tabs and Ribbon and is useful for reading long documents.

Reading view In Microsoft Edge, the display of a webpage that removes ads and most graphics and uses a simple format for the text.

Read-only An object property that indicates whether the object can read and display data, but cannot be used to change (write to) data.

Record A row of data in a table.

Record source The table or query that defines the field and records displayed in a form or report.

Recycle Bin A desktop object that stores folders and files you delete from your hard drive(s) and enables you to restore them.

Reference operators In a formula, symbols which enable you to use ranges in calculations.

Referential integrity A set of Access rules that govern data entry and help ensure data accuracy. Setting referential integrity on a relationship prevents the creation of orphan records.

Relational database software Software such as Access that is used to manage data organized in a relational database.

Relative cell reference In a formula, a cell address that refers to a cell's location in relation to the cell containing the formula and that automatically changes to reflect the new location when the formula is copied or moved; default type of referencing used in Excel worksheets. *See also* Absolute cell reference.

Removable storage Storage media that you can easily transfer from one computer to another, such as DVDs, CDs, or USB flash drives.

Report An Access object that creates a professional printout of data that may contain such enhancements as headers, footers, and calculations on groups of records.

Report Wizard An Access wizard that helps you create a report.

Responsive design A way to provide content so that it adapts appropriately to the size of the display on any device.

Restore Down button On the right side of a maximized window's title bar, the center of three buttons; use to reduce a window to its last non-maximized size. In a restored window, this button changes to a Maximize button.

Ribbon In many Microsoft app windows, a horizontal strip near the top of the window that contains tabs (pages) of grouped command buttons that you click to interact with the app.

Ribbon Display Options button A button on the title bar that is used to use to hide or show the Ribbon and the Ribbon tabs and commands.

Rich Text Format (RTF) The file format that the WordPad app uses to save files.

Right indent A type of indent in which the right edge of a paragraph is moved in from the right margin.

Right-align Alignment in which an item is flush with the right margin.

Right-click To press and release the right button on the pointing device; use to display a shortcut menu with commands you issue by left-clicking them.

Rotate handle A small round arrow at the top of a selected object that you can drag to turn the selected object.

Row heading The box containing the row number to the left of the row in a worksheet.

RTF *See* Rich Text Format.

Rule In Outlook, enables you to organize your email by setting parameters for incoming email; for example, you can specify that all email from a certain person goes into the folder for a specific project.

Ruler A vertical or horizontal guide that appears in Form and Report Design View to help you position controls.

Sandbox A computer security mechanism that helps to prevent attackers from gaining control of a computer.

Sans serif font A font (such as Calibri) whose characters do not include serifs, which are small strokes at the ends of letters.

Save To store a file permanently on a disk or to overwrite the copy of a file that is stored on a disk with the changes made to the file.

Save As Command used to save a file for the first time or to create a new file with a different filename, leaving the original file intact.

Save As command A command on the File tab that saves the entire database (and all objects it contains) or only the current object with a new name.

Screen capture An electronic snapshot of your screen, as if you took a picture of it with a camera, which you can paste into a document.

Screen clipping In OneNote, an image copied from any part of a computer screen.

Screen recording In Office Mix, a video you create by capturing your desktop and any actions performed on it.

ScreenTip A label that identifies the name of the button or feature, briefly describes its function, conveys any keyboard shortcut for the command, and includes a link to associated help topics, if any.

Scroll To use the scroll bars or the arrow keys to display different parts of a document in the document window.

Scroll arrow A button at each end of a scroll bar for adjusting your view in a window in small increments in that direction.

Scroll bar A vertical or horizontal bar that appears along the right or bottom side of a window when there is more content than can be displayed within the window, so that you can adjust your view.

Scroll bars Bars on the right edge (vertical scroll bar) and bottom edge (horizontal scroll bar) of the document window that allow you to move around in a document that is too large to fit on the screen at once.

Scroll box A box in a scroll bar that you can drag to display a different part of a window.

Search criteria Descriptive text that helps identify the application program (app), folder, file, or Web site you want to locate when conducting a search.

Search Tools tab A tab that appears in the File Explorer window after you click the Search text box; lets you specify a specific search location, limit your search, repeat previous searches, save searches, and open a folder containing a found file.

Secondary axis In a combination chart, an additional axis that supplies the scale for one of the chart types used.

Section A location of a form or report that contains controls. The section in which a control is placed determines where and how often the control prints.

Section break A formatting mark inserted to divide a document into sections.

Section tab In OneNote, a divider for organizing a notebook.

Select To change the appearance of an item by clicking, double-clicking, or dragging across it, to indicate that you want to perform an action on it.

Select pointer The mouse pointer shape that looks like a white arrow pointing toward the upper-left corner of the screen.

Selection box A dashed border that appears around a text object or placeholder, indicating that it is ready to accept text.

Selection pointer A pointer used to click a button or another element of the Word program window.

Sent Items When you send an email message, a copy of the message is stored in this folder to help you track the messages you send out.

Serif font A font (such as Times New Roman) whose characters include serifs, which are small strokes at the ends of letters.

Service provider The organization or company that provides email or Internet access.

Shading A background color or pattern that can be applied to text, tables, or graphics.

Share button A button on the Ribbon that is used to save a document to the Cloud.

Sheet tab scrolling buttons Allow you to navigate to additional sheet tabs when available; located to the left of the sheet tabs.

Sheet tabs Identify the sheets in a workbook and let you switch between sheets; located below the worksheet grid.

Shortcut An icon that acts as a link to an app, file, folder, or device that you use frequently.

Shortcut key *See* Keyboard shortcut.

Shortcut menu A menu of context-appropriate commands for an object that opens when you right-click that object.

Shut down To exit the operating system and turn off your computer.

Sign in To select a user account name when a computer starts up, giving access to that user's files. Also called log in.

Simple Query Wizard An Access wizard that prompts you for information it needs to create a new query.

Single-click *See* Click.

Single-factor authentication Security protocol in which an individual provides only one credential (password) to verify their identity.

Sizing handles Small series of dots at the corners and edges of a chart indicating that the chart is selected; drag to resize the chart.

Slide layout This determines how all of the elements on a slide are arranged, including text and content placeholders.

Slide Library A folder that you and others can access to open, modify, and review presentation slides.

Slide Notes In Office Mix, the written and displayed version of notes typically used to recite narration while creating a slide recording.

Slide pane The main section of Normal view that displays the current slide.

Slide recording In Office Mix, a video you create by recording action with a webcam, a camera attached or built into a computer.

Slide Show view A view that shows a presentation as an electronic slide show; each slide fills the screen.

Slide Sorter view A view that displays a thumbnail of all slides in the order in which they appear in a presentation; used to rearrange slides and slide transitions.

Slide thumbnail *See* Thumbnail.

Slide timing The amount of time each slide is visible on the screen during a slide show.

Slide transition The special effect that moves one slide off the screen and the next slide on the screen during a slide show. Each slide can have its own transition effect.

Slides tab On the left side of the Normal view, displays the slides in the presentation as thumbnails.

Smart Guides A feature in PowerPoint used to help position objects relative to each other and determine equal distances between objects.

SmartArt A professional quality graphic diagram that visually illustrates text.

SmartArt graphics Predesigned diagram types for the following types of data: List, Process, Cycle, Hierarchy, Relationship, Matrix, and Pyramid.

SmartArt Style A pre-set combination of formatting options that follows the design theme that you can apply to a SmartArt graphic.

Snap assist feature The Windows 10 feature that lets you drag a window to the left or right side of the screen, where it "snaps" to fill that half of the screen and displays remaining open windows as thumbnails you click to fill the other half.

Soft page break *See* Automatic page break.

Sort Change the order of, such as the order of files or folders in a window, based on criteria such as date, file size, or alphabetical by filename.

Source file In integration, the file from which the information is copied or used. An Excel file that is inserted into a file that contains a Word report is the source file.

Source presentation The presentation you insert slides from when you reuse slides from another presentation.

Spam Unwanted email that arrives from unsolicited sources. *Also called* junk email.

Spamming The sending of identical or near-identical unsolicited messages to a large number of recipients. Many email programs have filters that identify this email and place it in a special folder.

Sparkline A quick, simple chart located within a cell that serves as a visual indicator of data trends.

Spin box A text box with up and down arrows; you can type a setting in the text box or click the arrows to increase or decrease the setting.

Split form A form split into two panes; the upper pane allows you to display the fields of one record in any arrangement, and the lower pane maintains a datasheet view of the first few records.

SQL (Structured Query Language) A language that provides a standardized way to request information from a relational database system.

Start button A clickable button at in the lower left corner of the Windows 10 screen that you click to open the Start menu.

Start menu Appears after you click the Start button; provides access to all programs, documents, and settings on the computer.

Status bar The bar at the bottom of the Word program window that shows information about the document, including the current page number, the total number of pages in a document, the document word count, and the on/off status of spelling and grammar checking, and contains the view buttons, the Zoom level button and the Zoom slider.

Storyline In Sway, the workspace for assembling a presentation.

Style A named collection of character and paragraph formats that are stored together and can be applied to text to format it quickly.

Subdatasheet A datasheet that is nested within another datasheet to show related records. The subdatasheet shows the records on the "many" side of a one-to-many relationship.

Subfolder A folder within another folder.

Subject line Meaningful text in the subject text box of an email message providing recipients with an idea of the message content.

Subscript A font effect in which text is formatted in a smaller font size and placed below the line of text.

Subtitle text placeholder A box on the title slide reserved for subpoint text.

Suite A group of programs that are bundled together and share a similar interface, making it easy to transfer skills and program content among them.

Sum function A mathematical function that totals values in a field.

Superscript A font effect in which text is formatted in a smaller font size and placed above the line of text.

Sway site A website Sway creates to share and display a Sway presentation.

Symbol A special character that can be inserted into a document using the Symbol command.

Sync In OneNote, to save a new or updated notebook so that all versions of the notebook, such as a notebook on OneDrive and a copy on a hard drive, have the same contents.

Syntax Rules for entering information such as query criteria or property values.

System Clipboard A clipboard that stores only the last item cut or copied from a document. See also Clipboard and Office Clipboard.

System on a Chip (SoC) Consolidates the functions of the CPU, graphics and sound cards, memory, and more onto a single silicon chip. This miniaturization allows devices to become increasingly compact.

Tab A page in an application program's Ribbon, or in a dialog box, that contains a group of related commands and settings.

Tab Index property A form property that indicates the numeric tab order for all controls on the form that have the Tab Stop property set to Yes.

Tab leader A line that appears in front of tabbed text.

Tab order property A form property that determines the sequence in which the controls on the form receive the focus when the user presses [Tab] or [Enter] in Form view.

Tab stop A location on the horizontal ruler that indicates where to align text.

Tab Stop property A form property that determines whether a field accepts focus.

Table A collection of records for a single subject, such as all of the customer records; the fundamental building block of a relational database because it stores all of the data.

Table Design View A view of a table that provides the most options for defining fields.

Table styles Predesigned formatting that can be applied to a range of cells or even to an entire worksheet; especially useful for those ranges with labels in the left column and top row, and totals in the bottom row or right column. See also Table.

Tabs Organizational unit used for commands on the Ribbon. The tab names appear at the top of the Ribbon and the active tab appears in front.

Task In Outlook, an item in Tasks.

Task view A new Windows 10 area, accessible from the Task view button on the taskbar, that lets you switch applications and create multiple desktops (also called virtual desktops).

Taskbar The horizontal bar at the bottom of the Windows 10 desktop; displays icons representing apps, folders, and/or files on the left, and the Notification area, containing the date and time and special program messages, on the right.

Tasks In Outlook, the electronic to-do list, whereby each task has a subject, a start and end date, priority, and a description.

Tell Me box A text box on the Ribbon that is used to find a command or access the Word Help system.

Template A predesigned, formatted file that serves as the basis for a new workbook; Excel template files have the file extension .xltx.

Text Align property A control property that determines the alignment of text within the control.

Text annotations Labels added to a chart to draw attention to or describe a particular area.

Text box An area in a Windows program that you click to enter text.

Text concatenation operators In a formula, symbols used to join strings of text in different cells.

Text effect Formatting that applies a visual effect to text, such as a shadow, glow, outline, or reflection.

Text placeholder A box with a dotted border and text that you replace with your own text.

Text wrapping Formatting applied to a graphic to make it a floating graphic.

Text wrapping break Forces the text following the break to begin at the beginning of the next line.

Theme A predefined set of colors, fonts, line and fill effects, and other formats that can be applied to an Access database and give it a consistent, professional look.

Theme colors The set of 12 coordinated colors that make up a PowerPoint presentation; a theme assigns colors for text, lines, fills, accents, hyperlinks, and background.

Theme effects The set of effects for lines and fills.

Theme fonts The set of fonts for titles and other text.

Thumbnail A small image of a slide. Thumbnails are visible on the Slides tab and in Slide Sorter view.

Tick marks Notations of a scale of measure on a chart axis.

Tile A shaded rectangle on the Windows 10 Start menu that represents an app. See also App and Application program.

Title bar Appears at the top of every Office program window; displays the document name and program name.

Title placeholder A box on a slide reserved for the title of a presentation or slide.

Title slide The first slide in a presentation.

To Do tag In OneNote, an icon that helps you keep track of your assignments and other tasks.

Toggle button A button that turns a feature on and off.

Toolbar In an application program, a set of buttons, lists, and menus you can use to issue program commands.

Trash folder *See* Deleted Items folder.

Two-factor authentication (2FA) Security protocol in which an individual provides two credentials (often a pre-established password plus a one-time, randomly-generated code sent to a mobile phone) to verify their identity.

Ultraportable computer A type of laptop that is generally smaller and less powerful.

Unbound control A control that does not change from record to record and exists only to clarify or enhance the appearance of the form, using elements such as labels, lines, and clip art.

Universal apps *See* Windows 10 apps.

USB (Universal Serial Bus) Data communications standard designed to replace the need for earlier interfaces such as parallel and serial ports.

USB flash drive A removable storage device for folders and files that you plug into a USB port on your computer; makes it easy to transport folders and files to other computers. Also called a pen drive, flash drive, jump drive, keychain drive, or thumb drive.

User account A special area in a computer's operating system where users can store their own files and preferences.

User interface A collective term for all the ways you interact with a software program.

Username The first part of an email address that identifies the person who receives the email that is sent to this email address.

Vacation response An automatically-generated email message you can have sent in response to received emails when you are away; most email programs allow you to create a vacation response.

Value axis In a chart, the axis that contains numerical values; in a 2-dimensional chart, also known as the y-axis.

Values Numbers, formulas, and functions used in calculations.

Variant A custom variation of the applied theme that uses different colors, fonts, and effects.

Vertical alignment The position of text in a document relative to the top and bottom margins.

Vertical ruler A ruler that appears on the left side of the document window in Print Layout view.

Vertical scroll bar *See* scroll bar.

View Each Access object has different views for different purposes. For example, you work with data in Datasheet View. You modify the design of the object in Layout and Design Views. You preview a printout in Print Preview. Common views include Datasheet View for a table or query, or Design View for any Access object.

View buttons Buttons on the status bar that are used to change document views.

View Shortcuts The buttons at the bottom of the PowerPoint window on the status bar that you click to switch among views.

Wearables Computer devices that may be worn on a person's wrist or incorporated into clothing.

Web Layout view A view that shows a document as it will look when viewed with a Web browser.

Web Note In Microsoft Edge, an annotation on a webpage.

Web-based email Web site that provides free email addresses and service.

What-if analysis A decision-making tool in which data is changed and formulas are recalculated, in order to predict various possible outcomes.

Widow The last line of a paragraph when it is carried over to the top of the following page, separate from the rest of the paragraph.

Wildcard A special character used in criteria to find, filter, and query data. The asterisk (*) stands for any group of characters. For example, the criteria I* in a State field criterion cell would find all records where the state entry was IA, ID, IL, IN, or Iowa. The question mark (?) wildcard stands for only one character.

Window A rectangular-shaped work area that displays an app or a collection of files, folders, and Windows tools.

Window control buttons The set of three buttons on the right side of a window's title bar that let you control the window's state, such as minimized, maximized, restored to its previous open size, or closed.

Windows 10 apps Apps (application programs) for Windows 10 that often have a single purpose, such as Photos, News, or OneDrive.

Windows 10 desktop An electronic work area that lets you organize and manage your information, much like your own physical desktop.

Windows 10 UI The Windows 10 user interface. *See also* User interface.

Windows accessories Application programs (apps), such as Paint or WordPad, that come with the Windows 10 operating system.

Windows Action Center A pane that appears in the lower right corner of the Windows 10 screen that lets you quickly view system notifications and selected settings; also has Quick Action buttons to perform common actions in one click.

Windows app Small program available for free or for purchase in the Windows Store; can run on Windows desktops, laptops, tablets, and phones.

Windows Search The Windows feature that lets you look for files and folders on your computer storage devices; to search, type text in the Search text box in the title bar of any open window, or click the Start button and type text in the search text box.

Word art A drawing object that contains text formatted with special shapes, patterns, and orientations.

Word processing program A software program that includes tools for entering, editing, and formatting text and graphics.

Word program window The window that contains the Word program elements, including the document window, Quick Access toolbar, Ribbon, and status bar.

Word wrap A feature that automatically moves the insertion point to the next line as you type.

WordArt A set of decorative styles or text effects that is applied to text.

Workbook A collection of related worksheets contained within a single file which has the file extension xlsx.

Works cited A list of sources that you cited while creating a document.

Worksheet A single sheet within a workbook file; also, the entire area within an electronic spreadsheet that contains a grid of columns and rows.

Worksheet window Area of the program window that displays part of the current worksheet; the worksheet window displays only a small fraction of the worksheet, which can contain a total of 1,048,576 rows and 16,384 columns.

X-axis The horizontal axis in a chart; because it often shows data categories, such as months or locations, *also called* Category axis.

XML Acronym that stands for eXtensible Markup Language, which is a language used to structure, store, and send information.

Y-axis The vertical axis in a chart; because it often shows numerical values, *also called* Value axis.

Z-axis The third axis in a true 3-D chart, lets you compare data points across both categories and values.

Zoom level button A button on the status bar that is used to change the zoom level of the document in the document window.

Zoom slider A slider on the status bar that is dragged to enlarge or decrease the display size of the document in the document window.

Zooming A feature that makes screen information appear larger but shows less of it on screen at once, or shows more of a document on screen at once but at a reduced size; does not affect actual document size.

Zooming in A feature that makes a printout appear larger but shows less of it on screen at once; does not affect the actual size of the printout.

Zooming out A feature that shows more of a printout on screen at once but at a reduced size; does not affect the actual size of the printout.

Index